Phillippi
Thrace
(Gallipolli)
Bosphorus
Sea of Marmara
(Propontis)
Hellespont (Dardenelles)
TROAD PENINSULA
Phrygia
Troy
Tenedos
(AEOLIA)
Lyrnessos
Lesbos
(Sappho and
Alcaeus)
Messon
Eressos
Mytilene
Lydia
Aegean Sea
Sardis
Skyros
(IONIA)
Chios
(Homer)
Asia Minor
(Turkey)
Teos
(Anacreon)
Ephesus
Samos
Delos
(Oracle)
(DORIA)
Miletus
Paros
(Archilochus)
Naxos
Halicarnassus
(Herodotus)
Kos
Rhodes
Sea of Crete
Knossos
Crete
Map painting by
J. Craig Thorpe

## PRAISE FOR *THE LESBIAN LYRE:*

"A humanities degree between two covers. Brilliant."

– DAVID DUBAL, The Juilliard School, Author, *The Essential Canon of Classical Music*

"*The Lesbian Lyre* offers a bracing and very welcome challenge to the twentieth century dominance of 'personal voice' translations of Greek lyric, Sappho in particular, by translators with scant or no Greek but great self-confidence in their own intuition of what the Greek should say. The trend for 'poet-translators' to work from cribs and paraphrases has undoubtedly been deplorable, both in conception and results. The polemics of Jeffrey Duban's argument are very clear, with Ezra Pound the chief villain in the piece. The book promises both to resurrect some forgotten but remarkably effective translations of Greek lyric and to offer new renderings of Sappho in translations reflecting the simple and formal beauties of her lyrics while calling upon the full resources of the English poetic tradition."

– NIALL W. SLATER, Samuel Candler Dobbs Professor of Latin and Greek, Emory University, Atlanta

"Jeffrey Duban is one of the relatively few scholars and artists standing athwart the flood of modernism and yelling stop—if it is possible to characterize extraordinary erudition and the devoted advocacy of truth and beauty as 'yelling.'"

– MARK HELPRIN, Author, *A Kingdom Far and Clear: The Complete Swan Lake Trilogy*

"*The Lesbian Lyre* is scholarly in its overall plan, and well-informed and insightful. Interested readers will be accurately informed about the matters of Greek and Latin literature on which it touches; and in considering the themes of this literature from a modern viewpoint, they are also likely to be enlightened by some original judgments. Imperialism is not a cause which finds much enlightened support in the modern era, even within dominant powers such as the UK and the USA which consider themselves (and their quasi-imperial activities) to have been a net force for good in the world. But imperialism is an intrinsic theme of Classical Latin literature. It is a merit of this book that it considers these conflicts of value head-on. Taken as a whole, this book will certainly contain a feast of sound scholarship and challenging critical judgment."

– NICHOLAS OSTLER, Chairman, Foundation for Endangered Languages, Author, *Empires of the Word; Ad Infinitum; The Last Lingua Franca*

"A half-century ago Duban's views on the translation of Greek and Latin poetry would have been non-controversial. Now they may be as incendiary as they are desperately needed."

– VICTOR DAVIS HANSON, The Hoover Institution, Stanford University, Coauthor, *Who Killed Homer: The Demise of Classical Education and the Recovery of Greek Wisdom*

"Jeffrey Duban's *The Lesbian Lyre* is unique. It brings together the story of poetry (and also of the visual arts, and, in important ways, of music) from our first texts in ancient Greece up to the contemporary criticism of the Classics. It deserves comparison with Gilbert Highet's *The Classical Tradition* (1949) for its wide-ranging scholarship. The author is generous to the newcomer to the classical world: geography, cultures, the gods and their myths, the Greek language and its dialects, Greek poetic rhythms, are set as background. The writing is clear, and the essentials in all of this are reviewed quickly. The work is magisterial in its root sense: we enjoy good teaching.

Duban shows that the search for shock, or jagged impact—for energy— in English, often distorts the Greek model; similarly, that Marxist or feminist interpreters have made the Greek poets poster figures for their philosophical programs. I heartily applaud the patient and rational exposure of the way in which such ideologies wage war against the very excellent art already present in the Greek. Central to this book are the author's translations of Sappho and the Greek lyric poets, and of Catullus, who radically recast himself, a Roman lover, as Sappho. The translations and their comparison with other English versions are a strength of this book.

Every part of the work's huge trajectory helps build meaning for the reader. *The Lesbian Lyre* is a masterful synthesis of all the best arguments in classical scholarship for the past sixty or seventy years, illuminated by the changing cultural contexts of the past twenty-five centuries."

– WILLIAM R. NETHERCUT, Professor, Department of Classics, University of Texas, Austin

# The Lesbian Lyre

Reclaiming Sappho for the 21st Century

# The Lesbian Lyre

## Reclaiming Sappho for the 21st Century

Jeffrey M. Duban

CLAIRVIEW

Clairview Books Ltd.,
Russet, Sandy Lane, West Hoathly,
W. Sussex RH19 4QQ

www.clairviewbooks.com

Published in Great Britain in 2016 by Clairview Books



Sappho Fragments on Papyri, MS. Gr. class. c. 76/1 (P), reproduced with permission of The Bodleian Libraries, University of Oxford. (Displayed at the Morgan Library & Museum, New York City, June 6–September 14, 2014)



A CIP catalogue record for this book is available from the British Library

Print book ISBN 978 1 905570 79 9
Ebook ISBN 978 1 905570 80 5

Edited, designed, and typeset by Rachel Trusheim
Chariot illustration by Kati Gyulassy
Hand-painted map by J. Craig Thorpe
Printed and bound in Malta by Gutenberg Press Ltd.

*To the memory of*

Jeanne A. Petrek, *M.D. (1948–2005)*

*Loving wife and mother,*
*Healer and comfort to her patients.*

*Whatever of this work is worthy of her.*

# Contents

# Acknowledgments

I WISH TO RECORD sincerest thanks and appreciation to those whose tireless attentions have so increased the quality of this book. Most especially to my wife, Jayne Connell. Reading two drafts and more, she essentially set the work's foundation. A teacher of English critiquing my work, Jayne regularly took me to task on matters otherwise clear to me as a classicist. She further provided a grammatical and punctuation refresher on points I seemed long ago to have forgotten—corrupted after twenty-two years of practicing law. Through Jayne, the work progressed from its initial lumbering steps to its first balanced stride. References to *Jane Eyre* and to *Paradise Lost* and *Paradise Regained* were gleaned from our shared out-loud readings while this work was in progress. The perfect respite with the perfect companion.

Thanks also for the substantial contributions of:

My brother, James Duban, professor of English—wise in the ways of Melville, the Jameses, and Philip Roth. I have benefited from his instruction on Spenser and from his encouragement of some of my more audacious incursions. He knows, in true Hesiodic fashion, how much better the half is than the whole—the half-pound most of all.

Janice Benario, my former Georgia State University colleague, and since lifelong friend. During my years in Atlanta, Janice provided unstinting friendship, support, and encouragement, both as a classics colleague and then editor of *Vergilius.* A Horatian by temperament and academic preference, she has been the inspiration of my own high esteem of Horace, as especially evidenced in this book.

Michael Putnam, my undergraduate mentor and lifelong *exemplum,* for his knowing corrections and literary cross-references, and for his approvals throughout. Never did an undergraduate career in classics begin under such favoring auspices, and never was a professor's concern for his student, and former student, more biding.

Richard LaFleur, my former colleague at University of Georgia. Assuming the editorship of *The Classical Outlook* in 1979, Richard enlisted me as the journal's first poetry editor, a position I happily held for ten years. The *Outlook*'s submission requirements stated a preference for poetry of discernible form and content—rhyme in such cases the frequent adjunct. Richard has thus long been an impetus to this book.

Deborah Boedeker, who encouraged my travel to Lesbos.

Alfred Runte, stalwart friend and supporter in professional and personal matters alike. I have valued his steadfast encouragement of my work, his sympathies and humane understanding, his historical and political acumen, and, not least, his knowledge of the publishing trade.

My cousin Martin Mould, fellow pupil at The Boston Public Latin School, and student of beloved Greek "master" Patrick O'Callahan, "Oki." Martin provided insight on selected chapters and an extremity of impatience for the publication of this book.

My son, Paul Petrek-Duban, for making the *Odyssey* newer than it had ever been.

Elena Grigorenko for her enduring friendship, encouragement, and support, for her review of some of the book's earliest chapters, and for happily accepted guest-lecturing invitations at Columbia University.

Walter Levis and Stephen Sarnoff for insights on Chapter 1.

My indispensable editor and co-journeyer over the past three years has been Rachel Trusheim, who seven years ago "discovered" this book when it was far more in my head than on the page, and resolved to make it her editorial own. I thank Rachel for her sustaining presence throughout, for scrupulous focus on every page, for her retention of ever-increasing matter, for a manner at once authoritative and congenial, for fearlessness in taking me to task, and for ultimately shaping the work in ways I could not have imagined. Having studied Greek in college, she uniquely understood my purpose and passion.

My publisher, Clairview Books, and its chief editor, Sevak Gulbekian, for his grasp and full-hearted understanding of all things germane to this book, including its history, editing, and production.

I close by acknowledging the lifelong influence and inspiration of Gregory Nagy, with whom, on the steps of Gilman Hall as a graduate student at Johns Hopkins, I first read Sappho's great "Hymn to Aphrodite"—the two of us *fato profugi*.

# Abbreviations

GENERAL:

| | |
|---|---|
| Eng. | English |
| Fr. | French |
| Ger. | German |
| Gr. | Greek |
| Heb. | Hebrew |
| Lat. | Latin |
| ME | Middle English |
| OE | Old English |
| OF | Old French |
| PIE | Proto-Indo European |
| | |
| acc. | accusative (case) |
| c. | abbreviation, Lat. *circa* 'around' |
| cf. | abbreviation, Lat. *confer* 'compare' (imp.) |
| fr. | fragment |
| frr. | fragments |
| gen. | genitive (case) |
| imp. | imperative (mood) |
| lit. | literally |
| masc. | masculine |
| nom. | nominative (case) |
| n. | note |
| nn. | notes |
| n.s. | new series |
| n.f. | Ger. *neue folge* = n.s. |
| part. | participle (mood) |
| pass. | passive (voice) |
| perf. | perfect (tense) |
| pl. | plural |
| sing. | singular |
| * | indicates a hypothetical verbal root |
| ~ | indicates analogy or similarity |

CLASSICAL:

| | |
|---|---|
| *Aen.* | *Aeneid* |
| *Ann.* | *Annales* |
| *AP* | *Ars Poetica* |
| *Arg.* | *Argonautica* |
| *DRN* | *De Rerum Natura* |
| *Ec.* | *Eclogues* |
| *El.* | *Elegies* |
| *Ep.* | *Epistles* |
| *Epit.* | *Epitome* |
| *FQ* | *Faerie Queene* |
| *G* | *Georgics* |
| *IA* | *Iphigenia at Aulis* |
| *Il.* | *Iliad* |
| *Inf.* | *Inferno* |
| *Inst. Orat.* | *Institutio Oratoria* |
| *Met.* | *Metamorphoses* |
| *Od.* | *Odyssey* |
| *Or.* | *Orations* |
| *PL* | *Paradise Lost* |
| *PR* | *Paradise Regained* |
| *Prot.* | *Protagoras* |
| *Rep.* | *Republic* |
| *Sat.* | *Satires* |
| *Th.* | *Theogony* |
| *Thaet.* | *Thaetetus* |
| *Thes.* | *(Life of) Theseus* |
| *WD* | *Works and Days* |

BIBLICAL:

| | |
|---|---|
| Cant. | Canticles (Song of Songs) |
| 1 Cor. | First Corinthians |
| Deut. | Deuteronomy |
| 1 Sam. | First Samuel |
| Gen. | Genesis |
| Isa. | Isaiah |
| Num. | Numbers |
| Ps. | Psalm |

| | |
|---|---|
| KJB/KJV | King James Bible/King James Version |
| ESV | English Standard Version |
| RSV | Revised Standard Version |

# Guide to Pronunciation

DICTIONARIES GENERALLY PROVIDE phonetic pronunciations, using symbols of the International Phonetic Alphabet. For instance, the five principal poets discussed in this volume would be indicated as follows: Sappho, Sa′-fō; Alcman, alk′-mən; Anacreon, ə-na′-krē-on; Archilochus, ahr-kil′-ə-kəs; and Ibycus, i′-bə-kəs. It is a complex system, as the perusal of any manual of style and pronunciation would reveal. I do not use the International Phonetic Alphabet, largely because the names here discussed are not English names as such, but transliterations from Greek and Latin. Moreover, and in the case of ancient languages—especially Greek—we cannot be sure how the language actually sounded at any one time, in any one dialect, in prose versus poetry, or at all.

*Transliteration* entails the spelling of a word in one language with the alphabet of another. For example, μῆνιν ἄειδε θεὰ 'The wrath, sing, [O] goddess' (*Il.* 1.1) can be transliterated as *menin aeide thea* by substituting the most closely corresponding letters of the English alphabet for the Greek. Or, with markings, where helpful, to indicate equivalent vowel lengths: *mēnin aeide theā*. Transliterated Greek approximates the *appearance* of the original, but not necessarily its sound—among other reasons, because transliteration is pronounced according to the rules and conventions *not* of ancient Greek but of English. *Transcription*, on the other hand, entails the charting of *sound* from one language to another. Being purely sound-oriented, transcription generally distorts the original's appearance. For example, the Greek name Ἡρακλῆς can be transliterated as *Herakles* (or *Heracles*), with accent on the first syllable, but transcribed as *Hay-ra-klace′*, with accent on the last syllable, as in Greek. In fact, Greek names typically differ from their original accentuation when transliterated and pronounced in English. Where there is similarity of letters and sounds in both languages, transliteration and transcription may fairly well coincide, e.g., Κρόνος—*Kronos* (Zeus's father). However, because English is not always pronounced as spelled, transliteration may require transcription of its own, as in the case, again, of Ἡρακλῆς: transliterated, *Herakles*; transcribed, *Hay-ra-klace'*; transcribed from English transliteration (or pronounced), *Herakleez*.

Matters are not helped by the longstanding practice of Latinizing the transliteration of Greek (see further Chapter 21). For example, Latinization changes Greek kappa κ to Latin *c* (always hard), alpha/iota *ai* (as in *aisle*) to *ae* (as in see), and final omicron/sigma -*ος* to -*us*. Thus, *Kronos* is often Latinized as *Cronus* (cf. *Patroklos*/*Patroclus*), and *Alkaios* as *Alcaeus*. Latinization may also change alpha/iota *ai* to *e* (as in *see*), and where Greek omicron/sigma -*ος* serves as an adjectival rather than noun ending, it is typically rendered as the English suffix -*an*. Thus, Αἰγαῖος (Ai-gai'-os): *Aegean* (first *Ai* = *ae*, second *ai* = *e*, *os* = *an*). I generally follow the Latinizing practice.

In any number of cases, however, non-Latinized transliteration is preferable, e.g., *Herakles*/*Heracles* instead of *Hercules*, especially within the context of Greek rather than Latin literature or myth. And though Latinization otherwise favors the use of Latin names over their Greek equivalents (where they differ)—Jupiter or Jove for Zeus, Mercury for Hermes, Venus for Aphrodite—I resist the practice, preferring Greek names in Greek literary contexts. As there is clearly no formula governing these usages, the results can be puzzling. Even where transliterative spellings are consistent, pronunciations may vary from one to another speaker, owing to habit or local usage. For a prime example of just how tangled the transliteration and transcription of Greek and Latin proper names can be, especially where the different Greek dialects are involved, see the discussion of Sappho's own name (p. 118).

It thus little surprises to find a lack of pronunciation consensus. Seeking to streamline the inquiry, I offer a brief guide to vowel and other selected sounds, followed by recommended pronunciations of Greek and Latin names most often found in this volume.

VOWELS:

(In the case of alternative pronunciations, the choice may depend on whether the name is transliterated from Greek or from Latin.)

| | |
|---|---|
| *a* | as in *are* or *at* |
| *ā* | as in *say* |
| *e* | as in *elf* or *see* |
| *ē* | as in *say* or *see* |
| *i* | as in *it* |
| *ī* | as in *size* or *be* |
| *o* | as in *on* |
| *ō* | as in *zone* |
| *u* | as in *us* |
| *ū* | as in *loose* |
| *y* | as in *see, eye,* or *it* |

DIPHTHONGS:

| | |
|---|---|
| *ae* | as in *aisle* or *see;* sometimes an *a* sound like the *u* in *sun,* e.g., Aeneas |
| *ai* | as in *aisle* |
| *au* | as in *owl* |
| *ei* | as in *freight* or *see* |
| *eu* | as in *food* or *you* |
| *oe* | as in *see* or *soy* |
| *oi* | as in *soy* |
| *ou* | as in *food* |
| *es* | as in *breeze* or *ace* |

ALSO:

Latin *c* and *g* are always hard (as in *cat* and *get*).

Gr. *γ* (gamma) is always hard. It is transcribed as hard *g* initially, and as soft *g* internally when followed by *e* or *i*.

Gr. *η* (ēta), with *ay* sound in Greek, is transliterated as long *ē,* pronounced either *ay* or *ee.*

Gr. Θ (*theta*) is pronounced *th* as in *thin.*

Gr. *χ* (*chi*), a gutteralized *k* sound (like *ch* in Ger. *Buch*), is sometimes transliterated as *kh,* but more often as *ch* pronounced *k,* e.g., Ἀχιλλεύς, Achilles; Ἀρχίλοχος, Archilochus.

EXAMPLES:

| **Name (transliteration)** | **Pronunciation (transcription)** |
|---|---|
| Achilles | A-kil′-leez |
| Achilleus (Gr.) | A-kill′-yoos |
| Achilleid | A-kil-lee′-id |
| Aeacus | Ee′-a-cus (Achilles's grandfather) |
| Aeacidae | Ee-a′-ci-dee ('sons of Aeacus') |
| Aeacides | Ee-a′-ci-deez ('son of Aeacus', or Achilles) |
| Aegean | A-gee′-an |
| Aegina | Ai′-gi-na |
| Aelian | Ee′-li-an |
| Aeneas | A-nee′-us |
| Aeneid | A-nee′-id |
| Aeolia | Ai-o′-li-a or Ee-o′-li-a |
| Aeolis | Ai-o′-lis or Ee-o′-lis |
| Aeolic | Ee-o′-lic |
| Aeschylus | Ees′-ki-lus |
| Alcaeus | Al-see′-us |
| Alcmēnē | Alc-mee′-nee (or Alc-may′-nay) |
| Anacreōn | A-na′-cree-on |
| Annales | A-na′-lace |
| Archilochus | Ar-kil′-o-kus |
| Aristarchus | A-ris-tar′-kus |
| Aristophanes | A-ris-to′-pha-neez |
| Athenaeus | A-then-ee′-us |
| Aulis | Au′-lis |
| Atreus | Ay′-tree-us |
| | |
| Bacchylides | Bak-kil′-i-deez |
| Berenicē | Be-re-ni′-see |
| Boeōtia | Bee-ō′-sha |
| Briareus | Bri-ar′-yoos |
| Brisēïs | Bri-say′-is (or Bri-see′-is) |
| Brontēs | Bron′-teez |
| | |
| Callimachus | Cal-lim′-a-kus |
| Carmina Būrana | Car′-mi-na [*not* Car-mee′-na] Boo-ra′-na |
| Catullus | Ca-tul′-lus |
| Chīos | Kee′-os |
| Chīrōn/Cheirōn | Ki′-rōn/Kay′-rōn |
| *Chrestomathy* | *Kres-to′-ma-thee* |

| | |
|---|---|
| Chrysēs | Krī′-seez |
| Cinyras | Ci′-ni-rus |
| Clēïs/Klēïs | Clay′-is |
| Cliō/Clēō | Clee′-ō/Clay′-ō |
| Clōthō | Clō′-thō |
| Clytemnestra | Clī-tem-nes′-tra |
| Coeus | Coy′-us |
| Cottus | Cot′-tus |
| Cūretes | Coo′-re-teez |
| | |
| Deidamīa | Day-da-mee′-a |
| Dēlos | Dee′-los |
| Delphī | Del′-phi (or Del′-phee) |
| Diomēdēs | Di-o-mee′-deez |
| Diōnē | Di-ō′-nee |
| | |
| Ennius | E′-nee-us |
| Ephesus | E′-phe-sus |
| Euterpē | You-ter′-pee |
| | |
| Gaia | Gai′-a |
| Ganymēdē | Gan-i-mee′-dee |
| Geryonēis | Ge-ree-o-nay′-is |
| Gibōrim/Nephilim | Gee-bōr-im′/Ne-phil-im′ |
| Gorgias | Gor′-gee-us |
| *hamartia* | *ha-mar-tee′-a* |
| *Heautontimoroumenos* | *he-au-ton-ti-mōr-oo′-men-os* |
| Hecatē | He′-ca-tee |
| Hēosphorus | Hay-os′-pho-rus |
| Hephaistos | He-phais′-tos |
| Heraclitus | He-ra-cleye′-tus |
| Heroides | He-rō′-i-deez |
| *hērōōn* | *hay-rō-ōn′* |
| Hēsiod | Hee′-see-id |
| Hesperides | Hes-per′-i-deez |
| Hippocoōn | Hip-po′-co-ōn |
| | |
| Idaeus | I-dee′-us |
| Iphigenia | I-phi-gen-i′-a |
| | |
| Kronos | Kro′-nos |
| | |
| Laius | Lai′-us (or Lay′-us) |

| | |
|---|---|
| Laocoōn | La-o′-cō-on |
| Laomedōn | La-o′-me-don |
| Latium | Lay′-shum |
| Leschēs | Les′-keez |
| Leucippus | Loo-sip′-pus |
| Leukē | Loo′-kay |
| Lycomēdēs | Li-co-mee′-deez |
| | |
| Masoretes | Ma′-zor-eetz (or Ma′-zor-ites) |
| Menaechmī | Men-eyek′-mee |
| Moirai | Moi′-rai |
| Mytilēnē | Mi-ti-lee′-nee |
| | |
| Nausicaa | Now-si′-ca-a |
| Naevius | Nee′-vee-us |
| Neoboulē | Ne-o′-boo-lay |
| | |
| Oxyrhynchus | Ok-si-rink′-us |
| | |
| Pēleus | Pee′-lee-us (or Peel′-yoos) |
| Pēlēïdēs | Pay-lay′-i-deez ('son of Peleus', or Achilles) |
| Phaedrus | Phee′-drus |
| Phaeacia | Phai-ay′-sha (or Phee-ay′-sha) |
| Philoctētēs | Phil-oc-tee′-teez |
| Pīeria | Pi-e′-ri-a |
| | |
| Sappho | Sa′-phō |
| Semelē | Se′-me-lee |
| Steropēs | Ster′-o-peez |
| Stobaeus | Sto-bee′-us |
| Suidas | Soo′-das |
| | |
| Thersitēs | Ther-si′-teez |
| Thēseus | Thee′-see-us (or Thees′-yoos) |
| Thucydides | Thoo-si′-di-deez |
| Tyndareus | Tin-dar′-ee-us |
| Tyrtaeus | Teer-tee′-us |

The heroic books, even if printed in the character of our mother tongue, will always be in a language dead to degenerate times; and we must laboriously seek the meaning of each word and line. . . . The modern cheap and fertile press, with all its translations, has done little to bring us nearer to the heroic writers of antiquity.

– THOREAU, *Walden*

No man is capable of Translating Poetry, who besides a Genius to that Art, is not a Master both of his Authours Language, and of his own: Nor must we understand the Language only of the Poet, but his particular turn of Thoughts, and of Expression, which are the Characters that distinguish, and as it were individuate him from all other writers. When we come this far, 'tis time to look into our selves, to conform our Genius to his, to give his thought either the same turn if our tongue will bear it, or if not, to vary but the dress, not to alter or destroy the substance.

– DRYDEN, Preface, Ovid's *Epistles*

*The Joke* was translated into all the Western languages. But what surprises! In France, the translator rewrote the novel by ornamenting my style. In England, the publisher cut out all the reflective passages, eliminated the musicological chapters, changed the order of the parts, recomposed the novel. Another country: I meet my translator, a man who knows not a word of Czech. "Then how did you translate it?" "With my heart." And he pulls a photo of me from his wallet.

– MILAN KUNDERA, *The Art of the Novel*

# Preface

> Poetry is the place where language performs, and so poetry shows us most clearly what a language can do, and what it likes to do . . .
>
> – WILLIAM FITZGERALD

THIS WORK BEGAN nearly forty years ago with my translation of Ibycus, a Greek poet of the mid-sixth century BC. I was then a graduate student in Classics at Johns Hopkins University. Ibycus was a native of Greek-settled Sicily (a part of "Great Greece," or Magna Graecia). He was thus far removed—across the Ionian Sea, the Greek mainland, and the Aegean—from Sappho (7th–6th century BC) and her island home of Lesbos off the coast of Asia Minor (modern Turkey). The two ranked—according to the Hellenistic scholars of Alexandria, Egypt, in the fourth and third centuries BC—among "the Nine" great lyric poets of Greece. Their erotic poetry, the little we have of it, shares a like emotional intensity in its description of the catatonic effect of consuming passion. Ibycus was believed to have performed for the tyrant Polycrates on the island of Samos, located south of Lesbos (see map). Situated between Lesbos and Samos is the island of Chios, the frontrunner of seven locations claiming to be the birthplace of Homer. The poets of antiquity, as will be seen, traveled widely and enjoyed broad celebrity appeal. Sappho is known to have traveled to Egypt. She is believed to have committed suicide in a lovelorn leap from the Leucadian cliff, on the island of Lefkas off the western coast of Greece. Strange as it seems in retrospect, I found Sappho through Ibycus.

My translation of Ibycus—one of his two surviving love poems—was as follows:

> Love's melting look from eyes dark-browed
> has cast me into Cyprian chains

> unfailing, charmed in every wise.
> How I shake at his approach—
> as a horse once winner of the prize
> in later years must bear the reins
> and cart, unwilling, past the crowd.

Ibycus describes himself as one who in his late years can no longer run love's course ("Cyprian" referring to Aphrodite, born out of the sea onto the island of Cyprus). Trembling to be again harnessed, he finds that age offers no exemption. Like a once prize-winning horse put out to pasture, the poet has again been yoked—this time for humiliation, love's glory-day gone. The poem displays a sobering cognizance, powerfully conveyed with consummate control, as classical poetry knows neither blank nor free verse.

I was especially pleased with the translation's rhyme scheme, *a-b-c-d-c-b-a*, which is neatly emblematic of the poem's own lamented reversal of prowess: the balanced enjambments, the archaizing diction ("wise"), and the emphatic "shake at his approach" at the poem's unrhymed midpoint. I submitted it to Chauncey Finch, then editor of *The Classical Bulletin* (at the time a mere leaflet of a publication). When Finch responded that it would be published, I was ecstatic. Months later, however, when the piece appeared, I was crushed. The format, a too-narrow column, had caused first- and fifth-line carryovers, changing my perfect rhyme scheme and symmetry. I wrote to Finch and asked if he would kindly rerun the piece as originally submitted. Finch politely explained that carryover was common to verse publication, observed that the piece read nicely indeed, and respectfully declined.

The objection to carryover would, in time, prove the least of my cares concerning classical verse in translation. The field was even then filling with so-called poet-translators, i.e., translators who were ignorant, or only superficially informed, of the Greek or Latin from which they "translated." Poet-translators supposedly compensated for the deficit through their standing as "poets." Their understandings were comparable to what English professor and modernist avatar Hugh Kenner (1923–2000) said early in his career of James Joyce's Greek: It was "a magpie's hoard of details, sufficient to entertain Greek etymologies but not to write out the first line of the *Odyssey* accurately, let alone read with comfort." The poet-translators were being goaded, coached, and sponsored by classicists who knew, or should have known, better. The rationale was that stodgy classicists, though knowing Greek and Latin, lacked poetic instinct, while poets, being *poets*, compensated for the lack of classical training both with their innate gifts and the help of classicist friends.

The present work focuses on the results and implications of the poet-translator phenomenon, one that I have found to perplex non-classicists. Yet within the self-approving classics field of the past fifty years and more, this phenomenon has become commonplace. Reviewing such works for academic journals and other media, classicists rarely so much as note a poet-translator's lack of classical language training. Prior to the mid-twentieth century, such a situation would have been unthinkable. There have of course been rare and outstanding exceptions: witness Alexander Pope (1688–1744) who, with minimal Greek and an unfailing poetic sensibility, completed one of the most successful and enduring translations of Homer.

In contrast, the rare "classicist-translator" is the classics scholar with the temerity actually to *know* the languages from which he translates. While the classicist-translator looks to previous translations—one does, after all, work within a tradition—the poet-translator relies not merely on previous efforts, but on cribs and "coaches." Cribs are often crude, word-for-word, syntax-impervious renderings from which the poet-translator obtains meaning while *poetically* intuiting intent and feeling—be it of Sappho, Homer, Virgil, Horace, or any other classical poet. Coaches, in this context, are typically classics scholars who encourage and edit the poet-translator's work in progress. They may even write out rough translation drafts from which the poet-translator takes his lead. Coaches may also contribute introductions and favorably review the published work. Such practices are openly confessed, and the work of the poet-translator lauded "despite the lack of formal training." Indeed, the confession of ignorance may itself elicit praise. Says one reviewer, "Guy Davenport is sentimental. He is not ashamed of this, one imagines, for he can say of his translation of Sappho: 'my translation, therefore, is without any authority except the dubious one of sentiment.'"

I followed my first publication with the translation of Ibycus's only other surviving love lyric. I first memorized the Greek, seeking to determine whether internalizing the original benefited the process and result:

In spring the river streams bedew
the quinces in Cydonia,
where sacred stands the Maidens' grove
and shading bough vine-blossomed grows;
this love of mine no season knows
but races—northern Thracian blast
from Aphrodite's shrine outcast
ablaze with flash of lightning, black
with shameless fits of parching rage,
pain unrelenting, unassuaged.

One grasps from the poem's intensity how the poet, beset with years, trembles to reengage. None of that, however, seemed to register in the mechanistic modernist analysis by Hugh Kenner, *The Pound Era* (1971). This is the magnum opus that has, to this day, made modernist legends of Ezra Pound (1885–1972) and Hugh Kenner himself. In a chapter entitled "Words Set Free," Kenner promotes crib-based translation—Pound was openly and self-confessedly crib-reliant—by atomizing Ibycus, the words set out in Greek script, one by one, with word-for-word translation, as follows:

| | | | |
|---|---|---|---|
| *Eri* | *men* | *hai te* | *Kudōniai* |
| { Early<br>In spring | (on the<br>one hand) | the | Cydonian |
| *malides* | *ardomenai* | *hroan* | |
| { nymphs<br>fruits | are watered | streams . . . | |

Kenner's dissection of Ibycus is at root intended to suggest that the dry-as-dust literalism of an ancient text—not to slight its ambiguities—is all the poet-translator needs to translate from Greek into English. The approach works a significant refinement on the long-familiar adage—more effective in Italian than in English—*traduttore traditore* 'the translator is a traitor'. The adage indicates that translation, since always inexact, entails a betrayal of meaning. With the rise of the poet-translator, the adage evinces a greater treason yet.

The treason is apparent in the essentially Greekless Pound's version of Ibycus, titled "The Spring" (which Kenner quotes with approval). Pound anthropomorphizes "river streams," injecting "Maelids" (apple nymphs) and "water girls" who somehow "step beneath a wind from Thrace." Pound entirely misses, or simply glosses, the poem's pivotal antithesis: between Gr. *men* 'on the one hand'—the calm and seasonal regularity of spring—and *de* 'on the other hand', the random onslaughts of the poet's own passion. Invoking a "bewildered heart," Pound concludes with three entirely invented lines: "Though every branch have back what last year lost, / She, who moved here amid the cyclamen, / Moves only now a clinging tenuous ghost."

Kenner's Ibycus is an example of what John Dryden, famously distinguishing three types of translation, called "metaphrase," or literal translation. Metaphrase designates something "according to" or "following the utterance" (Gr. *meta* + *phrazo* 'speak'). Metaphrase provides a word-for-word rendering, as close to the original's word order and syntax as possible. For that reason, it is typically stilted, lacking any sense of idiom or coherence. Dryden's other types of translation are "paraphrase" (translation with latitude, or according to the spirit rather than letter of the original) and "imitation" (barely translation at all, or a free improvisation on the original). My own Ibycus is an example of paraphrase—in today's parlance, "literary translation"; Pound's rendering is an example of imitation. For the poet-translator, especially of Greek lyric, metaphrase is frequently the bridge to imitation, the only way anything of the original might be conveyed. Reliance on metaphrase, whether of Greek or Latin, is an exercise in sustained futility. A year's study of Latin, while not granting fluency, would render metaphrase and its crib convolutions unnecessary. Two years' study of Greek would similarly benefit the understanding of that language.

Students at The Boston Public Latin School of the 1960s were expected to keep up with their lessons, learning Latin enough to translate without the use of a crib. Accordingly, cribs were always a matter of high drama and trepidation, as they were the ultimate contraband. The cheating student, tearing out the day's translation and laying it into his Cicero or Virgil, would rise to recite. Stammering his way through, he trembled, responding *n-nothing* to the master's (pointing) *What's that you've got there*? There was no greater punishment than that for the use, or even possession, of a crib: the student's parents summoned to the headmaster, suspension or disciplinary censure following (two censures in a school year and you were *out*). For it was not simply cheating, it was *treason*—a betrayal of the core educational values and good citizenship embodied in the study of Latin at the Latin School. The severity of the sanction, the *opprobrium*, kept us well studied and respectful. The modernist intellectual community, by contrast, has known no such constraint or *aidōs* 'shamefastness', indulging with crib-based paraphrase or imitation in the erstwhile translation of classical texts. It is a pity that contemporary English-speaking culture must swallow it whole. As preservers of ancient languages in which the civilized world must still have a paramount interest, classicists have abrogated their responsibility. They (and the best of them) have collaborated in the fraud of translation—in the defrauding of the classical past—as further detailed herein.

Kenner and Pound will have no part of "the ease with which difficulties are mastered, the power of knowledge aptly arrayed, the lightning glance which perceives at once what the poet wants to say and how he must have said it." Offering his metaphrase of Ibycus, the atypically Greek-learned Kenner holds forth on possible ambiguities in what is a perfectly clear and simple and for that reason an uncommonly powerful poem, whether in Greek or in English; Kenner having culled the possibilities from Liddell & Scott, *A Greek-English Lexicon,* 1843 (1st ed.). Ambiguity is the modernist stock-in-trade; the emphasis always on the many rather than the one—on "multiplicities," "mergings of meanings," and that part of the larger enterprise concerned with the erasure or transgression of boundaries. One scholar, later discussed at length, contrives "boundarylessness" as a Marxist and otherwise radically infused approach to lyric poetry, and to Sappho in particular. One is sooner reminded that good fences make good neighbors.

However consummately conveyed the poem's passion, Kenner minces Ibycus into word-for-word components, these to be redeployed in whatever configuration the languageless poet-translator may want. The original Greek poem, no longer a meaningful text, has become a repository—a hat—from which words may be randomly pulled. Metaphrastic improvisation, for the modernist, is of a yet better world and place than any original. Such is Ibycus with his "words set free." Kenner, in brief, makes a glib and Poundian case for the modernist handling of Greek lyric and other classical texts. Not for nothing did English poet-novelist, critic, and classicist Robert Graves (1895–1985), who coined the term *modernist,* see fakery at the core of modernist poetry. "Pound's brand of 'new' was, for Graves and [poet-novelist Laura] Riding, the fakest of fakery."

The breakup of poems word by word has its analogue in the divvying of an author's body of work, poem by poem—a multiplicity of translators preferable to one. This is the approach of poet-editor J. D. McClatchy in *Horace, The Odes: New Translations by Contemporary Poets* (2002). As we have not recently entered upon a new golden age of Latin, the title's "contemporary" framework evinces a majority of Latinless translators. This is work of the team-translation variety, previously used for that most parceled-out of all poets, Dante (one Canto per player). Featured are various big hitters from among the poet-translator elite—Bly, Creeley, Hall, Merwin, Pinsky, Simic, and others. Editing the collection and himself participating in the translation, McClatchy, a professor of English (as are most poet-translators), shares the same disregard of source language that we find in Pound.

Each translation in *Horace, The Odes* appears with facing Latin text—to remind us what the translators (most of them) neither know nor understand: Latin. McClatchy, in his introduction, hedges mightily in this regard, never really making the admission. "Some poets worked close to the Latin bone," he says, "sometimes in the original meters," meaning: those who knew Latin tried to approximate Latin meters with English equivalents. "Others wrote more freely," referring to the Latinless and Latin-learned alike. Says McClatchy, "This book draws on three-dozen remarkable sensibilities, each in command of a formidable technique, yet able to submit that talent to Horace's own preoccupations. . . . But then each [participant] had been asked because of his or her mastery of English rather than of Latin in the enterprise 'to make the echo equal to the voice.'" This is the closest McClatchy comes to saying that source-language familiarity was irrelevant to "the enterprise." The echo equaling a voice unheard is but the echo's echo.

The volume exhibits other failings. First is the rationale for an All-Star team of "leading poets from America, England, and Ireland." McClatchy explains it by urging that Horace's "subtlety of tone and brilliance of technique have often proved elusive, especially when—as has usually been the case—a single translator ventures to maneuver through Horace's infinite variety." Since pre-McClatchy Horace has regularly been rendered by a "single translator," it has all apparently failed for want of the A-Team. Second, we are apparently to understand that the so-called "infinite variety" of a *single* poet is beyond the ability of a single translator, that no *one* person can translate what one person alone created. Last is the pairing of different odes with different translators by temperament or style. One wonders how and by whom such a determination can be made. Temperament now apparently joins the crib as a bridge to translation—the basic ability to read in the original gone.

The reception of McClatchy's *Horace, The Odes* is unsettlingly mixed. In an excellent essay on Horace, ending in a review of McClatchy, the estimable classicist Daniel Mendelsohn does not so much as mention that the majority of translators knows no Latin. Praising some of the results and faulting others, as if the translators were all equally equipped, Mendelsohn ultimately faults the volume as a whole, on both practical and conceptual grounds. Classicist John Talbot offers nothing short of a forty-page review in which he labors to determine which of McClatchy's Latinless translators do the best translations. This is all sadly beside the point. We seek the unerring ear and sensibility: authenticity, not stumbling imitation. One does better with esteemed classicist Cedric Whitman's *Fifteen Odes of Horace* (1980) than with the whole of McClatchy's *Horace, The Odes.*

We have in truth reached the point where translation, even by a classicist, is praised for its crib-like quality. Anthony Verity (b. 1939) "gives us English close enough to the lexical sense of the Greek that you could use it as a crib." This is the opinion, again, of John Talbot, favorably reviewing Verity's *The Iliad* (2011) for *The New Criterion.* The circle thus comes fully around from crib-made translation to translation made to sound like crib. Talbot observes:

> Nobody would call this poetry, and Verity in his preface disavows any poetic intentions. The line breaks create only the illusion of verse. . . . As a trustworthy contemporary account of Homer's sense in English, without embellishment or omission, that can be read pleasurably at length, Verity's *Iliad* is exemplary.

Reading for pleasure has surely taken a turn for the worse, as we cozy to a fine mediocrity in an age of diminished expectations. The same sentiment appears in Stephen Miller's *The Iliad* (2011), in which Miller speaks of "the sheer power of Homer's language even in the most prosaic or mediocre translations"—the most prosaic or mediocre now apparently sufficient. The downturn is early suggested by W. H. Auden, stating that "If Greek literature has to be read in translation, then the approach can no longer be an aesthetic one," since the aesthetic loss from Greek to English is "practically fatal." "One can almost say," continues Auden, "that the better a translation is as English poetry, the less like Greek poetry it is (e.g., Pope's *Iliad*) and vice versa." The "vice versa" is disconcerting to say the least, implying that the worse the translation, the more like Greek poetry it is.

The downturn is not merely accepted, but embraced; it is a *relief*. Reading Verity and other current translations of Homer, says Talbot,

> forces you to take stock how limited is the range of rhetorical registers in contemporary English, even in English poetry. Colloquial registers? No problem there. But the English of our day is not well suited to formal modes. . . . One reason for reading and cherishing Anthony Hecht is that he was one of the last poets in English who could achieve, elegantly, but without affectation, a lofty rhetorical pitch.

Hecht's success (discussed elsewhere in this volume) derives from his largely sequestered standing as a formalist poet, his use of rhyme and meter in an age of modernist penury. While the Shakespearean doublet ill fits our own poetic age, jacket and tie do help, for looking smart is a first step. Formality, by whatever degree, forces one to discriminate among alternatives, to be discriminating—from which follow standards and taste. That is the lesson to be learned from Hecht, whether applied to original or translated poetry. To instance Hecht as extinct ("one of the last poets in English"), rather than hold him up as an example, is to embrace impoverishment. Roman authors of the Republic, acknowledging the impoverishment—*egestas*—of their Latin tongue, looked ever to the formalities and refinement of Greek models, *atticizing* Latin to a perfection that assured its one-thousand-year survival as the language of Europe. The immediate results were apparent: Caesar and Cicero, then Virgil, Horace, Propertius, and Livy.

Is no manner of elevation possible? Apparently not. "Verity," says Talbot, "has created an idiom that minimizes the appearance of intervention: he has made his own hard work aggressively modest" (a fine oxymoron). Time was when English soared; it now barely hovers. If we hear neither the translator's voice nor the poet's original idiom, nor have a meeting or compromise of the two, we have truly little more than a crib. What Verity produces and Talbot endorses is a new category of translation, the "straightforward" one: "So, yes, we need straightforward translations such as Verity's, which I welcome as the best of its kind." The Best of the Achaeans would cringe to be so recollected.

It is, in the end, a fine appreciation of Pope—his aggressive immodesty, and the informed and heightened expectations of his day—that belies the recourse to mediocrity, as Talbot well knows and affirms:

> From Pope, a reader could gather that the *Iliad* is a poem not only of great conceptual but also poetically formal unity. Pope's English generates, and sustains for page after page, a musical cadence so marked that it is a kind of language in itself, from which readers may infer, by analogy, that a similarly powerful formal idiom pervades and sustains the ancient poem. The relish with which Pope dwells upon his description of a craftsman's polish is at one with the relish he takes in the craft of his own translation, shaping and joining each couplet, and leaving each one touched with a golden point.

It is for such reasons, among others, that Pope is, and will likely long remain, the most Homeric of translators. As Dr. Samuel Johnson considered Pope's Homer "a treasure of poetical elegances to posterity," it is to such treasure that we, as Pope's posterity, should sooner turn. In the hard cultural times on which we have fallen, it is to Pope we should aspire—to his exuberant one-of-a-kindness—rather than to a leveling "straightforward translation . . . the best of its kind." In the one way, lies supremacy; the other, collapse—the objective being what is conspicuously, not contemporaneously, best. The best Homer in English (by whatever criteria) will in its own way reflect what is best in the Greek—Homer in Greek being *the best*. We imagine Homer and Pope as two brilliant but differently constituted stars held fast across space within each other's view. Pope and classicism go hand in hand. Because we must maintain the classical ideal before our eyes, says Eliot, "we cannot afford either to reject or overrate the age of Pope. We cannot see English literature as a whole, or aim rightly in the future, without critical appreciation of the degree to which the classical qualities are exemplified in Pope."

This work endeavors to identify the criteria by which the best verse translation is known, be it lyric or epic. Such translation, I submit, is that which reads well as poetry in English, compensating for the original's essential incommunicability by whatever richness of features—rhythm, rhyme, diction, figures of speech, etc.—English may offer. The best translation further conveys the original's essential meaning and tenor—by which I mean tone, intent, and movement. The translations offered in PART III of this work aspire to that goal, as do my translations throughout. All, with minor exceptions and as noted, are mine.

Since Greek lyric and epic mark the start of the Western literary tradition and are the wellsprings of so much that followed, we cover far-ranging content. PARTS I and II provide literary and historical-mythological background to the five lyricists featured in the PART III translations, including critical review of the principal Sappho translators of the twentieth century, the near-deified Mary Barnard and prolific Willis Barnstone among them. Indeed, one scholar notes that "Barnard's Sappho is often read as if it *is* Sappho." But it most decidedly is *not* Sappho. PART IV deals in significant part with the broader themes of epic and lyric poetry. *Kleos* 'glory' is foremost among them, and we explore its various poetic formulations in the shaping of epic verse. PART IV offers a fresh understanding of some of the traditional views held in Greek mythology. For example, in Chapter 18 we examine whether Achilles would have married Helen of Troy. While the obstacle appeared to be his youth, in truth, age was no obstacle. The marriage, among other things, would have precluded the Trojan War, virtually nullifying Greek mythology. PART V, for the more stalwart reader, explains the basics of Greek poetic meter and accentuation.

PART VI provides a survey of Greek and Latin literature from the standpoints of translation, literary characteristics and influence, and the worldview of epic as a measure of Western thinking and orientation (including the delicate issue of colonialism). PART VII treats the major erotic poems of Sappho and her Roman imitator Catullus, establishing the concerns of my own work as they specifically relate to the union of form and content, the function of *art* in light of that word's own etymology, and the excesses of theorist scholarship as applied to Sappho. Chapter 25 includes a discussion of modernism as the antithesis of everything prized and achieved in the classical mode, including classicism's insistence on form and content, order and proportion.

PART VIII focuses on the shortcomings of the twentieth century's most heralded translations of Homer and Virgil, including those by Robert Fitzgerald, Robert Fagles, and Christopher Logue. It resurrects the Smith/Miller *Iliad* (1947), translated into an English verse-equivalent of Homeric meter. It pairs Smith/Miller with Pope as the two greatest and most Homeric of all *Iliad* translations, each excelling in its own way. PART VIII concludes with a lengthy discussion on the pernicious effects of modernism—and of Ezra Pound in particular—on translation, original poetry, and the arts overall in the twentieth and twenty-first centuries. Modernism in the arts was neither inevitable nor foregone, but won out over the period's otherwise dominant conservatism, owing largely to the outsize personality of Pound. The ability of a single personality to incline the masses is not without parallel in the worst political developments of Pound's own time.

The work's range of materials and observations, diffuse at first glance, is Herodotean in nature. The Father of History (5th century BC) broadly ranges over human experiences within a variety of settings, all while offering an overarching historical framework structured around the development of the Persian Empire. His is a worldview in which "everything is potentially important and interconnected." Proceeding in a logical yet skeptical manner, Herodotus weighs theories and accounts, citing sources as he goes. I do much the same, my framework being translation of the Classics and the Bible, with epic and lyric poetry the principal focus and illustration. If what I offer is not in each instance "potentially important," it is at least of interest, and memorable, if nothing else. Herodotus's *Histories* is also translatable as "inquiries," and it is in the latter sense that it falls short of an empirical model for writing of its kind (the task of Thucydides in the same century). The *Histories* was yet admired in antiquity for its persuasiveness, euphony, and charm. To the extent I have borrowed a page from Herodotus, I join with him in saying, "Digressions are part of my plan."

*JMD*
NEW YORK CITY, 2015

# I.

# Chapter 1

## Greek Lyric, Greek Epic, and Old Testament; the Quarrel of Ancients and Moderns

> Long before I undertook [the *Aeneid*],
> I was no stranger to the Original.
>
> – JOHN DRYDEN, Dedication, *Aeneid*

> Take my hand, I'm a stranger in paradise.
>
> – FORREST AND WRIGHT, *Kismet*

THE TRANSLATIONS HERE offered are of the archaic Greek lyricists Sappho, Alcman, Anacreon, Archilochus, and Ibycus (7th–6th centuries BC). They are all poems or fragments of an amatory or otherwise erotic nature, including verse on age and dying. This volume, now significantly expanded, takes its departure from my *Ancient and Modern Images of Sappho: Translations and Studies in Archaic Greek Love Lyric* (1983). Geared both toward the intellectually curious and the academic reader, it seeks to restore Sappho, no less than the translation of Sappho and archaic Greek lyric in general, to a level of realistic understanding and appreciation. Sappho has become unrecognizable in the translations and scholarship of the past fifty years and more. One wonders, were she alive today, whether she would at all recognize herself.

Popularizing translator Paul Roche noted in his 1966 translation of Sappho that "'imitations' have once again become fashionable. Poets up and down the land are writing their own Homers and Ovids and Virgils: some of them without reference to or even knowledge of the language from which they quarry their ore of gold." This statement, removed from Roche's 1998 edition, yet continues to resound. The regard for self over subject matter, which is to say, the disregard for works of art as they are or should be, reflects modernist tendencies, as will be amply shown. In sum, scholar and devoted amateur alike must gasp at the sham that has become the Classics in translation—the translation of fragile and fragmentary Sappho most of all. As translation has long been the lifeblood of continued interest in the Classics, the topic necessarily commands attention. Included are endnotes that should satisfy the scholar without proving burdensome to the general reader.

Homer's *Iliad* and *Odyssey* were originally oral compositions, the dominant parts of a comprehensive storytelling tradition developed over half a millennium before being written down: Trojan War, thirteenth century BC; Homeric Age, eighth century BC; transcription of Homeric epics, sixth century BC. It is worth emphasizing that however little of her work survives, Sappho was to lyric what Homer was to epic: Homer "the Poet" and Sappho "the Poetess." Greek epic and lyric poetry have been foundational in the development of Western literature. Both developed in and around the coast of Asia Minor (modern Turkey). Homer's reputed birthplace, as noted, was the island of Chios, just south of Sappho's birthplace, the island of Lesbos. When Athens was still a village, long before its glory-day in the fifth century BC, the poetry of Homer and Sappho was already the glorious achievement of a cosmopolitan Greek-settled eastern Aegean. The achievement was in significant measure shaped by the culture of an urbane and luxuriant Asia Minor.

The word *Lesbian* originally meant, as it does today, an inhabitant of Lesbos, while *lesbian,* referencing Sappho's love of women, now generally indicates sexual orientation. The distinction, however, is little observed. The word *sapphic* is sometimes used as a synonym for *lesbian,* and *sapphism* as a synonym for *lesbianism.* The word *homosexual* refers to *same* or *like* sexual preference (Gr. (*h*)*omoios* 'same, like, related', shortened to (*h*)*omo*- as prefix). The derivation is *not* from Lat. *homo* 'man' (in turn, from Lat. *humus* 'ground'; Eng. *human, humanity, humility*). *Homoerotic* thus describes contact between members of the same sex—male or female. Contact between members of the opposite sex is, of course, *heterosexual* (Gr. *(h)eteros* 'other'; Eng. *heterogeneous*). Same-sex relationships were not, as sometimes thought today, a matter of sexual preference or "lifestyle." Such notions were foreign to antiquity. Same-sex love, whether male or female, was, in the main, a socially sanctioned rite of passage. As such, it was largely transitory. Sappho's coterie, or *thaisos*, of adolescent girls, instructed by her in the refinements of music and womanhood, likely included a same-sexual right of passage, but with marriage the ultimate goal.

Sappho and the other lyric poets flourished against the backdrop of Homeric epic. The word *epic* comes from Gr. *epos* 'word, story', while *lyric* denotes poetry originally sung to the *luros* 'lyre'. Both epic and lyric evolved orally, to be later written down, though by Sappho's time composition likely also occurred by stylus on wax tablet or even papyrus. The themes of Sappho's poetry were both heterosexual and homoerotic love, and her poetry was uniformly praised during the millennium following her death. It was the homoerotic, however, that earned her the too-frequent sneer and, with the fourth-century AD advent of Christianity, increasing condemnation in official circles. About the ninth century AD, at the start of the Dark Ages, Sappho's poetry, estimated in the thousands of lines, disappeared. Its "sudden absence" gave rise to what Margaret Reynolds, collecting the evidence, calls "one of Sappho's most enduring legends": that her works "were destroyed, publicly burned, by the fanatical hands of the early Christians." The fate, as Reynolds further notes, is not without symbolic or metaphysical significance: the subtle self-consuming flame of Sappho's own poem *phainetai moi* 'He appears to me' (PART III, §2), "reaching out beyond her own time and space to light up the world with desire." Though other seventh- and sixth-century lyricists have largely disappeared from view, Sappho's is an extreme case, her situation unique. On the one hand, of female lyricists in antiquity, Sappho is the only one enamored and writing of women, and the only invoking Aphrodite in homoerotic loves. On the other hand, the sexual focus of her poetry is consistent with that of ancient Greek love poetry in general, written by men enamored of men. Neither focus, of course, is exclusive.

❧

Greek epic and lyric are as culturally connected as are the principles involved in their translation. Biblical translation is also germane because of the over one-thousand-year influence of Jerome's Vulgate (4th century AD), the first translation of the Old Testament into Latin directly from the Hebrew instead of from the Greek translation known as the Septuagint (3rd century BC). The Septuagint and Vulgate are noteworthy as the first translations into Greek and Latin from the original Hebrew by translators who knew Hebrew. The practice of more recent times, as noted, is for Greekless and Latinless translators to translate from classical languages of which they are either ignorant or have only passing familiarity. This largely accounts for the impermanence of much classics translation today. Anyone can do it; everyone does.

The Septuagint was the fabled translation of the Old Testament from Hebrew into Greek by seventy-two scholars (Lat. *septuaginta* 'seventy'). The translation, originally limited to the Five Books of Moses (or Pentateuch), was commissioned by Ptolemy II Philadelphus for inclusion in the Library at Alexandria—especially for the Jews of Alexandria, who were far more conversant with Greek than with Hebrew. The individually sequestered scholars, as legend has it, rendered identical translations in what is the greatest, if not only, example of unanimity in translation history. The Septuagint, in *Koinē* 'common' dialect, was intended for ready comprehension by the Greek-speaking masses.

Over five hundred years were required for a similar development in Latin. With the advent of Christianity, the need for liturgical texts prompted a new translation of the Bible into Latin, undertaken by Saint Jerome. The translation was known as the Vulgate, intended, by its simplicity, as a Bible for the masses (Lat. *vulgus* 'crowd, mass'; *vulgare* 'disseminate'; hence, Vulgar Latin). *Vulgar* in this context denotes what is 'common', without negative connotation. The Vulgate later included Jerome's translation of the Greek New Testament. From then on, Latin would essentially be Church or Christian Latin. The Vulgate was to the Bible in Latin what the Septuagint was in Greek. It was notably the first translation of the Old Testament into Latin from the Hebrew rather than from the (Greek) Septuagint.

Jerome undertook Hebrew tutorials and moved to Bethlehem to complete the Vulgate. What other translator has taken such pains to master a language? Not for nothing was Jerome a saint. As the Septuagint was the source of all *Latin* translations of the Old Testament until the Vulgate, the Vulgate was the source of all *English* translations of the Old and New Testaments until William Tyndale's early sixteenth-century translations directly from the Hebrew and Greek. The Vulgate enjoyed monumental influence for over one thousand years. The version for the Gutenberg Bible of 1456, the Vulgate had a critical impact on the religion, social fabric, literature, art, and music of the Middle Ages and Renaissance, infusing itself into every purposeful thought and activity—this, in equal parts because of Jerome's consummate abilities and the ultimate dissemination of his work through print. Commending Jerome, the translators of the King James Bible noted the muddiness of the secondhand Latin versions of Jerome's time. These "prompted St. Jerome, a scholarly Father and undoubtedly the best linguist of his age, or of any that were before him, to undertake a translation of the Old Testament from the sources themselves. This he accomplished with such evidence of great learning, judgment, industry, and faithfulness, that he has forever bound the Church to him in a debt of special remembrance and thankfulness."

Tyndale's Old and New Testaments were the most widely used Bible versions until the King James Bible (KJB) of 1611—on which Tyndale had a "commanding effect" (there being eight Bible translations in between). The King James Bible, also known as the King James Version or Authorized Version, was and remains the paramount example of great translation as great literature, a cornerstone (together with Shakespeare) of an exalted literary age, and a transformative influence on all that followed. Though significantly relying on both Tyndale and the Bishop's Bible (1568), the KJB was a source-language translation—i.e., a translation from the Hebrew by translators who knew the language. The KJB inevitably became a model for the translation of Homer.

The primary impetus to this development was Matthew Arnold, applying what one critic has tellingly called, "the somewhat blighting demands of unimpassioned common sense." Arnold (1822–1888) was a British poet, critic, classicist, and the Professor of Poetry at Oxford. His savagely sardonic, book-length *On Translating Homer* (1861) was and remains an unrivaled critique of Homeric translation and of translation practice in general. Arnold urged that "the Bible is undoubtedly the grand mine of diction for the translator of Homer; and, if he knows how to discriminate truly between what will suit him and what will not, the Bible may afford him also invaluable lessons of style." The *Iliad* and Old Testament have thus ever been bellwethers of what English translation should accomplish and be. Translation in these two instances transcends the mere conveyance of meaning, becoming a monument to religious and cultural preservation. "The centrality of the biblical, is most obvious in English-language literatures," observes literary critic George Steiner (b. 1929), who further asserts, "To speak English or Anglo-American is 'to speak the Bible.'" The biblical and classical precedent has a sense of persistent authority, and "has been one of the principal forces—perhaps *the* principal force—during some two millennia of Western sensibility. It has largely determined the Western image of reason and of form. The new design, the new utterance, are tested within and against the exemplary legacy." We here particularly note the emphasis on form.

Among the translations that followed Arnold's famous challenge and critique was the 1883 King Jamesian prose translation of the *Iliad* by Andrew Lang, Walter Leaf, and Ernest Meyers. This had been preceded by the 1879 prose *Odyssey* of Andrew Lang and S. H. Butcher. The biblicizing translators argued that "the Greek Epic dialect, like the English of our Bible, was a thing of slow growth and composite nature," and both, being exclusively literary, were never spoken; thus "the Biblical English seems as nearly analogous to the Epic Greek as anything our tongue has to offer." Biblicized Homer, in a pre-media, preelectronic, and thus significantly more literate age than our own, remained the most popular Homer well into the twentieth century. Though in time appearing dated, it evidences a proprietous sensibility the envy of *any* age. As *New York Times* columnist Charles McGrath noted in 2011, marking the four-hundredth anniversary of the King James Bible, "Not everyone prefers a God [or Zeus] who talks like a pal or guidance counselor. Even some of us who are non-believers want a God who speaketh like—well, God." Questionable preference is nonetheless characteristic of contemporary translators, though the problem predates them, and the modernizing tendency has ever occurred "at the usual risk of vulgarizing a Classic in the attempt to make it more popular."

It is, in sum, by repeated translation over time that the Classics retain their standing and appeal, an appeal nowadays more often enhanced by the translation's controversial nature than by any intrinsic merit. In discussing the translation of an ancient author, be it Sappho or any other, one thus necessarily begins with the translation of Homer. And as Homeric translation itself inevitably yielded to biblical translational impulses, one also looks to the Old Testament in English.

Whereas the literatures of the developed European nations have, with certain exceptions, only marginally influenced one another, it is otherwise with Homer and the Bible. The two works, including the classics devolved from Homer, constitute the West's "supra-national literary past." In fact, Homer and the Bible seem peculiarly, perhaps fatedly, to have "tracked" each other throughout time. Of comparable date are their (1) central events—the Trojan War and Hebrew Exodus, dated to the mid-thirteenth century BC; (2) formative phases—biblical prose development and Homeric oral tradition, dated to the ninth and eighth centuries BC; (3) most authoritative manuscripts—Venetus A (*Iliad*) and Masoretic Text (Old Testament), dated to the tenth and eleventh centuries AD; and (4) most renowned English translations—Chapman's Homer (the first complete Homer in English) and the King James Bible, both published in 1611. In both traditions, moreover, issues of authorship, origin, and development are misted in time, even as rational or anthropomorphic worldviews come to predominate over the more extreme elements of mythology (however much myth claims a correspondence with reality).

The connection between Homer and the Old Testament has always been pronounced. When Friedrich August Wolf in 1795 published his *Prolegomena ad Homerum,* challenging long-held beliefs on the origin and unity of the Homeric poems, he was said to have upset everything "for thousands of years accepted as the origin, construction and authority of the literary monument which approached nearest in claim of antiquity to the Hebrew scriptures." This monument "had exercised an influence second only to scripture in the religious belief of nations," one "directing and governing, far more than any other writings whatever, the general sentiment and taste of the cultivated world." More briefly and colloquially put, "Homer is the Bible of the Greeks":

> But Homer is a poet for all ages, all races, and all moods. To the Greeks the epics were not only the best of romances, the richest of poetry; not only their oldest documents about their own history,—

> they were also their Bible, their treasury of religious traditions and moral teaching. With the Bible and Shakespeare, the Homeric poems are the best training for life.

Or again, according to Ezra Pound, "A civilization was founded on Homer"—Greek civilization and, by way of Rome, our own.

I include basic discussion of the meters of Greek epic and lyric—original epic meter of consuming interest to Arnold, as will be shown, not only for translating Homer but for "producing a literature that would revitalize the aesthetic and moral standards of his age." Greek epic, though the earlier-appearing genre, derives its meter from lyric. This is to say that although Homeric epic first appeared, it derived its meter and compositional underpinnings from only later-attested lyric—there being no surviving evidence of pre-epic lyric poetry. The lyric-to-epic influence has nonetheless been adduced by resourceful scholarly inference.

Greek meter, though rarely or only superficially covered in books for the lay reader, is essential. Meter in classical poetry is not simply a question of this or that rhythm. It is of the essence of the poetry itself, what makes classical poetry *poetry*. There is *no* poetry apart from meter—which is to say apart from *form*—and there is as surely no classical blank or free verse. The form and content of classical poetry are fully merged, wherein lies its beauty, efficacy, and enduring quality.

It is by *fixing* rhythm that meter creates poetic form. Metered poetry, always presenting as "fixed" or "fitted" form, is ever *artistic* in the root sense of the word *art* (Gr. **ar-*; Lat. *ars* [stem *art-*], 'fix, fit, join'). What is fixed or fitted is, in turn, *sta*tionary and remains (Lat. *sta-* 'stand'). What is fixed, fitted, or "fit" creates *sta*ndards (that which stands or remains), even as it contributes to civilization (that which stands or remains over time)—civilization's hallmark being a sense of *permanence* (Lat. *per* 'through' + *manē-* 'remain'). What fits not only stands but *sta*bilizes (causing other things to stand), and again contributes to civilization. The fit or "fittedness" of art and civilization—art the *stay* of civilization, civilization an artistic design—is the natural outgrowth of the fit of form and content at the verbal (or plastic) level. We note in this connection that the Greek root **ar-* "is thematically appropriate for designating both social and artistic cohesion," and that the concept of fixity or fittedness—of *order*—is intrinsic to the Indo-European heritage of Greece and Rome as reflected in their languages. Of the Greek and Latin remains surviving over millennia, there are works of incomparable expressiveness to show for the union of form and content—in a word, *classics*. By contrast, modern, modernist, and postmodern tendencies have encouraged the free-verse approach—which is to say, free of form most of all and, by degree, of meaning and importance. Suffice it presently to say that free verse is a fundamental departure from the definition and intent of poetry, historically understood.

As the "essence of the artistic life is the production of effects permanently delightful and profitable to other people," civilization—its intended *permanence*—is the idealized goal and outcome of art; is *art itself* as an ideal fit of *constituent* elements (*con* 'together' + *sta*tuere 'set up' = *constituere*). As art endures, so do those who foster art and appreciate its underlying meaning and value. For Matthew Arnold and his generation, the comprehensiveness of epic's venerable and art-generative meter, dactylic hexameter, foretold the greatness and grasp of imperial destiny, of its civilizing and sustaining aims. These thoughts will be further developed.

This book contains an indictment, searing at times, of the past generation of translators—most of them modern or modernist and, as noted, without sufficient, if any, knowledge of Greek and Latin. They could not have succeeded on their own. Foremost among the abettors were William Arrowsmith (1924–1992) and D. S. Carne-Ross (1921–2010), principally through their journals *Arion* (still in print) and *Delos* (six volumes only). Notably, indeed surprisingly, involved was the renowned Bernard Knox (1914–2010). Knox's sixty-four-page introduction to the essentially Greekless Robert Fagles's *Iliad* (1990), to say nothing of Knox's esteemed imprimatur, propelled the translation to acclaims, awards, and prodigious commercial success. Needing no aiding and abetting, but himself the spur to translation run amok in the twentieth century, was Ezra Pound, primarily through his *Homage to Sextus Propertius* (1919). *Homage* confounded the distinction between translation and whatever else a derivative work might be or be called. It was the Greekless (and largely Latinless) Pound who encouraged the Greek-deficient Mary Barnard's translation of Sappho (1958), though it was from an Italian crib, as noted, that she ultimately made her translation. Barnard's *Sappho* introduced twentieth-century English-language readers to Sappho, remaining the most widely read Sappho to date (and always in print). Otherwise directly or indirectly influencing the translations or adaptations of others, Pound is ultimately responsible for the present morass. He was the modernist darling of William Arrowsmith, D. S. Carne-Ross, and *Arion*, including the Greekless *Arion* regular and Pound-stalwart Guy Davenport (1927–2005), well known for his translations of Sappho and Archilochus. All are discussed in the chapters that follow.

The practice of original-languageless translation was first noted—and lamented—thirty years ago by the long-lived classicist-translator L. R. Lind (1906–2008), past chairman of the Department of Classics at the University of Kansas. His words ring with the wisdom of the Heartland:

> Strange new theories are abroad these days about the technique and process of translation. Accuracy is now frowned upon and faithfulness to the original is regarded as at best an error in taste and at worst an anachronistic delusion. Even a nodding acquaintance with the original is no longer necessary; it is, in fact, looked upon . . . as a serious handicap to know Greek if you are setting out to translate Homer. . . . Structure, moreover, which means a handling of the original largely in terms of the movie-technique, the historical analogies of Pound's 'Cantos', and the use of staccato typography, is to be accepted instead of words, that is, words which accurately reflect Homer's Greek.

Original-languageless translation has only grown in audacity since first reproved by Lind. Behind the charade is the notion that the Greekless "poet-translator" is more likely to succeed than the assumedly unpoetic, or necessarily incompetent, classicist-translator; that the *poet* classicist-translator is so rare as to be dismissible. The bias may be dated to Dryden, who notes, "There are many who understand Greek and Latin, and yet are ignorant of their mother tongue." This, however, was not an invitation to those ignorant of Greek and Latin to give it a try, nor did it induce the practice as we have come to know it today. Greekless and Latinless translation of the Classics has persisted for more than half a century and is ever and perversely commended as the proverbial "making a virtue of necessity." The one translator's work is thus "beautiful despite the lack of formal training"; the other's, as most recently noted, is "particularly memorable for its candor about the fact that [the translator] did not know any Greek." Thus glossing the translator's failings—or perhaps even unaware of them—reviewers shower the works with praise.

We have reached the sorry point of having to distinguish among translators, among those who know their source language and those who—brazenly by self-confession—do not. Granted, acclaimed translators of the past have sometimes been less than firmly grounded in their originals. However, the dichotomy between learned and unlearned has never been as marked as it now is. Scribimus indocti doctique poemata passim, wrote Horace, 'We are everywhere penning poems, the learned and unlearned alike'. Or, in the rendering of politician and Classics translator Philip Francis (1740–1818), "Each desperate blockhead dares to write." The rebuke applies equally to original poets and poetry translators, as the line between them is frequently thin, and verse translation may often surpass original verse in quality. In sum, "poet" standing is no substitute for ignorance of the original, the assumption having arisen that classicists are somehow too stodgy and text-bound to soar; that for all their knowledge, love, and appreciation of classical poetry, they are incapable of poetry in English.

The failure to distinguish between learned and unlearned is the one shortcoming of George Steiner's magisterial—here as in everything he writes—"Homer in English" and *After Babel.* In his anthology essay "Homer in English," Steiner broadly speaks of Homeric "variants, re-creations, pastiches and travesties"—as though all of a kind in the great and ongoing venture that is Homeric translation. He nods equally to such disparate claimants as Rieu, Lattimore, Fitzgerald, Fagles, and Logue in what he calls "the unique radioactive tracer" that is the "sequence of translations from Homer." Steiner is not alone. The perceptive Richard H. Armstrong similarly speaks of the "translational *series,*" which over time "begins to constitute its own system."

Notes Steiner, "The radioactive tracer which these successive versions allow us to follow lights up not only the history of the English languages and their interrelations. It tells of the reciprocities 'in motion' as between different translators and readers of Homer. Each translator competes more or less openly with the great family of his predecessors." The problem is that there are no qualifying heats for the competition, and that the Greekless translator is bastard progeny in the "family of his predecessors." Nor do we rely on dabblers and dilettantes to illumine language and literacy appreciation, any more than we look to a "reciprocity" between translator and reader. What matters is the reader's intuition of something *beyond* the translator and to which the translator is ultimately irrelevant—even as the greatest art conceals its means. Steiner further observes that the translator in one way or another "'takes on' both Homer and the English or American 'Homers' already in the field." Adapting Steiner's colloquialism, I propose that we have mere *takes* on Homer—and those little worth the having. Steiner elsewhere proposes that "to understand is to decipher. To hear significance is to translate." What does the languageless translator hear or understand, that he might translate?

In *After Babel*, a seminal work on translation, Steiner displays near reverence for the languageless translator. With nods to Pound, Lowell, Logue, and others, Steiner maintains that "some of the most persuasive translations in the history of the *métier* have been made by writers ignorant of the language from which they were translating." Further skewed is Steiner's inclusion of Latin with Chinese, Japanese, and Mongolian as a rare or exotic language—Latin the language of Europe for more than a millennium. In many such cases, continues Steiner, it is not only the languageless "common reader . . . [who] feels convinced" but, as may be the case, "the original poet or native speaker to whom the English text is shown for judgement." Well, in some cases, perhaps—though such approvals are quite beside the point. Indeed, they ignore the searing critique that Nabokov leveled against Lowell's Mandelstam translations, and the highly disfavoring Italian reception of Lowell's Montale (see Chapter 34).

"In Pound's imitations of China [i.e., *Cathay*]," notes Steiner, "in Logue's Homer, ignorance of the relevant language is a paradoxical advantage. No semantic specificity, no particularity of context interposes itself between the poet-translator and a general, cultural-conventional sense of 'what the thing is or ought to be.'" Really? This but credits our gullibility and confirms our misunderstandings. Indeed, Steiner is not in the least dissuaded or deterred by the languageless translator, and certainly not by the likes of Pound, Lowell, and Logue—the most egregious of the lot. These, he says, succeed by a kind of "clairvoyance," the "insinuation of the self into otherness [being] the final secret of the translator's craft." In truth, these sooner succeed by dint of assumed, if not expected, reader heedlessness, encouraged by uncaring publishers and reviewer abettors. The reason for Steiner's unwillingness to distinguish among the qualified and unqualified is clear from his early deification of Pound, even before Pound's death: "If our age of poetic translation rivals that of Golding, Gavin Douglas and Chapman, it is because of the teaching and example of Ezra Pound." And, "Inevitably much of the translation in this book implies and was made possible by Pound's enlargement of the term." Bigger is apparently better. Its uncharacteristic fuzziness aside, Steiner's view is simply self-contradictory. Steiner notes, "Ninety percent, no doubt, of all translation since Babel is inadequate and will continue to be so." Languageless translation apparently adds nothing to the count.

❧

Historically viewed, my position constitutes a latter-day chapter in the *querelle des anciens et des modernes* 'quarrel of the ancients and moderns'. The quarrel first emerged in the late seventeenth century between those who believed the Classics should be faithfully represented as a linguistic, literary, and artistic model and those, believing in "progress," who argued that "updatings" and contemporary understandings were required for present consumption. The two camps were led by Boileau and Perrault, respectively. For those arguing the "modern" view, judgments concerning the works of antiquity were relative, reflecting the passage of time and perspective since the works' creation; and contemporary authors, because "modern," were of unequaled enlightenment. The failure of the modernist view, then as now, was its lack of appreciation of the constancy of human nature. As the young Mary Stewart so perceptively observed in her *Catullus, An Experiment in Translation* (1905): "Next to Horace, Catullus seems to us the most modern of the ancients—that is, if there is any *most*. They are all contemporaries when we get acquainted with them. It is amazing to find out how modern all these writers are, which is just another way of saying how ancient human nature is." The sentiment was lost on the likes of Ezra Pound and Robert Lowell, for whom the Classics were never modern enough. Indeed, the Classics were traduced and ruined in the effort to make them so.

The updatings tendency is evident in what has been called "personal voice theory"—described in a sympathetic assessment as "a very different kind of intervention into ongoing critical discourse . . . a practicum in a type of criticism that eschews the traditional scholarly stance of objectivity and detachment and incorporates 'the critic's own story' into the analysis of classical literature." Personal voice theory has otherwise, and more appropriately, been rebuffed as a "drive to subvert thinking and speaking on classics, to insist that the discourse [is] open to an Americanizing emphasis upon showbiz, commercialism, feminism," or what you will. Personal voice theory, in sum, parades the self and injects it into scholarship. However, in a quip most often ascribed to Mark Twain, "Be yourself is about the worst advice you can give some people."

A tributary of the *querelle des anciens et des modernes* was the so-called Homer War waged between Greek scholar, Homericist, and inveterate Sappho translator Anne Lefèvre Dacier (1674–1720) and the essentially Greekless Homer translator Antoine Houdar de la Motte (1672–1731). It was Dacier's prose translation of the *Iliad* (1699) that essentially introduced French readers to Homer. When in 1714 La Motte published a poetic version, abridged and altered to his own taste, he announced, "Ainsi, j'ai changé sans scrupule toutes les circonstances, pour rétablir la gloire des deux Héros de l'Iliade," that he had 'thus, and without compunction, altered all elements to reestablish the glory of the *Iliad*'s two heroes'. Not to establish or convey, but *rétablir* 'reestablish'.

The revisionist agenda, sacrificing original context to contemporary message, is clear:

> La Motte's words can be read to mean that the classical heritage could be exploited freely to one's own ends, and that its historical character had no value in itself, in the antiquarian or ethnographical sense. The view of translation as an act of communication was directly opposed by Mme. Dacier's idea, which regarded the original text as the perfect copy for the translation, save for the different language. La Motte treated Achilles and Hector as universal heroic types whose humanity had been obscured by the imperfect poetic language of Homer and the unfortunately crude moral code of

> their age. La Motte's main argument was that the original context could be sacrificed for a contemporary message.

The Homer War is as much with us today as ever, its twentieth- and twenty-first-century instances discussed in the chapters that follow. Equally the issue for this volume is what may be called the "Sappho War," with aberrancies the worse (by contrast to Homer) for the fragmentary state of Sappho's survival. Involving the corruption of taste (*corruption du goût*) in the service of a triumphalist feminism—via an often marked indifference to the limits of reasonable inference—"contemporary approaches" have augured ill for confidence in the Classics, whatever remains of them in the aftermath of political correctness. "Who Killed Homer?" ask Victor Davis Hanson and John Heath in the provocative book title of their 2001 publication subtitled, "The Demise of Classical Education and the Recovery of Greek Wisdom." The question is equally well posed of Sappho and lyric poetry.

We are reminded, by contrast, that Dryden "had long been a careful student of Virgil and above all of Virgilian expression and Virgilian metrical practice." In the dedication to his immediately and ever-renowned translation of the *Aeneid*, Dryden wrote:

> Long before I undertook this work, I was no stranger to the original. I had also studied Virgil's design, his disposition of it, his manners, his judicious management of the figures, the sober retrenchments of his sense, which always leaves somewhat to gratify our imagination, on which it may enlarge at pleasure; but above all, the elegance of his expressions, and the harmony of his numbers.

Coleridge provides a further example. Though translating little from Greek and Latin—looking more to modern languages, German most of all—Coleridge enjoyed a foundational relationship with the Classics. His understanding of Classical Greek was impeccable, while his affinity with classical authors "provided a comprehensive reference point and scale of values, beyond linguistic differences, for the way he thought about poetry and its place in the world." We have long since passed from Dryden's sense of "judicious management" and Coleridge's well-informed "reference point" to something exceeding hubris—call it flamboyant self-indulgence. If our poetic forebears could only see today's poet-translators—blithely self-confessed strangers to the original, hand-holding with scholar-coaches in starry-eyed stumbles through wonderland.

Seeking to flag and remedy this situation, I offer an aesthetic for the translation of classical poetry—lyric and epic most of all. The aesthetic—not to be confused with theory—is nowhere stated or encapsulated as such, but emerges from discussion and example. As further concerns theory, I follow E. M. Forster's caveat (1951) that "a theory in the modern world has little power over the fine arts, for good or evil. . . . A more practical activity for criticism is the sensitive dissection of particular works of art." I subscribe to the prescient outlook of W. S. Marris (1912)—then of the India Civil Service, formerly scholar of Christ Church, Oxford—in his often consummately rhymed and metered Horace: "This version of the Odes of Horace has not been written according to any theory. Metres have not been appropriated to metres . . . nor even to types of odes. I have simply tried to find the English into which each ode fell most readily, and for the rest to write readable verse, as faithfully as I could make it to the Latin consistently with being always English." Similarly disavowing theory, I neither reference nor make use of "translation theory" or "translation studies," as these oppress with their intractable jargon and after-the-fact considerations.

A return to pre-theoretical and once-unquestioned norms, my work is frightfully old-fashioned, making me, like George Steiner—to compare small with great—"a reactionary mastodon out of the lost past." Grounded in a philologically based understanding of the original, my aesthetic derives from considerations of (1) *form relative to content*—inextricably bound in classical poetry; (2) *diction*—in translation, the choice and arrangement of words; in classical poetry itself, the same—but with focus on the significance of words and their variants in related contexts, both within and outside a single work or author; and (3) *decorum*—the exercise in translation of artistic judgment in the use of diction and setting of tone, a tone appropriate to the original. Or as Robert Graves has said concerning decorum, diction, and tone, "A translator's first duty must always be to choose the appropriate level of his own language for any particular task." Today, alas, an appreciation of the connection between form and content is a dim memory, while diction and decorum—once the cornerstone and pillar of great poetry—are in ruins.

Much is also to blame in ideology-driven feminist scholarship. By feminist scholarship I mean *radical* feminist scholarship, which claims Sappho as its own and theorizes her beyond recognition. I examine the underpinnings of such scholarship, politically correct and Marxist in turn. My concern, to that extent, lies not only with classical and Western culture but with the culture wars and their crippling effects. Especially harmful to the treatment of Sappho is the union of theorizing scholar and Greek-deficient or Greekless translator. To encounter this combination is to answer the question posed in Sappho's great "Hymn to Aphrodite": "Who, O Sappho / Does you wrong?"

I aim, in biblical parlance, to "make the crooked straight," or at least fix some sign posts. Coincidentally, *diorthōtēs* 'one who thoroughly straightens' was the Greek word applied to the first systematic "editors" of classical texts in third- and second-century Alexandria. As the German-Anglo philologist Otto Skutsch (1906–1990) advised, "More than the Natural Sciences, the result of whose studies are perpetually checked against and corrected by their object, the Arts, if they are to maintain the standard of accuracy and honesty which alone makes such studies worth while, need, from time to time, a violent corrective to certain frailties of the human mind." To correct *and* reclaim—such is my uncongenial objective.

# Chapter 2

## Greekless Translators, Theorizing Scholars

> Sappho, like Shakespeare, has a remarkable quality of attracting idolators, pseudo-moralists, spinmeisters (mostly with a feminist agenda), and a wide range of crackpot theorists, ranging from the benignly dotty to the angrily obsessive. Her case has also been taken up ferociously by serious feminists of just about every persuasion.
>
> – PETER GREEN, *The New Republic*

As Homer is the earliest attested, most ambitious, most perfected, and most fully preserved and influential of all ancient Greek poets, he has long been a singular focus of translation and translation concern. Considerations of Greek lyric in translation are thus intertwined with those of Homer in translation. Although their themes, dialects, and meters differ, the translation of epic and lyric—or of any ancient Greek or Latin poetry—entails similar considerations of form and content. By polar contrast to poetry in English since Walt Whitman, form was inseparable from content in ancient poetry. The richness, insistent formality, and shared particularities of ancient Greek and Latin made it so.

Latin authors did not as a rule translate their Greek forebears, but imitated, incorporated, or transformed them. This is especially so in the case of Virgil. Emulation was the starting point. Indeed, the development of Latin literature is grounded in the ready assimilation of ancient Greek models and their adaptability to formal innovation, i.e., to Latin meter and a Roman, imperial worldview. The language of ancient Greek poetry, in its various meters and dialects, was a peculiarly literary and artificial language—artificial in the sense of developed and employed entirely for artistic purposes, and at no time spoken. It was *thus* appreciated by its authors and audiences from generation to generation throughout centuries of use. Such language was of the essence of the experience, at once facilitating composition, comprehension, and genre preservation. Its indebtedness to Greek aside, Classical Latin has a literary "artificiality" all its own.

This reality, however, goes largely unnoted by translators today with scant knowledge, if not an avowed ignorance, of Greek. Sidestepping the creative, taking unwarranted and often prosaic liberties with the text, struggling with rhythm, and all but incapable of rhyme, translators boast "straightforward" or "contemporary" renderings. These, as they suppose, best convey the spirit or feeling of the original. It is sooner the case that morphologically simple English—including the virtual absence of conjugations and declensions and, by consequence, a necessarily predictable word order—bodes poorly for capturing the precision and nuance of classical languages, even as the richness of English vocabulary helps offset the deficiency. For this reason, English must effectively use all devices at its disposal—rhythm, rhyme, alliteration, assonance, and its full lexical range (including selective older usages or archaism)—to convey what it may of ancient Greek or Latin beyond meaning alone.

It is amusing to note the extent to which the obvious has often required emphasis. The fifteenth-century Venetian humanist Ermolao Barbaro criticized contemporary Aristotelians for knowing neither Latin nor Greek, claiming there was no separating the eloquence of the original Greek from its philosophic content. Barbaro disparaged even the medieval Latin and Arabic commentators on Aristotle as being too far removed from Greek commentators closer in time and thought to their subject. In a letter of 1485 to fellow humanist Pico della Mirandola, Barbaro emphasizes the importance of studying Greek texts in the original, urging Pico to "become as thoroughly familiar with Greek" as with Latin, aware (as Pico is) that "for many centuries no Latin author has produced a monumental work without also knowing Greek." To separate Greek philosophy from the language in which it is written is to separate it from its inherent eloquence and philological underpinnings. Long intuited, the dictum equally applies to Greek literature. As Matthew Arnold has said, it is not "*fidelity* to an original to give its matter, unless you at the same time give its manner." More decidedly, it is "the union of the translator with his original, which alone can produce a good translation." These are self-evident propositions somehow lost on today's source-languageless translator, on the dilettante and dabbler.

Distinguished from the Greekless translators are the numerous Greekless or near-Greekless adapters or paraphrasers, those somehow taken by Greek poetry and wanting to convey their own sense of it. The circle comes fully round, however. Relying on translations or other assistance, such handlers ever distance the result from its original significance and power. Meanwhile, those knowing the original invariably pass on paraphrase or imitation as idle, except for the résumé enhancement that comes from reviewing it or writing edition introductions. That leaves the Greekless reader to suffer the results. This is not to dismiss the possibility of inspired or edifying imitation. To be sure, bonafide translation is *itself* a form of imitation—and most often imitation enough. What one wants in poetic translation is the at-once literate and literary conveyance of meaning and emotion. The key then is making clear what one is doing: translating, paraphrasing, imitating, adapting, transplanting, reconstructing, personalizing, abstracting, extemporizing, modernizing. The distinctions are little observed, with too much passed off as "translation."

❧

It is Sappho who most attracts the Greekless translator. Her antiquity, her name recognition, her sexual persona beckon, even as the fragmentary state of her poetry and its widely disparate translation invite meddling sans risk or exposure. The amateur wants to be "on board," imagining he can somehow improve on things, indeed, be definitive. "The monolithic nature of classic translations, the timelessness and immortality they confer, has always proved a very attractive proposition not just for translators but also for poets, who, like all writers, are of course concerned about the longevity of their work." Side by side with the amateur translator of lyric is the Greekless or marginally lettered translator of Homer and Virgil—sometimes also a translator of lyric and drama, sometimes perhaps with a year or two of college Latin or a bit of elective or self-taught Greek, most often a professor of English. His own vineyard apparently harvested, the English professor has wandered afield to do the classicist's work. Typically a self-professed or variously acclaimed poet, he is on that account a knowing and ready classics translator. One would think the epic undertaking too vast, the exposure too great, the folly immediately apparent. That, however, has proven no obstacle to plaudits, preferments, and sales in the millions of copies.

Aligned with the would-be translators are the academics, looking more to themselves—egos, theories, and predilections—than to Sappho's poetry. This follows, first, from notions advanced over thirty years ago by literary theorist Geoffrey Hartman (b. 1929). Hartman proposed that while traditional criticism had served and exalted literature, the then emerging criticism would privilege, or also privilege, the *critic*, resulting in a "literature of criticism." Quaint notions of the text's basic or apparent meaning would yield to the critics' readings or "interrogations"—the canonic work now secondary to the interpretive act; what the text says or means, secondary to what the critic says or means, or to what the critic considered or thought about during his work in progress. The most recent major example of this approach is Sappho translator Josephine Balmer's *Piecing Together the Fragments: Translating Classical Verse, Creating Contemporary Poetry* (2013).

The emphasis on one's self and one's own predilections further follows from the fragmentary state of Greek lyric, its sexual and personal nature, and the ideological temperament of politically correct and "postmodern" times. As the poetry itself is both first person and highly fragmented, it is as readily personalized as politicized in the course of "restorative" interpretation. Reviewing feminist writings on Sappho, Marilyn Katz writes, "Interpretation of Sappho's poetry . . . necessarily involves a great deal of reading between the lines and inevitably invites speculative reconstruction of poetic context, sociocultural situation, and biographical detail." If this is the "necessary" and "inevitable" result of Sappho's scant remains, the cause lies first with a lack of restraint. And further:

> As the principal female voice to survive from Greek antiquity, Sappho is pressed into service to speak for all women, and the history of ancient, modern, and contemporary commentary on Sappho devolves easily into a study of critical stereotypes of the ancient Greek woman. Sappho's 'I' seems always to precipitate our own: there is little discussion of her work that does not, willy-nilly, fall into the category of 'personal voice criticism.'

The process is hardly "willy-nilly," but programmatic, and if Sappho is "pressed into service to speak for all women," it is largely by feminist scholars that she is thus indentured. Such scholars constitute what classicist and Sappho scholar Thomas McEvilley calls "a contemporary academic *thiasos*," i.e., 'band' or 'coterie' of Sappho scholars (by analogy to the coterie postulated for the "Sapphic circle" itself). The resultant field, says McEvilley, "has almost become what it studies, a new 'female initiatory discourse . . . conducted in the sheltered atmosphere of the *thiasos*'—the thiasos in this case being the sheltered and cultic atmosphere of classical studies in academia." Finally, Sappho's "I" can only wishfully be thought "always to precipitate our [feminine plural] own," but is as distant and distinct from it as incorporeal from corporeal matter. What Katz offers is an apologia for a process which, as we shall see, "restores" both text and feminist interpreter—the former to middling advantage; the latter, more than anything else, to the interpreter's advantage alone. The process, seeking to establish the primacy of women's scholarship vis-à-vis the premiere woman poet of all time, is above all political.

The present work takes Sappho *at face value*, restoring her to common sense based on the meaning of her words in context. As David Mendelsohn wisely notes (his own predilections sometimes notwithstanding):

> As alluring and provocative to us today as the notion of 'the fragmentary' may be, it must be said that it has no meaningful relation to the presumed object of serious scholarly and translational energies, which is some kind of responsible representation of Sappho herself to the wider world—even if that representation must remain partial and unsatisfying to the world, eager as it is to see her in its own reflection.

The hyper-interpretation of Sappho is thus a matter of narcissism, individual and group—the preference of self over subject matter, of often belabored say-sos to the perfect and perfectly simple sentiments of antiquity, for therein lies their enduring beauty.

The greatness of Greek literature, notes Goethe, lies not so much in individual authors or artists, but in "the nation and the whole period." In other words, appreciation begins with the horizon, not the mirror. Choosing two of the classical host he admires, Goethe goes on to say that "beside the great

Attic poets, like Aeschylus and Sophocles, I am absolutely nothing." Like Socrates, Goethe professes to know only the *limits* of his own understanding—however much he (Goethe) was infused with Faustian striving and the "self-absorption required for [his] project of manifold literary, philosophic, and scientific mastery." An example unknown to politicized late twentieth-century scholars of Sappho, Goethe's self-humbling was instinctively appreciated by classicists of the early twentieth century—not that their eras were free of politics. Such scholars respected the boundary between politics and scholarship. Their interpretations were personal, to be sure—the source of their persuasiveness and charm—but not personalized and never theory-driven.

I do not track Sappho reception or offer a history of Sappho scholarship and translation. For better or worse, I have chosen, and in one case resurrected, two early and two late twentieth-century scholars, by their lives and works bridging the past one hundred and fifty years. These exemplify the extremes by which Sappho and the lyric poets have either benefited or suffered. They as surely exemplify the difference between academic discipline, including self-discipline, and the theory-driven self-indulgence of recent decades.

I focus first on Thomas George ("T. G.") Tucker (1859–1946) and Gilbert Murray (1866–1957), both hailing from the Antipodes. The since forgotten Tucker was one-time professor of Classical Philology at the University of Melbourne. Especially famed for his editions and commentaries on Aeschylus, he made one dazzling interpretive foray into Sappho, with a number of stunning translations. These are as alluring as they have been inaccessible—reminiscent, as it were, of Sappho's apple, past reach atop the highest bough (§17). The Australian-born Gilbert Murray was professor of Greek at Glasgow University, Regius Professor of Greek at Oxford, and Eliot Norton Lecturer at Harvard. Murray was prolific in many areas, including the politics of his day. I was pleased to find that his essay on Greek meter, read only after I had completed the translations of this volume, had much anticipated my approach. In the late nineteenth and early twentieth centuries, a broadly humanistic and thus *relevant* professoriate encountered a largely Classics-educated and thus receptive public. It was from public lectures as the Professor of Poetry at Oxford that Matthew Arnold, only a generation earlier, had written his epochal *On Translating Homer* (1861), even as leading Victorian art critic

John Ruskin (1819–1900) had invited his reader "to compare [Homeric passage] translations closely with the Greek version, which we will not insult him by supposing that he does not possess it."

Turning for comparative purposes to the late twentieth century, I consider Anne Carson and Page duBois. Anne Carson has taught Classics and Comparative Literature at the University of Michigan, New York University, McGill, Princeton, and Berkeley. She is a Canadian poet, essayist, and translator of Sappho and the Greek tragedians, and the recipient of many recognitions for her work. She is widely known for her *Eros the Bittersweet* (1986), described by *Slate* magazine as "a wittily epigrammatic analysis of the role of Eros in Greek culture." Carson, continues *Slate,* "marshals examples from Sappho, Plato, and lesser-known Greek poets, deftly explicating their vision of erotic love as temporary, contingent, and characterized by a thrilling sensation of lack. . . . Well-received among classicists, *Eros* quickly percolated into the living rooms of literary essayists. . . . Carson was singled out as a bracingly original writer by the likes of Harold Bloom, Susan Sontag, and Annie Dillard." Noteworthy for purposes of this study is Carson's emphasis throughout on edges, limits, boundaries, and separations. Such concerns flow naturally from *lack*—lack being separation, the divide between want and attainment—and are central to Carson's reading of Sappho and the Greek lyricists. Her inquiry on the whole is itself sharp-edged and revelatory, if sometimes teasing or oracular.

Page duBois, a professor of Classics and Comparative Literature at the University of California, San Diego, is the much-published author of *Sappho Is Burning* (1995). A radical feminist and tiresomely self-proclaimed Marxist, duBois offers what she calls "boundarylessness" as an interpretive approach. The result invites chaos—knowingly and inescapably. DuBois, as her reviewers note, writes not for the generalist, or even the undergraduate, but for the advanced student and like-minded professoriate. What will today's advanced student—tomorrow's teacher and professor—take away from this encounter with the pedagogy of oppression and resentment, this substitute for what Matthew Arnold famously called "the best which has been thought and said in the world"? The "best" is nowadays passé, elitist, oppressive—the casualty of Marxism, which is the *worst* that has been thought and *done* in the world. Katz's review essay (2000) of feminist approaches to Sappho awards pride of place and discussion to *Sappho Is*

*Burning*—"a sophisticated, challenging, and exciting book on Sappho and the difference Sappho makes." Katz, even so, includes a caveat, that the book "will be easy to criticize—even dismiss—since its style and rhetoric replicate both the fragmentation and excess of its subject matter, for example, 'Fragmentary Introduction.'" This, as will be seen, is the least of it. Having attained iconic status in the more than twenty years since its publication, the book even now warrants attention.

Marxism has everywhere been discredited and defeated, except in China, North Korea, Cuba, certain South American and African enclaves, and the college campus. The radical feminist/Marxist approach to Sappho is, not surprisingly, subversive, concerned more with ideology than with poetry. And yet, however much in earnest the approach may be, it cannot be taken seriously. Harold Bloom, the twentieth century's most traditionally appreciative and outspoken reader of Western literature, also belongs to the Marxist school of criticism—the Groucho Marx school, as he says, whose motto is "Whatever it is, I'm against it."

❧

As concerns Sappho's translators, their treasons are discussed in due course. We earlier noted the popular adage, based on Italian wordplay, that the translator is a traitor—*traduttore traditore*—meaning any translation is necessarily a betrayal of meaning and spirit. While articles and entire books have adopted this conceit, I mention it only to note its more recent reality. The betrayal is nowadays not that of the well-intended, though ultimately unsuccessful, translator but of those purporting to translate from a language they don't know or only wishfully understand. Such efforts are destructive of reader trust and experience, as a given translation will likely be its reader's only original author encounter. Such translation further compromises culture and our understanding of it, illustrating that we are unable to preserve what we purport to value. The motivation for such translation varies, though vanity predominates.

Thus, even as Sappho lived and loved some 2,700 years ago, the work of her latter twentieth-century interpreters removes us further from her still. Ideologically driven (and invariably recondite) interpreters do better to impart basic understandings to first-time readers, however little the effort garners collegial recognition or advancement. The Greekless translator, for his part, does better to prune his own vineyard. The present work is largely motivated by these concerns, if not by the special concern of returning Greek lyric to its expressive beauty and clarity of thought. The Greekless translator, more than the "boundaryless" interpreter, dominated the early 1980s, when my initial work on Sappho first appeared. The present work thus sharpens its critique of the translators while for the first time engaging with the interpreters.

# Chapter 3

## Selected Lyric Poets of Antiquity: Archilochus, Alcman, Anacreon & Ibycus

> Of all the poets of the world, of all the illustrious artists of all literatures, Sappho is the one whose every word has a peculiar and unmistakable perfume, a seal of absolute perfection and illimitable grace. In her art she was unerring. Even Archilochus seems commonplace when compared with her exquisite rarity of phrase.
>
> – HENRY T. WHARTON, *Sappho*

As concerns the poets other than Sappho included in this volume, I offer the following overviews. In so doing, I de-emphasize strictly biographical information. That Archilochus lived from 680–640 BC and was the son of a slave woman and an aristocrat from the island of Paros, or that Alcman is sometimes thought to have been a Lydian from Sardis, sometimes a Laconian from Messoa, is information as often mentioned as forgotten. What follows, then, are brief summaries to the extent relevant to erotic poetry or poetic persona (section marks indicating the poems as numbered in PART III).

### Archilochus

Archilochus of Paros (see map) is among the earliest Greek lyric poets. Though his diction is largely Homeric, he often deviates from the conventional epic outlook (e.g., §§82, 83). Archilochus's poems span a broad emotional range. He seeks to understand and adjust to the vagaries of life

(§81). He expresses the genuine emotion of the soldier-poet (§§78–80) in poems as much from the heart in their way as is his erotic verse. He is the most explicitly sexual (§§84–88). For all its constraint and veiled allusion, the lengthy Neoboulē fragment (§75) is without parallel. I omit two of Archilochus's poems only because their coarseness of tone is so unlike that of other pieces chosen for this volume.

As concerns poetic meter, Archilochus was the literary founder of the iamb—the repeated alternation of short and long syllables ( ◡ — )—conspicuous in English iambic pentameter. He was also the first extant Greek poet to use the trochee—an alternation of long and short syllables ( — ◡ )—less prominent in English, but found, for example, in Henry Wadsworth Longfellow's *Song of Hiawatha.* Iambic meter is considered by poet-critic Frederic Will (b. 1928), "one of the most 'heavily sensuous' of Greek meters," distinguished in its suggestiveness from the more stately dactylic hexameter of Homer (on which more below), marked by the varied alternation of dactyls ( — ◡ ◡ ) and spondees ( — — ). Archilochus's use and mixture of iambic and trochaic meter impart an "aural sensuousness [that] duplicates sensuous meaning." Notwithstanding the origin of iambic in early Greek religious invective (Gr. *iambo* 'assail'), the meter's adaptation to erotic ends exhibits a quality central to the appreciation of poetry as discussed herein: *decorum,* understood as "the proper harmony between manner and matter," i.e., between form and content.

The intrinsic qualities of his verse aside, a central event in the poet's life—reflected both in his work and in references by later writers—was his betrothal to one Neoboulē ('she of the new plan,' 'recently minded,' or 'new scheme') and her subsequent dispossession by her father, Lycambes, who married her off to a wealthier suitor (§§74, 75.21). The event is thought to have imparted the vehemence so characteristic of Archilochus's poetry. The legend, developed long after the poet's time, was that he so raged against Lycambes and his daughters that they hanged themselves in desperation.

Direct evidence of Lycambes or his daughters is, however, so scant as to call the event into question. Thus, if the verses do not reflect the poet's *own* person and situation, they serve an invective or vituperative function, which in turn determines both narrative and narrative persona. By *persona* we understand the poet's assumed or traditional role in a given genre. A piece like the Neoboulē fragment confirms what we also infer from other fragments, namely, an inherited tradition of vituperative poetry with stylized characters and themes. The issue is one of "assumed personality and the imaginary situation." Invective and its praise counterpart found social expression through the prime medium of verse. The genre's stylized characters include—as in the Neoboulē fragment—the betrayed or thwarted suitor, the wanton or wayward beloved, and the controlling father. The development of literary archetypes is in fact traceable to archaic Greek lyric, beginning with the conceits of vituperation and praise. We note that the relationship between invective and satire is often one of degree. Invective is aggravated satire, the difference between railing against and merely ridiculing. Invective is thus personalized, seeking to "search and destroy," while satire is generalized, blanketing current foibles. In either case, however, the character types have enjoyed a rich literary and performance afterlife.

Archilochean in its invective is the Old Comedy of Athenian Aristophanes (5th century BC), singling out, in fantastical plots, the politicos and sundry reprobates of the day. The New Comedy of Menander (4th and 3rd centuries BC), as shown by the title of his one surviving play—*Dyskolos* (*The Curmudgeon* or *Misanthrope*)—dealt not so much with individual characters as with types. As types act in predictable ways, the genre is known as "comedy of manners." It, in turn, influenced the Roman playwrights Plautus and Terence (3rd century BC). Roman comedy, e.g., *Menaechmi* (*The Menaechmus Brothers*) and *Miles Gloriosus* (*The Braggart Soldier*), further conventionalized Menandrean plot lines, even while recalling Archilochean themes of adultery, jealousy, and old age—the plots typically involving lovers pitted against disapproving elders. We have the "boor" of the Roman poet Horace (1st century BC), forever hallowed as the unflinching type he is, while the satirist Juvenal (1st and 2nd centuries AD) turns from Horace's gentle derisions to the invective-like denunciations of his own more profligate times.

The literary type is also a feature of Greek tragedy—a community-based religious experience in fifth-century Athens. Tragic characters often represent fixed ideas and positions: Creon, inflexible state authority and law; Hippolytus, steadfast and disdainful chastity; Ajax, insuperable and suicidal grievance; Philoctetes, inconsolable and isolating physical injury. Though tragic types helped to universalize the theater-going experience, they did not monopolize the stage. In marked contrast to the Creons and

Ajaxes is Orestes, uniquely and intractably duty-bound to slay his mother, thus avenging his father, whom she had murdered. As types are unchanging human nature writ large, their portrayals endure, which is to say, *they are always modern*; that they are *classic*—never "old" or outdated. Distinguished as types, they are necessarily exaggerated, caricatured. A primary vehicle of type-portrayal was sixteenth-century Commedia dell'Arte, its highly popular characters including Harlequin, Columbine, Pierrot, Scaramouch, and Pulcinella; "Pulcinella"—anglicized to "Punchinello"—begetting "Punch" of "Punch and Judy," with regional variants throughout Europe, including the principal character of Stravinsky's *Petrushka*.

Satire and vituperation seek to bruit a complaint to the world. What makes Archilochus's Neoboulē poem atypical, no less than significant, in this respect, "is the [unusual] absence of any attempt to give the narrator's experience a permanent or general significance, or to pass on a message to society. Even Archilochus, the archetypal misfit, usually felt moved to involve the community as a whole in his complaints and insults, and to give it the benefit of his advice." Such a view, urging a predominantly emotional response, is contrary to the idea, above stated, of the "poet's assumed or traditional role in a given genre." In fact, the issue of private versus public permeates archaic Greek lyric. Sappho's poetry is what a later age would deem predominantly private. Yet Sappho too is thought to offer a predetermined public persona, dictated by the assumed social context and function of her verse. Thus, when Sappho invokes Aphrodite or other gods, or mentions altars or religious festivities, her poems may have been taken as cult performances—real or imagined—her circle of friends the celebrants. In such a case, the personal is not only amplified through divine affiliation but made communicable as ritual in which others may share. "Quickly [you] arrived," says Sappho in the great "Hymn to Aphrodite" (§1), "a smile on your immortal face." The divine is thus summoned, as if by spell or incantation—indeed, by the incantatory language and structure of Sappho's very poetry—to intercede in human events. The goddess arrives, the ally of her summoning supplicant, even as she provides a sense of presence and reassurance to all.

Some urge that Sappho is "a feminine counterpart of Archilochus." However, Archilochus is sooner demonstrative and excoriating, whereas Sappho is contemplative and allusive. Archilochus shares his opinions forthrightly with his fellows; Sappho, only her most elusive emotions, in language often symbolic. Archilochus is more overtly sensual and self-centered, more autobiographical. He is at times unhinged. The perspective is unlike anything else in archaic Greek lyric, for example:

> Ever short of what she's lusting for,
> she's shown it all, the girl's a whore! (§75)
>
> And on that skin, insatiable, alight,
> hurling belly on belly, thigh on thigh. (§88)

Sappho, by contrast, reveals an awareness of her ability "to comfort and anchor others." Archilochus's "first remarkable intuition of self" is ultimately self-limiting as he relentlessly squares off against others, unaware of the give and take, the emotional interdependence that resides in human relationships. Aware of the rhythm that governs life (§81), he is yet incapable of emotional control. Sappho's voice, by contrast, is vulnerable and introspective, albeit confirmed in its pride. The audience suddenly shrinks from an entire city to a few close friends, whose problems and qualities she registers. Archilochus's intensity, whether of pleasure or pain, is instead his own rather than ours, and always suffered *alone*. He excels in the use of autobiography to make himself as distinct from everybody else as possible.

## Alcman

Alcman of Sparta is the earliest choral composer whose work survives in substantial fragments. The grace and gaiety of the scenes Alcman portrays accord with what archaeology and literary reference tell of Sparta in the seventh and sixth centuries BC: "Youth's mettle and the clear-tuned Muse bloom there." The phrase is ascribed to the musician and poet Terpander of Lesbos (7th century BC), believed active in Sparta at the time. Indeed, for all their geographical remove, mid-seventh-century Lesbos and Sparta vied as "centers of musical excellence." Only later, in the fifth century BC, did Sparta become a byword for severity and privation, leaving its namesake to our vocabulary. Where Archilochus addresses his fellow citizens, Alcman composes, more than any other, for his own city; and in such a way as to give his work a "strong, provincial, almost parochial" flavor. He is also fond of reference to obscure foreign tribes, both real and fabulous, to the puzzlement of scholars both ancient and modern.

The longest of Alcman's surviving poems is his *Partheneion* (*'Maiden Song'*), discovered in 1885 in an Egyptian tomb. The most problematic text of the Greek lyric period, it is riddled with uncertainties, from the smallest to the most comprehensive points of interpretation. As Greek lyric scholar-editor David Gerber has lamented, "No poem in Greek choral lyric has been the subject of so many different interpretations as Alcman's 'Partheneion,' and if the following commentary presents no clear or consistent view, the reason is very simply that I am seldom certain in my own mind of the correct solution to many of the problems involved. I have, therefore, often presented various interpretations without stating any preference."

Despite such diffidence, the poem has recently been tackled and translated anew by Gloria Ferrari in her intriguing, and quite technical, *Alcman and the Cosmos of Sparta* (2008). Ferrari argues that the *Partheneion* chorus members portray archetypal dancers in the form of an astral chorus: "Although it is performed by maidens, 'Partheneion' is not about maidens but about *kosmos*, both in the sense of political order—the constitution of the state—and in the order of the universe." The argument is persuasively couched in "music of the spheres" theory, first articulated by the Greek philosopher Pythagoras (570–495 BC). Ferrari's advancement of the poem's cosmic import, however, does not lessen its ostenstible appeal: "Here several female chorus members acclaim . . . one another's outstanding physical qualities graphically and lavishly; here too, they avow in sexually charged language an emotional investment in each other." I do not myself venture a new translation, instead reproducing Ferrari's, in her literal "bracketed" version, and Mary Lefkowitz's in a more fluid prose.

## Anacreon

According to Pausanias, the Greek traveler and geographer (2nd century AD), Anacreon of Teos (see map) was "the first poet after Sappho of Lesbos to write mostly love poems." For Sappho, love is a matter of recurrent helplessness. She calls repeatedly on Aphrodite for support (§1), though never views herself as diminished on that account. Like Archilochus in his calmer moments, Sappho appreciates the rhythm, the iterations, of emotional life

(§§1, 81). For Anacreon, love's recurrences—the game of it all—are less perturbing. Posterity assessed Anacreon as a drunkard and libertine. When one thinks of wine, women (or boys), and song, one recalls Anacreon. A court poet, like Ibycus, he composed at royal behest, with little recourse to historical, religious, or philosophic concerns. Anacreon's influence on later poets has been the greatest of any archaic Greek lyricist. A substantial body of poems known as *Ancreontics* was composed by various unknown authors from the period of the Roman Empire to Byzantine times. The poems are exquisite, as only elegant trifles can be. Their publication has often been the occasion for tasteful bookmaking.

## Ibycus

Ibycus came from Rhegium—at the southeastern extreme of Italy, across from the Straits of Messina and Sicily—in the Greek-colonized south of Italy. He was active at the court of the tyrant Polycrates of Samos, off the coast of Asia Minor (see map). As discussed in the Preface, there are only two surviving examples of Ibycus's love poetry (§§91 and 94). Their rich language, vivid imagery, and searing intensity set them off as among the finest examples of Greek poetry in any age. The poet, according to Cicero, excelled in this genre, surpassing Anacreon and Alcaeus (Sappho's contemporary). Indeed, Ibycus quite outdoes his compeers in conveying love's frightfulness. Sappho describes love, unnervingly enough, as a *(h)erpeton* 'crawler': "dissolver of limbs, bitter-sweet, irresistible, creeping in" (§36); again, she compares her love-smitten soul to mountain oaks "racked . . . by winds above" (§35). Anacreon figures love as a blacksmith, "again . . . striking the hammer's blow / plunging me / in Winter's torrent as I glow" (§46). For Ibycus, love's likeness to a "northern Thracian blast" is but the start: love's blast is "ablaze with flash of lightning, black . . ." (§91). For the archaic lyricists, Love, or *Eros,* is a primordial force, of a kind early recognized by Hesiod in his *Theogony*:

> Foremost of all then was Chaos born, followed by
> Broad-breasted Earth, the ever steadfast seat of all
> The gods atop snowy Olympus resident;
> Then murky Tartarus, creviced in spacious earth,
> And Eros, fairest among the immortal gods,

Looser of limbs, crushing in gods and humankind
Within their breasts all sturdy thought and mindfulness.

The Greeks of the archaic period had thus not yet imagined Love as the winged Cupid, what would come to be known as the quiver- and arrow-bearing child of Venus (the Roman Aphrodite). The malicious night visitant or elfish babe asleep in rosebuds, quick to his mother Venus's bidding, was the creation of Hellenistic and Roman times.

Though we have numerous references to Ibycus's narrative poetry, only a single fragmentary example survives, some forty-five verses. In this piece, Ibycus appears to have handled epic and mythological themes—Heracles, the Argonauts, the Trojan War—with a peculiarity perhaps owed to Stesichorus. Contemporary with Sappho and Alcaeus, Stesichorus was the first great poet of Magna Graecia (from which also Ibycus). Though considered in antiquity the "most Homeric" of poets, Stesichorus often departed from Homer and Hesiod in the details of his mythology. Ibycus was the second great poet of Magna Graecia and appears to have flourished some twenty-five years after Stesichorus's death.

Having briefly treated the poets with whom Sappho's erotic verse here keeps company, we turn to Sappho herself, arguably the greatest poet of all time.

# Chapter 4

## Sappho: Antiquity's Poetess and Ours

> Sappho, delectable glory of the Lesbians—
>
> – LUCIAN OF SAMOSATA

> I have woven in the flowers of Anyte, and many of Moero, and the few of Sappho, but roses all.
>
> – MELEAGER OF GADARA

SAPPHO'S LESBOS—well wooded, well cultivated, and well populated—lay within several hours of Sardis, the capital of the wealthy kingdom of Lydia in Asia Minor (§§4.16, 8.6, 27, 48.4). The island was active in seventh-century BC trade and colonization; it was torn by bouts of factionalism and political upheaval to which the aristocratic Sappho was sometimes prey (§28), although her poetry reflects little of this. As Aphrodite is Sappho's special goddess and herself apolitical among the contentious gods, so is Sappho's poetry apolitical. The women of Lesbos were famed for their beauty no less than for their sophistication. Beauty contests were a yearly event.

As we have sought to relate the ancient Greek and Old Testament worlds, we may briefly note that the principal biblical event occurring during Sappho's lifetime (c. 620–570 BC) was Nebuchadnezzar's siege and capture of Jerusalem and destruction of the First Temple; and, with the fall of the Kingdom of Judah, the start of the Babylonian Exile (587 BC). This pivotal event was preceded by the Old Testament prophecies of Ezekiel and Jeremiah. In the Greek and Roman worlds, contemporary with Sappho were the pre-Socratic philosopher Thales—considered by Aristotle the founder of natural philosophy—and Solon, the poet-statesman founder of Athenian democracy. In Rome, close to two and a half centuries of kingship (753–509 BC) would end within sixty years of Sappho's death, paving the way for the Roman Republic (509–27 BC).

Ancient criticism of Sappho finds its consensus in her poetic supremacy. In epigrams from the *Palatine Anthology* she is regularly counted as the tenth of the Muses: "Memory [mother of the Muses] herself was astonished when she heard the honey-sweet Sappho, wondering whether mankind possessed a tenth Muse." Sappho is deemed "the equal of any god" and the ultimate in her craft: "You have established the beginning and end of all lyric song." Also counting Sappho among the Muses, the Greek historian and biographer Plutarch (46–120 AD) elaborates: "Sappho utters words truly mingled with fire and gives vent through her song to the heat that consumes her heart." In so doing, she is said to "heal the pain of love with the Muses' melody." Again, in the *Palatine Anthology*, she is considered the "sweetest of love-pillows to the burning young"; a companion to Hymen, god of weddings at the bridal bed, and to Aphrodite, who laments Adonis in the sacred grove of the blessed.

Sappho was praised as well as derided in antiquity—the latter when critics focused on her sexuality rather than on her poetry. The Greek comic playwrights of the fourth century BC were particularly unsparing (and influential), notwithstanding their works are known in the merest fragments or by title alone. A key source is the poet Ovid, who espouses both sides of the issue, thus doing little to resolve it. Ovid asks, "What did Sappho of Lesbos teach but how to love maidens? Yet Sappho herself was safe." By 'safe' (*tuta*) Ovid apparently means that Sappho condoned, without herself practicing, homosexuality. Ovid's position appears to contradict the view taken in his famed "Sappho-Phaon Epistle":

> Not Pyrrha's coterie nor Methymna's girls beguile me now, nor any Lesbian maiden. Dazzling Cydro's of no account—Anactoria and Atthis, once embraced, are now disdained; and the hundred others, loved to my reproach, relinquished this their claim to callous you [Phaon] alone.

The rhetorician-philosopher Maximus of Tyre (2nd century AD) in an equally famous statement takes a more elevated view:

> But is not love of the Lesbian poetess (if one can compare older with more recent) in fact identical with Socrates' amatory art? It seems to me that each of them pursued a particular kind of affection, for women in the one case and men in the other. Both claimed to have many beloveds, and to be captivated by anyone who was beautiful. What Alcibiades, Charmides, and Phaedrus were to the one, Gyrinna, Atthis, and Anactoria were to the poetess of Lesbos.

Forests have fallen for the writing addressed to this comparison. We may for the present note that much of Sappho's surviving work is ambiguous about the type of love involved, and for that reason the more interesting. The love that Sappho's Aphrodite controls may be heterosexual or lesbian. Both types find expression in Sappho's work and life. The goddess is as responsible for Helen's adultery with Paris (§4) as she is for the departure of Sappho's beloved to Lydia (§6). Virginity is a cherished state (§17), but not to be cultivated (§20). Though its loss may be painful (§§18, 19, 21), marriage and the handsomeness of the groom find ready praise (§§22, 23, 24, 25), and sometimes ribald treatment (§§29, 30). Sappho's longest surviving work is a narrative poem celebrating the wedding of Hector and Andromache (§26). From what we may surmise, Sappho was married and had a daughter named Cleis (§27), though both points are disputable. According to Ovid (our primary source for the legend), Sappho ended her life in a suicidal leap for unrequited love of the ferryman Phaon.

This brings us to the most compelling and elaborate of the legends concerning Sappho: her leap from the Leucadian cliff. Cape Leucas, or the Leucadian Cliff, is a white-rock promontory of Leucas (or Lefkas), an island in the vicinity of Corfu and Ithaca, off the northwest coast of Greece (see map). Though there is report of Sappho's exile in Sicily and travel to Egypt, nothing except the legend of her death connects Sappho to far-off Leucas. The Leucas legend, moreover, is all we know of Sappho's death. Verses from the *Palatine Anthology*, however, proclaim a different location: "Aeolian earth, you cover Sappho, who among the immortal Muses is celebrated as the mortal Muse." Aeolia names the tribal-linguistic locale of ancient Lesbos (see map), whence Aeolic, the dialect of Sappho's poetry. The invocation of Aeolia may indicate that Sappho actually died on Lesbos. Even if not, a tomb may well have been erected there for antiquity's sightseers. The "localization" of Sappho's death appears to have extended into the present. Not to be upstaged by a remote and inessential Leucas, Eressos, the city on the south-central coast of Lesbos known as Sappho's birthplace, itself claims the privilege of Sappho's leap. A monument erected at the supposed promontory marks the site, making Eressos—fittingly—the place of Sappho's birth and death, alike.

Promontories may be either cultural or physical, as is anecdotally illustrated. The World War I singer-songwriter, poet, and playwright Théodore Botrel (1868–1925) specialized in popular songs about his native Brittany, the most famous of which was "La Paimpolaise" ("The Paimpol Girl"). Singing it for the first time and to great acclaim in 1895, Botrel launched himself as a popular singer. "La Paimpolaise," a lilting ballad about the quaint charms of the fishing village of Paimpol, became his signature song. The song's refrain, "J'aime Paimpol et sa falaise" ("I love Paimpol and its cliff"), was apparently coined because *falaise* rhymed with *Paimpolaise.* There being no cliff in the town, the nearby Pointe de Guiben was chosen. Similarly inventive were the inhabitants of Eressos. Unwilling to cede the location of Sappho's death to the far-off island of Leucas, they found their own promontory in the city of Sappho's birth.

Also noteworthy from the Homeric perspective was Botrel's appointment as official Chansonnier des Armées 'Bard of the Armies'. Botrel was authorized by the Minister of War "to enter all military depots, camps, and hospitals for the purpose of reciting and singing his patriotic poems." He traveled throughout the front line, performing for the troops. Botrel's most famous wartime songs were "Rosalie" (the nickname of the French bayonet) and "Ma P'tite Mimi" (about a machine gun). A monument to Botrel was erected in Paimpol (northern coast of Brittany), depicting the Paimpolaise gazing out to sea from the imaginary cliff. A statue of Botrel adorns the Pont-Aven (southern coast of Brittany). So also at Eressos, a metal abstract of Sappho adorns the beach near to the cliff of Sappho's putative leap.

The Homeric bard, by contrast, did not perform for or among the troops, but made their exploits known to others. The bard's military presence is nonetheless telling in both contexts—Botrel actually present to inspire the troops (though only by way of entertainment), the Homeric bard present through intercession of the Muse, herself witness to the events and inspiring the poet to sing them. Combining the roles of entertainer *and* warrior were the minstrels of British legend, both singing and accomplishing heroic deeds. The famed example is Taillefer in the Battle of Hastings (1066; the Norman Conquest). Appearing at the head of William's army, he inspired the troops with heroic poetry, reciting from *Le Chanson de Roland.* He possessed spear- and sword-handling dexterity attributed to the powers of enchantment. His maneuvers and recitations completed, he galloped among the English soldiers, giving the sign of battle, and was lost in the mêlée—knowing better than most the fame his sacrifice would win, both as combatant and reciter of combats. The bard's position as behind-the-scenes memorializer of combat is powerfully depicted in Anne-Louis Girodet's *The Bard* (1806). The subject of fame in combat—*kleos*—is otherwise a major topic of this work (Chapters 14–17).

According to a character in the comic playwright Menander's (4th century BC) *Leukadia,* Sappho "first leapt from the far-seen rock in wild love-chase of the proud Phaon." However, in Ovid's "Sappho-Phaon Epistle," the leap was supposed to cure love (that is, if it didn't kill you first). The epistle concludes with Sappho's intention of "seeking her fate in the Leucadian wave." Excerpts from Ovid's rhetorically charged epistle suffice to indicate the factors feeding Sappho's despair.

Ovid's Sappho laments her spurned condition, extravagantly elaborating on both Phaon's beauty and insensitivity:

> O neither yet man nor boy, but charmed in between, O ornament and glory of your time, return; entrust your beauty to my arms. Oh, take my love though not returning it. I write, and my eyes well up with tears, in drops that blur the page. Resolved though you were, more gracious yet your parting with a brief, "Farewell, my Lesbian maid." No tears did you take, no adoring kiss of mine; no hint had I of sorrow's swift approach. Thus were you gone, with no token of me; and no keepsake of yours, but this my pain, have I.

The poem contains the *locus classicus* for the idea that Sappho, in contrast to her beloved, was not especially physically graced:

> If spiteful Nature has denied me beauty's share, then balance my genius in beauty's place! Though my size is slight, my glory fills the earth; therein my pride and reputation's claim.

Sappho's self-reproach in no way blinded Phaon to her gifts. Sappho's recollection is one of ardent bliss:

> When I read my songs you found me fair enough, and vowed that speech thus never graced another. As I sang, I remember—lovers remember all—my lips surrendered kisses to your stealth. These were your praise and how much your pleasure! But then above all, when we labored at love, my playfulness was unaccustomed joy—the resourceful embraces, the whispered jests. . . . And when longing plunged to consummation—Ah then, the deep, deep languor of our wearied limbs.

Their happiness was but an interlude. Sappho views her suffering in the wake of Phaon's departure as the continuation of a traumatic childhood:

> Am I always to anguish, as ever from the start, and my life be endless pain? Six birthdays had I counted when my father's bones, too early gathered, moistened with my tears—while my witless brother burned for a harlot's love, enduring, with his every loss, debasement. Thus reduced, he endangers life and limb at sea, heedless to regain what heedlessly he lost, ever hating me for warnings I had offered. *This* the return for candor and concern. And if I lacked sufficient grounds for care, a young daughter now usurps my thoughts. And now yourself, most recent cause of my distress. I list to unfavoring winds.

The geographer Strabo (1st century AD), as Menander before him, notes an old yearly custom of the Leucadians at the sacrifice of Apollo, whose temple was atop the cliff. As an apotropaic, or averting, rite they would throw some guilty person from the cliff. Flapping birds and feathers were attached to the victim to break the fall. A large crowd waited in boats below to rescue and, if possible, take the victim beyond the frontier to safety.

Thus, what was to have been a curative—but was ultimately a fatal—leap for Sappho later developed into an expiatory offering, a communal scapegoat. It is difficult to say whether the "old custom" practiced by the Leucadians continued through Strabo's time, some five hundred years after Sappho. Curiously, by the time of the Virgilian commentator Servius (4th century AD)—five hundred years later—we find an attenuated version of the ritual. Servius, while not specifying the leap's purpose, speaks of the custom "now in vogue" of hiring people once a year to throw themselves from the cliff into the sea. The notion of hire would suggest some form of entertainment. The longevity of the myth and the practices associated with it attest to its grip on the popular imagination. The materials in fact have origins in myth and cult predating Sappho. Indeed, Strabo, citing the passage from Menander, indicates that Sappho was not first to make the leap.

Classicist Gregory Nagy, in a far-ranging discussion, probes the myth's cosmic dimensions. I here summarize and simplify his line of thought. Aphrodite first leaped in love for the dead Adonis, and later, in love for Phaethon, son of the Sun God. The names Phaon/Phaethon are related in Greek and mean 'bright'. We recall from the tale popularized by Ovid that Phaethon attempted to drive his father Helios's chariot and, in so doing, to be the Sun himself. He lost control and plunged into the sea. Aphrodite, in her astral guise of Hesperos ("evening/west")—the planet Venus, or Evening Star—dives ever after the sinking sun, here the falling Phaethon. She retrieves him the next morning in the guise of Heōsphoros ("dawn bearer")—also the Planet Venus, but this time the Morning Star. In the evening Aphrodite as Hesperos sets after sunset; in the morning Aphrodite as Heōsphoros rises before sunrise. Aphrodite thus pursues the sun at night and is pursued by him at daybreak, bringing on the day. The theme, as an instance of *amor versus*, appears in Sappho's poetry: "For if she flees at first, she'll soon pursue" (§1.21). Sappho loving Phaon is Aphrodite loving Phaethon. Thus projecting her identity onto the goddess, Sappho vicariously experiences Aphrodite's own love and its despair. The analogy between Sappho and Aphrodite is the mythic counterpart to that close association between them, seen everywhere in Sappho's poetry. Aphrodite is Sappho's special goddess, "a cosmic affirmation of Sappho's own eroticism."

An unrivaled female poet and lover of women in a man's world—where male poets typically wrote of homoerotic loves—Sappho has in turn been admired, derided, moralized, analogized, and, in her despair of a heterosexual rebuff, allegedly driven to suicide off an obscure island cliff. The analogy to Socrates intellectualizes, even as it seeks to redeem, Sappho's love of women, placing it on par with the love of man for man as propounded and practiced by the wisest man of all. It is, however, in the analogy to Aphrodite that Sappho transcends the mortal fray—its partisanship and judgmentalism—making of self-ideation a masterstroke of genius.

# Chapter 5

## Sappho's Eroticism

> Sappho's Muse . . . is passionately tender, and glowing; like oil set on fire, she is *soft* and *warm*, in excess.
>
> – EDWARD YOUNG, *On Lyric Poetry*

AMONG ISSUES OF CONCERN to the study of Sappho are her performance context or social setting and the poet's own sexual "preference." Even as the issue of context or setting abides, that of preference has well become passé. In our sexually expansive age, the poet's love of either sex neither surprises nor draws particular comment. We sooner care about the poetic expression of that love—of its intelligence and intensity which are indications alike of artistic and amorous fire, of poetic control in the face of erotic conflagration. Any shame that Sappho's sexuality might cast on her poetry does not arise from the poems themselves, "which are too frank and healthy to comfort any attempt to degrade them. It comes from those whose restricted sympathies are allowed to choke their pleasure in poetry."

Early seeking to free Sappho from negative imputation, the great German classical philologist Ulrich von Wilamowitz-Moellendorff (1848–1931) fixed on the idea of Sappho as "headmistress," running some manner of "boarding school" for girls (*Mädchenpensionat*). The idea, as so many of Wilamowitz's, carried the unquestioned allegiance his name alone commanded. The idea has since been largely abandoned, though not without a certain echo. We sometimes speak today of a *thiasos,* or quasi-religious band, group, or association devoted to the worship of Aphrodite and the Muses. In this scenario, Sappho is "priestess," binding her young devotées—*jeunes filles en fleurs*—in ties of intimacy and dedication;

or "teacher," through poetry and music, of the sole intimacies young girls might experience, before marriage, in a sexually segregated society. We do well to mention an essay titled "Sappho's Group: An Initiation into Womanhood"; the group more commonly called the "Sapphic circle." Given Sappho's poetic fame, this would include acolytes traveling from near and far to Sappho's side; and would otherwise provide a socially sanctioned forum for what, on its surface, was the erotically charged (and thus disfavored) verse of a female poet.

The social function of Sappho's poetry is apparent in its highly ritualized form, expression, and situation. In this context, invitation to the goddess (§§1, 3) and a companion's departure from the group (§§6, 8) present ritualized situations. Ritualized form is expressed in the incantatory, charming, or therapeutic effect produced, for example, by recurrent sound patterns, lulling rhythms, and sentence repetition (as in §1.21–24, which "almost seem to assure the success of a spellbound promise"). These effects are apparent in the epithalamia, or wedding songs (§§17, 19, 21, 23, 25), poems redolent with public statement and social function. Sappho's poetry is magical in the sense that "convincing someone without the aid or against the wishes of logic is a magical accomplishment. Sappho's personality and voice were capable of staging such events as the arrival of Aphrodite or communion with a friend over waters" (§§1, 8). Her lyrics are also "healing enterprises, linguistic attempts to spirit the mind suffering from desire or separation away, into a more satisfactory or pleasurable awareness, drawing upon the medicinal properties of daydream, memory, sensuality, Aphrodite and metaphor to accomplish this."

Thus does Sappho speak upon the departure of a beloved (§6):

> "Honestly, I wish I were dead"!
> She was leaving me, tears in her eyes.
>
> Much she said, this most of all:
> "Ah, Sappho, what we've suffered through;
> I swear, I leave not wanting to."
>
> And I made this reply:
> "Go then, yet remember me now
> and again. You know how

we have cared for you.
If not, I'd remind you [ ]
of joyous times which we once knew:

of rose wreaths and crocus,
of violets put on at my side,
necklaces flower-tied

[tossed] round your gentle neck;
how you anointed yourself
with [ ] a queen's costly scent

and on yielding beds
gentle [ ]
desire [of maidens] spent

and no dance [
no shrine [ ] where
we two were not found

No precinct [
] sound
]..."

To "spirit the mind . . . away" is to create a "private space." The poem (§6) thus becomes "the container of shared memories, hence itself the private space, the common world into which either can enter and find the other imaginatively. . . . The private space is the most important metaphor for love in the poetry of Sappho."

Private space and metaphor aside, how is Sappho's circle private or personally intimate relative to the worship or influence of Aphrodite? Ovid, as seen, claims Sappho taught girls to love but was herself "safe," that is, free from erotic involvement. Ovid nonetheless has Sappho, to her shame, lamenting her love of girls. No manner of disclaimer, however, has dampened the inquiry. The turn-of-the-twentieth-century reaction to Sappho was apologetic or appalled: first, as seen in the "headmistressing" of Sappho; and even more in the repudiations—disclosing dread and threatening censure—of "Sappho [as] a woman who has given herself up to unnatural and inordinate practices which defy the moral instinct . . . and harden and petrify the soul." Such response was grounded in what scholars identified as "two special difficulties": "the moral question: is Sappho fit to [be] read?" and "the aesthetic question: is Sappho worth reading?" Between the repudiations on the one hand and acceptances on the other stand those separating poetry from preference and practice. "Sappho's actual personal experience in sexual relationships is not in question. . . . [Of interest is] Sappho's imaginative projection of emotional life into aesthetically pleasing abstract shapes." And similarly:

> Whether or not Sappho was a practicing lesbian or just passionately attracted to women is superficial compared to the more basic fact that her love must include a woman. Here lesbian love and heterosexual love are combined to contrast with male homosexuality (about which she says nothing and implies almost nothing, probably because of lack of interest).

Another view has it that homosexual relations within the Sapphic circle were propaedeutic, or instructive, which is to say, limited in practice to Sappho and a *single* beloved. As for others in the circle, the communicative powers of Sappho's poetry would allow the collective emotionally to share in the tie between Sappho and one of their number—the objective being shared sensibility. *Propaedeutic* signifies that the tie, for the beloved, was an adolescent, or transitory, form of sexual engagement, preparing for the adult heterosexual expectations of marriage. The notion of a single physical relationship as group exemplum, however, seems strangely tepid and constrained. We know from ancient authors, Aristotle and Plutarch in particular, that Spartan noblewomen loved young girls and that it was customary for adult women in Sparta to have intercourse with girls before their marriage. What this suggests for the Sapphic circle is largely a matter of inference. There was also male pederasty, or boy love, in Sparta—to which the female practice may have conformed.

In a similar vein, emotional education, including spiritual communion, has been viewed as an element in the institutional affirmation of young girls before marriage, whether or not such education involved sexual attachment. Sappho, in this context, is a poet fulfilling a public function, that of instilling sensual awareness and sexual self-regard, and of easing the role adjustment for young women coming of age in a sexually segregated society. In such a society, young women were barred from the sexual attentions of their suitors as from any form of emotional gratification outside of marriage. They could turn only to other women for sensual awareness, thus meeting societal expectations and finding the sexual validation to satisfy their needs. As various sociocultural institutions appear to have served this precise function in the male sector of society, "it only stands to reason that Greek society would have similarly institutionalized the sensual education and affirmation of upper-class women." One posits the like distinction in male and female social circles between emotional or sensual appreciation and sexual appetite. The Greek religious, artistic, and poetic tributes to the male physical ideal are to be taken as "conventional public gestures [and not sexual overtures] intended to enhance the aesthetic appeal of their objects in a culture which placed a high premium on male physical beauty." So with Sappho, for whom—as often with her male poetic colleagues—a distinction may often exist between personal feeling and poetic *persona.*

Sappho as an enhancer of awareness to young females provides a reputational safeguard similar to the discredited notion of Sappho as "schoolmistress"—slighting the fact that those who poeticize love do so only by experiencing it. In the same defensive vein, one reads that Sappho's poems are "reputedly erotic" (*les poèmes reputés érotiques*) and that they serve a largely encomiastic, or praise-lavishing, function, since "the language of love lent itself to poetic praise owing to its affective power and not because of what it expressed." However, it taxes belief that "erotic admiration via poetry could be effective where the author dissociates herself from it." If the "praise of young men was undeniably based on sexual attraction" and the desire to possess a young man was socially acceptable, the same may be assumed for women—the role of pederasty having a similar educational and social role among males as among females in the Sapphic circle and elsewhere.

Our discussion proceeds with reference, first, to Plato's *Symposium,* in which Socrates and friends speak of the different kinds of love; and second, to Maximus of Tyre's well-known comparison between the Socratic and Sapphic "circles" (examined in part above). That the nature of this comparison may elude us today stems from the conventional misunderstanding of Platonic love. The term was not used in antiquity to designate the kind of relationship advocated by Socrates. Nor in antiquity was there any notion of Platonic relationship, understood today as a nonsexual bond between affectionate members of the opposite sex. The love advocated by Socrates, especially in Plato's *Symposium* (hence, Platonic love), has been defined as "a common search for truth and beauty by two persons of the same sex inspired by mutual affection." The relationship was ideally nonphysical. As the *Symposium* relates, physical attraction remains at the bottom of an aesthetic hierarchy consisting of physical beauty, moral beauty, the beauty of knowledge, and the supreme knowledge whose sole object is absolute beauty.

Plato conceives the hierarchy in terms of an ascent: from love of individual physical beauty, to love of all physical beauty as a single form of beauty, to love of all forms of beauty as the ideal of beauty—i.e., *to kalon* 'the beautiful'—to love of that supreme beauty that is wisdom and its acquisition through philosophy. The progression, in sum, is one from love of the physical (the body) to love of the intellect (ideas), from the immortality-driven impulse of physical procreation to the greater immortality of the mind's generative powers. The *Symposium* does not have Socrates hold forth on this progression. Plato, rather, ascribes it to the priestess Diotoma, who has thus instructed Socrates. That the last word on love as an ideal is systematically explained by a priestess—whereas all other discussion has been by male interlocutors, serious and droll—signals that philosophy is not an exclusively male domain.

Plato here, in a manner of speaking—or through Diotoma's speaking—"feminizes" philosophy, consistently with the Greek perception of wisdom as an embodiment of both the feminine and the divine—the priestess Diotoma partaking of both. Plato's searching inquiry into the nature of beauty and philosophical understanding thus bespeaks a male quest sustained by female insight. But the quest of wisdom is also an embodiment of both the masculine and the feminine—the goddess Athena partaking of both. Warrior-goddess of wisdom, Athena is born fully grown and armed from the forehead of her father, Zeus. Born mature and martially equipped, wisdom is immediately and capably combative. Emerging from Zeus's forehead, the goddess knows the mind of her all-knowing father, their thoughts coextensive. As female born solely of the male—the wisest and most powerful male—Athena peculiarly combines the best of male and female attributes while remaining free of male and female compulsions. Indeed, born without sex, the virgin goddess partakes of no sex. There could thus be no better symbol of the strength and composure that is wisdom attained—a wisdom ever ready to engage, yet one ultimately detached from the turmoil of sexual and all-too-human beginnings.

While the Socrates of Plato's dialogues vividly comments on how male physical beauty affects him, he remains committed in principle to abstinence. The same Socrates would dissuade other males from physical relations with desirable young men. He is nonetheless realistic enough to allow for human frailty, i.e., when physical attraction leads to consummation:

> But if they turn to a way of life more ignoble and unphilosophic, yet covetous of honor, then perchance in a thoughtless hour, or when the wine is flowing, the wanton horses in their two souls will catch them unawares and bring the two together who, choosing that part which the multitude consider blissful, will achieve their full desire. And once they have fulfilled this desire, they continue therein, though rarely, since their minds are not wholly intent on the undertaking.

On what undertaking, then, are their minds to be wholly intent? The goal of the lover (the *erastēs*) is the attraction and cultivation of youth for its physical, spiritual, and intellectual gifts; and that of the beloved (the *erōmenos*) to be so attracted, encouraged, and improved. As aptly noted by the German-American classicist Hermann Fraenkel:

> The Greek in general regarded homosexual love as more dignified and uplifting than love between the sexes. The untamed craving of that urge which finds fulfillment and satisfaction in the union of man and woman was not so celebrated in poetry as was homosexual love which feeds unquenchably on the sight, on the physical proximity and spiritual presence of another, and together with him seeks, by common action and united striving, the path to parallel self-fulfillment.

To be sure, practice, with many a variant, fell often short of theory.

By contrast, and despite the comparison by Maximus of Tyre, the focus of Sapphic love was neither the idealistic nor the intellectual, but the solace and communion derived through some manner of Aphrodite's excitation.

> Homosexuality was less repressed in the ancient world than in our own age, but it would be a mistake to say that the ancients had no prejudice against consummation of this love. The sacred band was a famous oddity, and the most admired milieu where homosexual love was unashamed and cherished—the Socratic circle of Platonic love—depended for its existence on non-fulfillment of these physical desires. For Plato, male homosexual love had as its ideal a rarified, non-physical, intensely exhilarating friendship which moved and was felt in a medium *of ideas*. Philosophy was its natural expression. Female homosexual love, on the other hand, lived in a medium of shared sensuality and sensibility, as Sappho shows us in her poems filled with rose chains falling on soft necks, apple boughs full of sleep, moonlit meadows, bowls full of wine, bodies full of glowing desire or harsh deprivation. Its special poignancy was that this love could not fertilize the womb, just as it could not engender philosophical discourse. Men identified with the world of ideas, as Freud argues; women don't; the most natural female communication is through some form of sensual awareness.

While the dichotomy, however nicely framed, cannot be steadfast, it does reflect the difficulty of separating an artist's life and work. Thus, our dependence on biography—specifically, the awareness of an artist's gender—leads to certain stereotyped assumptions about the creative process in men as opposed to the creative process in women. While it is assumed that male artists apply the full range of their intellectual powers in the creation of their art, the assumptions for female artists tend to be more narrowly defined. Creative women are deviant—thus tending to be either old maids or lesbians—whereas women with satisfactory home lives require no other creative outlet. Further to this point of view, "because women poets are emotionally disturbed, their poems are psychological outpourings, i.e., not intellectual but ingenuous, artless, and concerned with their inner emotional lives." As a result, criticism of two such different poets as Sappho and Emily Dickinson can sound remarkably alike.

In the end, one can neither deny Socratic and Sapphic homoerotic attachment nor explain it away. Attempts to do so bespeak inhibition and self-deception, an effort to correct or second-guess what is fully apparent on its face. Sappho, in sum, does not repeatedly love and call on Aphrodite for help in love (§1.13–20) without actually loving, any more than Socrates, without loving Alcibiades, praises him, or concedes the human condition. To lead is to lead by example not precept. The scholarly moralists, long since passed from the scene, "refused to recognize that Sappho, and the Greeks, and Aphrodite as well, knew more than they did about the kinds and inclusiveness of sex, and were honest about it." They have now been replaced by scholarly sensationalists who imagine such things as Sappho, the Greeks, and Aphrodite likely never considered—or would be loath to admit to if they had.

# Chapter 6

## The Loves of Men, Gods, and Primordial Forces

> . . . Eros, fairest among the immortal gods, looser of limbs, crushing in gods and humankind within their breasts all sturdy thought and mindfulness.
>
> – *Th.* 120–123

When it comes to the nature and inclusiveness of sex among the Greeks, Sappho's reputation as a woman who loved women can easily overshadow her artistic accomplishment, especially for those wanting a sexual pioneer instead of a poet. Such emphasis downplays the facts of Sappho's marriage and motherhood, and her poetic attentions to all things heterosexual. At the same time, the persistent focus on Greek homosexuality—even allowing for the compulsions of army life and the lesbian inducements of segregated female society—obscures heterosexuality as the norm. Heterosexual love—either desired, attempted, or consummated—drives classical storytelling and myth, though noteworthy exceptions occur.

It is Helen of Troy's abduction that triggers the Trojan War—the greatest cataclysm of antiquity and the focal point of its mythology. Indeed, the wooing of Helen brought suitors from far and wide in contest for her hand. Her father Tyndareus swore them all to an oath—the Oath of Tyndareus—that they would join in Helen's defense, should harm befall her or the chosen husband (Menelaus). The oath forestalled quarrels among the unsuccessful wooers and was responsible for the ships and hosts that later sailed for Troy. The oath also evidences, in the words of a recent critic, the "collective impairment caused by desire of Helen, which blinded each man with irrational hope . . . transforming the conflict from a dispute among men into a clash between armies." The same impairment disinclines the Trojans to rid themselves of Helen at any point in the ten years preceding the end of the war, for she is irresistible, even unto collective death. The *Iliad,* recounting events of the war's final phase, begins with the fallout of the Greek commander Agamemnon's seizing the daughter of a local priest. Achilles, in a speech before the army, urges her return. When finally required to make amends, Agamemnon seizes Achilles's concubine. His honor slighted, Achilles withdraws from battle, the better to contemplate his destiny as his comrades perish in his absence. The *Iliad* is thus impelled throughout by the wooing and taking of women.

The *Odyssey* presents a pack of boorish suitors wooing the "steadfast" Penelope in Odysseus's absence (as the story opens, he has been absent, returning from Troy, for ten years). Odysseus, for his part, enjoys sexual escapades during his homecoming with the nymphs or demigoddesses Circe and Calypso. But these are fantasy figures, "outside of human time" (and place), whom he doesn't and can't bring home as a slight or provocation to his wife (compare Agamemnon, below). Washed ashore on the never-never land of Phaeacia, Odysseus is saved by the Princess Nausicaa, who (it appears) would happily marry the seaweeded yet comely hero—a prospect of which Odysseus himself seems not unappreciative. The encounter is charged throughout with hints of marriage, despite the age disparity and Odysseus's already existing marriage to Penelope. It is an inversion of the scene back home in Ithaca: the wooing of a potential spouse by members of the younger generation. The double-sounded short *a*-ending of "Nausicaa" ("Miss Shipley," Gr. *naus* 'ship') imparts a diminutive girlish charm. And so she is in storybook life: a young but undaunted charmer, acknowledged by Odysseus as one he will ever remember for saving his life. What in the *Odyssey*-world's own reality would be a perilous, indeed, impossible courtship, is in make-believe Phaeacia a pageant for our amusement and speculation.

As further concerns heterosexuality, when Penelope makes her occasional appearances at the palace's upstairs balustrade, the suitors grow weak at the knees, as we learn, moaning aloud that they might lie with her. Returning from Troy and slaying the suitors, Odysseus hangs the female attendants who serviced them in his absence. The Greek commander Agamemnon returns from Troy with his concubine Cassandra, and is slain by his wife Clytemnestra—herself adulterous in his absence (like her half-sister, Helen, not so "steadfast"). Phaedra, spear bride of the Athenian prince Theseus, lusts for her stepson Hippolytus and commits suicide for want of him. Hippolytus is also a suicide (of sorts) for his resolve to live celibate. Such is the fate of those who seek to disavow Aphrodite. Paradigmatically worse, Oedipus sleeps with his mother, fathering his own siblings. Marrying another, Jason betrays Medea, who slays her own children by Jason. Under compulsion to found Rome, Aeneas—a Trojan War refugee—abandons his lover, Queen Dido of Carthage (another suicide).

These are some of the high points in the mythic course of heterosexuality. The gods of Olympus, whom the Greeks conceived so much in their own image, and who in early mythological time mixed freely among men, bide a similar norm. They do so without the pyrotechnics, however, as immortality takes little to heart. Gods enjoy predominantly heterosexual relations, and when they "mix" with mortal men and women, enjoy heterosexual relations with them. Zeus is the most philandering of the gods, even as his wife Hera oversees the sanctity of marriage and the labors of childbirth. Hesiod relates that Zeus married Hera "last of all," upon conclusion—or substantial conclusion—of his romp among the goddesses.

There are some exceptions. Foremost is the youth Ganymede (of Troy), whom Zeus, in the form of an eagle, swoops up to Olympus as his "cupbearer," though we hear nothing of Ganymede thereafter. Homer notes that Ganymede "was the most beautiful of mortals; the gods made off with him to pour wine for Zeus, on account of his beauty, that he might be among the immortals." The gods thus appear collectively to have coveted Ganymede as an inspirational presence. Ganymede is Zeus's sole homoerotic attachment (though, again, we are without details). He is further the only conquest Zeus transports to heaven instead of seducing and abandoning on earth. Contrary to her merciless pursuit and punishment of Zeus's female lovers, Hera remains muted in her objection to the Trojan Ganymede, vicariously venting her anger on the Trojan Aeneas in his effort to found Rome. There is Hylas, the occasional boy love of the demigod Heracles; the minor divinity Hermaphroditus; and, in some of his manifestations, Tiresias as bisexual seer. Ovid tells the tale of Iphis—a girl raised as a boy who fell in love with a girl and was gender-metamorphosed to be able to marry her. There is also the youth Hyacinthus beloved of

Apollo. Guiding Hyacinthus to the maturity of adulthood, Apollo acts as the older man/lover (the *erastēs*) to the younger man/beloved (*erōmenos*) in a Platonically idealized relationship.

Lacking the sanctions of such a relationship is the first homosexual abduction known to Greek myth, that of Chrysippus, son of Pelops, by the Theban king Laius, father of Oedipus. Laius is reported to have abducted his young charge on their way to the Nemaean games, where the youth was to compete, and to have raped him upon return to Thebes. In response, Pelops cursed Laius, and Hera sent the Sphinx to terrorize Thebes. The curse was fulfilled with Oedipus's slaying of his father and solving the Sphinx's riddle, the latter act ingratiating him to Thebes and facilitating his marriage to the king's widow—his own mother, Jocasta. Discarding the myth's crudeness, Sophocles's *Oedipus* ascribes its hero's fall to the inscrutable dictates of oracles, prophecy, and destiny, creating a dramatic high point in the West's understanding of self-delusion (see Chapter 27).

Somewhat more elaborate is the myth of Artemis (Lat. Diana) and Callisto. Artemis, chaste goddess of the hunt, keeps an entourage of nymphs, all sworn to chastity, one of whom is Callisto ("most beautiful"). Enamored of Callisto, Zeus, in a lesbian and, thus, hermaphroditic charade, disguises himself as Artemis and makes love to Callisto. Upon discovering Callisto's pregnancy, Artemis is enraged. In a fit of jealousy at the betrayal of one of her "own," Artemis transforms Callisto into a bear. The seduction has been many times depicted by, e.g., Boucher and Rubens (naturally) and Jacopo Amigoni (four times). By contrast is the marked female exceptionalism of the Amazons, the fiercely armed warrior queens of myth. Cutting off the left breast (an impediment to the level drawing of their bows), the Amazons repudiate men (except for purposes of procreation), give up their sons, and raise only daughters. Such exceptions, however, do not upset the heterosexual norm. Nor, with the teasing exception of nymphs sworn to chastity, are there suggestions of homoerotic attachment among female divinities.

Heterosexuality is also the norm at the pre-Olympian cosmic level. The Greek creation myth, told in Hesiod's *Theogony* (*Birth of the Gods*), relates that earth and sky assumed fixed positions only when father *Ouranos* 'Sky' ceased from his sexual depredations of mother *Gaia* 'Earth'. Ouranos's unceasing need for sex, his repeated descent to mate with Gaia, prevents their required division as separate realms of inhabited earth. Nonstop sexual activity is *chaotic*, in the initially mythic sense that earth, sky, and all creation are forever mixed and in flux. Differentiation occurs, as the *Theogony* relates, by Ouranos's castration during intercourse. This defeats the need for, and further possibility of, sex. The first significant act of creation is thus one of forced sexual differentiation, even as the most essential of human differentiations is that between the sexes. Ouranos's genitals are lopped off with a sharp-toothed sickle by Kronos, one of his children hidden in the womb of Gaia. (Kronos is the Titan father of Zeus, not to be confused with Gr. *chronos* 'time'.) Ouranos's conduct, we are told, made him hateful to Gaia and all their children.

Indeed, because of Ouranos's sexual impositions, Gaia cannot bring forth her children; cannot be the fruitful, bountiful earth of her calling. The myth accomplishes yet more, signaling the perception that male children come to hate their fathers as competitors for the mother, or hate them simply as authoritarian figures. The myth also entails vagina dentata (toothed vagina), the notion that intercourse, followed by detumescence, is castration. Male consummation is depletion and diminishment; it is recurrent death both at man's own generative source and at the source of his own begetting. The French tellingly refer to orgasm as *la petite mort* 'the little death'. (A similar idea appears in the coincidental soundalikes *womb/tomb*.) Once separated, Earth and Sky take form and position as earth and sky; their separation bounding them off, i.e., creating *boundaries* between them. The same is apparent from both Hesiodic and Homeric references to "broad-breasted Earth, the ever steadfast [Gr. *asphales* 'unslipping'] seat of all the immortals who hold snowy Olympus' peak," and to Ouranos as a physical element of bronze or iron, conceived as a solid roof to the earth.

This theme appears in the cosmogony sung by Orpheus in the *Argonautika* of Apollonius of Rhodes (3rd century BC):

> He sang how the earth, heavens, and sea, formerly intermixed in a single form, were sundered apart by deadly strife; and how heavenly stations, forever fixed, are held by the stars and the moon and the sun in their courses.

The abstraction "deadly strife" here substitutes, as a divisive force, for Hesiod's anthropomorphic doings of Earth and Sky. At the same time, the resultant separation is posited not by process, as in Hesiod, but as outcome:

the celestial bodies would lack fixed positions and courses save for the space resulting from separation through "deadly strife." In sum, the perception of separations, boundaries, and fixity is itself fixed in ancient Greek thinking—not least in the worldview of Sappho and the lyricists, as will be seen. How otherwise could Sappho summon Aphrodite to her "sacred grove"?

Heterosexuality is further manifest in the birth of Aphrodite. Ouranos's severed genitals are thrown into the sea. From the surrounding foam (read: semen) is born Aphrodite, goddess of love. Botticelli's iconic painting *Birth of Venus* (aka *Venus on the Half Shell*) depicts Aphrodite's progress, as she is blown shoreward by West Wind divinities and robed by flower-draped graces and nymphs. Contrary to the circumstances of her birth, Aphrodite is a 'modest, lovely goddess' (*aidoiē kalē theos*)—which is to say she knows *aidōs*, or 'shamefastness' (at least some of the time). Hesiod designates her allotted realms among the gods as: "maidens' whispers, smiles and schemes, love, sweet delight, and gentleness." She is married to Hephaistos, the lame and grimy smith god. Their relationship is rich, to say the least, in oppositional implications. In a lighter vein, she is the adulterous consort of Ares, god of war—also a richly oppositional relationship—with children *Erōs* 'Desire' and *Peithō* 'Persuasion'. Other than with Sappho, Aphrodite's concerns are always heterosexual.

As further concerns Lesbos, the island was not solely associated with lesbianism. The novelist Longus (1st or 2nd century AD) made Lesbos the setting of his *Daphnis and Chloe.* The work is a romance of innocent (almost excessively innocent) heterosexual awakening resulting in marriage. One imagines a locale other than Lesbos for a heterosexual rite of passage, notwithstanding Longus may have lived or written there. A Florentine manuscript of the novel contains the subtitle *Four Tales of Lesbian Loves* (*lesbiakōn erōtikōn logoi δ*), which more accurately translates as *Four Tales of Love on Lesbos.* It is of interest, then, that six to seven hundred years after Sappho, Lesbos might serve as the locale for a decidedly heterosexual awakening.

# Chapter 7

## Lesbos, Troy and Environs; The Principal Greek Genres and Dialects

> Lesbos, the centre of Aeolian culture, was the island of overmastering passions; the personality of the Greek race burned there with a fierce and steady flame of concentrated feeling. . . . Nowhere in any age of Greek history, or in any part of Hellas, did the love of physical beauty, the sensibility to radiant scenes of nature, the consuming fervour of personal feeling, assume such grand proportions and receive such illustrious expression as they did in Lesbos.
>
> – JOHN ADDINGTON SYMONDS, *Studies of the Greek Poets*

> With the emergence of Athens in the fifth century BCE as a cultural and artistic center, the Attic dialect, which is the great absentee in the age of archaic literature, makes its entree on the Greek literary scene. It is a grand entree: for Attic was soon associated with tragedy and oratory, the two new genres that most influenced Greek cultural life in the fifth and fourth centuries.
>
> – OLGA TRIBULATO, "Literary Dialects"

THE GREEKS WERE colonizers from early in their history, as any sea-girt peoples would be. They crossed the Aegean eastward to inhabit its multiple islands and the coast of Asia Minor (Turkey), and westward over the Ionian Sea, colonizing southern Italy and Sicily. Situated off the northwestern coast of Asia Minor was Lesbos, the third largest of the Greek Aegean islands (sixty-six square miles), boasting Mytilene as its capital. The city, in all its prosperity and strength, became virtually synonymous with Lesbos itself. Fabled both for Sappho's presence and the vigorous trade and military power that eventually made it the most influential of the Asiatic Greek cities, Mytilene (both before and during Sappho's lifetime) had been ruled by a succession of hereditary tyrants. The tyrant Pittacus, one of the "Seven Sages of Greece" (c. 640–568 BC), had successfully challenged the hereditary claims to tyrannic rule. A strong navy and network of outposts secured Mytilene's trade routes through the Hellespont.

Troy was situated at the entry to the Hellespont. The ancient site was located in northwestern Asia Minor, on the Troad Peninsula, just south and slightly inland of the Hellespont (see map). The distance between Lesbos and Troy was navigable by coastal reckoning. We learn from the *Iliad* that Achilles singlehandedly conquered Lesbos, the myth thus accounting for the subjection of Lesbos to Greek rule. Achilles is credited with similar exploits throughout the *Iliad*, including those against the islands of Skyros and Tenedos, and against adjacent Lyrnessos and Pedasos on the Troad. We also learn from the *Odyssey* that various contingents of Greek warriors, on their return from Troy, used Lesbos as an initial regrouping point. Controlling access through the Hellespont northward to the Propontis, or Sea of Marmora, and thence to the great hinterlands beyond, Troy was a strategic commercial center and military stronghold; in fact, the greatest and most fabled city of antiquity. As such, it was a magnet for conquest, much like Constantinople in the fifteenth century AD. The contest for Troy was inevitable. Herodotus at the outset of his *Histories* views the Trojan War as the beginning of antagonism between Asia and Europe, East and West. This is this same theme that governs his own treatment of Greece's (the West's) defeat of Persia (the East).

For all its political infighting, Lesbos was known foremost for its culture, both musical and literary (the combined political turmoil and artistic flourishing perhaps similar to that of Medici Florence). Sappho, born in Eressos (on Lesbos's southwest coast), and living and performing in Mytilene (southeast coast), has been Lesbos's greatest figure. Her elder contemporary was the famed poet Alcaeus, also of Lesbos, whose poetry (unlike Sappho's) was of a largely political—often caustically so—and civic inspiration. Significantly more of Alcaeus than of Sappho survives. A fragment attributed to Alcaeus speaks of "violet-chapleted, pure, honey-smiling

Sappho." Sappho for her part casts one of her poems as a brief dialogue with Alcaeus (§12). The two appear in performance mode on a Greek vase painting that dates to the fifth century BC. While there is no evidence of their actually having met, their works likely shared the stage. However, the wish to see Sappho and Alcaeus sharing each other's performance company is great. The classicizing British artist Lawrence Alma-Tadema depicts Alcaeus playing to an enthralled Sappho and company (*Sappho and Alcaeus*, 1881).

Lesbos further abounds in mythic and historic musical associations, the two often difficult to distinguish. Such associations are apparent in the figures of Arion, Orpheus, and Terpander. Arion was born in Methymna, modern Molyvos (northeast coast). He invented the dithyramb (etymology uncertain), a frenzied choral hymn and dance to Dionysus, which was the origin of Athenian tragedy, according to Aristotle. Herodotus credits Arion as the premier lyric musician (*kitharoidos*) during the time of the tyrant Periander of Corinth (late 7th century BC). Legend has it that Arion charmed the sea playing his lyre, thus escaping a perilous voyage on a dolphin's back. The scene, in Greek and Roman times (and since), has been the subject of numerous artistic depictions. Another musical miracle worker was Orpheus, charming Hades, ruler of the underworld, in an effort to retrieve the prematurely taken Eurydice. The venture failed when Orpheus broke faith by looking back to see if Eurydice followed. Orpheus was subsequently torn apart by Thracian Maenads—"the Raving Ones," attendants of Dionysus—for refusing Dionysus's worship. Orpheus's lyre and still-singing head were thrown into the river Hebros in Thrace and washed up on the shore of Lesbos, where they were gathered and enshrined. The "ensemble" is portrayed by the lurid Gustave Moreau in his *Thracian Girl Carrying the Head of Orpheus and His Lyre* (1865). Moreau also depicted various episodes from Sappho's life, including her death in *Sappho Leaping from the Leucadian Cliff* (1864) and *Sappho on the Rocks* (1869).

Musically active before Arion, Terpander is the "first human musician in Greek and Western music history," and otherwise the "prototypical itinerant professional songmaker." He is credited with the invention, or at least systematization, of ancient Greek music and with the creation of choral poetry (Gr. *terpo* 'delight'; the muse *Terpsichórē* 'delight in the chorus'). Born in Antissa, a town in the mountains of western Lesbos between Methymna and Sappho's Eressos, Terpander is said to have perfected the lyre (Gr. *kithára,* Lat. *cithara*) by converting it from a four- to seven-stringed instrument. This development, says Lawrence Durrell, was for the ancient world "as decisive as the jump from clavichord to piano." It was also at Antissa that Orpheus's memorial was established, known as a place where the nightingales never sang more sweetly. "Antissa could claim . . . the oracular head and lyre of Orpheus, the latter of which Terpander legendarily inherited." One sees in the name *Terpander,* with its root sense of "delight," the likely "retrojection" of a highly developed citharodic tradition—the name "a convenient symbol for Asiatic musical influence reaching Greece via Lesbos, for the excellence of music and poetry on the island which was to produce Sappho and Alcaeus." Traditions tend to invent their originators.

Similar invention is attributed to the name *Homer,* despite antiquity's committedness to his life and authorship. Modern scholars note the etymological meaning of *Homer* as a 'harmonizing' or 'fitting together' of song, or of the stages or layerings of epic recitation over time. Viewed as such, "Homer" is not so much the author of the *Iliad* and *Odyssey* as the summation of the process by which they were created: "a collective and not a personal name." The idea convincingly reflects what is now known of the lengthy oral development of Homeric epic, as briefly set forth herein.

Returning to Terpander, legend has it he was summoned to sing in Sparta to restore calm amid fractious infighting. From his unparalleled performance came the maxim, "next to the poet of Lesbos"—an expression indicating the secondary status of any other singer and the supremacy of Lesbos in all things musical. Lesbos "exported" its musicians, who gained fame both as entertainers and civic mediators through song. *Kitharoidia* 'singing to the kithara', came to be associated with good governance and, by extension, cosmic order. The *kitharistēs* 'kithara performer' became a celebrity, a "sex symbol," as are certain types of musical performers today. Terpander himself would become a "Pan-Lesbian axiom of *kitharoidia.*" Ironically, Lesbos was itself perennially riven with political strife, even as its *kitharistai* (or *citharodes*) mediated dissension abroad. A possible explanation resides in the power of poetry both to calm and inflame, in which case the upheaval on Lesbos is attributable to "the brilliant yet socially destabilizing musico-poetic counterculture exemplified by Alcaeus." Alcaeus's poetry, as noted, and to the extent surviving, was often abusively political.

Alcaeus covered the power struggles on Lesbos with partisan fervor, cursing his opponents and rejoicing in their deaths. Such poetry was nothing if not metered political rhetoric. By contrast, virtually all his love poetry has disappeared.

❧

Historian-essayist Tzvetan Todorov (b. 1939) asks, "From where do genres come? Why, quite simply, from other genres." He further explains, "A new genre is always the transformation of one or several old genres: by inversion, by displacement, by combination." We are thus not surprised to find, at the outset of the Western literary tradition, that epic, lyric, and tragedy were originally more of a kind than we today customarily imagine. Terpander is referred to, in epic manner, as a "praiser of heroic deeds." He is also said to have "lyricized" Homer, setting the latter's verse to the lyre. This has been taken to mean that Terpander's songs incorporated both dactylic hexameters, as used by Homer, and Homeric themes in lyric (rather than epic) dactyls. The same may be said of epic matter conveyed in elegiac couplets, elegy described as "a variation upon the heroic hexameter, in the direction of lyric." The foremost example of such elegy is what survives of the Spartan poet Tyrtaeus (late 7th century BC) and an extensive, recently discovered fragment of Archilochus. The *Iliad,* conversely, incorporates lyric materials in epic meter (specifically in women's songs of lament). The circle comes fully round, insofar as "the laments of [Hecuba, Andromache, and Helen] at Hektor's funeral represent the beginnings of the memorial of oral poetry that the heroes have won. Coming at the very end of the epic, they are also a reference to the composition which has just been performed." Indeed, to the extent Achilles's own use of language is "expressive" (self-validating) rather than "conative" (validating oneself to others), epic's most heroic protagonist may himself be viewed "as a lyric persona caught up in epic."

At the same time, it is in Achilles's "hyperstated mortality" that the origins of tragedy may be thought to lie. Achilles's "pathological, over-responsive character . . . drive[s] him, with a force rare in any epic, toward the existential immediacy of the tragic-dramatic character, or of the intense lyric *persona.*" Direct speech, with its affinities to tragic dialogue, also predominates throughout the *Iliad.* Achilles's situation is the "tragic situation *par excellence,*" replete with *peripeteia* ('reversal') and *anagnōrisis* ('recognition') in the service of painfully acquired self-recognition. "The fate of Achilles, who, as presented in the *Iliad*, became the ideal hero of Greek legend, was, by universal admission, 'tragic'—that is, it came about *di' hamartían tiná* ['through a certain flaw']. Moreover, as articulated by Achilles, the *Iliad*'s view that Zeus apportions good and evil irrespective of merit or desert, is what we acknowledge as a tragic view of the world." It is Plato who originates the idea of Homer as the first and greatest of the tragic poets, while Aristotle elaborates the structural similarity of epic and tragedy (the two essentially differentiated by scale and meter). Hector, in his way, is Achilles's tragic counterpart. Homer was a veritable storehouse of tragic plot development.

As further concerns genre mix, we turn to the paean, an early form of choral song-dance honoring Apollo as *Paean* 'Healer'. The paean was centered in Apollo's principal shrines at Delos and Delphi, and sung throughout the Greek world. The glens and ravines of Sappho's Lesbos surely resounded to it. The paean is twice prominently mentioned in the *Iliad*. The Greeks, Homer tells us, sing a paean to lift the plague (sent by Apollo) in Book One of the *Iliad*, and Achilles bids a paean be sung after slaying Hector (abandoned by Apollo). Although the paeans are themselves not recorded, the references alone show epic's awareness of the lyric genre (older than itself), a genre in which the *Iliad*'s own characters are well practiced. If, in a manner of speaking, Terpander's Homer is "lyricized epic," Homer's paeans are "epicized lyric." A form of non-dramatic choral ode, the paean was eventually adapted to Greek tragedy, which in its earliest form was largely choral. Just how this occurred is difficult to determine. The dramatic chorus yet reflects the paean's concerns of communal cohesion and stability. Further influencing Greek tragedy was the Mixolydian mode, said to have been invented by Sappho: "Thus when the tragedians took it over, they combined it with the Dorian mode, since the Dorian produces the effects of grandeur and dignity, and the Mixolydian that of passion, and tragedy is a blend of the two."

Complementing the musical myths and quasi-history of Lesbos is an historical record of philosophic and scientific achievement. Pittacus was among the devisers of the two maxims inscribed on the porch of the Delphic Oracle (*gnōthi s'auton* 'Know thyself'; *mēden agan* 'Nothing to excess'). Bringing the poet Alcaeus into his entourage, Pittacus reconciled with him, saying, "Forgiveness is better than revenge." Contemporary readers may experience a languid and lustrously imagined confluence of the poetic and political in Durrell's *Sappho: a play in verse* (1950), in which Pittacus is a major character. The polymath Theophrastus (4th–3rd centuries BC) was born in Sappho's Eressos. The "Father of Botany," he was the student of Plato and Aristotle, and for thirty-five years head of the Athens Academy. Aristotle himself taught briefly on Lesbos, as did the philosopher Epicurus.

Herodotus first distinguished three major tribes or peoples inhabiting Greece and its colonies: Ionians, Aeolians, and Dorians (see map). The three correspond to the major early Greek dialects: Ionic, Aeolic, and Doric, which literary remains show were intermixed. A dialect is a particular form of a language peculiar to a specific region or group. It is typically marked by distinctiveness of orthography, or spelling system, which differentiates it from the language's dominant form or from the language's other dialects (examples to follow). A dialect is not to be confused with (what we know as) an "accent." An accent, while also regional and identifying, is largely a matter of variant pronunciation (without change in spelling), intonation (the rise and fall of the voice), or occasional informality of usage. The complexities of archaic Greek dialects are here necessarily simplified.

**Ionia** was the central coastal region of Asia Minor. **Old Ionic, aka Homeric or epic Greek,** was the language of Homer and Hesiod. Homer, as earlier noted, likely hailed from the island of Chios, within the Ionic (as opposed to Aeolic) geographic parameter. Despite Hesiod's Boeotian origins on the Greek mainland near Athens, and despite the scattered locales of the various cyclic poets (Chapter 13), Old Ionic remained the dialect of epic, regardless the epic poet's habitation, own local dialect, or time period. Five hundred years after epic's heyday, Apollonius of Rhodes (3rd century BC), living in Alexandria, composed his *Argonautika* in Old Ionic. Homeric Greek, no less than Homeric themes, pervasively influenced the writings of Greek authors in general, epic and non-epic, poetic and prose. So nurturing were the origins of Greek literature.

**New Ionic** was the language of Ionia in the fifth century BC, best known today through the prose writings of Herodotus and Hippocrates (the "Father of Medicine"). Closely akin to **New Ionic** was **Attic Greek,**

such that linguists sometimes speak of **Attic–New Ionic** as a single dialect. Attica was the region of mainland Greece surrounding Athens; Attic Greek, the Greek of Athens during its fifth-century preeminence, and ultimately to be the standard. In enumerating the principal Greek dialects, we do, however, distinguish **Attic** from **Old Ionic**, bringing the dialects to four: Ionic, Aeolic, Doric, and Attic—the first three, again, admixed—urging less that ancient Greek had four dialects than that the four dialects *were* ancient Greek. The bulk of surviving ancient Greek is Attic, including the dialogue portions of Greek tragedy. Attic prose is typically intricate, polished, and refined. "Atticism" shaped the significant first-century BC reform of a corrupted Latin into what we even now recognize as "classical Latin." Atticism also shaped the early nineteenth-century reform of a then deteriorated Modern Greek into something of its former glory. "Attic" is a byword for perfection. "O Attic shape!" exclaims Keats, apostrophizing his Grecian urn.

**Aeolis** or **Aeolia** was an area comprising the northwestern region of Asia Minor, starting at the Hellespont to the north and extending southward to Ionia. This largely coastal area included several offshore islands, Sappho's Lesbos foremost among them. **Aeolic, in its Lesbian variant,** is the dialect of Sappho and Alcaeus. There were also Aeolic enclaves/dialects on the Greek mainland, in Thessaly (whence Achilles) and Boeotia (whence Hesiod).

A character in Plato's *Protagoras* disparages Aeolic as spoken by none other than the tyrant Pittacus, whose speech was somewhat slurred, since he was "a Lesbian and brought up in a barbarous dialect." Sappho was a younger contemporary of Pittacus. It is thus of interest that Plato deemed Sappho the tenth Muse for her Aeolic verse, even while disparaging the dialect in spoken form. This does not necessarily signal a marked difference between spoken and literary Aeolic, as Sappho's Aeolic is thought, in its constraint, to "reflect contemporary usage." Aeolic verse is thus a wonder for accomplishing so much with so little. Though too little Aeolic survives for generalization, Sappho's resort to common usage for supernal ends astonishes, the more so given the strictures of lyric meter. Sappho "rings as naturally as the spoken word," says classicist scholar and poet F. L. Lucas, "yet here are words such as few lips ever spoke." What Gilbert Murray has said of the language of Greek tragedy is equally applicable to Sappho's lyric poetry:

> The one reward which Greek tragedy reaps from its severe metrical rules is that the ear being satisfied and unconsciously thrilled by the meter, the language can at will cast away all ornament, and go straight for the drama. In the greater part of the *Oedipus* you will find scarcely any deliberate eloquence, and scarcely any poetical ornament. What you do find in every speech and in every line is dramatic relevancy. There is beauty of course, but it is not as it were a beauty that is deliberately sought and imposed upon the material. It is the beauty that necessarily results from clean well-balanced proportion, psychological truth, and intensity of feeling.

Given the interdependence of ancient Greek genres, as discussed, it does not surprise to find lyric and tragedy functioning by similar means.

The Dorians are believed to have originated in a small enclave known as **Doris** to the immediate north of the Peloponnese (see map). First mentioned in Homer's *Odyssey*, the Dorians primarily inhabited the Peloponnese with its principal city states of Corinth, Argos, and Sparta. Dorians also inhabited certain southern Aegean islands, such as Crete, Rhodes, and Kos, and between the latter two, the peninsula off the coast of Asia Minor. Westward, the Dorians settled parts of southern Italy. During the Age of Pericles, the Dorians and Ionians were the two most prominent peoples of Greece. Their enmity resulted in the protracted Peloponnesian War (431–404 BC), chronicled by Thucydides and ending in Sparta's defeat of Athens. Little of pure **Doric** survives. The language of the lyric poet Alcman shows Doric elements with an infusion of Homeric Greek. Doric, with varying elements of **epic Greek** (**Old Ionic**) and **Aeolic**, was used by fifth-century choral poets such as Pindar, Stesichorus, and Bacchylides. Doric elements also appear in the choral portions of the fifth-century Athenian playwrights. Theocritus (3rd century BC), the Sicilian inventor of Greek pastoral poetry, and of the Western pastoral tradition, used a Doric variant of his own making, even while sometimes composing entirely in Aeolic. The choice of dialect, however, was part of his literary sophistication, even as he may have sounded "more archaic than Homer himself."

With the exception of eventually standard **Attic**, one properly speaks of the other dialects largely in terms of predominance, given the blending of **Old Ionic**, **Aeolic**, and **Doric** as dictated, especially in Homer, by meter, poetic license, or inclination. Homeric Greek, itself an archaic dialect at the time of its transcription, contains borrowings from Aeolic, an archaic dialect in its own right believed to be epic's oldest stratum. The codification of literature of such form bespeaks the extreme flexibility and utility of ancient Greek poetic language. It is especially noteworthy that Aeolic was pervasively used for archaic Greek lyric, and freely incorporated into epic, while its spoken counterpart invited derision, as seen. **Attic–New Ionic** aside, the three dialects, as reflected in poetry, were literary constructs; i.e., non-spoken essentially artificial languages given to adaptable use and invention. The Athenians of the fifth century "were sensible that the variety of dialects, still infinitely varied by poetical license, constituted the riches of their language, and made the Grecian Homer the first of poets, as he must ever remain, until a language equally ductile and copious shall again be spoken." This has implications to which translators are most often impervious. In sum, "contemporary" translations of ancient Greek, though often proposed, little reflect the original's heterogeneity, however straightforward the original's meaning. By contrast, Attic Greek poetry and prose, though marked by structural formality, are little given to dialect contrivance. **Attic Greek** is the dialect of almost all surviving Greek prose, including that of Thucydides, Plato, Aristotle, and Demosthenes. Inscriptions aside, there is no surviving Ionic, Aeolic, or Doric prose.

Before considering the sound and accentuation of ancient Greek poetry, we note key differences in dialect, especially those between **Sappho's Aeolic, Homer's Ionic,** and what eventually emerged as standard **Attic**. Though the points must necessarily be few and for purposes of illustration only, they suffice to show the peculiarity that was the language of Lesbos and its Aeolic environs. We thus note that Aeolic uniformly uses *ā* where Ionic and Attic use *ē*. Where initial vowels in other dialects are either aspirated or non-aspirated—pronounced with an initial *h*-sound or without—Aeolic is never aspirated. Combining these two features, we find ***lēthē*** (Attic), but ***lāthā*** (Aeolic) 'forgetfulness'; ***(h)ēdomai*** (Attic), but ***ādomai*** (Aeolic) 'I am pleased'. Accentuation in Aeolic is typically recessive, meaning it goes as far toward the start of the word as possible; thus ***theós dunatós*** (Attic), but ***théos dúnatos*** (Aeolic) 'a mighty god'.

Diphthongs are also subject to change: ***ethelousa*** (Attic), but ***etheloisa*** (Aeolic) 'wanting, wishing'. Double consonants change as well; *dz*, represented by the Greek letter *zēta* (ζ), becoming *sd* in Aeolic: ***(h)idzanei*** (Attic), but ***isdanei*** (Aeolic) 'he sits'. The initial *zēta* is the only exception: ***Zeus*** (Aeolic and Attic). Such examples suffice to illustrate the insular peculiarities of Sappho's Greek, revealing the extent to which a single Aeolic poem might seem "foreign," yet nonetheless appreciable, to a non-Aeolic Greek of the period. The ancient Greek dialects, though quite marked in their differences, were still mutually comprehensible, at least in literary contexts. Alternatively, and as suggested, the dialects were literary languages, and collectively, the Greek language itself.

**Old** and **New Ionic Greek**, which is to say **Homeric** and **Attic,** differ most in vowel contraction, with Homeric Greek resisting it largely for metrical reasons: the fewer contractions, the more syllables. Thus, ***thaneein*** (Homeric), but ***thanein*** (Attic) 'die'; ***theoio*** (Homeric), but ***theou*** (Attic) 'of the god'; ***meneos*** (Homeric), but ***menous*** (Attic) 'of the strength'; ***eō*** (Homeric), but ***ō*** (Attic) 'I may be'. Homeric Greek may further double a consonant to create a metrically long syllable where a short vowel would otherwise govern, e.g., ***epessi*** (Homeric), but ***epesi*** (Attic) 'with words'; or even double a short vowel to create an additional metric beat: ***epeessi*** (Homeric), but ***epesi*** (Attic). The very name *Achilles* (Ἀχιλλεύς) is sometimes spelled with one *lambda,* sometimes two—depending on whether a short or long *iota* is wanted in the second syllable. The variants, in fact, appear in the two uses of *Achilles* in the seven introductory lines of the *Iliad.* In the first instance (short iota), the quadrosyllabic form of Achilles's name is emphasized on the penultimate syllable. In the second (long iota), the trisyllabic form is emphasized on the penultimate. The Homeric infinitive 'to be' may appear in five different forms: ***einai, emenai, emmenai, emen, and emmen,*** versus Attic: ***einai.*** To view a single word in all four dialects, we may look to the earlier discussed *Paōn*—an appellation of the god Apollo, and later the celebratory hymn, a paean: ***Paiēōn*** (Homeric), ***Pāōn*** (Aeolic), ***Paiān*** (Doric), ***Paiōn*** (Attic). One sees at a glance the different metrical possibilities and colorings, the rich and nuanced expressiveness for which dialect mixing allows.

We do well in this connection to recall Alexander Pope's summation in the preface to his *Iliad.* Pope notes, perceptively here as everywhere else, that Homer's Greek was not the language of any one part of Greece, but a purposeful mixing of dialects, to beautify and perfect his diction as required. Ionic, notes Pope, was the most preferred of the Greek poetic dialects for its

> peculiar sweetness from its never using contractions, and from its custom of resolving the diphthongs into two syllables; so as to make the words open themselves with a more spreading and sonorous fluency. With [Ionic] mingled the Attic contractions, the broader Doric, and the feebler Aeolic, which often rejects its aspirate, or takes off its accent; and completed this variety by altering some letters with the license of poetry. Thus [Homer's] measures, instead of being fetters to his sense, were always in readiness to run along with the warmth of his rapture, and even to give a farther representation of his notions, in the correspondence of his sounds to what they signif'd.

The outcome, as Pope noted, was "more sweetness, variety, and majesty of sound, than in any other language or poetry." To this may be added that Homer's handling of dialects—although not purposeful in the way Pope believed—served more than the beautification and perfection of his poetry. It also served the Panhellenicization of his poetry—making it in diction, theme, and outlook the religious and ethical patrimony of *all* Greeks (or Hellenes), rather than the property of any one group, and assuring its appeal and perpetuity. Homer's Olympian pantheon and religion thus supplanted the cultic practices of the various city–states, or relegated them to secondary status, even as his *Iliad* portrayed the Trojan War as "the first genuinely Panhellenic enterprise in Greek history." Moreover, as the "common Hellenic occasions" served by Homer's poetry were formal or religious, they called for a highly elaborate and exalted diction:

> Greeks of various dialects not only understood it, but accepted it naturally as the way a poet should express himself, lifting them to a vision of things that was strange and wonderful and truer, perhaps, than their own. If we call it 'artificial' we must remember that most poetical language is equally artificial. . . . Further, that while the spell of such poetry is on us, we are not conscious of its artificiality. That only comes with later reflection.

Homer in his own time was thus of all times and places, as he remains today—only exponentially so. Indeed, the fame is reminiscent of Ben Jonson's dictum upon the death of Shakespeare: "He was not for an age but for all time." Nothing less may be said of Sappho and perhaps more, had we even a dozen of her poems instead of her painfully exiguous remains. The poet Algernon Charles Swinburne (1837–1909) has come closest to the praises lavished on Homer and Shakespeare in deeming Sappho "simply nothing less—as she is certainly nothing more—than the greatest poet who ever was at all."

# II.

# Chapter 8

## Sappho and the "Lyric Nine," An Aesthetic for Lyric Translation

> I did not think it required to translate word for word, but have retained the spirit and force of the passage. For I saw it my duty not to count but weigh out the words for the reader.
>
> – CICERO, *On the Best Kind of Orators*

> . . . it is not [the translator's] business to translate Language into Language, but Poesie into Poesie.
>
> – SIR JOHN DENHAM, Preface, *The Destruction of Troy*

SAPPHO'S POETRY, BELIEVED to have once numbered nine books (or scrolls), has long existed in fragments only. "The flowers of Sappho, few but roses," records the *Greek Anthology*. Indeed, Sapphic fragments are of such beauty and charm as to prompt the notion that they were *composed* as fragments. As Anne Carson aptly notes of Sappho's three-line "apple bough" poem (§17), "The poem is incomplete, perfectly." According to one Tullius Laurea—of all people, a freedman of Cicero—the ancient collection of Sappho's poems, made or adopted by the Alexandrian editors, consisted of nine books (i.e., papyrus scrolls). The books were designated by metrical content with Book I containing poems in Sapphic meter as exemplified by the "Hymn to Aphrodite." Known to have been included in Book I, this is the only of Sappho's poems to have survived complete. Book I contained 1,320 verses, made up of 330 Sapphic stanzas—perhaps as many as sixty to seventy poems. There were eight additional rolls of approximately the same length (in other meters), meaning a total oeuvre of some five hundred pieces of which we have less than one percent. The sources of Sappho's present remains, from papyri and elsewhere, are reckoned (as of 2005) as follows:

> In modern editions the fragments are numbered up to 264. But many of these do not contain a single original word. Only sixty-three contain any complete lines; only twenty-one contain any complete stanzas; and only three—till now [including the 2004 "New Sappho"]—gave us poems near enough complete to appreciate as literary structures.

More recent discoveries (see Chapter 22) have not meaningfully altered these figures. The sparsity of Sappho's verse has generated commentary, dispute, and free invention in inverse proportion to what is known of her or remains of her work.

The fragmentary state reflects the hazards of preservation and what is thought to have been the prudery or bowdlerizing tendencies of later ages, including the possibility of book burnings by scandalized church leaders. In addition, and with the ascendancy of the Attic dialect, Sappho's difficult Aeolic fell to generalized neglect during Roman times, though the literati continued to admire and use her as a model. Sappho's two (and now four) principal surviving poems are a riveting reminder of what was lost. Papyri aside, the sources of the preservation of archaic Greek lyric are entirely random, consisting largely of quotations by later writers, some dating five hundred years and more from the poets they quote. Sappho's two principal poems survive in this way, quoted for their high polish and literary merit. Snippets are otherwise unceremoniously quoted to illustrate grammatical points or turns of phrase. Lyric fragments of this kind may vary in length, from a phrase, to several phrases or lines. A fairly complete poem can yet be "fragmentary" by virtue of missing words or lines in the invariably damaged papyrus or parchment on which it has been preserved.

There are any number of complete poems, most fairly brief, by lyric poets other than Sappho. The year 1973 saw the discovery of a lengthy erotic poem fragment by Archilochus (§75). The year 1992 witnessed the discovery of Oxyrhynchus papyri, allowing the reconstruction of upward of one hundred verses, attributable to Simonides, on the battle of Platea (479 BC). The year 2004 brought the discovery of a new piece by Sappho, believed to be fairly complete (§39) (for the 2014 discoveries, see p. 125). Such events are always the subject of dizzying scholarly activity, the last particularly noted in international news and literary media. Hope of lyric poem or fragment discovery thus springs eternal.

Commentary on Sappho focuses on three major concerns: context, reception, and relation. Context involves the occasion for Sappho's poetry; reception, the response to it beginning in the fifth century BC; and relation, the relationship between Sappho's poetry and other early Greek poetry—especially epic. One need not overly dwell on context, as the setting and audience of Sappho's poetry have been exhaustively treated. Reception, for its part, is a telling indication of intellectual, historical, and even personal history. Indeed, recent decades have shown a strong leaning toward the personal, which is to say a highly subjective response by those who study and comment on Sappho. Though personal poetry is likely enough to generate personal response, the outcome has little to commend it, as will be further apparent. The richest and most productive focus is that of relation, and of Sappho's relation to Homer most of all—be it her choice or alteration of epic diction or treatment of theme.

My own work, while examining relation, is of largely aesthetic concern. Its focus is on *who translates, how, and with what result.* It deals not only with the translation of archaic Greek lyric but also with the translation of ancient Greek and Latin poetry generally, and with attention to the Old Testament. The approach seeks to make the case for a formalist aesthetic, rooted in form and accompanied by the conventions traditionally associated with poetry—including rhyme, alliteration, appropriate diction, and judicious use of archaisms. This assumes a language—always somewhat artificial—appropriate both to the writing of poetry and its translation. Literary translation is or should be poetry in its own right, as necessarily determined by the resources and traditions of the language of translation. The translator "needs give to his work, in some respects, a high degree of excellence, of a kind not found in the original, to take the place of an excellence of another kind, which cannot be reproduced at all."

Translation at its best is thus an inspired work, "coauthoring" with the original to make its meaning known. Such assumptions concerning *translation,* however, especially from the mid-twentieth century on, run contrary to what has been the nearly virulent vernacularization of *original* poetry in the wake of Wordsworth and Coleridge's *Lyrical Ballads* (1798) and Walt Whitman's *Leaves of Grass* (1855)—poetry in everyday language, for and reflecting everyday people and concerns. The severity of this falling-off is apparent in the claim of *Leaves of Grass* to American epic status, "celebrat[ing] the heroic potential of all men"—with worse to follow in the Whitman-enamored Ezra Pound. If original poetry adheres to no particular standard, little more can be expected of poetry in translation. And as concerns both forms of poetry, the words of Samuel Butler still ring true: "There are a good many mediocre poets who are doing fairly well . . . publishers will tolerate nothing in a poet except mediocrity."

This volume, as noted, is novel as a collection largely of love lyrics composed for choral as well as for solo performance. Such lyrics more often appear in anthologies of Greek poems on all themes. Lyric subject matter may relate to politics or war; it can be devotional, admonitory, processional, or satiric. It can be sympotic (drinking songs for *symposia*), eulogistic (praise of the dead), encomiastic (praise of the living), epithalamic (praise of the newlywed), or epinician (praise of athletic victors). Lyric, as epic, often proceeds by way of mythological example or allusion, seeking to set the model for—or to discourage—a certain kind of behavior. The themes and their often hortatory tone show that lyric was composed not merely for the diary but for the informed elite.

One notes the almost sermonizing lyrics of the great lawgiver and social reformer **Solon** (7th–6th centuries BC), also the author of the famed Athenian constitution. Not wanting to be pestered, Solon decamped abroad for ten years, leaving the Athenians to implement the constitution on their own and sparing himself a thousand questions in the process. Solon was the first literary figure of Athens and the only such major figure before Aeschylus. He was deemed, with Pittacus tyrant of Lesbos, one of the Seven Wise Men of Greece. Also noteworthy in the sixth century is the lyricist **Theognis**, the "city poet" of Megara (see map) and spur to its civic conscience. Theognis's themes are justice and overreaching, as he inveighs against the depredations of a landed aristocracy. Theognis's complaints are of a kind with those of Hesiod in the *Works and Days*; indeed, with those Solon's constitution sought to remedy. Such poetry is public poetry, admonitory by default. Love poetry, by contrast, is confessional and self-revelatory, composed for the diary, though not without public-performance appeal.

The librarians of Alexandria (3rd century BC) compiled a list of nine lyric poets ("the Nine"), by analogy with the number of Muses. Four of the nine are included in this volume: **Sappho**, **Anacreon**, **Alcman**, and **Ibycus**. The fifth, **Archilochus**, was a lyric iconoclast, as noted—more self-centered and "up to date" in his loves and hatreds; not merely personal, but "taking things personally" and using significantly varied meters in the process. His poetry is more colloquial than that of his contemporaries and, thus, less clearly allied to the song and dance integral to Greek lyric performance.

The Nine's other five (some living into the 5th century BC) are **Alcaeus**, **Stesichorus**, **Simonides**, **Pindar**, and **Bacchylides. Alcaeus** wrote primarily on social and political themes. These reflected the turbulence of Lesbos under Pittacus, as noted, resulting in Alcaeus's and Sappho's exiles. **Pindar** and **Bacchylides** wrote celebratory odes at the behest of wealthy patrons for the victors at Olympia and other regional games. Celebratory odes were earlier written, though with less flourish, by **Simonides**, who also composed commemorative songs, dirges, and epitaphs for the fallen in Greece's battles: Salamis, Thermopylae, Artemisium, and Platea. **Stesichorus**, ranked with Homer in antiquity, is the least well preserved of the major lyricists. He wrote, among other things, narrative poetry on epic themes dealing with the sack of Troy and its aftermath. Born in southern Italy, Stesichorus was the first great poet of the Greek-colonized West. Another popular lyricist, included neither here nor in the Nine, is **Mimnermus,** especially famous for his query, "What is life, and what is joy, without golden Aphrodite?" His response: "Might I perish when these no longer concern me." Mimnermus's bent, as this couplet demonstrates, is more rhetorical than amatory.

# Chapter 9

## The Aesthetic of English-Language Prosody in the Translation of Classical Verse

There are so few translations which deserve praise, that I scarce ever saw any which deserved pardon.

– SIR JOHN DENHAM, *The Destruction of Troy*

What could be better than Homer, or worse than almost any translation of him?

– GEORGE SANTAYANA, *The Sense of Beauty*

BECAUSE OF SAPPHO'S REPUTATION and extraordinary appeal, and despite her fragmentary aftermath, she frequently takes center stage in books on ancient Greek lyric poetry. This can result in consecutive pages with no more than several words each, or in many pages of minimal content, with several unrelated verses or fragments printed together. Since the surviving papyri on which Sappho is sometimes preserved are by nature in tatters, editors and translators use brackets to indicate the numerous textual gaps, or *lacunae.* My own use of brackets is limited. In most cases, my rendering accounts for the fragmentary nature of the text, and seeks without embellishment or restoration to convey the sense. The occasionally bracketed word is based on conjecture.

When not dutifully bracketing *lacunae* or zealously enshrining isolated words, the translator of Greek lyric can be found at the opposite extreme, indulging pure invention. Such practice has followed from British classicist John Maxwell ("J. M.") Edmonds (1875–1958), who effectively spun an entire wardrobe of archaic Greek lyric from its remnant threads and patches. That the result was virtually all Edmonds/no Sappho has not deterred the Greekless and largely Greekless translators who have since relied on Edmonds. Edmonds epitomized a generation of scholars so proficient in ancient Greek that they could compose in it. And compose they did, dazzlingly and perversely. Edmonds's work was published in three bilingual volumes, in Harvard's Loeb Classical Library, as *Lyra Graeca: Being the Remains of All the Greek Lyric Poets from Eumelus to Timotheus Excepting Pindar* (1922). It was seized upon by those whose Greek "ran a poor second to their urge to put a recognizable and appealing Sappho on the contemporary literary map [and who] cheerfully included many of Edmonds' supplements as though they were Sappho's own." Thus, poet and popularizing translator Paul Roche (1916–2007): "The Greek text I have used is based on that edited by J. M. Edmonds . . . with emendations from [names] and others (and in a few instances my own)." We find more of Sappho "surviving" in Roche's translation than in any other translation of the last fifty years, a translation as popular as it is misleading.

Roche's problem was that he wanted it both ways. Disclaiming imitation, adaptation, or paraphrase, he maintained his renderings were "strictly a translation," while at the same time defending his reliance on Edmonds:

> Even in the most conjectural of the restored passages, where it is far from certain how Sappho expressed herself, there is seldom absolute doubt as to the gist of what she said. One does not question that in places where the records are blank it is foolish to fill in the gaps with fancy; but neither should one question that without recourse to "historical imagination" it is impossible to make any human sense of the records at all.

In the same vein, Roche fretted about "the perennial challenge of transferring the perfection of one language into the perfection of another" and, in that other, of dealing with a poetry "deprived of its original sound." Even so, he proposed to "give some idea of the variety within Sappho's verbal fabric: her flux of textures . . . to reflect a little of her elusiveness, shift of tempos, subtleties of echo within technique and mood." It is difficult to know what Roche was at all reaching for, or how he would ever take hold of it.

Some translators, gussying up texts that require neither improvement nor repair, have sought to do Sappho one better. A certain Sapphic fragment quite clearly translates as follows (§36):

> Love undoes me again—
> dissolver of limbs
> bittersweet, irresistible
> creeping in.

Guy Davenport offers the following:

> Percussion, salt and honey,
> A quivering in the thighs
> he shakes me all over again,
> Eros who cannot be thrown,
> Who stalks on all fours
> Like a beast.

Davenport, without acknowledgment, takes "salt and honey" from "H.D." (Hilda Doolittle) and turns Yeats's "A shudder of the loins" into "A quivering in the thighs." Davenport's fantasy on a Sapphic theme is hardly the translation it purports to be—to say nothing of the foreignness to Greek thinking of wing-borne Eros as a stalking quadruped. What will its reader know of the original's frightful simplicity? This is one of two translations of the fragment that Davenport provides: "Several times I have given alternate translations . . . since no English version of language so remote in idiom and estranged in culture can be in any sense wholly accurate or final." Such language is remote, indeed, from the translator ill-schooled in the language itself, as will be seen.

While translators may change their renderings over time, or from one edition to the next, as did Edward FitzGerald (1809–1883) in his *Rubáiyát*, they are initially called upon to *decide*. Remoteness of idiom, however much it results in differing translation, little warrants concurrent alternate versions by the same hand. These demonstrate only lack of conviction. And what do we make of such alternates from one whose stated intention is "everywhere . . . to suggest the tone of Sappho's words"? How many concurrent tones does she have? In the best of circumstances, those relying on translation have little idea of "what gets lost in translation and what gets retained or found." We care little enough from what possibilities the original poet chose, or what possibilities the informed translator considered. What should we care of indecisive alternates? It is, in the end, only the result that matters, a result *singular* in both senses of the word.

As previously mentioned, Dryden famously distinguished between three types of translation: metaphrase (literal translation), paraphrase (translation with "latitude"), and imitation (barely translation at all):

> All translation I suppose may be reduced to these three heads:
>
> First, that of Metaphrase, or turning an Authour word by word, and Line by Line, from one Language into another. . . . The second is that of Paraphrase, or Translation with Latitude, where the Authour is kept in view by the Translator, so as never to be lost, but his words are not so strictly follow'd as his sense and that too is admitted to be amplyfied, but not altered. . . . The Third way is that of Imitation, where the Translator (if now he has not lost that Name) assumes the liberty not only to vary from the words and sense, but to forsake them both as he sees occasion, and taking only some general hints from the Original, to run on the ground-work, as he pleases.

In metaphrase (literal translation), says Dryden, either "perspicuity or gracefulness will be wanting." Imitation, though "the most advantageous way of a Translator to shew himself, [is] the greatest wrong which can be done to the memory and reputation of the dead." (The translator's "shew[ing] himself," we note, is tantamount to the self-over-subject-matter tendency earlier identified in this volume.) These are "the two extreams, which ought to be avoided." Dryden's middle way is paraphrase (translation with latitude), what we today would call literary translation—our sense of the word *paraphrase*, i.e., a loose approximation, differing from Dryden's.

The notion of Greekless or Latinless translators would have been incomprehensible, even laughable, to Dryden. Yet, inasmuch as these have now usurped the work of cultural transmission, we do well to properly distinguish between literary translation, on the one hand, and imitation/adaptation, on the other, especially as the latter is practiced today. A literary translation is based on knowledge of the original. It seeks fidelity to the original and beauty in its own right—the conveyance of trustworthy meaning by effective poetic means. The goal is admittedly impossible, and one can succeed only by degree. Poetic effect must be that of the "target" language, as the original is essentially inimitable. Imitation, by contrast, proceeds with or without knowledge of the original, with or without attention to the original, and most often with the aid of existing translations and some extra-textual emphasis or "theme." The result is variation on a theme or pure invention. The less the translator knows, the more he invents. Invention may also occur within and around the original, as in the noted wholesale reconstruction of fragmentary remains. In such cases the reader is ever and further removed from a genuine experience. Fiction and original poetry are by nature inventive. Translation too is inventive, but properly only as concerns means and method. Invented meaning gives rise only to false impression, and to the liberty that feeds wayward and wasteful interpretation.

❧

The success of translation depends on aesthetic focus and steadfast commitment to English-language prosody. Prosody is the rhythm and sound of poetry, as well as its versification and stanzaic arrangement (Gr. *pros* 'to, toward' + *oidē* 'song, poem'; Eng. *ode*). As will be seen (Chapters 19 and 20), the prosody of Greek and Latin poetry—with their peculiar word order, quantitative as opposed to naturally accented stresses, and (in Greek) variable accents, pitches, and intonations—is entirely foreign to the qualities associated with poetry in English and other Western languages. Classical poetry neither knew nor needed rhyme as we know it, while its quantitative, or vowel-weighted, meter was of a kind unknown to succeeding cultures.

The translations of this volume (PART III), regardless the often fragmentary originals, are rhymed and accentually stressed—the better to communicate poetry in English. As Boris Pasternak has said, the "likeness" of a translation (as that of a portrait) can be achieved only by a "lively and natural method of expression. . . . Like the original text, the translation must create an impression of life and not of verbiage." Rhyme, as often claimed, is not an "imposition" on the translation of classical verse. Only by its stricter discipline does rhyme impose. The same applies to the consistent use of meter. It is the absence from classical poetry of rhyme and meter as we know them that fuels the pervasive freedom of form and content in translation. Though I discovered it late in the writing of this work, I welcome the formulation of the young Mary Stewart's *Catullus, An Experiment in Translation* (1905). Distinguishing three methods of translation—the purely scholarly, the scholarly-literary, and the purely literary—Stewart explains the second as follows:

> . . . the scholarly-literary . . . aims not only at an accurate transcript of ideas but at an appreciation of them in relation to their own setting. This means keeping the "flavor" of the original, translating oneself, so to speak, into the past rather than the original into the present.

Intending a literary, not social or other, "setting," Stewart speaks to the qualities that make poems *poems* by whatever means—or partnership, if you will—the original and translation allow. My own translations thus seek to recapture rather than contemporize a sense of the past. They are of the past, even as their translator is. As Stewart says, "We have written as we have read."

To grasp the challenge of scholarly-literary translation, we look to the key features of ancient Greek poetry, in which the aforementioned classicist Gilbert Murray (1866–1957) provides guidance as follows:

(1) **Quantitative meter.** Syllables are metrically either long or short, depending on the quantity—i.e., the pronunciational length or duration—of the vowels they contain. Vowel length is determined by set rules or conventions, as further discussed below. Greek metric duration sometimes coincides with, and sometimes plays against, the language's spoken or natural stress. The play is an essential feature of classical verse. English knows none of this. In English, as in modern European languages generally, meter is determined solely by spoken stress, regardless of vowel length or duration. What English observes of vowel length or duration tends to be randomly determined.

(2) **Inflection.** As those who have studied Latin recall (though the same applies to Classical Greek), nouns and adjectives are declined, verbs conjugated—a process in which personal, grammar-determinative endings are affixed to word stems. Western European languages, German in particular, retain significant declensional and conjugational features, including gender-assigned nouns, albeit far fewer such features than do Greek and Latin. English retains only the scantiest vestiges (e.g., plural *-s*/*-es*; 3rd pers. sing. *-s*; past tense *-ed*). Greek and Latin are thus called "inflected" languages (Lat. *flecto* 'bend, curve'). This suggests that words are not only "bent" or "curved" by their endings, but *inward* bent, or "inbent," one to the other, signaling relationship and grammatical function. Inflected words can appear

where they will, and without confusion, in the sentence, creating a rich and variable texture.

(3) **Polysyllabic, vowel-rich vocabulary.** A polysyllabic language given to the compounding of words, Greek is necessarily vowel rich. English by contrast is, or originally was, largely monosyllabic and consonantal. Greek polysyllabism, with personal endings designating grammatical function, requires pronunciational precision. As it is the Greek final syllable (the personal ending) that designates function, the final syllable must be heard. Leading to this heard-vowel "finale" must be the *clear* pronunciation of all preceding vowels. If the preceding vowels are slurred, there is little hope of clarity in the last. English by contrast relies on word order to designate function, even as it tends to swallow or de-emphasize final and grammatically unimportant syllables.

We further note that the English language began shedding its marked monosyllabism following the Norman Conquest of 1066 AD with its infusion into a then largely Germanic English of a richly Greco-Latinate, proto-French vocabulary. English may compensate for its shortcomings vis-à-vis the languages of antiquity by a synonym-rich vocabulary deriving from the Germanic, on the one hand, and the Greco-Latin on the other—e.g., ghost/spirit; rise/ascend; light/illumine—the former more clipped and consonantal, the latter longer and more vowel expressive. In the expressive realm of poetry, as in other areas, longer words are clearly of benefit. In the translation of Greek and Latin poetry, longer English words allow for the importation (or reimportation) of Greek- and Latin-based words as an aid to capturing Greek and Latin meanings or texture. This is a singular, yet largely unacknowledged, advantage—though traditionally heresy to those intent on a "pure" pre-Latinate English. The bias against polysyllabics nonetheless persists, even as flat and uneventful monosyllabics prevail. The problem is less pronounced in non-Germanic-based European languages, notably Italian, directly descendant from Latin.

There are scant means by which English can capture the essential features of Greek poetry. As Professor Murray notes, "The edges of words were more clear cut, and the value of each syllable more definite, than with us. Consequently, many metrical effects are possible and even easy in Greek which are practically impossible in English." Similarly, "speakers of a highly inflected language, like Latin or Greek, built their speech of clearly shaped marble blocks," whereas "our words pour out in a semi-liquid stream, melting into one another like wax." One must therefore look to the particular resources of "the thin liveliness of English" to make resonate in translation what first sounded and resounded in Greek.

The resonance will be of a different kind by different means, rhyme included, as "the condition [in English] for doing without rhyme is that the meter must be uniform and clear. . . ." Conversely, "Greek and Latin could do without rhyme because they had such clear meters." The logic is apparent. Rhyme principally serves English as meter did Greek, "to mark clearly the end of the line and provide the ear with a fixed resting place." Both serve better to fix or articulate, to *create*, meaning; to generally distinguish poetry from prose. Philosopher-poet George Santayana (1862–1952) notes that rhyme "gives an artificial relationship to the phrases between which it obtains"; that, without it, "phrases would run away from one another in a rapid and irrevocable flux." Artificiality, as we have noted, is a concomitant, a requisite, of poetic language. Similarly, asks formalist poet-metrist Anthony Hecht (1923–2004),

> does the matching of rhymes satisfy some curious but deeply human craving for a formal order that is meant in homage to some universal order we need to posit, if not out of reverence, then out of dread of its possible absence? Or is there something in the human psyche that delights in 'order for its own sake', wherever it may be found, in symmetries, harmonies, repetitions, and resolutions?

Santayana deems the sonnet "the most classic of modern poetical forms" for the way it "synthesiz[es] the phrase and make[s] the unexpected seem inevitable." This the sonnet does by the consistency of its metric and interlocking patterns of rhyme, analogous to the texture-enriching interlock of inflected classical diction.

# Chapter 10

## Translatability: Achieving Distinction and Charm

> The best lack all conviction, while the worst
> Are full of passionate intensity.
>
> – W. B. YEATS, "The Second Coming"

MANY ARE THE FALLACIES and pretensions surrounding the work of translation, the greatest that one may effectively or at all translate without knowing the original. Untranslatability begins not with words, notes Santayana, but with "the diversities of tongues and their irreducible aesthetic values . . . with the very sound of the letters, and with the mode of utterance, and the characteristic inflections of the voice." Impervious to this, as to what may at all be gleaned from the original, Greekless translators nonetheless propose to furnish a true sense, spirit, flavor, or tone, while actually boasting their ignorance of Greek, or their familiarity with its rudiments alone. Perhaps they are self-styled, passingly acknowledged, or prize-winning poets; know some French or Italian; are professors of English with undergraduate work in classics. Whatever the posture, any of the above suffice.

Following Mary Barnard's landmark *Sappho: A New Translation* (1958), the Edmonds-reliant Paul Roche joined the vanguard of popular translators with *The Love Songs of Sappho* (1966). We will have significantly more to say about Mary Barnard in the next two chapters. As for Roche, his reconstructed versions came accompanied by pencil sketches of pining women in various states of undress amid desolate antique ruins—these the trappings of authenticity. Noting that "'imitations' have once again become fashionable," Roche yet proposed that *his* Sappho was "strictly a translation." Roche further proposed, "Poets up and down the land are writing their own Homers and Ovids and Virgils: some of them without reference to or even knowledge of the language from which they quarry their ore of gold." And that the "best of them follow an old and lively tradition" was—in the mid-1960s, with the "tradition" merely aborning—less than accurate and not in the least consoling.

Admissions of ignorance or semi-ignorance of Greek are thus either veiled or shockingly avowed.

Here is the acclaimed writer-translator Guy Davenport on Sappho:

> My starting point was the poems and not the Greek language, my knowledge of which is functional rather than philological. . . . The reading of Sappho is surrounded by passionate dispute in which I am unqualified to join; my translation therefore is without authority except the dubious one of sentiment. . . . To approach the emotions of ancient poets is a matter helped along by more than halting Greek, dictionaries, and history books; my debt therefore extends to . . .

And Michael Ayrton on Archilochus:

> I do not know much Greek and so Geoffrey Kirk has made me a literal translation of the existing texts, all that can be comprehensibly transcribed of them. I took this and I acknowledge also a debt to Richard [sic] Lattimore, Guy Davenport, F. Lasserre, D. A. Campbell and others, whose translations and discourses I have read. But I rashly composed this text myself.

And the ubiquitous Willis Barnstone:

> In these often pained choices [i.e., of Greek transliteration into English] I have been helped hugely by my former colleague at Wesleyan University, William McCulloh, with whom I collaborated for both *Greek Lyric Poetry* (1961) and *Sappho: Lyrics in the Original Greek and Translations* (1965). Now, as in the past, it is his scholarship against my amateurism. I learn from him. McCulloh is absolute in making me note all sins. So what you find here may be enervating but not slipshod. Not on McCulloh's watch, for which I am endlessly grateful.

Davenport, as Roche, acknowledges his indebtedness to the reconstructions of J. M. Edmonds. For Davenport, however, the reliance is wholesale, if not particularly suited to his own fancy. Unlike Roche with his modicum of training, Davenport is quite the stranger to the original. Imputing authority to his effort even so, Davenport brings out the "heavies," asserting he has "generally followed the text as given by Lobel and Page, *Poetarum Lesbiorum Fragmenta* (Oxford, 1963), and additions from Page's *Supplementum Lyricis Graecis* (Oxford, 1974), and [is] indebted to [Page's] *Sappho and Alcaeus* (Oxford 1959)." Davenport likewise prefaces his endnotes with the claim, "Translated from Edgar Lobel and Denys Page, *Poetarum Lesbiorum Fragmenta,* etc." The cited works, with imposing Latin titles and Latin textual apparatus, are the *summa* of philological inquiry—inquiry in which Davenport elsewhere avers he is unqualified to participate. These same works belie Davenport's breezy assertion: "There is so little of Sappho that the reader with beginner's Greek can read the substantial fragments in an afternoon." If that is the case, what need has Davenport of such specialized textual resources—and what compelled their creation in the first place? Remaining undecided between the publication of his 1965 and 1980 (expanded) editions, Davenport again offers "alternate translations," as his knowledge of Greek *remains* "functional rather than philological," and his translation "without authority except the dubious one of sentiment."

The situation is equally apparent in the translation of modern poetry—and of some of the most challenging such poetry, that of twentieth-century Russian poet Osip Mandelstam. Thus does poet, translator, and *Poetry* magazine editor Christian Wiman admit,

> I don't speak or read Russian. I did these versions from word-by-word translations provided by Ilya [Kaminsky] or Helena Lorman (a scholar at Northwestern) as well as transliterations of the originals (the Cyrillic changed to the Roman alphabet) so that I could tell where the rhymes were happening and get a sense of the sounds. I also worked with a lot of scholarly sources to help me think about the context of individual poems.

Wiman is yet more unabashed in an excerpt from his book *Stolen Air: Selected Poems of Osip Mandelstam,* appearing in *The New Criterion*:

> I couldn't have written any of these poems without Ilya Kaminsky, who helped me every step of the way. I am also grateful to Helena Lorman for all kinds of intricate information about idiom, word choice, and formal detail.

The confession recalls the indebtedness of essentially Greekless *Iliad* translator Robert Fagles (later discussed): "To work with Bernard [Knox] on a translation of the *Iliad,* to receive his comments line by line, shaped the entire poem for me." What most amazes about Wiman's translations is his use of rhyme, which, though admirable, places greater strictures on a translator who is essentially second-guessing meaning, context, and tone. Pity the great poet. The Russianless Robert Lowell's translation of Mandelstam earned the searing rebuke of Vladimir Nabokov (later discussed).

To recall the lines of W. B. Yeats, "The best lack all conviction, while the worst / Are full of passionate intensity." Paraphrased for our purposes: those knowing *little* promise *all,* while those knowing much apologize. Among the latter, the notable Thomas George ("T. G.") Tucker, onetime professor of Classical Philology at the University of Melbourne, famed for his editions and commentaries on Aeschylus (these known to Charlotte Brontë and the Woolfs, Virginia and Leonard). His one foray into Sappho was in lecture form, published the year after its delivery as *Sappho: A Lecture delivered before the Classical Association of Victoria, 1913.* The lecture ranges over the key aspects of its subject, including translation, and is everywhere and to a fault intuitive. More than that, it is *sane* beyond contemporary imagining, a tribute to a bygone aesthetic and sensibility. Tucker intersperses the latter half of the lecture with his own quite marvelous translations of Sappho (reproduced herein, as noted). Tucker was that rarest of beings, the classical scholar-poet with true feeling for both his subject and his own language. Despite what may strike us a century later as a quaint or dated idiom, Tucker's translations escape the censure of words which, in the Earl of Roscommon's (1633–1685) formulation, "Rome admir'd in Caesar's time, / [but] neither suit our genius, nor our time." Tucker's idiom sooner shows, "The genuine sense, intelligibly told, / Shews a Translator both Discreet and Bold."

The issue for Tucker was not which translation, among many, was best, but which might "be nearer, less inadequate than another." His own translations are surely nearer than any before or since, with their all-but-flawless fidelity and felicity. For this he was yet *apologetic,* fearing the absence of that, to him, most crucial element: **charm** (key terms bolded in what follows). The word derives from Lat. *carmen* 'song, spell', and may be defined as *the attractive power of love* (*attractive* in the sense of that which *draws* or causes something to approach). One of the words for *charm* in Latin is *venustas* (the other, *lepos*), built on Venus's own name. Offering his version of Sappho's nearly complete *phainetai moi,* Tucker thus laments: "We can preserve, if we will, the directness, but the charm of its medium will inevitably vanish."

Focusing not only on charm but also on distinction—call it greatness, quality, excellence—Tucker continues at telling length:

> And here we are confronted with a supreme difficulty. While mere fact is readily translatable, and thought is approximately translatable, the literary quality, which is warm with the pressure and pulsation of a writer's mood and rhythmic with his emotional state, is hopelessly untranslatable. It can be suggested, but it cannot be reproduced. The translation is too often like the bare, cold photograph of a scene of which the emotional effect is largely due to color and atmosphere. The simpler and more direct the words of the original, the more impossible is translation. In the original the words, though simple and direct, are poetical, beautiful in quality and association. They contain in their own nature hints of pathos, sparks of fire, which any so-called synonym would lack. They are musical in themselves and musical in their combinations. They flow easily, sweetly, touchingly through the ear into the heart. The translator may seek high and low in his own language for words and combinations of the same *timbre,* the same ethical or emotional influence, the same gracious and touching music. He will generally seek in vain. In his own language there may exist words approximately answering in meaning, but, even if they are fairly simple and direct, they are often commonplace, sullied with "ignoble use," harsh in sound, without **distinction** or **charm**. He may require a whole phrase to convey the same tone and effect; he becomes diffuse, where terseness is a special virtue of his original.
> [emphasis added]

Tucker fears his translation lacks **charm**—the inherently *attractive* element of any poetry—equating charm with **distinction**. Tucker is mindful in this connection of the opening Prologue to Lucretius, *De Rerum Natura,* which highlights charm and distinction as Venus's special domain. Scholar and poet both, Tucker reveals a quite purposeful sense of association from which there is much to learn. The Lucretian passage is decidedly erotic and, on that account, relevant to Sappho and archaic Greek love lyric. We consider first

Lucretian *lepos* 'charm', then Lucretian *ornatum* (Lat. *orno* 'adorn')—that which has been rendered 'ornate' and thus given **distinction.**

Venus, goddess of love, is the most beautiful of the gods and irresistible. Her attraction is emotional, biological, and intellectual (heart, body, and mind). She is the generative force of both life and art. Lucretius bids Venus, quo magis **aeternum** da dictis, diva, **leporem** 'The more so, goddess, grant **charm everlasting** to [my] words'. "Charm everlasting" is the enduring godlike quality represented by Venus herself. Only with this quality will Lucretius's words attract the reader, engage him emotionally and intellectually, induce his understanding and own creative response. The engagement—by analogy to procreation in the natural world—is *generative*, begetting thought and understanding. Lucretius makes the entreaty with characteristic alliterative emphasis: quo magis **aeternum** *d*a *d*ictis, *d*iva, **leporem**. The pointedness of the plea shows Lucretius himself in thrall to Venus, his own imagination straining to her influence. All Nature submits to Venus. Sentient life thrills and quickens to her summons. Beasts in both senses *join* in her procreative retinue. Lucretius thus concludes: ita capta **lepore** / te sequitur quoquamque inducere pergis 'thus captivated by [your] **charm**, they follow wherever you seek to lead [them] each'.

As Lucretius is drawn to Venus, he hopes his readers will be drawn to *him*, that Venus's **charm** throughout his verse—her ***venustas***—will enthrall his readers to Lucretius's *own* lead. Thus, as charmed nature instinctively yields to love's generative impulse, the intellect is attracted to and seeks union with that to which Venus's **charm** is given—in this case a philosophical poem on the nature of things. "Mating" further occurs at the level of form and content. Suffused with the **charm** of artistically generative power, the *De Rerum Natura* is able to "wed" poetic form to philosophic content. This is a most unlikely and challenging union and, for the 7,500 lines of poetry that follow, a most successfully accomplished and *enduring* union. **Eternal charm** (***aeternum ... leporem***) thus also bespeaks the desired prolongation of all generative process, natural and artistic.

Lamenting the inevitability of translation—his own included—"without distinction or charm," Tucker finds in Lucretius's Prologue a reference point for the charm of poetry and translation alike, the line between them thin. If Tucker's translations of Sappho succeed—his diffidence notwithstanding–they do so because he has the proper frame of reference and mind, to say nothing of the proper training, including knowledge of the source language and an understanding of poetic discipline. Of course, a Lucretian perspective requires—of others—a certain nobility or liberality of mind, its ornamentation, its **distinction**—even as excellent music requires discriminating listeners. The Prologue singles out the poem's dedicatee, one Memmius, the stand-in for us all, as someone whom Venus wishes tempore in omni / omnibus **ornatum** . . . excellere rebus 'at every time to excel, **distinguished** in every way'. Responsive to Venus's charm, Lucretius will create, be creative. Emulating the all-encompassing distinction sought for Memmius, we, as he, will be positioned to appreciate both process and result.

**Distinction** and **charm** bespeak an ideal, here significantly poetic. But they are integral to any creative endeavor. The same desiderata, defined as *gravità* and *piacevolezza* 'dignity and charm', were essential to the ideal Italian vernacular discussed by Pietro Bembo, *Prose della Volgar Lingua* (*Writings on the Common Tongue*) (1525). *Prose,* in turn, provided a language and frame of reference for the social ideal of the perfect gentleman (and lady) in Baldassare Castiglione, *Libro del Cortegiano* (*Book of the Courtier*) (1528), the *Libro* being one of the most widely translated, distributed, and influential works of the sixteenth century. We recall, in this connection, the Roman architect Vitruvius's prescription for the ideal architecture: *firmitas, utilitas,* and ***venustas***—'solidity, utility, and **charm**'. All such usages variously center on the generative and sustaining power of **charm**—defined, again, as the attractive power of love and, thus, signaling the *decorum* in all things beautiful (Lat. *decus* 'right, fitting, befitting').

The same consideration is apparent in the Renaissance preoccupation (taken from Plato's *Republic*) with the Ideal City—the ideal urban layout of buildings, streets, and amenities, encompassing (and thus encouraging) the moral and spiritual values of good citizenship and, by extension, the stability of society and civilization itself. C. S. Lewis (1898–1963)—translator of Virgil, intimate of J. R. R. Tolkien, and author of *The Chronicles of Narnia* (1939)—deemed superlative translation a safeguard to the preservation of the past and of civilization itself. We come full circle to Lucretius and his craving for **charm** (*lepos*) in an epic positing the generative cause and rationale for the nature of *all things,* including the atom, biological and inanimate creation, the composition of the soul, the origin of language, the rise of civilization, and the cosmos itself.

Tucker ends his lecture as follows:

> There is, we may add, one quality besides beauty in verse which can never be analyzed. It is charm. Sappho is pervaded with charm. And this suggests that we may conclude by quoting the judgment of Matthew Arnold upon one defect at least which must make [Heinrich] Heine rank always lower than Sappho:—
>
> Charm is the glory which makes
> Song of the poet divine;
> Love is the fountain of charm.
> How without charm wilt though draw,
> Poet! The world to thy way?
> Not by thy lightnings of wit—
> Not by thy thunder of scorn!
> These to the world, too, are given;
> Wit it possesses and scorn—
> Charm is the poet's alone.

Such are the humbling thoughts that should guide our considerations of Sappho and Sappho in translation, of all poetry and poetry in translation. What we require are distinction and charm from a translator merged with the *original.* What we don't require are "tone, fabric, verbal flux," or other facsimile from one as nearly uncomprehending of translation as of the original itself.

# Chapter 11

## Translation as the Profession of Ignorance: Mary Barnard, Willis Barnstone, and Others

> Disputes about translation are always a pretext for disputes about poetry. Translation theory is poetics by a different name. If I am interested in a certain kind of translation, it is because I am invested in a certain kind of poetry.
>
> – CHARLES BERNSTEIN, *Attack of the Difficult Poems*

WE NOTED IN THE LAST CHAPTER the proclivity of Greekless, or only passingly qualified, translators to confess—even boast—their insufficiencies, as though laying claim to some great virtue. Their virtue has, for the most part, been embraced by the academic reviewing mill and media, to say nothing of unknowing readers. We now examine five such translators of Sappho. Though their outputs and reputations broadly differ, they all share a comparable amateur or dilettante status, one ultimately grounded in what may be called the profession of ignorance. Samples of the two most acclaimed—Mary Barnard and Willis Barnstone—are discussed in the following chapter.

### I. F. Stone

"He will generally seek in vain," says T. G. Tucker of one seeking translation equivalents. Such was the sense of the scholar-poet who by training and sympathy knew what and where to seek, and who, despite self-disavowals, *found* what he was looking for. It is now dilettantism that rules. No effort is too trifling for praise, with public profile and collateral credentials the stand-ins for facility. Famed investigative journalist I. F. Stone (1907–1989), author of the acclaimed *Trial of Socrates* (1989), took to the study of ancient Greek late in life. In 1979 he published five lyric translations (including two by Sappho) in *The New York Review of Books,* with a three-paragraph "Footnote in Explanation" stating, "These are the first verses I have translated from the Greek, a language I have begun to learn. I have no expertise but love of it, and these are a distant reflection of the originals." Whether Stone's translations are "a distant reflection of the originals" because of his admitted amateurism or due to the inherent difficulty of capturing *anything* of the original is difficult to say (and left for others to explore).

## Mary Barnard

Much the same may be said of Mary Barnard (1909–2001), the doyenne of Sappho translation. Barnard—an epistolary friend of Ezra Pound, William Carlos Williams, and Marianne Moore—became Pound's Sappho-translation protégée. "When I wrote to Ezra Pound in the fall of 1933, and asked for advice and assistance," says Barnard, "he took me on as an apprentice poet, God knows why, but perhaps the fact that I had been studying Greek had something to do with it." It was Sappho-enthusiast Pound who encouraged Barnard's 1958 translation, reading it twice in draft. Pound had early urged her, twice in 1934, to venture a translation in English Sapphics. Declining the advice, Barnard, more than two decades later, published the at-once critically and financially successful *Sappho: A New Translation* (1958). It was this work that introduced the twentieth century to Sappho. A rival translator heralded Barnard's work as "the best Greek translation in American Literature." Barnard's masterstroke was the word *new* in her title, which continues, despite the more than half-century since, to impress as contemporary and cutting edge.

Explaining the rationale of her translation, Barnard avers she was trying to find an equivalent for the "underlying cadence" of Sappho's verse, which she characterized as "belong[ing] to the speaking voice"—something which, "so far as [she] knew, no English translation had yet conveyed." Whether Barnard's translation achieved its goal or instead succeeded because of timing and sponsorship is debatable. Sappho's original "speaking voice" is highly regulated, marked by an exacting meter and other qualities peculiar to archaic Greek lyric, to say nothing of Sappho's Aeolic dialect. That such verse nonetheless retains a spoken quality is its singular achievement. Barnard's translation, by contrast, is dictionally challenged, her choice and arrangement of words lacking Sappho's fullness and finesse. Barnard in fact abandons any semblance of the original's form (and thus voice) for a haiku-like sparseness, even while sometimes relying, without acknowledgment, on J. M. Edmonds's expansive reconstructions. While Barnard's translation exhibits a certain spoken quality, it is mundane and unpoetic, nowhere evoking the voice in which Sappho spoke. Barnard's pronounced change of rhythm is nothing if not the *loss* of voice (see Chapter 12).

Barnard reveals that during a lengthy convalescence, she returned to Greek to help pass the time. Having re-honed her skills on liberal doses of Homer (twelve books each of the *Iliad* and *Odyssey*), she turned to Sappho upon receiving a slender volume from friends, with a side-by-side Italian translation by classicist-poet Salvatore Quasimodo. Barnard found Sappho's Aeolic more challenging than Homer's Ionic. She puzzled its meaning with "a crib, or notes, or a lexicon." Yet, her "efforts left [her] wondering what all the fuss was about." Sappho's Aeolic was clearly beyond her. Turning to the Italian as her primary source, Barnard essentially abandoned any pretense of translating from the Greek.

> The first thing Quasimodo's translations did for me was show me the text through the medium of a language that was not English, living or dead, leaving my mind free to balance between the Greek phrase and the Italian phrase while I searched for the truly equivalent phrase in living, not lexicon English. *This little book removed one of the chief obstacles to translation, so far as I was concerned, by showing me how to use a third language as a bridge.*
> [emphasis added]

From the translator of what became the most revered and enduring Sappho translation of the last century, this is an astounding admission. Knowing Homeric Greek enough, Barnard still felt insufficient in Aeolic to translate Sappho directly. She thus used, as would any Greekless reader, a "bridge"—in this case Italian. Indeed, before finding a bridge, she had resorted to a "crib," the first refuge of the desperate.

"I found the Italian translations very beautiful," says Barnard, "and wanted to match them, if I could, in my own language." Barnard states that the "spare but musical" style toward which she had been "groping" was one she "found here in Sappho's Greek, as revealed to [her] through the medium of Italian." In other words, she found little enough in Sappho's Greek itself. Barnard sought, more than anything else, to match or reflect Quasimodo's Italian. Matching an Italian translation is remote indeed from the credible rendering of an ancient Greek original. Any comparison of Sappho translations (as offered below) shows considerable divergence. So, which is "best" or least offensive? And how is one to trust one's chosen "bridge," the more so in a non-native tongue?

Tucker notes that "Lesbian Greek [is] perhaps the most 'singable' of [all the Greek dialects]. In several ways it is particularly like Italian. The aspirate is gone, the double consonants are brought out with an Italian clarity unique in Greece, the vowels are firm and musical." Whatever else Barnard labors to explain about her Italian-Sapphic inspiration, she expresses no awareness of such affinity—even as her translation fails to reflect it. Had she sooner happened upon a French translation, it would likely have served as well. Other questions arise. What made Barnard think a modern European language "bridge" was any more sound than the English translations already at her disposal? How could the Aeolic-challenged Barnard determine that no English translation—if any can—had "yet conveyed" Sappho's "inner voice"?

The task, not surprisingly, proved difficult. Barnard continues, "I kept on trying. Eventually I think most of the fragments and each stanza of the longer poems did go through about forty versions . . . different words and different arrangements of the words, asking myself over and over: what did she *mean*? Why did she say gold *sandals*?" Had the prolific F. L. Lucas needed forty versions to produce each of his consummate Greek lyric (and other) translations, he would have had time for nothing else. If, as earlier urged, the translator's task is to *decide*, one cannot fathom such numerous attempts for merely fragmentary remains. Barnard says, "If I had been leading an active life, I would never have had the patience to work so long over each fragment, or if I had, the job would have taken me ten years." It is a matter more of facility than of patience—and these are all very unwitting and self-compromising admissions.

## Robert Chandler

Barnard's bridge method, previously unexamined, is not without parallel; indeed, not without *marked* parallel in a far less heralded effort. Robert Chandler (b. 1953), almost exclusively a translator of Russian and Slavic works, points to the Sappho-crazed English poet Algernon Charles Swinburne (1837–1909) as the inspiration for his own translation of Sappho. No one before or since has written English Sapphics as has Swinburne (see Chapter 19). Reading these led Chandler, as he relates, to his own attempt at composition in the Swinburnian manner:

> Some six months later, without any conscious intention of reading Sappho, I decided to attempt to relearn the classical Greek I had studied as a child. Later I was to study more formally, but initially I just read *Teach Yourself Ancient Greek* on my own. After six weeks of this, I began to long for something less dry. I turned to the *Penguin Book of Greek Verse* and began, with the help of the prose crib, to read the "Ode to Aphrodite." This proved hard work—Sappho's archaic dialect is not easy even for a scholar to understand. In the fifth and sixth stanzas, however, as Aphrodite replies to the poet's entreaties, both language and meter become simpler. Suddenly I could hear a speaking voice, a voice that seemed, astonishingly, to speak to me from the page as clearly and vividly as anything I had ever read.

"Decided to attempt to relearn the classical Greek [he] studied as a child"? That must have been some small amount of childhood study, and a huge amount of adult retraining, for this one-time foray by an exemplar of the everyone-wants-a-piece-of-Sappho syndrome. For the rest, the coincidences in Barnard's and Chandler's "awakenings" are pronounced: from attempted reengagement with a language long unstudied or neglected, to various forms of self-help, including cribs, to the admitted struggle with Sappho's Aeolic, to the identically worded discovery by both translators of an inspirational "speaking voice." If my entirely chance encounter with this *one* of scores of Sappho translations bears such Barnard-like resemblance, we can only fear for a systematic comparison.

## Willis Barnstone

So also the plenteous Willis Barnstone's rendering of lyric authors from the eighth century BC to the sixth century AD (over six hundred selections). Still the most comprehensive undertaking of its kind, it occasions wonder as the product of a comparatist whose primary training is in Spanish, yet who has also translated from languages as divergent from one another—and from ancient Greek—as German (Rilke, *Sonnets to Orpheus*), Biblical Hebrew (Song of Songs), and Chinese (poems of Mao Zedong).

Unlike Mary Barnard and others, Barnstone seems not to have succumbed to Sappho's "speaking voice" or Aeolic fire. When Barnstone first translated Sappho (1962), Mary Barnard was the only other contender. So the issue was not even one of improving on one's predecessors. Rather, to quote Barnstone:

> For many years I have been interested in women's poetry. In 1962 I published a book of Sappho's poems in Greek, with a translation and study. My daughter, Aliki, and I did a large anthology called *A Book of Women Poets from Antiquity to Now* [1980]. I regularly teach a course in women poets for Indiana's women studies program, for which I am a faculty member. Most recently I published a book called *Sappho and the Greek Lyric Poets*. These are signs of a preoccupation with women's poetry, most of which began three decades earlier, when universities did not yet have women's studies programs. In other words, the signs that I lack a history as an insensitive sexist.

Barnstone's *Book of Women Poets*, etc., is eight hundred and eighty-two pages, containing all that survives of Sappho's work. If Barnstone's purpose was ingratiation with women's studies and the display of sympathetic credentials, he surely succeeded—his statement nothing so much as politically correct grandstanding before it was fashionable. For the rest, when journals and magazines regularly reject the submission of previously published poems, Barnstone's Sappho has since circulated in an inexplicable number of concurrent, or nearly concurrent, editions—six at last count. It is archaic Greek lyric as wallpaper.

Barnstone most recently authored *The Restored New Testament: A New Translation with Commentary, Including the Gnostic Gospels Thomas, Mary, and Judas*—an output of nearly 1,500 pages. Reviewer Frank Kermode notes,

> the languages one would need to know in order to do all this work are Hebrew, Greek—both classical and its 'marketplace' version *koine* (the language of the New Testament)—some Coptic, and some Aramaic (the Semitic vernacular used in Palestine and adjacent areas in the centuries when Hebrew was reserved for religious use). Add Latin, at the time of the New Testament the language of the Roman military occupation and later of the almost unchallengeably authoritative Vulgate, the Catholic Bible . . .

Kermode assumes Barnstone's proficiency in all of the above without suggesting how much "some" of a language might be. It is assuming a lot. Barnstone, in a 2006 edition of his *Sappho,* can say little more than "I have been tinkering with classical Greek for many decades along with Koine Greek and biblical Hebrew."

It is enough that Greek poetry, dating back millennia, makes us detectives of texts and meaning. However, one's knowledge of a source language is typically clear on the face of things. It need not be searched for. Search reveals that Barnstone, as he himself relates, studied not Classical, but Modern Greek at a time when contemporary Greek poets—Gatsos, Ritsos, Seferis, Elytis—"were in their prime." He wanted to write poetry, "to learn the landscapes of Greece and a language of symbolic images for poetry." Barnstone elsewhere relates:

> When I began to write poetry in 1948, I felt an affinity with the poetry of Spain, China, and India. I had studied Hebrew and knew Spanish and French. Then in 1949, near the end of Greece's civil war, I went to live and work a few years in Athens. There Greek joined the list, at first modern, then ancient.

These words come from an article suitably titled "How I Strayed into Asian Poetry." Indeed, Barnstone seems not so much to have studied languages as to have happened upon them. By comparison to European Romance languages, Classical and Modern Greek are difficult, each in its own way. Nor does Modern Greek at all "flow" from Classical. They are all but different languages. Such languages do not "join [a] list," but require years of dedicated study.

Barnstone's breezy absorption of languages can only astound. We have not seen its like since philologist and hyper-polyglot William Jones (1746–1794)—adept in Greek, Latin, French, Italian, Spanish, and Portuguese at age twenty, and, at the bidding of King Christian VII of Denmark, translator of Arabic and Persian into French. The truest assessment of Barnstone's claim to translation-level proficiency in Classical Greek comes in the following admonition: "Perhaps it is best to openly warn the reader against *Sappho: Lyrics in the Original Greek with Translations by Willis Barnstone* . . . which includes a Greek text so miserably riddled with errors as to be virtually worthless; and of course, the translation is based on it." Amen.

As concerns Barnstone's *Modern* Greek, he used it (with other help) as a bridge to the Hebrew in translating the Song of Songs (Heb. *Shir haShirim*). "The version," he relates, "was made from the Masoretic Hebrew Text. I also consulted the Septuagint . . . and George Seferis' consummate version in Modern Greek." One here senses more Seferis than Septuagint; and in Seferis's "consummate" version, the surrogate for Barnstone's Hebrew. Seferis himself did not know Hebrew, but found his 'attraction' (*élksī*) in 'the text of the Old Testament in the Septuagint' (*tó keímeno tís Palaiás Diathíkis tṓn Ebdomíkonta*). So Seferis relates in the Prologue to his 1965 edition of *Asma Asmatōn* (the Modern Greek title of the Song of Songs). That makes Barnstone's Song of Songs, to the extent reliant on Seferis, a translation four times removed from its source: Old Testament Hebrew, to Septuagint Greek, to Modern Greek, to English. We note that Septuagint Greek—*Koinē*, or common Greek—is a greatly simplified form of Classical Greek. To read Classical Greek with moderate ability is to read *Koinē* with ease—obviating the need for a significantly more difficult Modern Greek translation. Indeed, Barnstone's effort was but Seferis-worship, as any number of *English* versions, done directly from the Hebrew, would have put Barnstone *in his native tongue* yet closer to the biblical source. Barnstone's infatuation with Modern Greek resembles Barnard's with Italian.

That said, we may glimpse the opening of Barnstone's Song of Songs, as openings are invariably revealing. Instilling little confidence, Barnstone *again* announces, "I have been tinkering with classical Greek for many decades along with Koine Greek and biblical Hebrew." Barnstone's difficulties are apparent from the two-sentence outset of his translation: 'Kiss me with kisses from your mouth. Your love is better than wine' (*Yishakēni minshikōt pīhū, kī tōvim dōdechah miyayīn)*. Barnstone's opening 'kiss me' is not (in the Hebrew) a second- but a third-person command. Thus the King James Version (KJV): 'Let him kiss me with the kisses of his mouth'. The KJV continues, as do other translations, *not* with a new sentence, but with the conjunctive Heb. *kī* 'for, because': '. . . for thy love is better than wine'. In the Hebrew there is but one sentence. A new sentence in translation decidedly breaks the flow.

While the opening 'Let him kiss me' is sometimes rendered as a *second* person ('Kiss me'), the reason is recondite and without analogy in English. If such rendering is followed, an explanatory note is wanted. Challenges to the KJV, or to KJV revisions, show a similar uncertainty. The Revised Standard Version (RSV) thus uses the second person in the opening, but with a cross-reference to the KJV. The English Standard Version (ESV) reverts back to the KJV: 'Let him kiss me with the kisses of his mouth! / For your love is better than wine' (changing 'thy' to 'your'). Other versions, desperate for consistency, employ the third person in both clauses: 'Let him kiss me . . . for his love', etc. The issue is complex and ever changeable in English. Any choice requires explanation. And whatever the choice, a single sentence is needed.

Be that as it may, Barnstone's rendering is prosaic. It is, first, inelegant in its 'kisses *from* your mouth'. There is but one rendering for the Hebrew, and that is 'kisses *of* your mouth'. Even then, Heb. <u>*min*</u>*shikōt* is 'from [the] kisses'; not 'with kisses'. 'From the kisses' suggests an endless store from which any number is desired, with as many remaining; 'with kisses', a somehow finite and less exuberant supply. Barnstone follows the sometime practice of transliterating the Hebrew title as *Shir Hashirim.* While this illustrates that Heb. *ha* 'the' does not stand alone but attaches to the word that follows, the impression it creates for the title's meaning is misleading. The proper transliteration is *shir ha-shirim* (Hebrew has no capitalization); or, if capitalized, *Shir ha-Shirim, Shir haShirim,* or even *Shir HaShirim*—all of which convey that the definite article, despite appearances in Hebrew, is distinct from the noun that follows. The distinction fails with "*Shir Hashirim.*" Barnstone next takes Song of Songs in its secondary sense of a "Song [comprised] of Songs," ignoring the compelling superlative import of recognized biblical or liturgical usage, e.g., 'Holy of Holies' (*kōdesh ha-kōdoshim*), 'God of gods' (*elohā ha-elohim*), 'King of kings' (*melech ha-mamlachim*), and others. The preference has very long been settled: "For all the Writings are holy," asserts Rabbi Akiva (1st–2nd centuries AD), "but the Song of Songs is the Holy of Holies." The formulation Song of Songs is thus far better understood as a declaration of supreme worth than as a lyric anthology, and if as an anthology, surely not one in the conventional sense (for which one sooner looks to Proverbs or Psalms).

Barnstone's missteps, so soon out of the starting gate, belie his vaunted reliance on the scrupulously authoritative "Masoretic Hebrew Text." What is more, Barnstone thanks his Hebrew-language collaborators—first, a professor who helped "in interpreting the Hebrew texts" and who spent many evenings with Barnstone "checking each sentence of the translation"; then, the Israeli cultural attaché in Athens, who "help[ed] in the enigma of alternate meanings." The exegetical expertise of his helpers remains unevidenced. And what might a government attaché know of "the enigma of alternate meanings" that has not of old found its way into the existing biblical scholarship? Barnstone is not the first to have translated the most perplexing and frequently translated Songs of Songs. The work's interpretive dilemmas have long since been known and argued, and exceedingly so in the decades between the 1970 and 2002 editions of Barnstone's own rendering. While scholars may still differ over the precise meaning of particular words and phrases, the differences are generally over minutiae, and a translator who studies the commentary and applies his own good judgment is unlikely to stray. This makes meaning, again, a matter of *choice*—assuming the translator is sufficiently schooled to choose. Even the qualified might hesitate to choose in so problematic a work as the Song of Songs. Their discretion is the better part of valor. Barnstone, by contrast, has troubled over "enigmas" while wanting for the basics. Those conversant with biblical commentary do not seek amateur third-hand opinions, let alone advertise it. Barnstone's manner of collaboration and sentence-by-sentence compunction recalls Mary Barnard's "forty versions each."

Modern Greek is to Classical Greek, by analogy, what Modern English is to Old English: incomprehensible. Reading the opening lines of the *Iliad* in the "classic" Modern Greek translations of Iakovos Polylas (1826–1898), Alexandros Pallis (1851–1935), or Nikos Kazantzakis (1883–1957), or in even more current versions, poetic or prose, one finds little of Homer's vocabulary and syntax, to say nothing of simple elegance and concision. Barnstone's using Seferis's Modern Greek translation of Song of Songs as a bridge to his own translation of the Hebrew, when Seferis himself did not know Hebrew, thus assures little more than using

Italian as a bridge to archaic Greek, especially when the Italian translator, though knowing Greek, was as random in his prosody as was Quasimodo. In the end, it is not a bridge, crib, or dictionary, but *direct access* that is needed. Direct access comes not merely from knowing a language—for that is only the starting point—but from *internalizing* it through long exposure and extensive memorization. The sounds and rhythms become ingrained, imparting poetic wherewithal and closing the gap, if it exists, between scholar and poet. The difference between reading and memorizing poetry is the difference between viewing a Rembrandt at the museum and having it hang from your own wall.

The dilemmas confronting Barnard's translating of Greek, and the enigmas besetting Barnstone's translating of Hebrew combine in Barnstone's rendering of Chinese, which "obliges [one] to come up with ten or twenty solutions for each linguistic enigma." It is in his encounter with Chinese that Barnstone most fully proclaims his ignorance of the source language. His bridge for the translation of poems by Mao Zedong was not another language, but a muddled English translation he happened upon. "Behind the bombastic Chinglish," Barnstone advises, "I saw the work of a major poet." Barnstone further collaborated with a native Chinese graduate student in "retranslating" the poems. The student provided "literal, dictionary meanings—not equivalents or interpretations—for each word," and the thirty-seven (re)translations were in a month submitted to Harper & Row (which already had a book of Barnstone's own poems in the offing).

Though the manuscript sat idle at Harper's for four months, it was rushed to print within eleven days of Harper's learning that then President Richard Nixon was planning his epochal visit to China. Nixon subsequently toasted Mao with one of the poems. The book was next "selected as a Book-of-the-Month Alternate Feature, and poems were extracted for the editorial page of *The New York Times*. That Spring I was invited to impenetrable China as 'a friend of China.'" Barnstone's Mao, not so impenetrably, was a product of politics, fortuitous timing, and anticipated retail sales; of luck and publishing connections. These say nothing of the work's accuracy, quality, or authenticity—but much of laissez-faire publishers, the power of publicity, and a regularly inveigled reading public.

Barnstone clinches the matter when he admits that "apart from the Chinese experience, I have frequently translated from languages in which I had an imperfect knowledge of the tongue—or from languages . . . in which I could read nothing of the original." He laments that exotic languages are generally unknown to poets, and that scholars of those languages are themselves generally not poets. This is the supposed and much overstated conundrum in the translation of poetry, classical poetry included. In such cases, says Barnstone, "it is usually necessary, *faute de mieux,* to put a good poet together with a faithful informant," for "we should not read inferior translations, since they traduce the work of the author." *Traduttore traditore.* The troubling irony is that Barnstone not only believes and proclaims it, but has made a successful career of it. There is, of course, no arguing with success. But an original author is never more traduced (*traditore*) than by translation (*traduttore*) of Barnstone's kind. Native speakers of English would do far better to familiarize themselves with significant amounts of the best poetry in their own language than read Barnstone.

## Sherod Santos

Sherod Santos's *Greek Lyric Poetry: A New Translation* (2005) is among the more recent offerings by a Greekless translator. Far ranging in its breadth of lyric poets from 700 BC to 600 AD, *Greek Lyric Poetry* is often commended for its inclusiveness. Santos, as many translators before him, relies on J. M. Edmonds, referring to his Edmonds "trot" (or crib), but nowhere mentioning its excesses:

> A chance encounter with a fragment of Sappho's led me to track down, in our university's cavernous library stacks, a handful of English translations; and those, in turn, led me back to the originals in J. M. Edmonds' *Lyra Graeca,* a three-volume edition containing early Greek sources along with en face plain prose trots—the Virgilian guide to those of us who have little or no Greek save that received through translation.

Though Santos's book is subtitled *A New Translation,* it is not translation in any credible sense. Santos himself seems uncertain of *what* it is. His primary goal being "aural" effect, he claims not to have written

> proper translations, in the strict sense, but not exactly imitations or paraphrases or verse transfers either. I suppose I think of them

> as collaborations, for while they are firmly grounded in poems composed more than two thousand years ago . . . they still tend toward a certain self-sufficiency, or at least toward a kind of felicity that comes from pursuing more the tonal than the denotative meanings of the originals. In the end, this seemed faithful to the live, extempore spirit of an oral tradition, faithful, as well, to the special value the ancients assigned to the simple pleasures of hearing a poem. To evoke rather than mimic has been my general rule.

The emphasis on "tonal" over "denotative" meanings, i.e., on *sound* rather than meaning, is clearly suited to one who doesn't know the meaning.

The proposed capture of aural effect is of a kind with Paul Roche's doubtful intent to convey something of Sappho's verbal fabric, flux of textures, elusiveness, subtleties of echo, etc. In a curiously original and equally impossible formulation, Santos says that he "opt[s] for the grainy surfaces of unfinished wood, the rough pitch and raw materiality of the original," while rejecting archaic terms and phrasings as a "fad for 'antiquing' new furniture." Santos of course knows nothing of the original—its "materiality," "orality," or otherwise—and therefore cannot be concerned with the fact that Sappho's "Hymn to Aphrodite" was quoted in antiquity *not* for its "rough pitch and materiality" but for its smoothness and polish.

Santos's rejection of archaisms follows in this instance from his cavalier attitude in other respects. Curiously, and even while proposing to avoid the archaic, he regularly admits the arcane: *talus, dibble, caprocked, hornbeam, judder, aciculate, vireos, mattered, scrag, gurry, ragging, galled, comber*. Santos's recourse to the orality of archaic Greek lyric is, in any event, misplaced. Despite oral recitation—and even composition—of the poetry in question, the period is one of writing's emergence. The development heralded a consciousness in the choice of every word, versus the word groupings and formulae of the preceding age, highlighting the *particularity* of lyric emotion. The significance of this development is central to the analysis of Anne Carson, *Eros the Bittersweet* (see Chapter 28). The aural approach works, if at all, for lyric poets of the archaic period alone, having little or nothing to do with the many other lyricists included by Santos.

Translators lacking mastery of the original frequently have the longest explanations of how they go about their work and what they intend to accomplish. Santos's own explanation is reminiscent of that offered by other marginally proficient or entirely Greekless translators. He sets forth, from out of "cavernous library stacks," the numerous commentaries and past translations he has consulted—the notorious J. M. Edmonds above all. From these, as he explains, he gradually extracts a sense of each poem. It wasn't easy, as he "wrestled" with each. In one case he "worked on it for weeks, through countless versions, and . . . never came up with anything even vaguely satisfactory." "As you may gather," he adds, "the book proceeded at a glacial pace." This is Mary Barnard and Willis Barnstone combined. Toiling in his *own* academic vineyard, Santos would have had more to show for his time.

Noted classicist D. S. Carne-Ross, in a 1966 review of Barnstone and Davenport, observed that "a strong if vaguely focused interest in Greek civilization, coupled with a pervasive ignorance of the Greek language, has made classical translation a thriving industry. The demand is apparently so strong that the products are hustled to their market without benefit of criticism." However, what Carne-Ross laments as "a pervasive ignorance of the Greek language" in students, he happily allows and even encourages in translators, as will be seen. Davenport professed his ignorance of Greek in the very Sappho translation subject to Carne-Ross's 1966 review. Carne-Ross, however, gave Davenport a pass—and praises.

It is through friends in high places—university and commercial press editors, fawning reviewers, and interviewers—that the Greekless or quasi-proficient translator compensates for what he lacks. What other explanation for the trampling in translation of poems that first leapt dazzling from the lyre? Much is lost in translation, as poetasters and "from the Greek" translator-wannabes give it a try. The result lacks *authenticity*—the assurance that traditionally comes from the artist's signature, from knowing the work is a Rubens, not a period imitation. Though it is ideally by self-proclamation that great art is known, we often lack the confidence to trust our instincts. We require proof, a signature. Those relying on translation similarly lack the ability to judge. Authenticity begins with immersion at the source, in and within the language—words, structures, forms of expression, contexts comprising semantic range. The work cannot be overstated. "Even the simplest words, indeed, they especially," notes literary critic George Steiner, "carry a charge of specific energy, of historical association, social usage and syntactic tradition. They rise to the surface of speech from great depths of national or regional sensibility, barnacled with undeclared remembrance."

Robert Graves observes in an essay titled "Moral Principles in Translation": "A poem's emotional force depends on the strength and virtue of its component words; and the longer a word has been turned over by countless tongues and pens, and smoothed with use, the more powerfully will it strike home." It is the awareness of such matters that enables the determination of nuance, or the appropriateness of paraphrase or inventiveness in translation. As this is the philology, or *nurture,* with which authenticity begins, it is in intrinsic ability, or *nature,* that authenticity culminates. The two invariably exist on a sliding scale. Witness the nurture-deficient Alexander Pope—"It is not very likely he overflowed with Greek," notes Dr. Johnson—or, for that matter, Paul Valéry or T. S. Eliot. Dante knew no Greek. There will thus always be the exceptional case. Nurture and nature kept no better company than in Dryden.

Poor translation is a matter of poor diction, while good diction invariably lends luster and charm. Yet even those with both nurture and nature may miss the mark, as was apparent in a then true and prophetic assessment by Gilbert Murray:

> In English the condition for doing without rhyme is that the meter must be uniform and clear. . . . Of course, there is a strong spirit abroad which tries to throw off rules and exactitude. It is proud of trusting not to measured feet, but merely to its ear. . . . Unfortunately, it hates a correct ear almost as much as a measured foot . . . but it is difficult to expect good permanent results from [a method] which is based predominantly on contempt for the practice of good poets, on self-assertion rather than reverence, and on ennui rather than delight.

"Self-assertion" connotes translation from a language one admits to not knowing—the preference, as seen, of self over subject matter. "Ennui"? Translation as feather-in-cap and résumé enhancement, or nothing else or left to do.

My own translations herein offer both a correct ear and a measured foot. They revere and look to the practice of good poets—those herein translated, most of all. In a reversal of Pound's aphorism, they see in the poverty of translation today the counterpart to much of what passes for original verse. In these and other respects they march to their own drummer, even as they seek "good permanent results."

# Chapter 12

## Translations Compared

> Horace tells us that mediocrity in a poet is forbidden alike by gods, men, and publishers, but whether forbidden or no, there are a good many mediocre poets who are doing fairly well. So far as I can see, indeed, gods, men, and more particularly publishers, will tolerate nothing in a poet except mediocrity, and if a true poet by some rare accident slips in among the others, it is because gods and publishers' readers did not find him out. . . . Horace must have known perfectly well that he was talking nonsense.
>
> – SAMUEL BUTLER, *The Authoress of the Odyssey*

REVIEW OF FIRST-STANZA RENDERINGS of Sappho's "Hymn to Aphrodite" shows the bewildering variety of form and content confronting the general reader. My comparison focuses on five popularizing translators, all previously discussed: Richmond Lattimore, Mary Barnard, Guy Davenport, Willis Barnstone, and Paul Roche. To these I have added the recent rhymed translation of classicist Aaron Poochigian. There is finally the case of American poet and academic John Frederick Nims, which I discuss in a later chapter. Poochigian aside, only poet-classicist Richmond Lattimore has known Greek sufficiently to appreciate the importance of form and content (as did poet-classicist F. L. Lucas before him; Chapter 13). The first stanza translates literally as follows: 'Flower-robed, deathless Aphrodite, / child of Zeus, weaver of wiles, I beg you, / do not subdue me with distress or anguish, / lady, (in my) heart'. The original meter is three lines of eleven beats each ( — ⏑ — ⏑ | — ⏑ ⏑| — ⏑ — ⏑), followed by the five-beat ending ( — ⏑ ⏑ | — — ). This is believed to have been the opening poem of Sappho's nine books (or scrolls) of poetry. It is her only completely surviving poem and it has been universally admired. The expectations attending its translation are thus quite naturally high.

### Richmond Lattimore (1949, 1960)

— ⏑ — ⏑ | — ⏑ ⏑ | — ⏑—⏑
Throned in splendor, | deathless, O | Aphrodite,
child of Zeus, charm fashioner, I entreat you
not with grief and bitternesses to break my
spirit, O goddess . . .

Lattimore here recreates the original meter, a daunting task, given the steadfast polysyllabism of Greek. The disparity with English, as often noted, tends to result in padding and syllabic fill. But not here. The result is impressive and would be perfect, but for the metrically stressed final syllable of the plural 'bitternesses'. The disciplined fidelity of Lattimore's translation may, however, be lost on contemporary blank-verse readers, even as it is lost on erstwhile literati. Lattimore's Greek lyric translations are nonetheless credible, authoritative, and marked by a certain dignity, with frequent bursts of brilliance. My admiration and defense of Lattimore, throughout—in the translation of epic, lyric, and tragedy—warrant quotation of the following heartfelt obituary:

> Richmond Lattimore (1906–1984) . . . graduated from Dartmouth College, took a second degree at Oxford as a Rhodes Scholar, and later obtained a doctorate at the University of Illinois at Urbana, where he worked under W. A. Oldfather, a scholar who maintained the full rigor of the best German philological tradition. Rejecting offers from several great universities, Lattimore spent virtually his whole career as a professor at Bryn Mawr. He was a Greek scholar of great distinction, who could have achieved much in pure scholarship had he not felt it more important to provide modern readers with the best possible translations of Greek poetry. His decision was surely right. Lattimore was a genuine poet in his own right, and his poetic gifts combined with his excellent knowledge of Greek and his respect for the originals to produce translations of high quality.

We do well to keep such commendations in mind when considering the censures, and results, of those who would "make it new."

## **Mary Barnard (1958, 1986)**

Dapple-throned Aphrodite,
eternal daughter of God,
snare-knitter! Don't, I beg you,

cow my heart with grief! . . .

Barnard's short-line rendering barely captures or even approximates the original, even as it has little to commend it in English. The first three lines are the first of ten such stanzas, as compared to the original's seven. By further and significant contrast to Lattimore, Barnard's rhythm lacks any semblance of the Greek, or even of her Italian "bridge." Lattimore and Barnard thus exhibit extremes in translating Sappho. Lattimore's was the translation of record until Barnard's became the translation of choice.

In the Greek, Aphrodite is *Dios thugatēr* 'daughter of Zeus' (*Dios* the genitive or possessive form of Gr. *Zeus*). Barnard's rendering thus further misleads in its use of *God* for *Zeus* (a persistent translation error). What passes for *god/God* in translation is typically either Gr. *Zeus, theos,* or *daimōn* 'Zeus, a god, or divinity'. In the latter two instances, the reference is either to a specific god or divinity known from the context or, more broadly, to divine agency, when it is the equivalent of Zeus whose will is Fate. "Every great vicissitude," says Gilbert Murray, "every desire and emotion, seems to be referred to the mysterious action of tremendous and inscrutable laws or wills—something that a Greek would call *theos*." We can only wonder what motivates the use of *God* for *Zeus*. Even Quasimodo translates *Zeus* as *Zeus*.

Also, a more energetic diction would have alleviated the monosyllabic run: 'Don't, I beg you, / cow my heart with grief'—even as *cow* is less than felicitous diction (*crush* much better). 'Snare-knitter' appears as a playfully creative send-up of 'wile-weaver' (or 'weaver of wiles', the traditional translation of Gr. *doloploke*). 'Snare-knitter', however, lacks euphony, catching on the roof of the mouth. In addition to the shortfalls of structure and meter, the diction is unmindful of Sappho's polysyllabism and resultant texture.

Quasimodo's Italian is closer to Sappho's Greek than Barnard's English is to Quasimodo's Italian. However, not much else can be said for the Italian translator. While he provides no license for Barnard's clipped and haiku-like cadences, he supplies enough for her inattention to meter. Of the poem's seven stanzas, Quasimodo renders one stanza in five lines, one in three, and the others in four each. The lines are all of random length, conveying only the poem's meaning. While he offers some occasionally colorful diction—*ascoltasti, e lasciata la casa del padre* ('you listened, and left the house of your father'); *Leggiadri veloci uccelli / sulla nera terra ti portarano* ('graceful swift birds bore you onto the black earth')—nothing in the rendering overall justifies it as a "bridge" to Sappho's Greek. Lattimore would, again, have been a preferable guide.

In one necessarily if not purposefully bizarre locution, Quasimodo inverts a critical sequence. Sappho says of the disdainful girl, 'The love she flouts she'll soon long languish for / not wanting to' (stanza 6). That the girl will suffer the treatment she now inflicts would be justice enough. That she will love *against her will,* and even then be spurned, gives the reversal added force. The point catches us unawares in the Greek, coming as it does at the stanza's five-beat close, following three otherwise well-balanced propositions ('If . . . then', thrice). Quasimodo, however, inverts the order—*chi non ti ama, pure non volendo, / presto ti amerà* ('who loves you not, even not wanting to / soon will love you')—missing the point, losing the pointedness, and destroying the effect. Nor does Quasimodo make it clear that the object of Sappho's desire is female. Again, we can only wonder what Quasimodo had to do with Barnard's rendering—at once so unlike Quasimodo and Sappho both—and by what intrinsic merit Barnard has ever so captured the popular imagination.

## **Guy Davenport**

## **(1965)**

God's wildering daughter deathless Aphródita,
A whittled perplexity your bright abstruse chair,
With heartbreak, lady, and breathlessness
Tame not my heart.

**(1980)**

God's stunning daughter deathless Aphródita,
A whittled perplexity your bright abstruse chair,
Don't blunt my stubborn eye with breathlessness, lady,
To tame my heart.

**(1995)**

Aphródita dressed in an embroidery of flowers,
Never to die, the daughter of God,
Untangle from longing and perplexities,
O Lady, my heart.

Can the same Greek be behind these three renditions? We have already noted Davenport's self-professed unfamiliarity with Greek and his indecision in translation—here apparent in the use of 'stunning' (1980) to replace the superior 'wildering' (for 'bewildering') of his 1965 edition. 'Wildering' was at least consonant with Gr. *doloploke* ('weaver of wiles'). The same cannot be said of 'stunning', which by current understanding of the word is foreign to any such notion in the Greek.

For the rest, we again note in all versions the use of *God* for *Zeus*. Aphrodite's name, twice transliterated as 'Aphródita', is twice peculiar. It is not the general practice to transliterate Aeolic name forms. Why single out names when other Aeolic forms defy such rendering? Moreover, the *spoken* stress indicated for the second syllable is beside the point, as the syllable is not *metrically* stressed in Sappho's original. The transliteration of proper names into dialectic equivalents is a recent feature of epic translation as well. It is ultimately a form of pseudo-authenticity.

In Davenport's 1965 and 1980 versions, the second line ('A whittled perplexity', etc.) is an inexplicable elaboration of the original's first word; while the third line, with its gratuitous 'eye' and its proposed 'blunt[ing]' through alliterative 'breathlessness' leaves us breathless indeed. How 'tame my heart' might follow defies surmise. The line lengths—eleven, twelve, twelve, and four beats, respectively—are matched neither in sequence nor consistency in any of the remaining six stanzas. In fact, no two stanzas are alike, ranging from thirty to thirty-nine beats each. Davenport in his own way is as far afield as Barnard, though more imagistically outlandish. Is this what Davenport means by "suggesting the tone of Sappho's words"?

Davenport's 1995 version adopts, without explanation, the alternative meaning of the poem's opening word, which makes Aphrodite regally dressed instead of seated. 'Never to die' is a graceless substitute for Gr. *athanat'* 'deathless, immortal, undying'. 'The daughter of God' makes awkward use of the definite article in a direct address to Aphrodite (the figure of speech known as *apostrophe,* an address to an absent or imaginary character). The versification is as random as in the 1980 version, with the 'perplexity' of Aphrodite's chair now transferred to Sappho's state of mind—and ours.

### Willis Barnstone

### (1967)

On your dazzling throne, Aphrodite,
Sly eternal daughter of Zeus,
I beg you: do not crush my heart with grief.

### (2005)

On your dappled throne eternal Afroditi,
Cunning daughter of Zeus,
I beg you, do not crush my heart
With pain, O lady.

'On your dazzling throne', etc., commences the first of seven such stanzas in Barnstone's 1967 version, with fairly consistent syllabication. The third verse appears flatly monosyllabic. So also 'sly' as a rendering for the compound *doloploke,* again 'weaver of wiles'. 'Do not crush me with grief' lacks the fullness of the original's 'do not subdue me with distress or anguish, lady, (in my) heart'; and the substitution of 'pain' for 'grief' in the 2005 version is uneventful. Barnstone's 2005 rendition includes a fourth line, but to what effect is difficult to say. The 2005 rendition also peculiarly substitutes 'dappled' for 'dazzling' (throne). 'Dazzling' was the better choice (if one follows the 'throne' reading). 'Dappled' evokes blotches or mottled markings, as on an animal. Of 'dappled' classicist Carne-Ross notes as follows: "I find the diction trite; and I don't get the picture." Davenport's 'Aphródita' at least accurately transliterates the Aeolic Greek spelling of the goddess's name. However, we little know what to make of Barnstone's 'Afroditi', or elsewhere of his 'Kriti' for *Crete* (in a different poem). The spellings, nowhere found in Classical Greek, are Modern Greek-based hybrids—and the more confusing for that. Later in the "Hymn to Aphrodite" one similarly finds Barnstone's **Psapfo** for **Sappho** ('Who, O Sappho / does you wrong'?).

At the risk of technicality, we may note how far afield a translator may go for mere effect. The Attic-Ionic spelling of Sappho's name is **Σαπφώ,** which transliterates, and is typically rendered, as **Sappho.** However, the Aeolic spelling provides (1) initial **Ψ** (psi) instead of **Σ** (sigma) and (2) recessive accent (as earlier explained). Thus, **Ψάπφω,** transliterating as **Psappho.** However, because the phoneme **Ps** is not indigenous to English—appearing only in words of essentially Greek origin, e.g., *psyche*—the transliterated Aeolic form of Sappho's name typically remains **Sappho** (as in Attic-Ionic). Moreover, the fourth letter of Sappho's name, **φ** (phi), is a double consonant consisting of **p** with an **h**-aspirate, always rendered **ph** in English, e.g., **φιλοσοφία** 'philosophy'. Barnstone, however, even while injecting transliterated **Ψ** (**Ps**) at the start of Sappho's name, uses **f** for **φ** in his pseudo-Aeolic **Psapfo.** Why? Because Italian, Spanish, and other languages, as he explains, "do not aspirate their **φ**" (i.e., use **f** rather than **ph** in transliterating **φ**). This, to be sure, is a small point, but one revealing the idle reaching for effect where other matters were better tended to. It further highlights Barnstone's misplaced deference to Modern Greek and other languages over established English usage for the transliteration of ancient Greek.

### Paul Roche (1966, 1998)

Undying Aphrodite on your caparisoned throne,
Daughter of Zeus and weaver of ruses—
　　　　Now, I address you:

Queen, do not hurt my heart, do not harry it.

Roche begins the second stanza of his translation before completing the first of the original. As the shortfall will have somewhere to be compensated for, we find a concluding five-line stanza. 'Address' is too neutral for Gr. *lissomai* 'implore, beseech'; and 'hurt' too weak for Gr. *damna* 'subdue'. '[H]arry', straining as it does to alliterate, is a word little suited to matters of the heart. The desire for internal vowel rhyme seems to dictate the choice of 'ruses'—combining with 'Zeus' for a comical Broadway-lyric-sounding effect. The nicely alliterative and perfectly correct 'weaver of wiles', as noted, has been around for some time. There is no need to tamper with perfection when we can preserve it as part of the poem's traditional language-in-translation.

The poem's third and fourth lines, which Roche translates, 'Queen, do not hurt my heart, do not harry it', translate 'do not subdue me with distress or anguish, lady, (in my) heart'. Roche notes in these lines the emphatically repetitive choice of the words *asaisi, oniaisi* 'sufferings, sorrows', "which gives Sappho the opportunity [overall] of five splendid alliterations and one internal rhyme, making this one of the unforgettable lines of Greek literature." Perhaps so. But where is the splendor in English of a 'hurt' and 'harried' heart? There is in the end a significant discrepancy between the understanding Roche professes and his ability to convey it.

## Aaron Poochigian (2009)

Subtly bedizened Aphrodite
Deathless daughter of Zeus, Wile-weaver,
I beg you, Empress, do not smite me
With anguish and fever.

In a version appearing since the initial publication of my own, and apparently unaware of it, Poochigian adroitly adheres—as he does throughout the poem's seven stanzas—to interlocking rhyme in lines of fairly consistent length. One wonders, however, whether the insistent rhyme is too much of a good thing. Poochigian adopts, as do I, the "minority view," rendering the poem's colorfully opening *poikilothron'* to depict an enrobed rather than enthroned goddess. However, he nowhere notes the controversy or reason for his preference.

Yet even as the choice of epithet is preferred, the diction is taxing. 'Bedizened' (pronounced, *be-diz'-ened* or *be-dīz'-ened*) is recondite. The word means: dressed or adorned in a showy, gaudy, or tasteless manner. This is hardly the desired sense, and any such manner of dress would not be 'subtl[e]'. Also, the consonant-laden 'Subtly bedizened'—of a kind with Barnard's 'snare-knitter'—is not voiced, to quote Hamlet, "trippingly on the tongue." It is self-muting, with its run of short vowels inducing consonantal rattle. Dionysius of Halicarnassus, to whose quotation we owe the poem's survival, commends its "brilliant and finished" style. Characteristic of that style, he observes, is the blend of such letters as facilitates vocal flow and musical quality, the word arrangement in no way interfering with the smooth waves of sound. While this quality cannot be captured in every case, 'Subtly bedizened' runs the opposite extreme.

As concerns rhyme, Poochigian's gifts are apparent, though perhaps to a fault (viewing his translation of the poem as a whole). 'Wile-weaver', a translational "work horse," is here artfully rhymed with 'fever'—a resourceful and winning first. At the same time, 'Aphrodite' rhymes not simply with 'me', but with 'smite me', in rime-riche fashion. Were this not enough, the stanza internally (and doubly) rhymes 'deathless' and 'Empress' (and perhaps 'Empress' in near rhyme with 'anguish'). This too is highly resourceful, as Gr. *potnia* is invariably (and colorlessly) rendered as 'goddess, lady, queen'. Here, unlike examples from recent translations of epic (see Chapter 29), is engaging, purposeful innovation, not merely plundered phrasing.

Looking to Lattimore's rendering of Sappho's other (nearly) complete poem, *phainetai moi* 'He appears to me', we may note its glories, despite a certain monosyllabic excess (italicized).

> Like the very gods in my sight *is he who*
> *sits where he can* look in your eyes, who listens
> close to you, to hear the soft voice, its sweetness
> murmur in love and
>
> laughter, all for him. But it breaks my spirit;
> underneath my breast all the heart is shaken.
> Let me only glance where you are, the voice dies,
> I can say nothing,
>
> but my lips are stricken to silence, under-
> neath my skin the tenuous flame suffuses;
> nothing shows in front of my eyes, my ears are
> muted in thunder.

And the sweat breaks running upon me, fever
shakes my body, paler I turn than grass is;
*I can feel that I have been changed, I feel that*
death has come near me.

Here, too, Lattimore replicates Sapphic stanza and rhythm. There is some exceptionally fine phrasing—'its sweetness / murmur in love'; 'the sweat breaks running upon me'; 'Lips are stricken to silence'. Indeed, there are several highly effective whole-line renderings: 'underneath my breast all the heart is shaken'; 'under- / neath my skin the tenuous flame suffuses'. 'Under- / neath' effects a wondrous hyphenation, an unusual feature occurring twice in the original. This is accomplished translation with an eye—unblunted—to the Greek. However, in a poem where the torrent of runaway emotion is all, the pronouns and cumbersome auxiliaries (first and fourth stanzas, italicized) slow the pace.

Consecutive monosyllables may be *quite* eventful, as throughout Swinburne's "Sapphics." The likelihood, however, decreases with the piling-on of prepositions, articles, pronouns, and conjunctions. The little words accumulate, like so much flotsam, to impede the flow or, as may be the case, fill the line. Given the general felicity and high resonance of Lattimore's *phainetai moi,* it is sadly marred in this very respect. Barnard, for her part, and as noted, runs the opposite extreme, with lines of excessive brevity. She makes no attempt to engage with the original, or even with Quasimodo, but makes a full retreat. Her memoir, *Assault on Mt. Helicon,* is curiously silent about Lattimore, the dominant translator—in all genres—of her own generation.

Lattimore here uses *the* six times, *in* fives times, and *my* eight times—for a significant small-word instance, overall. In the last stanza alone, he uses seven pronouns, whereas the Greek has two expressed as direct and indirect objects, and two implied in first-person verb forms. Moreover, his three *can* + verb constructions (all monosyllabic) and four passives (all requiring auxiliaries) further attenuate momentum. That the Greek conjunction *de/d'* ('and' or 'but') appears no fewer than seven times in the original's last two stanzas is no obstacle to this analysis (see further Chapter 22). In the end, however, it is the translation by F. L. Lucas (PART III, §2) that avoids all monosyllabic excess and is the most felicitous of all in both diction and rhythm.

I have attempted to avoid commonplaces of diction and sentiment, the frequent companions of monosyllabism, and within such constraints have been as playful as the richest diction might allow. Such devising befits a theme of Greek lyric poetry (Anacreon and Archilochus especially): that of *play* itself (Gr. *paizein* 'to play', always with erotic connotation).

As I have sought before all else to render archaic Greek lyric poetically and with the requisite decorum, it is hoped my translations will provide a pleasure somehow comparable to that experienced by the originals' own Greek audience, though such pleasure is impossible to know. The pleasure, such as it is, results from English-language means that succeed in their own right, and not through the benighted hope of suggesting the original's tone, texture, flux, fabric, or the like—though *tenor* remains paramount. By "tenor" I mean structural and dictional formality, the "sense and flavor of [the translation's] words, insofar as good scholars are able to discern these." My PART III translations offer a haven from the willfulness of modern, post-modern, and invariably Greekless disregard. They are offered in the spirit of C. S. Lewis, whose literary taste is reported to have "stop[ped at] about 1890"—my own terminus exceeding Lewis's by some sixty-five years to embrace Lattimore. To be sure, newer has rarely meant better.

It is a truism that literary translation cannot be at once *faithful* and *beautiful*. The present volume stems from my perception, in 1983 as today, that the translation of archaic Greek lyric, no less than of Homer, has long been *neither*—indeed, that it has largely been a fraud. I have made the many choices I thought necessary to remedy the situation. I am, again in the spirit of Lewis, pleased to be "out of touch with all the dominant trends of contemporary literature"; and to prefer, with Edward FitzGerald, a flask of wine and book of verse to the mancel loaf and mutton haunch of Robert Graves.

# III.

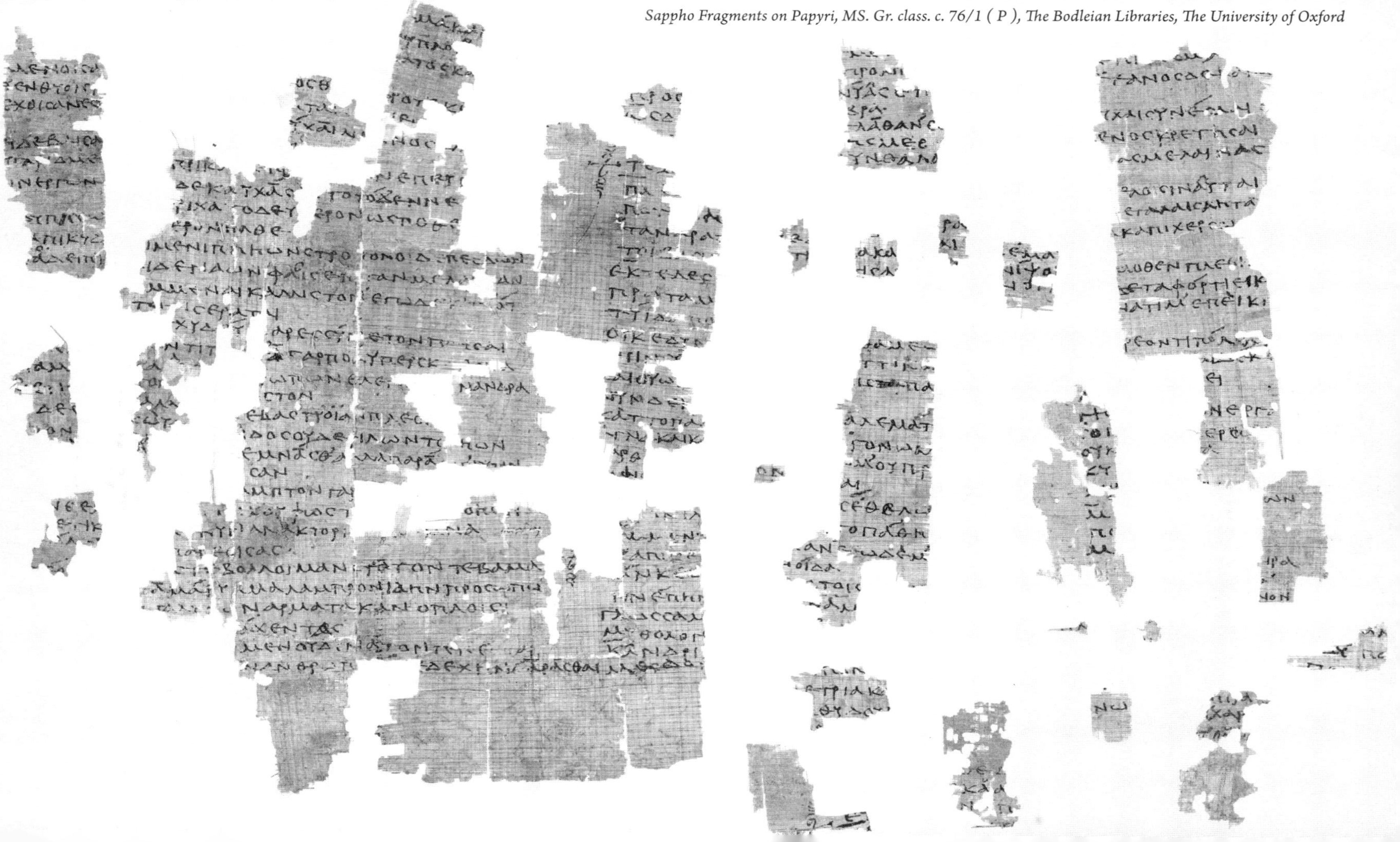

*Sappho Fragments on Papyri, MS. Gr. class. c. 76/1 ( P ), The Bodleian Libraries, The University of Oxford*

# Translations

> We may talk as we please about the beauty of the original and the impossibility of adequate translation, but the fact remains that for most of us it is translation or nothing.
>
> – MARY STEWART, *Catullus*

> The defence of translation has the immense advantage of abundant, vulgar fact. How could we be about our business if the thing were not inherently feasible, ask Saint Jerome and Luther with the impatience of craftsmen irritated by the buzz of theory.
>
> – GEORGE STEINER, *After Babel*

## SAPPHO

THE FOLLOWING TRANSLATIONS are essentially those of my 1983 work. The "New Sappho" aside (§39), the one exception is §2 *phainetai moi* 'He appears to me', retranslated for the present volume more closely to the line length of the Greek. The retranslation is followed by the earlier version (modified). The "New Sappho" refers to the poem on love and old age, first discovered in 2004. Verses or verse fragments by Sappho discovered as recently as 2014 are not included, since not conforming to the subject matter of this volume (the "Brothers Poem") or too scant for treatment. As discussed above, translators often use brackets (to excess) when the Greek is either missing (as on a papyrus), corrupt (mistranscribed by a copyist), or otherwise illegible. I use brackets sparingly, either to indicate a brief gap in an otherwise readable text or to venture a translation where the text is uncertain. Further, I have included translations by the much-neglected, if at all known, T. G. Tucker (1913) and F. L. Lucas (1956)—models of prosody for their time and ours. Sappho had another resourceful translator in the English poet and literary critic John Addington Symonds, whose "Hymn to Aphrodite" I also include (1883). Parenthetical references following each poem number are to the scholarly edition on which the poem's Greek text is based (see Bibliography). Thus, for example, "**§1 (1LP)**" indicates that the Greek text of my first translation appears as the first entry in E. Lobel and D. Page, *Poetarum Lesbiorum Fragmenta* (Oxford: Clarendon Press, 1955, 1968). The title of this seminal work translates as *Fragments of the Lesbian Poets*.

**§1 (1LP)** Our source text for the "Hymn to Aphrodite," the opening of Sappho's nine books of verse, is the Greek rhetorician and historian Dionysius of Halicarnassus, teaching in Rome (1st century BC). Dionysius, in his lengthy treatise *On Literary Composition,* quotes the poem in full as an example of the polished and exuberant style. The poem is discussed at length in Chapter 24.

Appareled in flowered allure, deathless,
Deceiver, daughter of Zeus, Aphrodite!
Subdue not nor destroy this heart, my lady,
  with distress.

But come to my side, if ever before
while listening alert from afar as I cried
you attended, and came leaving your father's
  golden door,

coupling lovely sparrows to the chariot's rein
that swiftly drew you down to darkened earth,
their wings awhirr along the way through aether's
  middle main.

Quickly they arrived, and you, O blessed one,
a smile on your immortal face, were asking
what I suffered this time, why this time did
  I summon;

And what it was my maddened heart did long
for most. "Whom this time shall persuasion lead

as captive to your love? Who, O Sappho,
  does you wrong?

For if she flees at first, she'll soon pursue;
the gifts she has spurned, she'll shortly bestow;
the love she flouts, she'll soon long languish for
  not wanting to."

Come even now to my side and free me
from crushing concern. Fulfill whatever
yearnings my own heart would fulfill, yourself
  my ally be.

◆

(T. G. Tucker)

Guile-weaving child of Zeus, who art
Immortal, throned in radiance, spare,
O Queen of Love, to break my heart
  With grief and care.

But hither come, as thou of old,
When my voice reached thine ear afar,
Didst leave thy father's hall of gold,
  And yoke thy car,

And through mid air their whirring wing
Thy bonny doves did swiftly ply
O'er the dark earth, and thee did bring
  Down from the sky.

Right soon they came, and thou, blest Queen,
A smile upon thy face divine,
Didst ask what ail'd me, what might mean
  That call of mine.

'What would'st thou have, with heart on fire,
Sappho?' thou saidst. 'Whom pray'st thou me
To win for thee to fond desire?
  Who wrongeth thee?

Soon shall he seek, who now doth shun;
Who scorns thy gifts, shall gifts bestow;
Who loves thee not, shall love anon,
  Wilt thou or no.'

So come thou now, and set me free
From carking cares; bring to full end
My heart's desire; thyself O be
  My stay and friend!

◆

(F. L. Lucas, in Sapphic meter)

Aphrodite, daughter of Zeus, undying
Goddess, throned in glory, of love's beguilements,
Do not now with frenzy and desperation
  Utterly crush me.

Hear and come!–if ever before Thou heardest
Cry of mine, that called from afar Thy succour;
Then, in haste, with chariot swiftly harnessed,
  Forth from the golden

Hall of Zeus, Thy father, to me Thou camest–
Then Thy lovely sparrows from Heaven swept Thee
O'er the dark-loamed earth, through the ether beating
  Swift wings together.

Fast they brought Thee hither; and Thou, most blessed,
With a smile of heavenly lips didst ask me,
What it was I suffered; and why I called Thee
  Hither to aid me.

'Tell me what it is, then, that most thou cravest,
Heart so full of madness?–who is it, Sappho,
Passion must awake to desire and love thee?
  Who is it wrongs thee?

'For, although she shun thee, she soon shall seek thee;
Though she scorn thy presents, herself shall bring them;
Though she love thee not, yet she soon shall love thee!–
  Yea, though she would not.'

Come again today, then, as once Thou camest.
Save my soul from sorrow, that grows too bitter—
Grant my heart's desiring—be Thou my helper,
Thou, Aphrodite!

◆

(John Addington Symonds, in Sapphic meter)

Star-throned incorruptible Aphrodite,
Child of Zeus, wile-weaving, I supplicate thee,
Tame not me with pangs of the heart, dread mistress,
Nay, nor with anguish.

But come thou, if erst in the days departed
Thou didst lend thine ear to my lamentation,
And from far, the house of thy sire deserting,
Camest with golden

Car yoked: thee thy beautiful sparrows hurried
Swift with multitudinous pinions fluttering
Round black earth, adown from the height of heaven
Through middle ether:

Quickly journey they; and, O thou, blest Lady,
Smiling with those brows of undying lustre,
Asked me what new grief at my heart lay, wherefore
Now I had called thee,

What I fain would have to assuage the torment
Of my frenzied soul; and whom now, to please thee,
Must persuasion lure to thy love, and who now,
Sappho, hath wronged thee?

Yea, for though she flies, she shall quickly chase thee;
Yea, though gifts she spurns, she shall soon bestow them;
Yea, though now she loves not, she soon shall love thee,
Yea, though she will not!

Come, come now too! Come, and from heavy heart-ache
Free my soul, and all that my longing yearns to
Have done, do thou; be thou for me thyself too
Help in the battle.

**§2 (31LP)** Our source text for *phainetai moi* 'He appears to me' is the rhetorician and literary critic Longinus (1st century AD), whose sole surviving work is *Peri hupsous* 'On the Sublime.' Longinus quotes the poem for its consummate marshaling of the emotions accompanying delirious passion. The poem is discussed at length in Chapter 22. The first translation was prepared for the present volume. It is informed by Sappho's words to Anactoria in Swinburne's poem of the same name (lines 74–75): "But thou—thy body is the song, / Thy mouth the music. . . ." The second, as modified, originally appeared in my 1983 work.

(2014)

Equal to the gods, or so he seems,
that man sitting opposite and near
to you, beguiled by your lyric voice
  upon his ear

and blissful in your laughter. My heart,
at that sight, I do swear, is distraught,
and of a sudden am I undone;
  my tongue untaught,

forgotten its skill; excruciate
flame enters racing beneath my skin,
recognition gone, and sight, and naught
  but deafening din–

a cold sweat commands me, a tremor
takes hold; more pallid than grass am I,
needing only, or so I seem, but
  little to die.

(1983)

Equal to the gods does he appear
to me, that man who sits close by you,
hears the sound of your sweet voice
  –intently near–

and your delightful laughter. That sight,
I do swear, does unsettle my heart;
The slightest glance at you puts my
  speech to flight!

My tongue unhinges, a delicate
flame slips racing neath my skin,
I see nothing, am blinded, my ears
  ring, pulsate,

a cold sweat commands me, fear
grasps at my heart. More pallid
than grass, nearly dead to myself
  I appear.

◆

(T. G. Tucker)

Blest as the gods, methinks, is he
Who sitteth face to face with thee
And hears thy sweet voice nigh,
Thy winsome laugh, whereat my heart
Doth in my bosom throb and start;
One glimpse of thee, and I
Am speechless, tongue-tied; subtle flame
Steals in a moment through my frame;
My ears ring; to mine eye
All's dark; a cold sweat breaks; all o'er
I tremble, pale as death; nay more,
I seem almost to die.

◆

(F. L. Lucas, in Sapphic meter)

Him I hold as happy as God in Heaven,
Who can sit and gaze on your face before him,
Who can sit and hear from your lips that sweetest
  Music they utter—

Hear your lovely laughter, that sets a-tremble
All my heart with flutterings wild as terror.
For, when I behold you an instant, straightway
  All my words fail me;

Helpless halts my tongue; a devouring fever
Runs in flame through every vein within me;

Darkness veils my vision; my ears are deafened,
  Beating like hammers;

Cold the sweat runs down me; a sudden trembling
Sets my limbs a-quiver; my face grows paler
Than the grass in summer; I see before me
  Death stand, and madness.

**§3 (2LP)** This poem, written on a potsherd in a hand assigned to the third century BC, is one of the two oldest surviving remnants of the text of Sappho. The only lyric fragment thus preserved, it was first published in 1937. The stanzas do not distinguish between lines. At the ends of the stanzas themselves a small space is left vacant. The text is highly corrupt, though the hand is quite legible. The copyist may have been less than fully comprehending of the Greek. Verses 5 to 8 are also known from Hermogenes (2nd century AD), author of *On Forms*. Verses 13 to 16 are from a version in Athenaeus (2nd and 3rd centuries AD), author of *Doctors at Dinner* (11.463e).

A word on Athenaeus, whose *Doctors at Dinner* (Gr. *Deipnosophistae also* 'Dinner-Table Philosophers' or 'Learned Banqueters') survives in fifteen books. The first two, and parts of the third, eleventh, and fifteenth exist only in summary. The work warrants mention, among other reasons, as a primary source for the preservation of the poems and poem excerpts herein. A vast compendium of information on matters of dining, the work contains remarks on music, dance, games, courtesans, and luxury. Athenaeus refers to nearly 800 writers and 2,500 separate works; one of his characters boasting to have read 800 plays of Athenian Middle Comedy. Athenaeus is our sole source for much valuable information about the ancient world, and many authors whom he mentions would be otherwise unknown. Book XIII is essential to the study of sexuality in classical and Hellenistic Greece.

Leaving Crete for this sacred enclosure
arrive! Here your pleasing grove
of apple trees, here altars breathing
  scents of myrrh.

Roses and shadows in this place abound;
cold water babbles neath apple bough

branches whose shuddering leaves sprinkle
  sleep to the ground.

Here a spring-flowered meadow
with horses agraze, where breezes
gently blow [ ]
  [ ]

Here then [ ] taking, Aphrodite,
with your exquisite touch admix
the nectar golden-cupped to blend with
  our festivity.

◆

(T. G. Tucker, 2nd stanza)

Through apple-boughs, with purling sound,
Cool waters creep;
From quivering leaves descends around
The dew of sleep.

**§4 (16LP)** Preserved on papyrus.

Some claim that infantry, cavalry corps,
or seas decked with fleets are the dark earth's
fairest sight. But I claim whatever
  you adore.

The fact is apparent, self-evident,
for Helen, far surpassing all mortals
in beauty, leaving a husband
  unmatched, went

sailing to Troy nor showed any remorse
for dear parents or child. [Aphrodite]
drove her to follow [obeying love's
  greater force]

[ ]
[ ] lightly [ ]
that makes me think of Anactoria
  though distant,

whose lovely step I would sooner see
and face gleaming radiant with light, than
Lydian charioteers or outfitted
  infantry.

**§5 (95LP)** Preserved on papyrus as verses 11 to 14 of a sixteen-verse fragment. In the beginning, Sappho apparently relates that her life has become unhappy, whereupon the god Hermes, guide of the dead to the underworld, appears.

I'm filled with desire to die,
see the dewy lotused shore
of Acheron [flow by . . .

**§6 (94LP)** Preserved on parchment and published for the first time in Berlin, 1907. The same parchment contains §8 and several other scraps.

"Honestly, I wish I were dead"!
She was leaving me, tears in her eyes.
Much she said, this most of all:
"Ah, Sappho, what we've suffered through;
I swear, I leave not wanting to."

And I made this reply:
"Go then, yet remember me now
and again. You know how

we have cared for you.
If not, I'd remind you [ ]
of joyous times which we once knew:

of rose wreaths and crocus,
of violets put on at my side,
necklaces flower-tied

[tossed] round your gentle neck;
how you anointed yourself
with [ ] a queen's costly scent

and on yielding beds
gentle [ ]
desire [of maidens] spent

and no dance [
no shrine [ ] where
we two were not found

No precinct [
] sound
] . . ."

**§7 (34LP)** Quoted by the churchman and scholar Eustathius of Constantinople (12th century AD) in his commentary to *Il.* 8.555.

The stars about the radiant moon
consider their brilliant orbs unsightly
when in her fullness she burns brightly
upon the earth . . .

**§8 (96LP)** From the same parchment as §6. Both are poems of departure or absence. Sappho comforts Atthis (see verse 13 and §§9 and 10) by assuring her that another girl, now in Lydia, has not forgotten her. Containing Sappho's most expansive surviving simile, the poem begins after three broken lines and trails off into nineteen highly fragmentary lines.

She thought you a goddess,
your song her special joy.

Among Lydian women
she now has her praise–
as the rosy-fingered moon,

shaming heaven's stars from sight
shines, ocean-enthroned,
over flowers in the night,

over fields where chevril grows lush,
where melilot and roses thrill
to evening's dewy touch;
ever wandering there, yearning
for tender Atthis, she languishes–
her gentle spirit crushed . . .

◆

(F. L. Lucas, elaborated)

Atthis, our own loved Anactória
In Sardis dwells afar,
And yet, there too, of us her memories are;

Recalling other days—how once you were,
To her, divinely fair,
And with your song no singing could compare.

Now among Lydia's daughters that dear head
Shines, as when day is fled
The risen moon, with fingers rosy-red,

Outshines the stars, and flings her glory wide
Across the salt sea-tide,
Across the many-flowered countryside,

While fair her dew falls on the flowering rose,
And where soft anthrysc grows,
And where in bloom the melilōtus blows.

Yet, Atthis, still of you her memories wake,
Where'er she goes, and make
That gentle heart grow heavy for your sake.

'Come back!' she cries. We know. For many be
The ears of Night; and She
Brings us that cry across the sundering sea.

**§9 (49LP)** The first line is quoted by the Greek metrist Hephaistion (2nd century AD), and the second line by the biographer Plutarch (1st and 2nd centuries AD). The version preserved by the Latin grammarian Terentianus Maurus (2nd century AD) suggests that the verses were consecutive.

I loved you, Atthis, once long ago;
a child to me then with little to show.

**§10 (131LP)** Quoted by Hephaistion with the preceding and likely to be grouped with it.

Atthis, now you regard me hatefully;
running off to Andromeda you flee.

**§11 (57LP)** Quoted apropos of Andromeda by Athenaeus (see §3), *Doctors at Dinner* (1.21b–c). The social standing of the girl in question would be much the opposite of the girl who spurns Anacreon (§50).

What country girl
dressed in country style
has turned your head around,
unable to keep
her hemline raised
from sweeping up the ground?

**§12 (137LP)** The quotation is introduced by Aristotle (*Rhetoric* 1367a) as follows: "They reproach what is shameful in what they speak, do, and intend, as even Sappho composed when Alcaeus said, 'there's something I'd tell you.'" On Sappho and Alcaeus, see Chapters 3 and 7.

*Alceaus to Sappho:*

"There is something I'd tell you
but shame [won't allow . . ."

*Sappho to Alcaeus:*

"If you had a desire for the noble and true,
and weren't stirring your tongue in some
   scurrilous brew,
then shame would depart your lowered brow,
not dawdling you'd speak your mind somehow."

**§13 (15bLP)** Preserved on papyrus, first eight lines illegible, Doricha unknown.

Be yet more severe with Doricha,
let her not boast thus in her pride,
that he came once again for the love
which at first he was denied.

**§14 (22LP)** Preserved on papyrus as verses 11 to 14 of a nineteen-verse fragment.

Longing floats round
the beautiful girl,
aflutter beholding the gown,
to my delight . . .

**§15 (21bLP)** Quoted by Athenaeus (see §3), *Doctors at Dinner* (15.674e). Two verses follow the quotation, appearing to indicate the Graces' preference for what is garlanded.

Dica, wreathe your hair, weaving garlands
of supple anise with tender hands.

**§16 (23LP)** Preserved on papyrus as verses 3 to 6 (restored) of a twelve-verse fragment. Hermione is Helen's daughter. See Chapter 18.

Such brilliant beauty as you possess
Does make Hermione's seem the less.
Rightly are you compared
to Helen golden-haired.

**§17 (105aLP)** Quoted by the philosopher and rhetorician Syrianus (5th century AD) in his commentary on the rhetorician Hermogenes (2nd century BC).

As the sweet apple reddens atop of the bough
by the tip at the furthest height,
the pickers forgot it, no they didn't, not quite,
but just couldn't reach it somehow.

◆

(T. G. Tucker)

On the top of the topmost spray
The pippin blushes red,
Forgot by the gatherers–nay!
Was it "forgot" we said?
'Twas too far overhead!

◆

(F. L. Lucas)

As the sweet apple reddens, high up against the sky,
High on the highest branch, where the pickers passed it by,
Forgetting–ah, no, not forgetting–they never could reach so
high.

**§18 (105cLP)** Quoted without attribution by the historian and literary critic Demetrius of Phaleron (4th and 3rd centuries BC) in his treatise *On Style*. The resemblance to the preceding poem suggests that the lines may have formed part of a wedding song. The Roman love poet Catullus (1st century BC) appears indebted to the image in his Poem 62.39–47.

As the hyacinth
on the mountain top,
trampling shepherds did
not see the purple flower drop.

◆

(T. G. Tucker)

The hyacinth so sweet
On the hills where the herdsmen go
Is trampled 'neath their feet,
And its purple bloom laid low–

◆

(F. L. Lucas)

As the hyacinth high on the mountains under the shepherds'
tread
Lies trampled, and to earthward bows down its purple head.
. . .

**§19 (114LP)** Quoted by Demetrius (see §18). Two verses in the Greek, transcription of the second uncertain.

"Maidenhood, maidenhood,
where go you leaving me?"
"I leave you for good,
you've outgrown my company."

**§20 (107LP)** Quoted by Apollonius Dyscolus (2nd century AD), Alexandrian grammarian at Rome under the Emperor Marcus Aurelius.

Do I yet long for virginity?

**§21 (104aLP)** Quoted by Demetrius (see §18), who notes that the charm of the verses lies in the repetition of the word *bring*. As in the case of §18, Catullus appears to have these verses in mind in his Poem 62.20–25.

Hesperus, restoring all that shining Dawn
has scattered far and wide,
You bring the sheep, bring the goat, bring
  every fawn
back to its mother's side.
  [Not so the bride–
who leaving home is forever gone.]

◆

(F. L. Lucas)

All things thou bringest, Hesper, that the bright Dawn did
  part–
Sheep and goat to the fold, and the child to the mother's
  heart.

**§22 (141LP)** Quoted by Athenaeus (see §3), *Doctors at Dinner* (10.425d).

A bowl of ambrosia had
there been blended,
for the gods Hermes poured,
all were attended.
They all raised their cups,
poured a libation,
wishing the bridegroom
his heart's elation.

**§23 (115LP)** Quoted by the Greek metrist Hephaistion (2nd century AD). Although the author's name is not given, the verses are believed (by Lobel and Page, among others) to be Sappho's. Subjecting the groom to multiple comparisons seems to have been a wedding pastime. The most eligible bachelor and maiden in Homer are compared to saplings, Achilles at *Il.* 18.56, and Nausicaa at *Od.* 6.163.

What likeness, O bridegroom, do you most bear?
To a tender sapling you best compare.

**§24 (30LP)** Preserved on the same papyrus as §4 (papyri sometimes containing the remains of more than one poem). My continuous rendering follows the restoration of classicist C. M. Bowra (see Bibliography).

May unwed maidens
the entire night long
make of you and your
violet-girt bride their song.

Awake, spread the call,
to your companions all,
that we such hours keep
as put the nightingale asleep.

**§25 (112LP)** Quoted by Hephaistion (see §23).

O blessed groom, now your wedding's complete
as you prayed; yours is the girl you've adored
as you prayed; her generous beauty, yours.
And the eyes of your bride are honey-sweet,
love's smile on the beautiful face, outpoured;
you are graced with Cyprian's honors.

**§26 (44LP)** Preserved on papyrus. The poem differs from Sappho's remaining poetry, being narrative instead of personal, and exhibiting the characteristics of epic dialect, meter, and style. See detailed discussion in Chapter 17. The first verse in translation condenses three fragmentary verses of Greek. A gap of one verse precedes verse 2.

Came the herald, Idaeus, swift messenger [
" . . . and of the rest of Asia, imperishable fame
Hector and his comrades bring a bright-eyed girl
from Holy Thebes, in ships on the salty sea,
from Placea's streams—exquisite Andromache.
Bringing purple robes, ivory, bracelets of gold,
oddly-tooled trinkets, silver cups untold."
Thus the messenger. His father quickly rose;
to his friends, through streets well paved, the tiding goes.
Trojan sons bend mules to rapid carriages,
the crowd surges, ascends; women, girls unmarried [
Priam's daughters, apart [and men unwed lead
horses to their carts, and greatly charioteers
[unknown number of missing verses]
] like to the gods
] holy, all together
set forth [ ] to Ilium,
the sweet-sounding flute [and lyre] blend.
Castanets clash; clear sacred maiden songs ascend,
the wondrous echo reaches the skies [
throughout the streets [
chalices, bowls, [
mingled frankincense, cassia and myrrh
elder women calling clamorously,
men's thrilling melody, shouted aloud
summons Paon, great archer, great lord of the lyre,
they sang of Hector, Andromache, like to the gods.

**§27 (132LP)** Quoted by Hephaistion (see §23). A papyrus line reads, "She [Sappho] had a daughter Cleis, named after her mother." The poem is three lines in Greek, the last of which requires a verb such as 'I would not take'. The rhythm of the words *chrusioisin anthemoisin* 'golden flowers' is especially appropriate with its girlish lilt.

A flower, golden petaled, is my child,
Precious Cleis, for whom all Lydia . . .

◆

(T. G. Tucker)

I have a maid, a bonny maid,

As dainty as the golden flowers,
My darling Cleis. Were I paid
All Lydia, and the lovely bowers
Of Cyprus, 'twould not buy my maid.

**§28 (98LP)** Preserved in fragmentary form on a papyrus dated to the third century BC. Among the oldest extant papyri of Sappho or Alcaeus.

She who bore me used to say
that in her youth a splendid sight
was hair adorned in a purple band,
but even better the strands
yet yellower than torch's light
wreathed in chapleted flower display.

**§29 (110LP)** Quoted by Hephaistion (see §23). At issue here and in §30 is exaggerated size; risqué abuse (or ribald humor) being a common feature of archaic Greek wedding songs.

The doorkeeper's feet are fourteen yards long,
his sandals are stitched five oxhides strong,
ten cobblers labored at fitting the thong.

**§30 (111LP)** Quoted by Demetrius (see §18). The opening line is the inspiration for J. D. Salinger's novella, *Raise High the Roof Beam, Carpenters* (1955, 1963).

Raise the roof higher
—sing joy to the groom—
carpenters, raise it,
give him more room.
Rivaling Ares he enters the door,
more duly endowed than you built it for.

**§31 (51LP)** Quoted by the Stoic philosopher Chrysippus (3rd century BC).

I know not what I want,
My every thought's a taunt.

**§32 (50LP)** Quoted by Galen (2nd century AD), court physician at Rome to the Emperor Marcus Aurelius.

Beauty is beauty as far as it goes,
a good man's beauty immediately shows.

**§33 (126LP)** Quoted in the *Etymologicum Magnum*, an extant lexicon of uncertain date, compiled from earlier works in Constantinople (12th century AD).

May you find rest
on a maiden's soft breast.

**§34 (102LP)** Quoted by Hephaistion (see §2).

Mother dear, no longer
does the loom delight—
sweet Love commands,
desire conquers me quite.

◆

(F. L. Lucas)

I cannot, sweetest mother,
My loom I cannot mind;
Delicate Aphrodite
With longing leaves me blind.

**§35 (47LP)** E. Lobel's generally accepted reconstruction of the paraphrase found in the Sophist and itinerant lecturer Maximus of Tyre (2nd century AD). Maximus writes: "Love racked her [Sappho's] heart, as a wind falling on oaks throughout the mountain." The comparison of love's violence to wind is reminiscent of §93.

My heart
was racked by Love—
like mountain oaks
by winds above.

**§36 (130LP)** Quoted by Hephaistion (see §23).

Love undoes me again—
dissolver of limbs
bittersweet irresistible
creeping in.

**§37 (48LP)** Quoted by Julian (aka Julian the Apostate, 4th century AD), and thought to be Sappho's.

You came, calmed my desire,
for you I raged;
my breast, a burning pyre,
is now assuaged.

**§38 (Fr. Adesp. 976P)** Quoted by Hephaistion without attribution to Sappho. Sappho's authorship, once doubted on dialect grounds, is now beyond question. Arguably not a fragment, but a complete poem, the work has inspired many translations.

The moon departs the sky,
the Pleiads pass from sight,
midnight's hour slips by,
and I lie alone tonight.

◆

(T. G. Tucker)

Sunk is the moon;
The Pleiades are set;
'Tis midnight; soon
The hour is past; and yet
I lie alone—

◆

(F. L. Lucas)

Moon's set, and Pleiads;
Midnight goes by;
The hours pass onward;
Lonely I lie.

◆

(A. E. Housman, *More Poems*, "XI," 1936)

The rainy Pleiads wester,
Orion Plunges prone,
The stroke of midnight ceases,
And I lie down alone.

The rainy Pleiads wester
And seek beyond the sea
The head that I shall dream of,
And 'twill not dream of me.

◆

(A. E. Housman, *More Poems*, "X," 1936)

The weeping Pleiads wester,
And the moon is under seas;
From bourn to bourn of midnight
Far sighs the rainy breeze;

It sighs from a lost country
To a land I have never known;
The weeping Pleiads wester
And I lie down alone.

**§39** The text of the "New Sappho" was first published in 2004 by Michael Gronewald and Robert W. Daniel in *Zeitschrift für Papyrologie und Epigraphik* (*Journal of Papyrology and Epigraphy*), a University of Cologne publication announcing the identification of a University of Cologne papyrus (see also §77) that contained poems of Sappho. The papyrus was recovered from Egyptian mummy cartonnage dated to the third century BC. Copied approximately three hundred years after Sappho's lifetime, the work is not only one of the earliest manuscripts of Sappho's poetry but also the longest after the "Hymn to Aphrodite" (§1). It is likely a complete poem, making it, again with the "Hymn," one of only two completely surviving poems by Sappho. It is noted that §2 may also be a complete poem. It certainly reads as one, but for the problematic verse 17, which appears to start a new (and final) stanza. I omit the verse from my own translation.

The "New Sappho," as it happens, was partially preserved on an Oxyrhynchus papyrus, first published in 1922 (58LP). That papyrus, however, contained only line-endings, preceded and followed by line-endings of other poems, without certainty of where one poem ended and another began. The line-endings of the verses published in 2004 were found to coincide with the isolated endings published in 1922—a most random, and rare, papyrological coincidence. The poem's last eight lines are virtually complete. The first four lack two or three words each at their beginnings, although the sense, if not exact wording, has been restored.

Dealing with the incapacities of advancing age, the poem makes telling reference to the myth of Tithonus. Tithonus, a beautiful Trojan youth, was beloved by the goddess Dawn (Gr. *Ēōs*, Lat. *Aurora*), who claimed and swept him away. Tithonus here shares the fate of the Trojan Ganymede, beloved and taken by Zeus. Asking Zeus to grant Tithonus immortality, Dawn forgets to request eternal youth as well. Tithonus was thus fated to live forever, growing ever older and more debilitated. It is an untenable situation for rosy Dawn—forever young and fresh, and without existence or thought past morning—who must rid herself of the increasingly hateful Tithonus. The account is also related in the *Homeric Hymn to Aphrodite* (that goddess, too, wedding a mortal named Anchises, father of Aeneas). As the *Homeric Hymn to Aphrodite* relates: "But when loathsome old age pressed full on [Tithonus], and he could neither move nor lift his limbs, this seemed to [Dawn] in her heart the best plan: to lay him in a room and fasten the shining doors. There he babbles endlessly, and no more has strength at all, such as once he had in his supple limbs."

As Tithonus bears the weight of advancing years, so, Sappho feels, does she. The poem bears a marked resemblance to Anacreon §72.

To the violet-bodiced Muses' gifts aspire,
dear children, to the gentle song-loving lyre.

But as for me, advancing years torment me quite,
skin earlier taut now slack, black hair turned to white.

Now is my heart all heaviness, now fail the knees
erstwhile startled to dalliance with fawn-like ease.

As fully futile, then, as bitter my lament,
that life's toil culminates in youthful beauty spent.

And once, they tell, enamored rosy-armèd Dawn
was to earth's furthest bourn with her Tithonus gone,

then young and trim. But hoary age did nonetheless
take hold of him—though with mate immortal blessed.

## ALCMAN

❧

**§40 (59D)** The Rhipean mountains, a far-northern legendary range, unvisited by the sun.

Forest
flowered
mountain,
Rhipē,
evening's
breast

**§41 (3D)** Preserved on papyrus dating to the end of the first century BC, and first published in 1957. The poem had at least one hundred and twenty-six verses, some sixty of which preceded the present segment. Of the sixty, only verses 1 to 10 provide any sense.

With longing that dissolves the limbs
Casting glances more melting than sleep and death
Her sweetness serves no idle whim

Astymeloisa makes me no reply
but holding a garland
like a glittering star
or golden shoot
or tender down
[ ]
] she has come on luxuriant stride

] the moist charm of Cinyras
which settles on maidens' hair

] Astymeloisa in the host
] people's darling
] winning praise

**§42(101D)** Quoted by Athenaeus (see §3), *Doctors at Dinner* (13.600).

Again sweet love
through Aphrodite's will
does melt and distill
my heart.

**§43 (36D)** Quoted by Hephaistion (see §23).

It isn't Aphrodite
but Eros, wild
as a child at play,
down over the flower tops
heading this way–
don't touch them, I pray.

**§44 (94D)** Quoted by Antigonus of Carystus, a philosophical writer of the third century BC, portions of whose work survive in Athenaeus (see §3) and other writers.

Maidens with honey tones
and voices of desire,
my limbs no more can
carry me. Ah, but to be
above the flowering wave–
a halcyon, a fearless flier
aloft on wingèd span,
a sprightly bird blue as the sea.

**§45 (58D)** Quoted by Apollonius the Sophist, the Alexandrian Homeric scholar (2nd century BC), to show that Alcman used the word *knōdalon* 'seamonster'.

Mountain peaks and gullies sleep,
ravines and headlands silence keep,
sleep forests and each quadruped
that dusky earth has ever bred,
sleep mountain breasts and swarming bees,
monsters in blue-chasmed seas,
birds that soar on wingèd spread.

**§46 (1P) *Partheneion* (*Maiden Song*)** The poem is preserved on papyrus datable to the mid-first century AD, and was first published in 1863. The papyrus was discovered in 1855 by a French Egyptologist at Saqqara, the burial ground serving as necropolis of the city of Memphis. For the Greek text, see Denys L. Page, *Alcman: The Partheneion* (Oxford: Oxford Univ. Press, 1951).

The poem's pervasive textual uncertainties do not warrant another translation. Those here provided are by Mary R. Lefkowitz and Gloria Ferrari. The first is a polished prose version; the second, a line-by-line translation.

As Lefkowitz notes, "A chorus of young girls describe themselves and their ceremonial role in a special song. . . . Emphasis on the beauty of face and hair suggests that they are involved in a ritual that marks the transition (hence perhaps the references to battle) from girlhood to womanhood: the running of races is also a feature of puberty rites. . . . Comparison to horses may suggest the imminence of marriage, which is often described in metaphors of taming and yoking." See, e.g., §51.

(M. R. Lefkowitz, 1982, 119)

I sing of Agido's light. I see her as the sun; Agido calls him to testify to us that he is shining. But our famous leader will not let me either praise or criticize her; for our leader seems to us to be supreme, as if one set a horse among the herds, strong, prize-winning, with thundering hooves—a horse of the world of dreams.

And don't you see: the race-horse is Venetic; but my cousin Hagesichora's hair blooms like unmixed gold. And her silver face—why should I spell it out? Here is Hagesichora. And she who is second to Agido in looks, runs like a Colaxian horse to an Ibenian. For the Doves bring the robe to the Goddess of the Dawn for us; they rise like the dog star through the immortal night and fight for us.

There is not enough purple to protect us, nor jewelled snake of solid gold, nor Lydian cap-adornment of girls with their dark eyes; nor Nanno's hair, no nor Areta who is like the gods; not Sylakis and Cleeisera. You wouldn't go to Aenesimbrota's house and say: let me have Astaphis; may Philylla look at me, and lovely Damareta and Vianthemis—no, it's Hagesichora who excites me.

For Hagesichora of the fair ankles is near her; close to Agido . . . she praises our festival. Yes, gods, receive [their prayer]. From the gods [comes] accomplishment and fulfilment. Leader, I could say—a young girl that I am; I shriek in vain from my roof like an owl, and I will say what will please Dawn most, for she has been healer of our troubles; but it is through Hagesichora that girls have reached the peace they long for . . .

◆

(G. Ferrari, 2008, 155–157)

. . . I sing
the light of Agido. I see it
like the sun, whom
Agido summons to appear and
witness for us. But the glorious chorus mistress
forbids me to either praise
or blame her. For she appears to be
outstanding as if
one placed among a grazing herd
a perfect horse, a prize-winner with resounding hooves,
one of the dreams that dwell below the rock.

Don't you see? That one is an Enetic
courser, while the mane
of my cousin
Hagesichora shines forth
like unalloyed gold.
Her face is of silver,
Why do I tell you explicitly?
There is Hagesichora herself.
Next will run Agido, her appearance
that of a Colaxian horse following an Ibenian.
For against us the Pleiades contend
at daybreak, carried aloft
like Sirius across immortal Night,
as we bring the season of the plow.

For surfeit of purple
does not help,
nor chased golden
snake-bracelet, nor Lydian
tiara, pride
of violet-eyed maids,
nor Nanno's tresses,
not even godlike Areta
or Thylacis and Cleesithera,
nor will you go to Ainesimbrota's house and say:
"let Astaphis stand by me,
  and let Philylla and Damareta
and lovely Hianthemis look upon me,
  but Hagesichora effaces me."

Nor does Hagesichora
of the beautiful ankles remain in place
to Agido. . .
and lauds our festival.
But [
accept. To the gods belong the fulfillment
and the end. Mistress of the chorus
I would say I myself
a maiden wail in vain from the sky,
an owl. But most of all I long
to please Aotis for she is ever
  the healer of our labors.
Away from Hagesichora, maidens
  enter upon delightful peace.
To the trace-horse
in the same way
to the steerman must
on a ship too [
the song of the Sirens
indeed more harmonious,
for they are goddesses, instead of [eleven]
children ten [
sings . . . on the streams of Xanthus
the swan. She of the lovely golden hair
[
[
[
    [

# ANACREON

**§47 (37G)** Quoted by the Alexandrian churchman Clement of Alexandria (2nd and 3rd centuries AD).

Exquisite Eros I'll not neglect,
I'll praise him, garlanded, flower-decked,
who over gods maintains his sway,
as over creatures of a day.

**§48 (25G)** Quoted by Hephaistion (see §23). This vivid description of love's assault derives from *Od.* 9.391–393: "As when a smith plunges an axe or an adz, hissing greatly, in cold water, and tempers it—for therein is the strength of iron . . ."

Like a smith–
again Love strikes the hammer's blow,
plunging me
in winter's torrent as I glow.

**§49 (46G)** Quoted by Hephaistion (see §23).

Again do I love, again love not,
this moment sane, the next distraught.

Compare Catullus, Poem 85:

Odi et amo. Quare id faciam fortasse requiris?
   Nescio, sed fieri sentio et excrucior.

I love and I hate. Wherefore you might inquire.
   I know not, but feel it, tormented entire.

**§50 (13G)** This complete poem is quoted by Athenaeus (see §3), *Doctors at Dinner* (13.599c), apropos of the untenable view that Sappho and Anacreon were contemporaries: "Chamaeleon in his *Concerning Sappho* declares that according to some Sappho was the subject of Anacreon's verses 'Again . . . agree.'"

Athenaeus then quotes, to disclaim, Sappho's supposed reply. This is the only archaic text showing an express link between Lesbos and homosexuality.

Again tossing his purple ball my way
blond Eros strikes calling me out to play
with a gaily sandaled girl.
But she's of Lesbian pedigree
and won't have any part of me
because my hair is grey,
and gapes that some other girl agree.

**§51 (78G)** Quoted by the pre-Socratic philosopher Heraclitus (6th century BC) as an example of allegory.

Thracian filly, why cast sidelong glances,
why flee as if I'd lost my senses?

I could easily bridle your head in place,
rein you in, run you round the race.

now grazing in meadows you lightly skip
with no nimble horseman to hug your hip.

**§52 (22G)** Quoted by Maximus of Tyre (see §35).

Boys by my words would be disarmed,
what I say, what I sing is charmed.

**§53 (15G)** Quoted by Athenaeus (see §3), *Doctors at Dinner* (13.564d), to illustrate the attention given by lovers to the eyes of their beloved.

Lad with the maiden's glance,
I wish only to have you near;
you give me not a chance—
my soul's unwitting charioteer.

**§54 (83G)** Quoted by a scholiast to Aristophanes's *Birds* (5th century BC).

To Olympus I wing my fragile way
to plead with Eros there,

that a lad no longer will delay
his youth with me to share.

**§55 (96G)** Quoted several times by Athenaeus (see §3), *Doctors at Dinner* (14.634a, 635c), vis-à-vis the precise type of lyre designated by the rare Greek word *magis.*

I pluck this lyre's twenty strings;
Ah, Leucaspis,
each with your youthful freshness sings.

**§56 (96G)** Preserved on papyrus, four fragmentary stanzas in the Greek. The "Cyprian" refers to Aphrodite, associated by birth with the island of Cyprus.

O lad with the lovely face,
another's look makes your heart race.
Your caring mother thinks that she

at home will nurse you constantly,
but you [ ] the meadows
of hyacinth, where the Cyprian

tethers her horses after they're run.
In the midst [ ] you darted down
setting hearts astir throughout the town.

**§57 (19G)** Quoted by Athenaeus (see §3), *Doctors at Dinner* (15.671d).

The season comes round;
Megistes, warm of heart,
is willow-crowned,
with honeyed wine assumes his part.

**§58 (99G)** Quoted in the *Etymologicum Magnum* (see §33).

I hate all who rant
and are given to riot.
Megistes you grant
the repose of the quiet.

**§59 (43G)** Quoted by the scholiast on Pindar's *Olympian* 7 (5th century BC) to illustrate the meaning of Gr. *propino* 'extend, yield, surrender, bestow'.

] but extend
Your tender thigh, my friend.

**§60 (28G)** Quoted by Athenaeus (see §3), *Doctors at Dinner* (9.396d), and others apropos of whether a doe has horns.

Gently, like a suckling fawn, newborn,
affrighted in the wood–
antlered mother gone, and he forlorn.

**§61 (76G)** Quoted by the scholiast to Sophocles's *Antigone* (5th century BC) in explanation of the verb "quivered." A single verse in Greek.

In dark-leafed bay
and green olive
he quivered.

**§62 (14G)** Quoted by the rhetorician Dio Chrysostom (1st and 2nd centuries AD) on the unseemliness of a king's calling on a god, as does Anacreon.

Master, with whom rosy Aphrodite,
blue-eyed nymphs and conquering Eros play,
whose mountainous empery
enthrones you over all that you survey,
I beseech you: come well disposed to me,
kind-hearted, attentive, as I pray
Kleoboulos be well advised
and the love I bear him not despised.

**§63 (5G)** Quoted by the Greek grammarian Herodian (2nd century AD) to illustrate the word *poluptoton* (lit. 'much falling'), namely, the repetition of "Kleoboulos" in different grammatical cases.

Kleoboulos I adore
for Kleoboulos I rage
on Kleoboulos I gaze.

**§64 (33G)** Quoted by Athenaeus (see §3), *Doctors at Dinner* (10.427a), to illustrate the proportion for mixing wine and water. Wine was mixed in antiquity. Giving it unmixed to the Cyclops, Odysseus gets the Cyclops drunk, blinds him, and escapes with his men.

Come, my lad, let the ladle abound
whose fifteen fathoms no thirst can sound;
ten measures of water, five of wine,
reveling yet would I walk a straight line.

Come, again, no longer let us pour
amid the din's riotous uproar;
no, let us intone sweet hymns instead,
raising our cups as men well bred.

**§65 (56G)** Quoted by Athenaeus (see §3), *Doctors at Dinner* (11.463a), for the correct conduct at a symposium. The translation expands on the four verses of the original.

I do not like the speakers
of strife and tearful war
whenever festive beakers
are filled and hold no more;
I'd rather one who mixes
sweet gifts of love and song
and, wistful, reminisces
of good times all night long.

**§66 (38, 65G)** Quoted by Athenaeus (see §3), *Doctors at Dinner* (11.782a), as evidence that the ancients when mixing wine poured the water into the bowl before the wine.

Bring water, bring wine, my boy,
flowered necklaces bring,
with Love would I enter the ring.

◆

I who sparred so painfully
can finally lift my head and see.

**§67 (111G)** Quoted by a scholiast on *Il.* 23.88 where the same word *dice* occurs.

> Love's dice, fully loaded for
> derangement and din of war.

**§68 (108G)** Quoted by Athenaeus (see §3), *Doctors at Dinner* (10.433ef). Spoken to a woman ('generous' feminine in the Greek).

> Generous to passers-by,
> Let one drink who's languished dry.

**§69 (94G)** Quoted by Hephaistion (see §23). See Chapter 4 for discussion.

> Drunk with love,
> again, up the Leucadian cliff I go
> and leap to the pallid brine below.

**§70 (84G)** The restoration by the nineteenth-century German philologist Theodor Bergk from a prose statement quoted in the rhetorican-turned-author Lucian (2nd century AD). For such reconstruction see also §§35, 89.

> Love who has seen my chin grow white
> wings past gold-gilded in his flight.

**§71 (74G)** Quoted by Hephaistion (see §23).

> Listen to me who am old
> fair-haired maiden, gowned in gold.

**§72 (36G)** Quoted by Stobaeus (4th and 5th centuries AD), author of an anthology of poets and prose writers, intended for his son, Septimius. Of a sober bent, Stobaeus considered this the only one of Anacreon's poems worthy to be included in his anthology. For Stobaeus and Sappho, see Chapter 27. The poem bears a marked thematic resemblance to the "New Sappho" (§39).

> Temples already white,
> gray thinning hair now slight,

graceless my aged plight,
my teeth have lost their bite.
Of life all but bereft,
brief is the sweet time left.

This then do I lament
by dread of Hades rent,
for death is a horrid pit,
and hard the path down to it.
Descend, and that descent
is fully infinite.

Commentators, while noting the idea is a commonplace, do not give Virgil's adaptation its due.

. . . facilis descensus Averno:
noctes atque dies patet atri ianua Ditis;
sed revocare gradum superasque evadere ad auras,
hoc opus, hic labor est. *Aen.* 6.126–129

. . . easy the descent to Hell:
All night and day its gates unfastened dwell,
But return regaining the upper air–
There's the task, therein despair.

## ARCHILOCHUS

**§73 (203T)** Quoted by Stobaeus (see §72).

I lie wretched, alone,
lifeless, pierced to the bone,
mercilessly pained,
thus the gods have ordained.

**§74 (197T)** Quoted by Stobaeus (see §72).

By love's desire fast possessed,
eyes misted, faint, at Love's behest,
frail spirit stolen from my breast.

**§75 (212T)** Quoted by Hephaistion (see §23). Compare §36.

But desire, dissolving my limbs,
undoes me, my friend.

**§76 (111T)** Quoted by Plutarch (see §9) apropos of the formulation used in beginning a prayer ("If only I might . . .").

Ah, could I but touch Neoboulē's hand . . .

**§77 (196aW)** The longest surviving fragment of poetry attributed to Archilochus—a poet otherwise only scantily preserved—the work survives on a first- or second-century AD papyrus discovered in the 1960s amid mummy wrappings from the Abusir el-Melek cemetery at the Faiyum Oasis (west of the Nile, just south of Cairo). As the mummy was then held at the University of Cologne, the poem is sometimes called the "Cologne Epode." The poem begins with a dialogue between an unidentified maiden (perhaps the sister of Neoboulē) and the poet. It ends with a negotiated erotic consummation, a compromise, so to speak. The poem is unique in theme and meter in ancient Greek poetry. First published in 1974, it generated a storm of controversy, most of it concerning the nature of the sexual act described in the final verses—though what happens is clear enough. On Neoboulē and the conventions of invective poetry, see Chapter 3.

". . . totally keeping yourself,
and in like fashion I'll forbear.
But if you are so very spurred,
with bed to all things else preferred,
we have at home a girl quite fair,
now most desiring to be wed;
her looks are quite beyond compare."
So much she spoke, and this I said:

"Daughter of Amphimedo
—a knowing mother nobly bred—

whom now dank earth conceals below,
many joys does the goddess grant
young men, aside from the divine;
of these some one will do just fine.
We'll better know the one we want
in parlance hushed, god-sped, lights low.
As you urge, so shall I go.
You think me eager, in a rush?
But by the gated portico
—don't be begrudging, don't say no—
I'll put in where the grass is lush.
Neoboulē!? the likes of such
assign to someone else's bed.
She's overripe, flower-fresh no more,
with grace of girlhood long since shed.
Ever short of what she's lusting for,
she's shown it all, the girl's a whore!

To hell with her, and far from me!
May never ruler Zeus decree
that I, possessed of such a cur,
become a neighbor's mockery.
It's you whom I do most prefer,
you're not a two-faced liar like her.
She, in a word, is too severe,
and many the man whom she holds 'dear.'
'Haste makes waste,' as often said,
avoid what ill you know is near."

I spoke, she followed as I led
to flowers, where I urged our rest.
Enfolded by my cloak outspread
(my hand positioned neath her head),
she hindered trembling like a fawn,
though I, undaunted, urged her on
and gently took hold of her breast.
Soon after was she all undressed—
Such maiden's charm in that fair skin
I scarce knew where I should begin—
I reconnoitered all her frame
released all my force and fell tame,
just touching on the tawny hair . . .

**§78 (109T)** Quoted by Athenaeus (see §3), *Doctors at Dinner* (10.433e). Compare §68.

With you love's battles to engage,
battle as drink when thirst does rage.

**§79 (190T)** Quoted by Plutarch (see §9).

Such did she conspire:
in one hand water; the other, fire.

**§80 (1T)** Quoted by Athenaeus (see §3), *Doctors at Dinner* (14.627c), as evidence of the poet's equal emphasis on civic and poetic activities.

Enyalius, lord of battles, I attend;
the Muses' lovely gift I also comprehend.

**§81 (2T)** Quoted by Athenaeus (see §3), *Doctors at Dinner* (1.30f). A good soldier's vigilance knows no unpreparedness.

I knead my bread with spear in hand,
pour my wine with spear in hand,
drinking aside my spear I stand.

**§82 (96T)** Quoted by Dio Chrysostom (see §62). The poet will have no part of a foppish or affected commander. Four verses in the Greek.

I hate the general, heavyset,
standing feet spread wide,
who most about his beard does fret,
whose hairdo is his pride;
I rather one who's spare and smart,
who walks firm-footed, full of heart.

**§83 (105T)** Quoted by Stobaeus (see §72). One of the more expansive examples of self-exhortation in archaic poetry. See, e.g., *Il.* 22.98; *Od.* 5.407, 20.18.

Heart, heart, overwhelmed with confusion past cure,
to adversities bearing yourself, endure.

Stand safely aside from the snare of a foe,
don't in victory overexultant grow,
nor bested, indoors bemoan your overthrow.
Temper triumph, be not grieving overwrought,
comprehending the rhythm of mankind's lot.

**§84 (8T)** Compiled from quotations in several authors; often referred to and imitated.

In my shield does some Thracian now rejoice,
which, flawless, I jettisoned, having no choice,
were I to escape alive. Let it go to Hell!
Another will serve me just as well.

**§85 (102T)** Quoted by Stobaeus (see §72). As in the preceding piece, the poet debunks an accepted notion, that glory is undying and worth dying for. See §26.2.

Deference and fame depart the dead,
dying is naught but dread;
let life and living be sought instead.

**§86 (16T)** Quoted by Athenaeus (see §3), *Doctors at Dinner* (13.594d). Figs and fishing were the mainstays of Archilochus's poverty-stricken Paros. So fragment §87T: "Good riddance to Paros, and those figs, and the life of the sea." The fig was known for its cheapness, while designating in Aristophanes (*Peace* 1350) the female genitalia.

A fig tree on its rock, feeding many crows,
accessible, loved by all, to all exposed.

**§87 (44T)** Quoted by a scholiast on Aratus (4th and 3rd centuries BC), best known for his still extant *Phainomena* (*Appearances*), a work in hexameters on the constellations and weather conditions.

Like a mating crow,
pleasured, perching low,
poised on a jutting peak,
slack pinioned, sleek.

**§88 (43T)** Quoted in the *Etymologicum Magnum* (see §33).

We have a sturdy ox at home,
knows how to plough, need not be shown.

**§89 (118T)** Second verse quoted by the Roman rhetorician Aelian (3rd and 2nd centuries AD). First verse reconstructed by F. Lasserre (1950 edition of Archilochus). For such "reconstruction" see §§35 and 70.

Gain gathered by long time and labor
often flows down the gut of a whore.

**§90 (112T)** Quoted by a scholiast on Euripides's *Medea*. Sometimes thought to be the sequel to §76 (both in the same Greek meter).

And on that skin, insatiable, alight,
hurling belly on belly, thigh on thigh.

**§91 (25, 26T)** The first two verses are quoted by Ammonius (3rd and 2nd centuries BC), who was the pupil and successor of the great Alexandrian grammarian and Homeric commentator Aristarchus. The last three lines (two in Greek) are quoted by Synesius (4th and 5th centuries AD), Christian Neoplatonist and orator, who says the poet is praising a courtesan's hair. Despite the vast chronological spread, the two fragments are often taken consecutively.

Her joy is a myrtle sprig
and a lovely flowering rose,
the long hair shades her
shoulders and neck,
all down her back it flows.

**§92 (27T)** Preserved on papyrus.

Breast and fragrant hair
to seize an old man with despair.

# IBYCUS

**§93 (6D)** Quoted by Athenaeus (see §3), *Doctors at Dinner* (13.601bc), as an example of Ibycus's love poetry. The poem strikes a contrast between the seasonal regularity of nature and the determined irregularity of the poet's passion; between the serenity of spring and the onslaught of the poet's frenzy. See Preface for discussion.

In spring the river streams bedew
the quinces in Cydonia,
where sacred stands the Maidens' grove
and shading bough vine-blossomed grows;
this love of mine no season knows
but races—northern Thracian blast
from Aphrodite's shrine outcast
ablaze with flash of lightning, black
with shameless fits of parching rage,
pain unrelenting, unassuaged.

◆

(F. L. Lucas)

Only in spring do the quince flowers quiver
Blossoming deep in the garden-close
Sacred to Maidenhood, where from the river
Many a quickening channel flows;
Only in spring do the vine flowers throng
Under the leaves; but all year long
No rest my passion knows.
Sent by the Cyprian (as from the north
Headlong the Thracian tempest breaks,
While from its gloom the lightnings shoot),
Raving it smites me in its wrath,
Shrivelling all—to the very root
My heart it shakes.

**§94 (JMD)** Variation on a theme from Ibycus.

Tamara demon of my brain
exquisite torment wreaking Cain
with seething song, incarnate fright,
my mind's disruption, mind's delight;
sing stinging strains that lash my brain
refrains of unrelenting pain
until my mind completely flayed
with scourge of Siren serenade
will bleed to have you far away
while pleading, stay, Tamara, stay.

**§95 (JMD)** Mill Song variation on a theme from Ibycus.

The murmured chant
"I want you now . . . "
pounds frantically
beneath my brow.
Your wanton nails
assail my back,
the tightening hold
impales me to the rack
where torn and tense,
resounding cadence
makes me crack–
a heathen din
a harrowing hymn
to crush my marrow
limb by limb,
confound the power
of my will, reduced to dust,
these two, within the mill
and ground with sweat and tears,
a mound to spill
insensate from the gears
of you . . .

**§96 (7D)** Parmenides, in the Platonic dialogue bearing his name (137a), paraphrases these verses, expressing his reluctance to embark on a lengthy exposition. The scholiast provides the actual poem, believed to be complete. The poet feels himself past the age for love and trembles at the prospect of being, once again, "harnessed" (see §53: "my soul's unwitting charioteer"). No more capable of running love's course than of resisting the yoke, he will be forced to stumble through love's paces. That the theme is commonplace with the lyric poets in no way detracts from Ibycus's unique expression of it. Compare §§45, 70–72, 92, and see Preface for further discussion.

Love's melting look from eyes dark-browed
has cast me into Cyprian chains
unfailing, charmed in every wise.
How I shake at his approach–
as a horse once winner of the prize
in later years must bear the reins
and cart, unwilling, past the crowd.

**§97 (JMD)** Chariot variation on a theme from Ibycus.

Love's glory day is past
and I to pasture placed
who in love's course held fast
nor equaled nor outpaced.

I mounted high the vale
descended the divide
and snorting did assail
love's rampart opened wide.

Yes, I who stayed love's course
to whom no steed drew near
am petted now perforce
a hayseed in my ear.

**§98 (JMD)** Affirmation on a theme from Ibycus.

Love's glory day be sung
resplendent to the lyre,
strings taut and neatly strung
aglow with bygone fire.

So range the bard's report
of epic ecstasies
wherein I did disport
once, nestled at your knees.

# IV.

# Chapter 13

## *Iliad, Odyssey,* and *Aeneid*: The Epic Cycle in Progress

I despise the cyclic epic
nor in the path delight
that leads the masses aimlessly,
proceeding where it might.

I loathe the sauntering lover,
shun the frequented spring,
detest coarse commonality's
hyped and deceitful ring.

Lykas, fairer than fair art thou!
To this my ardent vow
from afar responds the echo:
"Another has him now."

– CALLIMACHUS (JMD, tr.)

HOMER'S *ILIAD* AND *ODYSSEY*, each in twenty-four books (a division made by Alexandrian scholars of the third century BC), survive complete and perfected in over 27,000 verses combined. The *Iliad,* for all its length, relates a series of events occurring over approximately fifty days during the tenth and final year of the Trojan War, excluding the actual sack and fall of Troy (Gr. *Troiē,* also *Ilion*; Lat. *Ilium,* thus *Iliad*). The *Iliad* concludes with the funeral of Troy's principal defender, Hector, whose death at the hands of Achilles prefigures the death of Troy itself. The *Odyssey* relates the ten-year *nostos* 'homecoming' of Odysseus, after the fall of Troy, to his island kingdom of Ithaca, off the northwestern coast of Greece. The *Iliad* is antiquity's crowning jewel, greater (though less studied) than the *Odyssey*. The first-attested work of the Western literary tradition, developing, if not miraculously sprung, from centuries of oral recitation, the *Iliad* is a comprehensive, deeply tragic, and probing meditation on the human condition.

Other events of the Trojan War, including its prelude and aftermath, generated the various works of the later Epic Cycle, also referred to as cyclic epics. These were largely composed from the eighth to sixth centuries BC by poets other than Homer, though in Homeric meter and dialect. The poetry, however, was inferior, lacking Homer's craftsmanship and concision. Only fragments and brief excerpts survive in scattered references and quotations by later authors, though we know many of the poets' names and what parts of the Cycle they covered. The different poets cover the entire Cycle, which may be retro-constructed (theoretically at least) to the mythological beginnings of time, or forward-projected into Roman history, as in the case of Virgil's *Aeneid* (discussed below). Thus viewed, the Cycle is the Greek, and then Greco-Roman, mythological timeline itself. At the Cycle's center is antiquity's greatest catastrophe, the Trojan War, around which all else crystallizes.

The lost *Cypria,* in eleven books, is attributed to Stasinos of Cyprus. It treated the Judgment of Paris—leading to the abduction of Helen and start of the war—and events of the war's first nine years. The *Aethiopis,* in five books, attributed to Arctinus of Miletus (see map), related the events immediately following those of the *Iliad.* It included the death of Achilles by Helen's abductor, Paris—Achilles famously shot and killed by an arrow to the heel. The *Little Iliad,* in four books, attributed to one Lesches of Mytilene (on Lesbos), continued where the *Aethiopis* left off. According to ancient summaries, the *Little Iliad* began with the contest between Ajax and Odysseus for the arms of Achilles—following Achilles's death—and continued through the Trojan feast, held after the Trojans had brought the horse into the city, thinking it a tribute of the ostensibly departed Greeks. The *Little Iliad,* however, stops there, without proceeding to the actual sack of Troy.

Though not using the term "Cycle" or "Epic Cycle" as such, Aristotle famously criticizes the *Cypria* and *Little Iliad* as follows:

> Here again, then, as has been already observed, the transcendent excellence of Homer is manifest. He never attempts to make the whole war of Troy the subject of his poem. . . . He detaches a single portion, and admits as episodes many events from the general story of the war . . . thus diversifying the poem. All other poets take

> a single hero, a single period, or an action single indeed, but with a multiplicity of parts. Thus did the author of the Cypria and of the Little Iliad.

In sum, the *Cypria* and *Little Iliad,* with their "multiplicity of parts," contain too much plot. They do not and cannot "detach" and treat a "single portion" of the war because they function as gap-fillers, accounting for parts of the overall narrative covered by neither Homer nor competing cyclic poets. They are thus, as we would say, "all over the board." Granted, the cyclic poets did not "attempt to make the whole war of Troy the subject of the poem," but the significant parts they did choose were simply too great and too diverse for coherence.

Given their comprehensiveness, the cyclic epics abound in narrative-diverting profusions, e.g., "the fantastic, the miraculous, and the romantic, all exceed[ing]... the austere limits to which the *Iliad* confines them." Examples include the appearance of superhuman or exotic beings or creatures (only alluded to in Homer), the evasion of death (unthinkable in the *Iliad;* considered, but spurned, in the *Odyssey*), and love scenes between men and women (of no interest to Homer). Further, because Homer is "sparing in ascribing offspring to his characters," there are fewer "surplus children," and thus "no proliferation of intrigues." In sum, "The strict, radical, and consistently heroic interpretation of the world presented by the *Iliad* made it quite different from the Cycle, still content with monsters, miracles, metamorphoses, and an untragic attitude toward mortality, all seasoned with exoticism and romance, and composed in a flatter, looser, less dramatic style." Though narratively part of the Cycle, the *Iliad* and *Odyssey* are thus very much *outside* it. What excess the *Iliad* conveys focuses, to unparalleled effect, on Achilles's wrath and ferocity. Though excess of a human kind, it yet surpasses human scale, Achilles being a demigod.

To the extent that the Homeric epics themselves allude to events preceding or following their own narratives, they too are sources of cyclic material. Thus, as the war recedes to the background during Odysseus's ten-year wanderings, it is the Greeks' *nostoi* 'homecomings' on which the cyclic poets focus. Other than the *Odyssey,* none of the *Nostoi* survive, though we know of them both through the summaries and references of later writers and through the *Odyssey* itself. In Book One of the *Odyssey,* the bard Phemius, against his will, entertains Penelope's suitors with songs of the Greeks' ravaged returns. Such matter, following the *Iliad* and concurrent (up to a point) with the events of the *Odyssey,* is cyclic in nature. Phemius's song is a poignant reminder of Odysseus's still-unaccomplished return. Hearing the song from her upstairs quarters, Penelope is reduced to tears. There are also what may be called cyclic intimations. The *Iliad,* by its formulaic references to Odysseus as *polutlas* 'much suffering', "records the fact that Odysseus already has an *Odyssey* tradition about him"—a tradition still in the making, but not yet the *Odyssey* as ultimately known. That is to say, the *Iliad*'s use of *polutlas Odusseus* characterizes the hero in his belated and highly trying homecoming, as told in the *Odyssey*; there being nothing 'much suffering' about Odysseus in the *Iliad.* The storytelling tradition is fully known, regardless the part being told at any one time. All parts are *concurrently* known, whether Homeric, cyclic, or Homeric in the making.

Books Three and Four of the *Odyssey* contain cyclic materials relating to the sack of Troy and subsequent *nostoi.* In Book Three, the eldest of the Greek warriors, Nestor, receives Odysseus's son, Telemachus, in Pylos, where Telemachus travels (his own odyssey) to seek news of his missing father. As part of the hospitality, Nestor recounts the dispute on Lesbos concerning the sacrifices needed to assure safe passage home. Because it follows the events related in the *Iliad,* the homeward-bound Lesbos episode is cyclic material within the *Odyssey* itself. In Book Four, Helen and Menelaus, resettled in Sparta and entertaining Telemachus, relate an episode from the sack of Troy to which Helen bore particular witness. In Book Eight of the *Odyssey,* the bard Demodocus, at Odysseus's request, relates the tale of the wooden horse (Odysseus's invention). Odysseus weeps before his Phaeacian hosts to hear of events in which he prominently figures. He thus knows, even before his arrival home, that these events are already part of the epic storytelling tradition, here by cyclic allusion within the *Odyssey* itself.

Subject as it was to Aristotle's negative criticism, the *Little Iliad* was more recently tasked by indefatigable classicist-critic Daniel Mendelsohn in a searing review of Warner Brothers' *Troy* (2004)—Mendelsohn inveighing against the movie's narrative liberties and cyclic inclusiveness. The film, however, though freewheeling with events (as one would expect from Hollywood), was a cinematographic tour de force, splendidly evoking the aura and passions of the Trojan War and making them felt by millions otherwise knowing little of Homer. For all its precision, moreover, the review was also impervious to the movie's great merit, if also to its classically sanctioned design, of having Achilles (Brad Pitt) replace Helen as the supreme object of physical beauty and desire. Achilles's usurpation of Helen palliates the awesome threat of her beauty and power—even as ancient authors, in their own way, felt compelled to do (see further Chapter 18).

After the *Little Iliad* came the *Iliou Persis* '*Sack of Troy*' in two books, also by Arctinus of Miletus. The work, now lost, covered the story of the Trojan Horse, the actual sack, and other events of the city's destruction. The only fully surviving account of the sack of Troy, including the tale of the Trojan Horse, is Virgil's *Aeneid* (1st century BC). In Book One of the *Aeneid,* the Trojan Aeneas, destined to found Rome, has fled the fallen Troy. He arrives with what remains of his battered entourage at Carthage, on the west coast of Africa (the kingdom of Libya to Virgil; Tunisia today). Hosted by Queen Dido, Aeneas recounts the sack of Troy in Book Two of the *Aeneid,* the story fully told as post-banquet entertainment. The *Aeneid*'s Book Two underscores the vagaries of the preservation of classical accounts—the only fully surviving account of the sack of Troy (Virgil's) post-dating Homer by some seven hundred and fifty years. Similarly, the Roman poet Ovid (1st century BC–1st century AD) relates, in Books Thirteen and Fourteen of his *Metamorphoses,* the Greeks' arrival at Troy (also recounted in the *Cypria*) and the award, after Achilles's death, of his armor to Odysseus (also told in the *Little Iliad*). Cyclic narration continued well into the Common Era, again in Homeric dialect and meter, but with ever-diminished results. Quintus of Smyrna (4th century AD) wrote a *Posthomerica* (*After Homer*), accounting for events from Achilles's death to the end of the war. The Byzantine poet and grammarian Ioannis Tzetzes (12th century AD) wrote an *Antehomerica* (*Before Homer*), beginning with the birth of Paris and continuing to the Greeks' homecomings. The works of Quintus and Tzetzes have survived. In the twentieth century, one may look to Nikos Kazantzakis, *The Odyssey: A Modern Sequel* (1938; Kimon Friar, tr., 1958).

❧

Virgil is both a user and a fashioner of cyclic materials. As a user, he notably incorporates into his *Aeneid,* as seen, a narrative of the sack of Troy. As a fashioner, Virgil, by the escaped Trojan Aeneas, takes us from the sack of Troy to the founding of Rome. At this point on the cyclic continuum, myth changes from bygone tale to quasi-history. And as Virgil grounds Roman history aborning in the mythic past, the use and fashioning of cyclic materials go hand in hand. Thus, upon arrival at Carthage, Aeneas and his men make their way to the city, which is still under construction. The rising city presages Aeneas's own founding of Rome, tempting him to forget his purpose and join in Dido's enterprise. In a shaded grove in the middle of the city, they come upon a temple of Juno, the doors of which are engraved with scenes from the Trojan War, in which Aeneas sees himself portrayed. The sight brings tears to his eyes (and one of Virgil's most memorable and untranslatable lines to the page). The Trojan War is already epic history—as Aeneas gathers from the cyclic depictions on the temple doors—and Aeneas part of it in his own time. More than epic history, however, the war is now also a quasi-historical antecedent; it is Roman history in the making, moving Aeneas along the cyclic continuum and ultimately into Virgil's own time. Thus does Virgil not only use but fashion cyclic materials.

Aeneas before the temple of Juno harks back to Odysseus on Phaeacia, in tears before his hosts as he relates the sorry past, including his departure from Troy and subsequent adventures. Odysseus and Aeneas, a Greek and a Trojan, are *both* in transit from ruined Troy and both mournfully reminded en route of their epic pasts. They alone are destiny-bound—the one to restore his household and island sovereignty; the other to found a people marked for world dominion. The one to embody myth; the other to forge history. By way of further contrast, Odysseus's ego (no less than Achilles's) is boundless at the cost of others, while Aeneas's remains subservient throughout to a self-sacrificing mission. Virgil's *Aeneid*, extolling a Troy-risen Rome and the preordination of its empire, is thus itself a latter-day part of the Epic Cycle, even as it is Homeric through and through.

Integrating Homer as they do, the first six books of the *Aeneid* are known as the Odyssean *Aeneid* (for Aeneas's wanderings before reaching Italy); and the last six, as the Iliadic *Aeneid* (for his battles over the future site of Rome). Virgil could have translated the *Iliad* and *Odyssey* into what would have been dazzling Latin hexameter, and much is the pity he did not. He gave us the *Aeneid* instead: a story of supreme reinvention that has ever been the hallmark of Rome's literary indebtedness to Greece, even as it has been singularly influential during the millennia since.

The Greek tragedians also treated cyclic tales, many of them tied to the homecomings of Greek heroes after the Trojan War. The foremost narrative involves Agamemnon, brother of Menelaus and leader of the Greek host. When Agamemnon gathered the Greek forces to sail for Troy, the winds were still, preventing departure. To make amends with the goddess Artemis (for killing a deer within her sacred grove) and thus obtain favoring winds, Agamemnon was required to offer his daughter, Iphigenia, as a human sacrifice. When Agamemnon returns home from the war, it is with the Trojan princess Cassandra as his concubine. Agamemnon is then slain by his wife, Clytemnestra, on account of both Iphigenia and Cassandra. The story is told in Aeschylus's *Oresteia Trilogy*, the only Greek dramatic trilogy (of the many written) to have survived. Agamemnon's murder sets the stage for his son, Orestes, duty-bound in intractable dilemma, to avenge his father by slaying his mother. Nestor, the aged and garrulous Greek warrior, repeatedly alludes to this story in Book Three of the *Odyssey*, indicating what might befall should Penelope, in Odysseus's absence, go the way of Clytemnestra. The prospect is backed by the ominous family tree that makes the faithless Clytemnestra half-sister to Helen, and cousin of Penelope. Indeed, when Zeus at the outset of the *Odyssey* plans Odysseus's return, it is the thought of Clytemnestra's treachery that concerns him. Tragedies based on cyclic materials abound. The lyric poets, in turn, would have been familiar with both Homer and the cyclic tales.

The *Iliad* and *Odyssey*'s superior craftsmanship aside, the prestige enjoyed by Homer over the cyclic epics is also apparent in Homer's "greater Panhellenic orientation and diffusion." Homer not only surpassed the cyclic epics but rendered them largely irrelevant. The case is persuasively made that the *Iliad* and *Odyssey* "function as symbolic compendia of the entire history of the Trojan War and the Returns"; that Homer "meant the *Iliad* and *Odyssey* not simply to absorb the other [i.e., cyclic] traditions but to supersede them, thus claiming for them the unique status of metaepics." This Homer did by deftly incorporating, shaping, and—through his characters' abundant speeches—*dramatizing*, and thus decisively commenting on, otherwise stock cyclic materials. Examples include episodes which, chronologically viewed, belong to earlier parts of the war, e.g., the famed

Catalogue of Ships and Helen's identification from the Trojan rampart of principal Greek heroes, including her husband Menelaus (*Iliad,* Books Two and Three). To this may be added, among much else, the seduction of Helen by Paris and Aphrodite (*Iliad,* Book Three), serving as a "'reenactment of the original seduction', the proper context of which is . . . the *Cypria.*" What for the cyclic poets were largely transient events, occurring over a long time, became in Homer biding reflections on human values and the human condition. As Aristotle was no great admirer of the cyclic poets, the Hellenistic poet Callimachus would declare: "I despise the cyclic epic / nor in the path delight / that leads the masses aimlessly, / proceeding where it might." It is telling that the "path" of which Callimachus speaks is erotic, and that he is thus seen gathering his hatred of a too-inclusive Cycle into a complaint against indiscriminate eroticism. So had the loosely episodic Cycle—the tales of "those saying *then next*"—fallen into disrepute.

Having earlier noted the geographic proximity of Troy and Lesbos (Chapter 7), I add a word about the codification and dissemination of Homeric epic. The *Iliad* and *Odyssey* evolved orally over half a millennium at least, from approximately the mid-thirteenth to mid-eighth centuries BC. It is toward the latter point, circa 750 BC, that the *Iliad* and *Odyssey* are believed to have attained their essentially final form—though it would yet be some time before they were actually reduced to writing. The eighth century BC has thus been deemed "the era of the incipient Homeric audience" and "a watershed for the evolution of Hellenic civilization." The eighth century similarly witnessed the consolidation of Panhellenism, "formalized in such institutions as the Olympic Games, the Delphic Oracle, and the Homeric poems themselves." Because the storytelling tradition was oral, there are no rough, preliminary, or partial drafts. Rather, recitational versions of the *Iliad* and *Odyssey* were eventually written down and, from that point on, copied and recopied with such variants as scribal error or preference might occasion. There is, of course, nothing earlier with which to compare a perfected Homer. We are, however, better able to appreciate a perfected Virgil by comparison to the rough hewn, but always improving, hexameters of his predecessors (see Chapter 21).

As my discussions of Homeric formulae and meter suggest (Chapters 16 and 19), there was much trial and error in the development of the *Iliad* and *Odyssey*. In the process, the hexameter line and its trademark formulae became ever more flexible. Form and content grew to mutual accommodation, some formulae restricted, others adaptable. Some stories were codified, others rejected; the process conducive to increased recitational ease and lengthier, more refined and competitive versions. Indeed, the Homeric texts likely became the "last word" in epic storytelling through a competition-based process of elimination—Homer's recitations eventually deemed superior to those of other bards on similar themes. Musical competition is as old as the Homeric poems themselves. Hesiod relates in his other surviving epic, *Works and Days*, that there is not only an evil Strife (Gr. *Eris*), but a good or benign Strife that the gods have given mortal man. Thus contending, "the potter is the potter's foe, the artist the artist's rival, beggar competes with beggar, and bard with bard." Antiquity posits a *certamen*, or contest, between Homer and Hesiod. Hesiod himself tells of his travel to—and victory in—just such a contest.

The oral tradition is thought to have arisen in Greek-colonized western Asia Minor, also known as Ionia (the western coast of modern Turkey). The poetic dialect, as seen, is thus largely Ionic (or "Homeric") as opposed to Sappho's Aeolic (to the immediate north). What began as oral poetry, reaching full development in the eighth century BC, continued to be recited through the seventh and sixth centuries, the time of Sappho and the lyric poets. The tales were known throughout Greek-inhabited lands and islands, including Sappho's Lesbos—itself the reputed locale of the cyclic *Little Iliad* by Lesches of Mytilene. We know from Homer that Achilles once sacked Lesbos, and that it was conspicuous for the beauty and handiwork of its women; that Agamemnon sought to reconcile Achilles with the gift of seven Lesbian captives who "in their beauty surpassed the races of women"; and that Lesbos, Phrygia, and the "enormous Hellespont" marked the extent of Priam's kingdom before the Trojan War. Homer thus knew of Lesbos—without mention of its homoerotic traditions—even as Lesbos and the Greek-speaking world knew Homer. Of the seven locations claiming credit as Homer's birthplace, the island of Chios, closest to the south of Lesbos, is the most widely accepted. Chios is also believed to have been the source of the Homeridae, or "Children/Descendants of Homer," i.e., those perpetuating the oral tradition.

At some point in the early sixth century BC, under the sponsorship of the Athenian tyrant Peisistratos, the *Iliad* and *Odyssey* are believed to have been transcribed through dictation. The process or event is referred to as the "Peisistratid Recension." Transcription involved choosing what was best from among competing versions—some perhaps already in writing—and finalizing an arrangement. This process, though undocumented, persisted, because from the fifth century on, Homer dominates every aspect of Classical Greek thought and sensibility. Greek tragedy takes many of its themes from Homer and would not otherwise exist. Greek lyric, quite independently existing on amatory and political themes, also significantly borrows from Homer (though such poems are not here included). Accordingly, the notion of a Peisistratid Recension provides an historically appealing base for Homeric dissemination at a time when Athens was the "education of Greece" (according to Pericles), and when Greece owed its education to Homer (according to Plato, *Republic*). Of this event the estimable George Steiner remarks, "I believe our *Iliad* to be the product of an editorial recension of genius, of a wonderfully formative act of combination, selection and editing of the voluminous oral material. This recension would coincide with the techniques of writing and of the preparation of papyrus or hides in quantities sufficient for so extensive an inscription." The result: "Athens Hellenised Homer, and Homer through Athens moulded Hellas." Once transcribed, Homeric poetry began circulating as text, even while being performed "live" in a variety of versions or adaptations.

Only in the Alexandrian period (3rd–2nd centuries BC) do we have hard evidence for the collating and critical editing of Homeric texts (leading eventually to codification) by the scholars Zenodotus and Aristarchus, the latter's the standard edition of Homer for the ancient world. Codification involved comparison of different scrolls and a determination of the most reliable readings from among the different copyists. We imagine the existence at some early point of handwritten scrolls, their numerous parts containing the *Iliad* and *Odyssey* essentially as we know them today.

Zenodotus's edition of Homer was believed the first to divide the *Iliad* and *Odyssey* into twenty-four books each. With the increased availability of texts and the beginning of the end of the oral tradition, recitation became more a matter of memorized version than of improvisational composition. Indeed, the oral tradition was likely on the wane in Sappho's time, given the use of writing by then. Although written texts decreased the incentive and need for oral composition, performance continued long after, notably at the All-Athenian Festival or Panathenaia. The festival honored Athena as patron goddess of Athens and was Athens's greatest religious celebration. The Panathenaia was the perfect occasion for performances of the greatest poet by Greece's greatest city, a city with early claims to the dissemination of Homer throughout Greece.

# Chapter 14

## Cosmic Preservation and the Heroism of Heracles

> Every warrior hopes that a great death will find him.
>
> – ONE STAB, *Legends of the Fall*

ALTHOUGH THE EPIC CYCLE might be retro-constructed to creation itself, or indefinitely forward-projected, the events and immediate aftermath of creation only passingly touch on Homer's primary concern, which is martial heroism. It is Hesiod's *Theogony* that treats the mythological beginnings of time for their full epic worth. There is nothing more essentially heroic, assertive, or monumental than the establishment of physical foundation—the differentiation between chaos and order, flux and finitude. Creation is heroism at the cosmic level, involving elemental rather than social or human oppositions—the oppositions in either case implacable—and elemental rather than human triumphs and differentiations. Epic poetry, as a sustained creative undertaking for the ordering of heroic matter, is heroic beyond merely definitional considerations—which is to say heroic poetry *is* as it *does*.

Each new day, with its replacement of darkness by light, sleep by wakefulness, is creation's heroic recapitulation, even as the Book of Genesis bids "Let there be light" as creation's initial act. Henry David Thoreau knew as much, asserting that "Morning brings back the heroic ages." While creation seeks stability and finitude, it never fully achieves them. Anomalies persist. Relapse occurs. Chaos ever encroaches. The missed upriver stroke impels the skiff downstream. Heroism in its proximately post-creational phase protects civilization from the residuum of chaos. Heracles, in slaying primordial beasts (among other labors), exemplifies this kind of heroism, the "beneficent, regulatory force that fights against the disorderly and abnormal forces of nature which are in the process of being formed," or which have not yet entirely subsided. For his salvational efforts Heracles is deified, a singular occurrence. The event is forecast by his marriage to the divinity Hēbē 'Youth' and by Homeric references to Heracles's harrowing of Hell, when he both wounds Hades and makes off with the hellhound Cerberus. Pindar emphasizes Heracles's status with the singular locution *hērōs theos* 'hero god'.

The imperial/civilizing impulse has its mythological paradigm in Heracles. Our first imperialist, the deified Heracles is sanctioned by the gods as a protector of world order. At the same time, his inordinate strength and semidivine parentage make Heracles as much a force for evil as for good—between which he must ever choose. Heracles is thus a case study in ambiguity, even as are the putative benefits of imperialism: its ethos of the white man's burden, of civilizing mission, Westernization, and the like. Wringing order from chaos, preventing civilizational backslide, collapse, or implosion, Heracles must first subdue the beast within.

An illegitimate son of Zeus persecuted by Hera, the *Iliad*'s Heracles is the frequent source of Zeus and Hera's quarreling. The ongoing distemper between the king and queen of the gods concerning the destiny of the then-greatest hero of all time mirrors the earthly strife below, centered, as it is, on Achilles, the subsequent greatest hero of all time. When Heracles, as the *Iliad* recounts, was in the service of the Trojan king Laomadon (Priam's predecessor), he was cheated from his wages for building a city fortification. Heracles later conquered Troy—foreshadowing the success of the *Iliad*'s Greeks. At the same time, however, his conquest with a small contingent of six ships underscores the decline in heroism into the generation at Troy. Though exemplifying a different kind of heroism, Heracles is frequently referred to in the *Iliad* as an example bearing on Achilles's own situation. Achilles says, "For not even the strength of Herakles fled from destruction, / although he was dearest of all to lord Zeus, son of Kronos, / but his fate beat him under, and the wearisome anger of Hera. / So I likewise, if such is the fate that has been wrought for me, / shall lie still, when I am dead. Now I must win excellent glory." It is the death of Heracles, not his deification, that here concerns Achilles—deification being contrary to the heroic ethic. In the *Iliad* it is not deification but "win[ning] excellent glory" that defeats death.

It is argued that Heracles is "closer to an Indo-European model of the hero than is either Achilles or Odysseus." The difference is predicated on the fact that Achilles and Odysseus are several generations removed from the "best" that divine parentage has to offer. Thus, Heracles is a son of Zeus; Achilles, the son of the sea nymph Thetis, and a mortal; and Odysseus, the son of two mortals. In the same vein, the epic figures of Achilles and Odysseus result from a "split of characteristics" found in the single figure of Heracles. Heroism, in its subdued post-Heraclean guise, reflects a more settled state of nature. It is enacted on the battlefield "as the medium of human existence and achievement." Whereas Heracles strives to save the world, regardless the cost to himself, Homer's heroes seek to save themselves for what good it may do the world, and regardless the cost to others. Witness Achilles's and Odysseus's unthinking sacrifice of their battle companions to their own egos. Though sometimes contending with cosmic forces—Achilles with the river Scamander; Odysseus with the ocean, anthropomorphically depicted as the wrath of Poseidon—such encounters do not provide Heraclean opportunities or results. They rather reflect the sometimes chaotic quality of heroic impulse (Achilles) or test heroic mettle (Odysseus). Homeric heroes live secure enough from the encroachments of primal chaos to turn from the world at large to the world within—from cosmic preservation to self-perpetuation, the latter through transcendent glory.

# Chapter 15

## Self-Preservation and the Heroism at Troy

. . . wherefore deprive
All Earth her wonder at thy acts, thyself
The fame and glory, glory the reward
That sole excites to high attempts the flame
Of most erected Spirits, most temper'd pure
Ethereal, who all pleasures else despise,
All treasures and all gain esteem as dross,
And dignities and powers all but the highest?

– *Paradise Regained,* 3.23–30

FOLLOWING A GRIEVOUS INSULT by the Greek commander Agamemnon, Achilles withdraws from the combat, nurturing his *mēnin* 'wrath' against Agamemnon (*mēnin* the *Iliad*'s opening word). When in Book Nine of the *Iliad,* Odysseus, Ajax, and Phoenix arrive seeking to dissuade Achilles from his wrath, and have him rejoin the fighting, they find the most epic of epic heroes *himself* playing the bard. Achilles sings *klea andrōn* 'the glories of men'. These, more specifically, are *klea andrōn / (h)ērōōn* 'the glories of men who were heroes'. We marvel as the greatest epic hero of all time, semidivine of a goddess mother, seeks the consolations of epic poetry. The words and even the subject of Achilles's song are withheld, though the fact alone of his resort to epic poetry says much for the genre's development and for transcendent glory as its principal theme. Achilles is strategically the only Iliadic hero who sings epic poetry. Through him we enter a mirrored vestibule where the ancient hero reflects on heroes more ancient yet; the epic genre reflecting on itself.

Achilles sings epic poetry to find a reference point for his own situation. Achilles's fate, as he articulates it in the *Iliad,* is either die young but gloriously at Troy, or return home, living to a long but inglorious old age. This is in part to say that epic heroes do not merely seek *kleos* 'glory' but learn to *die young* for and with glory, as there is no fame in old age—whatever the solace of past exploits recalled. Disgraced by Agamemnon, Achilles will die young at Troy, as it seems, but without glory. He might as well return home without glory, but alive just the same. It is an option he early articulates, though perhaps more to gain his listeners' attention than anything else. Whether now dying young at Troy or living on at home, he will lack *kleos*. Instead of the better of two fates, he now faces the worst of both worlds. He will have lived in vain. Although Achilles articulates the option of returning home, "nowhere does Homer mention Achilles' own conscious decision to make the nobler choice" and remain. And well Homer doesn't, since either choice is a dead end. The decision is in any event mooted by Achilles's need to avenge Patroclus, all within the framework of the "Wrath"—now exponentially increased—that is the poem's theme.

Long but inglorious old age as an alternative to dying young with fame is, at this point in the *Iliad*'s narrative, a novel development. Elsewhere, the trade-off—a leitmotif—is simply one of glory for a short life. Not required to be at Troy, because unbound by the Oath of Tyndareus to join in rescuing Helen, Achilles reflects on the full dimensions of his crisis—a crisis unique in the annals of epic. This, however, does not mean that Achilles has lighted on the "unheroic truth" that "life is more precious than glory," thus "hijack[ing] the *Iliad* . . . onto thrilling new ground." Nor does it mean that for Achilles "the determination to live" is now paramount. Long life without glory is simply a newly conceived alternative, little embraced for being the lesser of two evils. Achilles vainly seeks to find solid footing *for himself*. The effort does not entail an upending of the heroic code as otherwise lived and died for.

Achilles is not merely offended, but mortally *pained* by Agamemnon's insult and by the dilemma it creates. If Achilles no longer knows his place in the scheme of things, he recognizes that epic poetry is not only an excellent reference point but superior medicine. For an affliction of that order, the "glories of men" go a long way. "He is blessed," says Hesiod,

> whom the Muses love, sweet speech flows from off his lips. For though a man despair in his heart's new pain, troubled, and withering within, the bard, servant of the Muses, intoning the glory of men gone by and the blessed gods who inhabit Olympus, make him soon forget his sorrow, remember nothing of his pain. For the Muses' gifts soon divert him from these.

So it is in Book Nine of the *Iliad* that Achilles's comrades, arriving to advise against continued anger, find him, lyre in hand, "delighting" his spirit as he sings "the glories of men." The theme—*klea* 'glories'—and its effect—*terpō* 'to delight'—signal the twin aspects of epic song, embodied in the names of the first two of the nine Muses: "Cleo" (Gr. *Kleio*; Eng. Clio) and Euterpe.

Epic heroes are thus compulsively mindful of their place and status in epic. From the standpoint of genre, they fight only nominally to win the war, and decidedly more to be enshrined in the songs it generates. The exercise, for the characters themselves, is significantly self-referential, as they famously strive in epic accounts to generate both greater fame and more epic proclaiming it. Though they seek to acquire glory through action, and express the hope of doing so, they are already heroes in the making, or heroes enough, by virtue alone of their inclusion in the *Iliad*. To be recounted in epic for one's *kleos*, or aspiration for it, is to enter the ultimate social register. Himself singing the "glories of men," Achilles consults precedent as he puzzles the impasse to his own glory quest. One cannot be a disgraced glory-seeker. Glory is assertive, not redemptive. What has epic to say of Achilles's dilemma? How will epic now treat him? That is Achilles's crisis; the rest of the *Iliad*, its resolution.

❧

Though the recurring wish of Greek and Trojan alike is to acquire the *kleos* that comes from battle, battle is not its only source. *Kleos* is broadly translated as 'glory, fame, report, repute, or reputation'. The word *kleos* derives from Gr. *kluo* 'hear'. What is *klutos* 'heard' is thus 'famous' (cf. Eng. *loud* and Old Eng. *hlūd*, related to Dutch *luid*, Ger. *laut*, from an Indo-European root related to *kluo/klutos* 'hear/heard'). The causative *kleiō* 'make heard', or 'recount, celebrate, make famous', indicates that it is song's 'recounting' (*kleiō*) that confers 'fame' (*kleos*). For present purposes, *kleos* may be rendered as "fame" via Gr. *phēmi/phaton* 'speak/spoken', from which Lat. *fama* 'report, rumor'. What is *phaton* 'recounted, spoken', thus becomes *fama* 'report, fame'. The Muses, moreover, are typically invoked to aid in the memory-intensive task of epic recitation. The first of nine Muses is Cleo (*Kleiō*), a name designating both the verbal (*kleiō*) and nominal (*kleos*) aspects of glory conferral. The semantic range of these designations signals, if you will, that *Kleio kleiei klea andrōn* 'Cleo recounts the accounts of men'. Descending Mt. Helicon after their birth, the Muses *kleiousi* 'recount' the reverent race of the deathless gods, inspiring the poet to do the same: *(h)ina kleoimi*, says Hesiod, 'that I might recount' (or 'confer *kleos on*'). Hesiod's *Works and Days* proclaims the same: "Pierian Muses, giving glory [*kleiousi*] through song, attend and tell of Zeus your father, hymning him; through whom mortals are either spoken of or not, named or anonymous, as great Zeus wishes it."

What, more precisely, does the epic hero gain by such account? If the hero prevails in battle, he acquires, as best reward, *kleos aphthiton* 'imperishable fame'. The fame is 'imperishable' because epic memorializes and monumentalizes the remembrance of what is everlasting: first, the Olympian gods, who live forever; and then the heroes, many of them demigods, who "are torn between divine aspirations and the certainty of mortality." They are godlike and would *be* gods, but for their mortality. If the heroes themselves cannot live forever, their fame may yet endure through song, which assumedly does. Which is also to say: if the heroes could live forever, an absolute immortality would be its own reward; they would not require the surrogate of imperishable fame through song, gotten at the cost of their lives in battle. The notion of fame as refuge from mortality surfaces in the words of the Trojan Sarpedon to his companion Glaukos:

> Man, supposing you and I, escaping this battle,
> would be able to live on forever, ageless, immortal,
> so neither would I myself go on fighting in the foremost
> nor would I urge you into the fighting where men earn glory.
> But now, seeing that the spirits of death stand close about us
> in their thousands, no man can turn aside or escape them,
> let us go and win glory for ourselves, or yield it to others.

Absent life everlasting, there is thus the immortality of *kleos* through song. Not vesting until death, however, *kleos* is measured not so much by the manner of the hero's death as by his success in having wrested *kleos* from others, i.e., by his battlefield career.

Given its transcendent concerns, epic operates on the conceit that it too is everlasting—including the belief that epic bards are themselves gloried or famed for reciting the glories of heroes. The Phaeacian bard Demodocus is described as an *aoidos . . . periklutos* 'broadly famed singer' in a clear nod to his own *kleos* (*peri* 'around' + *klutos* 'heard'). Odysseus elaborates:

> If you can tell me the course of all these things as they
> happened,
> I will speak of you before all mankind, and tell them
> how freely the goddess gave you the magical gift of singing.

The hero (here the listener) thus proposes to celebrate the bard, even as the bard celebrates the hero. Epic is again seen as self-reflective—song, singer, and subject matter all enduring on each other's account.

The epic undertaking is no less comprehensive and perpetual than its subject matter, as is clear from the epic poet's mission. Hesiod relates:

> They [the Muses] breathed within me voice divine to glorify [*kleioimi*] what was to be and what had been, and bid me hymn the race of everlasting gods, themselves both first and last forever to intone. . . . Come then, with the Muses let us start, who with their hymn delight the mighty mind of Olympian Zeus, speaking what is, what is to be, and what has been, their voices ablend, and from their lips the sweet strains flow with ease.

Singing the everlasting and bidding it be sung, the Muses both secure and mandate permanence. What better testament than the *Iliad* and *Odyssey*, as we continue, past millennia, to ponder Achilles's and Odysseus's heroics. Art historian Kenneth Clark (1903–1983) has famously noted that a sense of permanence is central to our concept of civilization: "Civilized man . . . must feel that he belongs somewhere in space and time; that he consciously looks forward and looks back." It is precisely this sense of civilization that the *Iliad* and *Odyssey* proclaim—Homer's heroes looking indefinitely forward to a time when men look ever back on them. Thus does Homer abide as the cornerstone of Western civilization 2,800 years later.

So much the reward of *kleos* for heroes prevailing in battle. However, should the hero fall, he is lamented as *penthos alaston* 'unforgettable grief'. Occupying a wishful middle ground is Hector. Delusional with death approaching, Hector wishes to die 'not without fame' [*akleiōs.* lit., 'famelessly'], but "doing some great thing to be reckoned by men to come"—as if "going out with a bang" sufficed for *kleos.* Earlier in the same scene, Hector proposes *olesthai eükleiōs* 'to perish famously'—the adverb *eükleiōs* appearing only here in Homer and marking the sentiment as peculiar to Hector. Far from fulfilling his wish, however, Hector flees trying to escape Achilles, who chases him around the walls of Troy, with all to witness his shame. And for all his glory in slaying Hector, Achilles's own death—shot by the cowardly Paris, from a distance with an arrow to the ankle (or heel)—is inglorious enough; hardly "the heroic 'good death' [that] is *supposed* to be violent, a sword death." Indeed, insofar as the tradition dictates the manner of Achilles's death (his ankle alone vulnerable), Achilles was peculiarly *fated* to die "unbeautifully," though with *kleos* to spare. It is accepted wisdom that the heroic code "demand[s] death in battle when the warrior is at his best," and provides that to be remembered at one's best is to be immortalized. The demand, however, is not always met, and in no case more notably than that of Achilles. Rather, what ultimately establishes *kleos* is one's "performance career," as reflected in elaborate funeral rites. To that extent, Hector and Achilles both fare significantly better than the manner of their deaths alone would warrant. We note in passing that Odysseus, in events narrated at the conclusion of the Epic Cycle, is unwittingly, and thus unheroically slain by Telegenos, his son by the nymph Circe.

Hector is also self-possessed in imagining his wife Andromache's fate without him:

> And some day seeing you shedding tears a man will say of you:
> "This is the wife of Hektor, who was ever the bravest fighter
> of the Trojans . . . in the days when they fought about Ilion."
> So will they speak of you; and for you it will be yet a fresh
> grief,
> to be widowed of such a man who could fight off the day of
> your slavery.

Though Hector is kind and well intentioned in this emotional scene, his posthumous reputation occupies him at least as much as his wife's widowed servitude. In fact, he uses the latter largely as a foil to the framing of his own renown. Craving *kleos*, Hector is slated for *penthos* 'grief'. And it will be no less *alaston* 'unforgettable' to friends and kin by his putatively "dying well." Fighting for the "perishable joys"—city, wife, and child; family and civic life; public approbation—Hector will be denied imperishable fame. This is the peculiar fate of a "defensive warrior," fighting for culture and a way of life rather than for glory at any cost. Hector knows he is doomed; his fate, in its way, as foregone as Achilles's. A practical and civilized man, Hector deals with his fate better than does Achilles with his own. Thus, whatever Hector's delusions of glory in defeat, we cannot begrudge him the self-consolation. As for the other extreme, the mere recounting of death in battle does not of itself confer *kleos*. That the *Iliad*'s many otherwise undistinguished fallen are named in the heroic register is at best a form of "honorable mention."

The battlefield aside, there is the vicarious *kleos* that comes from the public recognition of glorious parentage, as when Telemachus imagines that Odysseus's death with full honors—if Odysseus is actually dead—would also be *his kleos* as the great man's son. And there is the *kleos* that attaches to filial piety, i.e., that of Telemachus's personal, ongoing quest for his father, and the obligations that attend it; so, too, Hector, imagining that the *kleos* he gains will also credit his father, Priam. There is further an unspecified, or generic, *kleos* that Homeric characters wish on themselves and others, as does Nestor upon Telemachus, and then upon himself and his family in a kind of pre-bedtime benediction. This last is *kleos* "however you can get it"—so great is epic preoccupation with fame. In this same connection *kleos* may also be had for simply acting consistently with regard to group expectation, for "doing the right thing." Generic as well is *kleos* in the sense of "news," as when Telemachus asks the swineherd Eumaeus, "What news [*kleos*] from town?" And akin to this, *kleos* meaning "report," as when Homer invokes the Muses (*Iliad*, Book Two) for aid in reciting the assembly of ships and commanders that sailed to Troy, the famed Catalogue of Ships. The Muses, ever present and knowing all things, can help; but the poet, as he relates, knows only the *kleos*, or report. Even so, knowing the report is no small thing, since that is how epic endures. Though relying on hearsay, the poet may yet relate his tale "as if he had been there himself, or heard it from another."

❧

The *Odyssey* significantly reworks the *Iliad*'s idea of *kleos*. Odysseus's *kleos* is there largely unheroic in the Iliadic sense, and Odysseus himself untraditional for boasting of it. Indeed, he is the only Homeric character to do so. Introducing himself to his Phaeacian hosts, he says,

> Now first I will tell you my name, so that all of you
> may know me, and I, escaping death's pitiless day,
> may be your friend and guest, though living close enough by.
> I am Odysseus, Laertes' son, known to all men
> for craftiness and guile, and my fame reaches heaven.

This is *kleos* for being "best in your chosen field." Though Odysseus in the end displays a certain martial heroism—emerging from his beggar's rags, rearming, slaying the suitors, and reasserting control over Ithaca—we recall that the fabled Trojan Horse was Odysseus's idea, and that the *Iliad* generally plays not to his battlefield exploits, but to his persuasive abilities.

A still-disguised Odysseus credits Penelope for "fame that reaches broad heaven" on account of her conduct, including guile, which saved home and realm in his absence. The praise tacitly acknowledges Odysseus's appreciation of Penelope's likeness to himself. Guile so applied is *kleos*-worthy. "Both Penelope and Odysseus tread the fine line where *dolos* [trickery] can lead to 'glory' instead of 'shame.' In this respect, as in so many others, Odysseus and Penelope complement and parallel each other."

Penelope, though without boasting it, also speaks of her own *kleos*—a response to Odysseus's pride in his own: "Were he to return, looking after this life of mine, greater would my glory be and much the finer thus. But now I am grieved. . . ." Penelope's sole (though once identically repeated) mention of her own *kleos* bespeaks the expectation of reciprocity for diligence during Odysseus's absence. As she has cared or tried to care for their home and realm, so will she be cared for by Odysseus upon his return; and such care will inure to her *kleos*. However, such *kleos* is passive, as it derives from Odysseus's actions more than her own; moreover, it is tainted, since Odysseus has betrayed the trust on which it is based by ready and protracted infidelities while absent (the double standard in action). Granted, his paramours were divinities, and he didn't and couldn't bring them home. Still, one could not imagine the faithful Hector behaving this way.

It is important to note that although Helen is aware her actions have made her a subject of song, and thus singularly "exhibits a conscious relation to *kleos*," Helen is ascribed no *kleos* as such, the word never used by or of her in Homer (though used of her in the Hesiodic *Catalogue of Women*; see Chapter 18). It is to Penelope, alone of Homeric women, that *kleos* is ascribed. In his initial meeting (and first words) with Penelope, the disguised Odysseus addresses her as follows, in a comparison both telling and perplexing:

> Lady, no mortal man on the endless earth could have cause
> to find fault with you; **your fame goes up into the wide heaven**,
> as of some king who, as a blameless man and god-fearing,
> and ruling as lord over many powerful people,
> upholds the way of good government, and the black earth yields him
> barley and wheat, his trees are heavy with fruit, his sheepflocks
> continue to bear young, the sea gives him fish, because of
> his good leadership, and his people prosper under him.
> [emphasis added]

The passage, so amply probed, conveys many possibilities, given the delicacy, indeterminacy, and high drama of the moment. Odysseus perhaps suggests that Penelope has acted in his absence as he himself would have acted as king of Ithaca—had he not been long absent. Or, Odysseus "poses a question to Penelope": whether she has been working to preserve his kingship. In this sense, Odysseus's utterance "is essentially self-referential even though it is ostensibly about Penelope." Or, Odysseus's speaking of kingship in so knowing and kingly a manner intimates his own royal status, even as it anticipates Ithaca's restoration beneath his rule. What Odysseus here conveys is the "inherited cultural notion" of good governance, i.e., the "ruler's truth." When properly deployed, it depicts the speaker as a king.

But the kingship analogy does not quite fit. Yes, the household has survived through Penelope's resourcefulness, but it has hardly prospered. Penelope has not "rule[d] over many powerful people"; she has merely kept the suitors at bay. What fields, fruit trees, and sheepflocks have borne, the suitors have devoured. What *kleos* Penelope has earned is *kleos* for sufferance and resolve during Odysseus's absence—that which is typically *heard* (*kluo* 'hear') of the abandoned heroine left to cope. Such *kleos* connotes good 'report' or 'reputation' rather than 'fame' or 'glory'—however much Odysseus's imputation of *kleos* to Penelope intends to recall the *kleos* he elsewhere famously claims as his own. *Survival*, under the circumstances, is the heroine's *raison d'être*—heroic, in its own way, but less than *kleos*-worthy. As Lawrence Lipking decisively notes, "The figure of the abandoned woman seems historically not an *alternative* to heroic behavior, for women, but the ultimate sum and substance of being a hero."

Odysseus here makes the case for a domestic *kleos,* which, if not necessarily passive, is defensive—and the case falters (as does the case for Hector's *kleos* as a defensive warrior). The comparison may be intended to reflect awkwardness or hesitancy in the disguised Odysseus's first encounter with his wife and wily equal after a twenty-year absence. Similarly, Odysseus little commends Penelope *herself*. Odysseus's praise is analogized and indirect. It is presented in the form of a truncated Homeric "extended simile," truncated because not reverting to the initial point of comparison as extended similes typically do, i.e., "**as** (when) . . . **so** (did)." One may look, for instance, to the successive similes comparing a beleaguered Ajax first to a wild beast, then to an immovable donkey (emphasis added):

> He stood stunned . . .
> . . . like a wild beast,
> turning on his way . . .
> **as when** . . . [8 lines of comparison],
> **so Ajax** . . .
>
> . . . **as when**
> a donkey, stubborn . . . [3 lines of comparison]
> . . . and the children
> beat him with sticks . . . [2 lines of comparison]
> **so the high-hearted Trojans** . . .

The same format is apparent even in the shorter "extended simile," e.g.:

> Why are you simply **standing** there bewildered,
> **like** a young deer
> who . . . [2 lines of comparison]
> **Thus are you standing** there bewildered . . .

By contrast, Odysseus's kingship simile—'your fame goes up into the wide heaven, / **as of some king who** . . .'—does not so revert, leaving the issue of Penelope's *kleos* somehow unresolved, developmentally stranded, as it were. We would have expected, '**as** when a king . . . **so** have you. . . .' The simile can little do this, being inapposite from the outset.

Penelope's *kleos* is again elaborated—and again left-handedly—in Agamemnon's underworld evocation of Odysseus. In this scene, Agamemnon learns from the recently arrived suitors of their slaughter at Odysseus's hands (emphasis added):

> O fortunate son of Laertes, Odysseus of many devices,
> surely you won yourself a wife endowed with great virtue.
> How good has proved the heart that is in blameless Penelope,
> Ikarios' daughter, and how well she remembered Odysseus,
> her wedded husband. **Thereby the fame of her virtue shall never**
> **die away**, but the immortals will make for the people
> of earth a thing of grace in the song for prudent Penelope.
> Not so did the daughter of Tyndareos fashion her evil
> deeds, when she killed her wedded lord, and a song of loathing will
> be hers among men, to make evil the reputation
> of womankind, even for one whose acts are virtuous.

Agamemnon thus contrasts the 'fame . . . of [Penelope's] virtue' (*kleos . . . (h)ēs aretēs*) with the treachery upon his return from Troy of his own wife, Clytemnestra (daughter of Tyndareus). A *kleos* that 'shall never / die away' (*kleos ou pot' oleitai*), it is analogous to Iliadic *kleos aphthiton* 'imperishable fame'. Consistent with Odysseus's male-biased or "kingly" praise of Penelope, Agamemnon invokes and praises *Odysseus* for marriage to an excellent woman, *not Penelope herself for being one*. Women's *kleos* is further slighted by Agamemnon's "sexist" perception that one woman's bad repute—the case of Clytemnestra being admittedly extreme—can taint all, regardless the excellence of any one particular woman. Both Odysseus's and Agamemnon's commendations of Penelope confirm that *kleos* does not come easily to or sit quite naturally with Homeric women. Similarly, when Odysseus summons the spirits of famous (and infamous) women from the underworld, as many women came as were "wives and daughters of men who were best" (men referred to later in the same narrative as "heroes"). The female dead are thus esteemed less by their own worth than by their relationships to husbands and fathers.

Agamemnon's praise, however indirect, gives Penelope her due and more, even as it signals epic's self-referentiality. The "delightful song about constant Penelope" is the *Odyssey* itself. Epic, in its praise mode, is custom-made for just such a woman (as the *Iliad,* in its blame mode, is the song about Helen, which even she fears will be sung). Nor is Penelope alone. Panoplied with dazzling female characters, the *Odyssey* is as much an account of women's excellence, of their unbounded resourcefulness and control, as is the *Iliad* of male heroism. Working within traditional constraints that necessarily limit the notion of woman's *kleos,* the *Odyssey* yet does everything to exalt and expand it. What diction disallows, repeatedly insistent female characterization repairs. The epic vision is too capacious to be one-sided.

# Chapter 16

## Imperishable Fame and the Evolution of Greek Epic

> [I]f I stay here and fight beside the city of the Trojans,
> my return home is gone, but my glory shall be everlasting . . .
>
> – ACHILLES, *Il.* 9.412–413 (R. Lattimore, tr.)

THE EVOLUTION OF EPIC POETRY can be traced through the term *kleos* and its various metric shapings. The evolution proceeds from the word itself through increasingly expanded phrasings that contain it (the same applying to other key Homeric terms). Such phrasings come to serve as vehicles for fixed, or "formulaic," ideas. From a "synchronic" viewpoint, formulae fit the meter. From a "diachronic" viewpoint, formulae create the meter (metric considerations discussed in Chapter 19). At present, and for purposes of simplification, we deal solely with the formula as *phrase* with a variable syllable count.

A formula, as originally defined by Milman Parry (1902–1935), is "a group of words which is regularly employed under the same metrical conditions to express a given essential idea," e.g., "swift-footed Achilles." By this definition, Achilles needn't be running quickly when so described, as the phrase is simply a *set* phrase or formula describing Achilles, facilitating spontaneous composition with metrical "fill" of a predetermined length. Accompanying this idea was the "principle of thrift," positing "one formula and one only for a given idea within a given place in the line." However mechanistic his theory at first blush, Parry nonetheless "radically altered the course of Homeric studies in the twentieth century by demonstrating that many of the features of the *Iliad* and *Odyssey* derive from an oral technique of verse-making typically used by non-literate poets and claiming that Homer therefore was an oral poet." In support of the formulaic "oral technique of verse making," Parry highlighted significant amounts of set or predetermined phrasing on which the poet relied to facilitate live (and largely improvisational) composition. A seemingly mechanistic feature according to Parry, formulae seemed significantly to limit the prospect of Homeric originality (however that might be defined). However, studies after Parry have demonstrated a quite dramatic degree of formulaic flexibility, showing how utterly original a formulaic composition can be.

Indeed, post-Parry research has revealed that oral formulaic composition, far from being predetermined, was a sophisticated system; that Homeric poetry, while oral in origin and development, so developed over centuries of performance as to exhibit the precision and nuance associated with written composition. Or, if viewed from the standpoint of the poet rather than the tradition, "Homer may well have composed orally, but with so much occasion to think about and repeat his *Iliad* and *Odyssey* that they are in effect revised and improved final products, enjoying many of the same 'literary' qualities as written poems."

*Kleos* phrasings are a key example of formulae fitting a variety of metrically suited line positions. The "fit" of *kleos* phrasings into an already existing meter bespeaks a "synchronic" view, i.e., a present view (Gr. *syn* 'with' + *chronos* 'time'; Eng. *synchronize*); the "snapshot" of what we see of Homeric meter on the surface. We do equally well, however, to say that *kleos*, a key thematic concern, itself gives rise to the very phrases by which meter is ultimately determined. The creation of *kleos* phrasings that eventually shape meter bespeaks a "diachronic" view, i.e., a durational or developmental view (Gr. *dia* 'through(out)' + *chronos* 'time'). One necessarily looks to both views.

We thus begin synchronically, noting that "fit" is determined by the metrically set, yet flexible, alternation of long and short syllables, as will be shown. For now, however, we speak solely with reference to syllable count. At its most basically formulaic, *kleos* appears with a disyllabic form of the verb "to be" (a four-syllable phrase or formula):

> ***kleos esti/estai/eiē/einai***
> 'It is/will be/would be/(is) to be a *kleos*'

Similarly, with a disyllabic adjective:

> ***kleos euru*** 'broad fame' or 'fame broadly'
> ***kleos esthlon*** 'worthy fame'

The last phrase is expanded by a trisyllabic form of the verb "to be" (a seven-syllable phrase):

> ***kleos essetai esthlon*** 'it will be a worthy fame'

Such noun-adjective phrases may appear with a verb other than the verb "to be" (also seven syllables):

> ***kleos esthlon aroito/aroimēn*** '(that) he/I might win worthy fame'

Of comparable metric length are:

> ***kleos aphthiton estai*** 'it will be [or become] imperishable fame'
> ***kleos ouranon (h)ikei*** '(the) fame reaches heaven'
> ***asbeston kleos eiē*** 'it would be unquenchable fame'

And more elaborately yet (ten syllables):

> ***kleos ouranon eurun (h)ikanei*** 'the fame reaches broad heaven'

This formulation appears to collapse 'broad fame' (***kleos euru***) and assonantal 'broad heaven' (***ouranon eurun***) into the wanted, if not inevitable, composite. Both *kleos* and heaven are 'broad'. 'Broad fame' thus becomes formulaically coterminous with 'broad heaven' itself. The same idea is reflected in:

> ***(h)upouranion kleos esti /eiē*** 'it is/would be a glory beneath heaven' *or* 'it is/would be a glory reaching to heaven'

Again, it is not merely syllable count that governs. These phrases have metric shape. That shape, synchronically viewed, allows their "fit" into Homeric meter, as determined by the alternation of long and short syllables. Diachronically viewed, the emerging and ever-expanding shapes themselves create the meter. It is most arguably the centrality of *kleos* and of its metric shape that makes the *kleos* formulation a "favorite," "ideal," or "idealized grammatical" phrase. It is a model for the making of others, "setting the rhythmic mold for the meters in which they survive" and, ultimately, for epic meter overall. We let the matter stand, for purposes of illustration, on what may be considered a foremost and fully illustrative example. Other examples could, of course, be adduced.

# Chapter 17

## Imperishable Fame Denied: Sappho's "Wedding of Hector and Andromache"

> . . . Besides these [springs]
> in this place, and close to them, are the washing hollows
> of stone, and magnificent, where the wives of the Trojans
> and their lovely
> daughters washed the clothes to shining, in the old days
> when there was peace, before the coming of the sons of Achaians.
>
> – *Il.* 22.152–156 (R. Lattimore, tr.)

DESPITE WHAT LITTLE SURVIVES, Sappho's excellence as a poet belongs to no other woman in antiquity. The extent to which we would know this had all, or even a modest part, of her work survived is overwhelming. It is therefore astonishing and excellently fortuitous that the phrase "*kleos aphthiton*" 'imperishable fame' appears in Sappho's fragmentary thirty-four-verse cyclic narrative poem on the wedding of Hector and Andromache (§26). The poem fragment begins:

> Came the herald, Idaeus, swift messenger . . .
> and of the rest of Asia, imperishable fame . . .
> Hector and his companions bring a bright-eyed girl
> from Holy Thebes, in ships on the salty sea,
> from Placea's streams—exquisite Andromache.

The only surviving example of Sappho's narrative poetry, it combines lyric and epic elements and is composed in a predominantly dactylic meter, though not the dactylic hexameter of epic. Thus, while Sappho need not have borrowed "*kleos aphthiton*" from Homer directly, the phrase and subject matter clearly possess Homeric resonance. Sappho here composes conspicuously and ironically with reference to the *Iliad*'s climactic death of Hector.

First noted is Sappho's domestication of the theme. It is a wedding with its generative potential that signals "imperishable fame," not battlefield prowess resulting in death. The operative term is "generative": generation is an ever heroic, epic-worthy endeavor, occasioning, as noted, any of the meanings associated with *kleos*: 'fame, glory, renown, reputation'. Be that as it may, *kleos* will ultimately go to Achilles for killing Hector, not to Hector for marrying Andromache, nor to Hector for defending Troy or "dying well" in the process. Hector's death is *penthos alaston* and exponentially tragic. He is the *Iliad*'s family man par excellence; his death, typically brutal in the *Iliad*'s world of man-to-man combat, is exacerbated by the subsequent defilement of his corpse; he is Troy's prime defender, its (*h*)*erkos* 'bulwark'; and his death is the death of Troy, as he and all are aware. As between *kleos aphthiton* and *penthos alaston* in such a match, Achilles could have no greater *kleos*, and Hector occasion no greater *penthos*. When Hector's ransomed corpse reaches Troy, the city is drained of its inhabitants, who rush forth to greet it: "all were held in sorrow [*penthos*] past enduring."

The *kleos* of Sappho's wedding poem is therefore merely provisional. It is both knowingly and bitterly ironic, as Hector's fate is as fully known to Sappho as to us. Sappho's intent could be one of proleptic, or anticipatory, sorrow. One thinks of Michelangelo's *Madonna of the Steps*—the crucifixion prefigured in the nursing infant's limp and contorted right arm, the infant drawing sustenance even as he pre-enacts his death. The crucifixion is frequently prefigured in Christian iconography, but rarely so poignantly. The same applies to Hector's "crucifixion" in Sappho's setting and diction, prefigured in his wedding.

It is the Trojan herald Idaeus who announces Hector and Andromache's erstwhile joyous arrival by chariot, after an ocean voyage from Andromache's native Thebes, whereupon the chariot-borne Trojans hasten to greet them. In the *Iliad*, it is the boundary-crossing god Hermes, disguised as Idaeus, who makes the solemn nighttime journey with King Priam, by chariot across the same terrain, to ransom Hector's corpse. Upon Priam's return to the city, a grieving throng invades the scene, as had a joyous throng in the (earlier) time of Sappho's poem. The Trojan plain has been the scene of unrelenting death for ten years. Hector was slain there and, at the *Iliad's* conclusion, is himself in the no-man's-land of the unburied dead, the dead among the living. Hermes's guiding of Priam is an accompaniment through Hell on earth, recapitulating the *catabases* 'descents' of heroes into Hades, including the descents of Orpheus, Heracles, and Theseus. In the case of Orpheus, the (abortive) descent is specifically for the purposes of bringing back the dead Eurydice—even as Priam seeks in his own way to "bring back" Hector.

With the mention of Thebes as Andromache's birthplace, we recall from the *Iliad* that Achilles had previously sacked Thebes, killed Andromache's father and brothers, and enslaved her mother. Achilles had in fact once earlier almost killed Hector. Achilles's prior dealings with Andromache's family (Hector included) render Hector more poignantly Andromache's *everything*: "Ah Hector," laments Andromache, "in truth are you my father, my reverent mother / and kinsman; my most comforting husband too." What befell father and kinsmen at Achilles's hands will also befall Hector; and enslavement, her mother's fate, will befall Andromache. Narrative and dictional elements thus contribute to Sappho's reworking of the "Wedding of Hector and Andromache" into a forecast of the supreme epic catastrophe: Hector's death and the fall of Troy. Andromache's enumerated dowry items (§26.6–7) are ultimately destined for Hector's ransom.

The "Wedding of Hector and Andromache" shows Sappho conversant not only with Homeric narrative and diction but also with Homer's use of prolepsis, or anticipation, as a *gestalt* phenomenon, i.e., as a symbolic configuration or pervasive conceptual pattern. The pattern to which Sappho's prefigured death-in-marriage belongs is of a kind with the full chain of events through which Achilles and Hector fulfill each other's destinies.

Achilles is fated to die after killing Hector. That Achilles will die young is known and lamented from the outset of the *Iliad,* by Achilles and, most of all, his mother, Thetis (the poem's *mater dolorosa*). During his withdrawal from battle, the attentive but silent Patroclus emerges as Achilles's "alter ego," donning Achilles's armor, and ultimately being killed in it by Hector. The enraged and grieving Achilles at this point reenters the battle—not in service to Agamemnon but for personal revenge, and regardless his earlier pride or *kleos* concerns. For this purpose, Achilles is reoutfitted by Hephaestus, at Thetis's request, with new custom-made armor, magnificently described in a one-hundred-and-thirty-line proclamatory description, or "ekphrasis."

Patroclus's death in Achilles's old armor is a symbolic proxy for Achilles's death; the lament of Thetis and the Nereids for Patroclus, a mother's lament (by proxy) for Achilles himself. After slaying Patroclus and putting on Achilles's armor, Hector, initially fleeing, stands fast. Slaying Hector thus armored, Achilles in effect slays *himself*. The symbolic suicide is itself anticipated by the concern for Achilles's self-inflicted harm when grieving for Patroclus. The prospect of self-inflicted harm comes laden with resignation and death wish. Achilles is at this point so dehumanized as to be already dead, prey to his own absolutism. Killing Hector, he pierces the corpse at the ankles, attaches it to his chariot, and drags it three times around the walls of Troy—the two armies looking on in horror—one corpse dragging another.

Throughout the *Iliad* Achilles and Hector are essentially "dead men walking," which the epic tradition plays to full symbolic advantage. As Thetis submerged Achilles in the River Styx, imbuing him with immortality (but for his ankle/heel), Sappho has in a sense submerged her wedding song into River Scamander at Troy, imbuing it with epic *frisson*. "Thetis's excessive grief [over Patroclus's death] is an episode taken out of natural narrative sequence. But in a field of action where all is known, and in that sense everything has already happened, the grieving mother at the side of her as-though-he-were-dead son makes perfect sense. Time has been telescoped." A *gestalt*-minded Sappho also telescopes time, in keeping with the pervasive dictates of her theme.

Sappho's sole attested use of *kleos aphthiton* bitterly ironizes the traditional range and associations of this core epic concept. At the risk of generalizing from a single instance, we may venture that while "imperishable glory" may do for epic heroes, Sappho's sense of glory is decidedly personal, embodied, if you will, in her daughter *Kleïs* 'Gloria'. The name captures the personal sense in which *kleos* endures through children—indeed, through a *single* child in the generational continuum (§27). Personalization of the epic ethos is further apparent in Sappho's desire to be remembered not in the songs of men to come, but in the thoughts of a parting beloved (§6). To be remembered is to have one's loves recalled. "As Sappho so pointedly says, 'Someone, I say, will remember us in time to come. . . .'" According to Stobaeus, Sappho also correlates recollection and desire in the rebuke she makes to an uneducated woman: "But when you die you will lie there, nor will there ever be a recollection or any desire of you, since you share not in the roses of Pieria. . . ." For the epic poet, to be remembered is to have obtained *kleos*. For the lyric poet, it is to have desired and have been desired.

As further concerns her personalization of epic, Sappho seeks Aphrodite as an ally (*summachos* 'fellow fighter') not on the battlefield but in the battles of love (§1). Again rejecting military apparatus, Sappho prefers the sight and gentle step of her beloved Anactoria to Asia's trampling panoply (§4). Retaking Helen, the Greeks also seek Asia's fabled wealth. For Sappho, however, such treasure counts for nothing; her dear Kleïs is all (§27). Ignoring Helen's Iliadic self-reproaches as cause of the Trojan War, Sappho absolves her of all responsibility by condoning her passion as *absolute* (§4)—as is Helen herself absolute and all things connected with her (see Chapter 18). Given Helen's role as cause of the Trojan War—antiquity's singular cataclysm—Sappho's stance on Helen carries the force of manifesto: passion will *out*: "The fact is apparent, self-evident" (§4). Yet it is not passion in the abstract, but its precipitant, Helen in the flesh, so incomparably beautiful. "The dark earth's / fairest sight . . . [is] whatever one adores," but woe betide when the one who adores "far surpass[es] all mortals / in beauty." As absolute beauty is and can only be blameless, it is without censure: "To assail Helen with reproach was not less dangerous than to touch the Ark of the Covenant, for with the Greeks beauty was a holy thing." Sappho thus ironizes *kleos* in her singularly striking treatment of the theme, making personal tragedy the subtext of a famous wedding. She otherwise personalizes epic concerns, generally subverting the military ethos, and specifically grounding remembrance not in *kleos*, but in desire, and in the despotic claims of arrant beauty.

# Chapter 18

## Cataclysm Averted: Homer's Separation of Helen and Achilles

> It is not by some chance, arising out of her life's vicissitudes, that Helen has come to be the cause of the war and its stake; a deeper necessity has brought her there to join the apparition of beauty with the unleashing of rage.
>
> – RACHEL BESPALOFF, *On the Iliad*

> His beauty, his swiftness and ferocity, his unrivaled talent for killing his fellow men, his uncompromising commitment to honesty and to honor and, above all, the pathos of his freely accepted death, combine to invest him with an ineffable glamour.
>
> – LUCY HUGHES-HALLETT, *Heroes*

As Aphrodite incarnate, Helen possesses beauty that is at once absolute and irresistible. All are not merely responsive to it; they are conditioned, formed, and even fated by it. Achilles possesses a comparable beauty—in ways neither overtly apparent to Achilles himself nor fully acknowledged by the epic tradition. In her *The Evolution from Divine to Heroic in Greek Epic Tradition* (1976), a seminal work on Helen in the *Iliad,* Linda Lee Clader proposes that "in dealing with Helen's role in this epic . . . one must determine not so much what she has to do with the Trojan War, but specifically what she has to do with Achilles"—and, we must add, what the two have pointedly to do with each other. However, because Clader focuses on the evolution of Helen from a divine to an epic figure, the relationship between Helen and Achilles remains unprobed.

Their relationship crystallizes around antiquity's precarious claim that

Achilles, otherwise engaged, was unavailable for the wooing of Helen. So reads a significant fragment of the Hesiodic *Catalogue of Women:*

> Chiron was tending the son of Peleus, swift-footed Achilles, preeminent among men, on woody Pelion; for he was still a boy. For neither warlike Menelaus nor any other of men on earth would have prevailed in suit for Helen, if fleet Achilles had found her unwed. But as it was, warlike Menelaus won her before.

The operative verb is Gr. *kichano* 'happen upon, meet with, find'. The passage thus indicates that Menelaus won Helen *before* Achilles might have entered the scene, had he at all done so. It is not that Achilles is too young, since, had he found Helen unwed, he would have had her. Rather, being young, he was completing his apprenticeship with Chiron, and was for that reason absent. If not age, strictly speaking, it is a preexisting obligation, by definition age-related, that is meant to thwart the union. Achilles is "away" on (youthful) business.

By this rationale, and by all mythological accounts, Achilles and Helen never wed; in fact they remain separate throughout their lives. At the most basic level, the *dis*union of Helen and Achilles demonstrates the truism that opposites attract and likes repel. Comparably illustrious, the world's most legendary woman and most exalted hero are intended for a partnership *other* than marriage. In the end, however, the actual reason for Helen and Achilles's separation, as will be seen, is not that Achilles was "away," but that their marriage would have likely foreclosed the Trojan War, if not been the cause of some yet greater catastrophe. Their marriage might also have been taboo. Spiriting Achilles beyond the reach (or below the age) of marriage, the tradition is mindful of these possibilities, even while glossing them over. We examine the possibilities in turn.

The so beautifully and lethally congruent pair do not meet or even view each other in the *Iliad,* but remain apart—from each other and, each for different reasons, from the world at large. The epic *hērōs* 'hero', broadly conceived, is a unique and solitary figure "detached from cultural and social place." This is especially true of Achilles—by his divine birth in remote and fantastical Thessaly, upbringing by the centaur Chiron, choice of an early death in exchange for glory, inordinate anger, and withdrawal from combat at the cost of his comrades' lives. In this last regard, what Achilles has to say, reflecting and commenting on his own situation, has been deemed a "different language," removing Achilles further yet from his community. Marriage with its integrative and ideally workaday norms is incompatible with such circumstances and temperament. So, why does the epic tradition posit Achilles's marriage to Helen in so wishful and factually contrary a manner, saying he would have wed her, but for a youthful absenteeism?

Helen is a riveting paradox. Her beauty epitomizes the Greek ideal of beauty, even while negating the imperative of moderation: *mēden agan* 'nothing to excess'. Helen is excessively and thus perniciously beautiful. The same is true of Achilles, the most beautiful of the Greeks who came to Troy—whose very speech is "the most varied, beautiful, and powerful" of any speaker in the *Iliad*, and whose every act and aspect is overindulgent and unrestrained. Beauty exalts, even as it isolates. Beauty is willful, even as Achilles possesses an "absolute will," and Helen exhibits an erotic compulsion impervious to all else. The two are thus secluded, each introspective and self-aware as are no other Homeric characters. Helen is solitary in her bedchamber, away from the Trojan society that perishes on her account; Achilles is secluded beside his ships, apart from his companions who perish for want of him. Helen, in her lifelong succession of husbands and paramours, is estranged from meaningful family ties. Achilles, without family to speak of, is the only son of a divinity among the Greeks. As Helen commands unqualified male regard, Achilles has his "collection of beautiful captives who weep tractably on his command." Lacking integrative value, such attentions reinforce a sense of seclusion. Both have left young children behind: Helen, Hermione; Achilles, Neoptolemus. Isolation giving rise to introspection, Helen and Achilles display a consciousness of their participation in poetic tradition. Though isolated in life (and from each other), Helen and Achilles are yet aware of a shared afterlife as the subjects of song. Achilles is himself the stuff of epic, and, as seen, the *Iliad*'s only singer of epic. Helen, whose every appearance in the *Iliad* is associated with poetry, creates a piece of art. The artwork is a woven depiction of the battles, on Helen's account, beneath the walls of Troy. There is more than a touch of self-involvement and narcissism in the enterprise.

Helen's beauty is entirely attractive and sexual, making her the ultimate object of desire. Achilles's beauty, by contrast, serves only to enhance his prowess, making him the more outstanding. Beauty for Achilles is attribute, not essence. Nonetheless, Achilles, like Helen in her way, is both beautiful and lethal—exemplifying the splendor and savagery of warfare. Helen is agelessly beautiful, while Achilles is destined never to grow old. Whatever the complexities of their lives and choices, they are uniquely "forever young," envisioned and remembered as such, and thus existing only as idealized selves. Despite the long years at Troy on which Helen comments, Paris, after a near-death encounter with Menelaus, tells her that he never felt stronger passion for her than at that moment—illustrating "one of the fundamental laws of Homeric poetry, namely, once an actor is given or supposed to have a definite age or form he maintains each unchanged throughout." So, too, was the glimpse of Helen's breast that resolved Menelaus to take her back rather than slay her for her betrayal, as he had planned.

Achilles and Helen further share an affinity of divine birth: Achilles by Thetis, Helen by Zeus. Achilles is in no way diminished being born of a sea nymph rather than a god. Zeus, we recall, abandoned his courtship of Thetis—marrying her off to the mortal Peleus—upon prophecy that the union's male offspring would be mightier than its father. Zeus thereby avoids the overthrow he had visited on his own father, Kronos, and which Kronos had visited on *his* father, Ouranos. Thus is heavenly succession preserved and finalized in Zeus (notwithstanding the *Iliad*'s allusion to an uncertain interregnum). Almost Zeus's son *and* replacement, Achilles is preeminently descended from Zeus as great-grandson (Zeus > Aeacus > Peleus > Achilles). There is no slighting the technically lesser semidivinity of Achilles vis-à-vis Helen. Thetis, moreover, is privileged as foremost of the fifty Nereids (sea nymph daughters of Nereus and Doris) and, as often noted, enjoys a privileged relationship with Zeus. Thetis is privileged on Hera's account as well. Emphasizing Achilles's divine birth in contrast to Hector's mortal origins, Hera recalls (in *her* version of the tale) that she nurtured and raised Thetis before bestowing her on Peleus. That Thetis was nurtured by Hera and wooed by Zeus imparts increase of divinity to Achilles's parentage, making him the most *di(*ϝ*)os* 'godlike' of the demigods. Achilles fares equally well on the mortal side. Peleus is the "most worthy among mortal men," and Aeacus a giver of judgments to the gods themselves and the forebear of a line embodying the "civic" virtues.

As Helen is unspeakably beautiful, Achilles is unspeakably destructive and, in his beauty and destructiveness combined, "ineffably glamorous."

Though without overt awareness (in the narrative) of his reciprocity with Helen, Achilles is, tellingly, the only Greek to acknowledge Helen's destructive power, offering the "strongest and most emotional negative reaction to Helen in the entire epic." In his lament over Patroclus, Achilles refers to Helen as "chilling" or "shudder-inducing"—language matched in intensity by Helen's references to herself as a "horrid, evil intriguing bitch" before whom "all tremble." Such imagery recalls the dogs at the poem's start as the scavengers of the fallen dead. Achilles knows Helen as well as she knows herself, and one almost hears his execrations echoing in her bedchamber. Helen further, and singularly, refers to herself as *stugerē* 'loathsome' or 'hateful unto death'—the word in Homer frequently associated with death, and sharing the same root as Styx, the dread river of the underworld.

Achilles's claim to absolute beauty is apparent in his conquest of Lesbos itself—known in antiquity for the supreme beauty of its women. Agamemnon, trying to reconcile with Achilles, offers him nine Lesbian captives who "surpass the races of women in beauty." One of these is Briseis, whom Agamemnon had earlier taken, precipitating the quarrel with Achilles. Lamenting the fallen Patroclus, Briseis appears "like unto golden Aphrodite." The comparison, recalling Helen herself, validates Achilles's claim on beauty through a Helen-like concubine. Or, validating Achilles's claim on Helen, Briseis serves as her stand-in. Achilles compares Agamemnon's theft of Briseis to Paris's seduction of Helen, even as Briseis temporarily supersedes Helen as the *Iliad*'s source of contention—and death. The women of Lesbos "were superior *kallei* 'in beauty' to all other women from all other places in the whole world. . . . [Briseis] too, like the other Aeolian women, was captured—and captivated—by Achilles." The regard was mutual. We recall Achilles's origins in Aeolic-speaking Thessaly (known as Aeolia in the *Odyssey*) on the Greek mainland, and the dialect's spread to Lesbos and environs through pre-Homeric colonization. Taking Aeolian Lesbos and its women, Achilles is, as it were, "at home," taking what is his.

❧

Given Helen's and Achilles's heightened reciprocal natures, they are, symbolically, already united or wed—making conventional marriage irrelevant. As concerns such marriage, the preoccupations of age are ultimately beside the point; in fact, they are a pretext foreclosing marriage on other grounds. For one thing, while marriage that produces semidivine offspring abounds, marriage between the offspring themselves is anomalous. Nowhere could this be truer than in the case of Helen and Achilles—the beauty, strength, and sheer excess of their offspring unthinkable. Moreover, if Achilles's full divinity is thwarted because of his filial threat to Zeus, it little helps to make him Zeus's son-in-law. One also shudders to think what cataclysm yet greater than the Trojan War might follow from so startling a union. That possibility aside, the marriage of Helen and Achilles would have foreclosed cataclysm enough: the Trojan War itself. Since no one dare steal the Helen married to Achilles, there is no abduction of Helen and no Trojan War, no Armageddon, and no Achilles redeemed. There is, instead, the evisceration, at its core, of classical mythology. However, anyone dare steal the wife of doltish Menelaus, and the rest is epic history. As Helen and Achilles's marriage would have foreclosed the Trojan War, their offspring would have frustrated its primary goal: that of extinguishing the Age of Heroes, whereby to finalize the separation between human and divine. Second-generation demigods, they would have caused the Age of Heroes to live on in genetically adulterated form.

Achilles, since never a suitor of Helen, was unbound by the Oath of Tyndareus and thus not required to be at Troy. He is there solely for the *kleos* that will recompense his early death. Though Achilles does not fight on Helen's account, it is nonetheless her absolutism—her absolute beauty—that infuses his quest. This involves more than Helen as "simply a symbol of the epic quest, a symbol of the *kleos* which must be a hero's ultimate goal," and more than Helen as a "dangerous woman, with the same sinister beauty which *kleos* . . . portends for the hero." As the *Catalogue* relates: *mega gar kleos [eske gu] naikos* 'for the renown of the wo[man was] great'. Helen, in a manner unique to Homeric women, has her own *kleos,* which is the fabled report (Gr. *muthos* 'tale', Eng. myth) of her beauty. Among other factors distinguishing it from battlefield or heroic *kleos,* Helen's is not acquired but intrinsic, preexistent. It is the *kleos* of paradigmatic beauty, a Platonic form. It is, in sum, the unmitigated power of primordial physical attraction, the *Eros* described by Hesiod "which is most beautiful among the immortal gods, limb-loosening, subduing within their breasts, of all gods and men alike, their thought and well-considered plan."

Itself devoid of strife (since perfect), the *kleos* of absolute beauty, as contested object of attainment, is both strife-inducing and *kleos*-conferring. As any absolute, however, it can result only in destruction. We note, in this connection, the use of *lusimelēs* 'limb-loosening', which in epic poetry describes the outcome both of erotic affliction and battlefield death. In a related *Catalogue* reference to Helen's *kleos* (this one using the poetic plural *klea*), we find *tēs k]lea pasan epi chthona di(*ꜰ*)an (h)ikanei* 'whose fame reaches across all the glorious earth'. The formulation has its counterpart in the styling *kleos ouranon eurun (h)ikanei* 'the fame reaches up to broad heaven' (Chapter 16). The use in both formulations of verse-final *(h)ikanei* 'reaches' and of the correlative adverbials ('throughout the entire earth' and 'toward broad heaven') places Helen within a decidedly heroic framework.

For Achilles, the *kleos*-quest is outsize, owing to his nature and particular circumstances, including the certainty and acceptance of death. The quest, we might say, is as ferocious and uncompromising as is Helen beautiful; its rewards as bountiful. Helen's absolutism tautens Achilles's sinews; his life unstrung, unsung, without her. The people of Troy could have surrendered Helen at any time, ending the war and saving themselves; thus disenfranchising Achilles. But they too are willful in their own way, or willfully self-absorbed. They concede their doom over a ten-year period as inevitable, the all-but-welcome cost of infatuation with Helen. Priam—aged king of Troy, and father of Helen's seducer Paris—is no different: the war must be fought, as Helen can be neither denied nor dismissed. Such is the influence of Eros, "subduing . . . thought and well-considered plan." The *Iliad* alludes to a delegation by Odysseus and Menelaus that sought to regain Helen without hostilities. The overture was refused.

What mythology's most fabled woman accomplishes is not only the destruction of Troy, antiquity's most fabled city, but in the process the destruction of antiquity's most fabled hero. Theirs is a death-ridden alliance—Helen, the cause of death to thousands, wishing she had sooner died; Achilles, actively seeking death for the *kleos* only death confers; the two "unique in the *Iliad* as . . . wish[ing] fervently for their own death," both resolved to die, bringing the world down with them. As Helen and Achilles are not lovers, there is no self-immolation or death through erotic consummation: no *Liebestodt* 'love-death'. There is, however, love *of* death for which the two stand. All willingly perish round and about the willful pair. All perish vigorously, even as Helen and Achilles are unstinting in their dispositions. No deathly undertaking defies heroic bounds, as Achilles proposes that he (and Patroclus) *alone* take Troy. The totalizing death-drive at the individual level evinces, microcosmically, the totality of destruction—Troy, the Age of Heroes, Earth's excessive population (with biblical flood overtones)—that is ultimately the plan of Zeus. The hero *lives* in symbiosis with death, is paroxysmally enamored of death and death's reward. The hero thus functions under no better auspices than those of Helen and Achilles—the symbiotic incarnations of Eros and Thanatos, of Love and Death, of love's lethal spasm and deathlike sequel (*la petite mort*). It is noted that "Helen's submission [to Aphrodite, to the sex act] has the inevitability of a hero's death or the taking of a city." In antiquity, the concord of love and death is nowhere better sounded than in the biblical Song of Songs: "For love is dire as death, its grip the grave's, and grim; its flames a conflagration, God ablaze." This, on the Homeric battlefield, becomes the fusion of combat and copulation.

❧

To suppress even the prospect of marriage, the tradition tenuously assigns Achilles and Helen to different generations. In an article published one hundred years ago, entitled "The Assumed Duration of the War of the *Iliad*," Professor John A. Scott urges that "to sit down with paper and pencil for the purpose of auditing [Helen's] charms by her years is to fail to appreciate the very essence of Homeric poetry." The comment concludes an article that colorfully treats a number of chronological quirks and stretches in the *Iliad* and *Odyssey*. While the Old Testament handily reckons fantastical lifespans—Adam 930; Methuselah 969; Moses 120; Sarah 90 when bearing Isaac—Homer ventures no such count. For that and other reasons we do ill to calendar what the epic tradition leaves open. However, when the tradition makes an issue of age—sequestering an apprenticed Achilles, even while providing a number of year-specific referents (ten-year duration of war; Achilles fifteen at the war's start)—we may venture a surmise. The purpose is not to establish age per se, but its use in shaping the narrative.

When sent to Troy with his mentor, Phoenix, Achilles was a "mere child" ignorant of warfare, and—if destined to die young at Troy—not much past his early twenties at death (the *Iliad* beginning in the tenth year of the war). If old enough, even on the young side, to fight from year one of the war, he is old enough to woo and wed, compensating with godlike aspect for what he lacks in years. Even so, the age disparity constrains the possibility. One cannot have a "mere child," however divine, wed or convincingly love the world's most beautiful woman, making a mockery of her own divine, or divinely sentient, being. So why propose that Achilles would have wed Helen, had he been present, other than to suggest that their union is what the tradition wanted, determined as it was to subvert it?

The Athenian mythographer Apollodorus (2nd century BC) makes Achilles fifteen (and fleet commander under Agamemnon) when the Greeks sail for Troy. However, death at age twenty-five is on the older side of "dying young." Achilles's death at age twenty-five or older places him beyond the age of ephebic initiation, i.e., makes him an adult rather than the youth he is supposed to be at death. The *ephebe* (Gr. *epi* 'near' + *(h)ēbē* 'early manhood') is an adolescent of age seventeen to twenty undergoing military training and other preparations for civic life. It is the age depicted in the statuary representations of the male *kouros* 'youth', first appearing in the Archaic age and initially associated with Apollo (there being an abundance of Apollo *kouroi*). Achilles, always closely identified with Apollo, is *kouros*-like by association and, kindred to the archetypal *kouros* god, ever young. Notes one commentator, "Achilles is likewise the *kouros* who will never grow old, who will die without dedicating his shorn hair to the river Spercheios in the customary *rite de passage* of youths into manhood." At the same time, however, if Achilles, with the centaur Chiron, was "undergoing a mythic version of ephebic training," he was of quite accelerated maturity, though not "of age," reasonably to woo Helen. Here too the tradition struggles with itself.

Fearing for Achilles's life, Thetis disguises him as a girl while the troops marshal for Troy, and hides him on the island of Skyros (see map) at the court of King Lycomedes. Achilles there fathers Neoptolemus by the king's daughter Deidamia before being discovered and led to Troy, which could not be taken without him. Thus, with the ten-year duration of the war before him—and it is in the tenth year of the war that the *Iliad* begins—Achilles cannot have been much older than eleven or twelve when he fathered Neoptolemus (though by a different reckoning, below, he is closer to fifteen). Assuming that Achilles's marriage to Deidamia occurred after the second muster for Troy—presumably ten years after the wooing of Helen and the first muster—Achilles was barely born, or no older than five, when Helen was wooed. If we discount the ill-attested legend of a second muster, and posit an eleven- or twelve-year-old Achilles wedding Deidamia, Achilles was of sufficient age to have wed Helen during approximately the same time period.

The issue of generational divide is elsewhere apparent. The *Odyssey* presents both the persistent wooing of Penelope by men of a younger generation and—contrariwise—the flirtation of a long-married Odysseus with the nubile Nausicaa. Both scenarios suggest the possibility of an age-inappropriate union, the latter especially so. Odysseus must be forty, at the very least, to Nausicaa's fourteen or fifteen. Granted, it is the type of marriage that might occur only in the dreamland of Odysseus's wanderings, but it is a courtship nonetheless, played fantasy-wise for all its delicacy and restraint.

The suitors, for their part, and as generally viewed, were themselves at the time too young to sail for Troy. That would make them preadolescent at the start of the war and, unlike the semidivine Achilles, incapable of fighting. Grown to maturity in the interim, the suitors would be in their late twenties or early thirties upon Odysseus's return (Achilles dying ten years earlier in his early to mid-twenties). We do not know when exactly during Odysseus's ten-year absence the suitors beset the palace, nor how old they were at the time. Judging from the emphasis on their rapacity and waste of Odysseus's substance, they are not recent arrivals. As the *Odyssey* begins, then, the suitors are openly wooing an older woman—one who, if not old enough to be their mother, is older by at least a decade. In the normal course of wooing, the woman would be *younger* by as much. In this matter of intergenerational marriage, the example of Oedipus looms large: Jocasta does not blink to marry a man "young enough to be her son." However archetypal this example, it yet bespeaks the possibility of marriage despite a significant discrepancy of years. Achilles, vis-à-vis Oedipus and Jocasta, can hardly be "too young" for Helen, though ostensibly too young *at the time*.

Then again, the Oedipal significance perhaps lies elsewhere. Given the intimate (albeit non-consanguineous) kinship between Helen and Achilles, the tradition seems to have shunned the sibling-like incest with which the relationship came fraught (the *Nibelungenlied* showing no such reserve). Narcissism, as love of self, needs only incest—the consummated union of self with self—to be complete. The tradition thus sublimates and reconfigures the incest taboo by uniting Achilles and Helen not as husband and wife, and not as lovers, but as cause and agent of the war. If Patroclus is Achilles's *therapōn*—his alter ego or doppelgänger—Helen is, from a distance, his ersatz-betrothed (embodied, or bodied forth, in Briseis).

As in the tale of Oedipus and Jocasta, the issue of age at no time arises in the *Odyssey*. Telemachus is reckoned younger than the suitors. A baby or toddler at the start of the war, he is in his early twenties in the year of Odysseus's return—subject to the suitors' bullying and plots, disgruntled and stymied at home. But for Achilles's destiny—to die young, but with *kleos*—Achilles too might have stayed at home. In that case (never mind Helen), he could have surfaced as one of *Penelope*'s suitors. In the end, however, it is semi-divinity (offsetting youth) and destiny that take Achilles to Troy instead of Ithaca. The suitors, be it remembered, were not merely homegrown, but came from far and wide (as did Helen's suitors). Accordingly, those who had wooed Helen fought for Helen at Troy. The rest eventually fought over Penelope on Ithaca.

The marriage of Helen and Achilles, sooner precluding than causing the Trojan War, was disallowed for that reason, at least. The thought of Helen and Achilles's combined destructive potential is nonetheless intriguing, and imagination does not readily relinquish their union, however devised. An *Iliad* scholiast thus notes, commenting on the phrase *Dios d'eteleieto boulē* 'the plan of Zeus was being fulfilled' (*Il.* 1.5), that Zeus could and would have thinned the world's population with thunderbolts or any other manner of cataclysm, but yielded instead to two ideas of his advisor *Mōmos* 'Blame'. So yielding, he brought about (1) the marriage of Thetis to a mortal man; and (2) the birth of a beautiful daughter. The first of course alludes to Achilles, sole offspring of Peleus and Thetis; the second, to Helen, offspring of Zeus himself and Leda (or possibly Nemesis). "From these two events," says the scholiast, "war resulted between Greeks and barbarians, causing the lightening of Earth, with many killed." Thus does the plan of Zeus provide the "union" denied by conventional marriage—Achilles and Helen united not as spouses but as causes. In sum, Helen and Achilles's combined cataclysmic potential obliges some manner of partnership. From a narrative standpoint, however, the *Iliad*'s Helen and Achilles remain impervious to each other's larger powers—to their reciprocity both as causatives (*Cypria*) and characters (*Iliad*). Such matter is little reflected in overt epic-character awareness; it is *ur*-matter, the tradition's DNA.

Age signals transience and death; myth, what is constant and undying. Age-specific or human-age-based chronologies are thus of no concern to myth, which looks to stages, eras, and epochs; to the sweep of generations. A paradigmatic example is Hesiod's myth of the five human *genē* (sg. *genos*) 'races, breeds', tracing humankind from a fabled age of gold, via ages of silver and bronze, and the age of heroes, to a blighted age of iron—iron the avowedly worst of all ages, Hesiod's own, into which he wishes he had never been born. The myth strategically positions the Age of Heroes next to last. Being closest to Hesiod's (and Homer's) own, its epic accounts remain recent (relatively speaking) and readily accessible. Greek mythology is otherwise genealogy-driven, and, as the Old and New Testaments, awash in "begats."

On a literary level, "Hesiod's sequence provides an early parallel to the familiar 'exercise'—from Solon's ten ages of man to Shakespeare's seven—in which the human life span is segmented and characterized and its excellences age-graded." "Age-graded" in this sense means age not by year, but by stage of life—the latter determined by various "social markers," e.g., sexual maturity, marriage, the begetting of children, the assumption of household and civic responsibilities, deliberative skill, and counsel-giving readiness. The division of warriors into junior and senior grades is apparent in Homer. Agamemnon, Odysseus, and Patroclus represent an older tier as distinguished from the likes of the more impulsive Diomedes and Achilles. The division is sexually as well as tactically marked: the older tier usually married, the younger concubine-disposed; the younger often teamed with those of greater experience. The model's conspicuous features are: (1) relative lack of appreciation of childhood; (2) recognition of the excellence of maturity or middle age versus the immaturity of young manhood (characterizing the Age of Heroes itself); and (3) degeneration and vulnerability of old age. Though human beings die, humanity and the race endure. Long-term race survival supersedes age-based personal survival, myth being neither history nor biography.

There is, moreover, a looseness of time within Homeric epic's relation to its *own* epic past—what one writer handily calls the "epic plupast." Within this frame of reference, heroes mentioned from the generation preceding the fight at Troy are depicted at a "distance from the recent past," as "belong[ing] to a different world." The epic past thus "unfolds as a time *sui generis*"—the performance-present audience admiring epic heroes past, themselves admiring heroes more ancient yet, along a distantly retrojected continuum. Differences in the reckoning of human and divine time also come into play. The "correspondence between the time of men and the time of the gods in the *Iliad* [is] always indeterminate, and sometimes incoherent," with Homer's chronology being "so obscure that we can hardly determine the time taken by . . . events." Hesiodic chronology can be equally elusive, including the very sequence of events relating Achilles's ineligibility as suitor.

> . . . Tyndareus does not exact the oath from the suitors until just before the announcement of the winner. The result of the narrative delay, however, is a rapid succession of significant events: Tyndareus exacts the oath from the suitors; Menelaus is immediately declared the winner; a brief explanation is given as to why Achilles is not the winner . . . and Helen gives birth to Hermione, unexpectedly. And then, in the very same line that finishes the birth of Hermione, we learn that the gods were driven apart in strife and, following in rapid sequence, that Zeus plans to relieve the earth of humans and separate mortals from gods, as they were before. All of this takes place in about twenty continuous lines, with no obvious gaps or breaks in the papyrus.

Men and gods in the *Iliad* act within the inscrutable plan of Zeus, itself subject to temporal interruptions throughout the poem and never actually fulfilled within it. Adding to the uncertainty is chronologically fluid myth conscripted to cyclic sequence and arrangement—with the result that such material is "seen to belong together as part of a larger narrative, even if its consistency or temporal unity could not always be pressed." The lack of consistency is further apparent in the insertion of the Age of Heroes into an otherwise metallic sequence—gold, silver, bronze, heroes, iron—no less than in the *Iliad*'s masterful inclusion of tableaux pertaining more to earlier phases of the war (to say nothing of the poem's thematic digressions). Flouting chronology, such matter calls for the suspension of disbelief often accorded art. Further, as lifespans are shorter and marriages (and all other milestones) necessarily *earlier* in antiquity, age-specific reckonings invite a certain skepticism. Logically enough occurring, however, are the quasi-human delays in the lives of characters who fought the Trojan War—mythological cataclysm upending lives within its own real-world-like frame of reference (e.g., the marriage of Hermione, delayed to circa age twenty-eight).

That said, the following schema is based on whatever age-related detail the tradition or its commentators provide. To the extent such detail bespeaks an interest in age-specific chronology, we follow the lead—but only to establish childhood, and in Achilles's case, its special obligations—as a pretext for Achilles's not wooing Helen. By all accounts, Achilles was *not yet born* at the time, quite belying the idea that he would have taken Helen, had he found her of marriageable age. We may posit the following sequence, with some events doubtless overlapping, using information from the Homeric poems, from Proclus's summary of the *Cypria,* and Apollodorus ("Apoll"):

| EVENT | TIME PERIOD OR AGE |
|---|---|
| Birth of Helen | |
| Marriage of Peleus and Thetis | |
| Helen abducted by Theseus | Helen 12 (Apoll.) |
| Wooing of Helen | [Achilles likely not yet born] |
| Marriage of Menelaus and Helen | |
| Birth of Hermione | Helen 15 (?) |
| Birth of Achilles | |
| Judgment of Paris | |
| Helen abducted by Paris | Hermione 9 (*Cypria*); Helen 24 |
| First gathering of the Greeks at Aulis | 2-year prep. for gathering (Apoll.), Achilles 5 upon its completion |
| Abortive (initial) expedition to Troy | |
| Returns from initial expedition | 8 years (Apoll.) |
| Second gathering of the Greeks at Aulis | Achilles 15 (Apoll.), Helen 34, Telemachus 10 |
| Sacrifice of Iphigenia (under pretext of marriage to Achilles) | |
| Achilles on Skyros (with Deidamia) | Achilles 15 |
| Birth of Neoptolemus | |
| Second departure for Troy | |
| Arrival at Troy | |
| Trojan War (10 years) | Achilles 25, Helen 44, Neoptolemus 10, Telemachus 20 |
| Odysseus's homecoming (10 years) | Helen 54 |

From Apollodorus's mention of two years for the first muster and eight years for homecomings after the abortive first expedition, we reckon one decade between expeditions. If Achilles, according to the sole authority of Apollodorus, is fifteen at the start of the second expedition, he had to have been five (a decade earlier) at the first, and still under the care of the centaur Chiron. With Achilles fifteen at the second muster, Helen, already at Troy for a decade, is thirty-four. We extrapolate Helen at age thirty-four by moving backward from the *Cypria*'s and Apollodorus's views that Hermione was nine upon Helen's abduction. If her daughter was nine, Helen could not realistically have given birth earlier than fifteen. Thus, assuming Helen's abduction at age twenty-four (fifteen plus nine), Helen is thirty-four at the actual start of the war, forty-four when it ends, and close to fifty-four when resettled in Sparta (after Menelaus's eight-year homecoming). The nine months from conception and gestation to the birth of Hermione add approximately one year to all these ages.

From this we extrapolate the key juncture: *Helen is age thirty-four and Achilles age fifteen at the start of the second expedition.* Assuming Helen's marriage to Menelaus at age fifteen—the youngest reasonable child-bearing age for a woman leaving behind a nine-year-old daughter—Achilles, separated from Helen by nineteen years at the start of the second expedition, *was not even born when Helen was famously wooed.* This negates any age-related reason for Achilles's not wooing Helen. Clearly the tradition had something else in mind: to emphasize (1) the foregone union of Helen and Achilles, age permitting; and (2) the need, even with Achilles yet unborn, to *foreclose* that union, once and forevermore. The prospect of Achilles's taking a leave of absence from his apprenticeship to woo Helen does not enter the picture. By his innate superiority, Achilles would have eviscerated the wooing process, no less than Greek mythology, as noted.

A total of ten years' preliminaries, followed by a ten-year war is consistent with Helen's reference in the *Iliad* that it had been twenty years since her abduction. Such duration is troublesome, however, making a twenty-year ordeal of the Trojan War, and a thirty-year ordeal for Odysseus. And while the gods work in strange ways, one little imputes to the plan of Zeus an eight-year blunder—with its attendant dissipation of human focus and energy—by initial attack on the wrong city (Teuthrania in Mysia), followed by returns to Greece. More perplexing is why returns were at all required; why the Greeks did not simply regroup in Mysia, proceeding thence to nearby Troy. Whatever else happened during this decade of muster and misadventure goes unexplained, including the reasons for it.

At the same time, if, according to Apollodorus, Achilles were fifteen at the start of the second expedition, he would need have been approximately five upon muster for the first expedition, and, as noted, even younger, if at all born, when Helen was wooed. If he is fifteen at the start of the second expedition, Achilles is no less than twenty-five when "dying young" at Troy (*young* on the older side). And if, as suggested, Achilles is inappropriately young when Helen is being wooed, the idea that he would have taken her is fatuous—babies not reasonably "in the running." Not for nothing did classicist A. T. Murray, in his Loeb Classical Library translation of the *Iliad* (1924), note Helen's "astonishing statement" concerning the twenty years since her abduction. In truth, a first failed expedition adding ten years to the Trojan War adds nothing at all, but only confuses a sense of chronology and orderly development.

The passing reference to Hermione's age, moreover, is suspect because epic concerns itself, as seen, with reckonable time periods, not with age as such—and least of all for incidental characters (Hermione the only *dramatis persona* to whom age is assigned). A Hermione-based chronology is further tenuous because (1) Helen, already fairly young for childbirth at age fifteen, is but two or three years past her earlier, clearly underage abduction by Theseus (discussed below); and (2) we hesitate, in any event, to assign an age—for childbearing or otherwise—to the ageless beauty that is Helen's, to one whose "origins . . . are lost in fable, her end in legend." Curious in this connection is Helen's regret in the *Iliad*—without reference to Hermione's age—over having left "my adored child and the loveliness of girls my own age." The whiling of time with girls one's own age is a *premarital* pastime (cf. the "Sapphic circle") unbefitting the mother of a nine-year-old. Yes, Hesiod advises marriage for a man at age thirty (give or take), and for a woman at age eighteen. He further urges that the girl "live nearby." The time frame and limited geographical reach may suit life on the farm, but not the world of cataclysm and imperishable fame. Even then, however, there are limits.

The *Cypria*, in Proclus's second-century AD prose summary, passingly refers to a meeting, early held at Troy and at Achilles's request, between himself and Helen—presumably that he might see Helen with his own eyes and know what he is fighting for (the meeting arranged by Aphrodite and Thetis). If this was the meeting's motivation, it nicely corresponds to those of Helen's suitors who wooed her in advance by message, sight unseen, based on what they had heard of her beauty. We are told nothing more of the meeting, other than that Achilles next sought to dissuade the Greeks from an intended homeward voyage. From this we may infer maturity enough for Achilles to have wanted a look-see, and his heightened appreciation thereafter of Helen as his coequal and driving force. The encounter is *needed*; and how it smolders with destructive potential. Given their innate equivalence, it is difficult to sustain the prospect of Achilles and Helen's having not so much as once beheld each other.

We note, in closing, the myth of Helen's abduction by Theseus in a pact with his friend Pirithous to seduce the daughters of Zeus. The unreluctant-seeming Helen is depicted on a red-figure amphora (late 6th century BC), twirling Theseus's hair as he piggybacks her away. Having followed Apollodorus thus far, we follow him in making Helen twelve at the time—an age just old enough for sexual misadventure, though it yet taxes the speed of what follows—including Helen's wooing, marriage to Menelaus, and birth of Hermione, all by age fifteen. We briefly note two alternative versions. The Greek historian Diodorus of Sicily (1st century BC) makes Helen ten at the time of her abduction, noting she "excelled all women in beauty" and emerged from the encounter "still a virgin." The Greek chronicler Hellanicus of Lesbos (5th century BC) makes Helen seven (and Theseus fifty) at the time of the abduction, which is less a matter of rape than of kidnapping. Or, in the beneficent view of the esteemed Gilbert Murray: "we may well believe that [Theseus] only took her into safe keeping to protect the precocious princess from less scrupulous suitors." The Greek biographer Plutarch (1st–2nd centuries AD), referencing Hellanicus, notes that Theseus was already fifty when he "had his dealings with Helen." Not specifically mentioning Helen's age, Plutarch resorts to understatement: dealings *ou kath' ōran* 'not at the appropriate time'. Translators tend to be less coy: "Theseus was already fifty years old, according to Hellanicus, when he took part in the rape of Helen, who was not of marriageable age."

However young at the time, Helen was hidden away with Theseus's mother, that she might come of age, but was rescued by her brothers, the Dioscuri (a rescue reiterated at Troy by the brothers Agamemnon and Menelaus). That an underage Helen was being "saved" for marriage to Theseus suggests that the *ageless* Helen might have been allowed, at whatever length, to wait out an "underage" or generationally belated Achilles. Again, it is not age per se but a generational divide that hinders the marriage of Helen and Achilles. Thus, while a barely pubescent (or even younger) Achilles might be sexually mature enough to wed Helen, Helen's involvement with a "mere child" lacks fittedness and a certain propriety. It is an affront to her sexual maturity, experience, and desirability. Where she is raped in childhood by Theseus without say in the matter, that is one thing; but wooed and wed, quite another.

Nonetheless, so resistant was the mythic imagination to Helen and Achilles's separation that it made them "lovers after death, two *eidōla*—icons, images, shadows—consummating their secret, spiritual union on Leuke, the island in the Black Sea where Achilles was honored in cult after his death." Did this not suffice, the *Odyssey* recounts—with Helen and Menelaus at length resettled in Sparta—the preparations for Hermione's marriage to Neoptolemus: the daughter of Helen to the son of Achilles. Thus, and in strikingly compensatory fashion, the marriage in life denied Helen and Achilles is vouchsafed their children one to the other. This occurs in a way both recapitulating and correcting the ostensible grounds for Helen and Achilles's separation: age disjuncture. Hermione is belatedly, though credibly on the war's account, twenty-seven at marriage, which is to say she is nine when Helen is abducted, nineteen when the war ends, twenty-seven after Menelaus's eight-year homecoming. Neoptolemus, born on Skyros sometime toward the start of the war, is no more than ten when joining in its final phase—slaying Paris, his father's killer—and no more than eighteen upon marriage (following Menelaus's return). It was just such an imbalance that ostensibly disqualified Achilles as a suitor of Helen—the two beautifully destructive figures equals in every respect but age/generation.

We recall that Menelaus, married to Helen and son-in-law to Zeus, is spared physical death by reprieve to the Elysian Field—presumably with Helen. *Presumably* because Helen cannot be married in death to both Menelaus and Achilles. That, however, might just be the point: Helen as indeterminately wed in death as in life; eternal in her infidelities as in her surpassing beauty. For all his anguish in life, Menelaus gets a free pass in death, gaining the hallowed epic afterlife that only hard-won *kleos* confers on others. And in no case is afterlife more fittingly gained than by Achilles—a supplement, as it were, to the *kleos* for which he untimely perished. Menelaus and Achilles, each in his own way, are immortalized—the recompense for earthly anguish on Helen's account. As further recalled from Book Four of the *Odyssey,* Helen possesses magical powers, supporting the once fashionable view of her as a "faded goddess." If such were Helen's experiences, powers, and influence, she could have used them to overcome the age impediment to Achilles's suit—as the "godlike Achilles" could have applied himself to that endeavor. Age would then have been of no more importance to Achilles and Helen than to their children. "Beauty alone transcends all contingencies," says Rachel Bespaloff, "including those that brought it to flower." One would not know it from epic's determined separation of Helen and Achilles.

# V.

# Chapter 19

## Homeric and Sapphic Meter, Metric Formulae and Oral Composition, the Origins of Rhyming Poetry, Milton on Blank Verse

A metrical form of unsurpassed flexibility and beauty, the heroic hexameter, had been wrought out . . .

– JOHN W. MACKAIL

English verse has no measure which even remotely suggests the various flow of the hexameter.

– ANDREW LANG

THOUGH IT IS TEMPTING to think so, similarities between Homer and Sappho (and the lyric poets generally) do not reflect lyric's instinctive reliance on epic. Phraseology developed autonomously within the different constraints of epic and lyric meter. Though lyric, due to its less flexible meter, has been argued to *predate* epic, the first attested lyric poetry appears only *after* epic—which is to say that we have no lyric poetry predating Homer. "Sappho had at her disposal a tradition of inherited formulas which were parallel to the inherited meter of her verses. The rigid phraseological correspondences between her pentameter and the epic hexameter are due to parallel inheritance of related formulas from related meters. But the fact is, and it cannot be emphasized enough, that Sapphic pentameter is actually far more archaic in structure than Homeric hexameter." We now turn to the principal meters of Homeric and Sapphic poetry, noting that Sappho's use of *kleos aphthiton* is not necessarily, or at all, a borrowing from Homer.

For the *Iliad* or *Odyssey* to have developed orally, and been performed extemporaneously by the thousands of verses, a performance-facilitating language and meter were needed. The poems were likely never recited in full by a single bard in one or consecutive sittings, but rather recited over several days, in a festival setting, by teams or relays of bards. The meter was dactylic hexameter, later known as epic, heroic, or Homeric meter. It provided formulaic (though highly variable) phrasing to convey fixed or recurring ideas or events, even while allowing for colorful characterizations, grueling combat scenes, and reflections on mortality and mankind's wretched lot. In short, the full range of human emotion and experience.

Greek dactylic hexameter—and Latin hexameter, as adapted—runs as follows:

1 2 3 4 5 6
— — — — (—) ⏑
— ⏑⏑ | — ⏑⏑ | — ⏑⏑ | — ⏑⏑ | — ⏑⏑ | — —

NOTE: A dash indicates a long syllable; an "⏑" indicates a short. A dash above two shorts indicates the possible replacement of two shorts by a long. A dash in parentheses above two shorts indicates that the replacement is rare. An "⏑" atop a dash indicates a variable syllable (long or short). Vertical lines mark the end of each poetic foot. The need to place long and short marks directly above vowels or diphthongs can create an appearance of uneven spacing.

The meter is dactylic because it consists of six "finger-shaped" units (Gr. *daktulos* 'finger'), the basic unit, or foot, being one long and two short syllables. It is "hexameter" because there are six feet to the metric line. Lines typically exhibit a pause, or caesura (Lat. *caesum* 'cut'), often at word end *within* a foot, e.g.:

1 2 3 4 5 6
— ⏑ ⏑ | — ⏑ ⏑ | — — | — — | — ⏑ ⏑ | – –
Arma vir | umque ca | no || Troi | ae qui | primus ab | oris

Arms and the man I sing, who first from shores of Troy

A long syllable may replace any two shorts syllables, as a matter of metric equivalence. The resultant foot, a "spondee," may occur anywhere but in the fifth position. The final foot is always disyllabic, with a variably long or short final syllable. The line-ending rhythm is thus characteristically: — ⏑⏑ | — ⏓.

Classical poetry did not rhyme as we know rhyme. However, rhyme may be thought the later equivalent of line-ending dactylic rhythm for purposes of signaling line finality. Dante suggests as much, noting the arrival—some one hundred and fifty years before his own time—of vernacular poets in Italy: "And it is not so many years ago that such vernacular poets first appeared among us; for to compose vernacular rhyming verse is tantamount, in some measure, to writing Latin metrical poetry." Dante further notes the circumstance: "The first man who began writing as a vernacular poet was induced to do so because he wanted his words to be understood by a lady, for whom Latin metrical verse was hard to understand."

The first seven transliterated lines of the *Iliad* scan as follows. With the exception of the first line, and for visual simplification, I omit caesuras.

Greek:

> μῆνιν ἄειδε θεὰ Πηληϊάδεω Ἀχιλῆος
> οὐλομένην, ἣ μυρί' Ἀχαιοῖς ἄλγε' ἔθηκε,
> πολλὰς δ' ἰφθίμους ψυχὰς Ἄϊδι προΐαψεν
> ἡρώων, αὐτοὺς δὲ ἑλώρια τεῦχε κύνεσσιν
> οἰωνοῖσί τε πᾶσι, Διὸς δ' ἐτελείετο βουλή,
> ἐξ οὗ δὴ τὰ πρῶτα διαστήτην ἐρίσαντε
> Ἀτρείδης τε ἄναξ ἀνδρῶν καὶ δῖος Ἀχιλλεύς.

Translated:

> The wrath, Goddess, sing of Peleus' son Achilles,
> Accursed, which caused the Achaeans unnumbered pains.
> Many a hero's mighty soul did it hurl down
> To Hell, the mighty themselves making prey for dogs
> And banqueting for birds. Fulfilled was Zeus's plan
> When the two in strife first stood apart contending,
> Agamemnon king of men and lord Achilles.

Transliterated and scanned:

1 2 3 4 5 6
— ⏑ ⏑ | — ⏑ ⏑ | – – | — ⏑⏑ | — ⏑ ⏑ | — ⏑
Mēnin á | eide the | ā, Pē | lēïa | deō Achi | lēos

1 2 3 4 5 6
— ⏑ ⏑ | — — | — ⏑ ⏑ | — — | — ⏑ ⏑ | — ⏑
oulomen | ēn, (h)ē | mūri' A | chaiois | alge' e | thēke,

1 2 3 4 5 6
— — | — — | — — | — ⏑⏑ | — ⏑ ⏑ | — ⏑
pollas | d'iphthim | ous psu | chas Aï | di proï | apsen

1 2 3 4 5 6
— — | — — | — ⏑ ⏑ | — ⏑⏑ | — ⏑ ⏑ | — ⏑
(h)ērō | ōn, au | tous de (h)el | ōria | teuche ku | nessin

1 2 3 4 5 6
– – | — ⏑ ⏑ | — ⏑ ⏑ | — ⏑ ⏑ | — ⏑⏑ | — —
oiō | noisi te | daita, Di | os d'ete | leieto | boulē

1 2 3 4 5 6
— — | — — | — ⏑ ⏑ | – – | — ⏑ ⏑ | — ⏑
ex (h)ou | dē ta | prōta di | astē | tēn eris | ante

1 2 3 4 5 6
— ⏑⏑ | — ⏑ ⏑ | — — | — — | — ⏑ ⏑ | — —
Atreï | dēs te (ϝ)an | ax an | drōn kai | dī(ϝ)os Ach | illeus,

Depending on the number of substitutions of two shorts by a long syllable, a dactylic line contains anywhere from twelve to seventeen syllables; although in practice, thirteen to seventeen, as lines of six spondaic feet are rare (only five, all in the *Odyssey,* one of them repeated). For this reason, rhyming "fourteeners" have sometimes been thought the appropriate meter for translating classical epic into English: by Arthur Golding in his highly influential *Metamorphoses* (1567), read by Spenser and Shakespeare; by George Chapman in the first complete translation of the *Iliad* (1611); by William Morris, *Aeneid* (1875); and more recently by A. E. Stallings, *De Rerum Natura* (*The Nature of Things*) (2007). The operative term, however, is *sometimes,* as fourteeners have no epic monopoly.

Hexameter determines *poetic* stress according to vowel quantity, long or short, which is to say, according to syllabic weight and corresponding duration of pronunciation (twice the time for a long as for a short syllable). Quantity, in turn, is determined by set yet flexible rules and conventions. In hexametric meter, poetic stress and natural, or spoken, stress may coincide, though they should do so sparingly. The rhythm is otherwise singsong or prosaic. The basic unit of most English poetry is not the dactyl ( — ◡ ◡ ) but the iamb ( ◡ / ). It is the English iambic pentameter that has long been considered the functional equivalent of Greek/Latin dactylic hexameter:

1 2 3 4 5
◡ / | ◡ / | ◡ / | ◡ / | ◡ /
[If music be the food of love play on]

This is not to say, however, that iambic pentameter is invariably best suited to the *translation* of dactylic hexameter. On the contrary, the ten-beat pentameter ill corresponds to the upward-of-seventeen-beat hexameter, especially where line-for-line correspondence—one hexameter into one pentameter—is sought. However, when such correspondence is *not* the rule, pentameter works very well, since iambic rhythm is as indigenous to English as is hexametric rhythm to Classical Greek. The suitability of iambic rhythm in this last respect trumps all other considerations of difference between the two meters.

In iambic meter, poetic and spoken stresses regularly coincide. This is to say that spoken, or natural, stress *is*, or becomes, poetic stress, since English meter is but the sustained well-cadenced arrangement of natural stress in speech. Vowel quantity, in the classical sense, is of scant concern. (It is noted that early attempts at English verse according to the rules of classical quantity were abject failures.) In brief, a more polysyllabic Greek yields more unstressed vowels (i.e., vowels short by nature), whence the development of dactylic meter ( — ◡◡ | — ◡◡ , etc.). By contrast, a more monosyllabic English yields more stressed, i.e., long, vowels (whether or not long by nature), whence the development of iambic meter ( ◡ / | ◡ / ). It thus appears the case that the iamb is as natural to English as is the dactyl to Greek/Latin. It follows that dactylic hexameter is the heroic measure for Greek/Latin poetry, as iambic pentameter is the heroic measure for English poetry. But again, this but partially commends iambic for the *translation* of dactylic meter.

To take some examples from the famous soliloquy in Shakespeare's *Richard II*:

> Of comfort no man speak,
> Let's talk of graves, of worms, and epitaphs,
> Make dust our paper, and with rainy eyes
> Write sorrow on the bosom of the earth.

The disyllabic words are all emphasized consistently with their natural or spoken stress. So also trisyllabics and quadrosyllabics:

> Allowing him a breath, a little scene,
> To monarchize, be fear'd and kill with looks,
> Infusing him with self and vain conceit,
> As if this flesh which walls about our life
> Were brass impregnable . . .

Certain syllables may *sound* long because stressed, but they are not necessarily long for that. The *i* in *him* ("infusing *hím*") is neither long by nature nor long because stressed, any more than is the *e* in *imprégnable.* By contrast, the *u* in *infúsing* is long by nature (versus the *u* in *us*) and for that reason *should* be stressed. Hexameter, by contrast, and as noted, is a *quantitative* meter versus the stress-based, or pronunciational, meters of English and European languages. In other words, hexameter is determined by the poetically governed weight, pronunciational length, or *quantity* of syllables in lines of a variable syllable count, while iambic meter is determined by the alternation of naturally stressed and unstressed syllables in lines of equal syllable count.

The quantitative rhythm of hexameter (the amount of time it takes to enunciate each syllable) is superimposed, as it were, on the line's natural or spoken rhythm—on the words' natural beat—with the result that "[t]ime plays against beat." In other words, quantitative verse overlays spoken stress with poetic time/duration, the interplay being of the essence of the meter. In English, by contrast, there is no such play, since natural stress alone governs. In the process of hexametric composition, there is inevitably some amount of coincidence between time emphasis and natural stress emphasis. Thus, in the three-word opening of the *Iliad,* time and beat coincide in the first (μῆνιν) and third (θεὰ) words, as seen in the coincidence of their accent and scansion marks:

Greek:

— ⏑ ⏑|— ⏑ ⏑|–
μῆνιν ἄ|ειδε θε|ὰ

Transliterated:

— ⏑ ⏑|– ⏑ ⏑|–
Mēnin á|eide the|ā

Translation:

Wrath, sing, goddess

However, the second word's second-syllable time emphasis—the diphthong *ει/ei* being long by nature—preempts the word's otherwise naturally stressed first syllable (the stress indicated by its accent mark: ἄειδε/áeide). Again, care must be taken, since the excessive coincidence of time and beat submerges poetic rhythm, creating a singsong or prosaic effect. Where English and Western European languages are stress-based alone, the dangers of singsong or doggerel are more likely.

Latin was the spoken and literary language of Europe for a thousand years after the disintegration of the Roman Empire, starting in the fifth century AD (*disintegration* rather than *fall*). During the late twelfth century AD, as Dante notes, quantitative measure began yielding to simpler stress-based rhythms and to rhyme, even as Latin itself continued to surrender to vernacular, i.e., household, or local, tendencies. At the cost of oversimplification, the aggregate of such tendencies was a modern-European-language prototype called "Romance," because it derived from the Roman language, Latin. The dominant local tendencies morphed, in various instances, and in due course, into what are now considered Western Europe's Romance languages—the at-any-time-indeterminate progression being one from vernacular (a variant of Latin) to language (distinct, but indebted to Latin). Vernacular development followed from regional isolation after the breakdown of the communications system (and previously well-maintained roads) that had earlier spread and sustained Latin as the language of the Roman Empire.

The earliest vernacular verse forms were Christian hymns, in which natural stress and rhyme were especially conducive to singing.

At no time, however, did Classical Greek and Latin poetry rhyme, as English and European poetry have rhymed since the late Middle Ages. They did, however, exhibit (1) "internal rhyme," including alliteration (the repetition of the same or similar consonants at the starts of words or in a phrase's stressed syllables); (2) assonance or "vowel rhyme" (repetition of internal vowels); and (3) consonance (repetition of end consonants). The use of *end* rhyme in Latin verse, dating to the twelfth century, evolved from *internal* rhyme in rhythmically stressed poetry, bringing rhyme in poetry to its "final state." English and the classically derived vernaculars followed this development, with end rhyme the result, and internal rhyme the residuum.

Little recognized in this development is a balanced vowel-rhyming feature in the elegiac couplet composed in Sappho's own time (though none by her survive). An elegiac couplet consists of a dactylic hexameter followed by a dactylic pentameter; the pentameter resulting from a half-foot truncation in the hexameter's third foot and final foot, leaving two half-verses of two and one-half feet each. The meter is schematized as follows:

```
   1       2       3       4      5     6
   —       —       —       —     (—)    ‿
— ‿‿ | — ‿‿ | — ‿‿ | — ‿‿ | — ‿‿ | — —

   —       —               —     (—)
— ‿‿ | — ‿‿ | — ∧ | — ‿‿ | — ‿‿ | — ∧
```

Elegiac meter was the primary vehicle for melancholy or plaintive poems, especially lovelorn laments, with its alternating hexamaetric rise and pentametric fall reflecting the underlying emotion (Gr. *elegos* [derivation uncertain]; Eng. *elegy*). Unlike the hexameter's variable pauses, or caesuras, the pentameter's breaks (∧) are always symmetric, owing to truncation always at midpoint and verse end. The elegiac poetry of Theognis (6th century BC) was of a political-admonitory kind, the rise and fall suggesting precept and moral. It has been noted that one in seven of Theognis's pentameters (from among his 1,400 surviving couplets) exhibits rhyme at midpoint and verse end, "accentua[ting] the rhythmical symmetry of the elegiac pentameter vs. the asymmetry of the epic hexameter."

The following pentameters demonstrate the tendency, taken from a ten-line poem in which *each* of the five pentameters surprisingly rhymes at mid and end verse. The fourth and tenth read as follows:

(cliffs) (sheer)
riptein kai **petrōn** || Kyrne kat' **ēlibatōn**
(and to cast [himself], O Cyrnus, from sheer cliffs)

(harsh) (poverty)
ē zōein **chalepē** || teiromenon **peniē**
(than to live sorely crushed by harsh poverty)

In these two examples, the bolded nouns and adjectives rhyme internally, due to the replication of noun-adjective case endings in an inflected language. The replication allows noun and adjective to be separated without grammatical uncertainty. This same feature may also occur with "rhymed" verb endings. Though suggestive of consecutive end-verse rhyme, the feature is simply the balanced arrangement of inevitable assonance, or vowel rhyme. The balance, while highlighting sound and reinforcing rhythm, does little to create meaning, which is the higher office of rhyme. Indeed, it is the *unexpectedness* of English- or European-language end rhyme, occurring between different parts of speech, without grammatical parallel or anticipated soundalike *or* sense, that most delights or signifies, imparting a sense of the inevitable. Only in extraordinary hands does the anticipated, even facile, rhyme succeed, making Dylan Thomas likely the last to have triumphed with end rhymes: night-light-right-bright-flight-sight. Of the single feature of rhyme, Robert Graves observed, "It must come unexpectedly yet inevitably, like presents at Christmas, and convey the comforting sense of free will within predetermination."

It is thus from the inevitable internal rhymes of classical verse, notably those of Latin elegiac poetry, that end rhyme eventually developed. One might say that the internal rhyme of words in grammatical "agreement," or otherwise sounding alike, worked its way to line-end position, creating couplets, delimiting sense, and (at its best) creating meaning. Internal soundalikes, or assonances, were the "first glimmers of a movement toward rhymes," with full rhyme in the modern sense apparent by the twelfth century AD.

The emergent line-end rhyme in part repaired, or compensated for, loss of the metrically regularized and richly intonational features of classical quantitative verse. Though one would never know it from Walt Whitman on, end rhyme was not casually to be discarded as an encumbrance. It was, until John Milton, the essence of poetry itself. Though not the first instance of English blank verse, Milton's *Paradise Lost* (1667) first established it as a viable alternative for epic poetry.

Poets before Milton had railed against the "tyranny of rhyme," deeming rhyme a Gothic or Hunnish import in league with other destructive barbarian tendencies—brought first to Italy, then France and Germany and, finally, England. The abandonment of rhyme, it was thought, would return English to the classical standard, "raising the dignity of the English language by providing a workable English equivalent of the Latin hexameter as perfected by Virgil." Just as the Romans outgrew their primitive Saturnian meter in imitation of the Greek hexameter, the English would abandon the corruptive practice of rhyme for blank verse.

The faulting of rhyme on these grounds, however, is without historical warrant. First, end rhyme was neither arbitrary imposition nor "tyranny," but a development, as noted, from assonantal verse-balancing features already present in classical verse. Second, as spoken cadences usurped the field, rhyme compensated for loss of the inimitably marked rhythms of quantitative meter, and especially of the regularized hexametric close: — ◡◡ | — ⏓ (formula-laden hexametric rhythm, and rhyme, each in its way an aid to memory). Third, the relative simplicity of naturally stress-based iambics cannot be considered a "return" to classical standards, or an equivalent to the demands of the long-evolving and ultimately highly artificial classical hexameter. All that can really be said of English blank verse is that, like classical verse, it does not rhyme. Indeed, for all the *internal* rhyme apparent in classical verse, English blank verse is yet the more lacking, except in the most capable hands. Rhymed verse was thus not the corruption of a classical standard, but its logical (if not inevitable) development.

Milton himself takes a similarly ahistorical tack in the introduction to the "Revised and Augmented" version of *Paradise Lost*, published in 1674

(1st ed. 1667), noting (in his reactionary "The Verse"):

> The measure [of *Paradise Lost*] is *English* Heroic Verse without rime, as that of *Homer in Greek*, and *Virgil in Latin*; Rime being no necessary Adjunct or True Ornament of Poem or good Verse, in longer works especially, but the Invention of a barbarous Age, to set off wretched matter and lame Meter . . .

Implicitly faulting rhymed verse as "bad verse," Milton praises the poetry of Homer and Virgil as "good Verse"—because *unrhymed*—and proposes to conform to their example. But the proposal rings false, insofar as rhymed verse was not an option for antiquity, making its verse *good* for reasons having nothing to do with rhyme and its abandonment. The fallacy endures. Witness formalist poet and metrist Anthony Hecht (1923–2004): "Because much poetry secures its rich and powerful effects without rhyme—Homer, Virgil, *Paradise Lost*, William Wordsworth, Walt Whitman and many others—rhyme is relegated to the province of decorative adornment, and inessential luxury, etc." The cringe-worthy agglomeration of poets aside, the fact remains that Homer and Virgil secure rich and powerful effect *not* by discarding rhymed for unrhymed verse—as does Milton—but through a millennia-evolved medium made rich and powerful *without rhyme*.

Further noting in "The Verse" that "true musical delight" consists in "apt Numbers, fit quantity of Syllables, and the sense variously drawn from one Verse into another," Milton disavows the "jingling sound of like endings, a fault avoided by the learned Ancients both in Poetry and all good Oratory." The ancients, however, did not "avoid" rhyme. Again, they neither knew nor needed it; their poetry developing without it and validated by other means. Milton, moreover, ignores the distinction made by Dryden between the "vulgar tinkling rhyme that simply holds together language that would otherwise be hobbling prose and the developed art of rhyme that makes an appeal to the discriminating ear in complementing the subtle management of 'pauses, cadence and well vowell'd words.'"

His own *Paradise Lost*, in Milton's view, is "to be esteem'd an example set, the first in English, of ancient liberty recover'd to heroic Poem from the troublesom and modern bondage of Rimeing." Yet, however much Milton here purports to be freeing English poetry from rhyme, he is not returning it to a prelapsarian paradigm. English poetry had not (any more than vernacular poetry) *fallen* from classical usage, but had inexorably developed from it. Milton is instead composing in a form suggestive or reminiscent of poetry's rhymeless antecedents. It is thus *not* that epic poetry, being rhymeless in antiquity, should be rhymeless now. Rather, rhymelessness suits Miltonic epic, even as it naturally suited classical epic. Miltonic epic otherwise seeks the full expressiveness of its Greek and Latin forebears.

Milton further ascribes the use of rhyme to runaway "Custom," causing the self-punishing poet "to express many things otherwise, and for the most part worse than else they would have exprest them." Perhaps, though the stricture in no way impeded Pope, Keats, and Byron any more than it had proved an obstacle to Spenser and Dryden. Milton abandoned rhyme, knowing it an incident, not the essence, of poetry; certain that effective poetry could be written without it, that a *Paradise Lost* needed it least of all. Such certainty, however, does not account for Dante, with whose work Milton was intimately familiar and who was Milton's singular predecessor in the writing of theologic epic. Dante was not in the least stymied by the relentless demands of terza rima, having invented both the rhyme scheme *and* the proto-Italian in which he composed one of the West's greatest works. Spenser, for his part, invented the intricate stanza bearing his name, while Keats showed in his four-book epic *Endymion* that rhymed and highly enjambed couplets (hendecasyllabics in this case) precluded nothing whatever. And the Roman Lucretius, without abandoning the hexameter (were it possible), accomplished within its bounds a work of comparable scope, synthesis, and imagination to Milton's. Discarding rhyme, Milton not only wrote blank verse but devised an unrelentingly blank—indeed, a steroidal—iambic pentameter. Milton had previously composed in rhyme and could likely have rhymed *Paradise Lost.* Milton had written original Latin poetry in hexameters. By contrast, those condemning the "tyranny of rhyme" had, unlike Milton, become either incapable or undesirous of the *mastery* of rhyme and of poetry as resolutely known, practiced, and appreciated theretofore.

❧

The resort to blank verse was a strategic decision, impelled by the scope of Milton's work, and quite offset and sanctioned by its pervasive felicities. As concerns scope, the Invocation to *Paradise Lost* sets the tone: evoking

Adam, Christ, Moses, the Israelites, and Jerusalem; invoking the Muse (i.e., the Judeo-Christian Godhead); relocating the *situs* of classical inspiration from Parnassus and Helicon to Oreb and Sinai; and simulating the beginnings of Homer's *Odyssey*, Hesiod's *Theogony*, and Virgil's *Aeneid*. Milton's goal was to integrate while superseding them all, and to create the first biblical epic in English. Milton's accomplishment crowns the epic tradition that began with Homer. As concerns the work's felicities, these include a single-mindedly epic impulse synthesizing the classical and biblical origins of Western civilization; a tenaciously, often uncannily rhythmic work; an alliterative, freely archaizing, and sweepingly imagistic work; a work, though unique unto itself, in every way poetically sounding and adept.

It is the very amplitude of *Paradise Lost* that most urged the discarding of rhyme—a singular accommodation to Milton's twin-torrential influx of the biblical and classical traditions. This aligns Milton with no one so much as the often vexing but supreme lyricist of antiquity, Pindar (5th century BC), of whose style his lyric successor Horace famously said: "A river bursts its banks and rushes down a / Mountain with uncontrollable momentum, / Rain-saturated, churning, chanting thunder." It is with an eye toward such precedent that one finds in *Paradise Lost* a grandiloquently periodic style—its suspended syntax, subordinations, hypotaxes, and enjambments conveying the "sense variously drawn from one Verse into another." In such manner is the integrative rush, churn, and hurtle of Milton's advance conveyed, "dramatiz[ing] a mind which has dominated experience and reworked it to his liking." Thus, if Milton's syntax is sometimes "perplexed" and "difficult," and the poet "accused of forcing the language against its natural grain," such judgment must largely reflect the multivalent design of the enterprise itself—its human, mythic, cosmic, and theological dimensions. The tone is set from the opening sixteen-verse sentence of *Paradise Lost*, which may be properly designated an "exordium," since Milton's manner is as thoroughly oratorical—and annunciatory—as it is poetic. Milton had commended "the learned ancients" for their skill "in Poetry and all good Oratory." His opening sixteen verses, in all their rhetorical finesse, now announce his own poetical and oratorical endeavor (cf. "the learned Ancients in Poetry and all good Oratory").

Pope grasped Milton's qualities, noting that his "fire" or "poetic fury" "glows like a Furnace kept up to an uncommon ardor by the Force of Art."

Dryden, too, approved, even while adhering to the rhyming couplets that made his fame. (Keats, however, abandoned his epic poem *Hyperion,* dealing with Zeus's overthrow and ouster of the Titans from Olympus, because of its "too many Miltonic inversions.") Nonetheless, and in reproof of Milton's "the troublesom and modern bondage of Rimeing," Dryden produced a coupleted stage adaptation of *Paradise Lost* (*The State of Innocence,* 1674), the adaptation outselling the original until the century's end. Samuel Johnson precisely hit the mark, noting that "Poetry may subsist without rhyme, but English poetry will not often please; nor can rhyme ever safely be spared but where the subject is able to support itself." No subject had theretofore been as capably self-supporting as that of *Paradise Lost.*

Granted, the introduction of blank verse was a monumental event in the history of English metrics. But to credit Milton's achievement as a "liberation" is to misapprehend the otherwise *restrictive,* and for *that* reason liberating, qualities of *Paradise Lost.* Milton exchanged one constraint for another—the decorous constraint of rhyme for a consistent grandiloquence, a surge and thunder that only a rhyme-unfastened pentameter might allow. The heightened demand was more regulative in its way, and thus more enabling than the use of rhyme had ever been. Milton, in sum, intended more than what the strictures of traditional rhyme might previously have allowed; he intended, in Johnson's words, to *astonish* rather than merely please, and with variety enough to *engage,* not "tire by long continuance." Had Milton's epigones thus continued to "liberate" English poetry, we might have something other than the "free" verse of today. Milton was the last great epic poet of the English language, admitting—like Homer and Virgil—neither emulation nor transformance. He was the exalted height which others might only strain to glimpse, or turn from in despair. Departing from the heroic couplet, Milton showed it was not the medium but its mastery that mattered.

❧

Dactylic hexameter, to result in an *Iliad* or *Odyssey,* would need be highly flexible: the result of (1) protracted development allowing the substitution at will of two shorts by a long; and (2) flexible rules for determining short-and-long vowel lengths in the first instance. Thus, a syllable is long either "by nature," containing a naturally long vowel or diphthong, or "by position," containing a short vowel followed by two consonants in the same or adjoining words. A syllable with a short vowel followed by two consonants, one or both of them a "liquid" (*l, m, n, r*), is either long or short, depending on need. Thus, a short-vowel syllable, if naturally unstressed, acquires *metric* stress or *quantity* when followed by two consonants. A word-final diphthong (otherwise long) scans short when the next word begins with a vowel. Conversely, a naturally long vowel, expectedly stressed for metric purposes, is not necessarily stressed outside of verse (as 'sing'—*aeíde, Il.* 1.1; otherwise *áeide*). The interplay between metric and spoken stress—the latter more a matter of vocal pitch (depending on the particular accent mark) than of simple emphasis—was of the essence of ancient Greek poetry, and what made the poetry *poetry*.

In this way there developed, to quote Professor Mackail, "a metrical form of unsurpassed flexibility and beauty," one devoted to "the epic lays, the *klea andrōn* which had become a whole body of literature. . . . The heroic hexameter had been wrought out"—so overwhelmingly as to have "eclipsed all other poetical forms and subjects" and created the genre's potentialities. "The time was ripe for the great epic poet [and] the great epic poet came." Which is not to say that Homer happily arrived to seize the moment, but that conditions developed for the perfected recitations that we now know as Homer.

Dactylic hexameter encouraged the ready memorization and/or impromptu creation of metric phrases or units. It was in this way that oral composition proceeded, rather than word-by-word. The singer could thus think ahead, facilitating performance. A developed example appears in the *kleos* complex, reviewed above:

◡◡ | — ◡◡ | — —<br>
. . . kleos | aphthiton | einai<br>
(to be imperishable glory)

◡◡ | — ◡ ◡ | — —<br>
. . . kleos | esthlon a | roito<br>
(he would gain fine glory)

◡◡ | — ◡◡ | — ◡ ◡ | — —<br>
. . . kleos | ouranon | eurun (h)i | kanei,<br>
(the glory reaches broad heaven)

Somewhat more familiar perhaps are such metric phrases, or formulae, as "rosy-fingered dawn," "wine-dark sea," "earth-shaker Poseidon," and "swift-footed Achilles." The metric for the famed "swift-footed Achilles" is as follows:

⏑ ⏑ | — ⏑ ⏑ | — —
. . . podas | ōchus A | chilleus

The formula occupies two and one-half metric feet and could be relied on, without forethought, to fill that much of a line (always at line-end position). Formulaic flexibility is apparent in the variant "swift-footed Iris":

⏑ ⏑ | — ⏑⏑ | – ⏑
. . . podas | ōchea | Iris

There the adjective, in its trisyllabic feminine form (*ōchea*), modifies the disyllabic *Iris,* versus the disyllabic masculine *ōchus* with the trisyllabic *Achilleus.*

Then there is "king of men, Agamemnon":

⏑ | — — | — ⏑⏑ | — —
. . . (F)a | nax an | drōn Aga | memnōn

The phrase occupies three and one-third metric feet and could be thus relied on whenever Agamemnon was mentioned. Note that the *a* in *andrōn* and *e* in *Agamemnōn* are both naturally short vowels scanned long because followed by double consonants in each instance. Nor is Agamemnon exclusively "king of men, Agamemnon." An alternative formula of comparable metric length, beginning with a long syllable, makes him "wide-ruling Agamemnon":

— | — — | — ⏑⏑ | — —
eu | ru krei | ōn Aga | memnōn

Such are the simplest formulaic variations, consisting of proper name plus stock modifier (or epithet). This is in no way to understate the intricacy of formulaic usage overall, the ultimate result of which is the *Iliad* and *Odyssey.* Thus, with certain phrasings and recurrent descriptions largely predetermined, the poet could focus on story elaboration and nuance. As

C. S. Lewis notes of the illustrious one-hundred-and-three-line "Parting of Hector and Andromache" (*Iliad*, Book Six), "phrases, or whole lines, which occur again and again in Homer are twenty-eight times employed," while approximately "a *quarter* of the whole passage is 'stock.'" Here, as elsewhere, the bard does not simply recite what he has memorized, but composes from a variable formulaic repertoire. The repertoire is variable because it is not merely memorized but set within flexible parameters, making it ready for improvisation according to ability and occasion. As Albert Lord has noted,

> Even in pre-singing years rhythm and thought are one, and the singer's concept of the formula shaped but not explicit. He is aware of the successive beats and the varying length of repeated thoughts, and these might be said to be his formulas. Basic patterns of meter, word boundary, melody have become his possession, and in him the tradition begins to reproduce itself.

It is noted that approximately seven percent of the Homeric line-count contains words used once and only once. This too urges the extreme fluidity of formulaic composition, since it accommodates words which are ostensibly untraditional and thus lacking in formulaic associations. The bard composes as he recites and recites as he composes, the fixed inner rhythms of the formulae "join[ing] together in such a way as to produce a fixed overall rhythm," each performance of the whole or any part thereof producing a new, albeit familiar, composition. This is a *living* process—recitation neither purely from memory nor purely improvisational, but something between the two. "A truly 'oral' tradition is one in which every performance generates a new composition." The process is known as "composition-in-performance."

The medium allows for expansion, contraction, and variation while being grounded in formulaic repertoire within lines of twelve to seventeen syllables each—lines shaped by generous rules for determining vowel and syllable quantity. Formulaic repertoire would thus include everything from two- to three-word combinations to whole lines and pairs of lines, to set or recurring scenes—e.g., descriptions of daybreak and sunset, forms of address and response, the readying of sacrificial beasts, preparation of meals, yoking of chariots, launching of ships, elements of combat, and more. Whether a ship were "dark," "swift," or "hollow" may have been largely dictated by metrical convenience, but not necessarily so. Homer simply *worked* the medium, being neither its inventor nor slave.

It is for these reasons that contemporary translators err in seeking to vary or "diversify" Homeric formulae—thinking them static, repetitive, or lacking in ornament. They err in presuming to "improve" on an original that is both the *summa* of the Greek poetic tradition and the unique inspiration of all that followed. Theirs is yet another example of self over subject matter. It is sooner the case that Homer

> transformed the tradition, for . . . only a poet extremely conscious of the whole would have employed so much repetition, to which no other folk epic can offer a parallel. He saw the tradition could be exploited so as to turn its supposed defect into its greatest virtue. It gave him the means to combine the many and the one; display a massiveness that did not sacrifice delicacy; and thus achieve a balance between the generic and individual, uniformity and diversity, that has always been the despair of the inferior poets.

As C. S. Lewis remarks, the "unchanging recurrence" of Homeric diction is remarkable, "emphasizing the unchanging human environment." It is a diction that underscores the permanence and indifference—for better or worse—of the world as it is and how we confront it. "The sonorous syllables in which [Homer] has stereotyped the sea, the gods, the morning, or the mountains, make it appear we are dealing not with poetry about the things, but almost with the things themselves. . . . The general result of this is that Homer's poetry is, in an unusual degree, believable. . . ." Homeric pathos, says Lewis,

> comes from the clash between human emotions and the large indifferent background which the conventional epithets represent. . . . We must not think of Homer calculating [his] effects line by line as a modern poet might do. Once the diction has been established it works of itself. Almost anything the poet wants to say has only to be turned into this orthodox and ready-made diction and it becomes poetry.

Further, and by extension, notes classicist Charles Rowan Beye, "The hexameter line which ends invariably and so definitely with a disyllabic foot is as much a permanent facet of the poem as the invariable formulaic phrases. . . .

[T]he tension between the amorphous nature of human experience and the magisterial shape of the Homeric line is found everywhere repeated in Greek culture. . . ."

The flexibility of Homeric formulae is no less evident in the *Iliad*'s time span relative to its length. Though occupying approximately fifty days in the tenth and final year of the war—with several stretches narratively collapsed, e.g., "For nine days the god's arrows ranged throughout the camp"—the *Iliad* is over 15,600 lines long. Comparably short or shorter time spans could have been treated at equal length, resulting, hypothetically, in an Epic Cycle of staggering proportions—not unlike what has come to comprise India's two mammoth epics, the *Mahabharata* and *Ramayana* (the first alone at approximately 100,000 couplets, thirteen times greater than the *Iliad*). The *Iliad,* nonetheless, has a clearly defined beginning and end—the falling-out of Achilles and Agamemnon, and the funeral of Hector. Within such confines, it yet conveys a sense of the whole by seamlessly introduced retrospectives belonging to earlier parts of the war. These include the famed Catalogue of Ships (Book Two) and Helen's identification from the walls of Troy of principal Greek heroes, including her husband Menelaus (Book Three). For the epic treatment of an exceedingly brief time, we have James Joyce's *Ulysses,* based on Homer's *Odyssey,* and covering the events of a single day in the life of Leopold Bloom.

Audiences nurtured on oral storytelling were presumptively familiar, from one recitation to another, with the entirety of an epic narrative. A given narrative might begin at any point of the poet's choosing. Horace eventually codified the requirement as an epic conceit, noting that the Trojan War is not properly recounted "from the two eggs" (referring to Helen's birth). Rather, the poet "ever hurries to the action and, in the midst of things [*in medias res*], treating them as known, takes hold of his listener." The *Iliad* thus starts in the tenth year of the war, "from the time when the two [Agamemnon and Achilles] first stood apart in quarrel." Similarly, the *Odyssey* invokes the Muse to sing "of these events, from some point at least," so vast are the materials before the poet. The same applies to tales within the tale, as when Odysseus asks the Phaeacian bard, Demodocus, to sing a third song, *starting with* the Trojan Horse. "By directing his Muse to that place in the saga where he wishes to begin [Homer] reminds his auditors that the epic story is without beginning or end, that it is made of an infinite complex of events and people, all equally familiar to epic audiences." By contrast, cyclic narratives were generally far shorter, though covering greater time spans (and the more diffuse and flawed for that). Homer, assuming his historical existence, surpassed all others in delivering his narrative—at once perfectly composed and performed.

We now briefly consider Homeric meter with an eye toward archaic lyric, especially the lyric of Sappho. As mentioned earlier, though lyric is first attested only after Homer, Gregory Nagy persuasively argues that it is lyric meter that underlies Homeric hexameter.

The meter of what, until recently, were Sappho's two surviving poems (now four) is as follows:

Greek:

Ποικιλόθρον', ἀθάνατ' Ἀφρόδιτα,
παῖ Δίος, δολόπλοκε, λίσσομαί σε
μή μ' ἄσαισι μήδ ' ὀνίαισι δάμνα,
πότνια, θῦμον·

Translated:

Appareled in flowered allure, deathless,
deceiver, daughter of Zeus, Aphrodite,
subdue not nor destroy this heart, my lady,
with distress. . . .

Transliterated and scanned:

1 | 2 | 3
— ◡ — ◡ | — ◡ ◡ | — ◡ – –
Poikilóthron' | athanat' | Aphrodita,

4 | 5 | 6
— ◡ — ◡ | — ◡ ◡ | — ◡ — ◡
Pai Dios, do | loploke, | lissomai se,

7 | 8 | 9
— ◡ — ◡ | — ◡ ◡ | – ◡ — —
Mē m'assaisi | mēd' oni | aisi damna

| 10 | 11 |
|---|---|
| — ⏑⏑ | — ⏑ |
| Potnia, | thumon. |

Sapphic meter primarily consists of three lines of three feet each, each line eleven syllables, hence hendecasyllabic trimeter. The number of feet overall is also eleven. The first three lines of each stanza contain — ⏑ — ⏒ at the beginning and end, with an — ⏑ ⏑ in between. The fourth line replicates a hexametric close: — ⏑ ⏑ |— ⏒ . The meter is, further, *isosyllabic*, meaning it has an equal number of syllables in each foot, nowhere allowing the substitution of two shorts by a long, though the fourth and last syllable of any hendecasyllabic line may be either long or short. The rules for determining vowel quantity are the same as apply to the hexameter, earlier discussed. While the themes and diction of epic are older than those of lyric, the rigidity of lyric trimeter argues its own greater antiquity.

Epic hexameter, evolving over half a millennium, may itself have been isosyllabic at an early stage. Nagy shows that hexameter was likely an evolution from the Aeolic sixteen-beat, isosyllabic verse form preserved in the verse of Sappho's contemporary Alcaeus. Note that the line is predominantly dactylic, but without the hexameter's pervasive substitutions of a long for two shorts.

| 1 | 2 | 3 | 4 | 5 | 6 |
|---|---|---|---|---|---|
| — ⏒ | — ⏑ ⏑ | — ⏑ ⏑ | — ⏑ ⏑ | — ⏑ ⏑ | — ⏒ |

From the standpoint of substitution, the only flexible foot is the first, called the Aeolic base (Alcaeus coming from Lesbos, with its Aeolic dialect). The Aeolic base, in turn, was gradually restricted to — — and — ⏑ (rather than ⏑ — and ⏑ ⏑).

So, how might epic hexameter have developed from this predominantly hexametric but ultimately *lyric* line? The key is in a certain correspondence between the first foot of the lyric line and first foot of the epic line. In epic, observes Nagy, a first-foot spondee contains a full word on average once every ten lines. However, spondaic containment is far less common elsewhere in the line. The difference is apparent in the above-quoted third and fourth lines of the *Iliad*:

— — | — — | — — | — ⏑⏑ | — ⏑⏑ | — ⏑
pollas | d'iphthi | mous psu | chas Aï | di proï | apsen

— — | — — | — ⏑ ⏑ | — ⏑⏑ | — ⏑ ⏑ | — ⏑
(h)ērō | ōn, aut | ous de (h)e | lōria | teuche ku | nessin

Many a hero's sturdy soul did it hurl down
To Hell, the many themselves making meal for dogs
And banqueting for birds . . .

The spondaic *pollas* 'many' is contained in and by the first foot, whereas the following spondaic words *d'iphthimous psuchas* 'sturdy souls' extend from one foot to the next. So also is the extension from one foot to the next of the first word of the second line: *(h)ērō|ōn* 'of heroes'. The greater epic frequency of first-foot spondaic containment, Nagy urges, reflects the disyllabic Aeolic base of Alcaean meter. This same Alcaean meter eventually evolved through internal metric substitutions, i.e., the optional substitution of (1) a long by two shorts in the first foot; and (2) of two shorts by a long in the second, third, fourth, and fifth feet. The identical end rhythm — ⏑ ⏑ | — ⏓ shared by both Alcaean and Homeric verse, also closes Sappho's hendecasyllabic stanza (*potnia thumon* 'lady [my] heart'). The end rhythm was the likely bequest of a yet earlier metric source shared by both epic and lyric. We thus return to the initial proposition: lyric predates epic, though first attested only after it.

We have noted that classical quantitative verse seeks to avoid excessive coincidence between metric and spoken stress, between the emphases of time and beat. However, that such coincidence naturally results from English accentual verse need not render the result prosaic. Recall the "Sapphics" of Algernon Charles Swinburne (1837–1909), for whom Sappho was "simply nothing less—as she is certainly nothing more—than the greatest poet who ever was at all." There is a fine reciprocity in Swinburne's Sapphic imitations, of which Ezra Pound states: "The Greeks stimulated Swinburne; if he had defects, let us remember that, apart from Homer, the Greeks were often rather Swinburnian." We are not surprised that Swinburne's "Sapphics" caused a sensation when published:

1 2 3
/ ⌣ / ⌣ | / ⌣ ⌣ | / ⌣ / ⌣
All the night sleep | came not u|pon my eyelids,

4 5 6
/ ⌣ / ⌣ | / ⌣ ⌣ | / ⌣ / ⌣
Shed not dew, nor | shook nor un|closed a feather,

7 8 9
/ ⌣ / ⌣ | / ⌣ ⌣ | / ⌣ / ⌣
Yet with lips shut | close and with | eyes of iron

10 11
/ ⌣ ⌣ | / ⌣
Stood and be|held me.

Then to me so lying awake a vision
Came without sleep over the seas and touched me,
Softly touched my eyelids and lips; and I too,
Full of the vision,

Saw the white implacable Aphrodite,
Saw the hair unbound and the feet unsaddled
Shine as fire of sunset on Western waters;
Saw the reluctant

Feet, the straining plumes of the doves that drew her,
Looking always, looking with necks reverted,
Back to Lesbos, back to the hills where under
Shone Mytilene;

Heard the flying feet of the Loves behind her
Make a sudden thunder upon the waters,
As the thunder flung from the strong unclosing
Wings of a great wind.

The rhythm results from an ordering of words according to their natural stress, *eyelids* (1.1) always stressed on the first syllable, etc. Poetic and spoken stress thus coincide. However, the result is hardly prosaic, given the intensity of description and sense of the poet's own impassioned involvement. These are propelled by the large number of di- and polysyllabic words; conversely, by the absence of uneventful monosyllabic runs. There are monosyllables enough, but they are eventful, weighted; Swinburne breathing hard, rhythmically, throughout. The Sappho reincarnated in Swinburne is less an erotic than a "metrical essence." Swinburne's Greek, notes Rosanna Warren, "was excellent and, more than excellent, it was passionate, so that he writes the Sapphic stanza naturally, translating long and short syllables to stress with an ease scarcely ever matched in English."

Thus, in the literal sense of "translation" (*trans* + *latum*), Swinburne consummately "brings over" Sappho's quantitative meter into the only meter—a stress-based meter—English knows. Nor, of course, does it hurt that Swinburne, knowing Greek to a fare-thee-well, had internalized its rhythms. As in the case of Milton's blank verse, the driven, on-fire quality of Swinburne's metric, fueled by perfervid imagination, renders rhyme superfluous. Indeed, the Sappho translations surveyed in this volume—my own included—validate Warren's claim that "Sappho lives in English, not in any word-by-word reproduction of her texts, but in Swinburne's poems 'Sapphics' and 'Hendecasyllabics.'" Or, as put by one of Swinburne's contemporaries: "As the poet alone can truly interpret the poet for us, a study of Mr. Swinburne's paraphrases must remain our supreme guide to the character and writings of Sappho." Swinburne, however, is not the only claimant. "The silvery sweetness of [George] Herbert's [1593–1633] simple style," says author-critic Camille Paglia, "is exactly like Sappho's. If you want to know how Sappho sounds in Greek, don't read her pedestrian translators; read Herbert. Herbert discourages anything abrupt or emphatic—that is, masculine. Climactic speech is often ignored, restrained, or expelled. Herbert's world of contemplative serenity and whispery intimacies is androgynous." We do not normally think of Sappho in terms of androgyny, all indications pointing to her bisexuality. At the same time, grammatical indications of gender—in her two major surviving poems, at least—are postponed so as to render the poet/

speaker male *or* female only upon the near-final adjectival disclosures. Here too we are guided and beguiled by metrical considerations, since the masculine forms of the gender-disclosing adjectives are precluded by meter.

# Chapter 20

## Accentuation, Sound, and Word Order in Ancient Greek Poetry

> He lookd and saw a spacious Plaine, whereon
> Were Tents of various hue; by some were herds
> Of Cattel grazing: others, whence the sound
> Of Instruments that made melodious chime
> Was heard, of Harp and Organ; and who moovd
> Thir stops and chords was seen: his volant touch
> Instinct through all proportions low and high
> Fled and pursu'd transverse the resonant fugue.
>
> – *Paradise Lost*, 11.556–563

MUCH HAS BEEN WRITTEN about the accentuation and sound of ancient Greek, accompanied in recent decades by recordings thought best to convey it. Yet we will never really know how ancient Greek sounded, Greek poetry most of all, in which text, vocal intonation, music, and dance were all intertwined. We know even less how the different Greek dialects sounded to their own listeners; what a speaker of Attic in the fifth, fourth, or third centuries BC heard and appreciated in a poem of Sappho anywhere between one to three hundred years old; or even how much the original pronunciation might have changed in the interim. The strangeness to us of Greek or Latin poetic texts, especially lyric, is further apparent in the fact that an enlightened ancient listener or reader asorbed the experience as it unfolded, regardless the dialect or word order. Contemporary first-time readers of the Greek spend considerable time looking up words and sorting out syntax.

The closest we come to appreciating the effect of lyre-accompanied music is the description in the roughly contemporaneous *Homeric Hymn to Hermes*. The precocious trickster Hermes, at the tender age of one day old, steals Apollo's cattle and invents the lyre from a scooped-out tortoise shell. Hermes then connivingly assuages Apollo with his expertise on the newly invented instrument. The passage is unsurpassed in detailing the sound and effect of the lyre:

> Taking the lyre upon his left arm, he tested each string in turn with the plectrum; and the instrument resounded awesomely beneath his touch. Phoebus Apollo laughed, rejoicing; for the sweet throb of the wondrous sound did seize his heart and, as he listened, sweet longing possessed him. Then the son of Maia, strumming rapturously, took courage and stood to Apollo's left; and next, lifting his voice in song, played piercing melody. Beguiling was the sound that followed . . . and helpless the longing that seized Apollo's heart:
>
>> Slayer of oxen, meddler, contriver, comrade of the feast, you sing the worth of fifty cows, and I think our rift will be pleasantly mended. But come, tell me this, resourceful son of Maia, whether such wondrous works have been yours since birth or whether a god or some mortal gave you them—marvelous gifts—and taught you song divine. For wondrous is this sound new-uttered, the like of which I vow no man or god has ever known but you, knave, son of Zeus and Maia. What skill is this? What song for desperate cares? What way of song? In truth, one might at any time of three things choose—sweet slumbers, mirth, or love. For though I attend the Olympian Muses—whose love is twirling feet on the radiant path of song, enthralling chant, and the ravishment of flutes—yet never have I cared for skills as these at young men's revels as now I care for *this*. I marvel, O son of Zeus, at how sweetly you play!

Nonetheless, the sound of ancient Greek, to say nothing of ancient Greek poetry in performance, remains unknown. Further, though pronunciation varied with dialect and period, words in whichever Greek dialect were accentuated with either the acute (´), grave (`), or circumflex (^). In earliest times there was no spacing between written words. All words were printed in capitals and without accents, pronunciation being instinctive to native speakers. Introduced in the second century BC, accents and accentual terms guided foreigners in proper pronunciation. Greek accents originally indicated not so much a syllabic stress as a quasi-musical pitch. The acute signaled a rise in pitch; the grave, a fall; the circumflex (combining the two), a rise and fall. Accentuation of this kind was conducive neither to speaking nor to singing, but to the middle ground of intonation, or chanting, in the manner of a recitative. As ancient Greek shed its complexity, accents sooner indicated spoken stress than vocal intonation. Today, it is stress that predominates in the teaching and pronunciation of ancient Greek.

Ancient Greek poetry of all kinds was quantitative, its rhythm determined by the alternation of long and short vowel quantities, as seen—the longs, where falling, often overriding the intonational rise and fall of a word's natural or spoken accent; the shorts becoming long or the longs short, depending on subsequent consonants or word-initial vowels (all as earlier explained). Were this not enough, accents both changed and moved, depending on long-short vowel sequence within the same or adjacent words. Thus, a third-to-last-syllable acute (*ánthrōpos* 'man') changes to a second-to-last-syllable acute when the last syllable changes from short to long (*anthrṓpou* 'of the man'). In other cases, a circumflex changes to an acute; or an acute, if falling on a final syllable with a word immediately following, to a grave. There is thus a complex interplay among pitch/tone/accentuation and quantitative stress, here mentioned only briefly for purposes of basic explanation.

The point is that ancient Greeks were accustomed to hearing the same word differently pronounced in poetry versus prose, depending on vowel length and accent, and yet again differently pronounced or intoned from one dialect to another. These factors have placed the sound of ancient Greek poetry quite beyond reach or surmise—to say nothing of giving the lie to translators such as Paul Roche, who would "suggest the tone of Sappho's words"; or Guy Davenport, who would "give some idea of the variety within Sappho's verbal fabric: her flux of texture," or reflect "a little of her allusiveness, shift of tempos, subtleties of echo within technique or mood." To hear a reconstructed recitation of Sappho's poetry, as has been attempted, is to hear something beautiful indeed, if fittingly otherworldly.

The intricacies of Classical Greek abound, owing, among other things, to the richness of Greek verb formations. Ancient Greek verbs have six principal parts. The principal parts are the first-person singular forms that show the stems, or verbal roots, used in the different tenses, e.g., present active stem, future active stem, perfect passive stem, etc. This contrasts with four principal parts in Latin. For so-called regular verbs, the stems change under set rules. However, Greek verbs are frequently irregular in one or more principal parts. In such cases, the stem bears little or no resemblance to a preceding or following stem—as in *am, was, been,* one of the few English verbs exhibiting such peculiarity. Modern English, by contrast, is among the most regular of languages. Greek verbs have three different stems for the different aspects of past action: imperfect ('he was seeing'), aorist ('he saw'), and perfect ('he has seen'). The aorist (or past simple), both active and passive ('he saw'/'he was seen'), can have two different stems (so-called first and second aorist). Greek verbs undergo augmentation in past tenses, in the form of an *e*-prefix to stems beginning with a consonant—*luo* 'I free', *elusa* 'I freed'—or the lengthening of initial vowels (*a* or *e* to *ē*; *o* to *ō*). Verb stems otherwise reduplicate initial consonants—*leluka* 'I have freed', or augment reduplicated stems—*eleluka* 'I had freed'. Such constructions help to account for the polysyllabism of Greek, where English uses monosyllabic auxiliaries to establish tense and voice.

To the indicative and subjunctive moods, Greek adds a third: the optative, used for subordination in lieu of the subjunctive when the main verb is in a "secondary," i.e., past, tense. (In such cases Latin uses the imperfect instead of present subjunctive.) To the active and passive voices, Greek again adds a third: the middle, showing reflexive, self-interested, or frequentative action. To the singular and plural persons, Greek adds the dual, limited to two persons.

Ancient Greek also has a profusion of noun, adjective, and verbal inflections, or endings, designating grammatical function and relationship. This, as mentioned, allows the separation of adjectives from the nouns they modify, and the fairly at-will placement of verbs, all in a way unthinkable in English (though rather surviving in German). The opening two lines of the *Iliad* provide an example, at its simplest:

(wrath)
**Mēnin** | aeide, theā, Pēlēïadeo Achilēos

(accursed)
**oulomenēn** | (h)ē mūri' Achaiois ālge' ethēke.

> Sing, Goddess, the wrath of Peleus' son Achilles,
> Accursed, which caused the Achaeans unnumbered pains.

In the original, *wrath* and *accursed* appear at the start of their respective lines. It is yet clear, despite their separation, that they agree, both having a direct-object, feminine singular ending. At the same time, and unlike the "rhyming" endings in Theognis, these endings are not identical, since noun and adjective belong to different declensions. It is potentially unclear in English, however, whether *accursed,* so positioned, modifies *wrath* or *Achilles.* Translation of these dramatic opening lines thus invariably sacrifices the stand-alone emphasis of the original's *oulomenēn,* e.g., 'the/that accursed wrath'.

When the sacrifice does *not* occur, as in a recent line-for-line translation into iambic pentameter, the result can be stilted:

> Sing, goddess, of Peleus' son Achilles' anger,
> Ruinous, that caused the Greeks untold ordeals.

Here, *anger* appears at line-end position by default, given the lack of options in a foreshortened iambic pentameter—foreshortened because allowing only ten syllables per line for what Homer accomplishes in thirteen to seventeen. The resultant, and grammatically more certain, proximity of *anger* to *ruinous* (despite the effective alliteration) has been little worth the effort. The poem's key opening word—*anger*—is relegated to line-end position, while the clumped-together, proper-name possessives sit awkwardly on the ear and page. The line comes with the translator's special instruction: "When a polysyllabic proper noun ends in 's,' I form its possessive by adding only an apostrophe, which should not be read as adding a syllable or sound of any kind. For example, in the phrase 'Peleus' son Achilles' anger,' both names are read as if there were no apostrophes." This recent translation, by Herbert Jordan, sought to counter the "translation inflation" whereby "translators expanded the original [poem] by up to three thousand lines, which dilutes the immediacy of the original, one of its distinctive characteristics." However, the resultant iambic *constriction* does a disservice of its own, as Homer's thirteen-to-seventeen-syllable-per-line "immediacy" is of a quite different kind.

My own rendering is in twelve-syllable "alexandrines":

> The wrath, Goddess, sing of Peleus' son Achilles,
> Accursed, which caused the Achaeans unnumbered pains.

This version maintains a Greek-to-English line equivalence without awkward phrasing. It also clarifies grammatical relationships. It otherwise manages to keep the original's "Achaeans" instead of the usually more translation-friendly "Greeks." While "Accursed" might yet refer to Achilles, the alliterative forward movement allows for either construction, without delay or confusion to the first-time reader. Alternatively, the dramatically enjambed "Accursed" and ensuing relative pronoun urge the proper construction: "wrath . . . / Accursed, which. . . ." Were absolute clarity wanted, one might prefer, for example:

> The wrath, accursed, O goddess, sing, of Achilles,
> Peleus' son, the cause of countless Achaean pains.

But even that leaves it unclear whether *wrath* or *Achilles* is *the cause*. In any event, the lack of epic-opening drama in this formulation precisely illustrates the kinds of choices required in translation. It is, tellingly, as often at the cost of something in the original as in the target language that best advantage lies.

In sum, inflected languages allow for the intricate (yet always metric) interlocking of words, resulting in a richer texture than anything known to English verse or verse translation. The effect, in Nietzsche's famed formulation of the Roman lyricist Horace, "is in certain languages not to be hoped for":

> This mosaic of words, in which every word, by sound, by placing, and by meaning, spreads its influence to the right, to the left, and over the whole; this minimum in extent and number of symbols, this maximum thereby achieved in the effectiveness of the symbols, all this is Roman, and believe me, elegant par excellence.

And as amplified by Daniel Mendelsohn: "The energizing tension between the static 'mosaic' quality of the diction, which invites you to pause and admire every word, every stanza individually, and the forward-moving pull of his long arcs of thought is what gives Horatian verse its great distinction." What we lose in translating such poetry—is the original's "music, its cultural resonance, and the special pace at which it surrenders its information."

Finally, archaic Greek *poetry* was neither spoken nor sung, but intoned and chanted. The latter terms suit the congenial conflict between metric length/time/duration on the one hand, and natural stress/accent/beat on the other. The lyre player (*lurikos* 'lyricist') neither created lyrics nor set them to music. His melodies were not "accompaniment," but integral to the *poiēsis*, or 'making,' of the verse itself. The process—though the advent of writing was near, perhaps already at hand—was one of composition-in-performance, as with Homer. Performance was the verbal arrangement that partially but deftly superimposed metric length on natural stress, wherein lies the inimitable quality of ancient Greek poetry.

It is largely this tension that defines Greek poetry as *poetry*. The thrill is in hearing such poetry composed in and during performance, not in studying the result by midnight oil. Such poetry, hovering between speech and song, is addressed as much to the mind as to the ear. It was chant, of course, that aligned quantitative meter with music and music-in-performance. It was all one and the same. English and European poetic practice is far removed from such considerations, however much poems might ultimately be "put to music." Such being the impossibilities of capturing *anything* of ancient Greek poetry—its bare meaning aside—translator claims centering on the flow, spirit, mood, texture, or anything whatever of ancient Greek lyric ring hollow as the unstrung tortoise shell itself.

The caveat extends even to those who have studied and know the language well—for one can never really know ancient Greek. So contends Virginia Woolf in her essay "On Not Knowing Greek." Approaching the essay for the first time, one might think it a critique of the Greekless translator, or a lament for the general absence of Greek in school curricula. Woolf instead argues the impenetrability of ancient Greek (in particular Greek drama) even for those who claim to know it. As Woolf incisively observes,

> . . . [I]t is vain and foolish to talk of knowing Greek, since in our ignorance we should be at the bottom of any class of school boys, since we do not know how the words sounded, or where precisely we ought to laugh, or how the actors acted, and between this foreign people and ourselves there is not only difference of race and

> tongue but a tremendous breach of tradition. All the more strange, then, is it that we should wish to know Greek, try to know Greek, feel for ever drawn back to Greek, and be for ever making up some notion of the meaning of Greek, though from what incongruous odds and ends, with what slight resemblance of the real meaning of Greek, who shall say?

Woolf continues:

> We can never hope to get the whole fling of a sentence in Greek as we do in English. We cannot hear it, now dissonant, now harmonious, tossing sound from line to line across the page. We cannot pick up infallibly one by one all those minute signals by which a phrase is meant to hint, to turn, to live.

And, again, with specific reference to translators, and beyond:

> It is useless, then, to read Greek in translations. Translators can but offer us a vague equivalent; their language is necessarily full of echoes and associations.

A more sanguine view, perhaps, is taken by Woolf's contemporary Mary Stewart, opining on the necessity, if preferability, of translation. Even were it possible, claims Stewart, for everyone to study Greek, the pleasure of poetry in Greek would be nowhere comparable to that of Greek in good translation. Our own language is in every way as familiar to us as Greek is foreign, no matter how much studied:

> . . . no language can ever mean to us what our own language does, not even a modern, living tongue; and if this is true of a living tongue, what is to be said of a dead one. . . . For the English person the English language has a subtlety of meaning and richness of connotation that no other tongue can possibly have. It is bound up with experience, not only racial but personal. The power of a word is measured by myriad influences, drawn from every experience with which it may be associated in the mind of the individual. And the beauty of literature is so dependent on this unexpressed meaning of word and phrase we dare to say no original in a dead tongue could give to an English ear the aesthetic pleasure of a good translation.

Stewart's conclusion reflects the present and lasting state of affairs: "We may talk as we please about the beauty of the original and the impossibility of adequate translation, but the fact remains that for most of us it is translation or nothing."

# VI.

# Chapter 21

## Growing Latin from Greek Roots, Rome's Imperial Vision and Its Aftermath

> . . . our schoolmasters even today read Greek with Latin eyes. Greece, could we but approach it with eyes as young as its own, might renew our youth.
>
> – W. B. YEATS

IF HOMER AND THE LYRIC POETS are the *fons et origo* of Western literature, learning, and sensibility; if they have been constantly looked to, translated, and imitated from earliest times to our own, then it helps to know something of Greek literary influence and reception. I thus offer a brief discussion of Latin literature, from its beginnings—a translation of Homer's *Odyssey* (3rd century BC)—to its perfection in the Age of Augustus (c. 30 BC–14 AD). I emphasize Latin's *translatio* of Greek, which is not *translation* as we know it, but the transformative imitation of Greek models. More broadly, I emphasize the civilizing advances reflected in Latin *translatio* and in great literature generally. The topics range from Latin's signature use of alliteration to the Roman Empire as depicted in Virgil's *Aeneid* and beyond.

English-speaking culture has been influenced not so much by Greek directly as by Latin through its wholesale absorption of Greek. This has come to pass, notwithstanding Latin was still at a primitive stage when Greek reached its zenith in the fifth century BC. The influence is superficially, though tellingly, apparent in the conventional Latinization of Greek proper names—e.g., Callimachus rather than Kallimachos; Alcaeus rather than Alkaios—and in the generally favored use of Latin names instead of Greek, e.g., Jupiter or Jove for Zeus, Mercury for Hermes, Venus for Aphrodite, and the like. The Romanization of Greek antiquity, beginning with Rome itself, eventually achieved worldwide reception through the might, prestige, and administration of the Roman Empire. Here, according to British classicist F. L. Lucas, is what Rome initially lighted upon:

> Within seven centuries (c. 900–200 B.C., with most of it done in the last four) the [Greek] race invented for itself epic, elegy, lyric, tragedy, comedy, opera, pastoral, epigram, novel, democratic government, political and economic science, history, geography, philosophy, physics, and biology; and made revolutionary advances in architecture, sculpture, painting, music, oratory, mathematics, astronomy, medicine, anatomy, engineering, law, and war. One need not be a frenzied philhellene to find this a stupendous feat for a race whose home was only half the area of England and Wales (with a third of it barren) and whose most brilliant state, Attica [with its capital of Athens], was the size of Hertfordshire, with a free population (including children) of perhaps 160,000—less than Southampton.

Had Rome been unreceptive to Greek culture—as well it should have been, spurning the culture of a people it had conquered—we would have none of this. It is the counterintuitiveness of this unique development that underlies Horace's famous quip "conquered Greece her uncouth victor conquered, bearing arts to rustic Rome."

## I.

## Livius Andronicus: First Translator of Homer, First Translator of the West

According to the historian Thucydides, the Greek statesman, general, orator, and arts patron Pericles (c. 495–429 BC) was the "the first citizen of Athens." So great was Pericles's influence that the period in which he lived is known as the Age of Pericles. The Age of Pericles saw the flourishings of literature in the persons of Aeschylus, Sophocles, Euripides, Aristophanes, and Thucydides; and of Greek philosophical inquiry culminating in Socrates, Plato (429–347 BC), and others. Of the same age, though born in Asia Minor, was Herodotus, the "Father of History." Architecture and sculpture also reached extraordinary heights, Pericles turning a city of stone into marble. But what of Rome at this time? During the Golden Age of Greece, Rome was still in its political and cultural infancy, leaving us but "Old Latin" fragments of hymns, dirges, and epitaphs—and otherwise known for nothing more. Recall that the traditional foundation date of Rome, 753 BC—as supported by modern archaeological evidence—coincides with the flowering of Homeric epic. Rome was just aborning as the Homeric origin of both Greek literature and the Western literary tradition took root. Rome further had little to show for some centuries.

What Latin survived into the fifth century BC was likely incomprehensible to the earliest known Latin poet, the Greco-Italian dramatist Livius Andronicus (270–200 BC). Andronikos (in the Greek spelling) was a Greek brought to Italy as a prize of war, becoming the property of the Livii (i.e., members of the Livius family) and tutor of their children. Freed in exchange for his services, he followed custom by adopting his patron's name, and with his academic cast and Latin mastery, pursued a career in teaching.

While Homer was standard fare for the schools of Greece, there was nothing comparable in Rome. Livius thus prepared an abridged translation of Homer's *Odyssey*. The choice was well made. Homer had been a pervasive oral-poetic presence in Italic culture since the mid-eighth-century foundation of Rome itself, the presence supported by artistic evidence suggesting the then popularity of the Homeric poems. Moreover, in the story of Odysseus's return, Livius chose a subject with strong Italian geographic points of interest to Romans of the time. Predating the Trojan War itself was the founding of Pallantium, on the future site of Rome, by Evander of Arcadia in the central Peloponnese. Considered the first settler at Rome, Evander forged a legendary link between Rome and Greece. Before relocating to Italy, Evander had hosted Aeneas's father, Anchises, and a youthful King Priam of Troy, during their travels in Greece. Thus, by the time of Livius's Homer in the third century BC, Italy was receptive to all things Greek, which is to say to all things relating to the Trojan War, to its antecedents as well as its aftermath.

Livius's *Odussia*, however, was not in the dactylic hexameter of Homer, nor in any early Latin approximation of it, but in the unwieldy native-Italic Saturnian meter. "Saturnian" hints at the hoary antiquity of Saturn's reign (Saturn the Roman equivalent of Kronos, father of Zeus). The Saturnian was a perplexing meter of unknown origin, its principles no better understood by ancient grammarians than by scholars today. Its rhythm appears to have been *qualitative,* i.e., based on the patterned alternation of speech-stressed syllables, rather than *quantitative,* i.e., based on the alternation of long and short syllables. The Saturnian's eventual abandonment is generally ascribed to its difficulty and lack of prestige vis-à-vis the Homeric hexameter.

Approximately fifty lines of Livius's *Odussia* survive, together with various Saturnian epithets and inscriptions. Following Livius, however, and despite the success of his *Odussia,* the Saturnian fell into disuse. By the poet Horace's time in the first century BC, as we shall see, it persisted solely as a schoolboy torture. In the end, we must temper regret over Livius's choice of the Saturnian. An educated freedman and native speaker of Greek, Livius likely concluded that the Latin of his day was yet incapable of fully Homeric adaptation. Adapting the rhythm of inscriptional and official utterance—the Saturnian—to literary use, he gave his Homer a particularly Italic cast, while capitalizing on the fount of Greek literature. This was a strategic decision, marking a significant advance in Roman literacy and making Homer the source of Greek and Roman literature both. "Thus, part of the originality in translating epic is not just a matter of linguistic creativity, but also a matter of providing *origins* and strategies of legitimization for the current literary culture."

The first-known translator of the Western literary tradition, Livius grappled with the dilemma that would confront translators of the Classics to come: how best to render an ancient, highly regulated language into a different, less rigorous tongue? Adhere as closely as possible to the original's meter and form, or resort to whatever might yield the best result? If the latter, by what criteria has the effort succeeded? The issue today is yet more complex, embracing considerations of rhyme and translation from an inflected to a non-inflected language. Being unencumbered by such considerations, Livius's translation was also free of the idiomatic cast of his time. Of course, we have no way of knowing whether or in what way the Latin of Livius's day was idiomatic, or "current," compared to anything preceding it. More to the point, contemporaneity would not have been an issue. Homer's language was itself non-contemporary. It was in varying degrees *ancient* even in Homer's time—having developed over centuries—embedding archaisms, poeticisms, and various idiosyncrasies along the way. For this reason, as Livius would have appreciated, it was *artificial*—an amalgam of dialect forms, metric conventions, and phrases embedding well-established usages (i.e., formulae, as discussed). These were refined and customized over time for the composition and ultimately the preservation and transmission of Greek epic poetry—an *oral* poetry, improvisational within limits, relying on repeated performance for survival. Homeric language, codified as the language of epic, was as readily understood and serviceable in Livius's time as it had been in Homer's. Moreover, it retained the same serviceability for centuries to come—a language itself as timeless as the exploits and reputations it enshrined.

Homeric language, in all its stylization and artificiality, but at no cost to its simplicity, has long been termed a *Kunstsprache* 'art language'—that is, "an artificial idiom constructed out of archaic, dialectal, and invented forms, used both for their metrical utility and to give the effect of distancing the poetic language from everyday speech." So with Livius, and the earliest Latin poetry in general: one of the clearest compositional markers was "the exploitation of archaic morphology and lexicon, sometimes metrically motivated but also, as often in epic and tragedy, reflecting a desire to distance the language from everyday usage and to validate the enterprise through partial imitation of the stylized archaizing dictions of Homeric/Hellenistic epic and Athenian drama." Today's translators of epic and other classical genres have forgotten this lesson, intent on a "contemporary" idiom—or on how Homer would sound in English if he composed in English today. So much for timelessness.

Livius fully appreciated his place on the epic continuum. Little of his translation though we possess, we have enough to note artistic conventions reflecting Homer's own. Entirely new, Livius was engaged in an unprecedented venture. His method, however, was a reproach to what in the twentieth century would become the libertine injunction of Ezra Pound: "Make it new." Livius made it new precisely by making it old.

> When Livius Andronicus translated the *Odyssey* into Latin . . . he was extremely careful to keep Homer's "otherness" alive. To give the Romans an idea of the extent to which Homer's language was archaic, solemn and far removed from the present, he searched for words that were already considered old-fashioned in his own day. . . . Andronicus must have been a good scholar. Otherwise nothing would have

> prevented him from rewriting the Introduction to the *Odyssey*, putting in some Alexandrian Muses and making dozens of clever references to recondite Hellenistic poets. Andronicus had respect for the classics. He sensed that Homer's work was already something far removed from his own time, and he tried at every turn to emphasize Homer's otherness.

The first translator of the first literature into the first literary work of Rome appreciated Homer's pervasive antiquity, deeming it "of the essence." If Livius could not translate into Homer's hexameters, he could at least convey something of his author's manner through a judicious use of archaisms. Seeing how ingrained archaisms are and have been since the dawn of literature, we can only marvel, by contrast, at the cavalier attitudes of today's translators, with their colloquial, streetwise, or otherwise put-on idioms. Livius understood differently. He "bucked the trend," resisting the fashionable practices of Alexandria—then the literary center of the ancient world, the editorial center of the Homeric poems themselves, and disparager of Homer and Homeric-styled poetry as the literature of the future. Where Homer was concerned, Livius thus had a choice: adhere or renounce. Understanding both the needs and limitations of the moment, Livius adhered. He was not avant-garde, but derrière-garde—guardian of a precious tradition, the first anti-modernist, if you will (see further Chapters 25 and 34).

The translator into English must convey the vowel-rich polysyllabic cadences of Greek into an often brusque and consonant-laden English (Chapters 8 and 18). The problem, as suggested, is somewhat remedied by the use of Greek- and Latin-based vocabulary in English—a peculiar "giveback," allowing the Classics to be better conveyed and received in English. Livius, by contrast, was translating into a kindred Mediterranean language—already and ongoingly influenced by Greek—with its own inherent potential for Greek expressiveness. The surviving fragments of Livius's dramas are all in Greek meters, suggesting that Livius could have rendered Homer's *Odyssey*, however haltingly, into an equivalent Latin hexameter. Perhaps time and author were not yet right, or Latin not yet ready. Perhaps the need for what was essentially a school text preempted the more daunting task (which is not to credit the Saturnian for its ease). Choosing the Saturnian, Livius glossed what was inherently Greek in his Homeric original, launching Latin epic, whether by design or default, onto a distinctively Italic path. Its creation as a textbook notwithstanding, the *Odussia* was Livius's most famous work.

While Latin drama of the period is ever imitative of Greek models, Livius's *Odussia* is the first known *translation* of a literary—as opposed to legal or religious—text from Greek into Latin. Its loss is a loss for the history of the development of Latin, no less than for the appreciation of translation at the earliest known point in the Western literary tradition. It is further regrettable that no Roman poet ever ventured a more "contemporary" Latin translation of Homer into dactylic hexameters. The fact yet remains that Roman and subsequent Western literacy began with an act of translation, one returning to Homer at literature's very source. That the "Father of Latin Literature" began with translation is early validation of Ezra Pound's dictum that "a great age of literature is perhaps always a great age of translation," or in this case, that great or unprecedented translation is itself a great age of literature in the making.

## Naevius: First Author of an Epic Poem in Latin

Also living in the third century BC was Naevius, a dramatist and writer of epic. His scores of comedies, surviving only in fragments, were based on Greek models, but displayed a greater Italian infusion, since Naevius, unlike the Greek Livius, was native born. He was the first author of an epic poem in Latin, the *Bellum Punicum*—in Saturnian meter—concerning the first of Rome's three protracted Punic Wars with Carthage (264–146 BC). (The term *Punic* derives from Lat. *Punicus* 'Carthaginian', indicating the Carthaginians' Phoenician ancestry.) The contest was one for control of the Mediterranean, with Carthage (on the coast of modern-day Tunisia) facing Sicily (a major prize of the contest) and early controlling it. The Carthaginian commander of the First Punic War was Hamilcar Barca; and of the Second, his son Hannibal—famously crossing the Alps with elephants and occupying central Italy for the better part of fifteen years (until repelled). The Third Punic War ended in the destruction of Carthage itself (146 BC), fulfilling the battle cry of the Roman Senator Cato the Elder (234–149 BC): *Carthago est delenda* 'Carthage must be destroyed'. The threat of Carthage was threefold: size and strength, location, and governance. Aristotle in his

*Politics* (c. 330 BC), Book II, Chapter 11, singles out the constitution of Carthage as exemplary, placing it on a par with those of Sparta and Crete.

## Ennius: Rome's Homer Dreaming of Homer

The poet Ennius (239–169 BC) was the first author of Roman epic in hexameters. His *Annales* (*Annals*), of which some six hundred lines survive, covered Roman history from the fall of Troy to his own time. Ennius relates that Homer, appearing to him in a dream, said that Homer's soul now dwelt in Ennius's body. Roman critics exaggerated when they dubbed him a "second Homer," and, thinking as much of himself, Ennius was *nervosus* 'energetic' in preserving the posture. Though the poet Horace faults Ennius for his lack of gravitas, Cicero refers to Ennius as *ingeniosus poeta et auctor valde bonus* 'a creative poet and damn good author'. Ennius died secure enough in his reputation and at no time compromised by the use of his work as a school text. The *Annales* rendered hexameter the standard meter for Latin epic thereafter, with Ennius paramount in the genre until superseded by Virgil. Ennius had extensive knowledge of Alexandrian/Hellenistic works and, with Livius, is ranked a *grammaticus* in the teaching of Greek poetry. It is in this vein that Ennius obliquely refers to himself—by contrast to Naevius—as *dicti studiosus* 'learned of word', signaling philological self-awareness.

Though one senses an almost palpable relief in the long-awaited change from Saturnians to hexameters, the initial results, by later Virgilian standards, were far from spectacular:

> It goes without saying that Ennius wrote this difficult measure clumsily. Verse after verse jars on an ear trained by Virgil; some are pieces of prose, scanning in that they have the correct number of syllables, but totally devoid of rhythm.... Other lines are less atrocious than this, but offend the ear by too frequent coincidence of foot and word . . . or too much of that favorite Latin ornament, alliteration.... More instances of bad verses would be easy to find; yet the fact remains that Ennius, with no model to guide him, did manage, in a surprisingly large number of cases, to adapt the new meter to Latin, and at the same time, again and again, to hit on a happy arrangement of words, rhythmical and expressive, such as was in the future to form the vocabulary of Latin poetry. Horace, who was no admirer of early writers, had the good taste to point

> out that certain Ennian phrases were poetical in themselves, quite independently of meter.

Ennius thus effected a major advance in Latin prosody. His introduction of the hexameter so dominated that Livius was rewritten from Saturnians into hexameters, though we know not by whom. Of this effort, but five or six lines or line fragments survive in quotations from the grammarian Priscian (5th–6th centuries AD), with the attribution "Livius in his *Odyssey*."

Ennius's *Annales* set the precedent for Roman epic before Virgil and for the fundamental transformation of Roman epic that Virgil would accomplish. Indebted to Naevius's *Bellum Punicum*, Ennius's *Annales* was an "explicit and avowed attempt to create an Homeric epic on a Roman theme"—an "Homericization" of the early legends of Rome, replete with the story of Aeneas and its divine-heroic machinery; and from there, and with less mythologizing, an historical account down to Ennius's own time. The eighteen-book *Annales* was, in fact, predominately historical. Homer, remember, was not a historical author, making "the discrepancy between the Homeric and the historical aspects of the *Annales* [quite] glaring." Even as post-Homeric Greek epic from the Cycle onward marked a steady decline in quality (Chapter 13), there was yet no example combining history and myth in the jarring Latin manner.

"Ennius had simply ignored the problem of 'Homericizing' history: he had crudely joined Homeric mythology to an annalistic historical narrative (prosaic except for its hexameter rhythm) without apparently any feeling for the consequent clash of styles, epochs and ideas." To be sure, Ennius had a long string of epic-writing followers whose works have not survived. These continued, without aesthetic improvement, and with like disregard for the disparity between historical and epic styles, to "annalize" Roman history. As with the long-awaited change from Saturnians to hexameters, relief also arrived in the transition from Ennian to Virgilian epic. Virgil at last, and spectacularly, succeeded in both historicizing and Homericizing the Roman past. The *Aeneid*, as Brooks Otis announces on page one of his magisterial *Virgil: A Study in Civilized Poetry* (1963), was "a colossal *tour de force*, unprecedented in both its aim and execution"; a work astounding in its "novelty and . . . audacity." We will shortly return to this accomplishment.

## The Beginnings of Alliteration: Pounding the Hammer

We have just noted the criticism of "too much of that favorite Latin ornament, alliteration." The classic example of over-the-top alliteration is Ennius's own hexametric: *O Tite tute Tati tibi tanta, turanne, tulisti* 'Titus Tatius, with what travails have you tainted, O tyrant, your heart'; or in the idiom of an earlier time, 'Thyself to thyself, Titus Tatius the tyrant, thou tookest those terrible troubles'. It is alliteration of the Peter Piper variety, and one wonders whether Ennius himself could have taken it seriously. Alliteration of a similar kind was played to sidesplitting effect in the 1960s Broadway musical *A Funny Thing Happened on the Way to the Forum*. Upon the imagined death of his betrothed (actually a household slave in drag, strewn in a shroud before him), the *Miles Gloriosus* 'Braggart Soldier' proclaims, "And now my bridal bower is become a burial bier of bitter bereavement." Early Latin was indeed excessively alliterative, a feature with likely incantatory origins (Lat. *cano* 'sing') and, as always with alliteration, serving compositional and mnemonic ends. Marked alliteration also characterizes Old English *Beowulf* and other Germanic-based poetry. There is, however, nothing primitive or excessive about alliteration in *Beowulf*. Its three instances per line elevate alliteration to a compositional technique.

Early Latin alliteration resounds to the blacksmith's hammer. The verse is not "finished," but a work in progress, pounded out to the metric punctuation of its consonants. Homeric verse, by contrast, is of a seamless metric finish; "flow[ing] along freely and majestically, more like the great course of Nature, than any invention of man." It is "autochthonous," i.e., spontaneously sprung from the earth (as Athena, grown and fully armed from the forehead of Zeus). Overemphatic alliteration, as Ennius may have perceived, is quite absent from Homer—a poet conveying the burnished end product of the earliest, centuries-developed Greek poetry. Lacking no perfection when it first appeared, Homeric poetry had other, more subtle qualities both to commend it and to facilitate its composition-in-performance. The same also applies, with different considerations, to the lyric poetry first attested after Homer. Aware of and influenced by Homer, Greek lyric underwent a gestation before presenting *its* perfected fruits. Neither in Homer nor in the lyric poets is there evidence, as in Latin, of awkward developmental stages. The same applies to Greek Tragedy of the fifth century. No developmental stages and no models. As Sainte-Beuve has noted, "The Greeks, by peculiar good fortune and natural enlightenment of mind, had no classics but themselves."

## The Development of Alliteration: Plucking the Lyre

Effective alliteration is not slathered gloss or surface brightener. It *inheres* as a word-bonding element, mirroring or suggesting sympathetic association or analogy and, at its most effective, signifying or creating meaning. When alliteration suggests or creates analogy, it does so because the words, without necessarily sharing a common root, are themselves soundalikes, as so often in Latin: e.g., *flamma* 'flame'/*flumen* 'river'. The possibilities are immediately apparent in English, e.g., *flaming flow*. Another example is *aer* 'air'/*mare* 'sea'. Especially suggestive are the "foundational" soundalikes of *Rome*: *Roma* 'Rome'/*amor* 'love'/*Mavors* 'Mars' (*Mavors* with *m, a, o, r* = *amor/Roma; Mavors* with *M, ors* = *mors* 'death').

Such tendencies do not begin with Latin. "An interest in etymology, and especially the etymology of proper names, is found in all periods of Greek literature, reflecting a popular assumption that names are or should be somehow significant." In Plato's dialogue *Cratylus*, Cratylus urges that names, as all other words, exist by nature (*phusis*), and that there is thus an inherent relationship between the word (or sign) and what it designates (the signified). If this is not apparent in every case, the names/words have been corrupted over time (as explained by another of the dialogue's speakers). Following Plato (428–347 BC), the idea gains currency in Epicurus (341–270 BC) and his followers, including Lucretius (c. 99–55 BC), whose elaborate play between sound and meaning, revealing the inherence of a thing in its sound, has been aptly described as "atomistic poetics." Practicing what it preaches, Lucretius's *De Rerum Natura* abounds with verbal play and semantic association, as will be shown.

More than merely decorative or eye-catching, effective alliteration signifies or creates meaning. Thoreau notes a case in the especial pairing of *vir* 'man' and *virtus* 'virtue', since "the state of complete manhood is virtue." He notes in this connection that spoken language is too extemporaneous to yield anything of worth. On the other hand, "language in its settled form is the record of men's second thoughts; a more faithful utterance than they can momentarily give. . . . The analogies of words are never whimsical and meaningless, but stand for real likenesses." Being a "settled" similarity, the convergence of *vir* and *virtus* cannot be gratuitous. As words analogize to reinforce or create meaning, they signal or fulfill expectation. Such words are said to have a *semantic* association (Gr. *sēmaino* 'signal, signify'). This is a unique virtue (no pun intended) of Latin, which "offers words that simultaneously present themselves and their explanation. That should come as no surprise given that Latin is such a perfect language that it makes use only of words connected to the things they describe by a tie of complete and absolute necessity."

Thoreau's *vir/virtus,* and many other such etymologically derived examples, is association of one kind—*inbuilt,* as it were, because based on the same verbal root: a man (*vir*) shall always have virtue (*virtus*). The result is more compelling, however, in non-root-related words. First akin in sound alone, these become intrinsically kindred by contextual association. The effect reaches beyond soundalike coincidence or compatibility to associative resonance, indeed, to inescapable logic. And it is such logic, such *meaning,* that we regularly come to expect and relish.

A fine example at the start of the *Iliad* is *(F)anax andrōn Agamemnōn* 'Agamemnon king of men'. The amplitude of its five-times-recurring *a,* twice-recurring *ō* in word-final position, and five-times-recurring *n* conveys the desired sense and cadence of majesty. At the start of the *Odyssey* we find *all' oud' (h)ōs (h)etrarous erūsato* 'but not even thus did he save his companions', where Odysseus's 'companions' (*(h)etarous*) are semantically linked to their most grievous privation: that Odysseus did 'not' (*oud'*) 'save' (*erūsato*) them on their homeward voyage. The very name *Achilles* is a pronounced example of "thematic association between the Achilles figure and the notion of grief," premised on Proto-Indo-European **Akhí-lāuos* 'whose lāós [people] has ákhos' [pain]' = 'he who has the host of fighting men grieving'—which is precisely what Achilles "has" by withdrawing from battle. The association is apparent in the first two lines of the *Iliad,* beginning with the naming of the hero—"Sing, goddess, the wrath of Peleus' son *Achilles*"—followed by reference to (1) the *Achaeans,* i.e., Greeks (*Achaeans* also from *ákhos,* hence 'the Pained'); and (2) the thousands of *algea* 'pains' [sing. *algos* ~ *achos*] placed upon 'the Pained'. Thus, the *mēnin* 'wrath' of Achilles,

| | | | |
|---|---|---|---|
| (h)ē muri' | Achaiois | alge' | ethēke |
| which thousands | on the Achaeans | [of] pains | placed. |

The *Odyssey* also puns on its chief protagonist's name, but in a more "localized" fashion. As Odysseus is buffeted for a decade at sea, the presumption arises that he is scorned or hated by the gods. Seeking his safety, Athena ends her entreaty, early in Book One, with the question: *ti nu oi tosson* ***ōdussao,*** *Zeu;* 'Why have you so much **scorned** him, Zeus'? Or: 'Why, Zeus, has [Odysseus] been so **odious** to you?' The verbal play is based on Gr. *odussomai* 'I hate' (Lat. *Odi* 'I hate').

For purposes of Latin poetry, a consummate example is Lucretius's *It Ver et Venus et Veneris . . .* 'Comes Spring and Love and Love's [messenger, etc.]'. In the change of *Venus* (subject) to *Veneris* (possessive), Lucretius magically replicates, i.e., creates a resonance with, the preceding noun *Ver* 'spring': *Ver . . . Veneris.* The resonance is as much visual as auditory. The threefold alliterative *Ver . . . Venus . . . Veneris* alternates with the insistent *It . . . et . . . et.* How much more closely allied could the urgent arrival of Love and springtime be?

What follows amplifies the effect:

It Ver et Venus et Veneris praenuntius ante
pennatus graditur . . .

Comes Spring and Love; and Love's fore-messenger,
Wingèd, forges forth . . .

What panache. *Prae* 'before, ahead' here singularly combines with *nuntius* 'messenger' to richly alliterate *praenuntius* with *pennatus* 'wingèd'. *Praenuntius* 'fore-messenger' is a wondrously original locution for Venus's child, Cupid. *Pennatus,* containing the participle *natus* 'born' (from Lat. *nascor*), reinforces the kinship, both genial and generative, among Venus, Cupid, and Spring—as Cupid announces the season of Love and generative abundance. *Pennatus* further suggests *penitus* 'within, utterly, thoroughly' (Lat. *penetro* 'penetrate'), urging the reach, process, and completion of Love's work. Such associations are reinforced by a fragment attributed to Naevius: *penetrat penitus thalamoque potitur* 'he penetrates inward and takes charge of her bedroom'. Finally, the collocation *praenuntius ante /*

*pennatus*—the four letters of *ante* variously replicated to the adverb's either side—is no less remarkable than *It Ver et Venus et Veneris*. It is with a sense of release that we light upon the final aurally neutral *graditur*. The twelve-verse passage beginning with these words inspired Botticelli's *Allegory of Spring*, the only Lucretian-inspired painting of the Renaissance—the painting's right half seemingly based on Lucretius's description of seasonal progress.

Lucretius uses the words *praenuntius* and *pennatus* only here. Mindful of Lucretius, Virgil adapts the passage to describe the "generative" work of a negative kind; that of wingèd Rumor (*Fama*) generating fear and grief. In the process, Virgil drops the prefix *prae* and reduces the alliteration:

> interea pavidam volitans pennata per urbem
> nuntia Fama ruit . . .
>
> Meanwhile, the messenger, wingèd Rumor, flew
> ruinous through the fearful town . . .

and

> Et iam Fama volans, tanti praenuntia luctus . . .
>
> And Rumor, already aflight, fore-messenger
> of so much grief . . .

Indeed, the Latin poetry best reflecting these singular characteristics, and at such a qualitative remove from Ennius, is consistently that of Lucretius himself. His sound patterns teem with nature's own suggestive exuberance and interrelation, not merely creating meaning but providing auditory and structural analogues to cosmic principles. Thoreau the transcendentalist did not particularly warm to Lucretius the materialist. Adapting Lucretius to different ends, Virgil tempered his enthusiasms.

## Plautus and Terence: Comic Colloquial

The Roman playwright Plautus (254–184 BC), Ennius's older contemporary, has left us twenty comedies. Of these the two most famous are *Menaechmi* (*The Brothers Menaechmus*)—dealing with twins separated in youth—and the aforementioned *Miles Gloriosus* (*Braggart Soldier*). *Menaechmi*'s riffs on disguise, mistaken identity, cross-dressing, bumbling husbands and domineering wives, and conniving servants have left a rich dramatic legacy, including the plot of Shakespeare's *The Comedy of Errors* and *A Funny Thing Happened on the Way to the Forum. Miles Gloriosus* captures pomposity in a way unequaled since. It is just such a soldier who dominates in *A Funny Thing.* Early Roman comedy, as other Roman literary forms, was heavily indebted to Greek models and mores. Although the characters in *Miles Gloriosus* speak Latin, they are Greeks—with Greek names, clothing, and customs. The action occurs in Ephesus (see map), a Greek city on the central coast of west Asia Minor, famed for its Temple of Artemis (one of the Seven Wonders of the Ancient World). *Menaechmi* takes place in Syracuse, an early Greek-colonized city on the southeast coast of Sicily. Two major Mediterranean powers, Ephesus and Syracuse, lent highly cosmopolitan cachet to the farcical goings-on of Plautine comedy.

Although Plautus offers the earliest record of colloquial Latin, it may be misleading to dwell on Plautus's colloquialism. For one thing, his dialogue is metric (iambic: ⏑ — or trochaic: — ⏑ ), though less formally so than that of epic or tragedy. Further, there are many "poetic markers" in the colloquial mix. These include accumulated synonyms; archaizing, often for pseudo-tragic effect; the repetition of cognate or related words in close proximity (*figura etymologica*); and the perennial standbys, assonance and alliteration. Such features, it is thought, "often undermine any impression of real-life conversation"—of "colloquialism."

An "impression of real-life conversation" is, in any case, not especially comic, noteworthy, or ingenious, and may actually be beside the point. It is sooner noted that Plautus routinely adopted and adapted from Greek comedy, which places him squarely within present translational concerns:

> The chief significance of Plautine comedy is in demonstrating how far a "translator" can go in changing the form and content of his model. This is the first explosion of linguistic virtuosity in Roman literature, and Plautus' cavalier liberties taken with dramatic structure and characterisation are offset by the versatility of his lyric and dialogue metres and every kind of play on sound and sense in extravagantly stylised verbal fantasy. Translation as imitation has been superseded by exploitation of the model as vehicle for the Roman poet's personal idiom.

The point of comedy, in sum, and as exhibited at the earliest phase of Latin literature, is more *exuberance* than real-life similitude, exuberance confounding and re-creating the world in its own image. In this respect Plautus outdoes the staid (but perennially popular) "comedy of manners" of his predecessor Menander—the principal exemplar of Athenian New Comedy (4th–3rd centuries BC). Plautus rather harks back to the gamesomeness, though not the ethos, of the Old Comedy of Aristophanes (5th–4th centuries BC). Plautus, we might say, is comedy of manners on steroids.

The only other pre-Augustan playwright to survive in appreciable quantity is Terence (190–158 BC), who "by retreating from the unfettered verbal and stylistic exuberance of [Plautus], established a more restrained and formally consistent style that reflects, as far as we can tell, the Latin uses of the upper classes of the period." Though sharing certain Plautine features, Terence's style is marked, overall, by terseness, simplicity, and the absence of archaism. An early example of good Latinity, Terence was admired by Julius Caesar as *puri sermonis amator* 'lover of pure speech'. Whereas Plautus looked to Menander and New Comedy, Terence fully absorbed them. Terence is reported to have traveled to Greece for the express purpose of finding additional manuscripts of Menander.

Writing in an elevated style for a more sophisticated audience, Terence, on the one hand, "drained the color from comedy." This is early apparent from a "mixed review" in hexameters by Caesar—himself an acknowledged prose stylist, and for that reason often taught in high schools:

> You also, even you, are ranked among the highest, O diminutive Menander, and justly so, a lover of language undefiled [*puri sermonis amator*]. But would your graceful verse had force as well, to grow your comic verve in value equal to the Greeks'—and you, for that, escape all scorn. I am pained and torn, my Terence, for this one lapse of yours.

On the other hand, Terence gave Latin "*sermo*, informal conversation, and *contentio*, discourse streamlined for swift and forceful argument." In this last regard, Terence, as he is rhetorical, is also aphoristic and often quoted, even if unknowingly: e.g., *Fortes fortuna adiuvat* 'Fortune favors the brave'. His line *Homo sum: humani nil a me alienum puto* 'I am a man: I consider nothing of mankind foreign to me' has been translated into upward of one hundred languages and is often quoted by those espousing humanitarian causes. Its most famous incarnation is in John Donne (1572–1631):

> No man is an island, entire of itself; every man is a piece of the continent, a part of the main; if a clod be washed away by the sea, Europe is the less, as well as if a promontory were, as well as if a manor of thy friend's or of thine own were; **any man's death diminishes me, because I am involved in mankind**, and therefore never send to know for whom the bell tolls; it tolls for thee. [emphasis added]

Terence was a favorite of the eighteenth-century Enlightenment. President John Adams wrote his son (John Quincy) saying, "Terence is remarkable, for good morals, good taste, and good Latin. . . . His language has simplicity and an elegance that make him proper to be accurately studied as a model."

Terence had a running feud with his critics over charges of plagiarism. The feud is documented in the prologues to all six of his surviving plays, wherein the playwright self-defensively addresses his audience. One critic sees in these polemics—"offer[ing] the first body of systematic dramatic criticism in Latin"—the possibility of an implied criticism of Plautus. Under this scenario, Plautus's verbal pyrotechnics have blinded his admirers to his faults as a playwright—with Terence, the young, foreign-born parvenu, seeking to reform and refine the genre. The prologues in any event provide an early and well-developed record of an issue vexing authors to this day. This charge of plagiarism is of particular interest, coming in the second century BC, a century before the Latin imitation of Greek—with Latin's wholesale borrowings from and adaptations of Greek models—became the order of the day. We will never know what more than "plagiarism" was at the core of this ongoing and very public dispute.

### Fabled Alexandria in the Midst of It All

During the lifetimes of Livius, Naevius, and Ennius, the Egyptian city of Alexandria, the West's first metropolis (Gr. *mētēr* 'mother' + *polis* 'city') was the center of literature and of literary criticism and preservation. This followed from the conquests of Alexander the Great (4th century BC) and subsequent Hellenization of the ancient world. Founded in 331 BC, the city grew to become the largest in the known world, attracting an elite intelligentsia from all parts. Third-century Rome was to third-century Alexandria what seventh- and sixth-century Athens was to Lesbos and Asia Minor of the same period—a mere backwater.

Principal figures of the Alexandrian Age (3rd–1st centuries BC) included rival authors Callimachus of Cyrene (in Libya) and Apollonius of Rhodes; the Sicilian Theocritus, inventor of Greek bucolic poetry; and the critic-editor Zenodotus of Ephesus. The scholar-poet Callimachus was first to catalogue the holdings of the famous library at Alexandria, the catalogue a milestone in the preservation and study of Greek literature. The first librarian was the Greek grammarian and literary critic Zenodotus. Among other works on Homer, Zenodotus produced the first critical editions of the *Iliad* and *Odyssey*, based on a comparison of library manuscripts. None of his writings survives. His work on Homer was followed and improved on by Aristophanes of Byzantium (257–180 BC) and Aristarchus of Samothrace (c. 220–c. 143).

Apollonius, as noted, wrote the epic *Argonautica*. Four books in length, it is under 6,000 lines, compared to the more than 15,600 lines of Homer's *Iliad*. Apollonius thus complied, though writing epic, with the Alexandrian mandate of brevity. The *Argonautica* is the only completely surviving epic poem from the post-Homeric period until Virgil (a testament to its quality). And there is one surviving Roman *epyllion* 'little epic' in the highly mannered Alexandrian-influenced "Poem 64" of Catullus: a 408-hexameter epic treatment of the wedding of Peleus and Thetis. Written in hexameters and Homeric dialect some five hundred years after Homer, the *Argonautica* deals, by means of a lengthy excursus, with Jason's quest for the Golden Fleece. Jason, unlike his Homeric counterparts, is better in bed than in battle. His role as feckless user and amatory obsessive is apparent not only in his betrayal of Medea (though this occurs outside the *Argonautica*) but also in the very object of his quest, a golden sexually suggestive fleece (further spread on the bed when they consummate their union). Such change in emphasis bespeaks the change in outlook of the sophisticated, if jaded, metropolis that was Alexandria. Thus, while perpetuation of the lumbering Homeric ethos was out of the question, heroic exploits with a "modern" twist could be quite engaging.

Even so, the Alexandrian Age decidedly favored slighter or more modest poetic forms. Apollonius and his teacher Callimachus were in fact literary rivals: Apollonius the author of a Homeric-styled epic; Callimachus the author of smaller poetic forms, known especially for the adage *mega biblion mega kakon* 'a big book is a big evil'. Callimachus's major work *Aetia* (*Causes*) survives only in papyrus fragments and later quotations. A collection of elegiac poems in four books, it deals with the foundation of cities, religious ceremonies, and unusual local practices—all very recondite. The *Aetia* begins with a programmatic disavowal of epic and its themes. This literary conceit, first appearing in Callimachus, is called a *recusatio* 'refusal, declination'. It would be imitated by a number of Roman poets claiming to decline epic themes for more modest fare, all under Alexandrian influence. The *Aetia* concludes with the *Coma Berenices* 'Lock of Berenice', a fanciful narrative dealing with the ritual removal of a lock of hair from Berenice, wife of Ptolemy III of the then ruling Egyptian dynasty. The poem has been reconstructed from papyrus remains and exists in Latin translation, or adaptation, as "Poem 66" of Catullus. The theme has an early eighteenth-century incarnation in Alexander Pope's mock-heroic poem "The Rape of the Lock" (1712).

The Alexandrian poets are known as *neōteroi* 'neoterics', i.e., *new* poets, of which Callimachus was foremost. The period itself is known as neoteric. The practitioners were a Hellenistic avant-garde committed to small-scale (non-epic) poems on personal and sometimes recondite themes. Their concerns, following Athens's surrender to Sparta in the physically and morally draining aftermath of the Peloponnesian War (431–404 BC), were far removed from the "high confidence and established certainty" of fifth-century Athens and its empire. We sense in this an analogue to the rise of modernism following World War I (see Chapter 25). The key difference, however, is that the neoterics never abandoned form or formality, limiting their innovations to theme and treatment alone. The neoterics used varied meters; elegant, if contrived, diction and turns of phrase; and allusive imagery, all without surrendering form to content. Epic, too, if written, was, in good neoteric fashion, *subversive*, as in Jason's antiheroism and Apollonius's overall handling of traditional themes and language. The Roman poet Catullus was not alone in imitating Callimachus. Callimachus was extensively imitated and adapted over a two-hundred-and-fifty-year period by Roman poets ranging from Ennius to Ovid, the poet Propertius proclaiming himself the "Roman

Callimachus" and famously issuing his own *recusatio* of epic themes. The influence of Callimachus cannot be overstated, however much beyond the scope of this work.

## Recapitulation

Even as Latin literature was making its initial strides in the third century BC, the great ages of Homeric (8th century), lyric (7th and 6th centuries), and Classical Greek literature (5th century) had passed. Following the conquests of Alexander the Great (4th century), Alexandria became the literary and cultural center of the Mediterranean (3rd–1st centuries), the repository of Western learning, its editor and preserver. It is to the Alexandrian Age that we owe the first editings of Homer and preservation of much of the classical literature surviving today. Alexandria became the seat of neotericism, of "new" or "contemporary" poetic practice. Neotericism is especially evident in Catullus (1st century BC). The *neōteroi* were at once arcane and urbane in style. However, by contrast to the avant-garde of the last hundred years and more, they could not have conceived of content apart from form, or of other such free-verse aberrancies.

## II.

## Prelude to the Golden Age of Rome: Draining the Swamp

Latin did not reach its own golden age until the latter part of the first century BC with the poets Virgil, Horace, Propertius, Tibullus, and Ovid; and such prose writers as the historian Livy and architect-engineer Vitruvius. The period identified with this development is known as the Age of Augustus. It was Augustus, born Gaius Julius Octavius in 63 BC, who ended generations of bloody civil war with the defeat of Antony and Cleopatra at the battle of Actium (31 BC) (see map). Octavius (later called Octavianus) assumed the name Augustus in 27 BC, ruling as *imperator* 'emperor' until his death in 14 AD. The rule of Augustus effectively marked the end of the Roman Republic and start of the Roman Empire. The cultural groundwork for the Age of Augustus had been laid decades earlier, however, in and around the 80s BC, after Rome's conquest of Greece (146 BC). The same year also marked the victorious end of Rome's century-long conflict with Rome's challenger for control of the Mediterranean, Carthage. In short, the year was a milestone in Rome's consolidation of power, even as it marked Rome's turn to refinement. Horace directly correlates the end of the Punic Wars with the first serious Roman imitations of Greek literary models:

> For the Roman was late to turn his acumen to Greek, and after the Punic Wars began to ask, at ease, what Sophocles, Thespis, and Aeschylus might offer. He also made assay, if he might turn the matter out, and was pleased with the result, by nature keen and lofty-minded. For he has ample tragic spirit and derring-do, but sadly fears erasure and thinks it shameful.

Following 146 BC, Greek books and artifacts (most plundered) were readily available in Rome. Travel to Greece and the study of Greek language and culture became elitist pastimes. Greek tutors catered to those at home. Aware of its impoverishment in cultural matters, Rome became willingly subservient to Greece. The reality occasioned Horace's quip (as noted) that "conquered Greece her uncouth victor conquered, bearing arts to rustic Rome." Horace relates this development to what he metaphorically calls "drainage of the Saturnian swamp" (noting that the Saturnian meter yet lingered into his own time).

As classical Rome absorbed Greece, so English-speaking culture would eventually do the same through its own absorption of Rome. It was Dryden, Pope, Swift, Defoe, Addison, and Steele who defined the Augustan Age of eighteenth-century England, also known as neoclassicism, the Age of Reason, or the Enlightenment. It was an urbane time, a time of striving for harmony and precision through a second grand round of imitations of classical models—Virgil and Horace foremost among the imitated; Virgil and Homer foremost among the translated.

Classicization was also the goal of the sixteenth-century French Renaissance poets known as La Pléiade, who sought a vernacular literature based on Greek and Latin models, including the lyricists Alcaeus, Anacreon, Pindar, and Horace, and the epic poets Virgil and Ovid. The name *Pléiade* was based on the original "Pleiad" of seven Alexandrian poets and tragedians, corresponding to the seven stars of the Pleiades cluster. The French were at once emulatory and incorporative, as had been the Romans in their absorption of Greek authors and culture. The Renaissance further provided a bridge to the past, as noted by Ezra Pound (with a possibly Horatian echo), by the "determined attempts of the patriotic Latinists of Italy . . . to 'conquer' Greek by putting every Greek author effectively into Latin"—a process resulting in the proliferation of Latin cribs. By 1820, says Pound, the disuse of Latin cribs for the study of Greek resulted in "no end of damage to the general distribution of 'classical culture.'"

The Roman Augustan poets took inspiration from Greek models dating half a millennium earlier and more. The chronological reach can only amaze, underscoring as it does the centuries-long absence of anything closer in time or tongue. They conceded the shortcomings of Latin and its resources. Rome's admiration of Greece, combined with the admission of its own cultural impoverishment, became a literary conceit, as Latin poets sought to claim priority in doing for Latin what their Greek predecessors had done for Greek. The result was an Augustan Age comparable for Latin to what the Age of Pericles had been for Greek. Following the Augustan Age, Latin authors could look to their own models.

### Virgil: the Meaning and Method of *Translatio*

We turn first to Virgil (70–19 BC), the quintessence of Latin poetry, master imitator-transformer-creator, and fount of the English literary tradition to come. As Virgil was not a translator of Greek, we do well to note the meaning of *translation* (Lat. *translatio*), the better to grasp the nature of Virgil's accomplishment. Our own understanding of the word entails a rendering from one language to another, suitable in form and tenor, and, to the extent possible, combining faithfulness to the original with a fluency and distinction of its own. This is the literary—versus the literal or prose—translation of poetry. More than this, the word *translation* means 'brought across' (Lat. *trans* + *latum*).

Those who have studied Latin recall that verbs have four principal parts, each providing a particular "stem," stems allowing for the construction of verb forms in the various tenses (present, past, etc.), voices (active, passive), and moods (indicative, subjunctive, infinitive, etc.). Thus, for a regular verb of the first conjugation:

*porto,* I carry
*portare,* to carry
*portavi,* I carried
*portatum,* (having been) carried

However, the verb from which "trans*lat*ion" comes is the irregular verb:

*fero,* I bring
*ferre,* to bring
*tuli,* I brought
*latum,* (having been) brought

*Transfer* and *translate* derive from the same compound verb: *transfero/ translatum* 'bring over'/'brought over'. However, Latin *translatio* 'a bringing over', did not signify the transfer of meaning from one language to another, but the importation and reworking of materials from one culture to another, in this case from Greek to Latin. The process was essentially one of *transmutation*—spurred by the spirit of emulation. Virgil supremely emulated rather than translated Homer. In the Augustan period of eighteenth-century England, Dryden would supremely translate rather than emulate Virgil.

While we may regret that Virgil never translated Homer, his *translatio* is yet more impressive, involving not Homer's language as such, but Homer's materials and manner, and the historicizing of Homeric epic toward Roman and ultimately *civilizing* ends. That Virgil's *Aeneid* is civilizational is key to its understanding, as conveyed in the already referenced work of Brooks Otis, *Virgil: A Study in Civilized Poetry*. What Virgil first "brought over" was Aeneas, "transferring" him from fallen Troy to ascendant Rome. This is the sense indicated by the Italian Renaissance commentator Marcus Vida. Vida uses the third principal part of *transfero*—*transtulit* '(he) bore across (to)'—to indicate Virgil's transplantational success:

So Trees, that change their Soils, more proudly rise,
And lift their spreading Honours to the Skies;
And, when transplanted, nobler Fruits produce,
Exalt their Nature, and ferment their Juice.
So Troy's fam'd Chief [Aeneas] the Asian Empire bore [***transtulit***]
With better Omens to the Latian Shore . . .

*Translatio* in this sense is the *transfer* or transplant of traditional materials, the "cultivation and improvement" of one's native literary soil. As the Roman grammarian and Neoplatonist scholar Macrobius (4th–5th centuries AD) observed, "What the earlier poet [Homer] had uttered, he [Virgil], by bringing over [*transferendo*] made so much his own that it is believed to be his." Which is to say that Virgil, even as he emulated, imitated, and transferred, yet remained entirely original. The result, in Macrobius's view, was an *Aeneid* in Homer's image, an *Aeneid* crucially and creditably imbued with Homeric authority. Virgil worked the same process on his own Latin forebears, winning praise from Macrobius "for his artistic judgment in improving the old writers of Rome."

Virgil thus "grafted" from the works of Homer, Hesiod, and Theocritus in his *Aeneid, Georgics,* and *Eclogues,* respectively. For Aeneas's abandonment of Dido in Book Four of the *Aeneid,* Virgil looked to various accounts of Jason and Medea, including Apollonius's *Argonautica* and Catullus's Poem 64. In patterning his *Aeneid* on the *Iliad* and *Odyssey,* Virgil emulated Homer through an act of transformative imitation. His *Aeneid,* in just under 10,000 verses, relates Aeneas's founding of Rome after his flight from Troy and subsequent wanderings (the Odyssean *Aeneid*), and conquest of the inhabitants of a prehistoric Italy (the Iliadic *Aeneid*). The two themes are announced in the poem's opening words, *Arma virumque cano* 'I sing of arms and the man' (Gr. *andra* 'man' being the first word of the *Odyssey*: *andra moi enepe Mousa* 'The man to me sing, O Muse'). Virgil does not merely raise Rome from the ashes of Troy: he raises the greatest city *to be* from the greatest city that *was*; the world's greatest hope from its greatest catastrophe. Aeneas's survival of the ultimate catastrophe presages the survival, and ultimate success, of the resultant enterprise. Only survivors fulfill destinies. As the *Odyssey* charts its hero's homecoming voyage, and the *Aeneid* its hero's home-*founding* voyage, the Odyssean *Aeneid* is at once imitative and critically transformative of Homer.

The *Aeneid* conveys a supreme vision of empire as collective destiny. "That we refer our culture to [Virgil] and not to Homer is not an accident but a necessity of history. Ithaca is small, but Rome is Rome; and every nation that has sprung from Rome has always kept it in view." The slighting reference to Odysseus's island kingdom of Ithaca highlights the *Aeneid*'s more moral, historical, and civilizing vision. Odysseus returns home alone, having lost—much to his blame—all his companions. His mission then becomes one of entirely personal revenge against Penelope's suitors. His wanderings, all fictive, are forever gone and forgotten. Aeneas, by contrast, brings his past and future countrymen safely to Italy. His mission is to found a nation, fulfill a destiny—though the destiny, as with any great enterprise, is not untainted. Odysseus seeks the stability of home; Aeneas suffers the plight of building a new one. Odysseus is self-interested; Aeneas, self-sacrificing. Virgil's message and vision are thus paramount to the civilizing enterprise—albeit civilization at a cost to oneself and others. So is it ever.

In what way tainted and at a cost? At the end of the *Aeneid*, Aeneas slays Turnus—King of the Rutulians and Latium's mightiest defender—in a scene modeled on Achilles's slaying of Hector, defender of Troy. Hector of course is destined to fall to Achilles, as is Turnus to Aeneas. In narratively parallel terms, Achilles slays Hector to avenge Hector's slaying of Achilles's companion Patroclus; Aeneas slays Turnus to avenge Turnus's slaying of Pallas, the young son of Aeneas's ally Evander. The killing of Turnus in Book Twelve is the culmination of Aeneas's increasingly furious rampage after the death of Pallas in Book Ten. When Aeneas sees Pallas's sword-belt, taken as an ornament by Turnus, he drives his weapon home, giving vent both to revenge and a sense of duty to Evander. Killing Turnus, Aeneas has neglected the injunction of his father, Anchises, prophesying the greatness of Rome: "to spare the humbled, but strike the defiant down." The humbled Turnus, it is argued, deserved better of Aeneas, and Aeneas better of himself. The imperial enterprise is from the outset infused with the fury and rage it was intended to supplant. It is often noted in this connection that the Latin verb *condo* 'erect, found, store, place' is used at the beginning of the *Aeneid* to describe the 'founding' of Rome, and at the end to describe the 'storing' of Aeneas's sword beneath Turnus's heart.

Civilization is thus a conflictedly founded, if also a conflictedly beneficial, enterprise—particularly so in the case of Rome, as it would seem. In addition to Aeneas's arguable failure of self, Rome's beginnings were otherwise tainted. As the historian Livy records, the city was founded in an act of fratricide: Romulus killing Remus in an argument over the site of Rome itself. Rome was at first sufficiently populated only by an ingathering of riffraff and by the rape of the Sabine women. That the imperial enterprise was ultimately beneficial despite such sordid beginnings is further discussed below.

One thing is, however, certain: after Virgil our sense both of civilization and epic would never be the same. In response to Virgil's transformational achievement, C. S. Lewis coined the term "Secondary Epic." The term designates (without perjorative intent)

> a fundamental shift in the poetic understanding of epic composition. After the *Aeneid,* an epic worthy of that name had to take a single great theme, and, for that reason, Virgil's poetry could not be seen as merely derivative of Homer. Rather the *Aeneid* began a new tradition of epic that culminated in Milton's *Paradise Lost.*

The kind of greatness embodied in the *Aeneid* and *Paradise Lost* arises only when

> some event can be held to effect a profound and more or less permanent change in the history of the world, as the founding of Rome did, or still more, the fall of man. Before any event can have that significance, history must have some degree of pattern, some design. The mere endless up and down, the constant aimless alternation of glory and misery, which make up the terrible phenomenon called a Heroic Age, admit to no such design.

*Paradise Lost* would be the last great epic in the English language, the history of English poetry from Virgil to Milton charted with reference to the translation and adaptation of Virgil.

### Virgil: Epic Historicized for the British Empire

Virgil's great theme, unlike anything in Homer, is *historical*—empire, imperial family, worldwide battle, moral responsibility, national destiny—as it would continue to be for English epic thereafter. And if not empire, as in Milton, then empyrean, the Lord God of Hosts, Heaven's battles, moral culpability, and human destiny. With a more serious theme and more morally accountable hero, Virgil was preferred to Homer throughout the Middle Ages and Renaissance. "But a man, an adult, is precisely what [Aeneas] is: Achilles had been little more than a passionate boy. . . . With Virgil European poetry grows up." It grows up because it takes growth at the highest levels—historical growth, the destiny of nations, and the progress of humankind its themes.

Nowhere is such growth more firmly rooted than in Edmund Spenser's *The Faerie Queene* (1596), to which we will now briefly turn. Where Homer and Virgil (for all the latter's historicizing) seek inspiration by generic invocation of "the Muse" or "Goddess," Spenser's muse—"Helpe then, O holy Virgin, chiefe of mine"—is Clio, muse of history. Spenser's *The Faerie Queene* celebrates the Tudor dynasty and its stewardship of England, as Virgil's *Aeneid* celebrates the Julian clan and Roman *imperium*—the Tudors and Julians all divinely ordained and their histories idealized through poetry. Rome's glorious progeny is foretold Aeneas by his father, Anchises, in an underworld encounter, even as England's illustrious descendants are foretold by Merlin through Britomart (by marriage to Artegal). "The association of Britomart's name with British martiality, and thus her identification with Elizabeth I (the poem's "Gloriana") is unavoidable." Spenser further makes Brute aka Brutus, grandson of Aeneas, the founder of England and progenitor of the British monarchic line culminating in Elizabeth—thereby placing the mantle of imperial Rome on England's shoulders (the genealogy strengthened by the *Brut-/Brit-* wordplay, cf. *Britomart*). In Book I, Sir Guyon, embodying the virtue of temperance, is significantly modeled on Aeneas, to say nothing of the Proem to Book I, "suggest[ing] that the discovery of the New World provides the rationale for Spenser's entire poetic enterprise in *The Faerie Queene*." By these and other means, Spenser effects a *translatio imperii* 'transference of rule' from Rome to Britain, similar in literary-historical terms to Virgil's transference of Homer from epic tale to national narrative. Indeed, from Julius Caesar's initial incursions (55–54 BC) to the Emperor Claudius's first significant campaign of conquest (43 AD) to expansion and consolidation under Vespasian and Domitian (69–96 AD), and long thereafter (until c. 410 AD), Britain passed from a collection of self-protecting client kingdoms of Rome to an increasingly subject Roman province. Britain learned the lessons of imperial rule from its Roman rulers, themselves rulers of the known world. Thus was "colonization . . . almost hardwired into the English psyche. . . . Classical comparison functioned to legitimize the whole imperial project, from the military to the cultural."

Spenser dedicated the 1596 edition of *The Faerie Queene* to Elizabeth I (the "Virgin Queen"): THE MOST HIGH, MIGHTIE AND MAGNIFICENT EMPRESS . . . OF ENGLAND FRANCE AND IRELAND AND OF VIRGINIA. "The high idealism of this dedication is suggested by the inclusion of Virginia in the old formula of the monarch's 'empire.'" The question has thus long persisted of how much more than a mere ideal the notion of empire was during Elizabeth's reign, and what the poem's dedicatory inclusion of Virginia portends. Whatever else *The Faerie Queene*'s allegorical intent, Spenserian literary allusion evidences imperial prompting, if possibly ambition, in the years preceding the poem's publication.

We noted Merlin's foretelling England's illustrious pedigree to Britomart, as Anchises foretold Rome's to Aeneas. The scene in the *Aeneid* is situated in the underworld, albeit in Elysium, the part of Tartarus inhabited by the righteous. Merlin's abode of Cairmardin is as frightful as anything Virgil's Tartarus might offer, providing a comparable locale for prophecy. Aeneas and Britomart both journey to their respective prophetic rendezvous (such locales are never nearby). Merlin foretells Britomart's descendants ending in Elizabeth, as Anchises foretells Aeneas's descendants ending in Augustus. And as Aeneas is Trojan, so shall Britomart's offspring, by association, "spring, out of *Troian* blood." Britomart's issue will recollect the *Peres* 'champions' of Greece and Troy, and by extension, of the Rome that came from Troy (and absorbed Greece):

For so must all things excellent begin,
And eke enrooted deepe must be that Tree,
Whose big embodied braunches shall not lin,
Till they to heauens hight forth stretched bee.
For from thy wombe a famous Progenee
Shall spring, out of the auncient Troian blood,
Which shall reuiue the sleeping memoree
Of those same antique Peres, the heauens brood,
Which *Greeke* and *Asian* riuers stained with their blood.

In fact, Troy was first reborn when Aeneas founded Rome, and for a second time reborn when his grandson, Brute, founded New Troy, or *Troynouant*:

For noble *Britons* sprong from *Troians* bold
And *Troynounat* was built of old *Troyes* ashes cold . . .

And *Troy* againe out of her dust was reared,
To sitt in second seat of soueraine king,
Of all the world under her gouerning.

But a third kingdom yet is to arise,
Out of the *Troians* scattered offspring,
That in all glory and great enterprise,
Both first and second *Troy* shall dare to equalise.

Roman pedigree determines Britain's imperial destiny:

Renowned kings, and sacred Emperours,
Thy fruitfull Ofspring, shall from thee descend;
Braue Captaines, and most mighty warriours,
That shall their conquests through all lands extend,
And their decayed kingdomes shall amend:
The feeble Britons, broken with long warre,
They shall vpreare, and mightily defend
Against their forren foe, that comes from farre,
Till vniuersall peace compound all ciuill iarre.

Merlin here foresees "conquests [that] through lands extend," their goal being universal peace. The programme is precisely that urged by Jupiter to Juno, and by Anchises to Aeneas:

Jupiter to Juno (extent of conquest):
But now (since care consumes you, I shall speak
more fully and reveal Fate's hidden page)
he'll wage hard war in Italy; savage tribes
he must defeat, and give them towns and laws . . .

For [the Romans] I set no bounds of place or time;
rule without end I grant them. Juno, too . . .
shall come to better mind, and with me bless
the Romans, lords of the world, the toga'd race . . .

Anchises to Aeneas (mandate of peace):
You, Roman, remember: Govern! Rule the world!
These are your arts! Make peace man's way of life;
spare the humble but strike the defiant down.

The first English epic, Spenser's *The Faerie Queene* is designedly an epic of England. Rooted in the nationalism of Virgil's *Aeneid,* it is also galvanized by the words of Virgil's fourth Eclogue, words "which have never been forgotten in the history of the West": *iam redit et virgo, redeunt Saturnia regna* 'now returns the virgin, returns the Saturnian reign'. Written before the birth of Christ, the fourth Eclogue foretells the birth of a child, harbinger of a Golden Age. Under the child's tutelage, *magnus ab integro saeclorum nascitur ordo* 'the great order of ages is born anew'. The prediction looked, in the first instance, to Augustus's restoration of order in the aftermath of protracted civil war. Recalling Isaiah's prophecy of a "maiden who will give birth," the prediction was next deemed Christological. As concerns Elizabeth I (the "Virgin Queen"), the words sanctioned Tudor imperialism looking to a new world order through Elizabeth's own restoration of the Golden Age of the god Saturn.

From its first stirrings under Elizabeth, Britain would seek not only to imitate Rome but to stand unrivaled as its English competitor. Britain would be the largest empire in history and, for over a century, the world's foremost global power. By the early twentieth century it would rule approximately a fifth the world's population and cover a quarter of its total landmass—to be depleted in World War II, even as its onetime rival Spain was eclipsed in the Spanish American War (1898). Rome lived on in Britain, and British writers legitimized their empire by recourse to Rome. Spenser anticipated more than he could have imagined—and Virgil no less so.

The Rome of Virgil's day was *metropolis* 'Mother City': empire as a generative and nurturing source, teeming and eternal. "Its people were the people of God, their *maiestas* ['majesty'] indestructible." The preordained rise of the West's then greatest, and first great, city expands upon the Old Testament premise of Israel as a chosen people with an historical mandate—a "light unto the nations"—centered in the holy city of Jerusalem. Aeneas, like the biblical Israelites, is a foreign transplant overcoming a native population. So also the first English arrivals to America. Nor has Rome's trajectory lacked for recent example. Consistently with Spenser's *translatio imperii* from Rome's *imperium sine fine* 'rule without end', expansive power has fueled British no less than American notions of exceptionalism. It made Britain the greatest modern *imperium* since Rome, the "empire on which the sun never sets"; and America, by Manifest Destiny, a nation "from sea to shining sea."

## Virgil: Historicizing Empire for the World

Greece is the bedrock of Western civilization, and Rome its soil—the sources of the West's languages, literatures, laws, architecture, science, and philosophy. The American Founders, aspiring to the ideals of Republican Rome, established a constitutional democracy resulting in the freest and most enduring, most prosperous and powerful governance the world has ever known. The American republic, at first isolationist, aspired in time to empire—if not militaristic, then commercial, economic, or cultural. Its nineteenth-century acquisitions from Mexico and Spain aside, imperial America dates to the early twentieth century. A reluctant entrant into both World Wars, America had empire largely thrust upon it. What, then, of empire in a penitent "postcolonial" and politically correct age—and empire's vilification (and now, *self*-vilification), given its Roman paradigm?

Empire is motivated by the collective need of a sense of security and well being. Empire is to the nation, its growth and increase, what livelihood is to the individual. One can never have enough. "Greed was always more important than uplift in inducing the European diaspora," notes Arthur M. Schlesinger, Jr., "and what in earlier centuries was the rapacity of individual adventurers seeking spices, gold, and furs began in the late nineteenth century to be accounted as a blessing for the nation as a whole." On the upside, the abundances of wealth in expansionist/capitalist societies are often used for lifesaving, philanthropic, artistic, and other civilizational ends—there being scant resources otherwise.

The United States, for whatever criticism is brought to bear, has done more good for the world overall than have all the world's other countries combined. It also remains, not incidentally, the epic journeying point for those seeking freedom and new lives. This is neither to forget nor forgive the failures of U.S. policy, including post–World War II interventions, military and political, that have proven disastrous. Nonetheless, as the United States has been the most prosperous, it has also been the most altruistic and beneficent of imperialists—whether altruistic for "uplift" or strategic purposes is irrelevant. The complaint against American empire ignores this reality—as it ignores the fact that history is essentially a land grab, whether by design or default; that self-interest and the perception of threatened security are as inescapable as are the tolls they exact severe. Accomplishing much good and much evil, as does any assertive endeavor, empire, for the *good* it has done, has little for which to apologize. The modern case in point is colonized India, despite Britain's massive blunders and miscalculations along the way—and on the way *out*. At the opposite extreme is the Congo Free State (1877–1908) under the rule of Belgium's King Leopold II, standing at the exampled forefront of unredeemedly venal exploitation and murderous brutality. The mixed verdict on empire is reminiscent of the Choice of Heracles/Hercules (Chapter 14) and of the ultimately civilizing impulse embodied in Heracles as mythology's imperial paradigm.

"In the beginning," notes political philosopher Pierre Manent, "human beings gathered, fished, hunted, or even made war, which is a kind of hunting." Imperialism, in this light, is but the exportation of man's primal acquisitive impulse, and the use of force for its necessary satisfaction. Indeed, lacking viable economies and indigenous work forces, ancient—and, to a significant extent, preindustrial—societies lived by conquest, plunder, and enslavement. The choice was to conquer or be conquered, take or be taken, or otherwise take preclusively for fear of someone else's taking first and leaving nothing; or if leaving something, remaining behind as an obstacle or threat. They *take* who possess, and possess by the will and resources to keep others from taking. As noted by the early twentieth-century economist Joseph A. Schumpeter, (precapitalist) imperialism was "the survival within bourgeois society of a precapitalist warrior mentality, devoted, as in classical empires, to expansion for the sake of expanding, war for the sake of fighting, dominion for the sake of ruling." Even in economically viable times, "the imperialists were men who, because they inherited a code of physical risk and valor, could not find solid footing in the new commercial society." What neither expands nor grows perishes; what grows excessively collapses. Survival is the goal; expansion, the means. Either way, the need for growth at whatever cost is inborn and inevitable, reflecting "the perpetual and restless desire for power" posited by Hobbes for nations and individuals alike. Assuming, for argument's sake, a sixteenth- or seventeenth-century Native or Central American colonizing drive into Europe, the conflict and catastrophe would have been no different for what the assumption posits of insular and militarily inferior Europeans. The inroad, from one direction or the other, was in time inevitable—rapine and slaughter the outcome in either case.

It takes little to paint a negative picture of Roman imperialism. So Schumpeter, speaking of

> that policy which pretends to aspire to peace but unerringly generates war, the policy of continual preparation for war, the policy of meddlesome interventionism. There was no corner of the known world where some interest was not alleged to be in danger or under actual attack. If the interests were not Roman, they were those of Rome's allies; and if Rome had no allies, then allies would be invented. When it was utterly impossible to contrive such an interest—why, then it was the national honor that had been insulted. The fight was always invested with an aura of legality. Rome was always being attacked by evil-minded neighbors, always fighting for a breathing space. The whole world was pervaded by a host of enemies.

Critics of the Roman Empire have more recently been found within the upper echelons of classicists themselves, lamenting "the deepest unease" in the way "our traditional story [i.e., the traditional study of the Classics] has led us into connivance with Rome and its empire." This, however, is but politically correct and cant-ridden postmodernism, as shown in a trenchant (endnoted) rebuttal.

The complaints, however, are beside the point, given the acquisitive and self-preservational instinct of men and nations, and its exercise at all costs and by any means. *That* is the reality; and the only question: *What has been gained*? The answer in Rome's case is *much indeed*. Rome surely took—and as surely gave back. Rome's conquests resulted in the Pax Romana 'the Roman Peace', a period of over two hundred years (27 BC–180 AD) marked by relative harmony and greatly diminished Roman expansion. The period set the stage for the expansion of Latin as a unifying social, religious, and academic force for over a thousand years throughout Europe (and *that* despite the barbarian invasions and loss of empire). Rome further expanded through the grant of Roman citizenship to conquered peoples, even as Rome in both senses *settled* their territories. Rome was thus first to promote an expansive ideal of *civitas* 'citizenship' (Lat. *civis* 'citizen'), whence Eng. *civility*—the *sine qua non* of both personal and social prosperity, including the leisured dissemination of ideas through arts and letters.

Civility is the *sine qua non* of civilization itself, no less than the requisite of civilization is permanence—if not physically, then by legacy. Civilization arises not from those who are readily *taken* or live nomadic or migratory lives, but from the initially rapacious *metropolis*. Such was the Mother City of Western civilization, Rome, creating—through the brutal conquests of lunatic emperors backed by an impoverished Circus Maximus and gladiatorial culture of the masses—city, citizenship, civility, and civilization. In the last instance, Rome generated imperial patronage of the arts—whence Virgil, Horace, and others—both at Rome and in imperial cultures to follow, most notably Renaissance Florence. Western civilization is a Roman blessing, as surely as no blessing is unmixed.

Virgil sought to convey the essence of empire by way of contrast between the arts, on the one hand, and good governance, on the other. And yet, to the extent reliant on order and proportion, good governance is itself as much an art as any other—with Rome's absorption of the arts thus implied. Says father Anchises to Aeneas in the underworld:

> "Others will forge the bronze to softer breath,
> no doubt, and bring the sculptured stone to life,
> show greater eloquence, and with their rule
> map out the skies and tell the rising stars:
> you, Roman, remember: Govern! Rule the world!
> These are your arts! Make peace man's way of life;
> spare the humble but strike the defiant down."

"Others" refers to Greece, famed in the arts and intellectual pursuits, including astronomy ("map out the skies," etc.). Rome's mission, by contrast, is governance, to *rule*—as someone surely must and will. The objective of good governance is peace, including protection of the meek and humbling of the proud. That being the ideal, Virgil's inspirational formulation is half its attainment.

The more than one hundred years of brutal civil war preceding the rule of Augustus was a barbarous time, analogous in its way to that of the Homeric heroes, living to kill and be killed, with *kleos* hopefully in the bargain. Virgil, as Brooks Otis formulates the premise of his more than four-hundred-page opus, was "the first and only poet to recreate the heroic-age epic in an urban civilization"—epic poetry increasingly obsolescent—the *Aeneid*, "aspir[ing] to be both heroic and civilized, both remote and contemporary, both Homeric and Augustan." This is to say that even as Virgil heroicized the civilization of Rome aborning—Aeneas is a hero of the Trojan War—Rome's heroism would ultimately be *civilizational,* rejecting the barbarous and momentary impulses of battlefield *kleos* for the enduring benefice of peace. Enduring peace requires perpetual vigilance, which is to say, *imperium sine fine* 'rule without end'. To paraphrase the fifth-century AD military strategist Vegetius: *si vis pacem para bellum* 'if you want peace prepare for war'.

Rome's governance, in Virgil's account, is providential, preordained—as Augustus wished to believe both of himself and his mandate. To that extent, Virgil may be faulted, and often is, as propagandistic. But the underlying truth is this: good, but necessarily forceful, governance ends war—*by war* if necessary—to create and perpetuate the conditions of civilized life. Thus, with the transfer of Aeneas from Troy to Rome comes the change in outlook and direction from barbarous personal glory to enlightened national destiny. Aeneas—"by the acquisition of an historical perspective which includes Augustus and the *pax Romana*"—is effectively reborn from Homeric society to subdue the Homeric impulse embodied in the Italic Turnus and his allies, and perhaps even in himself. Aeneas's paradigm is Hercules/Heracles, recalled in Book Eight of the *Aeneid* as having rid prehistoric Italy of the *impius furor* 'unholy madness' that was the fire-breathing monster Cacus (Gr. *kakos* 'bad, evil')—"reasoned heroism triumphing over irrational, almost subhuman madness." Yet even as Hercules's heroism was itself not entirely reasoned, Aeneas's own victory, as seen, falls short of unalloyed good.

In the end, Virgil's accomplishment was one of "self-imposed difficulties [and] almost preposterous ambition." It was intrepidly and unprecedentedly *new*. New most of all was the ideal of *humanitas* 'humanity, humane understanding, universal empathy' with which Virgil opposed the narrow self-interest of Greek epic. *Humanitas* was the new standard, the ethical element, the "moral prerequisite" to peace. It was the sense of *lacrimae rerum* 'the tearfulness of things', which is to say, the "necessary sadness of success"; and relatedly, victory's ambivalence, the "feeling for what is humanly admirable in the 'bad' characters and for what is humanly blameworthy in the good." There was never a *pax Graeca*: for all else that the Greeks possessed and exemplified, they lacked humane intuition—"brutal self-seeking the hard reality." For want of *humanitas* the Greeks could not sustain durable empire and thus lacked enduring peace.

We have also known the Pax Britannica, the period of relative peace in Europe (1815–1914) from the defeat of Napoleon to the start of World War I, by which time the British Empire controlled most key maritime trade routes—there being nothing further to fight over. Accompanying this repose, however, was European adventurism abroad—"the Scramble for Africa" starting with the French annexation of Algeria in 1830 and continuing through the start of World War I. This "New Imperialism" was so named by way of contrast to earlier colonizations, as discussed, from the fifteenth to nineteenth centuries.

There has also been the Pax Americana, the term applied to the peace of the Western world resulting from preponderant American power in the twentieth century. Though most apparent after the end of World War II (1945), the Pax Americana historically dates to U.S. victory in the Spanish-American War (1898), resulting in America's interim control of Cuba, and purchase of Puerto Rico, Guam, and the Philippines. An American territory, Puerto Rico was "enfranchised"—its inhabitants gaining American citizenship and a dollar-based economy—to become the most prosperous island in the Caribbean.

These are matters to be pondered by those damning American "imperialism," burning their country's flag, and repudiating their American citizenship. Perceptions of self-interest, whether personal or national, make conflict man's natural predisposition; peace, the respite, however much the goal. Therein lies the ambivalence and the agony. All three *paces* 'peaces' were informed by notions of national exceptionalism—in the case of the United States, its standing as the world's first modern democracy. The inarguable evils of colonialism—be it military, economic, or cultural; be it benign or destructive—must thus in each case be weighed against the resultant good, its duration and subsequent influence. The paradox yields as much for thought as for regret. Heracles is its embodiment.

The prospect of entering upon that dark and savage forest, says Dante at the start of the *Divine Comedy,* was 'so bitter that death was little more' (*tant' è amara che poco è più morte*). He would yet know its evils 'because of the good that [he]also found therein of which to treat' (*ma per trattar del ben ch'i' vi trovai, / dirò de l'altre cose ch'i' v'ho scorte*). The ambivalence is perplexing, as seen in the conflicted response of classicist-historian Garry Wills:

> Building an empire does not much appeal to this postcolonial period, so those who would like to save Virgil from himself argue that he was subtly criticizing the empire—the thesis of the so-called "Harvard School." . . . This is like saying that we now consider hell an inhuman concept, so Dante must really have been undermining that concept while describing it in Inferno. After all, Dante was intelligent and humane, so how could he differ from us on such a fundamental matter? This complimenting of other cultures by saying they were really like us prevents people from meeting the challenge of real differences. Everything in Virgil's poem says that the costs of empire are very high but are decidedly worth paying.

Wills overstates the case, and is not as much at odds with the Harvard School as he might think. To say the costs are high but worth paying is but to acknowledge the ambivalence of the imperial enterprise. Not intending the *Aeneid* as a "one-dimensional panegyric" to Rome and Augustus, Virgil need not be "saved from himself" by those today thinking better of his vision. Nor was Virgil "subtly criticizing empire," but offering a "realistic, honest appraisal of [Rome's] present as mirrored in its past," and "hav[ing] us look clearly at what full power does to those who have it."

> Both Aeneas and Augustus need to resort to violence as they go about their careers—Aeneas in the establishment of a new foundation and in the securing of its integrity, Augustus in assuring his own position of authority as a bringer of peace and a renewer of wholeness after a century of civil strife. In so doing both reveal less attractive sides of their natures as they are forced by complicated circumstances to acts of injustice though their dispositions might be equally prone to pity and reconciliation.

So the imperial enterprise throughout history and to this day—and so the *Aeneid*'s own *imperium sine fine.*

### From Virgil to Dante and Beyond

Subsuming its Greek models, the *Aeneid* began the process that made Virgil (as Cicero in prose) the most studied and venerated Latin poet of antiquity. Having synthesized Homer (and other Greek authors in his lesser works),

Virgil would become both a primary vehicle for what we know of Greece and, with Jerome's Latin translation of the Old Testament, a basis for Latin's thousand-year reign as the language of Europe. Virgil, as no other author of antiquity, flourished during the Middle Ages—studied, allegorized, and venerated. Were the *Aeneid* not enough, its pedestal was shared by Virgil's fourth Eclogue, the Messianic Eclogue, as discussed above. For this reason among others—including his thorough absorption of Homer—Dante would make this "most Christian of pagans" his guide in *Inferno*. Virgil, as Homer before him, was a master of "infernal" discourse—Aeneas discussing reincarnation and Rome's future progeny with his father, Anchises, in Hades's Elysian Fields, even as Odysseus had discoursed on various topics with the underworld ghosts of family and fallen comrades. Virgil thus sustained thirteen centuries of interest until Dante's time, having been Dante's own intensive object of study. How joyous, then, and perfect their partnership, imbuing Dante with both the source and most purposeful realization of epic poetry, with Homer and Virgil both:

> O, of the other poets honour and light,
> Avail me the long study and great love
> That have impelled me to explore thy volume!
>
> Thou art my master, and my author thou,
> Thou art alone the one from whom I took
> The beautiful style that has done honour to me.

As the medieval attachment to a Christianizing Virgil impelled Virgil toward Dante's time and adoration, Dante has sustained the forward movement since.

### Horace: "A Porker in the Sty of Epicurus"

Equally creative and influential in his way, and often for the greater glory of Rome, was Horace (65–28 BC), Rome's greatest lyric poet, and its most autobiographical. Joining the army after the assassination of Julius Caesar (44 BC), Horace served under the leadership of Brutus, fighting *against* Octavius (the future Augustus) at the decisive Battle of Philippi in southern Macedonia (see map). Returning to Italy upon a declaration of amnesty,

Horace found his estate confiscated. He became in time a member of the literary circle that included Virgil and Lucius Varius Rufus, who introduced him to Maecenas, friend and confidant of Augustus. Maecenas became Horace's patron and friend, presenting Horace with an estate near Tibur in the Sabine Hills (modern-day Tivoli). For one having fought on the wrong side, it was a charmed existence. Horace lived at his Sabine villa, unvexed thereafter, referring to himself as "good for a laugh" and a "porker in the sty of Epicurus"—fat, sleek, and well complexioned. It is Horace who puts a human face on Latin poetry.

Horace relates his schoolboy travails with the long-lived Lucius Orbilius Pupillus (114–14 BC) aka *plagosus* 'the flogger'. The syllabus included the poetry of Livius Andronicus, doubtless Saturnians and all. Surviving the drill, Horace went on to do for Latin what Livius either would not or could not do; he assumed the mantles of Greek lyric predecessors Sappho and Alcaeus, asserting his own fame as "the foremost in adapting Aeolic [i.e., Lesbian] song to Italian measures." By this, Horace simply credited himself as the foremost (though not the first) in using Sapphic meter for the composition of Latin verse.

Complementing Virgil's *Aeneid* and its glorification of Rome and Augustus are Horace's six *Roman Odes,* three hundred and thirty-six verses in Alcaic quatrains, the opening poems of Horace's *Odes,* Book III (Books I–III published 23 BC). The meter is well chosen for its admonitory rather than amatory associations, Horace being of a generally admonitory temperament (even in his love poems). The *Roman Odes* are addressed not to any one person, as are others of his poems, but to all patriotic citizens. The poems emphasize the cardinal virtues that made Rome great and which, if followed, would assure its greatness for time to come. The virtues, in the order presented—and in sometimes explanatory translation—are: *frugalitas* 'simplicity of living', *patientia* 'endurance', *fides* 'fidelity', *iustitia atque constantia* 'steadfastness in a righteous cause', *virtus/fortitudo* 'martial courage', and *pietas/castitas* 'reverence for the gods and righteous doing'. To these Virgil's *Aeneid,* as seen, added a seventh: *humanitas*—forming a triad with *virtus* and *pietas* in the character of Aeneas.

The *Roman Odes* proceed not by way of systematic analysis, but by wealth of poetic illustration:

> Nowhere has the poet evinced more art than in the opening odes of this book; with fine instinct he has embodied the advocacy and enforcement of the loftiest ethical ideals in stanzas which, apart from the high purposes of his teaching, constitute some of the choicest verses he ever wrote.

The poet Joseph Brodsky opines that American poetry, and perhaps all poetry in English, is "by and large of Virgilian or Horatian denomination," which is to say, *contemplative*—a reflection of "pious resignation and its rewards" and of the cardinal virtues as guarantors of moral greatness. More broadly speaking of Horace, Ezra Pound notes that one "can study the whole local development . . . [,] the sequence of local fashion in British verse by studying the translations of Horace that have poured in uninterrupted sequence from the British press since 1650." This, however, is not quite the praise it appears to be. Pound's deprecation of Horace—what is ultimately Pound's cavalier lack of acquaintance and outright boredom with classical literature—is discussed in the concluding chapter.

## Catullus: Master and Imitator of Sapphic Verse

Horace's predecessor Catullus (c. 84–54 BC) is Rome's first love poet, even as Sappho is first among the Greeks. He wrote two poems, as we shall see, in Sapphic meter: one a translation, or adaptation, of Sappho; the other, by all accounts, composed with Sappho very much in mind. While unquestionably a classic of Latin poetry, Catullus does not properly belong to the Augustan Age. He is chronologically earlier, Alexandrian in outlook, one of the so-called neoteric, or new, poets. Still, and at his most strikingly direct, there is nothing arcane about Catullus. Moreover, by his famous couplet, beginning *Odi et amo* 'I love and I hate', Catullus was as equally "modern" in the first century BC as he is today—modernity an outlook at *any* time responsive to the contrarieties of human existence, to the acute realization of one's condition *sub specie aeternitatis* 'beneath the aspect of eternity'. We may note that the mandate of modernist avatar Ezra Pound to "make it new" is beside the point. In matters of perennial importance there is truly nothing new under the sun. What is truly important has always been important; so old it's new, never dated, classic.

## Lucretius: Master with Intimations of the Universe

Contemporary with Catullus in the first century BC was the epic-didactic poet Lucretius. Lucretius wrote in a rough-hewn, yet sturdy (indeed, unstoppable) hexameter. His *De Rerum Natura* (*On the Nature of Things*), in six books totaling almost 7,500 verses, expounds the doctrine of the Greek materialist philosopher Epicurus (4th–3rd centuries BC). Materialism posits the atom as the sole substance or matter of creation. Atoms are primordial, eternal, and infinite in number—though differing in size, shape and texture. They move endlessly throughout the void, assembling mechanically and largely at random through collisions and kindred associations (non-kindred atoms will not assemble). Atomism derives from various pre-Socratic philosophers (5th century BC)—to further credit the Age of Pericles—such as Leucippus (the "Father of Atomism") and Democritus (the "Father of Science").

Atomism posits the atomic structure of all things, from the physical universe, to the physical body, to the soul, and to the air we breathe. All partake of constant change, most of it indiscernible, as atoms randomly collide, attaching and detaching to and from each other, or to and from larger atomic compounds. Similarly, atomic compounds collide with other atomic compounds of whatever shape and size. The first process, as noted, is generally unseen, though Lucretius compares it to the movement of dust particles seen in sunlit windows. The second process is everywhere apparent when any two objects make contact. When, in this process, more of a compound's atoms dislodge than adhere, atomic dissolution, or death, occurs. Human death is thus a matter of atomic attrition—affecting body parts, organs, tissue, and breath itself. The diminution or dissolution of any one object returns its atoms, in whole or in part, to the *summa materiai* 'the sum of matter', whence the process recurs ad infinitum. The death or diminution of one thing thus always provides matter for the birth or increase of another—the sum total of matter always constant, the atoms alone indestructible. This is the dynamic of what a later age would call the Conservation of Energy.

The *anima* 'soul' is an ultimately fine and fiery atomic compound consisting of the smallest, roundest, and smoothest atoms in creation. Lucretius distinguishes *anima* 'soul' from *animus* 'breath'. The soul is not immortal, but destructible—suffering its own atomic collisions, its own atomic adhesions and dislodgements, its own increases and diminutions—until diminished to dissolution and death. Being mortal, the soul has no afterlife. There is accordingly nothing to fear in death. The soul's highly tenuous composition signals its very vulnerability. In his description of the soul's undoing through external force, Lucretius adopts Sappho's *phainetai moi* (see Chapter 23), a poem conveying the near-death experience of an amatory sighting from which the viewer, distraught, is excluded. Indeed, Lucretius's discourse on love's devastation in *De Rerum Natura* Book Four greatly elaborates on what Sappho conveys in brief. Lucretius no less than Sappho grasps erotic compulsion, though in Lucretius's case the compulsion governs not only personal destiny but all of nature.

Lucretius, as other Latin authors, thus also drew from Greek sources, albeit the prose sources of philosophy and natural science. While Virgil never mentions or invokes Homer as the source of his inspiration, Lucretius praises Epicurus outright and at length. Lucretius is a monument for all times to the merging of what we typically consider the opposites of poetry and science. Yet, to experience Lucretius is, in Lawrence Durrell's words, to know that "science is the poetry of the intellect and poetry the science of the heart's affections." Or as put by turn-of-the-century poetry critic and Old English scholar extraordinaire Albert Stanburrough Cook: "Poetry begins where matter of fact or of science ceases to be merely such, and to exhibit a further truth, that is to say, the connection it has with the world of emotion, and its power to produce imaginative pleasure."

Emotion is one thing, but what is the conceptual support for poetry as a vehicle for science? We have noted the richly oppositional relationship between Aphrodite/Venus and Ares/Mars, goddess of love and god of war. It is through this relationship that Lucretius bridges the putative divide between poetic form and scientific content. Lucretius seizes on the relationship in *De Rerum Natura*'s opening Invocation to Venus. Venus and Mars are there bodied forth, remade, as it were, from Homer's scamps into deadly earnest lovers—forces of nature no less than personifications of the atomic process. Lucretius's Venus and Mars represent benign and harmful Nature. In the pair's union, peace and war, love and hate, creation and destruction become one and indistinguishable. Goddess and god, representing the polarities of human emotion, become equally creative and equally destructive symbols of the principle that nothing in the universe (1) arises unhelped to life by the death of something else; nor (2) perishes unhelped to death by the birth of something else. "The names of Venus and Mars, not being essential to the poet's thoughts, disappear after the invocation and the actual processes for which they stand are described nakedly." We are again reminded in this connection of Rome's "foundational" soundalikes: *Roma* 'Rome'/*amor* 'love'/ *Mavors* 'Mars'—no less than of the primal connection between love (*amor*) and death (*Mavors/mors*).

The thrill of scientific revelation is riven with high emotion, wanting poetry for its conveyance. The confluence resounds in the phrase *naturae species ratioque* 'nature's aspect and reason', which Lucretius employs to designate the full scope of scientific inquiry. Nature's *species*, or outward appearance, is what meets the eye and generates visual appeal; Nature's *ratio*, or underlying principle, is what greets the mind, generating intellectual response. Nature's fullness is revealed neither to the emotions nor intellect alone, but to both, inescapably. Lucretius underscores this bond by praising Epicurus in the Invocation to *DRN* Book Three in language that all but makes him the counterpart to Venus in the Invocation to Book One. Epicurus stands for *ratio*; Venus, for *species*. Lucretius follows and thrills to Epicurus as does all of nature to Venus; he is in thrall to Venus, as is Mars.

For all Virgil's thematic indebtedness to Homer, Hesiod, and Theocritus, he yet drew heavily from Lucretian diction and phraseology, fixing and consecrating it as poetic language, even as he honed it to the perfection of his own hexameters. An example was seen in Virgil's adaptation of Lucretius's *praenuntius . . . pennatus*. Knowing Lucretius inside and out, Virgil is estimated to have adapted or reproduced upward of one thousand Lucretian usages. Such practice marks the ability of Latin authors to begin looking to models *of their own*, rather than to those of the Greeks. Being largely a matter of diction, however, and requiring knowledge of Latin, Virgil's Lucretian borrowings go largely unnoted by English readers. Rather, the emphasis for the reader of Virgil in translation is typically the *Aeneid*'s indebtedness to Homer. In his *Georgics*, however, Virgil sounded with counter-Lucretian resonance, praising the things of nature as opposed to the nature of things.

**Vitruvius: Architecture, Cosmic Order, and Bodily Form**

In prose, the Age of Augustus shone in the historian Livy and architect-engineer Vitruvius. Vitruvius (80–15 BC?) authored *De Architectura*, known today as *The Ten Books on Architecture,* dedicated to Augustus. Antiquity's only surviving work on architecture, building design, and construction, this work deeply influenced early Renaissance artists and thinkers, including Alberti, Leonardo, and Michelangelo. In fact, the next major work on architecture would be Alberti's own *De Re Aedificatoria* (*On the Art of Building*), in ten books modeled on Vitruvius. Published in 1452, it was the architectural standard into the eighteenth century, catapulting the cult of Vitruvius from one Augustan age to another. Vitruvius is famous for asserting that a structure must exhibit the three qualities of *firmitas, utilitas,* and *venustas* 'solidity, utility, and charm'. He cites the Greek invention of the Doric, Ionic, and Corinthian orders, their sense of proportion reflecting the understanding of an even greater work of art: the human body. The description of "Vitruvian Man" in *De Re Aedificatoria* Book Three was famously drawn by Leonardo as the human body inscribed in the circle and square, reflecting the fundamental geometric patterns of the cosmic order. The image is associated with the famed Pythagorean dictum (5th century BC): "Man the measure of all things."

**Livy: Champion of Republican Governance**

Livy (59 BC–17 AD) wrote a monumental history of Rome and the Roman people, *Ab Urbe Condita Libri* (*Accounts from the Foundation of the City*), covering the period from the earliest legends of Rome—predating Rome's own foundation in 753 BC—through the rule of Augustus in Livy's own time. It was a lifelong multivolume work, significant parts of which survive. Livy was considered a prose counterpart to Virgil and was equally extolled with him (and Vitruvius) in the Renaissance. Machiavelli, best known for his slender treatise *The Prince,* also wrote the voluminous *Discourses on the First Ten Books of Titus Livy* (comprising the early history of Rome). This work is a series of lessons on the structuring of republican government, including our own foundational ideas of checks and balances and a tripartite political structure. *The Prince* describes and offers famously cynical advice to the ruler of a principality, i.e., monarchy. The *Discourses,* motivated by Medici abuses in the Florence of Machiavelli's day, urges the superiority of a republic. Of the two works, the *Discourses* is considered more truly representative of Machiavelli's beliefs.

# VII.

# Chapter 22

## Equal to the Gods: Poetic Sublimity, Inner Collapse

> Hers is indeed a grand and mighty rhythm. No poet, with one half the success, has been able to confine within the well-ordered bounds of verse the whirlwinds of a passion at once so terrible and so real. This is her highest achievement, in this quality alone she "outstrips all praise and makes it halt behind her."
>
> – T. G. JOHNSON, *Sappho the Lesbian*

> . . . but as he climb'd the hill,
> Just where the prone edge of the wood began
> To feather toward the hollow, saw the pair,
> Enoch and Annie, sitting hand-in-hand,
> His large gray eyes and weather-beaten face
> All-kindled by a still and sacred fire,
> That burn'd as on an altar. Philip look'd,
> And in their eyes and faces read his doom . . .
>
> – ALFRED, LORD TENNYSON, "Enoch Arden"

PRIOR TO 2004 THERE was only one known complete—and one nearly complete—poem of Sappho. The two are commonly referred to as the "Hymn to Aphrodite" and, from the poem's opening words, *phainetai moi* 'He appears to me'. With the papyrus discovery of 2004, there is a second complete, or nearly complete, poem. And now, with the most recent papyrus discovery of 2014, we have a third complete, or nearly complete, poem and a two-line fragment. In the "Hymn to Aphrodite" (§1) Sappho summons the goddess as ally in dealing with a recalcitrant female beloved. In *phainetai moi* (§2) Sappho has a near-death experience upon witnessing an intimate conversation between her female beloved and a male admirer. The "New Sappho" of 2004 (§39) shows the poet ruminating on love, old age, and death, while the "newest Sappho" provides a nearly complete five-stanza poem in Sapphic meter. It has already been dubbed the "Brothers Poem," as it contains Sappho's prayer for her brothers' safe return following a commercial venture to Egypt. The same papyrus contains a couplet addressed to Aphrodite. This is the so-called "Kypris Poem," as Aphrodite, according to one legend, was born from the ocean onto the island of Cyprus.

In one of the few such surviving examples of ancient Greek poetry appearing in a Latin version, the poet Catullus is often said to have translated Sappho's *phainetai moi*. Latin authors, however, were concerned less with the translation of Greek than with its creative imitation or adaptation, as observed. It is thus as adaptation—a startling one—that we first consider Catullus's use of Sappho. Catullus was also mindful of the "Hymn to Aphrodite," adapting, and even comically subverting, its themes. We turn, then, in this and the following two chapters, to Sappho's two principal surviving poems and their treatment by Rome's premier, as he was its first, erotic poet. The focus is on inseparable form and content, an instructive focus in an age dismissive of both.

We owe the survival of *phainetai moi,* as previously noted, to the treatise of Longinus, *On the Sublime.* The treatise explores the qualities of thought and style that mark composition as "sublime." Although the work discusses oratory and its effects, its application to written poetry is clear, given the long oral nature of poetry in antiquity. As listeners predate readers, "ancient literary criticism often favors the vocabulary of listening and speaking over that of reading and writing, because the literature was thought of as primarily oral, and the sense of speeches and poems as auditory experiences was never lost."

Longinus quotes *phainetai moi*—and that poem alone—as an example of the sublime in poetry. This is a stunning tribute, and one surely intended for Sappho's poetry overall. Longinus's quotation underscores the accidents and incidents of the preservation of ancient texts—the poem known to Longinus some six hundred years after its composition and as a result to *us* some twenty-seven hundred years later. Longinus's own Greek is Attic, of the polished literary-critical kind. It is here used in praise of Sappho's quaint and antiquated Aeolic, unspoken and little familiar in the first century AD. The differences between Longinus's Attic and Sappho's Aeolic, insofar as relevant to *phainetai moi*, have been previously discussed (Chapter 7). To us they seem to signal two different languages. No matter. *Phainetai moi* was part of a classical heritage even in Longinus's time, and he treats it reflexively as such.

We do not know whether Longinus wrote out the poem from memory or transcribed it from a written source. Either way, his version reveals problems of meter and phrasing—not surprisingly, perhaps, in the transcription of Aeolic in Roman times. Modern editors have labored over these problems. For instance, it is uncertain whether sweat "takes hold" of Sappho or "pours down" on her, the two Greek words being similar in sound (and Longinus's spelling corrupted). Catullus's adaptation urges the latter sense. Nor is it clear—depending on the construction given the adverb *broche*(*a*) 'swiftly, briefly, shortly'—whether the poem's speaker "gazes only for a moment," is unable "for a moment to speak anything," or unable "to speak anything in a small voice' (i.e., constrainedly, chokingly). The poem's force and meaning are nonetheless clear. Longinus describes the poem as follows:

> Sappho . . . ever takes the pangs accompanying the pathology of love from love's attendant symptoms as they truly appear. And how does she thus show her excellence? In the skill with which she selects and combines the most striking and intense of those symptoms:
>
> > He seems equal to the gods, that man who sits across from you, who listens, attentive, to your sweet voice and your adoring laughter. It's that which blights the heart within my breast; and when I gaze on you but briefly, my tongue shatters, my voice no longer follows, but subtle flame steals instantly under my skin; my eyes see nothing, my ears resound, the sweat cascades, a tremor grips me through. I am paler than grass, and seem needing little to die.
> >
> > But all must be endured, since . . . [unfinished stanza]
>
> Is it not wondrous how she summons, all at once, soul, body, hearing, tongue, sight, skin, as though they all had strayed apart from her? She feels contradictory sensations, freezes, burns, raves,

> reasons, thus displaying not a single emotion, but a whole congeries of such. Lovers show all such symptoms, but what gives supreme merit to Sappho's art, as I have said, is the skill with which she takes up the most striking and combines them into a single whole.

In *phainetai moi* we witness Sappho in real time observing and reacting to the lovers: a woman of whom she is enamored, and the man of that woman's affections. Sappho's reaction is neither the culmination of growing forces nor a reflective postmortem, but death in the making—immediate collapse upon the merest glance. Like a moth to the flame, Sappho is instantly consumed. This is a poem about appearances. To Sappho, the man "appears equal to the gods." To herself, she "appears nearly dead," in a striking contrast between divine prerogative and human frailty. The man is equal to the gods because he can endure the beloved's beauty at close range and thrive in it. But for Sappho, the sight of him, of them, eviscerates her being. The sense is precisely captured in F. L. Lucas's translation (the use of "God" aside): "Him I hold as happy as God in Heaven, / Who can sit and gaze on your face before him, / Who can sit and hear," etc. *He* can do so; Sappho cannot.

*Phainetai moi* contains many instances of elision, that is, of words joined and pronounced together when one ends and the next begins with a vowel (Eng. "I'm" for "I am"). The poem also contains many instances of asyndeton (Gr. *a-sun-dein* 'not-together-bound'), that is, of absent or omitted conjunctions (Eng. "He laughs, weeps, despairs" for "He laughs, weeps, and despairs"). Condensing language, elision and asyndeton hasten thought. In *phainetai moi*, the two devices combine to extraordinary effect. Thus, because the recurrent conjunction *de* 'and, but' is often elided to *d'* before a vowel, one hears only the *d* sound as part of the following word. With the conjunctions reduced from word to sound, the syntax, while technically not asyndetic, *seems* so. Which is to say, the elided conjunctions, seeming absent, create an asyndetic effect. Stanzas three and four thus read as follows:

> Transliterated Greek:
>
> all' akan men glōssa eage, lepton
> ***d'*** autika chrō(i) pur upadedromēken
> oppatessi ***d'*** oud' en orēmm' epirrom-
> beisi ***d'*** akouai;

kad ***de*** m' idrōs psychros echei, tromos ***de***
paisan agrei, chlōrotera ***de*** poias
emmi, tethnakēn ***d'*** oligō 'pideuēs
phainom' em' auta.

Translation:

but my tongue breaks in silence, **and** delicate
flame steals instantly under my skin; **and** my eyes
see nothing, **and** my ears resound, **and** the sweat
cascades, **and** a tremor grips me through, **and** I
am paler than grass; **and** seem to myself needing
little to die.

Four of the no fewer than seven times it appears, the conjunction *de* is elided to *d'* (before words beginning with a vowel), eliminating, or "collapsing" a syllable, and thus speeding the pace. Though Longinus does not discuss the omission of conjunctions in *phainetai moi,* what he says elsewhere of asyndeton applies:

> . . . the phrases tumble out unconnected in a sort of spate, almost too quick for the speaker himself. . . . The phrases being disconnected, and yet none the less rapid, give the idea of an agitation which both checks the utterance and at the same time drives it on. This effect the poet has achieved by his use of asyndeton.

Though verbal collapse here serves to reinforce inner physical collapse, it is nonetheless required by the meter, which would not tolerate the unelided syllables. In other words, the requirements of form, however demanding, in no way *impede* content, but *create* it—form and content in synchrony. The result of these elisions is the joinder of the sound *d'* with the syllable or metric beat that follows. And again, since the conjunctions actually remain, there is no asyndeton as such, though the elisions have an asyndetic effect. The conjunctions, moreover, are so distributed as not to appear twice in the same metric position, a feature allowed by the flexibility of Greek word order. This further "submerges" the conjunctions by de-emphasizing their placement. In the English, by contrast, the regularity of conjunctive placement is necessarily apparent.

Collapsing the diction, the elisions speed the description of Sappho's own collapse, thus creating meaning. The effect is signaled from the outset by elision and contraction combined. 'Equal to the gods he seems **to be, that man**': *phainetai moi kēnos isos theoisin* / ***emmen' ōnēr.*** The bolded Greek—for a shortening of two syllables—is first elided, then contracted from

> ***emmenai*** [to be] ***o*** [the] ***anēr*** [man]

to

> ***emmen' ōnēr***
> [ ***o*** + ***a-*** = ***ō*** ]

This prepares the way for six shortenings in the second stanza, and ten in stanzas three and four, for a total of seventeen elisions or contractions in all. The second and third appearances of elided *de* offer

> *oppatessi* ***d'****oud' en orēmm' epirrom- / beisi* ***d'****akouai*
> **and** with my eyes I see nothing, **and** my ears whirr

Here, *de* is first elided with *oud'* = ***d'*** *oud'*, while *oude* ('not') is in turn elided with *en* ('one'). Next, *orēmm'* (i.e., *orēmmi* 'see') is elided with soundalike *epirrom-* ('whirr'), and the following *de* with *akouai* ('ears') = ***d'****akouai*—for a total of four elisions in that enjambed line and one-third alone. Noteworthy as well is the dictional, or emblematic, confounding of senses—sight and hearing—as the soundalike verbs, as noted, elide: ***orēmmi*** ('see') elided with ***epirrom-*** ('whirr') = *orēmm' epirrom-*.

This is all quite remarkable for so short a poem. But it is not all. The verbal compression, as noted, is marked by pervasive enjambment (including hyphenated enjambment) signaling run-on thought; by racing polysyllabics signaling physical and sensory agitation; by words conveying a sense of imminence or proximity. There is a possibly orgasmic quality to it all. It began quietly—the man sitting, Sappho watching. It will end quietly—Sappho expiring, or nearly so. Indeed, for all the poem's freneticism, an eerie repose frames the whole. The repose lies in the opening "He appears to me," and in the closing "I appear to myself." The formulations connote not what is, but what *seems* to be. There is a detachment in it all, a sense of experience not entirely of this world.

Even while collapsing and hastening rhythm, Sappho once allows facing vowels to stand *unelided,* a feature known as hiatus (or "gap"). Sappho is not only emotionally but *verbally* shattered, her 'tongue breaks' (*glōssa eage*). For a poet in an oral society, this is tantamount to death (reinforcing the poem's concluding near-death). The *break* occurs, at the dictional level, in the confrontation of words that should, but do not, elide: *glōssa eage.* The vowels face off in a dictional confrontation signaling the rupture of Sappho's tongue and speech. The hiatus is unique in attested Lesbian poetry. Often considered a textual infirmity, the hiatus is "the very factor that creates the special effect, namely, that the form is arranged in such a way that it symbolizes what it means." So is it ever in the best poetry.

Similarly serving the forward motion of poetry is enjambment, that is, the carry-over of thought from one verse to another. Whereas a single thought per line would result in a wooden and sing-song effect, enjambment keeps verse fluid and forward-moving. True to the instantaneity and racing urgency of *phainetai moi,* we find enjambments in all but one of its sixteen lines—including two highly unusual hyphenated enjambments. Speed is further conveyed by five- and six-syllable verbs—the first verb describing the 'fire [that] has run beneath' Sappho's skin (*pur upadedromēken*); the other, the 'whirring' that besets her ears (*epirrom- / beisi d'akouai*). Quadrosyllabics abound, though these of themselves are not unusual in Greek. The fire, moreover, 'immediately' (*autika*) sets to, accelerated, as it were, by the flurry of words indicating physical proximity: the man sits 'opposite' (*enantios*) and 'close by' (*plasion*) Sappho's beloved, listening 'attentively', i.e., 'from under' (***up**akouei*)—Sappho needing but 'briefly' (*broche'*) to view the intimacy. The nearness of death is also speed related, as Sappho's consistently enjambed verses hasten us toward the perception that she "needs but little to die."

❧

The selection and combination of poetic elements, as posited by Longinus, is not the sole criterion of the sublime. Longinus's fuller context instructs as follows:

> The sublime consists in a consummate excellence and distinction of language, and . . . this alone gave the greatest poets and prose

> writers their preeminence and clothed them with immortal fame.
>
> A well-timed flash of sublimity shatters everything and reveals the full power of the speaker at a single stroke.
>
> The true sublime naturally elevates us: uplifted with a sense of proud exaltation, we are filled with joy and pride, as if we ourselves produced the very thing we heard. . . . For what is truly great bears repeated consideration; it is difficult, nay, impossible, to resist its effect; and the memory of it is stubborn and indelible.

Longinus further mentions the power of grand conceptions and consuming emotion, for the most part one and the same (i.e., *authigeneis* 'congenital'); figures of thought and speech; nobility of language, including choice of words, use of metaphor, and elaborate diction; and the dignified and elevated arrangement of words. These derive 'through art' (*dia technēs*).

Again without specific reference to *phainetai moi*, but fully illustrative of the best poetry, Longinus speaks as follows of *phrasis* 'diction' in relation to *noēsis* 'thought':

> The choice of the right word and the fine word has a marvelously moving and seductive effect upon an audience and . . . all orators and prose writers make this their supreme object. For this of itself gives to the style at once grandeur, beauty, old-world charm, weight, force, strength and a sort of luster, like the bloom on the surface of the most beautiful bronzes, and endows the facts as it were with a living voice. Truly beautiful words are the very light of thought. However, their majesty is not for common use, since to attach great and stately words to trivial things would be like fastening a great tragic mask on a little child . . .

The dictates of diction inhere since, for the Greeks, as noted, readers were still very much listeners, and the auditory habit long persisted despite writing. These dictates ideally apply to all poetry and poetry in translation, as the latter must be poetry in its own right. Yet, so little of today's poetry, original or in translation, has any of these commended qualities. From democratized poetry has come debased diction, and lead from burnished bronze (see Chapter 25).

For all its attributes and varieties, the sublime need not take voice.

"Sublimity," Longinus proclaims, is 'the echo of a noble mind' (*hupsous megalophrosunēs apēchēma*) and "even without being spoken the bare idea often of itself wins admiration for its inherent grandeur." Such, according to Longinus, is the silence of Ajax in the *Nekyia*, "more sublime by far than any speech." Longinus here refers to Book Eleven of the *Odyssey*, where Odysseus summons ghosts from the underworld, including those of his companions slain at Troy. Ajax—eternally aggrieved over the award of Achilles's armor not to himself, the mightiest of the Greeks after Achilles, but to Odysseus, the most clever—declines to speak with Odysseus. As a result of the slight against him, Ajax had gone mad and committed suicide (as described in Sophocles's *Ajax*). "The Silence of Ajax" has thus become a byword for inarticulable contempt. Longinus uses the episode as the example par excellence of sublimity by intimation or, as he says, "the bare idea."

Silence is thus not merely golden; it can be sublime. Ajax neither rages nor howls, though well he might. His portrayal is also consistent with the sublime in Greek representational art, requiring that the everyday disfigurements of pain, rage, or despair be "softened" to create a figure "inspir[ing] compassion in its beauty and suffering." Ajax suffers beautifully, extravagantly; his torment is both exquisite and eternal. The satisfaction he takes in displaying it makes his death, as it were, worthwhile. Ajax's silence in its way reflects the remove Homer maintains from his own poem. No matter how impassioned the activities he describes, Homer's tone is pervasively the same. "It is the tone," says Erich Auerbach, "of narrative neutrality, a kind of sublime serenity, equable, untroubled, almost playful, and by virtue of evenness and unbiased serenity, almost divinely sublime." It is a dispassionate sublime, far from the wrenching articulation of Sappho's self-consumption.

# Chapter 23

## Equal to a God: Form and Content in Convulsive Union

> Sappho remains a supreme example of the Greek gift, so lamentably rare today, of combining subtlety and simplicity, plainness and dignity, in a style so tense, yet terse, as to defy the translator. It rings as naturally as the spoken word—yet here are words such as few lips ever spoke.
>
> – F. L. LUCAS, tr., *Greek Poetry*

NOTWITHSTANDING LONGINUS'S CHOICE of *phainetai moi* and his forceful analyses overall, renowned classicist Denys Page (1908–1978) dismisses the idea of "contradictory sensations" and, similarly, the notion of selection—as one cannot properly speak of selection when "nothing of the least importance is omitted." Nor, claims Page, is there "any special art in the combination of elements into a whole," since "each element is described in turn, and the whole—the total emotion which each symptom partly attests—could not possibly, in the circumstances, fail to be implicit." Page instead emphasizes:

> The uncommon objectivity of [Sappho's] demeanor toward her own extremity of passion; the accurate definition of its physical symptoms; the rare gift of vivid, brief, and precise expression. These thoughts could hardly be put into words more candid, apt, and luminous. . . . Despite the fact that everything possible is packed into a few lines—the dumbness, deafness, numbness of the heart, the sweat and shiver and pallor and fainting—the description is free from exaggeration and self-pity. There is certainly no lack of control in the expression, whatever there may have been

> in the experience. . . . The listener recognizes his potential, in the artist's actual portrait; therein lie both the immediate appeal and the abiding interest of the poem, in that creative power which gives universal validity to the details of a personal experience.

Whatever the basis of our appreciation, the poem has persistently had its imitators. Catullus translated (imitated or adapted) it some five hundred years later in one of his two poems in Sapphic meter (Catullus the first known Roman poet to use it, and the first Roman love lyricist; as Sappho was first among the Greeks). Meter aside, his poem further evokes Sappho/ Lesbos through the naming of *Lesbia* 'woman of Lesbos' as his love interest (a woman named Claudia in real life). Catullus plays the male to Sappho's female poet, thus changing the original triangle from two women and a man to two men and a woman (as have many of Sappho's imitators over the years, wanting to sidestep the poem's lesbianism). Numbered 51 in modern editions, the poem is typically referred to as "Catullus 51":

Latin:

Ille mi par esse deo videtur,
ille, si fas est, superare divos,
qui sedens adversus identidem te
  spectat et audit

dulce ridentem, misero quod omnis
eripit sensus mihi; nam simul te,
Lesbia, aspexi, nihil est super mi
  [*words missing*]

lingua sed torpet, tenuis sub artus
flamma demanat, sonitu suopte
tintinant aures, gemina teguntur
  lumina nocte.

Otium, Catulle, tibi molestum est:
otio exultas nimiumque gestis:
otium et reges prius et beatas
  perdidit urbes.

Translation:

That man to me seems equal to a god; that man—if it befits—to surpass the gods, who sitting opposite, repeatedly sees you and hears you

sweetly laughing, which from my wretched self does seize the very senses. For, as soon as I look on you, Lesbia, there is nothing in me [*words missing*]

but my tongue grows torpid, flame descends beneath my fragile limbs, my ears tinkle to sounds within, my eyes are covered in double night.

Indolence irks you, Catullus, in indolence you exult and enthuse too much—indolence, the ruin of kings aforetime and prosperous cities.

Catullus's last stanza is perplexing, having no counterpart in Sappho, despite her one-line start of a new stanza: "But all must be endured, since . . ." In an article as brief as it is penetrating, Richmond Lattimore proposes, first, that the start of Sappho's new stanza and the entirety of Catullus's fourth conform to a poetic conceit, beginning with a "description, complete in itself, of a personal experience . . . followed by a generalization, which is set to counteract the suffering which precedes." The goal is to acknowledge the limitations in human affairs. Second, and conversely, Lattimore suggests that *otium* is here: "the idleness that leads to daydreaming, to thoughts of making what is impossible come true, or of dissolving facts by fancy." Sappho's stark "But all must be endured" is thus broodingly met by Catullan idleness: "the refusal to endure what is the case because it is the case." Whatever the interpretation, Catullus "continues in his last stanza to follow Sappho, but with greater freedom than heretofore. His transition is, however, so abrupt, as to make the sequence of thought obscure." And so it is.

There is in fact a pervasive freedom in Catullus's Sapphic adaptation, appearing as follows. Catullus, first, compresses Sappho's four stanzas into three—exclusive of his own last stanza (which continues to elude). In the last, he idly indulges the denial of reality, though the indulgence is harmful (*otium . . . molestum est*) and self-destructive (*otium . . . perdidit*). The poet's *otium* 'indolence, leisure, sloth' is both a moral and poetic predicate. Moral, because Catullus by indirect allusion to Paris, Helen, and Troy—"indolence, the ruin of kings aforetime and prosperous cities"—cautions against the epic-catastrophic dimensions of lyric eroticism. Catullus elsewhere (Poem 68) more overtly makes the connection, lamenting the fate of Greek manhood at "obscene Troy," that "Paris not enjoy his stolen debauch, pursuing unchallenged leisure [*libera* . . . / *otia*], secure in his bedroom." Catullan *otium* serves as a poetic predicate, first, because leisure is the accustomed prerequisite of poetic composition; and second, because excessive leisure becomes sloth, as perilous to the individual as to the collective. The poet thus takes a sullen, self-reproaching turn—noting his sloth-induced torpor and, as may be the case, the futility of venting dudgeon through an exercise in translation. The exercise is *otiose,* the product of indolence. It allows the poet, peculiarly, and to no purposeful avail, to evoke bygone Sappho. Catullus, the man of action, "vacations" in Sappho, chafing all the while.

How does Catullus "peculiarly" evoke bygone Sappho? We begin by noting that there is a certain detachment in Catullus's treatment, signaled by the parenthetical *si fas est* 'if it befits' (second line). The phrase, with its sense of compunction—'if it is right', 'should it be appropriate'—conveys skepticism toward doing Sappho one better, the man in Catullus's poem seeming not merely "equal to the gods," but to "surpass the gods." What is gained? If Sappho says the man is "equal to the gods," that is surely measure and godliness enough. Sappho is in any event not one for compunction, either in her own loves or, as in the case of Helen, those she condones. Alternatively, it is not Catullus's poetic exercise that is *otiose,* but love itself—love being its own preoccupation, and the lover inert, but for love's behest. One thinks of Shakespeare's love-in-idleness, the flower inspiring romantic love.

Catullus's tone is everywhere different from Sappho's. By contrast to Sappho's runaway emotion, Catullus is slower paced, if not deliberative. His parenthetical 'if it befits' restrains rather than hastens emotion; it expresses reserve, a "second thought" quite absent from his original. So also the protracted visual incitement of the quadrosyllabic *identidem* 'repeatedly': "that man . . . who sitting opposite, *repeatedly* sees you and hears you sweetly laughing." The adverb is strikingly quadrosyllabic, its alliterative iterations—combined with the words that follow (*identidem te / spectat et audit*)—underscoring the adverb's meaning. Catullus has *otium* enough to view a scene, *itself* one of repetitive viewing, whereas Sappho passes from first sighting to immediate collapse. Catullus's experience is thus more voyeuristic or, if you will, *indolent*—in a way for which only the surfeit of *otium* might allow. It is, perhaps, not so much a matter of "premature climax" as of flaccidness—Catullus replacing Sappho's death by climax with death by boredom. Catullus uses *identidem* but once elsewhere, to describe the *repeated* debaucheries of Lesbia in Poem 11: *identidem omnium / ilia rumpens* 'repeatedly busting their balls, one and all' (alliterative *m* and *n* instead of the *d* and *t*). Poem 11, as noted, is the only other Catullan verse in Sapphic meter—the supposed complement of Poem 51: beginning of relationship in 51, end of relationship in 11. *Identidem* 'repeatedly' thus injects an appetitive or compulsive note into both contexts, whether in the viewing (Poem 51) or doing (Poem 11), as if to signal Lesbia's not only ready but repeated reciprocation of viewing and doing.

Catullus 51 further lacks the original's quickening elisions, as noted in the last chapter, except for the last stanza (likely Catullus's own) in which final *-um*, without dropping, twice elides with the vowel-initial words that follow. The poem seems more about *leisure* than *seizure*; its pace *otiose*, consistent with the last stanza's focus on *otium* itself. By his handling of Sappho, Catullus in fact goes from torrid to torpid: his tongue does not, as Sappho's, "break" but 'grows inert' (*torpet*)—a notion itself prefiguring inertia (*otium*); a flame does not, like Sappho's, "race beneath" his skin, but 'descends, flows down' (*demanat*) 'beneath limbs' (*sub artus*) already 'frail' (*tenuis*); his ears do not "whir" with head-splitting sounds but merely 'tinkle' (*tintinant*) to sounds within. By contrast to Sappho, who endures instant apoplexy, Catullus displays a dreamlike trudge through quicksand. Both experience paralysis: Sappho at once; Catullus in slow motion.

Further removed from the manner of his Sapphic original are Catullus's neoteric, or new poetic, indulgences, some of which may be noted as follows. Instead of *sonitu suo* ('with its own sound'), Catullus uses a sometimes suffixed and emphatic form of the possessive adjective: *sonitu suopte*. The phrase *geminā teguntur / lumina nocte* ('my eyes are veiled in double night') features the word *lumina* ('lights'), which can also mean eyes, but only in a secondary sense. *Lumina,* as an abstracted reference to an organ of sensory perception, seems to acknowledge Sappho's *akouai*—'hearings, tidings, sounds'—for ears (*akouomai* 'hear'; Eng. acoustic). *Geminā . . . nocte* ('in double night') is an instance of "transferred epithet"—the transfer (often for metrical reasons) of an adjective from one to another noun in a phrase. The phrase literally translates: "my lights are veiled in a twin night" (meaning "my twin eyes are veiled in night"). With the transferred epithet, Catullus peculiarly conveys the notion of night in twain divided—a portion for each eye. Of the poem's more traditional qualities, abundant to a fault, we note that the last two stanzas are richly and liquidly *m- n-* and *l*-alliterative, even as *sonitu suopte*—*s*-alliterative, and *o-* and *u*-assonantal—sounds the very tintinnabulation described. The last two stanzas, heavily *t*-sounding, mark the progression toward *o̱tium*, the poem's latent touchstone.

> . . . torpet, tenuis . . . artus
> . . . demanat, sonitu suopte
> tintinant . . . teguntur
>   . . . nocte.
>
> otium, Catulle, tibi molestum est:
> otio exultas . . . gestis:
> otium et . . . et beatas
>   perdidit . . .

All such features are significantly removed from Sappho's unstudied simplicity, i.e., from her immediacy. Catullus has written a pretty poem—as neoterically contrived as is the (twin) night long. Nor would he call it Sappho.

I began by noting that Catullus in Poem 51 plays the male to Sappho's female poet-viewer, thus changing the original triangle from two women and a man to two men and a woman. So he does—and *there*, essentially, is an end to it. The two texts have surely enough to offer without theorizing efforts to square the triangle. This, however, is what "personal voice" criticism now offers. Notes Sappho translator Josephine Balmer (b. 1959): "How then could this new poem—a male heterosexual version of a female homosexual desire—be rendered into English by a woman who had herself previously worked on Sappho's original"? And if the same woman has *not* already worked on Sappho's original, but pleads some other circumstance, what then? And what might sexual preference have to with any of this? The effect of such discussion is deadening (see endnote). It is the *result*, not the personal-information-spangled process that counts. I myself translated

Sappho's *phainetai moi* a second time, some thirty years after the first, specifically for this volume. It is the only time I have ever translated the same poem twice, doing so because I sought a line length closer to that of the original. Res ipsa loquitur. Readers will judge the two versions on their merits, apart from any other factor.

❧

Catullus's older contemporary Lucretius offers the following adaptation of Sappho's *phainetai moi* in his *De Rerum Natura.* Lucretius's subject is the interconnectedness of mind, body, and soul (I quote the excellent metrical translation of W. E. Leonard, Random House, 1921):

> But when the mind is moved by shock more fierce,
> We mark the whole soul suffering all at once
> Along man's members: sweats and pallors spread
> Over the body, and the tongue is broken,
> And fails the voice away, and ring the ears,
> Mist blinds the eyeballs, and the joints collapse,—
> Aye, men drop dead from terror of the mind.
> Hence, whoso will can readily remark
> That soul conjoined is with mind, and, when
> 'Tis strook by influence of the mind, forthwith
> In turn it hits and drives the body too.

Lucretius has broadened the inquiry. It is not simply emotional paroxysm, but the severity of any mental shock that can result in death. Lucretius makes the Sapphic point in his exposition on the interconnectedness of mind (*animus*), soul (*anima*), and body (*corpus*). The non-amatory context is further apparent from the inclusion of the passage in Book Three of the *DRN* (dealing with the nature and composition of the soul) rather than in Book Four (dealing with the pathologies of love). Lucretius, more than Catullus, is thoroughly transformative of Sappho. He perceives Sapphic symptomology as a thing not solely amorously induced, but resulting from any mental trauma.

In the *Aeneid*'s climactic death of Turnus—Turnus is Aeneas's fated adversary, as Hector is Achilles's in the *Iliad*—the mental trauma is fear of approaching death. For this climax, Virgil combines Homeric and Lucretian (but ultimately Sapphic) elements. Such features include, among others, the *Iliad*'s dreamlike frame of reference: "And as in a dream a man cannot pursue the one who flees—the one cannot flee, nor the other pursue—so he [Achilles] could not overtake the other, nor the other [Hector] escape." In Virgil's handling, the chase is ended, with Turnus's psychological and physical states the focus. Showing the physical effects of psychological anguish, Virgil traverses Homer, Sappho, and Lucretius (I quote the excellent verse translation of F. O. Copley, Bobbs-Merrill, 1965):

> Just as in dreams, when weariness and sleep
> press night on our eyes, we seem to try to run
> eagerly, vainly, and in mid-trial we fail
> and fall—our tongue is useless, every sinew
> forgets its force; no word, no sound will come;
> so Turnus: no matter how bravely he attacked,
> the Dira [female demon] denied success. . . .
>
> [ac velut in somnis, oculos ubi languida pressit
> nocte quies, nequiquam avidos extendere cursus
> velle videmur et in mediis conatibus aegri
> succidimus; non lingua valet, non corpore notae
> sufficiunt vires nec vox aut verba sequuntur:
> sic Turno, quacumque uiam virtute petivit,
> successum dea dira negat.]

"We seem to try to run" translates *avidos extendere cursus / velle videmur,* lit: "we seem to wish to press our determined course." "Seem to wish" reflects Sappho's "He seems to me . . . I seem to myself"—even as *videmur* 'we seem' recalls Lucretius's *videmus* 'we mark' (present passive and present active forms of *video* 'to see'). Especially noteworthy is Virgil's *videmur* 'we seem'—a narrative "first-personalization" emphatically and empathetically involving us, as readers, in Turnus's fate. The effect surpasses that of the direct address, or apostrophe, by which the epic poet conventionally elicits concern for his characters. Indeed, while second person *apostrophe* "turns [us] away from" the narrative (Gr. *apo* 'away from' + *strepho* 'turn'), the first person positions us in its very midst. We *seem* to be there, by Turnus's very side. Adapting the *seeming* perceptions of Lucretius and Sappho, Virgil personalizes, indeed lyricizes, the *Aeneid*'s most arduous ending. Finally, where Sappho's several physical reactions culminate in near-death, Virgil focuses on speechlessness alone, condensing Sappho's pathologies into a single bodily response: '. . . every sinew / forgets its force' (*nec corpore notae / sufficunt vires*).

Notes Margaret Reynolds, the "symptoms of 'love's madness', and the pervasive physicality of Sappho's description of desire . . . have become the standard repertoire of love's effects recited throughout Western culture, from high to low." Johann Wolfgang von Goethe, in his signature *The Sorrows of Young Werther* (1774, 2nd ed. 1787), writes, without attribution, of Werther's love for his dear Lotte (Goethe's work an epistolary novel addressed to his friend Wilhelm). To the examples generally cited may thus be added the following:

> Ah, Wilhelm, what my heart often urges me to do!—When I've sat with her for two or three hours, enjoying her figure, her demeanor, the heavenly expression in her words, and all my senses then gradually become tense and there's darkness in front of my eyes, I can hardly hear anymore, and I am seized at the throat as if by a strangler, when my heart then tries in all its wild beating to give vent to my oppressed senses but only increases their confusion—Wilhelm, I often don't know whether I am still in the world. . . . Adieu! I see no end to this misery except the grave.
>
> [Ach Wilhelm! Wozu mich mein Herz oft drängt!—wenn ich bei ihr gesessen bin, zwei, drei Stunden, und mich an ihrer Gestalt, an ihrem Betragen, an dem himmlischen Ausdruck ihrer Worte geweidet habe, und nun nach und nach alle meine Sinne aufgespannt werden, mir es düster vor den Augen wird, ich kaum noch höre, und es mich an die Gurgel faßt wie ein Meuchelmörder, dann mein Herz in wilden Schlägen den bedrängten Sinnen Luft zu machen sucht und ihre Verwirrung nur vermehrt—Wilhelm, ich weiß oft nicht, ob ich auf der Welt bin! . . . Adieu! Ich sehe dieses Elendes kein Ende als das Grabe.]

The passage, not intended as translation, spools out what Sappho far more concisely says, even while suggesting Sappho's asyndetic breathlessness. Reaction is not instantaneous—"when I gaze on you but briefly"—but protracted: "When I've sat with her two or three hours" (Goethe focusing on *sitting*, as does Sappho). Sappho's "attentive to your sweet voice and adoring laughter" becomes "enjoying . . . the heavenly expression in her words." Sappho's "it's that which maddens the heart within my breast" supplies "when my heart then tries in all its wild beating to give vent to my oppressed senses." And "I seem but needing little to die" yields "I often don't know if I am of this world." Following a detailed description of how he seeks relief—"roaming far and wide outdoors"—the young Werther concludes, clinching the Sapphic thought: *Adieu! Ich sehe dieses Elendes kein Ende als das Grabe* 'Adieu! I see no end to this misery except the grave'.

*Phainetai moi* also extends to Charlotte Brontë's *Jane Eyre*. The terrified young heroine is locked by her guardian, Mrs. Reed, in the infamous Red Room. Jane sees what she concludes is not moonlight penetrating an aperture in the blind, but lantern light stirring on the wall and gliding toward the ceiling:

> . . . but then, prepared as my mind was for horror, shaken as my nerves were by agitation, I thought the swift darting beam was a herald of some coming vision from another world. My heart beat thick, my head grew hot; a sound filled my ears, which I deemed the rushing of wings; something seemed near me; I was oppressed, suffocated; endurance broke down . . .

The description, as in Lucretius, is generalized to *any* severely emotional ordeal. "My head grew hot" describes the state preceding Sappho's "the sweat cascades"; "endurance broke down" recalls Sappho's "needing little to die"; "something seemed near me" conveys Sappho's "that man who sits close by you"; "a sound filled my ears, which I deemed the rushing of wings" synthesizes Sappho's ears awhir, and palpitating heart.

Also noteworthy is Racine's drama of sexual obsession, *Phèdre*:

> I saw him, I reddened, I blanched at his sight,
> Misgiving arose in my soul's grievous plight;
> No word could I utter, no vision behold,
> I felt all my frame though on fire grow cold. . . .
>
> [Je le vis, je rougis, je palis à sa vue,
> Un trouble s'éleva dans mon âme éperdue;
> Mes yeux ne voyaient plus, je ne pouvais parler,
> Je sentais tout mon corps et transir et brûler. . . .]

And finally, the classically hyper-learned Tennyson's "Fatima," lines 15 through 19 (1833), with its riveting notion of the soul in consumptive transit through the flesh:

> Last night, when some one spoke his name,
> From my swift blood that went and came
> A thousand little shafts of flame
> Were shiver'd in my narrow frame.
> O Love, O fire! once he drew
> With one long kiss my whole soul thro'
> My lips, as sunlight drinketh dew.
>
> [Compare Marlowe, *Doctor Faustus*, 5.1.90:
> "Her lips suck forth my soul; see where it flies—"]

Considered among the most erotically charged of Tennyson's poems, "Fatima" was prefixed upon publication with a transliterated version of the opening verse of Sappho's *phainetai moi*, the title "Fatima" later added. Tennyson's assumption of the female voice ("when someone spoke *his* name") is noteworthy, though beyond the scope of this study. At the cost of repetition, however, biography is irrelevant. Reading "Fatima" and believing the poet female, the reader is none the worse, and none the less enraptured.

# Chapter 24

## Frenzied Emotion, Expressive Control: Form and Content Bound

> 'Meaning' and 'form' are not apprehended separately, but operate together. There is 'a resonant meaning or a meaning resonance'—two expressions for one and the same thing. It is only in later reflection that the 'formal' aspect of true poetry can, by fiction, be detached from the aspect of 'meaning.'
>
> – HIGHAM AND BOWRA, *The Oxford Book of Greek Verse in Translation*

ITS BURSTING EMOTION WITHIN rigid confines makes *phainetai moi* a spectacular poem. That same quality is sure to have characterized much of Sappho's non-surviving works. Scholar Denys Page notes of Sappho's charged response: "There is certainly no lack of control in the expression, whatever there may have been in the experience." In the more expressive parlance of the early twentieth century, "the essential fires of sincerity, spontaneity, imagination, and passion were flaming with undiminished heat behind the fixed forms and restricted measures." More recently, says critic Rosanna Warren, the "haunting shape" of Sappho's meter "plays release against restraint with unrivaled cunning: the poem runs from stanza to stanza like water pouring from basin to basin down a trout stream, twisting and flashing, unfurled and checked" (though the notion of a *stream* is rather tame). "If we consider Sappho as a myth," says Warren, "it must be as a myth not of love, but of form." In classical poetry form and content are inseparable. Content crystallizes around form and is absent without it.

Catullus's acclaimed Poem 11 is an object lesson in the union of concise form and boundless content. It is, as earlier noted, sometimes considered the complement of Poem 51—Poem 11 marking the end of the relationship begun in Poem 51 (notwithstanding the earlier position of Poem 11 in the sole surviving manuscript of Catullus). Gone, however, are the reserve and deliberation of Poem 51 and all its learned manner. Emotionally and geographically unhinged, Catullus summons companions to deliver a blighting rebuke:

Furius, Aurelius, Catullus' friends—
Should India beckon from earth's far ends
Where thundering Ocean batters the shore,
  Echoing evermore;

Should Persia, Caspia or soft Araby
Or the Parthians' mobile archery
Or waters brown with Nilotic silt
  From mouths twice-seven spilt;

Should the lofty Alps yield to being crossed
And the vistas of Caesar's advance;
The Rhine engineered and arched from France
  And channeled Britain's coast—

Prepared to bestride the world entire
Wheresoever the gods require
Relate but this to the darling girl
  Whom I adored erstwhile:

May she live and prosper a practiced whore,
Clutching three-hundred strong at her door,
Draining each lout of his overload
  Till his balls explode—

Nor may she count on my love as before
Which has dropped by her fault like a flower
Once touched on the distant meadow's floor
  By the passing plough.

[Furi et Aureli comites Catulli,
sive in extremos penetrabit Indos,

litus ut longe resonante Eoa
   tunditur unda,

sive in Hyrcanos Arabesue molles,
seu Sagas sagittiferosue Parthos,
sive quae septemgeminus colorat
   aequora Nilus,

sive trans altas gradietur Alpes,
Caesaris uisens monumenta magni,
Gallicum Rhenum horribile aequor ulti-
   mosque Britannos,

omnia haec, quaecumque feret uoluntas
caelitum, temptare simul parati,
pauca nuntiate meae puellae
   non bona dicta.

cum suis viuat valeatque moechis,
quos simul complexa tenet trecentos,
nullum amans vere, sed identidem omnium
   ilia rumpens;

nec meum respectet, ut ante, amorem,
qui illius culpa cecidit velut prati
ultimi flos, praetereunte postquam
   tactus aratro est.]

This is palpable rage, of world-entire and brutalizing magnitude, a world both known and mythological. The known world extends from the oozing sunbaked estuarial Nile, northward to the towering snowbound Alps; from Caesar's savagely conquered Gaul and Britain, eastward to louche and dissolute Arabia and central Asia Minor. India, the furthest east of lands known to Rome ("Earth's far ends"), evokes the mythological world of the rising sun and of Ocean (Gr. *Okeanos*), the fabled river encircling Earth, the source of all terrestrial waterways, the father of all created life.

This fully epic itinerary with its male-penetrative brio (v. 2, *penetrabit* 'will penetrate'; v. 4, *tunditur* 'is pounded') sits in peculiar though purposeful counterpoint to the personal expressiveness of Sapphic meter. Catullus's

Sapphic meter serves as a reproach to the markedly *un*-Sappho-like Claudia, who, Michael Putnam observes, "far from being a brilliant combination of poetess and lover, able to transmute intense emotion into rigorous word—to combine felicitously elegance of mind and body . . . is in reality one of the most notoriously vulgar and degraded women of Roman history." Similarly, "the enormity of Rome's political ravening [is] resumed in Lesbia's careless, cold, gluttonous physicality."

Evoking this expansive itinerary, Catullus summons two friends, Furius and Aurelius, for the fully *limited* undertaking—as crosstown messengers—of cursing his faithless lover. The anticlimax underscores the plunge from exalted to commonplace, from boundless vista to livid fixation. But it isn't rage alone. The poet concludes, in a surprising shift, by revealing his vulnerability and isolation. *He* has kept faith; *she* has not. Distance now contracts from the remote male-marauded world of his imagination to the remoteness of a space both isolated and enclosed. Posturing aside, his own love has been a distant and solitary flower, delicate and worthy of attainment, yet heedlessly shorn and ploughed under. How so "worthy"? In the words of Sappho imaginer Carman Bliss (1861–1929): "But thou alone shall gather / This fragile flower of beauty,— / To crush and keep the fragrance / Like a holy incense." Catullus wants to be gathered up, his essence kept and cherished. His concluding image is feminizing—Sapphic—and the fragile counterpoise to the poem's blighting assault. For all his execratory vigor, the poet is cut down and unsexed, *de-flowered*. He no longer ploughs, but is himself ploughed under. Having withdrawn from the "world entire," he finds his place is a sorry piece of earth. Situated at the meadow's furthest reach, he recalls—and may have had in mind—Sappho's mountain hyacinth, trampled by heedless shepherds (§18). How different his plight from that of Sappho's reddened apple—a symbol of intact virginity, topmost upon the bough (§17).

The extreme and rapid shift from vulgarity to delicacy, from bravura to bathos, from the mythological and known-inhabited worlds to Lesbia's lecherous doorstep and, ultimately, to an isolated field—all is conveyed, *articulated*, in measured Sapphic stanza, boldly chosen for coarse albeit well-calculated subject matter, the likes of which it had never previously known. Thus did Catullus "make it new." It is the best and most effective rage—*controlled*, pressure-cooked in the cast iron of form and hissing stridently. We are reminded, in this connection, of Longinus's formulation, above, of the "agitation" that "both checks the utterance and at the same time drives it on."

We have previously noted the hundred years of civil war and anarchy that preceded the publication of Virgil's *Aeneid* (19 BC): the murderous proscriptions, rampant thuggery, and massive confiscations of land; the decades of bloodshed, treachery, and near-total social dissolution that especially followed the assassination of Julius Caesar (44 BC). Catullus (84–54 BC) wrote during this period, while Virgil and Horace, ages twenty-six and twenty-one upon Caesar's assassination, were already embarked on the peerless careers that would make them the "common currencies of civilization." The times could have been no worse; the poetry, no better. Relentless social upheaval did not lead to "free verse" (were it an option), any more than did extended, brutalizing army service and fighting, always *mano a mano*, for any number of Greek and Roman soldier-poets. "Horace's lifetime belonged to the most tumultuous age of Roman history.... It was also the finest age of Latin Literature." Indeed, the flowering of Latin literature in the age of Augustus astounds all the more as the ultimate, and superior, accomplishment of a people perforce hardened by history—first, for survival, then dominance, 'the achievement of a people which', as Livy reminds us, 'had been eight hundred years at war' *(populi iam octingentesimum bellantis annum res)*. We do well to keep such matters in mind when considering the modernist premise that war and the horrors of war are inimical to the production of coherent verse or art.

❧

The Sapphic element in Catullus, Poem 11 extends beyond the formal and feminizing elements observed to thematic contrast with the "Hymn to Aphrodite"—Catullus, as Sappho in the Hymn, summoning help in an amatory impasse. A verse translation of the Hymn appears in PART III of this volume. For present purposes I translate literally as follows, the poem's seven stanzas rendered as prose paragraphs of three or four lines each:

> Flower-adorned, O deathless Aphrodite,
> Zeus's daughter, weaver of wiles, I beseech
> you, do not with madness or folly subdue,
> O Lady, my heart;

But come to this place, if ever at other times,
hearing my voice from afar, you listened, and
leaving your father's golden house, came,

yoking your chariot; swift the lovely sparrows
that drew you to dusky earth, fast-circling their
wings in the midst of clear-skied heaven.

Quickly they arrived, and you, O blessed
one, immortal visage smiling forth, asked
what again I suffered, and why again I called,

and what in my maddened heart I most desired
to happen. "On whom, again, do I prevail to take
you back in love? Who, O Sappho, wrongs you?

"For if now she flees, she will soon pursue;
if refusing gifts, she will give them soon;
if by love unmoved, she will quickly love,
though not wanting to."

Come again to me now, and free me from crushing
concerns; as much as my own heart would fulfill,
*fulfill*; yourself my ally be.

In the Hymn's final verse, Sappho summons the goddess as an "ally." In the first verse of his Poem 11, Catullus addresses Furius and Aurelius as "companions." As Poem 11 unfolds, we see that Catullus has summoned them on other occasions, even as Sappho has repeatedly called on Aphrodite. Catullus, however, summons his friends not to *win* but to *berate* a faithless lover. The companions' destination is Lesbia's house; Aphrodite's starting point in the Hymn is her father Zeus's house. Willing for Catullus's sake to traverse "the world entire," as Aphrodite traverses heaven for Sappho, the companions will answer his summons. They will do so, however, only as crosstown conveyors of prurient tidings. No amorous flight or pursuit as in the Hymn, but ready and repeated consummations—the housebound Claudia *consuming* her lovers.

Catullus, needless to say, is in dead earnest, while the Hymn, as further discussed below, is parody through and through, "visuals" included. Sparrows, known for their lasciviousness, draw Aphrodite's chariot in a mawkish epic send-up of a horse-drawn conveyance. With its comic implications for Aphrodite's size, just how does one envision this epiphany? Sparrows being but sparrows, a towering Aphrodite (gods always larger than humans) miniaturizes them from view. Or Aphrodite is herself somehow miniaturized for purposes of the poem. The yoking of sparrows, as if draft animals, is further incongruous. A sparrow-drawn chariot is thus either precious or ridiculous—either equally suited to the poem's mock-heroic manner. As the Hymn is mock-heroic, and even maudlin, so is Catullus's Poem 11. The latter nonetheless stands as a consummate example of poetic control in the service of fevered emotion, of form and content bound—more like *phainetai moi* in that respect than like the Hymn to which Poem 11 also refers; and much by way of contrast to the lethargic Poem 51.

As concerns its parodic elements, the Hymn's summons to Aphrodite is fully déjà vu. Sappho has many times called on Aphrodite, even as the goddess acknowledges the iterations and gently chides her for them ("what again . . . why again. . . . On whom, again"). Sappho's own appreciation of the to-do is apparent in her ready repetition of Aphrodite's rebuke, through both indirect and direct questioning ("you asked what . . ." and "'Who, O Sappho . . .'"). The iterations—of Aphrodite's visits and of her questions on each occasion (as posed by Sappho)—bespeak a close relationship between Sappho and her protector: "the poet ventriloquates the goddess in dialogue with herself, producing a fusion of their voices."

Speaking Aphrodite's rebuke, Sappho essentially rebukes herself. Indeed, with the change from indirect to direct questioning, the rebuke intensifies. Sappho knows what Aphrodite will say and spares her the trouble. Aphrodite promises reversal, with the sweetener that the recalcitrant girl will eventually love, unable to keep from doing so, and *quite* knowing as much. Whether the girl will unwillingly love Sappho or another is unclear, as the verse lacks a second-person pronoun. The line reads: "if by love unmoved, she will quickly love" (*not* ". . . she will quickly love *you*"). The object of the recalcitrant girl's pursuit may thus be one other than Sappho, with Sappho the observer rather than instrument of Aphrodite's justice. We note in passing that the sole indication of the beloved's gender in the Greek is the delayed feminine participle in the concluding line of the second-to-last stanza: (*k'ōuk*) *etheloisa* '(though not) wanting'. Only at this point does the stanza—as if by afterthought—reveal its lesbian affection.

The Hymn resonates not only by comparison to Catullus 11, but to *phainetai moi*. While detailed comparison of Sappho's only two—and randomly—surviving poems may seem suspect, the poems yet depict polarities of emotional response. We noted in *phainetai moi* Sappho's immediate collapse—emotional, psychological, artistic—upon viewing "that man" close by her beloved. Also pronounced was a reinforcing dictional speed, the result of multiple elisions producing a hurried, breathless effect. No Aphrodite to the rescue there, pledging a better, brighter day; instead, apoplexy and near-death. No humorous iteration of an all-too-frequent travail, but a scene as equally beyond reversal as recurrence.

The Hymn takes a detached and expansive view. Sappho is there the self-ironic observer of her own repeated plight. The proximities of *phainetai moi*—the observed lovers in intimate conversation, Sappho voyeuristically looking on, the imminence of death—stand opposed to the distances of the Hymn: a beloved in flight, Aphrodite traversing heaven, and grammatically indirect questions. There is much conversation in both situations. In *phainetai moi* it is intimate, undisclosed, and enduring. In the Hymn it is openly (if mawkishly) spoken for all the world to hear, in clearly numerable questions. It is Sappho not once and for all besieged, as in *phainetai moi*, but merely *again* beset. Where there is conversation, there are smiles and laughter. Hearing the girl's "sweet laughter," Sappho would construe it either as a rebuke to her affections or an incitement to jealousy, but only to the extent that Sappho covets the man's proximity to his—and her own—beloved. (Contrary to some interpretations, Sappho wishes neither the man's gender nor genitalia.) In the Hymn, however, laughter by Aphrodite is beside the point, as Sappho essentially mocks herself. Aphrodite's knowing smile ("immortal visage shining forth") is laughter enough.

Though *phainetai moi* was not then the subject of Longinus's remarks, we noted his observation—no less true of that poem—that phrasing can "tumble out unconnected in a sort of spate, almost too quick for the speaker himself. . . . The phrases being disconnected, and yet none the less rapid, give the idea of an agitation which both checks the utterance and at the same time drives it on. This effect the poet has achieved by his use of asyndeton." The same cannot be said of the Hymn, which lacks any such agitation. The poem, instead, unfolds with the ease suggested by Aphrodite's sweeping descent—with time enough for questions, all previously asked and answered. The situation is born not of the explosive moment, but of tiring experience. Indeed, the benign "immortal visage shining forth" signals divine understanding *sub specie aeternitatis*. The Hymn's emotion is well rehearsed, answering to expectation rather than dictated by necessity.

Longinus further notes concerning the Hymn (though without specifically mentioning it): "emotion is always more telling when it seems not to be premeditated by the speaker but to be born of the moment." The emotion of the Hymn, as noted, is not born of the moment but of recurrence. In the next sentence, Longinus concludes that "questioning and answering one's self counterfeits spontaneous emotion." Sappho here peculiarly counterfeits emotion. Her self-deprecating posture is conveyed (and the poem's action delayed) not by questions she asks Aphrodite or Aphrodite asks her but, at a remove, by questions *Sappho has Aphrodite ask her*. Sappho in effect questions only herself. The emotion is counterfeit, but endearingly so.

Catullus's two poems in Sapphic meter, the first such in extant Latin literature, reveal him in a Sapphic themes-and-variations mood—all prompted by, and thoroughly meaningless without, Sapphic *form*. In sum, form/manner is always fully bound to content/meaning—form and content the proverbial two sides of the same coin. Examples could be multiplied. For the present, however, the two Sapphic and two Catullan poems suffice to show what the strictures of form impart to the making, meaning, and pleasures of poetry.

But that was once upon a time. The early modernists, largely abandoning form, consigned content to the leveling winds. With form abandoned, most any content would do, making controlled, and thus *intelligible*, content increasingly anachronistic. Western poetry, originating in Homer, preceded both prose and writing. It did not at some arbitrary point "put on" form—a thing to be later "put off"—but made its epiphany *as* form, thus shaping the West's literary consciousness. With the start of the twentieth century, however, over 2,500 years of tradition were ready for the scrap heap. There is, notes pianist-critic Charles Rosen (1927–2012), a "neutralizing interaction" between "established practice" and "radical modernization" that "has so far warded off the final verdict of death for our inheritance of the past." Yes, so far.

# Chapter 25

## Modernism Wins Out: Form and Content Abandoned

> Hundreds of people who had never written poetry, decided free verse must be easy, and committed one of the grandest conglomerate blunders in our literary annals.
>
> – ARTHUR KREYMBORG, "The Free Verse Revolt"

> *Some* good! If there is not *all* good, there is no good . . . all inferior poetry is an injury to the good, inasmuch as it takes away the freshness of rhymes, blunders upon and gives a wretched commonality to good thoughts; and, in general, adds to the weight of human weariness in a most woeful and culpable manner.
>
> – JOHN RUSKIN, "Two Orders of Poets"

MODERNISM, AS IT DEVELOPED from the mid-nineteenth through early twentieth century, was a self-conscious artistic break with the classical past, seeking to disclaim traditional forms and beliefs in accordance with what were considered modern ideas. The movement quickened in the aftermath of World War I. The war's unspeakable carnage and devastation, defying logic, seemed the death of Western civilization itself and all its traditions, values, beliefs, and rules. Reason, proven false, had outlived its usefulness, yielding to doubt and free association. Unity, an illusion, yielded to fragmentation and multitudinous possibility; beauty, to the mundane, unsightly, and repellent—all welcome in its stead as better reflecting reality. "Behind this extreme subjectivity," notes American literary and social critic Irving Howe (1920–1993), "lurks an equally extreme sense of historical impasse, the assumption that something about the experience of [the] age is unique, a catastrophe without precedent." The catastrophe of World War I induced an extreme response: the rejection of what was then considered an inconstant and seditious past, including the traditions and wisdom of the ages. The goal: to deconstruct, reconstruct, and build anew; to "make it new"—what Howe called modernism's "improvisation of 'the tradition of the new.'"

We earlier noted an analogy between the upsurge of modernism following the cataclysm of World War I (1914–1918) and the rise of neotericism (Gr. *neos* 'new'; *neoteros* 'newer') following the physical and moral depletion of the Peloponnesian War (431–404 BC). The analogy is suggestive and merits further thought, as the desire for renewal, for the new and ever newer, typically follows cataclysm. The question is, at what cost to the old.

In words that resonate for the rise of twentieth-century modernism, the *Columbia Encyclopedia* entry for "Ancient Greek Music" states the case as follows:

> After the fall of Athens in 404, an anti-intellectual reaction took place against the classical art, and by about 320 it was almost forgotten. The new style, which resulted in the rise of professional musicians, was marked by subjective expression, free forms, more elaborate melody and rhythms, and chromaticism. The chief musical figures were Phrynis of Mytilene (c. 450), his pupil Timotheus of Miletus, and the dramatist Euripides. Finally, ancient Greek music lost its vitality and dwindled to insignificance under the Roman domination [starting in 146 BC].

A brief overview of the three above-named musicians helps close the more than 2,300-year divide between the Peloponnesian War and World War I, and the modernist impulses arising from each. The comparison is instructive, tending, again, to illustrate that the more things change, the more they stay the same; here, that there was nothing especially new in the early twentieth-century mandate to "make it new."

Of the shadowy Phrynis (c. 490–420 BC), hailing from but doing little to credit Sappho's own Mytilene, Plutarch relates: "In short, the style of singing to the cithara instituted by Terpander continued to be quite simple down to the period of Phrynis [approximately two hundred years]; for in ancient times it was not permitted to sing to the cithara as at present." Phrynis then marked a turn away from the acknowledged tunefulness and simplicity of Terpander (Chapter 7). Other sources relate that Phrynis's innovations included the combination of hexameter "with loose meter" (or rhythm) and the use of *more* than the seven strings that Terpander had introduced, but which Terpander himself, as seen, preferred *not* to use. Though there was little stopping such novelties, they came not without objection. At a performance in Sparta, the ephors, or city overseers, asked Phrynis whether he wished to have the two extra strings cut from the top or bottom of his lyre. And Aristophanes in his *Clouds* (423 BC) makes the following slighting reference: "And if any of the boys fooled around or performed the kind of twist they perform nowadays, one of those real twisters, Phrynis-style, he would get a thorough hammering for doing away with the Muses" (Gr. *tas Mousas aphanizōn* 'making the Muses unseen'). An eclipse of the Muses, or upending of music as it was known, has a twentieth-century counterpart in the abandonment of tonality (tonal music being fixed by key and the relationship between notes). None of Phrynis's works survives.

Timotheus of Miletus (446–357 BC) extended Phrynis's radical "new music" practices, adding a tenth and eleventh string and making "the old fashion music more effeminate." This time gesturing with a knife, the ephors are reported to have posed the same question of Timotheus concerning a reduction in the number of his strings. Timotheus is also among a number of poets deemed "more vulgar and fond of novelty, aiming for what is now called the popular and money-spinning cithara style: the use of few strings and simplicity and dignity in music hav[ing] dropped out of fashion completely." Analogies with twentieth-century modernism are apparent. Following Phrynis's practice of combining hexameter "with loose meter" (Gr., *tō*(*i*) *lelumenō*(*i*) 'with the loosened [meter]'; perf. pass. part. of *luō*), Timotheus is also credited, in a singular reference by the Greek metrist Hephaistion (2nd century AD), with "free verse" itself, or such as it was then known (Gr. *apolelumena;* perf. pass. part. *apoluo* = *apo* 'away' + *luo* 'loose, loosen'). Verse that is *apolelumena* is written "at random and without definite meter." Only fragments of Timotheus's works survive.

Of the famed late fifth-century tragedian Euripides (480–406 BC), of whose more than one hundred known dramas barely one-tenth survives, the classicist Glen Bowersock (b. 1936) observes:

> No writer of this turbulent time understood better than Euripides that the brutal dissolution of traditional social and political norms allowed, even required, a new kind of drama. He took one risk after another in subverting traditional tragedy by rethinking myths, reimagining familiar characters, and exploring new possibilities for music outside the choral odes. It is hard not to see all this as somehow induced by the war.

The difference, among others, is that Euripides's innovations did not seek to nullify dramatic form or metric convention, or make dead letter of the literature, however battered by war. To the contrary, in the year of the defeat of Athens, it is the weightier Aeschylus (525–456 BC), not the trendy Euripides, that Aristophanes's *Frogs* (405 BC) retrieves from the underworld. Athens *in extremis* requires the classic, not the avant-garde. Aeschylus, in departing, urges that his place in Hades be taken by Sophocles, not by Euripides.

Thus was antiquity's "modernism" born of distrust of the past following the trauma of protracted war and Athens's demise as political and cultural capital of the ancient world. A complete break with tradition, however, was neither advocated nor sought. Then modernist practice, as noted, became centered in Alexandria during the third and second centuries BC, exerting its influence on Latin literature aborning in the third century through to the publication of Virgil's *Aeneid* (19 BC). Following World War I, a "loosening" of literary standards—the rejection of a now dated past—would also take hold of English poetry. The change, epitomized in the farrago that is Pound's *The Cantos,* is announced in the second section of his *Hugh Selwyn Mauberley* (1920):

> The age demanded an image
> Of its accelerated grimace,
> Something for the modern stage,
> Not, at any rate, an Attic grace;
>
> Not, not certainly, the obscure reveries
> Of the inward gaze;
> Better mendacities
> Than the classics in paraphrase!

> The "age demanded" chiefly a mould in plaster,
> Made with no loss of time,
> A prose kinema, not, not assuredly, alabaster
> Or the "sculpture" of rhyme.

The rejection of "Attic grace" (line 4) signals the obsolescence of Attica—the region of Greece containing Athens (see map)—and its achievements. Knowingly or not, Pound here aligns the Classical Greek and early twentieth-century postwar periods, urging that classic forms no longer suit the latter, even as they declined in the former. Yielding instead to the "accelerated grimace" of his time, Pound proposes a "modern[ist] stage" from which the recognizable poetry of the past—rhymed, metered, attentively sculpted—is, Phrynis-like, "made unseen." Reflex superseding reflection, the goal is no longer a considered rendering or communicable understanding, but a kind of plastered slapdash "made with no loss of time." The end product is apparent in the "mendacity" that is Pound's *Homage to Sextus Propertius* (1919). (The work, composed in a year's time, is the subject of Chapter 34.) "*Mauberley*," notes Michael Schmidt in his voluminous *Lives of the Poets*, "is the last poem by Pound which English readers at large will tolerate. Many seem to part company with the poet after this point, seeing the later work as a wild aberration in its form, language, allusiveness, and in its politics." And yet, if readers no longer tolerate the post-*Mauberley* Pound (they do!), the influence of Pound as "problematic, polyphilo-progenitive ancestor" of modernism has persisted over the years.

❧

Modernist promptings were anticipated in the acceleration, both cultural and industrial, of the years preceding World War I: Monet's *Impression, soleil levant* (1872)—from which impressionism took its name—the first telephone call (1876), the first controlled powered airplane flight (1903), the first mass-produced automobile (1908), Pound's *Personae* (1909), the New York Armory Show, Stravinsky's *Rite of Spring*, D. H. Lawrence's *Sons and Lovers*, Proust's *du Côté du Chez Swann* (the first volume of *À la Recherche du Temps Perdu)*, the opening of the Woolworth Building and of Grand Central Terminal (all in 1913), Joyce's *Dubliners* (1914), Eliot's "The Love Song of J.

Alfred Prufrock" (1915), and Joyce's *A Portrait of the Artist as a Young Man* (1916). The unspeakable savagery of World War I, however, appeared to both heighten and restrict response, rendering it too intense for containment—be it in words or in musical notation, or in plastic or architectural form, as traditionally known and nurtured. Love and death were themselves now other than what they had once and always been. They were *new*, or had to be newly considered and conceived. A *modern* sensibility was needed, and modernism was aborning. Art would now *historically* evolve, "keeping up with the times [as] a sign of its good behavior and its worthiness to be incorporated among the material evidences of progress." The modernist fallacy was that civilization is always developing toward an absolute and perfect end. The artist need only keep up with the times.

Though modernism blossomed with the war, its inception dates to the Industrial Revolution (c. 1760–c. 1830). The change was one from farming and hand production to machine, with a demographic shift from countryside to city. Pride in urban progress was subsequently exalted in a multitude of world expositions, beginning with the Crystal Palace Exhibition; Hyde Park, London (1851), styled: "Great Exhibition of the Works of Industry of All Nations." However, teeming city life—its possibilities and depravations—came burdened with busyness, impersonality, and neuroses. Cubism (c. 1910) perfectly reflected this malaise. With its fractured and flattened surfaces, i.e., its rejection of traditional perspective and near abandonment of recognizable subject matter, cubism reflected a lack of spatial and emotional depth, a lack of human scale and relationship. *La Ville* (*The City*) by Fernand Léger (1919) famously rendered the rush and confusion of city perceptions as a cubist collage (the work, like many of its kind, likely inviting a good deal of puzzlement). The city's alienating effects would figure into much of T. S. Eliot's work, including "The Love Song of J. Alfred Prufrock" (the city as "abyss") and *The Waste Land* (read as a poem of the modern city). Reflecting in his essay "What Dante Means to Me" (1950) on the stimuli that inspired his work, Eliot cites the legacy of "the more sordid aspects of the modern metropolis," bequeathed him by Laforgue and Baudelaire. Early critics of modernism fulminated against "the unmetrical, incoherent banalities of the literary Cubists," doing so with specific reference to "Prufrock." Indeed, the poem comes laden with cubist compression: "When the evening is spread out against the sky

/ Like a patient etherized upon a table" equalizes high and low, flattens the depth of sky "upon a table," draining the very empyrean of perspective (and turning it upside down). The sky's life-sustaining aether becomes sense-numbing ether. The circumambient is localized, creating a sense of spatial and sensory suffocation.

Following the war, Léger became transfixed with the tubular and machine-like weaponry he had experienced at close range (almost dying in a mustard gas attack). Indeed, World War I was history's first mechanized war—the lethality of its weaponry an engineering and artistic fascination. Thus began Léger's "mechanical period." Meanwhile, the best known work of avant-garde composer George Antheil (1900–1959), in which Léger collaborated, was *Ballet Mécanique*, "scored for countless numbers of player pianos. All percussive, like machines. All efficiency, no love. Written without sympathy. Written cold as an army operates. Revolutionary as nothing has been revolutionary." In the composer's own words: "brutal, contemporary, hard-boiled, symbolic of spiritual exhaustion, the super-athletic, non-sentimental period commencing the 'The Long Armistice.'"

In the manner of his idol Stravinsky's *Le Sacre du Printemps* (*The Rite of Spring*), Antheil's *Ballet Mécanique* was an "essentially *romantic* work, breaking all the barriers, the rules, and thriving upon it." Also like *Sacre*, *Ballet* was a work inviting performance riot—with riot at the Paris (1926), but not Carnegie Hall (1927), premiere. The headline of the *New York Evening Post* (April 11, 1927) read, "Expected Riots Peter Out at George Antheil's Concert—Sensation Fails to Materialize." Antheil himself registers disappointment with the less-than-riotous Carnegie Hall reception: "Such reported 'rioting' as might have occurred . . . seemed—at least to me—synthetic." In truth, much that transpired in the early avant-garde had a "three-ring circus" aspect. Antheil applies the phrase to the Carnegie Hall debut of *Ballet*—owing to a series of performance miscalculations and mishaps. These included his publicist's last-minute deployment of a real airplane propeller to supplement the score's wind machine. Antheil—whose *oeuvre* shows him capable of far better—shamelessly primped and promoted *Ballet*, courting audience stupefaction in hopes of a Stravinsky-like *succès de scandale.*

The beat goes on, Stravinsky in tow, but nowadays with mechanized sex instead of machinery. "Scandalous Opera Bares All" reads a 2003 review of composer Thomas Adès's "Powder Her Face" (1995). The performance "jolted the New York City Opera's brief spring season to a sizzling start"—with twenty-five nude males taking the stage as "the gym-toned spirits of one-night stands past" and a "nerve jangling score, which sounds like Stravinsky, Ravel and Alban Berg run through a Cuisinart." "Observ[ing] all this debauchery with hardly a snicker [the audience] exploded in bravos for cast and director." Nothing has changed in the twelve years since. Ours is a post-scandalous age: no riots, just riotous good fun. Irving Howe predicted in 1953 that modernism would *not* die, however rattling its death throes then seemed, but would encounter "the kind of savage parody which may indeed be the only fate worse than death." He was wrong. Though early lampooned by some, modernism has been little parodied in the more than sixty years since Howe wrote. Nor has it become more shocking, our age being as equally beyond scandal as shock. Modernism has become increasingly and more outlandishly *self*-parodic. The band plays on; the jaded rejoice.

❧

"Make it new" exhorted Ezra Pound in an even then pointless directive—and the goad ever since to feckless self-indulgence. Renewal is the precondition of life and art both. Everything from the mundane to the exhilarating is *new* upon inception. The best of what is new endures, aging without growing old. Remaining fresh, inviting, and revivifying, it becomes classic, traditional.

Each day *renews* the day before. Thus is the goddess Dawn, Aurora, depicted as eternally young. The ancient Greek poets, as seen, were *originally* new, even as the Latin poets were *imitatively* new. Bach and the Beatles were initially *new*—following no directive to *be* or make it so—as were all the literary, artistic, and musical traditions that Pound and the modernists proposed for the scrap heap. The issue, then, is whether "the new" *renews* or rejects the past; whether it nurtures, negates, or possibly supersedes tradition—tradition itself once inspirationally new, periodically renewed, and retaining a presumptive claim to allegiance. Modernism's pervasive rejections and negations proceed from the false belief of progress in the arts, the belief that the arts and the society they reflect necessarily improve and grow better, the new necessarily better than what preceded. The goal of continuous improvement—of *progressivism*—is perfection in a utopian future. The goal, being absolute, is *transformative* at any and all costs and by whatever means. Hence that key strain of European modernism known as futurism—its founder Filippo Marinetti an early fascist and Mussolini supporter—with its aggressive push toward a utopian past-unencumbered future.

Pound's "make it new" was a call for negation. What had once made a work new, and how the lesson might be appreciated or applied, was of little interest. "Out with the old, in with the new" was the order—the disorder—of the day, and the result for the most part pernicious. "One goes on year after year getting the disorder of one's own mind in order," said Yeats, "and this is the real impulse to create.'" But not so with Pound who, as Yeats further observes, "'has made flux his theme; plot, characterization, logical discourse, seem to him abstractions unsuitable to a man of his generation." It is thus small wonder that in 1949, more than thirty years later, "nobody seems to have discovered in the *Cantos* the structure which Pound thought he had realized in them." Of his unfinished lifelong opus, Pound himself lamented: "I cannot make it cohere." The only order discernible in Pound's *Cantos* is the "total order culminating in [Mussolini], who derives his prestige ultimately from the power of his example and from his intelligence." Pound arrogated much of his own power from the self-centered cachet of his own example and intelligence, imagining himself the artistic counterpart to Mussolini's *Il Duce*. Not for nothing has *The Cantos* been deemed Pound's "Fascist Epic." Mussolini, as protagonist of *The Cantos*, is Pound's *deus ex machina*—at once the savior of disordered civilization and orderer of the unorderable in Pound's own mind—or what remained of it during *The Cantos*' more than fifty-year gestation.

Walt Whitman (1819–1892), the "Father of Free Verse," predated Pound's promptings, making it astoundingly new with the 1855 publication of *Leaves of Grass*. Ralph Waldo Emerson aside, the self-published twelve-poem work was harshly received. Containing "Song of Myself," it set the maniacally egocentric tone of Whitman's free-verse extravaganza: *self* the center of existence; Whitman's self—as he declares in the work's preface—a "kosmos." And everyone's self a kosmos/cosmos, etc. The publication was excoriatingly reviewed by Dante translator and Harvard art historian Charles Eliot Norton (1827–1908). Although fame largely evaded Whitman during his lifetime, America would eventually grow into Whitman—wearing him like an oil-softened glove. Pound, not surprisingly, came to admire him.

In 1919 Pound sought to make the Roman love elegist Propertius *new*, misapprehending how entirely modern Propertius was and had always been, which is to say, how much a *classic*. T. S. Eliot, by contrast, made it new to startling effect (with Pound's encouragement and sponsorship) in *The Waste Land* (1922), a lament for post–World War I civilization. The work evoked a sensation "due in part to its intrinsic beauty, in part to its musical despair, and in part to its controversial inspiration aroused by its obscurity." If Pound lacked one of these qualities, it was intrinsic beauty. The same year saw James Joyce's *Ulysses*, also under Pound's sponsorship, which "had a similar effect in the world of literature and was destined to parallel in prose the influence 'The Waste Land' exerted in poetry. . . . Postwar despair and disillusionment found themselves heroically sung, in a bold spirit of tragi-comedy, in the perfectly cadenced lines of the patrician Eliot and hurly-burly and hullabaloo of Rabelaisian Joyce."

Commentaries aside, *The Waste Land* and *Ulysses* engendered a host of pretenders and wannabes, as had Whitman. Whitman's influence, however, was more harmful, given his greater comprehensibility, his homoeroticism, exoticism, and poetic lack of inhibition. An early Whitman pretender was Pound himself, whose *Personae* (1909)—with its "unmetrical sprawling lengths"—English poet Rupert Brooke (1887–1915) deemed to have fallen under Whitman's "dangerous influence." At his best inimitable, Whitman at his frequent worst drove poetry over the brink. Significantly, it was not a post–Civil War lament for America that provided the initial impetus to the dissolution of form and content in Whitman; three editions of *Leaves of Grass* had appeared *before* the war, and as many and more after. Egotism aside, Whitman shared one indispensable quality with modernism: shock value. This, for Whitman, was the artless byproduct of audacity. For the modernists, it was a stratagem. In both cases, it assured success.

Though modernist parallels to Pound and Eliot are apparent in music (Stravinsky), painting (Picasso), and sculpture (Brancusi), the endgame that conferred the victory on modernism was not necessarily foregone. As author, poet, and literary entrepreneur extraordinaire James Atlas (b. 1949) notes recounting the early travails of modernism:

> What was it about these books that made the public so nervous? D. H. Lawrence's *The Rainbow* was banned in England; *The Waste Land* was derided in the Press. From the vantage of the early

> Twenties, things looked grim indeed. "With the *Egoist* finished, Vorticism over, Pound self-exiled from London, Lewis almost silent, Eliot faintly praised, *Ulysses* effectively banned from publication, it must have been tempting to think in 1921 that what its enemies regarded as the lunacies of modernism were over."

To be sure, Stravinsky, Picasso, and Brancusi could, at their pleasure, be as traditionally as they were experimentally innovative, *renewing* tradition rather than "making it new." Witness Picasso's progression from his largely representational Blue and Rose Periods to cubism—and cubism run rampant—and the often grotesquely self-parodic work of his later years. So also Stravinsky's *Sacre,* a pulsating modernist icon, versus his *Pulcinella Ballet* (1919), a neoclassical work based on eighteenth-century *commedia dell'arte* (Chapter 3); a work that Stravinsky considered "the epiphany through which the whole of my late work became possible[,] . . . a backward look, of course—the first of many love affairs in that direction." Stravinsky tellingly considered that *look* "a look in the mirror, too," as if to indicate the viewing of his truer self. In his "backward look" Stravinsky was perhaps more forward-looking than he realized, since commedia "types" are never old, but always new—as *modern,* in a word, as anything early twentieth-century modernists might want.

Other post–World War I "gems of the repertoire"—tonal, introspective, recognizably rhythmic, achingly beautiful—include Frank Bridge's *Sonata for Cello and Piano* (1918) and Edward Elgar's *Cello Concerto* (1919), however much the latter reflects a postwar melancholy and the war-altered mood of Elgar's declining years. Composed between 1913 and 1917, the Bridge sonata is no less fixed, constant, or classical for the chaos of the period of its gestation. (A similar constancy prevails in the post–World War II creation of Richard Strauss's *Oboe Concerto* in 1945 and Sergei Prokofiev's *Cello Sonata* in 1949.) Especially telling of classicism's dominance in wartime is Maurice Ravel's *Le Tombeau de Couperin,* composed between 1914 and 1917 (François Couperin, 1668–1733; French composer, organist, harpsichordist). As an ambulance driver at the Verdun front, Ravel saw the worst of the war's butchery. His *Tombeau* ("memorial piece") was written as a suite for solo piano in six movements, each dedicated to the memory of a fallen friend. The idiom in which Ravel paid homage was that of the

Baroque French keyboard suite, with its ornamentations; bygone modal harmonies; and, in the third suite, neoclassical elements. Ravel did not fixate on the war or repeatedly plummet into its darkness, but, as a "master of logic and reason, looked back with yearning to an earlier age of aristocratic elegance." When criticized for the *Tombeau*'s lightheartedness, Ravel is reported to have said, "The dead are sad enough, in their eternal silence."

Accordingly, Ravel did not resort to chaos to convey chaos or its toll. With *Tombeau* he chose intelligibly to celebrate lives tragically lost, instead of inconsolably or incoherently mourning them. So also in his *Piano Concerto for the Left Hand* (1929–1930), commissioned by pianist-friend Paul Wittgenstein—brother of philosopher Ludwig—who lost his right arm in the war. The seventeen-minute one-movement piece is tonal throughout; its moods in turn somber, sonorous, agitated, aspirational, idyllic, or subdued. The low-register orchestration (English horn, bass clarinet, two bassoons, contrabassoon, four horns, three trombones, and tuba) provides the appropriate depth and melancholy. A percussive *marche-militaire* rhythm begins toward the concerto's midpoint, punctuated by staccato piano and brass. The section insistently progresses, in a way reminiscent of Ravel's similarly orchestrated *Boléro* (1928). The piano predominates in the concluding two and one-half minutes, sounding graceful, sounding optimistic, even as it seems to signal—before a *Boléro*-like ending—not one arm lost, but *one* playing with the beauty of *two*.

Is not the loss of a pianist's arm comparable to the "breaking" of the poet's tongue seen in Sappho's *phainetai moi*? Sappho paradoxically conveys the experience of vocal rupture in a uniquely articulated and resourceful poem—one affirming the artistic process even as it conveys the artist's near-death experience. Ravel for his part determinedly plucks *new* life from artistic near-death, indeed from near-death itself. Thus did Ravel "make it new" by renewing artistic life and hope precisely when they seemed ended. Both in his *Tombeau* and *Concerto*, and despite wartime trauma endured, Ravel sought life's reaffirmation through traditional life-giving forces. The war profoundly affected, but *did not defeat*, Ravel—"a Classicist by temperament . . . an elegant Apollonian, and exquisite jeweler." As for Ravel's *Boléro*, it is in C major, three-quarter time, progressing from *pianissimo* to *fortissimo*, built on an unchanging rhythmic snare-drum *ostinato*. As straightforward as it is mesmerizing, *Boléro* shows—*cause célèbre* though it was—that a work, even in the aftermath of war, could hew to entirely traditional resources, not needing scandal to succeed. It was, as much as anything else, the classic high-water mark of *simplicity*—call it iterative or insistent simplicity—that commended *Boléro.*

Although Ravel's *Tombeau* is admired to this day, it is Alban Berg's *succès de scandale,* the atonal and *Sprechstimme*-infused *Wozzeck*—the twentieth century's first avant-garde opera (composed 1914–1922)—that attracts the sold-out audience. It is, for shock value, the direct descendant of Stravinsky's scandalous *Sacre.* Berg, too, witnessed the war as a soldier in the Austrian army. And what Berg took away from it resonates in his *Wozzeck,* even as it resonated with postwar audiences: expressions of rage, madness, and alienation—all amplified and conveyed through a cacophonous break with the past. Thus, despite the example of Ravel and the classicism of many of Stravinsky's own works, it is Stravinsky's most audacious work, *Le Sacre*; the audacities of Berg's *Wozzeck*; and, in painting, the outlandishness of Picasso's late works that prevail. The modernist triumph demonstrates three things. First, the force of personality and its cult—Pound's especially—in determining taste: the more *outré,* the more transgressive, the better. Second, the public's craving for astonishment (*il faut épater le bourgeois*), and relatedly, its herd mentality. And third, the public's predilection for a buzz, even in the early twentieth century, driven by unrelenting media, to say nothing of Pound's own calculated merchandising.

Even as totalitarianism takes root in the cult of personality—the infallible leader, his total control over every aspect of life, and the conformity required of the perfected individual in the perfect society—we note the obeisance afforded Pound, and the prescriptive, if sacrosanct, nature of Pound's own example. Most *welcomed* Pound as the messiah of laissez-faire poetics—embracing his idiosyncratic persona and liberating message—for only through Pound would they be poetically enfranchised. They could scrap the tradition to which they themselves were unequal and which, in the end, they little understood. All they had to do was "make it new." Nor was Pound unaware of the appeal he exerted, noting at age thirty-five in a letter to Ford Madox Ford: "Any damn thing I put down is susceptible of being made into a new academicism." Pound quite believed this, dispensing "gists and piths" (as Michael Dirda too approvingly refers to them) from the singular repository of his own eclecticism, from what the unteachable disdainer of professors dubbed the "Ezruversity." Indeed, the entire Pound phenomenon comes within what

Leon Botstein (b. 1946) calls "the preference of the marketplace, the dynamics of fashion . . . and the propagandistic talents of a few darlings of the elite taste-makers . . . to explain how and why some artists, writers, and composers become heralded as . . . the prophetic voices of the age."

Fascist in his poetic heart of hearts, no less than he would prove to be in his politics, Pound exerted an inordinate influence as "Poetic Leader" of modernity. Indeed, his control over poetic sensibility was and has long been as great as any fascist dictator's control over the conditions of life, Pound's gists and piths well suited to a Chairman Ezra's *Little Red Book*. "Intellectual intolerance, striking at all simplicity of form[,] . . . now rides the world," noted *Books Abroad* editor Gilbert Malcom Fess in 1952. Citing publisher hostility to any submission that makes sense, and its preference for the difficult and relatively unintelligible, Fess lamented the duration of modernism into the early 1950s—its having behaved "like a totalitarian dictator gone to seed." Fess continues:

> Modernists were said to have 'stood on the rostrum and shouted themselves hoarse,' like any political zealots. They used precisely the Big Lie tactics preferred by absolute governments: 'If we tell the people often enough it's poetry, and get critics to tell them it is poetry, in the end they'll disregard the testimony of their own sense, and believe it is poetry.' . . . Modernists operate 'with an intolerance which denies others the right to exist.' The editors of *Pinnacle,* the magazine of the League for Sanity in Poetry, described modernism as genocide: poets were being exterminated. ('The actual mandate, to be precise, prescribes not that all poets be exterminated, but only those who respect the literary traditions of three thousand years.')

One thing is thus certain: the 'middle class' (*le bourgeois*), once 'shocked' (*épaté*), relishes the condition. Better vociferous disbelief than awe-struck reverence. Indeed, in the new art ideology to which modernism gave rise, originality had nothing to do with beauty or tradition but was tantamount to shock value alone. Only the rebellious was original and creative, regardless "the technical ability to express something new, and . . . the possession of something worthwhile new to express"—something of "transcendent worth," something appreciable *sub specie aeternitatis*. Innovation without these qualities is willful self-assertion, there being, in Goethe's words 'nothing more frightful than imagination without taste' (*nichts fürchterlicher als Einbildungskraft ohne Geschmack*); or, as the artist Donner says in Tom Stoppard's *Artist Descending the Staircase* (1972), "Imagination without skill gives us Modern Art." And if the repellent prevailed over the beautiful, it was (and is) because beauty is both rare and debatable, leaving the beauty-minded artist vulnerable, while ugliness is pervasive, unmistakable, and artistically self-insulating. Thus, if the modern is evolution from traditional forms and values—"worthwhile art grow[ing] out of other art"—modernism has been revolution, deformation, and the shock inhering in those occurrences (whence "shock value," understood as the value of shock in sustaining the modernist enterprise). Where the modern bespeaks appreciable change, modernism too often signals willful overthrow. The difference, to borrow from Aristotle's *Poetics,* is one between that which occurs by probability or necessity, and that which occurs at random—a difference ultimately between civilization and chaos.

❧

New classics are ever emerging. Sainte-Beuve has said that "such a classic may for a moment have been revolutionary; it may at least have seemed so, but it is not; it only lashed and subverted whatever prevented the restoration of the balance of order and beauty." The notion is of a kind with that previously voiced by critic Charles Rosen concerning the "neutralizing interaction" between that which is "established" and that which is "radically modern." To few might this have better applied than to the "Father of Modern Music" Claude Debussy (1862–1918). Debussy "demanded new forms that reflected the revolutionary poetry and painting of the new century. His mature music showed almost no resemblance to the past; balance and regularity no longer mattered. The diversity, irregularity and discontinuity of his forms were entirely different in each work." Debussy, however, was what would prove to be a conservative, or tonal, modernist who made it new without excess or idiosyncrasy, without bombast, grotesquerie, or escapist primitivism. To be sure, modernist escapism sought refuge—from the nostrums of history and religion—in the mutability of myth, the escape often embodied in notions of African primitivism: Stravinsky's *Sacre,* Picasso's *Demoiselles* and *Guernica,* Gaugin's Polynesia, Rousseau's jungles.

The escape is otherwise apparent in the retreat into childhood or bygone times, as seen in the color-flamboyant Matisse and *les Fauves* 'wild beasts'.

Debussy's mesmerizing free-chordal technique (the restrained opposite of Whitman's untempered free verse) made the *new* familiar, if instinctively appreciable, because it was essentially tonal. It also made Debussy at once logical and unpredictable as no other composer. Debussy "effortlessly broke any rule he needed to break. The first performance [1894] of *Prélude à l'après-midi d'un faune* [*Prelude to the Afternoon of a Faun*] opened new vistas for music." His *Pelléas et Mélisande* [1902] "was the last word in refined music and used the most sophisticated harmonic palette." With its "pages of unearthly beauty," it was a favorite of Proust—Debussy himself recording that he "tried to follow a law of beauty" during the ten years he spent composing it. *Pelléas* was a work—not surprisingly—of which Ezra Pound was contemptuously dismissive.

Composers become significant for the vistas they open and for our ability to enter them with a sense of familiarity and security. Beethoven and his predecessors aside, much the same may be said of Chopin and other Romantic composers, each in his way transcending the constraints of received classical form. Schoenberg, by contrast, would sanctify travesty—first with atonality, then with the systemized and contrivedly rules-bound atonality that was serialism—abandoning the tonal hierarchies that had defined European music for centuries. Markedly devoid of emotion, the New Music, as it developed, was largely "head music," fed and thriving on theory. The more famed of the latter-day "complexity boys," reviving Schoenberg's discredited serialism, include Milton Babbitt (1916–2011) and Pierre Boulez (1925–2016). Also noteworthy are Luciano Berio, Elliott Carter, György Ligeti, and Iannis Xenakis. The extremes of these composers are apparent in the Greek Xenakis (1922–2001), who sought to improve upon modernist formularity by generating "pitch sets" from mathematical formulae. Of interest for purposes of the present volume is his rebarbative *Psappha* (1975), written in unique graphic notation for six groups of instruments—three of woods and/or skins and three of metal—with instrument choice ultimately left to the musicians. Such excitements have since somewhat yielded to a "New Tonalism" (dominated by post-1945 composers), a return to traditional values, to fullness over minimalism, to heart over head. Though suffering charges of "conventionalism," the return evidences nothing so much as the constraints—indeed, the appeal—of reality. The excesses of early modernism had themselves occasioned a similar "Return to Order" (*le rappel à l'ordre*) in the years following World War I. The movement even then resisted outsize avant-gardism and sought a return to the traditions of classicism and realistic painting. As modernism's pervasive influence to this day attests, the movement was unsuccessful.

Among Debussy's (and Ravel's and Milhaud's) formative influences was Erik Satie (1866–1925). Satie's early works, *Gymnopaidiai* and *Sarabande,* evidenced "startling innovations in harmony"—"delicate, almost imperceptible melodies; an air of reticence . . . an eerie, almost unearthly simplicity and purity . . . an economy and control." Satie's work "did for music something of what the cubists were to do for painting and sculpture. Yet, because of its built-in orderliness and simplicity, it was less disruptive, less explosive, more sympathetic, more positively creative." Here too, perhaps, one distinguishes as a matter of degree between *modern* and *modernist*—between "effortlessly [breaking] any rule he needed to break" (Debussy), and being, at certain stages in his career, "so violently opposed [to] all limiting rules except those which he made and destroyed daily for himself" (Stravinsky). The extent to which rules may be broken is judged only by the result—by the greatness of what is produced or the divinity of instinct that produced it, as John Ruskin well understood. The assessment of course varies with the taste of the time.

It is enormously curious that Debussy was the first to hear Stravinsky's *Sacre,* playing it through with the composer—over one hundred years ago—in a four-handed piano version. The "Father of Modern Music"—admiring Stravinsky more as orchestrator than composer—remained ever ambivalent about the mother of all musical audacities that was Stravinsky's *Sacre.* In a decided rebuff to modernism, piano virtuoso Arthur Rubinstein (1887–1982) declined Stravinsky's *Piano Rag Music*—which Rubinstein had himself commissioned—as unsuited to his musical taste. Stravinsky responded by composing *Three Movements from Petrushka* for solo piano (1921), dedicated to and avidly played by Rubinstein thereafter. Rubinstein upheld a standard of taste, and Stravinsky complied. What was missing from the early avant-garde were sufficient nay-saying Rubinsteins—and, during the same period, Conrad Aikens.

Reviewing D. H. Lawrence's *Birds, Beasts and Flowers* for *The Dial* magazine (1924), Conrad Aiken—American poet and novelist, T. S. Eliot intimate, and United States Poet Laureate (1950)—had this to say during modernism's still-formative phase:

> If there is any selection or arrangement at work at all, it is not enough in any poem here printed to make of it a work of art. It remains simply a kind of amusing chatty comment, under which one perceives that Mr. Lawrence's aim is simply the assertion of his personality. Perhaps he caught this from Whitman? At all events, it is a common form of aesthetic error at present . . .

And focusing on the issue of intelligibility in art:

> . . . it is easy to see that in what we are accustomed to call the "disintegration" of the arts during the last decade we witness a very marked movement away from the objective [what is intelligible to others] and toward the subjective [what is intelligible only to the artist]. In Cubism, Vorticism, Expressionism, and Dadaism, the emphatic common factor is the marked increase in the solipsism of the artist, accompanied as we should expect, by a more or less complete breaking up of established forms and symbols, and a conscious contempt for manifest intelligibility.

Referring to the "stammerings" of Pound, among others, Aiken prophetically equated the worst of modernist poetry with "the art of the definitely insane," but one step removed from "the compulsive iterations of religious mania."

It is thus apparent that not everyone was fooled or taken in—though sufficient, or sufficiently influential, numbers *were* to assure modernism's ascendancy and triumph. Debussy, *resisting* the modernist juggernaut, ultimately laid claim to the rebirth of classical music in the twentieth century, while the modernists, *making it new*, engendered often unwieldy and overweening offspring: a Chthonian versus an Olympian dispensation. In the year of his death (1971), Stravinsky—himself arguably a father of modern music—asserted, "Debussy is in all senses the century's first musician." Stravinsky and others would have been impossible without Debussy's example.

Pound himself straddling many lines and fences sought "pure" or "significant" form, clear language, and precise imagery as the early 1920s leader of the "imagist" movement (Pound contriving a variety of catchy labels, e.g., "vorticist," as he progressed). He nonetheless composed *The Cantos* over half a century, in a relentlessly obscurant fashion—the obscurantism not as "new" as he might have thought—making Joyce, by contrast, an easy read. Pound was a jack of many languages (haplessly deployed throughout *The Cantos*) but master of few—Latin and Greek among them. He edited *The Waste Land* down to half its original length for publication. Equally welcome would have been half a Pound.

The modernists were, from the movement's inception, a small and incestuous albeit explosive circle. Pound and Eliot were both influenced by the short-lived Jules Laforgue (1860–1887), one of the first French poets to write in free verse, himself influenced by Whitman and French impressionism. Pound conflictedly admired Whitman. Impressionism, breaking the rules of academic painting—"any rule it needed to break"—was both controversial and ascendant as Debussy reached his teens, and the composer was instinctively influenced by it. Matured to acceptance by the early twentieth century, impressionism was on display with yet newer and more controversial European and American offerings at New York's epochal International Exhibition of Modern Art—aka the Armory Show of 1913 (the same year as Stravinsky's *Sacre* and other cultural milestones).

The *New York Times*, in its editorial of March 16, 1913, styled "Cubists of All Sorts," was nothing if not prescient concerning what the Armory Show portended. Having been proven largely correct in the more than one hundred years since, the piece warrants quotation in substantial part (but how the *Times* has since changed its tune):

> . . . The cant of these people already fills the air. We all know too well that judgment of their silliness by common-sense methods will not avail to silence them. They may all be arrant humbugs, or some of them may be weak-minded persons who really believe their unintelligible markings and scratches signify something.
>
> . . . But it should be borne in mind that this movement is surely a part of the general movement, discernible all over the world, to disrupt and degrade, if not to destroy, not only art, but literature and society, too. There is a kind of insanity extant which had its remote origin, it must be said, in the earlier developments of the democratic spirit. Its kinship to true democracy and to real freedom in thought, action, or expression, however, is slight and indefinite. . . .

> . . . Their only need seems to be that all that is old is bad, all that has been proved is false, all that has been cherished should be destroyed, all that is beautiful should be despised, all that is obvious should be ignored. Their power is wholly negative, they have nothing to replace the things they would exterminate.
>
> They have no true message to impart, but there is no room, nevertheless, to doubt the potency of their appeal to many of the disheartened, embittered, and discontented, as well as the mentally ill-balanced. Of course, they will not destroy art, supplant literature with ribald nonsense, abolish economic law, or permanently retard the growth of nations. But we have no present hope that their influence will not grow and produce evil results. The mirth they cause encourages them, the ridicule they receive actually strengthens them. The only influence that can overcome them is sound education. What the cubist artists show is false art. The reasoning of their brothers in other fields is false. In fighting cubists of all sorts the trustworthy weapon is the truth.

The rush to scrap tradition was on—the Armory Show's more traditional pieces so many irrelevancies. What credibility the avant-garde and its sundry "isms" may have garnered was subsequently dashed by yet another *succès de scandale*: Marcel Duchamp's *Fontaine* (*Fountain*) (1917). This was the instantly iconic porcelain urinal, signed "R. Mutt," offered up as sculptural art (or protest to art). It thenceforth added secretional and fecal matter to the artist's palette, setting the stage for the likes of Andrea Serrano, Chris Ofili, and Damien Hirst, and making the Venice of Titian, Tintoretto, and Veronese the romper room of Jeff Koons and the Venice Biennale. The idea behind *Fountain*, apparently, was that anything removed from its natural setting and function, set apart and offered for display or observation, was "art."

The influence has been pervasive. Indeed, we are recently reminded, "To a large extent, the art world today represents the institutionalization of Duchamp's early twentieth-century pranks." Yet few saw *Fountain* as the practical joke it was—the piece attracting, and tantalizing, rather than repelling with its outsize outlandishness. Indeed, humor, or "irony," was a core value of early modernism, signaling the divide between probity and caricature, norm and deviance (not that the divide was necessarily new). A form of denigration, *Fountain* is the ridicule of standards by those unequal to attaining them. Worse yet, *Fountain* would in time eclipse Duchamp's visionary *Nu descendant un escalier n° 2* (*Nude Descending a Staircase, No. 2*)—the most frequented and controversial (and then caricatured) work of the Armory Show, relegating it to secondary status. The joke was thus on Duchamp and on art itself—the world sooner agog at his buffoonery than at his tangible genius. What is *new* is not necessarily important, and what is important is not necessarily new. The lesson was lost on the early modernists and their followers, even as it has all but vanished amid the aggressively meaningless innovations (technological and other) of a later age. "For it is necessary to make a choice," says Sainte-Beuve, "and the first condition of taste, after obtaining knowledge of all, lies not in continued travel, but in rest and cessation from wandering. Nothing blunts and destroys taste so much as endless journeyings. . . ." When at the start of the *Odyssey* Telemachus admonishes his mother that men celebrate the song most newly heard, he is speaking solely of epic subject matter, not of hexametric obsolescence.

Those resisting modernism, or at least still beholden to tradition, were by far outnumbered, as it is easier to discard than preserve. However, as fixity conveys the root sense of art (Gr. *arariskō* 'to fix, set'), *preservation* is precisely the artist's calling, and as regards decline, the chronicling of decline for salutary ends (not the joining of hands in a drop to the bottom). Modernist though he was, American poet, playwright, and literary editor Alfred Kreymborg (1883–1966) showed himself a thinking man's modernist with the following view of the artist's fortifying role in crisis:

> The decline of an age has been set to high literature hitherto. European cultural history is full of notable examples: Tolstoy, Chekhov, Thomas Mann, Proust. The golden rattle has been torn from the hands of young America and he stands at the street corners weeping and bellowing. His incorrigible optimism can support him no longer. . . . The average American digs a terrified hole, and the average artist follows him thither. . . . It was never the artist's business to be shaken off without a fight, even against the inevitable. . . . He

> is an escapist in the sense he fashions a world of his own out of the world about him. But it is this world of his the human world reproduces or harks back to in an effort to reshape itself on firmer feet and broader wings.

The artist is thus ideally a standard bearer, especially in the worst of times. No matter how clear the illogic or regression, or grievous the fall, the standard—*a* standard—is the footing for ascent ("firmer feet and broader wings"). The ascent is as rightly boundless as the fall. Notes United States Poet Laureate and T. S. Eliot critic Stephen Spender (1909–1995): "So he [Eliot] was driven back on the position that in times of the breakdown of civilization the individual becomes peculiarly responsible to himself, has to remember that he lives not just in this time of collapse, these disrupted cities, but also in eternity, in the city of God."

It is on the wings of ascendant thought and example that the journey is made, be it by sonnet or epic. Wilfred Owen (1893–1918) honed his sonnet-writing skills during World War I: "To concentrate meaning and metaphor within that enduring form was no doubt a pleasure to him," said contemporary war poet and critic Edmund Blunden, "a trial of art, even if the topic was pain and grief." Owen was among the soldier-poets who "upheld the honor and necessity of poetry where hard times threatened to annihilate it and its inheritors." If such poets wished to register the heart-sickness of the times, they did so not by abandoning the traditional forms and incidents of poetry, but as in Owen's superlative instance, by introducing, as Blunden puts it, "some discord in the utterance." Thus, in his "Strange Meeting," a poem exuding the pity of war, Owen has an underworld encounter with one he greets as "friend"—actually, with the ghost of the enemy soldier he had bayoneted. The twenty-four finely metered decasyllabics (and occasional hendecasyllabic) proceed, atypically for the times, in near-rhymed couplets (e.g., "grained/ground," "years/yours," "laughed/left"). "Discord in the utterances" conveys the deformity in the times. Yet the message is clear, as it must be, even as the method is designedly irregular. In Owen's "Strange Meeting," we are firmly in the realm of Virgil's *sunt lacrimae rerum* (replete with epic underworld encounter).

As further concerns ascendant thought and example, this time through epic, acclaimed American classicist and archaeologist Emily Vermeule

(1928–2001) has noted: "Epic offers a set of memories of a deep past in a time of crisis, which, while fictitious in a poetic sense, sets values and aspirations, and embodies issues of courage, pride, reflectiveness, skill in speaking and persuasion, and acceptance of death." The case is vividly illustrated by the Nikos Kazantzakis/Ioannis Kakridis translation of the *Iliad* into Modern Greek (dimotiki) during the German occupation of World War II:

> The period of the occupation was among the hardest times for Greece, especially for the population of Athens: more than 200,000 Athenians died from famine and malnutrition during the winters of 1942 and 1943. In an environment of physical and mental abuse, a project centered on translating Homer was a refuge and a consolation, a way to keep the mind of an intellectual productive and occupied. The translator's choice to focus on Homer . . . signifies a recourse to Homer and, more generally, to epic poetry in a time of crisis. Kazantzakis and Kakridis desired to communicate through their translation of the ancient epic a part of their own contemporary epic, Greece's struggle for liberation in WWII, and also to describe the *erga* [deeds] as well as the *algea* [pains] of Greece during the forties.

High art—the archetypally high art of epic, in fact—serves not only to commemorate glories past but also to instill future assurance. It is no less the case with Virgil:

> Virgil's profound sense of order, which enabled him to perceive a pattern and direction in human history while acknowledging the necessity of evil as a factor in that process, captured the attention of readers who had been sensitized to disorder by the events of their own times. Recognizing a response in Virgil's work to the violence of the late [Roman] Republic from which the *imperium* emerged, they began to appreciate for the first time his relevance for the modern world.

Such relevance was lost on Pound as a father of modernism. One wonders the outcome, had Pound been less enamored of "modernizing" Propertius and more attentive to the perennial modernity of Virgil. The former, as will be seen, he ill understood; the latter he understood not at all, and peremptorily dismissed.

There were more than a few early twentieth-century artists who maintained traditional standards, in verse as in the other arts. Indeed, the British literary homefront waged its own war during World War I to maintain a "high diction" and "exalted rhetoric"; to seek a "regeneration of traditional values" in the service of the national morale. The object was "a comprehensible art, based on emotions accessible to all, which, like 'faith,' could be 'mobilized' in the service of the nation." Leading the drive was the Poetry Society's *Poetry Review*, founded by Harold Monro (1879–1932). Its stance (after a brief flirtation with Ezra Pound and the "Futurists") was "that the language and attitudes associated with 'bardic' poetry were useful tools in combating avant-garde ideas and the modern world in general." That world included the industrialized modernity and barbarism of World War I. *Poetry Review* increasingly became a bulwark of anti-modernism. A 1913 editorial stated: "That poetry will remain unaffected by the extravagances of what is mistakenly called 'Futurism' we may safely assert; but it may be well to remember that this perversely styled craze for notoriety is a species of debased megalomania." Despite the crisis of World War I, which induced the abandonment of traditional forms and styles, *Poetry Review* continued to promulgate the spiritualized "high diction" of the prewar period. It was lofty sentiment and high diction that sustained "the boys in the trenches" during the worst of the war, as historian Paul Fussell elaborates in his magisterial book chapter "Oh What a Literary War."

As the war dragged on, casting doubt on traditional sentiment and manners of expression, *Poetry Review* grew increasingly outspoken in its rejection of the avant-garde. In 1917 Paul Valéry (1871–1945) published his masterpiece (composed throughout the war years, as was the Frank Bridge sonata), *La Jeune Parque* (*The Young Fate*). Written in five hundred and twelve rhymed alexandrines, the work drew on classical authors—especially Aeschylus and Sophocles—in its meditation on the perennial themes. Recognized as a major French poet and genius, Valéry adhered to a lifelong orthodoxy of rhymed and metered poetry, notwithstanding his profession of moral crisis over World War I. Pound, Eliot, and Joyce had not been present at the Western Front to replace the "available language of traditional literature" with "new idioms" better conveying the war's indescribable horror. They had communicated no such idiom to Valéry, and no such idiom to Owens, who writes, "Do you know what would hold me together on a battlefield?: The sense that I was perpetuating the language in which Keats and the rest of them wrote! I do not know in what else England is greatly superior, or dearer to me, than another land and people." Nor were the influences of Pound and Eliot otherwise yet established (Pound thirty-three and Eliot thirty at the war's end).

The above-mentioned English poet, author, and critic Edmund Blunden (1896–1974), who *did* serve in World War I, miraculously survived two years on the front to record his experience. He did so in rhymed and metered verse and had this to say of Eliot: "I don't know why Eliot should feel so badly about things. There is no reason why he should have to write in that 'I-cannot-be-gay' manner. He did not have to go through the war." As for Pound, his "wars were literary, and he took only desultory interest in the progress of fighting in France, except as it interfered with his friends." His *Cantos,* begun in 1915, in the vortex of war, "inevitably suffer when we judge their fortunes of war by the letters from the front Pound received in his snug apartment in Kensington." Thus, while soldiers and soldier-poets were sustained by as traditional and elevated a poetry as ever existed, finding it adaptable to a new and ghastly range of undreamed-of experience, the homebound *littérateurs* across the channel issued their dicta and manifestos, surrendering to the barbarism of which they learned second-hand and—fifth columnists all—inviting its advance. Similarly in World War II, while intellectual exiles such as Theodor W. Adorno in California assuaged aching consciences with announcements of "no poetry after Auschwitz," concentration-camp prisoners were writing poems by the thousands. "Rather than condemning poetry, [they] turned to aesthetic expression as an escape from the horror of the camps." Indeed, "highly structured forms like the sonnet and terza rima were preferred by prisoners who sought some order [to] oppose to the chaos of their daily lives."

It would in fact take World War II before the early twentieth-century modernist frame of reference "would force itself up from below and propose itself for use." The process, however, was already underway, with the futurists and dadaists both (1915, 1916)—the former despising everything "old," the latter (in response to World War I) proclaiming everything null. The contemporaneous example of Valéry urges that there was nothing foregone in modernism that would or was even then forcing itself "up from below," and nothing foregone in the "proposal" for its use. Modernism in the end prevailed, however, as Dada proved a more persuasive influence than

Valéry, and the mind's disorder a more inviting template than disciplined application. The controversy would be largely muted by the rise of pop culture in the 1960s, the "Men of 1914" yet secure in the curriculum.

In 1929 Monro published his *Twentieth Century Poetry,* an anthology seeking "to make 'this warlike and tragic age' speak as clearly and authentically as it can through the mouth of its own poetry." Consisting largely of rhymed and metered verse, the anthology takes a hands-off approach to the emergent modernism, noting:

> A discussion of what is known as *free verse* must not here be broached. The matter is controversial and subject to much misunderstanding. The influence, however, will be clear in the following pages and the tendency definite. I will refer the reader to Mr. T. S. Eliot's Introduction to the Poems of Ezra Pound.

Monro includes seven poems by Pound—Pound's "Apparuit" ("She Appeared") an imagistically vivid six-stanza Sapphic poem with intimations of the "Hymn to Aphrodite," but marred, as it seems, by its disdain of Swinburne's dynamism and flow.

Full censure would not be long in coming, however. In the 1936 introduction to *The Oxford Book of Modern Verse (1892–1935),* William Butler Yeats, the modern master of traditional form for the twentieth century, lambastes Pound (despite their friendship), tasking his sometimes better qualities for being "constantly interrupted, broken, twisted into nothing by [their] direct opposite, nervous obsession, nightmare, stammering confusion." Yeats similarly reproves the "loss of self-control" in Pound, who is "content . . . to leave unbridged transitions, unexplained ejaculations, that make meaning unintelligible." Of the poems Yeats anthologizes (Monro's and Pound's included), the better part is in traditional form. As an indication of his own taste, Yeats is especially partial to the consummately rhymed and metered poetry of the short-lived Ernest Dowson (1867–1900), which was expressly omitted from Monro's anthology on chronological grounds. Yeats at the same time could be exceedingly difficult to please, regarding the poignantly expressive Wilfred Owen as "unworthy of the poet's corner of a country newspaper," and dramatically banning the trench poets from his seminal *The Oxford Book of Modern Verse* on the ground that their passive suffering was unsuited to art.

It is Yeats who further notes Pound's "great influence, more perhaps than any contemporary except Eliot," and who cites Pound as the probable "source of the lack of form and consequent obscurity" in other poets—thus suggesting how reputation may substitute for merit, and self-presentation for substance. Yeats was little kinder to Eliot ("unexaggerated plainness that has the effect of novelty") and especially critical of Pound's *Cantos,* then in progress ("His belief in his own conception is so great that since the appearance of the first Canto I have tried to suspend judgement"). Feeling the sting, Pound vented in correspondence, e.g., "God damn Yeats' bloody paragraph. Done more to prevent people reading Cantos for what is on the page than any other one smoke screen." In fairness to Eliot, however, according to David De Laura, "The events surrounding the first world war seemed to evoke . . . a poetry filled with the menace of the declining West, whereas the events of the years *entre les deux guerres* and the events, above all, of the second world war, moved him . . . [to] openly speak for the maintenance of tradition and civilized standards in the face of engulfing barbarism." At the same time, "his poetry and drama were steadily progressing, in a new serenity, to uplands of the spirit where personal and social relations could be cultivated and, in some degree, protected from the collapse of standards in the world at large." Eliot, unlike Pound, sought "to prove the efficacy and vitality and flexibility of classicism in a world of uncertain values."

If the standard bearers did not emerge atop the modernist mêlée, or were slow to emerge thereafter, it is because a decided *non*-standard was wondrously stupefacient for *le bourgeois—épaté* beyond recall and wanting nothing so much as something to talk about. Embracing heady notions of formlessness and of marginal or esoteric comprehension, the modernists succumbed to the very chaos its generation had fought to defeat in World War I, and later in World War II. A famed war memorial erected in Les Eyzies (la Vallée de la Dordogne, Périgord, southwest France) reads: *A tous ceux qui sont morts pour la civilisation 1914–1918* (*To all who died for civilization*). The stay-at-home part of the generation that so bled for civilization would in the war's aftermath disown it and proudly declare victory. The betrayal is peculiarly apparent in Pound. Notwithstanding incisive prose essays and aperçus, the "delicate lyricism of his middle period," and his selflessly tireless promotion of others—including Eliot, Joyce, and Frost—Pound in World War II, as seen, proved a fascist partisan accused of treason. He was spared trial and virtually foregone execution only by a judgment (such as it was) of insanity. Both in the arts and in politics, Pound was ultimately, and decidedly, allied with anti-civilizational forces, "his adopted ideology compel[ing] Pound to besmirch all struggles for liberty, and the fraternal heroism engendered in democratic wars of defense, past and present. . . ."

Eliot, famously allusive or recondite, signaled in a revived classicism the hope for cultural regeneration. His poetry "combined plunging into a world of chaos and absurdity with a '*rappel à l'ordre.*'" His essay "Tradition and the Individual Talent" acknowledged the need for adherence to the past, for poetic craft over poetic personality, and for wariness against "new human emotions to express"—the "search for novelty in the wrong places" likely ending in poetry's discovery of the perverse. For Pound, by contrast, and in his own words, "The sorting out [and] the *rappel à l'ordre*" ended in the "new synthesis, the totalitarian." Thus would Pound "make it new." Proudly obscurant to the end, and in the end declared insane, Pound signaled civilization in decay. The difference between Eliot and Pound crystallizes, in significant part, in their divergent views of Virgil: for Eliot, the very heart of Western civilization, as primarily set forth in his signature essay "What is a Classic?" (1944); for Pound, "a second-rater, a Tennysonianized version of Homer," an author that Pound is "chucking out . . . without the slightest compunction." The dismissiveness is astounding, given Virgil's Renaissance standing as the ideal poet; Dante's adoration, as seen, of Virgil and his style; and Dante's choice of Virgil as guide through *Inferno* and *Purgatory*. It is the more astounding, given Virgil's creation of a *new* epic tradition (yes, Virgil had "made it new") centered for the first time on an entirely earth-changing theme—the founding of Rome—that would remain unmatched until Milton's fall of man.

Pound could theoretically distinguish and categorize, but not morally discriminate. Italy's importance, he divined, lay in two decisive developments: the Renaissance and fascism. Pound saw in Italian fascism, through its restoration of a Renaissance-empowered Italy, the cornerstone of a "balanced Europe"; he saw in Mussolini the Great Leader called for by Dante for the regeneration of the corrupt and fallen Italy of Dante's own day. Mussolini would renew civilization, would "make it new." With Mussolini's March on Rome (1922), the modern era, for Pound, became the fascist era and a new age for the world—"the leader . . . known by his capacity to imagine and execute a new and superior design." The connection between modernism and fascism is thus far from casual. Pound's make-it-new credo was anti-civilizational, not merely in being opposed to the sense of permanence, central, in art historian Kenneth Clarke's view, to our concept of civilization. The credo's ultimate instantiation was, for Pound, the new era of fascism—a *novus ordo seclorum*—with its barbaric conduct and suppression of civilizing values. Ever dismissive of Virgil, Pound, here too, missed the boat. The 1930 bimillennial celebration of Virgil, in Italy at least, had co-opted Virgil into the national agenda, "offer[ing] a favorable opportunity to emphasize the parallels between ancient Rome and Mussolini's Italy." The emphasis was on authoritarian strongmen—Augustus and Mussolini—as restorers of order from social chaos. Many were the celebratory works viewing "modern Italy as moving in the footsteps of the past." Pound could not love Virgil—even for all the wrong reasons.

Pound would be rewarded for his apostasy. In 1949 the Bollingen Prize committee of the U.S. Library of Congress, comprised, among others, of Conrad Aiken, W. H. Auden, T. S. Eliot, Robert Lowell, Katherine Anne Porter, Allen Tate, and Robert Penn Warren, outrageously bestowed the inaugural 1948 award on Pound's *Pisan Cantos* (*Cantos* 74–84), a lament over the death of Mussolini at the hands of Italian partisans. The virulently anti-Semitic work was written by a delirious Pound while in Italy, near Pisa, under U.S. arrest (1945)—initially in a steel-caged enclosure—for treasonous wartime broadcasts over Rome's radio. Having escaped trial by judgment of insanity, Pound, at the time of the award, had already spent four of twelve years at St. Elizabeth's Hospital. Though not commenting, he probably relished the award's presumptive vindication of his wartime conduct. The award, in fact, was an unsuccessful ploy by the then literary establishment to embarrass the Department of Justice into releasing Pound. The establishment may have been unaware that the prize was "named in honor of Dr. [Carl] Jung, whose country place [was] in Bollingen [Switzerland], and who was 'an ardent Nazi Collaborationist.'" Even so, the association is ironically, if entirely, fitting. To be released in the wake of the Bollingen Prize would have been a reward exponentially conferred on flagrant wartime treason—the supreme irony that the award, in its first year at least, was made under the auspices of an agency of the United States government.

The eventual defeat of Mussolini was, perversely for Pound, the defeat of Western civilization itself—or, as Pound may have hoped, Western civilization in thrall to fascism. Misguided and unrepentant to the end, Pound absorbed the wrong lessons both from Dante's totalizing politics and comprehensive artistic vision. Pound's "imitation of Dante's epic design [was] a disastrous failure" and his aspirational role as artistic *duce* or *führer,* alongside Mussolini, defeated. Here too, in Dante as in Virgil, Pound, though more influential by his misapprehensions and waywardness, was dramatically bettered by the equanimous Eliot.

We may in the same vein anticipate Pound's antipathy toward Horace. Ford Madox Ford viewed Horace as a bulwark against the "savage brutes we have made ourselves today." Observes Ford, "The essence of civilization consists in its domination by a mood of frugal happiness: we are the best citizens who most have been tamed by the Horatian note." Relatedly, notes Richard Weaver, citizenship is in part dependent on "a due respect for the canons of grammar." In his disdain of these concerns, which is to say, in his intellectual profligacy and poetic obscurantism, Pound evidenced his abrogation of both political and literary citizenship: political citizenship in his embrace of fascism; literary citizenship for the rebarbative style of his major works—hermetic, petulant, and obscurant, in turn; in a word, *regressive.* The political or content-based abandonment of citizenship we relegate to the endnotes. As concerns literary citizenship, however, Pound was dramatically regressive as measured against the universally acknowledged clarity, maturity, and purposefulness of the West's own literary origins in Homer.

The primal, indeed, the primordial, standard against which Pound faltered was articulated by R. C. Jebb (1841–1905), acknowledged the most brilliant classical scholar of his day, as follows:

> The capital distinction of Homeric poetry is that it has all the freshness and simplicity of a primitive age,—all the charm which we associate with the 'childhood of the world'; while on the other hand it has completely surmounted the rudeness of form, the struggle of thought with language, the tendency to grotesque or ignorable modes of speech, the incapacity for equable maintenance of a high level, which belong to the primitive stage in literature.

Jebb first published these words in 1886, the year following Pound's birth, in his incisive *Introduction to Homer*, Chapter 1: "General Literary Characteristics." The words, as Jebb goes on to note, recapitulate what Matthew Arnold had deemed the four principal characteristics of Homer's style: "it is rapid; plain in thought; plain in diction; and noble." Walter Leaf (1852–1927), the foremost Homericist of his day, reviewed Jebb's book in the 1887 inaugural issue of *The Classical Review* (the journal of the Classical Association of Great Britain). Leaf praised Jebb's opening chapter as follows:

> . . . we find a clear and lucid statement of the most approved results of [Homeric] criticism, informed and illustrated by their passage through a mind of similar tact and delicacy of judgment. In no part of the book is this more conspicuous than in [Jebb's] first chapter on "General Characteristics," which is full of acute and instructive remarks on the position of the Epic . . . in the history of literature. The whole chapter is a model of quiet and luminous criticism.

Erstwhile classics student that he was, Pound resisted the best qualities of the best literature at their very source, as well as the best professorial assessments of his day. He resisted the *dolce stil novo* 'sweet new style' of his own Dante. Amid such renunciations did his own style smolder. As for Matthew Arnold, Pound refers to him but once in over four hundred pages of collected literary essays. Indeed, in his own essays on translating Homer—collectively edited as "Translators of Greek: Early Translators of Homer"—Pound shows scant appreciation of the Homeric original, even while confessing himself "very ill-taught in Greek." Pound's disregard of the professors is understandable. As he disdained Western civilization, so did he disdain its transmitters and intermediaries, being otherwise too obdurate and self-assured to suffer formal instruction. As Pound took all the wrong lessons from Dante—those of his politics, artistic purpose, and style—he proved impervious to the best in Homer and had no use for Virgil. There would have been no Pound, and no self-willed alienation, otherwise.

The "democratizing" Walt Whitman unleashed the whirlwind, leveling the formal traditions of British verse for a young and expanding America, and eclipsing William Cullen Bryant (1794–1878)—the first American poet to bear comparison with British rivals and, by 1832, the unrivaled poet of America. "The old forms we saw about us, handled in the most stilted style, were bloodless," says poet and chronicler of his age Alfred Kreymborg. "They had nothing to do with our own lives, and evaded the racial call of Walt Whitman, the legendary hero of our youth." (By *racial* Kreymborg means *American* or *national.*) Despite Whitman's struggle for popular recognition during his lifetime—he was yet the darling of Emerson and assorted Europeans—the free-verse revolution was sadly foregone. Whitman's younger contemporary, and only other major "modern" poet of the mid to late nineteenth century, was the famously reclusive Emily Dickinson (1830–1886). Yet, of her over 1,800 poems, fewer than a dozen appeared in her lifetime. Dickinson worked in a sparse and highly formal style, with the artist's rather than the barn painter's brush. Requiring discipline, education, and time, her poetry reflected the life of the mind rather than life's adrenalized gusto. Even had she been better known in her lifetime—let alone as shamelessly self-promoting as Whitman—Dickinson would not have won the palm. More congenial to the times were the wide outdoors and the up-winded scent of one's armpit. Dickinson was fine wine to Whitman's beer. Why sip and savor when you can guzzle?

❧

Great poets of the past—Bryant, Dickinson, Emerson, Longfellow, Thoreau, and others—could be counted on for consistency; some poems preferable to others, but all of a similar quality. So Petrarch in his three-hundred-and-sixty-six-poem *Laura Cycle,* as critic Eric Ormsby observes: "Remarkably, though there are inevitably *longuers* in such a work, there are no weak poems; the intensity, and the elegance of expression, remains at highest pitch throughout." Precisely the opposite, however, for Whitman, as critic William Logan states: "There are some passages of most vigorous and vivid writing, some superbly graphic descriptions, great stretches of imagination,—and then passages of intolerable coarseness,—not gross and licentious but simply disgustingly coarse." The critic generally passes from here to the increasingly dogged search for the passable poem or mere *handful of verses*: "When considering Ashbery the Romantic, one is forced to look not at whole books or poems, but at passages and excerpts, often no more than a few lines long"; or, "To read Ashbery is to plod through a dismaying expanse of trivia, jokes, bent grammar, and nonsense so that the poet can finally bring in his five or ten lines of epiphany." It is no less the case with the master himself: "Apart from rare passages of controlled translation or passionate rhetoric . . . what most people remember in the *Cantos* are its images, and when the *Cantos* are spoken of as great art it is often on the basis of scattered lines of description, the discreet evidence of Pound's *phanopoieia,* his 'scattering of light.'" A light sparsely scattered, to be sure, and by light years remote from "What in me is dark / Illumine."

Poet-critic Randall Jarrell (1914–1965) searched out the epiphanies in Whitman, combing through *Leaves of Grass* for its admittedly dazzling lines. The cream skimmed, what does one make of the rest of it—of Whitman's chocking inclusiveness and rampant pilings-on, of his congested comparisons and analogies with their predisposition toward gear-changing wreckage? And the insufferable "Song of Myself," characterized by William Carlos Williams as "man at his worst—but most typical." And then there is Whitman, by his own lights cosmic creator and godhead, and by the lights of those revering him the Second Coming itself (O, how he embraces the "common prostitute" together with all the human race). And then the fanatic egalitarianism and boundless ego (for his apologists, not his own ego, but that of the collective of his fellows). It is all too credulous and fantastically accepting.

Philosopher George Santayana has been among the many conflicted over Whitman—on the one hand praising his "charm of uniformity in multiplicity," his "resolute marshaling of nullities," his "effort to show us everything as a momentary pulsation of a liquid and structureless whole [by which] he profoundly stirs the imagination." The commendation is, however, ambivalent. Santayana continues:

> We may wish to dislike this power, but, I think, we must inwardly admire it. For whatever practical dangers we may see in this terrible leveling, our aesthetic faculty can condemn no actual effect; its privilege is to be pleased by opposites, and to be capable of finding chaos sublime without ceasing to make nature beautiful.

If such leveling were the rule, there would be no hierarchy of values (i.e., no taste), no discrimination in beauty and no sense of beauty, and no *The Sense of Beauty* by George Santayana. Further, to approve on the ground of nothing to disapprove—"our actual aesthetic faculty can condemn no actual effect"—is faint praise, indeed. As concerns chaos, it may be found sublime—"capable of finding chaos sublime"—only from the standpoint of an eventually emergent and ordered whole. Chaos is sublime *being pregnant with order*, and by the epic struggle through which order is wrought and maintained (Chapter 14). This is the lesson of Genesis, of the Hesiodic creation account, and of comparable creation myths worldwide. It is not a lesson to be discarded for sufferance of Whitman.

Santayana seems more fairly to engage with Whitman in a context having nothing to do with the poet per se. For an "untrained" public, as Santayana labels it,

> it becomes a point of pride . . . to understand and appreciate everything. And our art, in its turn, does not overlook this opportunity. It becomes disorganized, sporadic, whimsical, and experimental. The crudity we are too distracted to refine, we accept as originality, and the vagueness we are too pretentious to make accurate, we pass off as sublimity. This is the secret of making great works on novel principles, and of writing hard books easily.

The case for Whitman—indeed for Pound himself—could have been no more truly made. In sum, poetry (as all art) is not an agglomeration but a refinement: the one extracted from the many; the essence from the excess; gold, to adornment crafted, from ore. Art is not the smelter's, or butcher boy's, or blacksmith's apron. This dictate, however, is today everywhere flouted.

As ever in the critical discussion of such poetry, there is the effort—working ever against itself—to make a blessing of adversity:

> It is perfectly legitimate for the poet to make the road to his truths a difficult one, and in Ashbery's best poems the game is worth the candle. But the Romantic perplexity that animates his work—the dilemma of having to communicate in words, a feeling that is beyond words—also drags it down, requiring or at least permitting a great deal that is insubstantial, inessential, insufficiently formed, tedious.

"In Ashbery's best poems," says critic Adam Kirsch (b. 1976). Is this to ignore or forgive Ashbery's worst? And "requiring or at least permitting"? Is this not hedging of the first order? The law knows no clearer distinction than that between *must* (requiring) and *may* (permitting)—and many the case that turns on that distinction. There is no such thing as "must, or [at least] may." And the Romantics themselves? Were *they* ever stymied by the "dilemma" of verbal communication? If Ashbery's "game is worth the candle," the phrase is apt for poetry so devoid of light and ill-reckoned significant (except perforce by reviewers with little else "out there" to review). The real candleholder is the estimable Adam Kirsch. A modern-day Diogenes with his lamp, Kirsch seeks an honest poem—alas!

This then is the common mode of modern poetry review: lamentation for the poetry's impoverishment overall, with hosannas for selected verses and the occasional image. It is the mode of Kirsch's very book—reviewing some twenty-five modern poets—in which the Ashbery example appears. The book, always discerning, is by a polymath who, though knowing what real poetry is, judges *modern* poetry against a merely middling standard. By contrast, and taking no prisoners whatever, poet-critic William Logan has a deservedly *mauvais mot* for everyone. In one of his milder rebukes, Logan says of former United States Poet Laureate Billy Collins, "He's the Caspar Milquetoast of contemporary poetry, never a word used in earnest, never a memorable phrase. . . . If such poems look embarrassing now, what are they going to look like in 20 years?" The assessment is peculiarly reminiscent of Sappho's rebuke of an uneducated contemporary: "But when you die you will lie there, nor will there ever be a recollection or any desire of you, since you share not in the roses of Pieria."

With only twenty years intervening between the World Wars, modernism's dour view of an eviscerated humanity and of the art needed to reflect it could only deepen—the search *on* for some miraculous, i.e., grandiose, way of reordering, repairing, and setting all right. Thus did the chaos of World War II "create an opening for cultural ideologues with comprehensive world-ordering systems, and serialism filled the bill to perfection." An exception was the American poet Anthony Hecht (1923–2004). Within a year of enlisting in 1944, Hecht not only saw combat in Germany and Czechoslovakia, but was in the Seventy-Ninth Infantry Division that helped liberate Flossenbürg concentration camp, an extermination and slave-labor annex of Buchenwald. "When we arrived," reports Hecht, "prisoners were dying at the rate of five hundred a day from Typhus. . . . The place, the suffering, the prisoners' accounts were beyond comprehension. For years after I would wake shrieking." And yet, in the "familiar dramaturgy of culture versus barbarism," notes Kirsch, Hecht's poetry is unusual for the way in which it "reflects on the shattering of humanism . . . [even while] continu[ing] to pay homage to it":

> Hecht's regular meter and rhyme, his formal diction and clear expository sentences betray none of the uncertainty or extremity his subject seems to demand. . . . For more than fifty years Hecht's poetry maintained this disciplined disjunction between form and subject [i.e., content]. He often wrote about the forces of dissolution—evil, chaos, lust, slovenliness—but always in a decorous, ornate style, as though these subjects were explosive chemicals that could only be handled with tongs.

There followed Hecht's second volume of poetry, *The Hard Hours* (1956), maintaining the high style for the anguish of his war experiences. Says Kirsch,

> The allure of such strictness [of the high style] is easy to understand, for Hecht's writing life . . . coincided with a universal abandonment of strictness, not least in the poetic sphere. In an essay on Richard Wilbur, Hecht writes of "this poetic era of arrogant solipsism and limp narcissism—when great, shaggy herds of poets write only about themselves, or about the casual workings of their rather tedious minds."

One of many obituaries credited Hecht as "the epitome of formalism in poetry," "a classicist if ever there ever was one, for whom rhyme and metric schemes constitute poetry's very music." Hecht, notes the obituary, is a poet citing Flaubert for the proposition that "'One must not always think that feeling is everything. Art is nothing without form.'"

Though forthright in his commendation of Hecht, Kirsch backpedals, surmising that poems on evil and degradation, when "always formal, reasonable, and good[,] . . . do not really engage with evil and degrading things. They do not allow them to rise to speech, only to be spoken about." The critique falters, first, on the facile linking of *formal* with *reasonable* and *good*. Also faulty is Kirsch's observation that Hecht, by the formalist treatment of chaotic subject matter, long maintained a "disciplined disjunction between form and subject." This implies that certain subjects are unsuited to (or incapable of) formal expression—that Hecht, formally treating them, could not truly confront them, whence the disjunction of form and content. Conversely, were form and content truly united, the chaos of the subject matter would reflect in that of the form. The same notion appears with reference to "explosive chemicals that could only be handled with tongs," the tongs the formality of Hecht's verse. This is to say that Hecht is either wary or incapable of directly handling the explosion, the conflagration that was the Holocaust, but had to formalize and make it pretty, instead. Having taken chaos as his theme, Hecht's putative failure "to accede to that chaos, to allow it into his very speech," is (Kirsch surmises) what "sets the limit to [Hecht's] achievement" and turns readers to others—e.g., Lowell, Berryman, and Plath—"for a sense of what it was like to live, and suffer, in the late twentieth century." Thus, even as he praises him, Kirsch reproaches Hecht for not being sufficiently "modern," i.e., for not matching putative incoherence of content to comparable incoherence of form.

Truth be told, it was not only poets such as Hecht, who fought in and saw the worst of the war, but those who suffered its extremist torments who adhered to form, as if to salvation itself:

> Facing the mental and physical ultimates, the prisoners of Nazi death camps would often express in poetry their gropings for a sustaining moral order; and this in such demanding structures as sonnet and terza rima; and this is while interrupted by torture and terror. It seemed the human thing to do.

As in the classical model, form never yields to intensity of content but is conditioned, *created*, by it—the only "disjuncture" being that of modernism's sense of superannuated past and redemptive present (i.e., "out with the old, in with the new").

The lesson, so very old, is tiresomely new. "If . . . 'form is never more than an extension of content,' then the decisions poets make about what forms to write in are ultimately of less importance than the things they have to say." We may qualify and reword as follows: form is not an extension of content, but coextensive with it, the two inter-determinative and mutually reinforcing. The rule equally applies to the best modernist poetry. As Stephen Spender notes of Eliot, "the poetry, beautiful as it is, is forced into very narrow channels of vivid spiritual experience. This narrow and concentrated poetry is intensely beautiful, intensely expressive, with a command of language that is absolute: In its expression in controlled language with a rhythm inseparable from a translucent imagery to which it adds force, this is great poetry."

The final word goes to poet-critic J. D. McClatchy, writing that a Hecht poem is more than

> ravishingly beautiful stanzas. . . . His is a responsible art, an art that responds to history, to political and domestic tragedies and persistent problems. . . . And the beauty of a Hecht poem, the very skill with which its material is worked often throws into an even stronger, more pathetic light the isolation and helplessness of the human condition that is his subject.

There is thus little in Hecht to decipher, puzzle about, or be befuddled by; rather, there is *meaning*, artfully and—dare we imagine in a postmodern age—comprehensibly conveyed. To take two examples:

> We move now to outside a German wood.
> Three men are there commanded to dig a hole
> In which the two Jews are ordered to lie down
> And be buried alive by the third, who is a Pole.
>
> Not light from the shrine at Weimar beyond the hill
> Nor light from heaven appeared. But he did refuse.
> A Luger settled back deeply in its glove.
> He was ordered to change places with the Jews.

Or this, in a lighter more intimate vein, with rhyme scheme *a-b-c-b-c-a*:

> We rise together to the second floor.
> Outside, across the lake, an endless wind
> Whips against the headstones of the dead and wails
> In the trees for all who have and have not sinned.
> She rubs against me and I feel her nails.
> Although we are alone, I lock the door.

What more could one want for whatever foothold chaos, including the Holocaust, might allow. Hecht's is an art, which by the precision that is formality itself glimpses "the detail, the quaking heart, in the very midst of the muddle." Let others muddle on.

Approximately six hundred years earlier, Dante had seen bodies burn and suffer torments unspeakable. *That* inferno he confronted in terza rima, a new and unprecedentedly demanding meter. His ordered verse and voice "concentricized" and wrought order from his subject's chaos, and from the disorder and anarchy that were the Florence of his day. Also, and for the first time since written epic in antiquity, Dante sidestepped Latin (in which he was expert) for the Tuscan dialect of Vulgar Latin, making it the earliest form of Italian. He further absorbed the classical tradition into a work at once the cornerstone of the Italian Renaissance and of the subsequent Western humanistic tradition. The *Divine Comedy* was no less a literary narrative of Catholicism and its doctrine of life beyond the grave. Neither Dante's fearsome subject, his frightful social and political milieu, nor his own tumultuous private life or exile impeded his verse's flawless flow or obscured its vision. In form, content, and depth Dante "made it new," *monumentally* new, even as Virgil, Dante's inspiration, had done in the *Aeneid*. Pound in his *Cantos* gorged on Dante and made of him a muse, yet without digesting his craft or inspiration. Virgil was decidedly better served as Dante's guide than was Dante as Pound's.

❧

The Romantic era, at its peak in Europe from approximately 1800 to 1850, found the source of aesthetic experience in heightened emotion. The dilemma, then, for latter-day Romantics is apparently one of "having to communicate in words, a feeling that is beyond words." Classical poetry, as seen, knew no such dilemma, because *form* shaped and enabled any and all expression. The latter-day Romantic's remedy is *freedom*—allowing the maximum space and freest rein for bursting emotion. The more room the better—as though ballet were the better staged on a football field. The function of art, however, is to transcend time and space, not merely fill it; to fashion and *fix*, not dissolve and release. Such, precisely, is the problem with the Beat poet Allen Ginsberg's "Howl" (1955–1956): it howls rather than articulates. "A habitual indulgence in the inarticulate," observes Santayana, "is a sure sign of the philosopher who has not learned how to think, the poet who has not learned to write, the painter who has not learned to paint, and the impression that has not learned to express itself." Santayana nonetheless proposes that all of these "are compatible with an immensity of genius in the inexpressible soul." And yet, genius thus bound and mute is but fetal order within chaos—of no account or practicality.

The delight of its own time, "Howl" will be of no moment to posterity. It sooner shares in an assessment of Horace's early poetry, the *Epodes*, written in imitation of the rage-inflamed Archilochus: "no one wants to read twice the poems which he [Horace] designs to look like the proper explosion of rage—at least you would hardly read them a second time for pleasure." Achieving a similar though more affable effect than Ginsberg's howl is Whitman's "barbaric yawp." At his most careening and multitudinous, Whitman boundlessly vociferates, leaving nothing unsaid and nothing to the imagination. He is tiresomely, interminably, inclusive—fill rather than fit, effusion and unchanneled flood. Ginsberg was an early acolyte of Whitman, and the latter's yawp is writ large over "Howl." Oedipus howled, as did Lear, but their moments endure.

It is not enough to say that in Whitman form yields to magnitude of spirit. Whitman's magnitudes are by many magnitudes too great and too idiosyncratic. Whitman's enormities tell us too much of *Whitman*, of what *Whitman* knows and aspires to, little enough of ourselves and what is reasonably, or even ideally, within reach. Whitman is an outsize tutelary presence, too much with us—in our face—a caricature. We live and die for the most part privately and alone, our friendships typically few and passing. The poet thus claiming voice and kinship with everyman is for that reason alien to any man. Whitman is no man that others find in themselves, even as his peerlessly egalitarian America is and will be nowhere found, is *utopia* 'no place'. Whitman is too often merely ridiculous, and more than a little harmful.

Equally flagrant, by way of contrast to the yawp and howl, is the muted voice of trivial perception. This is typically either a formless affair, or one in haiku; dullness and superfluity by and large. "Passionate observation of the ordinary," says Kirsch, "is a way to endow it with significance it otherwise lacks." And if not of the ordinary, then of the secondary or unimportant. "The business of the poet," says Imlac to Rasselas, "is to examine not the individual, but the species; to remark general properties and large appearances: he does not number the streaks of the tulip, or describe the different shades in the verdure of the forest." Nor, for that matter, does he reckon the leaves of grass.

There are many flowerings of this phenomenon. Kirsch on poet Sharon Olds (b. 1942) is illustrative:

> Olds has no interest in abstracting from the contingent details of her life a larger, more universally valid idea or symbol. And she does not see this as a deficiency; it is rather a kind of principle, as she has said: "just being an ordinary observer and liver and feeler and letting the experience get through you into the notebook with the pen, through the arm, out of the body, onto the page, without distortion. And there are so many ways I could distort. If I wrote in a sonnet form, I would be distorting. . . . It's kind of like ego in a way, egotism or narcissism."

What it *is* is the combination of self-centering modernism (objective reality unknowable), postmodernism (personal reality paramount), and political correctness (self- and group-affirmation)—a Triune self-immersion reducing all to the first-person pronoun. Note especially how Olds—cutting to the very root of English poetic form—eradicates the sonnet. Assessing Olds, Kirsch precisely identifies the "deficiency":

> This lamentably common attitude toward poetic form simply means that the poet is exempting herself from the difficult dialectic of art, and indeed all thought. . . . The belief that one need not engage in this process is the greatest and most limiting egotism; and of course Olds, so far from being free of distortion, has such a fixed vision that everything she sees looks the same.

What began as the enervating disillusionment of World War I continued in the wake of World War II and in the aftershocks of Vietnam and beyond. In the words of critic-connoisseur Hilton Kramer (1928–2012)—as true today as when first penned in 1981—the contemporary artistic agenda reflects "the values and outlook of the radical counterculture that had nurtured the rejection of permanence and 'success.'" Art, he laments, "in order to remain spiritually uncontaminated by the evils of a wicked society, must henceforth take only the most perishable forms." This agenda, as seen, is inimical alike to culture and civilization. The rejection of permanence, of a recognized or clearly self-declaiming excellence, is the rejection of the past and its essential traditions. It is chronic fidgeting in the service of making it new.

# Chapter 26

## "Freedom, Freedom, Prison to the Free": The Obfuscatory Unfettered

> Artists always seek a new technique, and will continue to do so as long as their work excites them. But form of some kind is imperative. It is the surface crust of the internal harmony, it is the outward evidence of order.
>
> – E. M. FORSTER, "Art for Art's Sake"

THE ROMAN SATIRIST JUVENAL (1st and 2nd centuries AD) wrote scathingly of everything from royal family incest to the filth and chaos of the Rome of his day. He did so in challenging, dictionally rich hexameters, ever finding the *mot juste* and perfect turn of phrase—form never the obstacle but the catapult to outrage. Epic hexameter was perfectly suited to Juvenal's epic indignation and his "heroic" stand against circumambient depravity. The polished Propertius (1st century BC) wrote allusively of love—recondite mythological references riding the surge and retreat of his elegiac couplets. The singular Lucretius—in hardy, unhalting hexameters—expounded the atomic foundation of all things from the cosmos to the individual soul; from the rise of civilization to love's obsessions and the dread of death. He wedded emotion (poetry) to reason (philosophy), transforming the arid reaches of Epicurean philosophy into almost 7,500 verses of torrential and often tormented epic. In each such highly varied instance, form and content are one and unthinkable apart—the discipline of classical verse its liberating constraint.

Discipline, and the function it serves, has long been anathema both to poetry and poetry in translation. In an earlier time, discipline was self-imposed, and poetry unthinkable apart from form. Poet, philologist, and Anglican archbishop Richard Chevenix Trench (1807–1886) notes that poets who choose the sonnet form do so precisely for its constraints, for "the advantage of that check to diffuseness, that necessity of condensation and concentration which these narrow limits impose." Trench, a contemporary and disciple of William Wordsworth (1770–1850), made the observation in a prefatory essay to his edition of Wordsworth's sonnets. Trench appears to have gotten the idea directly from Wordsworth's sonnet beginning, "Nuns fret not at their convent's narrow room," in which constraint is deemed a remedy to "the weight of too much liberty."

> In truth the prison, unto which we doom
> Ourselves, no prison is; and hence for me
> In sundry moods, 'twas pastime to be bound
> Within the Sonnet's scanty plot of ground;
> Pleased if some Souls (for such there needs must be)
> Who have felt the weight of too much liberty,
> Should find brief solace there, as I have found.

"Often," continues Trench, "a poem which, except for these [constraints], would have been but a loose nebulous vapour, has been compressed and rounded into a star." By contrast, much of today's poetry, original or in translation, is facile, nebulous. Alternatively, it is arcane and incommunicable. Blank verse, frequently indistinguishable from prose, is one thing; free verse, for William Carlos Williams, "a contradiction in terms," and for T. S. Eliot, nonexistent ("*Vers libre* does not exist"). Many of the worst examples of free verse are receptacles of self-indulgence—the "indispensable garbage-disposal unit" wanting for felicitous rhyme, diction, or figures of speech. If nothing else, *express thyself*. It comes down to the lack of "fixity." "No one, or practically no one," says Robert Graves, "has any fixed beliefs: except that all traditions must be broken because they hamper freedom of expression, and that what is brand-new must necessarily be good while it lasts. The whole corpus of art from Aurignacian cave-paintings to Picasso is now finally 'out' . . . and thrown [away]. There are no standards left."

Adherence to discernible form—or regimen of any kind—shows that real freedom lies only in that to which we willingly submit. Real freedom is not freedom *from*, but *through*. The idea informs the medieval belief in perfect freedom through perfect obedience, and pervades the Shakespearean vision of social authority, i.e., of freedom within limits as the ideal and always restorative status quo. Great poetry validates this truth—a truth so long apparent to serious artists and thinkers as to stupefy by its more recent neglect.

Goethe, at middle age, made the point poetically:

> Unfettered spirits will strive in vain to the pure heights of perfection. He who wills great things must gird himself; only in limitation is mastery revealed, and law alone can give us freedom.
>
> [Vergebens werden ungebundene Geister
> Nach der Vollendung reiner Höhe streben.
> Wer Grosses will, muss sich zusammenraffen;
> In Beschränkung zeight sich erst der Meister,
> Und das Gesetz nur kann uns Freiheit geben.]

The point is cosmically illustrated in the myth of Phaethon, son of the Sun god, who insists on driving his father's chariot (a symbol of the sun itself). Control of the vehicle is beyond his small build and youthful years. "The weight was light," says Ovid, "nor what the Sun's horses might recognize, for they lacked the yoke's accustomed gravity." The tumbling, runaway horses fly too high and low, scorching heaven and earth, drying rivers as they go. The unfettered Phaethon is free to rule the Sun, free to ascend the "pure height of perfection." But freedom alone is insufficient. He lacks the strength and discipline; he has not "gir[t] himself" for the task, nor does he know the "limitation[s]" that reins and yoke provide. The excess of the horses' *unbridled* energy results in the loss of control and in his failure.

It is from the yoke, literally and figuratively, that constructive energy issues. It is displayed by the horses of Dawn, converting twilight to fire in Tennyson's "Tithonus" (39–42):

> . . . and the wild team
> Which Love thee, yearning for thy yoke, arise
> And shake the darkness from their loosened manes
> And beat the twilight into flakes of fire.

Ostensibly opposed to such submission, Robert Herrick (1591–1674) in his six-line poem "To Love" claims to be free of love at last:

> I'm free from thee; and thou no more shalt heare
> My puling Pipe to beat against thine eare:
> Farewell my shackles, (though of pearl they be)
> Such precious thraldome ne'r shall fetter me.
> He loves his bonds, who when the first are broke,
> Submits his neck unto a second yoke.

His shackles, since "of pearl they be," are for that reason always inviting. One might compare Catullus, assuring his faithless love that he is *already* getting over her. "Farewell, my girl, Catullus already endures" (Lat. *obdurat* 'endure, hold out, be hard'; the range of meanings quite suggestive in context). One thus senses in Herrick's wistful disavowal that he will again take the yoke, and sooner than he thinks. The yoke as willing servitude connotes the *freedom of submission*—alone the source of integrity and sustaining energy. As Jane Eyre pleads, wanting liberty after eight grim years at Lowood School, but not knowing what liberty to seek: "'grant me at least a new servitude!'"

Submission also resides in that to which we are inexorably resigned. So Dylan Thomas (1914–1953) in "Fern Hill":

> Oh as I was young and easy in the mercy of his means,
> Time held me green and dying
> Though I sang in my chains as the sea . . .

The freedom of which Thomas here sings is that which comes from the reverberant acceptance of mortality. The poem itself, at first seeming free verse, displays a metrical balance of imagistically lavish lines at regular—though not immediately apparent—intervals. Such method is characteristic of the often-inscrutable Thomas, who shows consummate control, despite appearances, *concealing* artistry, which is the highest art.

As further concerns personal freedom, Igor Stravinsky (1882–1971), a composer credited with putting modernism on the map, paradoxically said:

> My freedom consists in moving about within the narrow frame that I have assigned myself for each of my undertakings . . . the more constraints one imposes, the more one frees oneself of the chains that shackle the spirit.

Hamlet makes a similar point saying, "... I could be bounded in a nutshell, and count myself a / king of infinite space."

For Gotthold Lessing (1729–1781), explicator of the "Father of Art History" Johann Winckelmann (1717–1768), form was beauty, and beauty form, meaning that beauty was the lack of *de*formity. What *deforms* renders the content repulsive and inartistic:

> ... among the ancients beauty was the supreme law of the imitative arts.... Rage and despair disfigured none of their works.... Anguish was softened into sadness.... [The] concealment [of pain] was in short a sacrifice to beauty; an example to show, not how expression can be carried beyond the limits of art, but how it should be subjected to the first law of art, the law of beauty.... Screams must be reduced to sighs ... because they would deform the countenance to a repulsive degree.

Though the consideration is here enlarged, the issue remains one of *constraint.* The artistic "soften[ing]" of pain (or deformity) presents a figure "to inspire compassion in its beauty and suffering." Only beauty can "turn our pain into the sweet feeling of pity for the suffering object." (We have encountered this idea in the indignation of Ajax.) Form does not surrender to runaway emotion or imagination, but channels its flow, keeps it bounded and directed, and makes it appreciable. Form is conduit no less than valve. In a caveat lost on Allen Ginsberg's "Howl," Lessing asks, "Cannot a god foretell the future without screaming? Would a more becoming posture of the lips cast suspicion upon his prophecies?"

In the same vein, Lawrence Durrell (1912–1990) has his Sappho state the following. It is one of the sole rhymed passages in his *Sappho: a play in verse*:

> O Freedom which to every man entire
> Presents imagined longings to his fire,
> To swans the water, bees the honey-cell,
> To bats the dark, to lovers loving well,
> Only to the wise may you
> Restricting and confining be,
> All who half-delivered from themselves
> Suffer your conspiracy,
> Freedom, Freedom, prison to the free.

The point is that true freedom is but *half*-freedom, and this a "conspiracy" to which the wise alone are privy. To have everything is to have nothing, which is the true prison. The sentiment is as old as Hesiod, who laments: "Fools, who know not how much better the half is than the whole / or how great the advantage in bread and cheese." Freedom from all need is enervating satiety, the want of desire and aspiration. Need, absence, and limitation spur desire and attainment. They fool themselves who think otherwise. It is in this sense that Durrell's *freedom* presents only "imagined longings to [man's] fire."

The aforementioned Richard Chevenix Trench, noting the vast numbers who have attempted the sonnet form since its thirteenth-century debut, concludes that only one in a thousand sonnets has been worth the effort. Even so, the sonnet form, for those who use it best, provides restraint against aspirational overreach:

> Then, too, while it is quite true that ampler space and larger room are needful for a full display of power, that the Sonnet has not the capabilities of the epic poem, nor even of the ode; this, while it limits the glory which may be acquired in this province of verse, also limits the hazards of him who adventures himself therein.

It amuses to imagine a time when the constraints of an already demanding form, though mastered, were yet considered a check on overreaching design. In today's age of rampant license, use of the accomplished sonnet, to say nothing of sonnet collection, is virtually nonexistent; indeed, it is a literary throwback. The most accomplished sonneteer of the past century was Edna St. Vincent Millay (1892–1950), author of one hundred and thirty-eight sonnets and substantial poetry in all forms and meters. She is seldom taught, however, as wariness attaches to her ease and felicity of expression, to her effortless dispatch of a demanding and bygone-seeming medium. "It can't possibly be that easy," is the response. Here, for example, is Millay on the poignantly fatal moment of reckoning in a May–December relationship (Sonnet "X"):

> Oh, my beloved, have you thought of this:
> How in the years to come unscrupulous Time,
> More cruel than Death, will tear you from my kiss,
> And make you old, and leave me in my prime?
> How you and I, who scale together yet

A little while the sweet, immortal height
No pilgrim may remember or forget,
As sure as the world turns, some granite night
Shall lie awake and know the gracious flame
Gone out forever on the mutual stone;
And call to mind that on the day you came
I was a child, and you a hero grown?—
And the night pass, and the strange morning break
Upon our anguish for each other's sake!

Note also American lyric poet Sara Teasdale (1884–1933), and the crystalline artistry by which she achieves profound and affecting ends. Here is Teasdale's Sonnet I in praise of the Italian actress Eleonora Duse (1858–1924).

Oh beauty that is filled so full of tears,
Where every passing anguish left its trace,
I pray you grant to me this depth of grace:
That I may see before it disappears,
Blown through the gateway of our hopes and fears
To death's insatiable last embrace,
The glory and the sadness of your face,
Its longing unappeased through all the years.
No bitterness beneath your sorrow clings;
Within the wild dark falling of your hair
There lies a strength that ever soars and sings;
Your mouth's mute weariness is not despair.
Perhaps among us craven earth-born things
God loves its silence better than a prayer.

Moderns and postmoderns, however, have put away such sonnet-toys, preferring self and inscrutability, the cryptic and belabored to the effortless and clear. Indeed, we find in Millay and Teasdale, both capable of classical references and themes, the very models of constraint, simplicity, and translucence—a reproach to the obfuscatory unfettered.

# Chapter 27

## Sappho Unbound and Boundaryless—Theorized, Personalized, Politicized

> Who, O / Sappho does you wrong?
> – SAPPHO

> The fascination of what's difficult
> Has dried the sap out of my veins, and rent
> Spontaneous joy and natural content
> Out of my heart. There's something ails our colt
> That must, as if it had not holy blood
> Nor on Olympus leaped from cloud to cloud,
> Shiver under the lash, strain, sweat, and jolt
> As though it dragged road-metal. . . .
> – W. B. YEATS

CRITICS HAVE SOUGHT OVER the years to cleanse Sappho of sexual imputation in order to make her "safe"—as schoolmistress, spiritual leader, mistress of ceremonies, or the like. For instance, here she praises the groom in a ceremonial rather than erotic setting; there she bids an "acolyte," not a lover, farewell; elsewhere she merits Alcaeus's praise as "pure" or "chaste." Moreover, her aristocratic provenance puts her beyond reproach. More recently, though, Sappho has been a sounding board for grievance. The focus nowadays is on her political utility rather than her moral fitness, the mandate ideological rather than exonerative. The sexual or sociopolitical manner of such discussion is often no less comical than gratuitous. Whence this pathology?

Paul Roche's translation of Sappho, originally published by Mentor in 1966, was reissued by Prometheus Books in 1998 with a new introduction by feminist and classicist Page duBois. The 1998 introduction is abridged and adapted from the first chapter of duBois's acclaimed *Sappho Is Burning* (1995). Both the 1998 introduction and chapter subject the fragile and fragmentary Sappho to the heft of philosophers and theorists like Jacques Derrida, Michel Foucault, Jacques Lacan, Friedrich Nietzsche, and Walter Benjamin, among others. How can Sappho, caryatid-like, bear the mass and weight of twentieth-century sexual, psychoanalytic, and, ultimately, Marxist theorizing? Such emphases are not entirely self-willed but reflect the American inferiority complex vis-à-vis all things European—Europe old, venerable, culturally rich, and given to tyranny; America callow, culturally challenged, and democratic. In the intellectual sphere, America has been especially taken with the self-obsessive French, as earlier in the twentieth century with the blighted German Bauhaus. The combined academic progeny is what Harold Bloom calls the "clones of Gallic-Germanic theory." The most recently lauded entrant is the French Thomas Piketty, a Marx-reviving utopian visionary whose prognostications on inequality, *Capital in the 21st Century* (2014), has the left agog.

France and Germany, themselves the source of European cataclysm for one hundred and fifty years and more, have made a cultural export of the thinking that informs their respective experiences. The two countries, imposing or enduring oppression through their own savage wars and political tyrannies, have long been discourse-driven in such matters. The "matrix" of such discourse is power in its various guises. Second only to military or political power is the sexual power expressed through the dichotomy of male "oppressor" and female "oppressed." Sexual power, the argument goes, is a "social construct" rather than a physical, biological, or even cosmic imperative. As a "construct," it can, of course, be *de*constructed; which is to say made or theorized into something else, something more congenial. It may be corrected to comport with contemporary political imperatives or desiderata—i.e., political correctness. Within this framework, sexual intercourse as pervasively practiced (heterosexually) is but a social construct for domination by "the penetrator" of "the penetrated" (in Foucauldian parlance). The scheme works well for those aggrieved by the belief that oppression has ever been women's sexual and historical lot—in theorist terms, their "narrative."

Following World War II, the meaning of "France" as a conquered nation was clearly open to dispute. The focus and insistence were on the permanence, the "irreducibility," of French national character even as France's history suffered eclipse. And as there was no controverting reality, the discourse became more abstract, "part of a larger verbal strategy, half mystifying and half genuine, to insist on French superiority and distinction in the face of defeat."

Of note as part of this postwar "verbal strategy" was the rise of the French Annales School of historical writing. The school focused on neither individuals nor chronologies, nor even on cause and probable effect, but on *la longue durée* 'the grand duration', i.e., the grand and gradual sweep of geopolitical and climactic forces over the expanse of time. Within this framework, problems of the year, decade, or century might be "contextualized," resolved, or simply forgotten. The approach came packaged in words made famous by the former president of France, François Mitterrand, himself a participant in France's World War II defeat: *Il faut laisser le temps au temps* 'one must give time to time', meaning things will work out in the end; time will make them right. The phrase later became a popular song title with lyrics by Didier Barbelivien (b. 1954), further ingraining itself in the social consciousness. Likewise the notion of *l'étrange defaite* 'the strange defeat' as a moniker for France's wartime catastrophe; *l'étrange defaite* the title of a 1940 book by Annales School historian Marc Bloch (emphasizing an overall change in the rhythm or tempo of warfare between the two wars). "Strange Defeat": strange we were ever defeated. Did it really happen? Denial was likewise at the heart of the French reaction to the brutal and utterly ruinous Algerian War (1954–1962)—denial "eating away like a cancer" at the French who "had to forget in order to live." Heedless of the facts on the ground, the French outlook was utopian—a come-on to the defeated, disaffected, or dissatisfied. This outlook has been embraced by radical feminist scholarship. Under the ensign of twentieth-century French theorists, radical scholarship prefers the facts that aren't, might, or should have been to those that *are*. To read Sappho, or read about her, in this vein is of itself oppressive. Theories often conform to a priori assumptions, such as those of male sexual dominance and oppression. It is not male contrivance but biological fact that sexual intercourse is penetrative, invasive. Penetration, however, is not necessarily violative, nor is it archetypal domination.

Alternatives exist only in science fiction. Today, one thinks of the Na'vi of James Cameron's *Avatar*, who mate by intertwining tendrils of their hair queues. It is the direct linking of minds and nervous systems of which physical sex is but biological paraphrase. It is to know another in the biblical sense, but without the intermediacy of sex. In Robert Heinlein's 1961 cult classic novel *Stranger in a Strange Land,* Martians *grok*—meaning "drink, drink in," and thus "understand" (water being scarce on Mars)—and figuratively "know, love," or "be with." Those who share water, whether by drinking or submersion, have *grokked* and become "water brothers." To *grok,* according to Heinlein, is to "understand [another] so thoroughly that you merge with it and it merges with you"; "*grok* means 'identically equal.'" The fluid lack of discernible difference or boundary, allowing sexual or some higher form of union without penetration, and resulting in ready assimilation or equality, recalls Milton's description of angelic intercourse. It otherwise obtains only through the interpretive fluidity to which theory is given. Back on planet Earth, one thinks of Woody Allen's Orgasmatron from his movie *Sleeper* (1972): step in, sexually refresh, step out.

Science fiction infuses the radical feminist gestalt. Inhering in both, as a matter of both form and content, is the transgression of boundaries:

> Probably more so than any other genre, science fiction defies definitional closure, if only because the transgression of genre boundaries is already part of its unique tradition. Fantasy, romance and elements from other forms such as utopian writing have always been used by science fiction writers.

As specifically concerns non-penetrative sex, there is a utopian strain of feminist science fiction that posits an alternative way of being, a selfhood separate and apart from matters of sex and gender and, thus, autonomous. As sex-role differences create the model for a relationship in which one person "masters, dominates or controls another," the elimination of such differences levels the playing field, as it were, by creating alternative horizontal models. The leveling is not merely sexual, but extends to all difference-based hierarchies. In the feminist utopia, there are thus no distinctions between "humyn beings" and no dichotomies. It is a Marxist utopia with women of the world (rather than workers) uniting. The utopia disavows distinctions, as these invite invidious comparison. Inequalities are removed and edges rounded. However, as "Women and Gender" specialist Mary Louise Roberts reminds us, "The blurring of the boundary between 'male' and 'female'—a civilization without sexes—serves as a primary referent for the ruin of civilization itself."

Also gone is the emotional edge that generates both love and poetry. Gone too is the need for deconstruction—the dismantling of a thing to reveal its hidden inequity, since equality ideally removes all complaint, in which case one must be careful what one wishes for. Indeed, if one cannot hope to attain the stated objective—however defined—it is only partly because the objective is unattainable. The dynamic that drives radical feminism, as noted, is the imagining of a different future. "In Lacanian terms, it is an operation of desire, unsatisfied by any particular object, 'constant in its pressure,' ever in search of a fulfillment that is elusive because attaining the utopian aim of abolishing sexual difference altogether would mean the death of feminism." It is the core dilemma of any special interest: what happens when the call is heard and heeded? As with any trip, "it's about the journey not the destination." And it is easier to complain than contribute.

Radical feminist scholarship is to high culture what feminist science fiction is to low (or lower) culture. To appreciate the analogy, we look to the conditions that have radicalized the study of literature on the contemporary college campus. At one extreme, for purposes of Sappho's poetry, is classicist Page duBois's *Sappho Is Burning* (1995); at the other, classicist Anne Carson's *Eros the Bittersweet* (1986). Carson's work precedes duBois's by almost a decade. While duBois cites Carson in the bibliography to *Sappho Is Burning,* there is no discussion or even mention of her in the book itself. DuBois does the same in *Trojan Horses: Saving the Classics from Conservatives* (2001). The reason is apparent: Carson's starting point—the very word *bittersweet*—is a sharply dichotomous reproach to the muddle duBois would make of things. There is "bitter" and there is "sweet." The opposites do not merge in the compounded word, but work in tandem and alternation to establish and maintain *difference,* to create the tension of life's equipoise. This reality, as we shall see, is inimical to duBois's thinking.

Moreover, the larger issue of feminist criticism as it relates to Sappho cannot be sidestepped. It has from the 1960s on sought to reclaim Sappho (and literary studies generally) from years of scholarship that, because predominantly male, was "inherently opposed to Sappho." The "reclamation" has been especially marked in campus English departments. As recently noted, "A group of primarily female scholars has come of age and claimed a special right to the field. They comprise what may be called a contemporary academic *thiasos* [i.e., 'band' or 'coterie'] of Sapphic studies. . . . Indeed, the field has almost become what it studies: a new 'female initiatory discourse . . . conducted in the sheltered atmosphere of the *thiasos*'—the *thiasos* in this case being the sheltered and cultic atmosphere of classical studies in academia."

Within this theorizing precinct, notes classicist-polymath Thomas McEvilley (1929–2013), Sappho has become many things, including a "proto-queer" or sexually "dominant" or "phallic" aristocrat. To such readings of Sappho, gay and lesbian theorists and historians, no less than classicists, believe they have much to contribute. The highlights of this treatment are provided in the final chapter of McEvilley's magisterial four-hundred-and-sixty-three-page *Sappho* (2008) and needn't here be rehearsed. McEvilley's opus shows that serious work on Sappho is still possible in "postmodern" academe. His work is a reproach to the radical reclamation and "problematization" of Sappho; it is a credit to what is instinctive or primal in Sappho's outlook and, thus, to what is eminently simple and straightforward. We know and have always *intuitively* known Sappho's predicament: "Love and sorrow are re-born with every human being. Time and civilization make little difference. But those touches are only weakened by . . . recondite conceits and ambitious psychology."

Enter Page duBois, who slips the moorings from page one of her *Sappho*. She speaks of the "model of an eternal postmodern present, chaotic and fluctuating, [which] permit[s] a sense of boundarylessness, an exhilarating new way of conceiving of community that imagines an endless process, multiplicity of ties, and mergings with others." What does this mean? And what does it portend for duBois's view of Sappho? In truth, the statement's immediate appearance smacks of manifesto, with implications extending far beyond Sappho and lyric poetry. In duBois's scheme, Sappho is but a conduit or prop, something incidental to an enterprise at once both political and personal. The aforementioned quotation is nothing if not the theorized concentrate from which follows the modernist Big Bang. As Irving Howe presciently noted:

> The traditional values of decorum, both in the general ethical sense and strictly literary sense, are overturned. Everything must now be explored to its outer and inner limits. And then, since learning seems often to be followed by ignorance, there come the demi-prophets who scorn the very thought of limits; so that they drive themselves into the corner of wishing always to go beyond while refusing to acknowledge a line beyond which to go.

Which is, again, to say, be careful what you wish for. DuBois's statement urges a return to Chaos, to the world remade through wishful thinking. Like any utopia, it is eternal—outlasting, even as it supersedes, the past. However, as the past has been male dominated and chronicled, it is flawed and must be replaced. It can be dismantled, deconstructed—the process ideally entailing (for those who urge it) the erasure of history and progress as we have known them. Being "eternal"—a kind of *longue durée*—the postmodern present provides for "endless process," processing, or interpretation, the one giving way to the many ("multiplicity of ties"), the many lacking distinction (in both senses of the word), all merged. Within this framework, difference is illusory, a "social construct," since we are all essentially the same or aspire to be.

It is worth repeating: duBois calls for the "model of an eternal postmodern present, chaotic and fluctuating." This is ultimately not even a return to Chaos, but a *rebirth* into Chaos, i.e., a "new way of *conceiving* of community." The newly conceived community—both as an entity and in the manner of its begetting—has messianic overtones; it is a *novus ordo seclorum* 'a new order of generations'. And the conception, notes duBois, is "exhilarating." The word is sexually charged, as words frequently are in feminist discourse: conception "exhilarates"; ideas "excite" or "tantalize"; debate concerning the meaning of Gr. *olisbos* 'dildo' is "vigorous." Such uses purposefully tease, as neutral alternatives are readily available. The "new order" is strikingly heralded by the new word, or neologism, "boundarylessness," with reference to Marx at its heels.

Such notions are right out of the radical sixties. The 1960s and 1970s thrived on the razing of boundaries—the drug culture, free love, coed dorms and bathrooms, the abolishment of curricular requirements and prerequisites. Interdisciplinary studies repealed the "disciplines" as traditionally drawn. A potpourri of programs, inquiries, and "studies" took their place, many of which would previously have been laughed off campus. The joke continues, even as it intensifies today, making a virtual oxymoron of "higher education." "Studies" are mostly located in "centers" instead of departments, *self*-centeredness the key. *This* to effect the work of "boundarylessness"—the merging of high and low, serious and ludicrous, prerequisite and random selection (i.e., logical sequence or *order*); all laws revocable and refashionable according to one's own will in a world of *limitless* possibility. English majors, in this brave new world, can graduate without reading Shakespeare. It makes no difference. All is merged, equal and the same. Colloquially reflecting the morass was African-American literature professor Houston A. Baker, Jr.'s signature pronouncement that choosing between Shakespeare and Jacqueline Suzanne was "no different from choosing between a hoagie and a pizza." This is the playing field of moral and aesthetic equivalences, the idea that there is no reason to prefer anything to anything else. Everything and everyone is totally equal, and totally undifferentiated, in the totalitarian state.

Moving from the ridiculous to the tragic, the larger tale is told by twentieth-century "isms," including fascism, communism, and Nazism. These movements have been self-annihilating collectives in the service of unbounded power and world dominion. Such "isms" have emerged anew across the humanities through anti-Western and anti-Semitic ideology masquerading behind the beneficent guise and euphemism of "postcolonial studies." First demonize, then destroy. The objective of each "ism" is one of collective, transcendent, and undifferentiated will; individuals ideologically merged and made one, for a common purpose, regardless difference or distance—"boundarylessness," in a word, the heady and totally licensed sweep of values, and surrender to the immediate. Nor is physical limit an obstacle—be it the limits of a country's borders or those vanquished by the eugenics and self-confidence of totalitarian man. The confidence is especially reflected in triumphalist fascist architecture, and, at the other end of the spectrum, the revisionist and new-societal Bauhaus. Totalitarianism is a supreme leader's *total* control of every aspect of life, even as it is total surrender to the leader, channeled through the "cult of personality." Totalitarians know no bounds, boundaries, or constraints. All is merged and the same, including life and death—so long as the death is someone else's. We shall return to these concerns in connection with Ezra Pound and Mussolini.

Back on campus, students traditionally learned from their professors (who once sought to profess something meaningful), while professors often benefited from student response. But in the brave new world of boundaryless academe, professors and students have merged to become "partners in learning." As such, they overstep—i.e., transgress—that once revered boundary between master and disciple. "Disciple" derives from Lat. *discipulus* 'student', from which also *discipline*. Academic disciplines were once the markers of a sound curriculum and education. It is now punitive discipline that rules under ever-expanding politically correct enforcement codes. Everything is allowed on the progressive campus, and anything is punished.

Where there are no boundaries, one thing leads not to another, sequentially, but flows into another, chaotically. All is relative, nothing "defined" (Lat. *finis* 'end'; Eng. finite, definite, definitive). Things mean what one wants them to mean. Standards and hierarchies—which create order by degree of merit or importance—are *out*. Standards are judgmental and hierarchies "oppressive," as tending to establish the superiority of one thing to another (and doubtless hurting someone's feelings). The would-be egalitarian society brooks no such injustice. Enter Liberation Theology, defined by the principal dichotomy of "oppressor" and "oppressed." Enter Paulo Freire's pervasively influential *Pedagogy of the Oppressed* (1968), proposing that students are "oppressed" by "official knowledge," and should, with their teachers, cocreate the curriculum. Such dichotomies derive from the *Communist Manifesto* (1848), which opens as follows: "The history of all hitherto existing society is the history of class struggle. Freeman and slave, patrician and plebeian, lord and serf, guild-master and journeyman, in a word, oppressor and oppressed, stood in constant opposition to one another."

The struggle, notes the *Manifesto*, ends "either in a revolutionary reconstitution of society at large, or in the common ruin of the contending classes." However, if revolution cannot presently reconstitute democratic society, semantics and semiotics will—starting with a revolutionized vocabulary and frame of reference, progressing thence to settled formulations of grievance, and substituting verbal momentum for force of arms (the pen mightier than the sword). The result is a world reconstituted, if nowhere else than on paper and campus. The one-time barricade-burning zeal of present-day college administrators has continued unabated, though now recalibrated to *laissez-faire* education in the service of social justice and other forms of right thinking. In the process, academe has nurtured many a hothouse flower, of which radical feminism—i.e., feminism of the peculiarly academic kind—has been among the hardiest.

Within this climate, certain classicists and English professors have appropriated Sappho as *cause célèbre* and literary icon-in-chief. I earlier noted that the response to Sappho's poetry—its "reception" from the fifth century BC to date—was a telling indicator of intellectual, historical, and even personal history. The work of Page duBois, in my view, is the *locus classicus* for the personalized—in this case, radicalized—interpretation of Sappho and archaic Greek lyric. DuBois is the most outspoken, and conflicted, of radical feminist strategists. *Feminist* is not the least of her labels: "As well as a historicist, Marxist, classicist, historian of sexuality, I am also a feminist." And again, "I am a psychoanalytic female subject, an academic, a Marxist historicist feminist classicist, split, gender-troubled, in the midst of a book about Sappho." By her self-proclaimed allegiances and tenor throughout, duBois is a latter-day adherent of one of the most repressive, murderous, and utterly failed ideologies in human history. She contemns Western culture, dominated as it has been by the male sex (and male scholarship). The word is *misandry*. In sum, Western "patriarchal" culture has all been a big and as yet uncorrected mistake. The remedy, being everywhere and nowhere, is utopian (Gr. *ou* 'no' + *topos* 'place'). Among duBois's other calling cards, then, is a utopianism that allows her to be favorably reviewed by the like-minded professoriate.

Feminist scholarship subjects Sappho to crushingly deconstructive analysis. By *deconstructive* I mean an approach that deprecates, as a reflection of supposed misunderstanding or bias, most of what male scholarship has had to say about Sappho. A correct (or corrected) understanding of Sappho, and of the liberation she has long required, is possible only through those, like duBois, who divest themselves of "ahistorical essentialist assumptions about women," i.e., of generally accepted understandings mistaken for want of historical basis.

Feminist interpretation has its own lexical scaffolding. Again taking duBois as example, we find: "Eurocentric past," "postmodern, multi-ethnic reality," "postmodernity," "subjective body," "instrumentalization of the erotic body," and "a self with interiority, with a silent, private consciousness." As concerns theory process, we have: "implicit narratives," "poetics" (instead of "poetry"), "matrix" (instead of "way" or "manner"), etc. Of the last three, *implicit* connotes only suggestion, while *narratives* bespeaks ongoing, indeterminate discussion. The more one talks it up, the more "problematized" (and impenetrable) it becomes—and the better suited to publication. We live in a post-intelligible world, one looking to the "problematic" as modernity's mirror image. To paraphrase Howe's discussion of the modernist novel, the problematic nature of experience tends to replace the experience of human nature as the dominant subject of Sappho's poetry. Abandoning the assumption of a text that is knowable, the critic turns to the problem of establishing a bridgehead into knowability as the precondition for portraying any text at all. And further: statement yields to supposition, the text only temporarily validated, the problem and its discussion persisting.

"Poetics" is a term of theory and literary discourse, rightly designating, insofar as poetry is concerned, poetic method, process, or presentation. The problem nowadays is that *poetics* too often substitutes for and eclipses *poetry*. Why? Because *poetics*, unlike *poetry*, implies fluidity, flexibility, indeterminacy—something yet subject to analysis and verbal strategy, yet another opportunity for talk (thus did *The Journal of Narrative Technique* change its name to *The Journal of Narrative Theory*). A mathematical "matrix" urges comparison to a steam-engine rotary, or turnstile—trains entering from one direction and "roundabouted" in whichever new direction they may go. It is the language of theory that makes theory possible, and the obfuscation or debasement of language that impedes thought and action and corrupts civilization. This truth has been apparent from Thucydides to George Orwell. As Ezra Pound has said of "the damned and despised *literati*," "when their very medium, the very essence of their work, the application of word to thing goes rotten . . . the whole machinery of social and of individual thought and order goes to pot. This is a lesson of history, and a lesson not yet half learned." As later discussed, there was ever a significant gap between Pound's theory and practice.

Part of the new "matrix" involves the restyling of traditional terms. Aphrodite, forever the goddess of love in English, is now the goddess of sexuality, *sexuality* being to love what *poetics* is to poetry—an enlargement of theorizing possibilities. Aphrodite, as noted, is associated with all generative processes—physical, intellectual, and artistic. The association is predicated on charm, defined as the attractive power of love. Aphrodite is thus more than sexuality and its possibilities—sex being one thing, sexuality another, and fullness of heart and mind another yet. As Tom Stoppard observes, "There are some among us who think knowledge is advanced when we give something a new name. Goodbye, Eros; hello, libido."

The new matrix further encourages the distracting tease so characteristic of feminist theorizing. Erotic poetry does not raise, prompt, elicit, or suggest comment or interest, but *excites* them, as in: "the issues of sexuality that Sappho's work excites for many readers"; and "we must conclude that [Sappho's] expressions of love for women were completely acceptable to her readers in ancient Greece, since they excite no comment, neither praise nor blame." This last statement, moreover, posits a suspect conclusion based on silence—that conduct is condoned by lack of preserved objection. Sappho's poetry generated abundant comment in antiquity, all of it praise, even as the comic playwrights and others snickered. But, O! could they have penned just one of Sappho's verses. Then again, male sexual practices, both homoerotic and heterosexual, were equally subject to comedic barbs. Whether Sappho's expressions of love for women were "acceptable," let alone "completely acceptable," is irrelevant, as it ever is in the assessment of genius. Thus does feminist scholarship labor to validate its Sappho, to rehabilitate her from the centuries, the millennia, of imputed manhandling. Having done so, it will seal her off, impenetrably theorizing the fortress.

Where validation resides, self-esteem is not far off. Here too the banner unfurls: "Through imaginative identification with the first-person speaker, a girl would have absorbed survival tricks for living within a patriarchal culture: formulas for resisting misogynistic assumptions and so protecting self-esteem." The rallying cry of the multiculturally oppressed, self-esteem is defined by Ambrose Bierce in his *Devil's Dictionary* (1911), as "an erroneous appraisement." And so it is. It is for *others* to appraise—granting or withholding esteem. One's self-regard, self-respect, or sense of self-worth is the starting point.

Language empowers. DuBois's introduction to Roche further informs us that Sappho "reconfigures" the Homeric ethos. Sappho does so, and it is well she does, since that ethos includes (duBois reminds us) the distribution of women as spoils of war. This is merely an anachronistic, politically correct reproof of antiquity. That conquered males were uniformly slaughtered or enslaved *en masse* in warrior cultures does not figure into the argument. DuBois further tells us that Sappho, in the "Hymn to Aphrodite," "reinscribes her probable source, Homer's *Iliad,* making hers a poem of homoerotic courtship." The reference is to Achilles's pursuit of Hector around the walls of Troy (*Iliad,* Book Twenty-Two), which Sappho possibly glosses in positing fruitless amatory pursuit by a girl who had earlier scorned Sappho's affections. The Hymn is, first, grammatically ambiguous concerning whether the pursuing girl will actually pursue Sappho. Having rejected Sappho, the girl may suffer the unrequited love of one other than Sappho, male or female. The notion of "courtship" is in any event tenuous. The "reinscription" supposedly alters or corrects the *Iliad*'s male militaristic perspective; it tells us in so many words to make lesbian love, not war. At the same time, the notion of "homoerotic courtship" is overly prettified for what is merely same-sex amatory pursuit, and there is ultimately nothing in amatory pursuit to conjure the archetypal and most deadly pursuit of Homer's *Iliad.*

To similar effect does duBois speak of amatory pursuit in connection with Sappho's verses about a country girl. In a delightful fragment Sappho asks,

> What country girl
> dressed in country style
> has turned your head around,
> unable to keep
> her hemline raised
> from sweeping up the ground? (§11)

With the words "turned your head around" I translate Gr. *thelgei nöon* 'charms, enchants, bewitches (your) mind'. That said, it is unclear whether Sappho here chides a third party (male or female) or *herself* for being enchanted by the country girl. What reproach there is, however, is not aimed *at the girl* (as duBois believes). Why should the girl not be *charming,* thus rustically clad and mannered? If she is the head-turner Sappho makes her, why should Sappho not be expressing her own jealousy, protesting too much? The poem's character or cast of mind—down to the notion contained in Gr. *thelgei* 'bewitch'—is suggested by Robert Herrick's "Delight in Disorder":

> A sweet disorder in the dress
> Kindles in clothes a wantonness:—

> A lawn about the shoulders thrown
> Into a fine distractión,—
> An erring lace, which here and there
> Enthrals the crimson stomacher,—
> A cuff neglectful, and thereby
> Ribbands to flow confusedly,—
> A winning wave, deserving note,
> In the tempestuous petticoat,—
> A careless shoe-string, in whose tie
> I see a wild civility,—
> Do more bewitch me, than when art
> Is too precise in every part.

A similar effect obtains in Giuseppe di Lampedusa's (1896–1957) description of the lovely Angelica in peasant attire:

> . . . from behind the door was heard a subdued 'May I?' It was Angelica. In the rush and excitement she had snapped up, to protect her from the pouring rain, one of those huge peasants' capes of rough cloth called a *scappolare* . . . under the wet hood her green eyes looked anxious and bewildered, eagerly sensuous.
>
> The sight of her, and the contrast between the beauty of her face and the rusticity of her clothes, was like a whiplash to Tancredi; he got up, ran to her without a word, and kissed her on the mouth.

Sappho's verses about the country girl are an exercise in unadulterated simplicity. "The perfection of the Greek style is fine simplicity," asserts T. G. Tucker, ". . . illustrated by Sappho in that region of verse which preeminently demands it, the lyric of personal emotion." Simplicity inheres in the very origins of Greek poetry. Terpander, though the inventor of the seven-string lyre, denied himself its use and variety. His simpler compositions for fewer strings were so far superior that that compositional style remained preeminent. Simplicity in matters Greek has become an article of faith. Winckelmann famously emphasized the "noble simplicity and quiet grandeur" of ancient art, as did Friedrich Schiller (1759–1805), noting that "poetry, when most fully developed, must . . . surround us with supreme clarity." It was for its "directness and simplicity," its "exalted solemnity," as well as its "charm," that his learned reviewer praised William Cullen Bryant's *Iliad* (1870). In the same vein, though preaching mightily more than he practiced, Ezra Pound: "One 'moves' the reader only by clarity. In depicting the motions of the 'human heart' the durability of the writing depends on exactitude. It is the thing that is true and stays true that keeps fresh for the new reader"; and more, "the Tuscan poets gambol through the complicated Aquinean universe with an inconsequent preciseness which bewilders one accustomed to nothing more complex than modern civilization."

That Sappho might initially be "charming indeed in the simple directness of [her] expression," is a point that goes begging in feminist scholarship. Her "country girl" lyric is explained by duBois as follows: "Perhaps class power was expressed in terms of sexual domination, and Sappho best understood as one of those who had the right of pursuit in sexual relations, the power to read, to write, to lay out her desire in literary forms of seduction." Or perhaps not. Which will it be: charm or classist reproach? It is, in any case, clear that the "right of pursuit in sexual relations" is variable. As the Hymn makes clear: "If at first she flees, she'll soon pursue," the lead ever changeable. DuBois's surmise about the country girl follows on little more than a single page invoking Hegel, Foucault, Nietzsche, Bataille, Marxism, French communism, class struggle, and the victory of the proletariat. As Pope trenchantly observed, "Men of a right understanding generally see at once all that an Author can reasonably mean, but others are apt to fancy two meanings for want of knowing one."

We further learn that a certain fragment "typifies Sapphic poetics and allows us to thematize the act of reading itself as a recording of the experience of absence . . ." or that "Sappho's poems present a powerful challenge to what has often been seen as a monolithically phallic economy, an untroubled history of heterosexuality triumphant through all of Western culture." Sappho's poems present no such thing. There are, needless to say, reasons—imperatives—for the so-called triumph of heterosexuality. Insofar as we are all born of heterosexual union, heterosexuality is the very prerequisite of homoeroticism. As for the theoryspeak, it plays with language as surely as with itself. "Monolithically phallic," to give the devil its due, is a triumph of verbally suggestive profligacy. Hard to top.

Where there's patriarchy there's the obdurate phallus, object alike of disdain and delight—and not merely the cudgel of women's sexual and economic oppression, but a metaphor, if one pleases, for Sappho's *own* status as a member of Lesbian aristocracy. "The fact that Sappho is an aristocrat, dominant, if not 'phallic,' may be more significant than the fact that . . . the adjectives that modify the 'I' in her poetry have feminine endings." In this hermaphroditic composite, the female (whom Sappho embodies) becomes, or is equipped with, the emblem-in-chief of male empowerment. The empowerment, so goes the argument, trumps the female identity inhering in Sappho's language.

DuBois's sexually metaphoric flight unwittingly perverts (without mentioning) the Roman poet Horace's reference to *mascula Sappho* 'manlike Sappho'.

> Temperat Archilochi Musam pede mascula Sappho,
> Temperat Alcaeus, sed rebus et ordine dispar.
>
> The manlike Sappho tempers Archilochus's Muse with her meter;
> Alcaeus tempers it too, though different in matter and arrangement.

The reference appears in Horace's *Epistles* amid discussion of the development and uses of lyric poetry. These quoted lines were deemed by Eduard Fraenkel (1888–1970), a preeminent classicist of the twentieth century, "one of the most controversial passages in Latin poetry." The choices may be reduced to the propositions that Sappho is "masculine" because excelling in the male sphere of poetry; because showing resolve in leaping (lovelorn) from the Leucadian Cliff, as believed; or because excessively aggressive as a lesbian lover. Horace, viewing himself as the Roman lyric successor to Sappho and Alcaeus, likely meant the first—the imputation of tribadism being ill-suited to the context of a literary epistle and otherwise nowhere documented (however hyperactively imagined).

Reverse gender change (male to female) is also argued. DuBois ascribes a kind of transvestism to the Socrates of Plato's *Phaedrus,* where Socrates paraphrases the description of emotional turmoil in Sappho's *phainetai moi.* "Delicate and allusive as the [transvestism] is," it nonetheless prompts duBois to another sexually outrageous riff: "To echo [Sappho's] response so deftly is to be possessed by her, to become the lyric poet possessed by the lyric poetess, to blur once again the line between the sexes by dressing oneself in the words and images of the other." Words, we recall, are for *addressing* not dressing *in.* One quotes another to evoke, aptly apply, or even identify with another's words, not to cross-dress in them. *Phainetai moi* has since antiquity been the classic example of emotional seizure and, since its initial appearance, seizure affecting either sex. It quite suffices as such. While recent scholarship has credibly elaborated on the essentially sexual nature of Sappho's vocabulary and frame of reference, such theorizing of Sappho's sexuality from whole cloth is quite beyond the pale.

Finally, there is that fragment, sometimes attributed to Sappho, appearing to include the word '*dild*[o]' (Gr. *olisb-*). Garry Wills recently notes:

> A prurient thrill ran through the scholarly world when *olisb-* ("dild[o?]") appeared (partly) in an unattributed fragment in Sappho's (Aeolic) dialect. Was Sappho the den mother of the vibrated? But every one of the extant five letters of the incomplete word is unclear, the context indeterminate, and other parts of the badly damaged papyrus may be more appropriate to the other Aeolic poet from Lesbos, Alcaeus.

Undeterred, duBois urges

> some analogy, posed or suggested, between the playing of the lyre with the *plektron* ['pick'], the plucking or striking of the strings, and the sexual activity of striking or rubbing with the dildo—the connection of the *olisbos* with the *plektron* implicit, but present. . . . We find a possible connection between two 'instruments,' tools, devices to produce a certain result.

Exasperation aside, we hesitate to venture what that "certain result" might be. The connection between the lyre pick and dildo, claims duBois, is "implicit," "possible"—much as the suggestion of Socrates's transvestism is "delicate and allusive." Nothing is too tenuous for "sexing." It had in any event been shown, years before duBois's surmise, that *olisbos*—if the word is thus properly reconstructed—did not mean *dildo* in Sappho's time, if it ever did. In his admirably researched "A Note on the *olisbos*," Max Nelson concludes that the word *olisbos* seems originally to have been a term for a musical instrument, i.e., a "slider" run along strings, and only later "a rare comic euphemistic term for the dildo" (indeed, a by no means common designation for it). As in Latin, concludes Nelson, ancient Greek had no characteristic designation for the implement.

Delicate and allusive duBois is not. It is the inartfully vigorous discussion of dildos, female masturbation, and the phallus—the last of whatever material or length, in whatever state of readiness or repose—that enables duBois's outlandish reach. I say "inartful" because the art in art, as Horace famously notes, is concealment. Knowing as we do of such matters, we little need them so deliciously up close, especially given their tenuous relation to the matter at hand. Absent from duBois's frame of reference, in a word, is *aidōs* 'shamefastness', i.e., compunction or restraint. Where there are no boundaries there is, of course, no restraint. Greek comedy is a different matter.

The purpose of radical feminist scholarship is to liberate Sappho from male presuppositions from antiquity to date; to render her valued in a sexually liberated age, hip to "the new work on sexuality." Or, in duBois's words: "although Sappho's Lesbian desire has proven intolerable to generations of male classical scholars, it never affected her high reputation as a poet in antiquity." The views of nineteenth- and twentieth-century scholars are, of course, irrelevant to Sappho's fame in antiquity. Nonetheless, if Sappho's lesbian desire has been "intolerable" to male classical scholars, feminist classical scholars will "teach tolerance," beginning with the truism that Sappho's personal life had no effect on her literary reputation. The notion of (Sappho's) desire "proven intolerable to generations of male classical scholars" is of a kind with a female's "resisting misogynistic assumptions" and so forth—the emphasis on oppression rather than on poetry.

Even while significantly shortening her book's first chapter for use as the introduction to Roche, duBois adds the following:

> Sappho's poem 53 exemplifies some of the wonders of her poetics. The poem transforms inherited material of ancient culture, in particular the theme of the woman's body as a field to be plowed by her husband, a field in which his planted seed will grow and be harvested as a crop for new male citizens for the city. It speaks of loss, of the absent beloved one, now far away in Lydia, etc.

Sappho's poem 53 (Roche's 53; §11 herein) does no such thing, not even in Roche's fancifully reconstructed version. The purpose of duBois's comment is, again, to (politically) correct the record, to credit Sappho's "poetics" (versus her poetry) with the salutary "transform[ation]" of woman from the routinely penetrated to the touchingly sentient. But it is rhapsody on a nonexistent theme. DuBois's Sappho does not *burn* but crumbles beneath the weight of it all.

At the close of her introduction, duBois proposes, analogizing sex to agriculture, that the poem,

> set under the sign of the moon, a goddess, rather than under the light of Helios, the sun god, celebrates not labor, the nourishing crops of grain, productive of wealth, of new sons for the city, its sustenance, but rather flowers, pleasure for its own sake—this great poet, lover of women, shines like a moon over Western culture; she is the lost one herself, shining in the darkness, speaking of desire for the same, speaking of difference.

This is merely a romanticized touch with which to close the Roche introduction. The view ignores Sappho's worship of the sun and all things bright, and of things both feminine and masculine. Sappho is quoted by the Greek rhetorician and grammarian Athenaeus (2nd–3rd centuries AD), as saying, "I love the exquisite—that and yearning for the sun have won me brightness and beauty." In another of her poems, Sappho longs for Anactoria, saying she would rather see her "face sparkling radiant with light, than / Lydian charioteers and outfitted / infantry" (§4). The picture conjures a changing or variegated brilliance in the beloved's face, superior to the panoplied sun-reflected blaze of Lydian infantry. Special pleading for Sappho's moon will not do. Sappho is devotee of sun and moon alike, no less than she is a mother enamored of women.

Roche's *Sappho,* reissued with duBois's introduction, gives us the worst of both worlds: the alliance of fancifully reconstructed texts and rampantly deconstructive theory. The match in its twisted way could be no better. However, insofar as Sappho's actual poetry is concerned, the match is a no-man's-land; and for those relying on Roche/duBois as a meaningful introduction to Sappho and the lyric poets, a muddle. Be it remembered that the classical authors responsible for preserving Sappho's two complete (or nearly complete) poems quote them *solely for their poetic merit,* not for their political or socio-sexual implications—and not because Sappho spoke in code, fancying decipherment by latter-day theorists.

Over a thousand years after Sappho's time, the Macedonian Greek anthologizer Joannes Stobaeus (5th century AD) related an event supposed to have occurred at a symposium, or drinking party. Hearing his nephew sing one of Sappho's poems, the Athenian lawgiver Solon (7th–6th centuries BC) wished to learn it. Asked why he should thus waste his time, Solon replied, "That I might learn it and die." The anecdote is thought to reflect the introduction of Sappho's poetry into Athens. More than this, it conveys the effect Sappho's poetry had on her near contemporaries, such as Solon. Thus may we perish all, free from death by theory.

❧

There is a pop-cultural association of Sappho with sexual tawdriness, or forms of suspect or salacious behavior, that dates to Roman times. The term *Sapphic* has been luridly popular in media titles—too numerous to mention—relating to pulp fiction or live stage performances. Bypassing the lurid for the merely wishful, we note the following in *Sappho Was a Right-On Woman: A Liberated View of Lesbianism* (1972), one of the first contemporary works to popularize Sappho's name:

> If Sappho could literally be regarded as the archetypal Lesbian, much of the concern about the Lesbians in the women's movement would disappear. Sappho was an educated woman at a time when most women could not read or write, a political exile, a mother, and one of the finest poets who ever lived. When virtually all women apparently lived to serve the male hierarchy and died anonymously without leaving a trace of their uniqueness, she said her name would live through history, and it has. Today she would be called a Feminist.

In other words, if Sappho were the "archetypal Lesbian," then the kind of success she enjoyed—including the apparent cachet of exile—helps ease the way for lesbians in the 1970s, boosting their standing in society. But Sappho was not the "archetypal Lesbian" nor could her manifold accomplishments assure the "mainstreaming" of lesbians today, in the 1970s, or at any other time. Sappho's standing, singular and irreplicable, little lends itself to collective assimilation or partisanship. Would a 1970s Sappho have been called a "Feminist," as authors Abbott and Love propose? The question is sooner whether she would have wanted or even understood the designation.

Nor is Sappho's status as "tenth Muse" any longer secure. "The grand gesture of describing Sappho as the Tenth Muse," says Margaret Williamson, "is perhaps double-edged. As well as paying her an extravagant compliment, it may also indicate a difficulty in thinking of real women as poets: in order to write as she did, Sappho has passed beyond the bounds of ordinary humanity." "Perhaps double-edged"; perhaps not. Skepticism begins with the redundant "ordinary humanity." Nor is this an "extravagant compliment." It is *deification,* of a kind with Sappho's own deification of the man sitting across from her beloved, the man "seem[ing] equal to the gods" (§2), or with the status frequently evoked by such epithets as *di(*F*)os* or *theoeikelos* 'divine' or 'godlike'. Deification was a religious practice in antiquity—a convention, not a compliment. Since the nine Muses, inspirers of poetry and the arts, are themselves female, it little surprises that Sappho should join their ranks as one, if you will, who "seems equal to the Muses."

In truth, there is no "difficulty in thinking of real women as poets." There is instead a tendentious need to impugn the supposed inability of men, from antiquity onward, to "deal" with Sappho as both woman and poet. Williamson thus posits a spiritualization—or spiriting away—of the male-venerated Sappho. In sum, to reconcile themselves to the accomplishment of Sappho as a woman, men have transformed her into a Muse, removing her "beyond the bounds of ordinary humanity." Thus is she sequestered in the divine *seraglio,* fantasized.

This is simply new packaging of an old product. Male scholarship of previous generations had already "decorporealized" Sappho, rendering her a schoolmistress or finishing school proprietress, as seen. As the argument goes, girls came to her from throughout Greece for instruction in the arts—though surely not the art of love—en route to maturity and marriage. Their departures caused Sappho sadness, which prompted her poetry. The male discomfort reflected in *this* fiction, however, had less to do with Sappho's status as female poet than with the imputations of her love for women. The aim, however, was much the same: Sappho's removal from the realm of flesh and blood.

What most astounds about feminist interpretation of Sappho is the free pass it gets from the rest of academe—though one little expects a soil to fault its flowers. None of four consulted reviews of *Sappho Is Burning* (three by members of the *thiasos*) raises the issue of radical interpretation, other than to note (in one case), "This heady mix of theory, literary criticism, cultural history, and polemic is characteristic of the book." One review, without criticizing the book's radicalism, wishes it had been somewhat less trumpeted. Classicist Thomas McEvilley merely registers the phenomenon as one belonging to its own generation—as if a logical development on the scholarly continuum. And one review simply misstates or misapprehends the facts: duBois "cautiously approaches Sappho without a cultural agenda, be it literary, historical, or socio-sexual." This last review claims that duBois "wants the texts to speak for themselves, and so offers introductory chapters on the methodological problems of the interpretation of so tantalizing a series of fragments." Texts that speak for themselves have no "methodological problems of interpretation" and require no explanatory Chapters I and II.

Moreover, the entirely random fragments through which Sappho so sparingly speaks have now become "so tantalizing a series": *tantalizing* not in the traditional sense of implying more than is said, nor of leaving just enough to the imagination, but because consolidated into a *series*. It is now the *series* that tantalizes for its theorizing potential—for the interpretive stretch allowed from one to the next of the series, for a feminist Sappho resurrected from papyrus shreds. The exercise recalls biblical prophecy: "Lord God, think you these bones may live?" Sappho translator Jim Powell apparently thinks so:

> In the absence of any compelling reason to do otherwise, in *Sappho: A Garland* I have taken the opportunity to arrange Sappho's extant poetry in an integrated collage or mosaic, playing off modernist techniques of poetic sequence, fragmentary montage, and stream of consciousness to treat a cumulative movement that points to the integrity of her work as the surviving fragments disclose it.

"Integrity of her work"—as disclosed by what is thought to be the merest three-percent survival? *That* is the compelling reason *not* to do what Powell has done. The practice has most recently surfaced in reviewer approval of a translator who "organizes the fragments into thematic sections . . . making Sappho's lost oeuvre seem less distant and more imaginable as a whole." No, such notions merely invite "reader response" and encourage free association.

The exiguous texts spark a panoply of "problematics." Sappho will no longer be read, but "theorized" and "contextualized" into dubiously more than the sum of her parts. Most recently, Josephine Balmer, by a "strategy of juxtaposition" and "policy of recontextualization," provides "emotive section headings" as a framework for the organization of Sappho's fragmentary remains. The headings, she concedes, "speak far more for my interaction with the texts than for Sappho's now impenetrable, unknowable intent." This is certainly true, as classical verse did not use titles to orient reader expectation. However, what we want is the translator's *reaction to* the text, not *interaction with* it; the *result,* not the process or byproducts, and not the "why I did it," "felt," or "went about it" with which Balmer overflows. Balmer believes that "such interaction seems inevitable for any translator/versioner of Sappho's problematic work." Why? Because previous translators have similarly interacted, grouping their translations by theme or under one or another heading. Many wrongs apparently make a right. The fact that Sappho's once voluminous work survives mostly in fragments does not make it "problematic." Problematizing theorists make Sappho problematic, as does the suspect notion of "versioner."

"Contextualization," far from reflecting concerns germane to an author's work, is a matter of critical predisposition—what the critic brings to Sappho, and, greater yet, *what she wishes to find.* This is the "personal voice theory" earlier discussed in this volume. In the case of feminist scholarship, contextualization is utopianist. It is, first—though not designated as such—what has long passed as "reader response" criticism. The approach makes the reader "an integral part in the creation of meaning." This merely states the obvious—that we bring our own perceptions or biases to what we read. A cornerstone of deconstructionism, reader response "unloosens" meaning, "relative-izes" it, creates and even *re*-creates it. The text itself, contrary to its status even under the New Criticism, now lacks core meaning or intent. It has only what the reader brings to it, what the reader finds. As the reader thus constructs meaning, she reconstructs herself, breaking free of the ahistorical view of antiquity found in the scholarship of dead white males. The males among us who have neither acknowledged nor pondered their own relation to the big postmodern theoretical debates at the heart of this transformation remain "unreconstructed"—i.e., unrehabilitated, lacking in grace and salvation.

From the outset of *Sappho Is Burning,* duBois queries, "why not a master narrative, say one by Marx . . ."? She "contemplat[es] a new relationship between ourselves and the archaic past . . . [and the] kinds of empowerments or utopias or imagination of the future it enables." We note the connection between utopia and "empowerment," as utopia is always coercive. The possibilities are apparently as variable as the imagination one brings to Sappho's poetry. DuBois thus argues for "a historical materialist historicism . . . that engages with the past in order to generate some vision of a utopian future." Where does this come from? What *ever* does it have to do with Sappho?

True to its root meaning of "no place," utopia is the perfect society, the absence of all ills and injustice—those of oppressive heterosexuality most of all. DuBois posits the "utopian, heterogeneous, fluid, 'queer' postmodern" as opposed to "the installation of masculinity as the sovereign." The "'queer' postmodern" erases difference, subordination, and hierarchy, resulting in a "deterritorialized [i.e., boundaryless] utopia free of homophobia, racism, and sexism." The goal is as ultimately unattainable as it is irrelevant to Sappho and her poetry. Utopia's perfect, perfectly regulated, and perfectly oppressive society is a culture blindly idolatrous of its own vision as embodied in a Supreme Leader, whence the Cult of Personality—be it that of Marx, Lenin, Stalin, Mussolini, Mao, Kim, Castro, or any number of African luminaries. The cultic personality dominating duBois's vision is Michel Foucault. Despite his poor reception in some quarters (as she notes), duBois will continue "to look to Foucault as an exemplar of a certain utopian model of eroticism." Thus do feminist scholars theorize Sappho's fragmentariness, seeking a wholeness at once refused and afforded by the texts. We have emphasized that "The perfection of the Greek style is fine simplicity." Admitting no simplicity, feminist scholarship complicates and problematizes Sappho, ignoring what Gilbert Murray posited as the touchstone of Arnoldian criticism: the "somewhat blighting demands of unimpassioned common sense."

Dubois's *Sappho Is Burning* (1995), though published twenty years ago, remains a touchstone of radical feminist interpretation. More recently, Arion Press published *Poetry of Sappho,* "introduction by Page duBois, with wood engravings by Anita Cowles Reardon, in Greek with English translation by John Daley with Page duBois, interspersed with twenty prints by Julie Mehretu, November 2011." The work is an irrelevance. "English translations by John Daley with Page duBois" signals Daley's status as a Greekless translator. Daley's sole publication appears to be a slender volume of unremarkable verse titled *Not Guilty* (2005), containing such gems as: "Right wing banality bores the shit out of me." Daley's *Not Guilty* dedication reads, "for Page" (as duBois's *Slaves and Other Objects* dedication reads, "for John"). At the same time, the Ethiopian-born radical artist Julie Mehretu is of a kind with the radical Page duBois, like finding like. *Poetry of Sappho* is fortunately—and at $1,700 per copy necessarily—a "limited edition." It is the summation of everything blameworthy in the classics in translation today. By contrast in the deluxe publications arena, one looks to *The Iliad and Odyssey of Homer as Translated by Alexander Pope* (Chestertown: Chester River Press, 2009). The dust-jacketed slipcased set, with facing Greek text, priced at three hundred and fifty dollars, comes with an introduction by the estimable Steven Shankman and with fifty-two original color drawings by Avery Lawrence. Though Pope would disapprove the to-do, the volumes are an impressive and timely reminder of what is enduring in the Classics and their translation—and how it is done.

# Chapter 28

## Boundaries, Artistic Fit, and What "Art" Means and Does

> It is the power of the imposition of form which liberates the ancient Greek or Roman from the horror of the chance, random, or accidental life. We have a theology, they had art.
>
> – CHARLES ROWAN BEYE, "Horace in English"

ANNE CARSON'S POPULARLY RECEIVED *Eros the Bittersweet,* as mentioned, is the counterpoint, indeed, the antithesis, to *Sappho Is Burning.* Where duBois confounds, Carson—if sometimes puzzling—seems often to mean more than one can rightly say. *Eros the Bittersweet* has a quasi-oracular quality. Poetry, Carson appears to say, is the structural analogue to amatory yearning. The emphasis is on *structural,* Carson everywhere emphasizing delimited form, edges, bounds, and borders. Borders are necessarily fixed, and the space between them protected. No mergings or boundarylessness here. The concept is hardly new, though Carson wondrously reformulates it in relation to archaic Greek lyric. In what follows, I gather and order key elements of her argument for summary presentation. As the references are many, I include page numbers from her text.

Poetry, as all art warranting the name, is a process of critical selection, of delimiting or *fixing* form and content, with more typically suggested than expressed. One begins with words—their very sounds and syllables—proceeding to lines, and stanzas, all purposefully distinct and differentiated. Comparing Greek and English, classicist Gilbert Murray, as seen, adverted to Greek's more clearly cut verbal edges, more definite syllabic values, and greater metric flexibility, allowing for richer texture and expressiveness. As further concerns the fixing of form and content, a contemporary scholar aptly notes that "time and limit are the stuff of which poetry is made," poetry consisting of *measured* syllables, accents, and metrical feet. It is *limit* that determines a poem's measure and reach, and imparts its sense of time, including *allotted time* and the sense of *self-limitedness* that is death. "Bounded time, time hedged and underwritten by its terminus, death," is poetry's essential frame of reference. "It is this boundedness that gives time its value and its measure, that gives the poem, like other forms of consciousness, its poignancy and proportion."

Poetic meter, then, is that which is *measured* (Gr. *metron* 'measure') and that which is fixed or determined by time (Lat. *determinare* 'enclose, bound, set limits to'; from *de* 'off, from' + *terminus* 'end, limit'). Meter, though fixed, takes the measure of time with a certain flexibility. It is by correption (Lat. *corripio* 'snatch away') that an otherwise long final vowel or diphthong becomes short when the following word begins with a vowel; otherwise, the long would overreach its allotted space, hyperextending the line. It is, for the same reason, by elision that certain final syllables combine with the initial vowel of the word that follows, making one syllable of two. In erotic poetry, Carson implies, the constraint imposed on syllabic overreach signals the constraint by which the lover himself is inevitably *bound*: always held back, never quite attaining the object of desire. In ideal circumstances, reach is thus necessarily limited or constrained:

> Both correption and elision may be regarded as tactics to restrain a unit of sound from reaching beyond its proper position in the rhythm. (One might think of correption as a sort of metrical décolletage, in contrast to elision which bundles the too tempting vowel right out of sight.) One gets the sense as the poem proceeds, of a gradually imposed constraint. The reaching action of [a poem's depiction of] desire is attempted again and again in different ways through the different lines; with each line it becomes clearer that the reach will not succeed (28).

Why should the reach not succeed? Because desire attained is desire ended. "What does the desirer want from desire," asks Carson, but "to keep on desiring?" (130). "As all paradoxes are, in some way, paradoxes *about* paradox, so all eros is, to some degree, desire *for* desire" (109). The lover's goal is to "freeze the beloved in time"—by which I understand, to have her ever the object, rather than consummation, of desire. Scenes of amatory pursuit on Greek vases depict the objective (25). However, Keats's "Ode on a Grecian Urn" gives it voice, describing a lover's pursuit in bas-relief:

> Bold Lover, never, never canst thou kiss,
> Though winning near the goal—yet, do not grieve;
> She cannot fade, though thou hast not thy bliss,
> For ever wilt thou love, and she be fair!

Greek vase painting and Keats's poem both depict amatory pursuit. Though Carson does not adduce "Ode on a Grecian Urn," it perfectly illustrates her point: "The reach of desire is defined in action: beautiful (in its object), foiled (in its attempt), endless (in time)" (29).

Distinguishing oral from written poetry, Carson marks "the entrance to written language and literate thinking" that is the alphabet, and the alphabet's uniqueness "unfolding directly from its power to mark the edges of sound" (55). Carson further notes that "words . . . written or read place in sharp, sudden focus the edges of the units of language, and the edges of those units called 'reader' and 'writer'" (108). It is thus *edge*—differentiation, demarcation, *boundary*—that governs; *edge* that marks delimited, unbridgeable space. Delimitation is both physical and emotional. 'Shamefastness' (Gr. *aidōs*)," says Carson, "is a sort of voltage of decorum discharged between two people approaching one another for the crisis of human contact, an instinctive mutual sensitivity to the boundary between them. . . . The static electricity of erotic 'shame' is a very discreet way of marking that two are not one" (20, 21). Indeed, it is in the act of reaching, in desire itself, that intervening space is bodied forth, and "the space must be maintained or desire ends" (26).

With the spatial, or flesh-bound, divide between lovers comes the heart's own division. "The erotic code is a social expression of the division within a lover's heart. Double standards of behavior reflect double or contradictory pressures within erotic emotion itself" (24). Eros is thus "bittersweet," underscoring the conflicted emotion of love and hate combined (*Odi et Amo*) (25). And finally:

> Eros is an issue of boundaries. He exists because certain boundaries do. In the interval between reach and grasp, between glance

> and counterglance, between 'I love you' and 'I love you too,' the absent presence of desire comes alive. But the boundaries of time and glance and I love you are only aftershocks of the main, inevitable boundary that creates Eros: the boundary of the flesh and self between you and me. And it is only, suddenly, at the moment when I would dissolve that boundary, I realize I never can (30).

As the bodily boundary is indissoluble, the physiology that poets suggest for erotic experience—melting, singeing, grinding, and the like—bespeaks an "intense concern for the integrity and control of one's own body. The lover learns, as he loses it, to value the bounded entity of himself" (40–41). That entity is endangered in the reach or desire for intellectual as well as physical knowledge:

> There would seem to be some resemblance between the way Eros acts in the mind of a lover and the way knowing acts in the mind of a thinker. . . . Stationed at the edge of itself, or of its present knowledge, the thinking mind launches a suit for understanding into the unknown. So too the wooer stands at the edge of his value as a person and asserts a claim across the boundaries of another. Both mind and wooer reach out from what is known and actual to something different, possibly better, desired. Something else (71).

"Eros," in sum, "is always a story in which lover, beloved, and the difference between them interact"—the difference being spatial, physical, and emotional (169).

❧

Poetry, as mentioned, entails the *fixing* of form and content—*fixing* in the sense of *delimiting,* of *setting* or *securing* matter beyond flux and mutation. Little noted in this connection is the derivation of the word *art* from the verb root **ar-* as in the Greek *arariskō, artuō, artunō, artaō,* all meaning to 'fix, fasten, fashion, set'; 'arrange, prepare, make ready' (see also *areskō* 'adapt, reconcile'). The number of Greek derivatives urges the notion's primacy. Other derivatives are *artios* 'complete, perfect, exactly fitted'; *arti* 'just, exactly, closely'; and compounds, e.g., *artinoos* 'sound minded'; and—describing Hesiod's Muses—*artiepeiai* 'word fitting' or 'word fitters', often in a mildly negative sense: 'ready of speech, quick with words, glib', and thus translated, e.g., 'mistresses of words' (Lattimore), 'sure of utterance' (West). Cognate with the Greek root (from a common Indo-European source) is Lat. *ars* (gen. *artis*), lit., 'the craft of fitting things'; in a word, *art*. Related is Lat. *arto* or *artio* 'to closely fit, compress'; 'contract, control, *limit*'. Also attested is Lat. *artio* 'to endue with art' and *artitus* 'imbued or instructed in the arts'. A key element of classical thought, *fixity* is further apparent in the aspirated (*h)arm-* (preserving Gr. **ar-*)—from which *harmony* and even *arm/arms/armor* (all precisely *fitted*). Fixing, fitting, (de)limiting: the issue is one of *articulating* (from *articulus*, diminutive of Lat. *artus* 'limb, joint'), of extracting equipoise and permanence from chaos. Such are the linguistic and conceptual underpinnings of *art* as conceived by the West's first and most exalted practitioners. Boundarylessness is the storm; art, the eye.

To the extent it limits, compresses, or fixes, art ideally *perfects*, extracting an essence and discarding the chaff. The German art historian Johann Winckelmann argued that Greek art—i.e., statuary art—far from imitating nature, captures the perfectible in nature. Less diffuse and more harmoniously united (*mehr in eins vereiniget*), art immediately discloses the essence of what is otherwise dispersed throughout all nature. To start with nature is to go the long way around. Greek art distills the best in nature, providing ideal images of beauty, "if not from more beautiful bodies, then from a daily opportunity to observe beauty in nature—an opportunity which we do not have every day, and rarely in a manner that an artist would desire." Winckelmann's view accords with the Greek etymological import of the word *art* and its ideal, or essential, function as "essence" (Lat. *esse* 'to be'), i.e., that which ultimately *is*, apart from any externality. By this postulate, art does not imitate nature but perfects it. The idea is of a kind with that earlier expressed by Winckelmann's contemporary Joshua Reynolds (1723–1792), British portraitist extraordinaire and first president of the Royal Academy: that the achievement of Greek sculpture lay in its idealization of beauty. Ballet, as an art form, epitomizes this ideal.

Similar views continued into the early nineteenth century. English literary critic and essayist William Hazlitt (1778–1830), seeing the Elgin Marbles (Greek statues also known as the Parthenon Marbles), first displayed in London 1807, stated, "Art is the imitation of nature, and the Elgin Marbles are in their essence and their perfection casts of nature—from fine nature, it is true, but from real, living, and moving nature; from objects in nature, answering to an idea in the artist's mind. . . ." Hazlitt's notion of "fine" nature posits another grosser or "inartistic" nature. Saying that art in fact imitates nature, albeit only fine nature, Hazlitt maintains (with Winckelmann) that art distills the best in nature, providing ideal images of beauty ("the idea in the artist's mind"). The ideal for Hazlitt is the perfected "cast" of Nature embodied in such forms as the Elgin Marbles. "For most Victorian and Edwardian critics, the ideality and not the realism or naturalism of Greek art constituted its foremost excellence and virtue." We are reminded in this connection of Ben Jonson's (1572–1637) aphorism: "Without art, nature can ne'er be perfect; and without nature, art can claim no being."

Poetry exists within the same rubric. The view of Greek tragedy as an essence or distillation from the transient vitality and volatility of life prevailed in English author and intellectual Thomas De Quincey (1785–1859). Tragedy, he said, seeks the idealized, using idealized or "fixed" characters to portray it. The fixity of tragedy is, for De Quincey as well, analogous to statuary. Idealization of the human condition is best conveyed through suffering, itself essential and enduring. And as suffering endures, it begets endurance, "fixing" response and heightening catharsis:

> Certain great situations—not passion in states of growth, of movement, of self-conflict—but fixed, unmoving *situations* were selected. . . . The [tragic] mask, with its monotonous expression, is not out of harmony with the scene; for the passion is essentially fixed throughout, not mantling and undulating with the breath of change, but frozen into marble life. . . . And all this is both explicable in itself, and peremptorily determined, by a sort of idealized life—life . . . translated into a neutral world of high cloudy antiquity. . . . Had real life offered to [the Greeks'] conceptions a just field for scenic exhibition; in that case they must have been thrown upon conflicts of tempestuous passion. . . . But being . . . imperiously driven to a life more awful and still[,] . . . they felt it possible to present this mode of being in states of *suffering,* for suffering is enduring and indefinite; but never in states of *conflict,* for conflict is, by its nature, fugitive and evanescent.

Greek tragedy thus offers fixed character, fixed facial expressions, and fixed situations. It was, moreover, set in bygone ages, says De Quincey, as these were both ennobling and immutable. Such ages, he notes, were suited to "abstracting the individualities of a character," relieving dramatic situations of "molding and determining power," i.e., assuring the stasis for what De Quincey elsewhere calls *tableaux vivants* 'living pictures'. Such pictures, exhibiting a "statuesque attitude," are immutable. So also the dialogue—largely undevelopmental—which seems but "an additional exposition of the interest—a commentary on the attitude originally assumed." The story, for its part, is without background or character development, "told by implication."

A prime example of situational or attitudinal character is the *Antigone*'s Creon, "pretty uniformly exhibited as tyrannical and cruel," as De Quincey further notes, his conduct "purely official and ministerial." Creon, moreover, is characterless, but for "the mere blank expression of tyranny in a public cause." Such portrayal "abstracted all petty details of individuality and local notoriety[,] . . . all that would have composed a character[,] . . . reduc[ing] the historic person to that sublime state of monotonous gloom which suited the views of a poet who wanted only the *situation*." The tragic persona has its origins in the *Iliad*; the comic, in the *Odyssey*. "The tragic hero [Achilles] has character, the comic hero [Odysseus] personality. The one is stamped with certain attributes and cast in a single mold; the other wears as many masks as he needs. . . . The tragic hero enters into an 'irreversible reaction,' and 'there's an end'. . . . Achilles made his way into his death, Odysseus talked his way out of his." Achilles is the archetypal tragic figure, his condition dictated by fate (Lat. *fatum* 'spoken') and thus unavoidably "fixed" or "set." As there is no escaping fate, only its embrace proves tragic heroism. If Achilles is himself "a work of art," it is because he is all essence—*essential* in the root sense—embracing a life compelled by necessity and enduring its necessary suffering.

Nothing so characterizes Greek thought as the sense of limit and boundary through portion, proportion, and apportionment. This is reflected in the formality of classical poetry, verse after individual verse, ordering recitation to represent ordered creation and society. These concerns are most apparent in the Invocation to Hesiod's *Theogony* 'Birth of the Gods'. The need for boundary is first apparent in the forceful and at-last permanent separation of Earth and Sky and, with the ascendancy of Zeus, the division of functions and honors among the gods. The gods are "sorted out" as a predicate to religious observance or ritual—this the means by which worshipers separate the sacred from the profane, and themselves from others. Differentiation extends to things that are not of themselves divisible, such as the ocean. The *Theogony*'s Nereid catalogue thus isolates oceanic *attributes*, including coastlines and climates, by bringing each within the control of a name-suggestive deity. To name is to identify, set apart, and control (as Odysseus learns in his encounter with the Cyclops). Following procreative order out of primal chaos comes the tripartite division of the cosmos into Olympus/earth (Zeus/earthly kings), waters (Poseidon), and underworld (Hades). Olympus, earth, and Hades are, respectively, the inviolate realms of eternity, mortality, and death. Heroic encounters with the underworld—as in Odysseus's summoning of its ghosts —are notably perilous and few. The possibility that the underworld might be breached and revealed by divine distemper is loathsome, portending merger of living and dead. The boundary is sacrosanct.

The privilege of mediating these realms is, we might say, limited. The epic bard recreates the past in the present and, to that extent, brings what is dead to life: "And they [the Muses] breathed within me voice divine to glorify what was to be and what had been." Thus, "In removing the barrier that separates the present from the past, [memory] makes a bridge between the world of the living and that world beyond[,] to which everything that has left the light of the sun must return." The bard is privileged to freely enter and return from this world. The record of the illustrious past depends on it.

Also mediating these realms is Hermes. Among his numerous functions is that of messenger of the gods and sole boundary-crosser of Olympus, earth, and Hades. Speed and winged sandals ease the passage and mitigate the sense of trespass. Hermes thus also functions as "psychopomp" (Gr. *psuchos* 'soul' + *pempo* 'send'), he who accompanies souls to the underworld. Hermes is depicted on the exquisite Euphronios Krater, preparing to accompany the soul of the fallen Sarpedon, a son of Zeus. Painted in the late sixth century BC, the bowl (for mixing wine with water) is the only fully intact example of the two dozen or so surviving vases painted by the renowned Euphronios. The legendary Greek musician Orpheus ill-fatedly enters the underworld to reclaim Eurydice, charming Hades with his music. A marble relief at the Museo Nationale in Naples depicts Hermes guiding Orpheus and Eurydice back—Eurydice's hand on Hermes's shoulder, his same arm bent gently from under, his fingertips touching her wrist. Hermes, as earlier seen, makes death-symbolic crossings on earth as well—such as in the last book of the *Iliad*, where he accompanies Priam across the plain of Troy to ransom Hector's body.

Greeks of the classical period positioned "Herms" as field, boundary, or crossroad markers. The statues were believed to have an apotropaic effect, i.e., the ability to "turn away" evil or bad luck at crossing points where they most might loiter, including household entrances. So sacrosanct was the respect for apportioned space that the fifth-century Athenian general Alcibiades was sentenced to death *in absentia*—and without convincing evidence—for Herm desecration. Although the conviction was politically motivated, the imposition of such sentence underscores the transgression's severity and taboo.

The *Iliad* itself begins on just such a boundary-transgressive note. Agamemnon's taking of Achilles's spear-bride Briseïs, while on one level a slight to Achilles's honor, also violates the protocol of the Greeks' having "apportioned" her as a merit-based prize of war. Battlefield apportionment further extends to the division of meat, the best parts going to the most meritorious, i.e., those distinguishing themselves from others. Achilles's own time is apportioned to early death, as is the elderly Nestor's to advanced old age. Greek mythology assigns life-span apportionment to the three Fates: Clotho, Lachesis, and Atropos: 'Spinner', 'Apportioner', and 'Not Turning (Away)'. Clotho spins the thread of life, Lachesis measures it, and "she who cannot be turned" inexorably cuts what is measured. Collectively they are known as the Moirai 'parts, shares, allotted portions'. Things sought, attempted, or occurring *(h)uper moiran* 'beyond what is apportioned' are slated for disaster. Although the Moirai's parentage varies in antiquity and beyond, Hesiod suitably makes them the offspring of Zeus and Themis—*Themis* 'law' designating what is morally 'fit' or 'set' (Gr. *the-*, 'place, put'; Eng. theory). When one does things appropriately, it is *(h)ē <u>the</u>mis esti* 'as is right, or lawful'. The opposite is *(h)uper moiran* 'beyond what is apportioned'. The ancient Greek notion of apportionment, limit, and law, is thus ingrained and layered at every turn. Beyond such boundaries lies retribution or Nemesis (Gr. *nemō* 'distribute, apportion')—the goddess who punishes immoderation.

❧

We note, relative to boundaries, the golden age of Old French (Provençal) during the eleventh and twelfth centuries, when the troubadours, with an indifference to Latin, composed love songs in their own or one another's vernaculars. An excellent argument has been made by María Rosa Menocal for "the explicit lack of boundaries" in an "essentially atemporal 'Romania'" (not the Romania of today, founded in 1877). The fictitiously named entity harks back to an ahistorical, pre-nationalist Europe suffused with the emergent linguistic variations aborning from Rome/Latin (hence *Romania*). Romania in this sense is the cradle of Romance—a single language at this point, call it proto-Romance. The language's dialects reflect a common still-remembered Latin source. Proto-Romance "is without nation—indeed, it is the product of the explicit scattering of a nation [Roman Empire]—and it is, concomitantly, written in all languages and at all times." Regional dialects and texts are not yet correlated with national boundaries. "The Romance model . . . begins with the premise that the universe has exploded and that its remnants are dispersed everywhere and may appear at any time or place."

"Boundarylessness," though Menocal does not use the term, works well within the context of the Romance languages' development—the languages widely exploded pieces of a preexisting whole now coalescing, region by region; eventually becoming distinct and autonomous; taking fixed form and position in a linguistic recapitulation of order from chaos. The new languages are eventually bound and *boundaried*, preserving those who preserve them. A lack of boundaries, thus supposed, is not the theorist's sleight of hand. Signaling a primitive stage of formation, such lack seeks no erasure of what—both presently and for the foreseeable future—is distinct, proved, and accredited; of what is created rather than chaotic.

❧

The anathema of indistinction is also apparent in the biblical tradition, with reference to knowledge and longevity approximating the divine. Genesis

6:1–4 speaks of marriages between the *bnei ha'elōhim* 'sons of God'—"divine beings who belonged to the heavenly court"—and the "fair daughters of men." Their offspring are the "mighty men of old"—the *gibōrim* (some manner of hero)—also called *Nephilim* 'fallen ones' (perhaps because compromised by mortality). A threat to gods and man alike, the boundary-crossing semidivine cannot endure in the order of things. The biblical concern over the *gibōrim* is similar to epic's concern over the *andrōn (h)ērōōn* 'the men who were heroes' aka *(h)ēmitheoi* 'demigods'. To kill them off, the biblical tradition conceives the flood; the Greek tradition, war.

Both the *gibōrim* and heroes are "larger than life," whether in body or temperament. They are unbounded and thus without limit—"absolute," so as to encroach on divine prerogative. The biblical concern is, initially, the mating free-for-all (resulting in hero births) between the "sons of God" and mortal women ("and they took to wife such of them as they chose"). The concern thereafter is one of excessive and thus godlike longevity ("My spirit shall not abide in them forever"). And if not excessive longevity in the Greek tradition, then the tradition's excessive, and thus destructively disordering temperament, as in the supreme case of Achilles. Achilles, however short-lived, is an absolute and thus godlike will—epic's paradigmatic illustration both of the limits of personal behavior and of the clearly intended distinction between gods and men. Indeed, it is the *Iliad* itself that emblematizes the limits and transgressions of power. Despite Achilles's depiction as "a perfect paradigm for the transgression of boundaries," limitation will prevail in a cosmos where, like Achilles's fate, all is fixed and boundaried.

The imperative of limitation also underscores the concept of *hamartía*. Though commonly deemed "a tragic flaw," *hamartia* is actually 'a miss, mistake, error'—what authoritative work on the subject calls "an ignorance or mistake as to certain details." *Hamartia* is invariably associated with *(h)ubris* 'hubris, hybris', commonly rendered as "pride." Thus, according to popular understanding, *hamartia* is an outgrowth of hybris; i.e., one is flawed, and thus prone to tragic consequence, as the result of excessive pride.

*Hamartia*, however, is nothing quite so definite. Aristotle's *Poetics* speaks only of *hamartian* <u>*tina*</u> 'some mistake', signifying unintentional wrongdoing or error in judgment resulting in disaster. Only in later Greek religious or philosophical thought does the word connote "sin" or "guilt," as later strengthened by Judeo-Christian authority. The verb *hamartano* in its earliest Homeric use means to 'fail in one's purpose' or 'miss the mark', as when casting a spear. The noun itself indicates a generic "failure" or "fault" (the latter without the moral implications of "flaw"). Nor will the "fault of fragility" do, as fragility implies weakness, and thus helplessness, whereas *hamartia* connotes a certain *willfulness*—the mistake or failure being one of *hybris* 'overreach, insolence'. *Hybris* is in this sense "pushing the envelope," *failing to know one's limits or the limit in things.* The most compelling example, as Aristotle appreciates, is Oedipus—the archetypal embodiment of error, of the avoidable ignorance at the heart of *hamartia.*

Oedipus was a pre-Homeric early hero, renowned and prosperous, before becoming a "tragic hero." He sought to flee a prophecy that he would slay his father and wed his mother. Fleeing Corinth (where he was raised and thought he had been born) for Thebes (where he was actually born and abandoned, his ankles fastened), he confronts the Sphinx; solves her riddle at peril of his life; saves Thebes; and marries the then recently widowed queen Jocasta (his mother). Oedipus, in his flight, murders King Laius—Jocasta's husband/Oedipus's father—over the right of way at a Thebes-bound crossing. The play opens many years later with Oedipus securely enthroned, but with Thebes plague-stricken from the rot within. The play progresses through Oedipus's gradual acquisition of the facts and ends with Jocasta's suicide and Oedipus's self-inflicted blinding and exile. Oedipus succumbed to "some mistake": the avoidable ignorance of his birth and related events.

Had Oedipus been wiser, i.e., less "mistaken"; had he at any time before fleeing Corinth inquired into his ankle scars, which were the key both to his birth and name (Gr. *Oedipous* 'swollen foot'); had he otherwise consulted his genealogy (the Greeks were genealogical obsessives), he would, theoretically at least, have learned that Jocasta was his mother. Indeed, had he not forgotten, upon triumphant arrival at Thebes, the identity issues that had initially motivated his flight, the outcome might have been otherwise.

In that case, however, he would have outwitted and defeated the Oracle—an unthinkable feat even for the Sphinx's great riddle solver. Alternatively, and though *not* learning his true parentage, Oedipus would never have fled Corinth to avoid the heinous prophecy. He would instead have refrained from killing or marrying anyone, or at least anyone "of a certain age." This too, however, would have been to outwit and defeat the Oracle, but perhaps more plausibly in such a case by self-restraint, by self-*limitation*. Believing, however, that he might flee his destiny, Oedipus "pushes the envelope." This is an act of *unbounded* presumption, one disdainful of the limit in things, one pitting human contrivance against divine will or fate. In a word, it is *overreach*. In killing his father and wedding his mother (and begetting children by her), Oedipus indeed oversteps the greatest boundaries and commits the greatest taboos of all: parricide and incest. We speak metaphorically of "outdoing" or "surpassing" ourselves, of "knowing no limits," and the aspiration, metaphorically speaking, is worthy. Even so, there remains a limit. Oedipus, to be sure, outdid himself, both ironically and profoundly, trying so hard to circumvent fate as to have seemingly brought it to pass, to have acquired an ownership in the result, to have gotten his just deserts.

Ceding the palm, Richmond Lattimore notes that "Professor [Gerald] Else has demonstrated with what I think complete and sensational success that the famous Aristotelian *hamartia* can mean neither fault, or flaw, in character, nor yet an error in judgment, but simply a mistake about the identity of a person." *Hamartia* in this sense is a "functional element in a complex plot," a plot defined by Aristotle as one involving a change from ignorance to understanding—*hamartia* the ignorance from which the change begins. This formulation is consistent with the above, insofar as the misidentification is initially of *oneself*—the failure to "Know Thyself." Oedipus's misidentification of his father and mother directly follows on his failure of self-knowledge—and on the limits such knowledge imposes.

The structural requirements of tragedy make the mandate of limit yet more apparent. However self-evident the basics may seem, they remain foundational. Aristotle writes:

> Now, according to our definition, Tragedy is an imitation of an action that is complete, and whole, and of a certain magnitude; for there may be a whole that is wanting in magnitude. A whole is that which has a beginning, a middle, and an end. A beginning is that which does not follow anything by causal necessity, but after which something is or naturally comes to be. An end, on the contrary, is that which itself naturally follows some other thing, either by

> necessity, or as a rule, but has nothing following it. A middle is that which follows something as some other thing follows it. A well constructed plot, therefore, must neither begin nor end at haphazard, but conform to these principles.
>
> Again, a beautiful object, whether it be a living organism or any whole composed of parts, must not only have an orderly arrangement of parts, but must also be of a certain magnitude; for beauty depends on magnitude and order.

After discussing the appropriate length or *oros* 'limit' of a tragedy, Aristotle casually, but pointedly, concludes:

> And to define the matter roughly, we may say that the proper magnitude is comprised within such limits that the sequence of events, according to the law of probability or necessity, will admit of a change from bad fortune to good, or good fortune to bad.

We here have, by one of the West's greatest minds, a perfectly reductive, essentialist approach, taking nothing for granted. The approach bespeaks the centrality of proportion not only to tragedy, itself the consummate expression of the human condition, but to all things worth consideration as determined by their beauty—beauty being a function of proportion and orderly arrangement. These in turn are functions of the clearly discernible beginning, middle, and end of any created thing, organism, or work of art. Random occurrence, being unordered or chaotic, is exempt from the inquiry. A tragic plot must thus exhibit causality, as dictated by necessity or probability. This in turn is but the ordering of expectations according to what is morally right or divinely appointed. In Greek tragedy, proportion and orderly arrangement emerge from the ordered sequence of metrically consistent verses—typically 1,100 to 1,500—advancing toward and receding from a cathartic change of fortune. The concision is more remarkable yet, as choral refrain (i.e., "the chorus") is a substantial part of any tragedy. Commenting on but not advancing the action, choral song occupies a quarter or more of the line count.

In all ways integral to the above, as Richard Wagner noted, is concision of form, itself reflecting concision of myth:

> Greek Tragedy is the artistic embodiment of the spirit and contents of Greek Mythos. As in this Mythos the widest-ranging phenomena were compressed into closer and ever closer shape, so the Drama took this shape and re-presented it in the closest, most compressed of forms. The view-in-common of the essence of things, which in Mythos had condensed itself from a view of Nature to a view of Men and morals, here appeals in its distinctest, most pregnant form to the most universal receptive-force of man; and thus steps, as Art-work, from Phantasy into reality. As in Drama the shapes that had been in Mythos merely shapes of Thought, were now presented in actual bodily portrayal by living men: so the actually represented Action now compressed itself, in thorough keeping with the mythic essence, into a compact, plastic whole.

Accordingly, we see the thoroughgoing emphasis on limit and proportion, on the resultant separation and integrity of space and all that transpires within it, which is central to the Greek (and Hebraic) way of thinking. It applies to the rudiments of language, the structure of poetry, social interaction, the erotic encounter, and the physical cosmos. It is further evident in the compulsory differentiation between living and dead, human and divine. Paramount in the rites of religious observance, limit and proportion are the "essence" or "placement" of things by which Greek tragedy corrects human overreach. All is summed up in the gnomic inscriptions at the Delphic Oracle: "Nothing to excess" and "Know thyself." In a word, *boundary, containment.* Such to be sure are the lessons learned by Achilles, who was the "perfect paradigm for the transgression of boundaries," the hard way. The inscriptions were penned, among others, by Pittacus, tyrant of Lesbos and one of the seven sages of the ancient world. *Boundarylessness,* by such reckoning, is some surely as yet unknown and passing wondrous phenomenon in the Greek and biblical traditions alike.

# VIII.

# Chapter 29

## Not Making It New (or Better): Recent Iliads and Aeneids

> With short, sharp, violent lights made vivid,
> To southward far as the sight can roam;
> Only the swirl of the surges livid,
> The seas that climb and the surfs that comb.
> Only the crag and the cliff to nor'ward,
> And the rocks receding, and reefs flung forward,
> And waifs wrecked seaward and wasted shoreward
> On shallows sheeted with flaming foam.
>
> – ADAM LINDSAY GORDON, "The Swimmer"

NO CONTEMPORARY TRANSLATION of archaic Greek lyric has run the gamut of both rhyme and meter as do the translations of this volume (PART III). First appearing in 1983, such translation, or manner of translation, was clearly not of its time—though it may have been ahead of its time. Indeed, we have since witnessed the lament of formalism's demise, with Penguin Books publishing A. E. Stallings's rhymed and metered translation in coupleted fourteeners of Lucretius's *De Rerum Natura* (2007). The translation is a Drydenesque, even a Chapmanesque, undertaking in the early twenty-first century. Penguin has also published Aaron Poochigian's rhymed and metered *Sappho* (2009). By contrast, the epigrammatic sting of the Roman Martial (1st century AD) has always been unthinkable apart from rhyme, as most recently evidenced by the renderings of Garry Wills (Viking, 2007) and English professor Susan McLean (Univ. Wis. Press, 2014). Of course, Roman epic poetry, as noted, no sooner knew our rhyme and meter than did Homer or archaic Greek lyric. And yet, A. E. Stallings's and Aaron Poochigian's rhymed and metered translations rise as high ground from the quicksand of modernist self-infatuation. "How did things for poets come to seem so unhinged," asks Joseph Epstein, "so that so much of what they write, not being memorable, doesn't seem much to matter, at least not in the way that poems written fifty and more years before seem to matter?"

The errancy predates the last fifty years. Adam Kirsch distinguishes between "courteous" and "discourteous" poets: the courteous poet "aspires to be a part of literature, and appeals to the generally educated reader." The courteous poet thus "approaches language as a medium of communication, which must be brought to a height of precision and eloquence in order to move and delight the reader. . . . Such a poet will naturally gravitate toward meter and rhyme, which knit the poem to the traditions of English verse and provide a pattern to guide the reader's expectations." The courteous poet is the serious or meaningful poet. The discourteous poet prefers free form and random association to intelligible communication. Writing more for himself than for others, he deems obscurantism worth the game. He is uncaring, even disdainful, of his readers. The discourteous poet is the self-absorbed and often meaningless poet, his exercise hermetic. The discourtesy of translation has gone hand in hand, as noted, with the impoverishment and inscrutability of original verse. If, as Ezra Pound surmises, "A great age of literature is perhaps always a great age of translations; or follows it," the reason for a poor age of translations is apparent—the famed Pound himself to blame. Speaking of the fourth-century Ausonius—poet-rhetorician, politico, and tutor to the heir-apparent Gratian—Edward Gibbon quipped, "The poetical fame of Ausonius condemns the taste of his age."

❧

As generally concerns translation of the Classics, the output of Sapphos, Iliads, Odysseys, and Aeneids (Gilgameshes and Beowulfs) is tireless and unrelenting. Nor do the results necessarily or at all "make it new." In 2010 the University of Michigan Press published Rodney Merrill's translation of the *Iliad*—an unnecessary labor that imagined itself an improvement on centuries of accepted English usage. It renders *Pelēïadeō Achilēos* (verse 1) as "Achilles, scion of Peleus" instead of "Achilles, son of Peleus"; "Achilles, Peleus' son"; or "Peleus' son, Achilles"; and similarly, *Atreïdēs* (verse 7) as "Atreus' scion" instead of "Atreus' son" (i.e., Agamemnon). Is the translator here perversely playing with a son/scion soundalike? If so, it is an unprofitable game so soon in the poem, given the reader's likely unfamiliarity with the dated term of lineage. In fact, Merrill's verse 7 is typical of the heedless non-improvement of his work. Verse 7 originally reads:

> Atreïdēs te (F)anax andrōn kai di(F)os Achilleus

It is traditionally, and accurately, rendered:

> Son of Atreus, king of men, and godlike Achilles

However, Merrill translates:

> Atreus' scion, the lord of the people, and noble Achilles

Gr. *di(F)os* (Lat. *divus,* cf. Eng. divine) means 'godlike, divine'. The word reflects Achilles's semidivine parentage (son of the sea nymph Thetis) and intemperate or divinely wrathful disposition (*mēnin . . . oulomenēn* 'wrath . . . accursed'). In fact, *mēnis* 'wrath', the poem's opening word, is typically used of *divine* wrath, and as concerns those of lower status, only of Achilles. Merrill's "noble" softens these attributes away. Agamemnon, for his part, is supreme commander of the Greeks at Troy. Himself rapacious, he is "king of men"—rapacious, *fighting* men. "Lord of the people" makes him a presiding spirit or beneficent social presence. There is nothing gained, and much lost, by these changes.

In his dedication and acknowledgments, Merrill writes: "I must also acknowledge the indispensable contributions of commentators, translators, and lexicographers listed in the bibliography. I have constantly had at my side the versions of Richmond Lattimore [1906–1984] and A. T. Murray [1886–1940]—the latter revised [in 1999] by William F. Wyatt—and have plundered them freely for felicitous phrasing." This, if other than humorous, is a self-indictment. Translators typically reference and judiciously borrow from their predecessors, but without "plundering" them. Pope's indebtedness to Dryden is of this kind, even as the King James translators looked to the earlier Wycliffe and Tyndale Bibles. But if a new translation does not provide abundant felicitous phrasing of its own, why bother? Why even suggest that it does not? The contributions of others being "indispensable," Merrill admits that *his* best is *their* best.

Another troubled translation is the *Aeneid* of Frederick Ahl (2007). Also an improver, Ahl batters established use by translating *litora* as "coastlines" (pl.) in the poem's third verse, the word typically translated "coast, shore(s)" or even "littoral":

> Arma virumque cano, Troiae qui primus ab oris
> Italiam fato profugus Lavinaque venit
> **litora** . . .

This translates as:

> Arms and the man I sing, who first from shores
> of Troy to Italy, fate's outcast, came and
> to the Lavinian **coast** . . .

Lavinia is Aeneas's Italian wife-to-be; hence, *Lavinaque . . . litora* 'and / to the Lavinian coast'—a circumlocution for Italy. Now, Latin *litora* is a "poetic plural"—at the risk of simplification, a plural form used with singular force. Translating it "coastlines," Ahl gives *plural* meaning to a plural noun. Yet even the singular "coastline" is ill suited to the context, suggesting geographic expanse rather than the specific point of Aeneas's arrival. Ahl's "coastlines" is thus doubly inapt, to say nothing of unnecessary after centuries of translation getting it right. "Coast" or "shore(s)" is what's needed.

Ahl, like Merrill, is determined to make a difference from the opening verse. Instead of, "Of arms and the man I sing, who first from shores of Troy," Ahl translates: "Arms and the man I sing of Troy, who first from its seashores." We note, compounding the infelicity of Italy's plural "coastlines," the further pluralized "seashores" of Troy. Why *is* this? Latin *ora* (a first-declension feminine noun) means "boundary-line, bound, border, edge, shore(s), seashore"—notably as in Lucretius's signature phrase *dias in luminis oras* 'into the divine shores of light'. Virgil's *oris* [dat.], a poetic plural, designates the land's border or edge that fronts the sea, i.e., the shore or seashore. But "seashores"?

Ahl further imperiously notes: "*of Troy*: I delete the traditional comma after 'I sing' [*cano*]. Troy refers back to 'arms and the man' as well as forward to 'seashores.'" Ahl provides no authority for the deletion of this long-respected editorial comma—"editorial" because Latin was originally written without punctuation—nor for the Janus-like duty imposed on *Troy*. The "traditional comma" is simply a latter-day indication of the natural pause, or caesura, following *cano* 'sing', a pause precisely modeled on the opening of the *Iliad*:

— ⏑ ⏑| — ⏑ ⏑| –
Arma vir|umque can|o Troiae qui primus ab oris

— ⏑ ⏑| — ⏑ ⏑| –
Mēnin a|eide the|a Pēlēiadao Achilēos

The caesura dictates the proper sense, which is construction of *cano* solely with what precedes—*Arma virumque*. What is more, the Roman rhetorician Quintilian (1st century AD) makes of the *Aeneid*'s opening lines the *locus classicus* for the figure of speech called *hyperbaton* (Gr. *(h)uper* 'beyond' + *baino*/*bat-* 'step, stepped')—i.e., the means whereby word order, as characteristically in classical poetry, does not *keep step* with the sequential unfolding of thought. This, as earlier discussed, results from the freer word order allowed by an inflected language (Chapter 9). Quintilian takes *Arma virumque cano* 'Arms and the man I sing' as the proper and intended phrasing. "Arms and the man I sing of Troy" is thus both strained and erroneous. The intended reading gives the better sense, and leaving well enough alone makes the best sense of all. One generally knows from the first five to ten lines of any translation—epic most of all—just how it will go, and the examples of Merrill and Ahl are in this respect telling.

Equally telling is Robert Fagles's translation: "Wars and a man I sing—an exile driven on by Fate, / he was the first to flee the coast of Troy, / destined to reach the Lavinian shores and Italian soil." One reviewer, noting that "We like our heroes to be first in war, first in peace, and first in the hearts of their countrymen," observes: "'first to flee' doesn't sound so good. In fact it sounds decidedly bad, and 'decidedly bad' is not Virgil's way. . . . [I]t's not as if there were a lot of escapees to be the first of, after all." Otherwise put, Latin *qui primus* goes with *venit*: 'who first came' (to Italy). That Aeneas "came" as "fate's outcast" or "fugitive" (*fato profugus*, cf. *fugio* 'flee') does not mean, in Virgil's telling, that he *fled* Troy, or was first to do so. Although *flee* is what Aeneas in fact did, had Virgil determined to express the idea, he would have sooner said *escaped* (Troy).

Also different for its own sake is Fagles's *Arma virumque cano* 'Wars and a man I sing'. First, nothing is gained by Fagles's insistently novel *arma* 'wars' instead of 'arms'. Second, though some translate *virumque* as "and *a* man" (e.g., Copley, Lombardo, Ruden), the *Aeneid*'s famed opening is correctly rendered, as by those knowing better: 'Arms and *the* man I sing' (Dryden). Granted, because Latin has no definite or indefinite article, *virum* may, technically at least, be rendered either 'a man' or 'the man'. But Aeneas, notably both "first" and "fate's outcast," is *known*, and thus "*the* man." We think in this connection of the opening of Homer's *Odyssey*: *andra moi enepe, Mousa* 'Sing to me, Goddess, the man', or in Fagles's own *Odyssey*, "Sing to me the man, Muse. . . ." Unlike Latin, Greek *does* have a definite article: *(h)o* (nom. masc.)/*ton* (acc. masc.) 'the'—which, though absent at the start of the *Odyssey*, is invariably supplied in translation. Who would think to translate: "Sing to me, goddess, a man," or for that matter, "Sing, goddess, a wrath"? The proper choice, appealing to common sense and better translational usage, in fact dovetails with Greek linguistic development:

> Homeric Greek preserves a linguistic stage prior to the development of the demonstrative pronoun [i.e., *this/that*] into a definite article [*the*]. Hence, in Homeric Greek, semantically definite noun phrases often lack the article where it would be mandatory in later Greek. Examples of this are the first words of the *Iliad* and *Odyssey*, i.e., μῆνιν 'wrath' and ἄνδρα 'man' . . . introducing the basic topic of both epics, which is assumed to be known to the audience and is consequently definite.

Homeric Greek did not yet have a definite article, and none was needed. Latin never had a definite article, and surely none was needed here. Virgil and Dryden knew as much in composing and translating the *Aeneid*'s famously opening line. This is but the beginning of such matter as today's translators find beyond their grasp.

Finally, Fagles's "driven on by Fate" (uppercase *F*) offers an unnecessary and misleading personification. "Destined to reach" for *venit* 'came' unnecessarily enlarges on the idea already present in Fagles's "driven on by Fate" (*fato profugus*), while "Italian soil" for "Italy" (*Italiam . . . venit*) is *fill*, creating a faux balance with "Lavinian shores." How the esteemed Bernard Knox, who wrote the introduction to Fagles's *Aeneid,* as to his *Iliad* and *Odyssey,* could have endorsed this translation is past wondering.

❧

Virgil has also entered the gender-in-translation fray. Sarah Ruden's *Aeneid* (2008), appearing the year *after* A. E. Stallings's *Lucretius, The Nature of Things,* has been incorrectly hailed the first translation of classical epic by a woman (though it *is* the first of the *Aeneid*). It has, in any event, decidedly overshadowed Stallings's most noteworthy and superior achievement. Ruden little needed such billing, as the merits (and shortcomings) of her translation, as with any translation, have nothing to do with gender. Translation, as all great art, is essentially gender-neutral, by which we mean *indifferent* both in motivation and result to male or female authorship, the end product devoid of gendered indication. (I say so acknowledging an entire literature to the contrary.) The event of Ruden's translation nonetheless came freighted with feminist pleading. Ruden has been quoted as saying she believes "women, not men, are the natural translators for the great book," that a sense of "personal connection"—to Virgil's tenderness, as she proposes, to his feeling for landscape and human emotions, to his pity for the human condition—"gives female translators an edge over their male counterparts"; that women have the "right attitude"; that "women get more involved. The authors are more real to us. We develop relationships with them." Is *this* what it comes to—the self-help mantras of attitude, personal involvement, and relationships? One may of course question how women have greater access to the emotions of works first authored by men. If male authors instill feelings of pity and tenderness, male translators can do quite the same. The fully appreciable pities of war and human transience reside in a decidedly male Homer; and pity for the human condition, in Virgil. The translation that makes them known and felt is entirely gender-neutral. Ruden's special pleading is regressive, a backward step from the gender-neutrality that feminists have long sought.

Ruden's work is generally praised for its line-for-line correspondence to the original, even while using iambic pentameter (the meter of Shakespeare and Milton) in lieu of something approximating Latin's longer hexameter. In a marvel of concision, Ruden features ten (or eleven) beats per line where

Virgil himself, and most translators, have up to seventeen. The result is impressively disciplined. More than anything else, it imparts a sense of Virgil's extreme compression—inhering from the outset in Latin as a language—despite Virgil's longer line. Less can be more.

Without using a comparable meter, Ruden is nonetheless succinct. At the same time, however, she is necessarily short on texture—her line significantly shorter in English than is Virgil's in Latin:

> A long way out, with nothing in our sight
> Anywhere but the ocean and the sky,
> A blue-black mass of rain and stormy midnight
> Loomed in; the water bristled in the dark wind.
> All that colossal surface rose in arcs,
> Flinging and strewing us across itself.
> The storm clouds muffled day, the sky was hidden
> In soaking night, fire shattered on and on.
> Slammed off our course, we groped through blinding waves.
> The sky could not show even Palinurus
> The time; he said he'd lost his way in mid-sea.
> For three long days (we thought—the gloom confused us)
> We wandered, and as many starless nights.
> On the fourth day at last we saw land rising:
> Some distant mountains and a curl of smoke.

The outspoken Garry Wills adduces this passage in support of the fabulous claim that "This is the first translation since Dryden's that can be read as a great English poem in itself." No, we must not call it Dryden and not merely because it is composed in blank verse rather than in rhyming couplets. Wills further proposes that Ruden "comes very close to Virgil's mark, with a kind of quiet power even in the tumult of a storm." But she doesn't, as the passage has little tumult; and it is *great*, not quiet, power that suits a storm.

The passage is largely monosyllabic and thus flat, especially "[t]he sky could not show even Palinurus / The time; he said he'd lost his way in mid-sea." It contains some twenty articles, conjunctions, and prepositions (a, in, but, the, of, and)—sometimes four to the line—and ten pronouns (he, his, we, us, our). These are largely uneventful monosyllables, needed more to convey than create meaning. Thus, of the passage's one hundred and twenty-five English words, the *thirty* uneventful monosyllabic articles, conjunctions, prepositions, or pronouns comprise nearly twenty-five percent, while ninety-two monosyllables overall comprise nearly seventy-five percent. The passage utilizes but fourteen disyllabics, two trisyllabics, and one quadrosyllabic (a proper name). We recall that conjunctions, prepositions, and pronouns are frequently conveyed in Latin not by separate words, but by noun and verb endings. Even where a preposition might be expressed, it is readily sacrificed to meter, with case ending alone to signal function. This option does not exist in English. Thus, where so much of Ruden's line is given over to words merely implied in the original, the deadening monosyllabic effect is yet more pronounced.

As Ruden has been compared to Dryden, it does to compare her rendering to his—Ruden's a blank iambic pentameter, Dryden's rhymed. The passage is *Aeneid* 3.192–206:

> Now from the sight of land our galleys move,
> With only seas around and skies above;
> When o'er our heads descends a burst of rain,
> And night with sable clouds involves the main;
> The ruffling winds the foamy billows raise;
> The scatter'd fleet is forc'd to sev'ral ways;
> The face of heav'n is ravish'd from our eyes,
> And in redoubled peals the roaring thunder flies.
> Cast from our course, we wander in the dark.
> No stars to guide, no point of land to mark.
> Ev'n Palinurus no distinction found
> Betwixt the night and day; such darkness reign'd around.
> Three starless nights the doubtful navy strays,
> Without distinction, and three sunless days;
> The fourth renews the light, and, from our shrouds,
> We view a rising land, like distant clouds;
> The mountain-tops confirm the pleasing sight,
> And curling smoke ascending from their height.

Detailed analysis is unneeded, given Dryden's richer diction and manifest flow. Dryden has eighteen lines to Ruden's fifteen. He is decidedly more polysyllabic, even while providing *eventful* monosyllables. And he has greater sound-to-sense correspondence, despite the strictures of both meter and rhyme. Were there ever a case of freedom in constraint, Dryden is it. Ruden, by contrast, is short on cadence and texture, having trimmed them away to corset a necessarily more wordy English into a line-for-line corresponding translation; the English line, as noted, already significantly shorter than its Latin counterpart. However much a tour de force, such manner of translation is without aesthetic benefit. Extra lines, if reasonably tailored to the translation's needs, provide breathing room, a sense of amplitude reflecting epic's own fullness. Dryden's rhymed pentameter aside, the technique is also apparent in William Cullen Bryant's *Iliad* (1870)—like Ruden's, a blank iambic pentameter, but not in line-for-line correspondence. If the goal of translating dactylic hexameter into iambic pentameter with line-for-line correspondence is concision achieved through avoidance of Latinisms, the strategy ill befits Virgil's, or any classical epic's, layered expressiveness. This is epic, not epigram. As earlier suggested, the Latinization of English happily allows the recapture of some part of the original's texture and effect. In the end, one does not tally Ruden's monosyllables hoping to disparage, but only to identify the clutter. The issue is ultimately one of decorum, defined as "the proper harmony between manner and matter," or what is aptly called "imitative harmony."

Beginning the same review, Wills announces, "Just two years ago, Robert Fagles . . . set the bar very high for translating Virgil's Aeneid. Yet already the scholar-poet Sarah Ruden has soared over the bar." It was Robert Fitzgerald who earlier set the bar for Fagles, and it was then *Fagles* who reputedly soared. Virgilian translation is in truth a perpetual round of leapfrog, the subject of books unto itself. The King James Bible, as noted, stood for nearly three hundred years unchallenged. Where is our Virgilian equivalent? It is and has always been Dryden, the consummate conveyor of Virgil and English poetic craftsmanship combined, the beacon of millennial classicism.

❧

The age in which Dryden lived would, eponymously, be his *own*, the "Age of Dryden." His *Aeneid*, poetry of no less an English caliber than that of Virgil's Latin, was richly textured and inventive, everywhere evocative, memorable, and decorous. It could not be otherwise, given both the original's theme and magnitude and the poetic climate of late seventeenth-century England

(Dryden born in 1631, thirty-two years after Spenser's death, fifteen after Shakespeare's). Dryden is effortlessly formal, even as he is *contemporary* without being colloquial, obscure, or debased. Had Virgil written in English, Dryden is what we would have. Conversely, the English eighteenth century was a second Augustan Age, and Dryden its English Virgil. Alexander Pope praised "the long majestic march, and energy divine" of Dryden's verse. Dryden himself implicitly "claims to have done for English poetry what Virgil did for Latin in refining its metre and cultivating its expression." Here is the achievement credited Dryden by Dr. Johnson: "The veneration with which his name is pronounced by every cultivator of English literature, is paid to him as he refined the language, improved the sentiments, and tuned the numbers of English poetry." Through the great translations that dominated the last phase of his career, Dryden ultimately established his fame as a translator, shaping an age in which great translation—his own most of all, and *that* in preference to original works—was the great literature of the day. Dryden effaces what line exists between poetry and the translation of poetry; between poetic creation and re-creation.

Unfazed by whatever passes for current preference or dogma, Robin Sowerby notes Dryden's "consistent metrical fluency, syntactic clarity, and rhetorical emphasis," stating: "Until there is a strong poet of comparable ability using blank verse, his couplet translation will remain the best available, whatever is the prejudice, for or against his couplet form." The assessment, recalling Shankman's concerning Pope, advises against the facile comparison of *any* contemporary translator to Dryden. Dryden sooner begot translators of his own kind—Pope greatly indebted to Dryden, and both to the King James Bible (influences entirely lacking nowadays). A blank-verse translator comparable to Dryden would need be a Milton of sorts, Milton's verse "imperishably associated with the highest imaginative products of our literature." As Virgil never translated Homer, we may further regret that Milton never translated Virgil, or that the "age" of such translation has now decidedly passed. Virgil and Milton sidestepped translation, responding to the greater enticements of imitative transformation. One cannot argue the results. In the end, we must render unto Dryden the things that are Dryden's. Classicist Charles Rowan Beye strikingly observes that "The figures carved above the doors at Chartres derive their monumentality from the stone in which they are carved. It is eternal. Virgil's characters and their actions gain the same immanence from being lodged in a contrived formulary which implies eternal propriety." Dryden's propriety, his "fittedness," is equally enduring.

A translation that Ruden and others disapprove on formalist grounds is C. S. Lewis's rendering of parts of the *Aeneid*. According to its editors, Lewis's work, in rhymed alexandrines (twelve-beat couplets), "restores the archaism and poetic diction of our preindustrial literary inheritance. . . . The rhyming alexandrines immediately give us the sense of a classical poem, and the diction is essentially simple, yet poetic." And that grates on contemporary sensibilities. Lewis begins heraldically as follows:

> Lo, I who in the woodland blew an oaten reed
> Of old and taught the neighboring tilth anon to feed
> The hunger of keen husbandmen who loved my lay,
> Now of the god of battle and his rough array,
> Of arms and of the exile I must sing, of yore
> Guided by fate from Troy to the Lavinian shore
> And Italy. Much travelled upon land and sea
> By powers in heaven for angry Juno's sake was he,
> And proved in war, still endeavoring in our soil to place
> His gods and build a city. Whence the Latin race
> Comes, and the Alban fathers and the walls of Rome.

Fully rhymed and metered, this is a masterful opening. Frequent enjambment assures seamless movement, blunting the pauses that tend to accompany rhyming couplets. Movement is further apparent in omission of the classical French alexandrine's standard mid-line pause (caesura). The result, by a born scholar-poet and storyteller, is triumphant. C. S. Lewis's circumvention of the alexandrine's mid- and end-verse pauses is a show of form overcoming inherent limitation, and a certain "liberation" within a still-rigorous framework. The result is one unmatched in contemporary Virgilian translation. The evolution is reminiscent, in its way, of the hexameter's development into a generously accommodating verse form from what might once have been its isosyllabic beginnings (Chapters 19, 21). *Tilth* is tilled soil (Old Eng. *tilian* 'strive for'; perhaps here also suggesting Lat. *tellus* 'earth'; *Tellus:* Roman agricultural and fertility goddess). The archaism is well chosen, reinforcing the sense of bygone time evoked by "of old" (line 2) and "of yore" (line 5). *Tilth* also conjures a literary past, namely, Virgil's own as a pastoral and georgic poet, even while recalling the great antiquity of Earth herself. Indeed, Tennyson's "To Virgil" invokes the Roman poet as "Thou that singest wheat and woodland, / tilth and vineyard." The use of archaism thus secures "a natural habitat for the alien presence which [the translator] has imported into his own tongue and cultural setting. By archaizing his style he creates a sense of *déjà-vu.* The foreign text is felt to be not so much an import from abroad . . . as an element out of one's native past. It has been there 'all along' waiting reprise. It is really a part of one's own tradition temporarily mislaid."

There are passing quirks or infelicities, to be sure. One winces at "I must sing" for "I do sing"—suspecting the slip would have been repaired in Lewis's later revisions. Still, Lewis stands as a reproach to contenders and pretenders alike, worthy to be considered best after Dryden. In the words of one reviewer:

> Lewis was ideally qualified to translate Virgil. In an era when all educated men and women still learned Latin, Lewis was *primus inter pares* ['first among equals']. He not only read the language, he composed letters in it. We have a correspondence entirely in Latin between Lewis and an Italian priest who spoke no English. Lewis also saw Virgil through a Medieval rather than a Renaissance lens, putting him more in touch with the ancient author's mindset than any translator since the 16th-century Scot, Gavin Douglas. And the *Aeneid* itself was singularly important to Lewis. It was a work he knew intimately and which he read and returned to again and again, perhaps second only to the Bible.

Nor is Lewis's familiarity with biblical idiom to be slighted (Chapter 1).

❧

Classicists may have preferred a pause-laden alexandrine instead. The *Aeneid,* composed over an eleven-year period, at an average rate of four lines per day, is deeply contemplative, a necessarily "slow read." It differs in this key respect from the orally composed and recited *Iliad* and *Odyssey,* which sweep their audiences up in rapid, bravura performance. Yet despite the original's retarding pace, the *Aeneid* has succumbed to every possible poetic measure, fast and slow: the eight-beat rhyming couplets of Conington (1886), the ten-beat rhyming couplets of Dryden (1697), the ten-beat blank verse of Ruden (2008), the twelve-beat rhyming alexandrines of Lewis, and the rhymed fourteeners of the medievalizing William Morris (1875). All have their merits. The issue, as earlier framed, is not which is best, but which least offends or most engages. It is also a matter "not so much [of] what is absolutely best as what is best for the individual translator." Leavening the latter concern is variable reader preference and contemporary taste. Reader preference need not coincide with the times, dubious as they may be.

We have already noted the role of translation in refining and even forging language, in creating an "age" and serving as its benchmark. Translation has also been used to prove a point, as it were, or to signal a language's flexibility. The form in such a case is one to which the translator is personally sympathetic, regardless its likeness to that of the original or the likelihood of its pleasing. The result may be yet more gratifying, and more successful, than that of stricter adherence to convention. Distinguished scholar-poet Philip Stanhope Worsley (1835–1866) was thus to do—with marked Roman literary bravura—what no one else had previously dared. Where Virgil, through Dryden's prosody, "entered the eighteenth century an English Gentleman," Worsley's *Odyssey* and first half of the *Iliad* endeavored to make Homer a Spenserian, even as E. Fairfax Taylor's *Aeneid* (1907) sought to make Virgil a Spenserian. Such practice has a Renaissance-painting analogy in the depiction of classical or biblical figures in Renaissance-period dress, our pleasure and interest unimpaired for that.

Worsley's translations of Homer into Spenserian stanza were largely judged in their time as leaving no room for improvement. Though the situation sadly differs today, as the examples of Christopher Logue, Stanley Lombardo, and others attest (Chapter 33), translation so widely divergent from the form and spirit of an original could not become the standard version. (To be sure, the best is rarely standard.) Such attempts have nonetheless validated the power and resourcefulness of the English language. Worsley was unsurpassed in grace, diction, and musicality by any other translator using the Spenserian stanza, of which form Shelley fretted, "You must succeed or fail." The canonic Matthew Arnold, though fixing on the hexameter, retained a soft spot for Worsley, remarking that he "ma[d]e the stanza yield to him what it never yielded to Byron, its treasures of fluidity and sweet ease, above all bringing to his task a truly poetical taste and skill." Then contemporary metrist T. S. Omond enthused about the "lingering lusciousness of [Worsley's] Spenserian stanza."

Here then is a Worsley stanza, splendidly conveying the famed watch fires scene from the close of the *Iliad*'s Book Eight:

So they, with high thoughts on the bridge of war,
Sat through the night, their watch-fires blazing nigh.
As when the moon and every shining star
Beam loveliest, when the winds in slumber lie,
And in clear outline stand revealed thereby
Sharp peak and sunken valley and rifted hill,
Deep beyond deep unutterable the sky
Breaks open, and the night spreads calm and still,
  All the stars shine, and joy the shepherd's heart doth fill . . .

Arnold did not always get it right, however. Tennyson—responding to Arnold's gibe that Homer in blank verse "must not be [in] Mr. Tennyson's blank verse"—penned the following translation of the same watch fires scene:

And those all night upon the bridge of war
Sat glorying; many a fire before them blazed:
As when in heaven the stars about the moon
Look beautiful, when all the winds are laid,
And every height comes out, and jutting peak
And valley, and the immeasurable heavens
Break open to their highest, and all the stars
  Shine, and the shepherd gladdens in his heart . . .

The two versions—at nine and eight lines each—are equally apposite, and one can imagine reading large swaths of either translation. If Worsley's greatest fault in the service of Spenserian form was to flesh a word or phrase into a line, the fault is lost in the result overall. It is, then, not form alone that governs, but felicity in its use.

If Worsley's *Odyssey* was more successful than his *Iliad*, it is because the *Odyssey*'s character was sooner adaptable to the romantic sweep of the

Spenserian stanza. His *Iliad,* half finished at his death, was completed by John Conington, and the contrast between the resultant *Iliad*'s two halves is instructive. However remarkable Conington's command of language, he was a poet made, not born—his mechanical stanzas lacking the "grandeur and the bloom" of his predecessor's. This much seems evident in Conington's rendering of the passage indicating Hector's doom:

> How then should Hector his death-doom have fled,
> Had not Apollo that worst hour and last
> Come near him, and his limbs with vigor sped?
> Nodding, Achilleus signalled as he passed
> That none at Hector dart or spear should cast,
> And, rashly meddling, bear his fame away.
> But when again they reached the springs, at last
> Zeus did his golden scales in heaven display,
> And in them the death-fate of either champion lay . . .

However Conington's *Iliad* may be judged, one can only marvel at the combined *pietas* ('piety') and ability that impelled an avowed Latinist—who would translate the *Aeneid* into rhyming octosyllabics—to translate half the *Iliad* into a form he would never himself have chosen. A similar *pietas* is noted in Walter Miller's completion of William Benjamin Smith's 1944 translation of the *Iliad* into hexameters (Chapter 30). Such circumstances more readily urge appreciation than severity. *Pietas* characterized Worsley as well, who touchingly inscribed and saw to the delivery of his *Iliad* to Robert E. Lee, whom he compared to Hector in the noble cause. The gesture initiated a heartfelt correspondence. The *pietas* of a former age has since yielded to posturing, to original-languageless translation, to indiscriminate endorsement and publication.

# Chapter 30

## So Old It's New (and Better): The Smith/Miller Hexametric *Iliad*

> If great difficulties are opportunities for great successes, the immeasurable obstacles to Homeric translations are but so many demands for every kind of and degree of excellence in attempting it.
>
> – CHARLTON T. LEWIS, 1871

> Allow me to add, the reading of the translation of your Iliad has been a real joy. It is truly imagistic. Through it all glows the great soul of the translator who masterfully, lovingly, and tenderly weighs and chooses his colorful words. I appreciate it keenly and thank you for it.
>
> – ALICE WITHERSPOON, 1946

THE MOST AGREEABLE QUALITY of Richmond Lattimore's *Iliad* (1951) is, perhaps, its lack of pretension. It does not strive for the effect of the Greek-impaired "poet-translator" or, for that matter, of the classicist seeking novelty for its own sake. Lattimore, as regularly noted, was a rare combination of classical scholar and poet. As he knew Homer's Greek—its simplicity, tenor, and compass—he had no need for contrivance. Of course, no translation is beyond criticism. In Lattimore's case, however, the work's aptness and honesty far outweigh its occasional lapses. Lattimore's aim was to render the *Iliad* to "best convey the meaning of the Greek in a speed and rhythm I find in the original." Toward that end, he adopted "a free six-beat line" to be read "with its natural stress, not forced into any system." Though Homer, as noted, used a poetic dialect, Lattimore did not, employing instead "the plainest language I could find which might be adequate, and mostly this is the language of contemporary prose." The operative terms, however, are "which might be adequate" and "mostly," for at no time does Lattimore's seemingly plain diction lapse into colloquialism or vulgarity.

Lattimore shunned "poetic dialect" because he said it might immerse him in the idiom of Spenser or the King James Bible. Yet if Lattimore's own idiom was not "poetic dialect," neither was it "plainest" nor merely "contemporary prose." The following few lines, taken at random from his *Iliad*, make the point:

> And Teukros with an arrow struck the strong son of Hippolochos,
> Glaukos, as he was swarming aloft the wall's high bastion,
> where he saw the arm was bare of defence, and stayed his warcraft . . .

"[S]warming aloft the wall's high bastion" and "stayed his warcraft" are hardly the language of Everyman (even in 1951), while "bare of defence" (for *exposed*) has a clearly archaizing ring. Of such features Lawrence Venuti has said: "It is the archaism that gives [Lattimore's] translation its poetic qualities, joining with the Greek and Latinate names and the close renderings of the epithets . . . to elevate the tone to a slight formality and make the verse seem 'noble' or lofty." In fact, even "[w]ithout using archaism, Lattimore is dignified, indeed noble, and . . . keeps appreciably nearer to the meaning of the original." Lattimore's idiom is the "plainest . . . which might be adequate," the adequacy reflecting Lattimore's sense of decorum before an original which he both knows and respects. It is an idiom not of high but of middle nobility—nobility enough and more vis-à-vis Lattimore's poet-translator successors.

Having but recently compared the "watch fire" lines of Worsley and Tennyson, we may note a similar elegance almost a century later in Lattimore:

> So with hearts made high these sat night-long by the outworks
> of battle, and their watchfires blazed numerous about them.
> As when in the sky the stars about the moon's shining
> are seen in all their glory, when the air has fallen to stillness,
> **and all** the high places of the hills are clear, **and the** shoulders outjutting,
> **and the** deep ravines, as endless bright air spills from the heavens
> **and all** the stars are seen, to make glad the heart of the shepherd . . .
> [emphasis added]

One notes the concluding chiastic "and all . . . and the / and the / and all," which quickens the sense of the night sky's magnitude and the shepherd's joy-at-heart in viewing it. The passage has been praised for the superiority of understanding and method that Lattimore as scholar-translator brings to the work of translation. It is translation deemed superior overall—e.g., to the since much-lauded *Iliad* of Robert Fagles—in its dignity, nobility, clarity, and superiority of rhythm owing to length of line. This is work by the old master, Lattimore, who "still remains in possession of the field."

Active in the 1940s and early 1950s, Lattimore wrote, "when the canon of verse form had loosened up greatly and allowed for less regular lines . . . [I was] free to adopt a loose six-beat line that was dactyloid without being pure dactylic hexameter." However, whether Lattimore actually felt "free" is questionable, given his translation of Greek lyric, four years *after* his *Iliad,* into stress-based approximations of the original meter. Lattimore's *Iliad* is aptly described as "oddly occup[ying] a place between poetic and prose translation: loose poetry in the plain language of prose." Thus far, at least, it contrasts with the excessively heralded Iliads of Robert Fitzgerald (1975) and Robert Fagles (1990), which are loose poetry in the often affected idiom of contemporary verse. Lattimore's "prosy verse" followed on a long period of prose translations alternating, in turn, between King Jamesian sublimity and the colloquial language of the day.

Dactyloid without being pure dactylic hexameter is apt (but for the superfluous "pure"). English meter, as noted, is based not on syllable length or quantity, but on natural stress. As previously noted, the preferred rhythm of English is iambic ( ◡ — ) rather than dactylic ( — ◡ ◡ ); its favored poetic line, iambic pentameter rather than dactylic hexameter. Otherwise stated, because English lacks a tradition of quantitative verse-making, the stress-based approximation of such verse is challenging and most often unsuccessful. A prominent example of original English stress-based hexameter is Longfellow's *Evangeline* (1847). Arnold in *On Translating Homer* provides examples of Homer in English hexameter, including fair examples of his own. Arnold generally approves of Longfellow's *Evangeline* but deems it too "tenderly elegant," which is to say excessively "lumbering," or dactylic.

We should recall in this connection that Lattimore's dactyloid *Iliad* was only shortly preceded by the now ignored William Benjamin Smith and Walter Miller's *The Iliad of Homer: A Line for Line Translation into Dactylic*

*Hexameters* (1944). This was the third complete translation of the *Iliad* into stress-based hexameter. The canon of verse form had thus not entirely "loosened up," nor was it perceived to have done so. The Smith/Miller dactylic *Iliad* was published only seven years before Lattimore's "dactyloid" *Iliad,* and eleven years before Lattimore's own lyric hendecasyllabics. Of his own Iliadic meter, Lattimore sparingly says, "It is less regular than that of Longfellow, or the recent Smith/Miller translation."

Arnold believed that epic hexameter was *ordained* as the meter of English poetry, starting with the then still-elusive translation of Homer into hexameters. In this he differed from the equally Classics-learned Tennyson, with whom he (Arnold) competed as the voice of Homeric authority in English. For Arnold, the hexameter was more than a matter of poetic pedigree: it was the embodiment of national persona in verse.

> If, as Arnold implied, modernity was the demand of the right measure and if, as Arnold believed, England was a nation in need of measure, then perhaps, as Arnold hoped, hexameter would be a way to measure up to these modern times. . . . Mediating between . . . the complex past and the complex present, hexameter became Arnold's measure of, and for, the present time.

For a "present time" brimming with the potentials of empire, the hexameter and its associations were custom-made. Arnold was fifteen when Queen Victoria ascended the throne, beginning the sixty-four-year rule (1837–1901) that would take her name. In 1858, three years before *On Translating Homer,* India came under British rule, marking an extraordinary expansion and rule over lands and peoples. Indeed, the notion of "Rule, Britannia" had become ingrained as a patriotic song since its composition in 1740 by the Scottish poet and playwright James Thomson. The Virgilian resonance was clear: *tu regere imperio populos, Romane, memento* 'Roman, remember: Govern! Rule the world!' That the Homerically based hexameter had been the measure of empire and its mandate since Virgil's *Aeneid* was not lost on Arnold. Nor for that matter was it lost on Tennyson, his "To Virgil" crediting the Roman poet as "Wielder of the stateliest measure / ever moulded by the lips of man"—whose "ocean-roll of rhythm / sound[s] forever of Imperial Rome." A *translatio imperii* 'transference of rule' from Rome to Britain was no less apparent in Tennyson than it had been in Spenser. In his "Epilogue: To the Queen," concluding *Idylls of the Kings*, Tennyson heralds, "Our ocean-empire with her boundless homes / For ever-broadening England and her throne / In our vast Orient, and one isle, one isle, / That knows not her own greatness . . ."

But it was not the *Aeneid* alone that mandated empire. The *Aeneid*'s Homeric antecedents were themselves monumental structures—idealized through size, comprehensiveness, and arrangement—"manag[ing] to incorporate and orchestrate something of practically everything that was once thought worth preserving from the Heroic Age." Which is to say: in the beginning was the hexameter. In its regularity, stateliness, and accommodation; in the permanence of its narrative matter, be it the creation and ordering of the cosmos (*Theogony*), the world's greatest cataclysm (*Iliad*), its most enduring quest (*Odyssey*), or greatest foundational and civilizing endeavor (*Aeneid*); the hexameter brooked no comparison. Although the decidedly non-hexametric Rudyard Kipling (1865–1936) emerged as the "Poet of Empire," it was the hexameter that informed Arnold's hopes and world-poetic view.

Through a slow but inexorable process, Rome had adopted the Greek hexameter, perfected in the *Aeneid*'s tale of national destiny. Britain too would adopt the hexameter, aided by the rhythmic suitability of a plethora of hexametrically conducive Greek and Roman loan-words. Britain recalled its status as a colony of Rome and of the Roman Empire in the making. Geoffrey of Monmouth had early rooted British beginnings in the progeny of Aeneas. Spenser, as seen, had cast Elizabethan destiny in Rome's imperial image. Epic hexameter, the West's earliest vehicle of heroic aspiration, had been half a millennium and more in the making for Greece; it had been hard-won by Rome. Adopted by Britain, it would buttress, by metric rule and regulation, all manner of heroic endeavor, including Britain's succession as master to unruly multitudes. Early sensing its own imperial promise, and ultimately destined to rule one-quarter of the earth's surface, Britain would rule the initially recalcitrant six-beat hexameter. Imperial governance and metric regularity were civilizationally bound counterparts—imperialism aspiring to order, and by order to duration and the sense of permanence we associate with civilization;

meter, of venerable pedigree, enshrining all worth preserving, and assuring its continuity. Thus wrote Henry Purcell upon the 1685 ascension of James II: "Oh, how blest is the Isle to which Caesar is giv'n / The glory of Earth, and the darling of Heaven! / His name shall the Muses in triumph rehearse / As long as there's number or music in verse."

Inspirited by Arnold's *On Translating Homer*, the mid-nineteenth century was a period of marked interest in the translation of Homer into dactylic hexameter. The hexameter debates "went to great lengths to pronounce or denounce English limitations of classical meter," or to determine whether the essentially foreign hexameter could be adapted to English-language use. The debates were the cultural or aesthetic counterpart, as has been argued, to the then emergent British Empire's struggle to "accommodate foreignness both within and beyond its national borders" and consolidate "a common language out of heterogeneous elements." Signaling cohesion, ordered process, and compelling narrative, the consolidation of English poetry within the traditions of epic hexameter would enhance British culture and national self-identity. As with Attic Greek in the aftermath of the Persian Wars, as with Latin throughout the Roman Empire and beyond, as with French in the eighteenth century and American English today, language and literature have invariably been a projection of power.

The 1860s saw at least six hexametric translations of the *Iliad* in England, four in 1862 alone (the same year as Worsley's Spenserian *Odyssey*). In 1862, the year after Arnold's *On Translating Homer*, and in response to it, astronomer John Herschel published a dactylic translation of the *Iliad*, Book One, in the May issue of *Cornhill Magazine* (reissued in book form, 1866). The publication was cryptically disparaged by Tennyson (*Cornhill Magazine*, December 1863) in a remark preceding his rejoinder to Arnold, in which he urged blank verse as the only suitable vehicle for Homeric translation:

> Some, and among these one at least of our best and greatest have endeavoured to give us the *Iliad* in English hexameters, and by what appears to me their failure, have gone far to prove the impossibility of the task. I have long held by our blank verse in this matter, and

> now after having spoken so disrespectfully here of these hexameters, I venture, or rather feel bound, to subjoin a specimen, however brief and with whatever demerits, of a blank verse translation.

The year 1862 also saw John Ingles Cochrane's dactylic *Iliad,* Book One (followed in 1867 by private publication in book form). In 1865 the *Iliad* saw two complete dactylic translations, by Edwin W. Simcox and J. Henry Dart. Dart's, the superior, was issued in two installments, the first (Books One–Twelve) also in 1862. It is uncertain what belated precept Dart or others might at any time have taken from the 1861 appearance of Arnold's book-length treatise. In 1862, Arnold published his concluding thoughts on the subject, *Last Words.* In it he footnotes Dart as "meritorious." When Dart released his complete *Iliad* in 1865, it was presumptively with the full benefit of Arnold's thoughts. From what Arnold had seen, however, Dart was not the answer to Arnold's dactylic wish fulfillment. Nor can more be said of H. B. Cotterill's 1911 *Odyssey* in English hexameters, overly praised at the time (to judge from its opening verses) as "com[ing] out with every advantage of stately form and artistic dress." The same reviewer concluded, however, that insofar as the successful hexametric translation of Homer was concerned, "We have hardly got beyond mere versifying; the bones are not clothed with flesh and blood."

"Clothing" was at last provided by William Benjamin Smith and Walter Miller (Smith/Miller) in the last dactylic Homer (*Iliad,* 1944) that we are likely to see—a Homer magnificently appareled and finally successful. Though at first quite favorably reviewed, it has since passed into obscurity, or at best survives as a source of curiosity or jaded disparagement. This, to be sure, discredits a work of singular manner and result, as much an improvement on Dart as was Dart on Simcox and others. In fact, it is fair to say that the Herschel–Simcox–Dart–Smith/Miller progression, within a smaller time frame, was to English stress-based hexameter what the progression of Naevius–Ennius–Lucretius–Virgil was to Latin quantitative hexameter. Though Latin was intrinsically more receptive to hexameter than is English, gains in Latin's adaptational battle were, nonetheless, slowly made. Of further importance is Smith/Miller's pedagogic value. Since one wonders how Arnold would have received this *Iliad,* its neglect in these pages would be a major omission.

When judging translation, especially epic, we begin not *in medias res,* but *ab initio,* since the beginning usually tells all. In Smith/Miller, it inspires great confidence:

> Sing, O Goddess, the wrath of Achilles, scion of Peleus,
> Ruinous Wrath, that afflicted with numberless woes the Achaeans,
> Hurling headlong to Hades souls many and brave ones—of heroes
> Slain—ay, gave unto dogs, unto all birds lonelily flying
> Them as prey; and the counsel of Zeus moved aye to fulfilment
> E'en from the time when first stood parted in quarrel asunder
> Atreus' son, the monarch of men, and the godlike Achilles.

The metric, based on considerations already discussed, is as follows:

| 1 | 2 | 3 | 4 | 5 | 6 |
|---|---|---|---|---|---|
| — — | — ⏑ ⏑ | — ⏑ ⏑ | — — | — ⏑ ⏑ | — — |
| Sing, O | Goddess, the | wrath of Ac | hilles, | scion of | Peleus, |
| — — | — ⏑ ⏑ | — ⏑ ⏑ | — ⏑ ⏑ | — ⏑ ⏑ | — — |
| Ruinous | Wrath, that af | flicted with | numberless | woes the Ac | haeans, |
| — — | — ⏑ ⏑ | — ⏑ ⏑ | — ⏑ ⏑ | — ⏑ ⏑ | — — |
| Hurling | headlong to | Hades souls | many and | brave ones—of | heroes |
| — — | — ⏑⏑ | — ⏑⏑ | — — | — ⏑⏑ | — — |
| Slain—ay, | gave unto | dogs, unto | all birds | lonelily | flying |
| — — | — ⏑ ⏑ | — ⏑ ⏑ | — — | — ⏑ ⏑ | — — |
| *Them* as | prey; and the | counsel of | Zeus moved | aye to ful | filment |
| — ⏑ ⏑ | — — | — — | — ⏑ ⏑ | — ⏑ ⏑ | — — |
| E'en from the | time when | first stood | parted in | quarrel a | sunder |
| — — | — — | — ⏑ ⏑ | — ⏑ ⏑ | — ⏑ ⏑ | — — |
| Atreus' | son, the | monarch of | men, and the | godlike A | chilles. |

Typical of Smith/Miller disparagement was classicist William Arrowsmith (1924–1992).

> What is interesting is not so much the curious diction, but the extent to which the exigencies of the meter has [sic] demanded that the diction be curious; that birds should fly "lonelily" is not only appalling, but also gratuitous. It was good perhaps that the

> experiment was made but the waste of devotion is the more terrible because it could have been predicted.

To which we can only say there is no pleasing some modernists, especially one whose reviewer-puffed *Greek Tragedy in New Translations* would pedestrianize Greek drama beyond recognition (Chapter 33). Arrowsmith's response to Smith/Miller was simply reactionary, ignoring the undertaking itself and the incidents of poetry traditionally deemed those of *good* poetry.

Smith/Miller creates—in the best sense of *poiēsis*—an excellent facsimile of the original meter. Given that dactylic hexameter is for English a foreign and unfriendly meter, the result marvelously recreates the original, at once catching up meaning, spirit, word order, and archaisms. In the last regard, we have already urged that archaizing is *desired* in translation, as Greek epic itself archaized and was appreciated *as* archaic from its very origin—indeed, even as it was an artificial, traditionally determined construct. Smith/Miller, in short, is uncannily authentic. While the Greekless reader would require several hundred lines to begin assimilating the strange but unerring rhythm, the learning curve would be worth the effort. Most of all, Smith/Miller's adherence to meter requires, even as it necessarily allows for, poetic *license,* of which archaisms are an inevitable part. The result quite effectively evokes a bygone time and place: "mak[ing] it new" precisely by making it old.

Accomplishing the impossible, these opening lines possess a peculiar beauty and precision. Allowing near line-for-line correspondence to the original, the Smith/Miller hexameters are also a scaffolding to fidelity. In fact, the work is a rebuke to the accepted wisdom concerning the incompatibility of beauty and fidelity in translation, however exotic the beauty. The first seven lines warrant particular attention:

> (1) Sing, O Goddess, the wrath of Achilles, scion of Peleus.

The first line rings perfectly true.

> (2) **Ru**inous **wr**ath that afflicted with num**er**ous woes the Achaeans.

The second line exhibits interlocking soft and hard alliterations, with the added internal rhyme, "Ruinous" and "numerous."

(3) **H**ur**l**ing **h**ea**dl**ong to **H**a**d**es sou**l**s many an**d** brave ones—of **h**eroes.

The third line provides an alliterative flurry of interlocking *h, d,* and *l,* while *heroes* echoes *woes* in the preceding verse and *souls* in its own. The resultant *woes–souls–heroes* is a semantically significant sound pattern (i.e., one helping to create meaning). At the same time, the delayed "—of heroes" approximates the enjambment of the Greek word *hērōōn* 'of heroes' in the original. Were there any doubt of the intended effect, the next verse makes it clear through the actually enjambed modifier *Slain*:

(3–4) . . . many and brave ones—of heroes / Slain—

Both *ones* and *slain* are, of course, pleonastic (Gr. *pleō* 'fill')—used not to convey sense, but filling it out for metrical reasons. They do so unobtrusively.

(4) Slain—ay, gave unto dogs, unto a**ll** birds **l**one**l**i**l**y f**l**ying.

Here, the alliterative *lonelily flying,* with its unusual adverb, depicts birds of prey flying languorously overhead. The Greek more simply reads *oiōnoisi te pasi* 'and for all birds', or in a preferable variant, *oiōnoisi te daita* 'and a feast for birds'—without mention of their circling. But the Smith/Miller addition neither obtrudes nor distorts. It merely conveys a notion latent in the original. It is the kind of license for which a demanding metrical form allows, especially given the work's effectiveness overall.

(5) *Them* as prey; and the counsel of Zeus moved aye to fulfilment.

At the start of the fifth line, "*Them*" (italicized), emphatically in the same line-position as the Greek pronoun *autous* 'them', precisely evokes the original's contrast: between, on the one hand, the heroes' souls (hurled to Hades) and, on the other, the men *them*selves, i.e., their bodies (made prey for dogs and birds). The "*Them*" further conveys the force of the Greek pronoun with oppositional particle: *autous d'* '*but* them', i.e., the men themselves (as opposed to their souls). This is all precisely as it should be—a confluence of meter, meaning, and means.

We pause for a moment on Greek particles—the translator's bane, the source of despair and lengthy explanation. Particles, as their name implies, are recurring "little words"—often two- and three-letter vowel-final monosyllables. Dropping the final vowel—*de* to *d'*—when followed by a vowel-initial word, particles are reduced to non-syllabic consonantal sounds (Chapter 22).

Omitting one or more syllables in lines where they occur, elided particles are critical to regulating meter (Chapter 28). Adding nuance, they are typically untranslatable. It is more a sense or shading that they convey.

Smith/Miller, here as elsewhere, comes laden with "particular" emphasis. In "—of heroes / Slain—ay, gave unto dogs," the archaic interjection *ay* expresses regret or sorrow, even while adding emphasis. Though translating nothing in the Greek, it injects, particle-wise, a telltale remorse. There follows in "the counsel of Zeus moved aye to fulfilment" an element of verbal play—*aye* here meaning "always, still, ever" (Gr. *aiei* 'always'). But play alone is not the object. The adverb *aye,* though translating nothing in the Greek, clarifies the import of the *Iliad*'s fateful words, *Dios d'eteleieto boulē* 'the plan of Zeus was being fulfilled'.

*Aye* underscores that the verb is imperfect "was being fulfilled," not perfect "was fulfilled" (as often translated). This is to signal that when the *Iliad* begins with the argument between Achilles and Agamemnon, the *Dios boulē* 'the plan of Zeus', is still a work in progress (as we would say today). The argument and all that follows are not *alone* the plan of Zeus. Were that the case, we would translate "the plan of Zeus was fulfilled." Rather, and as signaled by the imperfect tense, the argument is only a stage in some other, more comprehensive plan. In other words, the *part* or *phase* of Zeus's plan conveyed by the *Iliad* starts with the quarrel of Achilles and Agamemnon. The greater plan—nowhere alluded to in the *Iliad* itself, but known from other sources—is the depopulation of an overburdened Earth by the death of the *Iliad*'s generation of heroes. It is, then, not the *Iliad* alone that begins *in medias res;* here, "from the time the two first stood asunder quarreling." Rather, the *Iliad* is itself *in medias res* for purposes of Zeus's larger plan. All of which is to say (reverting from macro- to microcosm) that the imperfect tense—"was being fulfilled"—conveys past continuous rather than past completed action. This critical sense of continuity is conveyed by *aye*/ever: "and the counsel of Zeus moved aye to fulfilment." Smith/Miller could just as metrically have used *ever,* creating a dactyl in the fourth foot instead of a spondee. Compare:

| 1 | 2 | 3 | 4 | 5 | 6 |
|---|---|---|---|---|---|
| | | | (dactyl) | | |
| — — | — ⏑ ⏑ | — ⏑⏑ | — ⏑⏑ | — ⏑ ⏑ | — — |
| *Them* as | prey, and the | counsel of | **Zeus ever** | moved to ful | filment |

and

| 1 | 2 | 3 | 4 | 5 | 6 |
|---|---|---|---|---|---|
| | | | (spondee) | | |
| — — | — ◡ ◡ | — ◡◡ | — — | — ◡ ◡ | — — |
| *Them* as | prey, and the | counsel of | **Zeus moved** | aye to ful | filment. |

The former is galloping and singsong; the latter, markedly emphatic—a significant gain won by archaism.

We return to our overview of Smith/Miller, the first seven lines.

(6) E'en from the time when first stood parted in quarrel asunder.

The sixth line both faithfully *and* poetically translates the Greek, lit., "from the (time) when first the two stood apart quarreling" (*diastētēn erisante*). For all the redundancy of "asunder," the word is aptly emphatic: this, after all, is no petty spat.

(7) Atreus' so**n**, the **mon**arch of **men**, and the godlike Achilles.

In the seventh and final line, the alliterative "monarch of men" does good metrical service for the more traditional "king of men," while Achilles, contrary to the inclinations of today's poet-translators or affected classicists, remains, as we like to see him, "godlike."

A final touch secures the whole. Achilles is described as "scion of Peleus" (first line), a usage elsewhere in these pages disparaged. The rendering, however, is here sanctioned because

| 5 | 6 |
|---|---|
| — — | — — |
| . . . son of | Peleus |

would create a rare spondaic verse-ending. Smith/Miller thus adheres to the traditional metric, albeit with less traditional diction:

| 5 | 6 |
|---|---|
| — ◡ ◡ | — — |
| . . . scion of | Peleus. |

While spondaic end-rhythm is allowed, it is infrequent. It thus poorly suits the *Iliad*'s famed opening verse, as one does not want to begin by way of exception. By contrast, the last line's more traditional

1 2<br>
— — | — —<br>
Atreus' | son, the . . .

in line-*initial* position, is spondaic where fully allowed. Unneeded for the meter, the earlier used "scion" is absent. The scion/son variance is here, in its way, reminiscent of the earlier-observed name of Achilles in the first and seventh lines of the Greek: appearing once with single lambda (λ) to provide a short syllable:

3 4 5 6<br>
— | –⏑⏑ | — ⏑ ⏑ | – ⏑<br>
. . . Pē | lēïa | deō Achi**i** | **l̲**ēos (line 1)

And once with double lambda (λλ) to create a long:

4 5 6<br>
— | — ⏑ ⏑ | — —<br>
. . . kai | di(F)os A | chi**l̲l̲**eus. (line 7)

Here, too, there resides in Smith/Miller a deep empathy with the Greek and its resourcefulness in sustaining meter.

Another excerpt, again typical of the whole, merits passing mention. It describes Apollo's dramatic descent, in anger, to the Greek encampment, and his slaughter by bow and arrow of the Greeks and their pack animals (a poetic depiction of the ravages of plague):

> Such was the prayer of the priest, old Chryses. Phoebus Apollo
> Harkening, wroth in his heart, from the heights of Olympus descended
> Bearing his bow on his shoulder, a close-shut quiver beside it.
> Clanging, rattled and rang on his shoulder the shafts of the godhead,
> Striding along in his wrath, like nightfall fearful advancing.
> Off from the galleys he sat; then loosed an arrow amid them.
> Fearfully came the clang of the bent bow's shivering silver.
> First at the mules, at the swift-footed dogs, he directed his onset,

> But thereafter, discharging his biting missiles against them,
> Men too, smote he; and aye burned pyres close-crowded of corpses.

The metric and alliterative speed of these verses convey the speed of Apollo's own descent, even as their fidelity reflects the accuracy of Apollo's aim. A minor lapse, no doubt, where the *dogs*—"wild" in the Greek—become "swift-footed" (for meter's sake), recalling the stock epithet of Achilles himself. No matter. Wild dogs are swift-footed, and the sweeping meter affords scant occasion for quibble.

Dactylic hexameter was early deemed unadaptable to English, largely because of the predominance in English of monosyllables, which "make our verses unapt to slide"; and of polysyllables, few of which are "by reason of their heaviness, willing to serve in place of a *Dactile*." This assessment, too often proven true, is belied by Smith/Miller, a version singularly supporting Arnold's belief in the English hexameter as best suited to Homer. If we do not yet have a hexametric *Iliad*, asserts Arnold, it is but a matter of time and application; indeed, though not one of "our established metres," the hexameter is simply too well suited to lie forever dormant:

> I know all that is said against the use of hexameters in English poetry; but it comes only to this, that, among us, they have not yet been used on any considerable scale with success. *Solvitur ambulando* ["it is solved by walking," i.e., by practical experiment]: this is an objection that can best be met by producing good English hexameters. And there is no reason in the nature of the English language why it should not adapt itself to hexameters as well as the German language does; nay, the English language, from its greater rapidity, is itself better suited than the German for them. The hexameter . . . possesses a movement, an expression, which no metre hitherto in common use amongst us possesses, and which I am convinced English poetry, as our mental wants multiply, will not always be content to forego. Applied to Homer, this metre affords to the translator the immense support of keeping him more nearly than any other metre to Homer's movement; and since a poet's movement makes so large a part of his general effect, and to reproduce this general effect is at once the translator's indispensable business and so difficult for him, it is a great thing to have this part of your model's general effect already given you in your metre, instead of having to get it entirely in itself.

While the English hexameter might ultimately not prove best for translating Homer, the message is yet clear: to forego the best meter is to forego the better part of a poetic translation and have to find it elsewhere. Such is the lesson of Fitzgerald, Fagles, and other Greekless blank-versifiers. Smith/Miller, by contrast, would doubtless have been Arnold's hexametric epiphany. As Arnold further prophesied:

> . . . it is to be wished that by the efforts of poets like Mr. Longfellow in original poetry, and the efforts of less distinguished poets in the task of translation, the hexameter may generally be made familiar to the ear of the English public; at the same time that there gradually arises out of all these efforts, an improved type of this rhythm; a type which some man of genius may sign with the final stamp, and employ in rendering Homer. . . . I am inclined to believe that all this travail will actually take place, because I believe that modern poetry is actually in want of such an instrument as the hexameter.

❧

Even as Smith/Miller is the final hexametric "stamp," its instructional value could yet, belatedly, make the hexameter "familiar to the ear of the English public." Imagine the following classroom scenario. Students studying classics in translation are first taught a simplified dactylic hexameter. They next recite aloud Longfellow's *Evangeline,* followed by Smith/Miller, doing so both individually and in groups. This instills both an appreciation of oral recitation and a sense of proximity to the original. The professor, in turn, recites Homeric passages in Greek.

The class is taught the Greek alphabet to allow for the use of individual Greek words and phrases, then of lines and brief passages. Name-epithet combinations and other simple formulae are highlighted on the board, the reading slowed to facilitate recognition and emphasis. Seeing formulae thus function in context, students have the rhythm from three sources: *Evangeline,* Smith/Miller, and Homer's Greek. Each student next memorizes a sufficient number of Smith/Miller verses to provide for the relay recitation of *Iliad,* Book One (six hundred and eleven lines)—recreating the experience of Iliadic recitation in antiquity. The course would thus be neither an abstraction nor a distribution requirement, but a studied and participatory encounter. The exercise ideally leads to Greek-language study and Homer in the original.

An epic poem in dactylic hexameter, *Evangeline* is the first such poem in American literature. It relates the tale of the Acadian expulsion from Nova Scotia and the heroine Evangeline's wanderings in search of Gabriel, her lost beloved. Expulsions and wanderings are the stuff of epic, as the *Odyssey* and *Aeneid* demonstrate. Using *Evangeline* as an entrée to Smith/Miller, the student thus encounters the primary epics of Greece and Rome, and the first of America—all in dactylic hexameter. Longfellow made a point of composing *Evangeline* in hexameters, saying even as he feared rebuff that he "could not write it as it is in any other [meter]; it would have changed its character entirely to have put it into a different measure." Longfellow's wife, Frances "Fanny" Appelton shared her husband's sense of "imitative harmony": "It enables greater richness of expression than any other [meter], and it is sonorous like the sea which is ever sounding in Evangeline's ear." Longfellow and Arnold shared a hexametric compulsion. Those who have followed, only to disapprove, have not been half their equals in advancing a contrary rationale or example, or even prospect, for success. Encountering the archaisms of Smith/Miller, students are initially perplexed, shortly enough receptive, and eventually enthralled, marveling at, and then possessing, the new-old vocabulary—like archaeologists stumbling upon long-buried artifacts. They come to appreciate that archaic language was already integral to the *Iliad* as the work was being composed. Their connection to the content has dramatically increased—to a level far exceeding Homer in Greekless poet-translator knockoff.

❧

What amazes and confounds about the Miller/Smith translation is its standing within the poet-translator arena. William Butler Smith (1850–1934), professor emeritus at Tulane University, was neither classicist nor poet, but a Bible critic and professor of mathematics. He wrote extensively on the New Testament and knew Greek, it would seem, from that source. Walter Miller, Smith's literary executor, held the emeritus chair of Philosophy at the University of Missouri, where the two were originally colleagues. Smith had been inspired by the famed German hexametric translation of Johann Voss

(1751–1826). As related in Miller's preface, Smith's translation "after much happy labor on his [Smith's] part," was submitted to various classical scholars for criticism and suggestions. These were so abundant as to result in full revision before Smith would even look for a publisher. At his death, Smith left the unfinished manuscript to Miller, his lifelong friend and colleague, to edit, finalize, and see to publication. Miller did not falter.

It is noteworthy that Smith here uniquely assayed a verse form that classicists would themselves be loath to consider. Yet the result impresses and inspires. It was a lifetime's work, and more impressive yet as the only work in the Classics that Smith and Miller ever undertook. The result—for all its fidelity, resolute beauty, and pedagogic value—has since been sadly ignored. Today, by contrast, Greekless blank- and free-verse translators thrive, seeking not precision but preciosity and sales. Their outputs, often embracing the better part of epic, tragedy, and lyric, have a mechanistic quality. How unknowingly correct was Carne-Ross in decrying classical translation as a thriving industry, the demand "apparently so strong that the products are hustled to their market without benefit of criticism"—and yet, how culpable Carne-Ross in facilitating the worst of it. Unlike the publication-shy Smith, today's translators work under contract with advances. After Pope, and possibly allowing for Cowper, it is Smith/Miller alone, and as line for line as can be, that provides consistently poetic translation. Largely Greekless translators that they are, Smith and Miller embody what is the exception to every rule. It is translation as *deus ex machina*.

Smith/Miller's *Iliad* was very well reviewed in its time. It was thought destined, on two accounts, to replace the then long-reigning King Jamesian prose translation of Lang, Leaf & Myers. There were, first, Smith/Miller's many archaisms, "which in the popular mind have become as inseparable from Homer as King James English is from the Bible" and, second, illusion of metrical equivalence provided by a line-for-line translation. Here then was an "age," seventy years past, which understood the essence of a foundational work and the means for conveying it. Their intrinsic appeal and suitability aside, archaisms would further regulate or help establish meter. The synergy is perfect, recreating in English the linguistic-metric *artifact*—the thing "*fitly made*"—that was and is the *Iliad* in Greek.

Smith/Miller was further praised as a precarious balancing act "through an alien and nearly impossible rhythmic pattern"—a work of "Herculean resourcefulness" exhibiting "difficulties surmounted" and "positive literary excellence." Similarly *Time* magazine wrote:

> The newest translation of the Iliad stands among the best ever made. . . . [I]t suggests the rhythmic quality of Homer better than Chapman, better than Pope, and a great deal better than the King James prose of the Lang, Leaf & Myers translation. . . . [The] meter, rarely used in English, the translators have maintained through 15,693 lines, and have made it clear, resonant, and readable.

The prediction for Smith/Miller was that "the longstanding allegiance to the archaizing prose of Lang, Leaf & Myers [would] be dissolved in favor of this new and reliable version which appears to add the ancient music as well." The prediction, however, failed with the fast-approaching debut of Lattimore's "dactyloid" *Iliad.* The eclipse of Smith/Miller was more lamentable yet, given the attainments of its inspiration. Goethe considered Voss's hexametric *Odyssey* (1781) and *Iliad* (1793) "one of the glories of European translation and a principal instrument in the creation of German Hellenism." Voss's epigones would not garner a similar regard and result.

# Chapter 31

## Leaving Well Enough Alone: Rejecting Lattimore for R. Fitzgerald

> I remember saying to Anatole that translation was an impossible thing. . . . He replied: "Precisely, my friend; the recognition of that truth is a necessary preliminary to success in the art."
>
> – J. LEWIS MAY, "Concerning Translation"

THE AFOREMENTIONED WILLIAM ARROWSMITH (1924–1992), classicist and prolific translator, could not sufficiently praise Lattimore:

> The problem of meter has gone a good step toward solution in Richmond Lattimore's new translation. But before discussing that, I should like to put it down firmly at the outset that this is to my mind the finest translation of Homer ever made in the English language. It could be improved only by Lattimore's revision of his work, a revision which I very much hope he will have the opportunity to make. For the meantime, it is quite enough that we should have an *Iliad* which again and again gives one the feeling of the Greek on the page, which, when it reads itself, is a creation as exciting as we can hope for in translation and which allows us to have the *Iliad* as a classic in the English language.

The "problem" and "solution" which Arrowsmith initially mentions are the presumptively failed metric of Smith/Miller and the then recent Lattimore translation, respectively. Arrowsmith's dismissiveness of Smith/Miller (Chapter 30) may in fact be fueling his enthusiasm for Lattimore. The praise is too expansive to forego a single word. Having discussed several faults, as any critic must, Arrowsmith concludes:

> Against these criticisms, one can more than balance the achievement: a line-for-line translation in a meter which often gives the feel of reading the Greek; an absolute fidelity to the original, in both spirit and letter; a diction which is almost without exception true and proper and whose effect, in conjunction with meter, is what Arnold could have called "noble"; a superb freshness in a genuine English; success in conveying the special effects of the particles, the effect of the significant Homeric run-on, and sweep of the Greek. The introduction to the translation is a superb essay on Homer. If we can have more translations like this (and the hope of its own improvement) I, for one, have no fear for the continued life of the classics in their new ground.

The enthusiasm lasted one generation, the critics next flocking to the *Iliad* of Robert Fitzgerald (1974). Prominent classicist C. John Herington (1924–1997), praising, even while back-stepping from, Lattimore, deemed Fitzgerald the *dernier mot*; indeed, the first "truly poetic translation" after Pope. As all superlatives had earlier been depleted on Lattimore, a new vocabulary and approach were needed. These Herington supplied in a taxing biological analogy, beginning with what praise of Lattimore could yet be mustered:

> What Lattimore has done for Homer will not need to be done again (and indeed could not be done again with anything like the same sensitivity and fidelity) so long as the English language keeps its present idiom. Nevertheless I cannot count his translations [*Iliad* and *Odyssey*] as English poems. In their very faithfulness to the details, the epidermis, of Homeric poetry, they distract the eye from the vast heroic anatomy itself. In time, I believe, Lattimore's translations will be more clearly seen and respected for what they are—the crowning achievement of modern professional Homeric scholarship, very much as Pope's were the crowning achievement of the immemorial humanistic tradition which that scholarship displaced.

The critique fights with itself. Will a work garner deserved and lasting fame, show sensitivity and fidelity, yet be unpoetic because faithful to detail? Did the same detail detract from the original? Is oral detail incapable of written transmission millennia later? If so, must it be changed or omitted consistently with our own aesthetic? Objecting to Lattimore's "details," Herington faults his adherence to Homeric formulae—to their literal and consistent renderings—whenever formulae appear. It is a tall objection.

In fairness, all manner of proposal has been made for dealing with formulae—from noun/epithet combination to entire lines and passages—including their case-by-case omission or alteration. Translations utilize both approaches, though, to borrow a phrase, "we cannot call them translations." In one instructive case, David Reck, using a roughly iambic ten-syllable line, notes: "I translate [the *Iliad*] almost line for line, often word for word, treating only the epithets freely. These I add or omit at will for reasons of metric, as the Homeric singers themselves did." Of course, there is no boasting a line-for-line translation when the thing most likely to impede it is omitted. Further, while we know what epithets Homeric singers included, we know nothing of what they might have omitted in any instance. In sum, it is for the translator *to account for what epithets exist,* not omit them because, in some hypothetical case, they might have gone equally missing.

Herington, as seen, first refers to formulaic particularity—the "details" to which Lattimore adheres—as "epidermis," i.e., "the outer nonsensitive and nonvascular layer of the skin . . . that overlies the dermis." The dermis in turn is "the sensitive vascular inner . . . layer of the skin," composed of connective tissue, blood and lymph vessels, sweat glands, and the like, with an elaborate sensory nerve network. By this analogy the Homeric detail of Lattimore's translation is something of a coating or veneer concealing the complexity of life within. The devil, however, is precisely in the details, invariably hard to capture. We sooner emphasize the essential nature of Homeric formularity—of epithets as much as any other detail—namely, its function as a staple of Homeric reality, the indicator of a world beyond time and change, of immutability itself. "The translator who omits some epithets," notes Charles Rowan Beye in his review of Fitzgerald's *Iliad*, "is exercising a reckless poetic license that leaves the Homeric world diminished, more nervous and fragmented. The Homeric epics have a devastating finality which may be in fact their greatest legacy, something which a translator certainly should not avoid."

Herington, however, would scrub Homer's detail away, though the "connective tissue" he prefers in Fitzgerald is *not* of Homer's world, but an alien organism. In sum, Fitzgerald's translation of formulae—not the epidermis but the *backbone* of Homeric composition—is too often "poeticized" to misleading effect. Herington flags such usages, only to forgive and ultimately embrace them. Why? Because Fitzgerald, unlike Lattimore, has (behold!) composed a *poem*, and Herington enthuses about telling us how. His validation of Fitzgerald, however, comes laden with ad hoc justification. Suffice it to consider three of Fitzgerald's approved poeticisms.

Fitzgerald first translates the epithet *di(F)os* 'godlike'—as applied to Achilles and other characters—as "vivid and beautiful" when used of Paris, and as "in majesty" when used of Priam. Both translations ring homerically untrue. "Vivid and beautiful" suggests an energetic object of admiration. Paris, however, is energetic only in bed. In Fitzgerald's context, Paris leaps from the Trojan ranks, sword at his side, bow slung from his shoulder, twin spears in hand, wearing leopard skin rather than battle gear. Effeminate, degenerate, and all show, he immediately shirks Menelaus's onslaught "as a man, coming upon a snake in a mountain vale, suddenly leaps back, and shivers take hold of his limbs." Paris escapes into the Trojan ranks, to be upbraided by Hector as a feckless pretty boy. The incident is not drama, but farce. Accordingly, the epithet *di(F)os* 'godlike', is merely stock, as there is nothing here either godlike or, for that matter, "vivid and beautiful" in Paris's manner. Rather, like his paramour Helen, Paris is consummately beautiful and "godlike" *for that*. That is what the epithet here designates: an inherent attribute regardless of circumstance. "Vivid and beautiful" seeks only to improve on Homer while proving false to Homer's idiom and intent.

*Di(F)os* rendered "in majesty" sounds false, as would "Your Majesty" in formal Iliadic address. In the relevant context, a distraught and sorrowful Priam prepares to play suppliant to Achilles—to grovel at risk of his life, begging the return of Hector's corpse. It is a king *in mourning*, of former majesty perhaps, but not "in majesty." Priam yet endures. Surpassing human limit, he is "godlike" in resolve and resignation. It is the perfect stock modifier for the *Iliad*'s man of sorrows.

Achilles, Paris, and Priam are all "godlike" for different reasons: birth, beauty, and endurance, respectively. The same Homeric epithet, used unvaryingly of each, is intended, even as it is understood, to capture the essence of each character—the element idealizing and transfiguring each, the element making each "godlike." This is the meaning and intent of "godlike," variously used. It is such traditional aspects of Homeric composition and intent that the translator should address. Knowing Greek is an excellent starting point.

As concerns the women of Troy, Fitzgerald translates the epithet *eükolpoi* 'well-' or 'deep-bosomed' as "deep-breasted." This is not so much an example of tampering with the Greek as of tampering with translation tradition. "Deep-breasted" is simply odd, rather evoking cleavage than that resting place of yore ("I reign in Jeanie's bosom," Burns; "Come rest in this bosom, my own stricken deer," Moore; "I would in that sweet bosom be," Joyce). Finally, and in a hyper-elaboration of the original, Fitzgerald translates *klutōpōlōi* 'Hades, horse-famed' as "the lord of nightmare, Death." How *very* removed from Homer's frame of reference. Hades, lord of the underworld, is "horse-famed" because horse and chariot are his conveyance (as when abducting Persephone). Hades is ill personified as Death. While Homer can personify an abstraction—as he famously personifies Prayers and Repentance—the abstraction of a personified god is not Homer's manner. "Lord of nightmare, Death" makes Hades a Horseman of the Apocalypse; Albrecht Dürer rather than Homer. Further, and as Matthew Arnold warns those who render Homer, "They must expel their nature with a fork, and keep crying to one another night and day: 'Homer not only moves rapidly, not only speaks idiomatically; he is, also, *free from fancifulness*.'"

"Lord of nightmare, Death" further suffers from what appears to be a sophistic translingual pun. "Nightmare" contains OE/Ger. root *mar* (from PIE **mer-* 'rub away, harm, seize'), originally meaning "evil spirit, goblin, incubus." The same root appears in Fr. *Cauche<u>mar</u>* 'nightmare' (OF *caucher* 'press, oppress'; Lat. *calcare* 'trample, oppress'). A *cauchemar* is an 'unpleasant dream with the sensation of oppressive weight' (*rêve pénible avec la sensation d'un poids qui oppresse*). The same sense is reflected in Eng. "incubus," above (Lat. *incubare* 'lie upon'; cf. *incubate*). The oppressive weight is sexual, evoking a woman's nightmare of demonic sex.

ME *mare* 'goblin' eventually became associated with English *mare* 'female horse', resulting in nightmares depicted as equine visitations. The association is vividly portrayed in the breakthrough painting of Henry Fuseli (aka Johann Heinrich Füssli) called *The Nightmare* (1781). The work depicts a pensive goblin perched atop the belly of a sleeping sexually languid woman, a grinning horse's head seen peering from behind a background curtain. Equine imagery also predominates in the Four Horsemen of the Apocalypse—Doomsday as nightmare. Fitzgerald's "lord of nightmare, Death" (for "Hades, horse-famed") transforms Homer's mythologically workaday horses into phantom "(night) mares." This is all quite resourceful, but foreign to Homer's thought and frame of reference—and misleading in the extreme.

Commending all (eleven) such examples, Herington concludes:

> In most every one of these instances—which of course could be multiplied by the thousand—it will be seen that Fitzgerald has put the formula to work *in its context*, selecting in translation the appropriate facet of the polysemous word-group. The result is almost always effective for the reader conditioned to English poetry, without obscuring anything of great importance in Homer's Greek. . . .

The high-flown "polysemous word-group" raises a flag. "Polysemous" means with a "variety of meanings" (Gr. *polu* 'many' + *sēmainō* 'signify, designate'; Eng. semantics). But Homeric formulae are not polysemous. What they are is multivalent, as shown in the case of *di(F)os* 'godlike', immediately above. A formula, as noted, is "a group of words which is regularly employed under the same metrical conditions to express a given essential idea." Formulaic wording remains by definition essentially the same, save for grammatical or other variations from one context to another. Nothing in or about such contexts warrants the translator's "putt[ing] the formula to work *in its context*." Usable in a variety of contexts, formulae do not have a like variety of meanings. They serve instead to suggest a timeless aspect in the person or thing described, or the antiquity or ritual nature of a given activity. If "godlike" or other epithets seem (to us) sometimes nondescript, the original audience is unlikely to have taken note amid the recitational rhythm and speed. In the end, Herington's full-throated approval of Fitzgerald sits oddly with the praise of Lattimore by Herington's equally prominent contemporary Arrowsmith: Lattimore "lacks the common *hybris* of the poet, his temptation to improve upon the original by slightly changing the meaning or charging a word which is neutral in the Greek; there is equally no sign of the pedant-translator."

Herington errs in crediting Fitzgerald for "treat[ing] each formulaic expression ad hoc, exploiting one or another of its latent possibilities at each occurrence in such a way that it will give piquancy and color to the verse at hand, without slowing down the narrative." He is similarly incorrect in proposing that Fitzgerald's twentieth-century inventiveness speeds the reader along, as Homer sped his listeners with formulae. What is formulaic in the original cannot properly be ad hoc in translation. Nor do we conclude that the original, for all its formulism, lacks "piquancy and color."

If faithfully translated formulae, unlike their originals, seem retarding, it is because we lack appreciation of oral composition and its indebtedness to formulaic phrasing. We are a literate, not oral, culture; we do not look to ready-made phrases, but to word-for-word precision and the purposeful variety that come with writing. We thus imagine, as concerns Homeric formulae, that "making it new" each time repairs our failing patience. Lattimore's formulae, claims Herington, are unfamiliar and retarding when literally translated, defeating Homer's rapidity. No, they are familiar enough, or likely in time to become so. We all know and relish "swift-footed Achilles," "rosy-fingered dawn," the "wine-dark sea," and the like; it is their beauty and very uncommonness that intrigue. The notion of "Homer's rapidity" in translation is, in any event, beside the point when even those reading Homer in Greek today read largely line by line. Barring the study of Greek, it remains Homer in translation, not Fitzgerald's Homer, that we wish to consult. The translator's job, especially in blank verse, is to convey epic formulae as seamlessly in English as did Homer in Greek, *not* to provide eye-popping improvements. It is *these* that slow the reader. To the extent unconstrained by rhyme or meter, it befits the blank-verse translator to convey this essential element of Homeric verse.

There are other ways to deal with the issue. We may assume, for instance, that in name/epithet combinations the "entire phrases are but names" and are used in the rapid flow of oral composition "as proper names without regard to the context[,] . . . the singer's rounded line a full compensation for the frequent repetition of familiar epithets." Thus, where Hector is *phaidimos* 'illustrious', *koruthaiolos* 'beaming-helmeted', *chalkokorustē* 'bronze-armored', or even *di[F]on* (acc.) 'godlike'—depending on the nominative, genitive, dative, or accusative use of his name—he might, in translation, be *any* of these interchangeably, with the net Homeric effect preserved. Otherwise, while some epithets may be omitted, the translator may still "properly retain enough of them to suggest the effect of lavish fulness and large simplicity which they there help to give." *This* is the needed compromise: not discounting, but accounting for, one's source materials; preserving flavor, not seasoning it away.

This approach, however, takes us only halfway. David Shive, in his *Naming Achilles* (1987) "discern[s] such subtle delicacies" in Homer's compositional style as one would have anticipated "only in the literary refinement of self-conscious Hellenistic and Roman epic." Shive, in fact, subjects Hector's also grammatically variable protagonist, Achilles, to such chapter headings as "Unique and Equivalent Formulae for Achilles: Nominative Case," "Unique and Equivalent Formulae for Achilles: Genitive Case," etc. The analysis everywhere dazzlingly posits Homer's sensitivity to the use of epithets, and the hyper-development of archaic Greek hexameter that allowed it. Yet not even this is determinative. As Shive concedes, "Some in Homer's audience learned this sensitivity: others doubtless remained indifferent to ornamental epithets and praised Homer for other reasons."

Herington concedes that he himself was initially "troubled by what seemed the too-high proportion of intrusive simile and metaphor in Fitzgerald generally." "Nonetheless," he continues, "further reading and reflection have convinced me that in most [cases] the gamble with Homer's art has paid off; the modern reader's imagination (more jaded, I suspect, than that of his archaic forerunner) is needled, the texture of the English line is enriched, and the substance of Homer's meaning is not seriously affected." One rejects the notion of Homer in translation as a prod to the jaded—Homer the jade in Fitzgerald's translation. While the substance of Homer's meaning may not be "seriously affected," his tone and manner are. For those knowing better, Fitzgerald's tone and manner are affected to distraction, their sacrifice to his "triumphant diction" yielding an essentially altered and misleading experience. Herington had remarked (riffing Bentley on Pope) that "Lattimore has given us a very pretty Homer, as the professionals would like Homer to be; but they mustn't call it poetry." Fitzgerald has given us a rather tony *Iliad*, as the poet-translators would like it to be, but they must not call it Homer.

We may end, as we began, with Herington's comparison of Fitzgerald to Pope. As we have "Pope's Homer," so have we Fitzgerald's. The difference, however, is this: Pope's *Iliad*, though labeled a translation, is nothing of the kind. It is so much a transformation as to be "Homer's *Iliad* by Pope"; "Pope's *Iliad*"; or "The *Iliad* by Homer and Pope." Its non-Homeric qualities were the product of an eighteenth-century aesthetic, now lost. These included a heightened, more literate expressiveness; respect for tradition, including the use of rhyme and meter; and the quite intended perfection, through his *Iliad,* of the verse form ever Pope's thereafter. Translation within such constraints requires—even as it permits—significant license. Pope's *Iliad,* moreover, enjoyed a literary-historical privilege, being but the second complete *Iliad* after Chapman's (over a hundred years earlier), to say nothing of being fundamentally different from it. Moreover, Pope's readers, knowing Greek, could appreciate what Pope was doing: ingeniously recreating Homer within the best traditions of a highly literate age. Fitzgerald, by contrast—laboring in the spaciously forgiving workshop of blank verse—had and needed no such licenses. Fitzgerald's importations are insufficient to be transformative, yet sufficient to mislead. Rendered by his *own* lights and imagery, Homer remains genuinely himself and poetry enough. Yet Herington's accolades were not an isolated phenomenon.

# Chapter 32

## Pope's *Iliad* and E. FitzGerald's *Rubáiyát*; Pope on Chapman's *Iliad*

> . . . nothing could serve the classics more than superbly free translations—backed of course by the thoroughest knowledge—accompanied by the strict text. The original supplies the corrective or the guarantee; the reader, *I* find, understands the depths of his Greek or Latin much better for the free rendering—again, I think of a chaste freedom, a freedom based rigidly on a pre-servitude. . . . In other words, a good free translation can I think be proven to be much nearer to the original than most literal translations.
>
> – STEPHEN MACKENNA, letter to Ernest Debenham, April 1919

SUGGESTIVE IN WAYS OF Pope's *Iliad* is Edward FitzGerald's famed and justly beloved rendition of *The Rubáiyát of Omar Khayyám* (1859), from the Persian, eleventh century AD. FitzGerald referred to his work as "transmogrification," remarking to his Persian teacher and clergyman E. B. Cowell on its lack of literalness. FitzGerald's approach aspires to the best result:

> My translation will interest you from its form, and also in many respects in its detail: very unliteral as it is. Many quatrains are mashed together: and something lost, I doubt, of Omar's simplicity, which is so much a virtue in him.

> I suppose very few People have ever taken such Pains in Translation as I have: though certainly not to be literal. But at all Cost, a Thing

> must live: with a transfusion of one's own worse Life if one can't retain the Original's better. Better a live Sparrow than a stuffed Eagle.

FitzGerald expanded on the latter sentiment some twenty years later, distinguishing between the translation of drama and epic. The less literal, he said, the more in the translator's image—and more so the worse. FitzGerald, however, would rather have the fame of the inventive Pope than the obscurity of William Cowper, Pope's blank-verse competitor:

> I am persuaded that, to keep Life in the Work (as Drama must) the Translator (however inferior to his Original) must re-cast that original into his own Likeness, more or less: the less like his original, so much the worse: but still, the live Dog better than the dead Lion; in Drama, I say. As to Epic, is not Cary still the best Dante? Cowper and Pope were both Men of Genius, out of my Sphere; but whose Homer still holds its own? The elaborately exact, or the "teacup-time" Parody?

FitzGerald here finds a counterpart in Santayana's "What could be better than Homer, or worse than any translation of him?" FitzGerald's correspondence with Cowell signals the belief that his *Rubáiyát* was of a kind—in design and effect—with Pope's *Iliad*. FitzGerald's formulations recall Pope's own: "of the two extremes, one could sooner pardon frenzy than frigidity."

Condensed, and offering inventive paraphrase and additions, FitzGerald's *Rubáiyát* was sometimes called "The Rubáiyát of FitzOmar." His biographer tellingly speaks of FitzGerald's "concentrating the scattered rays" of the original's world-weariness "into his burning glass." His readers did not realize "how much of the poignant sadness, the rich beauty of the thought had been overlaid upon the barer texture of the original writer by the far more perceptive and sensitive mind of the translator. It was as though FitzGerald had found some strict and solemn melody of a bygone age, and enriched it with new honed and honeyed harmonies, added melancholy cadences and sweet interludes of sorrow." Similarly, the biographical preface to an undated edition of FitzGerald notes the "fancies," both lyric and philosophic, and "vivid brilliance of imagination" that colored FitzGerald's thoughts to such a degree that "even when he oversteps the largest licence allowed to a translator, his phrases reproduce the spirit and manner of the original with a nearer approach to perfection than would appear possible." Such praise is equally allowed of Pope, the two translators in league to the exclusion of all others.

A translator of Greek tragedy, the plays of Calderón, and other Oriental works, FitzGerald was the first to translate Khayyám after being sent the manuscript by Cowell, who discovered it in the Asiatic Society library in Calcutta. FitzGerald proceeded without precedent or peer in a late medieval Persian, as little known then as now. He thus had free rein to use Khayyám not as text for translation, but as inspiration for a work his own. Such work might be exempt from established poetic convention, thus allowing a high degree of originality. Adapter-interpreter more than translator, FitzGerald was groundbreaking in more ways than one. The work's enduring beauty aside, "Our contact with Oriental poetry," notes Pound, "begins with Fitzgerald's Rubaiyat." George Chapman, the first translator of Homer, complete, into English, took prodigal liberties with similarly self-fashioned results—omitting, loosely paraphrasing, and sometimes significantly enlarging his original. Pope, in a translation of considerably more exacting form, not unlike FitzGerald in that regard, produced a classic, relegating Chapman to largely antiquarian interest (John Keats excepted).

What did Pope think of his illustrious predecessor, and how do the two compare? Pope's critique of Chapman is actually no less applicable to Homeric blank-verse translation in the twentieth century. Confessing himself "utterly incapable of doing Justice to Homer," Pope sought to offer "a more tolerable copy of him." And so he did, especially insofar as appreciable form and coherence were concerned. Chapman, in a word, was nebulous and unfocused. As Pound observes, "Chapman remains the best English 'Homer', marred though he may be by an excess of added ornament, and rather more marred by parentheses and inversions, to the point of being hard to read.... Pope is easier reading, and, out of fashion though he is, he has at least the merit of translating Homer into *something*." "Something" was the heroic couplet, a form far more readily grasped than Chapman's free-wheeling fourteeners, rhymed though they were. Pound further commends Pope for "a definite idiom within the limits of the rhymed pentameter couplet," and the "fine accomplishment" of certain phrasing. Pound here approves Pope's manner (much of it self-invented)—the consistently impressive figures of speech and turns of phrase that make Pope memorable, and the quality that makes his *Iliad* a "pretty poem" without its necessarily being or trying to be Homer. The appreciation is one of Pope on his own imitative or transformative merits, not on his fidelity as translator.

If Pope succeeded by the above and other criteria, Chapman, insofar as Pope was concerned, succeeded far less. Pope faults Chapman for having "taken the advantage of an immeasurable length of verse, notwithstanding which there is scarce any paraphrase more loose and rambling than his." Pope is saying that Chapman squandered a length of verse that should sooner have advantaged him with greater adherence, and thus fidelity, to the original. By contrast, Pope's "brevity of verse"—the need to do more with less—would require greater license. Four hundred years after Chapman's *Iliad,* the "freedom of blank verse" should offer not modernist airs or contrivance, but an idiom better conveying Homer's dignity and manner; an idiom conveying the precision for which such freedom of form—one would think—allows.

Pope further notes that Chapman is "often mistaken in so bold a manner, that one might think he deviated on purpose." Here too, today's blank-verse renderings are brashly removed from Homer's idiom and imagery; from the formality that, for all Homer's speed and directness, is the essence of his nobility. Wanted before all else is the *sense* of Homer—or any other classical author—that comes from long study, memorization, and cumulative appreciation of the exception or the exceptional. Also applicable to blank-verse translation is Pope's critique of a certain willfulness in Chapman, of his "strong affectation of extracting new meanings out of his author, insomuch as to promise in his rhyming preface, a poem of the mysteries he had revealed in Homer: and perhaps he endeavored to strain the obvious sense to this end." Even Pope's single compliment of Chapman is left-handed:

> But that which is to be allowed, and which very much contributed to cover his defects, is a daring fiery spirit that animates his translation, which is something like what one would imagine Homer himself would have writ before he arriv'd at years of discretion.

Chapman captures Homer's essential fire (also essential to Pope's view of Homer). But the fire is excessive, something that might have blazed from the page of a less artistically mature poet (Pope and his age as yet unaware of Homer's origins in oral poetry). Pope, by contrast, will provide a more temperate translation, suggesting a Homer come of age. The issue with

Chapman, as with most contemporary translators, was and persists as one of excessive invention and self-regard. As Pope also speculates of Chapman, "The nature of the man may account for his whole performance; for he appears from his preface and remarks to have been of an arrogant turn, and an enthusiast in poetry." *Plus ça change, plus c'est la même chose.*

Edward FitzGerald, like Pope, created an enduring work, one with no pretense of fidelity. Pope embraced consecutively rhymed iambic pentameter (the heroic couplet); FitzGerald, also iambic pentameter, famously rhymed *a-a-b-a*.

> The Worldly Hope men set their Hearts upon
> Turns Ashes—or it prospers; and anon,
> Like Snow upon the Desert's dusty face
> Lighting a little Hour or two—is gone.

FitzGerald's overarching *a*-rhyme ends each quatrain with a sense of iterative closure; with a sense of finality, even resignation. Reflection, not speed, is the goal. The effect is epigrammatic, one thought per quatrain. The third line, a blank, "seems to lift and suspend the Wave that falls over the last," as the quatrains, in alternating succession of "Grave and Gay," "trac[e] in vague outline a soul's progression." FitzGerald, as no other, belies the notion of rhyme's tyranny.

Pope's couplets, like FitzGerald's quatrains, can also be epigrammatic. They do not, however, result in speed-inhibiting closures of thought, as Matthew Arnold believed. Indeed, George Steiner rather sees them *confirming* Arnold's priorities, as in the following passage, where Achilles addresses his horses:

> Be swift, be mindful of the Load ye bear,
> And learn to make your Master more your Care:
> Through falling Squadrons bear my slaught'ring sword
> Nor, as ye left *Patroclus*, leave your Lord.

Steiner here observes, "That speed which Matthew Arnold will place foremost among the requisites of Homeric translation, gathers pace towards the laconic climax: 'Nor, as ye left *Patroclus*, leave your Lord.'" Steiner similarly notes "the tensed energies of Pope's Homer" and the "concision and supple flow [that] prepares the ripening of modern prose." The best writers of couplets, in any event, compose not in individual couplets, but in "paragraphs." The notion of Homer's rapidity may in any case be overstated, as individual Homeric lines tend toward self-containment. This owes to the virtually invariable line-ending rhythm — ⏑ ⏑ | — ⏓, a closing that tends to mark line-by-line advance, enjambments notwithstanding. Pope's thought, advancing by couplets, is none the slower for that:

> Monarch awake! 'tis *Jove*'s command I bear,
> Thou, and thy glory, claim his heav'nly care,
> In Just array draw forth th'embattl'd train,
> Lead all thy *Grecians* to the dusty plain;
> Ev'n now, O King! 'tis giv'n thee to destroy
> The lofty tow'rs of wide-extended *Troy*.
> For now no more the Gods with Fate contend,
> At *Juno*'s suit the heav'nly factions end.
> Destruction hangs o'er yon' devoted wall,
> And nodding *Ilion* waits th' impending fall.
> Awake, but waking this advice approve,
> And trust the vision that descends from *Jove*.

If Pope's sculpted couplets lack Homer's speed, they possess their own. Pope was fully aware that Homer's verse was the "most rapid, and yet the most smooth imaginable." Pope, however, conveyed it "heroically," in coupleted rather than hexametric cadence. The choice was foregone, his genius as a poet being inseparable from his mastery of the rhyming couplet. Pope's control of the rhyming couplet is complete, no less than is Homer's of the dactylic hexameter.

Or, because Pope supremely handled the poetic codes and conventions that he largely invented, he was a tradition unto himself, even as Homer was the perfection of the tradition in which he himself labored. The perfection of Pope's form, though vastly different, nonetheless parallels Homer's—the formalities and diction of Pope's translation (artificialities and all) resonating with Homer's own technique and effect. Indeed, the alignment extends, in Dr. Samuel Johnson's view, to the use by both poets of formulaic language (though Johnson does not speak of formulae as such): "By perpetual practice, language had in his mind a systematical arrangement; having always the same use for words, he had words so selected and combined as to be ready at his call." It may surely have been this that Byron intended when he said to Marguerite Gardiner, Countess of Blessington, "Translators almost always disappoint me; I must however, except Pope's 'Homer,' which has more of the spirit of Homer than all other translations put together." Conversely, there was never more erroneous a judgment than that of Coleridge, who deemed Pope "the main source of our pseudo-poetic diction." Such judgment, on the one hand, surprises, coming as it does from a poet thoroughly versed in Greek and thus aware of the essential Homeric qualities to which Pope responded; aware of the Homeric *Kunstsprache,* or artificial idiom, one of whose purposes was to give the effect of distancing poetic language from everyday speech. Such judgment, on the other hand, does not surprise, given Coleridge and Wordsworth's *Lyrical Ballads'* promotion of prosaic language for the poetry of everyman. As Homer was the father of poetry, he was also the father of poetic diction. Pope's *Iliad,* in content and diction alike, was singularly Homeric.

Samuel Johnson deemed Pope's *Iliad* "the noblest version of poetry the world has ever seen" and "a performance which no age or nation could hope to equal." Mentioning neither Homer nor translation, it is Pope's English *Iliad* that Johnson commends. Pope's *Iliad,* however designated, is what no other literary translation aside from Dryden's *Aeneid* has been: a work of genius at once singularly elevated, disciplined, and resourceful—no less so than Homer's. It is in *these* respects that Pope is most Homeric, and in these respects that we may "call [his poem] Homer." Otherwise stated, Pope's *Iliad* "give[s] the impression that to read Homer is to read great poetry." Had Homer been three and four times the length, Pope's couplets would have risen with the tide. Pope's *Iliad,* while young by comparison to Homer's, is yet the product of a literary culture and sensibility as exacting in its way as was the oral tradition of Homer. The permanence of Pope's *Iliad* was recognized in his lifetime. Dr. Johnson called it "a poetical wonder" and said that Pope "cultivated our language with such diligence and art that he has left in his *Homer* a treasure of poetical elegances to posterity."

The decline to come was both swift and assured, from Pope's heroic couplet—through the continued slighting of diction and poetic line—to blank verse; and from there to prose and all but amorphous modern-verse translation in the latter part of the twentieth century. Dead-on accurate and prophetic in discerning a process that others are loath to acknowledge, if they at all comprehend it, Steven Shankman's offers the following:

> Not long after Pope completed his versions it would become increasingly difficult for the translator to recreate the disciplined energy of Homeric verse, as English poetry would become increasingly stripped of many of its traditional resources. First to disappear would be the diction associated with the elevated style, a diction which would come to be seen as "artificial." And next to go would be the integrity of the poetic line itself. Blank verse would, for a while, replace the couplet as a means of translating the Homeric hexameter. . . . Then blank verse would be further diluted to prose, resulting in readable versions, such as that of Samuel Butler (1898); but prose is, by its very nature, incapable of simulating what Pope described in the *Iliad* preface as "that unequal'd Fire and Rapture, which is so forcible in *Homer*, that no Man of true Poetical Spirit is Master of himself while he reads him." And when modern verse translations would appear in the latter half of our own century, so profound would be the lack of consensus as to what constituted the poetic line that the approximation of Homer's formal grandeur would be beyond the resources of English poetry. But in Pope's version we find, for the last and perhaps the only time in the history of English verse, a traditional and viable poetic style that can be held answerable to the demands of the Homeric hexameter. And it was a style that was managed by a poet—great imitator and verbal genius that he was—who was very nearly equal to the impossible task.

Sadly, Shankman's 1983 summation is a virtually express disavowal of all Homeric translation following (and likely to follow) Pope, to say nothing of those translations next discussed.

# Chapter 33

## Versions and Perversions of Homer: R. Fitzgerald, Fagles, and Logue

> This is my essential criticism of modernism, whether perpetrated by Parker, Pound, or Picasso: it helps us neither to enjoy nor endure. It will divert us as long as we are prepared to be mystified or outraged, but maintains its hold only by being more mystifying and more outrageous: it has no lasting power.
>
> – PHILIP LARKIN, *All What Jazz: A Record Library*

> Poems swim free of their age and live in ours; but if we understand them on their own terms rather than conform them to ours, they take on a fuller life, and so do we.
>
> – MICHAEL SCHMIDT, *Lives of the Poets*

POPE'S PERMANENCE IN THE ANNALS of translation is secure. And the more challenging his English becomes to successive generations, the more his *Iliad* will stand revered as the poetic height of its age. The "Age of Pope" will endure as a high-water mark of literate culture—Pope's *Iliad* ageless, then as now, even as subsequent translations have and will continue to age and fade. Pope's only rival, of a quite different kind, is Smith/Miller in English hexameters—every bit as disciplined, resourceful, and marvelous in its way—the two inviting contrast of appreciation. Robert Fitzgerald's *Iliad*, however, has now been two and three times superseded, while Lattimore's, praised only to be maligned, was reissued in 2011 on the sixtieth anniversary of its initial publication. Fitzgerald, Fagles, and the like are less poets in their Iliads than poetasters (the word implying unwarranted pretensions to artistic ability). Their contemporary English flourishes are not of such quality or quantity as to *transform* their Iliads and make them truly *theirs.* It is for this reason that scholar C. John Herington strained in approval of Fitzgerald.

Nowhere noting the paucity of Fitzgerald's Greek, Herington praises Fitzgerald for his Homer-imitative rapidity. Rapidity, however, is but a single part of Arnold's nucleus, inseparable from simplicity and directness, and from *nobility* most of all. Speed alone, or in significant part, does not forgive all. In fact, the critics are hopelessly at odds. Twenty-two years before Fitzgerald's *Iliad,* William Arrowsmith took precisely the opposite view of speed in translation, lamenting: "We are today flooded with translation which, in the name of 'rapidity' and 'directness and plainness' sacrifice [sic] the poem to the story, or ruthlessly excise epithet and detail as otiose. . . . A translation which sacrifices detail to rapidity misses the whole tension of the poem's movement."

As concerns the state of his Greek, Fitzgerald makes self-incriminating admissions similar to those of Mary Barnard and Willis Barnstone, though he is more artful in not "giving away the store." Pope, as noted, was himself in less than full command of Greek—there being exceptions to every rule, even as in the case of Smith/Miller. Yet Pope, the consummate poet of his own age and beyond, made Homer his *own* in an act of supremely imaginative appropriation (like FitzGerald and his *Rubáiyát*). "Homer was [to Pope] the 'what' of Pope's dictum: 'what oft was thought, but ne'er so well expressed.'" In *expressing* Homer as he did, Pope communicated the heroic ethos in transcendent language, producing not a translation—though the work presents itself as such—but an *original* work that he, no sooner than Bentley, would have called "Homer." As for Bentley and his ilk, they "were either devoted classical scholars or critics brought up in the rigorous Aristotelian tradition, who, as men of the past, belittled the artistic element in Pope's intentions." We recall in this connection that in Pope's time classical education was still the rule, and most readers were still acquainted with the Latin and Greek originals. Fidelity in translation was thus not as much the object as was "the tasteful embellishment of the original according to contemporary poetic fashion: ingenious variations on a well known theme." The result was one of transformative imitation, not, as with today's "poet-translators," imposture and charade.

The point is made by Pope's prefatory embrace of a passage from the start of Book Three of Lucretius's *De Rerum Natura.* Lucretius there proposes not to translate Epicurus but to imitate him:

> Te sequor, O Graiae gentis decus! inque tuis nunc
> Fixa pedum pono pressis vestigia signis:
> Non ita certandi cupidus, quam propter amorem,
> Quod te imitari aveo . . .
>
> You I follow, O ornament of Greece!
> And in your step impressed repose my own,
> Not wanting to compete, but for love's sake
> And wish of imitation . . .

The "ornament" is the philosopher Epicurus, on whose doctrines Lucretius elaborates and, by his poetry, utterly transforms. No "anxiety of influence" here, as Lucretius seeks not to compete with Epicurus but to indulge the sincerest form of flattery. The result is a work distinctively Lucretius's own. In the same vein, Pope speaks of Homer's poetic fire as *vivida vis animi* 'the quickening power of mind'. The phrase is that originally used by Lucretius of Epicurus. For Pope, then, Homer no less than Epicurus possesses "a quickening power of mind"; both are "firsts," originals. Pope will imitate Homer as Lucretius did Epicurus—to the point where the respective originals are but distant, yet always audible, echoes. Pope's is a pretty poem indeed; one never intended to be called Homer.

❧

Of Robert Fagles's Homer we may briefly note the following. In a well-known passage from the *Odyssey,* earlier referenced, Telemachus admonishes his mother concerning the bard Phemius's choice of subject matter, the Greeks' return voyages from Troy:

> τὴν γὰρ ἀοιδὴν μᾶλλον ἐπικλείουσ' ἄνθρωποι,
> ἥ τις ἀκουόντεσσι νεωτάτη ἀμφιπέληται.

"Men sooner and especially glorify the song," says Telemachus, "that encircles its listeners as newest." Fagles translates: "Men like best a song that rings like morning on the ear." Fagles translates the prefix-intensive ἐπικλείουσ'—*epikleious'* = *epi* + *kleiousi* 'they especially celebrate'—as 'like'. The rendering is inexplicably bland for so key an epic concern as *kleos*. This, moreover, is the sole occurrence of the Homeric compound, the unprefixed verb *kleiō* 'make famous' itself appearing only once in Homer. No less singular is ἀμφιπέληται—*amphipelētai* = *amphi* + *pelomai* 'move round about, encircle, hover'—the sole Homeric instance of the compound verb. Such usages surely rang as morning on the ear of *Homer*'s listeners. However, that they "ring" for contemporary readers falsifies *Homer*'s idiom, especially in the translation of a *kleos*-compounded word, *kleos* of the essence of Homer. Such instances abound. Fagles typifies the modern translator of whom Professor Lang warned over a century ago: "Translators who employ verse give us a feeble Homer, dashed off with their own conceits, and moulded to their own style. Translators who employ prose 'tell the story without song,' but, at least, they add no twopenny 'beauties' and cheap conceits of their own." While Fagles, as Fitzgerald, won reviewer plaudits, the more discerning were less enthused.

The state of Fagles's Greek, intermediate at best, emerges from the several interviews he (as Fitzgerald) granted. Because Fagles began the language late, as he relates, he "always felt behind and struggled to catch up. That's not false modesty. It's just fact." A Ph.D. in English (with his dissertation on Pope's *Odyssey*), Fagles professes to have "smuggl[ed] in Greek on the side." Fagles collaborated throughout with one of the twentieth century's premier classicists, Bernard Knox (one of his Yale professors and lifelong friend thereafter). Knox wrote lengthy introductions and notes to Fagles's translations of the *Iliad*, *Odyssey*, and *Aeneid*, lending them credence and escalating sales. Of the partnership Fagles remarks, "To work with Bernard on a translation of the *Iliad*, to receive his comments line by line, shaped the entire poem for me." No doubt it did. Fagles's "smuggling" of Greek recalls Willis Barnstone's "tinkering" with Greek and Hebrew, and David Slavitt's "on the train" training in Greek, while the line-by-line review by Knox recalls Barnstone's professor-friend "checking each sentence of the translation."

In one startling interview response Fagles reveals, "I'm always asking myself, if Homer lived in the nineties, how would he say this or that?" Precisely the wrong question, of course. Homer's language, as observed even by Knox in his introduction, was already traditional in Homer's time—traditionally *archaic*—and welcome as such in his own age and ever thereafter. In his *Iliad* preface, Fagles similarly proposes to "lend Homer the sort of range in rhythm, pace and tone that may make an *Iliad* engaging to a modern reader." This Fagles will do by expanding his own line to accommodate "the big reach of a [Homeric] simile or some vehement outburst in the discourse," or by contracting it for added "point" or "stress." One might as handily translate into decently cadenced prose, as Fagles merely *slackens* the Homeric line—which is to say, the hexameter's centuries-long-developed *fittedness* to every narrative, dialogue, or imagistic contingency. "Engag[ing] the modern reader," Fagles looks to a Homerically uncongenial no-size-fits-all.

C. S. Lewis, in a wilting late 1950s attack on modern translations of the Classics, "express[ed] little sympathy," in the words of a newspaper correspondent, "with the new idea that translations should try to be 'what the author would have written if he lived in our own day.'" Lewis found much of the problem in the inclination of modern translators to fault the use of archaisms as a "cardinal sin," to say nothing of poetic diction overall. We still preserve archaism and ritual elsewhere in life, reminded Lewis, because there could be no better way of heightening effect. "Modern translations of the classics," he continued, "apparently sprang . . . from 'a very real hatred' of what most poetry, other than that of relatively recent times has been." Over fifty years ago Lewis witnessed the start of the breakup of classics in translation. We live today amid the shards.

Especially peculiar is Fagles's start as a translator of Aeschylus and Sophocles, turning finally to Homer, as he relates, in his reach for "the source." One wonders how Fagles's smuggled Greek sufficed for the two tragedians, and for Aeschylus in particular—loftily (if not cryptically) elevated, decidedly more challenging than Homer, and one of the most difficult Greek poets overall. Fagles's early efforts also included Pindar (no less difficult than Aeschylus) and Bacchylides (somewhat easier). Fagles collaborated with the best of them—a scholarly Argo oared by Bernard Knox, Maurice Bowra, W. B. Stanford, and Adam Parry. But if he returns to the source, he should drink with his own lips, not, as it were, through a funnel. Indeed, Fagles's fawning adulation of Knox bespeaks unseemly dependence. Otherwise expounding the challenges overcome, Fagles acknowledges the help of some seventy-five divers persons, enabling leaves of absence, fellowships, and "roofs of some great houses [that] extended welcome shelter to the translator." We feel the huff and the puff, the *tantae molis erat*. . . . Fagles curiously singles out "several [eight] classicists [who] lent a steady hand," as though that were the extent of his help from classicists. Yet the immediately preceding list of thirty-six thank-yous contains any number of classicists preeminent in the field. There follow, in Iliadic-catalogue fashion, the names and functions of over twenty-five people involved in every aspect of publication, production, marketing, and the like. *Annuit coeptis*. Everyone is on his side.

❧

What we thus witness is a translation-impairing dichotomy between the scholar and so-called poet—the palm and preference given the unstudied "poet-translator." The best (and most ambitious) classical scholars are nowadays disinclined to spend a decade rendering Homer or adding to the droves of tragedians in translation. The greater reward and recognition come from original research. Lattimore, of course, was a singular exception—not that abundant translation foreclosed an appreciable scholarly output. The poet-translator thus reigns, lauded in turn for his "success, despite the lack of formal training." In the end, it taxes belief that scholars immersed in Latin and Greek—with the French, German, and Italian needed for research—have not the wherewithal for blank-verse translation and better. The dominant part of any poetry is rhythm, and those living in the complex world of classical meter can surely turn an iamb or two. Nor will classicists steeped in the Greek and Latin etymologies of English lack for diction, which is simply the disposition and movement of words. If the words are right, their movement follows, even as a sense of movement tends to sweep the right words up. His Homer aside, Lattimore was a standout in the translation of Greek drama. More recently, poet Anne Carson, rightly described as a "rigorously trained . . . classical scholar," has won similar praise: "In translating the choral lyrics of Euripides' plays, Carson is able to combine her excellent control of ancient Greek metric with her own personal experience as a poet. The result comes as close as could be imagined to the verbal music of the original text." One may also look to the classically trained formalist Daryl Hine (1936–2012) and his *Ovid's Heroines* (1991) and *Works of Hesiod and the Homeric Hymn* (1972, 2005); similarly, to James Michie's (1927–2007) *Horace, Odes* (1963, 2002) and *Poems of Catullus* (1969, 2001).

The fifty-four translators of the King James Bible were all academics and clergymen, Oxford and Cambridge University professors and scholars versed in Hebrew, Greek, and Aramaic, and conversant in Latin from childhood. Discretion being the better part of valor, they did little translating, but much tweaking in the interests of increasing the euphony and musicality of the then reigning Bishop's Bible (1568), even while consulting the run of translations preceding it. They were not "poet translators," nor even poets in any recognized sense. Nonetheless:

> Time and again the language seemed to slip almost unconsciously into iambic pentameter—this was the age of Shakespeare . . . and right from the beginning the translators embraced the principles of repetition and the dramatic pause: "In the beginning God created the heauen, and the Earth. And the earth was without forme, and voyd, and darknesse was vpon the face of the deepe; and the Spirit of God mooued vpon the face of the waters."

If such results elude scholars today, it is, to say the least, because we no longer live in the age of Shakespeare, but in the most Iron(ic) Age of all. Despite more recent disregard of him, we yet have sufficient appreciation of Shakespeare, and feel enough for his cadence, to fashion iambic meter—English, after all, being inherently iambic. So why encourage pretenders?

The outsourcing of translation to the ill-equipped became an article of faith with the thirty-three-volume *Greek Tragedy in New Translations* (Oxford, 1973), edited by William Arrowsmith and Herbert Golder, both of Boston University. The series "manifesto," so flatulently self-approving, appeared in an editors' foreword to each volume:

> The Greek Tragedy in New Translations is based on the conviction that poets like Aeschylus, Sophocles, and Euripides can only be properly rendered by translators who are themselves poets. Scholars may, it is true, produce useful and perceptive versions. But our most urgent present need is for a re-creation of these plays—as though they had been written, freshly and greatly, by masters fully at home in the English of our own times. Unless the translator is a poet, his original is likely to reach us in crippled form: deprived of the power and pertinence it must have if it is to speak to us of what is permanent in the Greek. But poetry is not enough; the translator must obviously know what he is doing, or he is bound to do

> it badly. Clearly, few contemporary poets possess enough Greek to undertake the complex and formidable task of transplanting a Greek play without also "colonializing" it or stripping it of its deep cultural difference, its remoteness from us. And that means depriving the play of that crucial otherness of Greek experience—a quality no less valuable to us than its closeness. Collaboration between scholar and poet is therefore the essential operating principle of the series. In fortunate cases scholar and poet coexist; elsewhere we have teamed able poets and scholars in an effort to supply, through affinity and intimate collaboration, the necessary combination of skills . . .

One such fortunate case, in which scholar and poet coexisted, was that of series founder and coeditor William Arrowsmith, a premier translator with numerous works and awards throughout a dazzling career. How he ever so lost his way can only amaze.

Not content to let the matter lie, the foreword continues:

> Finally, the reader should perhaps be aware that no pains have been spared in order that the "minor" plays should be translated as carefully and brilliantly as the acknowledged masterpieces. For the Greek Tragedy in New Translations aims to be, in the fullest sense, *new*. If we need vigorous new poetic versions, we also need to see the plays with fresh eyes, to reassess the plays for ourselves, in terms of our own needs. This means translations that liberate us from the canons of an earlier age because the translators have recognized, and discovered, in often neglected works, the perceptions and wisdom that make these works ours and necessary to us.

Was it total evisceration that Pound intended by "make it new"? The blighting self-centeredness is otherwise apparent. It is, again, the self-over-subject-matter syndrome, the *contemporary* "colonialization" (to borrow Arrowsmith's own term) of antiquity. The "needs" sooner addressed by Greek tragedy in translation are those of its original audience—those not merely watching but vicariously engaged in a religious community ritual. Greek tragedy was played in large inclining amphitheaters seating an estimated twelve to fourteen thousand viewers (at Epidaurus). Knowing what tragedy meant to its original audience is the *only* basis for knowing what it means to us.

For Wagner, surveying what he deemed the frivolity of opera in his day, Greek tragedy was the *Gesamtkunstwerk* 'total work of art' combining all the arts: poetry, drama, costumes, mime, instrumental music, dance, and song. As such, it surpassed any single art in scope and expressive power. Tragedy's subject matter derived from myth, penetrating and inexhaustible in every age, and revealing in universal terms the core of human experience. Tragedy was enormous spectacle—the actors costumed, on high-soled shoes (or buskin), speaking through large painted masks. Because the mask concealed the actor's own face, the fated anguish of the tragic character was "common-denominatored"—i.e., projected to the back of the theater as the anguish at once of everyman and the entire community. The anguish of everyman was not, however, conveyed *in the language* of everyman, but in a formal and highly stylized idiom integral to the tragic experience and properly reflecting the religious festivals for which tragedy was written. Opera, then, was potentially the greatest art, for it alone (as did Greek tragedy) combined all arts into one. On the model of poetic drama, Wagner created a music drama uniquely his own and since without rival. Taking the old opera, he "made it new," generally grounding it in mythological themes and bypassing the aria/recitative divide for a middle ground of continuous and deeply felt expressiveness (so much of it in the orchestral part). *This* was Greek tragedy, or a use of Greek tragedy, which, to paraphrase the series editors, "[aimed] to be in the fullest sense *new*."

*Greek Tragedy in New Translations* was the culmination of a tendency decried fifteen years earlier by C. S. Lewis in his lecture "Translations of the Classics," a lecture described as a "withering attack," delivered to the Classical Association at Cambridge, August 7, 1958. (Because Lewis lost the script of his lecture, we rely for its substance on the next day's report of the *Times*'s special correspondent.) The *Times* reported:

> In spite of the unlikely hour (immediately after breakfast) the hilarity of Professor C S Lewis in his most mischievous mood proved irresistible this morning when he delivered to the conference of classical teachers here a withering attack on modern translations of the classics. . . . They apparently spring, he declared, from "a very real hatred" of what most poetry, other than that of relatively recent times, has been.

> According to the Special Correspondent Lewis expressed little sympathy with the idea that a translation should try to be what the author would have written if he had lived in our day. He denied that "poetical language" was only fit for "toffs" and "cissies" pointing out how we still kept archaisms and ritual elsewhere in life "because there could not be a more effective way of heightening the effect." Lewis thought "the only safe way was to seek as closely as possible the effect a translation would give a reader if he was really a tiptop modern classical scholar."

C. S. Lewis was here taking a swipe at C. Day Lewis's *Aeneid* (1952), which proclaimed, "A translation which is not somehow based upon the language of its own time will never begin to come near the poetic quality of the original." In support of his position, C. Day Lewis adduces "Dryden himself [who said], 'I have endeavored to make Virgil speak such English as he would have spoken, if he had been born in England, and in this present age.'" The short answer is that when translators are such as to define and have ages take their names, they may have classical authors speak a "contemporary" idiom in translation, the idiom being far removed from that of the street.

Similarly revealing are C. S. Lewis's 1955 letters to his former Greek professor Gilbert Murray (then age eighty-nine):

> I wish you might feel inclined to give (and then print) a course of lectures on modern translations of the classics. For there are really a dark conspiracy and concerted attempt (by men of whom some must know better) to convince the modern barbarian that the poetry of the past was, in its own day, just as mean, colloquial, and ugly as our own.

And further:

> The poetical situation seems to me still without one spark of hope. And the cunning devils are now translating Virgil and Sophocles into the modern style so as [to] make people believe that poetry *always was* the same sort of muck it is now. And some of the worst are schoolmasters, and boys are being brought up on the muck.

In something the obverse of Pound's "a great age of literature is perhaps always a great age of translation," Lewis saw poor translation as threatening an appreciation of the civilized past. The time had come, he urged Murray, for one with his (Murray's) indisputable qualifications to forever trample the "increasingly popular lie that Homer wrote the language of the streets." The translations of his time, Lewis felt, were doing more to detach readers from the roots of Western civilization than could any neglect. Better to let the ancients be than remake them after the commonplace prescriptions of the preface to *Lyrical Ballads* (1800). The topic was one that Murray should seriously consider for "mak[ing] a delightful book out of it" as much as for anything else—*ne quid detrimenti.*

For their desecration of Greek tragedy, editors Arrowsmith and Golden merited the following:

> In the past[,] poetic transmutations of Greek Tragedy, like those of Yeats or Pound, have been left to the promptings of the Muses: here we have, however, the first four of a series in response to a publisher's contract. The end product will probably be the most lavish and expensive collection of "The Greek Tragedy" on the market—and quite possibly the worst. With the notable exception of Lattimore's *Iphigenia,* they expand, elaborate, and distort unrestrainedly in the attempt, inevitably doomed to failure, to give the impression the plays were written yesterday. They hardly begin to convey the tone, the immediacy and theatricality of the originals, but spend all their strength on self-indulgent, often obscure imagery and subtext patterns. These translations (always excepting Lattimore's) are too idiosyncratic and tendentious to be suitable for students, even had they not adopted their own line-numberings, and even if the introductions and glossaries were not so superficial.

Lattimore and colleague David Grene had earlier published *The Complete Greek Tragedies* (Univ. of Chicago Press, 1959), which was hailed as "a major event in American scholarship, a historical event in the translation of the Classics, and far from a minor event in American poetry"; an endeavor "assimilat[ing] the past on a noble level." The translations became the most successful and widely used of their generation and beyond (as had Lattimore's *Iliad*) and contained Lattimore's own translations of Aeschylus, considered excellent. Lattimore's acumen and agility reflected not only his innate poetic gift but also his *philology* as author of *The Poetry of Greek Tragedy* (1958) and *Story Patterns in Greek Tragedy* (1964). An inspired and principled translator of Greek epic, lyric, and tragedy, Lattimore was in each genre followed by hacks and pretenders.

Just when one thought it could get no worse, enter the *Penn Greek Drama Series* (David R. Slavitt and Palmer Bovie, eds., 1998). The series proposed "translations . . . loyal to the Greek originals" that would become "the standard for decades to come." The offerings were anything but, and the prophecy as brazen and commercially motivated as it was ultimately idle. The first six of a projected twelve volumes were early faulted by the watchful Daniel Mendelsohn as "providing neither the intellectual satisfactions of the original nor . . . the compensatory pleasures of really distinguished English poetry. Indeed, the strained and unconvincing efforts at novelty that are the series' hallmark suggest that the real goal was . . . 'to create a publishing event.'" The series, more specifically, was deemed vain, vulgar, gimmicky, dumbed-down, gussied up, superficial, trivializing, and effusively self-congratulatory in its autobiographical prefaces. The series was further cited for lack of purpose other than that of novelty, and, given its pretensions as the next "standard," for its rampant inconsistencies. Finally, it exhibited a "dismaying lack of curiosity, or of an incitement to curiosity, about the foreign context of these old plays, about differences of history, of language, of belief."

We are not surprised to find that the *Penn Greek Drama* authors were virtually all Greekless poet-translators working from earlier English versions. The goal of this self-congratulatory entourage was to strike a "deceptively neat opposition between the 'literary' ambitions of the series and 'the literalism that has made many previous translations unusable in the classroom and inaccessible to general readers.'" Deceptively neat—and absurdly unfair to previous translations. Palmer Bovie died in 1999, the year following the series debut. He was an eminent classicist and classicist-translator. It is indeed hard to imagine why in the twilight of so illustrious a career he should squander good name and prestige on so dubious an enterprise as the *Penn Greek Drama Series*, or ally himself with poet-translator and translation omnivore David R. Slavitt.

Accordingly, the flaw in contemporary translation of epic is the gussying-up of Homer with customized epithets, overly ambitious imagery, and personalized stylings overall. In the translation of lyric, it's the make-whole personalization of fragmentary verse. And in the translation of tragedy, a flattened contemporaneity or outlandish novelty for its own sake. As noted by Edward FitzGerald's biographer, "The whole essence of the culture which depends upon familiarizing oneself with the best products of the human spirit, is that one should try to put oneself in line with the old. To admire a Greek play for the modernity which may be found in it, is, I believe, to misapprehend the situation altogether."

More recently, and in a more jocular vein, the issue of false contemporaneity has been perfectly conveyed by a columnist for the *New York Times*. Addressing the idiom of the King James Bible, Charles McGrath's column is titled "Thou Shalt Not Be Colloquial," and subtitled: "The King James Bible is 400 years old. But it still speaks to current debates over how best to translate sacred texts." McGrath parodically drives the point home with a mock-contemporary biblical translation in large quasi-Gothic letters:

> **& God sed**
> ***Let there**
> **b lite: &**
> **there wuz**
> **lite!**

McGrath notes that the King James Bible, by no means an easy read, is the more devotional and inspiring precisely because of its unusual language, its ability to be "at once recognizably English and also a little bit foreign." Even in its time, the King James Bible was "deliberately archaic in grammar and phraseology." The translators avoided contemporary usage, knowing it would quickly date. McGrath, in words equally suited to classical texts, observes that the procedure followed in most new Bible translations today is precisely the opposite, seeking to convey *not* the language or majesty of the Bible, but its meaning alone in "current terms." In the aesthetic decline, "through a glass darkly" becomes "a dim image in a mirror."

There is mystery in religion and its texts and, as concerns the Classics, texts of religious import, such as those of Greek tragedy. The language of tragedy is solemn—often referred to as hieratic (Gr. *hieros* 'sacred'). Such solemnity is fittingly conveyed, notes McGrath, in language "often a little elevated and incantatory, even ambiguous, or just plain hard to understand." The Greeks and Romans were rhetorically minded, appreciative of the *mot juste*, the turn of phrase, the periodic sentence. Different manners of verbal expression were early distinguished. Homer's Menelaus speaks rapidly, in few but exceedingly lucid words, not wasting a one; Odysseus, by contrast, "in words drifting downward like snow." Ajax, Odysseus, and Phoenix, in their embassy to Achilles, speak each with character-appropriate emphasis in favor of Achilles's return to battle: Ajax as comrade in arms, Odysseus as the "man of words," and Phoenix as the doting caregiver of Achilles's youth, charged (among other things) with teaching Achilles to be a "doer of deeds and speaker of words." We have then in Phoenix a tailor-made speaker whose instruction of Achilles itself involves speaking. Such emphases bespeak the precision that is Homeric verse itself. The same should be evident in Homeric and other classical translation. And yet we are adrift on the bilge of Thersites—the *Iliad*'s sole "man in the ranks"—disparaged and derided, "whose head held many words, disordered and unavailing."

❧

Arrowsmith's defection to a workaday idiom by poet-translators was further ironic, as his own translations of Greek tragedy had earlier graced the highly praised Lattimore series. Arrowsmith, however, was not alone. His equally prominent contemporary, classicist-translator and translation theorist D. S. Carne-Ross (1921–2010) also advocated and actively encouraged the same, with express dislike for the best that classicist-translators had to offer.

A fawning review of Carne-Ross's *Classics and Translation* (2010) pegs Lattimore's *Iliad* as "chief" in the "spate of depressingly flat and lifeless mid-twentieth century translations." The "spate" supposedly ensued, in carriage-before-horse fashion, from the need for "reliable" classroom translations to service Lit. 101–type requirements. These were being taught by Greekless professors, goes the argument, at a time when the falloff in original-language study made classics in translation the Classics' "bread and butter." Asserts reviewer-classicist John Talbot (quoting Carne-Ross), "The main reason for buying Lattimore's translation has always been that you had to take—or teach—a survey of Greek or world literature. [Lattimore's translations] came at exactly the right time, a time when Greek literature, read in translation, was starting to play an important part in undergraduate education all over the country. Since the instructors for the most part knew nothing of the ancient world, the need was for translations of a certified philological accuracy."

This smacks of *post hoc* fallacy. An inveterate, accomplished, and enthusiastically received classical scholar and translator, Lattimore would cringe to find himself described as precipitating a "spate" of market-driven translations, however much the market may have warmed to *him* as translator. Lattimore translated from love of craft, unmindful of college distribution requirements or commercial markets. Lattimore's *Iliad* (1951) neither anticipated nor happily coincided with the emphasis on "Greek or world literature." (How different Barnstone's *Mao,* which was rushed to press on the eve of Nixon's visit to China.) The turn to classics in translation came in response to the post-Sputnik (1957) cry for "relevance," to which Greek and Latin language study was losing its claim. Moreover, classics in translation was taught only in small part by those unfamiliar with the ancient world or its languages. It sooner became the jobs- and Classics Department-saving "port in the storm." As the original-languages galleon slipped perilously out to sea, students were floated on the in-translation raft that was Lattimore.

Talbot joins his prophet in inveighing against the stiff-necked multitude:

> Carne-Ross thought Lattimore's dedication to literal, word-for-word accuracy [this mischaracterizing Lattimore]—the very quality for which the translation is ordinarily praised—had produced a perverse and unreadable distortion of Homer. He was right. Lattimore's *Iliad* is tone-deaf and often unclear, and Carne-Ross, in various reviews and articles, challenged the fashion of praising Lattimore.
>
> But Carne-Ross could also see, with great clarity, a larger point—the reason why such an undistinguished translation was just what the age demanded.

Well, if an age of great literature can be an age of great translation, it now seems that a debased age is not merely an age of undistinguished translation, but one that somehow *demands* it. Perhaps it was Carne-Ross who was tone-deaf, imagining, as he did, that praise of Lattimore was "fashion" rather than creed.

Carne-Ross entertained a utopian vision of poet-translators, believing them so immersed in English poetry as to quote or reference the best of it instinctively. If Odysseus's crew, for example, sat ranged at their oars, dashing them into the surf, the poet-translator would immediately bethink himself of Tennyson's "Ulysses": "Push off, and sitting well in order / smite the sounding furrows." Such cognizance would assure that translation stood "in a responsible relation not only to its original but also to the literary situation of its day." The process, Carne-Ross seems to imply, is cumulative and comprehensive, entailing "interact[ion] with the development of poetry in English." The *entire* development. The process would make new translations part of a literary-cultural continuum embracing future original *or* translational poetry. An impossibly tall and, in our time, ultimately distortive exercise.

Such may have been the expectation in the glory-day of translation, when it possessed, in the words of Garry Wills, "the shared cultural language, imagery, and feeling of great things at stake that made past translations from antiquity resound throughout the culture." The present day, by contrast, reckons otherwise. It is *decultured,* with instructors who know nothing of the ancient world, using "translations" by those equally ill-equipped. It was, to be sure, not only the bygone *formality* of certain renderings that imparted the "feeling of great things at stake," but those renderings' *status*—Chapman and Pope the "firsts" in intellectually agile periods given to purposeful programmatic endeavor. These were ages far more closely connected to their pasts than is ours to any past of its own. Chapman's age, after all, was that of the Renaissance, itself newly discovering and appreciating the past—an urgent, instructive, and immanently useful past.

Wills further observes that "Chapman and Pope and Dryden made Homer and Virgil central figures of their time." Their translations "expressed a living connection with the past, integral to the culture because developing from within it." With the sprawl of today's translations, however—each responsive to the culture only in the culture's lower reaches, each rapidly superseded—none is of sufficient quality to take root, despite market hype and pedigreed introductions. Indeed, in a now multiculturally driven world, the definition of culture itself is up for grabs. Translation today is less prize than enterprise; the emphasis more on the translator than on his work. One thinks of high-profile TV anchormen of recent decades—Dan Rather, Peter Jennings, Brian Williams, and the like—wanting to *be,* rather than report, the news.

In a particularly alchemic instance of poetic transformation, Carne-Ross credits Robert Fitzgerald's importation of a translated Virgilian phrase as "letting the Latin speak through the Greek because [Fitzgerald's] vision is synoptic." According to John Talbot, "Fitzgerald's departure from literal accuracy brings his translation into expressive relationship with the whole epic tradition in Greek, Latin, and English, and makes his translation resonate through time." Translation of the *Iliad* or the Second Coming? We are not told how such resonance is attained by the poet-translator sans Greek and Latin, propped and prompted by experts and cribs. The contest is thus, apparently, between poet-translator *without*—or with only middling—classics (Fitzgerald, Fagles), and the classicist-translator *with* poetry, including the original poetry (Lattimore). Laurels, it would seem, to the former.

The classicist-translator, in Carne-Ross's view, is the rare bird. Scholarship, after all, has its limits. Its business, says Carne-Ross, is "with those many and complex questions which only an exact scholarship can handle." It cannot by itself handle the nuances of literary translation, which call for the related but distinct gifts of poetry and critical judgment. Talbot further quotes Carne-Ross on a dichotomy—as overdrawn as it is misleading—between cribs and translations. "Yet poetry," says Talbot, "must take into account other standards of accuracy no less stringent than the scholar's." And then, "If we are looking for a faithful account of the letter of the original, we should use a crib, not a translation. . . . The accuracy of a translation is of a very different kind."

Of course it is, compared to a crib. But cribs are not the only option. Carne-Ross had himself advocated *prose* translations, while *encouraging the study of Greek* if more were wanted: "But what is the matter with prose? A prose translation can very well give you the plot of a poem: without the distortions of second-rate verse. If you want more, learn Greek." Whose verse, then, is both distortionless and first-rate? Only that of the poet-translator, especially if prodded by Carne-Ross. And yet, the poet-translator cannot have it both ways—first-rate results with secondhand understanding. Authentic translation is already sufficiently secondhand.

It is on the poet-translator's "insight" that we now attend. The inventions of the poet-translator are not "license," asserts Talbot, but "necessary freedoms." The distinction baffles. As opposed to the "schoolman's literal linguistic equivalence," continues Talbot, these freedoms "must be 'dictated by insight into the original.'" Being devoid of the original, however, such *insight* is either intuitive or quasi-mystical. Also perplexing is how "a translator of original powers could register an insight into the Greek that a professional scholar might miss." Might or might *not*—even as the scholar's supposed number of "misses" must pale by comparison to those of the poet-translator. It is a scenario in which some manner of autochthonous power, Prospero-like, trumps basic approaches and understanding. Might the requisite original-language study possibly impair such power? The poet-translator will doubtless have a take on the original, but we must not call it insight.

The following insight is, however, offered the skeptical. Says Talbot, again quoting Carne-Ross: "Even a poet with little classical training, but with acute linguistic instincts, may produce an insightful translation, given a proper crib, and a chance to get a feel for the original by 'nosing around the Greek on his own. . . . Poets pick up a good deal this way.'" And so on. Carne-Ross was dead wrong, and Talbot's nonsense but fawning adulation to a literary hoax. The casualness, the cumulative lie and self-deception astound. It is, if anyone, the *classicist,* with a bare minimum of Greek, Latin, French, German, and Italian who has the "acute linguistic instinct," not the invariably monolingual—though Carnac-like "borderline divine and mystical"—poet-translator. When it comes to translation, the classicist does not "nose around" his native English, knowing it better than most. Moreover, he has direct recourse to the literary traditions of his *own* language in a way the poet-translator can never have to those of Greek and Latin.

There is finally the Carne-Ross puppeteer. "It was Carne-Ross who first persuaded Christopher Logue to try his hand at translating the *Iliad,* and supplied him with trots, transliterations, and advice on how to understand Homer's Greek." It was also Carne-Ross "who set David Ferry to work at translating Latin poetry"—English professor David Ferry's *Odes* of Horace (1997), Virgil's *Eclogues* (1999), and *Georgics* (2005) appearing in short order. Carne-Ross in lieu of the Muse, the benevolent birch in lieu of the laurel branch.

Even as Carne-Ross is described as setting David Ferry to work, Ferry himself characterizes the work as "assignments":

> I had another friend [Carne-Ross] a classicist at Boston University, and he liked what I'd done and began to give me assignments, translating some of the odes of Horace. So I did some of those and then I got hooked and I did more. Because I'd done those, I then

> got into The Epistles of Horace. But meanwhile I got into doing The Eclogues of Virgil, because pastoral poetry figures so much in English poetry. So I did The Eclogues and I guess I got into The Georgics because I'd done The Eclogues and by then I was not only crazy about Horace, I was crazy about Virgil.

Such casualness is reminiscent of Willis Barnstone's breezy explanations of how he came to do his own "translations." And Ferry's language, even in an interview: "what I'd done. . . . So I did . . . then I got hooked and did more. Because I'd done those, I then got into. . . . But meanwhile I got into doing." In the same interview, Ferry admits with graceless ease to having never studied Latin or Greek and to having "no confidence in reading Latin aloud"—this last admission in response to being asked to read aloud a bit of the Latin he had translated. And the etymology of *Georgics*? "It comes from the Latin word that means 'farmer.' The farm." And so on. Needless to say in today's literary climate, Ferry has garnered broad acclaim from the learned and unlearned alike.

Horace, as earlier noted, is notoriously difficult to translate, even literally, because of his metric complexity, interlocking word order, and compact expressiveness. Nor are the urbane concerns of Virgil's shepherds a model of simplicity. If translations of Horace once "interacted with the development of poetry in English," such development is fully skewed of late by the Latinless or otherwise under-studied translator. We do better reading consummate classicist Cedric Whitman's (1916–1979) *Fifteen Odes of Horace* than all of Ferry and others combined, as well as Horace in the translation of Classics-learned four-time British Prime Minister extraordinaire William Ewart Gladstone (1809–1898). One has to know where to look for these—finding Whitman's *Horace* and Palmer Bovie's *Georgics*; knowing of Gladstone. The merry pranks of amateurs, encouraged to "nose around" and "try their hand" by those who should know better (and could themselves likely do better) is a sham. In the end, says John Talbot, "Carne-Ross has instigated or abetted many other important translations of our time." The operative term is "abetted." The word's use in a presumptively positive sense is here quite Freudian. The law recognizes "aiding and abetting" as a criminal offense. What then shall be the consequence for "instigating and abetting" in translation? Pray tell.

Carne-Ross's final word on the translation of Horace is to "force English into the Latin mold" through "poetic speech—of a new kind." Yet another variant of "make it new":

> We must hope, translators in the days to come will learn to write, in the process of giving us, sometimes (the word should be stressed), not English Horace, but difficult, foreign Horace through whose intricate stanzas we make our careful way as we do with the originals.

Thankfully, only "sometimes"—as an English Horace thus Latinized would be gibberish, little better than word-for-word crib translation. In his quest for novelty, if not something ever yet more outlandish on which to place his imprimatur, Carne-Ross forgets the failure of Wordsworth's similarly Latinized *Aeneid*; and, even while looking to Pound, forgets the Wordsworthian lesson that Pound imbibed: "I ruined my English prose for five years, trying to write English as Tacitus wrote Latin. Very Bad. However, I may have learned something by it. I know now that the genius of the two languages is not the same."

Finally, there is Professor Talbot's extravagant praise of bad boy Christopher Logue: "Forty years on, Logue's Homer is now widely regarded as the most important version of the Iliad since Pope's, and has taken on the status of a classic in its own right. (One of the finest essays in the collection is Carne-Ross's study of Logue's art.)" I quote the parentheses only by way of noting Carne-Ross's discreditable partisanship. One does not encourage and nurture an endeavor to praise and promote the finished product: it is called conflict of interest. If Logue's *Iliad* is a classic in its own right, it is only as cult classic, while the claim for Logue's scant and outlandish rendering as "the most important version of the Iliad since Pope" is simply fatuous. "Pope is not lightly to be rivaled by a modern translator," remarked Professor Lang over a century ago—and least of all by the likes of Logue. The best translation of the *Iliad* since Pope is Smith/Miller. No other *Iliad* since Pope's has exhibited such resolute adherence to a chosen form, in this case—uniquely—Homer's own, and pursued it so resolutely and effectively to conclusion. Moreover, Smith/Miller perfectly displays what George Steiner has noted of Pope: an "idiom . . . most fully committed to the fact that the *Iliad* is a poem, that its design and effect are poetic." Pope's *Iliad* remains the greatest imitation or version of Homer; Smith/Miller's, the greatest translation.

If Logue's Homer is "widely regarded" the "most important version of the *Iliad* since Pope's," we are not told how or by whom. The unacknowledged source of Talbot's Logue-to-Pope comparison is the estimable Garry Wills in his own review of Logue—*Wills* calling Logue "the best translation of Homer since Pope's," Wills previously flattering Ruden by comparison to Dryden. Logue is sooner to Homer what Louis Zukofsky is to Catullus—a mind-numbing assault.

For a sense of what the putatively "most important version of the *Iliad* since Pope's" entails, we turn to a *Slate* magazine reviewer. *Slate* endorses Logue's version, but only in sweeping terms as the imposing oddity it is:

> . . . thrilling and somewhat exhausting, like watching the first reel of Saving Private Ryan . . . presented as a grueling short . . . nevertheless, exciting and possessed of a very terrible beauty. In fact, it's some of the best poetry being written in English today, and it should be read widely and with great pleasure by anyone still interested in the art of verse.

The praise is conclusory—the fashionable exaltation of radical or downmarket chic. We have here and elsewhere the kind of praise only a *succès de scandale* can generate. *Slate*'s praise is praise of a supreme oddity, for reasons *Slate* itself provides:

> . . . he has modernized [the Iliad] without compunction, bringing to bear all the techniques of contemporary poetry—mixed line length, tricks with typeface, fragmentation, allusions to the literature of the last century or so; and the kicker is: Logue can't read Ancient Greek, not a word of it. He fashions his Iliad by consulting pre-existing translations, getting a sense of what the thing is about, and then setting off to write his own version—inventing new episodes, ignoring others, renaming characters, and occasionally drifting off into narrative entirely of his own making. . . . On the face of it, his is a task of monumental foolishness, and you can't help but laugh at the very idea: It's like learning of a deaf man who prepared himself to conduct Stravinsky by watching Fantasia. So, is Logue a genius or a joke? Is his Iliad sheer hubris, humbug, or one of the Wonders of Modern Literature?

The short answer is: when the choice is one of extremes—genius or joke—the joke is on us for genuflecting. Logue is the Jeff Koons of Homeric translation, a balloon-metallic canine baying at Tintoretto. He is the "bad boy," and the critics love him for it. Indeed, for the forty-four years he spent "translating" only a small portion of the *Iliad,* dribbling it forth as he went, Logue made no effort to learn even a modicum of Greek. Carne-Ross apparently made no such suggestion, any more than he "assigned" Latin language study to Ferry. Why impair the "insight"? The critics are simply gaga for Logue, showing their chic appreciation for scandal. Comparisons to Pope are not uncommon.

Little more may be said for Stanley Lombardo's *Iliad,* with its "Yo, Achilles" colloquialisms, touted as "brave departures" from previous translations. Both Logue and Lombardo have their greatest fun with Homeric epithets: Logue in one laughable instance renders "white-armed Hera," with its statuesque associations, as Hera, "Heaven's creamy queen." Sounds like a bisque porcelain figurine, or a soft ice-cream treat.

The twentieth century's Second Coming of Homer, Logue is all the rage and all respectability—as seen in the title of Matthew Reynolds, *The Poetry of Translation: From Chaucer & Petrarch to Homer & Logue* (2011). While the book overall has much to commend it, my objections to the bizarrely styled chapter "Epic Zoom: Christopher Logue's Homer (with Anne Carson's Stesichorus and Seamus Heaney's *Beowulf*)" are too numerous to entertain. Suffice it to mention, as example, Logue's total ignorance of Greek. Reynolds approvingly reports that in 1959, at the start of his work, Logue "wanted to know *exactly* what it was Homer said in the first instance," and that Carne-Ross replied, "There is no exactly, no first instance." A quasi-oracular response to a foolish question. Carne-Ross should have answered: "Hard to say, but why not take Greek 101 and see what you can learn."

What so distresses about these travesties is the distraction they constitute from a genuine encounter with Homer—such as generations obtained from Lattimore—including, in a debased age, a sense of the decorum traditionally associated with epic. Decorum is "the proper harmony between manner and matter," between form and content. It begins with the choice of grand manner for grand matter. Ill suited—and indecorous—to the translation of epic are haiku, limerick, iambic trimeter, ballad meter, or "mixed line length [and] tricks with typeface." It is that simple. Decorum is further a matter of diction and portrayal. Diction, as noted, is the choice and arrangement of words; portrayal, the propriety of presentation—the latter often noted in the allusive consummation of love by Dido and Aeneas, and the offstage deaths of Greek tragedy. The softening of physical expressions of pain and suffering reflects a similar concern, as seen in our discussion of Winckelmann and Lessing. Decorum, then, is "refined critical judgment," "the chief requirement for the judicious disposition of the poet's material." To observe decorum is to "keep to a standard of artistic fitness." In Barnum & Bailey translation, by contrast, Homer comes fitted with red suspenders and a bulbous nose; the squirting carnation's a hoot, and everyone loves the circus.

Garry Wills, so often correct, errs here as well (as in his review of Ruden). Fleshing out the role of Carne-Ross—and the many peculiarities of Logue's "version," "account," "translation," "cultural translation"—Wills makes a Pope of Logue, even while claiming that Logue shares much with Chapman. Wills concludes that, despite what may seem the extremity of his (Wills's) claims, Logue's work is "in the service of Homer, trying to be true to him." The comparison to Pope confounds; the likeness to Chapman misleads. Pope, with one begrudging exception, as seen, rather negatively assesses Chapman. As the writer of introductions to contemporary editions of Chapman, Wills knows this.

Wills concludes:

> Colonial wars with "natives" are clearly echoed in Logue's British verse—but Americans will think, inevitably, of Korea and Vietnam, of war with "gooks" and "slopes." These brutal militarisms are part of all war poetry for us, and Logue's obscenities, violations of epic "decorum," share a modern sensibility. . . . But seeing Homer from our standpoint is what cultural "translation" always entails.

Here again is the "from our standpoint" fallacy. We also note the scare quotes around "decorum." Although recent books have instructively compared Troy and Vietnam, we should not be thinking of Vietnam when reading the *Iliad*, but of Troy and the Trojan War, and of the latter's centrality to Greek and Western culture. "Cultural translation" in the service of "modern sensibility" traduces these essential concerns. Nor should we be thinking of "all war poetry" but, again, of the Trojan War and *Homeric* poetry. As human nature never changes, it is Homer's *already* "modern sensibility"—his unchanging resonance over millennia and for every age—that makes him a classic. Homer need never be colloquialized, brutalized, or obscenified to be relevant or appreciated. These merely render the classic commonplace. Homer's own audiences needed no such effects. To prefer our own sensibility to Homer's, to view him "from our standpoint," or remake him in our image, is yet another instance of self over subject matter. It is similar to the misdirected efforts of tragedy translators "to see the plays with fresh eyes, to reassess the plays for ourselves, in terms of our own needs." The issue, as noted, is the need classical works served for their *original* audience, and how our understanding of that need validates them for ourselves.

Wills finally notes, as an offset to Logue's "daring and risky choices," the fact that Logue's *Iliad* was initially commissioned to be read as part of a BBC broadcast; his *Iliad*'s "vocal delivery and performance" reflecting the original's composition and purpose. (The same excuse had been offered for C. Day Lewis's execrable *Aeneid.*) However, and by contrast to Homer's formulaic and comprehension-speeding language, Logue's bizarre diction and frame of reference defy ready understanding. Take a Logue passage that Wills especially esteems:

> They passed so close that hub skinned hub.
> Ahead, Patroclus braked a shade, and then,
> And as gracefully as men in oilskins cast
> Fake insects over trout, he speared the boy,
> And with his hip his pivot, prised Thestor up and out
> As easily as later men detach
> A sardine from an open tin.

Who would understand this upon first reading? What, without pause or dictionary, is "braked a shade" or "prised . . . up"? Yes, "men in oilskins" are fishermen in the here unhomeric activities of trout-spearing and sardine-prying. But they are little appreciable as such in the course of recitation (leaving aside the sudden shift from trout to sardines). Most of all, the proleptic "later men" is simply chronological legerdemain on which to hang an anachronistic comparison.

Of such "freedoms" Carne-Ross characteristically observes that Logue

> reproduces Homer's action while responding to it in his own terms. He knows, for instance, that Homer's war is not play-acting and hence makes no attempt to keep out his own disgust at the fact of war. This involves violent changes of tone, abrupt juxtapositions of attraction and revulsion which are not to be found in Homer. They are however inescapably part of our reading of Homer and the translator who seeks to make the *Iliad* live in the modern world cannot exclude them.

Lucky the redeemed, on Logue's account, who have thought that Homer was merely play-acting. What is "inescapably part of our reading of Homer" has in no way escaped Homer's audience for over 2,700 years—whence his status as a classic. Carne-Ross's Logue-over-subject-matter adulation is head on backward, the kind of modernist bravura that credits latter-day sensibility as the sole measure of experience.

George Steiner for his part early commends Logue's "ferocious re-statements of the *Iliad*—in which every modern line seems . . . explicitly directed toward Homer's survivance, towards the presentment and 'presentness' of his songs. . . ." It is difficult to know what this means. Especially noteworthy is *survivance*, by which Steiner cannot possibly mean *survival. Survivance* is an archaic legal term relevant to the transfer of estates. Its only other recognized use relates to *La Survivance*, for which one perforce consults Wikipedia, learning of "an expression used by French Canadians denoting the phlegmatic survival of francophone culture, typically in the face of Canadian anglophone or Anglo-American hegemony." What Logue's ferocious *re-statements* have contributed to Homer's *survivance* is anyone's guess. This is nothing but muddled praise of the indefensible. Logue's heroes, in the end, are neither heroically cast nor armed. Logue may write whatever homerically inspired poem he likes, but what he and others call it, or how they promote it, is a different matter. In that regard, sense and sensibility have long been outrun, leaving Pope standing, and very much intact.

Thus do major publishers and university presses turn out their own Sapphos, Homers, or Virgils. It is a matter of prestige, regardless the need, merit, or translator qualification. Robert Fitzgerald (1910–1985) and Robert Fagles (1933–2008)—professors of English with middling or no Greek, and with no philology—*both* translated the "trifecta": *Iliad, Odyssey,* and *Aeneid.* The two were actually friends, Fitzgerald publishing his *Iliad* while Fagles's was still in progress. Fitzgerald in his lifetime was deemed the last word in epic translation, as was Fagles in his. Reader memories are short, infatuation with the new and next persistent, and the translations—by contrast to their source—ephemeral.

Moving from one travesty to another, we note *Homer* by Wilder Publications (2007), with a stunning disclaimer:

> This book is a product of its time and does not reflect the same values as it would if it were written today. Parents might wish to discuss with their children how views on race, gender, sexuality, ethnicity, and interpersonal relations have changed since this book was written before allowing them to read this classic work.

The assumptions, and all manner of assumption, in this statement are staggering. It is noteworthy that the volume contains prose translations of the *Iliad* and *Odyssey* both, a publication rarity reserved for special editions (though the same editorial caveat appears on the title pages of Wilder's separately published *Iliad* and *Odyssey*). Most telling is the absence of translator's name, signaling indifference to the matter at hand, the *caveat* being paramount. In truth, that's precisely the point: the wholesale politically correct vilification of Western culture at its source. Homer is but the vehicle for this torpedo to the engine room. As the ulterior motive is clear, the absence of translator name does not surprise.

This disclaimer is what has since become known as a "trigger warning." Such warnings, with ideological roots in multicultural thought, are now a campus-wide phenomenon providing explicit alerts that curricular subject matter might somehow be "upsetting." As an Oberlin College advisory puts it:

> Triggers are not only relevant to sexual misconduct, but also to anything that might cause trauma. Be aware of racism, classism, sexism, heterosexism, cissexism, ableism, and other issues of privilege and oppression. Realize that all forms of violence are traumatic, and that your students have lives before and outside your classroom, experiences you may not expect or understand.

Professors teaching such potentially traumatic matter are presumably immune to the accompanying trauma or, with the acquisition of years and life's experience, impervious to it. Again, the assumptions are staggering—though we would not want to make anyone in any way "uncomfortable." What of a class in which everyone is subject to a different "ism"—including, perhaps, openminded-ism or anti-ismism? As with so much of politically correct doublespeak, trigger warnings contradict the equally prescribed notion of being or doing things "outside one's comfort zone." And what if, despite all warnings, a student experiences trauma or begins to feel it coming on? At Brown University, the student adjourns to a "safe space" to "recuperate." The room is "equipped with cookies, coloring books, bubbles, Play-Doh, calming music, pillows, blankets and a video of frolicking puppies, as well as students and staff members trained to deal with trauma." The safe space is a "live action version of the better known trigger warning"; it is "where a brain used to be" (as one pundit has put it). Faint and fail rather than buck up is the order of the day, as young people resort to cookies and coloring books in preparation for adult life.

# Chapter 34

## Ezra Pound: Damage to Sextus Propertius

> There for the first time I met Erik Satie and a Mephistophelian red-bearded gent who turned out to be Ezra Pound. . . . Ezra was at the time the world's foremost discoverer of genius; in fact he frankly called himself "an expert in genius."
>
> – GEORGE ANTHEIL, *Bad Boy of Music*

> Pound never had more than a smattering of Greek. . . . In Latin, he knew enough to let him follow the general sense of a simple sentence and to grasp some of the more obvious effects of sound and rhythm, but not enough to permit him to understand or even approach the greatest Roman poets or to save him from making coarse antipoetic blunders in interpreting Roman poetry. Worse than that, he would not learn. He would not admit his deficiencies and cure them through humility and industry. Nor would he avoid those areas where a display of ignorance would be damaging.
>
> – GILBERT HIGHET, *Horizon*, 1961

### 1. Propertius: A "Modern" Without Pound; Pound's Scrupulous Mistranslation

As Logue was an acolyte of Ezra Pound, we would be remiss to omit Pound's greater influence on the translation of the Classics. Our discussion focuses on Pound's ever-controversial *Homage to Sextus Propertius* (1919)—a "modernization" of the Roman elegiac poet Propertius (c. 50–15 BC). *Homage* was Propertius "made new" by a Pound either bored or baffled by the Classics as they are: *Propertius really* is *modern,* Pound might have said. *What the professors have obscured, my insightfully modified and ironized Homage will convey.* Pound would "liberate" Propertius. If Pound had it in for the professors, "in reality he had it in for the Classics . . . criticiz[ing] them for not being modern." Pound would "make everyone understand what Propertius was really like: thoroughly modern." Four years earlier, in 1915, the young and recently graduated classicist Mary Stewart, from her first teaching outpost at the University of Montana, had intuited the fallacy of modernizing the Classics. Briefly quoted at the outset of this book, her words merit reprise: "Next to Horace, Catullus seems to us the most modern of the ancients—that is, if there is any *most*. They are all contemporaries when we get acquainted with them. It is amazing to find out how modern all these writers are, which is just another way of saying how ancient human nature." Truly and perceptively said.

Indeed, the twentieth-century critic, journalist, and belletrist George Sutherland Fraser (1915–1980) adduces Catullus's famed love-hate couplet as quintessentially modern:

> Odi et amo. Quare id faciam fortasse requiris?
>   Nescio, sed fieri sentio et excrucior.
>
> I love and I hate. Why I do this perhaps you inquire?
>   I know not, tormented, but feel it transpire.

Furthering Fraser's assessment, critic Irving Howe (1920–1993) notes that in modernist literature "perversity—which is to say: surprise, excitement, shock, terror, affront—becomes a dominant motif"; and that "the modern poet" Catullus, as opposed to the traditional poet (e.g., Robert Bridges), is "our twin." In sum, the couplet evinces a modern sensibility in its startling lack of both rational predicate and logical development—which is to say, in its situational acuity, irresolvable dilemma, and sense of fragmentation. The love-hate relationship is of course symptomatic of love at any time, Propertius's or our own. Pound at one point intimates an awareness of antiquity's modern likeness: "The value being that the Roman poets are the only ones we know of who had approximately the same problems as we have." The insight, however, passes as quickly as it surfaces, unreflected in Pound's treatment of the Classics, and of Propertius most of all. For Pound, moreover, shock is not what flares from the exultant acuity of contrary sensation; it is sooner the parlor trick of "comment by juxtaposition." Pound regularly "uses both his quotations and original phrases in bizarre juxtapositions. Again and again phrases are violently yoked to others not akin to them. This is the overly exploited technique of literary shock, already exhausted by the latter 1930's." The method's intent and facile result is vilification—the stock-in-trade of a man steeped in disapprovals and needing abundant *non bona dicta* in which to voice them.

Propertius needed no remake. Pound was simply blind to the poet's "newness"—to what made and always kept him "modern"; and to what he, Propertius, and other classical and even more contemporary authors had quite in common. As early as 1895, Professor Mackail had rhapsodized on Propertius as "a genius of great and, indeed, phenomenal precocity" and on his "feverish self-consciousness" and "want of good taste and sense"—all characteristics traditionally associated with modernism. Most significantly, Mackail dilated on Propertius's "*new* power of versification accompanied by a *new* spirit even more remarkable [and] of profound import as the precursor of a whole school of *modern* European poetry" (i.e., the "neurotic young man" of Rousseau, Goethe, and de Musset).

In an article entitled "Propertius, Kin to the Romantics" (1923), English teacher, Latinist, and Mary Shelley scholar Elizabeth Nitchie makes the proto-Romantic of Propertius, deeming "Romantic" the "whole school of modern European poetry" to which he gave rise. Nitchie notes:

> The Roman [Propertius] is akin to the romantic in every period and every nation, in character and ideas . . . in his use of color, glamorous and musical proper names; in his unconventionality and innovations in language and meter; in his very youth . . .

And in words apropos of Pound:

> Romantics are usually rebels and innovators. Believers in individuality, they carry their individualism into their style. They rebel against restraints of metre and of language and try experiments with new rhythms, new words, new images. Propertius is no exception. To be sure, he used one metrical form, the elegiac couplet, but with that he tried experiments. . . . He carries to extremes certain Latin idiomatic tendencies, such as that toward conciseness. He is fond of . . . unusual meanings of prepositions, of rare ellipses, of peculiar sentence structure, of strange word order. His vocabulary,

> too, is peculiar. In addition to his use of archaisms and of proper names full of recondite and exotic suggestion, he employs his large vocabulary with a freedom that, with the fresh meaning often given to a much-used word or the peculiar construction of it, lends to his poetry variety and individuality. It is not that he coins words, but that he puts them to new uses.

We read in this description of Propertius as rebel, innovator, and experimenter the better part of Pound. Propertius had, in his own way and time, made it *singularly* new—even before Virgil and Horace had realized their own full inventive potentials. Not truly understanding Propertius (for want of sufficient Latin as of anything else), and thus having no inkling of the Propertius within, Pound reduced the Roman to pastiche. Indeed, Pound's avowed attraction to Propertius—the analogy he perceived between the latter's anti-Augustanism and his own contempt of British imperialism—is simply irrelevant. By this I mean that Propertius's *recusatio* 'disavowal' of martial/epic themes, in preference for erotic or other more modest matter, is merely a literary trope—a conceit—not an anti-Augustan broadside. The classical *recusatio* first appears in Callimachus's *Aetia* prologue, to be imitated by Virgil, Horace, Ovid, and Propertius himself (the self-styled "Roman Callimachus," as noted). Had Pound better grasped Propertius—his indebtedness to Callimachus, and what in the Roman poet was *new avant la lettre*—Pound's *Homage* would have been worthier of its subject, or perhaps not written at all. In a passing reference at the close of her article, Nitchie notes that "Among our contemporaries, Ezra Pound has 'translated' into modern idiom four of [Propertius's] poems, but his interest can scarcely be said to be romantic." Which is to say that Pound simply missed the point.

In the years immediately preceding the *Homage*, Propertius was referred to as a "modern" by Johns Hopkins University professor Kirby Flower Smith. In an article titled "Propertius: A Modern Lover in the Augustan Age" (1917), Smith presents Propertius as "an amatory sport, a modern lover born into the world more than sixty generations before his time." Smith's reading of Propertius was as only a Latinist could read him, which is to say, without the modernist upending. American poet, translator, and essayist Kenneth Rexroth (1905–1982) passingly notes that Propertius "is one of the few classic writers, possibly the only one, afflicted with the modern temper." Goethe himself found contemporaries in Propertius and the other

Roman elegists, revisiting and recapitulating the genre in *Erotica Romana*, published in 1795 as *Elegien* (*Elegies*) in Friedrich Schiller's influential literary journal *Die Horen*. Such lessons are lost on those who think Propertius modern only by Pound's doings.

The Classics' perennial modernity, i.e., that which makes them *classic*, is broadly acknowledged. Mary Barnard notes that Sappho "was riding the crest of her own wave; her own world seemed as modern to her as ours does to us, and just about as troubled." Euripides was sensationally, indeed shockingly, modern. Similarly, "Lucretius is not only one of the most inspired but he is also surely the most modern of the ancient poets." And R. L. Lind, in the excellent introduction to his own translation of the *Aeneid* (1963), finds Aeneas "modern as a lover, strange as this may sound to those who dislike him for deserting Dido. . . . [T]he love . . . was genuine and his parting from her a great and sincere sorrow. . . . " Nor was Matthew Arnold, in his signature essay "On the Modern Element in Literature" (1868–1869), impervious to such concerns:

> And what past literature will naturally be most interesting to such an age as our own? Evidently, the literatures which have most successfully solved for *their* ages the problem which occupies ours: the literatures which in their day and for their own nation have adequately comprehended, have adequately represented, the spectacle before them. . . . Such an epoch and such a literature are, in fact, modern; they are founded upon a rich past and upon an instructive fullness of experience.

There being no solution to the problem of passion or amorous despair, Propertius nonetheless adequately comprehended and represented his own predicament—a modernist today no less than yesterday and the day before. Pound didn't get it. "I am tired," said Yeats in a letter to Dorothy Wellesley. "I have spent the day reading Ezra Pound for the [1936 Oxford] Anthology—a single strained attitude instead of passion, the sexless American professor for all his violence."

Says political philosopher Pierre Manent (b. 1949), "We have been modern for several centuries now. We are modern, and we *want* to be modern; it is a desire that guides the entire life of Western societies. That the will to be modern has been in force for centuries, though, suggests we have not *succeeded* in being truly modern." From a synchronic versus diachronic perspective, ages measure their modernity from their own standpoints in time, while posterity measures it against time's continuum. In sum, every age, thinking itself possessed of some new insight or advance, believes itself modern. Witness the late seventeenth-century *querelle des anciens et des modernes* 'the quarrel of the ancients and moderns', discussed at the outset of this book, or Milton's disparaging reference in the introductory note to *Paradise Lost* to "some famous modern poets." Having ultimately failed to realize the transformative ambition of the modern project, which is the progressive transformation of the conditions of life itself, we abandon modernism's utopian pretense for an even more nebulous postmodernism. Proclaiming the ineffectiveness of political action and its irony, postmodernism yields to the post-ironic, the post-ironic declaring a heightened or now somehow genuine perception of irony with its muddling of earnest and ironic intent. All this results from the failure to appreciate who and when in time we are, as measured against the constancy of human nature.

We note in this connection that blindness to what is always modern in the Classics has led to the wholesale rejection of Greek itself for understanding Homer. In 1973, Peter G. Snyder proudly proposed—relying solely on Robert Fitzgerald's translation—a "personal and perverse reading of the *Odyssey* that will repel all right-thinking classical scholars." *Il faut épater le bourgeois* 'You have to shock the provincials'. The very thought was grist for the progressive journal *Arion*'s mill, which published "Homer's Apocalypse," at nearly fifty pages, as the lead article of its new series. Adopting Fitzgerald's misadventurous translation, Snyder was "concerned with . . . the *Odyssey* as it is read today by someone with modern poetry and poetic." Fitzgerald's translation, Snyder continued, "both imitates and represents the essentially modern preoccupations of the heroic poem. The presence of this modern mode too easily escapes us if we approach it via the tradition of classical scholarship." In other words, we can now thank Fitzgerald, and Fitzgerald alone, for a translation disclosing what is modern in the *Odyssey*, since the *Odyssey* in Greek was never sufficiently modern to do so itself. As R. L. Lind observes, "The logical implication of this approach . . . is clear: the 'modern mode' would escape us entirely if either the Greek text were used or any . . . translation, including presumably Pope's." Any translation excepting Fitzgerald's, that is. Snyder proceeded on the fully contestable conclusion that Fitzgerald's *Iliad* is "so genuine a recreation and yet so faithful to the original." Rejecting the original, *Arion* put itself squarely in the *querelle* camp of those impugning the "imperfect poetic language of Homer."

The *Odyssey*'s modern preoccupations, however, have always been apparent, notwithstanding their conveyance in a long-ancient tongue, archaic even in its own time: homecoming after protracted absence at war, the perils and allurements en route, sexual wish-fulfillment or erotically charged possibility, dream vision and altered states of consciousness, encounters with the dead, a wife's perseverance, a son's devotion and coming of age, elaborate disguise and the risk of sudden detection, planning of the perfect revenge and its execution, the merciless slaying of accomplices, reunion and family reintegration, a return to the marital bed—to say nothing of sardonic exchanges, witty repartee, and consummate wordplay throughout. Such themes and devices are so old they are new. There is nothing ultimately newer than the *Odyssey* (not even Joyce's *Ulysses*); and the *Odyssey*—for lack of anything to "make new," improve on, or modernize—is and remains enduringly modern. Nothing of this escapes us by knowing it through Homer's Greek, the medium of the *Iliad* and *Odyssey*'s centuries-long gestation, the DNA of what makes Homer *Homer*, then as now. To treat the *Odyssey* "as though it had been written not in the 720s BC by Homer, but in the 1950s AD by Robert Fitzgerald," and to proceed in largely unfootnoted fashion, as though Homer had never previously met with comment, is a presumption for which Zeus keeps a special thunderbolt.

We return to Propertius. Failing to find him modern, Pound made him a modernist. Chancing only on a "dead man," Pound saw it his job to bring him to life and present a living figure. Had Pound understood Propertius aright—and cared about Latin more—he might have spared both himself and a thankful posterity from the *Homage* and its grandiose conceits.

Propertius, to the mind of classicist-scholar, humanist, and public intellectual Gilbert Highet (1906–1978) is one of the most "difficult" and "strangest" Latin poets, filled with "jagged ideas and obscure references" in a "cabalistic type of poetry." Given the obstacles to understanding, Pound little understood Propertius as Propertius might be understood—assuming of course that Pound had any such desire. What he did understand was that Propertius was *difficult*, and therein lay the attraction. Pound enthused more about the idea of Propertius's difficulty than about the felicities and innovations of his poetry; so even was he enamored more with the idea of languages than with any one of them.

Pound converted that which a recent Propertius translator has called Propertius's "willful strangeness" into something stranger yet. His libertine *Homage* was from the outset maligned as poor translation and worse. Pound disdainfully denied that *Homage* was translation—he had written an "*English* poem"—and subsequently withdrew the word *translation* altogether. Whatever the state of Pound's Latin (he himself conceded it was middling), neither precision nor correctness was of concern. Pound committed glaring errors or took monstrous liberties, incomprehensible even in a work intended other than as translation. Among them was the misapprehension of look-alikes, e.g., *canēs,* second person future of *cano* 'sing', rendered by Pound as the plural of *canis* 'dog', with other words in the same passage also recklessly mismatched. Thus, Propertius's *nocturnaeque canes ebria signa fugae* 'and you will sing the drunken tokens of nocturnal flight' became Pound's "Night dogs, the marks of a drunken scurry"—the original not transformed but travestied. Enthusiasts would make a virtue of Pound's ignorance, willfulness, or both, explaining that "the 'Homage' is also a linguistic joke, the fruit of Pound's imaginative use of Lewis-Short's *Latin-English Dictionary* or simply reflecting his delight at the superficial similarity between Latin and English words." Great minds, however, do not delight in superficialities, and what delight could possibly warrant so unedifying a subversion of the original? Another reviewer notes, "Yet the seven major blunders in [*Homage*] No. 12 and the five in No. 5 are enough to show that Mr. Pound refuses to make a fetish of pedantic accuracy." Pound, as Carne-Ross proposes, "refuses to look up words in the dictionary because he doesn't want his image of the poem to be sullied by what professors claim the words mean." And so on. Curative in the matter of Pound's "elementary school-boy blunders" is the surgical precision of medievalist Margaret Schlauch (1889–1986): "Either the linguistic forms are wrong or the passage is nonsensical. In either case, it is time to strip the author of claims of exemption or special consideration because of a putative eminence in humanistic culture. He simply doesn't have it." "Eminence" aside, Pound was merely a shoddy autodidact, concealing ignorance with bravura.

Critic Robert Graves saw through the charade and, and through Pound's gullible champions, in his brief and biting essay "Dr. Syntax and Mr. Pound."

Noting Pound's penchant for inventive translation regardless of syntax, Graves's interlocutor sarcastically concludes what every Pound scholar lives earnestly to confirm:

> Breathtaking, Magnificent, Pound. . . . You are, I see, deliberately distorting the strict sense in order to bring out vividly Propertius' latent irony. I would go further: I would say that you have expanded a facile and rather petty pair of elegiac couplets into what must surely prove to be a durable addition to, and influence upon, original poetry in the English language in this century.

If Pound knew better, he was supremely indifferent, writing to his undergraduate mentor Felix E. Schelling, then head of the University of Pennsylvania English Department: "As if, had one wanted to pretend to more Latin than one knew, it wdn't have been perfectly easy to correct one's divergences from a Bohn crib. Price 5 shillings." The Latin-accomplished Graves, moreover, has characterized Latin as "the most sober, economical, and unambiguous of languages"—everything Pound was not. Perhaps we ought to think less of Pound's Latin mistakes than of the mismatch, from the outset, between the rigors of Latin and the aesthetic profligacy of Pound.

## 2. Pound and His Propertius by Proxy

Given Propertius's difficulty, *accuracy*, however passé to the excitable mind, remains the needed starting point. The difficulty, as often held, stems from the corrupt and uncertain state of the manuscripts in which Propertius survives. As John Swinnerton Phillimore famously proclaimed in his *Oxford Classical Text of Propertius* (1901), *quot editores tot Propertii* 'for every editor a different Propertius'. The caution and self-restraint that Phillimore's caveat induced among subsequent interpreters had no effect on Pound, the headstrong disdainer of professors and systematic inquiry. But *that* is what modernism was all about—the contempt of authority, of established form and meaning, of tradition itself.

The manuscripts of Propertius are thought to reflect the peculiarities of his Latin—what critic Elizabeth Nitchie calls Propertius's "abnormal Latinity"—including novel usages, a complex word order, abrupt transitions, and a highly associative or allusory train of thought. The more the poems were copied and recopied over time, the more numerous the variants and errors. The peculiarities are otherwise believed to reflect the tortuousness of the poet's emotions—a dubious proposition, to judge from our discussions of Sappho and Catullus. Editions to this day vary concerning the end of one poem and start of the next, and also on line sequence within individual poems. Propertius in antiquity seems to have suffered by comparison to his contemporary the elegist Tibullus (c. 55–19 BC): "We also challenge the Greeks in elegy," said Quintilian (1st century AD), "as an author of which Tibullus to me seems especially terse and elegant. There are those who prefer Propertius." Admiring him as "terse and elegant," Quintilian admires Tibullus's "formal perfection and his sureness of taste." Propertius, being less transparent in both diction and direction, is, by Quintilian's lights, neither as terse nor as tasteful. Of a more insulated temperament and approach, Propertius, to paraphrase Gilbert Highet, wrote for the coterie of friends and poetic puzzlers who were his following. Had he wished to be more readily understood, he would have written differently. As Propertius was by reputation difficult, Pound had hit on a soul mate—whom the twice-difficult Pound would make more difficult yet.

As concerned his view of Pound, Highet himself underwent an abruptly Propertian change of temper. Discussing Propertius in his *Poets in a Landscape* (1957), Highet noted that Propertius's manner "also resembles the technique of the difficult modern poets such as Eliot and Pound. It has brought them much abuse, but it has made many readers study their poetry with a more earnest attention, and take it more seriously than the work of simpler and easier writers." The abuse it brought Pound, however, would soon include Highet's as well. Publishing a review of Pound's *The Cantos* in *Horizon* (Jan. 1961), Highet had this to say of the *Homage*:

> Homage to Sextus Propertius is an insult both to poetry and to scholarship, and to common sense. It consists of twelve free-verse poems which try to follow, very closely, the themes and wording of certain love elegies by Propertius. On every page Pound displays his ignorance, as though confident that, for scholars, his verse will be too subtle, and, for amateurs, his knowledge of foreign tongues will be overpowering. But he can grasp neither the important little details nor the large essentials; and the suave and delicate rhythms of Propertius' poetry are quite beyond his grasp. . . . The

> misinterpretation of Propertius' words is disgusting but explicable and even, from some points of view, amusing. What is more disgusting is that Pound, himself a poet, should have so degraded the sensitive thoughts of another poet. Propertius gracefully explained that he could not handle epic themes and listed the noblest. Pound made him say that he could not discuss a mineowner's dividends—a subject far from high poetry and far beneath Propertius' attention and utterly irrelevant. This is not a mistake in language. It is fundamental failure of taste.

Even classicist and Pound supporter Dudley Fitts became disgruntled, in a manner recalling Coleridge's chastisement of Wordsworth for his "unenglish" *Aeneid*. "When he fails," writes Fitts, "he fails because he has chosen to write a no-language, a bric-a-brac archaizing language, largely (in spite of his excellent ear) unsayable, and all but unreadable." Although Fitts conceded Pound's archaisms as an evocation of the past from ancient texts (here Provençal), he remained ambivalent toward Pound and modernist translation. In the words of translation specialist Lawrence Venuti, Fitts "yet rejected any discursive strategy that did not assimilate [modernist] texts to prevailing English values, notably current standard usage, because the resulting translation was not sufficiently transparent to produce the illusion of originality."

Pound's stance toward what became the *Homage* was as seemingly rushed as it was cavalier. The work, completed between 1916 and 1917, was preceded by a remark in 1916 correspondence as follows: "If you CAN'T find *any* decent translations of Catullus and Propertius, I suppose I shall have to rig up something." And so he did. Pound's regard for Latin and other languages he had dabbled in was equally casual: "Really one DON'T need to know a language. One NEEDS, damn well needs, to know the first few hundred words in the few really good poems that any language has in it. It is far better to know the POIKILOTHRON [Sappho's "Hymn to Aphrodite"] than to be able to read Thucydides without trouble. . . ." Pound's "shortcutting" is also apparent in the view, further apropos of "the POIKILOTHRON," that "he prize[d] the Greek more for the movement of the words, rhythm, perhaps than for anything else." In fact, exposure based on third-party recitation was apparently enough. "No," writes Pound, "I do not regret not having learned greek [sic] better in school. A fellow named Spenser recited a long passage of *Iliad* to me, after tennis. That was worth more than grammar when one was 13 years old." Pound quite believed it, writing, "You might learn Latin if it isn't too much trouble. If it is, I shall have to read a few Latin and Greek things aloud to you, and possibly try to translate 'em."

Pound's reliance on such proxies is apparent in the following of his "precepts": "Let the candidate fill his mind with the finest cadences he can discover, preferably in a foreign language, so that the meaning of the words may be less likely to divert his attention from the movement." Pound, as just seen, was quick to divert his own attention from the meaning of words. Yes, movement, but in what direction and to what end? Pound is here saying, think *form* rather than content; divide and divorce the two. It is just such habitude that licenses the Greekless translator's reach, at the expense of Sappho's words and meaning, for some will-o'-the-wisp called "verbal fabric," "flux of textures," "elusiveness," "subtleties of echo," or—in Pound's terminology—"movement." Poetry may have originated in incantation, "communicating before it is understood." That, however, little allows for the alienation of meaning in the course of poetry's long development, for the disparagement of what has been perfectly said and should strive to be as near perfectly said in translation.

If the translator knows and appreciates his source language, he has no need of Pound's recommended "cadences" or of "Saxon charms and Hebridean Folk Songs" as preparation for his task. Pound's "let the candidate fill his mind" smacks of today's hucksterish infomercials promising language fluency in ten days. And while a poem's "first few hundred words" are all well and fine, they little suffice for epic enterprise of the kind to which Pound aspired. At least not if he intended it as comprehensible or meaningful to anyone but himself.

Pound's borderline-comprehensible *Homage* met with the scholarly adulation of careerists on the cutting edge. They, as he, were bored with the old—guessing at Pound, as Pound guessed at Propertius; seeking to make Pound coherent, as Pound had made Propertius abstruse. Pound was *himself* something new—an outspoken, self-styled original, of striking appearance and demeanor, posing à la "Whistler's Mother" for *Pavannes and Divisions* (1918). The chic was irresistible. If one seeks irony in Pound—his name synonymous with it—it is his wholesale consignment to the very professors from whom he sought to free the Classics. Highet's disgust centered on the fact that Pound, "himself a poet, should have so degraded the sensitive thoughts of another poet." The view has a pedigree in the seventeenth-century poet Sir John Denham's lament against translators "so unhappy, as to rob others, without enriching themselves, pulling down the fame of good Authors, without raising their own." The irony is that Pound's own fame surged as he defiled what he little enough knew to hold dear. Would that Pound had actually translated or paraphrased Propertius, or created a credible imitation. But translation was beyond his interest (because beyond his ability), while "imitation" in the classical sense was not "making it new" enough. Ever the great disdainer, Pound disdained *imitatio,* calling Virgil, in a foolish bit of anachronism, "a second-rater, a Tennysonianized version of Homer." That Tennyson was Virgilianized does not Tennysonianize Virgil.

## 3. Pound's Apologists Forgiving All

Much, however, tends to be forgiven Pound, save his overt support of fascism during World War II and treason against his country—though his acolytes soft-pedal both. That he was notoriously anti-Semitic appears among the lesser of his faults. There *was* genius in him, and its irresistible concomitant: madness. He worked tirelessly and selflessly to advance the careers of others, T. S. Eliot included. And he "undoubtedly had a powerful instinct for the essence of poetry. And also . . . for the essence of life." We see an acute example of Pound-forgiveness in a recent formulation by Latin poetry translator Charles Martin. Indeed, Martin's wry self-assessment as an expert in translating Horace—since he's been "doing it for quite a while with remarkably little success"—rings far more honestly than his assessment of Pound:

> For every language from which Pound translated, there was an expert hiding behind a bush, waiting to pop up and inform you that Pound just didn't know what he was doing. Often enough the expert was right; Pound did not know Chinese when he published *Cathay*—or at any time after; Hugh Kenner finally admitted that Pound knew no Greek either, and I have come to the reluctant conclusion that Pound's knowledge of Latin was tenuous at best. Nevertheless, there is a sense in which this really doesn't matter at all, at least for the best of his translations, where what does come through, whether supplied by Pound or his original, lifts the hair on the back of one's neck as it is read.

Through how many of the *worst* must one wade before happening upon one of "the best of his translations"? This, again, is the school of hit and miss in the valuation of modernist poetry (Chapter 25). At the same time, the lifting of neck hairs—conspiratorially suggesting hair on end—has apparently replaced poetry's once hallowed office of tingling the spine or stirring the soul. Think, by contrast, of Solon—hearing Sappho's poetry and next content to die. Martin continues:

> The problem with imitation, however, is that the art that shapes it is often not part of the original. Pound's art, not Propertius's, shaped his *Homage*. . . . There is a sense, though, in which this matters not at all; when the hairs rise on the back of the neck, it may be ungenerous to ask who created this effect.

However, sound effects are not music, and effect alone does not suffice. The question is, *to what effect?*

In sum, too much Pound, too little Propertius. And yet, the issue is not even what we owe Propertius and what Pound. Pound did not know Propertius well enough to do much of anything except learn how to read him—for which he lacked both patience and interest. End-running any kind of study or apprenticeship, Pound showed indifference and a basic lack of understanding of what his Propertius required. *Homage* was a penthouse without a ground floor, a big idea with no frame to contain it. Worse yet, it was the precursor to Pound's equally obscurant *The Cantos,* hailed (alas) as a twentieth-century American epic. "The Homage," notes Pound apologist J. P. Sullivan, "has directed the attention of non-classical readers to Propertius in a way no classical scholar ever could." But, again, to what purpose? How the reader, with or without Latin, may genuinely benefit from *Homage,* or what the reader may even understand of it, is anyone's guess—whatever its serviceability to "cutting edge" scholarship. We recall in this connection that T. S. Eliot omitted *Homage* from his *Ezra Pound: Selected Poems* (1928), explaining in his preface: "I was doubtful of its effect on the uninstructed reader, even with my instructions. If the uninstructed reader is not a classical scholar, he will make nothing of it; if he be a classical scholar, he will wonder why this does not conform to his notions of what translation should be." This, to be sure, was an audacious statement by the co-patron saint of modernism, whom Pound had championed to prominence.

The "instructions" that have since accompanied Pound are nothing if not themselves obscurant and defensive:

> The book [*The Poetry of Ezra Pound*] is not so much exposition as argumentation, a running active defense, right down to the line, of almost everything Pound has written, said, or done. The result is, as it seems to me, an unfair drawing up of Pound as a kind of Pooh-Bah of poetry. Unfair, because no man ought to have to support this kind of deification. . . . It does little good . . . to remark that in view of his "undeviating sincerity," which no one knowing him could doubt, "Pound's local imprudences" are rendered "not only comprehensible but nugatory." . . . When Kenner talks about "our present hypertrophied neuro-muscular sensitivity to the morphologies of racial sensibility," or when he writes about Pound's "tone of flexible urbanity" as something which "can depersonalize exasperation into a reified scrutable marmoreality,"—and quite a bit of the book is like this—the language parodies itself out of meaning, and is likely to exasperate the most willing reader.

And there we have it: the decipherment of those deciphering Pound. There is sounder footing than this alluvium, such as Latin study, to the intermediate level, at least. Pound's *Homage,* no less than his *Cantos,* defies art's mandates (so E. M. Forster) of freshness, surprise, and the receptiveness of "eternal virginity." Art, notes Forster, "does not expect to be studied, still less does it present itself as a crossword puzzle, only to be solved after much re-examination. . . . [I]t is, to that extent, not a work of art, not an immortal Muse, but a Sphinx who dies as soon as her riddles are answered." To be sure, the essential nature of modern poetry may be thought to reside in its "suggestive indefiniteness" (so Poe, Mallarmé)—in the "overtones and undertones of implication which lie parallel with the surface meaning." But that implies discernible surface meaning to begin with. "Certain poets," says Paul Valéry, "insist that the mind shall work for its pleasures. They propound riddles to us." "Work," however, is one thing; indentured servitude, another. "Riddles," one thing; unfathomable obfuscation, another.

Pound was too busy faking Chinese to learn Latin; his Propertius a plaything, not poetry. So why toy with Pound as he toyed with Propertius, or be importuned by the turgid exuberances of his defenders? Why suffer accounts of Pound's Latin or Greek transcription errors as the likely result of quotation from memory, Pound "misspelling words with the freedom of one who has them by heart"? Is it really "bad memory, not bad Latin that in one of [Pound's] letters transformed Dante's *De Vulgari Eloquentia* into *De Volgari Eloquio*"? So botched a rendering of so crucial a work results only from bad Latin.

Whatever the typically Latinless reader garners of Propertius via Pound can only confuse and mislead. "Scruples concerning philological accuracy," offers Maurizio Bettini with fine understatement, "were fairly low on Pound's list of priorities." In what does the excellence of a poem reside? Poe argues, "It is *not* excellence if it requires to be demonstrated as such:—and thus, to point out too particularly the merits of a work of Art, is to admit that they are not merits altogether." And again, says Poe, "the proper 'profundity' is rarely profound—it is the nature of truth in general, as of some ores in particular, to be richest when most superficial."

There is perhaps no better, or better positioned, example of Pound apologetics than the response to Canto I with which Pound "begins his journey through history." The canto begins with Pound's translation of verses from *Odyssey,* Book Eleven, in which Odysseus journeys to the seer Tiresias in the underworld. Pound "translates" from the Renaissance translation of the *Odyssey* into Latin by one Andreas Divus (aka Andrea Divo) (1538). He does so adopting the poetic conventions of Old English.

These doings, according to Pound's most ardent advocate, Guy Davenport, are part of the master plan:

> And look at Canto I. It is a translation of the most archaic part of the *Odyssey*: the descent of Odysseus into Hades, a motif that goes all the way back to the Gilgamesh epic. And how does Pound translate it? Not from the Greek, but from the Latin of Andreas Divus, the first Renaissance translator of Homer, thereby working another archaic fact into his symbol. And into what kind of English does he translate it? Into the rhythms and dictions of *The Seafarer* and *The Wanderer*: archaic English.

Davenport's Pound-worship aside, his is but one Greekless translator's praise of another. Pound, of course, could not possibly have thought Divus worth the effort—more the failing if he did. It was, however, not effort but effect that Pound wanted, and *that* the stammering Divus provided. Highet hits the mark:

> Now, if a more modest or more dedicated poet did not know Greek and yet wished to use a passage from Homer in his poetry, he would take five or six versions of Homer in languages which he understood . . . and by combing them and extracting their essence, he might come fairly close to the original. Or—reflecting that Art is long—he would set out to learn Greek. Pound did neither. He used a line-for-line, word-for-word translation from Homer's Greek into flat literal Latin prose which was published in 1538 by a hack named Andrea Divo. . . . The affectation of using a Renaissance Latin pony for a Greek poem caused him more trouble than it was worth. Not only did Andrea Divo sometimes get Homer's meaning wrong, but Ezra Pound sometimes got Andrea Divo's meaning wrong. The result was a double layer of misunderstanding spread, like a Cimmerian cloud, between the radiant sun of Homer and Pound's wretched readers beneath.

Beginning his *Cantos* with a translation of Homer, Pound, notes Highet, was "putting himself into competition, or close connection, with one of the greatest poets in the world"—charting his own poetic odyssey. And what a presumptuous mess he made of it: "not poetry but confetti"—"pure fakery: a mere pretense of learning, cynically manipulated to look like the product of deep knowledge and intense poetic imagination."

Pound was admittedly cavalier about his entirely derivative crib-reliant enterprise: "Why write what I can translate out of Renaissance latin [sic] or cribs from the sainted dead. Here are [sic] a list of facts on which 9,000,000 other poets have spieled endlessly: (1) Spring is a pleasant season," etc. Pound took no cue from Pope's "What oft was thought but ne'er so well expressed," there being "nothing new under the sun"—nothing, apparently, except the endless drive to *make* it new. Pound himself might have taken a lesson from Ecclesiastes, of the sort experienced by novelist Thomas Wolfe:

> Of all I have ever seen or learned, that book seems to me the noblest, the wisest, and the most powerful expression of man's life upon this earth—also the highest flower of poetry, eloquence, and truth. I am not given to dogmatic judgments in the matter of literary creation, but if I had to make one I could say that Ecclesiastes is the greatest single piece of writing I have ever known, and the wisdom expressed in it the most lasting and profound.

*That* is homage, with preconditional humility.

### 4. Pound's Assaults on Dryden, Milton, Spenser, and Western Tradition

Clearly no imitator (or imitative transformer) in the Virgilian sense, Pound neatly fits Dryden's sense of imitation as "an Endeavour of a later Poet to write like one who has written before him on the same subject: that is, not to Translate his words, or to be Confin'd to his Sense, but only to set him as a Patern, and to write, as he supposes, [what] that Authour would have done, had he liv'd in our Age, and in our Country."

The Age of Dryden, however, provided a significantly different frame of reference than Pound's or our own. It was one of neoclassicism, of decorum and refinement in the arts; the Pound Era one of modernism, adulteration, and artistic indirection. The Age of Dryden had Dryden, and flourished in the literary afterglow of the King James Bible. The Pound Era was the repudiation of tradition in the aftermath of war, combined with successive dumbings-down of the King James Bible—an age of iron(y) relative to any that had preceded. For all the panegyric posterity lavished on Dryden, Pound was contemptuously dismissive, referring to the poet as "Johnnie Dryden," castigating his "outstanding aridity" and calling him "by nature a lunk-head." The opprobrium appears in a brief essay critical of A. E. Housman—another master of form and content—and is of a kind with Pound's contempt for the master of them all, Horace.

As Dryden did more than any other critic of his time to establish Milton's poetic reputation, we are further unsurprised to have noted Pound's scant regard of Milton. Disparaging Milton, Pound failed to appreciate what was "new" in him, either thematically or prosodically: the making, in *Paradise Lost*, of the first biblical epic in English; the unprecedented license and skill Milton brought therein to the use of blank verse; the integrality to the work of the Latin periodic style; and perhaps most especially of all, that "Nearly everything that happens in Paradise happens for the first time." Milton, in sum, could not have made it newer, proceeding, as he did, by way of a "series of related improvisations," making "Baffling dreams, angelic visitations, and discussions with the author of one's own being . . . seem part of the normalities of Paradise." Milton proclaims his originality from the outset: "Things unattempted yet in Prose or Rhime". For these reasons, and despite the inventiveness of his recourse to blank verse in an unprecedented endeavor, Milton—by manner, theme, and learned predisposition—was "never a contemporary poet." Making it new by making it old, Milton, to twentieth-century modernism aborning, was a fossil.

Milton, moreover, was fluent in Latin, Greek, and Hebrew, imparting a supreme credence (and cadence) to the synthesis that was *Paradise Lost*. He was the classicist Pound in a millennium would never be, and he was *learned* (if Pound at all wished to be so). Milton's learning, moreover, was ordered—he wrote "perhaps the most militantly organized [poem] in the language"—in a way Pound's learning, and *The Cantos* into which he poured it, would never be. While Pound foundered on *The Cantos* for over half a century, Milton composed *Paradise Lost* in a concerted effort over a discrete number of years. The consummate artist and poet—to say nothing of political provocateur—Milton was everything Pound was not. The same by degree applies to other artists who were the objects of Pound's disparagement—Horace and A. E. Housman in particular, as will be seen. It was perhaps a latent sense of his own inadequacy vis-à-vis Milton and Milton's preeminence in the Western literary tradition that fueled Pound's antagonism.

Pound was not yet done with Milton. Blank verse, traditionally consisting of five iambic feet ( ⌣ / ), is essentially iambic pentameter. Apparently concluding that the pentameter was "outworn" and incapable of new effects, Pound resolved "To break the pentameter, that was the first heave." Thus heaving the pentameter, Pound assembled the modernist chaos of *The Cantos*—hoisting yet another banner, and a significant one, over his denigration of the Western literary tradition. His heaving and "chucking" of the centuries-old metrically regular pentameter was nothing less than the overthrow of order itself, of the "traditional norm of our poetry." Shakespeare, farewell. Were it architecture, one might as readily topple the column; or flatten perspective in painting, as the Cubists did; or abandon tonality, as the Serialists in music. Pound struck, in both senses, at the *heart* of Western poetry, and of our very lives as experienced in poetry—for the iamb denotes the heart's own beat: *da-dum*. Presumptive Latinist that he was, Pound condemned Milton's Latinate style, failing to see both its relevance and monumental *newness* within Milton's design. He further ignored the brilliance wrought from Milton's pentameter, even as he was impervious to the pentameter's as yet "untapped resources." Out with old.

Indeed, as Dryden and Milton were equally devotees of Virgil, Pound's dismissal of the better part of Western literature, including its English "poetic norm," is apparent. His Western disdain predates Virgil. Pound targets Socrates, calling him a "distinguished gas-bag in comparison with Confucius and Mencius," and adding that "Greek philosophy . . . mostly a mere splitting, [is] an impoverishment of understanding." Pound then descends on Aristotle: "that old (or middle-aged or whatever he was) bastard [who] had 'got hold of something' from Plato, from Plato's gossip of Socrates." For Pound, Aristotle's thought was "syllogistic" and thus obsolete. Better the Eastern representational ideogram than the Western reasoned thought. The leave-taking of deductive reasoning and logical inference was congenial enough to the prescriptive, fiat-minded, and borderline comprehensible Pound. The ideogram delimits Pound's idiolect and idiosyncrasy alike.

Himself so much the dilettante, Pound consigns Aristotle to the "higher dilettantism" with which one might "monkey" in the leisure hours of one's fifties or sixties. No, ignoring Aristotle's most painfully basic definition of a "whole" as "that which has a beginning, a middle, and end," the ever-fragmented Pound intermittently labored for over a half-century on the fragments comprising *The Cantos*—over their "multitudinous discontinuities" and "indeterminacies," their "unceasing flow" and incoherence. Further underscoring his rejection of Aristotelian aesthetics, Pound denigrates Sophocles's *Oedipus.* "Certainly the whole Oedipus story is a silly lot of buncombe [*bunkum*]—used as a peg for some very magnificent phrases. Superbly used." The fact aside that Pound was incapable of recognizing the half of such magnificent phrases, Aristotle in his *Poetics* refers to and praises *Oedipus*—of the thousands of Greek tragedies then before him—more than any other tragedy. Hand in hand with Pound's disdain of Aristotelian aesthetics goes his disdain of the kindred aesthetic in Horace's *Ars Poetica.* Though the authority of Aristotle and Horace reigned for two centuries in literary criticism from Italy to England, Pound would have nothing of it.

"*Once* the classics could be studied in certain extent," said Pound, "but to try to make room in a full life that is needed for Chinese and for Frobenius research, is no go." Pound was thus prepared to let go the remainder of Western classics for the Chinese he never mastered and a scholarly German beyond his ready grasp. The preferences were decidedly anti-Western, the Chinese speaking for itself. For the rest, Leo Frobenius (1873–1938) was a prolific German anthropologist who traveled to Africa to study primitive myth and folklore. Anticipating the discredited Martin Bernal's *Black Athena: The Afroasiatic Roots of Classical Civilization* (1987), Frobenius believed that European culture originated in Africa, moving northward. Pound warmed to this revisionist view of Western origins and autonomy (even as he sought to vilify the outcome of the Battle of Salamis, 480 BC, credited with saving the West from Persian domination). Frobenius's anti-Westernism permeated the dour outlook of Oswald Spengler's *Decline of the West* (1918), a work rejecting a Eurocentric view of history and announcing the West's demise in its final "winter" season. Pound further equated Frobenius's fascism with that of his own literary favorite, the Florentine heretic Guido Cavalcanti (1250–1300), "reconfigured by Pound into Cavalcanti the protofascist saint."

Though Eliot, by contrast, exalted the West through his appraisals of Virgil, Dante, Dryden, and others, so-called modern poets would know little more than what Pound, Eliot, and first-generation modernists taught them. Modern poets "approach their problems without knowing which poetical problems have been tackled before, or indeed that any poetical problems have ever been tackled." True in 1952 and truer yet in the more than sixty years since. The same applies to the study and practice of contemporary art. The premium being on originality, absent merit or taste, students nowadays "are taught and know very little of art history. This is all part of the programme of radical disconnection from the past, of making them free-floating molecules in the vast vacuum of art." Filling the void is Roy Lichtenstein as exemplum of Western art appreciation. "As satire would be impossible," says Theodore Dalrymple, "so commentary would be superfluous." The same may be said of Ezra Pound.

Pound, by his silence, was also dismissive of Edmund Spenser, and of the "new" in what critic J. Isaacs called "The New Poet":

> Although "New Poetry" has turned up at various times, and at increasing speed in the past hundred and fifty years, there has only once been a poet hailed as "The New Poet," announced and finally accepted as such by his generation, and that was Edmund Spenser, and he may well be taken as the type of the Modern Poet, in our modern conception of him. He was the starting point of more

> than two hundred years of poetry . . . he taught all our great poets, Marlowe, Shakespeare, Milton, Dryden, Pope, and Keats . . .

Spenser's work, as critic Andrew Hadfield similarly observes,

> is notable mainly for its ceaseless experimentalism. Ezra Pound demanded that a true writer had to "make it new" and no one in English literary history made more things new than Spenser. He invented his own stanza; his own styles of poetic language; the romance-epic, a weird combination of English, Italian and Classical poetry; wrote strange and misleading commentaries to his poetry; and was the first poet to write a marriage hymn about his own wedding.

Spenser, as Propertius, was, or should have been, a poet "after Pound's own heart." But here too was an awareness renounced. Spenser's poetic persona and career are insistently suggestive of Pound's own, leading Pound intimate and *Guide to Kulchur* co-dedicatee Basil Bunting to note "an extraordinary parallel" between the two, and to predict (incredibly) that they might eventually have a comparable influence. (Note that Spenser was as virulently anti-Irish as was Pound anti-Semitic.) Yet, works by and about Pound are virtually silent on Spenser. To take but one example, George Bornstein's *Ezra Pound among the Poets* (1985) contains no "Pound and Spenser" chapter, and only an isolated reference to the latter. Nor have journals lighted on the subject.

All of which suggests that Pound was, again, impervious to his own literary antecedents, to "poetical history's . . . habit of repeating itself," to "poetry's having always been modern"—and to the ultimate lack of anything "new" under the sun, at least insofar as the impulse toward novelty is concerned. Pound shows himself unknowing of innovation at the source, in Homer himself; of how Homer outdistances the tradition in which he works. The Beethoven rather than Mozart of the epic tradition, says classicist Joseph Russo, Homer "represents not the perfection of all that went before him but the eruption of a mighty and singular talent into wholly new realms of expression . . . a creative departure from the tradition, or innovative playing with the tradition, that points to a freedom not found in the tradition-bound oral poet." Classicist Lorenzo Garcia sees this innovation in the setting of a particular "mood" for the poem. Homer himself "makes it new"—which is to say, the Homeric tradition, until codified, is itself ever aborning.

Pound was also contemptuous of Charles-Augustin Sainte-Beuve (1804–1869), whose studies of French literature from the Renaissance to his own time made him one of the most powerful and respected critics in nineteenth-century France. "The evil done by St. Beuve," says Pound in the gratuitous opening to his eulogy of Harold Monro, "is considerable and incalculable. It has allowed every parasite and nitwit to present himself as a critic, and thousands of essayists incapable of understanding a man's work or his genius have found opportunity in a discussion of wash lists." Again on the French side, and as seen, Pound expressed heartfelt disdain for Debussy's epochal *Pelléas et Mélisande.* His scorn, in general, is otherwise apparent in his mocking references to the "Amurikan langwidge" (letters to Mary Barnard) and use of "iggurance" and "deh Awts" (i.e., the Arts), among other such persistent and tiresome lexical drolleries. To these may be added the subversive spellings "Amerika" and "Kulchur," anticipating both the anti-Americanism of the '60s counterculture and Pound's own apostasy (Franz Kafka's novel *Amerika* written between 1911 and 1914; posthumously published, 1927). Indeed, *Guide to Kulchur* (1938), the "Adams Cantos" and "Chinese History Cantos" (1940), and the wartime broadcasts over Rome Radio—the last not merely "controversial," but "Nazi," "genocidal," and "treasonable"—have been deemed to constitute Pound's "totalitarian synthesis." Given the cultic allegiance Pound has fostered, and the academic-industrial complex grown about his person and work, Pound's indiscriminate assessment of Sainte-Beuve is sooner epitaph to Pound himself: "evil . . . considerable and incalculable."

## 5. Pound's *Homage*, Lowell's *Imitations*, and the Art of the Hoax

Imitation, as defined by Dryden, injects the translator into his subject matter—to the point of usurpation. It is more recently defined as "hyperbolic translation," wherein Pound is said to have excelled:

> Hyperbolic translation is one of the most fruitful apprenticeships around for the aspiring poet, one that all the ancients recommended under the name of *imitatio.* . . . [The] period was most decisively shaped, perhaps, by Ezra Pound, probably the greatest hyperbolic translator of our time: by creating "modernism" out of Sappho in Greek, Sextus Propertius in Latin, Arnaut Daniel in

> Provençal, Guido Cavalcanti in Italian, Li Po in Chinese, and so on—by finding in each writer that spark, that Poundian touch, that Paterian glow of isolated moments, and fanning it into a TL [Target Language] flame—Pound shaped his period into what Hugh Kenner calls the "Pound Era."

What manner of "shape" that leaves is debatable. We have spoken of Roman poetry as a matter of increasingly creative or transformative imitation. However, whereas Roman imitation was grounded in the total assimilation of Greek originals, and in the purposeful development and programmatic redirection of existing traditions, the "Pound Era" merely dabbled in languages and would likely have translated more and "imitated" less had it known its languages better. Its "modernity" was thus largely a matter of linguistic parlor trick and literary-historical legerdemain. One must accordingly disagree with the above characterization of "hyperbolic imitation" as "one that all the ancients recommended under the name of *imitatio*," as there was nothing "hyper" in ancient *imitatio*. At the same time, one regretfully acknowledges *imitatio* as serviceable apprenticeship for the aspiring poet: if original inspiration fails, toy with the Classics until it arrives. Or, as critic John Simon comments in a magisterially negative review of Pound intimate and fellow modernist Robert Lowell, "One uses this [adaptation] as a surrogate for whatever creativity one finds oneself lacking. A poet runs out of creativity of his own, so he makes it out of someone else's. . . . It is all part of that most terrible contemporary phenomenon in the arts that mistakes for inspired innovation what is merely lack of respect."

Pound's *Homage* was inspiration to the equally contumacious *Imitations* (1961) of Robert Lowell and to the execrable "homophonic" *Catullus* (1969) of the Zukofskys, Louis and Celia (Louis Zukofsky the other dedicatee of *Guide to Kulchur*). We will pass over Zukofsky, saying but this much for the also Propertius-influenced Lowell. Lowell's manner of "imitation"—to critic John Simon, "perverse as translation and unpalatable as poetry"—was early named the "New Sensationalism" (the moniker recalling the "hyperbolic translation" of Pound):

> The pressure of the new sensationalism is clearest in [Lowell's] translations of Horace, where nothing warrants it. Horace has been so exquisitely translated in English by Pope, Housman and

> others, that Lowell's deliberate hysteria and violence shock not only the reader of Latin but even the reader of previous translations. Horace's fine decorum in the ode to Spring (I, 4) becomes flashy, and gratuitous sentences are inserted for effect, etc.

Invoking the fashionable here-and-now fallacy of artistic transference, Lowell explains that his renderings were not translations, but imitations—one and the same for Lowell—seeking, by his "many licenses," to convey "what [his] authors might have done if they were writing their poems now in America." But *that* is of no importance or interest. If not writing then and in his own country, a poet is ideally writing for all times and places—the specific time and place but scaffolding to a "monument more enduring than bronze." The "transculturalization" of poetry is sooner derivative aberrance, compensating with garish show for what it lacks in authenticity.

Lowell limited his Russian *Imitations* to Boris Pasternak:

> Pasternak has given me special problems. From reading his prose and many translations of his poetry, I have come to feel he is a very great poet. But I know no Russian. I have rashly tried to improve on other translations, and have been helped by exact prose versions given me by Russian readers. This is an old practice; Pasternak himself, I think, worked this way with his Georgian poets. I hope I caught something worthy of his all-important tone.

Hope springs eternal, even as Lowell, in a published work, contents himself to *think* his source serves as precedent. And what does Lowell at all know of Pasternak's "all-important" tone? And whence Lowell's inference that tone is somehow "all-important" in Pasternak, or more important than in other poets? This is haste and insouciance straight out of the Pound playbook. Asked in an interview by Carne-Ross whether he "get[s] someone to read [him] the poem in the original," Lowell responds, "No, it just bores me to hear a language I don't understand. People have sometimes read me Russian and so forth. But the worst Russian poet would sound like the best, I couldn't tell." We earlier posited boredom as requisite to Pound's creating *Homage*.

It is Pound and Lowell who set the tone for what I initially urged as the sorry state of classics in translation during the past fifty years and more.

Whether or not Pasternak and Georgian poetry serve as precedent for Lowell's cavalier doings, others clearly took their cue from Pound and Lowell alike: Lowell's "this is an old practice" (1958) has its counterpart in Paul Roche's *Sappho*: "Imitations have once again become fashionable" (1966). And Lowell's "but I have rashly tried to improve on other translations" (1958) is echoed by Greekless Archilochus translator Michael Ayrton: "I rashly composed this text myself" (1977). Earlier yet, Dudley Fitts, in his *Poems from the Greek Anthology in English Paraphrase* (1938), mimicked Pound's revisionary method of creating "English poems." The volume was published by New Directions (founded in 1936), the initially Pound-championed experimental imprint and publisher of Pound's own works. It was Fitts who wrote the introduction to Mary Barnard's *Sappho* (1958), published, as seen, with Pound's encouragement. And it was Fitts and his onetime Choate student the Greekless Homer translator Robert Fitzgerald who collaborated on then-acclaimed translations of Greek tragedy. Meanwhile, Guy Davenport, one of the most egregious of the Greekless translators, befriended Pound and annually visited him at St. Elizabeth's Hospital from 1952 until his release in 1958 (describing one such visit, in 1953, in his story "Ithaka"). Davenport—whose doctoral dissertation was on Pound's *Cantos*—wrote a plangent eulogy for Pound and was otherwise friends with the modernist "Who's Who."

Ten years after his "go" at Pasternak, Lowell produced a series of "adaptations" from Osip Mandelstam in a bilingual volume by Olga Carlisle, *Poets on Street Corners: Portraits of Fifteen Russian Poets* (1968). Of the hundreds of poems contained, Vladimir Nabokov saw fit to task but one, and that by Lowell—doing so with the erudite indignation only Nabokov could summon. It is censure of a kind with Highet's of Pound. After discussing Lowell's spectacular subversion of Mandelstam, the Russian mightily concludes:

> What, then, is there especially adaptive or adaptational in an obvious travesty? This I wish to be told, this I wish to comprehend. "Adapted" to what? To the needs of an idiot audience? To the demands of good taste? To the level of one's own genius? . . . What we do have are crude imitations, with hops and flutters of irresponsible invention weighed down by the blunders of ignorance.

Nabokov continues in wondrous *de te fabula narrabitur* fashion, imagining a Lowell who reaps as he has sown:

> If this kind of thing becomes an international fashion I can easily imagine Robert Lowell himself finding one of his best poems, whose charm is in its concise, delicate touches ("... splinters fall in sawdust from the aluminum-paint wall... wormwood... three pairs of glasses ... leathery love") adapted in some other country by some eminent, blissfully monolingual foreign poet, assisted by some American expatriate with a not too extensive vocabulary in any language. An outraged pedant, wishing to inform and defend our poet, might then translate the adaptation back into English (". . . I saw dusty paint split and fall like aluminum stocks on Wall Street . . . six glasses of absinthe . . . the football of passion"). I wonder on whose side the victim would be.

Nabokov's vision of Lowell—done unto as he himself had done—is wickedly Aristophanic, pointing up the brazen absurdity of the "adaptive" or "transcultural" enterprise. Had Nabokov or others taken similar note of Lowell's *Imitations*, the work might have fared less well. But no. *Imitations* was awarded the 1962 Bollingen Poetry Translation Prize by those as unconcerned with any of the above as was Lowell himself. *Kirkus Reviews*, praising some of Lowell's imitations, canning others, noted, "Sappho, we must admit, escapes him, as does most of Villon, Leopardi, and the rotund Hugo." Here again is the poetic school of hit and miss: *some* good is good enough. We especially marvel to see Lowell—the undergraduate Classics major—missing closest to home with Sappho. Perhaps it has to do with his rendering of Sappho's "Equal to the gods does he appear / to me, that man who sits close by you, / hears the sound of your sweet voice /—intently near—" (§2) as: "I set that man above the gods and heroes—/ all day he sits before you face to face, / like a cardplayer." Writing four years after *Imitations*, and perhaps intending Lowell, even if not naming him, Robert Graves notes the translator's principal duty as follows: "to treat the other man's work with as much respect as if it were his own and present it with loving care—which means . . . he must never foist new ideas on the original." The Bollingen Prize notwithstanding, Oxford University had the good sense to pass on Lowell as a 1964 candidate for its chair of Professor of Poetry. In succession to Auden and Graves himself, the chair went as deservedly to prolific World War I poet, author, and critic Edmund Blunden (1896–1974).

The infatuation with Lowell persists, however. In a recent review of Arrowsmith's posthumously published *The Collected Poems of Eugenio Montale: 1925–1977*, poet, poetry translator, and publishing mogul Jonathan Galassi (b. 1949) plays both ends against the middle. (Himself a translator of Montale, Galassi is president and publisher of Farrar, Straus and Giroux, which published Lowell's 1961 *Imitations*). Galassi notes that the appearance of eleven Montale "texts" in *Imitations* "effectively presented Montale as the great inheritor of Europe's symbolist tradition . . . tacitly anointing him, in true Lowellian style, a modern classic." Really?

Judging from Galassi's assessment—everywhere at odds with its erstwhile laudatory intent—Lowell's consecration is not in the least hallowed, but quite hollow. Galassi relates that:

(1) Lowell's "familiarity with languages other than English was spotty" (spottiness in Russian, perhaps; but Italian?);

(2) Lowell "eventually made versions" of the poems with the help of two Italian translators and *The Penguin Book of Italian Verse* (crutches and wheelchair both);

(3) Lowell's first translator tried in vain to help him but was soon disabused of Lowell's interest in accuracy;

(4) Uninterested either in accuracy or translation, Lowell was instead "devouring and assimilating a new experience according to his poetic physiology" (one cringes); and

(5) Lowell "chose to exercise his own 'powerful' tone, over the Italian's more gnomic and inward briefer lyrics"—but, "despite the *Imitations*' excesses and awkwardness, something of the originals' austere grandeur does come through."

Montale of course was less than thrilled, while the Italian reception took a page from Nabokov on Lowell's *Mandelstam*: "Lowell was accused of betraying Montale's poetry, not only for being unfaithful to its meaning but also for 'the screeching and dissonance . . . the harsh reality of the images which upset, disfigured and violated the delicate structure of Montale's compositions.'" The Bollingen Prize was not far off.

## 6. *The Cantos*: A Dump Containing Some Beautiful Fragments

Scholars remain in thrall to the modernist take, and with the academic rewards attending the outrageous. No better way to become an early tenured "superstar professor" than to dangle long and acrobatically from a neo-interpretive limb. Translation and intercultural studies guru Anthony Pym remarks that Pound and Lowell—through the many "personal acknowledgments and copious citations" in their works—"might thus be said to have had adequate if not privileged access to quite extensive accumulations of knowledge, and it would thus be difficult to treat their translational works as the results of simple ignorance or indeed as bizarre curiosities in need of correction." Little, however, is so often abused as privilege. And "quite extensive accumulations of knowledge" merely defy credible focus or synthesis. Multiples aside, what manner of wonderment is a *single* "quite extensive accumulation of knowledge," and how is it taken in? The very idea is laughable, as reflected in Highet's view of Pound's *Cantos*: "a dump containing some beautiful fragments of antique and Oriental sculpture (often disfigured by careless handling), some outrageous fakes, loads of personal trivia, some bits of filth, many promising but embryonic artistic sketches, and a huge spree of pure rubbish." And more demurely, "Never perhaps has poetic material been collected so indiscriminately." It is thus not surprising to hear Pound spoken of—even by those sympathetic to him—as "prepared to mount an assault on meaning."

Indeed, farraginous innovation—"make it *especially* new"—has, since Pound, become the poet's calling card, from the neophyte to the recently deceased. The debut collection of one Adam Fitzgerald (b. 1983) is praised for the piled-on opulence of its images (seven within a twelve-line sample) and cultural references—ranging from Hieronymus Bosch to English philosopher John Locke, to the character John Locke from the television drama *Lost*, to the Abkhazian culture of the eastern Black Sea area and early modernist Marcel Duchamp. "Fitzgerald's mash-ups," asserts kindred poet-spirit and reviewer David Kirby, "make a kind of sense that is brainy and, as they accumulate, explosively funny." The Adam Fitzgerald phenomenon is a throwback to Pound's early imagism—the image, or accretion of images paramount, regardless the sense or context (whence also the prominence of haiku).

Pound in his own words professes an accumulative predisposition, no less than the tenacious disdain of actually *learning* something:

> I resolved that at 30 I would know more about poetry than any man living, that I would know what was accounted poetry everywhere, what part of poetry was "indestructible," what part could not be lost by translation and—scarcely less important—what effects were obtainable in one language only and were utterly incapable of being translated. In this search I learned more or less of nine foreign languages, I read Oriental stuff in translations, I fought every University regulation and every professor who tried to make me learn anything except this, or who bothered me with "requirements for degrees."

In the same vein is Pound's letter of 1917 to James Joyce: "I have begun an endless poem, of no known category. Phanopoeia or something or other, all about everything."

Pound's linguistic-cultural catchall found voice in *PAIDUMA: A Journal Devoted to Ezra Pound Scholarship* (later *PAIDUMA: Studies in American and British Modernist Poetry*). First published in 1972 under the editorship of famed Pound-explicator Hugh Kenner (1923–2003), the journal came to have an editorial staff of close to forty. The number, huge for any journal, reflected the "multiplicity" of all things associated with modernism, to say nothing of the outsize attention his explicators and editors lavished on the self-engorged holy man. In the 1994 Mary Barnard issue (earlier cited), Hugh Kenner ("University of Georgia at Athens") and Eva Hesse ("Munich, West Germany") sit in strange senior coeditorial proximity. The credits end in a list of twenty-six "associates"—all, with the exception of two from Ireland, from different countries. Impenetrable as he is to most speakers of English, one can only wonder what Pound meant to this global miscellany of "associates," or what they might possibly contribute to his afterlife.

The damage done Propertius by Pound within the field of Propertian studies itself is apparent in the following doozy of an opening to a 1998 article titled, "A Book Made New: Reading Propertius Reading Pound. A Study in Reception." The emphasis, recalling our earlier discussion of "boundarylessness," is again on the *many*—as many as humanly possible:

> That there is more than one way of reading an individual poem is readily accepted today. It would seem only logical to extend this approach to a collection of poems, to possible patterns of connection, juxtaposition and balance of poems in a book. For it seems not inherently unlikely that there should be such patterns discernible in a book, that recontextualization of an independent poem in a collection would generate new and different meanings, contribute to a variety of patterns. At the same time, it seems inconsistent with other ways of reading to assume only one pattern rather than several. Not a pattern, therefore, that is inert, mechanical, univocal. Not a means of closing down meaning, as is often the case with the concept of the book, the static concept that is a standard weapon in the critical armoury: single, authorial, a one-way process disdainful of the reader. Rather the book as part of an interpretative dialogue, the book as dynamic release for a plurality of meanings. This article proposes only one of many possible patterns in Propertius to which the reader might respond.

We are thankful, then, for author Michael Comber's (1944–2004) self-imposed restraint in an eighteen-page article containing one hundred and twenty-two largely substantive footnotes. All the author is saying, and would be saying, but for Poundian sway, is that a poem within a book of poems is read both in isolation and as part of the whole; that the whole throws light on the individual poems and their relation to one another, individually and severally; that the process creates meaning. The same is eminently true, say, of Browning's *Sonnets from the Portuguese.* But we can little imagine such theoretical to-do for its appreciation. We note in passing that British classicist Michael Comber, in predisposition and manner, was a virtual cutout of Pound, the difference being that Comber knew the Classics.

### 7. John Frederick Nims and Damage to Sappho

Let us briefly turn from the mischief done Propertius to the damage done Sappho. The latter comes not so much from Pound—who never published a translation of the "Hymn to Aphrodite"—as from his Greekless acolytes who have. One such was Guy Davenport, as discussed. The harshest assault, however, came from American poet and English professor John Frederick Nims (1913–1999). What makes the result so deplorable is Nims's decision—far beyond his means—to translate into English Sapphic meter. He is the only Greekless translator, the only "poet-translator," to venture this high ground. His efforts stand in vivid contrast to those of Lattimore, Lucas, and Powell, three twentieth-century Greek-proficient translators to have done the same. The three, as seen, convey accurate meaning in frequently vivid phrasing. Nims, by contrast, delivers distortive and baldly colloquial fill. **Nims in fact gives the lie to the very poet-translator fallacy that the Greekless poet, because a poet, succeeds where the presumptively unpoetic classicist fails.** Nims is entirely Poundian in his disregard of original meaning and tone, even while ignoring Pound's advice (to Mary Barnard) that English Sapphics refrain from "fill" or what Pound calls "trype." Nims, as Pound, presents his "imitations" as translations—*Sappho to Valéry: Poems in Translation* (1971)—though they are nothing of the kind. The designation is all the more misleading in Nims's first edition, given the inclusion of "An Essay on the Art of Translation."

The opening stanza of the "Hymn to Aphrodite," we recall, reads literally as follows:

> On embellished throne, deathless Aphrodite,
> daughter of Zeus, weaver of wiles, I beg you,
> do not with distress or despair subdue me,
> lady, (in my) heart.

Lattimore, as seen, provides the following:

> / ⏑ / ⏑ | / ⏑ ⏑ | / ⏑ /⏑
> Throned in splendor, | deathless, O | Aphrodite,
> child of Zeus, charm fashioner, I entreat you
> not with grief and bitternesses to break my
> spirit, O goddess.

And Lucas:

> / ⏑ /⏑ | / ⏑ ⏑ | / ⏑ /⏑
> Aphrodite, | daughter of | Zeus, undying,
> Goddess, throned in glory, of love's beguilements,

Do not now with frenzy and desperation
Utterly crush me.

And Powell:

/ ⏑/⏑| / ⏑ ⏑|/⏑ / ⏑
Artfully a|dorned Aphro|dite, deathless
child of Zeus and weaver of wiles I beg you
please don't hurt me, don't overcome my spirit,
goddess with longing.

Nims offers:

/ ⏑ / ⏑| /⏑⏑|/ ⏑ /⏑
On your throne, a|marvel of|art, immortal
Aphrodite, daughter of Zeus, amused to
lead us on through folly and pain—you'd doom me
body and soul now?

"Amused to / lead us on through folly and pain" is fill for *doloploke* 'weaver of wiles'. And while Sappho shows Aphrodite to be sympathetic, even amused, Nims's *calling* her *amused* defeats the poem's means and timing for making this information known. Moreover, "you'd doom me / body and soul now?" (1) unnecessarily dichotomizes Gr. *thumon* 'spirit, heart'; (2) makes for singsong with "folly and pain"; (3) introduces a disagreeable contraction ("you'd"); and (4) tastelessly converts Sappho's suppliant command—"do not with distress or despair subdue me"—into a quizzical interrogatory. And this is the *best* of the poem's seven translated stanzas. Nims, in fact "interrogatizes" three other declarative statements, thus significantly diluting the effect of the five questions already written into the poem (e.g., "Running off now?" for "If at first she flees").

Nims betrays not only the original's meaning but, curiously, its dialect—as if seeking to outdo himself as spoiler. Aeolic, as noted, disallows *h*-aspirated vowels: Attic ***(h)imeros*** = Aeolic ***imeros*** ('desire'), etc. Nims, nonetheless, heavily inclines toward *h*-based alliteration: "help . . . heard and hurried . . . home . . . harness . . . / Had" (all within five lines), and—for shame—"What's your wild heart heaving to have . . ."? Such uses are reminiscent of Paul Roche (Chapter 13): "Do not hurt my heart, do not harry it." Aeolic non-aspiration aside, the exhalatory *h*-sound is simply unappealing.

In the same vein, the gratuitous—if not risible—"Even so, though!" (beginning the final stanza). The translation is otherwise steeped in colloquial contractions—no fewer than a dozen: *what's* (twice), *you'd* (twice), *she'll* (twice), *won't, I'm, she's, you'll, can't, now's.* Sounding, next, like a British nanny, Nims has Sappho ask: "What's it now, love?" (similarly, "like it or not, dear"). Such term of address—"What's it now, *love*?"—is especially unfortunate in a poem where the word *love* twice appears in the expected sense: "Whom this time shall persuasion lead / as captive to your love?" and "the love she flouts, she'll soon long languish for."

And Sappho's chariot? Drawn not by *swift*, but by 'gamy' sparrows (rotisserie fare). These have not *quickly* arrived, but "flew you quick as a wink"; and have arrived not *through heaven's mid-aether*—but, "sky-high / diving through cover / spiraled down here" (bombardier-style). One may contrast Aphrodite's sparrow-drawn descent in the 1883 Sapphics (revised, 1893) of John Addington Symonds:

> . . . thee thy beautiful sparrows hurried
> Swift with multitudinous pinions fluttering
> Round black earth, adown from the height of heaven
> Through middle ether . . .

The intrinsic superiority of Symonds's metric aside, the abrupt change from lilting polysyllabics in the second line, to weighted monosyllabics in the third, conveys the contrast between avian busyness and the focused search for a landing spot—the chariot hovering helicopter-wise, as it were, "[r]ound black earth." The hovering, the *heaviness*, is underscored by the assonantal and markedly stressed "[r]ound . . . adown"—suggesting *ground* and virtually forcing a descent. That is the way it is done.

So much suffices. Nims's rendering appears in an overreaching volume of "translations" from various languages—ancient, medieval, and modern. Nims, in his introduction, renders the necessary obeisance to Arrowsmith and Carne-Ross, while extending his "Greekless" thanks to those who shepherded his efforts, including the Greek-deficient Robert Fitzgerald. In the manner of translators relying on help from others, Nims professes, "No man is an island, the translator least of all," and then lists the many persons, language by language, who, let us say, *insulated* him. "With Greek and Latin poetry," notes Nims, "all I know about classical verse owes much to the generosity and learning of. . . ." This flies in the face of Nims's "opener," that "One should translate only poems he cares very much for; poems he has been living with . . . for many years." The inference, in Nims's case, is that one can long live with a poem, not caring enough, even so, to actually learn it.

Matters are otherwise "clarified" in Nims's "Essay on the Art of Translation." Nims's introduction to the "Hymn to Aphrodite" itself—citing a "40-times" Mary Barnard-reminiscent failure rate—is bonafide muddle, e.g., "Aphrodite is mournfully amused, or rather is remembered as having been mournfully amused on other occasions." With the compensatory false precision that the Greekless translator ever brings to his task, Nims proposes that the subject/nominative *k'ōuk etheloisa* 'though not wanting to', if read as an object/accusative (which, despite the thinnest possibility, *never is)* might refer *to Sappho.* In other words, the recalcitrant girl, rather than being made to love against her will (whether loving Sappho or another) will love *Sappho* against *Sappho*'s will. *That* is not quite the justice Sappho seeks. Finally, and as Greekless translators before him, Nims parades the heavies, purporting to base his Greek text on E. Lobel and Denys Page, eds., *Poetarum Lesbiorum Fragmenta* (1955), while "taking some readings" from Page, *Sappho and Alcaeus* (1955). Lobel and Page would question their role in any of this.

The aforementioned classicist-translator Dudley Fitts, who objected to Pound at his most strident, is the complacent dedicatee of Nims's first edition. The pedigree is clear. Nims is a largely Greekless translator in the manner of Ezra Pound, Robert Lowell, W. S. Merwin, and Willis Barnstone. Nims served as editor (1978–1984) of the influential avant-garde *Poetry*, whose premiere issue relied on Pound's "To Whistler, American" to create the wanted modernist buzz and provocation. Nims has admired and reviewed books by Lowell and Merwin, and, in his *Sappho to Valéry* produced just such another. As concerns Merwin, his "mature style" is described as "his own kind of free verse, he layer[s] image upon bright image, allowing the lines to hang in space, largely without punctuation, without rhymes . . . with a kind of graceful urgency." Like Pound, Merwin looks to the poetic forms of multiple eras and cultures—devouring all, digesting none. Not content to leave bad enough alone, Nims later published *Poems in Translation: Sappho to Valéry, Revised and Enlarged Edition,* with identical acknowledgments and introduction, but with a significantly expanded number of translations, including those of Sappho, Catullus, and Horace.

Pound considered the opening of the "Hymn to Aphrodite"—*poikilothron' athanat' Aphrodita*—a poetic *summa*; anything less a mere warm-up or preparation, either for oneself or others:

> No man ever writes very much poetry that 'matters'. In bulk, that is, no one produces much that is final, and when a man is not doing this highest thing, this saying the thing once for all and perfectly; when he is not matching ποικιλοθρον' αθανατ' Αφροδιτα, he had much better be making the sorts of experiment which may be of use to him in his later work, or to his successors.

Despite his exaltation of the "Hymn to Aphrodite," Pound, as noted, never ventured a translation, however much tempered our thanks by Nims's homage. Otherwise, Pound's deleterious effect on Sappho and the lyricists persists. Josephine Balmer "continue[s] in Pound's imagist tradition, using free modernist verse forms which allow lines to wander across the page like splintered conversations, incomplete declarations of love, intensifying the impact of a hanging, isolated image, of metaphor in its purest form, crystallized into a single line or even word, echoing the broken nature of the text." For Balmer, this must necessarily entail "inventive translation strategies," including a "strategy of juxtaposition" (Chapter 27). Balmer's descriptions of these strategies occasion pause, such as "Jumping their Bones: Translating, Transgressing, and Creating," the name of her chapter in S. J. Harrison's *Living Classics: Greece and Rome in Contemporary Poetry in English* (2009) (cover showing antique bronze bust with earbuds). Reading Nims and Balmer, what has one truly read of Sappho?

## 8. Pound's Assaults on Horace and Housman

We have quoted Pound to the effect that one "can study the whole local development . . .[,] the sequence of local fashion in British verse by studying the translations of Horace that have poured in uninterrupted sequence from the British press since 1650." The statement ultimately reads as one of regret rather than tribute, since nothing so captures Pound's lack of classical sympathy or understanding as his disdain of Horace (and of Virgil as "second rate"). The fashioner of numerous lives in the course of his afterlife, Horace, for Pound, was little more than the barometer of "local fashion in British verse" and thus merely transient.

The novice need only read Gilbert Highet in the recently reissued *Poets in a Landscape* (1957, 2012) to be quickly acquainted with Horace—his warmth and worth—and, more recently, Daniel Mendelsohn, "The Strange Music of Horace" (2004, 2012), to appreciate the poet's caliber and technique. Add to these (Latin poetry amateurs though they be) T. R. Glover, *Horace: A Return to Allegiance* (1932); Peter Levi, *Horace: A Life* (1997); V. G. Kiernan, *Horace: Poetics and Politics* (1999); and most recently, by a Horatian in our times, Harry Eyres, *Horace and Me: Life Lessons from an Ancient Poet* (2013). Eyres's is an absorbingly sympathetic work by one steeped in his author's time, place, and poetry—by one who has *lived* and acutely conveys his own sense of the Horatian life (the book's sole fault and anomaly being the Poundian translation of Horace). It is, finally, a book showing, through the life of a thinking, classically educated man, that *Orazio è sempre attuale* 'Horace is always relevant'. "I have adored Horace in the simplest manner," says Peter Levi, "since I was fifteen, and as undiscerning about poetry as anyone else, but he keeps pace with our years as he does with the ages of the world. Without being deep oneself, one can see depth in him, and he is one of the very few poets who always leaves one feeling wiser, better and more relaxed, with no diminution of energy or appetite." Most recent are the disarmingly astute insights of classicist William Fitzgerald's "Horace: The Sensation of Mediocrity," in *How to Read a Latin Poem (If You Can't Read Latin Yet)* (2013). Thus, where other classical authors generate critical studies, Horace often generates appreciations, and those by writers at first lacking the means to grasp him.

Pound would have none of this, his view both boorish and uninformed. In an article first published in T. S. Eliot's *The Criterion*, IX.30 (1930), Pound began by calling Horace a "liar of no mean pomposity when he claims to have been the first to bring in the 'Aeolic modes,' for Catullus preceded, and Catullus wrote better Sapphics." For Pound, Catullus was thus not only first; *he was better* (which we assume clinches it). However, Horace positions himself in relation to Sappho as *princeps* 'foremost' not *primus* 'first'. The thought that the author of *Ars Poetica* would so falsify a matter of literary pedigree is laughable. Pound really missed the boat on this one, heedless of Propertius's own opening lesson in vocabulary. It was Cynthia, as Propertius says, who 'first' (*prima*) snared him with her eyes; and being his 'first' (*prima*) would be his 'last' (*finis*). Pound further notes that Catullus "improves on Greek style." What does that mean? He next says, "Horace lifts passages; incorporates lines; I doubt if he improves on Alcaeus." Horace, of course, does significantly more than "lift" and "incorporate"—as classicist extraordinaire Brooks Otis (1908–1977) has shown of Horace's great ode in Alcaic meter to his patron Maecenas. It is a poem in which "the mature Horace is attempting to summarize and define his poetical purpose and meaning. Here, if anywhere, his definitive statement and achievement are to be found." As for improving on Alcaeus, does the Greek- and Latin-deficient Pound thus imagine the Roman Horace's intent by contrast to his five-hundred-year-old Greek predecessor? Pound in his essay ultimately avoids saying anything specific about Horace—least of all about how Horace made Alcaeus "new." Pound instead invokes such unknown Horatian commentators/translators as John Hanway (1712–1786), Jacques Mondot Velaunois (*Horace*, 1579), and one Auguste Étienne Xavier de la Chabeaussière (*Horace*, 1803)—citing the last two by last name only and without date. Why belabor the obvious? Surely *tout le monde* is as *au courant* as Pound.

Similarly, Pound considered the Greek lyric poet Pindar—Horace's self-proclaimed inspiration—"the prize wind-bag of all ages," a poet, together with Virgil, that he was "chucking out . . . without the slightest compunction." Impervious to Pindar's ancient reputation as the height of lyric imagination, or to Horace and Pindar's standing as the twin pillars of classical lyricism, Pound (mimicking Thomas Grey) disparagingly calls Pindar the "Theban Eagle." Nor could Pound appreciate how similar Pindar and Propertius were, despite differences of meter and genre, in their regular use of allusive, and perhaps even jarringly interposed, mythology—by which they exalted the objects of their praise (Pindar) or love (Propertius). It is further noteworthy that Pound, even while lamenting Propertius's one-meter limitation, disparages the singular metric diversity he yet acknowledges in Horace. Horace, in sum, gets no credit for "making it new." Rather, "He had the art of writing, as much as can be learned, and the knack of incorporating Greek treasure-trove in pseudo-Greek meters." Indeed, Pound entirely missed that "Horace was often venerated precisely to be modernized: many poetic imitations treated subjects of the present day, even referring to recognizable contemporaries under Latin pseudonyms." Finally, and despite his clarity of thought, Horace in his way is as challenging to read as Propertius. Horace, for that reason as well, was beyond Pound's patience and ability. If Horace (as one critic claims) had been a significant influence in the composition of Pound's *Cantos*, he would recoil to discover it.

Dealing with Pound's major poetry, we do not feel, as we do with Horace, "wiser, better and more relaxed, with no diminution of energy or appetite." Pound rather drains and satiates. Pound's disenchantment with Horace extends to factors quite beyond the Roman's Greek meters. These include subject matter largely "outside the range of [Pound's] interest," an "evasive[ness]" vis-à-vis "new ways of treating things directly," and "distrust" of Horace's "lack of individuality." At a deeper level Pound's distaste reflects the antithesis he himself embodied of everything ever admired in Horace. This includes the unfailing orderliness of Horace's thought and rhythm and, relatedly, his marked poetic economy and restraint. It further includes, deriving from these, Horace's sense of proportion and personal limit, and his grasp of reasonable expectation. There is also Horace's urbanity and understated common sense, his scorn of pomp and self-inflation. And finally, his consummately well-turned truisms (or "commonplaces," if you will) reflecting a sense of the permanence of human nature versus the evanescence of life—*this* all so inimical to the experimentalist credo of "make it new." Indeed, these same Horatian characteristics were also the hallmark of the pre–World War I Georgian poetry that Pound and the modernists would resolutely "chuck."

Let us note Professor Mackail's 1895 summation of Horace's skill, apropos of, and by contrast to, Pound's:

> [Horace's] unique power of compression is not that of the poet who suddenly flashes out in a golden phrase, but more akin to the art of the distiller who imprisons an essence, or the gem-engraver working by minute touches on a fragment of translucent stone. With very great resource of language at his disposal, he uses them with singular and scrupulous frugality; in his measured epithets, his curious fondness for a number of very simple and abstract words, and the studious simplicity of effect in his most elaborately designed lyrics, he reminds one of the method of Greek bas-reliefs, or, still more . . . of the sculptured work of Mino of Fiesole, with its pale colours and carefully ordered outlines.

One again finds in Horace the fullest antithesis of Pound: distillation versus excess, focus versus flash, translucence versus opacity, studious simplicity (*simplex munditiis*) versus studied complexity, and so forth. Summarizing Horace's worth, the Roman critic Quintilian notes that he is *plenus . . . iuncunditatis et gratiae et varius figuris et verbis felicissime audax* 'full . . . of grace and charm, and resourceful in figures of speech, and in diction felicitously bold'. Here too Pound failed to appreciate how Horace had "made it new," or how his thought, "long since . . . absorbed in the common thought of the world," is ever memorable for the singular form of its expression. By contrast, and as often noted, Pound's epic form was designedly expansive to accommodate the scope of an unprecedented epic reach. This is only to say that Pound's lack of form accommodated an indiscriminate, indeterminate, and unorganizable subject matter—one largely memorable for such qualities alone.

One might have hoped for a different relationship: Pound, like Horace, a devotee of companionable friendship (befriending and helping others—as Horace himself had been befriended and helped). Pound, like Horace, an advocate of authority, with this difference: Horace preferred severe though restorative governance to chaos, and found it in Augustus; Pound preferred companionable chaos and found it in Mussolini. "Linguistic accuracy," observes Harry Eyres, "is not merely an end in itself but an essential way of learning moral distinctions." Pound ultimately knew neither—unable to distinguish order from chaos, freedom from tyranny, noun from verb.

If any English poetry collection captures Horace's laconic wit and economy, it is A. E. Housman's *A Shropshire Lad* (1896), followed some twenty-five years later, in a similarly rueful mood and manner, by his *Last Poems* (1922). The Horatian in Housman has been noted and elaborated on: witness Brooks Otis, "Housman and Horace" (1967) and Richard Gaskin, *Horace and Housman* (2013). Without overt reference to Horace, John W. Stevenson, reappraising *A Shropshire Lad*, discusses Housman's steadfastly traditional form and lack of interest in new artistic theories, as well as his belief in the consoling comfort of once-known friends and places—their *physicality*—which "defines what is real, what is true." Housman preferred "not the thing said, but a way of saying it" (Pope's "What oft was thought," etc.). It is by means of the "way" that the poet fulfills his obligation "to recover that which is as old as mankind's beginnings, to define again the knowledge felt along the bones."

The key here, as with Horace, is to define *again*—not redefine, modernize, or revolutionize, but define *again* what is enduring (the "bones") and ingrained ("*felt* along the bones"), that we may savor and take comfort in what *abides*, even as our individual lives flit by. "We want," says Yeats in a critique of Pound, "not a new technique, but the old passion felt as new." Acceptance of mortality is the key; reminder—not revision or reinvention—the mandate. There is thus no "making it new" in Housman, other than as a matter of verbal formulation. There is, instead, "a compelling insistence of simplicity and sincerity. . . . In uncomplicated meters, in the language of everyday life, he expressed the elemental themes of love and death." Thus, and despite his modest output, Housman strongly influenced an entire generation of poets and was one of several poets most in demand in the trenches of World War I. Pound responded to Housman more pithily, but no less disdainfully, than he did to Horace. Pound's lame twelve-line parody "Song in the Manner of Housman" begins: "O woe, woe, / People are born and die, / We also shall be dead pretty soon / Therefore let us act as if we were dead already."

Pound especially missed a certain Sapphic perfection in Housman's use of the "language of everyday life," a quality captured in classicist-translator F. L. Lucas's 1924 review of Housman's poetic output, appropriately entitled, "Few, but Roses." Lucas praised Housman's poetry as "English of a quality English literature has not surpassed." He found in Housman one of three British poets (with Matthew Arnold and Walter Savage Landor) in whom "the spirit of Greece, Rome, and England found that happy mixture of their elements which lives in them—the grace and lucid sadness of the flutes of Hellas, the proud glitter and the stab of the Roman sword, the sweetness and strength of the English countryside." Here as elsewhere, though specifically in Housman's case, Pound missed what was *new*—precisely because it was lucid rather than opaque, which is to say, under his very nose. Says Lucas of Housman's versification, "It is a curiosity of literature that so late in the development of English poetry it should have been possible to bring harmonies so new, so invariably perfect out of some of its most hackneyed meters." And finally:

> Some rejecting [Housman's] interpretation, will yet recognize, if they are human, that in moods, at least, they too have felt the same, and will hope, if they are wise, that though differing they enjoy him none the less; and some, sharing his view of life, will enjoy him yet the more. And nobody will deprecate.

Nobody except Ezra Pound. The contemporary appreciation of A. E. Housman is most fully realized in Tom Stoppard's *The Invention of Love* (1997), a play portraying Housman's life (recollected from the viewpoint of the aged poet-scholar) and considered Stoppard's finest.

## 9. Pound and *Arion, A Journal of Classical Culture*

Pound's take on Horace enjoyed a second life, reprinted (1970) in the modernist hotbed that is *Arion, A Journal of Classical Culture* (est. 1962). The journal was founded by William Arrowsmith, D. S. Carne-Ross, and J. P. Sullivan (all previously mentioned), and by the Whitmanesque Frederic Will, a classicist-comparatist omnivore and founding editor of *Micromegas, A Journal of Poetry in Translation* (1965–1975). Translation was, not coincidentally, the passion of all four. A University of California "In Memoriam" (1993) to J. P. Sullivan called *Arion* "brashly revisionary."

*Arion* has suffered from the Promethean egos of its editors. Their agenda for the radical transformation of the Classics, and of the educational system itself, proceeded on the penthouse-without-ground-floor assumption that students could be made as instantly energized and cross-culturally appreciative as they themselves (the editors) had become. This applies in particular to Arrowsmith, whose unrealized "distinctively American version of the study of the classics" was nothing if not the humanities writ large in his own self-image. At the same time, however, Arrowsmith's "rage for new ideas was not matched by a patience for implementation," even as his own drummer was so loud as to be deafening. More than a mover and shaker, Arrowsmith was a restlessly conquering Alexander, a prophet unheeded in his own country, a Coriolanus defiantly proclaiming "There is world elsewhere."

The tumult and torrent of Arrowsmith's persona are manifest in all that *Arion* sought to accomplish. *Arion*'s opening mission statement initiated the capacious and uncompromising search for

> that *tertium quid* which is neither scholarship nor popularization nor any compromise between them . . . [, requiring] that whole ensemble of skills, approaches and possibilities which are neglected in current philological practice and whose encouragement we consider vital for the survival of the classics as anything other than an esoteric and insignificant branch of learning.

Posited on the misleadingly extreme dichotomy of "scholarship" and "popularization," the quest was quixotic from the outset, the rejected "compromise" anyone's guess. Upon the inaugural of the journal's third series (1990), *Arion* issued a multipage editorial statement announcing that the *tertium quid* 'third something'—*Arion*'s goal, as previously—was *now* not merely the search for a non-compromising median between "pedantry and vulgarization," since these were "no longer the only barbarians." Rather, "The new human sciences now present another leveling threat to the classics. The assault is not simply against literature but against language, against *meaning.*" *Really*? The extravagantly wishful *Arion* had itself become the new pedantry—cultural instead of philological—having from the outset, and quite independently of the "new sciences," worked its own assault on literature, language, and meaning. What else was *Arion*'s Pound-pedaling but the hammer by which these blows were dealt?

What Arrowsmith, Carne-Ross, and *Arion* failed to appreciate was that understanding is *itself* first measured one step (and one declension) at a time—from the ground up, not from the aether down. This is precisely the lack of understanding that turns the pleasant meadows, forests, towns and cities of the world inside Pantagruel's mouth into Pound's expansive dump. Learning precedes understanding; and understanding, knowledge. But as Highet noted of Pound, "He would not learn." Intuitive understandings are the exception not the rule.

Modernism has always gone hand in hand with cronyism at *Arion*. An Arrowsmith protégé, Herbert Golder was a freshly minted Ph.D. (1984) when he became, as noted, coeditor with Arrowsmith of the monumentally misguided *Greek Tragedy in New Translations* (1986–1992). Still an assistant professor when he became editor of *Arion* (1990)—two years before Arrowsmith's death—Golder still serves in that position. A charmed career, it was jump-started by singular preferment. Preferment of one or another kind has from the outset compromised *Arion*'s standing as a refereed journal.

Carne-Ross wins the biggest-offender award for "Scenario for a New Year" (1969)—an "essay" of one hundred and fifteen pages "concerned in various ways with learning," and bumptiously footnoted as: "The opening and no doubt provisional chapters of a work in progress" (Carne-Ross dons his thinking cap, and we are all invited to gather round and watch him make it snug). There was also Carne-Ross's "Classics and the Intellectual Community" (1973), in which the author, despite his demonstrated indifference to a translator's familiarity with original languages, proposed that the time for learning Modern Greek is only after one has learned "French, German, Italian, Spanish and presumably Russian." Arrowsmith published his longest article, on Aristophanes, at close to fifty pages, in *Arion* (1974). Such examples raise the question of whom an academic journal is for: its editors or the profession at large, especially where publication and the availability of publication are critical to academic survival. As concerns the self-promotion that *Arion* allowed its editors, there is no arguing the benefit, to paraphrase Virginia Woolf, of "a journal of one's own." *Arion*'s editors also published elsewhere, of course—but rarely at such length when *others* were keeping page-count. In the space consumed by the above three pieces, approximately fifteen articles at fifteen pages each could have been published—each a needed showing for any promotion and tenure hopeful (promotion versus self-promotion). Fully half those fifteen were outed by Carne-Ross's "no doubt provisional chapters of a work in progress."

*Arion* favorite John Talbot published a thirty-pager in 2004, noteworthy—with nods to Carne-Ross and J. P. Sullivan—for its Poundian drumbeat and lockstep. The occasion was a new translation of Callimachus that "does homage to Pound doing homage to Propertius doing homage to Callimachus." This is not to disparage Talbot's masterful discussion of the arcana of Callimachean diction, which would decidedly have eluded Pound. Talbot ends his article with the apocalyptic suggestion—the more frightful for being made in earnest—that "what is needed now is for some resourceful poet to . . . reinvent Callimachus in English in some way that goes beyond translation; someone to do for Callimachus what Pound did for Propertius, or what Lowell did with the European tradition in his *Imitations,* or what Christopher Logue is doing for Homer." Indeed, Talbot's "English Ghosts of Callimachus" is also the conjuring of Pound's ghost at the start of the twenty-first century. Pound may have preferred his "Era" ended—freeing his hated academics to make something new of something else.

The year following Talbot's article, *Arion* published a forty-page review by the consummate gloves-off reviewer Steven J. Willett of *Ezra Pound, Poems and Translations,* Richard Sieburth, ed. (New York: Library of America, 2003). The review was suggestively titled "Wrong Meaning,

Right Feeling: Ezra Pound as Translator." Signaling a possible change in direction—a Lucretian swerve, as it were—the piece characterized Pound's "ostensibly original poetry" as the "brittle, jumbled, inhumane, monomaniacal, and spiritually desiccated work of a very limited, but fatally authoritarian mind." Willett, without saying as much, was calling Pound the fascist he ultimately proved to be. Willett similarly decried Pound's inclination to "bully his reader into submission." On the modestly positive side, said Willett, Pound's importance as a "literary theoretician, stylistic innovator, and selfless promotor of talent" would ensure him "little more than standing room on the lower slopes of Parnassus." Pound's translations and adaptations would constitute his true poetic legacy as "surely the greatest minor poet in English of the twentieth century." All this on *page one*. Highlighting Pound's Chinese/Confucian translations and his translations of Sophocles's *Elektra* and *Women of Trachis*, Willett further notes,

> I have grouped two very different sets of translations in the last category . . . —nearly half the volume—because they present decades of misplaced, largely worthless effort. They are a testament to the lethal effects of a linguistic ignorance that refused to correct itself, a false belief that unaided poetic genius could see into the heart of an alien culture without the need of scholarship, and a knot of crackpot aesthetic, social, and economic theories that blocked honest introspection or self-reflection.

Highet knew as much over forty years earlier. Willett otherwise takes a dim view of *Homage*, and no longer is Pound all forgiven:

> In some cases he was able through his genius for rhythm and verbal music to turn errors into happy mistakes, but in many others philological incompetence nullified his efforts both at poetry and fidelity. A poetic translation based on a serious misunderstanding of the original language is still a failure no matter how effective the English may seem to be. If we separate accuracy from invention, as so many Poundians do, then we are implicitly claiming that the cultural heart of the poem need make no substantive contribution to the translation. It takes a very happy mistake for me to ignore fidelity.

It is good to awaken. For as we slept, volumes filled with pretzeled exegesis; with plaudits and acclamations; with the homage to Pound which is Pound ever expounded, its better part a disordering and enervation of thought. The time had been better spent—and less the damage to Sextus Propertius, the Classics, and classics in translation.

The crack in the façade of vested academic interest has been long in developing. Outspoken American poet and political thinker Peter Viereck (1916–2006) noted in 1953 (Pound already eight years at St. Elizabeth's) that Pound was the keystone of the school of New Criticism: "If he goes out of fashion, then the whole structure becomes shaky." As Viereck noted a generation later in 1986, albeit prematurely: "Modernism . . . is now the outdated Royal Academy it once rightly fought. A book should be written . . . about the road not taken." The road not taken "would have led—can still lead," not through Eliot and Pound, but through a variety of rhymed and metered verse forms "reform[ing] our language's traditional meters from within and thereby mak[ing] unnecessary the free-verse revolution from without." Had it only been so. Modernism may in many ways have been a cruel joke—"a tale told by Eliot, full of Pound and fury, signifying Williams"—but the joke is still, and will long be, on us.

*Arion* is currently presented as a journal "Celebrating and Redefining the Classics for 20 Years" (fifty is more like it). It is not *we* who redefine the Classics, but we who are defined and redefined by them. And we best divine their meaning and relevance by trying to grasp what they meant to their original audiences. Pound's assessment of Horace as "a liar of no mean pomposity," "such a humbug," and overall vexation to the progress of literature sooner applies to Pound himself and to so much of the modernist enterprise as has "redefined" the Classics by mucking the means to their survival—which is to say, their translation and level-headed instruction. When my son, Paul, was eight, I read him the *Odyssey* at the rate of one hundred lines a night before bedtime. The sight of him, as I read, peering wide-eyed from atop his bunk bed has long endured. And how he chafed when I urged that we skip the *Catalogue of Women*. During those several months of reading, I had *made it new*, finding an *Odyssey* I seemed not to have known before. *That* is how we make it new for ourselves, by making it new for others—not by boredom-assuaging reinvention or agenda-driven theory. With reference to art, "The objects themselves," says E. M. Forster, "are eternally new, it is the recipient who may wither." Or in the words of a medieval Latin lyric describing perfect and perfectly endless lovemaking:

*hoc non deficit, incipitque semper* 'And here no end shall be / But beginning everlastingly'.

### 10. The Swamp Draining, the Derriere Guard

Elegance, notes Horace, first entered Latin upon drainage of the Saturnian meter:

> Then drained that rude Saturnian measure,
> and elegance vanquished the viral scent.
> Yet for years did the rustic trace remain,
> remaining to this day . . .

You *can* go home again—"to the old forms and systems of things which once seemed everlasting but which are changing all the time." It will, however, require a certain draining-off of modernism, however much the residuum keep. The work is already underway in the New Formalism, developed in response to modernism's "debasement of poetic language" and the related ills of contemporary verse. As the New Formalism has ever waged an uphill battle, the work is arduous—like learning to walk again. The process proceeds apace in music, "now that the wreckage of serialism and the nihilist avant-garde have been cleared away," and our sights realigned with the genius of tradition.

Spearheading the new focus is the Hungarian-born American composer Stefania de Kenessey (b. 1956), founder and artistic director of the "Derriere Guard," an alliance of traditionalist, i.e., antimodernist, contemporary artists, composing neoclassical contemporary music. The alliance's best-known member is author Tom Wolfe (b. 1931) whose *The Painted Word* (1975) and *From Bauhaus to Our House* (1981) are brief (for Wolfe) but laser-penetrating indictments of modernist painting and architecture. It was Wolfe who gave the Derriere Guard keynote address upon both its 1997 founding and its ten-year anniversary. De Kenessey's chamber music album "Shades of Light, Shades of Dark" (North/South Records) received rave reviews in *Fanfare* magazine as "fully worthy to share a program or disc with the masterpieces by Mozart or Brahms." Therein lies the difference nowadays between sympathetic pairing—let us also call it "fit" or "decorous" pairing—and that which so often imposes or intrudes, though briefly enough to result in passing indisposition alone.

We earlier noted the cool reception, despite numerous official recognitions, of formalist poet and literary translator extraordinaire Richard Wilbur (b. 1921). Wilbur was largely eclipsed in the 1960s and 1970s by the "Howl" crowd and the form- and meter-discarding confessionalism of Robert Lowell (*Life Studies*, 1959), Sylvia Plath, Anne Sexton, and numerous other self-as-subject-matter obsessives. Coming of age in the heyday of modernism and serving in World War II, Wilbur declined shock and novelty for their own sake, or for any reason. Also suffering grudging praise is neoclassical sculptor Frederick Hart (1943–1999), whose monumental deep relief *Ex Nihilo* (*From Out of Nothing*) graces the west facade of Washington National Cathedral. Depicting the emergence of man and woman from the swirl of Chaos, it is the twentieth century's answer to Ghiberti's *Gates of Paradise.* Yet its dedication and afterlife have gone largely unnoticed, Hart himself dying a virtual unknown. *Ex Nihilo,* indeed. When the nihilists, minimalists, and assorted theorists have gone their dreary way, Hart will yet have his recognition—*himself* emerging from the swirl.

A similar neglect essentially veils classical realist painter Jacob Collins (b. 1964), whose focus on beauty, order, and harmony smacks too much (for modernist tastes) of European academicism. Alexandre Cabanel's seductively glancing-eyed *Birth of Venus* (1863) is a prime example of academic art—of the beauty in art first arising in Greece and Rome, resurrected in the Renaissance, and perpetuated by the beaux arts academics of the nineteenth and twentieth centuries. The exactingly representational nature and period-eroticized allure of such art would succumb to mid-nineteenth-century impressionism and all that followed. Poet-scholar and former *Kenyon Review* editor Frederick Turner (b. 1943) notes that modernism's "each new shocking novelty could only bounce the rubble of an already devastated culture," while Collins himself deems modernism "a simple virus with a simple replicating system to destroy the western tradition." Collins's "simple virus" peculiarly echoes Horace's *grave virus*—which I have translated 'viral scent'—designating the ruinous Saturnian meter of his day.

The swamp, to be sure, drains grudgingly. As the searing social critic Heather Mac Donald reminds us:

> New York's Metropolitan Opera triggered an outpouring of critical contempt this winter by reviving a traditional production of Antonin Dvořák's fairy-tale opera *Rusalka*. The press's enraged reaction to the Met's sylvan setting starkly revealed the pressures on the house to embrace nihilistic European-style directing. But the critical bile was even more alarming as a sign of the shriveling aesthetic imagination among our purported guardians of culture.

And equally at the close of her review:

> The assault on opera is not an isolated phenomenon. It is part of a larger attack on the humanistic tradition. The same solipsistic impulse that drives an opera director to ignore a composer's intentions and force a work to ape his own shallow obsessions is also behind the gutting of humanistic study in the academy and its replacement by facile identity politics. Both travesties grow out of an adolescent insistence on making everything revolve around the self. The revisionist director and the identity infatuated academic are destroying the promise of the arts: the possibility of losing oneself in beauty and in the radical difference of the past.

It is in this vein that the New York Philharmonic, with a 2014 (inaugural) "biennial" of its own, apes the Venice Biennale as local avatar of the contemporary. So begins, under the baton of the Philharmonic's music director Alan Gilbert, an eleven-day, twenty-one concert "Let's Go Beyond" festival, styled: "A Musical Playground of the Here and Now." But as this work has emphasized, serious art is not the romper room, and it is not the here and now, but eternity, that concerns it. Meanwhile, New York's Metropolitan Museum, housing more than two million works of high art, deems its collection incomplete without woolly rooftop installations—including Jeff Koons's balloon-dog metallics—to distract its visitors. Staged, perhaps not coincidentally, at the Metropolitan was the Philharmonic's biennial inaugural, H. K. Gruber's "Gloria—A Pig Tale." The anarchic opera concerns a preening pig with golden hair, ostracized for her loveliness by her porcine companions—in the Poconos, no less. And the mainstream media? As approving as it was critical of Dvořák's *Rusalka*.

What transpires within museum walls and atop their roofs these days is reflected in the new museum construction and old museum façade renovation of recent decades. Of lasting imposition is the now everywhere in-demand "blob architecture" of Frank Gehry & Co. "The rapturous reception of [his Guggenheim Museum Bilboa, Spain, 1991–1997] led to the so-called Bilboa effect, a salubrious influence on the city's economy that in turn has spurred countless other municipalities to fund avant-garde architectural schemes to attract cultural tourism." This is museum-going as building-gawking. Similarly the depredations of Renzo Piano (b. 1937), with his congeries of girders and glass (2006) athwart Charles Follen McKim's Morgan Library & Museum (formerly the Pierpont Morgan Library, NYC); his new wing and adjoining corridor (2012) at the fifteenth-century Venetian palazzo-styled Isabella Garner Museum (Boston); and his seventeen-year, under-one-roof consolidation of the Harvard Museums (2014)—Palladian and other bygone elegance boxed in Bauhaus packaging.

All such panderings to the masses further lower both bar and standards. *Further,* because even at entirely classical performances, Lincoln Center and Carnegie Hall patrons are now seen in sneakers, T-shirts, and jeans; the arts establishment having long since abandoned cachet for cash. Truth be told, it is precisely the sense of *elitism*—a certain snob appeal, if you will—that best generates the patronage and donor dollars on which the arts depend. And there is no elitism without good example, good taste, and the adherence to standards that reflect them.

Wanted, in sum, is the replacement of degenerate exhibitionism and self-regard by the mastery, elegance, and humane concern of a bygone era. *Mais où sont les neiges d'antan?* One may start with Gilbert Highet himself: *The Outline of Homer* (1935); *The Classical Tradition: Greek and Roman Influences on Western Literature* (1949); *The Art of Teaching* (1950); *People, Places and Books* (1953); *Man's Unconquerable Mind* (1954); *A Clerk of Oxenford: Essays on Literature and Life* (1954); *Poets in a Landscape* (1957, 2010); *Talents and Geniuses: The Pleasures of Appreciation* (1957); *The Powers of Poetry* (1960); *The Anatomy of Satire* (1962); *Explorations* (1971); *The Immortal Profession: The Joys of Teaching and Learning* (1976).

Such are the sources and resources of reclamation, *Horatio operi instante* 'Horace guiding the work'.

– *finis* –

# Addendum

> Perhaps adequate translation of [Sappho's] fragments is ultimately impossible, and the hard demand that they make, first and foremost, is familiarity with their original Greek.
>
> – PETER GREEN (2015)

FOREMOST AMONG THE WORKS appearing while this book was in press is Page duBois, *Sappho* (London and New York: I.B. Tauris, 2015). Part of the publisher's Understanding Classics series, the work largely succeeds in its introductory purpose.

This concise five-chapter, 185-page primer contains most everything the beginner might want, in a narrative adroitly interweaving all the poems or poem fragments. Gone are the Marxist, radical feminist, and other liberal perspectives; gone the heady notion of boundarylessness and the conflicted self-confessions of duBois's *Sappho Is Burning* (1995). Gone the classist pleading for the "country girl" (§11), of whom duBois now simply says, "Urban elegances, finery imported from Asia, these escape the poor country girl" (71). An overly compact style, however, is the occasional price of abundant information, for example, "But [Phaon] now pursues the girls of Sicily. Sappho begs help from the goddess of Eryx, a settlement in Sicily, which had a temple dedicated to Astarte, the Phoenician form of the goddess, and in her manifestations as Aphrodite and Venus, an Italian goddess who was eventually identified with the Greek Aphrodite" (108).

Chapter I, "Understanding is a Process, and One Poem," parses the "Hymn to Aphrodite," explaining the poem's translated words and phrases with reference to the original Greek. It bears the following caveat: "For readers who may find this sort of thing tedious, I advise moving on to later chapters that set Sappho in her ancient and modern contexts" (8). This is peculiar advice for an opening chapter discussing Sappho's principal poem. The disclaimer is equally apt to Chapter II, "Sappho of Lesbos," which applies the same parsing method to Sappho's other poems. And yet the method, highlighting verbal meaning vis-à-vis literary context or myth, is helpful to the beginner.

DuBois's offerings can be prolix. The meaning of Aphrodite *doloploke* 'weaver of wiles' ('deceit, trickery') is apparent on its face. The two and one half pages adducing other occurrences of the words *deceit* and *weave* are belabored (12–15). Matters are sometimes ungainly put, as when duBois explains that Sappho "compares the lovely step and shining face of Anaktoria to the chariots of the Lydians" (52). What Sappho says of her beloved is that she (Sappho) would sooner see Anactoria's "lovely step . . . / and face gleaming radiant with light, than / Lydian charioteers or outfitted / infantry" (§4). The key to Sappho's poetry is *radiance*: light, luster, brilliance—their increase and intensity. Sappho, as earlier seen, is quoted by Athenaeus as saying, "I love the exquisite—that and yearning for the sun have won me brightness and beauty." The picture here conjured is one of a variegated brilliance in the beloved's face, superior, by comparison, to the panoplied resplendence of Lydian chariots; the luster of a beloved's face outshining myriad infantry ranged against the sun; her merest footstep more stunning than armies on the march.

Otherwise duBois skillfully explains the "complex set of associations" of Gr. *thumon*—'heart, life, breath, spirit, life itself, mind, appetite, courage', and more (16)—where Sappho beseeches Aphrodite not to subdue her *thumon* with anguish. Equally welcome is duBois's suggestion of two meanings—where most argue one or the other—for the poem's controversial opening epithet, *poikilothron'*: "The goddess is remote, on her highly wrought throne *or* garlanded with flowers" (17, emphasis added; see p. 602).

DuBois insightfully treats "Sappho in Ancient Greece and Rome" in Chapter III, ending with "Queer Sappho" in Chapter V. However, given our prevailing emphasis on translation, it is duBois's Chapter IV, "Trying to Translate Sappho," that most merits attention. DuBois does well to highlight the little known work of Sir Granville Bantock (1868–1946), *Sappho, Nine Fragments for Contralto* (1907). Noting the work's Wagnerian influence, duBois errs in saying that the songs were *translated* by Bantock's wife, Helen (135). Poet Helen Bantock did not know Greek—granted, no obstacle to today's poet-translators—and did not purport to translate from the Greek. She instead paraphrased, combined, and otherwise elaborated on the prose translations of polymath Sir Henry Thornton Wharton (*Sappho*, 1885). Wharton's was the first complete translation into English of all Sappho's then known works. He was doubtless the impetus to the Granvilles' *Sappho* composition. *Sappho* and Edward Elgar's *Sea Pictures* are considered the two most virtuosic contralto song cycles in the English language.

"Trying to Translate Sappho" is largely a panegyric to erstwhile translator John Daley. Having collaborated with Daley in his translations for the earlier-referenced deluxe *Poetry of Sappho* (Arion Press, 2011), duBois uses the same translations throughout *Sappho* (2015). DuBois's *Sappho* is dedicated "To John, for us." The dedication of Daley's one book of poems reads "for Page." The promotion of her favorite, her present and past dedicatee, is of a kind with the noted promotion of *his* favorites by Carne-Ross.

We have had occasion to remark on the theoretical doublespeak, or translational *programmes,* of those who least know the languages from which they "translate." The most aggravated example thus far has been that of Greekless translator Sherod Santos (Chapter 11). That, however, pales by comparison to duBois's exorbitant take on Daley (quoting interview excerpts):

> John Ashbery too has had his impact on Daley's thinking, a model of liberating verse from the constriction of thought; Ashbery's fragmentary, dispersive style, embedding in a whole poem allusions, thoughts and a wide variety of cultural materials, also appealed to Daley. With regard to Sappho's fragments: 'One can hear them, not need to forge them into coherence, allow for fractures of time.' Reading Ashbery with Sappho, Daley noted that Ashbery calls all art 'surreal'; Sappho's fragments created for him a 'surreal', super-real surface. Yet 'the voice still wants its coherence—it drives toward that—even in language poetry, the language drives toward that'. So Daley, in the deconstruction and reconstruction of Sappho's verses, sensed a person in the words, understood a body behind the Greek. His technique was, in consultation with me, to establish a field of possible English meanings of the Greek, alternatives for any particular phrase, and from that to develop 'a thread of the voice'. The Greek was preserved in the English translation, as a 'base meaning', as syllabic presence in metre, a 'tightness' that was maintained there, almost as a mathematical object. He saw his

> task as not producing a text 'the same' as Sappho's Greek, not 'rendering it', but rather keeping 'the count' as close as possible to the Greek metres, without insisting on replication of the stresses, the rhythmic shape of the fragments in Greek. He said at one point in the interview, echoing Flaubert: 'I am Sappho; I hope she doesn't mind' (145).

Enough has been earlier said of the execrable Ashbery, like finding like. As for the wink at Flaubert, hope ever springs eternal.

Published in the same year as Peter Green's *Iliad,* is Caroline Alexander, *The Iliad: A New Translation* (New York: HarperCollins, 2015). Alexander translates into prosaic lines of random length. This, she maintains, is "unrhymed verse, with a cadence that attempts to capture the rhythmic flow and pacing, as well as epic energy, of the Greek, and which like the Greek varies from verse to verse" (xl). Such variance between the hexameter's highly regulated thirteen-to-seventeen-beat line and Alexander's unfitted seven-to-seventeen- or nine-to-nineteen-beat line (e.g., *Il.* 4.332–333, 347–348) is too great to sustain comparison. Closer to the truth is Alexander's claim that the translation is "meant to follow unforced rhythms of natural speech"—which is to say it is cheerless prose. Translations of the *Iliad* proceed briskly apace, regardless of quality or need. See James Romm's article in *The Daily Beast* called "Translating the 'Iliad'? Who Isn't" (1/1/2016). This is in no way to discredit Alexander's excellent *The War that Killed Achilles: The True Story of Homer's Iliad and the Trojan War* (New York: Viking, 2009). Similarly, who isn't writing introductions to and "new translations" of Sappho? To Rayor and duBois in the Sappho-101 category may now be added popularizing classicist (thirteen books in as many years) Philip Freeman, *Searching for Sappho: The Lost Songs and World of the First Woman Poet* (New York: W. W. Norton, 2016). Acknowledging the difficulty of translating "a poet as subtle as Sappho," Freeman "trie[s] to let Sappho speak to us through the centuries with her own voice" (174). But whose voice is, "Who should I persuade this time?"

The undermining of the diction appropriate to Greek tragedy is apparent in recent translations by the well-intentioned and narratively compelling, but only sporadically Greek-learned, Bryan Doerries (*The Theater of War: What Ancient Greek Tragedies Can Teach Us Today* [New York: Alfred A. Knopf, 2015]). Laying no claim to literary intention or result, Doerries makes "adaptive attempts to convey the drive and action of Greek drama, clearly and directly, for contemporary readers" (8). Contemporary chic is apparent in the two-to-four-words-per-column layout of the Doerries translations. This makes a four-hundred-and-eighty-three-page paperback of three tragedies by Sophocles and of Aeschylus's *Prometheus Bound* (*All That You've Seen Here Is God: New Versions of Four Greek Tragedies* [New York: Vintage Books, 2015]). Doerries disavows any approximation to the Greek, calling his columns "a visual representation of how the words appear when filtered through [his] synapses." Like Sappho scholars intent on the interstices of Sappho's remains, Doerries probes "how omission creates an opportunity for the reader or performer to imbue the space between words with meaning." Not surprisingly, then, does the layout of these four surviving and already fully meaningful tragedies resemble half-torn papyrus sheets.

The trend toward colloquial language in the translation of epic and Greek tragedy is also apparent in recent treatments of Shakespeare. Deeming the Bard's language too difficult for today's audiences, the Oregon Shakespeare Festival will commission thirty-six playwrights over the next three years to "translate" all the plays into modern English. For the future it portends, the prototype, *Timon of Athens,* has been deemed "a hodgepodge, neither Elizabethan nor contemporary, and . . . dismal reading" in a *New York Times* op-ed called "Shakespeare in Modern English?" (10/7/2015). In stark contrast is British playwright Mike Bartlett's acclaimed teleplay *King Charles III,* written and performed in pentameters. Bartlett presents serious subject matter, decorously conveyed, with shadings of *Henry IV, Part I; Macbeth*; and *Richard II*—no less than of the British TV series *House of Cards* (1990). Resourceful pentameter and moderate archaisms, in the service of contemporary issues and references, strike a balance between old and new in this four-hundred-year anniversary of the Bard's death. As Stefania de Kenessey in music and the late Frederick Hart in sculpture, Bartlett demonstrates it is high artistic precedent—the repeatedly acknowledged best—that maintains the arts as safeguards of civilization. Such instances of hope, however, continue to battle the lowest common denominator.

# Notes

NOTES ARE ARRANGED by chapter paragraphs, italicized beginnings preceded by the number of the page on which the paragraph appears. The text to which a note attaches is in bold.

Works cited only once, or of secondary interest, appear in full below. Works cited more than once, or of primary interest, are listed in the Bibliography, appearing here by author and page number alone. Exceptions may occur. Authors of more than a single cited work are distinguished by date of publication.

PREFACE

xxvi *The objection to carryover*

**"a magpie . . . with comfort."** Hugh Kenner, "Homer's Sticks and Stones," *James Joyce Quarterly*, 6.4 (1969), 286–287.

**"[Guy] . . . of sentiment."** Beye (1981), 201.

xxvii *I followed my first publication*

**from the poem's intensity.** Ibycus was especially known in antiquity for his love of boys (pederasty). However, his two surviving love lyrics offer no indication of whether his beloved is male or female. In Sappho's great "Hymn to Aphrodite," it is only by a single feminine participle, delayed to the poem's end, that we know the beloved is female. In Sappho's other major surviving poem, *phainetai moi* 'He appears to me' (§2), it is again participial endings alone that signal a female beloved. The better part of the period's erotic poetry is, in fact, homoerotic.

xxix *The treason is apparent*

**essentially Greekless Pound's.** As Kenner himself concedes; see pp. 519, 716.

*Kenner's Ibycus is an example*

**three types of translation.** See further pp. xvii, 83.

xxx *Kenner and Pound will have*

**"the ease with . . . said it."** Spoken by classicist Otto Skutsch of classicist-poet A. E. Housman (1859–1936). Skutsch speaks of Housman's "fastidious sense of accuracy, the revolt against the vague and high sounding, which tends to disregard what is clearly ascertainable"; the antipathy toward "dishonesty, intellectual laziness, and presumption." Skutsch, 2, 6, 7. Such qualities made Housman anathema to Pound; and as Housman was of a kind with Horace, made both Housman *and* Horace anathema to Pound. See pp. 525, 547. Skutsch praises the "perfect harmony of mood and expression" that places Housman's original verse—e.g., *A Shropshire Lad* (1896)—in the "realm of great poetry." The wellspring of most of Housman's poems, observes Skutsch, was "'simply the imposition of a pattern upon a mood, . . . the mood melancholy and the pattern rigid . . . and the conscious mind . . . not mediat[ing] between them.'" Skutsch, 12. This is nothing more and nothing less than the natural conjunction of form and content.

**transgression of boundaries.** The erasure of boundaries may be said to have originated in the mid 1960s with "free love," coed dorms, and the heady notion of "interdisciplinary" and now "trans-disciplinary" studies. Such studies replaced requirements and prerequisites with a mix-and-match approach.

*However consummately conveyed*
**"Pound's brand . . . fakery."** Janine Utell, "Virtue in Scraps, Mysterium in Fragments: Robert Graves, Hugh Kenner, and Ezra Pound," *Journal of Modern Literature,* 27.1&2 (2003), 101 (referencing Robert Graves and Laura Riding, *Survey of Modernist Poetry,* 1927). Pound had the exceeding good fortune to find in Kenner a soulmate as equally imperious and unruly. On the frequent dogmatism and insufficiencies of Kenner's ex cathedra pronouncements, see Bruce Bawer, "Hugh Kenner: a sinking oeuvre," review of Hugh Kenner, *A Sinking Island, The New Criterion,* 6.6 (1988), 63–68.

More recent anti-modernists have included Philip Larkin and Martin Amis. It is otherwise noted, vis-à-vis the personalization—the self-centeredness—of modernist scholarship discussed herein, that modernism offers "a salvation by, of, and for the self"; it "declares itself as an inflation of self, a transcendental and orgiastic aggrandizement of matter and event in behalf of personal vitality." Relatedly, "A modernist culture . . . respect[s], even cherish[es], signs of division. It sees doubt as a form of health. It hunts for ethical norms through underground journeys, experiments with sensation, and a mocking suspension of accredited values. . . . It cultivates, in Thomas Mann's formulation, 'a sympathy for the abyss.'" Howe, 4–5. The tendency of modernism toward nihilism is apparent. First published in 1962, Howe's *Decline of the New* was premature in its assessment that "modernist literature seems now to be coming to an end." It was further impervious to "postmodernism" and its progeny. Kenner's *The Pound Era* (1971) would raise Pound to cult status, giving modernist studies a decades-long infusion. Howe locates the period of modernist literature "in the past hundred years," i.e., 1862–1962, thereby rightly dating it to Walt Whitman and the literary aggrandizement of self at its source.

xxxi *Each translation in Horace*
**"some poets . . . Latin bone."** McClatchy, *Odes of Horace,* 6 (other paragraph quotations also from *Odes of Horace,* 6).

*The volume exhibits other*
**"subtlety of tone . . . variety."** Quoted here from the front flap. Even if the publisher writes the copy, the author has likely approved it.

*The reception of McClatchy's*
**estimable . . . Mendelsohn.** See Mendelsohn (2004 and 2012).
**classicist John Talbot.** See Talbot (2003).

*We have in truth reached*
**favorably reviewing Anthony.** Anthony Verity, tr., *The Iliad* (Oxford: Oxford Univ. Press, 2011), reviewed by John Talbot (2012).
**"Nobody would . . . exemplary."** Talbot (2012), 25.
**"the sheer . . . translations."** Stephen Miller, tr., *The Iliad* (New York: The Free Press, 2011), xvi.
**"If Greek . . . and vice versa."** W. H. Auden, ed., *The Portable Greek Reader* (New York: Penguin Books, 1948), 4.

xxxiii *The downturn is not merely*
**"forces . . . rhetorical pitch."** Talbot (2012), 25–26.

xxxiii *Is no manner of elevation*

**The Best of the Achaeans.** The Best of the Achaeans—*aristos Achaiōn*—is Achilles, protagonist of the *Iliad*. Achaea is the district of Greece (northern Peloponnese) in which the royal city of Mycenae was located. In the second millennium BC, Mycenae, a military stronghold, was a major center of Greek civilization. The period of Greek history from circa 1600 BC to 1100 BC is called *Mycenaean*, coinciding with the Greek Bronze Age (the flowering of Homeric epic dated to 750 BC). It is from Mycenae/Argos that came Agamemnon, leader of the Greek expedition to Troy. *Achaioi'* 'Achaeans' is one of several Homeric designations for Greeks. The two others are *Argeîoi* 'Argives' (after the city of Argos) and *Danaoi'* 'Danaans' (after the earliest inhabitants of Argos, named for the city's founder Danaus). The three are used interchangeably in Homer for metrical reasons. Though the term *Greeks* is never used in Homer, I use it throughout this work, following the accepted practice. My phrase "The Best of the Achaeans" adopts the title of a seminal work on ancient Greek heroism. See Gregory Nagy, *The Best of the Achaeans: Concepts of the Hero in Archaic Greek Poetry* (Baltimore: Johns Hopkins Univ. Press, 1979; 2nd ed. 1999, with new introduction).

xxxiv *It is, in the end, a fine*

**"From Pope . . . point."** Talbot (2012), 29.
**As Dr. Samuel Johnson.** See further pp. 110, 478.
**"we cannot . . . in Pope."** Eliot (1944), 17.

xxxv *Since Greek lyric and*

**"Barnard's Sappho . . . Sappho."** Prins (1996a), 63. The most recent hagiography is that of Sarah Barnsley, *Mary Barnard, American Imagist* (New York: State Univ. of New York Press, 2013). Barnsley makes a tenuous case for Barnard's "sand poetics," arguing that the "sawmills and seashore" of Barnard's home in Ocean Park, WA, were "physical and geographical expressions of the kind of spare plainness to be found in Japanese haiku form or Sappho's fragments." Barnsley, 59, 130. Ocean Park is a far cry from Lesbos. What we ultimately have in Barnsley is an English professor writing on a sparsely Greek-learned Barnard, whose *Sappho: A New Translation* (1958) was done more with reference to an Italian crib than with any true grasp or appreciation of Sappho's Greek (see Chapter 11).

xxxvi *The work's range of*

**"everything . . . interconnected."** Herodotus, xxvii (Waterfield, tr.).
**admired . . . and charm.** W. Kendrick Pritchett, tr., *Dionysius of Halicarnassus, On Thucydides* (Berkeley and London: Univ. of California Press, 1975), §23, 16.
**"Digressions . . . my plan."** Herodotus 4.30. See Aubrey de Sélincourt, tr., *Herodotus, the Histories* (New York: Penguin Books, 1972), 280.

PART I, CHAPTER 1

3 *The translations here*

**Sappho, Alcman, Anacreon, etc.** Pronounced (emphasis bolded): **Sa**-fō, **alk**-mən, ə-**na**-krē-on, ahr-**kil**-ə-kəs, and **i**-bə-kəs). The poetry of Homer and the lyric poets (8th–6th centuries BC) is properly called archaic Greek poetry (Gr. *archaios* 'old'; Eng. *archaeology*). The terminus for the archaic period may be placed at the landmark of Xerxes's invasion of Greece, 480–479 BC. Snodgrass, 212. Archaic literature is generally distinguished from the classical literature of the "Golden Age" of Athens (5th century BC), followed in turn by Hellenistic literature in the aftermath of Alexander (4th century BC). Writers nonetheless often use *classical* or *ancient* to include *archaic*, though *archaic* provides a significant chronological and cultural referent.

*Popularizing translator*
**"'imitations'... their gold."** Roche (1966), xviii.

4 *The word Lesbian originally*
**inhabitant of Lesbos.** The play between "Lesbian" (an inhabitant of Lesbos) and "lesbian" (a female lover of women) has persisted since antiquity. The latter meaning—to the recent displeasure of Lesbos residents—has of course enjoyed the greater recognition. In 2008, Lesbians brought suit to limit use of the term to residency alone. They further sued to have the "Homosexual and Lesbian Community of Greece" drop the word "lesbian" from its title, claiming it offended island identity. One witness testified, "My wife is a Lesbian, my daughter is a Lesbian, and I am a Lesbian." The testimony elicited courtroom laughter, which the witness used to confirm the truth of his claim: that the term was one of shame and ridicule. On the other hand, the chief complainant, one Dimitris Lambrou, characterized the suffering of Lesbians as "psychological and moral rape." The Mayor of Lesbos dissociated himself from the case, and several witnesses testified that the island's economy had benefited from the term "lesbian" (as it surely does, the tourism industry most of all). The lawsuit failed, of course, as there is no deleting 2,700 years of history and historical association, though many have been the attempts to manipulate them.

The observations and quotations in the above paragraph are indebted to Sophie J. V. Mills, "Lesbians and lesbians in the Garden of Sappho," a paper delivered at the annual meeting of the Classical Association of the Middle West and South, Oklahoma City, March 25–27, 2010. I am grateful to Professor Mills for providing me with a copy of her paper. See also Hauke Goos, "The Lesbian Man: A Greek's Crusade to Protect His Island's Name," *Spiegel Online International*, 7/11/2008 (Christopher Sultan, tr.).
**distinction ... little observed.** In the groundbreaking *Sappho Was a Right-On Woman: A Liberated View of Lesbianism* (New York: Stein and Day, 1972), authors Sidney Abbott and Barbara Love capitalize *Lesbian* throughout, making a proper name of a sexual type. The usage comports with their capitalization of *Feminism, Gay Liberation,* and *Women's Liberation,* which the authors were then championing as movements. The book's title comes from the concluding line of a poem called "Thinking Back Lesbian," written by a friend of the authors and quoted in the book's acknowledgments. The book itself has nothing to do with Sappho, other than by its token formulation of the poet as feminist ideal. It is rather "a very practical book for women who have, or are about to, come out. It is politically correct and deeply unsexy, though the British Library still sees fit to catalog it as a 'private case book.'" M. Reynolds, 359.
**sapphic ... lesbianism.** A survey of the term *lesbian,* as defined in mid-twentieth-century dictionaries, appears in Hallett, (1979) 452, n. 19, and may be summarized as follows: "erotic" is the chief non-geographic meaning of *Lesbian*; "female homosexuality" (as a medical term) is the chief meaning of *lesbianism*; *no* sexual meaning is given the word *Lesbian*; "erotic," ahead of "pertaining to female homosexuality," is the meaning of *Lesbian*. A history of the term *Sapphism* appears in Hallett (1979), 451, n. 17, and may be summarized as follows: *Sapphism*, according to the *Oxford English Dictionary* (1933), first appears in *Billings's National Medical Dictionary* (1809). A June 1901 issue of the British medical journal *Lancet* notes that *Sapphism* and other vices have been treated in French but not yet in English novels.

Hallett also notes that the French view of Sappho as a homosexual owes much to the publication of Pierre Louÿs's *Les Chansons de Bilitis* (*Songs of Bilitis,* 1895). These "purport to be translations of an ancient Greek manuscript, the autobiography of a peasant girl who had belonged to Sappho's homosexual circle and later became a temple prostitute." For discussion, see Venuti (1998), 34–46; Apter, 162–167; DeJean, 276–280.

For exhaustive bibliography on "what it means to identify oneself as lesbian, the relationship between lesbian and gender constructions, and in which way lesbian existence challenges social arrangements," see Brooten, 18–21 and n. 38. On lesbian history and the history of female homoerotic attraction from medieval times to the present, see Brooten, 20, n. 38.

***(h)omoios* '. . . like, related'.** The parenthesized *h* represents a non-alphabetic *h*-sound, represented by a *c*-shaped "rough breathing" mark atop an initial Greek vowel. The Greek word *(h)omoios* is thus written ὅμοιος, with rough breathing and acute accent, both on the first vowel. I parenthesize the *h*-sound, except in proper names.

**was largely transitory.** "We are dealing with an institutionalized type of sexuality, in which the preferences of those involved may have been of little consequence. . . . [I]n the establishment of relationships between Sappho and her girls alliances between prominent families probably played a larger part than her own heart. Our sources about the pederastic relationships of men indicate that they were primarily a mark of honour, and the whole practice may ultimately go back to an initiation ritual." Lardinois (1989), 30.

5 *Sappho and the other*

**to what Margaret Reynolds.** Quotes and paraphrases from Reynolds, 81–82.

*Greek epic and lyric*

**Biblical translation . . . germane.** For elaboration on the roles of the Bible and Homer in the formation of Western culture, see George Steiner's rhapsodically erudite "Preface to the Hebrew Bible," and "Homer in English," in Steiner (1996), 40–87 and 88–107, respectively.

6 *The Septuagint was the*

**Greek by seventy-two scholars.** The history of biblical translation into English is beyond the scope of this work, notwithstanding my discussion of it vis-à-vis the translation of Homer and Greek lyric. For an excellent introduction to the Bible in English (in an entirely absorbing book), see Barbara W. Tuchman, Ch. 5, "The Bible in English," in *Bible and Sword: England and Palestine from the Bronze Age to Balfour* (New York: Ballantine Books, 1956). See also Bruce M. Metzger, *The Bible in Translation: Ancient and Modern Versions* (Grand Rapids: Baker Publishing Group, 2001); Glen G. Scorgie, Mark L. Strauss, and Steven M. Voth, eds., *The Challenge of Bible Translation: Communicating God's Word to the World* (Grand Rapids: Zondervan, 2003); and David Lawton, "The Bible," in Roger Ellis, ed., *The Oxford History of Literary Translation in English, Vol. 1: to 1550* (Oxford: Oxford Univ. Press, 2008), 194–233.

**unanimity in translation history.** See the account of the Hellenistic Jewish Philosopher Philo of Alexandria (1st century AD), *On the Life of Moses*, 2.25–44. The legend also appears in the Talmud: "King Ptolemy once gathered 72 elders. He placed them in 72 chambers, each in a separate chamber, without revealing why they were summoned. He entered each one's room and said: 'Write for me the Torah of Moshe, your teacher.' God put it in the heart of each to translate identically, one with the other." Mishnah, Order *Moed*, Tractate *Megillah*, pages 9a–9b.

*Over five hundred years*

**translation . . . Saint Jerome.** Jerome, more accurately, translated the Old Testament—except for the Apocryphal books of Baruch, Ecclesiasticus, Wisdom of Solomon, and First and Second Maccabees—while revising existing Latin versions of Psalms and the

Gospels. The Latin into which selected parts of the Old Testament had been translated prior to Jerome's Vulgate was known as Old Latin (*Vetus Latina*).

*Jerome undertook Hebrew*
**monumental influence.** See further Steiner (1996), 47.
**"prompted . . . thankfulness."** Rhodes and Lupas, 73.

7 *Tyndale's Old and New*
**a "commanding effect."** Steiner (1996), 49.
**(together with Shakespeare).** On the relationship between Shakespeare and the KJB, see p. 486.

*The primary impetus to*
**"somewhat . . . common sense."** Murray (1912), 8.
**savagely sardonic . . . general.** See Simon Goldhill, *Who Needs Greek? Contests in the Cultural History of Hellenism* (Cambridge: Cambridge Univ. Press, 2002), 224 ("Arnold made his name as a polemicist through his savagely sardonic critique of translations of Homer while he was Professor of Poetry at Oxford.").
**"The Bible is . . . of style."** Arnold, 220. Arnold distinguishes between diction and style. As concerns diction, the Bible in translation is an excellent source of diction for the Homeric translator. As concerns style, the Bible, of many genres and periods, has little of Homer's stylistic uniformity. The Homeric translator must accordingly "discriminate truly between what will suit him and what will not." On the difference between Homeric and Old Testament style, see Erich Auerbach's seminal introductory essay "Odysseus' Scar" in the equally seminal *Mimesis: The Representation of Reality in Western Literature* (1953). For the language of Homer as "comparable with yet radically different from that of Scripture," see Steiner (1996), 95.
**"To Speak . . . 'speak the Bible.'"** Steiner (1996), 83.
**"has been . . . exemplary legacy."** Steiner (1975, 1988), 488.

8 *Among the translations*
**Arnold's famous challenge.** For Homeric translation in the immediate aftermath of Arnold's *On Translating Homer*, see pp. 450–451.
**"the Greek . . . nature."** Andrew Lang and Samuel Henry Butcher, *The Odyssey of Homer Done into English Prose* (New York: Macmillan, 1893, 3rd ed; first pub. 1879), Preface, ix. For a discussion of prose translations of Homer, see Edward S. le Comte, "Homer Transposed," *Classical Journal*, 45.7 (1950), 315–321.
**"the Biblical . . . to offer."** Lang and Butcher, ix.
**"Not everyone . . . well, God."** Charles McGrath, "Thou Shalt Not Be Colloquial," *New York Times*, 4/24/2011.
**"at the usual . . . popular."** Higham & Bowra, c.

9 *Whereas the literatures*
**"supra-national literary past."** Otis, 22 (as adapted).
**mid-thirteenth century BC.** Herodotus 2.145 (dating the Trojan War to approximately eight hundred years before his own time, or c. 1250 BC). Cf. George W. Shaw, "The Period of the Exodus," *The Monist*, 16.2 (1906), 207–208 (dating the Exodus to c. 1240 BC). See also Walter Burkert, "Lydia Between East and West or How to Date the Trojan War: A Study in Herodotus," in Carter and Morris eds., 139–148.
**Venetus . . . Masoretic Text.** See pp. 599, 606.
**rational or anthropomorphic.** See Griffin, 40–42 ("the fantastic, the miraculous, and the romantic" treated within "austere limits" in the *Iliad*); Webster, 292–293 ("belief

in human reason," "manageable way of thinking about the gods," "rejection of ecstatic and magic elements"). The *Odyssey*, of course, to the extent expressly dealing with the fantastic, differs. The contrast between the *Iliad* and *Odyssey* thus illustrates early Greek literature's ability to distinguish between realism and fantasy. The Old Testament for its part preserves mythological traces alone, as in the reference to the bygone "Sons of God" marrying mortal women (Gen. 6:1–4), and such discretely staged and self-contained episodes as Saul's visit, following the death of Samuel, to the witch of Endor (1 Sam. 28). While Hesiod's *Theogony* fully depicts Zeus in the final phase of succession, battling the mythic beast Typhoeus, the *Iliad* only alludes to the episode (Zeus helped by the *Theogony*'s hundred-handed Briareus, *Il.* 1.396–406). Similarly, the Old Testament only alludes to God's victory over Leviathan (Ps. 74, 104, Isa. 27.1, Job 41.1–34). See further Shinan and Zakovitch, *From Gods to God* (2012), and Herbert Gordon May, "Pattern and Myth in the Old Testament," *The Journal of Religion*, 21.3 (1941), 285–299.

*The connection between*
**"for thousands of . . . world."** Anonymous review of William Mure of Caldwell, *A Critical History of the Language and Literature of Ancient Greece*, Vols. I–III, *Quarterly Review*, 87 (1850), 437. Wolf argued brazenly, and to devastating effect, that there was no historical "Homer," that the *Iliad* and *Odyssey* were a composite of poems sung by different bards, and that the poems' original forms were hopelessly beyond reach. This, of course, long preceded oral-compositional awareness or analysis. We would now say that "Homer," if not an historical person, was the summation of, or designation given, centuries of oral storytelling tradition; that the Homeric poems came to incorporate the best the tradition had to offer; and that given the perfection in which they have reached us—the appreciation of which long postdates Wolf and those arguing his thesis—their original or intermediary versions are of no account.
**"But Homer . . . for life."** Lang, 84. And further, "Homer, in truth is to be matched only with Shakespeare, and of Shakespeare he has not the occasional willfulness, freakishness, and modish obscurity. He is a poet all of gold, universal as humanity, simple as childhood, musical now as the flow of his own rivers, now as the heavy plunging wave of his own ocean." Lang, 87–88.

10 *I include basic discussion*
**"producing . . . of his age."** Markley, 20.

*It is by fixing rhythm*
**sense of the word *art*.** For the derivation of the word *art* from the Greek root **ar-*, see pp. 415–416.
**civilization's hallmark being.** Art historian Kenneth Clark has famously noted that a sense of permanence is central to our concept of civilization: "Civilized man . . . must feel that he belongs somewhere in space and time; that he consciously looks forward and looks back." Clark, 14, 17.
**"is thematically . . . cohesion."** Nagy (1979/1999), 9, n. 7.
**reflected in their languages.** See Emile Benveniste, *Le vocabulaire des institutions indo-européennes* (Paris: Les Editions de Minuit, 1969), tome 2, 100–101.

11 *As the "essence of*
**"[t]he essence . . . other people."** Albert Stanburrough Cook, "The Artistic Ordering of Life: An Address (1898)" (Whitefish: Kessinger Legacy Reprints, n.d.), 10. Cook, an Old English scholar and philologist, has added the notion of permanence to Horace's much-adapted formulation:

> Aut prodesse volunt aut delectare poetae
> aut simul et iucunda et idonea dicere vitae . . .
> omne tulit punctum qui miscuit utile dulci
> lectorem delectando pariterque monendo.
>
> Poets wish to be either profitable or delightful,
> or to speak what is at once pleasant and suited to
> life. . . . He hits the mark who mingles useful with
> agreeable, equally admonishing and delighting the reader.
> [*AP* 333–334, 343–344]

*This book contains an*
**Pound . . . present morass.** Though the quoted author intends it as commendation, the following reads equally well as indictment. Not surprisingly, Pound is the *fons malorum*:

> Clearly related to this question is the vexed issue of poetic diction, always an important and tricky factor in translations or adaptations of classical poetry. The campaign for the modernization of poetic diction associated with modernism has been extremely successful. Though 'conventional' translations—translations relying on metre, standard syntax, homogeneous vocabulary, and perhaps even rhyme—are by no means an extinct category, it is now absolutely normal for a translator of Sappho or Callimachus to discard metre altogether, use fragmented syntax, simplify the vocabulary so as to exclude any references that might be obscure to a modern reader, and imitate the forms of modern poetry; in other words, to employ techniques associated with Pound's procedures as a translator and imitator. [Svensson, 113–114]

12 *The practice of original-languageless*
**"Strange new . . . Greek."** Lind (1983), 69–70.
**"There . . . mother tongue."** Preface to *Sylvae,* Walker ed., 246–258.
**"Particularly . . . any Greek."** Balmer (2013), 6 (of Christopher Logue).

13 *We have reached the*
**Scribimus . . . poemata passim.** *Ep.* 2.1.117.

*The failure to distinguish*
**Steiner's . . . "Homer in English."** Quotations in this and the following paragraph from Steiner (1996), 90, 93, 98–99.
**"the unique radioactive tracer."** The coequal listing of learned and unlearned translators persists to this date, more than forty years following Steiner's *After Babel.* In Greek epic and lyric, Sappho translator Josephine Balmer recently offers Richmond Lattimore, Mary Barnard, Robert Fitzgerald, Willis Barnstone, Guy Davenport, and Robert Fagles (all discussed below) as proof that "The late 1950s and 1960s saw a flowering of confident work." Balmer (2013), 35–36, 37–38. Lattimore, in the translation of epic, lyric, and tragedy, is in a class of his own, while Barnstone and Davenport lack all credibility. Balmer, moreover, finds "clear precedents" in the authors least favored in the present work: Ezra Pound, *Homage to Sextus Propertius* (1919), Christopher Logue's Homeric pastiches (1963, 1981, 1995, 2004), and Alice Oswald's "version" of the *Iliad* (2011). These allow her to feel "liberated both from and by the text." Balmer (2013), 182–183.
**the "translational *series*."** Armstrong (2008), 171–172. The saving grace of Armstrong's list (cf. preceding note), is its omission of Christopher Logue.

*Notes Steiner, "The radioactive*
**"to understand . . . translate."** Steiner (1998), xii.

14 *In After Babel, a seminal*
**In *After Babel* . . . reverence.** Quotations in this and the following paragraph, unless otherwise noted, are from Steiner (1998), 375–380.

*"In Pound's imitations*
**"If our age . . . Pound."** Steiner (1966), 32.
**"Inevitably . . . the term."** Steiner (1966), 34.
**"Ninety percent . . . be so."** Steiner (1998), 417.

15 *Historically viewed, my*
**quarrel first emerged.** For discussion see Simonsuuri, Chs. 1–3. The controversy soon surfaced in England in Jonathan Swift's "The Battle of the Books," a satire published as part of the prolegomenon to his *A Tale of the Tub* (1704). See also Levine, Ch. 1 ("John Evelyn and the Education of Antiquity") and Ch. 2 ("Evelyn between the Ancients and Moderns").
**"Next to Horace . . . is."** Stewart, 17. Mary Stewart joined the faculty of the University of Montana in 1905 as an instructor in English and Latin, where she also served as Dean of Women for eight years. Her selected translations from Catullus were completed in 1904, at or around the time she received her B.A. from the University of Colorado. They were published in 1915. Stewart's collection begins on a plangently Catullan note with a moving poem to her deceased sister, beginning, "Oh, Sister of mine, so beloved." One chills reading it.

16 *The updatings tendency is*
**"personal voice theory."** See Judith P. Hallett and Thomas Van Nortwick, eds., *Compromising Traditions: the personal voice in classical scholarship* (London and New York: Rutledge, 1997).
**"a very . . . literature."** M. Katz (2000), 510.
**"drive to . . . feminism."** See Charles Rowan Beye, "A response," in Hallett and Van Nortwick, eds., 160–161. Beye's generally balanced response does not prevent his noting "the great danger and weakness in the personal voice theoretical approach: that it leads into endless speculation about the critic rather than the text. To the extent that the personal voice theory derives from the feminist movement and to the extent that women (in the USA at least) are acculturated to analyze other persons—what dismissive males call 'gossip'—such endless speculation can perhaps please the one sex and repulse the other." Personal voice theory, in a word, is divisive—in a way and at a time it can ill afford to be. Serious study does not come packaged in a professor's biography or personal views. It may well reflect them, but that is for the student to discover, not be hammered with. Feminist-inspired personal voice theory was subject to a searing review by Victor Davis Hanson, "'Too Much Ego in Your Cosmos,'" *Arion*, 3rd series, 6.1 (1998), 137–168 (characterizing its grievance-peddling as smug, careerist, calculating, and pusillanimous). The most recent personal voice practitioner is Sappho translator Josephine Balmer, *Piecing Together the Fragments* (2013).

*A tributary of the*
**the so-called Homer War.** Simonsuuri, 46. See also Julie Candler Hayes, "Meaning and Modernity: Anne Dacier and the Homer Debate," in *Translation, Subjectivity & Culture in France and England, 1600–1800* (Stanford: Stanford Univ. Press, 2009), 121–140.
**inveterate Sappho translator.** Four editions of Anacreon and Sappho, translation and commentary, over thirty-five years: 1681, 1696, 1699, and 1716.
**Ainsi . . . Héroes de l'Iliade.** Simonsuuri, 51 (as quoted).

*The revisionist agenda*
**"La Motte's words . . . message."** Simonsuuri, 51.
**taste *(corruption du goût)*.** Simonsuuri, 53.

17 *We are reminded, by*
**"had . . . metrical practice."** Sowerby (1986), 2.
**"Long . . . of his numbers."** Sowerby (1986), 2 (quoting Dryden's "Dedication of the *Aeneis*"; *Aeneis* Lat. for *Aeneid*).
**"provided . . . in the world."** James C. C. Mays, *Coleridge's Experimental Poetics* (London and New York: Palgrave Macmillan, 2013), 164.

18 *Seeking to flag and*
**aesthetic . . . lyric and epic.** The translation of tragedy, while also requiring a mastery of Greek, involves considerations of staging and verbal projection. Projection and audience comprehension are thus additional factors in any modern translation. See Simon Goldhill, "Translations: Finding a Script," in *How to Stage a Greek Tragedy Today* (Chicago and London: Univ. of Chicago Press, 2007), 153–188.
**"a theory . . . of art."** Forster, 109.
**"This version . . . English."** Marris, v.

*A return to pre-theoretical*
**"a reactionary . . . past."** Steiner's self-description, in Peter Applebome, "A Humanist and Elitist? Perhaps," *New York Times*, 4/18/1998.
**philologically based.** Philology (Gr. *phil-* 'love' + *logos* 'word') is the study of literature with reference to word usage and syntactic structure in comparative contexts. One speaks in this connection of "semantic range," meaning the fullness of interpretive possibility based on the aggregate of a word's attested usages. Philology is essential to sound interpretation. It is essential to translation as an interpretative art.

The term *philologus* 'philologist' is of Alexandrian origin. The term "lies halfway between scholar and critic and denotes a man with sufficient learning in language and literature to evaluate and give permanent form to poetic text." Fantham, 222. Originating in German universities, Classical Philology was introduced to this country by the American-born, German-educated Basil Gildersleeve (1831–1924). After a twenty-year teaching career as professor of Greek at the University of Virginia, Gildersleeve was wooed to The Johns Hopkins University, newly founded in 1876, where he introduced the philological method to graduate study. In 1880, he founded the *American Journal of Philology*, to date the oldest and among the most highly regarded classics journals in North America. During the Civil War, Gildersleeve fought for the Confederacy and was discharged after being severely wounded in the leg. Of further interest is the brief appendix "The Art of Philology," in Bruno Gentili, *Poetry and Its Public in Ancient Greece*, A. Thomas Cole, tr. (Baltimore and London: Johns Hopkins Univ. Press, 1988), 223–233.
**"A translator's first . . . task."** Graves (1965), 54. As further concerns decorum, we may note the formulation of Lane Cooper (1875–1959), a classics-trained professor of English:

> The doctrine of "decorum," growing out of Aristotle's demand that tragic character should be "good," "true to type," "true to life," and "self-consistent," drew to itself other elements from the *Poetics*: that character should suit the action, and the parts of this should suit each other—all should be *appropriate*. Reinforced by Horatian maxims, and by the counsels of Roman rhetoric, the doctrine becomes an art of poetry in itself. Decorum, says Milton, "is the grand masterpiece to observe" (114).

For a recent appreciation of the redoubtable Lane Cooper, see Michael Dirda, "Learning from Lane Cooper," *The New Criterion*, 32.6 (2014), 14–19. Cooper was everything today's classics-deficient professors of English and classicist-wannabes are not.

*Much is also to blame*
***radical* feminist scholarship.** For purposes of simplification, I sometimes refer to *feminist* and *feminism* as shorthand for *radical feminist* and *radical feminism*. This is neither to overlook nor slight the legitimate concerns of *normative* feminism. Radical feminism, largely the product of college campuses, speaks little to the concerns of women outside of academe. Such women may be little aware of their campus counterparts' thinking (or language), or of the literary, historical, and philosophical groundings of radical feminist thought. The dichotomy is largely one between theorists and activists, thinkers and doers.

Recent feminist theory, to paraphrase a feminist critic, has been criticized for its inability to address the needs of non-academics in a language accessible to people who do not have a Ph.D. in philosophy. Feminist work influenced by post-structuralism especially, is largely incomprehensible to people who are not at home with the rhetoric of Western philosophy. Cortiel, 6. It was not always so. See, e.g., Jean Curthoys, *Feminist Amnesia: The Wake of Women's Liberation* (London and New York: Rutledge, 1997), tracing feminist theory from demands for equality in the 1960s to abstractions divorced from reality.

19 *I aim, in biblical parlance*
**"More than . . . human mind."** Skutsch, 10.

CHAPTER 2

21 *This reality, however*
**morphologically simple.** Despite peculiarities of spelling and pronunciation, and a richly redundant vocabulary, English might be considered the simplest and most widely used of modern languages. Simplification of morphology—the form and structure of a language—is the general rule of linguistic development. Sanskrit, the earliest well-attested Indo-European language, is the most complex of all; ancient Greek, for all its difficulty, less so; Latin, even less so than Greek; and the modern "vernacular" languages that developed from Latin—Italian, French, Spanish, Portuguese, and others—simpler yet than Latin. English, deriving from Anglo-Saxon, with an infusion of Latinate French following the Norman Conquest (1066), has evolved from the now unintelligible Old English of *Beowulf*, through Chaucer, Spenser, Shakespeare, and Milton, to a model of verbal and grammatical simplicity, becoming the "international language."
**older usages or archaism.** For the function and effect of archaism see pp. 67–68, 77, 267–268, 693–694, 709–710.

*It is amusing to note*
**humanist Ermolao Barbaro.** The paragraph is adapted from Jill Kraye, "Pico and the Relationship of Rhetoric and Philosophy," in M. V. Dougherty, ed., *Pico della Mirandola: New Essays* (Cambridge: Cambridge Univ. Press, 2008), 13–36. I am grateful to the late Marion Leathers Kuntz (1924–2010), classicist and Renaissance scholar, for urging this book upon me.
**"*fidelity* to an . . . manner."** Arnold, 150.
**"the union of . . . translation."** Arnold, 153.

22 *Distinguished from the*
**distinctions . . . "translation."** See discussion, pp. 107–109, of Sherod Santos, *Greek Lyric Poetry: A New Translation* (2005).

*It is Sappho who most*
**"The monolithic . . . work."** Balmer (2006), 184.
**Greekless . . . and Virgil.** Greekless translators generally self-excuse the deficiency, their banner-waving backers doubling as line checkers and introduction writers to the finished product. See pp. 11–12, 89, 91, 434, 481, 483–484 (discussing Robert Fitzgerald and Robert Fagles, among others). The most shameless instance is Dennis Hall's *Odyssey* (Greenwich, 1978). With a riff on Shakespeare's "Little Latin and less Greek," Hall boasts, "So, knowing little English [poetry] and less Greek, I decided to do it [i.e., translate Homer] myself."

23 *Aligned with the would-be*
**Hartman proposed that.** See Geoffrey H. Hartman, "How Creative Should Literary Criticism Be?" *New York Times Book Review*, 4/5/1981; cf. Mark Bauerlein, "What Dido did, etc.," *The New Criterion*, 32.4 (2013), 4–5.
**major example . . . approach.** The personalization of fragmentary sources is of Victorian pedigree. Charlotte Brontë's academic writings are noted for their "potential for imaginative free play extended by popular Greek's discourse of fragmentation." Similarly, Brontë's "regard for the ancient Greek past as a malleable narrative space derived not from Aristotle but from her exposure to the discourse of fragmentation constitutive of her popular Greek sources. . . ." Fiske, 67, 76. More recently, "Even the fact that these poets came down to us in fragmentary form promoted their 'marginal' image, as Pound and H.D., Hugh Kenner and Guy Davenport created an aesthetic of brokenness and silence around these partial texts." Wills (2005), 55.

*The emphasis on one's*
**"Interpretation of . . . detail."** M. Katz (2000), 520.
**"As the . . . voice criticism."** M. Katz (2000), 520.
**The process . . . programmatic.** The programmatic nature of the process is apparent in Katz's detailed description, almost chapter by chapter, of works employing "contemporary" or "new critical" approaches to Sappho—a "variety" or "broad spectrum" of such approaches, to be sure. These are variously "innovative, subtly argued, and complex"—involving "feminist perspectives," the "function of gender," the "intensity and specificity of [the poems'] sexual passion," women's "active negotiation with social norms," "intersubjectivity" in the "construction" of the "specific character of Sappho's erotics," "narrativization," "archaic anteriority to the classical norm," and "radical alterity." See Katz (2000), 520–525 (discussing books—see bibliography herein—by Greene, L. Wilson, Stehle, Snyder [1997], Williamson, and duBois). On the nature of theoryspeak, see pp. 397–398.
**"a contemporary . . . *thiasos*."** McEvilley, 383.
**"has almost . . . in academia."** McEvilley, 383 (and n. 6 for quotation). See further p. 392.

24 *The present work takes*
**"As alluring . . . own reflection."** Mendelsohn (2003), 28. I quote, here as elsewhere, from Mendelsohn's earlier version, finding it more outspoken (and helpful) than its 2012 revision (cf. "which is some kind of responsible representation of Sappho herself to the wider world" [2003] versus "which, you might think, ought to be," etc. [2012]).

*The greatness of Greek*
**"the nation . . . whole period."** Johann Peter Eckermann, *Conversations of Goethe with Johann Peter Eckermann*, John Oxenford, tr. (New York: Da Capo, 1998), 201.
**"self-absorption . . . mastery."** See Algis Váliunas, "Goethe's Magnificent Self," *Commentary* (January 2008), 48.

25 *I focus first on*

**of stunning translations.** In an effort to make these better known, I reproduce in PART III as many as Tucker offers. Also reproduced for their éclat (though in fewer numbers) are the translations of English classicist-poet-critic-novelist F. L. Lucas (1894–1967), and several by English poet and literary critic John Addington Symonds (1840–1893).

**"to compare . . . possess it."** Ruskin, 289. It was Arnold's dissatisfaction with Ruskin's 1860 "The English Translators of Homer" (published in the *National Review*) that led to his own *On Translating Homer* (1861).

26 *Turning for comparative*

**"a wittily . . . Greek culture."** Meghan O'Rourke, "Hermetic Hotties: What is Anne Carson doing on The L Word," *Slate*. Web. 2/11/2004. A review and high commendation of Carson's many works appears in classicist Glen Bowersock's (b. 1936) 2007 review of Carson's Euripides translations.

**lack being . . . and attainment.** Compare Germaine Greer, *The Female Eunuch* (New York: HarperCollins, 1970), positing the stereotypical concept of femininity as one of "lack" and constructing woman as a castrated man. Carson's is surely the more productive approach.

*Page duBois, a professor*

**pride . . . and discussion.** M. Katz (2000), 524–525.

**"a sophisticated . . . makes."** M. Katz (2000), 525.

27 *Marxism has everywhere*

**China, North . . . campus.** On April 1, 2011, New York University held a conference titled "Academic Freedom in the 1960s," sponsored by the university's Frederic Ewen Academic Freedom Center. The bland academic language could not mask the conference's true agenda: vindication of Stalin, whitewash of communism, and wholesale leftist reappraisal of the recent past. See Ronald Radosh, "University's Soft Spot for Stalinists," *New York Post*, 3/23/2011. The apologists, however, persist: see Terry Eagleton, *Why Marx Was Right* (New Haven & London: Yale Univ. Press, 2011). See also Anthony Grafton, "Our Universities: Why Are They Failing?" *New York Review of Books*, 11/24/2011 (drawing on eight recent publications).

**"Whatever . . . against it."** Adapted from Charles McGrath, "Loose Canon," review of Harold Bloom, *The Western Canon*, *The New Yorker*, 9/26/94 (see Bloom, 486). Bloom further laments:

> I have very little confidence that literary education will survive its current malaise. . . . Finding myself now surrounded by professors of hip-hop; by clones of Gallic-Germanic theory; by ideologues of gender and of various sexual persuasions; by multiculturalists unlimited, I realize that the Balkanization of literary studies is irreversible. All of these Resenters of the aesthetic value of literature are not going to go away, and they will raise up institutional resenters after them. [Bloom, 483]

CHAPTER 3

29 *Archilochus of Paros*

**epic outlook (e.g., §§82, 83).** On Archilochean deviance from the Homeric outlook, see further Barker and Christensen, "Flight Club," etc. (2006).

**I omit . . . two poems.** Translated and discussed by H. D. Rankin, *Archilochus of Paros* (Park Ridge: Noyes Press, 1977), 61–64.

30 *As concerns poetic meter*
**"one of the most . . . meters."** Will, 94.
**"aural . . . sensuous meaning."** Will, 94.
**poetry as discussed herein.** See pp. 18, 438, 501–502, 571, 711.

*Direct evidence of*
**Lycambes and his daughters.** Paragraph summarized from Nagy (1976). The phrase "assumed personality and the imaginary situation" is Gerber's (1964), 212–216.
**"assumed personality . . . situation."** Even as "Archilochus" may be a literarily "assumed personality," Lycambes, it is suggested, is "a character constructed to question the value and status of the iambist [i.e., the vituperative poet in iambic meter] within the social space of contemporary Paros." Tom Hawkins, "Out-Foxing the Wolf-Walker: Lycambes as Performative Rival to Archilochus," *Classical Antiquity*, 27.1 (2008), 93–114 (Lycambes being "a voice that rivals" Archilochus's own; "reject[ing] Archilochean poetics in an invective voice of his own").

31 *Archilochean in its*
**Roman playwrights Plautus.** See further pp. 276–279.
**"boor" . . . poet Horace.** See *Sat.* I.9, and pp. 300–302.

*The literary type is*
**Stravinsky's *Petrushka*.** For Stravinsky's *Pulcinella Ballet* (1920) as a retreat from modernism, see p. 348.

32 *Satire and vituperation*
**"is the . . . of his advice."** Snodgrass, 173.
**taken as cult performances.** On this aspect of Sappho's poetry, including the private versus public nature of Sappho's poetry, see Segal (1996), 63–64; Hallett (1996), 139–142, Winkler (1969), 89–109 (public/male versus private/female spheres), and Petropoulos (1993) (focusing on the Hymn's "affinities with magical discourse"). See also Cameron (1939), 9 (arguing the Hymn's religious import and sacral style, but concluding that "Love is above all a sphere of private interest in which religion and magic are hard to distinguish").
**provides a sense of presence.** Aphrodite's smile is "the gracious smile with which the gods are called on to appear to reassure their worshippers." Cameron, 5 (citing Euripides, *Bacchae* 1021).

*Some urge that Sappho*
**"feminine . . . of Archilochus."** Bowra, 240; Gerber, 161.
**Archilochus . . . demonstrative.** Comparisons between Archilochus and Sappho from Bagg, 44–46.

33 *Alcman of Sparta is*
**believed active in Sparta.** Terpander was reportedly the first winner of lyre-accompanied song at the Spartan Feast of the Karneia (founded sometime between 676 and 672 BC). The Karneia, the oldest established festival of the Spartans, was thus reckoned on the basis of Terpander's victory there. See Nagy (2004b), 35.
**"centers of musical excellence."** See Ferrari, 8–9.
**"strong . . . parochial" flavor.** Campbell (1967), 194.

34 *The longest of Alcman's*
**"No poem in . . . preference."** Gerber, 85.

*Despite such diffidence*
**"Although it is . . . universe."** Ferrari, 17.
**"music . . . spheres" theory.** Ferrari, 4–6.
**"Here several . . . other."** Hallett, 462. For a summary of views concerning what the chorus members are doing or celebrating, see Ferrari, 11, n. 36.
**Ferrari's . . . Lefkowitz's.** See pp. 150–152.

*According to Pausanias*
**"the first . . . love poems."** Pausanias, 1.25.1 (in Levi, Vol. I, 70).
**occasion . . . bookmaking.** See, e.g., *The Odes of Anacreon,* Thomas Moore, tr., with fifty-four illustrative designs by Girodet de Roussy (London: John Camden Hotten, 1896); *ANACREON,* Thomas Stanley, tr., illustrations by J. R. Weguelin (London: Lawrence & Bullen, 1893).

35 *Ibycus came from Rhegium*
**Their rich language, vivid.** My overview takes its departure from Symonds, Vol. I, 326–327.
**"Foremost . . . mindfulness."** *Th.* 116–122. On Chaos, see pp. 583–584. On Gr. *lusimelēs* 'limb-loosing' as used by the lyric poets, see West (1966), 196 and p. 212.

CHAPTER 4

37 *Sappho's Lesbos—well*
**Sappho's poetry apolitical.** See Friedrich, 108.
**were famed for their Beauty.** See *Il.* 9.129–130, 664.
**Beauty contests . . . event.** See §26.19.

38 *Ancient criticism of*
**epigrams . . . *Palatine Anthology*.** Also known as the *Greek Anthology,* a collection of poems, mostly epigrams, spanning Greek literature in the classical and Byzantine periods.
**Adonis in . . . the blessed.** The reference is to Adonis, son of Cinyras (king of Cyprus) by an incestuous union with his (Cinyras's) daughter (Ovid, *Met.* 10.298–559, 708–739). Adonis was beloved by Aphrodite for his exceptional beauty. See further Friedrich, 69–71; Grigson, 55–62; and Boardman/LaRocca, 132–133, 142.

*Sappho was praised as*
**particularly unsparing.** "Seeing that six comedies are known to have been written under the title of *Sappho,* and that her history furnished material for at least four more, it is not strange that much of their substance should in succeeding centuries have been regarded as genuine." Wharton, 22–24, 37–39.

Wharton's *Sappho* (1885, 1887, 1895)—memoir, Greek text, literal translation, selected renderings, and bibliography—was the first edition of Sappho written not "solely by scholars for scholars," but for "those who have neither leisure nor power to read her in the tongue in which she wrote" (xix). The volume, of biding interest, is readily available in reprint. Wharton himself could have been no more eminent a Victorian: a master of arts (Oxford), Member of the Royal College of Surgeons, a fellow of various medical associations, Honorary Surgeon of Kilburn Dispensary and of Queen Charlotte's Convalescent Home, the writer of various scientific papers (on e.g., ornithology and mushrooms), *and* the author of *Sappho*—collecting and translating all her extant writings.
**"What did . . . Lesbos teach."** Lesbia quid docuit Sappho nisi amare puellas? / tuta tamen Sappho . . . (*Tristia* 2.365–366). The *Tristia* are five books of poems addressed to

the Emperor Augustus, to Ovid's wife, and to other unnamed persons at Rome. Ovid wrote these highly autobiographical materials while in exile at Tomis on the Black Sea. Somewhat monotonous in tone, they reflect the poet's preoccupation with the miseries of banishment.

**condoned . . . homosexuality.** The notion of theory versus practice is difficult to maintain, as those professing love are wont to practice it. Comment on the nature of Sappho's relationships with women does not begin until Hellenistic times (4th century BC) and may derive from fifth-century Athenian social, moral, and cultural attitudes. See Dover, 174, 182.

**"Sappho-Phaon Epistle."** The fifteenth (and most famous) of fifteen *Heroides* of Ovid. The *Heroides* (*Heroines*) is a collection of poems in letter, or "epistolary," form, composed in elegiac couplets (see pp. 63, 234–235). They are presented as though addressed by various aggrieved mythological heroines—Penelope, Dido, Helen—to their heroic lovers who have abandoned or in some way mistreated them. They are highly rhetorical and somewhat overwrought, though compelling in their sympathetic portrayals of "hearts submissive to the power of love." See G. Showerman, *Ovid Heroides and Amores* (Cambridge and London: Harvard Univ. Press, Loeb Classical Library, 1963).

Of particular interest in the "Sappho-Phaon Epistle" is the unusual opening: three questions addressed to Phaon—two direct, one indirect—by which Sappho teases out her authorship. See Albert Baca, "Ovid's Epistle from Sappho to Phaon (*Heroides* 15)," *Transactions and Proceedings of the American Philological Association*, 102 (1971), 32–35. The epistle closes with two additional questions (both direct). The interrogatory framework necessarily recalls the five questions (three indirect, two direct) that Sappho's "Hymn to Aphrodite" ascribes to the goddess. As the Hymn is reputed to have been the opening poem in the first of Sappho's nine books of poetry, the epistle's interrogatories appear quite purposeful. The indirect questions in both the Hymn and the epistle are introduced by the verb *ask* (Gr. *ēre'*; Lat. *requiras*).

The *Heroides*' male authorship is often noted, especially in the case of the *Sappho-Phaon Epistle,* where the woman—Sappho—is the collection's sole historical figure and herself a poet much admired by Ovid. Further noted is the "shift from the frankly mythical to notionally biographical material." See Joseph Farrell, "Reading and Writing the *Heroides,*" *Harvard Studies in Classical Philology,*" 98 (1998), 310 (and bibliography); also Lipking, 67–68 ("It is amazing how many later poets have preferred Ovid's Sappho to Sappho herself, as if not even the feelings of a woman could be authenticated except through the witness of a man."). See also Efrossini Spentzou, *Readers and Writers in Ovid's Heroides: Transgressions of Gender and Genre* (Oxford: Oxford Univ. Press, 2003). Of further note is the preface to his rhyme-coupleted translation of the *Heroides* by classicist-poet Daryl Hine, beginning as follows:

> Heroines in name only, the passive but vocal victims of Ovid's epistolary elegiacs might better, if less neatly, be termed women of the Heroic Age, dames, or famous females. In lieu of an anachronistic feminism, they display, from Hypermnestra to Sappho, a wounded femininity, ambiguous because imagined by a man—and an avowedly heterosexual man at that. Never is the feminine mystique more cruelly traduced, indeed parodied, than in the singular instance of Sappho, the sole subject in the gallery to have a self-portrait, less fragmentary in Ovid's first century than in our twentieth. [Daryl Hine, *Ovid's Heroines: A Verse Translation of the Heroides* (New Haven and London: Yale Univ. Press, 1991), ix]

Ovid may not have authored the "Sappho-Phaon Epistle." See J. R. Tarrant, "The Authenticity of the Letter of Sappho to Phaon (*Heroides* XV)," *Harvard Studies in Classical Philology*, 85 (1981), 133–153 (effectively demolishing the case for Ovidian authorship). The Ovidian authorship of other *Heroides* has also been impugned. The "Jason-Medea

Epistle" is viewed with salutary skepticism by Stephen Hinds, "Medea in Ovid: Scenes from the Life of an Intertextual Heroine," *Materiali e discussioni per l'analisi dei testi classici*, 30 (1993), 9–47 ("I am less concerned to *identify* the author per se than defend the author's workmanship—whether he [or she] be Ovid or not"). That the "Sappho-Phaon Epistle" may not be Ovid's diminishes neither its interest nor influence. See, e.g., Clyde Furst, "Sappho and Phaon," *The Classical Weekly*, 1.15 (1908), 114–116 (reviewing Percy Mackaye, *Sappho and Phaon: A Tragedy* [New York: Macmillan, 1907], and noting high points of the epistle's influence to the end of the nineteenth century). Thanks to Professor Joseph Farrell for alerting me to Hinds's article.
**"Not Pyrrha's . . . you alone."** Pyrrha is located in central Lesbos; Methymna, on the northeast coast. Sappho herself came from Mytilene, on the southeast coast. For Atthis and Anactoria, see §§4.15 and 10. At line 200 of the poem, Sappho invokes the "Daughters of Lesbos whom I have loved to my disgrace."

38 *The rhetorician-philosopher*
**"But is not . . . of Lesbos."** M. B. Trapp, tr., *Maximus of Tyre: The Philosophical Orations* (Oxford: Clarendon Press, 1997), *Or.* 18.9, p. 167. Cf. Campbell (1982), 21.
**Forests have . . . comparison.** The topic is yet the subject of an excellent master's thesis by Elizabeth Baxter, "Sappho and Socrates and the Nature of Eros" (Dalhousie University, 2007).
**reason the more interesting.** What follows is adapted from Friedrich, 115–117.
**Both points are disputable.** The name of the merchant—"Cercolas"—to whom Sappho was supposedly married is of late provenance and comically derived. See Parker, 309–310. For early skepticism on the identity of "Kleïs" as Sappho's daughter, see Prentice, 348–349. Those otherwise disinclined to see Sappho as married and with child look to the word *pais*, which Sappho uses to designate her daughter. The word means 'child', and, as in many languages, either in the biological or affectionate sense. In the latter case, *pais* may also designate a sexual playmate. Sappho, in what remains of her poetry, uses *pais* in both the biological and affectionate sense. The word is used in an expressly homoerotic sense by Anacreon (§52; there translated 'lad'). Plato regularly uses *pais* with reference to the object of homoerotic desire, i.e., an *erōmenos* 'beloved' (young male). In any poetic context, considerations of meter might dictate the preference for *pais* over *thugatēr* 'daughter'—though the Muse is prominently invoked as *thugatēr Dios* 'daughter of Zeus' at the start of the *Odyssey*, and the formula is otherwise frequently used of Aphrodite and Athena and once, tellingly, of Helen. See Clader 43, 53. The above-mentioned Maximus of Tyre refers to Cleis as Sappho's *thugatēr*. In the *Iliad*, Hector wishes he were a *Dios païs* 'son of Zeus' (*Il.* 3.825), or is otherwise accused of too proudly wishing such parentage (*Il.* 13.54).

In the opening stanza of Sappho's "Hymn to Aphrodite," the goddess is invoked as *pai dios* 'child [i.e., daughter] of Zeus'. This last reference is to the union of Zeus and the obscure goddess Dione (an alternate parentage, less vaunted than that of Aphrodite's birth from Ouranos's severed genitals). In the penultimately discovered Sapphic poem (on love, death, and dying, §39), Sappho invokes her *paides* (pl.)—'dear children, companions, friends'—in the generic sense. A similar flexibility is apparent in the English word *mate*. For other views and attestations supporting a mother-daughter relationship, see Hallett, "Beloved Cleis" (1982).

A sexually quixotic interpretation takes *Kleïs* as a by-form of Gr. **klei-tōr* 'closer, door-keeper', the equivalent of *clitoris*. Reviewing the linguistic data, Holt Parker (2006) concludes: "Sappho's daughter was her daughter, not her clitoris, not her girlfriend." *Contra* Parker, and seeking to "dismiss the putative daughter," is Bennett, "Concerning 'Sappho Schoolmistress'" (1994).

39 *This brings us to the*
**"Aeolian earth . . . mortal Muse."** See Campbell (1982), 27–28 (quoting Antipater of Sidon; Greek poet, 2nd century BC). See also Wharton, 15 ("The story of Sappho's . . . leap . . . so long implicitly believed, does not seem to rest on any firm historical basis. . . . [M]ore than one epigrammatist in the Greek Anthology expressly states that she is buried in an Aeolic grave"). See also Prentice, 349. Notes one commentator with a fine skepticism:

> She followed Phaon, failed to gain his love, and so travelled from Sicily to the west of Greece and threw herself off the two-thousand-foot-high rock of Leucadia on the coast of Epirus, a favorite point of adieu for lovers keen to cure themselves of desire. . . . Quite apart from the implausible geography—that she pursued him from Sicily to the east [sic] coast of Greece—judging from the poems that survive, this is unlikely. If Sappho died around 550 BC, as most scholars believe, her suicide would have taken place when she was in her seventies, by which time she might have been expected to have learned restraint. [Schmidt (2005), 181–182]

That Sappho leapt from a Lesbian promontory, if she leapt at all, is thus entirely possible.
**a tomb . . . for sightseers.** See Campbell (1982), 26, n. 1.

40 *Also noteworthy from the*
**"to enter all . . . poems."** *New York Times*, 7/19/1915: "Botrel, the Trench Laureate: France's Unique Poet, Who Is at the Front Singing His Patriotic Songs to the Soldiers."

*The Homeric bard, by*
**intercession of the muse.** So Homer, at the start of the *Iliad*'s Catalogue of Ships, relates that the inspiring Muses are at once everywhere and know everything:

> Tell me now, you Muses who have your homes on Olympos.
> For you, who are goddesses, are there, and you know all things,
> and we have heard only the rumor of it and know nothing.
> Who then of those were the chief men and lords of the Danaans?
> [*Il.* 2.484–487, R. Lattimore, tr.]

**famed example is Taillefer.** See Edward Augustus Freeman, *The History of the Norman Conquest of England: Its Causes and Its Results* (New York: Cambridge Univ. Press, 2011; 1st pub. Oxford: At the Clarendon Press, 1896), Vol. III, 477–478.

41 *Ovid's Sappho laments*
**"O neither . . . have I."** *Ep.* 15.93–104. The remaining paragraph quotations are from *Ep.* 15.31–34, 41–50, 59–72.

43 *Classicist Gregory Nagy*
**summarize and simplify.** See Nagy (1973), 173–175; (1990b), 258–260.
**for the dead Adonis.** For Aphrodite and Adonis, see Boardman/LaRocca, 132–133, 142.
**popularized by Ovid.** *Met.* 2.1–400.
**by him at daybreak.** An instance, *pace* Ferrari (54), when Aphrodite is the pursued.
**"a cosmic . . . eroticism."** Stigers (1981), 57. On Phaon, Phaethon, and Aphrodite, and a suggestive parallel between Phaethon and Hippolytus (both willful, both drawn to their deaths by horses), see Ferrari, 53–67.

## Chapter 5

44 *Among issues of concern*
**"which are . . . in poetry."** Bagg, 47.

*Early seeking to free*

**since been . . . abandoned.** The critical and much cited study is by Parker (1993), "Sappho Schoolmistress"; *contra* Bennett (1994) and Lardinois (1994).

**sometimes speak . . . *thiasos*.** See Roche, xvi. The word *thiasos* appears in neither Sappho nor Alcaeus. "Sappho instead uses the word (*h*)*etairai* ['companions'] to connote a close bond between individuals—a bond which conveys the relationship in which one sleeps on another's bosom." West (1970), 324; cf. §33. The same obtains of the female lyric choirs of archaic Greece—as in Alcman's *Partheneion*, below—consisting of young girls bound to their leader through ties defined by the term (*h*)*etairai*, and finding their primary activity in song and dance. Calame (1977), 367–369. See further *pro* and *contra*: Russo, 721–722 and Segal, 141. The difficulty lies in defining the activities of a *thiasos*. On these issues, see further Poochigian, xix–xxviii.

**"Sappho's . . . Womanhood."** See article of same name by Calame (1996).

**a socially sanctioned forum.** See further Mendelsohn (2003), 26–27 (recapping recent views on the public/social versus private/amatory nature of Sappho's poetry).

45 *The social function of*

**The social function of.** Paragraph summarized from Segal (1974), 141, 145, with addition of translation references herein. Segal's scrutiny of sound and rhythmic patterns shows the extent to which there is no substitute for the original. See further Friedrich, 121.

**"convincing . . . over waters."** Bagg, 63.

**healing . . . accomplish this.** Bagg, 74.

*Thus does Sappho speak*

**"the container . . . Sappho."** Stigers, 59–60.

46 *Private space and*

**"Sappho [as] . . . the soul."** Robinson, 44.

**"two special difficulties."** Davison, 226.

**"Sappho's . . . abstract shapes."** Stigers, 49.

**"Whether or not . . . interest."** Friedrich, 117.

47 *Another view has it*

**limited . . . *single* beloved.** Paragraph adapted from Calame (1977), 430–431, 434–436, 438 (referencing Plutarch and Athenaeus).

**Aristotle and Plutarch.** For Aristotle's and Plutarch's accounts of female homosexuality in Sparta, see Susan Cavin, *Lesbian Origins* (San Francisco: Ism Press, 1985), 244–245.

**pederasty . . . conformed.** Jan Bremmer, "An Enigmatic Indo-European Rite: Pederasty," *Arethusa*, 13 (1980), 292–293. See also Dover, 189–190.

*In a similar vein*

**In a similar . . . marriage.** This and the following paragraph adapted from Hallett (1979), 450–461.

48 *Sappho as an enhancer*

**are "reputedly erotic."** Lasserre, 27–31 (speaking of *les poèmes reputés érotiques* and noting, as quoted in English, that "le langage de l'amour se prêtait à la louange poétique en raison de son pouvoir affectif et non à cause de ce qu'il exprimait").

**"erotic admiration . . . it."** Stigers, 468.

**"praise of . . . attraction."** Stigers, 468.

**role of pederasty . . . circle.** Calame, 431.

*Our discussion proceeds*
**"a common . . . affection."** W. Hamilton, *Plato, Symposium* (New York: Penguin Books, 1975), 26.
**As the *Symposium* relates.** Reference is made in what follows to Hamilton and Cairns, eds. (Plato, *Symposium* 209e–211a, 216d–219d), 561–562, 568–570, and (*Phaedrus* 236d–241d, 244a–257b), 484–488, 491–502.

49 *Plato conceives the hierarchy*
**in terms of an ascent.** So also Milton, distinguishing love and carnal desire, *PL* 8.585–594.
**was ideally nonphysical.** Insofar as the nonphysical ideal was *not* maintained, an extensive literature encompasses the topic of "Greek love" (i.e., male homosexual love)—much of it centered on active and passive roles in lovemaking and on attendant social expectations.

> The model of socially validated homosexuality was *paiderastia* [or pederasty; Gr. *paid-* 'child, youth' + *eraō* 'to love'], the love of an older man for a youth [the "older man" generally in his twenties, the youth an adolescent]. . . . An elaborate ritualization of appropriate conduct on the part of both participants was designed to give the relationships a "beautiful" form, one that would honor the youth's ambiguous status. . . . [The] reciprocal desire between men of the same age was almost unknown and . . . the distinction of the man who takes on the active penetrating role (the *erastes)* and the youth who accepts the passive role (the *eromenos*) was a rigid one. "Virtually no male both penetrates other males and submits to penetration at the same stage of life" (although a youth engaged in a passive relationship with a man might at the same time be taking on the active role vis-à-vis the female. . . . [Downing, 173, quoting Dover (1987)]

For the referenced "ritualization of appropriate conduct," see Downing, 174–175. Pederasty, as opposed to homosexuality, was also the norm of the warrior class. See D. Miller, 115.

Classicist Hermann Fraenkel (1888–1977) provides a comparably elegant formulation:

> The Greeks in general regarded homosexual love more dignified and uplifting than love between the sexes. The untamed craving of that urge which finds fulfillment and satisfaction in the union of man and woman was not so celebrated in poetry as was homosexual love which feeds unquenchably on the sight, on the physical proximity and spiritual presence of another, and together with him seeks, by common action and united striving, the path to parallel self-fulfillment. [Fraenkel (1963), 175–176]

See also William Armstrong Percy III, *Pederasty and Pedagogy in Archaic Greece* (Urbana and Chicago: Univ. of Illinois Press, 1996); Thomas K. Hubbard, ed., *Homosexuality in Greece and Rome: A Sourcebook of Basic Documents* (Berkeley and Los Angeles: Univ. of California Press, 2003); Beert C. Verstraete and Vernon Provencal, eds., *Same-Sex Desire and Love in Greco-Roman Antiquity and in the Classical Tradition of the West* (Binghamton: Haworth Press, 2005).

50 *While the Socrates of*
**committed . . . abstinence.** See Cantarella, Ch. 3: "Homosexuality and Heterosexuality Compared in Philosophy and Literature," on the evidence in Plato, Xenophon, Aristotle, and Plutarch.
**"But if . . . the undertaking."** Plato is less permissive in *Laws* 7.837c, 841d–e. The extent of Socrates's own homosexual activity is a matter Plato little clarifies. Opinion

varied in antiquity on the nature of Socrates's relationship with the famous and famously handsome Greek general Alcibiades (who makes a sudden and riotous appearance at the end of the *Symposium*).

Contemporary discussion of Socrates's sexuality has been as fumbling as that of Sappho's. According to the more generous view, "Given the acceptability and wide practice of pederasty in Socrates' circle, and Socrates' erotic nature, it would be most unusual if he did not engage in it himself. Plato's ambiguity and the abhorrence of Judeo-Christian thought to homosexuality, until recently, has led [others] vehemently to deny Socrates had homosexual relations." R. J. Littman, "The Loves of Alcibiades," *Transactions of the American Philological Association,* 101 (1970), 270–276. For social convention in fifth-century Athens and the codification of law with respect to homosexuality, see Kenneth J. Dover, "Eros and Nomos (Plato, *Symposium* 182a–185c)," *Bulletin, Institute of Classical Studies of the University of London,* 11 (1964), 31–42.

**"The Greek . . . self-fulfillment."** Hermann Fraenkel, *Early Greek Poetry and Philosophy,* Moses Hadas and James Willis, trs. (New York: Irvington Publishers, 1984), 175–176 (German, 1975).

**practice . . . short of theory.** See Cantarella, 44–49 (subtitled, "Making oneself a woman" as an adult: social sanction and the vocabulary of infamy).

*By contrast, and despite*

**"Homosexuality . . . awareness."** Bagg, 80, n. 10.

**difficulty . . . life and work.** Paragraph adapted from Lefkowitz (1973), with my own equating of "biography" with gender awareness.

**dependence on biography.** The dependence on biography involves, first and foremost, the recognition of gender—whether the artist is male or female. The discussion dramatically changes when the artist's gender is unknown. Gender of course does not necessarily or at all determine artistic result.

**different . . . remarkably alike.** Lefkowitz proceeds with criticism of an interpretation by (1) John Cody—*After Great Pain: The Inner Life of Emily Dickinson* (Cambridge: Harvard Univ. Press, 1971)—of Emily Dickinson's "I had been hungry all these years" and (2) Denys Page (1979) of Sappho §2, as "vivid illustration of the special criticism applied to female artists." In the first instance, Cody is criticized for his dream-interpretive reading of Dickinson, along canonical Freudian lines, whereby *sexual* hunger is the determining metaphor in a poem primarily concerning sex. In the second instance, Page is criticized for his reading of Sappho's poem as a direct outpouring of emotion, a reading similar in its way to Cody on Dickinson.

51 *In the end, one*

**"refused to . . . about it."** Grigson, 109.

CHAPTER 6

53 *It is Helen of Troy's*

**"the collective . . . armies."** Blondell (2013), 31.

54 *The Odyssey presents*

**"outside of human time."** See Felson and Slatkin, 109–110.

*As further concerns*

**spear bride . . . Theseus.** A "spear bride" is a woman taken in battle and wed or made concubine by the victor.

55 *These are some of the*

**relates that . . . goddesses.** *Th.* 921.

*There are some exceptions*

**"was the most . . . immortals."** *Il.* 20.231–235.

**vicariously . . . found Rome.** See *Aen.* 1.23–33 (recounting the Judgment of Paris and abduction of Ganymede as the reasons for Juno's anger toward Aeneas and her resistance to his founding Rome).

**Tiresias as bisexual seer.** See Luc Brisson, *Sexual Ambivalence: Androgyny and Hermaphroditism in Graeco-Roman Antiquity,* Janet Lloyd, tr. (Berkeley: Univ. of California Press, 2002), 115–130; also Loraux (1995), 211–226 ("What Tiresias Saw"). In the nineteenth and twentieth centuries, see Guillaume Apollinaire's play *Les Mamelles de Tirésias* (*The Breasts of Tiresias*) and the *opéra bouffe* of the same title by Francis Poulenc (1917).

**Ovid . . . tale of Iphis.** *Met.* 9.666–761.

**idealized relationship.** See pp. 48–50.

56 *Lacking the sanctions of*

**the myth's crudeness.** For further discussion of Sophocles's *Oedipus,* see pp. 423–424. The crudeness of early myths associated with Oedipus extends to the Pelopian family line overall. Pelops, through his son Atreus, was founder of the accursed House of Atreus. Pelops himself was killed by his father (Tantalus), cut up as stew, and served to the gods.

*Somewhat more elaborate*

**hermaphroditic charade.** Though the subterfuge results from the demands of the myth, this is the sole instance of Zeus in female disguise. On Callisto's receptiveness to Zeus in female disguise, and the spiritual versus physical nature of the relationship between the "chaste" Artemis and her nymphs, see Downing, 189. Zeus typically disguises himself to seduce mortal women, both to escape the notice of his wife Hera and to spare his mortal partners the insuperable revelation of his divinity. The disguise, often in animal form, is one of male machismo (bull, satyr) or majesty (eagle); otherwise, of phallic suggestiveness (long-necked swan), or opulence (shower of gold)—the last with pre-ejaculatory suggestiveness. At his most prosaic (as when wooing Alcmene), Zeus takes the form of Alcmene's husband (Amphitryon). On the uniqueness of this instance, see Philips, 433. Zeus's acquiescence to Semele's request, that he take her undisguised, results in her death by thunderbolt—such is the power of unmediated divinity. Zeus, at *Il.* 14.312–328, enumerates the women involved in these escapades. The list includes several goddesses. Its comical aspects aside, the list signals Zeus's sexual dominance as elaborated at *Th.* 886–923. Once enthroned in the *Theogony,* Zeus sets the procreational pace. He otherwise enjoys a sexual prerogative unlimited but for Hera.

*Heterosexuality is also*

***Theogony* (*Birth of the Gods*).** Hesiod is considered a contemporary of Homer (8th century BC). His two principal surviving works are the *Theogony* and the *Works and Days,* both in epic meter and dialect, though considerably shorter than either the *Iliad* or *Odyssey*. The *Theogony* deals, as noted, with the birth of the gods and ordering of the cosmos; the *Works and Days,* with the ordering of earthly existence through farming cycles, the administration of justice, and related moral precepts.

**sexual activity is *chaotic*.** Primordial chaos—things mingled and in flux—is different from Gr. *Chaos,* posited by Hesiod as the first created entity: *prōtista Chaos genet'* 'first before all was Chaos' (*Th.* 116). Hesiod's Chaos is the "Gap," the "yawning space," or "chasm" (Gr. *chasko* 'gape') that separates Earth and Sky, following Ouranos's castration. See further West (1966), 192–193, and Muellner, 55–56. A *New York Times* writer surprisingly captured the ancient Greek sense of the term vis-à-vis the confusion preceding Greece's July 5, 2015 austerity referendum: "The ancient Greek term for all this is khaos, and the vast chasm or void of coherent decision making appears to extend well beyond [Greece's] borders." Andrew Higgins, "Mixed Messages and No Progress in Greek Crisis," *New York Times*, 7/2/2015.

The biblical account is otherwise, depicting a state more like the chaos we typically imagine. Genesis describes *ha'aretz* 'the earth' as initially *tōhū vavōhū* 'welter and waste', the spirit (or breath) of God *mirachephet al p'nāy ha-mayīm* 'hovering on the face of the waters'. The felicitous rendering "welter and waste" is that of Robert Alter, *Genesis: Translation and Commentary* (New York & London: W. W. Norton, 1996), 3.

A *chasma* also separates earth and the underworld (*Th.* 700). Chasms maintain the boundary separations of sustainable creation—between heaven and earth, earth and the underworld. As space alone provides tenuous division, the mythic imagination furnishes physical support. Atlas was originally imagined as standing at the western edge of earth, supporting heaven on his shoulders. He thus kept heaven and earth from resuming their primordial embrace. Holding the celestial sphere, Atlas was ultimately popularized as holding the earth. In Homer "baleful-minded Atlas" is water-bound, "knowing the depths of the sea in its entirety, and holding the mighty pillars which keep earth and heaven apart" (*Od.* 1.52–54). This depiction conflates the notions of Atlas himself as pillar, and Atlas as bearer or positioner of pillars. For other Atlas/pillar associations, see West (1997), 148–149; for further discussion, Nagy (2009) 594–599 and (2010), 366–372. Figures modeled on Atlas, called *atlantes* (Lat. *telemones*), have been in use since antiquity as elements of architectural and decorative support. The *caryatid* is a female precursor of this form, i.e., an effortlessly standing woman in lieu of column or pillar (e.g., the caryatids of the Erechtheion on the Acropolis at Athens).

**castration . . . intercourse.** The biblical account, by contrast, as in all else, dispenses with anthropomorphisms and any such manner of gory dealing. It announces differentiation as simple fact, predicated on God's six days of creation: "In the beginning God created the heaven and the earth."

57 *Indeed, because of*

**soundalikes *womb/tomb*.** Cf. *PL* 2.911 ("The Womb of nature and perhaps her Grave") and Milton, "On Time" (speaking of what Time's "womb devours" and "entomb[s]"). Entombment as a return to the womb, for the male at least, is a biological homecoming of sorts, anticipated by every instance of sexual intercourse with its resultant 'little death' (*la petite mort*). See further pp. 213, 625 and Kazantzakis, *Odusseia* 16.1369–1370.

"**broad-breasted . . . peak.** *Th.* 117–118.

**as a physical element.** *Il.* 17.425, "bronze heaven"; *Od.* 15.329, "iron heaven."

*This theme appears*

**"He sang . . . courses."** *Arg.* 1.496–500. For Apollonius in the Greek literary tradition, see pp. 280–281; and for excellent discussion, Beye (2006).

58 *Heterosexuality is further*

**"maidens' . . . gentleness."** *Th.* 205–206.

**consort . . . god of war.** The bard Demodocus in Book Eight of the *Odyssey* sings of an illicit assignation between Aphrodite and Ares. Hephaestus, learning of it, traps the two *en flagrante*, inviting the other gods to view and comment on the disgrace. The lovers are made a laughingstock, Hephaestus is vindicated, and the incident passes in mirth.

As many a truth is told in jest, the episode reflects the adultery theme running throughout the *Odyssey*: Clytemnestra's adultery in Agamemnon's absence, and what it might presage for the absent Odysseus upon return. It was Helen's adultery that precipitated the Trojan War.
**oppositional relationship.** See discussion at p. 608.

*As further concerns Lesbos*
**"Four Tales of . . . Love."** The delta ($\delta$) is the fourth letter of the Greek alphabet, equivalent to the number four.

CHAPTER 7

59 *The Greeks were colonizers*
**They crossed the Aegean.** Greek colonizations gave rise to *ktsis* 'foundation' poetry, reflecting the Greek preoccupation with beginnings, first causes, and etiologies. See Nagy (1990), 73–74, and Carol Dougherty, "Archaic Greek Foundation Poetry: Questions of Genre and Occasion," *Journal of Hellenistic Studies,* 114 (1994), 35–46.

60 *Troy was situated at the*
**Asia and Europe . . . West.** Herodotus, however, is highly critical of the Homeric version of the Trojan War. See James W. Neville, "Herodotus on the Trojan War," *Greece and Rome,* 24.1 (1977), 3–12. If the Trojan War marks the start of hostilities between East and West, Virgil's *Aeneid* marks the actual "transition in the world-order, the shift of civilization from the East to the West." C. S. Lewis (1942), 36.
**Achilles . . . conquered Lesbos.** *Il.* 9.129, 271, 664. On the centrality of Lesbos, see further pp. 37–43, 60.
**against Skyros and Tenedos.** Skyros (*Il.* 9.668), Tenedos (*Il.* 11.625), Lyrnessos and Pedasos (*Il.* 19.60, 20.90–92, 188–194) (see map).

*For all its political infighting*
**works likely . . . stage.** Sappho and Alcaeus likely performed together on Lesbos during the festival at Messon, and at symposia and the musical competitions of the Panathenaia in Athens during the sixth and fifth centuries BC. See Nagy (2009), 225, 263, and Nagy (2002); cf. Dimitrios Yatromanolakis, *Sappho in the Making: The Early Reception* (Cambridge, Mass. and London: Center for Hellenic Studies, 2007), 73–81 ("Two Singers—Together"). With its temple dedicated to Zeus, Dionysus, and Hera (ruins surviving), Messon was the center of ancient Lesbian worship for the federation of cities dominated by Mytilene. Meaning "middle space," Messon is appropriately located in central Lesbos north of the Gulf of Kalloni. Messon may be the site of the annual beauty contests celebrated by Alcaeus. See further Robert, 245; Nagy (2013), 117, 124; cf. Athenaeus, *Doctors at Dinner* (13.610a).

61 *Lesbos further abounds*
**according to Aristotle.** Butcher (*Poetics* 1449a, IV.12), 18–19.
**lyric musician (*kitharoidos*).** Herodotus 1.23.
**attendants of . . . worship.** Also the fate of Theban Pentheus, vividly depicted in Euripides's *Bacchae.*

*Musically active before*
**"first human . . . history."** Martin van Schaik, "Terpandros of Lesbos in Medieval and Renaissance Music Theory Reconsidered," *Utrecht.* 2007, rev. 2009. Web. 2/17/2013 (beginning with a helpful collection of principal ancient references to Terpander).

**"prototypical . . . songmaker."** Nagy (2004b), 35.
**perfected . . . instrument.** Aristotle calls the kithára "a *tekhnikon ergon*, an instrument designed for use by the *tekhnitēs*, a master technician of instrumental performance, typically a professional virtuoso." Power, 5 (citing Aristotle, *Politics* 8.1341a18–19).
**"as decisive . . . to piano."** Durrell (1978), 185.
**"Antissa could . . . inherited."** Power, 388.
**in the name *Terpander*.** See Power, 327, nn. 33–34 (summarizing earlier scholarship).

62 *Similar invention is attributed*
**note . . . meaning of *Homer*.** *(h)óm-ēros*: interpreted as a compound meaning 'he who fits [the song] together,' built from the Indo-European elements **som-* 'together' and **ar-* 'fit, join' (as in *arariskō* 'fit, join'). See Nagy (1979/1999), 296–300 (citing others); Nagy (2010), 255. So also the name *Hesiod*—*(h)ēsí-odos* 'he who sends forth [his] voice'. Nagy (1979/1999), 296–300. A form of the verb *(h)omēreō* 'fit together' appears in Hesiod's *Theogony* Invocation. The Muses—singing of things past, present, and future—are described as *(h)omēreusai* [fem. part.] *phonē* 'according [or harmonizing] in voice', i.e., singing tunefully or in unison (*Th.* 39). *Hómēros* and *Hesíodos* are thus not so much, if at all, authors per se, as descriptions of authorial process, signaled by the diction of epic itself. See Vermeule, 695, n. 9 (for the German philologist W. A. Wolf's view to the same effect), to which may be added the formulation of Sainte-Beuve, 127 (Lee, tr.). For other views on the name *Homer*, see Nagy (1996), 21; Nagy (2010), 254–266; and M. L. West, "The Invention of Homer," *The Classical Quarterly*, 49.2 (1999), 364–382. See also Garcia, 15, n. 29. On **ar-* and *ararisko*, etc., as applying to the meaning and function of *art* (i.e., that which 'fits' or is 'fixed'), see pp. 415–416.
**"collective . . . personal name."** C. T. Lewis, 342. In the same vein, *Homer* was "expressing not himself but the material at hand," whence his renowned objectivity. See Reck, ii. Similarly, when speaking of Homer, we mean the *Iliad* and *Odyssey*, just as "When we say Shakespeare we mean the plays." Mackail, 24.

*Returning to Terpander*
**summoned . . . fractious infighting.** "Now music was first organized at Sparta, under the direction of Terpander." Also, "that . . . the best regulated states have taken care to concern themselves with music of the grand style we could show by many examples, especially Terpander, who settled the civil strife that had broken out in Lacedaemon" (i.e., Sparta). Einarson and De Lacy, trs., *Plutarch, On Music* §9, 371; and §42, 449. For a suggestive contemporary parallel, see Sebnem Arsu, "Music in Istanbul Is Intermission for a Protest: The Pianist David Martello Calms Istanbul Tensions," *New York Times*, 6/14/2013.
**"exported" its musicians.** Sappho, however, appears to have remained on Lesbos. See generally Ian Rutherford, "Aristodama and the Aetolians: an itinerant poetess and her agenda," in Richard Hunter and Ian Rutherford, eds., *Wandering Poets in Ancient Greek Culture: Travel, Locality and Pan-Hellenism* (Cambridge: Cambridge Univ. Press, 2009).
**associated . . . governance.** Power, 220.
**"Pan-Lesbian . . . *kitharoidia*."** Power, 388.
**"the brilliant . . . by Alcaeus."** Power, 383–384.
**Alcaeus's . . . abusively political.** On the sympotic, or "drinking party," setting for the recitation of Alcaeus's poetry, and the poetry of other lyricists (including Sappho), see Nagy (2004b), especially n. 23 (collecting sources for the singing of Sappho's songs at symposia). See also E. L. Bowie, "Early Greek Elegy, Symposium and Public Festival," *The Journal of Hellenic Studies*, 106 (1986), 13–35 (distinguishing symposium—a social institution, involving both ritual and relaxation, that strengthened group identity—from public festival: "an institution where the city as

a whole defined its corporate identity and paraded its internal structure—likewise with a blend of ritual and relaxation").

63 *Historian-essayist Tzvetan*
**"From where . . . genres."** Tzvetan Todorov, "The Origin of Genres," *New Literary History*, 8.1 (1976), 161. Reprinted *Genres in Discourse*, Catherine Porter, tr. (Cambridge: Cambridge Univ. Press, 1990).
**originally more of a kind.** "For epic contains within it a whole encyclopedia of genres and repertoires deceivingly linked by the formal unity of the verse, which lie like virgin timber to the ambitious translator." Armstrong (2008), 173. Linguistic analysis further shows that Homeric similes "are affiliated with, and may be taken from, the epic performer's prior knowledge of *nonepic* Greek genres." R. Martin, in Bakker and Kahane, eds., 139. For genre mix in *Paradise Lost*, especially that of epic and tragedy, see Rajan, 114–118.
**Terpander is referred to.** Power, 386 (citing Plutarch, *Laconian Institutions*).
**Terpander is also said.** "Thus he says that Terpander also . . . set to music in each nome [i.e., regulated tuning; Gr. *nomos* 'law'] hexameters of his own and Homer's and sung them in contests." Einarson and De Lacy, trs., *Plutarch, On Music* §3, 358–359. See also *On Music* §4, 360–361 (for other non-epic compositions in heroic hexameters).
**(rather than epic) dactyls.** See Power, 243–249 ("Terpander's Homer"). For the difference between the lyric dactyls of early Greek poetry and dactylic hexameter, see James W. Halporn, Martin Ostwald, and Thomas Rosenmeyer, *The Meters of Greek and Latin Poetry* (London: Methuen, 1963), 17–20.
**epic . . . elegiac couplets.** For elegy and the elegiac couplet, see pp. 234–236.
**"a variation . . . of lyric."** Campbell (1993), xxiv–xxv (citing W. R. Hardie, *Res Metrica*, 49).
**fragment of Archilochus.** See Barker and Christensen, "Flight Club," etc. (2006).
**The *Iliad* . . . incorporates.** See Nagy (1996), 7–8; Nagy (2010), 241–253 (especially 251: "Homeric poetry represents Aeolian women in the act of performing choral lyric poetry.").
**"the laments . . . performed."** Clader, 11. For Helen's funeral lament over Hector in connection with her own sense of shame and wish to die, see Ebbott, 11–14.
**"as a lyric persona . . . epic."** MacCary, 57.

*At the same time*
**"hyperstated mortality."** Alexander, 96.
**"pathological . . . *persona*."** Will, 57.
**"tragic situation *par excellence*."** Whitman, 182.
**with *peripeteia* . . . *anagnorisis*.** Whitman, 202.
**"The fate of Achilles . . . *tiná*.** Samuel Eliot Bassett, "The *Hamartía* of Achilles," *Transactions and Proceedings of the American Philological Association*, 65 (1934), 47.
**Moreover . . . *Iliad*'s view.** The observation is summarized and condensed from Kullmann, 11.
**It is Plato who originates.** *Rep.* 595b, *Thaet.* 152.
**while Aristotle elaborates.** Butcher (*Poetics* 1459b, XXIV.1–9), 91–97. See also Butcher (*Poetics* 1453a, XIII.4–7), 47 (distinguishing the well-constructed tragic plot as single, rather than double, in its issue; and associating the *Odyssey* with the latter, and the *Iliad*, implicitly, with the former).
**Hector . . . tragic counterpart.** See Whitman, 108 ("Both men are, in one sense of the word, tragic: both experience action, recognition, and doom; both are moved by noble motives and both are caught in the consequences of their own decisions.").

64 *As further concerns genre*
**in Book One of the *Iliad*.** *Il.* 1.472–474:

> The Greeks made supplication to the god,
> All day in beauteous song, chanting a paean,
> Hymning the Archer; he, well pleased, gave ear.

The quoted verses frame Plutarch's dialogue *On Music.* They emphasize, at the beginning of the dialogue, the "piety and principal concern of man to sing hymns to the gods, who have granted articulate speech to him alone." The same verses, closing the dialogue, praise the efficacy of music in ending a pestilence at Sparta, even as "the pestilence that attacked the Greeks [in Book One of the *Iliad*] came to an end in Music." See Einarson and De Lacy, trs., *On Music* §2, 355, and §42, 450 (including Homeric translation).
**Achilles . . . slaying Hector.** *Il.* 22.391–394.
**Hector (abandoned by Apollo).** *Il.* 22.202–213.
**lyric genre (older than itself).** On the relative chronology of epic and lyric, as determined by meter, see pp. 247–248. Again, though lyric is older, epic is first attested—which is to say, we have no archaic Greek lyric poetry predating Homer, though we know it existed.
**"lyricized epic"/"epicized lyric."** On the development of epic meter from lyric meter, see pp. 247–248.
**tragedy . . . largely choral.** This is apparent from the predominance of choral lyric in the oldest surviving Greek drama, Aeschylus's *Persians,* 472 BC (dramatizing the Persian response to news of their defeat at the Battle of Salamis, 480 BC).
**Just how this . . . determine.** For possible determinants, see Ian Rutherford, "Apollo in Ivy: The Tragic Paean," *Arion,* 3rd series, 3.1 (1995), 118–121. See also Acosta-Hughes and Stephens, 105–108 ("The Paean"). Power distinguishes choral and citharodic performance as follows:

> The chorus was the musical expression of social collectivity par excellence, a metonymy [a part used to designate the whole] of the *polis* [city state], performing before the *polis* a gracefully idealized version of its communal solidarity and cooperation—ideology in perfectly synchronized motion and sound. [Citharodic performance, by contrast,] entailed a more passive and top-down, yet less effective mode of group manipulation. The charismatic virtuoso ideally produced a kind of collective *katharsis* through the *terpsis* ['joy'] he created; he could mobilize and align the divergent moods and temperatures of his listeners under the spell of an expert combination of music, text, and visual spectacle, stimulating a common effect among the civic audience that would become in turn conducive to amity. [Power, 401–402]

**"Thus when . . . the two."** Einarson and De Lacy, trs., *Plutarch, On Music* §16, 386–387 (as adapted; also noting: "Aristoxenus says that Sappho was the first to invent the Mixolydian and that the tragedians learned it from her").

65 *Herodotus first distinguished*
**Ionians, Aeolians, and Dorians.** Herodotus 1.141–144 (Waterfield, tr.).
**complexities . . . simplified.** For more detailed discussion of the Greek dialects, including the standardization that resulted in Attic Greek, see Stephen Colvin, "Greek Dialects in the Archaic and Classical Ages," and Olga Tribulato, "Literary Dialects," both in Egbert J. Bakker, ed., 200–212 and 388–423, respectively.

***New Ionic** was the*
**four dialects *were* . . . Greek.** "In the Archaic and Classical periods the Greek lan-

guage is an abstract notion in the sense that there was no standard language, but a collection of dialects that we think were mostly mutually intelligible. One should not overstate the 'abstractness' of Greek at this period, however: the notion that a language is a standard with a set of variations (dialects) is a later idea, reflecting the linguistic and sociolinguistic history of languages such as English, French, and Spanish." Colvin, above, in Bakker (2014), 200.

***Aeolis** or **Aeolia** was*

**Aeolic in its Lesbian variant.** For the geographic parameters of the Lesbian variant of Aeolic Greek, see Nagy (2011), 134; Vol. 1.1 (2012), 1.
**Thessaly . . . and Boeotia.** For the geographic parameters of the Thessalian and Boeotian variants of Aeolic Greek, see Nagy (2011), 134; Vol.1.1 (2012), 1.

66 *A character in Plato's*

**"a Lesbian . . . dialect."** Hamilton and Cairns, eds. (Plato, *Prot.* 341c), 335.
**"contemporaneous usage."** Page, 327.
**"rings as naturally . . . spoke."** Lucas, 56.
**"The one . . . of feeling."** Murray (1912), 22–23.

67 *The Dorians are believed*

**"more . . . Homer himself."** Shankman (1994), 190.

*With the exception of*

**be epic's oldest stratum."** Robbins, 10 (noting that Aeolic in Homer "normally survived only where the Ionic could not displace it in the same position in the line"). See further Richard Janko, *Homer, Hesiod, and the Hymns* (Cambridge: Cambridge Univ. Press, 1982), 89–92.
**"were sensible . . . spoken."** Thomas Jefferson, letter to John Waldo (1813), as quoted in Vermeule, 690.
**little given to contrivance.** Thucydides is a special case, "writ[ing] his *History of the Peloponnesian War* in almost impossibly difficult Greek" (even for ancient readers) and making the translation of his work particularly contentious. See Mary Beard, "Which Thucydides Can You Trust?" review of Donald Kagan, *Thucydides: The Reinvention of History* (2010), *New York Review of Books,* 9/30/2010; adapted and updated in Mary Beard, *Confronting the Classics: Traditions, Adventures, Innovations* (New York and London: W. W. Norton, 2013), 32–41.

***Old** and **New Ionic***

**the fewer . . . more syllables.** Where Attic is given to vowel contraction, Doric exhibits *word* contraction—e.g., *dō* for *dōma* 'house'; (*h*)*o* for (*h*)*o ti* 'that'; *trein* for *tremein* 'tremble'.

69 *We do well in this*

**"peculiar sweetness . . . signif'd."** Pope, Preface, 9–10. A generous number of dialect-mixing examples appear in the *Essay on the Life and Poetry of Homer,* by "Pseudo-Plutarch" or [*Plutarch*] (1st–2nd centuries AD), §§8–14, 71–81: "mustering the dialects [*phōnas,* 'voices/sounds'] of all the Greeks, he produces [*apergazetai* 'works up'] an embellished account [*poikilon . . . logon*]." The use of *poikilon* 'embellished, variegated', both here (§14) and at the beginning of the account on dialect mixing (§8), is reminiscent of the richly evocative Sapphic epithet *poikilothron'*.

As the naming locutions indicate, Plutarch's authorship is doubtful. The *Essay* is, nonetheless, our most valuable source concerning the view of Homer during the

Roman Empire. It was used as prefatory material by Renaissance editors of Homer, beginning with the first printed edition of Homer (1488), and thus greatly influenced Renaissance and later readers who considered Plutarch an authority on Homer.
**"the first . . . Greek history."** Finkelberg (2002), 85 (citing Thucydides 1.3).
**"Greeks of . . . reflection."** Higham & Bowra, lxxii–lxxiii.
**"simply . . . was at all."** Swinburne, 228.

Part II, Chapter 8

75 *Sappho's poetry, believed to*
**"The poem . . . perfectly."** Carson (1986), 27. See further Mendelsohn (2003), 27 (discussing the postmodern appeal of "wholeness-in-fragmentation").
**Tullius . . . of nine books.** For the division of Sappho's works into books, see Page, 112–116; Campbell (1982), 29–31; and Green, 38.
**"In modern . . . structures."** West (2005), 1.
**parchment . . . preserved.** Most Greek-inscribed papyri were discovered, starting at the end of the nineteenth century, at Oxyrhynchus, Egypt, about one hundred miles southwest of Cairo. Oxyrhynchus was an ancient rubbish dump, and the Greek and Latin manuscripts discarded there over a one-thousand-year period themselves number in the thousands. These include, among biblical and other materials, fragments ascribed to Sappho and other ancient Greek lyric poets. The papyri date from the time of the conquest of Alexander the Great to the end of Roman rule in Egypt (4th century BC–3rd century AD).

76 *There are any number of*
**fragment by Archilochus.** See Fondation Hardt, *Entretiens, Tome X: Archiloque* (essays and discussion in English, French, and German).
**on the battle of Platea.** The final land battle in 479 BC of the Persian Xerxes's invasion of Greece. For the Simonides discovery, see Deborah Boedeker, ed., *The New Simonides, Arethusa* 29.2 (Baltimore: The Johns Hopkins Univ. Press, 1996), and Boedeker and David Sider, *The New Simonides: Contexts of Praise and Desire* (Oxford: Oxford Univ. Press, 2001).
**international news . . . media.** The discovery was announced by eminent Greek scholar Martin L. West, "A new Sappho poem," *Times Literary Supplement*, 6/21/2005. See also Greene and Skinner, 1, n. 1 (citing other media announcements). West published the text and translation of the then newly reconstructed poem. Part of the poem was first published in 1922 from an Oxyrhynchus papyrus (no. 1787). Most of the rest of the poem has since been found on a papyrus housed at Cologne University.

77 *My own work, while*
**"must give to . . . at all."** C. T. Lewis, 353.

*Translation at its best*
**"coauthoring" . . . original.** The translator, in E. M. Forster's formulation, would ideally be a "cocreator" with the original author, "actually enter[ing] his space." The poem/translation, as any work of art, has "the power of transforming the person who encounters it towards the condition of the person who created it." The process involves "a change analogous to creation." Forster, 117.
***Leaves of Grass* . . . status.** See McWilliams, 217–237 ("An Epic of Democracy?").
**"celebrat[ing] the . . . men."** McWilliams, 218–219. If every man has a heroic potential, its lack of realization makes any man a tragic hero. Enter everyman, Willy Loman.

**Worse to follow . . . Pound.** See Chapter 34 (and Pound's poem—"A Pact"—to Whitman: "We have one sap and one root— / Let there be commerce between us").
**"There are . . . mediocrity."** Butler, 264.

78 *One notes the almost*
**Solon decamped abroad.** Herodotus 1.29 (Waterfield, tr.).

79 *The librarians of*
**The librarians of Alexandria.** On the library at Alexandria and the Alexandrian period, see pp. 6, 79, 279–283.

CHAPTER 9

80 *Because of Sappho's*
**translators use . . . *lacunae.*** Tributes to what Sappho composed, no less than to what is lost, continue apace, as in the staging of Anne Carson's *Bracko.*

> The title "Bracko" alludes to the many brackets that mark the fragmentary texts of Sappho's poems, whose incomplete nature becomes obvious in live performance. . . . Carson['s] . . . larger point is that our idea of this Greek poet is shaped by what we don't know, and what we choose to imagine about her. . . . Carson's text becomes an overlay of voices, brackets, words, possibilities—as a dance full of beauties, hints, ideas, alternatives, possibilities.
> [Alastair Macaulay, "Translating Poetry to the Stage, With or Without Words," *New York Times* (Dance), 7/21/2010]

Carson's *Bracko* comes as no surprise. Despite the excellence of her *Eros the Bittersweet,* Carson is Bracket Offender in Chief. Her *If Not, Winter: Fragments of Sappho,* running close to four hundred pages, offers page after nearly empty page of one-line or several-word translations, with brackets everywhere indicating gaps. Notes Garry Wills, the "cult of the fragmentary has led to an absurd printing of half-lines and half-words as if they were poems." Wills (2005), 57. There is also Carson's *Autobiography in Red* (1999), in which she "grew a volume of fragments of the *Geryoneis*" of Stesichorus, "find[ing] a place for her poetry in the gaps created by the ravages of the manuscript tradition." M. Reynolds, 231. The *Geryoneis* is the *Song of Geryon* (Geryon a mythological beast slain by Heracles).

*When not dutifully*
**Loeb Classical Library.** The Loeb Classical Library (LCL), published and distributed by the Harvard University Press, was founded in 1912 by German-born American banker, Hellenist, and philanthropist James Loeb (1867–1933). Its purpose was to provide bilingual access (original texts with facing translation) to Greek and Roman authors. Edmonds's *Lyra Graeca* (in three volumes), first published in 1922, was reprinted in LCL through 1963. David A. Campbell's LCL *Greek Lyric* (in five volumes) replaced Edmonds starting in 1982, incorporating all significant editorial work to date.
**"ran . . . Sappho's own."** Green, 35.
**"The Greek text . . . own."** Roche (1966), 164. "Paul Roche's version . . . is absurdly dependent on Edmonds's inflated text, but nonetheless has charming versions of the hymeneal fragments." McEvilley, 280.
**"surviving" in . . . fifty years.** Roche was among the last surviving members of the Bloomsbury Group, the artists and writers congregating about Virginia Woolf. Personally dashing and well attired, he led a venturesome and far-ranging life. He studied Latin and Greek at an English boarding school, but apparently no further. The

author of many original works, his translation of Sophocles's *Oedipus* was for many years the standard.

81 *Roche's problem was that*
**were "strictly a translation."** Roche, xviii.
**"Even in . . . records at all."** Roche, xxiii.
**"deprived . . . original sound."** Roche, xix.
**"give some idea . . . mood."** Roche, xx.

*Some translators, gussying*
**"Percussion . . . beast."** Davenport, 95.
**"Several . . . or final."** Davenport, 14. Davenport's unique two-for-one translations find an admirer in classicist Elizabeth Vandiver: "Occasionally Davenport includes two very different translations of the same poem; they are such fascinating commentaries on the difficulties and treacheries of the translator's art that I would have liked more of them." Vandiver, 73 (note). Preferable, of course, is the translator who gets it right the first time. Reviewers are especially enamored of Davenport, dismissing his many flaws—e.g., "These reservations aside" (Vandiver, 71)—to point up his "gift." None dwells on the inadequacy of his Greek.

82 *While translators may*
**"everywhere . . . words."** Davenport, xx.
**"what gets lost . . . found."** Lawrence Rosenwald, "On Not Reading in Translation," *The Antioch Review*, 62.2 (2004), 316.

83 *As previously mentioned,*
"**All translation . . . pleases.**" The Dryden quotations in this paragraph may be found in John Dryden, *Ovid's Epistles, Translated by Several Hands*, Preface, 91–119 (in Hooker and Swedenborg). See also Gillespie (2001). For helpful discussion of Dryden's terms, see Steiner (1998), 267–272 and 318 ("The perennial distinction between literalism, paraphrase and free imitation, turns out to be wholly contingent").

*The notion of Greekless*
**The less the . . . he invents.** Sapphic literary inventions are too numerous to name. The topic has been exhaustively treated; see works by Bremmer, DeJean, Donoghue, Prins, and Reynolds.

84 *The translations of this*
**"lively and . . . of verbiage."** Boris Pasternak, "Translating Shakespeare," in *I Remember* (Cambridge and London: Harvard Univ. Press, 1983), 125.
**"the scholarly . . . present."** Stewart, 13.

85 *To grasp the challenge*
**essential features . . . poetry.** Parts of the following, including quotations, are indebted to Gilbert Murray (1930), 80–121, especially 92, 95, 98, and 103.
**tends . . . randomly determined.** See G. Thomson, *Greek Lyric Meter* (Cambridge: Cambridge Univ. Press, 1929), 130–138; M. L. West, *Introduction to Greek Meter* (Oxford: Clarendon Press, 1987). Also Philip Hobsbaum, *Metre, Rhythm and Verse Form* (London and New York: Rutledge, 1966); Paul Fussell, *Poetic Meter and Poetic Form* (New York: McGraw-Hill, 1979); and John Thompson, *The Founding of English Meter* (New York: Columbia Univ. Press, 1988), 128–138.

87 *The resonance will be*
**"gives . . . which it obtains."** Santayana (1896), 131.
**"phrases would run . . . flux."** Santayana (1896), 131.
**"does the . . . resolutions"?** Hecht (2003), 264.
**"the most classics . . . forms."** Santayana (1896), 131.
**"synthesizes . . . inevitable."** Santayana (1896), 131. As further concerns making the "unexpected seem inevitable," see p. 235.
**interlocking patterns of rhyme.** See Higham & Bowra, cvii.

CHAPTER 10

88 *Many are the fallacies*
**"the diversities . . . voice."** Santayana (1896), 129.

*Following Mary Barnard's*
**"best of them . . . tradition."** Roche, xviii.

89 *Admissions of ignorance*
**"My starting . . . extends to."** Davenport (1980), 14–16.
**"I do not know . . . myself."** Ayrton, 3.
**Geoffrey . . . existing text.** Geoffrey Kirk (1921–2003), a renowned British classical scholar and Regius Professor of Greek at Cambridge University (1974–1982). One wonders how the estimable Professor Kirk could have lent his prestige to so ill conceived a venture. Alas, his role as "aider and abettor" is all too typical.
**to Richard [sic] Lattimore.** *Richmond* Lattimore (1906–1984), classicist-poet and translator extraordinaire.
**"In . . . endlessly grateful."** Barnstone (2006), xlvii; Barnstone (2009), xlv.

*Davenport, as Roche*
**Davenport . . . indebtedness.** For the quotations in this paragraph, see Davenport (1980), 11–14, 234.
**"There is . . . an afternoon."** Davenport appears to have lifted the idea from Ezra Pound: "There is so little Sappho that that won't take long, after you buy a crib." Letter to Mary Barnard, 1/22/1934; Paige, 252. Davenport has further taken it upon himself to translate the sayings and fragments of the Greek philosophers Heraclitus (6th–5th centuries BC) and Diogenes (5th–4th centuries BC). The inscrutable Heraclitus was known as *(h)o skotos* 'the Obscure', while Diogenes was a founder of the Cynic school. For all the originals' pith, Davenport's translations are imagistically overwrought—the two philosophers the perfect grist for Davenport's Greekless mill.

Davenport has fooled the best of them. Notes Eric Ormsby in a recent review of *The Guy Davenport Reader* (2013), "In Addition, the *Reader* gives us selections of Davenport's translations from Ancient Greek poetry (Sappho, Anacreon, Archilochus)—he was trained as a classicist—as well as his versions," etc. See Eric Ormsby, "Glide of Eye and Sizzle of Tongue," review of *The Guy Davenport Reader, The New Criterion*, 32.5 (2014), 78–81. One further notes poet-essayist Rosanna Warren, commending Davenport's "long and honorable engagement with archaic Greek poetry." Warren (2008), 296, n. 30. For Warren's defense of the Greekless Sherod Santos, see p. 596.

90 *The situation is equally*
**"I don't speak . . . poems."** See Austin Allen, "The Man Who Died for Poetry": *A Q&A with Christian Wiman, Translator of* Stolen Air. www.bigthink.com/book-think/the-man-who-died-for-poetry. Web. 3/23/2012.

**"I couldn't . . . formal detail."** Christian Wiman, "Osip Mandelstam: new versions," *The New Criterion*, 29.8 (2011), 30.
**Fagles (later discussed).** See pp. 433–434, 482–485, 504–505.
**Nabokov (later discussed).** See pp. 532–534.

91 *To recall the lines*
**"Rome admir'd . . . time."** See Wentworth Dillon, *An Essay on Translated Verse. By the Earl of Roscommon.* (London: H. Hills, 1709), 11 (Gale ECCO Print Editions).

*The issue for Tucker*
**"be nearer . . . than another."** Tucker, 80.
**"We . . . inevitably vanish."** Tucker, 71–72 (with translation). The translation appears at p. 131.

92 *Focusing not only on*
**"And here . . . his original."** Tucker, 74–76.
**mindful . . . Prologue to Lucretius.** For an overview of Lucretius, *De Rerum Natura*, see pp. 303–305. Given the present focus on the opening Prologue, I here include my own translation, as modified, initially appearing in *The Classical Outlook*, 57.1 (1979), 11.

***De Rerum Natura* 1.1–43**
Mother of Rome, of men and gods
Ravishment, nurturing Venus,
Who under heaven's zodiac
Makes ship-decked sea and fruitful earth
To teem with life, since through you are
Conceived all forms of living things
Which risen, contemplate the sun—
Before you, goddess, flee the winds,
Your presence hails the clouds' retreat,
And daedal earth makes spring to you
Its flowered scent. Upon you smile
The ocean plains, and placid skies
Shine offerings of outpoured light.

For when the day dons spring attire,
And western breezes rush to take
All living things to their embrace,
The birds from heights ethereal
First herald, goddess, your approach,
Thrilled and quickened by your allure.
Then beasts maddened with desire
Fast overleap their fertile fields
And swim across the swirling tides—
Thus all bound by your sorcery
They crave to follow where you lead.

At length through oceans and mountains,
Throughout rapacious river streams
And leaf-encircled homes of birds
And greening fields, do you make each
New generation grow afresh,
Instilling in the hearts of all
The eagerness of luring love.

Since you alone hold sway of life,
And nothing, wanting you, ascends
To reach the splendid shores of light
Nor has its share of joy or charm,
I ask for your companionship
In writing verse to clarify
The cosmos for our Memmius,
For whom, goddess, you have wished
All ornament of excellence
In all respects at every time—
The more so, Venus, may you grant
Grace everlasting to these words.

And as I write make works of war
To slumber soundly throughout earth.
For you alone with limpid peace
Dispel the pain by man endured,
Since Mars, renowned in weaponry,
Takes refuge on your sacred breast,
Subdued by love's enduring wound;
And tilting back his tapered neck,
With gaping parted lips regales
His eyes ablaze with love on you—
His breathing lingering 'round your mouth.

Pour down a sweet complaint on him
Reclining on your sacred breast
To bring, clear goddess, peace for Rome!
For strife, our state's iniquity,
Drives thought of writing verse away,
And noble Memmius must be free
To serve its causes as he may.

93 *As Lucretius is drawn*

**Venus's charm—*venustas*.** *Venustas*, as noted, also meaning "charm," is a word built on Venus's very name. The use of *lepos* 'charm' (gen. *leporis*) is dictated by meter. Without Venus, nothing either "ascends / To reach the splendid shores of light / Nor has its share of joy or **charm** . . ."—*charm* here connoted by the word *amabile* 'love-worthy' (nec sine te quicquam dias in luminis oras / exoritur neque fit laetum neque **amabile** quicquam) (*DRN* 1.22–23).

**the intellect is attracted.** For the complementarity of physical and intellectual attraction in Plato, of whom Lucretius was doubtless mindful, see pp. 49–50.

**prolongation of . . . process.** Lucretius designates Venus as *Aeneadum genetrix* 'begetter of the line of Aeneas' (*DRN* 1.1), i.e., begetter of all Romans and of Rome in perpetuity.

***Distinction** and **charm***

**defined as . . . *piacevolezza*.** Adapted from V. Cox, 55–56.

***decorum* . . . things beautiful.** See further pp.18, 30, 438, 501–502, 571, 716.

94 *The same consideration*

**"There is . . . poet's alone."** Tucker, 90–91.

Chapter 11

96 *"He will generally*
**(including two by Sappho).** I. F. Stone, "From the Greek," *New York Review of Books,* 2/22/1979.

97 *Much the same may*
**doyenne of . . . Translation.** "Barnard's version of Sappho has become iconic . . . 'often read as if it is Sappho.'" Balmer (2013), 49 (quoting Yopie Prins, "Sappho's Afterlife in Translation," in Greene, ed. [1996b], 63).
**"When I wrote . . . with it."** From an unpublished letter to Pound, 12/2/1933; *PAIDEUMA,* 147.
**urged her, twice in 1934.** See Letters to Mary Barnard, 1/22/1934 and 8/30/1934; Paige, 252, 261. Himself a translator-by-crib, Pound urges a crib on Barnard in the first of the two letters. On Pound's two letters, and Barnard's correspondence with Marianne Moore and William Carlos Williams, see Barnard (1984), 54–66. For Barnard on metrics (which are nowhere reflected in her *Sappho*), see *PAIDEUMA,* 141–179.
**"the best . . . Literature."** The untraceable quote appears to this day on the back cover of Barnard's *Sappho.* To similar laudatory effect is Burton Raffel: "Sappho now enjoys as nearly perfect an English translation as one can find, a great translation, an immensely moving translation, complete, beautiful, deserving of endless praise." Raffel (1965), 236. However, the Greek-challenged Raffel, with no reference whatever to the Greek text, merely compares several Barnard renderings to those of other translators. Even the wary have been taken in: "Without being able to judge directly, I cannot imagine a fine poet like Barnard (whose Sappho I admire) to be anything but at the same time a careful classicist." George, 39 (adverting to Barnard's serviceable "A Footnote to These Translations," *Sappho,* 95–106).

Nor are classicists immune to over-reliance on translation, to the Mary Barnard mystique, or both. Yopie Prins uses disparate translations spanning a four-hundred-year period to bolster her highly theoretical interpretation of Sappho's *phainetai moi* 'He appears to me' (§2). Instead of telling us what the Greek reasonably conveys, Prins tell us, first, what various translations (Barnard's included) suggest about the *translators'* understanding of the Greek, and next, how those understandings validate Prins's own. Nor is it certain in each case that the chosen translators are well enough versed in Greek to at all appreciate the subtleties that Prins ascribes to them. This is especially so in Barnard's case. Despite Barnard's cited deficiencies—"the short lines and the shortened stanzas, . . . the spare diction and the fragmentary ending"—Prins proposes an interpretive finesse surely beyond Barnard's means. In the process, Prins nowhere adverts to the shakiness of Barnard's Greek, to her reliance on an Italian crib, or to her numerous struggles with each fragment. No matter, though, so long as the doyenne of Sappho translation may be suitably aligned with feminist theorizing about the "engendering" of Greek lyric. See Prins, 54, 63, in Greene, ed. (1966b).

*Explaining the rationale*
**"so far . . . unconveyed."** Barnard (1984), 284.
**is dictionally challenged.** See discussion at pp. 114–115.
**haiku-like sparseness.** Sparseness of form in American poetry, essentially unrelated to *haiku,* appears to have originated with "imagism" in the early twentieth century. This particular "ism" offered up isolated images as (necessarily sparse) poems. See Isaacs, 29–30, 41–42. For Barnard as imagist, see p. 564.
**expansive reconstructions.** "Mary Barnard's *Sappho*. . . also includes several long poems written primarily by Edmonds and must be criticized sharply for indicating

nowhere in her text or notes the extent of the restoration, and I for one do not find her short lines a suitable vehicle for Sappho's characteristic long ones." McEvilley, 280.
**it is mundane and unpoetic.** "Barnard keeps Sappho's simplicity of diction, but when the poem is stripped of her characteristic meter, the shape of her stanzas, her alliteration and assonance, what remains is an impression or a paraphrase of content, with no trace of Sappho's unique style. . . . The essential Sapphic combination of sharp-edged, jewel-like words and intricate rhythmic patterns is missing; Barnard's stanzas, with their three repetitive lines of seven syllables and three or four stresses, are completely misleading." Vandiver, 68.

98 *Barnard reveals that during*
**to help pass the time.** The following quotations and examples are from Barnard (1984), 281–284.
**poet Salvatore Quasimodo.** Focusing on Barnard's connection with Pound, critics tend to overlook the more influential Quasimodo. Thus Balmer (2013), 49. In her "A Footnote to These Translations" (1958), Barnard nowhere mentions Pound, Quasimodo, Italian, or the arduousness of her translation effort. An oblique reference to Quasimodo appears in Barnard's *Sappho* dedication "to Douglas and Marie Paige in return for the little volume of *Lirici Greci*" (Paige the editor in due course of Pound's *Selected Letters*, 1907–1941). Barnard otherwise notes that "In translating and annotating these poems I have followed Bowra." Barnard (1958), 100. The reference is to Bowra's *Greek Lyric Poetry* (1936, 2nd ed. 1960, corrected 1967) with its serviceable prose translation of all Greek verse translated by Barnard.
**equivalent . . . lexicon English.** "This brief, but telling remark," notes a reviewer, "helps explain why [Barnard's] translation of Sappho's poetry has been continuously in print for more than 40 years and has sold more than 100,000 copies." Walter Englert, "The Words She Commands," *Reed Magazine*, August, 1999 (Barnard attended Reed College). Barnard's *Sappho* was again reissued in 2012.

99 *Tucker notes that*
**"Lesbian Greek . . . musical."** Tucker, 14–15. See also Higham & Bowra, xlvii ("Greek is one of the most fluid and musical of all languages. Latin cannot approach it in these respects; and in the Western world of today it is rivalled only by Italian.").
**English . . . "yet conveyed."** Barnard (1984), 284.

*The task, not surprisingly*
**forty versions to produce.** Sappho's own choices were, of course, immeasurably more complex, the emphasis being on *finality*, on what genius irreducibly and thus permanently *fixes*. As Tucker notes:

> Where song was for generations so abundant, it follows that there was floating about among the people many an old ballad or favorite ditty whose author has been long forgotten. Numbers of these *Volkslieder* ['folk songs'], or snatches of them, lay, sometimes with consciousness and sometimes unrealized, in the memory of every child of Lesbos. The artistic poet did not scorn them; he feared no charge of plagiarism if he adopted and adapted them; he often acted as Burns acted with the ballads of Scotland; he took them, *gave them that marvelous and inexplicable touch of finality which only genius can impart, and so made them his forever.* This also did Sappho do, and her verses, when she deals with well-worn themes, are beyond question often fed with hints of older nameless songsters. [Tucker, 30–31 (emphasis added)]

On fixity and finality in art, see pp. 10–11, 415–416.

100 *Barnard's bridge method*
**"Some six . . . ever read."** Robert Chandler, tr., *Sappho* (London: J. M. Dent, 1998), xv.

101 *Unlike Mary Barnard*
**on one's predecessors.** To the contrary, as others came to occupy the field, Barnstone lent blurbs and approvals, even as his own translations were successively reissued. Barnstone's back-cover blurb to Davenport (1980) proclaims that Davenport's "exciting original versions are appropriately an immediate modern classic." Barnstone's blurb to Santos (2005) states that Santos "takes fragments and epigrammatic stanzas and makes each a singing erotic, caustic or descriptive lyric." Barnstone elsewhere refers (1966) to "the almost miraculous beauty of Miss Barnard's poems from Sappho" and to "Mr. Paul Roche's exquisite versions of Sappho"—as free in his assignment of praise as in his claim to langauge competence.
**"For many . . . sexist."** Barnstone (2000), 116.
**editions—. . . last count.** *Sappho and the Greek Lyric Poets* (Schocken Books, 1988), revised edition of *Greek Lyric Poetry,* originally published by Bantam in 1962 and Schocken in 1972; *Sappho: Lyrics in the Original Greek with translations by Willis Barnstone* (Anchor Books, 1965; facing Greek texts); *Sappho, Poems—a New Version* (Green Integer, 1999); *Sweetbitter Love: Poems of Sappho* (Shambhala, 2006; facing Greek texts); *The Complete Poems of Sappho* (Shambhala, 2009; without facing Greek texts); and *Ancient Greek Lyrics* (Indiana Univ. Press, 2010).
**It is archaic . . . wallpaper.** Translations and mega-anthologies of poetry are a Barnstone family industry. See "Willis Barnstone's Complete Bibliography," *BSM, LLC.* 2011. Web. 2/17/2013. There is Barnstone's *Modern European Poetry—French, German, Greek, Italian, Russian & Spanish* (Double Day, 1966), purporting to convey Barnstone's mastery of the languages in question (and surely conveying an expansive notion of Europe). Who really reads poetry in such an assemblage? The same year also saw Barnstone's *Modern European Poetry: The Most Comprehensive Collection of Contemporary English Translations Ever Published in One Volume* (Double Day, 1966). This is poetry as "The Greatest Show on Earth." Since 2003 there has been a Willis Barnstone Translation Prize. The prize is awarded for the best translation of a poem into English *from any language,* Barnstone the final arbiter. A commentator notes the Barnstone phenomenon as "poetry's answer to Thomas Kinkade" (the mass-marketing Home Shopping Network purveyor of painterly kitsch). One cannot disagree. See Dan Schneider, "The Stricture of Structure: Willis Barnstone's Successful Sonnets." N.p., 29 Sep. 2002. Web. 2/17/2013.

*Barnstone most recently*
**"the languages . . . Bible."** Frank Kermode, "A Bold New Bible," review of Willis Barnstone, *The Restored New Testament: A New Translation with Commentary, Including the Gnostic Gospels Thomas, Mary, and Judas* (2010), *New York Review of Books,* 7/15/2010.
**"I have been . . . Hebrew."** Barnstone (2006), xlvi.

102 *It is enough that Greek*
**"to learn . . . for poetry."** Barnstone (1995), 70.

*Barnstone's breezy absorption*
**"Perhaps it . . . based on it."** McEvilley, 280.
**"Tinkering with classical Greek . . ."** Barnstone (2006), xlvi.

103 *As concerns Barnstone's*
**"The version . . . Greek."** Barnstone (2002), 15.

**Masoretic Hebrew Text.** The Masoretic Text is the authoritative Hebrew text of the Old Testament. Its oldest manuscript dates to the ninth century AD. The MT was copied, edited, and distributed from the seventh to tenth centuries AD by a group of Jews known as the Masoretes. The MT both defines the books of the Jewish canon and establishes precise letterings with vocalizations and accentuation. These markings, with accompanying marginal notes (primarily in Aramaic), are preserved both in MT manuscripts and later-printed editions. The critical apparatus, with its emphasis on precise spellings, is known as the *Masorah*—Heb. *msr* 'hand down, transmit'—hence *Masoretic/Masoretes.*

*That said, we may glimpse*

**"I have been . . . Hebrew."** Barnstone (2006), xlvi.

**The KJB continues.** For some of the abbreviations used in referring to editions and versions of the Bible, see p. xvi.

104 *While the opening 'Let*

**The reason is recondite.** Note Bloch and Bloch (137): "The shift from the third to the second person typically occurs in direct addresses to persons of a higher social standing, as in Gen. 44:7 'Why does my lord speak [third person] such words as these? Far be it from your [second person] servants. . . .'" Whether this isolated instance supports typicality of usage is questionable, given that the third person is traditional in addressing majesty. Bloch and Bloch otherwise seek to *incorporate* the element of majesty, suggesting as "the most plausible explanation" that "the courtly, ceremonious tone of the [woman's] address to her lover belongs to their phantasy world, in which he figures as her 'king,' her very own 'Solomon,' as it were. . . ." For this interpretation Bloch and Bloch adduce Cant.1:4 and 1:12 (translations mine): "The king has brought me to his chamber [saying]: 'we will rejoice and exult in thee'" and "while the king was on his couch, my nard gave forth its scent." Alternatively, the issue is resolved with reference to the lover's "phantasy world," or dreamlike perception. She begins by invoking her beloved in the third person, as if he were absent, and next addresses him directly, as if suddenly appeared.

*Be that as it may,*

**"For all . . . of Holies."** See Marc Hirshman, "Love and Holiness: The Midrash on Song of Songs and Origen's Homilies," in *A Rivalry of Genius: Jewish and Christian Biblical Interpretation in Late Antiquity* (Albany: SUNY Press, 1996), 83. The most recent study documents the work's title as an expression of supreme worth, adducing a secondary, less supported sense of "anthology" or "compilation" (a song consisting of songs). See *The JPS Bible Commentary: Song of Songs שיר השירים*, The Traditional Hebrew Text with the New JPS Translation, Commentary by Michael Fishbane (Philadelphia: The Jewish Publication Society, 2015), 24. The Soncino Books of the Bible series makes no mention of "anthology," noting: "***the song of songs.*** The repetition of the noun in the genitive expresses the superlative; e.g., *most holy* (Exod. xxix.37, lit. 'holy of holies')." See A. Cohen, ed., The Song of Songs, in *The Five Megilloth* (London: The Soncino Press, 1946, 1974), 1. Cf. Sanskrit *Maharaj Adhiraja* 'King of Kings'.

106 *The dilemmas confronting*

**"obliges one . . . enigma."** The quotations and facts supporting my discussion of Barnstone's *Mao* appear in Barnstone (2000).

107 *Sherod Santos's Greek*

**"A chance . . . translation."** Santos, 19.

**"Proper . . . general rule."** Santos, 23.

108 *The proposed capture of*
**"opt[s] for . . . original."** Santos, 24.

*Santos's rejection of archaisms*
**admits the arcane: *talus*.** The list, excepting the last three, is by Wills (2005), 60.

*Translators lacking mastery*
**Santos's own explanation.** For the method, see interview by Bryan Narendorff, "The Continued Life: A Conversation with Sherod Santos," *Meridian* 16 (2005).
**"As you . . . glacial pace."** Santos was reviewed, largely negatively, and surprisingly with no mention of his lack of Greek, by classicist, prolific author-essayist, and translator Garry Wills (2005). Highly flowered rebuttals came from Willis Barnstone—"fresh originals," "unparalleled versions," "a shrewd and compelling craft," "amazing book of evenly beautiful poems"; and Rosanna Warren—"subtle formality," "artistic achievement," "living poems in English," "has not betrayed the originals so much as amplified them in his imagination." Rosanna Phelps Warren is the daughter of late illustrious parents, Poet Laureate Robert Penn Warren and poet-author Eleanor Clark (*Rome and a Villa*). Until July 2012 professor of Humanities at Boston University, she is the author of well-received original poetry. Though there is no ready indication of her training in Greek, she is a sometime translator of Euripides (with former husband, classicist Stephen Scully) and mentions in her Santos rebuttal that she herself has "translated a few poems by Sappho, Alcaeus, and Alcman . . . working closely from the Greek."

109 *Noted classicist D. S.*
**"a strong if . . . criticism."** D. S. Carne-Ross, "Prima Donna," review of Barnstone and Davenport, *New York Review of Books*, 5/3/1966.

*It is through friends*
**"Even the . . . remembrance."** Steiner (1966), 22. Steiner elsewhere observes, "Because all human speech consists of arbitrarily selected but intensely conventionalized signals, meaning can never be wholly separated from expressive form. Even the most purely ostensive, apparently neutral terms are embedded in linguistic particularity, in an intricate mold of cultural-historical habit." Steiner (1998), 252.

*110* *Robert Graves observes*
**"A poem's . . . strike home."** Graves (1965), 48.
**As this is . . . culminates.** On philology, see p. 571.
**nurture-deficient . . . Pope.** Johnson in his *Life of Pope* responds to critics impugning Pope's credentials. Noting "it is not very likely he overflowed with Greek," Johnson observes, "When he felt himself deficient, he sought assistance, and what man of learning would refuse to help him? Minute inquiries into the force of words are less necessary in translating Homer than other poets." Pope, as Johnson further explains, also likely relied on various Latin cribs then generally available. Johnson, *Lives of the English Poets*, III.114.
**Paul Valéry or T. S. Eliot.** "The French poet himself remarks with characteristic modesty, *quant au grec, je suis malheureusement un écolier des plus médiocres*—'As for Greek, I'm sadly about as middling a student as they come'—but he knew the language and his poetic talents and intuitions no doubt helped to give him deeper insight into the meaning of Pindar's poem than, say, a dogged but uninspired scholarly interpreter of the poet." Shankman (1994), 143–144 (with citations). As for Eliot, "although he deprecates himself among 'those who . . . have not remembered enough to read the

originals with ease' . . . a contemporary classicist has noted that the range and subtlety of Eliot's classical borrowings and echoes . . . as well as his sensitivity to linguistic and textual matters, argue 'an intimate and learned acquaintance with the ancient classics.'" De Laura, 155–156 (with citations). Of his own Greek, Pound says, "I wish I knew more Greek, but I envy Cocteau *his* greek as I shd. never envy Swinburne his probably ampler acquaintance." Pound (1938), 312.

*Poor translation is a*
**"In English . . . delight."** Murray (1930), 98, 121. Murray succeeded better as an expositor than translator of poetry, his Euripides translations eliciting the rebuke of T. S. Eliot's "Euripides and Professor Murray" (1921).

CHAPTER 12

113 *Lattimore here recreates*
**lost on erstwhile literati.** Burton Raffel, quoting Lattimore's translation of *phainetai moi* (also into *Sapphic* meter), notes: "This is very good, it is very moving; it does not, I feel, sound much like the poet of whom the commentators speak." Raffel (1965), 240–241. Raffel in no way adverts to Lattimore's use of an English Sapphic meter—if Raffel is at all aware of it. No wonder, then, that Lattimore, to Raffel, does not sound quite as Sappho should. Raffel, as elsewhere seen, can judge a translation only as English compared to other English translations.
**"Richmond . . . high quality."** Lloyd-Jones, 8.

114 *In the Greek, Aphrodite*
**"Every great . . . call *theos*."** Murray (1912), 14.

*Also, a more energetic*
**inattention to meter.** Quasimodo's first stanza reads as follows:

> Immortale Afrodite dal trono fiorito,
> figlia di Zeus, tu che intrecci inganni,
> ti supplico, o potente,
> non piegare l'anima mia
> con affanni e con dolore. . . .

Salvatore Quasimodo, *Lirici Greci* (Casa Editrice Mondadori, 1944). Barnard would have done better with the consummate Italian Sapphics of Ugo Foscolo (1778–1827)—the third and best of Foscolo's three translations of *phainetai moi* appearing in an appendix to his *Essays on Petrarch* (1821). For Foscolo's translation, see Lipking, 85–87 (describing Foscolo as a kind of Italian Swinburne: "Foscolo views himself as a reincarnation of the classical lover [i.e., of Sappho], "her spirit lives in him"). Foscolo's version is noteworthy for the multiple elisions that hasten the Italian (comparable to the elisions in Sappho's original), e.g., *Serpe la fiamma entro il mio sangue, ed ardo*. See pp. 313–314. Born on the Ionian island of Zacynthos—off the western coast of Greece, near Odysseus's Ithaca (see map)—Foscolo (poet and writer) knew both Modern and Classical Greek. Barnard similarly took no note of the Sapphics of Italian classicist Gennaro Perròtta (1900–1962): *Afrodite immortale dal bel trono*, etc., *Lirici Greci* (Milano: Garanzi, 1976).

116 *For the rest, we again*
***the use of God* for *Zeus*.** For the highly misleading impression this substitution caused in Benjamin Jowett's famed translation of Plato (1871), see Steiner (1988), 362–363

("Plato's cosmic builder is resolutely conceived in the image of a human craftsman, not an omnipotent Deity in the Judaic-Christian vein.").

117 *Davenport's 1995 version*
**Sappho's state . . . ours.** Davenport has always had his admirers. I note, with due regard, the highly favorable review by my mentor Charles Rowan Beye (1981).

*'On your dazzling throne'*
**"I find the . . . picture."** Carne-Ross (reply to Barnstone), *New York Review of Books,* 5/26/1966.

118 *At the risk of technicality,*
**"do not aspirate their φ."** Barnstone (2009), xlv. The explanation here provided significantly summarizes a taxing full-page footnote on Greek phonology in Barnstone's 2006 edition. The footnote (as he acknowledges) was written with the help of—i.e., essentially *by*—classicist William E. McCulloh, the author of introductions to Barnstone's 1967 and 2005 editions (and of the latter's metrical addendum).

119 *The poem's third and*
**emphatically repetitive.** Roche (1966), 145–146; Roche (1998), 145.

*In a version appearing*
**"enrobed . . . than enthroned."** There are persuasive arguments for either reading. An early proponent of the minority review is Michael Putnam, "*Throna* and Sappho 1.1," *Classical Journal,* 56 (1960–1961), 79–83. Thus, "the epithet, if indeed it is derived from *throna* 'embroidered flowers' rather than from *thronos* 'throne', can be translated 'with varied embroidered flowers'. For those who reenact her, the goddess of love is as limitlessly varied as the limitless varieties of flowers embroidered on her exterior." Nagy (1996), 101. Sometimes noted is the alternate reading, *poikilophrēn* 'diversely minded'.

Though differing in result, Poochigian proceeds in full sympathy with the premise and approach herein. Noting that previous translations have all but neglected form for content, he notes: "Since form and content are inseparable, the translator must find not only appropriate words for the original words but an appropriate form for the original form. Sappho did not compose free verse, and free verse translations, however faithful they may be to her words, betray her poems by their very nature." Poochigian, xiv. Poochigian otherwise offers an excellent introduction covering major points of interest to the lay reader.

*Yet even as the choice*
**Characteristic . . . style, etc.** Paraphrased from Stephen Usher, tr., *Dionysius of Halicarnassus: Literary Composition, Critical Essays II* (Cambridge: Harvard Univ. Press, Loeb Classical Library, 1985), 199.

120 *Looking to Lattimore's*
**whole-line renderings.** Such renderings, of which more were desired, are comparable in effect to Swinburne's "Sapphics" (pp. 248–249). Lattimore's "Hymn to Aphrodite" is also worth a studied reading. Sappho has since been rendered into Sapphics by Jim Powell, *The Poetry of Sappho* (Oxford and New York: Oxford Univ. Press, 2007). For earlier renderings into Sapphics, see Wharton (1895), 49–69 (among which John Addington Symonds's *phainetai moi* [1883] is especially noteworthy).

121 *Consecutive monosyllables*

**little words . . . the line.** The defect, as specifically applied to English hexameter, has long been noted. "Thus in English hexameter, not only is quantity, the essential principal of the hexameter, wholly unknown, but the multiplicity of little words destroys the metrical value of the pauses, on the proper adjustment of which the harmony of the heroic Greek verse depends, and delays and breaks up the movement; while finally, the accumulation of rough consonant sounds in our words adds vastly to these defects." C. T. Lewis, 366.

*Lattimore here uses*

**Greek conjunction . . . analysis.** For fuller treatment, see pp. 312–315.

122 *I have attempted to*

**Gr. *paizein* . . . connotation.** Cf. Rosenmeyer, "Girls at Play, etc." (2004).

*As I have sought*

**"sense and flavor . . . these."** Reyes, 17 (paraphrasing C. S. Lewis).
**have "stopp[ed] about 1890."** David Cecil, in a 1978 letter to C. S. Lewis scholar and editor Humphrey Carpenter (as quoted in Reyes, 18, n. 55).

*It is a truism that*

**"out of touch . . . literature."** Reyes, 18 (quoting C. S. Lewis, "Introductory Letter," xix, in *The Collected Poems of C. S. Lewis*).

Part IV, Chapter 13

172 *The lost Cypria, in*

**Cypria, in eleven books.** The *Cypria,* which does not survive, is the major source of events preceding those of the *Iliad.* What we know of the *Cypria* comes quite indirectly—such are the vagaries of preservation—from a summary by the Byzantine Neoplatonist Proclus (5th century AD) in his handbook titled *Chrestomathy* (Gr. *chrēstos* 'useful' + *mathein* 'to know'). The summary in turn is preserved by the patriarch Photius I of Constantinople (9th century AD) in a work titled *Bibliotheca* (*Library*). The *Library* is a unique Byzantine compendium on the history of literature, summarizing works read by Photius himself and containing many notices of works since lost. Photius ostensibly wrote the *Library* (per its introductory letter) to both console and instruct his (absent) brother Tarasius concerning the books they had been unable to share in each other's presence. Proclus's summary of the *Cypria* appears as *Library* summary number 239 of 280. References to the *Cypria* are, accordingly, to Proclus's summary of the *Cypria* as preserved in Photius. The *Cypria* is today most accessible in the Loeb Classical Library editions of H. G. Evelyn-White (1914) and M. L. West (2003). For more detailed discussion of the relationship between Proclus and Photius, see West (2013), 1–11.

*Though not using the*

**"Cycle" or "Epic Cycle."** It is in his *Rhetoric* that Aristotle first devises the notion of an "Epic Cycle," establishing it "as a literary quantity." See West (2013), 23–26.
**"Here again . . . Little Iliad."** Butcher (*Poetics* 1459a–b, XXIII.3), 89–90. The idea is echoed by Wagner in *Opera and Drama*:

> An action which consists of many parts is either over-weighted, redundant, and unintelligible when all these parts are of equally suggestive, decisive importance;

> or it is petty, arbitrary and meaningless when these parts are nothing but odds and ends of actions. The content of an action is the idea that lies at the bottom of it: if this idea is a great one, wide of reach, and drawing upon man's whole nature in any one particular line, then it also ordains an action which shall be decisive, one and indivisible; for only in such an action does a great idea reveal itself to us. [Ellis, tr., 156]

173 *Given their comprehensiveness*
**"The fantastic . . . them."** Quotations and summary in this paragraph are from the excellent discussion by Jasper Griffin. For qualification of Griffin's view, see Nagy (1979/1999), 7–8, n. 4, and Nagy (1990), 72, n. 99 (Allowance of the fantastic does not so much indicate the inferiority of the Cycle vis-à-vis a superior or "unique" Homer as "the religious ideology of local cults, reflecting the more localized interests of individual city-states or groups of city-states."). See also Burgess, 158–159 (with reference to Griffin's "well-known article").
**excess the *Iliad* conveys.** For supernatural or surreal occurrences in the *Iliad* and *Odyssey* (aside from those of Odysseus's wanderings), see Duban (1980). As there noted, such occurrences tend to intrude only at climactic moments, as when Achilles rampages before the walls of Troy or Odysseus prepares to slay the suitors.

*To the extent that the*
**"records the fact . . . him."** Nagy (2009b), 25. Nagy explains that "the prime regulator of the Homeric epithet in particular [here *polutlas*] and formula in general [here *polutlas di(*F*)os Odusseus*] is traditional *theme* [here "homecoming"] rather than current meter [dactylic hexameter]." Such analysis employs a diachronic perspective. On the diachronic/synchronic distinction, critical alike to the study of linguistics and oral poetry, see pp. 197–198, 512, 604, 616–617.

174 *Subject as it was to*
**indefatigable classicist-critic.** See Mendelsohn (2004).
**usurpation of Helen palliates.** Blondell (2009), 4, 8–9, 17; see further Chapter 18.

175 *After the Little Iliad*
**tale of the Trojan Horse.** A reference to the Trojan Horse, focusing on Achilles's son Neoptolemus (hiding within), appears at *Od.* 11.523–540.
**works of Quintus and Tzetzes.** Also extant is the early fifth-century *Dionysiaca* of Nonnus of Panopolis (upper Egypt). This is an extraordinary epic on a non-cyclic theme: the labors and final triumph of Dionysus. Composed in the dactylic hexameter and epic dialect of Homer, and comprising forty-eight books and over 20,000 lines, the *Dionysiaca* is the fancifully degenerate product of its age and milieu.

*Virgil is both a user*
**most untranslatable lines.** Sunt lacrimae rerum et mentem mortalia tangunt (*Aen.* 1.463), lit., 'There are tears of things [i.e., things have their tears] and mortal [matters] touch the mind', or: 'Life is tears and mortality touches the mind." Compare C. S. Lewis, "Life has its tears and men's mortality its sting;" and Wordsworth (in two verses): "Tears for the frail estate of human kind / Are shed; and mortal changes touch the mind." A. E. Housman offers a poignant adaptation: "They say, my verse is sad: no wonder; / Its narrow measure spans / Tears of eternity, and sorrow, / Not mine, but man's." Dryden curiously omits the line. See also David Wharton, "Sunt lacrimae rerum: An Exploration in Meaning," *Classical Journal*, 103.3 (2008), 259–279.
**is already epic history.** Epic's self-memorialization can be more immediate yet, as seen in Helen's weaving ". . . the numerous struggles / of Trojans, breakers of horses,

and bronze-armoured Achaians, / struggles that they endured for her sake at the hands of the war god." *Il.* 3.126–128 (R. Lattimore, tr.). Helen's medium is more transient, however, suggesting a certain lack of finality in the formation of what has but recently transpired.
**marked . . . dominion.** See further pp. 293–299.

176 *Integrating Homer as they*
**Odyssean *Aeneid* . . . Iliadic.** Nor should we be unmindful of the marked similarity between the *Aeneid* and Old Testament story of the Exodus from Egypt. "In each tale a leader obedient to a divine command leads his people, often protesting, to a land which has not only been promised them but was the original home of their forebears." Lind (1963), xiv–xv.
**supreme reinvention.** On Virgil's "translation" of Homer, see further pp. 284–288.

177 *The Illiad and Odyssey's*
**"greater . . . and diffusion."** Nagy (1982), 72.
**"function as . . . the Returns."** Finkelberg (2002), 78.
**"meant the . . . metaepics."** Finkelberg (2002), 79.
**stock cyclic materials.** Materials to which "the [c]yclic poets had very little to add." Finkelberg (2002), 86.
**added, among much else.** For examples, see Finkelberg (2002), 76–78.
**"reenactment of . . . *Cypria*."** Finkelberg (2002), 76 (quoting source).
**"I despise the . . . it might."** The Callimachean poem is discussed in Acosta-Hughes and Stephens, 79, 96–97. Further on Callimachus, see pp. 280–282.

178 *Having earlier noted the*
**"the era . . . audience," etc.** Nagy (1979/1999), 9–10. Further on Panhellenism, see Nagy (1990a), Ch. 2 ("The Poetics of Panhellenism and the Enigma of Authorship in Early Greece") and Ch. 3 ("The Panhellenization of Song"); also Nagy (1990b), Ch. 3 ("Hesiod and the Poetics of Pan-Hellenism").

179 *As my discussions of*
**"the potter . . . with bard."** *WD* 24–26.
**victory . . . such a contest.** *WD* 646–661.

*The oral tradition is*
**Ionic . . . Sappho's Aeolic.** For the Greek dialects, see pp. 65–71.
**Achilles once sacked Lesbos.** *Il.* 9.128–130.
**"in their beauty . . . women."** *Il.* 9.130 (R. Lattimore, tr.).
**Lesbos, Phrygia . . . Hellespont.** *Il.* 24.543–545.
**as Lesbos . . . knew Homer.** "Lesbos must have known epic poetry ever since its colonization from Boeotia and Thessaly in the eleventh or tenth century." West, "The View from Lesbos," 207.
**Homer's birthplace . . . Chios.** See also the *Homeric Hymn to Apollo* 166–176, where the anonymous poet refers to himself as "a blind man who lives on rocky Chios, all of whose songs excel in aftertimes." Chios is also the birthplace of Mikis Theodorakis (b. 1925), Greece's greatest songwriter and orchestral composer of all time.

The so-called Homeric Hymns—both designations problematic—survive as thirty-three hexametric compositions of greatly varying lengths and different dates and origins. They are variously addressed to different deities and share certain formal aspects. The earliest of the hymns is dated to the seventh century BC. Despite the Homeric authorship apparently inscribed in the cited *Hymn to Apollo*, the issue was contested

even in antiquity. See generally Bruno Currie, "Hymns, Homeric" in Finkelberg, ed. (2011), Vol. II, 383–385.
**source of the Homeridae.** See T. W. Allen, "The Homeridae," *Classical Quarterly*, 1.2&3 (1907), 135–143; and Nagy (2010), 59–65 ("The Homeridae of Chios").

180 *At some point in*
**"I believe . . . an inscription."** Steiner (1996), 100–101.
**"Athens Hellenised . . . Hellas."** Mackail (1919), 20. Though writing before Milman Parry (1902–1935) founded the discipline of oral composition (see pp. 197–198, 616–617), Mackail exhibits an instinctive ease and appeal:

> The effect of the re-emergence and dominance of Homer on the literature and life of the whole Greek world was swift and profound. From 550 BC, or some years earlier, the whole of Greek literature implies Homer, is founded on Homer, is in organic connection with Homer throughout. . . . The Attic drama was the creation of a Homericised Hellas with its Hellenised Homer. So, in varying measure, was the whole of classical Greek literature: not only the dramatists, not only the poets, but the orators, the historians, the philosophers.
>
> Thus the touch of Homer upon Hellas had something of the same awakening and vivifying effect that the touch of Hellas has had, again and again, on other countries and later ages. The movement of the sixth century BC, which brought Homer fully into the life of Hellas, was the first Renaissance. In the course of that movement the Homeric and Hellenic genius were incorporated and became indissolubly one. Jointly they created what we mean by Greece; they created ideals toward which the human race has ever since turned its eyes. [Mackail (1919), 20–21]

*Only in the Alexandrian*
**Alexandrian period.** During the third and second centuries BC, Alexandria, in Egypt, became the center of ancient learning and new refinements—or affectations—in the writing of Greek poetry. Neoteric poetry would make inroads into the Latin poetry of the first century BC. See further pp. 282, 302, 322–323.
**handwritten scrolls . . . *Odyssey*.** The most famous (and reliable) manuscript of the *Iliad*, known as Venetus A, dates to the tenth century AD. Taking its name from the library in Venice where it is housed, Venetus A preserves not only a text of the *Iliad* but also annotations and commentaries known as the "A scholia," along with a valuable summary of the early Epic Cycle. The manuscript was first published in 1788 in a Latin edition by Jean Baptiste Gaspard d'Ansse de Villoison. See Casey Dué et al., *Recapturing a Homeric Legacy: Images and Insights from the Venetus A Manuscript of the Iliad* (Washington and Cambridge: Center for Hellenic Studies and Harvard Univ. Press, 2009).

*Zenodotus's edition of*
**"All-Athenian Festival."** See Plato's dialogue *Ion* and Nagy (2002).

## Chapter 14

182 *Each new day, with*
**"Morning brings . . . ages."** Jeffrey S. Cramer, ed., *Walden* (New Haven: Yale Univ. Press, 2004), 55 (page references below also to Cramer). Thoreau prescribes the reading of Homer and Aeschylus in Greek. Such activity requires that readers "in some measure emulate their heroes, and consecrate morning hours to their pages." The classic

authors, says Thoreau, are "as beautiful almost as the morning itself" and singular in "their elaborate beauty and finish," the "lifelong and heroic literary labors of the ancients" (98, 101).

The association of dawn (Aurora), morning, creation, divinity, and heroism is pervasive in Thoreau. *Walden* is framed by such concerns, from the dedicatory invocation of the "chanticleer in the morning" to the work's closing words:

> The light which puts out our eyes is darkness to us. Only that day dawns to which we are awake. There is more day to dawn. The sun is but a morning star (81, 325).
>
> The morning wind forever blows, the poem of creation is uninterrupted; but few are the ears that hear it; Olympus is but the outside of the earth everywhere (82).
>
> That man who does not believe that each day contains an earlier, more sacred, and auroral hour than he has yet profaned, has despaired of life. . . . All memorable events, I should say, transpire in morning time and in morning atmosphere. . . . All poets and heroes. . . . are children of Aurora, and emit their music at sunrise (87).
>
> We must learn to reawaken and keep ourselves awake, not by mechanical aids, but by an infinite expectation of the dawn, which does not forsake us in our soundest sleep (88).

And from Thoreau's journal comes the following stunning passage:

> July 4 [1840]. 4 o'clock a.m. The Townsend Light Infantry encamped last night in my neighbor's enclosure.
>
> The night still breathes slumberously over field and wood, when a few soldiers gather about one tent in the twilight, and their band plays an old Scotch air, with bugle and drum and fife attempered to the season. It seems like the morning hymn of creation. The first sounds of the awakening camp, mingled with the chastened strains which so sweetly salute the dawn, impress me as the morning prayer of an army.*
>
> And now the morning gun fires. The soldiers awakening to creation and awakening it. I am sure none are cowards now. These strains are the roving dreams which steal from tent to tent, and break forth into distinct melody. They are the soldier's morning thought. Each man awakes himself with lofty emotions, and would do some heroic deed. You need preach no homily to him; he is the stuff they are made of.
>
> *I have heard a strain of music issuing from a soldiers' camp in the dawn, which sounded like the morning hymn of creation. The birches rustling in the breeze and the slumberous breathing of the crickets seemed to hush their murmuring to attend to it. [Written in pencil on a fly-leaf of the Journal.]
>
> [Bradford Torrey and Walter Harding, eds., *The Journal of Henry D. Thoreau* (In Fourteen Volumes Bound As Two): 1837–October, 1855 (New York: Dover, 1962), Vol. I, 58]

**upriver . . . downstream.** See *G* 1.198–203.
**"beneficent . . . being formed."** Mills, 39.
**with the hellhound Cerberus.** *Il.* 5.395–397; 8.362–369; *Od.* 11.623–626.
**locution *hērōs theos* 'hero god'.** Pindar, *Nemean* 3.22. The *(h)ērōs* 'hero' is any warrior who strives for glory in battle. The *(h)ēmitheos* 'demigod' is a hero of half-divine parentage, though the distinction is not always observed. Heracles is the only *(h)ērōs theos.*

183 *The imperial/civilizing*

**between which . . . choose.** The seminal work is that of G. Karl Galinsky, *The Herakles Theme* (1972); and more recently, Thalia Papadopoulos, "Heracles in Perspective," in *Heracles and Euripidean Tragedy* (Cambridge: Cambridge Univ. Press, 2005), 1–9. Papadopoulos notes the "extreme ambivalence concerning the nature of Heracles's *aretē*, 'virtue' or 'excellence'. On the one hand, Heracles is portrayed as the invincible hero and civilizer of mankind, an exemplar of virtue; on the other hand, he is presented as the megalomaniac and hubristic conqueror, a representative of excess." See also F. Carter Philips, "Heracles" (1978), with particular reference to Heracles in Homer and Hesiod.

For the "Choice of Heracles," first formulated by the fifth-century Sophist Prodicus, see Galinsky, 101–104. There are a dozen and more old artist depictions of the "Choice of Heracles," typically in the form of the hero choosing between two women, one representing virtue and duty, the other pleasure and vice. Two of the better known are by Paolo Veronese, "Wisdom and Strength" (c. 1580) and *Allegory of Virtue and Vice (the Choice of Heracles)* (c. 1565), flanking an interior gallery entrance at the Frick Collection, New York City. Handel composed *The Choice of Hercules*, an Oratorio in One Act (1751).

*An illegitimate son*

**Heracles . . . quarreling.** See especially *Il.* 19.85–133, where Agamemnon, after reconciling with Achilles, awkwardly relates the birth of Heracles in a way suggesting Achilles's subservience to Agamemnon—even as Heracles, by delayed birth, was subservient to King Eurystheus (for whom he accomplished his Labors). For discussion with reference to the name *Heracles* = '*kleos* of Hera' (Gr. *hērōs* 'hero' cognate with *Hērā*), and the "unseasonality" of the hero's life, see Nagy (2013), 33–47 (Heracles's birth delayed, Achilles's death hastened; seasonality restored in cult worship after death). In sum, Achilles, as a latter-day Heracles, adheres to his predecessor's key aspiration and namesake: the *hero's kleos = Heracles*. On heroic "withering," based on the etymological and thematic relationship between (*h*)*ērōs* 'hero' and (*h*)*ōra* 'season', see Garcia, 23, n. 50. For further comparison between Heracles and Achilles, see Fantuzzi, 8–9: both "born to kill," both "display the most brazen and fierce awareness of the killer's disposition and of their unbeatable superiority," both cross-dress for a period of their lives "for reasons that are totally unheroic"; cf. Loraux (1995), 116–139 ("Herakles: The Supermale and the Feminine").

**Heracles later . . . Troy.** *Il.* 5.640–651; 14.250–251.

**"For not even . . . glory."** *Il.* 18.117–121.

**death . . . his deification.** As Heracles's situation is unique, it is marked by a certain indecision. Heracles is the last of the heroes whom Odysseus encounters in the underworld: "After him I was aware of powerful Herakles; / his image, that is, but he himself among the immortal / gods enjoys their festivals, married to sweet-stepping Hebe, / child of great Zeus and Hera of the golden sandals. . . ." *Od.* 11.601–604 (R. Lattimore, tr.).

**deification . . . heroic ethic.** The evasion of death is unthinkable in the *Iliad* (see p. 183).

184 *It is argued that*

**"closer to . . . or Odysseus."** Nagy (1979/1999), 14.

**several generations removed.** Nagy (1979/1999), 14–15.

**"split of characteristics."** Nagy (1979/1999), 14 (a split in characteristics based on language signaling both Achilles and Odysseus in the contemporaneous *Homeric Hymn to Heracles*).

**"as . . . achievement."** Schein, 68.

**Achilles with . . . Poseidon.** See Mills, Chs. 3 and 4.

## Chapter 15

185 *Following a grievous insult*

**Achilles sings *klea andrōn*.** *Il.* 9.189: "With [the lyre] he was pleasing his heart, singing the glories of men." The topic of heroic glory or fame, here treated in brief, is immense. The topic "occupies a central place not only in Greek epic but in the entire Indo-European epic tradition as well." Segal (1994), 85–109 (with bibliography); also Nagy (1974), 244–255, and Nagy (1979/1999), 15–25, 94–117.

Odysseus too plays the bard, relating the tale of his wanderings—thus do we know of them—at the banquet of his Phaeacian hosts (*Odyssey*, Books Eight through Twelve). Heroism, as depicted in the *Iliad* and *Odyssey*, differs widely. See Segal (2001), Ch. 5.

**'the glories . . . were heroes'.** *Il.* 9.524–525: "Thus do we also hear of the glories of men who were heroes in days gone by."

*Achilles sings epic poetry*

**reference point . . . situation.** In sorting through *klea andrōn* (*Il.* 9.189), Achilles lights on the story of Meleager, emphasizing the themes of rage and reconciliation (the story told later in Book Nine by Phoenix). It is the paradigm most suited to Achilles's own situation and for that reason, perhaps, saved for recitation by Phoenix. Achilles reflects on the tale, while Phoenix expressly draws its moral. This possibility is urged by the only Iliadic recurrence of the phrase *klea andrōn*—at the start of Phoenix's recitation (*Il.* 9.524). One scholar notes, over-restrictively, that "Achilles [now] contentedly play[s] the role of bard—a singer of the glorious deeds of other men, not the performer of his own," and that "Achilles has crossed into new territory, where stories of what moved the men of old—*kléa andrōn*—have no force." Alexander, 86, 102. *Klea andrōn* sooner seem to have *paradigmatic* force, and it is for that reason, not because he has somehow changed *métiers*, that Achilles consults them. Milton effects a comic inversion of the famed Iliadic scene—the newly defeated satanic host singing to the harp "Thir own Heroic deeds and hapless fall / By doom of Battel." See *PL* 2.546–550.

**articulates it in the *Iliad*.** See *Il.* 9.410–416.

**there is no fame in old age.** Nestor is the oldest and wisest of the Greeks at Troy (and the only such warrior of his generation). Nestor's own pre-Iliadic deeds of glory, which he ever recalls, serve largely to bolster his credibility as advisor to others (age having its prerogatives). As others once heeded Nestor, those presently quarreling at Troy, he urges, should listen and be reconciled. The "garrulous" Nestor, played to somewhat comic effect, has no *kleos* for having outlived his heroic past. One must rather, and should sooner, die in battle for the assurance of fame. Such death, however, is not inevitable. Thus does the storm-tossed Aeneas, fearing an inglorious death at sea, invoke as "three-and-four-times blessed" those fallen at Troy—wishing the same had been his lot (*Aen.* 1.94–101). Nestor appears in the *Odyssey*, as seen, having outlived the Trojan War—even as he had earlier outlived his own heroic past. The exhaustive study is Douglas Fame, *Hippota [Horseman] Nestor* (Washington and Cambridge: Center for Hellenic Studies and Harvard Univ. Press, 2009).

**option he early articulates.** See *Il.* 1.169–171; also 9.393–400, 417–420.

**"nowhere . . . nobler choice."** Snell, 1, 21 (vis-à-vis Aeschylus's treatment in the lost Achilles trilogy, apparently the only ancient tragedy centering on Achilles).

186 *Long but inglorious old*

**Long but . . . alternative.** See *Il.* 9.410–420 and cf. 1.352–354. The development of this alternative is deftly explained by Floyd, 180.

**the Oath of Tyndareus.** See pp. 53, 211, 619.

**"life . . . precious than glory."** Alexander, 98.
**"the determination to live."** Alexander, 103.

*Achilles is not merely*
**"He is blessed . . . these."** *Th.* 96–103.
**find him, lyre in hand.** There are numerous artistic representations of Chiron's instructing Achilles in archery, e.g., Donato Creti, *The Education of Achilles by Chiron* (1714); or on the lyre, e.g., Pompeo Batoni, *The Education of Achilles by Chiron* (1746). Such images also endure in Roman frescoes.
**"delighting" his spirit as.** *Il.* 9.186–191.

187 *Though the recurring wish*
**be rendered as "fame."** "The usual translation of *kleos* as 'fame' is inadequate, for 'fame' indicates only 'the consequences rather than the full semantic range [of *kleos*]' whereas, in fact, the relationship between the actual fame of the hero and the medium that preserves that fame is more complex: 'The actions of gods and heroes gain fame through the medium of the singer, and the singer calls his medium *kleos*.'" Segal (2001), 88–89 (quoting Nagy [1974], 248–250).
**first-listed . . . is Cleo.** *Th.* 75–79.
**'that I might recount'.** *Th.* 31–32, 65–67.
**Pierian . . . Zeus wishes it.** *WD* 1–4. The Pierian Spring, located in southern Macedonia, near Mt. Olympus (see map), was sacred to the Muses. Said Pope in his "Essay on Criticism" (1709), "A little learning is a dang'rous thing; / Drink deep, or taste not the Pierian spring."

188 *What, more precisely,*
**acquires *kleos aphthiton*.** *Kleos aphthiton* 'imperishable fame' is a unique Homeric locution (though not without analogues), appearing only once in words spoken by Achilles, as further discussed below. Playing on the word *aphthiton* 'imperishable, unwithering', Homer calls Achilles's kingdom in Thessaly (northern Greece) *Phthiē* (Gr. *phthino*, 'perish, decay, wither'). The punning name of this ill-defined locale highlights the perishability of Achilles's life measured against the acquisition of imperishable fame. See Nagy (1979/1999), 174–185, and Garcia, 244 and n. 10. Or, one might say: to be home in *Phthiē* 'Perish' is to *perish*—slowly and without fame—to wither away. Forms of the word *aphthiton* 'imperishable' describe, e.g., objects of divine manufacture (Agamemnon's kingly scepter, Hephaestus's house), Zeus's thoughts (*aphthita mēdea eidōs* 'knowing imperishable thoughts'), and the vines, 'unwithering', on the Cyclopes' island. See further Garcia, 236 and 239–258.

The inquiry has of late undergone a persuasive notional change. "Achilles's *kleos aphthiton* is not 'imperishable fame', for there is nothing in the world of the *Iliad* that would allow us to comprehend what 'imperishable' means. Instead, we should interpret is as 'unwithered fame,' fame that is temporarily conditioned, though projected into an indefinite future." Garcia, 237. By "temporarily conditioned," etc., Garcia appears to mean *singled out for long-durational value or expectation.* In other words—and despite the projected or supposed perpetuity of, e.g., fortifications, tombs, epic poetry, and epic memory itself—nothing lasts forever. As Homer's imagery makes clear, all organic matter eventually withers, perishes. And the non-organic disintegrates; is lost, misplaced, or eventually forgotten. What informs Garcia's interpretation of *kleos aphthiton,* then, is the notion of an as-yet unwithering, and hopefully long-to-be unwithered, fame.

For purposes of discussion herein, I nonetheless adhere to *kleos aphthiton* 'imperishable fame'.
**"are torn . . . of mortality."** MacCarey, 166.

**"Man, supposing . . . others."** *Il.* 12.322–328 (R. Lattimore, tr.). The reader should note that the twice-used *glory* in Lattimore's translation does not render the Greek word *kleos,* but the related words *kudos* and *euchos.* The dictional preferences, however, impede neither meaning nor theme. In the lines immediately preceding, Sarpedon imagines what he believes men will someday say of him and Glaukos, venturing that men will not consider them *akleës* 'without *kleos*'.
**wrested *kleos* from others.** See further pp. 190–191.

*Given its transcendent*
***aoidos . . . periklutos.*** *Od.* 8.83.
**"If you . . . of singing."** *Od.* 8.496–498 (R. Lattimore, tr.). See further (without reference to *Od.* 8.83, 496–498), Irene J. F. de Jong, "The Homeric Narrator and His Own *Kleos,*" *Mnemosyne,* 4th series, 59.2 (2006), 188–207.

189 *The epic undertaking is*
**"They [the Muses] . . . ease."** *Th.* 31–33, 36–40.
**"Civilized . . . looks back."** Clark, 16–17. See also p. 366.
**Western civilization . . . later.** Indeed, while hundreds of classical works are known by title only, and others have survived thanks to a single manuscript, or in mere fragments, the manuscript tradition of the *Iliad* and *Odyssey* attests to unflagging interest and copying, to say nothing of translation.

*So much the reward*
**lamented . . . 'unforgettable grief'.** The *kleos aphthiton/penthos alaston* dichotomy has been formalized by Nagy (1974), 261. For the numerous discussions of *kleos* through 1991, see Goldhill (1991), 72, n. 12. Though Achilles alone speaks of *kleos aphthiton,* and only once (*Il.* 9.413), it remains the ultimate desideratum.
**Delusional . . . approaching.** Hector's delusionism is elsewhere buttressed by the hubristic wish to be "immortal and unageing forever" and to have the same honor as Athena and Apollo. See *Il.* 8.538–541, 13.825–826; Nagy (2009b), 204, n. 10; also Nagy (1979/1999), 142–150 ("The Death of Hektor").
**"doing something . . . come."** *Il.* 22.304–305 (R. Lattimore, tr.).
**proposes *olesthai eükleiōs.*** *Il.* 22.110.
**adverb *eükleiōs* . . . Homer.** Lit., 'with good *kleos,* well-gloried', or 'well reported'. Homeric *eükleiōs* appears in Greek tragedy (as does *akleiōs* 'famelessly'). Also appearing are noun and adjective counterparts *eukleia* 'good report' and *eukleēs* 'of good report'. A certain Hectorian taint or defeatism marks the treatment of women's *kleos* in Greek tragedy, the taint usually deriving from mortal self-sacrifice or some less-than-praiseworthy action (e.g., Medea's slaying her children). Like Penelope in the *Odyssey* (see pp. 194–195), women in Greek tragedy lack an affirmative, self-emanating *kleos.* See **Aeschylus:** *Agamemnon* 1098; **Sophocles:** *Antigone* 502, 695, 817; *Electra* 973, 985; **Euripides**: *Children of Herakles* 534, 623; *Alcestis* 150, 447, 938; *Hippolytus* 47; *Phoenician Women* 1742; *Suppliants* 1015; *Medea* 415; *Iphigenia at Aulis* 1376, 1383, 1504; *Helen* 135; *Electra* 1084. I thank Anne Rabe, then of Brown University, for her help in researching these uses.

Though the notions of a 'beautiful death' (*kalos thanatos*) or 'well-gloried' or 'well-reported death' (*eukleēs thanatos*) would eventually evolve, the ethos and terms describing it are absent from Homer—though Hector appears as an emerging case. See Dova, 51, n. 54 (applying the term 'beautiful death' to Homeric deaths, "even though [the term] is directly related to the Classical *pólis* [city state])"; also Goldhill (1991), 123–128 (on "the increasing involvement of the state and in particular the *polis* in the language of praise"); also Loraux (1995) 63–74 ("The Spartans' 'beautiful Death'");

and Loraux (1995), 75–87 ("The Warrior's Fear and Trembling"). To be spared mangling or disfigurement in death means only to retain a certain beauty (see *Il.* 22.71–73, 24.757–759), not to *have* a "beautiful death." It is mistaken to argue that the enemy's admiration of a corpse—'They marveled at Hektor's size and at his admirable beauty' (*Il.* 22.370–371)—either renders death *kalos* or *eukleēs,* or confers *kleos aphthiton.* Thus, mistakenly, J. P. Vernant, "A 'Beautiful Death' and the Disfigured Corpse in Homeric Epic," in *Mortals and Immortals: Collected Essays* (Princeton: Princeton Univ. Press, 1991), 67 (speaking of "the hero's beautiful death, which grants him eternal glory"); Mackie, 102 ("the poem embodies the *kleos* of Achilles, but concludes with the celebration of Hektor's 'beautiful death'"); and Monsacré, 282 ("when Hecuba sees 'in the corpse of her son a beauty comparable to that of dew and flowers,' she is summarizing the ideal of the warrior's heroic death: to die, after a great exploit, at the height of one's youth and beauty"). Such conclusions misstate the heroic ethos, even as they generalize from the unique case that is Hector, his death, and the gods' intervention in preserving his chariot-dragged and disfigured corpse. Dying "intact"—rare in the *Iliad*'s world of mano-a-mano savagery—renders death neither beautiful nor glorious. Were that the case, an otherwise inglorious warrior, dying physically unscathed (or relatively so) would—for that alone—have *kleos.* Rather, because death is integral to heroism, meaning that the hero *perforce* dies—his *kleos* a *penthos* to those who love him—it befits to die well; witness Hector's proposing to die "doing some great thing" (*Il.* 22.303–305). Cf. Goldhill (1991), 71, 93, 99 (arguing the possibility of *victim kleos* and the "establishment of *kleos* in death").
**"the heroic . . . sword death."** D. Miller, 121.
**(his ankle alone vulnerable).** Mortal only at the ankle/heel, Achilles is otherwise invulnerable and thus *cannot be heroically slain*—by *any* weapon. Achilles's baptism in the river Styx in fact rules out a heroic death, even as it solves the problem of who might be heroic enough to kill him. "How to kill a hero? Even if [Achilles] accepts death, his extraordinary prowess, his exceptional physical qualıties and manifest perfections, must make this no easy task." D. Miller, 122. The *Iliad*—equipping Achilles with heroically prescribed armor, and pairing him in "mortal" combat with Aeneas and Hector—glosses the issue of Achilles's essential invulnerability, even as it stops short of his less-than-heroic death. Neither story element properly serves the *Iliad*'s dramatic purpose. Otherwise, see the thorough and highly suggestive treatment by Jonathan Burgess, "Achilles' Heel," etc. (developing the idea of Achilles's "imperfect invulnerability" and explaining [239] that Homer does not portray Achilles as invulnerable in the *Iliad*). See further p. 618 (on Achilles's suicide).
**"demand[s] death . . . best."** MacCarey, 196.
**remembered at one's best.** MacCarey, 203 (discussing the Homeric *aristeia* [Gr. *aristos* 'best'], conveying the sense of "battlefield excellence in action").
**elaborate funeral rites.** See Dova, 9–15.

190 *Hector is also self-possessed*
**"And some day . . . slavery."** *Il.* 6.459–463 (R. Lattimore, tr.).
**for the "perishable joys."** For Hector as "guardian of perishable joys," See D. Miller, 119–120 (quoting Bespaloff, 39).
**denied imperishable fame.** At least insofar as Homer is concerned. However, for the Greek lyric poet Tyrtaeus (late 7th century BC), there is a *kleos esthlon* 'fair repute' for one who lives on *athanatos* 'undying', having fallen in defense of city and child:

> Nor ever perishes his fair repute or name,
> and though to earth recalled, undying lives,
> whom excelling, foremost, and standing firmly fast
> for land and child, the might of Ares breaks.

Greek text quoted by Campbell (1967), 11–12. By contrast, the once-weeping Odysseus is compared to a woman prostrate over the fallen body of her husband, "who before his city and people falls, from town and children averting a pitiless day" (*Od.* 8.524–525). In Homer, then, a defensive death occasions no "fair repute"—only sorrow and the misfortune of loved ones left behind.

191 *The battlefield aside*
***kleos* that . . . recognition.** *Od.* 1.230–240.
***kleos* that . . . filial piety.** *Od.* 1.93–95; 3.75–78.
**obligations that attend it.** Nestor says, "And you, dear boy. . . be brave, that one born of later times may praise you"; to which Telemachus responds: "He [Orestes] exacted a fine revenge, and the Greeks will bear his fame (*kleos*) abroad, a song for men to come" (*Od.* 3.199–204).
***kleos* he gains . . . his father.** *Il.* 6.441–446.
**There . . . unspecified *kleos*.** *Od.* 3.380–381.
**"What news [*kleos*] from town?"** *Od.* 16.461.
**poet . . . the *kleos*, or report.** *Il.* 2.485–486.
**"as if he had . . . another."** See *Od.* 8.487–492. Odysseus here commends Demodocus for the accuracy of his song about the otherwise unelaborated quarrel between himself and Achilles at Troy (*Od.* 8.72–83). It is perhaps not expecting too much that Demodocus get it right, as it is relatively recent epic history. Odysseus, as protagonist in the events described, is well positioned to commend the story's accuracy. The three songs of Demodocus have occasioned significant interpretation and debate. See, e.g., Nagy (1979/1999), 17–25; Nagy (2003), 12–19; and Yoav Rinon, "*Mise en Abyme* and Tragic Signification in the *Odyssey*: The Three Songs of Demodocus," *Mnemosyne*, 59.2 (2006), 208–225.

*The Odyssey significantly*
**"Now . . . reaches heaven."** *Od.* 9.16–20.

192 *A still-disguised Odysseus*
**"fame . . . broad heaven."** *Od.* 19.19–20.
**"Both Penelope . . . other."** Segal (2001), 93. As Segal further notes, it is Clytemnestra who exemplifies trickery leading to destruction of home and realm, and resulting in shame rather than *kleos*.

*Penelope, though without*
**"Were he to . . . grieved."** *Od.* 19.127–129, cf. 18.251–256. "The extent of a woman's *kleos* is thus linked to the presence by her side of a husband who 'takes care of her life (*bios*)' in the most concrete sense of the term, that is, of the wealth which is at the root of the prosperity and the reputation of a house." Saïd, 312.

*It is important to note*
**made her a subject of song.** *Il.* 6.354–358.
**"exhibits a . . . to *kleos*."** Deborah Lyons, *Gender and Immortality: Heroines in Ancient Greek Myth and Cult* (Princeton: Princeton Univ. Press, 1997), 56.
**Homeric woman . . . *kleos*.** There is, however, a reference to Helen's *mega kleos* 'great fame' in the Hesiodic *Catalogue of Women*, on account of which suitors offered many and lavish gifts. See MW fr. 199.4–9, p. 98, and M fr. 154d.4–9, p. 224. As the context makes clear, *kleos* there indicates reputation—what is *heard* or reported. Blondell perhaps goes too far in equating "what people say" of Helen with the beginning of her "special association with *kleos* 'renown' or 'reputation', a word that is most often used

for the glory sought by warriors in battle." Blondell (2013), 30. Helen cannot have a "special association" with *kleos*, as that is Achilles's preserve. The word *kleos*, as noted, is never used of Helen in the *Iliad* (and is twice peculiarly used of Penelope, as discussed).
**"Lady, no . . . under him."** *Od.* 19.107–114 (R. Lattimore, tr.).
**"poses a question to Penelope."** Foley (1978), 11. See Foley's seminal "'Reverse Similes' and Sex Roles in the Odyssey," discussing Odysseus's comparison of Penelope to a king as a primary example of "reverse simile," i.e., a situation where a woman is described in masculine terms and vice versa. I differ from Foley in two key respects: the suitability of the kingship simile in the first instance, and the conclusion that Penelope's reply "shows a clear perception of and assent to the model of kingship suggested by Odysseus." Penelope sooner says that what *kleos* she had departed when Odysseus left for Troy, and that only his return and "caring for [her] life" will restore the loss (*Od.* 19.124–129).

I suggest that the simile may be purposefully askew, weighed against comparable contexts and the poet's intent to create a "particularly surprising effect." Moulton (1974), 392. The larger issue is one of "ad hoc invention," suggested "by consideration of [the] immediate context, rather than consistency with the poem as a whole." Floyd, 150 (explaining the *Iliad*'s once-referenced *kleos aphthiton* in relation to the immediate context). Similarly, "The place of comparison and simile in immediate and remote contexts is so infinitely variable that each one must be examined as an individual poetic creation in its own right." Michael Coffey, "The Function of the Homeric Simile," *American Journal of Philology*, 78.2 (1957), 132. On "reversal" in similes see further Moulton (1977), 128, and Anthony J. Podlecki, "Some Odyssean Similes," *Greece and Rome*, 18.1 (1971), 82 (speaking not of "reversal," but of "unique feature[s]" in certain Odyssean similes "by which the poet reminds us of an important theme in the poem, but with a *slight difference of focus or point of view*"). Of the simile here discussed, however, Podlecki merely notes, "The details of the just king's rule read like a programme of what Odysseus's own rule will be, if he can survive the test ahead and reestablish his authority in Ithaca" (87). Cf. Goldhill (1991), 97 (citing Foley and commenting only on what a "reverse simile" does).

Indeed, Penelope and Odysseus appear to converse in similaic uncertainties. As concerns Penelope's famed nightingale comparison, also in Book Nineteen, "Odysseus ignores the analogy with which Penelope began. . . . A close look at the simile suggests that its relationship to the narrative is anything but straightforward. . . . Whether it conveys ambivalence or variety or some combination of the two, the simile nevertheless appears somewhat inappropriate to Penelope's situation." Indeed, even as does Odysseus's kingship simile. See Emily Katz Anhalt, "A Matter of Perspective: Penelope and the Nightingale in *Odyssey* 19.512–534," *Classical Journal*, 97.2 (2001–2002), 145, 147.
**"is essentially . . . Penelope."** See Levaniouk, 27–28 (as quoted and paraphrased in the remainder of the paragraph), and Levaniouk, 258–262. So also Moulton (1977), 131–132 (noting that the *Odyssey* elsewhere compares Odysseus to a good king, and that the imputation of kingship to Penelope, while ostensibly underscoring *her kleos*, is in fact self-referential).

193 *But the kingship analogy*
**analogy does not quite fit.** For a different view, ". . . a noble queen keeping fidelity to her lord absent from the palace has kleos as does a warrior facing his enemies on the open field of battle." Segal (2001), 92.
**however much . . . his own.** Compare Odysseus to Penelope: 'your fame ascends wide heaven' (*Od.* 19.108), with Odysseus's boast to the Phaeacians of his consummate guile (Gr. *dolos*): 'I am Odysseus, son of Laertes, by all manner of wiles renowned among men, and my fame ascends the heavens' (*Od.* 9.19–20). The two contexts, as

often noted, resonate with the Odyssean, rather than Iliadic, *kleos* in which Odysseus and Penelope both share. Thus, to the extent Penelope's guile has preserved hearth and realm, she is Odysseus's true and queenly equal. It is on this level that Odysseus's crediting Penelope with *kleos* best works.
**"the figure . . . a hero."** Lipking, 67.

194 *Odysseus here makes*
**'as (when) . . . so (did)'.** For other such instances, see *Il.* 4.141–147, 422–456 (three extended similes); 5.84–94, 596–599; 6.506–511; 8.555–561; 11.473–484, 492–496; 17.389–395; 24.477–484; *Od.* 5.394–399; 8.521–531; 13.28–35.
**similes . . . comparing Ajax.** *Il.* 11.543–564.
**shorter . . . "extended simile."** *Il.* 4.243–246 (note second-person-based simile, as at *Il.* 4.141–147, above).

195 *Penelope's kleos is again*
**"O fortunate . . . virtuous."** *Od.* 24.192–202 (R. Lattimore, tr.).
**the fame of her virtue.** Though translators typically render the gender-neutral possessive as "her," Nagy takes it as masculine ("his" fame), "understanding the *kleos* at verse 196 as belonging primarily to Odysseus himself, and that it is his *aretē* 'merit' to have won a Penelope (rather than a Clytemnestra)." Nagy (1979/1999), 36–38. Goldhill tellingly notes, "Where *kleos* is mutually implicative, any ambiguity may be significant." Goldhill (1991), 100, n. 101. Singing Penelope's *kleos* in *Od.* 19.107 (above), Odysseus thus implicitly sings his own. Moulton (1977), 150. Husband and wife are of a kind, the one's *kleos* the other's. The decisively gender-neutral pronoun at *Od.* 19.196 signals as much.
**Agamemnon's "sexist" perception.** The taint of all by the taint of one is actually a quite gender-neutral proposition. "Often even the entire city suffers for a bad man, who sins and devises intolerable deeds; and the son of Cronus brings great trouble upon the people, famine and plague together, so that the men perish, their women bear no children, and their households decrease" (*WD* 239–245). This is precisely the situation at the start of Sophocles's *Oedipus*: Thebes suffering the weight of Oedipus's still unrevealed parricide and incest. Plague and death beset the Greek camp at the opening of the *Iliad* as a result of Agamemnon's abuse of Chryses, priest of Apollo. The theme of collective inculpation, with the Oedipal plot in reverse, is poignantly captured in the companion films *Jean de Florette* and *Manon of the Spring* (Orion Pictures, 1986).

*Agamemnon's praise, however*
**What diction disallows.** *Arete* is a quality attributed solely to Penelope among Homeric women. Bergren, 207. *Arete* 'excellence, virtue' is analogous to *kleos* 'reputation, fame', and for Penelope, its functional equivalent. Accordingly, the locution combing the two—*kleos* . . . (*hēs*) *aretēs* 'the report/reputation of her excellence'—is extraordinarily reinforcing of all the best qualities Penelope possesses. It is of course context that governs such considerations. When in Book Two of the *Odyssey* the suitor Antinous complains that Penelope, through calculated delay, "creates a *mega* . . . *kleos* for herself, but the want of much sustenance for you"—i.e., for Telemachus (*Od.* 2.125–126)—*kleos* is here understood in the more neutral sense of "report." Indeed, the systematic loss of household wealth negates the best sense of 'reputation' inhering in the notion of *kleos*.
**dazzling female characters.** See, e.g., Beth Cohen, ed., *The Distaff Side: Representing the Female in Homer's Odyssey* (Oxford: Oxford Univ. Press, 1995); also Saïd, 259–314. See also *Oscar Wilde, The Women of Homer,* Thomas Wright and Donald Mead, eds. (London: The Oscar Wilde Society, 2008); and, for its antiquarian value, Walter Copland Perry, *The Women of Homer* (London: William Heinemann, 1898).

CHAPTER 16

197 *A formula, as originally*

**"a group of words . . . idea."** Parry (1930), 80. Parry first published his ideas in a 1928 University of Paris doctoral dissertation, *L'Epithète traditionnelle dans Homère: Essai sur un problème de style homérique* (*The Traditional Epithet in Homer: Essay on a problem of homeric style*), followed by a supplementary thesis, *Les Formules et la métrique d'Homère* (*Homeric Formulae and Meter*), the latter work emphasizing the strictures of formulaic diction. Here and elsewhere Parry saw a functional rather than creative method of composition. Homer, in this light, was "the cumulative creation of a tradition rather than the product of an individual poetic genius." Russo, 629. The latter view is now widely accepted, though on grounds of a since-revealed Homeric flexibility rather than functionality. Parry's theses were followed by fieldwork comparisons with still-current South Slavic oral traditions. He was assisted in this work by his then student and colleague Albert Bates Lord. Their combined endeavors resulted in what is often called the "Parry-Lord Theory" or "oral-formulaic theory," revolutionizing the study of Homer in the twentieth century and beyond.

Parry's collected writings were published in 1971 as *The Making of Homeric Verse*, edited with an introduction by his son, classicist Adam Parry. The readiest relatively non-technical guide to the oral development and nature of Homeric epic (with South Slavic analogies) is Albert B. Lord, *The Singer of Tales* (1960). A second edition, edited by Stephen Mitchell & Gregory Nagy, appeared in 2000 (with audio CD). Lord continued Parry's work after the latter's untimely death, in 1935. The work was then significantly advanced by Gregory Nagy, Lord's student and, until Lord's death in 1991, his lifelong disciple. See also Albert Lord, *Epic Singers and Oral Tradition* (Ithaca: Cornell Univ. Press, 1991); Mary Louise Lord, ed., *The Singer Resumes the Tale* (1995) (posthumous publication of Lord's sequel by his widow); and Nagy (2003), 4–7, 49–50, 60–69, 79 (addressing both Parry-Lord critics and Nagy's own, explaining the disservice to Milman Parry done by son Adam's 1971 introduction, and otherwise correcting the record).

More recently, see Barbara Graziosi, "Homer in Albania: Oral Epic and the Geography of Literature" in Graziosi and Greenwood, eds. (2007), 120–142. Persuasive with increasing refinements over time, the Parry-Lord theory has nonetheless been recently impugned. A. P. David, *The Dance of the Muses: Choral Theory and Ancient Greek Poetics* (Oxford: Oxford Univ. Press, 2006), asserts that epic originally derived from dance and was thus choral rather than oral (a thesis generally dismissed by reviewers). See also Steven Schwartz, "Bartok, Parry & Lord: A Flawed Legacy," *The New Criterion*, 28.3 (2009), 76–80.

**"one formula . . . the line."** Paraphrased from Page, 224 (as quoted and discussed by Nagy [1990b], 21–22). See further Roger Dunkle, "Swift-Footed Achilles," *The Classical World*, 90.4 (1997), 227–234 (dwelling on the "affirmative redundancy of Achilles's speed epithets").

**"radically . . . an oral poet.** Russo, 629.

198 *Indeed, post-Parry research*

**"Homer . . . written poems."** Russo, 631.

*Kleos phrasings are a key*

**Both views . . . full perspective.** ". . . reconstruction cannot yield all the answers. What is also needed is a thorough description of the structure of a language as it exists at a given time and place. Since the influential work of the linguist Ferdinand de Saussure, such a perspective on language has been called 'synchronic,' in contrast to the 'diachronic' perspective, where we see the structure of a language as it evolves through time. For solving most problems of language, it is now generally recognized that both perspectives are needed." And further, "These concepts of synchronic and diachronic are readily applicable to the study of oral poetry." Nagy (1997b/2009b), 19–20. Nagy (1976b/1990b) marks a significant advance in Parry-Lord aesthetics, arguing, diachronically, that traditional theme rather than meter is the conditioning factor of formulaic diction. On the synchronic/diachronic antithesis, see also Nagy (2003), 1–2, 39–48, 83–84. It was Parry's South Slavic fieldwork in a still-living oral tradition that provided synchronic "leaven" (my term) to what had theretofore been the strictly philological, i.e., diachronic, research into the origins of the Homeric poems.

199 *Again, it is not merely*
**"setting . . . they survive."** Nagy (1974), 143–146.
**ultimately . . . meter overall.** "The epic hexameter consists of formulas which have fixed inner rhythms and which are joined together in such a way as to produce a fixed overall rhythm." Nagy (1974), 9. The formulaic network generated by the notion of *kleos* early crystallizes epic's preoccupation with fame.

The wording *emoi kleos aphthiton estai* appears at *Il.* 9.413 (Achilles speaking), and translates, 'for me it will be [or become] imperishable fame'; or 'for me there will be imperishable fame' (*aphthiton* designating an attribute of *kleos*; hence attributive); or 'my fame will be imperishable' (*aphthiton* designating a property of *kleos* [following the verb *to be*]; hence predicative). See further Garcia, 4, n. 3. The combination *kleos aphthiton* appears only here in Homer, though once in Sappho (see Chapter 17), and several times elsewhere. Whether *kleos aphthiton* is a traditional formula (Nagy [1974], 109, 229–265; Nagy [1979/1999], 16, 95) or part of the expression *kleos aphthiton estai* (which is a unique expression, as some argue, but not a formula) is irrelevant to my discussion of the word "*kleos*" as part of an expanding metrical combination. For the controversy, see Floyd (1980), Nagy (1981) (responding), Finkelberg (1986) (*kleos aphthiton* not a Homeric formula), A. Edwards (1988) (responding), R. Friedrich (2002) (agreeing), Volk (2002) (responding), and again Finkelberg (2007). See also M. Katz, 26, n. 13, and Garcia, 5, n. 5.

Chapter 17

201 *Despite what little survives,*
***Iliad*'s climactic death of.** Sappho, in fact, "rewrites" Homer in much of her surviving poetry. See Winkler, 96 ("insofar as her poems are a reading of Homer they set up a feminine perspective on male activity that shows more clearly the inner structure and motivation of the exclusion of the feminine from male arenas").

202 *First noted is Sappho's*
**"all were . . . past enduring."** *Il.* 24.708.

*It is the Trojan herald*
**through Hell on earth.** For systematic treatment, see Miguel Herrero de Jáuregui, "Priam's Catabasis: Traces of the Epic Journey to Hades in *Iliad* 24," *Transactions of the American Philological Association*, 141 (2011), 37–68.

203 *With the mention of*
**Achilles . . . killed Hector.** *Il.* 1.364–366, 6.413–424, 9.352–355.
**"Ah, Hector . . . husband, too."** *Il.* 6.429–430.
**Narrative and . . . elements.** For instance, the last word of Sappho's poem is *theoeikelois*

'equal to the gods', referring to Hector and Andromache. The epithet is used only twice in the *Iliad*, both times of Achilles. Its application to Hector and Andromache is ill omened at the end of a wedding song. This and other examples are provided by Nagy (1974), 135–139. Marriage and death are archetypical counterparts. When mourning the fallen Enkidu, Gilgamesh covers his face "with a veil like the veil of a bride" (Tablet VIII).

Though it is Achilles who is *theoeikelos* 'like a god', Hector peculiarly shares the trait. In the lament over his fallen son, Priam notes:

> Hector, who was a **god** among men, nor **seemed**
> to be the child of mortal man, but of **a god**. (*Il.* 24. 258–259)

The bolded words in Greek are ***theos*** ('a god') and ***eōikei*** ('he seemed'), the latter from the same root appearing in ***theoeikelos*** 'seeming like a god'/ 'godlike'. The Trojan women elsewhere pray to Hector in language uniquely suggesting his divinity. See Nagy (1979/1999), 149 (citing references). Thus, and though we have noted that *kleos,* not deification, is the epic desideratum, and that Hector will particularly lack *kleos,* epic appears to divinize him out of high regard.

**dowry . . . Hector's ransom.** Lawrence P. Schrenk, "Sappho Frag. 44 and the *Iliad*," *Hermes*, 122.2 (1994), 144–150.

203 *The "Wedding of Hector*

**death-in-marriage belongs.** See e.g., Rush Rehm, *Marriage to Death: The Conflation of Wedding and Funeral Rituals in Greek Tragedy* (Princeton: Princeton Univ. Press, 1994).

**prefigured death-in-marriage.** See Kazantzakis's description of "That black snake, Death, digesting slowly, coiled on sands / . . . / with piles of golden wedding rings stacked in his guts" (*Odusseia* 9.535–537); cf. *Odusseia* 10.1238–1250; 11.1091–1092; 12.685. See generally Rush Rehm, *Marriage to Death: The Conflation of Wedding and Funeral Rituals in Greek Tragedy* (Princeton: Princeton Univ. Press, 1984).

*Achilles is fated to die*

**That Achilles . . . outset.** The passages supporting this paragraph appear at *Il.* 1.413–418; 9.409–420; 18.95–96, 114–121.

**one-hundred . . . "ekphrasis."** See *Il.* 18.478–608. Ekphrasis (Gr. *ek* 'out, from' + *phrasis* 'utterance'; *ekprazein* 'to proclaim, call by name') is the highly graphic description of a visual work of art, though it can refer to the description of any thing, person, or experience that causes a break in the narrative flow. The "Shield of Achilles" in Book Eighteen of the *Iliad* is antiquity's prime example. Other famed examples are the gates of the Temple of Juno in Book One of the *Aeneid* (discussed above), and the Homerically inspired armor made for Aeneas later in the poem.

204 *Patroclus's death in*

**(by proxy) for Achilles.** See *Il.* 18.35–77.

**Hector thus armored.** The climactic scene occurs in Book Twenty-Two of the *Iliad*. For the elaboration of points here made in brief, see Duban (1980), 8–10.

**The symbolic suicide.** *Il.* 18.32–34: "On the other side Antilochos mourned with him, letting the tears fall, / and held the hands of Achilleus as he grieved in his proud heart, fearing Achilleus might cut his throat with the iron" (R. Lattimore, tr.).

*Throughout the Iliad*

**"Thetis's . . . been telescoped."** Beye (1975), 45–46. The telescoping of time is, in this sense, also characteristic of Greek tragedy. The plays cover a significant amount of plot in approximately 1,150 to 1,350 lines (including choral odes, which do not advance the plot). The characters and stories of Greek tragedy, deriving largely from Greek epic, were essentially known to the original audience—though variously adapted, sometimes considerably. The audience did not have to sit through the play to know that Oedipus killed his father, married his mother, and blinded himself—though how this would be revealed in the particular instance was another matter. In the case of Oedipus, see Lattimore (1964), 3–6. For a recent concise discussion of tragic plot development vis-à-vis the liberty-taking Euripides, see Mendelsohn (2013).

I say "how this would be revealed" instead of "how this would happen" because, "The *Oedipus* is almost unique among Greek tragedies in telling its story in reverse. Nearly every crucial event in the action has already happened. The action is therefore almost all retrospective action—that is, how the characters (and the spectators too) see and understand in the present events that took place far in the past." Segal (2001), 60.

*Sappho's sole attested*
**"As Sappho . . . to come."** Quotation (and internal quotation) from Dio Chrysostom (1st and 2nd centuries AD). See Campbell (1982), 158.
**"But when you . . . Pieria."** Quotation from Stobaeus (4th and 5th centuries AD). See Campbell (1982), 99.

205 *As further concerns her*
**"To assail . . . holy thing."** Symonds, Vol. I, 127.

CHAPTER 18

206 *As Aphrodite incarnate,*
**"in dealing . . . Achilles."** Clader, 5.

*Their relationship crystallizes*
**"Chiron was . . . her before."** M frr. 154–156, pp. 218–239; MW fr. 204, pp. 99–105; E-W fr. 68, pp. 193–203 (quote herein from p. 199). The operative terms in Greek are the gender-neutral *pais* 'child' (used of Achilles; see Sappho's use vis-à-vis Cleis, p. 578) and *parthenos* 'unwed, maiden' (here used of Helen). Likely following the Hesiodic *Theogony*, the *Catalogue of Women* is a fragmentary poem in five books recounting the deeds, marriages, and genealogies of famous women. It is further considered "something approaching a compendious account of the whole story of the [Greek] nation from the earliest times to the time of the Trojan War or the generation after it." West (1985), 3.
**for the wooing of Helen.** What is known as the "Catalogue of Helen's Suitors" is thus a catalogue within the *Catalogue of Women*. Positioned toward the end of the *Catalogue of Women*, it anticipates Helen's adultery, leading to the Trojan War and, through the war, to the end of the Age of Heroes, all according to the *Dios boulē* 'plan of Zeus', as explained below. Recent years have witnessed a dramatic increase in Hesiodic catalogue research. See Ziogas (2013) and Ormand (2014); also Cingano and Osborne in R. Hunter, ed. (2005), Most (2007), and González (2010). See also West (1985).

207 *The so beautifully and*
**"detached . . . social place."** D. Miller, 163. The broader extent of Achilles's isolation is apparent in the folkloric elements of his origins "on the fringes of the Greek world, in remote Thessaly," thereby highlighting, among other factors, his originally "outsider" status vis-à-vis epic. Alexander, 95–96 (marshaling other significant factors). For the hero's "solitary state" vis-à-vis what only the hero or the hero alone can do, see Kahane, in Bakker and Kahane, eds.

On the other hand—but for his semidivine birth and vastly superior ability—Achilles initially differs little in his assumptions and chivalric conduct from other glory-seeking princes at Troy. His isolation is not something he necessarily brings to the epic, but what develops from it, "through various phases of disillusion, horror, and violence, to a final detachment which is godlike indeed." To be sure, "Homer has subordinated all characters to Achilles, and all incidents of the Trojan War to [his] Wrath." Whitman 182–183, 187–189, 200. Given Achilles's utter centrality to the *Iliad,* it is thus difficult to imagine him as an epic "import." Whitman further traces Achilles to the earliest strata of Greek epic: ". . . Homer has built his conception [of the heroic vision] out of the old materials, and made his first tragic hero from assumptions and qualities inherent in the earlier heroes of more primitive epic." Whitman, 220. This notion is consistent with epic's focus on *kleos,* Achilles's extreme need of *kleos,* and the posited shaping of epic verse vis-à-vis expanding *kleos* formulations.

208 *Helen is a riveting*

**excessively . . . beautiful.** For literary testimonials to the excess of Helen's beauty, see Macguire, 35–38.

**Achilles, the most beautiful.** "Nireus, the most beautiful man who came beneath Ilion / beyond the rest of the Danaans next after perfect Achilleus" (*Il.* 2.673–674, R. Lattimore, tr.).

**Achilles . . . whose very speech.** "For the most part, Achilles speaks a different language again. He constitutes the voice of Hesiodic wisdom within the *Iliad,* casting himself in the role of resident alien . . . who gives instruction, from an original point of view, to the rest of the community." Mackie, 2; see next note. Of course, much of Achilles's speech is an interrogation of the heroic code, to that extent suggesting his status as an outsider, or at the very least, his increasing alienation.

**"the most varied . . . powerful."** Vermeule, 697. For the centrality of face-to-face conversation in the *Iliad,* see Mackie, 45. For Achilles's "showing himself a master of language," see MacCary 57–58. For Achilles's "inventing" a language by borrowing from the conventions of wisdom literature (i.e., Hesiod), see Mackie, 141–142. And for some of the numerous studies investigating the features unique to Achilles's style, see Mackie 150–151, and n. 87. That Odysseus, as craftiest of the Greeks, is a supremely gifted speaker, comes as no surprise (see *Il.* 3.216–224). Given Odysseus's character, however, such ability is of an entirely different order. Hector, for his part, is the *Iliad*'s most poetic, balanced, and deliberative speaker. See Mackie, 11, and Duban (1981).

**possesses . . . "absolute will."** The phrase *absolute will* is Cedric Whitman's, 213. See also Whitman, 187 (". . . Achilles's own nature seeks the absolute in all its concerns. His feelings aspire to exist free of all secondary reference, even as his actions aim at utter supremacy"). See also Benardete (1963), 1 ("Achilles is a hero in a world of heroes; he is of the same cast as they, though we might call him the first impression, that has caught each point more finely than later copies"). In a similar vein, Fantuzzi speaks of the epic past as an "absolute past," by which he accounts for the Iliadic absence of romance or love. Being "far too human or commonplace," they are essentially irrelevant to the *Iliad*'s prevailing values and concerns. Fantuzzi, 3.

**"collection . . . his command."** Bespaloff, 55.

**consciousness . . . tradition.** See *Il.* 6.358–359; 9.189.

**singer of epic in the poem.** *Il.* 9.189 (Achilles sings *klea andrōn* 'the glories of men'; see pp. 185, 609).

**is associated with poetry.** See Clader, 6 *et passim.*

**itself suggestive of poetry.** Clader, 8.

*Helen's beauty is entirely*

**Achilles's . . . more outstanding.** Hughes-Hallett, 28.

**destined never to grow old.** "Destined never to grow old, he has a young man's

splendor and a young man's energy. His emotions are extreme, his responses passionate, his actions devastating. For all these reasons he is unique among the Homeric warriors." Hughes-Hallet, 18. Similarly, "Achilles, constantly under the influence of and protection of Thetis and the other maternal goddesses, simply refuses to mature and accept the sexual and political role society demands of him." MacCarey, 168.
**long years at Troy.** The Trojan War is traditionally of ten years' duration. Helen's one-time reference (*Il.* 24.765) to her *twenty* years at Troy significantly adds to the combined duration of war and homecomings, as further discussed below.
**never felt stronger passion.** Scott, 453 (citing *Il.* 24.765 and 3.442–446). See also *Il.* 14.312–317, where Zeus, to comic effect, avers that he has never desired Hera more.
**"one of the . . . throughout."** Scott, 453; cf. Scott, 454 on the passions of the suitors (citing *Od.* 1.365, 18.212), and 455 on the aged Nestor, who "has added to his years, but has grown no older . . . unchanged in body and mind."
**glimpse of Helen's breast.** The literary afterlife of this stunning scene is provided by Macguire, 53–56.

209 *Achilles and Helen further*
**upon prophesy . . . offspring.** Pindar, *Isthmian* 8, and in Aeschylus's lost plays *Prometheus Bound* and *Prometheus Unbound.* Achilles surpasses his *earthbound* father, Peleus. Peleus's folkloric origins are thought partly responsible for his "striking absence from the *Iliad,*" in which he is known only as Achilles's father. "In this way, as benefits his unique destiny, Achilles is in fact proved to be greater than his father; alone of the heroes at Troy, it is he who defines his sire." Alexander, 95. The surpassing of one's father is not always a negative. In his leave-taking of Andromache, Hector wishes to be surpassed by his child, Astyanax (*Il.* 6.476–481).
**avoids the overthrow.** Achilles is the "last contender in the struggle for succession." Mayer, 14. Avoiding marriage with Thetis, Zeus secures the succession won from his own father, Kronos, as he (Zeus) had earlier done by swallowing the goddess Mētis (also prophesied to bear a child mightier than its father). The battle for succession, as recounted in Hesiod's *Theogony,* took ten years. Foiling Achilles's own assault on Olympus through Thetis's marriage to a mortal, Zeus "displaces strife" from the divine to the human sphere, "causing not only the Trojan War in particular but the human condition in general." Mayer, 2 (quoting Nagy [1979/1999], 220).
**uncertain interregnum.** The reference is to the episode, mentioned by Achilles, of certain gods trying to bind and overthrow Zeus, with Thetis subverting the plot (*Il.* 1.393–407). See generally, Noriko Yasumura, *Challenges to the Power of Zeus in Early Greek Poetry* (London: Bristol Classical Press, 2011).
**There is thus no slighting.** Cf. *Il.* 20.203–209, where one sees a slighting reference to Thetis-born Achilles by the Aphrodite-born Aeneas.
**sea nymph daughters.** For Thetis and the Nereid catalogue, see *Th.* 240–264.
**privileged relationship.** See *Il.* 1.493–530 and Slatkin, *The Power of Thetis.*
**she nurtured and raised.** *Il.* 24.59–60.
**Aeacus . . . "civic" virtues.** See Helen North, "Pindar, Isthmian, 8.24–28," *The American Journal of Philology,*" 69.3 (1948), 304–308. The *Aeacidae* 'sons of Aeacus' are frequently praised by Pindar in connection with athletic victories on the island of Aegina, where the line originates. There are a dozen such odes in all. Aegina, the island's eponym, was daughter of the river god Asopus. Aegina, seduced by Zeus, gave birth to Aeacus, Achilles's grandfather. Achilles is thus sometimes referred to in the *Iliad* as *Aeacides* '(grand)son of Aeacus', though more frequently as *Peleïdes* 'son of Peleus'.

*As Helen is unspeakably*
**"ineffably glamorous."** See Hughes-Hallett, 15–16.

**Helen . . . 'shudder-inducing'.** Gr. (*h*)*rigedanē* (*Il.* 19.325); for context, Blondell (2010b), 4–5. Though the word appears only here, the root (*h*)*rig-* is frequently found in verbal forms. In its various Homeric contexts, the root "seems to imply shuddering from fear of death through warfare, or fear of the gods, or fear of the consequences of a violation of trust." Clader, 22.
***stugerē*** **. . . 'hateful unto death'.** Helen refers to herself as *stugerē* at *Il.* 3.404. See Clader, 19–21, for the possibilities related to the meaning of the root **stug-*.
**"horrid, evil intriguing bitch."** *Il.* 6.344.
**before whom "all tremble."** *Il.* 24.775. The Greek verb in this case is *phrissō* 'bristle, shiver with fear'. See Clader, 21–22.

210 *Achilles's claim to absolute*
**conquest of Lesbos itself.** On Achilles's conquest of Lesbos and Agamemnon's conciliatory offer of eight Lesbian captives, see *Il.* 9.128–131, 270–273, 663-664; 19.245–246. The captive women, Briseis included, had been taken by Achilles during his sack of Lesbos—one of many island or coastal campaigns either preceding or during the ten-year siege of Troy. The campaigns were apparently not lacking in "R & R"—Menelaus recalling Odysseus's well-applauded wrestling victory on Lesbos (*Od.* 4.341–344). The present discussion of Achilles and his conquest of Lesbos has its point of departure in Blondell (2010a), 350–352 (focusing on the not surprising interest of Lesbian poets in Helen). For Greek heroic exploits against other Aeolic settlements at the time of the *Iliad*, all featuring Achilles, see Nagy (1979/1999), 139–141. For the broader territorial, political, and artistic interests served by the incorporation of the sack of Lesbos into the *Iliad*, see Nagy (2010), 142–146, 241–253. The mythographer Apollodorus (2nd century AD) makes Achilles a one-man conquest-machine throughout Asia Minor and its coastal islands. *Epit.* 3.3.32–33 (Head, 152); cf. Oliver Taplin, "Homer's Use of Achilles' Earlier Campaigns in the *Iliad*," in J. Boardman and C. E. Vaphopoulos-Richardson, eds., *Chios: A Conference at the Homereion in Chios, 1984* (Oxford: Oxford Univ. Press, 1986), 15–19.

Apollodorus is author of the *Bibliothēkē* (*Library*) and *Epitomē* (*Summary*), providing overviews of traditional Greek myth and legend, starting with creation as set forth in Hesiod's *Theogony*. Genealogically well structured, the *Epitomē* is far from comprehensive. A helpful tool from a later time, it is written in a handbook, facts-only style, assuming no prior familiarity with its subject matter. It is of particular interest when providing information elsewhere unattested. My discussion looks to those parts of the *Epitomē* involving chronology. The *Epitomē* appears, in part, based on Proclus. See West (2013), 11–16.
**"like unto . . . Aphrodite."** *Il.* 19.282; also "resembling the goddesses" (*Il.* 19.286).
**theft of Briseis . . . Helen.** *Il.* 9.334–343. However, "whereas Agamemnon, as general, has authority over Achilles, Paris has flouted the *xenos* ('guest, host') relation, and hence his crime is more heinous." Suzuki, 22.
**temporarily supersedes.** Suzuki, 23 (noting that Helen unites the Greeks, Briseis divides them).
**"were superior . . . Achilles."** Nagy (2010), 242. In addition, Sappho's contemporary, Alcaeus, describes the beauty contests among Lesbian girls; see p. 585.

*Given Helen's and Achilles's*
**what cataclysm . . . Trojan War.** After Menelaus prevails as Helen's husband, cataclysm is sounded in a catalogue fragment, with teleological overtones, in which Zeus produces a cosmic storm upsetting the sea, destroying vegetation, and draining men's strength. See Ziogas, 20.
**no abduction of Helen.** "Marriage to Achilles would eliminate [Helen's] story."

Blondell (2013), 46.
**evisceration . . . mythology.** The evisceration of mythology might have occurred at an even earlier point, had Achilles, however young, and not away training with Chiron, been available for marriage to Helen. Their encounter would then presumptively have obviated the need for a wooing contest and all that followed (cf. Ormand 198–200). Be that as it may, the prospect of Achilles as suitor contradicts the Hesiodic narrative, which makes wealth, not merit, the criterion of selection. For the Euripidean narrative, see further pp. 625, 629.

211 *Achilles, since never a*
**unbound . . . Oath of Tyndareus.** See pp. 53, 186, 632. Pausanias reports a legend that either Achilles *or* Patroclus wooed Helen, noting "the fact that Achilles is not one of Helen's wooers in the *List of Women* is no evidence that he never asked for her, but Homer in the very beginning of his poem [*Il* 1.158] writes that Achilles came to Troy to please the sons of Atreus, not because he was obliged by [Tyndareus's] oath." Pausanias, 3.24.10; Levi, Vol. II, 92. Pausanias's jumbled account glosses the real point: that the *Catalogue*'s exclusion of no less a one than Achilles is a compelling indication of his non-participation, especially when youth as the reason for exclusion is elsewhere attested. It was thus the glory-quest alone, in all its absolutist menace, that brought Achilles to Troy. Being there to "please" Agamemnon and Menelaus is merely Achilles's ad hoc sarcasm. Pausanias otherwise peculiarly notes that Helen's abduction by the much older Theseus makes it "utterly inadmissible that Achilles was Helen's wooer." When Helen is asked in Euripides's play of the same name whether she has ever heard of Achilles (but of course she has), she passingly responds that "he once came to woo Helen, as I have heard" (*Helen* 99). It is unlikely that so passing a response to so idle a question intends "to 'normalize'. . . Achilles's participation in the war." Fantuzzi, 13, n. 28. There is nothing normal either about Achilles or his situation.
**"simply a symbol . . . goal."** Clader, 10–11.
**"dangerous . . . for the hero."** Clader, 12.
***mega gar kleos [eske gu]naikos.*** See E-W fr. 68.39, p. 194; MW fr. 199.9, p. 98; M fr. 154d-(9)39, p. 224.
**Helen . . . has her *own* kleos.** The situation, as noted, is unique among Homeric women. The *kleos* imputed Penelope is less assured.
**fabled report . . . of her beauty.** See excellent discussion by Ziogas, 20–29.
**Eros described by Hesiod, etc.** *Th.* 120–122.

212 *Itself devoid of strife*
***tēs k]lea pasan . . . dian (h)ikanei.*** The reconstruction, creating a second *kleos* context for Helen, is that of E-W fr. 68.74, p. 198. Others more recently read *muthon* 'tale' for E-W's *kleos* (among other changes). See MW fr. 204.60(23), p. 100; M fr. 155.63(23), p. 228.

*For Achilles, the kleos-quest*
**infatuation with Helen.** For Helen's self-recriminations and the Trojans' hapless infatuation, see *Il.* 3.146–180 (esp. 171–176). The point is well taken that Helen's self-blame serves in lieu of blame from the opposing sides. Were she blameworthy in the combatants' eyes, she would be less worth fighting for. See Blondell (2009), 7; Blondell (2013), 60; Ebbott, 19–20. At the narrative level, Homer has Hector suppress whatever blame of Helen might arise (*Il.* 24.767–772). In Book Four of the *Odyssey*, Helen, re-settled in Sparta with Menelaus, recounts her regretful past with a certain ambivalence.

While Helen accepts a certain responsibility for her actions and their consequences, hers is a unique case. The *Iliad* is otherwise impervious to personal responsibility. Conduct is instead imputed to divine agency—to the "will of the gods"—as when Agamemnon, for instance, explains that Zeus, Destiny, and the Furies are to blame (not himself) for his affront to Achilles (*Il.* 19.85–89; 137–138). It was *they* who filled his mind with *agrian atēn* 'savage delusion' (*Il.* 19.87, 136). Helen would not have acted as she did (believes Penelope) had she foreseen the consequences; and "it was a god who moved her to do the shameful things she did" (*Od.* 23.217–224). Priam similarly refuses to blame Helen, even as the elders of Troy—"men of counsel"—refuse to blame themselves (*Il.* 3.155–165). The *Odyssey* from the outset marks a turn by personalizing blame and responsibility. Zeus there reflects that mortals, though faulting the gods for misfortune, have only themselves to blame (*Od.* 1.32–34). With the appearance of lyric, the personalization of blame is complete. For the association of *atē* 'delusion' with (what would later be called) *hamartía* 'flaw', see R. D. Dawe, "Some reflections on Ate and Hamartia," *Harvard Studies in Classical Philology*, 72 (1968), 95–96, 101–103. For the *Iliad* and *Odyssey* as mutually exclusive religious explanations of the world, see Kullmann (1985). For the "Greek idea of a diffuse guilt [as] represent[ing] for Homer and the tragic poets the equivalent of the Christian idea of original sin," see Bespaloff, 63–64.

**alludes to a delegation.** *Il.* 3.205–206. According to *Epit.* 3.3.28 (Hard, 151), the embassy was sent after the fleet had put in offshore at the island of Tenedos (see map).

212 *What mythology's most*

**death-ridden alliance.** The alliance is not entirely morbid. Even as Achilles sings *klea andrōn* 'the glories of men' (*Il.* 9.189), Helen weaves the many combats being waged for her sake beneath the walls of Troy (*Il.* 3.125–128). "Lyre and loom, singer and weaver—Achilles and Helen are two impersonations of the poet, transmuting nature into art, Being into Meaning." N. Austin, 38.

**wishing . . . sooner died.** *Il.* 3.173–174; 24.764.

**"unique in . . . own death."** Mayer, 12 and *Il.* 3.173–176, 6.345–348; 18.98–107. As Achilles and Helen are unique, they are necessarily marginalized: Achilles, sitting apart from his companions, nursing his indignation; Helen, apart from Trojan society, nursing her shame. See N. Austin, 28–29.

**he (and Patroclus) alone.** *Il.* 16.97–100.

**ultimately the plan of Zeus.** As set forth and at pp. 216–220, 455, 619, 628–630, 688. On the totality of the contemplated destruction, see Scodel (1982) and Buchan, 108–110.

**symbiotic . . . Eros and Thanatos.** "War . . . stands at the very heart of the Eros-Thanatos polarity. Eros and Thanatos provoke the same psycho-psychological transformations. Love's passion, like death, envelops those it afflicts; it conquers them, loosening their limbs." Monsacré, 282 (citing *Il.* 3.442, 24.294 [Eros] and *Il.* 5.68, 16.350 [Thanatos]). Love and death are both absolute forms of taking, often forcible, as well as of loss, reversion, or dissolution (especially for the male). Sexual abduction often has deathly consequences, as in the paradigmatic case of Helen. And sexual separation or privation is often tantamount to death itself. See, e.g., the following examples from Sappho:

> a cold sweat commands me, a tremor
> takes hold; more pallid than grass am I,
> needing only, or so I seem, but
> little to die. (§2)
>
> I'm filled with desire to die,
> see the dewy lotused shore
> of Acheron [flow by . . . (§5)
>
> "Honestly, I wish I were dead"!
> She was leaving me, tears in her eyes.
> Much she said, this most of all:

"Ah, Sappho, what we've suffered through;
I swear, I leave not wanting to." (§6)

See also Lanata (1969a), 19 ("Nothing is more frequent in amatory lyric than the topos of 'love and death,' and even in Sappho it recurs with particular insistence"), and Meagher, 44 ("*Eros* has *thanatos* as an overtone; when the one note is struck, the other is heard"). See further Jonathan Dollimore, *Death, Desire and Loss in Western Culture* (New York: Routledge, 1988), Introduction, ix–xxix (with detailed reference to Camille Paglia's *Sexual Personae*), and Ch. 1 ("Eros and Thanatos, Change and Loss in the Ancient World").

In a more contemporary vein, one notes novelist Dan Simmons's *Lovedeath* (New York: Warner Books, 1993): "I had considered writing something superficially profound here about the themes of Eros and Thanatos which circle through these five tales like hungry sharks in a crowded pool, but truth be told, almost all successful stories include some element of the twin themes of love and death." Simmons's greatest sense of lovedeath emerges form his World War I story "The Great Lover." Speaking with reference to the war's savagery, Simmons says, "I do not believe that those who witnessed these events and wrote about them so eloquently, in prose and poetry, did seem to come closer to the terrible beauty and terror of combat than most of the war chroniclers since Homer." Simmons, xiv, xx.

As earlier noted, there is also the swoon and deathlike enervation that follows orgasm, whence the euphemism *la petite mort* 'the little death'. Sappho herself, nearly catatonic in a state of sexual exclusion (see *phainetai moi*, §2), "needs but little to die." One may also look to Anthony Hecht's "Death the Whore": "We both seemed to like sex for the same reason. / It was, as they used to say, a "little death," / A tiny interval devoid of thought." The operative term is "devoid": freedom from thought being oblivion—the *void*—akin to death.

**"For Love is dire . . . ablaze."** Cant. 8.6. The Hebrew is highly alliterative:

ki azah ka'mavet ahavah,
Because strong as death [is] love

kashah k'shōl kinah,
hard as Sheol [is] possessiveness,

rishīphehah rishīphāy āysh shalhevetyah.
her flames [are] flames of fire, the blaze of God.

The complementarity of love and death is an admittedly vast topic. A number of observations are yet in order. One may look to Elizabeth Barrett Browning (1806–1861), *Sonnets from the Portuguese* (§1):

. . . Straightway I was 'ware,
So weeping, how a mystic Shape did move
Behind me, and drew me backward by the hair;
And a voice said in mastery, while I strove, —
"Guess now who holds thee?" — "Death," I said. But, there,
The silver answer rang, — "Not Death, but Love."

One wonders whether Browning is here relieved to find escape from Death or merely mindful of Love's deathliness, of the absolutism it shares with Death as with nothing else.

Central to such understanding is *Liebestod* 'love death' (see preceding note), meaning erotic death or the consummation of love in death, e.g., *Tristan and Isolde*, *Romeo and Juliet*. The connection between love and death is suggested by the French soundalikes *l'amour* and *la mort* (cf. Lat. *amor* and *mors*). The French wordplay surfaces in copies of the *Liebestod* aria itself, from Wagner's *Tristan und Isolde*, sometimes marked "*Liebestod* (*mort dans l'amour*)." Cf. Goya's *El amor y la muerte* (*Love and Death*) in *Los Caprichos*—the two often pictured as dancing together (comically in the final scene of Woody Allen's *Love and Death*, 1975). The grammatical allocation of death to the feminine, e.g., in French and Spanish, is inconclusive—*death* being masculine, e.g., in German (*der Tod*) and of course genderless in English. Personifications of death, with rare exception, are male (the "Grim Reaper" also usually male). See further Karl S. Guthke, *The Gender of Death: A Cultural History in Art and Literature* (Cambridge: Cambridge Univ. Press, 1999), 26. See also Mina Curtiss, *Olive, Cypress and Palm: An Anthology of Love and Death* (New York: Harcourt, Brace, 1930).

For the word *elegy* and its "veiled origins, and auspicious dual associations with death and with love," see Warren (2008), 12–13. Note also the morbid eroticism of Walt Whitman's care of the Civil War dead and dying (Peter Collier, ed., *Walt Whitman's Memoranda During the Civil War* [Oxford: Oxford Univ. Press, 2004]), xxxi–lii, and Théophile Gautier's (1811–1872) attachment to the trappings of literary decadence, including the intimate bond between death and eroticism (esp. *La Morte Amoureuse* [1836] and *La Comédie de la Mort* [1838]).

Correlative to *eros* 'love' and *thanatos* 'death' (consider also Eng. womb/tomb) are the Greek soundalikes *eros* 'love' and *eris* 'strife'. Indeed, "The antipodal *erōs* and *eris* . . . share a common root in linguistic prehistory, as they do so often in the human psyche." Michael Weiss, "Erotica: On the Prehistory of Greek Desire," *Harvard Studies in Classical Philology*, 98 (1998), 47.

**"Helen's submission . . . city."** Kenneth J. Reckford, "Helen in the *Iliad*," *Greek, Roman, and Byzantine Studies*, 5 (1964), 15.

**of combat and copulation.** "The deep-psychic confusion involved in combat and copulation, of what is acceptable and non-acceptable in sex and violence, appears in the epical contexts often enough to attract remark" (apropos of Achilles's rumored necrophilia with the Amazon queen Penthesilea, whom he slew). D. Miller, 109. Later traditions would deal with Achilles's "temporary erotic compulsions" and his fury as a lover no less than as a warrior. Fantuzzi, 9–11. Such fury is also apparent in Shakespeare's *Antony and Cleopatra*. The "combative" nature of sex is, of course, a universal trope. Though of deadly earnest and import in the heroic context, the trope has its lighter, more transparent moments. Escaping a near-fatal battlefield encounter with Menelaus, Paris is sexually aroused, wanting immediately to bed Helen (*Il.* 3.420–446). The analogy between military and sexual campaigning is a conceit of Roman elegiac and other amatory verse. For the equation of military and sexual control in Catullus and Virgil, see Putnam (1966), 90.

213 *To suppress even the*

**tradition . . . different generations.** Presumably too old for Achilles—her ideal and equally destructive counterpart—Helen marries the loutish gift-lavishing Menelaus, only to run off with Paris, the most effeminate and ineffectual of the Trojans. The ideal marriage (or partner) not surprisingly eludes Helen. Paris, like Helen, is a favorite of Aphrodite. The ship that carries Paris to Sparta, whence he abducts Helen, is built from Aphrodite's blueprints (an otherwise singular pastime for the goddess), with Aphrodite herself onboard. So the scholiast to *Il.* 3.443; W' fr. 8, p. 89. In Book Three of the *Iliad*, Menelaus and Paris duel one on one, winner take all. They are as much mismatched combatants as they are ineffectual husbands of Helen. The duel is both comical and inconclusive.

*When sent to Troy with*

**a "mere child" . . . warfare.** As Phoenix himself reminds Achilles (*Il.* 9.438–443). A "mere child": Gr. *nēpios* (*nē-* + *epos*) 'not speaking' (which is not to imply infancy). Phoenix's reminder contains another of the *Iliad*'s best-known lines. Achilles was sent to Troy *muthōn te (h)rētēr' emenai prēktēra te ergōn* 'to be a speaker of words and a doer of deeds' (*Il.* 9.443). This sums it up. The key words in Greek—*speaker* and *doer* (underlined)—are complementary soundalikes. The line is not merely window dressing: "During his withdrawal from battle, Achilles's words replace his deeds as he criticizes the heroic code." Suzuki, 44. Sooner a doer of deeds, Achilles becomes, perforce, a speaker of words—starting with searing invective against Agamemnon; proceeding thence to an existential examination of the heroic code; and ending, with Priam, in a profound articulation of the futility of revenge and pervasiveness of grief. See further Cedric Whitman, Ch. 9 ("Achilles: Evolution of a Hero").

**for what he lacks in years.** Achilles's youthful career bears comparison with that of the handsome and youthful Alexander (before he was "Alexander the Great"), reared to identify himself with Achilles as his putative ancestor and already king of Macedonia at age twenty. Alexander was tutored by Aristotle until age sixteen. At age eighteen he led the critical cavalry assault (under his father, Philip) at the Battle of Chaeronea (338 BC) (see map), resulting in the subjugation (Athens) or destruction (Thebes) of the southern Greek city-states. At age twenty, following his father's assassination, Alexander found himself king of Macedonia and prospective leader of the great Persian/Panasian expedition. This would feed his insatiable lust for conquest and become his legacy. He died at age thirty-three (cause still disputed), quickly lapsing into the stuff of legend. Alexander is said to have kept a copy of the *Iliad* at his bedside and to have actively modeled himself on Achilles. When visiting the site of Troy, he conducted elaborate rituals to Achilles and the Greek heroes. See further Ada Cohen, "Alexander and Achilles—Macedonians and 'Mycenaeans,'" in Carter and Morris, eds., 483–505.

214 *The Athenian mythographer*

**"Achilles is . . . manhood."** Robbins, 20.

**in Book Twenty-Three.** *Il.* 23.140–153; cf. 23.45–46, 135–136 (knowing he will not return home to the Spercheios, Achilles dedicates a lock of his hair to the fallen Patroclus). On Achilles and Apollo, see Nagy (1979/1999), 62–63, 120–122, 289–295.

*Fearing for Achilles's life*

**island of Skyros . . . Lycomedes**. On the conflicting legends, see Griffin, 43–44; on Achilles and Deidamia, Fantuzzi, Ch. 2 ("Deidameia").

**there fathers Neoptolemus.** Achilles's longing references to Neoptolemus validate the legend of his (Achilles's) paternity. See *Il.* 19.321–327; *Od.* 11.491–493, 538–540.

**"undergoing . . . training."** Ormand, 150.

215 *Then again, the Oedipal*

**Narcissism, as love of self.** "He is an absolute rule unto himself and though [his fellows] might use him as a model by which to judge themselves, he uses none but himself to judge himself. This we call narcissism: one seeks not the completion of the self in the other, but the assurance and definition of the self in the mirror image(s) of the self in the other." MacCary, 58.

**reconfigures the incest taboo.** The case differs with divinity, Zeus and Hera brother and sister/husband and wife.

**his alter ego or dopplegänger.** That Achilles and Patroclus are not lovers in the *Iliad* is no obstacle to inferences and depictions elsewhere, starting with the Epic Cycle itself and with Greek drama, and extending throughout Latin literature. See Fantuzzi, 7–20 (referring to the "post-Homeric eroticization of their especially powerful bond"). The lost *Myrmidons* of Aeschylus portrayed Achilles as *erastēs* 'lover' to Patroclus (the play, without being named, is referred to in Tom Stoppard's *The Invention of Love*). While Achilles as the "youth," and Patroclus as the older, more tutelary companion are age-appropriate to pederasty, one cannot press the point, both because Achilles is a demigod and because the younger of a homoerotic pair is the expectedly passive partner—the *erōmenos* 'beloved' rather than the *erastēs* 'lover'. Achilles as *erōmenos,* subject to intercrural or possibly penetrative sex, is problematic, to say the least. See further Downing, 173–174; Snell, 14–15. In Plato's *Symposium,* Phaedrus argues that Aeschylus cannot have portrayed *Achilles* as the *erastēs* and Patroclus as the *erōmenos,* precisely because Achilles is the younger and more beautiful of the two. The relationship, taking Plato as its starting point, is the subject of Madeline Miller's novel *The Song of Achilles* (2011).

216 *As in the tale of*

**A baby or toddler.** "Snatched from Penelope's bosom" and threatened with death. The action is taken to dissuade Odysseus from his refusal (he has feigned madness) to join the Greek expedition to Troy. See West (2003), 71–72. Penelope does little to clarify Telemachus's age, referring to her *païs* 'son' as "already a 'man' [*anēr*] capable of caring for the house" (*Od.* 19.159–161).

**over Penelope on Ithaca.** For comparative discussion of the folkloric and saga elements in the wooing of Penelope, see W. Crooke, "The Wooing of Penelope," *Folklore,* 9.2 (1898), 97–135.

*The marriage of Helen*

***Iliad* scholiast thus notes.** W' fr. 1; pp. 81–82. For the Trojan War as a means of population control (analogous to the biblical flood story), see pp. 213–216. Being more than human and seeking more than human prerogatives, the heroes and demigods present a continuing threat to Olympus. The plan for disburdening an overpopulated earth is thus principally aimed at *this* population, marked for death in epic combat either at Troy or Thebes, or otherwise reassigned to the ends of Earth. See the Races of Man parable, *WD* 109–201. Once the heroes and demigods have been dispatched, the gods have the "carefree existence" befitting divinity. This process provides the stability coming only from the full separation of human and divine. In other words, *stability,* to abide, must be free of intercourse between gods and humans with its production of semidivine and divinity-challenging offspring. Men and gods once lived together (*Th.* 535). Their separation in the Heroic Age reiterates, as it consolidates, the separation of Earth and Sky in the Mythic Age (pp. 56–58). Both separations establish limits and boundaries. See further the incisive comments querying (1) the source of the archaic Greek belief in overpopulation as a cause of the Trojan War (Reeves 1966), and (2) the dormancy of that belief in the Western world for 2,000 years following Euripides (Reeves 1967).

**'plan of Zeus . . . fulfilled.'** The *Dios boulē* 'plan of Zeus' is a plan of overarching mythological scope and of ultimately indeterminate purpose and implementation. It is "the master plot of archaic mythology." Murnaghan, 25. The key phrase *Dios d'eteleieto boulē* 'the plan of Zeus was being fulfilled' appears at the start of the *Cypria* in verses quoted by an *Iliad* scholiast vis-à-vis the identical phrase at the start of the *Iliad.* As used in the *Cypria,* the phrase appears to designate (according to the *Iliad* scholiast) a plan to disburden the earth of excessive population. As used in the *Iliad,* the phrase appears to signal Zeus's intent to glorify Achilles through the slaughter of the Trojan War (or the part of it that concerns the *Iliad*). A massive death toll seems the means in both cases, the *Iliad*'s plan of Zeus a phase of the plan overall. In this sense, the *Iliad* figures as "one more chapter in Zeus's endless scheme." Murnaghan, 36. For other instances of Homeric and Hesiodic language identifying parts of the overall myth as *boulai* 'plans', see Murnaghan, 25, n. 3.

The scholarship on this topic is immense, the more so because it dovetails with the Hesiodic Myth of the Five Races. The latter also evidences the destruction of the Age of Heroes in battles at Troy (the *Iliad*) and Thebes (a different epic cycle) as part of the plan to lighten the earth's population and finalize the separation of men and gods. The following are especially noteworthy: Reeve (1966), Murnaghan (1979), Scodel (1982), Falkner (1989), Koenen (1994), Scaife (1995), Marks (2002), Wilson (2007). See also Hendel (1987) (the demigods and Genesis 6:1–4).

**advisor *Mōmos* 'Blame'.** Though an obscure god or *daimōn* 'spirit', Mōmos and his siblings conjure forth every negative aspect of war, making him the perfect advisor on the subject. The mother of *Mōmos* is *Nyx* 'Night'. His siblings are *Eris* 'Strife', *Moros* 'Doom', *Ker* 'Violent Death', *Oizys* 'Misery', the *Moirai* 'Fates', the avenging *Keres* 'Death-Fates', *Nemesis* 'Retribution', *Apatē* 'Deceit', *Gēras* 'Old Age' (*Th.* 211–225).

**Zeus himself and Leda.** According to the more popular myth, Zeus, in the form of a swan, impregnated Leda. The egg hatched Helen and her twin brothers, Castor and Pollux—the Dioscuri, or "Zeus's boys." Leda, in turn, is the wife of Helen's nominal father Tyndareus, the father by Leda of Clytemnestra (p. 637). Clytemnestra and Helen are thus half-sisters, keeping perfidy all in the family.

The myth features many permutations, one positing Zeus and Nemesis 'Retribution' as Helen's parents. See W′ fr. 11, pp. 91–92, and Graves (1988), 125–127, 206–208. For *nemesis* 'retribution' and Helen's sense of self-shame and the opinions of others (i.e., the basis of *nemesis*), see Ebbott, 12–19. Parentage from Zeus and Nemesis is clearly allegorical, since it would render Helen fully divine. It is Helen's semidivinity that explains her divine afterlife and the afterlife divinity she confers on Menelaus as her husband. Such is Menelaus's reward for tribulations on Helen's account, no less than for the singular privilege of marriage to the world's most beautiful woman. The daughter of Zeus and Leda—that version first recounted, to our knowledge, by Euripides (*Helen,* 16–23)—Helen is significantly the only mortal daughter of Zeus. Further, and for all her eventually five (later expanded to eleven) husbands, Helen is neither courted nor seduced by a god and never gives birth to a demigod. Though Helen's parentage by Nemesis is more persuasive, her birth as a swan's hatchling is more picturesque—even as the Judgment of Paris is more picturesque than the advice of Mōmos as a cause of the war. It is the picturesque that predominates. The sources concerning Helen's birth are otherwise "ambiguous and possibly self-contradictory." See Mayer, 9–12; N. Austin, 43, 46, n. 32; Clader, 71–72.

**"From these . . . many killed."** For views on the birth of Helen's daughter, Hermione, as a precipitant of the Trojan War, see González, 392–394.

217 *Age signals transience*

**myth of the five . . . *genē*.** See *WD* 174–178: "Thereafter, would that I were not among the men of the fifth generation, but either had died before or been born afterwards. For now truly is a race of iron, and men never rest from labour by day, and from perishing by night; and the gods shall lay sore trouble upon them" (Evelyn-White, tr.). In translating *genē* as 'races' or 'breeds' (instead of 'ages' or 'generations'), I follow Currie, 36–51, whose chapter "Hesiod on Human History" is otherwise recommended.

*On a literary level*

**"Hesiod's . . . age-graded."** The paragraph's quotations and paraphrases are from Thomas M. Falkner (1989; 47, 56, 60) and (1990).

The relative lack of appreciation for childhood has an exception in the case of Achilles, for whom childhood and young adulthood constitute the better part of life. The Roman epic poet Statius (c. 45–c. 96 AD) wrote an *Achilleid* focusing on Achilles's youthful training with Chiron and subsequent encounter with Deidamia. In that case, Achilles's youthful life, excepting Troy, is essentially all there is. The *Achilleid*—surviving in 1,200 lines—is thus episodic, unconcerned with age or personal development as such. Mythology otherwise relates a number of baby episodes: the infant Heracles strangling snakes, or the newly born Hermes rustling cattle and inventing the lyre. These are largely anecdotal, illustrating early predisposition (strength, cleverness, etc.) more than early age as such.

*There is, moreover, a*
**"correspondence . . . incoherent."** Purves, 201 (paraphrasing sources).
**"so obscure that . . . events."** Will, 53.
**"Tyndareus . . . the papyrus."** Ormand, 198.

218 *Men and gods*
**plan of Zeus . . . interruptions**. For the suspension of "temporal verisimilitude" in the *Iliad,* see the excellent article by Ann Bergren, "Helen's Web: Time and Tableau in the Iliad." In the *Odyssey,* by contrast, "narrative is relatively unproblematic because time is unproblematic." Segal here contrasts time in the *Odyssey* with time in Greek tragedy, and especially in Sophocles's *Oedipus* where time is "constantly bending backward and forward with mysterious gaps and discontinuities. The dangers and limits that surround human life in tragedy make both generational time and narrative time uncertain, unreliable, and complicated." Segal (2001), 62.
**"seen to belong . . . be pressed."** Burgess, 173.
**masterful inclusion of tableaux.** "The art of the *Iliad* is the art of the tableau. The two conventions of realistic narration and temporal suspension produce a verbal version of what we would see in Helen's tapestry [*Il.* 3.121–128], i.e., the action of struggle in stasis, both movement in time and metatemporal permanence, both at once." Bergren, 23.

219 *That said, the following*
**whatever age-related detail.** Reference is made to the following for attested chronological or age-related data: **Hermione age nine when Helen abducted by Paris**, *Cypria* (West [2003], 69), *Epit.* 3.3 (Frazer, 174–175; Hard, 147); **Achilles age fifteen when sailing for Troy, taking command of fleet**, *Epit.* 3.16 (Frazer, 185–186; Hard, 149); **Helen age twelve when abducted by Theseus**, *Epit.* 1.23 (Frazer, 153; Hard, 142–143 ); **Agamemnon musters Greek forces**, *Il.* 11.766–770, *Epit.* 3.6 (Frazer, 177; Hard, 147–148); **two-year muster for first expedition, eight years of return voyages following its failure**, *Epit.* 3.18 (Frazer, 187–188; Hard, 149); **twenty-year duration of Trojan War (ten at Troy)**, *Epit.* 3.18 (Frazer, 187; Hard, 149), *Il.* 24.765; **Iphigenia summoned to Aulis on pretext of marriage to Achilles**, *Epit.* 3.22 (Frazer, 191; Hard, 150); **eight-year return of Menelaus from Trojan War**, *Od.* 4.81–82.

220 *A total of ten years'*
**(Teuthrania in Mysia).** *Cypria* (West [2003], 73); *Epit.* 3.3.18 (Hard, 149). A papyrus from Oxyrhynchus, attributed to Archilochus and written in elegiac couplets, narrates a pre-Trojan War battle between the Greeks and Telephus, King of Mysia (the Greeks decisively routed). It is the first known instance of an epic narrative from the archaic period in a meter other than dactylic hexameter. See www.papyrology.ox.ac.uk/POxy/ papyrus number LXIX 4708. Web. 1/25/2015.
**by returns to Greece.** According to this legend, Achilles was blown off course returning home, landed at Skyros, and only then took up with Deidamia.

*The passing reference*
**"origins . . . in legend."** Bespaloff, 67.

**"my adored . . . own age."** *Il.* 3.175.
**Hesiod advises marriage.** Being contemporary with Homer, Hesiod is a good source for the matters discussed herein. Hesiod advises as follows: "Bring home a wife at the right time of life, when you are not far short of thirty nor much older; this is the age for marriage. Let your wife mature four years and be married in the fifth" (*WD* 695–698). To "mature four years" means to be four years post-puberty—puberty then deemed to have occurred at age fourteen. By this reckoning, Helen appears to have borne Hermione pretty much *at* puberty. The ancient testimonia relating to the age of puberty and marriage are gathered by M. L. West in his commentary to the cited passage of the *Works and Days.* See West, ed. (1978), 326–327. A girl's marriage between ages twelve and sixteen was also possible, and "Hesiod seems, to our way of thinking, to have been ahead of his time in advocating a later age." See T. A. Sinclair, *Hesiod Works and Days* (Hildesheim: Georg Olms, 1966), 71 (citing sources).

222 *The Cypria, in Proclus's*
**a meeting . . . at Troy.** See West (2003), 79.
**wooed . . . sight unseen.** Such suitors "not seeing her form, but hearing the word (*muthon*) of others . . . for great was the woman's *kleos*" (i.e., what was *heard* of her). See MW fr. 199.0–9, pp. 97–98, and M fr. 154d.0–9, p. 224.
**are told nothing more.** The Byzantine Ioannis Tzetzes (p. 175) discounts as nonsense the assumption that Achilles and Helen had sex during this encounter. The disclaimer appears in a notation of Tzetzes to the *Alexandra* 'Cassandra' of the Hellenistic poet and grammarian Lycophron (3rd century BC). See Edwin L. Brown, "Achilles and Deidamia on the Portland Vase," *The American Journal of Archaeology*, 76.4 (1972), 382, n. 25.

*We note, in closing*
**abduction by Theseus.** See Graves (1988), 362–364 (full account and sources).
**Diodorus of Sicily.** See C. H. Oldfather, tr., *Diodorus Siculus, Library of History* (Cambridge: Harvard Univ. Press, Loeb Classical Library, 1939), 18.
**Hellanicus of Lesbos.** See Henry J. Walker, *Theseus and Athens* (Oxford: Oxford Univ. Press, 1995), 200 (citing source).
**"we may . . . suitors."** Murray (1954), 50–51 (further noting that Hellanicus "formed the most convenient and most frequently used authority on early history for mythographers like Apollodorus and commentators on the poets").
**"Theseus was . . . age."** Bernadotte Perrin, tr., *Plutarch, Life of Theseus*, in *The Parallel Lives of Plutarch* (Cambridge: Harvard Univ. Press, Loeb Classical Library, 1914), 71. Plutarch further entertains the possibility that Helen's father, Tyndareus, himself gave Helen to Theseus for safekeeping, "for fear of Enarophoros, the son of Hippocoön, who sought to take Helen by force while she was yet a child." Plutarch notes earlier in his *Life of Theseus* that Theseus's "rape of Helen is said to have filled Attica with war" (*Thes.*, Perrin, tr., 67). It appears from these accounts that Helen, from earliest age, had talismanic value. Theseus, by Plutarch's account, was a serial rapist—Helen's early fate at his hands heralding her rape-victimization throughout life. For Helen's "consistently being raped" as an aspect of her origin as a fertility goddess, see Clader, 71–72. For the serial liaisons of Achilles, see D. Miller, 423, n. 235.

223 *However young at the*
**she might come of age.** So Plutarch (indirectly): "With this mutual understanding they cast lots, and Theseus won [i.e., over Pirithous, with whom he abducted Helen], and taking the maiden, who was not yet ripe for marriage, conveyed her to Aphidnae. Here he made his mother a companion of the girl, and committed both to Aphidnus, a friend of his, with strict orders to guard them in complete secrecy." *Thes.*, Perrin, tr., 73.

**Agamemnon and Menelaus.** Rescuing Helen after her second abduction (to Troy), Agamemnon and Menelaus substitute, as it were, for the Dioscuri. In a mythological bow to the earlier incident, Helen notes (when surveying the Greek forces) that the Dioscuri are absent. (They are dead, the poet tells us, and buried in Sparta.) See *Il.* 3.236–244. For Agamemnon and Menelaus as the Homeric hypostases of the Dioscuri, see Clader, 49–52.
**to wait out . . . Achilles.** Charles Rowan Beye, in his acclaimed and highly insightful fictional biography *Odysseus: A Life* (New York: Hyperion, 2004), 23–25, creates the following age-rectifying scenario: Odysseus espies and is impressed with Penelope, age ten, at the wooing of Helen (Penelope Helen's younger cousin). He has traveled to Sparta for the event out of curiosity alone, knowing Tyndareus would not award his fabled daughter to an Ithacan bumpkin. Ever the great deviser, Odysseus proposes that the suitors swear an oath of assistance to whoever is chosen as Helen's husband, should harm befall her. The Oath of Tyndareus, as just such an oath, will preempt dissension among the losing contenders. In return, Tyndareus accedes to Odysseus's request to wed Penelope. Odysseus, however, departs on his own for Ithaca, leaving Penelope to come of age. He returns eight years later, taking her back to Ithaca. Beye further visualizes Odysseus at age twenty-one the ruler of Ithaca in all but name—delaying marriage first to consolidate his hold, then to wait out Penelope's maturity. (His belated marriage at age twenty-nine to an eighteen-year-old Penelope curiously conforms to Hesiod's age-appropriate prescriptions). The scenario is entirely tenable. If Odysseus, in Beye's words, considered Penelope "worth waiting for," and waited eight years, Helen (or Tyndareus) could have appreciated the potential of an Achilles come of age, and also waited. That this did not happen shows, again, that the union was impossible. For another instance of marital deferral, one may compare the biblical story of Jacob, who worked for Laban seven, then a total of fourteen, years for the right to marry Rachel (Gen. 29).

*Nonetheless, so resistant*
**"lovers after . . . his death."** N. Austin, 26. As concerns spiritual union on Leuke, both Achilles and Heracles, the two greatest demigods of their respective generations, are granted a kind of immortality: Achilles with Helen on Leuke, and Heracles with wife *Hēbē* 'Youth' on Olympus. Both, however, also reside in Hades through their *eidōla* 'ghosts, simulacra', and both wretchedly so (*Od.* 11.465–540, 617–626). Leuke, or White Island, is located in the Black Sea off the Danube Delta. Originally sacred to Apollo, it became the sanctuary and cult center of the dead Achilles and his companion, Patroclus. It is one, and perhaps the most prominent, of the Isles of the Blest (p. 632). On Leuke and the Black Sea, see also Burgess, 160–167.
**Hermione's . . . Neoptolemus.** The wedding plans are underway when Telemachus arrives in Sparta to question Helen and Menelaus concerning Odysseus's whereabouts (*Od.* 4.1–14).
**marriage in life . . . children.** Kazantzakis works to similar effect in having Odysseus, upon his return to Ithaca, marry the Phaeacian princess, Nausicaa, to his son, Telemachus. Odysseus's encounter with the fairyland Nausicaa (during his Homeric wanderings) teems with marital potential; but the encounter remains chaste. Kazantzakis's Odysseus thus eventually sublimates his desire for Nausicaa by her marriage to his son (*Odusseia* 2.559–618)—even as Hermione and Neoptolemus are proxies for the frustrated union of Helen and Achilles. Nausicaa's arrival by ship and reception at Ithaca (*Odusseia* 2.1131–1284) is rhapsody on the theme of Andromache's arrival at Troy in Sappho's "Wedding of Hector and Andromache" (Chapter 17; §26). Moreover, in marrying Telemachus to a fairyland princess, Kazantzakis ignores the distinction between the real and fantasy worlds, everywhere maintained in Homer's *Odyssey*. Similarly, the magical amulet, originally given him by Calypso, which Kazantzakis's Odysseus gives

Helen (*Odusseia* 3.599–621), whom he later abducts. Such early confoundings of real and unreal prepare for the *Odusseia*'s pervasively hallucinogenic quality.
**Neoptolemus . . . final phase.** *Od.* 11.489–540 (Odysseus tells Achilles in the underworld how he and Nestor retrieved Neoptolemus from Skyros, and how Neoptolemus excelled in the concluding phases of the war).
**slaying Paris . . . father's killer.** Neoptolemus finishes the work his father had left undone. Appearing in the Epic Cycle (not in the *Iliad* itself), Neoptolemus also slays Hector's son, Astyanax, and enslaves Hector's wife, Andromache. Achilles, we recall, had himself been the bane of Andromache's family. See *Od.* 11.513–540.

*We recall that Menelaus*
**to the Elysian Field.** Located at the "limits of the earth" (*Od.* 4.561–569), i.e., at the western edge of the earth by the earth-encircling Ocean (*Okeanos*, the source of all life). The Elysian Field is also imagined as a subdivision of Hades, reachable, according to Virgil, by a split in the road within Hades itself (*Aen.* 6.535). It is there that Aeneas meets with his father, Anchises. Elysium was early equated with the Isles or Islands of the Blest (later consolidated into a single island). "In the tradition outside the Homeric texts the major heroes of the Trojan expedition have passed through the mortal state to a quasi-divine state. Many were thought to have reached islands far at sea . . . where they became the tutelary spirits of their respective islands. These were collectively the Islands of the Blest. 'Blest' here refers to the hero whose cult was maintained on the island." N. Austin, 26, n. 4.
**view . . . "faded goddess."** Clader (1976) and (without mention of Clader) Skutsch (1987).
**used them to overcome.** Euripides entertains the possibility that Helen was free to choose which suitor she wished, wealth being no criterion. See Ziogas, 22, n. 6 (citing *IA* 68–69).
**"Beauty . . . it to flower."** Bespaloff, 66–67.

Part V, Chapter 19

227 *Though it is tempting*
**"Sappho . . . Homeric hexameter."** Nagy (1974), 134.

229 *Classical poetry did not*
**"And it is not . . . poetry."** "E non è molto numero d'anni passati, che appariro prima questi poete volgari; chè dire per rima in volgare tanto è quanto dire per versi in latino, secondo alcuna proporzione." Dante, *The New Life: La Vita Nuova*, Ch. 25, pp. 61–62 (Appelbaum, tr.).
**"The first . . . understand."** "E lo primo che cominciò a dire sì come poeta volgare, si mosse però che volle fare intendere le sue parole a donna, a la quela era malagevole d'intendere li versi latini." Dante, *supra*, Ch. 25, p. 62. For the "cult of women as the ideal audience for vernacular literature" (as they were assuredly not for Latin literature), see V. Cox, 44–45. Women, says Cox, were considered "possessed of an innate *intelleto d'amore*" in an age greatly influenced by medieval Provençal culture and the traditions of courtly love. To that extent, "women were concretely important as patrons and even poets themselves."

*The first seven transliterated*
**(ϝ)anax . . . di(ϝ)os Achilleus.** The ϝ in (ϝ)anax and di(ϝ)os is the Greek letter digamma, with sound approximating the letter *w*. Already obsolete in Homer's time—i.e., before the Greek language became fixed by writing—digamma was (re)discovered by

famed British classicist Richard Bentley (1662–1742). Bentley intuited its presence in certain words, since its omission left the meter defective (an issue glossed by the poems' transcribers over the centuries). The digamma attests the Homeric poems' exceeding antiquity. The letters *v* or *w* sometimes reflect the digamma, e.g., Gr. *di*(F)os, Lat. *divus* 'divine'; cf. Gr. (F)*oinos,* Lat. *vinum* 'wine'.

231 *In iambic meter, poetic*
**It follows . . . heroic measure.** See Sowerby (2006), 63–64, quoting Roger Ascham distinguishing *Carmen Exametrum* from *Carmen Iambicum.*

232 *To take some examples*
**"of comfort . . . impregnable."** *Richard II,* 3.2.144–147, 164–168 (*The Riverside Shakespeare* [Boston: Houghton Mifflin, 1974]).

*The quantitative rhythm*
**"[t]ime plays against beat."** My own formulation has benefited from Beye (1987), 171: "Latin prosody is contrapuntal, based first upon the fact that some vowels take longer to pronounce, then on the fact that Latin words have a slight stress accent. The metrical scheme of the long and shorts refers to the length of time it takes to enunciate each syllable. Time plays against beat. English has only a stress accent."

233 *Latin was the spoken*
**communications system.** See further Ostler, 51–52, and on the Christian hymns, Ostler, 122.

234 *At no time, however, did*
**bringing . . . "final state."** Ostler, 182–183.

*Little recognized in this*
***elegos* [derivation uncertain].** See "The Origin of Elegy as a Literary Form," in Georg Luck, *The Latin Love Elegy* (London: Methuen, 1959, 2nd ed. 1969), 25–46. Cf. Warren (2008), 12–13.
**"accentuat[ing]. . . hexameter."** Nagy (1974), 100–101; on the archaism of rhyme in Greek versification, Nagy (1972), 730–733.

235 *The following pentameters*
**The fourth and tenth.** See Theognis 173–182 in Campbell (1967), 81–82, 356–359. For rhythm as the functional equivalent of rhyme in Homer, see p. 229.
**or anticipated soundalike.** A flagrant example of sense anticipating rhyme appears in a recent poem by Vikram Seth (b. 1952) in *New York Review of Books,* 3/20/2014. In each case, one can well enough guess the rhyme before it appears. The first of two stanzas reads as follows:

> Through love's great power to be made whole
> In mind and body, heart and soul—
> Through freedom to find joy, or be
> By dint of joy itself set free
> In love and in companionhood:
> This is the true and natural good.

**night-light-right-bright.** Dylan Thomas, "Do Not Go Gentle into That Good Night," considered his best-known and most successful poem. The same rhyme scheme escapes censure in the first quatrain of Edward FitzGerald's *Rubáiyát,* its exquisite imagery and intense alliteration predominating:

> Awake! for morning in the Bowl of Night
> Has flung the Stone that puts the Stars to Flight:
> And Lo! the Hunter of the East has caught
> The Sultan's Turret in a Noose of Light.

**"it must . . . predetermination."** Hecht (2003), 262, quoting Robert Graves, *The Common Asphodel: Collected Essays on Poetry, 1929–1949* (London: Hamish Hamilton, 1949), 5.

*It is thus from the*
**notably . . . elegiac verse.** See also apropos of Horace, and especially *Odes* 4.1: "A pathetic echo of the final sound of *bonae* in the noun it modifies, *Cinarae,* comes close to the effect of modern rhyme, for *Cinarae* is placed at a significant break in the metrical line. The sentence has a dying fall." W. Fitzgerald, 126–131.
**"first glimmers . . . rhymes."** See further Ostler, 122–124. Or as put in an earlier day: "The Greek inflections give an effect of assonance that is sometimes deliberately exploited, especially in the pentameter. . . . Rhyme after all, is only a kind of assonance disposed in regular places of incidence." Higham & Bowra, cvii.

236 *Poets before Milton had*
**Poets . . . "tyranny of rhyme."** For the disparagement and abandonment of rhyme, see Sowerby (2006), 62–63, 131 (quoting Elizabethan scholar Roger Ascham, *The Scolemaster* [1570]: "our rude beggarly ryming, brought first into Italie by *Gothes* and *Hunnes. . . .*" ). The "barbarianization" of Latin, for its part, was viewed as a contaminant of the barbarian invasions themselves. See V. Cox, 62. For Proust, however, the "tyranny of rhyme forces [great poets] into the discovery of their finest lines." Marcel Proust, *Swann's Way,* C. K. Scott-Moncrieff, tr. (New York: Henry Holt, 1922), 30.
**"raising the dignity . . . Virgil."** Sowerby (2006), 62.
**primitive Saturnian meter.** See pp. 265–271, 283, 301, 553–554.

*Milton himself takes a*
**reactionary "The Verse."** Samuel Daniel's *Defence of Rhyme* (1603) "founds the defence of the native metres on a broader basis than any had so far envisioned, and achieved a victory for rhyme so complete that the first readers of *Paradise Lost* were, the printers tell us, 'stumbled as to why the poem rimed not.' Hence the Preface *On the Verse.*" Wilcock, 6.
**"Because much . . . luxury."** Hecht (2003), 261. Perpetuating the fallacy of rhyme as a rejected option in antiquity, another writer speaks of rhyme's having been "shunned by versifiers in all major literatures of classical antiquity" and wonders why "this pariah, once regarded as a blemish of prose, should, in a relatively brief period, become a nearly indispensable component of lyric poetry." William Harmon, "English Versification: Fifteen Hundred Years of Continuity and Change," *Studies in Philology,* 94.1 (1997), 26.

237 *Further noting in "The Verse"*
**"vulgar tinkling . . . words.'"** Sowerby (2006), 146; see Dryden, Epistle V: To the Earl of Roscommon, on His Excellent Essay on Translated Verse.

238 *Milton further ascribes the*
**an obstacle to Spenser.** Samuel Johnson, somewhat unfairly it seems, felt that Ben Jonson's summation of Spenser—"he wrote no language"—was equally suited to Milton. Pope had earlier said that "Milton's style in the *Paradise Lost* is not natural;

'tis an exotic style." See Shankman (1983), 142 (citing sources). Of course, the same applies, by degree, to Pope's own *Iliad*. Such views slight the fact that the language of classical epic, through and through, was an unspoken, highly artificial construct. Epic language, in its way, was "no language": unnatural, exotic, and tailor-made to and within the genre.

**incapable or undesirous.** Ezra Pound makes the same point vis-à-vis Provençal, noting that "the English 'poets' en masse had simply said: 'these forms are *impossible* in English, they are too complicated, we haven't the rhymes.' That was bunkum, usual laziness of English, and hatred of craft." Letter to Felix E. Schelling, 7/9/1922; Paige, 179.

**practiced, and appreciated.** See Paul J. Hunter, "Seven Reasons for Rhyme," in Clymer, ed. (2006). In his rhymed translation of the Latin epigrammatist Martial (1st century AD), Garry Wills refutes the notion that translators "to be modern, to be authentic, must not resort to things as forced, now, and artificial, as regular meter, stanzas, and rhyme." Wills believes (as his translation affirms) that such features are at least "partial recompense" for the loss in translation of Latin's peculiar artifice. This he defines as "the endlessly interlockable verbal patterns of an inflected language." Epigram is all about bang for the buck. Delivering much in a narrow scope (*multum in parvo*), it relies on what Wills calls a "studied formality." Wills (2007), 4–5. Epigram's pointed or even predatory nature—the final verse *zapping* its unsuspecting subject—is no better conveyed in English than by rhyme (so Wills). To be sure, each classical genre has a "studied formality" of its own, formality being the pith of classical poetry. Varieties of rhyme and meter may thus serve, in their several ways, to enhance the translation of classical verse into English.

239 *It is the very amplitude*

**"A river bursts . . . thunder."** *Odes* 4.2. *The Odes of Horace*, James Mitchie, tr. (New York: Penguin Classics, 1976).

**"dramatiz[ing] . . . his liking."** Richard A. Lanham, *Analyzing Prose* (New York: Continuum, 2nd ed., 2003), 49.

**"accused . . . natural grain."** Sowerby (2006), 142.

**"in Poetry . . . good Oratory."** On the connection between poetry and oratory in classical Latin verse, see Coleman, 28, 57.

*Pope grasped Milton's*

**"glows like . . . Force of Art."** Pope, Preface, 4–5.

**Dryden, too, approved, even.** Sowerby (2006), 144.

**"too many Miltonic inversions."** Letter to John Hamilton Reynolds, September 22, 1819. See Sidney Colvin, ed., *Letters of John Keats to His Family and Friends* (London: Macmillan, 1891), 319.

**"Poetry may subsist . . . itself."** Sowerby (2006), 146 (quoting Johnson's *Life of Milton*).

240 *Granted, the introduction*

**monumental . . . metrics.** Sowerby (2006), 63.

***Restrictive* . . . reason liberating.** On constraint as the catalyst to artistic freedom, see pp. 380–386.

***astonish* . . . merely please.** "He that thinks himself capable of astonishing may write blank verse, but those that hope only to please must condescend to rhyme." Johnson, *Lives*, Vol. 1, 194.

**"tire by long continuance."** "Blank verse makes some approach to that which is called the 'lapidary style'; has neither the easiness of prose nor the melody of numbers, and therefore tires by long continuance." Johnson, *Lives*, Vol. 1, 193.

*In this way there*
**quote Professor Mackail.** Mackail quotations in this paragraph from Mackail (1919), 10.

242 *Such are the simplest*
**"Parting . . . Andromache."** C. S. Lewis (1942), 20 (citing *Il.* 6.390–493).
**"Even in . . . reproduce itself."** Lord (1960), 31, as quoted and discussed by Nagy (1990b), 24–25.
**used once and only once.** Such words are known as a *hapax legomena* 'once spoken' (sing. *hapax legomenon*). The number of such words was early estimated at close to 2,000 (1,097 in the *Iliad*; 868 in the *Odyssey*). See Clyde Pharr, *Homeric Greek, a book for beginners* (Lexington: D. C. Heath, 1920), xxii. There are approximately 27,000 lines in the *Iliad* and *Odyssey* combined; hence a seven percent frequency. In terms of total Homeric vocabulary, the frequency of such usages is placed at approximately twenty-seven percent. R. Friedrich, 12, n. 5 (with bibliography).
**"join[ing] . . . overall rhythm."** Nagy (1974), 9.
**"A truly . . . composition."** Nagy (1974), 16 (citing Lord, 1960).

244 *It is for these reasons*
**"transformed the . . . poets."** Benardete, 7.
**As C. S. Lewis remarks.** Paragraph quotations and paraphrases from Lewis (1942), 22–24.
**"The hexameter . . . culture."** Beye (1975), 141.

245 *Audiences nurtured on*
**"ever hurries . . . his listener."** Nec gemino bellum Troianum orditur ab ovo; / semper ad eventum festinat et in medias res / secus ac notas auditorem rapit (*AP* 147–149). The two, or twin, eggs refer to the births of Helen and, possibly, Clytemnestra, following Zeus's mating as a swan with Leda.
***starting with* the Trojan Horse.** *Od.* 8.487–498.
**"By directing . . . audiences."** Beye (1966), 18.

246 *We now briefly*
**Nagy persuasively argues.** What follows derives from and simplifies Nagy (1974), 49–55.

248 *We have noted that*
**"simply nothing . . . at all."** Swinburne, 228.
**"Greeks . . . Swinburnian."** Pound (1937), 185–186.

250 *The rhythm results*
**"All the night . . . wind."** From Swinburne's "Sapphics," the first five of twenty such stanzas. For Sappho's influence on Swinburne, see further David McKay, *The Works of Algernon Charles Swinburne: Poems* (Philadelphia, n.d.), 82–84, and M. B. Raymond, *Swinburne's Poetics: Theory and Practice* (The Hague: Mouton, 1971), 57–86. "Sapphics," I submit, is Swinburne's own *phainetai moi* 'she appears to me'—appears not 'equal to the gods', of course, but actually appears, as the goddess Aphrodite herself. The epiphany unnerves him.
***uneventful* monosyllabic.** For "the stunning effect of monosyllables" in the poetry of Shakespeare, Hopkins, and Yeats (powerful lines composed entirely of monosyllables), see Edith Grossman, *Why Translation Matters* (New Haven and London: Yale Univ. Press, 2010), 97–98. See also Haynes (2003), 65–72, referring to Swinburne as "one of the most monosyllabic of all English poets," and sensibly concluding: "Monosyllabic lines, monosyllables in verse, are simply too common, too various, to be helpfully discussed by reference to the intrinsic virtues or limitations of the

monosyllable." Homer's first translator into English, George Chapman, strongly favored monosyllables over the "bastard" rhyming polysyllabics of French and Italian. See George Chapman, "To the Reader" (ll. 163–177) in Nicoll, 11.
**monosyllables . . . *weighted.*** Midway between monosyllabic fill and monosyllabic weight is monosyllabic indecorousness. Dryden decried clergyman, critic, and poet Bratten Holyday's translation of Juvenal as teeming with "ill-sounding monosyllables, of which our barbarous language affords him a wild plenty." Haynes, 68. Dryden himself defends against charges of monosyllabic "harshness" in the opening of his own *Aeneid*: "Arms, and the Man I sing, who forc'd by Fate." Haynes, 66.
**"was excellent . . . in English."** Warren (2008), 22–23 (including the notion of Swinburne as a "metrical essence").

*Thus, in the literal*
**"Sappho . . . 'Hendecasyllabics.'"** Warren (2008), 22–23.
**"As the poet . . . of Sappho."** T. G. Johnson, Preface.
**"is exactly . . . androgynous."** Paglia, 228.
**are precluded by meter.** See p. 661.

CHAPTER 20

252 *The closest we come*
**"Taking the lyre . . . play."** *Hymn to Hermes* 435–455, H. G. Evelyn-White, tr. (as adapted). For the pleasures derived from poetry in Homer, see recently (without reference to the *Hymn to Hermes*), Saïd, 129, n. 58 (the listeners "feel pleasure [*terpsis*] which is almost physical, the same word being used to evoke the 'pleasures' of food, drink, sleep, sex, conversation, playing, or hunting").

254 *Ancient Greek poetry*
**here mentioned . . . explanation.** The books on Ancient Greek accent and pronunciation are too many and too specialized to enumerate. One may start with Philip Hobsbaum, *Metre, Rhythm and Verse Form* (London: Routledge, 1996) and D. A. Carson, *Greek Accents: A Student's Manual* (Grand Rapids: Baker Books, 1985).

*The point is that*
**"suggest . . . Sappho's words."** Roche (1966), xx.
**"give some idea . . . mood."** Davenport (1980), 14. One wonders what Davenport ever meant by "subtleties of echo within technique or mood" or how such subtleties might be conveyed. This, from a translator who openly professed his ignorance of Greek, even as he was favorably reviewed.
**a reconstructed recitation.** For recitations of a variety of ancient Greek texts, including Sappho's "Hymn to Aphrodite," see Stephen G. Daitz, *The Pronunciation and Reading of Ancient Greek* (2nd ed.), Audio Forum. *Society for the Oral Reading of Greek and Latin* (*SORGL*). 2002–2010 (www.rhapsodes.fll.vt.edu/links.htm). Web. 7/18/2012.

256 *When the sacrifice*
**"Sing, goddess . . . ordeals."** Herbert Jordan, tr., *Homer: The Iliad* (Norman: Univ. of Oklahoma Press, 2008).
**clumped together . . . possessives.** We have noted Herbert Jordan's clumped-together proper-name possessives as follows:

> Sing, goddess, of Peleus' son Achilles' anger,
> ruinous, that caused the Greeks untold ordeals.

To this may be compared the most recent rendering by classicist Peter Green (2015):

> Wrath, goddess, sing of Achilles Peleus's son's
> calamitous wrath, which hit the Achaeans with countless ills.

This combines ungainly possessives—in lines unconstrained by metric uniformity—with the unnecessary repetition of the poem's opening word *mēnin* 'wrath'; cf. Fagles (1990): "Rage—Goddess, sing the rage of Achilles Peleus' son / murderous. . . ." If anything, a comma is needed after *Achilles.* Alternatively, and better (if *wrath* is repeated): "Wrath, goddess, sing of Achilles, Peleus's son, / that calamitous wrath." And *hit*? This is dull diction.

**"When a . . . no apostrophes."** Jordan, ix.

**"translators . . . characteristics."** Jordan, ix. The year 2008 also saw the translation into iambic pentameter of Sarah Ruden's *Aeneid.* See pp. 435–442.

258 *Finally, archaic Greek*

**integral to the *poiēsis.*** Dance, too, was integral to performance, especially in the choral odes of Greek tragedy. Choral lyric is distinguished from individual lyric, or "monody" (Gr. *monos* 'alone' + *oidē* 'song'; Eng. *ode*). Since the time of Horace, *lyric(al)* has been genericized to mean poetry of a personal nature.

*The caveat extends*

**"[I]t is vain . . . to live."** For the Woolf quotations, see Woolf (1925), 23, 35, and 36. The point is similarly made that the unevenness of the same translator from one passage of Homer to another "suggests that modern knowledge of ancient Greek is inescapably fragmentary, even in the case of those fluent in the language." Fiske, 102.

259 *A more sanguine view,*

**"no language . . . translation."** Stewart, 9–10.

Part VI, Chapter 21

263 *English-speaking culture*

**wholesale absorption of Greek.** T. S. Eliot exalted the West's Greek legacy over its Latin counterpart and derivative. The primacy of Greek over Latin, for W. B. Yeats at least, is amusingly illustrated in a draft letter to the teacher of his son, Michael (1930 diary entry):

> Dear Sir,
>
> My son is now between nine and ten and should begin Greek at once and be taught by the Berlitz method, that he may read as soon as possible that most exciting of all stories, the *Odyssey,* from that landing in Ithaca to the end. . . . As he grows older he will read to me the great lyric poets and I will talk to him about Plato. Do not teach him one word of Latin. The Roman people were the classic decadence, their literature form without matter. They destroyed Milton, the French seventeenth and our own eighteenth century, and our schoolmasters even to-day read Greek with Latin eyes. Greece, could we but approach it with eyes as young as its own, might renew our youth. Teach him mathematics as thoroughly as his capacity permits. I know that Bertrand Russell must, seeing that he is such a featherhead, be wrong about everything, but as I have no mathematics I cannot prove it. I do not want my son to be as helpless. Do not teach him one word of geography. He has lived on the Alps, crossed a number of rivers and when he is fifteen I shall urge him to climb the Sugar Loaf. Do not teach him

a word of history. I shall take him to Shakespeare's history plays, if a commercialized theatre permit, and give him all the historical novels of Dumas, and if he cannot pick up the rest he is a fool. Don't teach him one word of science, he can get all he wants in the newspapers and in any case it is no job for a gentleman. If you teach him Greek and mathematics and do not let him forget the French and German that he already knows you will do for him all that one man can do for another. If he wants to learn Irish after he is well founded in Greek, let him—it will clear his eyes of the Latin miasma. If you will not do what I say, whether the curriculum or your own will restrain, and my son comes from school a smatterer like his father, may your soul lie chained on the Red Sea bottom.

[Vareen M. Bell, *Yeats and the Logic of Formalism* (Columbia and London: Univ. of Missouri Press, 2006), 100–101]

**"conquered Greece . . . Rome."** Graecia capta ferum victorem cepit et artis / intulit agresti Latio" (*Ep.* 2.1.156–157).
**"Within seven . . . Southampton."** Lucas, xxx.

264 *According to the historian*
**"the first citizen of Athens."** Thucydides 2.56.

265 *While Homer was standard*
**had hosted Aeneas's father.** *Aen.* 8.151–168.
**The choice was well made.** The success of Livius's translation earned him state-sponsored commissions as a playwright. In what is our best source for the origins of Roman literature, Cicero relates that the Roman Senate commissioned Livius to compose translations of a Greek tragedy and comedy for the Great Games (240 BC). Cicero, *Brutus* 72–73. The Roman historian Livy records that Livius, a generation later, was commissioned to compose a hymn honoring Juno. See *Ab Urbe Condita* 27.37.7.
**supported by . . . evidence.** Farrell, 427–428.
**Italian geographic points.** Goldberg, 430.

*Livius's Odussia, however,*
**dactylic hexameter of Homer.** Quantitative meter accentuates syllables according to vowel length, not spoken beat. For Homer, dactylic hexameter, and the conventions of quantitative meter, see pp. 227–233. For the derivation of Homeric meter from lyric meter, see pp. 246–248. For Sappho's sole surviving dactylic poem and its knowing use of Homer, see pp. 201–205.
**native-Italic Saturnian meter.** See Gabriele Erasmi, "The Saturnian and Livius Andronicus," *Glotta*, 57.1&2 (1979), 125–149.
**meter of unknown origin.** We consign the dread Saturnian to this discussion alone. For key readings see W. M. Lindsay, "The Saturnian Metre. First Paper," *American Journal of Philology*, 14.2 (1893), 139–170, and "The Saturnian Metre. Second Paper," 14.3 (1893), 305–334 [reviewed by F. F. Abbott, *American Journal of Philology* 17.1 (1896), 94–97, and A. S. Wilkins, *Classical Review*, 8.3 (1894), 108–110]; Thomas Cole, "The Saturnian Verse," *Yale Classical Studies*," 21 (1969), 3–73; Jed Parsons, "A New Approach to the Saturnian Verse and Its Relation to Latin Prosody," *Transactions of the American Philological Association*, 129 (1999), 117–137; and Ernst Pulgram, Ch. 8, in *Latin-Romance Phonology: prosodics and metrics* (Munich: Fink, 1975).

266 *Approximately fifty lines*
**"Thus . . . literary culture."** Armstrong, 193.

*The first-known translator*

**how best . . . rigorous tongue.** The concern of this volume is the translation into English of ancient, and thus more grammatically complex, languages. Different concerns attend the translation of modern Romance languages into English, and of Romance languages one into the other.

267 *Homeric language, in all*

**In Livius's . . . Homer's.** Contemporary with Livius in the third century BC was Apollonius of Rhodes, an Alexandrian. His fully surviving *Argonautika,* written in Homeric dialect and meter, remains the epic high point of the period. For the Alexandrian (or Hellenistic) period, see pp. 279–282. Alexandrian literary practices in all their sophistication were known to the inventors of Roman literature. See Fantham, 221–222.
**"an artificial . . . speech."** Chadwick, 176, citing K. Meister, *Die homerische Kunstsprache* (Leipzig, 1921). It has long been acknowledged that Homer composed in a blended artificial language, i.e., the Homeric dialect, created over centuries of recitation. As concerns the objectives of "art language," my book is predicated on the distancing of poetic language from everyday speech, whether in original or translated verse, whether in an "art language" or not.
**"the . . . Athenian drama."** Clackson and Horrocks, 175 (with examples of forms obsolescent or already obsolete in the time of the earliest Latin poetry).

*Livius fully appreciated*

**Pound . . . "Make it New."** In Pound's poem "Against Form" (the injunction a folly and source of endless mischief).
**"When Livius . . . otherness."** Bettini, 74–75. Bettini notes the following examples of Livius's archaisms: *puera* for *puella* ('girl'), *dacrimae* for *lacrimae* ('tears'), *topper* for *cito* ('quickly').

269 *While Latin drama of*

**no Roman . . . ever ventured.** An impressive rendering into Latin hexameters by David Cunningham of the *Odyssey*'s first fifty lines appears in *Classical Outlook,* 74.1 (1996), 21. I cite the first five lines:

> Musa, virum memora vafrum, qui multa diuque
> Errabat, Troiae sacram cum verterat arcem.
> Multum hominum vidit sedes mentem quoque novit;
> Multos inque mari passus de corde dolores
> Si qua animamque suam ferret reditumque suorum.

Horace, referring to Homer as the poet "who does nothing ineptly," translates the *Odyssey*'s first two lines as follows:

> . . . Quanto rectius hic, qui nil molitur inepte:
> "dic mihi, Musa, virum, captae post tempora Troiae
> qui mores hominum multorum vidit et urbes."

See Fairclough (citing *AP* 140–142), 462–463.

One may further note the *Ilias Latina,* or *Latin Iliad.* The work is a reduction of the *Iliad* to 1,070 Latin hexameters, with many Virgilian and Ovidian stylings, by one Publius Baebius Italicus writing in the reign of Nero (54–68 AD). The work was the primary access to Homer in the Middle Ages—and the only Homer available to Dante. On the *Ilias Latina* and other renderings of Homer during the "Trojan frenzy" at the court of the Emperor Nero, see Armstrong (2008), 187–190.

270 *The poet Ennius*

**Homer . . . him in a dream.** Ennius relates the episode at the outset of his *Annales*, utilizing the conceit of poetic inspiration via divine encounter. The *locus classicus* is Hesiod's *Theogony*, where Hesiod relates the Muses' descent from Mt. Helicon and their "breath[ing] into [him] voice divine," that he might recount creation (Gr. *en* 'in' + *pneō* 'breath'; Lat. *in* + *spiro* 'breath'; Eng. inspiration). Ennius's dream sequence is also indebted to the similarly inspirational encounter related in the Alexandrian Callimachus's *Aetia*. See Acosta-Hughes and Stephens, 208–209.

**dubbed him a "second Homer."** Ennius et sapiens et fortis et alter Homerus / ut critici dicunt 'Ennius, wise and valiant, a second Homer, as the critics say' (*Ep.* 2.1.50–51).

**was *nervosus* 'energetic'.** As conveyed by Porphyrion (2nd–3rd centuries AD), the Latin grammarian and commentator on Horace.

**for his lack of *gravitas*.** Non ridet versus Enni gravitate minores? 'Does not [Lucilius] mock Ennius's verses as lacking in dignity'? (*Sat.* I.10.54; Lucilius, a pioneer of Latin satire in hexameters). Horace elsewhere credits Ennius for enriching Latin with new coinages (*AP* 56–58), even while criticizing him for a dramatic ponderousness verging on haste or ignorance of craft (*AP* 259–262). One surmises from this last notice that Ennius's use of Greek meter in his dramas little evidenced the readiness for his translation of Homer into Latin hexameters.

***ingeniosus poeta . . . bonus*.** Cicero, *pro Murena*, 30.

**Ennius had . . . Greek poetry.** See Fantham, 222–223. For concise stylistic analysis of Naevius and Ennius, based on one passage each, see Clackson and Horrocks, 177–179.

**obliquely refers . . . *studiosus*.** The reference *dicti studiosus*, by which Ennius favorably compares himself to Naevius, comes from a jumbled quotation in Cicero. "The lines are obviously incomplete, but it seems more likely that Cicero himself selected from familiar verses brief suggestions of the ideas he wished to convey, rather than that the missing words have been lost." See Hendrickson, *Cicero: Brutus, Orator* 66–67 (§ xviii.71 and note a).

*Though one senses an*

**"It goes . . . of meter."** Rose, 36–37.

**rewritten from Saturnians.** See Edward Courtney, ed., *The Fragmentary Latin Poets* (Oxford: Oxford Univ. Press, 1993, 2003), 45–46.

271 *Ennius's Annales set the*

**set the precedent for Roman.** Paragraph quotes and paraphrases from Otis (1963), 21–23.

*"Ennius had simply*

**"Ennius had . . . and ideas."** Otis (1963), 23.

**"a colossal . . . and execution."** Otis (1963), 1.

**"novelty and . . . audacity."** Otis (1963), 5.

272 *We have just noted*

**"Thyself . . . terrible troubles."** *Ann.* 109; E. H. Warmington, *Remains of Old Latin I: Ennius and Caecilius* (Cambridge: Harvard Univ. Press, Loeb Classical Library, 1935, 1961), 37.

*Early Latin alliteration*

**"flow[ing] . . . invention of man."** C. C. Felton, ed., Ὁμήρου Ἰλιας. *The Iliad of Homer, From the Text of Wolf. With English Notes and Flaxman's Illustrative Design* (Boston: Hillard, Gray, 1833), ix. The analogy of Homer to a force of nature recurs throughout

Homeric scholarship.
**"autochthonous" . . . sprung.** Gr. *auto* 'self' + *chthōn* 'earth'. The gods of the underworld, or those associated with primal or mysterious forces, are known as Chthonian (versus the Olympian gods, atop their bright and airy mountain). The Chthonians include, among others, Hades, Persephone, the Furies, Hecate, Styx, Sleep, Night, and Death.
**"The Greeks . . . but themselves."** Sainte-Beuve (Lee, tr.), 121–122.

273 *Effective alliteration is*
**"foundational" soundalikes.** See further pp. 304–305.

*Such tendencies do*
**"An interest . . . significant."** Kennedy, 86.
**In Plato's dialogue *Cratylus*.** Hamilton and Cairns, eds. (Plato, *Cratylus* 383b), 422.
**inherent . . . (the signified).** Kennedy, 86 (as paraphrased).
**the idea . . . in Epicurus.** The Letter to Herodotus, 75–76.
**verbal play . . . association.** See Phillip DeLacy, "The Epicurean Analysis of Language," *American Journal of Philology*, 69 (1948), 85–92; and Paul Friedlander, "The Pattern of Sound and Atomistic Theory in Lucretius, *De Rerum Natura*," *American Journal of Philology*, 62 (1941), 16–34 (both seminal articles). See esp. Lucretius, *DRN* 5.1028–1090 (on the development of language).

*More than merely*
**"the state of complete . . . virtue."** For this and following quotations, see Elizabeth Hall Witherell et al., eds., *Henry D. Thoreau, Journal Vol. 1* (1837–1844) (Princeton: Princeton Univ. Press, 1981), 92. To the semantic couple *vir/virtus* may be added the non-root related, but suggestive, *vireo* 'to be green' (Eng. *verdant*).
**"offers words . . . necessity."** Bettini, 57.

274 *Thoreau's vir/virtus,*
**on the same verbal root.** While *virtus* stands for all that is best in the physical and moral nature of man—including strength, bravery, and courage—it typically denotes 'manliness' or 'manhood' in the moral, social, or ethical sense. For 'manliness' in the *virile* sense, Latin uses *virilitas* 'manliness', *virilis* 'manly', *viriliter* 'manfully, courageously'.

*A fine example at the*
**"thematic association . . . grief."** On the name of Achilles, here too briefly treated, see Nagy (1979/1999), Ch. 5: "The Name of Achilles"; on the association between Achilles and Achaeans, Nagy, Ch. 5: "Supplement: The Name of the Achaeans." See further Nagy (2004), Ch. 6: "The Name of Achilles: Questions of Etymology and 'Folk-Etymology.'"
***algea* [sing. *algos* ~ *achos*].** As Nagy also shows, the meaning of Achilles's name is conveyed within the Homeric complex of words for pain, including *achos, algos, penthos, and pēma*; also, that fighting men have *kratos* 'might' when they win, and *achos* 'pain' when they lose. On *penthos alaston* 'unforgettable grief' versus *kleos aphthiton* 'imperishable fame', see pp. 189–190, 202, 610.
***ti nu* (ϝ)*oi . . . ōdussao, Zeu*;** *Od.* 1.62.

275 *For purposes of Latin*
***It Ver et Venus et Veneris.*** *DRN* 5.737. Lucretius is further discussed below. Though removed from the principal concerns of this book, Lucretius's pull is persistent—with the present author, as it seems, no less than with the resurrected T. G. Tucker.

**as much visual as auditory.** Another deft example appears in the first and last lines of Catullus 46: ***ver***... *referet / Diversae*... *reportant* (with other *er* sounds between). I am indebted to Michael Putnam for this example.

*What panache. Prae*
***penetrat... thalamoque potitur.*** Quoted in West (2003), 93. The context further suggests Lat. *pēnis* 'penis', the long *ē* notwithstanding. Cf. Catullus 11.2 (*sive penetrabit*).
**Botticelli's *Allegory of Spring.*** For the Lucretian influence on Botticelli, see Charles Dempsey, *The Portrayal of Love: Botticelli's "Primavera" and Humanist Culture at the Time of Lorenzo the Magnificent* (Princeton: Princeton Univ. Press, 1992), 36–49; and Aby Warburg, "Sandro Botticelli's *Birth of Venus* and *Spring*: An Examination of Concepts of Antiquity in the Italian Early Renaissance," in Kurt W. Forster, ed., *The Revival of Pagan Antiquity*, David Britt, tr. (Los Angeles: Getty Research Institute for the History of Arts and the Humanities, 1999), 88–156.

The passage is a Lucretian highlight. I provide it from the rhymed A. E. Stallings translation (170–171):

> Spring and Venus come, and wingèd Cupid leads the way,
> And mother Flora, in Zephyr's footsteps, scatters a bouquet
> Of blossoms coloured bright to catch the eye, and smelling sweet,
> Carpeting the path that stretches out before their feet.
> Scorching heat comes next, with Ceres head to toe in dust,
> Attended by the Northerlies that in the summer gust;
> Next in the annual procession, we see Autumn traipse,
> Swaying arm in arm with Dionysus, lord of grapes,
> The other seasons follow, and the other winds blow past:
> Volturnus the sky-thunderer, the South-wind's lightning blast.
> And then, with snow and frost in tow, the Solstice of the year,
> While Winter, his teeth chattering with cold, brings up the rear.

276 *Lucretius uses the words*
**"Meanwhile... much grief."** *Aen.* 9.473–474 and 11.139.
**auditory and... analogues.** See articles by DeLacy and Friedlander cited at p. 639.
**Thoreau... not particularly.** See Ethyl Seybold, "Thoreau: the Quest and the Classics," in Harold Bloom, ed., *Henry David Thoreau* (New York: Infobase Publishing, 2007), 27.

277 *Although Plautus offers*
**are many "poetic markers."** Clackson and Horrocks, 176 (with examples here simplified and explained).
**"often... conversation."** Clackson and Horrocks, 176.

*An "impression of*
**his predecessor Menander.** Menander is known to have written over one hundred comedies, though only the *Dyskolos* 'Curmudgeon', first published in 1957, survives in full. Cf. Molière, *Le Misanthrope*.

278 *The only other pre-Augustan*
**"by retreating... period."** Clackson and Horrocks, 177.
**terseness, simplicity, and.** Clackson and Horrocks, 177.
***puri sermonis amator.*** For the end result in Latin (via Greek), see p. xxxiii.

*Writing in an elevated*
**"drained... argument."** Fantham, 226.

**"You also . . . of yours."** As quoted by the Roman grammarian and rhetorician Aelius Donatus (4th century AD) from a lost *Life of Terence* attributed to Suetonius. Suetonius is the Roman historian (1st–2nd centuries AD) whose most popular work, *De Vita Caesarum* '*Concerning the Lives of the Caesars*', or *The Twelve Caesars*, survives to this day.
**"Fortune . . . the brave."** Terence, *Phormio* I.4.25.
**'I am a man . . . to me.'** Terence, *Heautontimoroumenos* 'Self-Tormentor' I.1.25.
**"No Man is . . . for thee."** *John Donne, Devotions Upon Emergent Occasions,* Andrew Motion, ed. (New York: Random House, 1999), from "Meditation XVII."
**"Terence is . . . as a model."** David McCullough, *John Adams* (New York: Simon and Schuster, 2001), 259.

279 *Terence had a running*
**One critic . . . the genre.** Fantham, 224 (as paraphrased or quoted).

*During the lifetimes*
**Aristarchus of Samothrace.** The dean of Alexandrian Homeric editors, parts of whose commentary survive. See Nagy (2004), Ch. 5: "Aristarchean Questions: Emerging Certainties about the Finality of Homer's Text."

280 *Apollonius, as noted,*
**"high confidence . . . certainty."** See Higham & Bowra, xxiii.
**extensively . . . and adapted.** See detailed discussion by Acosta-Hughes and Stephens, 204–269 (Ch. 4: "In my end is my beginning"). The authors date the "historical intersection of Callimachus and Rome" to as early as 273 BC, when Alexandria and Rome exchanged embassies (pp. 205–206). By this chronology, the "Father of Latin Literature," Livius Andronicus (c. 284–c. 204 BC), is subject to Alexandrian influence.

282 *Latin did not reach*
**"For the . . . it shameful."** *Ep.* 2.1.161–167.

283 *Following 146 BC*
**"conquered Greece . . . Rome."** Graecia capta ferum victorem cepit et artis / intulit agresti Latio (*Ep.* 2.1.156–157). The last word, *Latio* (nom. *Latium*), designates Rome's foundation site on the west-central coast of Italy. It is the eponym, or namesake, of *Latin*. The codification occurs in Virgil: ". . . until he [Aeneas] might found a city and bring his gods to Latium—whence the Latin race, the Alban fathers, and mighty walls of Rome" (*Aen.*1.5–7).
**"drainage . . . Saturnian swamp."** Sic horridus ille / defluxit numerus saturnius, et grave virus / munditiae pepulere; sed in longum tamen aevum / manserunt hodieque manent vestigia ruris 'Then drained that rude Saturnian measure, and elegance vanquished the viral scent. Yet for years has the rustic trace remained, remaining to this day' (*Ep.* 2.1.157–160).

*Classicization was also*
**"determined . . . culture."** Pound (1937), 187. Despairing of the lack of an acceptable English translation, Pound advocated reading Homer "in full" through Latin cribs and the French Homer-translator Hugues Salel (1504–1553), with Chapman "as reference." Pound otherwise dismisses Chapman and Pope as having "left Iliads that are of interest to specialists." Pound (1937), 185, 189.

A poet and translator of the *Iliad,* Salel was praised in his day by Pléiade leaders Pierre de Ronsard and Joachim du Bellay; also by the lesser Pléiade Etienne Jodelle (who compared Salel to Homer himself). This did not prevent published rumors that Salel had translated from a Latin crib. Ronsard touted the primacy of Salel's translation in the development of the French language, referring to Salel as the one *qui des premiers tira notre langue d'enfance* 'who initially extracted our language from infancy'. See Hélène J. Harvitt, "Hugues Salel, Poet and Translator," *Modern Philology*, 16.11 (1919), 595–605.

284 *Those who have studied*
**the meaning of *translation*.** I focus on the meaning of the word *translation* (from Lat. *transferre*) because it is the word most familiar to readers of works in translation. For other Latin terms describing the process, see Balmer (2013), 8–11.
**Dryden would supremely.** Dryden's and Pope's "curatorial" concern for *preserving* epic, rather than composing it, may be explained with reference to Milton's *Paradise Lost* and the controversy attending its reception. Doubts over the viability of "modern" epic were expressed by adherence to and preservation of the old. See Johns-Putra, 83–99.

285 *While we may regret*
**Renaissance commentator.** Vida, *De Arte Poetica* (1517), written in Latin hexameters; the first (modern) "Art of Poetry" since Horace's own *Ars Poetica*. My explanation of *translatio*, focusing on Vida and Macrobius, derives from Sowerby (2006), 48–50 (as summarized).
**"So trees . . . Latian Shore."** Sowerby (2006), 49, quoting Vida, *De Arte Poetica*, iii. 296–303. Virgil's transplant of Homer, horticulturally analogized by Vida, is also apparent in Edward FitzGerald's (1809–1883) *translatio* of Omar Khayyám's quatrains (11th century AD) into FitzGerald's own *The Rubáiyát of Omar Khayyám* (see Chapter 32). FitzGerald is thus credited with having created a poem far superior to his Persian original, infusing it with English heartiness. Indeed, "Very rarely do we have the good fortune to light on a work which, like Fitzgerald's . . . 'is much too good to be a good translation.'" F. Smith, 33. FitzGerald's poetic *translatio* was earthly reenacted in the transplant of a rose bush from Omar Khayyám's grave in Naisházpúr to FitzGerald's grave in Boulge, Suffolk. "The Persian plant was too weak for England; so that it might survive, it had to be fused with an English rose." Drury, 49. The process is apparent at the level of civilization itself. We are, in the first instance, generally indebted to Rome's absorption of Greece for what we know of Greece. At the same time, ancient Greek culture has been little transmitted by the Greeks themselves; rather, by the adaptive cultures of England, Germany, and France. "Especially in the Victorian Era, classical antiquity was England's 'consuming passion' and classical studies were not just an Englishman's prerogative but . . . one that entitled him to feel more truly 'Greek' than the Greeks themselves." Spiropoulou, 1.
**"cultivation and improvement."** Sowerby (2006), 49.
**"What . . . believed to be his."** Sowerby (2006), 50, quoting Macrobius, *Saturnalia* V. iii: hic [Virgil] opportune in opus suum, quae prior vates dixerat [Homer], transferendo, fecit ut sua credantur.
**"for his . . . writers of Rome."** Sowerby (2006), 48.

286 *Virgil thus "grafted" from*
***Aeneid, Georgics,* and *Eclogues*.** Virgil's *Aeneid* is further discussed below. His *Georgics*, or farming poems (Gr. *gē* 'earth' + *erga* 'works, activities'), were modeled on Hesiod's *Works and Days* (*Erga kai Hēmera*), though far exceeding it in scope and resonance. Virgil's *Eclogues* 'selections' (Gr. *ek* 'from' + *legō* 'choose') depict herdsmen in a pastoral setting, albeit with highly urbane concerns. They are modeled on the *Idyllia or Idylls* 'vignettes' of the Alexandrian poet Theocritus. The *Eclogues* are also known as *Bucolics* ('on the care

of cows'). Especially noteworthy is Virgil's artistic progression from idealized setting (*Eclogues*); to husbandry, civilization, and the arts (*Georgics*); to empire (*Aeneid*).
**founding of Rome . . . flight.** Aeneas figures prominently in the *Iliad*—at one point stunning Achilles with the force of his spear, as the two face off: "The son of Peleus with his heavy hand held the shield away / from him, in fright, since he thought the far-shadowing spear / of great-hearted Aeneas would lightly be driven through it" (*Il.* 20.259–262: R. Lattimore, tr.). No small feat to affright Achilles. More than this, Aeneas, later in the same scene, is actually saved from Achilles by Poseidon, an ardently anti-Trojan god who foretells Aeneas's and his progeny's survival for generations to come. See *Il.* 20.288–339; Nagy (1990b), 27–29 (arguing a "variant epic tradition" in the *Iliad*, centering on Aeneas). It is similarly Venus who informs her son, Aeneas, that more is involved in the destruction of Troy than he realizes; that a destiny greater than his slaying of Helen awaits (*Aen.* 2.795–812). Finally, Aeneas's being the son of the goddess Aphrodite/Venus, Rome's founding could have befallen no better a Trojan survivor.
**(the Odyssean *Aeneid*).** See Otis (1963), 215–312, Ch. VI: "The Odyssean *Aeneid*."
**(the Iliadic *Aeneid*).** See Otis (1963), 313–382, Ch. VII: "The Iliadic *Aeneid*."

*The Aeneid conveys a*
**"That we refer . . . view."** Kermode (1983), 16–17 (paraphrasing the opening of Sainte-Beuve, *Étude Sur Virgile* (Paris [1857]).

287 *In what way tainted*
**"spare the humbled . . . down."** *Aen.* 6.853.
**infused with fury and rage.** For the poetic progress and significance of these events, see Putnam (1966), Ch. 4: "Aeneid Book XII: Tragic Victory"; also Putnam, "The Virgilian Achievement" (1972/1995), 53–70/9–26; "Pius Aeneas and the Metamorphosis of Lausus" (1981/1995), 139–156/134–151; and other collected essays (1995). The culminating work in this series of probing explorations is Putnam, *The Humanness of Heroes: Studies in the Conclusion of Virgil's Aeneid* (2011).
**the Latin verb *condo*.** Cf. *dum* ***conderet*** *urbem* 'until he should **found** a city' and *tantae molis erat Romanam* ***condere*** *gentem* 'so great was the task of **founding** the Roman people' (*Aen.* 1.5 and 33), and *ferrum adverso sub pectore* ***condit*** 'he [Aeneas] **stores** his sword beneath [Turnus's] waiting heart' (*Aen.* 12.950).

*Civilization is thus a*
**Romulus killing Remus.** The killing subject to "idealizing revision" at *Aen.* 1.292 (a formulation owed to Michael Putnam).

288 *One thing is, however*
**riffraff . . . Sabine women.** See *Ab Urbe Condita* 1.7–9.
**"a fundamental . . . *Lost*."** Reyes, 9 (summarizing C. S. Lewis [1942], Ch. VI: "Virgil and the Subject of Secondary Epic").
**"some event . . . such design."** C. S. Lewis (1942), 29–30.
**English poetry . . . of Virgil.** See e.g., Elizabeth Nitchie, *Virgil and the English Poets* (New York: AMS Press, 1966), and Tanya M. Caldwell, *Virgil Made English: The Decline of Classical Authority* (New York: Palgrave Macmillan, 2008).

*Virgil's great theme*
**Virgil was thus preferred.** See Simonsuuri, 3–16 (noting the appreciation of Homer's "originality, sublimity and 'fire,'" but the greater appreciation of Virgil's "elegance, regularity, discretion, judgment, and humanity").
**"But a man . . . grows up."** C. S. Lewis (1942), 37.

289 *Nowhere is such growth*

**"Helpe . . . chiefe of mine."** *FQ* 1.2.1. For identification of Spenser's muse as Clio (here not specifically named), see Webb, 71–72. Cf. "Begin, O *Clio,* and recount from hence / My glorious Soueraines goodly auncestrye" (*FQ* 3.3.4). All Spenser quotations from *Spenser: The Faerie Queene,* A. C. Hamilton, ed. (rev. 2nd ed.) (London and New York: Longman, 2007).

***Faerie Queene* . . . Dynasty.** "That Spenser was steeped in the theory of imitation and considered Virgil his master in epic poetry is apparent from the opening lines of *The Faerie Queene.*" Webb, 71–72. See also Tanya M. Caldwell, *Virgil Made English: The Decline of Classical Authority* (New York: Palgrave Macmillan, 2008), 4–6; and Philip Hardie, "Spenser's Vergil: *The Faerie Queene* and the *Aeneid,*" in Farrell and Putnam, eds. (2011), 173–185.

**foretold Aeneas . . . by Merlin.** *Aen.* 6.676–885; *FQ* 3.21–50. "Spenser perceived Vergil's intention and found in the *Aeneid* epic precedent for his functional use of British history." Webb, 74.

**"The association . . . unavoidable."** A virgin knight of Chastity, Britomart symbolizes Elizabeth. *Britomartis* is originally a minor classical divinity of Cretan origin. Spenser happily associates "Britomart" with British martiality by way of folk etymology.

**"suggest[ing] that . . . *Queene.*"** Walter Cohen, "The Literature of Empire in the Renaissance," *Modern Philology,* 102.1 (2004), 17 (the mention of the Virginia colony in the Proem to Book Two, recalling the prominence of its inclusion in the title-page dedication of 1596).

**grandson, Brute . . . *Troynouant.*** The idea by Spenser's time was traditional, appearing in Geoffrey of Monmouth, *Historia Regum Britanniae* (*History of the Kings of Britain*) (12th century AD), and identifying Britain's first king as Brutus, a far-wandering descendant of Aeneas.

**"colonization . . . to the cultural."** Toner, 33. See also Toner, 40 ("The British Empire had . . . been built by great men such as Clive of India, and foundational texts such as the *Iliad* shone with examples of the kind of hard-fighting, high-minded heroes that many British imperialists felt themselves to be").

*Spenser dedicated the*

**"The high idealism . . . 'empire.'"** David Read, *Temperate Conquests: Spenser and the Spanish New World* (Detroit: Wayne State Univ. Press, 2000), 29.

**empire . . . Elizabeth's reign.** I join with David Read (above) in seeking "to retrieve Spenser's engagement with colonialism . . . at the level of poetic composition," a position opposed to the New Historicism's (1980s/1990s) "generalized version of 'imperial' Spenser functioning almost independently of his poetic output." If *The Faerie Queene* bespeaks imperial concern, says Read, it is for reasons other than Stephen Greenblatt's "general critique of the colonial-in-the-literary and the literary-in-the-colonial." Read, 12, 18.

In his *Renaissance Self-Fashioning: From More to Shakespeare* (Chicago: Univ. of Chicago Press, 1980), Greenblatt presents as postcolonial apologist of colonialism. Though Greenblatt disavows the blanket condemnation of Spenser as "our originating and preeminent poet of empire," he nonetheless speaks of Spenser as "beari[ing] witness to the deep complicity of our moral imagination even in the noblest and most hauntingly beautiful manifestations in the great Western celebration of power." Greenblatt, 174. Whatever this may mean, it smacks of inculpation. Greenblatt sees the excesses of sixteenth-century imperialism reflected in Spenser's description of the ruthless destruction of the Bower of Bliss (*FQ* 2.12.83) and in the marauding activities described in Elizabethan voyager accounts. *Faerie Queene* episode, canto, and verse are rare in Greenblatt's discussion, colorful comparisons to Freud serving in their stead. At the same time, Greenblatt's reliance on Virgil is misplaced, as the *The Faerie Queene*'s imperialism is still a work in progress, while the *Aeneid*'s is fait accompli. (The *Aeneid* composed from 29–19 BC, the Greek Polybius [c. 200–117 BC] begins his *Histories* with the confounding observation that Rome had subdued the inhabited world within fifty years.) A breviary of Greenblatt's stances on empire is found in Walter Cohen, "The Literature of Empire in the Renaissance," *Modern Philology*, 102.1 (2004), 4, n. 3.

We need not look to Freud. Aware of the preeminence and threat of Spain, Spenser made "imperial gestures" in *The Faerie Queene* and "a place for colonial matters within his larger allegorical design," at the same time confronting "the difficulty of depicting a 'truth' that ha[d] yet to be revealed." Spenser's was thus "an embryonic notion of 'empire' [that] gradually made its way from the pages of Spanish chronicles into the pages of English poetry, including those of *The Faerie Queene*." Spenser dwelt on "the glories and failings of England's nascent imperialism." Read, 15, 17, 25, 34. My own discussion fleshes out these tendencies with reference to Spenserian and Virgilian chapter and verse, not to mention the patent historical record. Such considerations—the Spanish Armada in particular—go unnoted by David Armitage, "The Elizabethan Idea of Empire," *Transactions of the Royal Historical Society*, 14 (2004), 269–277 (largely disavowing Elizabethan imperial intent or result).

Read further urges that *empire* was an ill-defined term in the sixteenth century, fairly well limited to religion, i.e., "Holy Roman Empire." He further adverts to the extensive library of expedition-related literature—to which Spenser had access—owned by "eclectic mathematician, occultist, cosmographer, court philosopher, and 'projector' extraordinaire John Dee." Read, 25–28 (*projector*: one who projects colonial prospects). Of significance, then, is the case that "to Dee and his friend Edmund Spenser, who drew extensively on Dee's occult theories in evolving the allegory of *The Faerie Queene*, the 'British Empire' was not only a dreamed-of geopolitical entity, it was also a new Golden Age characterized by freedom, purity, and the union of all nations in the radiance of true (Protestant) faith." See Hughes-Hallet, "Francis Drake," in *Heroes* (2004), 214–217. And further, "We know that Spenser strongly supported the Virginia settlement and those like Raleigh who advocated imperial expansion. Faery [i.e., Fairyland] is thus a dream of empire," and "the where of faery is anywhere that human beings exit"—i.e., imperialism is instinctive. Michael Murrin, *The Allegorical Epic: Essays in Its Rise and Decline* (Chicago and London: Univ. of Chicago Press, 1980), 139, 141. Spenser's imperial views toward Ireland were of a decidedly less radiant sort, as set forth in his genocidal tract, "A View of the Present State of Ireland."

290 *We noted Merlin's*

**foretells Britomart's descendants.** The scene has a counterpart in the Italian epic of Ludovico Ariosto, *Orlando Furioso* (1516, 1532), where Merlin reveals Bradamante's lineage (Canto 3). Virgil is the common source for both Ariosto and Spenser. Spenser's other major epic source was Torquato Tasso, *Gerusalemme Liberata* (*Jerusalem Delivered*) (1580).

**Cairmardin . . . might offer.** *FQ* 3.7–10.

**descendants ending in Elizabeth.** So also:

> Well worthie stock, from which the branches sprong,
> That in late yeares so faire a blossome bare,
> As thee, O Queene, the matter of my song,
> Whose lignage from this Lady I deriue along. [*FQ* 3.4.3.]

**"spring, out of *Troian* blood."** Spenser is here likely thinking of the Amazons Penthesilea and Camilla. Penthesilea in the Epic Cycle is a late arriving Trojan ally, appearing

on the scene after the funeral of Hector (with which the *Iliad* concludes). Virgil in Book One of the *Aeneid* highlights her warrior aspect. Camilla, on the other hand, is a Rutulian ally of Turnus, fighting to defeat Aeneas in Italy (*Aeneid*, Book Seven). Spenser here seems to be equating Britomart with Trojan epic warrior queens in general rather than establishing a bloodline per se.
**"For so must . . . blood."** *FQ* 3.3.22.
**"For noble . . . ashes cold."** *FQ* 3.9.38.
**"And *Troy* . . . equalise."** *FQ* 3.9.44.
**"Renowned . . . iarre."** *FQ* 3.3.23.

291 *Merlin here foresees*
**"But now . . . and laws."** *Aen.* 1.261–264 (F. O. Copley, tr.). For the implications of *imperium sine fine* 'rule without bound', and the progress, if inevitability, of Roman empire until Virgil's own time, see Shankman (1994), 241–243.
**"For [the Romans] . . . race."** *Aen.* 1.278–282 (F. O. Copley, tr.).
**"you . . . the defiant down."** *Aen.* 6.851–853 (F. O. Copley, tr.).
**"which have . . . the West."** Frances A. Yates, *Astraea: The Imperial Theme in the Sixteenth Century* (London: Routledge & Kegan Paul, 1975), 33.
**"iam . . . Saturnia regna."**

> magnus ab integro saeclorum nascitur ordo.
> iam redit et virgo, redeunt Saturnia regna;
> iam nova progenies caelo demittitur alto.
> Tu modo nascenti puero, quo ferrea primum
> desinet ac toto surget gens aurea mundo,
> casta fave Lucina: tuus iam regnat Apollo.
>
> The great order of ages is born anew. Now returns the Virgin, returns the Saturnian reign; a new progeny is now from high heaven sent. But you, chaste Lucina [goddess of childbirth], favor the child at birth, by whom, first, the iron age will end, and a golden race arise throughout the world. Already your Apollo reigns.
>
> [*Ec.* 4.6–10 (cf. Manlius, *Astronomica* 4.542–546)]

**Recalling Isaiah's prophecy.** Cf. Is. 7.14: "Behold the maiden [Heb. *ha'almah*] will conceive and bear a child and his name will be *emanuēl*" [with us God]. Latin commentators from late antiquity on understood Virgil's *virgo (iam redit et virgo . . . )* to mean *iustitia* 'justice', which they equated with Maria (both of them incorruptible). In Greek mythology, the celestial virgin Astraea 'star maiden' (see preceding note) was last of the gods to live among mortals, starting in the *Saturnia regna* 'Saturnian reign' or Golden Age. Ovid has her finally abandoning earth during the most wicked Iron Age (*Met.* 1.149–150)—which is to say that the absence of justice marks man at his most depraved. The virgin Astraea is believed to have become the constellation Virgo, positioned near Libra ('weighing scales') to reinforce her ties with justice. Some Latin editions capitalize (*iam redit et Virgo . . .*) by way of suggesting the identity of Virgil's *virgo* with Astraea as the personification of "Justice," and thus the tie of Justice with the *Saturnia regna*. Some translators apostrophize *Virgin* and *Justice* to achieve a strictly Roman as opposed to Christian messianic emphasis. So E. V. Rieu:

> Time has conceived and the great Sequence of the Ages starts afresh, Justice, the Virgin, comes back to dwell with us, and the rule of Saturn is restored. The Firstborn of the New Age is already on his way from high heaven down to earth. With him, the Iron Race shall end and Golden Man [*aurea gens*] inherit all the world. Smile on the Baby's birth, chaste Lucina [the Roman goddess of childbirth], your own Apollo is enthroned at last.

[E. V. Rieu, tr., *Virgil: The Pastoral Poems* (Baltimore: Penguin Books, 1949), 53 (*Ec.* 4. 5–10)]

**British writers . . . to Rome.** For the British legitimization of empire by recourse to Rome, see Phiroze Vasunia, "Greater Rome and Greater Britain," in Barbara Goff, ed., *Classics and Colonialism* (London: Duckworth, 2005), 38–64.
**—and Virgil no less so.** The West Roman Empire ended in 476 AD with the capitulation of Romulus Augustulus to the Germanic Odoacer. The East Roman Empire did not end until almost a thousand years later with the fall of Constantinople in 1453.

292 *The Rome of Virgil's*
**"Its people . . . indestructible."** Kermode, 31.

*Greece is the bedrock*
**ideals of Republican Rome.** That is to say, rule by the Senate and Roman people, headed by two co-consuls. The initials are well known: SPQR, *Senatus Populusque Romanus.* Rome enjoyed republican rule for approximately five hundred years until the assassination of the Julius Caesar, ensuing civil wars, and the emergence of Octavian (aka Augustus) as emperor.
**empire's . . . Roman paradigm.** A mythological paradigm is argued in Odysseus's foray into the land of the Cyclops (*Odyssey*, Book Nine). See e.g., Edith Hall, "Colonial Conflict," in *The Return of Ulysses: A Cultural History of Homer's Odyssey* (I.B. Tauris: London and New York, 2008, 2012), 89–100. Hall's chapter is at odds with the stance taken herein, that the assertion of power, typically with mixed results, is a human and historical inevitability. Hall thus notes what "is always the conundrum of empire—that its justification . . . is inevitably cancelled by the physical or cultural violence required to impose it" (94–95). However, violence (or coercion) toward a better, if arduous, end, is the paradox of empire, not the undoing of its justification. The betterments, including standards of living, literacy, and resultant cultural refinement, are what distinguish empire from foreign tyranny.

293 *Empire is motivated*
**"Greed was . . . as a whole."** Arthur M. Schlesinger, Jr., "America and Empire," in *The Cycles of American History* (Boston and New York: Houghton Mifflin, 1986, 1999), 120. My thanks to Alfred Runte for bringing this work to my attention.

*The United States, for*
**empire . . . which to apologize.** On the need, benefit, and inevitability of empire, see Niall Ferguson, *Colossus: The Rise and Fall of the American Empire* (New York: Penguin, 2004). For Ferguson "the best case for empire is always the case for order"—a perspective recalling Heracles's role in subduing the vestiges of both natural and societal chaos. "Liberty is, of course, a loftier goal," continues Ferguson, "but only those people who have never known disorder fail to grasp [that order] is the necessary precondition for liberty." The case for American empire is, thus, "simultaneously a case against international anarchy or to be more precise, of a proliferation of regional vacuums of power." Ferguson, xxviii. Or, as the radical economist Joan Robinson once put it: "The misery of being exploited by capitalists is nothing compared to the misery of not being exploited at all" (as quoted by Ferguson, 123). Or, as Robinson might have added, *to the misery of being exploited by native tyrants from Genghis Khan to Bokassa and Idi Amin.*

As Ferguson also persuasively notes, it is not imperialism per se that is necessarily the culprit—assuming an imperialism not of plunder but of civil order—but the withdrawal of imperial troops which, when announced, "unleashes a struggle between rival power elites for control of the indigenous armed forces." Ferguson, xi. Viewed in this light, imperialism's biggest failing is not the exploitation of its subjects, but its indifference to their post-imperial well being. See recently Keith Windschuttle, "Pax Americana," *The New Criterion*, 30.5 (2012), 1–21 (discussing Ferguson and others), and Windschuttle, "The Burdens of Empire," in Kimball and Kramer, eds., 9 ("In short, history shows imperialism, rather than being a force of oppression, has often been the engineer of civilization.").

294 *"In the beginning," notes*
**"In the beginning . . . hunting."** Manent, 49.
**take preclusively . . . threat.** Schlesinger lists the following examples of "preclusive imperialism": "The Louisiana Purchase eliminated the French from the North American Continent. The annexation of Florida eliminated the Spanish. The Monroe Doctrine warned European powers not to meddle in the western hemisphere. The annexation of Texas and Oregon snuffed out British intrigue in North America. The war of 1846 eliminated Mexican obstacles to the transcontinental drift." Schlesinger, 143.
**They take . . . from taking.** As National Parks historian Alfred Runte reminds us, "In a world of seven billion people, everyone original to the land has been dispossessed at some point." See Runte, "The Book That Launched A Thousand Parks: Wilderness and The American Mind [1967, 5th ed. 2014]," *National Parks Traveler*, 2/23/2014 (at www.nationalparkstraveler.com). The perennial method and rationale of such dispossession, or "supplantation," on legal, effective, and moral grounds worldwide, is the compelling subject matter of David Day, *Conquest: How Societies Overwhelm Others* (Oxford: Oxford Univ. Press, 2008). *Taking*, argues Day, has ever been the way of the world. A society owns or keeps its territory only by defense against the claims of others. Ownership is never in perpetuity. "It is clear that no society has been in continuous occupation of the land that it has come to regard as its own. . . . Even the ancestors of those we regard as indigenous people originally came from somewhere else and . . . continued to move or be pushed by others across their ancient lands." Day, 236–237.
**economist . . . Schumpeter.** Schumpeter here paraphrased (in quotations) by Schlesinger, 126.

295 *It takes little to*
**in a trenchant rebuttal.** See Steven J. Willett, "Postmodernist Classics" (2004) (rebutting the January 4, 2004, address to the American Philological Association of its then president-elect, James J. O'Donnell). The speech called on classicists "to embark on a heady notion of self-demolition" on account of the sins of the Roman past.

*The complaints, however*
**The requisite . . . permanence.** See Clark, 16–17.
**impoverished Circus-Maximus.** "To read the ancient historians' account of the period is to be repeatedly astonished by the contrast between the grandeur and efficacy of Rome's rule over its expanding empire and the rowdiness and violence at the very heart of it." Hughes-Hallett, 87.

296 *Virgil sought to convey*
"**Others will . . . defiant down.**" *Aen.* 6.847–853 (F. O. Copley, tr.).

> "excudent alii spirantia mollius aera
> (credo equidem), uiuos ducent de marmore uultus,
> orabunt causas melius, caelique meatus

describbent radio et surgentia sidera dicent:
tu regere imperio populos, Romane, memento
(hae tibi erunt artes), pacique imponere morem,
parcere subiectis et debellare superbos."

Copley's translation (Virgil would have approved) nicely puns on the imperative: *regere* 'rule'! (l. 851). In what precedes, "and with their rule / map out the skies," *rule* connotes physical measurement (Lat. *radio*, cf. Eng. radius). The translation conveys the connectedness of heavenly measurement (*caelique meatus / describent radio*), on the one hand; and the earthbound-measured social regulation (to *regere imperio populos*) that is good governance, on the other—heaven and earth coterminous as an ordered whole. These associations, if not as verbally apparent in Virgil's Latin, nonetheless inhere. We recall that the fame of ancient warriors ideally "reaches broad heaven," and that when Roman emperors are deified, the heavens receive them. Virgil elsewhere imagines the deified Augustus taking his position as a constellation, with Scorpio "even now contracting his pincers to receive you" (*G* 1.32–35).

*The more than one*
**"the first . . . urban civilization."** Otis (1963), 2.
**"aspir[ing] to . . . and Augustan."** Otis (1963), 2–3.

297 *Rome's governance, in*
**"by the acquisition . . . *Romana*."** Otis (1963), 384.
**reborn from . . . even in himself.** Otis (1963), 384–385 (as paraphrased).
**"reasoned heroism . . . madness."** Putnam (1966), 134 (132–134 for the Cacus episode overall).

*In the end, Virgil's*
**"self-imposed . . . ambition."** Otis (1963), 2.
***Humanitas* . . . new standard.** The remainder of my paragraph on Virgilian innovation quotes and paraphrases from Otis (1963), 316–317, 381–382, 391. Looking ahead, we may note that Ezra Pound had no understanding of how utterly *new* Virgil had made it. It is Pound's dramatically failed appreciation of Virgil and of other classical authors which, as nothing else, belies his prestige. See Chapter 34.

298 *These are matters to*
**those damning . . . "imperialism."** Schlesinger rightly maintains that by contrast to the Roman, Napoleonic, and even British empires, the American Empire of the 1980s, for want of ultimate control over its "subjects," was "no empire at all." Schlesinger, 161–162.

*The prospect of entering*
**"Tant' è . . . ch'i' v'ho scorte."** *Inf.* I.2–3.
**"Building . . . worth paying."** Wills (2009).
**"one-dimensional panegyric."** Putnam (2011), 15.
**"realistic, honest . . . its past."** Putnam (2011), 15.
**"hav[ing] us . . . who have it."** Putnam (marginal note to manuscript draft).
**"Both . . . and reconciliation."** Putnam (2011), 15.

299 *Subsuming its Greek*
**Having synthesized Homer.** Virgil's concision in combining "two epics in one" further commended him to future generations of Greekless readers. The *Aeneid* is under

10,000 verses (in twelve books). The *Iliad* is 15,693 verses, and the *Odyssey* 12,110 (each epic divided into twenty-four books).
**Virgil . . . the Middle Ages.** See Comparetti (1996); also Ziolkowski and Putnam, eds. (2008), and Farrell and Putnam, eds. (2010).
**"O . . . honour to me."** *Inf.* I.82–87 (H. W. Longfellow, tr.):

> O de li altri poeti onore e lume,
> vagliami 'l lungo studio e 'l grande amore
> che m'ha fatto cercar lo tuo volume.
>
> Tu se' lo mio maestro e 'l mio autore,
> tu se' solo colui da cu' io tolsi
> lo bello stilo che m'ha fatto onore. . . .

Longfellow was the first American translator of Dante, and it is with Longfellow that the Dante tradition at Harvard (Norton–Grandgent–Singleton) begins. See Eric Griffiths and Matthew Reynolds, eds., *Dante in English* (New York: Penguin, 2005). Longfellow also wrote at length on *Beowulf*, translating some seventy verses that he thought particularly heroic.

300 *Equally creative and*
**"porker . . . sty of Epicurus."** "When you want to smile, come visit me. I'm sleek and fat, well cared-for—a hog in Epicurus's herd" (*Ep.* 1.4.15–16).

301 *Horace relates his*
**doubtless Saturnians and all.** The reference is to *Ep.* 2.1.69–71.
**"the . . . to Italian measures."** Princeps Aeolium carmen ad Italos / deduxisse modos (*Odes* I.30.13–14). Horace makes a somewhat more aggressive claim to priority vis-à-vis Archilochus and Alcaeus, *Ep.* 1.19.21–35.

*Complementing Virgil's*
**frugalitas . . . pietas/castitas.** Horace's *Roman Odes* (*Odes* 3.1–6), praising Roman ideals after Augustus's post-civil wars ascendancy (Augustus equated with Jupiter, *Odes* 3.5), resound in Milton's praise of Oliver Cromwell ("Lord Protector") following the English civil wars. See *Second Defence of the English People* (1653), quoted in W. Carlos Martyn, *Life and Times of John Milton* (New York: American Tract Society, 1866), 208–217. Milton caps his praise with a "quotation" of Horace's famed *Exegi monumentum aere perennius* 'I have sculpted a monument outlasting bronze': says Milton, "I had almost said to erect a monument, which will not soon decay, to deeds of greatness and of glory almost transcending human panegyric." Martyn, 215. The *Roman Odes* open *Odes*, Book III; *Exegi monumentum* closes not only Book III but Books I–III, published together in 23 BC (four years after Augustus's ascendancy). *Odes*, Book IV, written at Augustus's request, did not appear until 13 BC.
***humanitas* . . . of Aeneas.** "The ancient Roman *virtus*, with its implied sense of duty, manly decision, and courage, is combined with a new feeling of compassion and attachment to his comrades. . . . [I]t is in the figure of Aeneas that *humanitas* attained the glowing and satisfying embodiment which a truly creative imagination could give it." Lind (1963), xi.

*The Roman Odes proceed*
**"Nowhere has . . . wrote."** Charles E. Bennett, ed., and John C. Rolfe, rev., *Horace Odes and Epodes* (New York and Boston: Allyn and Bacon, 1934, 1965), 285–286 (to which the paragraph is otherwise indebted).

**"by and . . . denomination."** Joseph Brodsky, "On Grief and Reason: Is Robert Frost America's most misunderstood poet?" *The New Yorker,* 1/26/1994.
**"can study . . . since 1650."** Pound (1937), 185.

302 *Horace's predecessor Catullus*
**Catullus . . . among the Greeks.** For detailed discussion of Catullus and Sappho vis-à-vis their major poems, see pp. 318–323, and for other considerations, Willard Connely, "Imprints of Sappho on Catullus," *Classical Journal,* 20.7 (1925), 408–413.

304 *Lucretius, as other Latin*
**"science . . . heart's affections."** Lawrence Durrell, *Balthazar* (1958) (*The Alexandria Quartet,* Vol. 2), endnotes, "Consequential Data (g)."
**"Poetry begins . . . pleasure."** Albert S. Cook, ed., *Leigh Hunt's What Is Poetry (including Remarks on versification)* (Boston: Ginn, 1893), 4.

*Emotion is one thing*
**"The names . . . nakedly."** Santayana (1910), 42. Given the subject matter and scenario, Santayana's use of *nakedly* cannot be accidental.

305 *The thrill of scientific*
**the counterpart to Venus.** See Duban (1983).

*For all Virgil's thematic*
**diction and phraseology.** For the pioneering work on this intriguing subject, see W. A. Merrill, "Parallels and Coincidences in Lucretius and Virgil," *Univ. of California Publications in Classical Philology,* 3 (1918), 135–247; and the critique by Cyril Bailey, "Virgil and Lucretius," *Proceedings of the Classical Association,* 28 (1931), 21–39. Also, W. Liebeschuetz, "The Cycle of Growth and Decay in Lucretius and Virgil," *Proceedings of the Vergilian Society,* 7 (1967–1968), 30–40.
**Praising . . . nature of things.** "Where Lucretius' interest had led him to the nature of things, to man's subordination in the material universe, Virgil's led him to the things of nature, to the purpose, duty, and powers of man, to the centrality of man in the whole scheme." Smith Palmer Bovie, *Virgil's Georgics* (Chicago & London: Univ. of Chicago Press, 1956), xix. Bovie's *Georgics,* unsurpassed in its own right, is a model for the translation of classical hexameter into English blank verse.

*In prose, the Age of*
***De Re Aedificatoria . . .* Vitruvius**. As often noted, however, Vitruvius was descriptive, explaining why past architecture had been great, whereas Alberti was prescriptive, urging how future architecture might be great. His lessons were not lost on the Renaissance.
**"man the measure of all things."** The proposition was taken up in the widely read treatise of Luca Pacioli, *Divina Proportione* (1509), echoing "fashionable opinion of the day by declaring that our body measurements express 'every ratio and proportion by which God reveals the innermost secrets of nature.'" Leonardo provided illustrations for the Pacioli treatise, having "long been fascinated by the concept of man as a microcosm of the universe." See Jonathan Lopez, "The Measure of All Things," reviewing Toby Lester, *Da Vinci's Ghost: Genius, Obsession, and How Leonardo Created the World in His Own Image,*" in *New York Times Book Review,* 2/5/2012; also, Indra Kagis McEwen, *Vitruvius: Writing the Body of Architecture* (Cambridge and London: The MIT Press, 2003).

306 *Livy (59 BC–17 AD)*
**checks . . . political structure.** "In fact, when there is combined under the same

constitution a prince, a nobility, and the power of the people, these three powers will watch and keep each other reciprocally in check" (*Discourses* 1.2).

Part VII, Chapter 22

309 *Prior to 2004 there*

**papyrus discovery of 2004.** See Ellen Greene and Marilyn Skinner, *The New Sappho on Old Age* (2009).

**papyrus discovery of 2014.** See Dirk Obbink, "New poems by Sappho," *Times Literary Supplement*, 2/5/2014, and Dirk Obbink, "Two New Poems by Sappho," *Zeitschrift für Papyrologie und Epigraphik*, 189 (2014), 32–49. Translation and commentary for the lay reader in the expanded and updated translation of Diane J. Rayor and André Lardinois (2014), 154–164 (cf. Rayor 1980 and 1991). Mendelsohn (2015) notes that Rayor lacks metric appeal; and Hall (2015), that she offers "neither idiomatic English nor inherent beauty."

310 *In one of the few*

**Sappho's two . . . poems.** For treatment vis-à-vis divine epiphany and the shared communal experience of the people of Lesbos, with Sappho as choral leader and "prima donna," see Nagy (2013), 118–126, 132–135.

*We owe the survival*

**"ancient literary . . . lost,"** Fyfe (*Longinus, On the Sublime*), 163, editorial note "b."

311 *We do not know*

**Nor is it clear—depending.** The choices are painstakingly discussed by Lidov, 513–514, 524–525 (taking the adverb as measuring space rather than time).

**"Sappho . . . single whole."** Fyfe (*Longinus* 10.2), 199. For Sappho's "contradictory sensations" as a "litany of affliction" (here eroticized) with Near Eastern (i.e., West Asiatic) precedents, including the biblical Psalms, see West (1997), 527–528. In an intriguing article, ethnologist/psychoanalyst George Devereux argues that "clinically, Sappho's symptoms are not *primarily* manifestations of an ordinary, if extreme, love-sorrow and/or jealousy, but those of an anxiety attack, *stricto sensu*, elicited—quite specifically—by the abnormal nature of her love": in short, a "homosexual anxiety-attack." George Devereux, "The Nature of Sappho's Seizure in Fr. 31 LP as Evidence of Her Inversion," *Classical Quarterly*, n.s. 20.1 (1970), 17–31. *Contra*, M. Markovich, "Sappho Fr. 31: Anxiety Attack or Love Declaration," *The Classical Quarterly*, n.s. 22.1 (1972), 19–32. The discussion resumes in Odysseus Tsagarakis, "Some Neglected Aspects of Love in Sappho's Fr. 31 LP," *Rheinisches Museum für Philologie*, n.f. 122.2 (1979), 97–110 (adducing parallels from modern Greek folk song). ("Fr. 31 LP" is the fragment number assigned to *phainetai moi* by lyric fragment editors Lobel and Page.)

312 *In phainetai moi we*

**because he can endure.** The endurance is tantamount to "invulnerability"; so Lipking, 61. This reading is preferable to, e.g., "*fortunate* as a god (privileged to woo the girl)" or "*potent* as a god (capable of loving her as a woman never could)"—the latter giving rise, as Lipking further notes, to unfounded notions of penis envy, "imply[ing] the presence of a man in every erotic relation between women."

**F. L. Lucas's translation.** Quoted in full, PART III, §2.

*Phainetai moi contains*

**"the phrases . . . asyndeton."** Fyfe (*Longinus* 19), 235.

313 *Collapsing the diction,*
**"the very factor . . . means."** Nagy (1974), 45. See also B. B. Ford and E. Christian Kopff, "Sappho fr. 31.9: A Defense of Hiatus," *Glotta*, 54 (1976), 52–56 (surveying early emendation efforts and concluding that Sappho here adapted hiatus as a Homeric onomatopoetic device. "Read the line out loud and you will yourself reproduce the effect sought so long ago by the Lesbian poetess.").

315 *Similarly serving the forward*
**i.e., 'from under' (up*akouei*).** The man 'listens' to the girl, somehow 'from under' (Gr. ***up****akouei*: Aeolic, *up*; Attic, *(h)up*; Eng. *hyp*[*o*] 'beneath' + *akouei* 'hear, listen'). The woman's head is thus somehow positioned *above* the man's, as if he were looking up, head hovering about her upper torso. The composite tableau, further suggested by the man's position 'opposite' (*enantion*) the woman, is one of head on elbowed knees, craning forward.

*The selection and*
**Longinus's fuller . . . follows.** For the examples provided, see Fyfe (*Longinus* 1.3, 1.4, 7.3, 8.1), 163, 179, 181. Of art itself (*technē*), Longinus tellingly reminds us that Nature is to good fortune what good judgment is to art. Fyfe (*Longinus* 2.3), 167.

316 *Again without specific*
**"The choice of . . . child."** Fyfe (*Longinus* 30), 257–259.

*For all its attributes*
**'the echo of a noble mind'.** Fyfe (*Longinus* 9.2), 184.
**"even without . . . grandeur."** Fyfe (*Longinus* 9.2), 184.
**"more sublime . . . any speech."** Fyfe (*Longinus* 9.2), 184.
**Ajax—eternally aggrieved over.** See further pp. 31, 117, 384.
**of sublimity by intimation.** Next in effect to intimation alone is "an eloquence of least means, as in the shock of understatement, where one's excitement arises from the surprise of finding something said so barely yet so definitively." Donoghue, 3. The point is one of artistic economy, the maximum through minimum means.

317 *Silence is thus not*
**"inspir[ing] . . . suffering."** Lessing, 13.
**"It is the tone . . . sublime."** Auerbach (1965), 231.

CHAPTER 23

318 *Notwithstanding Longinus's*
**"The uncommon . . . experience."** Page, 27–28.

319 *Whatever the basis of*
**Numbered 51 . . . editions.** We have had occasion to note the "accidents and incidents" of the survival of classical literature, and of Sappho's poems most of all. It is noteworthy that a *single manuscript* once separated Catullus's 116 known poems from oblivion. The manuscript, discovered around 1300 in Verona, was called "V" for "Verona codex." Two copies were made from the V manuscript, which was subsequently lost. One of the copies was itself copied twice, after which it was lost in turn. Catullus's works thus depend on three surviving copies of the single V manuscript. The first printed edition appeared in Venice in 1472.

320 *Catullus's last stanza*

**Richmond Lattimore proposes.** Quotations in this paragraph from Richmond Lattimore, "Sappho 2 [now 31] and Catullus 51," *Classical Philology*, 39.3 (1944), 184–187. The poems, by Lattimore's account over seventy years ago, have already been much discussed. See also J. A. Woodman, "Some Implications of *Otium* in Catullus 51.13–16," *Latomus*, 25 (1966), 217–226 (with reference to the "inertia" of the Roman love elegists Propertius and Tibullus); Garry Wills, "Sappho 31 and Catullus 51," *Greek, Roman and Byzantine Studies*, 8.3 (1967), 167–197 (*otium* more than mere "weakness," but a "moral term" related to the duty of bearing the ecstasies of love); Charles Segal, "Catullan *Otiosi*: the Lover and the Poet," *Greece and Rome*, 2nd series, 17.1 (1970), 2–31 (the poet struggles with *otium*, but "the superb first three stanzas illustrate what his *otium* can produce"); and William H. Race, "'That Man' in Sappho fr. 31 L-P," *Classical Antiquity*, 2.1 (1983), 92–101 ("jealousy" not the issue; "that man" merely a "contrast-figure" or "foil" to Sappho's emotion). See also Lidov, 520–521 (stanza two purposefully incomplete, the missing words reflecting Catullus's appreciation of the uncertainties of the Greek text even in Roman times; the finesse of his treatment appreciated by Catullus's own audience).

*There is in fact a*

**Sappho's four . . . into three.** See Brent Vine, "On the 'Missing' Fourth Stanza of Catullus 51," *Harvard Studies in Classical Philology*," 94 (1992), 251–258.

**"lest Paris . . . bedroom."** ne Paris abducta gavisus libera moecha / otia pacato degeret in thalamo (68.104–105). The connection with Poem 51 is strengthened by the parallels: *exultas* (51.14) / *gavisus* (68.104) and *gestis* (51.14) / *degeret* (68.105). The verbs *exultas* and *gestis* (*gestio* a reiterative or intensive form of *gero*) "primarily refer to physical restlessness and both imply riotous emotion." C. J. Fordyce, *Catullus: A Commentary* (Oxford: The Clarendon Press, 1961), 221 (with examples). There is, then, a heightened or pernicious pursuit of leisure—"leisure with a vengeance," as we might say. My thanks to Michael Putnam for alerting me to Poem 68.104–105.

**"vacations" in Sappho**. Lipking, 66.

321 *Catullus's tone is*

**of Lesbia in Poem 11.** For discussion of Poem 11 and its Sapphic model, see pp. 322, 333–335. Claudia, though known to be Catullus's real-life beloved, is nowhere mentioned in his poetry. She is referred to as "Lesbia" in Poem 51, consistent with the poem's Sapphic theme and meter, and is the presumptive subject of Poem 11. Lesbia is the addressee of Poems 5 and 7; she is mentioned in Poems 43, 58, 83, 86, 87, and 92.

**of "premature climax."** Lipking, 65.

**replacing death by climax.** "The association of 'dying' and 'coming' is so deeply ingrained in so many languages that not even the most literal translation of the [poem] can avoid it." Lipking, 65 (cf. *la petite mort*, pp. 57, 213, 584, 625).

322 *Further removed from*

**neoteric . . . indulgences.** See pp. 281–282, 339, 606.

323 *I began by noting*

**"How then . . . original"?** Balmer (2013), 152.

**The effect . . . deadening.** As in the following: "As we have seen," says Balmer, "such cross-gendering versions of Catullus's poetry [here, Poem 41] moved my own work on from the feminist considerations of *Sappho: Poems and Fragments* and *Classical Women Poets* to those of post-feminist criticism, where gender difference becomes more a point of focus than any assumptions and analyses, negative or positive, about the nature of women's writings. It was also clear that the aims and points of reference of the volume would be very different to [sic] its predecessors, which had excavated forgotten works or offered a response to past critical judgments." Balmer (2013), 163–164.

324 *Catullus's older contemporary*
**"But when . . . body too."** *DRN* 3.152–160 (W. E. Leonard, tr.).

*In the Aeneid's climactic*
**Such features include.** My discussion, injecting more of the Sapphic element, is otherwise indebted to Putnam (2011), 95–97 (from whose wealth of detail I selectively borrow and paraphrase). Putnam is especially noteworthy on the richness of the scene's specialized diction.
**"And as in . . . escape."** *Il.* 22.199–201; see Duban, "Distortion as a Literary Device," etc. (1982).
**"Just . . . denied success."** *Aen.* 12.908–914 (F. O. Copley, tr.).
**personalizes . . . lyricizes.** Putnam (marginal note to manuscript draft), further noting that Catullus Poem 51 shows lyric eroticism shading into epic by indirect allusion to Troy and Helen. On the lyric in epic, see further Putnam (1995–1996) and pp. 63–64, 247–248.
***notae / sufficunt vires.*** An example of Virgilian diction tailor-made for the occasion; cf. *mediis conatibus* 'in mid-effort', and others. See Putnam (2011), 95–97.

326 *Notes Margaret Reynolds,*
**"symptoms . . . high to low."** Reynolds, 21. See also the discerning analyses by Lipking, 57–96 (including adaptations by Theocritus, Catullus, Ovid, Ronsard, Scudéry, Boileau, Racine, and others).
**"Ah Wilhelm . . . the grave."** Stanley Appelbaum ed. and tr., *Johann Wolfgang von Goethe, The Sorrows of Young Werther: Die Leiden des jungen Werther* (Mineola: Dover, 2004), 84–85 (letter, 30 Aug. 1771).

327 *Phainetai moi also extends*
**"but then . . . broke down."** Charlotte Brontë, *Jane Eyre* (New York: Heritage Press, 1942), Ch. 2, p. 11. Though Brontë (1816–1855) did not know Greek, she may well have known *phaintai moi* through translation. There was a marked emphasis on education in the Brontë household and an array of scholarly books and journals, including Latin and Greek texts, in her father's library. Brontë labored to acquire as much knowledge of antiquity as she might, incorporating her learning into her novels. In the wake of F. A. Wolf's highly controversial *Prolegomenon ad Homerum* (1795), Brontë showed herself conversant with the Homeric Question (concerning the unity and composition of the *Iliad* and *Odyssey*) and assiduously followed and contributed articles to the ongoing debate. She tried her hand at Homeric translation (from a French version) and had much to say about Greek tragedy. See "Charlotte Brontë and the Discourse of Popular Greek" in Fiske's excellent *Heretical Hellenism*.
**". . . the rushing of wings."** Compare Brontë's "a sound filled my ears, which I deemed the rushing of wings" with Swinburne (Chapter 19):

> Heard the flying feet of the Loves behind her
> Make a sudden thunder upon the waters,
> As the thunder flung from the strong unclosing
> Wings of a great wind.

**"Fatima" later added.** At or around the same time, perhaps the year before, Tennyson composed a more expansive adaptation of *phainetai moi* in "Eleänore," ll. 122–144 (c. 1832, rev. 1842).

CHAPTER 24

329 *Its bursting emotion*
**"the essential . . . measures."** Roberts, 8 (introduction to Carman). By contrast, an earlier renowned scholar, John Addington Symonds (1840–1893), commended Sappho's perfected form not as the accelerant of her passion, but as its wanted containment: "All is so rhythmically and sublimely ordered in the poems of Sappho that supreme art lends solemnity and grandeur to the expression of unmitigated passion." Symonds, 173. The view is consistent with the since-repudiated tendency to regulate or somehow tame the poet. Symonds is of the "Sappho schoolmistress" school.
**"plays release . . . checked."** Warren (2008), 17.

330 *Catullus's acclaimed Poem*
**"Furius . . . the passing plough."** Translation (as modified) by Jeffrey Duban, first appearing in *The Classical Outlook*, 75 (1998), 136.

331 *This is palpable rage,*
**world-entire . . . magnitude.** Michael Putnam incisively traces Virgil's "refractions" of Catullus 11 throughout the latter books of the *Aeneid*, finding allusions in both authors to the recent history of Roman power, and a "scrutiny" (proper to lyric) "spread . . . out as a larger glow over a grand stretch of epic time":

> Catullus 11, in Virgil's adoptions . . . proffers an important intellectual and spiritual map of the *Aeneid*, showing how the Augustan poet utilizes his great predecessor to make us turn from idealizing vistas of Roman glory to the lived horrors of human brutality. Or, to put the matter in terms of genres, by his linear survey of Catullus 11 Virgil in a special way personalizes the *Aeneid*, putting final stress, as Catullus does, on the immediacy of the problematics of human emotionality, not on the impersonal prowess of empire and its dream of future glory. It is with stress on man's passional side, not on Rome's achievement, that the epic ends. [Putnam (1996), 92]
>
> In both instances, as lyric leaves behind its foray into epic impersonality and vastness, and as epic absorbs lyric's concentrated affectivity, apparent eulogy of *imperium* yields to acknowledgment of human emotions and to the particulars of loss. [Putnam (1996), 93]

Putnam's emphasis on the losses entailed in Roman *imperium* is consistent with his treatments elsewhere. See p. 647.

*This fully epic itinerary*
**its male-penetrative brio.** Lat. *sive in extremos penetrabit Indos* 'whether he penetrate deepest into India'; *litus ut . . . / tunditur unda* 'where the shore . . . / is pounded by the wave'. "We revel in a boundless, public sphere of topographical grandeur where omnipresent activity and dynamism is couched in terms of sexual mastery (*penetrabit* ['will penetrate'], *tunditur* ['is pounded']) and conveyed in grandiloquent language (*sagittiferos* ['arrow-bearing'], *septemgeminus* ['seven-twinned']) that pushes lyric to the boarders of epic." Putnam (1996), 88. For another instance of geographic ambition counterpoised by unhappy love at home, see Propertius 1.6.
**"far from . . . Roman history."** Putnam (1982), 17–18.

**"the enormity . . . physicality."** Putnam (1996), 88.

332 *Evoking this expansive*

**remoteness of a space.** The word *ultimus* is used to describe both Britain (toward the start of the poem) and the field (at the end). Putnam notes the "remarkable correspondence" between *ultimos Britannos* 'to farthest Britain', *prati / ultimi* 'of the farthest field', and *extremos Indos* 'deepest [into] India'. He observes that Catullus has contracted the view to "an object both generic and universal, though fragile and far removed. And the poet, instead of initiating and executing his vibrant journey to the extremes of the known world, becomes himself an 'extreme' to be seen, incapable of motion, not a strange tribe [as he might encounter in his travels] but something less worthy perhaps, yet infinitely more precious." Putnam (1982), 21–22. Claudia, for her part, is as dangerously exotic as anything Catullus might have hoped to see abroad.

**"But thou . . . holy incense."** Bliss Carman, poem XXIV, ll. 5–8.

**ploughs . . . ploughed under.** On plough (male) and flower (female) symbolism in ancient literature, see Putnam (1982), 29, n. 13 (citing references). The sexual conceit, in English poetry, is poignantly conveyed in A. E. Housman's poem "Is My Team Ploughing?"

333 *We have previously noted*

**civil war and anarchy.** For contemporary readers, the sweep and brutality of the times is majestically conveyed by Hughes-Hallett, "Cato," 76–130 (her chapter on the Roman politician and statesman Cato the Younger, a contemporary of Catullus).

**"common . . . civilization."** The designation originally applied to Horace alone. See V. G. Kiernan, *Horace: Poetics and Politics* (New York: St. Martin's Press, 1998), ix.

**"Horace's . . . Literature."** Kiernan, x.

**'the achievement . . . war'.** Ernest Rhys, ed., *Livy, the History of Rome* (London: J. M. Dent & Sons, 1905), Book 9, §18. Recall that the traditional founding date of Rome is 753 BC.

**inimical to . . . verse or art.** We note in passing that the Black Death (1348), horrifically eliminating at least half Europe's population and any semblance of social order, did not subvert the nascent Renaissance; that the physically and psychologically catastrophic Sack of Rome by troops beholden to Charles V (1527), though accelerating mannerist tendencies and bringing the High Renaissance to a close, did not subvert the Renaissance example.

334 *Catullus, needless to say*

**Sparrows . . . incongruous.** For these and other elements of Aphrodite's peculiar epiphany, see Harold Zellner, "Sappho's Sparrows," *Classical World*, 101.4 (2008), 435–442.

335 *As concerns its parodic*

**"the poet . . . their voices."** Blondell (2010a), 173.

**sole indication . . . gender.** The third-person subject of the verbs in the Greek stanza—*flees, pursues, receives, gives, loves*—is contained in the verb endings and may be either *he* or *she*. This serves to conceal gender (e.g., Gr. *philei* 'he/she/it loves'; cf. Lat. *amat*). It is thus the feminine participle alone—(*k'ōuk*) *etheloisa* '(though not) wanting'—that reveals it. Delayed appearance aside, the participle's strategic function is also apparent as a trisyllabic feminine, since the disyllabic masculine—(*k'ōuk*) *ethelān*—is metrically unsuited to the line. While the phrase (*k'ōuk*) *ethelān* could be used elsewhere in the stanza, the change in position would destroy stanza and poem alike. Only the feminine participle will do, and only at that line- and stanza-end position. The poem's homoeroticism is thus, as it were, metrically predetermined.

336 *The Hymn takes a*

**man's gender nor genitalia**. The possibility of penis envy in the poem is a frequent feminist preoccupation. See p. 656.

**Aphrodite's knowing smile.** In the Hymn, Aphrodite is described as *meidiaisais' athanatō prosōpō* 'immortal visage shining forth'. In epic, one of Aphrodite's stock epithets is *philommeidēs* 'smile-loving' (*philo* + *meidiaō* 'smile'). Hesiod calls Aphrodite 'genital-loving because she appeared from genitals': *philommeidea (h)oti mēdeōn exephaanthē* (*Th.* 200). The play is based on the punning *meidiao* 'smile' and *mēdea* 'genitals'. Gr. *mēdea* also tellingly means 'plans, schemes, cunning, craft'. See Deborah D. Boedeker, *Aphrodite's Entry into Greek Epic* (Leiden: E. J. Brill, 1974), 18–42. Zeus's *mēdea* are, in both senses, and not surprisingly, *aphthita* 'imperishable' or 'unwithering'.

*Though phainetai moi*

**"tumble out . . . asyndeton."** Fyfe (*Longinus* 19), 235–237.

337 *Longinus further notes*

**"emotion is . . . the moment."** Fyfe (*Longinus* 18), 233–235.

**"questioning and . . . emotion."** Fyfe (*Longinus* 18), 235–237.

*But that was once upon*

**With form . . . anachronistic.** Rhymed and structured verse, both good and bad, appeared during and following the cataclysms of the American Civil War and World Wars I and II. See especially the elegant two-part review by early modernist critic, poet, and author Alfred Kreymborg (1883–1966), "American Poetry after the War." Robert Bridges—classicist, formalist, and British Poet Laureate (1913–1930)—edited a volume of prose and poetry, *The Spirit of Man* (1915), intended to appeal to readers in wartime (his own son was wounded in battle). It is a designedly consolatory collection of poetry and prose, the former rhymed *to a poem* (or of Shakespearean blank-verse quality). Composer Benjamin Britten's *War Requiem* (1962) is based, *inter alia*, on nine poems by famed World War I poet Wilfred Owen. Also noteworthy is Ivor Gurney, poet, composer, and one of World War I's most prolific letter writers. See especially Ivor Gurney, *Seven Sappho Songs, for Soprano and Piano* (to poems by Bliss Carman; see Bibliography), and the poetry collection, *Severn and Somme* (London: Sidgwick & Jackson, 1917).

The abundance of rhymed and metered, i.e., "traditional," war poetry belies the modernist injunction "make it new." The volumes are too numerous to mention—supplemented, during the 2014 World War I centennial, by a new "Poets of the Great War" series from Faber & Faber, and many other works from numerous publishers. For the American Civil War, one does no better than Edmund Wilson, "Poetry of the War," in *Patriotic Gore: Studies in the Literature of the American Civil War* (Oxford: Oxford Univ. Press, 1966), 466–507. See also Paul Negri, ed., *Civil War Poetry: An Anthology* (New York: Dover, 1997). For World War I, see John Bremer, "The Poets, 1914–1918," in *C. S. Lewis, Poetry, and the Great War: 1914–1918* (Lanham and New York: Lexington Books, 2012), 13–35 (including chapter bibliography). For World War I and Homer, see Elizabeth Vandiver, *Stand in the Trenches, Achilles: Classical Receptions in British Poetry of the Great War* (Oxford: Oxford Univ. Press, 2010), and Vandiver, "Homer in British World War One Poetry," in Lorna Hardwick and Christian Stray, eds., *A Companion to Classical Receptions* (Chichester: Blackwell, 2011), 452–466. See also Jonathan Shay, *Odysseus in America: Combat Trauma and the Trials of Homecoming* (New York: Charles Scribner's Sons, 2002). The tally (if such can be made) of British and German World War I poets, poems, and poetry volumes is staggering. See Bogacz, 647, n. 15, and Bremer, 13 (est.

50,000 poems a day in August 1914).
**"has so far . . . the past."** Rosen, 397.

CHAPTER 25

338 *Modernism, as it developed*
**disclaim . . . forms and beliefs.** Whereas the carnage of World War I appeared to change long-held perceptions and to challenge the poetic forms in which they had long been expressed, the atrocities of World War II, and the Holocaust most of all, challenged the ability of poetry itself to make *any* accommodation with events. Philosopher-aesthetician Theodor W. Adorno (1903–1969) thus advanced the popularized view that there should be "no poetry after Auschwitz." By this he meant *not* that poetry could not be written, but that the bestowal of form and meaning upon the atrocity would seem either to condone or trivialize it. See Ziolkowski, "The Literature of Atrocity" (1977).
**"Behind . . . without precedent."** Howe, 5.
**"improvisation . . . of the new."** Howe, 30.

339 *In words that resonate*
**"After the fall . . . domination."** See "Greek Music," *The Columbia Encyclopedia,* 6th ed., Paul Lagassé, ed. (New York: Columbia Univ. Press, 2000), 1182.
**"In short the style . . . present."** The references (from a variety of ancient sources) to Phrynis, Timotheus, and Aristophanes, in this and the following paragraph, are from Campbell (1993), 62/2, 67/4–6, 73/2, 77/7–8, and 81/11. See also Martha Maas, "*Polychordia* and the Fourth-Century Greek Lyre," *The Journal of Musicology,* 10.1 (1992), 78–81, and Eric Csapo and Peter Wilson, "Timotheus the New Musician," in Budelmann, ed., 277–293.

340 *Of the famed late fifth-century*
**"No writer . . . by the war."** Bowersock (2007).

341 *Thus was antiquity's*
**"*Mauberley* . . . in its politics."** Schmidt, 615.
**"polyphilo-progenitive ancestor."** Schmidt, 619.

342 *Modernist promptings*
**too intense for containment.** For lack of words, or "the lacking word," as part of the "modernist crisis" in the aftermath of World War I, and prior thereto, see Steiner (1998), 184–215 (with emphasis on *private* language and its impenetrability).
**"Keeping up . . . progress."** Graves and Riding, 162.
**absolute and perfect end.** Graves and Riding, 162 (as paraphrased).

343 *Though modernism*
**"the more . . . metropolis."** Eliot (1965), 126–127.
**"the unmetrical . . . Cubists."** Isaacs, 13–14; cf. Isaacs, 36 ("Futurist and Cubist poetry").

344 *Following the war,*
**"scored . . . revolutionary,"** Carol J. Oja, "George Antheil's Ballet Mécanique and Transatlantic Modernism," in Towsend Ludington, ed., *A modern mosaic: art and modernism in the United States* (Chapel Hill: Univ. of North Carolina Press, 2000), 185.
**"brutal . . . Long Armistice."** Antheil, 139.

*In the manner of his*
**"essentially . . . upon it."** Antheil, 140.
**"Expected . . . Materialize."** Olga Samaroff, *New York Evening Post*, 4/11/1927. See further John K. Kasson, "Dances of the Machine in Early Twentieth-Century America," and Carol J. Oja, in Ludington, ed., *supra*, 153–174 and 175–202.
**"such reported . . . synthetic."** Antheil, 195.
**"three-ring circus" aspect.** Antheil, 193.

*The beat goes on*
**"jolted . . . sizzling start."** James Jorden, *New York Post*, 2/19/2003.
**"the kind . . . than death."** Howe, 33.

345 *"Make it new" exhorted*
**"Make it new" . . . Pound.** The phrase *make it new* appears for the first time in Canto 53 (written in the early 1930s, first published 1940). The phrase is also used for an eponymous book, *Make It New* (1934), the essays of which, largely dealing with translation, date back twenty to twenty-five years. Thus, although "make it new" is frequently associated with the advent of modernism, its published appearance came somewhat later. Nonetheless, the *idea* inspirited the movement.

*Each day renews the*
**progress in the arts.** See Dalrymple, 134–135, on the contrast between science (measured by discernible progress) and art (not so measured).
**founder Filippo Marinetti.** See recently Jonathan Galassi, "Speed in Life and Death" (Italian Futurism, 1909–1944: Reconstructing the Universe: an Exhibition at the Solomon R. Guggenheim Museum, New York City, 2/21–9/1/2014), *New York Review of Books*, 6/9/2014. See also Todorov, 9–14.

346 *Pound's "make it new"*
**"One goes . . . mind in order."** Haeusermann, 452 (quoting Yeats).
**"has made flux . . . generation."** Haeusermann, 443 (quoting Yeats). Pound apologists take this statement not as a criticism but as a vindication of Pound's technique. Pound himself insisted that *The Cantos* have no "structure" and no "key," his apologists maintaining that "his work is not to be understood through paraphrase or conventional analysis. It is the quintessence of Imagist practice, a tissue of juxtapositions of historical fact, poetry, politics, vocal registers, music, satire." Schmidt, 617–618.
**"nobody . . . realized in them."** Haeusermann, 443.
**"I cannot make it cohere."** Canto 116. Pound's correspondence intermittently reveals his struggles with the issue of clarity in *The Cantos*. See Rajan, 272, n. 2 for references.
**"total order . . . intelligence."** Lauber, 9. (Lauber's persuasively argued "Pound's *Cantos*: A Fascist Epic," is ineffectually rebutted by David Murray, "A Reply," etc., *Journal of American Studies*, 13.1 [1979], 109–113.) See also Louis Menand, "The Pound Error: The elusive master of allusion," *The New Yorker*, 6/9/2008 ("Pound's politics are not incidental to his achievement. Italian fascism is integral to 'The Cantos'").
**counterpart to Mussolini's.** See further Todorov, 55–56 (totalitarian dictators and avant-garde artists "emerged from the same womb," both setting out to "make it new," be it society or art; both knowing no limits and intoxicated by self-importance).

*Walt Whitman (1819–1892)*
**Charles Eliot Norton.** "Review of *Leaves of Grass* (1855)," *Putnam's Monthly: A Magazine of Literature, Science, and Arts* (1855), 321–323.

347 *In 1919 Pound sought*
**"due in part . . . obscurity."** Kreymborg, 22.4 (1933), 263.
**"had . . . Rabelasian Joyce."** Kreymborg, 22.4 (1933), 263–264.

*Commentaries aside*
**"unmetrical sprawling lengths."** Rupert Brooke, *Cambridge Review*, 31 (1909), 166–167, in Betsy Erkkila, ed., *Ezra Pound: The Contemporary Reviews* (Cambridge: Cambridge Univ. Press, 2011), 13–14 (an excellent review that should be read in full).
**with modernism: shock value.** At the time of Whitman's death in 1892, shock value was in vogue in fin-de-siècle Europe. Early twentieth-century modernism could thus look, in England for instance, to such self-styled decadents as Aubrey Beardsley and Oscar Wilde, and to the aesthetic of Beardsley's *The Yellow Book*.

*Though modernist parallels*
**Stravinsky, Picasso, Brancusi.** Accounts of the rise of modernism are legion. For firsthand accounts, and the pervasive postwar despair that fueled the movement, see the autobiographies of modernist composer George Antheil, *Bad Boy of Music*; and Ernest Hemingway, *A Moveable Feast* (New York: Simon & Schuster, 1964). See also Roger Shattuck, *The Banquet Years: The Origins of the Avant-Garde in France—1885 to World War I* (New York: Random House, 1955). Also, Julian Symons, *Makers of the New: The Revolution in Literature, 1912–1939* (New York: Random House, 1987); Ian Dunlop, *The Shock of the New* (New York: McGraw-Hill, 1972); and *MAKE IT NEW: The Rise of Modernism* (Austin: Harry Ransom Humanities Research Center, Univ. of Texas, 2004) (exhibit catalogue).
**"What was . . . were over."** Atlas, xx.
**"the epiphany . . . direction."** Igor Stravinsky and Robert Craft, *Expositions and Developments* (Berkeley: Univ. of California Press, 1981), 285.
**Commedia "types" . . . new.** See p. 32.

348 *Other post–World War I*
**"master . . . aristocratic elegance."** Dubal, 551.

349 *Is not the loss of a*
**"a Classicist . . . jeweler."** Dubal, 546.

350 *Although Ravel's Tombeau*
**Pound's . . . merchandising.** See Timothy Materer, "Make It Sell! Ezra Pound Advertises Modernism," in Kevin J. H. Dettmar and Stephen Watt, eds., *Marketing Modernisms: Self-Promotion, Canonization, Rereading* (Ann Arbor: Univ. of Michigan Press, 1996). Cf. Atlas, xx ("his [Pound's] genius was more entrepreneurial than literary").

*Even as totalitarianism*
**"Any . . . academicism."** Letter to Ford Madox Ford, 9/7/1920. See Brita Lindberg-Seyersted, ed., *The Correspondence of Ezra Pound, POUND/FORD: The Story of a Literary Friendship* (New York: New Directions Books, 1982), 43.
**too approvingly refers.** Michael Dirda, Introduction: *Pound, ABC of Reading* (1934, 2010).
**"the preference . . . age."** Leon Botstein, Conductor, "Against the Avant-Garde: Romanticism of the 1920s," *American Symphony Orchestra Dialogues and Extensions* (concert notes to a performance of the same name, Avery Fisher Hall, New York City, December 7, 2008). The program included works by Joseph Marx (1882–1964), Walter Braunfels (1882–1954), and Hermann Suter (1870–1926). Botstein further notes

that the challenge for such composers was "to create new music by engaging tradition and the past in an overt manner, not to declare fealty to a progressive ideology that rendered the surface of tradition irrelevant."

351 *Fascist in his poetic*
**"like a . . . gone to seed."** Filreis, 166 (citing sources).
**"Modernists were . . . years."** Filreis, 166 (citing sources).

*One thing is thus*
**in the new . . . alone.** Paraphrased and quoted from Dalrymple, 135–136.
**"*nichts . . . ohne Geschmack.*"** Goethe, *Maximen und Reflexionen*. www.wissen-im-netz.info/literatur/goethe/maximen/1-24.htm (xxiv.1247). Web. 7/2/2013.
**"Imagination . . . Modern Art."** I owe the Stoppard reference to author Tom Wolfe (correspondence, 4/23/2010).
**beauty is . . . self-insulating.** Paraphrased from Dalrymple, 136.
**"[w]orthwhile . . . other art."** Dalrymple, 135.

352 *New classics are ever*
**"such a classic . . . beauty."** Sainte-Beuve (Lee, tr.), 124. The term *classic/classical,* connoting a work of timeless value, with its clearly *classist* frame of reference, derives from the Latin author and grammarian Aulus Gellius (2nd century AD). Gellius speaks of *classicus assiduusque aliquis scriptor, non proletarius* 'a first-class, responsible author, not some low-class type'. See Armstrong (2008), 174. Seminal works addressing the nature of a classic are those herein cited by Sainte-Beuve, Eliot, and Kermode.
**"demanded new . . . work."** Dubal, *Wall Street Journal* (2012).
**conservative, or tonal, modernist.** The terms are Teachout's (2000), 73.
**or escapist primitivism.** The primitivism—the primeval hysteria—that so offended at *Sacre*'s premiere centered on the work's visual and choreographic aspects, all of them disturbingly contrary to audience expectation of ballet. The work's score, by contrast, enjoyed a relatively unperturbed, albeit musically challenging, afterlife. *Sacre* nonetheless became a byword for modernity, and the most frequently discussed of modern works—discussion never omitting the riot of opening night. And while composers are often celebrated upon the significant anniversaries of their lives or deaths, *Sacre* itself received such tribute in 2013, the hundredth-year anniversary of its premiere. For further aspects of the opening night (within the context of the Paris of 1913), see Thomas Forrest Kelly, *First Nights: Five Musical Premieres* (New Haven and London: Yale Univ. Press, 2000), 256–334.

Truth to tell, *Sacre* is more revered than loved. One may compare Carl Orff's scenic cantata *Carmina Burana* (1936)—of all Orff's voluminous works the only one now really performed, and performed regularly; a work insistently rhythmic, percussive, and primitive in its own right. A signature twentieth-century creation—and for many the gateway to classical music—*Carmina*'s attraction resides, simply enough, in its formal balance of rhythm, melody, and libretto; of soloists, chorus, and orchestra. *Carmina* is not modernist, but *modern,* because its inspiration—medieval, primarily Latin poems of the wine-women-and-song and mutability-of-fate variety—speaks across the ages. The poems were as modern when composed as when first gathered for *Carmina,* because poignantly reflecting the concerns of *their* day and every day. (The proper pronunciation is *Cármina,* not *Carmína.*)

353 *Debussy's mesmerizing free-chordal*
**mesmerizing free-chordal.** Music critic Anthony Tommasini speaks of Debussy's writing "hauntingly restrained, ethereal, time-stand-still works," which "after 300 years

of pulsating Germanic music [were] a shock to the system." Tommasini, "Top 10 Composers," *New York Times* (Arts), 1/12/2011.
**free-chordal technique.** "With Debussy, the chord itself was freed of its necessity to move and became an experience in itself. With this concept, harmonic progression was no longer required in the traditional sense. Yet Debussy's work is not a formless mass, relying merely on sensation." Dubal, 444. "For his new soundscape [Debussy] made chords into building blocks, shifting and juxtaposing them for contrast rather than resolution. Harmonic progression was no longer a necessity as it had been since J. S. Bach." Dubal, *Wall Street Journal* (2012). Frédéric Chopin (1810–1849) had earlier effected ground-changing innovation, creating music, in the words of pianist-critic Charles Rosen, "as destructive of the tonic-dominant polarization of eighteenth century style as Schoenberg's of late nineteenth century chromaticism." Rosen, *Arnold Schoenberg* (New York: Viking, 1957), 27.
**"effortlessly . . . for music."** Dubal, 443.
**logical and unpredictable.** "Unpredictability and logic combine as in no other composer." Dubal, *Wall Street Journal* (2012).
**"was . . . harmonic palette."** Dubal, 446–447.
**"pages of unearthly beauty."** Dubal, 447.
**"tried to . . . law of beauty."** Dubal, 447, 737 (citing source).
**contemptuously dismissive.** "Sat through the *Pelléas* the other evening and am encouraged—encouraged to tear up the whole bloomin' era of harmony and do the thing if necessary on two tins and wash-board. Anything rather than that mush of hysteria. . . . Very much encouraged by the *Pelléas*, ignorance having no further terrors if that DAMN thing is the result of what is called musical knowledge." Letter to Agnes Bedford, 4/?/1921; Paige, 167.

*Composers become significant*
**latter-day "complexity boys."** The sobriquet derives from critic-composer Virgil Thomson. See generally Terry Teachout, "The New Tonalists," *Commentary* (12/1997), and "Music: Back to the Future," *Time* (3/6/2000)—the former an excellent overview of musical trends since Debussy. The juggernaut of an in-creeping and cumulative complexity was early apparent to music critic Henry Pleasants, *The Agony of Modern Music* (New York: Simon and Schuster, 1955), 87–96. Some of its argument since proven wrong, the polemic retains an incisive thrust with valuable discussion, e.g., the distinction between a theme and a tune. See Pleasants, 113–121.

354 *Among Debussy's (and Ravel's*
**"startling . . . and control."** Highet (1971), 226–227. As concerns "almost unearthly simplicity and purity," these qualities are of the essence of art, as further discussed below vis-à-vis ancient Greek poetry and the Classical Greek aesthetic overall. We may further note in this connection composer Virgil Thomson's appraisal of Satie: "Satie's music is as simple as a friendly conversation and in its better moments exactly as poetic and as profound." Quotation from Dubal, 637.
**"did for music . . . creative."** Highet (1971), 229
**"so violently . . . for himself."** Antheil, 103.
**Ruskin well understood.** "A good composition can be *contrary* to the rules. It may be contrary to certain principles, supposed in ignorance to be general; but every great composition is in perfect harmony with all true rules, and involves thousands too delicate for ear, or eye, or thought, to trace; still, it is possible to reason, with infinite pleasure and profit, about these principles, when the thing is once done; only all our reasoning will not enable any one to do another like it, because all reasoning falls infinitely short of divine instinct." Ruskin (1855), 109–110.

**Wagner's *Die Meistersinger.*** As one recent critic succinctly puts it concerning the opera's singing contest, "The organizers know what kind of song they like; it must have a certain form and structure. But along comes an outsider with a new song that enlarges their horizons, opens up the old forms (without totally destroying them) and gets the girl; the just reward of measured progress." Michael White, "Wagner's Playful Paean to Culture," *New York Times* (Arts), 2/11/2015. As further concerns the opening of old forms without totally or at all destroying them, see Andrew Butterfield, "The Magic of Donatello," *New York Review of Books,* 4/23/2015. What is radical in its time may, in this way, become the norm, Beethoven the case in point.

*It is enormously curious*
**Debussy was first to hear.** See Jeremy Noble, "Portrait of Debussy—I: Debussy and Stravinsky," *The Musical Times,* 108 (1967), 22–25; and Eric Walter White, et al., "Stravinsky and Debussy," *Tempo,* n.s. 61–62 (1962), 2–5.
**virtuoso . . . Rubinstein.** Example from David Dubal, "Claude Debussy and the Piano," a lecture series upon the 150th anniversary of the composer's birth, aired August 20–24, 2012, on New York City's WQXR.

*Reviewing D. H. Lawrence's*
**"If there is . . . at present."** Aiken, 537
**"it is easy . . . intelligibility."** Aiken, 537–538.
**"the compulsive . . . mania."** Aiken, 538.

355 *It is thus apparent that*
**"Debussy is . . . musician."** Quoted by Dubal, 445.

*Pound himself straddling*
**not as "new" . . . thought.** On the literary precedent for Pound's obscurantism, see Isaacs, 6–7 (quoting, e.g., Ben Jonson: "Now nothing is good that is natural. . . . That which is writhed and tortured is counted the more exquisite.").
**Pound . . . *Waste Land.*** For the method of Pound's editing of *The Waste Land,* see Thormählen (1987), 23–27.

356 *The modernists were,*
**conflictedly admired Whitman.** Pound ultimately resolved the conflict. For Pound's admiration of and indebtedness to Whitman (a vast topic), see especially Herbert Bergman, "Ezra Pound and Walt Whitman," *American Literature,* 27.1 (1955), 56–61 (containing the full text of Pound's then unpublished 1909 manuscript "What I Feel about Walt Whitman"); and Clarence A. Brown, "Walt Whitman and the 'New Poetry,'" *American Literature,* 33.1 (1961), 33–45.

357 *The influence has been*
**"To a large . . . pranks."** *The New Criterion,* 32.7 (2014), 3.
**the practical joke it was.** A keen observer in all things, President Theodore Roosevelt penetrated the foolery. "Probably we err in taking most of the [Armory Show] pictures seriously. It is likely that many of them represent in the painters the astute appreciations of the power to make folly lucrative which the late P. T. Barnum showed with his faked mermaid." Conceding that the exhibition "contained so much of extraordinary merit," Roosevelt nonetheless chides the "European extremists," the "rather cheap straining after effect," and the "lunatic fringe among the votaries of any forward movement." Roosevelt most tellingly attributes modernist failings to the artistic "self-conscious[ness]" that makes the artists "ridiculous by pretentiousness."

This is a manifestation of self over subject matter early identified herein. See Theodore Roosevelt, "A Layman's View of an Art Exhibition," *The Outlook*, 3/29/2013, later appearing in *For and Against: Views on the Infamous 1913 Armory Show* (The Association of American Painters and Sculptors, 1913); also *For and Against*, etc. (Tucson: Holart Books, 2009), 49–54.

**agog at his buffoonery.** The Duchamp legacy, as noted, is very much with us today. Yves Klein (1928–1962), "one of the leading heirs of Marcel Duchamp's Modernist wit," composed his *Monotone Symphony* in 1947–1948. The work had its New York City debut to a sold-out audience on September 18, 2013. "The sound, a D major chord produced by an orchestra and a chorus begins abruptly, full force, and fills the air for 20 minutes, like a sonorous foghorn with a stuck switch. It ends as suddenly as it begins, but there is no applause because the orchestra is only half finished—its members sit without playing or even moving, 'performing' silence for just as long." Randy Kennedy, "A Sound, Then Silence (Try Not to Breathe)," *New York Times*, 9/18/2013 (Arts). Polymath Thomas McEvilley (1939–2013), whose scholarly book *Sappho* is cited herein, also curiously wrote *Yves the Provocateur: Yves Klein and Twentieth-Century Art* (Kingston: McPherson & Company, 2010).

**"For it is . . . journeyings."** Sainte-Beuve (Lee, tr.), 132. The idea is reprised by Nikos Kazantzakis (see p. 175):

> The risks of youth are good, but when time's firm foundations
> steady a man at length, it's time he put to port;
> boundaries are sacred: woe to the mind that crowds them close!
> [*Odusseia*, 2.714–716]

**the song most newly heard.** *Od.* 1.351–352.

358 *Those resisting modernism,*

**(Gr. *ararisko* 'to fix, set').** For the derivation of Eng. *art* from root **ar*- in Greek and Latin, see pp. 415–416.

**"The decline of . . . wings."** Kreymborg 22.4 (1933), 272–273. The saving grace of tradition in adversity is also poignantly conveyed by Robert Bridges—then Poet Laureate of England—in the preface to *The Spirit of Man* (1917), his consolatory compilation of poetry and prose in wartime:

> From the consequent miseries, the insensate and interminable slaughter, the hate and filth, we can seek comfort only in the quiet confidence of our souls. . . . Common diversions divert us no longer; our habits and thoughts are searched by the glare of conviction that man's life is not the ease that a peace-loving generation has found it or thought to make it, but the awful conflict with evil which philosophers and saints have depicted; *and it is in their abundant testimony to the good and beautiful that we find support for our faith, and distraction from a grief that is intolerable constantly to face,* nay impossible to face without trust in God which makes all things possible. [emphasis added]

**"So he [Eliot] . . . of God."** Spender, 13.

*It is on the wings*

**"To concentrate . . . and grief."** Blunden, 35.
**"upheld the . . . its inheritors."** Blunden, 36.
**"some discord . . . utterance."** Blunden, 35.

359 *As further concerns ascendant*

**"Epic offers a . . . death."** Vermeule, 696.

**The period . . . the forties."** Sophia Papaioannou, "Translating Homer in 20th Century Greece: the 'Silent' Voice of a Revolution" (1998), §IV. www.class.uh.edu/mcl/faculty/armstrong/papa.draft.html#f10. Web. 8/14/2013.
**"Virgil's profound . . . world."** Ziolkowski, 238.

361 *There were more than*
**"a comprehensible . . . nation."** Bogacz, 660. There was a call at the time against extreme individualism in poetry; for comprehensibility based on a "communal standard in verse writing." See *Contemporary Verse: The All-poetry Magazine for America*, May 1920.
**"that the language . . . general."** Bogacz, 653.
**"That poetry . . . megalomania."** Bogacz, 655.
**"Oh What a Literary War."** See Paul Fussell, "Oh What a Literary War," in *The Great War and Modern Memory* (Oxford: Oxford Univ. Press, 1975), 155–190. Fussell notes (174) that Pound, Joyce, Eliot, and others "were not present at the front to induct [those later recalling the war] into new idioms" which might have better succeeded in conveying the "indescribable nature of the war." For the dichotomy, with further reference to Fussell, between the "trench poets" and the modernists, see Margot Norris, "Teaching World War I Poetry: Comparatively," *College English*, 32.3 (2005), 136–153.

*As the war dragged*
**As the war . . . avant-garde.** Bogacz, 655–656.
***Poetry* . . . outspoken.** For more detailed treatment of the antimodernist *Poetry Review* and other publications, see Filries, "Poetry in the Hour of Need" (Ch. 7), in *Counter-revolution of the Word* (2008).
**"available . . . literature. "** Fussell, 174 (as paraphrased).
**"Do you know . . . people."** Harold Owen and John Bell, eds., *Wilfred Owen: Collected Letters* (Oxford: Oxford Univ. Press, 1967), letter 302. For the broader implications of Owen's statement vis-à-vis the importance to the poetry of World War I of established literary models and genres, see Nils Clausson, "'Perpetuating the Language': Romantic Tradition, the Genre Function, and the Origins of the Trench Lyric," *Journal of Modern Literature*, 30.1 (2006), 104–128.

362 *The above-mentioned*
**"I don't know . . . war."** Quoted by Spender, 6. See also Blunden, 9–11 (noting that "Old War Poetry"—that written during the eighteenth and nineteenth centuries—was typically the product of the non-soldier poet).
**"wars were . . . his friends."** Logan (1995), 58.
**"inevitably . . . in Kensington."** Logan (1995), 60.
**"Rather than . . . daily lives."** Ziolkowski (1977), 139.

*It would in fact take*
**"would force . . . for use."** Fussell, 174.
**secure in the curriculum.** "The Men of 1914 began in obscurity and ended up part of the curriculum." Atlas, xx.

363 *In 1929 Monro published*
**"to make . . . own poetry."** Monro, 7.
**"A discussion . . . Pound."** Monro, 11.

*Full censure would not*
**"constantly . . . confusion."** Yeats, xxv. For Yates's 1936 critique of Pound and Eliot, see further Donoghue (2010), 575–579.

**"content . . . unintelligible."** Yeats, xxv.
**poetry of . . . Ernest Dowson.** Yeats, xxxiv ("I have indeed read certain poems by Turner, by Dorothy Wellesley, with more than all the excitement that came upon me when, a very young man, I heard somebody read out in a London tavern the poems of Ernest Dowson—that too living history").
**"unworthy of . . . newspaper."** Kathleen Raine, ed., *Letters on Poetry from W. B. Yeats to Dorothy Wellesley* (London and New York: Oxford Univ. Press. 1940), 113 (letter of 12/21/1936).

364 *It is Yeats who further*
**"great influence . . . Eliot."** Yeats, xxv–xxvi.
**"source of the . . . obscurity."** Yeats, xxvi.
**"unexaggerated . . . novelty."** Yeats, xxi.
**"His belief in . . . judgment."** Yeats, xxv.
**Feeling the sting, Pound.** On Yeats's editing of *The Oxford Book of Modern Verse*, see Brater, 670–674.
**"God damn Yeats' . . . screen."** Letter to Hubert Creekmore, 2/?/1939; Paige, 321. Also, "ole Uncl. William Yeats" (Paige, 257), and "If Yeats knew a fugue from a frog . . ." (Paige, 293).
**"The events . . . barbarism."** De Laura, 157.
**"his . . . uncertain values."** De Laura, 157.
**"to prove . . . uncertain values."** De Laura, 162.

*If the standard bearers*
**"delicate lyricism . . . period."** Viereck (1953), 4 (i.e., the post-imagist and pre-*Cantos* period).
**"his adopted . . . and present."** Schlauch, 268.

365 *Eliot, famously allusive*
**Eliot, famously allusive.** For concise comparison between Eliot and Pound (to the latter's marked detriment), see Kreymborg (1934), 342–343.
**"combined . . . *rappel à l'ordre.*"** Spender, 6.
**His essay . . . acknowledged.** See "Tradition and the Individual Talent," in Eliot (1932), 3–11.
**"new . . . the totalitarian."** Pound (1938), 95.
**civilization in decay.** Pound, of course, had a quite different view of himself, e.g., "My problem is to keep alive a certain group of advancing poets, to set the arts in their rightful place as the acknowledged guide and lamp of civilization." Letter to Harriet Monroe, 1/?/1915; Paige, 48.
**"a second-rater . . . Homer."** Letter to Iris Barry, 7/20/1916; Paige, 87.
**a *new* epic tradition.** The distinction, now classic, is that of C. S. Lewis (*Preface to Paradise Lost*, 1942) between the "primary epic" of Homer and "secondary epic" of Virgil, the latter the forefront of epic poetry to come. For discussion see Ziolkowski, 129–134.

*Pound could theoretically*
**the Renaissance and fascism.** See Timothy Redman, *Ezra Pound and Italian Fascism* (Cambridge: Cambridge Univ. Press, 1991), 76.
**Mussolini the Great Leader.** See Dasenbrock, 187–188.
**Mussolini's march . . . world.** Lauber, 5.
**"The leader . . . design."** Lauber 17.
**connection . . . from casual.** See e.g., Roger Griffin, *Modernism and Fascism: The Sense of a Beginning under Mussolini and Hitler* (London and New York: Palgrave Macmillan, 2007).

**the defeat of . . . civilization.** Lauber, 7.
**"offer . . . Mussolini's Italy."** Ziolkowski, 18.
**"modern Italy . . . the past."** Ziolkowski, 19.

366 *Pound would be rewarded*

**Bollingen Prize committee.** The literature surrounding the award to Pound is vast. For a summary, see Viereck (1986), 131–133.
**"named . . . Collaborationist."** Wertham, 587. Dr. Frederick Wertham further (and articulately) battled the Pound apologists in the pages of the *Saturday Review of Literature.* See especially *SRL,* 7/30/1949 (and preceding issues). The *Review*'s then editors, Norman Cousins and Henry Seidel Canby, little needed Wertham's promptings for their own critique, citing Pound's "grotesque pseudo-scholarship [and] his counterfeit Greek and Chinese classicism," and concluding that his values were incompatible with a society in which culture is possible. Debunking the judgment of insanity that spared Pound his life, they noted that Pound's "insanity" in no way interfered with his poetry. *SRL,* 7/30/1949.
**exponentially confirmed.** Paraphrase from Wertham, 594.

367 *The eventual defeat of*

**his "imitation . . . failure."** Dasenbrock, 214. The failure is further explicable with reference to *The Cantos*' lack of historical knowledge and sensible judgment about what can start a war, virulent anti-Semitism (belying Pound's erstwhile humanism), paranoid simplifications (i.e., leaps from facts to conclusions), recourse to repetition over logic, and the "attempt to explain everything." See Lauber, 16–17.
**artistic *duce* or *fürer*.** See Lauber, 20–21. Pound, I submit, would be Mussolini's counterpart, even as Hitler was Wagner's apotheosis. See Todorov, 36–44.
**Here too, in Dante . . . Pound.** For Eliot's more sanguine, believing, and apprehending view of Dante, see Dasenbrock, 217–219. See also Eliot's essays "Dante" (1929) in Eliot (1932), 199–237; and "What Dante Means to Me" (1950) in Eliot (1965), 125–135.

*We may in the same*

**Pound's . . . toward Horace.** Notes Pound in oracular fashion, "A specialist may read Horace if he is interested in learning the precise demarcation between what can be learned about writing, and what cannot. I mean that Horace is the perfect example of a man who acquired all that is acquirable, without having the root." Pound (1937), 173–174.
**"savage brutes we . . . today."** Ford, 200.
**"The essence . . . Horatian note."** Ford, 200.
**"a due respect . . . grammar."** Richard Weaver, *The Ethics of Rhetoric* (Chicago: Henry Regnery Company, 1953), 142.
**relegate to the endnotes.** The matter is incisively discussed by Peter Viereck, who sees the fascist anti-Semitism of Pound's *Pisan Cantos* as a challenge to civilization itself: "All human beings, including poets, who enjoy the privileges of a free society, ought to make their freedom-enjoying privileges be equaled by their freedom-defending duties." In other words, with rights come responsibilities. Viereck further notes that the *Pisan Cantos,* being "politics, not serious poetry," are "not exempt from ethical, as well as aesthetic, considerations." The mandate, then, is as follows: "*Poetry must never be judged by politics.* But on grounds that *our entire civilization,* including poetry, depends almost completely on our constantly maintaining a moral heritage which Nazi anti-Semitism would destroy." Viereck, 5, 14, 15. Societal and artistic joint responsibility for the maintenance of civilization is further apparent as follows:

> Pound's Bollingen award is an example of the estrangement of art and life in our society. His "insanity" is an example of how we are trying to explain away

> profound defects in society by placing them outside society, in the sphere of individual pathology. Ezra Pound has no delusions in any strict pathological sense. But we have let ourselves be deluded—into the belief that responsibility is not responsibility, guilt not guilt, and incitement to hate not incitement to violence. [Wertham, 600]

And finally, the indomitable Margaret Schlauch: "Pisan Cantos is an anti-human document, convicted by the major themes it chooses to exploit. . . . Great poetry has something to do, they say, with the greatness of the human spirit. And Ezra Pound is anti-human and anti-humanistic." Pound's failure, as Schlauch further explains, resides in his inability to "rise above creed or dogma," to "give us something of universal validity for all men's aspirations," to fashion a "constructive world view," and to support "a common belief in the dignity of man as a special and responsible creature" in nature. Schlauch, 268, 269. The issue, otherwise viewed, is one of values. See Todorov, 57–58 (quoting Simone Weil).

For the nascent bibliography on the relation of the artistic to politics, following Pound's Bollingen Prize and during his own lifetime, see Ferkiss, 176, n. 12. A recent instance of politicized and morally indefensible art involves the Metropolitan Opera's staging (October 2014) of John Adams's *Death of Klinghoffer* and the opera's effort to elicit sympathy for a murderous and psychopathic "point of view."

**"The capital . . . literature."** Jebb, 12.

**Arnold . . . characteristics.** For Arnold's formulation, see pp. 368, 702.

**"We find a . . . criticism."** Walter Leaf, review of R. C. Jebb, *An Introduction to the Iliad and the Odyssey, Classical Review* 1.1 (1887), 12.

**"Translators of . . . Homer."** in Pound (1968), 249–279.

**"very ill-taught in Greek."** Pound (1968), 249.

368 *The "democratizing" Walt*

**bear comparison . . . rivals.** For perspective and background, see Bryant's Lectures on Poetry, including: (1) "On the Nature of Poetry," (2) "The Value and Uses of Poetry," (3) "Relation of Poetry to Time and Place," and (4) "On Originality and Imitation"; also "Early American Verse" and "On Trisyllabic Feet in Iambic Poetry," all in Parke Godwin, ed., *The Prose Writings of William Cullen Bryant, Volume First: Essays, Tales, and Orations* (*The Life and Works of William Cullen Bryant, Vol. V*) (New York: D. Appelton, 1889), 3–68. Bryant and Whitman, the classic and radical founders of American poetry, straddled the nineteenth century. They were sometimes seen together. See further Kreymborg (1934), 206.

**"The old . . . our youth."** Kreymborg (1934), 339.

369 *Great poets of the past*

**"Remarkably . . . throughout."** Eric Ormsby, "A confusion of harmonies," *The New Criterion*, 30.8 (2012), 17–20.

**"There are some . . . coarse."** William Logan, "The unbearable rightness of criticism," *The New Criterion*, 30.8 (2012), 22 (quoting from a letter of Charles Eliot Norton to James Russell Lowell).

**"When considering . . . long."** Kirsch, 45.

**"To read Ashbery . . . epiphany."** Kirsch, 51.

**"Apart from . . . of light."** Logan (1995), 68.

370 *"Poet-critic Randall*

**its admittedly dazzling lines.** Randall Jarrell, "Some Lines from Whitman," in Brad Leithauser, ed., *No Other Book: Selected Essays* (New York: Harper Collins, 1999),

98–111. Poet and literary critic Herbert Read (1893–1968), similarly (i.e., contradictorily) praises Ezra Pound. Says Read, "there are passages of the purest lyricism which in themselves, if extracted, would constitute a body of poetry for which there is no contemporary parallel. In the complex structure of the Cantos, these passages are relatively rare . . ." (speaking elsewhere in the essay of the "terrible warning" provided Pound by Walt Whitman). See Herbert Read, "Ezra Pound," in *The Tenth Muse: Essays in Criticism* (New York: Horizon Press, 1957), 265, 272–273.

For a quite balanced assessment of Whitman, published during Whitman's lifetime by a younger contemporary and Trinity College-educated poet, see Roden Noel, "A Study of Walt Whitman," in *Essays on Poetry and Poets* (London: Kegan Paul, Trench, 1886), 304–341. Most surprising, perhaps, is the book-length tribute by classicist, Renaissance scholar, and poet John Addington Symonds, *Walt Whitman* (New York: Benjamin Blom, 1893). The work is rhapsody on the theme of "the enormous variety of knowledge, the broad sympathies, the just perception of relative values, and the serene wisdom that distinguish *Leaves of Grass*" (xxxi). That Whitman, like Symonds, was homosexual may have contributed to Symonds's admiration. Symonds especially extols Whitman's leveling, all-inclusive, and democratic tendencies. Little quoting actual passages of Whitman's poetry, Symonds generally extols Whitman's language, e.g., for its "passionate glow, a warmth of devotion, beyond anything to which the world is used . . ." (71). It is thus for his themes that Symonds extols Whitman, at no time commending, or even discussing, his form or poetic qualities. Symonds's work is ultimately a panegyric "in duty to my master Whitman" (34–35), in whom he sees "deliverance and saving grace from deepest affliction"—though he doesn't quite say what that affliction may have been.

Similarly adulatory is American poet-critic Arthur Kreymborg, "Whitman and the Democratic Cosmos" in *A History of American Poetry* (1934), 206–230. Kreymborg's treatment (enfolding Whitman's shortcomings into asides and subordinate clauses) is outright hagiography, seen in such characterizations as: "a magnificent man, a large imperturbable animal, compact of passion and serenity" (208); "the huge, ingenious child in Whitman" (209); "the native, athletic, continental giant of Walt's vision" (210); "the imperturbability of a prehistoric mammal" (212), "closer to the soil than any poet before him," (212); and "Walt, child of man" (213). Romantic nature worship and the celebration of childlike sincerity are key elements of hagiography. See T. J. Jackson Lears, "The Image of Childhood and the Childhood of the Race," in *No Place of Grace: Antimodernism and the Transformation of American Culture 1880–1920* (Chicago and London: Univ. of Chicago Press, 1981), 144–160.

**"man at his . . . typical."** William Carlos Williams, Letter to Mary Barnard, 3/19/1935 (quoted in Barnard [1984], 73).

**collective of his fellow.** Kreymborg (1934), 225.

*Philosopher George Santayana*

**"We may wish . . . beautiful."** Santayana (1896), 85–86.

**no discrimination in beauty.** Santayana (1896), 79. Santayana is here quite aware of the nullifying effect, wrought by excessive leveling, on all discernment. The awareness is, however, peculiarly unexercised in the case of Whitman.

371 *Santayana seems more*

**"it becomes . . . books easily."** Santayana (1896), 101.

**today everywhere flouted.** As in the case of the "revered" Swiss-German Dieter Roth (1930–1998):

> Roth was a multiple-medium madman who blithely tackled music and poetry as well as nearly every art form you can name. Inspired by the self-destructive

mechanical sculptures of Swiss artist Jean Tinguely, he favored organic materials like chocolate, dough and sausages to make works that were as mortal and decay prone as humans. He constantly blurred the division between art and life and tended to push his work to the brink of chaos. Process—as disorderly, random and natural as possible—was his overriding interest.

[Roberta Smith, "Large Visions in a Large Space," *New York Times* (Weekend Arts II), 2/8/2013]

*As ever in the*
**"It is perfectly . . . tedious."** Kirsch, 51–52.

372 *This then is the*
**"He's the Caspar . . . years?"** See William Logan, *Our Savage Art: Poetry and the Civil Tongue* (New York: Columbia Univ. Press, 2009), as reviewed by Mark Ford, "Samurai Critic: Choosing the way of the sword, a poet cuts others down to size," *New York Times Book Review*, 4/29/2009. Of Sherod Santos (whose *Greek Lyric Poetry: A New Translation* I discuss): "The verse of Sherod Santos makes Logan want to put his hand into the whirring blade of a lawn mower." His intolerance of folly aside, Logan yet warms to Ezra Pound. In an article twice the length of those typically allowed by the journal, Logan relates how Pound, "sometimes slow to change," could, during a certain period in his life, "be goaded into brilliance." Logan otherwise dignifies Pound's *phanopoeia, logopoeia,* and *melopoeia.* See "Pound's Metro," *The New Criterion*, 33.8 (2015), 4–13. See further Chapter 34 and, on the dubious *logopoeia*, p. 711.
**"But when you . . . Pieria."** See pp. 188, 372.

*With only twenty years*
**Anthony Hecht (1923–2004).** For Hecht's place in the Auden-influenced generation of "New Critics" and "postwar formalists," see Beach, 144–151. For the "New Formalism" (the revival of metered and rhymed poetry in the 1980s), see Beach, 151–153.
**"create an . . . to perfection."** Teachout (1997), 54.
**"When . . . wake shrieking."** Philip Hoy, *Anthony Hecht in Conversation with Philip Hoy* (London: Between the Lines, 1999; 3rd ed., 2004), 26.
**"familiar . . . homage to it."** Kirsch, 160.
**"Hecht's regular . . . tongs."** Kirsch, 160.
**"The allure . . . tedious minds."** Kirsch, 160.
**"a classicist . . . very music."** Dinitia Smith, "Distilling the Music of Poetry: A Half-Century as a Bulwark of Rhyme and Meter," *New York Times*, 1/21/2003.

373 *Though forthright in*
**"always formal . . . about."** Kirsch, 162–163.
**"for . . . twentieth century."** Kirsch, 169.

374 *Truth be told, it was*
**"Facing . . . thing to do."** Viereck, 222.

*The lesson, so very old*
**"If . . . they have to say."** Beach, 153 (quoting Black Mountain poet Robert Creeley [1926–2005]).
**"the poetry . . . great poetry."** Spender, 13 (Spender here quoting Agatha in *The Family Reunion*, "It is possible that a sin may strain and struggle").

375 *The final word goes to*

**"ravishingly beautiful . . . subject."** J. D. McClatchy, ed., *Anthony Hecht, Selected Poems: A New Selection* (New York: Alfred A. Knopf, 2011), x–xi.
**"We move . . . with the Jews."** From "More Light! More Light!" *Collected Earlier Poems* (New York: Alfred A. Knopf, 1990).
**"We rise . . . lock the door."** From "The End of the Weekend," *Collected Earlier Poems* (New York: Alfred A. Knopf, 1990).
**"the detail . . . of the muddle."** McClatchy, *supra*, x.

376 *The Romantic era, at*

**"A habitual . . . itself."** Santayana (1896), 101.
**"are compatible . . . soul."** Santayana (1896), 101.

377 *The delight of its own*

**"no one . . . for pleasure."** Glover, 47.
**Ginsberg was . . . of Whitman.** For a searing, yet intermittently sympathetic, indictment of Ginsberg, see Norman Podhoretz, "My War With Allen Ginsberg," *Commentary* (August 1997), 27–40.

*It is not enough to*

**form . . . magnitude of spirit.** Paraphrase from Kreymborg (1934), 228.

*Equally flagrant, by way*

**"Passionate . . . otherwise lacks."** Kirsch, 268 (on the mundanity of a poem by Czeslaw Milosz). In an early review of new poetry for 1965–1966, poetry doyenne Helen Vendler, by contrast, commends John Woods (1926–1995) for keeping "precious tokens of reality from disappearing unrecorded in verse." And she commends Allen Ginsberg for showing that "verse, no less than the novel, has the power to salvage the details of American life. . . ." Vendler's then endorsement of contemporary poetry was significantly more accepting than Kirsch's today. Like him, however, she can hedge mightily, affording herself *carte blanche* for whatever position, e.g., "Since poets have to create the taste by which they are enjoyed, a review of contemporary poetry runs the risk of being wrong in preference and wrong in emphasis, but even with suspect judgments, descriptions can perhaps be accurate." Vendler, 541, 552. At the same time, however, Vendler was unequivocal in her rejection of the "new sensationalism" of Robert Lowell's Horace translations. See Vendler, 558–559 and pp. 530–531.
**"The business . . . the forest."** *Rasselas*, Ch. 10, 352, in Donald Greene, ed., *Samuel Johnson, The Major Works* (Oxford and New York: Oxford Univ. Press, 1984).
**reckon the leaves of grass.** Santayana puts it thus, again helping to resolve his Whitman quandary; ". . . when various objects have many common characteristics, the mind is incapable of keeping them apart. It cannot hold so great a multitude of distinctions and relations as would be involved in naming and conceiving separately each grain of sand, or drop of water, each fly, or horse, or man that we have ever seen. The mass of our experience has therefore to be classified, if it is to be available at all. Instead of a distinct image to represent each of our original impressions, we have a general resultant—a composite photograph—of those impressions." Santayana (1896), 90. See also Santayana (1896), 95 (speaking of our "experience which we are incapable of retaining and surveying in its multitudinous immediacy").

378 *There are many flowerings*

**"Olds has . . . narcissism."** Kirsch, 275.

**how Olds . . . the sonnet.** See pp. 87, 381, 385–386.
**"This lamentably . . . same."** Kirsch, 275.

*What began as the*
**"the values . . . and 'success.'"** Hilton Kramer, "Art View: An Artist Emerging from the 60's Counterculture, Chicago," *New York Times*, 12/13/1981. See also "Hilton Kramer, Art Critic and Champion of Tradition in Culture Wars, Dies at 84," *New York Times* (Obituaries), 3/28/2012.
**in order to . . . forms.** See pp. 189, 295, 366, 386, 568 (with reference to art historian Kenneth Clark's notion of permanence as the predicate of civilization).

CHAPTER 26

380 *Discipline, and the*
**"the . . . limits impose."** Trench, xi.
**"In truth . . . have found."** These are the concluding lines of Wordsworth's sonnet beginning, "Nuns fret not at their convent's narrow room." For poems reflecting on poetic form, see John Hollander, *Rhyme's Reason: A Guide to English Verse* (New Haven: Yale Univ. Press, 1989, 2001), 71–86.
**"a poem . . . into a star."** Trench, xi.
**indistinguishable from prose.** See Shankman (1983), 134–139.
**"*vers libre* does not exist."** For Williams and Eliot on free verse, see Chris Beyers, *A History of Free Verse* (Fayetteville: Univ. of Arkansas Press, 2001), 13–16.
**"indispensable . . . unit."** Viereck (1986), 128.
**"No one . . . standards left."** Graves (1967), 159.

381 *Adherence to discernible*
**"Unfettered . . . us freedom."** This passage marks the conclusion of the nineteenth act of Goethe's 1802 drama *Was wir bringen* (*What we bring*).
**'The weight was . . . gravity'.** Leve pondus erat nec quod cognoscere possent / Solis equi, solitaque iugum gravitate carebant (*Met.* 2.261–262).

382 *It is from the yoke,*
**"'grant me . . . servitude!'"** Charlotte Brontë, *Jane Eyre* (New York: Heritage Press, 1942), Ch. 10, p. 77.

383 *As further concerns personal*
**modernism on the map.** Dubal, 570.
**"My freedom . . . spirit."** Igor Stravinsky, *Poetics of Music* (Cambridge: Harvard Univ. Press, 1942), 65.
**". . . I could . . . space."** *Hamlet* 2.2.274–275.

384 *For Gotthold Lessing*
**"among the . . . degree."** Lessing, 11–12.
**"turn . . . suffering object."** Lessing, 11–15.
**"Cannot . . . prophecies?"** Lessing here negatively comments on an eighteenth-century French scholar's identification of a bearded wide-open-mouthed old man as Jupiter delivering an oracle.

*In the same vein,*
**"O Freedom . . . the free."** Durrell (1950), 69. Durrell's "Freedom, Freedom, prison to the free" is the converse of Wordsworth's "In truth the prison, unto which we doom

/ Ourselves, no prison is." The enumeration in Durrell ("To swans the water, bees the honey-cell, etc.") recalls the opening of Wordsworth's sonnet (a reference to bees in each):

> Nuns fret not at their convent's narrow room;
> And hermits are contented with their cells;
> And students with their pensive citadels;
> Maids at the wheel, the weaver at his loom,
> Sit blithe and happy; bees that soar for bloom,
> High as the highest Peak of Furness-fells,
> Will murmur by the hour in foxglove bells:
> In truth the prison . . .

**Fools, who . . . and cheese.** Bread and cheese being a poor man's food; in Greek, "mallow and asphodel" (*WD* 40–41).

385 *The aforementioned*

**"Then, too . . . himself therein."** Trench, xi–xii.

**"Oh, my beloved . . . sake!"** Norma Millay, ed., *Collected Poems of Edna St. Vincent Millay* (New York: HarperCollins, 1945), 581. See further Artemis Michailidou, "Why Always the Greek Dance? Edna St. Vincent Millay's Address to Sappho," in Tatiani G. Rapatzikou, *Anglo-American Perceptions of Hellenism* (Newcastle: Cambridge Scholars Press, 2007), 214–227 (Millay the '"greatest woman poet since Sappho'"). Women poets are often compared to Sappho, e.g., the short-lived American Anne Reeve Aldrich (1866–1892): "Passion and agony, the one because of the other, are the keys to [her] nature and verse. This woman is of the few who nearest share the moods of Sappho and her talents." *Springfield Republican* (c. 1892), as quoted in *The Book Buyer*, X. 3 (April, 1893). Greek poet Kiki Dimoula (b. 1931) has been called "the best Greek woman poet since Sappho." Samples of her work appear in Rae Dalven, tr., *Daughters of Sappho: Contemporary Greek Women Poets* (Rutherford and Madison: Fairleigh Dickinson Univ. Press, 1994). Millay, be it noted, was also a translator—to her own great surprise—of Baudelaire. She holds forth, commandingly, on the subject in her preface to a 1956 volume coauthored with translator George Dillon (see Bibliography).

**Note . . . Sara Teasdale.** The lustrous and aching nostalgia of Durrell's *Sappho: a play in verse* is also apparent in Teasdale's poetry, e.g., *Sonnets to Duse and Other Poems* (1907), *Helen of Troy and Other Poems* (1911), and *Rivers to the Sea,* V: "Sappho" (1915). In the same vein, Franz Grillparzer, *Sappho: Tragedy in Five Acts* (1818), Arthur Burkhard, tr. (1953); and Marcus Holland, *Sappho: A Drama in Verse* (1948).

In "The Strange Victory of Sara Teasdale," an introduction to Teasdale's *Collected Poems,* poet Marya Zaturenska (1902–1982) suggestively notes that

> the people around her became transfigured into poetry. Her inner world provided an escape from the warm, adoring world of her comfortable family mansion. It transmuted the everyday world in which she lived into a shimmer of color, glittering imagery and warm, intense feeling. She had the art of drawing a seemingly artless beauty out of simple things—a walk in Central Park or along Riverside Drive on a windy day; or two lovers occupied only with each other among the splendors of the Metropolitan Museum. [xxi–xxii]

**"Oh beauty . . . than a prayer."** Sara Teasdale, *Collected Poems of Sara Teasdale* (New York: Macmillan, 1937), 3.

## Chapter 27

388 *Following World War II,*

**Following World War II.** The following paragraph is partially indebted to Catharine

Savage Brosman, "French Intellectuals in the Americas during World War II," *The Sewanee Review,* 118.2 (2010), 241–258 (especially 244 and 246). The article deals with the traditional equation of culture and history at the core of French national identity. The treatment of French intellectual and political mutability is endless. See Richard Wolin, *The Wind from the East: French Intellectuals, the Cultural Revolution and the Legacy of the 1960s* (Princeton: Princeton Univ. Press, 2010); Theodore Dalrymple, *The New Vichy Syndrome: Why European Intellectuals Surrender to Barbarism* (New York: Encounter Books, 2010); and Alan Riding, *And the Show Went On: Cultural Life in Nazi-Occupied Paris* (New York: Alfred A. Knopf, 2010). Riding concludes, "Probably no other country better illustrates the perils assumed by a population that is educated to revere theories." He is critical of the political doctrines promulgated by French writers and intellectuals and those doctrines' failed "mirages of Utopia" (350).

389 *Of note as part of*

**Denial was likewise . . . heart.** See Scott Sayare, "A Life Spent Remembering a War France Has Tried to Forget," *New York Times* (Saturday Profile), 3/28/2014.
**"It doesn't . . . studies courses."** Naomi Schaefer Riley, "Trial By Fury: Columbia mattress rape case is not justice—it's shaming without proof," *New York Post,* 2/8/2015.

*Alternatives exist only*

**Martians . . . identically equal.** For the erotic effects of water and scope of *grokking* in general, see Robert Heinlein, *Stranger in a Strange Land* (New York: Ace Books, 1987), 93–94, 148–150, 213, 284–286, 419–420.
**of angelic intercourse**. *PL* 8.618–629.

390 *Science fiction infuses*

**"Probably . . . fiction writers."** Cortiel, 3.
**utopia . . . "humyn beings."** Adapted from Carol Pearson, "Women's Fantasies and Feminist Utopias," *Frontiers: A Journal of Women Studies,* 2.3 (1977), 50–61; also, Ellen Morgan, "The Feminist Novel of Androgynous Fantasy," *Frontiers,* 2.3 (1977), 40–49. Prominent examples of the genre are Marge Piercy, *The Woman on the Edge of Time* (1979); Ursula K. Le Guin, *The Left Hand of Darkness* (1969); and Le Guin, *The Dispossessed* (1974). See also Suzy McKee Charnas, *Motherlands* (1978) (imagining a parthenogenic all-female society), and Joanna Russ, "Recent Feminist Utopias," in *To Write Like a Woman: Essays in Feminism and Science Fiction* (Bloomington and Indianapolis: Indiana Univ. Press, 1985), Ch. 7.

Mary Wollstonecraft Godwin Shelley, child-bride of the then adulterous Percy Bysshe Shelley, is generally thought to have invented science fiction with the publication of *Frankenstein* (1818)—a story that "lends itself to strong feminist interpretations." Veronica Hollinger, "Feminist theory and science fiction," in Edward James and Farah Mendelsohn, eds., *Cambridge Companion to Science Fiction* (Cambridge and New York: Cambridge Univ. Press, 2003–2009), 128. Science fiction's clones, androids, cyborgs, and other such quasi-human life forms are also descendants of *Frankenstein.*

Mary's riotous relationship with Shelley (she seventeen, he twenty-two) included the death of three of their four children. It is perhaps not coincidental that the world's first science-fiction novel was written by a woman whose life was as fully escapist as it was nomadic. Further noteworthy are Mary's childhood influences. Her parents William Godwin and Mary Wollstonecraft were philosophers, writers, liberal political activists, and early advocates of women's rights. See generally William St. Clair, *The Godwins and the Shelleys: a Biography of a Family* (New York: W. W. Norton, 1989), Chs. 12, 28, and 38. See also Russ, *supra,* Ch. 10, "On Mary Wollstonecraft Shelley," in *To Write Like a Woman.* Mary Wollstonecraft's *A Vindication of the Rights of Woman:*

*with Strictures on Political and Moral Subjects* (1792) is considered the "founding feminist text in English." It describes women in highly negative terms, even as it seeks to assert their value. See Susan Gubar, "Feminist Misogyny: Mary Wollstonecraft and the Paradox of 'It Takes One to Know One,'" in Elam and Robyn Wiegman, eds., *Feminism Beside Itself* (New York: Routledge, 1995), 133–154.
**women of . . . uniting.** "Workers of the world unite!"—the *Communist Manifesto*'s famous rallying cry—is predicated, without using the term, on (geographic) "boundarylessness." "Integrism," or the transcendence of separations, is among the predicates of totalitarianism, as is the revocability of all laws and precedent (societal and cultural boundarylessness) and the resultant shaping of the world to one's own will (through the unbounded recourse to power and violence). See Todorov, 9–10, 19, 28, 32, 40, 52, 55–58.
**"The blurring . . . itself."** Mary Louise Roberts, *Civilization Without Sexes: Reconstructing Gender in Postwar France, 1917–1927* (Chicago: Univ. of Chicago Press, 1994), 4 (summarizing the view of World War I veteran-novelist Pierre Drieu la Rochelle).
**case for a "third gender."** See Julie Scelfo, "The Third Gender," *New York Times* (Education Life), 2/8/2015 (explaining *genderqueer*: "A gender identity that falls outside of the male/female binary," and *trans**: "Short for transgender, with the asterisk meant to indicate the wide range of identities beyond the norm"). Binaries are by definition oppositional. Foremost, indeed foundational, among binary oppositions is that of male and female, owing not only to its pervasiveness but also to its social and sexual disparities, both real and perceived. The "queering of the binary"—to borrow the article's language—seeks to soften, mitigate, indeed eradicate sexual difference, which is to say, the differential, the definitional edge, confirming ordered existence (see Chapters 2 and 28). The result is, again, "boundarylessness," the topic of this Chapter 27. The queering of the binary, moreover, is an attack on straight white males as the male/female binary's "privileged" half. It is, by extension, an attack on Western civilization, itself the singular result of predominantly male inspiration, accomplishment, and control. The sexes are sooner complementary than oppositional, as recognized by the cardinal Chinese precept of yin and yang.

One could conclude from Scelfo's article that the accommodation of gender preferences or self-determinations, as each presents for accreditation, is the current job description of most university administrators. And so it is, at Barnard (Women's) College at least, which now admits transgender women—i.e., "those who live and consistently identify as women, no matter their gender at birth"—with the full array of administrative and potentially legal issues involved. See Mike Vilensky, "Barnard Accepts Applications from Transgender Women," *Wall Street Journal*, 6/4/2015.

391 *Also gone is the*
**"In Lacanian . . . feminism."** Joan Wallach Scott, *The Fantasy of Feminist History* (Durham: Duke Univ. Press, 2011), 34. Despite its title and preoccupation, including discussion of feminist utopias, the book makes no reference to science fiction. Its cover bears one of the Holofernes beheadings by Artemesia Gentileschi.

*Moreover, the larger*
**"A group of . . . academia."** McEvilley, 383 and n. 6. A broader net was earlier cast by Peter Green: "We need to clear our minds of the clamorous new ideologies, from post-colonialism to post-structuralism, from political feminism to queer theory, that have been busily putting their own enthusiastic spin on Sappho and her world in a vigorous campaign of appropriation." Green, 35.

392 *Within this theorizing*
**"Love and . . . psychology."** Tucker, 86–87.

*Enter Page duBois, who*

**"model of . . . with others."** DuBois (1995), 1–2. DuBois's "sense of boundarylessness, an exhilarating new way of conceiving of community that imagines an endless process, multiplicity of ties, and mergings with others" suggests no one so much as Walt Whitman. It otherwise gives rise, based on figurative notions of "boundless" imagination, to such academic contrivances as Christa Jansohn, Lena Cowen Orlin, and Stanley Wells, eds., *Shakespeare without Boundaries* (2011). The work "offers a wide-ranging collection of essays written by an international team of distinguished scholars who attempt to define, to challenge, and to erode boundaries that currently inhibit understanding of William Shakespeare, and to exemplify how approaches that defy traditional bounds of study and criticism may enhance understanding of a dramatist who acknowledged no boundaries in art." Which is to say: the work offers a freewheeling collection of essays by line crossers with strength in numbers who take—we may be comforted—a moderate approach to the destruction of limits (they only "erode" them). It is blinkered boundaries that have "inhibited" our understanding of Shakespeare. Being "distinguished," the team can indulge whatever practice it likes, including the dismissal of empirical analysis (its approach "defy[ing] traditional bounds of study and criticism"). All the while, it enhances our understanding of Shakespeare. Although Shakespearean drama is typically either restorative of the norm or punitive of its transgression, the claim that Shakespeare "acknowledged no boundaries in art" provides modernist grounds for turning him on his head.

**"The traditional . . . to go."** Howe, 24.

393 *It is worth repeating:*

**ideas "excite" or "tantalize."** See further below, and for "vigorous" with reference to *olisbos* 'dildo', duBois (2008), 90. The association of vigor with sex needs no elaboration. It has been used to good effect in cinema: "No, but he was young and vigorous. He was *very* vigorous, father." The line is spoken, breathlessly, by Elena (Catherine Zeta-Jones) to her father after the sexually charged swordplay in which Zorro (Antonio Banderas) "offs" the slip from her very form (*The Legend of Zorro*, 1998).

*Such notions are right*

**graduate . . . Shakespeare.** Perhaps some English professors and their deans subscribe to Pound's view—cavalier here, as often elsewhere—on Shakespeare in the curriculum: "For the purpose of general education we could omit . . . study of Shakespeare for thirty [years] on the ground that acquaintance with these subjects is already quite diffused, and that one absorbs quite enough knowledge of them from boring circumjacent conversation." Pound (1937), 190.

**Shakespeare . . . Suzanne.** Baker made the remark in a 1988 interview with *The New York Times*. See Emily Eakin, "Black Captive in a White Culture," *New York Times*, 5/5/2001. The comparison is sometimes given as that between Pearl S. Buck and Virginia Woolf. For the context of Baker's remark—"illogic, linearity and form are only white male ideology"—see Alvin B. Kernan, *In Plato's Cave* (New Haven: Yale Univ. Press, 1999), 274–275. Kernan further notes the defection of professors from departments of English to cultural studies, "a fragmented field that no longer had any center or any boundaries." Minority-interest complaints against Western culture (and the proposed remedies for them) have very much paralleled those of radical feminism.

395 *Where there are no*

**"The history . . . another."** Frederic L. Bender, ed., *Karl Marx, The Communist Manifesto* (New York and London: W. W. Norton, 1988), 55; Paulo Freire, *The Pedagogy* *of the Oppressed,* Myra Bergman Ramos, tr. (New York: Herder and Herder, 1970; Portuguese, 1968).

396 *Within this climate,*

**DuBois . . . locus classicus.** See pp. 16, 23, 25, 323–334, 409.

**"As well . . . also a feminist."** These and duBois's other professions of Marxism appear, in unsettling proximity, in duBois (1995), 147, 154, 162. DuBois is also the author of *Slavery: Antiquity and Its Legacy* (New York: Oxford Univ. Press, 2009), in which she relates slavery in the ancient world to California factories and Asian sweatshops and, with exemplary Marxist overbreadth and condemnation, to the enslavement of immigrants to globalized corporatism and exploitative capitalism. This is liberation/postcolonial theology based, again, on the Marxist social dichotomy of "oppressor" and "oppressed," of Caucasian male and everyone else. It has a sexual counterpart in the perceived inequality of the "penetrator" and "penetrated."

A similar perspective informs duBois's *Slaves and Other Objects* (Chicago: Chicago Univ. Press, 2003), arguing that ancient Greek achievements are over-idealized at the cost of an awareness of slavery in the ancient world. Also among duBois's publications is *Trojan Horses: Saving the Classics from Conservatives* (New York: New York Univ. Press, 2001). The volume was dashed off in response to Victor Davis Hanson and John Heath, *Who Killed Homer: The Demise of Classical Education and the Recovery of Greek Wisdom* (New York: Encounter Books, 2001). The latter refers once, but pointedly, to duBois.

**(and male scholarship).** The dissatisfaction persists. Noting that "the echoes of Sappho in poets from Ovid to Baudelaire to T. S. Eliot create an extraordinarily rich afterlife for her across the millennia," a recent author adds: "Sappho's afterlife has been largely in the hands of men." Belinda Jack, *The Woman's Reader* (New Haven: Yale Univ. Press, 2012), 33 and 297, n. 23.

*Feminist interpretation*

**own lexical scaffolding.** The examples that follow are taken, with minor exception, from duBois's introduction to Roche (1988), 11–22.

**"instrumentalization . . . body."** "Instrumentation of the body" in the Roche introduction; "instrumentation of the eroticized body" in the book chapter; "female body instrumentalized in heterosexual ideology" in *Sowing the Body* (1988), 58.

**To paraphrase Howe's.** Howe's statement reads as follows: "The problematic nature of experience tends to replace the experience of human nature as the dominant subject of the modern novel. Abandoning the assumption of a life that is knowable, the novelist turns to the problem of establishing a bridgehead into knowability as the precondition for portraying any life at all. His task becomes not so much depiction as the hypothesizing of a set of *as-if* terms, by means of which he may lend a temporary validation to his material." Howe, 26.

*"Poetics" is a term*

**"when their . . . learned."** Pound (1937), 164.

397 *Part of the new*

**"There are . . . libido."** See also pp. 403–404.

398 *The new matrix further*

**Erotic . . . but *excites* them.** "Excitation" has escaped the politicized classroom to become a jurisprudential force. Supreme Court Justice Stephen Breyer disavows the principal of original intent, noting that the Constitution, like a literary, i.e., living text, should not be rigidly interpreted. "It is the practical application of the Constitution that makes its interpretation such an *exciting* thing." See Kyle Smith, "A Philosopher-King on the High Court," *New York Post*, 11/20/2013 (Smith's emphasis). The promise of excitement, notes Smith, prompts skepticism and fright. Or, as the *Post's* Internet byline puts it (11/20/2013), "Justice Mistakes the Constitution for Modernist Art."

*Where validation resides,*
**"Through . . . self-esteem."** Skinner, 135 (quoted and discussed by duBois, introduction to Roche, 17, with tie-in to Foucault).

*Language empowers.*
**"reinscribes . . . courtship."** The relevant reading of the Hymn vis-à-vis Homer is that of Winkler, who notes that it metaphorically transfers the language of soldiery to "the experience of women in love" through "a multiple identification" with Homer's characters, specifically Diomedes and Aphrodite in Book Five of the *Iliad*. Winkler, 94. As Sappho does not "reinscribe" the *Iliad* for homoerotic ends, she does not "reject" its martial-heroic ethos nor "ingeniously redefine" it "based on what may be described as a feminine prerogative." See Johnson, 67–69. Sappho does not "deconstruct" Homer, but, as Winkler suggests, imbues epic contexts with differing points of view.

399 *To similar effect does*
**Why . . . not be *charming*?** The argument for the girl's *charm* in rustic attire runs contrary to the accepted wisdom: "It is striking that the déclassée [girl] is criticized here not for being too free with her favors but for not knowing how to present herself in an enticing manner." Poochigian, xxiii.
**"from behind . . . the mouth."** Giuseppe di Lampedusa, *The Leopard*, Archibald Colquhoun, tr. (New York: Pantheon Books, 1960; Italian, 1958), 177–178.

400 *Sappho's verses about*
**"The perfection . . . emotion."** Tucker, 85.
**style remained preeminent.** "Witness the compositions of Olympus and Terpander and of all the composers who resemble them. These compositions, although confined to three notes and simple, are better than those that make use of a variation and many notes, so that no one is able to copy the style of Olympus, and all the composers of many notes and a variety of styles are his inferiors." Einarson and De Lacy, trs., *Plutarch, On Music* §18, 390–391.
**"noble simplicity . . . grandeur."** From *Gedanken über die Nachahmung der griechischen Werke in der Malerei und Bildhauerkunst* (1755), translated (in a facing bilingual edition) by Elfriede Heyer and Roger C. Norton as *Reflections on the Imitation of Greek Works in Painting and Sculpture*, 3–25, 33–39. In the finest imagistic turn of this work, Winckelmann notes:

> The general and most distinctive characteristics of the Greek masterpieces are, finally, a noble simplicity and quiet grandeur [*edle Einfalt und stille Größe*], both in posture and expression. Just as the depths of the sea always remain calm however much the surface may rage, so does the expression of the figures of the Greeks reveal a great and composed soul even in the midst of passion [*bei allen Leidenschaften*]. [Winckelmann, 33]

For the fuller context of this passage, and the exception taken by the Enlightenment philosopher and critic Gotthold Lessing, see Victor Anthony Rudowski, "Lessing contra Winckelmann," *The Journal of Aesthetics and Art Criticism*, 44.3 (1986), 235–243. On the origins of the notion of classic simplicity, and the compromises it makes with contemporary literary norms or expectations, see Fred Parker, "Classic Simplicity,"

in Lianeri and Zajko, eds., 227–242. Considered the founder of German classicism, Winckelmann, who spent most of his life in Italy, was a child of the European Enlightenment. He was a contemporary of Voltaire, Diderot, and Rousseau. Bach and Handel (both born in 1685) were thirty-two when Winckelmann was born. Winckelmann's work was an immediate success, though initially published as a mere pamphlet in fifty copies.
**"poetry, when . . . clarity."** Friedrich Schiller, *Essays*, Walter Hinderer and Daniel O. Dahlstrom, eds., Dahlstrom et al., trs. (New York: Continuum, 1993), 150.
**"directness and simplicity."** C. T. Lewis, 361–362.
**preaching . . . he practiced.** The divide between Pound's theory and practice little helps:

> In fact, Pound's and other modernists' influence has been so pervasive that we sometimes forget that they were far from consistent in their own theory and practice. Thus, in both his 'major personae'—poetic appropriations so free as to be virtually new poems—and the works he labelled 'translations', Pound makes frequent use of archaisms, dialectal expressions, convoluted syntax, and so forth in order to signal the foreignness of the appropriated text, though his reasons for doing so may not be the same in his personae as in his translations. [Svensson, 114]

**"One 'moves' . . . reader."** Pound (1937), 165. Poundians have capitalized on the master's lip service to clarity, e.g., "Guy Davenport brought the Poundian-imperative of clarity to bear on his long and honorable engagement with archaic Greek poetry." Warren (2008), 296, n. 30. Cf. "Pound never relinquished the demands for clarity, precision, and brevity which are so characteristic of his writings in the Imagist period." Thormählen (1978), 21. How Pound's major works sustain this view is a mystery.
**"the Tuscan . . . civilization."** Pound (1952), 104.

401 *That Sappho might*
**"charming . . . expression."** Cameron, 1 (of the "Hymn to Aphrodite").
**"Perhaps . . . seduction."** DuBois (1998), 150.
**"Men of right . . . one."** Shankman, ed. (1996), 47 (Pope's "Observations on the First Book" [of the *Iliad*]).

*Where there's patriarchy*
**"fact that . . . endings."** DuBois (1998), 155.

402 *DuBois's sexually metaphoric*
***Sappho* 'manlike Sappho'.** *Ep.* 1.19.28–29:
**"one of . . . Latin poetry."** Eduard Fraenkel, *Horace* (Oxford: Oxford Univ. Press, 1957), 342. The full sense is best captured as follows: "Sappho, although she had the spirit of a man (i.e., of Archilochus), and employed the measure of Archilochus, yet dulled the keen edge of his Muse; so did Alcaeus, but unlike Sappho, he differed widely from Archilochus both in matter and arrangement." See M. B. Ogle, "Horace, *Epistle* I, XIX, 28–29," *American Journal of Philology*, 43.1 (1922), 59. See also Lipking, 58 ("she joins a masculine power or readiness to make demands with a feminine openness of feeling"), and 90 (for Baudelaire's *la mâle Sapho*). But does Sappho really "warn all women, everywhere and for all time, how much they hazard by trying to rise above their sphere"? So Lipking, 58. The perfection of Sappho's verse sooner removes it from remonstrance.
**imputation of tribadism.** Gr. *tribo* 'rub', Eng. *tribad* and *tribadism*, referring, according to Porphyrion (3rd century AD), to the "monstrous desire for intercourse with females" (commentary to Horace, *Epode* 5.4). Says Porphyrion, 'Sappho, moreover, was masculine either because engaged in poetry, more often a male pursuit, or because defamed

as a tribad' (mascula autem Sappho vel quia in poetico studio est, in quo saepius mares, vel quia tribas diffamatur fuisse). See generally Williamson, 32–33; Brooten, 23–26. On *mascula Sappho* and the "Amazonian 'virility' the Renaissance likes to attribute to classical womanhood," see V. Cox, 48–49.

*Reverse gender change*
**transvestism . . . *Phaedrus*.** The passage is discussed at length by Carson (1986), 141–167.
**"To echo . . . the other."** DuBois (1995), 85–87 ("Sappho in the Text of Plato").
**essentially sexual nature.** See, e.g., Winkler (1996a), 102–109 (*Numphē* 'nymph, young woman', also meaning "clitoris" and "bride"), and compare the more reserved analysis of an earlier time by Cameron (1939), 12–13 (discussing the Hymn's "numerous traces of conventional erotic vocabulary"). See also Lanata (1969a), 19 ("Nothing is more frequent in amatory lyric than the topos of 'love and death,' and even in Sappho it recurs with particular insistence").

403 *Finally, there is that*
**"A prurient . . . Alcaeus."** Wills (2005), 58.
**"some analogy . . . result."** DuBois (2008), 91–93.
**Max Nelson concludes.** Nelson, "A Note on the *olisbos*," Glotta, 76.1&2 (2000), 75–82.

406 *Over a thousand years*
**Solon wished . . . learn it.** See Campbell (1982), 13. We earlier noted that Athens was only a village at the time of Homer's and Sappho's flowerings. J. M. Edwards thus plausibly relates Stobaeus's anecdote to the introduction of Sapphic song into Athens, where it was first known to the younger generation, i.e., Solon's nephew. Edwards (1912), 4. See also Nagy (2004b), 33 (adducing the incident as evidence of Sapphic recitations at symposia). It is unnecessary to place a feminist spin on Sappho's reception in Athens, e.g., Sappho "a woman in a fiercely patriarchal society, whose poetry was extravagantly praised even in fifth century Athens, a bastion of male dominance if ever there was one, as among the greatest ever written in Greek." Vandiver, 60. That Sappho's was among the greatest poetry ever written places it beyond special pleading.

*There is a pop-cultural*
**to pulp . . . performances.** See, e.g., Mark Blankenship, "Sapphic Pulp Fiction, Live Onstage: from Women about Women," *New York Times* (Theater), 9/30/07; also Margalit Fox, "Tereska Torrès, 92, Writer of Lesbian Fiction, Dies," *New York Times*, 9/25/2012 (Torrès's *Women's Barracks* [1950] "America's first lesbian pulp novel").
**"If Sappho . . . a Feminist."** Stanley Abbott and Barbara Love, *Sappho Was a Right-On Woman* (1972), 158.

407 *Nor is Sappho's status*
**"perhaps double . . . humanity."** Williamson, 15. This same remark, with obeisance to duBois, is approvingly discussed by Eva P. Lester, MD, "Sappho of Lesbos: The Complexity of Female Sexuality," *Psychoanalytic Inquiry*, 22 (2002), 170–181.

408 *Moreover, the entirely*
**"In the absence . . . disclose it."** Powell (1993), 37–38.
**"organizes the . . . a whole."** Rachel Hadas, "The Tenth Muse," review of Aaron Poochigian, in *The New Criterion*, 28.7 (2010), 76–78.

409 *The exiguous texts*
**"strategy of juxtaposition."** Quotations in this paragraph from Balmer (2013), 96.

410 *From the outset of*
**"... then ... by Marx"?** Quoted references to utopia in this and the following paragraph from duBois (1995), 53–56, 92–93, 97, 162.

*True to its root*
**"somewhat ... common sense."** Murray (1912), 8.

CHAPTER 28

412 *Poetry, as all art*
**more clearly ... flexibility.** Paraphrasing Murray (1930), 92 ("The edges of words were more clear cut, and the value of each syllable more definite, than with us. Consequently, many metrical effects are possible and even easy in Greek which are practically impossible in English.").
**"time and limit ... made."** This, and the balance of the paragraph, either quoted or adapted from Linda Gregerson, "Mortal Time," in David Baker and Ann Townsend, eds., *Radiant Lyre: Essays on Lyric Poetry* (Saint Paul: Graywolf, 2007), 247–263.

414 *With the spatial, or*
**love and hate combined.** For Catullus's *Odi et amo* ('I hate and I love'), see pp. 153, 302, 414, 508, and compare §§46 and 47 herein. For *Odi et amo* as "the most remarkable case in Latin of a sequence of prosaic words combining to create a powerful poetic effect," see Adams & Mayer, 55.

415 *As the bodily boundary*
**control of one's own body.** For far-ranging discussion of bodily integrity, the feeling of security, and the basic instinct for survival, see Segal (1990), 94–170.

*Poetry, as mentioned,*
**root *ar ... ararisko.** For parts of what follows, I have consulted Henry George Liddell and Robert Scott, *A Greek-English Lexicon* (Oxford: The Clarendon Press, 1976), and Charlton T. Lewis and Charles Short, *A Latin Dictionary* (Oxford: The Clarendon Press, 1966). I am a grateful to Gregory Nagy for his contribution to this paragraph.

416 *To the extent it limits,*
**Winckelmann ... statuary art.** What follows either summarizes or quotes Heyer and Norton, trs., 18–21. For a critique of Winckelmann's "interpret[ing] everything through the statues," see Murray (1912), 13.
**Joshua Reynolds ... portraitist.** Reynolds's *Discourses* gave rise to protracted debate concerning the value of the Greek artistic achievement.

*Similar views continued*
**William Hazlitt (1778–1830).** A. R. Waller and Arnold Glover, eds., *William Hazlitt, The Collected Works of William Hazlitt in Twelve Volumes* (London: J. M. Dent, 1903), Vol. 9, 490.
**"For most Victorian ... virtue."** Frank M. Turner, *The Greek Heritage in Victorian Britain* (New Haven: Yale Univ. Press, 1981), 45. Turner further notes the connection between naturalism and sensuality, both inimical to the ideal of Greek art. In this vein, Winckelmann: "Sensual beauty provided the artist with all that nature could give [*gab dem Künstler die schöne Natur*]; ideal beauty provided him with sublimity [*(gab ihm) die erhabenen Züge*]—from the one he took the human element, from the other the divine." Heyer and Norton, trs., 17.

**"Without art . . . no being."** Ben Jonson, *Discoveries*, Maurice Castelain, ed. (Paris, n.d.), 127.

417 *Poetry exists within*
**distillation from . . . of life.** De Quincey quotations and paraphrase in this and the following paragraph are from Thomas De Quincey, *Theory of Greek Tragedy*, William Dallam Armes, ed. (San Francisco: William Doxey, 1893), 8–12.
**or "fixed" . . . to portray it.** On the fixity of tragic character as embodied in types, see pp. 31–32.

418 *A prime example of*
**"The tragic hero . . . his."** Benardete, 134.
**only . . . tragic heroism.** Benardete, 134 (as paraphrased).
**Achilles . . . "a work of art."** Benardete, 134.

*Nothing so characterizes*
**the tripartite division, etc.** See further Louden, 98–99.
**Olympus . . . earthly kings.** Kings on earth are the counterparts of Zeus on Olympus, from whom they derive their authority. This is the germ of the theory of the divine right of kings, which surfaced in Europe during the Middle Ages. See Duban, "Poets and Kings" (1980).
**as in Odysseus's summoning.** *Odyssey*, Book Eleven.
**possibility . . . living and dead.** *Il.* 20.61–67.

419 *The privilege of mediating*
**"what was to . . . had been."** *Th.* 31–33. The poet is described as knowing past and present; the Muses, as knowing past, present, and future (*Th.* 36–40). The Muses' song thus shares in prophecy. The seer Calchas, knowing past, present, and future, is credited with guiding the Greeks to Troy (*Il.* 1.86–87).
**"In removing . . . return."** Segal (2001), 103, n. 45 (translating Jean-Pierre Vernant, "Aspects mythiques de la mémoire et du temps," in *Myths et pensées chez les grecs* [Paris, 1974]), Vol. I. 87.

*Also mediating these*
**death-symbolic crossings.** See pp. 202–203.

420 *The Iliad itself begins*
**offspring of Zeus and Themis.** *Th.* 901–906, though at *Th.* 217 Hesiod makes them the parthenogenic offspring of Night (a rare internal variance).

421 *We note, relative to*
**excellent argument . . . Menocal.** For quotations provided and argument summarized in this paragraph, see Menocal's highly thoughtful *Shards of Love: Exile and the Origins of the Lyric*, 108–111.
**Romania . . . a single language.** Pei makes a similar point with reference to what he calls the "Romance area": "There is also evidence of a trend toward change, with phenomena that point in a general Romance direction rather than toward any specific Romance language." Pei, 74–75.
**"Boundarylessness." . . . works well.** Kazantzakis variously views "boundarylessness" (though he does not use the word), depending on the needs of his narrative. Sometimes he insists that boundaries be maintained; sometimes he greets their dissolution. In the latter instance, a grandly inclusive aesthetic is in play, as when Odysseus communes with God

(*Odusseia*, Book Fourteen) or becomes a renowned ascetic (16.1270–1394; 18.1145–1219); otherwise, when socialist leanings predominate (15.548–573). Alternatively,

> The mind to conquer me, great king, has not been born!
> I am the Law, father of virtue, thorny hedge
> That guards man's ordered way, the sacred boundary line
> Behind which spreads the desert with no hope or god!
> [*Odusseia* 19.853–856; cf. 2.714–716]

While linguistic boundaries tend to be porous, territorial boundaries are a different matter. The recent flood of Muslim immigrants into Europe (summer, 2015) is of clear border-eradicating import. As one commentator notes, "The European Union has been devoted to eliminating borders, and now finds itself functionally with none amidst its worst refugee crisis since World War II." Richard Lowry, "Europe's Folly and the Refugees," *New York Post*, 9/9/2015. And as concerns ISIS and the New Caliphate, "The global order that held since Hitler was defeated is disintegrating before our eyes. Borders are erased and entire populations are put to the sword or forced to flee the new tyrannical monsters." Michael Goodwin, "The Bigger Picture behind the European refugee Crisis." *New York Post*, 9/6/2015.

*The anathema of*

**the *bnei ha'elōhim*.** Earlier discussed at p. 567; elsewhere mentioned in Job 1.6, 2.1, 38.7; Ps. 29.1, 89.6; Deut. 32.8.

**"divine beings . . . court."** RSV, Gen. 6 (note), p. 8. "This whole passage is obviously archaic and mythological." Robert Alter, *The Five Books of Moses: Translation with Commentary* (New York: W. W. Norton, 2004), 38.

**'men who were heroes'.** The term *(h)ēmitheoi* appears only once in the *Iliad*, in the account of the gods' postwar destruction of the Greek fortification at Troy—nearby rivers made to rise and wash it away. The rivers roll up helmets, shields, and (bodies of) *(h)ēmitheōn genos andrōn* 'the race of men who were demigods' (*Il.* 12.1–23). The unique usage, in context, strikes a decidedly retrospective, even nostalgic, tone.

**To kill them off . . . war.** The problem was not simply the indiscriminate proliferation of demigods, but excessive population in general. A scholiast on the phrase 'the plan of Zeus was being fulfilled' (*Il.* 1.5) quotes from the cyclic poem *Cypria* to the effect that "countless tribes of men, though wide-dispersed, oppressed the surface of the deep-bosomed earth"; that Zeus took pity, determining "to relieve the all-nurturing earth of men" through the Trojan War; that "the heroes were slain and the plan of Zeus fulfilled." See W′ fr. 1 (*Cypria*), pp. 81–82; and E–W fr. 3 (*Cypria*), p. 497. For the Hesiodic *Catalogue*'s view of the Trojan War as a means toward human/divine separation, see M fr. 155, pp. 231–239; MW fr. 204, pp. 99–105; E–W fr. 68, pp. 193–203; and Nagy (1979/1999), 215–221 (on other aspects of the permanent separation of men and gods). The *Iliad* scholiast notes in a prose introduction to his quotation from the *Cypria* that, according to the myth Homer followed, Earth asked to be relieved of her multitudes, "there being no piety among humankind." The Greek tradition thus posits not only excessive population, but—as the biblical flood tradition—impiety and lawlessness.

The scholiast's account is corroborated by the Races/Ages of Man narrative of Hesiod's *Works and Days*: Gold, Silver, Bronze, Heroic, and Iron. The Iron Age, as Hesiod laments, is his own—debased and marked for destruction—into which Hesiod wishes he had never been born. In the Heroic Age, preceding Hesiod and Homer's own, Zeus created "a divine race, better and more just [than the preceding Bronze Age] of 'men who were heroes' [*andrōn (h)ērōōn*] called 'demigods' [*(h)ēmitheoi*]." To this age belonged Achilles (born of the mortal Peleus and sea nymph Thetis); and Aeneas (born of the mortal Anchises and goddess Aphrodite).

The *Works and Days* goes on to explain that the heroes perished in battles at Troy and Thebes (the latter a different epic saga; see Aeschylus's *Seven Against Thebes*). The *Works and Days,* however, provides no motive for the heroes' destruction. Thus, while the heroes to which Hesiod refers may have been "better and more just" than their Bronze Age predecessors, they were yet sufficiently wanting, according to the *Iliad* scholiast, to merit destruction. See *WD* 106–201, Lattimore, tr. (1972), 31–43; see also West (1990), 172–204 (overview, bibliography, and commentary).

**The Greek tradition, war.** A Greek flood tradition may precede the Trojan War as the means of the demigods' destruction, as evidenced by Poseidon's eventual water-borne destruction of the Greeks' wall fortifications at Troy. See Scodel (1982). The flood tradition associated with Deucalion and Pyrrha is of later vintage, dating to the fifth century BC. See González, 387–390 and West (1997), 377–382.

422 *Both the gibōrim and*

**Both . . . "bigger than life."** RSV, Gen. 6 (note), 8 (citing Num. 13.33 and Deut. 2.10–11). See also Deut. 3.11. Milton refers to the Sons of God on more than one occasion. See *PL* 5.443–450; 11.573–597, 683–688; *PR* 2.172–190.

**clearly intended distinction.** On the "hierarchical distinction between gods and men that is tested by the heroes," or the "limit that keeps mortals from becoming gods," see Muellner, 15–18, 26, 50–55.

**"a perfect . . . of boundaries."** Fantuzzi, 7.

*The imperative of limitation*

**"an ignorance . . . certain details."** Else, 383. Alternatively, "an ethical flaw or some grave misjudgment in a crisis." Cooper, 78.

*Hamartia, however, is*

***(h)amartian tina* 'some mistake'.** See Butcher (*Poetics* 1453a, XIII.3), 45–46 (though Butcher translates "a certain flaw"). Several sentences later, Aristotle refers to it as *hamartian megalēn* 'a great mistake' (*Poetics* 1453a, XIII.4), as it must be to have tragic consequence.

***hybris* 'overreach, insolence'.** To such notions of "overreach" and "insolence" may be added "a series of offenses unified and characterized by a particular psychological attitude on the part of the perpetrator: a desire to damage the victim's honor and diminish the victim's social prestige through an offensive action, of whatever sort." This too is *hybris.* Among such actions would be "outrageous behavior which, while failing to reach the extremes of sexual violence, induces the victim to accept a dishonorable sexual relationship." See Cantarella, 43.

**avoidable ignorance . . . *hamartia*.** Aristotle mentions Sophocles's *Oedipus*—for him, perfectly constructed—more than any other Greek tragedy. We recall, however, that Aristotle had access to hundreds of Greek tragedies—over one hundred each by Aeschylus, Sophocles, and Euripides alone—while we have all of thirty-two by the three combined. It is noteworthy, then, that Aristotle's *(h)amartia* pattern is only marginally apparent in surviving Greek tragedy. See Lattimore (1964), 18–26 (discussing *(h)amartia, hybris,* and *nemesis* 'retribution').

Butcher (a preeminent Aristotelian prior to Else) distinguishes *hamartia* by the following "shades of meaning": (1) error, as applied to a single act, due to inadequate knowledge of particular circumstances (which might have been known); (2) error due to unavoidable ignorance; (3) error involving a conscious or intentional, but not deliberate, act, i.e., acts committed in anger or passion (the "moral *hamartía* proper"); and (4) a human frailty or moral weakness (i.e., "flaw" of character) not tainted by vicious purpose. Butcher, 317–319. *Hamartia* likely includes a combination of the above, "which in English cannot be covered by a single term." Butcher, 320.

424 *Ceding the palm, Richmond*

**"Professor . . . of a person."** Lattimore (1967), 10, 74, n. 32, citing Else, 376–379. Else deems the following interpretations of *hamartia* "misleading and beside the point": error, moral failing, moral culpability, intellectual error, error of judgment, moral flaw.

**"functional . . . complex plot."** Else, 379. Aristotle distinguishes simple and complex plots. A complex plot is one in which a change of fortune is accompanied by a reversal, a recognition, or both—Sophocles's *Oedipus* the best example. See Butcher (*Poetics* 1452a–b, X–XI), 38–43. For a highly readable précis of simple and complex plots in Aristotle, see the opening paragraphs of Mendelsohn (2013).

***hamartia* . . . change begins.** Else, 379.

*The structural requirements*

**"Now, according . . . order."** Butcher (*Poetics* 1450b, VII.1–4), 31.

**"And to define . . . to bad."** Butcher (*Poetics* 1451a, VII.7), 33.

425 *In all ways integral*

"**Greek Tragedy . . . whole.**" Ellis, tr., 157. For other aspects of compression and condensation, with reference to Shakespeare and Racine in the development of drama, see Ellis, tr., 125–130. (Wagner further speaks in this connection of the "narrowed stage.")

426 *Accordingly, we see that*

**"perfect . . . of boundaries."** Fantuzzi, 7 (noting that Achilles's heroic status "is synonymous with his ability to cross over divisions that other men cannot surmount: human/god, human/beast, male/female [i.e., Achilles's cross-dressing on Skyros], life/death").

**Greek and biblical traditions.** On the confusion of categories and overstepping of bounds in the early Genesis narratives, see Hendel, 24–26. See further the pithy remarks in "The Order of Things" and "The Tragic Flaw Concept" in Timothy Sharkey, *The Art of Tragedy and the Battle Against It* (Chicago: Deus ex Machina, 2012), Chs. 3 and 4. The often transgressively minded Daniel Mendelsohn (2014) scoffs at the idea of boundaries, noting of Pentheus's fate in Euripides's *Bacchae* (he is torn limb from limb by his crazed mother and other bacchantes): "It is a horribly apt punishment for the king who had so vehemently insisted on self-containment, on maintaining, as we would say today, 'boundaries'"—as though "boundaries" (in Mendelsohn's scare quotes) were a recent imposition on excess, sexual or otherwise.

Part VIII, Chapter 29

429 *No contemporary translation*

**of formalism's demise.** See David Yezzi, "The Fortunes of Formalism: Formalism versus free verse, revisited," *The New Criterion*, 23.8 (2005), 21–24. Despite its revival, or "re-appreciation," formalism appears destined to remain suspect. Poetry critic David Orr has recently observed of poet-translator Richard Wilbur (b. 1921) that he "has been for decades a Grand Old Man of American poetry, and he's spent most of his career alternately praised and condemned for the same three things. First, he's widely agreed to be a formal virtuoso. One might think this would be an indisputable virtue, but in certain quarters, working in meter can still earn you skeptical looks." Other issues involving Wilbur include his "civilized or old-fashioned" manner, and resistance "to certain tendencies in American poetry, most notably the conspicuous self-dramatization associated with Robert Lowell and Sylvia Plath, and the even more self-conspicuous self-dramatization associated with Allen Ginsberg." See David Orr,

"The Formalist," review of Richard Wilbur, *Anterooms: New Poems and Translations* (2010), in *New York Times Book Review*, 1/9/2011. In a similar vein—Wilbur's critics "have lived within the tensions of his poetry by an ignorant celebration of his faults or gleeful damning of his perfections"—see William Logan, "Richard Wilbur's Civil Tongue," review of Wilbur's *New and Collected Poems* (1988), *Parnassus: Poetry in Review*, 21.1–2 (1996), 90–110.
**Stallings's . . . translation.** A. E. Stallings, *The Nature of Things* (New York: Penguin, 2007). Penguin's last edition of Lucretius was the wondrously metered blank-verse translation by R. E. Latham (1951).
**"How did things . . . matter."** Joseph Epstein, "'The Literary Life' at 25," *The New Criterion*, 26.1 (2007), 4–11.

430 *The errancy predates the*
**"courteous" . . . "discourteous."** Discourteous poetry, notes Kirsch, sees itself "as a part of 'contemporary poetry'—almost a separate endeavor—and appeals to readers whose taste is formed on the poetry of the last hundred years." For the full and telling comparison, see Kirsch, 113–114.
**"A great age . . . follows it."** Pound (1935), 101.
**"The poetical fame . . . age."** Edward Gibbon, *The History of the Decline and Fall of the Roman Empire*, J. B. Bury, ed. (New York: Fred de Frau, 1906), Vol. III, 134, n. 1.

*As generally concerns*
**translation of the *Iliad*.** Rodney Merrill, tr., *The Iliad of Homer* (Ann Arbor: Univ. of Michigan Press, 2010).
***mēnis* 'wrath' . . . Achilles.** The principal work is by Muellner (1980).

432 *Another troubled translation*
***Aeneid* of Frederick Ahl.** *Virgil Aeneid* (Oxford: Oxford Univ. Press, 2007).
**the risk of simplification.** See Maurice P. Cunningham, "Some Poetic Uses of the Singular and Plural of Substantives in Latin," *Classical Philology*, XLIV.1 (1949), 1–14 (with specific discussion of Lat. *litus*); cf. Adams & Mayer, 75.

*Ahl, like Merrill, is*
**"into . . . shores of light."** Cf. "Glad we return'd up to the coasts of Light." *PL* 8.245.

*Ahl further imperiously*
**Roman rhetorician Quintilian.** See *Inst. Orat.* 11.3.36–38. Quintilian otherwise validates the point, discussing the metrical requirements of the phrase "*Troiae qui primus ab oris.*" *Inst. Orat.* 1.5.27.
**leaving well enough . . . all.** Not that Ahl does. The following three extravagances are culled from the start of Book One:

> ***Aen.* 1. 28:**
> *rapti Ganymedis honores*, lit. 'the honors of seized Ganymede', meaning the preferential treatment given Ganymede (p. 55), once snatched up by Zeus in eagle's form. Ahl translates: "Ganymede, raped and exalted."
>
> ***Aen.* 1.94–96:**
> . . . o terque quaterque beati,
> quis ante ora patrum Troiae sub moenibus altis
> contigit oppetere . . .
>
> which translates:

... O three and four times blessed
who chanced before their fathers' eyes to die
beneath Troy's soaring walls ...

This is Aeneas's prayer as he fears capsizing in storm-tossed seas. Ahl expatiates as follows:

... Greater by three, even four times the blessing
Chance gave those with the fortune to die beneath Troy's
mighty ramparts
Under their fathers' gaze.

***Aen.* 1.128:**
*Aeneae ... classem*: 'Aeneas's fleet' (as always translated); Ahl: "Aeneas's navy."

433 *Equally telling is*
**"we like ... after all."** Hayden Pelliccia, "Let Virgil Be Virgil," review of Robert Fagles, tr., *The Aeneid*, and Stanley Lombardo, tr., *Aeneid, New York Review of Books*, 4/12/2007.

434 *Also different for*
**"Homeric Greek ... definite."** Olav Hackstein, "The Greek of Epic," in Bakker, ed., 405.

435 *Virgil has also entered*
**Sarah Ruden's *Aeneid*.** *The Aeneid, Vergil* (New Haven: Yale Univ. Press, 2008).
**Ruden ... quoted as saying.** Ruden quotations are from an interview with Jennifer Howard, "Measuring the 'Aeneid' on a Human Scale," *Chronicle of Higher Education*, 5/15/2008.
**from the gender-neutrality.** See, e.g., Luise von Flotow, *Translation and Gender: Translating in the 'Era of Feminism'* (Manchester: St. Jerome Pub., 1995), 57–66 (on Sappho).

*Ruden's work is generally*
**line-for-line correspondence.** An early example of dactylic hexameter rendered into iambic pentameter is the *Iliad* (1870) of famed American poet-attorney and editor William Cullen Bryant. Bryant's translation, with a somewhat shorter (and thus stricter) metric—ten beats per line to Ruden's ten *or* eleven—maintains a near, but not exact, line-for-line correspondence. The "breathing room" makes all the difference. Bryant's translation was one of several composed following Matthew Arnold's *On Translating Homer* (1861) and seeking to employ Arnold's standards. Bryant's was the superior translation of a prelapsarian age, by a poet-translator who knew Greek. It was commended for its Miltonic cadences in a magisterial review by Charlton Thomas Lewis (of Lewis and Short *Latin Dictionary* fame). See C. T. Lewis (1871).

437 *As Ruden has been compared*
**sound-to-sense correspondence.** "In neoclassical theory it is axiomatic that words be decorously related to the things they are seeking to express and describe; this is the ultimate criterion by which to judge the validity of the aesthetic entailed in Dryden's desire for the 'ornament of words.'" Sowerby (2006), 124.
**case of ... in constraint.** See pp. 380–386.
**what ... "imitative harmony."** The point is made by Pope as follows: "But when loud Surges lash the sounding Shore, / The *hoarse, rough Verse* shou'd like the *Torrent* roar." See Sowerby (2006), 56 (quoting Pope, *An Essay on Criticism*, ll. 362–373). So also *Aen.* 4.632–652 (Aeneas battered by Anna's complaints as trees by a storm): "All the [prior] translators have sound effects ... but there is much more sound and fury in

Dryden not only in relation to the wind and tree with the additional line in which the sound echoes in the valleys but also in the storm of complaint raised by the women." Sowerby (2006), 104–105. The alliterative crash and tumult of the sea and its effects are no better captured than by poet Adam Lindsay Gordon (1833–1870), "The Swimmer."

438 *The age in which Dryden*
**eighteenth century . . . Virgil.** See pp. 283, 285, 442.
**"the long . . . energy divine."** Alexander Pope, "Imitation of Horace, *Ep.* II.1," in Mark Pattison, ed., *Pope: Satires and Epistles* (Oxford: Clarendon Press, 1881), 61–75.
**Had Virgil written in English.** Says Dryden in his preface to the *Aeneid*: "I have endeavor'd to make Virgil speak such English as he would himself have spoken, if he had been born in England, and in this present age." See Dryden, tr., *Virgil's Aeneid* (1909), 64. This, of course, is not a plea for translation in a contemporary, or somehow colloquial, idiom (as the terms are now understood)—"this present age" being Dryden's poetically refined and elevated own. Dryden's "formula" has *not,* as most recently proposed, "at once licensed any Anglicization, however inappropriate." Green (2015), 19. Even assuming their familiarity with Dryden, translators nowadays contemporize not by his license, but because irretrievably removed from Dryden and his intellect.
**"claims to . . . expression."** Sowerby (2006), 2 (quoting Johnson, *Lives,* Vol. 1, 419, and Dryden's 1697 *Aeneid*):

> . . . I have added to both of them [the English language and poetry] in the choice of Words, and Harmony of Numbers which were wanting, especially this last, in all our poets, even in those who being endu'd with Genius, yet have not cultivated their Mother-Tongue with sufficient Care; or relying on the Beauty of their Thoughts, have judg'd the Ornament of Words, and Sweetness of Sound unnecessary. [Dryden, *Works,* Vol. 6, 807]

**"The veneration . . . poetry."** Donald Greene, ed., "Dryden," in *Samuel Johnson, The Major Works* (Oxford: Oxford Univ. Press, 1984), 707.

439 *Unfazed by whatever*
**"Until there . . . couplet form."** Sowerby (2006), 140.
**"imperishably . . . literature."** C. T. Lewis, 354–355.
**"The figures . . . propriety."** Beye (1984), 220.

440 *A translation that Ruden*
***Aeneid* by C. S. Lewis.** All of Book One (758 lines), Book Two (516 lines), and Book Six (253 lines).
**"restores . . . yet poetic."** Ross, xix, xxi.
**"Lo, I who . . . rough array."** These first four lines (of disputed authorship) refer to Virgil's earlier *Eclogues* and *Georgics* (see p. 286). Spenser opens his *Faerie Queene* with an adaptation of the same lines.
***Tilth* is tilled soil . . . chosen.** See Milton: "His eyes he open'd and beheld a field, / Part arable and tilth, whereon were Sheaves / New reapt. . . ." *PL* 11.429–431.
**"a natural habitat . . . mislaid."** Steiner (1998, 3rd ed.), 364 ("Archaism internalizes. It creates an illusion of remembrance which helps to embody the foreign work into the national repertoire."). Similarly, Steiner on the King James Bible, speaking of "an unequalled feeling of 'at-homeness' . . . a native presence in what is, in obvious truth, a remote entirely alien world of expression and reference. By choosing or achieving almost fortuitously a dating some two to three generations earlier than their own [i.e., grounded in Tudor rather than Jacobean usage], the translators [of the KJB] made of a foreign, many-layered original a life-form so utterly appropriated, so vividly

out of an English rather than out of a Hebraic, Hellenic, or Ciceronian past, that the Bible became a new pivot of English self-consciousness." Steiner (1998, 3rd ed.), 360, 366–367.

441 *There are passing quirks*
**"Lewis was . . . the Bible."** Jason Fisher, "C. S. Lewis's Lost Aeneid," *Mythprint*, 48.5, #346 (May 2011), online publication of Mythopoeic Society, www.mythsoc.org/reviews/lewis-lost-aeneid. Web. 5/17/2015.

*Classicists may have*
**All have their merits.** Variously metered translations appear as follows:

**Conington (1855), *Aeneid*, rhymed octosyllabics**
(rhymed iambic tetrameter)
Arms and the man I sing, who first,
By Fate of Ilian realm amerced,
To fair Italia onward bore,
And landed on Lavinium's shore:—
Long tossing earth and ocean o'er,
By violence of heaven, to sate
Fell Juno's unforgetting hate:
Much labored too in battle-field,
Striving his city's walls to build.

**Taylor (1907), *Aeneid*, Spenserian stanza**
Of arms I sing, and of the man, whom Fate
First drove from Troy to the Lavinian shore.
Full many an evil, through the mindful hate
Of cruel Juno, from the gods he bore,
Much tost on earth and ocean, yea, and more
In war enduring, ere he built a home,
And his loved household-deities brought o'er
To Latium, whence the Latin people come,
Whence rose the Alban sires, and walls of lofty Rome.

**Dryden (1697), *Aeneid*, rhymed decasyllabics**
(rhymed iambic pentameter)
Arms, and the man I sing, who forc'd by Fate,
And haughty Juno's unrelenting hate,
Expelled and exil'd, left the Trojan shore.
Long labors, both by sea and land, he bore,
And in the doubtful war, before he won
The Latian realm, and built the destined town.

**Ruden (2008), *Aeneid*, blank decasyllabics**
(unrhymed iambic pentameter)
Arms and a man I sing, the first from Troy,
A fated exile to Lavinian shores
In Italy. On land and sea, divine will—
And Juno's unforgetting rage—harassed him.
War racked him too, until he set his city
And gods in Latium. There his Latin race rose,
With Alban patriarchs, and Rome's high walls.

**Lewis (1952), *Aeneid,* rhymed dodecasyllabics**
(rhymed alexandrines)
Of arms and of the exile I must sing, of yore
Guided by fate from Troy to the Lavinian shore
And Italy. Much travelled upon land and sea
By powers in heaven for angry Juno's sake was he,
And proved in war, still endeavoring in our soil to place
His gods and build a city. Whence the Latin race
Comes, and the Alban fathers and the walls of Rome.

**Morris (1875), *Aeneid,* rhymed fourteeners**
I sing of arms, I sing of him, who from the Trojan land
Thrust forth by Fate, to Italy and that Lavinian strand
First came: all tost about was he on earth and on the deep
By heavenly might for Juno's wrath, that had no mind to sleep:
And plenteous war he underwent ere he his town might frame
And set his Gods in Latian earth, whence is the Latin name,
And father-folk of Alba-town, and walls of mighty Rome.

**Stallings (2007), *De Rerum Natura,* rhymed fourteeners**
Life-stirring Venus, Mother of Aeneas and of Rome,
Pleasure of men and gods, you make all things beneath the dome
Of sliding constellations teem, you throng the fruited earth
And the ship-freighted sea—for every species comes to birth
Conceived through you, and rises forth and gazes at the light.
The winds flee from you, Goddess, your arrival puts to flight
The clouds of heaven. For you, the crafty earth contrives sweet flowers,
For you the oceans laugh, the skies grow peaceful after showers,
Awash with light.

442 *We have already noted*

**Translation . . . prove a point.** This and the following paragraph are adapted, with interpolations, from Richard Garnett, *Dictionary of National Biography* (London: Smith, Elder, 1885–1900), Vol. 63, 36; reissued 2004 as the *Oxford Dictionary of National Biography* (print and online).

*Worsley's translations of*

**"ma[d]e . . . taste and skill."** Arnold, 281–282.
**"Lingering . . . stanza."** Omond (1912), 260.

443 *Here then is a Worsley*

**"So they . . . doth fill."** *Il.* 8.542–549. For the continuation of this signature passage in Matthew Arnold's hexameters, see p. 697. Worsley's translation did not, of course, escape censure, especially as concerned "foreign matter" to fill out the Spenserian form (e.g., "And in clear outline stand revealed thereby"—conveyed by a single word in the original). The *Spectator*'s editors concluded, condescendingly, that "Mr. Worsley has succeeded better than we should have expected in dealing with the unmanageable meter to which he has enthralled himself, but we cannot say he has achieved a success." It is an echo of Bentley's reproof, popularized by Matthew Arnold: "Pretty poem, Mr. Pope, but you cannot call it Homer." *The Spectator* further criticized Worsley's form as "too foreign" and his movement as retarding. The critique was addressed more to the translation's "spirit" than to its abundant "nobility" (that most elusive Arnoldian quality). See, further, *The Spectator* 39 (1866), p.

220 ("Current Literature"). The *Spectator,* curiously, ignores Matthew Arnold's high praise of Worsley only six years earlier. It instead invidiously compares Worsley and the then still-popular blank-verse translation (1864) of Edward Smith-Stanley, 14th Earl of Derby. See further *Notes and Queries,* 60 (1872), 314.

443 *Arnold did not always*
**responding to Arnold's gibe.** See Markley, 99–102.

*If Worsley's Odyssey*
**"How then . . . champion lay."** *Il.* 22.201–210.

444 *However Conington's*
**The gesture . . . correspondence.** Robert E. Lee's appreciation of Worsley's *Iliad,* and the heartfelt correspondence the offering engendered, is of literary-historical moment: "Among the many tokens of respect and admiration, love, and sympathy which my father received from all over the world, there was one that touched him deeply. It was a 'Translation of Homer's Iliad by Philip Stanhope Worsley, Fellow of Corpus Christi College, Oxford, England.'" The gift was transmitted with a letter designating Lee as "the hero, like Hector of the Iliad, of the most glorious cause for which men fight." Lee responded, in significant part, as follows: "My Dear Sir: I have received the copy of your translation of the Iliad which you so kindly presented to me. Its perusal has been my evening's recreation, and I have never more enjoyed the beauty and grandeur of the poem than as recited by you. The translation is as truthful as powerful, and faithfully represents the imagery and rhythm of the bold original." See *Recollections and Letters of General Robert E. Lee,* by (his son) Captain Robert E. Lee (St. Petersburg: Red and Black, 2008), 162–164 (originally, New York: Doubleday, Page, 1905).

CHAPTER 30

445 *The most agreeable*
**Lattimore's aim . . . render.** See Lattimore (1951), 55 ("A Note on the Translation").

446 *Lattimore shunned*
**"And Teukros . . . warcraft."** *Il.* 12.387–389 (passage chosen by randomly opening to Lattimore's *Iliad*).
**"It is the archaism . . . lofty."** Venuti (1998), 100–101.
**"[w]ithout . . . the original."** Lloyd-Jones, 13.

*Having but recently*
**passage has been praised.** For full appraisal, see Lloyd-Jones, 13–14.
**"still remains . . . the field."** Lloyd-Jones, 17.

447 *Active in the 1940s*
**"when . . . dactylic hexameter."** Armstrong, 189.
**stress-based approximations.** The reference is to Lattimore, *Greek Lyrics* (1955).
**"oddly occup[ying] . . . prose."** Armstrong, 188.
**Lattimore's "prosy verse."** For a brief review of the "alternating" history of Homeric translational styles, see Lloyd-Jones, 7–9.

*Dactyloid, without being*
**fair examples of his own.** See Arnold, 226 (translating *Il.* 8.560–565):

> So shone forth, in front of Troy, by the bed of Xanthus,
> Between that and the ships, the Trojans' numerous fires.
> In the plain there were kindled a thousand fires; by each one
> There sat fifty men, in the ruddy light of the fire:
> By their chariots stood the steeds, and champed the white barley
> While their masters sat by the fire, and waited for morning.

**too "tenderly elegant."** Arnold, 214.

*We should recall in*
**stress-based hexameter.** A residual longing for past glory, in original and translated verse alike, had earlier persisted in the sometimes attempted "English hexameter," i.e., hexametric rhythm determined by spoken stresses alone. In its more demanding and inevitably failed attempts, English hexameter sought to approximate the syllabic quantities of Latin poetry (themselves adapted from the Greek). However resourceful such attempts, they were necessarily inexact and invariably disappointing, the Smith/Miller *Iliad* (1947) an exception. This owed to the lack of a native tradition of dactylic verse in English, given the language's monosyllabic weight, which "makes our verses unapt to slide." As concerns polysyllables, their "heaviness" makes few of them "willing to serve in place of a *Dactile*." Sowerby (2006), 65 (quoting Thomas Campion, *Observations on the Art of English Poesie*, 1602). See further G. D. Wilcock (1934), 6 (the late sixteenth-century ascendancy of the Elizabethan sonnet essentially brought hexametric verse-making to an end); and Robert Bridges, *Ibant Obscuri* (1916). See also John Thompson, *The Founding of English Meter* (New York: Columbia Univ. Press, 1961), 128–138; H. Gross, *Sound and Form in Modern Poetry* (Ann Arbor: Univ. of Michigan Press, 1964), 32–38; and C. O. Hartman, *Free Verse* (Princeton: Princeton Univ. Press, 1980), 33–39. For concerns amplifying those of the present chapter, see Martin, 5, 112–130, 143–158.
**"It is less . . . translation."** Lattimore (1951), 55.

448 *Arnold believed that*
**"If, as . . . present time."** Prins (2005), 231.

449 *But it was not the*
**But it was . . . arrangement.** Paraphrase from Nagy (1979/1999), 18.
**"manag[ing] . . . Heroic Age."** Nagy (1979/1999), 18 (speaking of epic's "amplitude and comprehensiveness"). And again, Homer speaks

> for the Athenian Empire—as far as Athenians in the fifth century BC were concerned. In that age, Homer was a classic, an Athenian classic, and Homer's poetry gave meaning not only to civilization in general but to the Athenian empire in particular. The Athenian version of Homer is shaped by the idea of a unified text of Homer, a Homeric Koine. This idea of a Homeric Koine, a text that is both 'common' and 'standard', matches the idea of a society that is both democratic and imperial. [Nagy (2009), 1–2]

*Through a slow but*
**adopted the Greek hexameter.** See pp. 268–269, 282.
**hexametrically conducive Greek.** I paraphrase C. B. Cayley, "Remarks and Experiments on English Hexameters" (1862), as quoted in Prins, to the effect that English was a language of "intermediate cadence" between Greek and Latin that had "'many words accented after the Greek model . . . and many, of course, after the Latin model.'" English, "being composite, could combine different accentual structures with some sense of duration in syllables," etc. Prins (2005), 239–240.

**Geoffrey of Monmouth . . . Aeneas.** See p. 648.
**Spenser . . . imperial image.** See pp. 289–292.
**"Oh, how blest . . . in verse."** Purcell, "Why, why are all the Muses mute?" Zimmerman, 343.

450 *Inspirited by Arnold's*
**"accommodate . . . elements."** Prins (2005), 239.

*The 1860s saw at least*
**The 1860s . . . in England.** And from 1860–1900 there appeared more than fifty British and American translations of Homer. See Prins (2005), 252, nn. 7, 8 (with bibliography).
***Cornhill Magazine* . . . 1866.** Sir John F. W. Herschel, *The Iliad of Homer Translated into English Accentuated Hexameters* (London and Cambridge: Macmillan, 1866).

451 *The year 1862 also saw*
**When Dart released . . .1865.** J. Henry Dart, *The Iliad of Homer in English Hexameter Verse* (London: Longman's, Green, 1865). Dart's inspiration, as he relates in his preface, was Charles Kingsley, "Andromeda" (1852), a lengthy poem in hexameters.
**"com[ing] out . . . dress."** Omond, 257.
**"We have hardly . . . blood."** Omond, 261.

452 *When judging translation*
**"What is . . . been predicted.** Arrowsmith (1952), 438.
**pedestrianize . . . recognition.** See pp. 490–491, 503.

453 *Smith/Miller creates*
**marvelously recreates . . . archaisms.** The opening of Dart's *Iliad,* by comparison—and however commendable—supports Arnold's dismissiveness:

> Sing, divine Muse, sing the implacable wrath of Achilleus!
> Heavy with death and with woe to the banded sons of Achaia!
> Many the souls of the mighty, the souls of redoubtable heroes,
> Hurried by it prematurely to Hades. The vultures and wild dogs
> Tore their tombless limbs. Yet thus did the will of the Highest
> Work to an end—from the day when strife drove madly asunder,
> Atreus' son, king of men; and the Godlike leader Achilleus.

454 *We pause for a moment*
**shading that they convey.** The slightness of particles is inversely proportionate to the exhaustiveness of their study. The seminal work (672 pages upon initial publication) is John Dewar Denniston, *The Greek Particles* (Oxford: Clarendon Press, 1934; 2nd ed., 1954), known in the trade as *Denniston's Particles.*

455 *Aye underscores that*
**depopulation . . . overburdened.** See further pp. 213, 216, 688.

457 *Another excerpt, again*
**Such was the . . . of corpses.** *Il.* 1.43–52.

458 *Dactylic hexameter was*
**"by reason of their . . . *Dactile.*"** Sowerby (2006), 65, quoting Renaissance poet and

musical composer Thomas Campion (1567–1620), *Observations on the Art of English Poesie,* in G. Gregory Smith, ed., *Elizabethan Critical Essays,* 2 Vols. (Oxford: Oxford Univ. Press, 1904), Vol. 1, 333. Roger Ascham (1515–1568), the leading Greek scholar of his day, had earlier professed that the predominance of monosyllables in English, most of them long, was ill suited to Heroic song, because dactylic rhythm is seldom found in English; that English sooner "stumbles than stands" upon its monosyllables; and further, that the iamb—as natural to English as the dactyl to Greek or Latin—was the appropriate vehicle for heroic song in English. Sowerby, 63–64, quoting Ascham, *The Scolemaster* (distinguishing *Carmen Exametrum* and *Carmen Iambicum*) in Smith, *supra,* Vol. 1, 30.

**"I know all . . . in itself."** Arnold, 210–211. I call particular attention to the following part of the quotation: "The hexameter . . . possesses a movement, an expression, which no metre hitherto in common use amongst us possesses, and which I am convinced English poetry, as our mental wants multiply, will not always be content to forego." Arnold falsely prophesied. Our mental wants have not multiplied but decreased, and we have all but given up the store. Arnold elsewhere elaborates on his hope for the development of a non-*Evangeline*-esque English hexameter, noting: "[We] turned to [the hexameter] because we required certain Homeric characteristics in a translation of Homer, and because all other rhythms seemed to find, from different causes, great difficulties in satisfying this our requirement." Arnold, 284–285.

**"it is to be . . . hexameter."** Arnold, 159–160.

460 *An epic poem in*

**"could . . . different measure."** Edward Wagenknecht, *Henry Wadsworth Longfellow, Portrait of an American Humanist* (New York: Oxford Univ. Press, 1966), 129.

**"It enables . . . Evangeline's ear."** Cecil B. Williams, *Henry Wadsworth Longfellow* (New York: Twain, 1964), 155. As for the sea's resounding in Evangeline's ear—and the sea's hexameter-like rhythm—one thinks of Pound's oft-cited preference for Gavin Douglas's Old Scots translation of the *Aeneid* to Virgil's original, "as Douglas had heard the sea." Pound (1937), 185. Longfellow was reading Homer while writing *Evangeline* and had earlier done a translation from the Swedish, using the same meter (151). Highly popular in its time, *Evangeline* was the most financially remunerative of all Longfellow's works. One thinks in this connection of Pope's *Iliad,* which secured its author a lavish income for life. For Longfellow as the first American translator of Dante, see p. 654.

461 *It is noteworthy that*

**"apparently . . . of criticism."** Full quotation and context at p. 109.

**Carne-Ross . . . worst of it.** See pp. 493–498.

*Smith/Miller's Iliad was*

**Smith/Miller . . . in its time.** Reviewer quotations in the following paragraphs from Blake, review of Smith and Miller, and *Time* (Books), "First Great War Book," 12/11/1944.

*Smith/Miller was further*

**"one . . . German Hellenism."** Steiner (1998, 3rd ed.), 272. And more: "The evolution of modern German is inseparable from the Luther Bible, from Voss's Homer, from the successive versions of Shakespeare by Wieland, Schlegel, and Tieck. Thus the theory of translation takes on an unprecedented authority and philosophic texture." Steiner (1998, 3rd ed.), 280. Because of German's far greater syntactic approximation to Greek, Voss attained a "Greek-Germanness" the counterpart of which was generally lacking in

English. See further Steiner, 280. For Voss within the context of a strong German hexametric tradition in both original and translated verse, see Ziolkowski (2000), 559–560. **similar regard and result.** Smith/Miller was published in 1944 by Macmillan. The dark-blue hardcover is adorned with a circular golden emblem displaying Zeus and his eagle; gold lettering on the spine. The text contains no lengthy discursive introduction, but begins after a sparing preface, a glossary of names, and a note on the illustrations by John Flaxman (1755–1826). Flaxman—English draftsman-sculptor extraordinaire and ornamental designer for Josiah Wedgwood—spent time during his early thirties in Rome, then in thrall to the great Winckelmann. Thus did one of the most gifted sculptors of English art come under the influence of the "Father of Art History," the two men towering figures of eighteenth-century Enlightenment. Thirty-nine full-page drawings, in all their simple beauty and art-historical resonance, grace and dignify the Smith/Miller *Iliad.* (Twenty-nine of those drawings had graced the 1943 Heritage Press publication of Pope's *Iliad.*) The drawings "multiply the enjoyment of this translation for the reader." Then there are the first-word capitalizations of every verse, a sign certain of poetry not yet in decline. In sum, and for all else the translation has of merit, it also has a classical *aesthetic.* It is of classical *moment,* in a way Homer since Pope has not and will never again be.

The understated "multiply the enjoyment" quotation is from a Memphis newspaper review by "P. F." My own secondhand copy of Smith/Miller concealed both the review and a handwritten letter addressed to "Dr. Miller" from one Alice Witherspoon, dated March 6, 1946. The volume, then, apparently once belonged to Miller. His former student Witherspoon extends condolences upon the passing of Miller's wife. Witherspoon concludes, "Allow me to add, the reading of the translation of your Iliad has been a real joy. It is truly imagistic. Through it all glows the great soul of the translator who masterfully, lovingly, and tenderly weighs and chooses his colorful words. I appreciate it keenly and thank you for it."

## Chapter 31

463 *The aforementioned*

**"The problem of . . . language."** Arrowsmith (1952), 440.
**"Against these . . . new ground."** Arrowsmith (1952), 443.

464 *The enthusiasm lasted*

**next flocking . . . Fitzgerald.** "The multiplicity of British and American Homers is near to bewildering. . . . What remains arresting, and not totally explicable, is the readiness of publishers to commission and print new 'Homers' on both sides of the Atlantic. Kitto follows immediately on Rieu, Robert Fitzgerald on Lattimore, Fagles on Fitzgerald, Mandelbaum on Fagles, Martin Hammond on Mandelbaum, etc." Steiner (2004), 372. Similarly, Steiner (1996), 104. The situation is no less pronounced with translations of the *Aeneid,* as noted above.
**Indeed, the first . . . Pope.** By contrast, Carne-Ross (1974)—peculiarly praising Pope as a foil to Fitzgerald—faults the latter for not producing a modern Popian version of the *Iliad.*
**praise . . . yet be mustered.** See Herington (1975), whose review is quoted without further page references.

465 *Herington, as seen, first*

**Lattimore adheres . . . "epidermis."** Definitions of *epidermis* and *dermis* from Merriam-Webster's Collegiate Dictionary (11th ed.), Frederick C. Mish, ed. (Springfield: Merriam-Webster, 2003).

**We sooner emphasize the.** Remainder of paragraph paraphrased and quoted from Beye (1975), 145.

*Herington, however, would*
**"poeticized" to misleading effect.** See, e.g., Lloyd-Jones (1991), 8: "Unlike Lattimore he [Fitzgerald] often rates the word of his own choice ahead of the word that translates the Greek. . . . He is a good deal less successful than Lattimore in making an impression like the impression made by Homer." Lloyd-Jones does not consider that this may reflect Fitzgerald's lack of Greek. Reviewers of Homeric or other classical translation seldom focus on translator familiarity with the original language. To do so would vitiate poet-translator license.

466 *Fitzgerald first translates*
**Paris leaps from . . . ranks.** See *Il.* 3.1–57.

*Di(ϝ)os rendered "in majesty"*
**prepares to play suppliant.** See *Il.* 24.299–301.

467 *As concerns the women*
**Prayers and Repentance.** *Il.* 9.505–507.
**abstraction . . . Homer's manner.** C. T. Lewis (reviewing William Cullen Bryant's *Iliad*, 1870) criticizes a comparably fanciful example in the Earl of Derby's *Iliad* (1864), which Lewis considers the best before Bryant's: "Homer says that Paeon 'was not made mortal,' but Lord Derby introduces an unpoetic personification, and tells us 'death on him was powerless.'" Lewis broadly criticizes the Earl of Derby's "offend[ing] so constantly in this way that he has given his pages a thoroughly modern tone. . . ." Lewis, 360.
**"They . . . *from fancifulness.*"** Arnold, 222.

*"Lord of nightmare, Death"*
**rêve . . . poids qui oppresse.** *Dictionnaire Génèral de la Langue Française*, Hatzfeld, Adolphe, et al., eds. (Paris: Librairie Delagrave, 5th ed., n.d.).

468 *Commending all (eleven)*
**formulae . . . variety of meanings.** The contextual "variety of meanings" in Stanley Lombardo's *Iliad* has likewise found an advocate: "Another remarkable feature of this 'Iliad' is its handling of stock epithets and phrases. Rather than rendering these exactly the same way every time they appear . . . Lombardo translates each in a slightly different way depending on context, vivifying what can be the poem's most deadening bits." Mendelsohn (1972). One cringes at the notion of "deadening bits." As others more telling note, "Noun-epithet formulae do not simply refer to a character. Rather, they invoke an epic theme, creating what we might call 'an epiphany.'" Kahane (quoting Bakker) suggests that an epithet is a "miniature-scale myth, a myth summoned to the narrative present of the performance," one needing "a proper (one would say 'ritual') environment for reenactment." Kahane, in Bakker and Kahane, eds., 114.
**"lacks the . . . pedant-translator."** Arrowsmith (1952), 440.

469 *There are other ways*
**"entire phrases . . . names."** My paragraph is indebted to C. T. Lewis, 355–356.

470 *This approach, however,*
**David Shive, in his *Naming*.** See David Shive, *Naming Achilles* (New York & Oxford:

Oxford Univ. Press, 1987), Preface.
**"Some in Homer's . . . reasons."** Shive, 37.

*We may end, as we*
**perfection, through his *Iliad*.** The perfection entailed the virtual avoidance of enjambment, resulting in a complete thought per couplet. For the opposite technique, see, e.g., Keats, *Endymion* (1818) ("A thing of beauty is a joy forever," etc.).
**not an isolated phenomenon.** See Robert Bagg, "Translating the Abyss: On Robert Fitzgerald's Odyssey" (1969), commending Fitzgerald for making "declarative something the Greek only implies" and otherwise praising the work based on the second-guessing of what an original audience would have liked in Homer's Greek. Bagg otherwise draws too clean a distinction between "literalist" scholars and poet-translators and, with no comment on the state of Fitzgerald's Greek, excessively credits Fitzgerald's "intuitive sense of the translator's responsibility." See esp. Bagg, 58–60.

CHAPTER 32

472 *(Epigraph)*
**"nothing could . . . translations."** Stephen MacKenna (1872–1934), the first (largely Greekless) translator into English of the philosopher Plotinus (3rd century AD), from a letter of April 1919 to his businessman-benefactor Ernest Debenham. *Journal and Letters of Stephen MacKenna*, Edited with a Memoir by E. R. Dodds (New York: William Morrow, n.d.), letter 9 (155); cf. letter 51 (241); letter 31 (194–195). In his journal entry of June 27, 1908 (126–127), MacKenna calls himself a "trifler" in languages and bemoans the inadequacy of his prose style (a complaint everywhere belied by his eloquence). His "trifling," if credited, is belied by a lifetime's single-mindedness, under exiguous circumstances, to Plotinus.

*Suggestive in ways of*
**"Suggestive . . . Pope's *Iliad*."** The far better analogy is that between Pope's *Iliad* and FitzGerald's *Rubáiyát*, not that between the latter and Pound's *Homage to Sextus Propertius*, as proposed by Sullivan (1961), 465, 467; (1964), 14–16. For one thing, Pope and FitzGerald display, each in his way, a beauty, efficiency, and comprehensibility that Pound could only dream of.
**"My translation . . . him."** Letter to E. B. Cowell, 9/3/1858, in W. A. Wright, ed., Vol. I, 346.
**"I suppose . . . stuffed Eagle."** Letter to E. B. Cowell, 4/27/1859, in W. A. Wright, ed., Vol. II, 5. FitzGerald also dwells on his translation method in the prefaces to his *Translations of Six Dramas by Calderón* (1853) and Aeschylus's *Agamemnon* (1869).
**Cowper, Pope's . . . competitor.** The reference is to *The Iliad of Homer, Translated into English Blank Verse by William Cowper* (1791). Undertaken by the most acclaimed poet of his day, Cowper's *Iliad* was the most significant translation since Pope's, earlier in the century. Cowper's preface offers a spirited rationale for his own effort vis-à-vis Pope's. Though consigned by his predecessor to obscurity, Cowper reads marvelously well, and is faithful to the original in a way Pope could never be (or want to be). Cowper is better than any number of contemporary translations of Homer, including those discussed herein. Here is Cowper's opening:

> Achilles sing, O Goddess! Peleus' son;
> His wrath pernicious, who ten thousand woes
> Caused to Achaia's host, sent many a soul
> Illustrious into Ades premature,

To dogs and all ravening fowls of prey,
When fierce dispute had separated once
The noble Chief Achilles from the son
of Atreus, Agamemnon, king of men.

[Cowper, *Iliad*; Southey, ed.]

and here Pope's:

*Achilles'* Wrath, to *Greece* the direful spring
Of woes unnumber'd, heav'nly Goddess, sing!
That Wrath which hurl'd to *Pluto*'s gloomy reign
The Souls of mighty Chiefs untimely slain;
Whose limbs unbury'd on the naked shore
Devouring dogs and hungry vultures tore:
Since Great *Achilles* and *Atrides* strove,
Such was the sov'reign doom, and such the will of *Jove*!

[Pope, *Iliad;* Shankman, ed.]

Cowper is arguably more "classic" than Pope. Known in its own age, Pope's language becomes less familiar to each succeeding generation. Cowper's language, by contrast, exemplifies Sainte-Beuve's notion of a "true classic": written "in no matter what form, only provided it be broad and great, refined and sensible, sane and beautiful in itself; has spoken to all in peculiar style, a style which is found to be also that of the whole world, a style new without neologism, new and old, easily contemporary with all time." Sainte-Beuve (E. Lee, tr.), 124. To this may be compared a telling (and often quoted) observation concerning the composer Ralph Vaughan Williams (1872–1958): "The work is wonderful because it seems to lift one into some unknown region of musical thought and feeling. Throughout its course one is never quite sure whether one is listening to something very old or very new. . . . it cannot be assigned to a time or a school but is full of the visions which have haunted the seers of all times" (the word *seers* especially apropos, the seer knowing past, present, and future; see *Il.* 1.70). J. A. Fuller Maitland, "Three Choirs Festival," *Times* (London), 9/7/1910 (reviewing the premiere of *Fantasy on a Theme by Thomas Tallis*).

Cowper wrote equally well (and prodigiously) in rhyming couplets, among other verse forms. His blank verse was criticized as too much under Milton's spell. There are worse failings.

**"I am persuaded . . . Parody."** Letter to J. R. Lowell, 12/22/1878, in W. A. Wright, ed., Vol. II, 262.

**"What . . . translation of him."** Santayana (1896), 129.

**"of the two . . . than frigidity."** Pope, Preface, 16.

473 *Condensed, and offering*

**"how much . . . of sorrow."** Benson, 97.

**"coloured . . . appear possible."** FitzGerald (n.d.), 12 (from the Biographical Preface by M.K.)

474 *A translator of Greek*

**"Our contact . . . Rubaiyat."** Pound (1937), 186.

**Chapman . . . prodigal liberties.** "In Chapman's . . . *Iliad,* English is spendthrift, inebriate with waste motion, at times precocious and as yet uncertain of its coruscating force. . . . Homer, as Chapman construes and misconstrues him, makes the English language know itself and impels it to cast its lexical-grammatical net over a thronging prodigality of life." Steiner (1996), 95. Chapman (as Pope) will ever be subject to mixed reviews, e.g., "Chapman's version has golden qualities as an English poem which no other poem does or even can possess, but it is not the best translation. On the contrary, considered strictly and solely as translation, it is probably almost the worst. As a 'notable' translation, however, it perhaps takes precedence of every other book in the whole of this bibliography. . . ." F. Smith, 16–17. Much the same might perhaps be said of Christopher Logue's *Iliad*; see Chapter 33. For similarly mixed reviews of Dryden and Pope, see F. Smith, 33–37.

*What did Pope think*
**What did Pope . . . predecessor.** The following quotations are from Pope, Preface, 19.
**"Chapman remains . . . *something*."** Pound, "Early Translators of Homer," in Eliot, ed. (1918), 249–251. See also Pound on the difficulty of proceeding with Chapman: "You plunge into adjectival magnificence and get stuck. You have two or more pages of admiration, and then wait to regather your energies, or acquire a definite impression of Chapman's language. And very little of Ilion [i.e., Troy]." Pound, "Hell," in Eliot, ed. (1918), 207.

475 *Pope further notes*
**"The nature . . . in poetry."** Pope, Preface, 19.

476 *Edward FitzGerald, like*
**Pope . . . (the heroic couplet).** The sobriquet "Heroic Couplet" aside, it was early noted that the iamb (⏑ /), being as natural to English as is the dactyl (— ⏑⏑) to Greek or Latin, is the appropriate vehicle for heroic song in English. See Sowerby, 63–64.
**"seems to lift . . . progression."** Benson, 101.
**successions of "Grave and Gay."** The effectiveness of this rhyme scheme may be gauged against the "abcb" scheme of adventurer-Orientalist Richard Burton (1821–1890) in his *Kasîdah* (*Testament*). Though offered as a translation, the *Kasîdah* is in fact an original work and, though written independently of FitzGerald's *Rubáiyát*, resembles it in content, tone, and format:

> The light of morn has grown to noon,
> Has paled with eve, and now farewell!
> Go, vanish from my life as dies
> The tinkling of a Camel's bell. (I. 17)

The sense of each quatrain is here more open-ended, the rise and fall less apparent, the melancholy less pronounced; there is less a "vague outline of the soul's progression" than a statement of its present condition. As a sustained effort, however, running many quatrains beyond the *Rubáiyát*, it is unparalleled.

Burton's *Kasîdah* is the only poetical work of its kind in English. It is not a creative translation or adaptation like FitzGerald's *Rubáiyát*, but an entirely original creation. Burton was inspired to the task years before perusing Omar's quatrains in either Persian or English. See *The Kasîdah of Hâjî Abdû El-Yezdî*, Translated and Annotated by His Friend and Pupil Sir Richard Burton, Introduction by Dhan Gopal Murkerji, Illustrated by Willy Pogany (New York: David McKay, 1931). Burton was a prodigious polyglot and translator of exotic languages, as well as a published ethnographer and sexologist. See Fawn M. Brodie, *The Devil Drives: A Life of Sir Richard Burton* (New York: W. W. Norton, 1967); and Dane Kennedy, *The Highly Civilized Man: Richard Burton and the Victorian World* (Cambridge: Harvard Univ. Press, 2005).

*Pope's couplets, like*
**George Steiner . . . *confirming*.** For discussion of this and the following two quotations,

see Steiner (1996), 96–97.
**"That speed . . . your Lord."** Steiner (1996), 136.
**"concision . . . modern prose."** Steiner (1996), 137.
**the best . . . in paragraphs.** Sowerby (2006), 145.
**Homeric . . . self-containment.** Classicist Geoffrey Kirk has observed that the Homeric hexameter "tends to be more or less self-contained in meaning; its ending usually coincides with a major or minor pause, the end of a sentence or clause or at least the point at which a predicate is divided from its subject." Kirk, 60.
**"Monarch awake! . . . *Jove.*"** Pope, *Iliad*, 2.31–42 (Shankman, ed.).
**If Pope's . . . Homer's speed.** Arnold concedes rapidity to Pope, but one "not of the same sort as Homer's rapidity." He further allows that "Pope's translation of the Iliad is more Homeric than Cowper's, for it is more rapid." Pope otherwise "renders [Homer] ill because he is artificial both in his style and in his words." Arnold, 153, 200.
**"most rapid . . . imaginable."** Pope, Preface, 10.
**Pope's . . . rhyming couplet.** Shankman (1983), 133.

477 *Or, because Pope*
**Pope supremely . . . invented.** Paraphrase of Manguel, 134.
**even as . . . himself labored.** Paraphrase of Beye (1975), 149.
**"By perpetual . . . at his call."** Manguel, 134, quoting Johnson, *Lives*, Vol. 3, 219. Johnson intended much the same by noting, in his detailed comparison of Dryden and Pope, that "Pope contains his mind to his own rules of composition." Johnson, *Lives*, Vol. 3, 222.
**"Translators . . . put together."** See "Conversations with Lord Byron," by Lady Blessington, in *The New Monthly Magazine and Literary Journal*, 37.146 (1833), 217; later published as Marguerite Gardiner, *Journal of Correspondence Between Lord Byron and the Countess of Blessington* (Cincinnati: Lorenzo Sratton, 1851), 133. The view, despite Byron's authority, has carried little weight. Lady Blessington herself footnotes the comment as follows: "This was indeed carrying his [Byron's] admiration of Pope to an extreme. It is impossible to conceive anything more foreign not only from Homer, but from the spirit of all Greek poetry, than Pope's translation—in fact, it has the air of an imitation from a French paraphrase!" We have already noted Arnold's disfavor, and Bentley's pithy dispatch. Though considering the heroic couplet "now too much derided," Santayana notes that "its compactness and inevitableness make it excellent for epigram and adequate for Satire, but its perpetual snap and unvarying rhythm are thin for epic, and impossible for song." Santayana (1896), 83. This is a thin view of the matter, given the combined epic-translational achievement of Dryden and Pope (neither of whom Santayana expressly mentions), and the heroic couplet's extensive epistolary service.
**"the main . . . poetic diction."** Samuel Taylor Coleridge, *Biographia Literaria* (London: George Bell and Sons, 1905), 19.

478 *Samuel Johnson deemed*
**"noblest version . . . ever seen."** Johnson, *Lives*, Vol. 3, 119.
**"give[s] the . . . great poetry."** Higham & Bowra, xxxv.
**"cultivated our . . . to posterity."** Johnson, *Lives*, Vol. 3, 238.

*The decline to come was*
**"Not . . . impossible task."** Shankman (1983), 163–164. It is with these words that Shankman recaps the argument of his Pope's *Iliad*: *Homer in the Age of Passion* (1983).

CHAPTER 33

481 *Nowhere noting the*

**inseparable from . . . of all.** Arnold identifies, and repeatedly returns to, four qualities the translator of Homer must convey. His initial formulation provides that Homer "is eminently rapid; that he is eminently plain and direct, both in the evolution of his thought and in the expression of it, that is, both in his syntax and in his words; that he is eminently plain and direct in the substance of his thought, that is, in his matter and ideas; and, finally, that he is eminently noble." Arnold (1861, 1883), 149. Nobility being "of all others the most impalpable, the most irreducible to rule" (Arnold, 225), Arnold essentially concludes that it is known when seen by one of requisite sensibility. Arnold (1861, 1883), 225. Alternatively, it is the sum of Homer's other eminent qualities. "Eminent nobility," moreover, has its gradations, as the narrative rises and falls in the manner of any sustained work of art, each grade exhibiting the requisite level. Failing to convey one or more of these qualities, all translators of Homer, in Arnold's view, have failed, including Chapman ("the mist of the fancifulness of the Elizabethan age, entirely alien to the plain directness of Homer's thought and feeling"), and Pope ("mist of Pope's literary artificial manner, entirely alien to the plain naturalness of Homer's manner"). Arnold (1861, 1883), 150, 200.

For serviceable discussion of Arnold's "four outstanding qualities of Homeric verse," see Lillian E. Doherty, "On Teaching Homer from Translations," *Classical Journal*, 81.2 (1985–1986), 161–166.

**"We . . . poem's movement."** Arrowsmith, 434–435 (also containing insightful qualification of the four essential qualities that Arnold finds in Homer). Speed appears to be the principal virtue of the epithet-omitting *Iliad* of David Reck (1994), but at the cost of "nobility." See Rachel Hadas, "Reader's Notebook: New Iliads," review of Reck, Fagles, and others, *New England Review*, 18.3 (1977), 160–172.

*As concerns the state*

**admissions against interest.** See interview of Robert Fitzgerald by Edwin Honig. *Poets.org.* Academy of American Poets. n.d. Web. 2/18/2013.

**exceptions to every rule.** So also Keats who, though "the most Homeric of modern men could not read Homer." Lang, 80.

**than full command of Greek.** For the scholarly assistance on which Pope relied, see Simonsuuri, 58 and n. 3.

**"Homer . . . 'so well expressed.'"** Simonsuuri, 58.

**"were either . . . intentions."** Simonsuuri, 59.

**Pope's time . . . Greek originals.** Green, 188.

**"the tasteful . . . known theme."** Simonsuuri, 59.

482 *The point is made*

**"You I follow . . . imitation."** *DRN* 3.3–7.

**'quickening power of mind.'** Preface, 4.

**"a quickening power . . . firsts."** *DRN* 3.1–2 (*qui primus*).

*Of Robert Fagles's*

**"men sooner . . . as newest."** *Od.* 1.351–352; see p. 358.

**"Translators . . . of their own."** Lang, 88. Fagles, moreover, as others before him in both epic and lyric, translates "the/a god" as "god": "Nine days the arrows of god swept through the army" (*Il.* 1.53; Fagles, 1.61). The god is here Apollo, and the needed translation: "the arrows of *the* god." And if "god," why not uppercase? The word *God* raises misleading Judeo-Christian associations.

**more discerning among them.** See, e.g., Willett (1997–1998), 203, reviewing Fagles's *Odyssey:* "He avoids both accentual meter and strict stress meter while larding his verse with the wildest range of colloquial American English to be found in any translation of the *Odyssey.* The consequences have been fatal for his version, which makes no advance over earlier ones and in many cases executes some notable retreats. . . . Against the massive adulation lavished on the work, a little reality is in order."

483 *The state of Fagles's*

**several interviews . . . granted.** The following interview quotations and attributions are from (1) *Online NewsHour* (3/3/1997): "Immortal Tale: The *Odyssey*—the Fagles Translation," by Elizabeth Farnsworth; (2) *Paris Review* 151 (1999): "Robert Fagles, The Art of Translation, No. 2," by Edwin Frank and Andrew McCord; and (3) *New York Times* (4/13/2004): "A Bridge Between the Classics and the Masses," by Chris Hedges.

*In one startling*

**Knox wrote . . . introductions.** Knox, 11–12.
**"lend . . . a modern reader."** Fagles (1990), xi.
**"the big reach . . . discourse."** Fagles (1990), xi.

484 *C. S. Lewis, in a*

**"express[ed] . . . own day."** From a lecture delivered August 7, 1958, to the Annual Conference of the Classical Association. The text of the lecture, while not surviving, was largely conveyed in the *Times,* as paraphrased by Lewis's biographers and reproduced in part herein. See Reyes, 15–16.

*Especially peculiar*

**fawning adulation of Knox.** Fagles, *Iliad,* Preface, xi–xii.
***Tantae molis erat. . . .*** Tantae molis erat Romanam condere gentem 'So great was the task of founding the Roman people' (*Aen.* 1.33).

485 *What we thus witness*

**Lattimore . . . Greek drama.** See pp. 113, 121, 490–491, 493, 569.
**"rigorously . . . scholar."** Bowersock (2007).
**"In translating . . . text."** Bowersock (2007).
**formalist . . . Daryl Hine.** For an excellent appreciation, see "A Neglected Master in Our Midst: Bill Coyle on Daryl Hine," *Contemporary Poetry Review,* 12/19/2011.

486 *The fifty-four translators*

**"Time and again . . . waters."** McGrath (2011).

488 *For Wagner, surveying*

**the . . . 'total work of art'.** My paragraph is in part indebted to the summary of Wagner's theory of opera (*Opera und Drama*), in Bryan McGee, *Aspects of Wagner* (Oxford: Oxford Univ. Press, 1968, 1988), 5–7. The notion of a "total work of art" would assume pernicious dimensions in the totalitarian impulse to mold, unify, and control all aspects of life. "Projects concocted in small avant-garde journals could suddenly be applied on the scale of an entire country." See Todorov, 3–9, 17–20, 25, 48.

*Greek tragedy in New Translations*

**"In spite . . . classical scholar."** *C. S. Lewis, Collected Letters,* etc. Vol. III, 967–968, and 968, n. 136 (Letter, 8/29/1968, to Arthur Conan Doyle scholar and C. S. Lewis biographer, Roger Lancelyn Green).

*C. S. Lewis was here*
**"A translation . . . original."** C. Day Lewis, tr., *The Aeneid of Virgil* (Garden City: Doubleday, 1952), 7. For a belabored defense of C. Day Lewis's technique, see Patrick Cheney, "C. Day Lewis's Translation of Virgil's *Aeneid*: 'A Living Contemporary Language,'" *Comparative Literature Studies*, 20.4 (1983), 435–445.

489 *Similarly revealing are*
**"I wish you . . . as our own."** *C. S. Lewis, Collected Letters*, Vol. 3, 648–650 (as quoted in Reyes).
**"The poetical . . . the muck."** *C. S. Lewis, Collected Letters*, Vol. 3, 416–417 (as quoted in Reyes) (Letter, 1/25/1954, to English poet and critic Herbert Palmer). The references to Virgil and Sophocles are, again, to C. Day Lewis, *Aeneid* (1952) and Edward Fairchild Watling, *Antigone* (1954).

*In something the obverse*
**Lewis . . . *ne quid detrimenti.*** *Ne quid detrimenti* 'lest anything of harm', i.e., *ne quid res publica detrimenti caperet* 'lest the Republic suffer any harm'. The words are from the Roman historian Sallust (86–35 BC), author of *Bellum Catilinae* (*The War with Catiline*). In the original context (Chapter 29), the Roman Senate votes to empower the consuls in an emergency situation "lest the Republic suffer any harm." The Emperor Augustus, *Res Gestae* (*Accomplishments*) §1, similarly explains that he acted *res publica ne quid detrementi caperet.* Mindful of the present threat to the Republic of Letters, C. S. Lewis would have Murray thus empowered.

490 *For their desecration*
**"In the past . . . superficial."** Oliver Taplin, "Tragedy in Translation," review of Arrowsmith, etc., *Classical Review*, n.s. 26.2 (1976), 168–170.
**"a major . . . American poetry."** Kenneth Rexroth, review of Richmond Lattimore and David Grene, *The Complete Greek Tragedies*, in *The Nation*, 12/12/1959, reprinted in Rexroth, "Greek Tragedy in Translation" (in *With Eye and Ear*), 141–144.

491 *Just when one thought*
**"providing neither . . . event."** See Mendelsohn, "Brush Up Your Aeschylus" (1998); remainder of paragraph quotations from Mendelsohn *passim.*
**The series was . . . deemed.** Descriptions paraphrased from Mendelsohn (1998).
**"dismaying lack . . . belief."** Adrian Poole, review of "Aeschylus, 1: The Oresteia by David R. Slavitt" (and other volumes of the *Penn Greek Drama Series*), *Translation and Literature*, 8.1 (1999), 60–61.

*We are not surprised*
**"deceptively neat . . . readers."** Poole (above), 61.
**omnivore David R. Slavitt.** David R. Slavitt (b. 1935) is the wildly successful and generally adored author of more than one hundred books, including novels, poetry volumes, and translations. With little or no training in classics (M.A. in English, Columbia), his translated works—Barnstone-like and better—include numerous Greek and Latin authors, some inhabiting the obscurest reaches of the inventory. Modern European authors aside, his translations also include the Hebrew books of Lamentations, Psalms, and the Twelve Prophets, and most recently—even in its abridged immensity—the Sanskrit *Mahabharata* (Evanston: Northwestern Univ. Press, 2015). The most prestigious university presses compete to publish him, while reviewers and prize-committees stand generally enthralled. One supposes there is no arguing with success.

More than Willis Barnstone—though with equal abandon and desultory grasp of his originals—Slavitt seems intent on translating *everything*. "I learned Greek," says Slavitt, "on the train on the way to New York to go to screenings. It was a way of maintaining my self-respect. What grown-up gets up in the morning, shaves, brushes his teeth, and goes off to see an Annette Funicello movie?" "David R. Slavitt, The Per Contra Interview by Miriam N. Kotzin," www.percontra.net/archive/20slavittinterview.htm (n.d.). In the words of one reviewer, Slavitt "often seems to forget all about the Latin in his haste to scribble over the text with slavittries." Willett (2002), 397. For his *Eclogues*, Slavitt is faulted for "evading any extensive translation" and *thoroughly* simplifying and vulgarizing Virgil's original. Philip Murray, "The *Eclogues* of Virgil by David R. Slavitt," *Poetry*, 120.5 (1972), 304–306. More critical yet is Lee Fratantuono, reviewing Slavitt's *De Rerum Natura*. In a list of over one hundred gaffes and deficiencies, Fratantuono systematically "sample[s] only some of the numerous problems." *Bryn Mawr Classical Review*, www.bmcr.brynmawr.edu/2008/2008-12-41.html. In his Propertius, Slavitt is cited for "baggy versification, never-ending slang and rampant invention"; for needlessly "obscure vocabulary"; for "howlers" reflecting an "ingrained lack of respect for the text." Willett (2002). Not one for understatement, Willett begins as follows: "In a long career of defacing Greek and Latin poetry with the graffiti he likes to pretend are translations, David R. Slavitt has finally turned to Propertius and vandalized him so effectively that the poet lies invisible beneath the smear." His lifelong imposture notwithstanding, there is no classicist Slavitt, only classic Slavitt—by Tiber's bank forty years ago and the Gangetic Plain today.

As concerns the latter, Slavitt's inelegantly produced 577-page *Mahabharata* contains a two-page translator's preface, followed by the series editor's two and one-half page introduction. Not a single explanatory note accompanies this highly exotic work, nor a single page of back matter. (One may compare classicist Peter Green's 2015 translation of the *Iliad*, with bottom and endnotes both.) The front matter, though brief, suffices to confuse. The cover reads, "adapted and edited by David R. Slavitt," while the introduction speaks, similarly, of Slavitt's "retelling" or "retelling and editing." And yet, Slavitt offers a translator's preface, and the title page grants him an "English translation and preface copyright." Tellingly enough, Slavitt says, "I should probably explain that my adaptation of this work is not a translation directly from the Sanskrit (which I am not competent to undertake) but rather a recasting of Ganguli's [prose] version." Yes, probably *should*. We have earlier encountered translator avowals of ignorance (see pp. 12–13, 89–91, 706).

What we have, then, is Slavitt's poeticization of a prose translation, the prose "leav[ing] altogether too much to the reader's literary imagination." After all, "a poem wants to be 'Poetry,'" says Slavitt, "which is to say, in a form that presents itself to the reader as entailing some minimal degree of linguistic activity beyond the basics of exposition and description." True to form, and within a maximum page-count, Slavitt offers up his minimum. "I just wanted to suggest the feel of chanting and produce a text that doesn't just plod along but dances, at least a bit." Drivel.

*Accordingly, the flaw*
**"The whole . . . altogether."** Benson, 123.

492 *More recently, and in a*
**"deliberately archaic . . . phraseology."** For concise treatment of the method and significance of archaism in the King James Bible, see Steiner (1998, 3rd ed.), 366–367. He notes that "this 'ingestion' and transmutation [through archaism] of Hebrew, Greek, and Latin sources into English sensibility, where it continues to play a part more immediate than that of Scripture in any other European community, more linguistically central and theologically diffuse, would not have occurred had the [KJB] scholars and

editors . . . laboured to be modern. It was by looking back that they justified the proud definition contained in the preface: 'Translation it is that openeth the window, to let in the light; that breaketh the shell, that we may eat the kernel.'"
**"through a glass darkly" becomes.** 1 Cor. 13. The phrase has been frequently adopted or adapted for film, television, music, and literature. See also Royal Skousen, "Through a Glass Darkly: Trying to Understand Scriptures," *Brigham Young Univ. Studies*, 26.4 (1986), 3–20.

*There is mystery in*
**speaks rapidly . . . words.** For the contrast between Menelaus and Odysseus, see *Il.* 3.205–224.
**Ajax, Odysseus . . . Achilles.** *Il.* 9.338–444 and pp. 609, 626–627.
**"whose head . . . unavailing."** *Il.* 2.212–214.

493 *A fawning review of*
***Classics and Translation* (2010).** Reviewed by John Talbot (2011), further cited herein without page numbers.

495 *Such may have been*
**"the shared cultural . . . culture."** Wills, review of Sherod Santos (2005).

*Wills further observes*
**"Chapman . . . of their time."** Wills, review of Sherod Santos (2005).

497 *Even as Carne-Ross is*
**"I had another . . . Virgil."** See review and interview by Judith Moore, "The Georgics of Virgil: Bilingual Edition" (A Translation and Introduction by David Ferry), *San Diego Reader*, 7/28/2005.
**"It comes from . . . farm."** For the etymology of *Georgics*, see p. 646.
**garnered broad acclaim.** Rosanna Warren notes that in David Ferry, "Horace has found . . . a single voice for our time." She explains by noting that "Ferry's ear is as finely tuned to English as Horace's to Latin." That Ferry's ear, by his own admission, is stone deaf to Latin, is apparently irrelevant. Warren makes no reference to Ferry's Latinless estate nor to his coaching by Carne-Ross and others. She thus creates a misleading picture of Ferry as a Latinist doing yeoman's work. See Rosanna Warren, "A Symposium on Translation," *The Threepenny Review*, 70 (summer, 1970), 15. Warren elsewhere mounts a spirited defense of the Greekless Sherod Santos. See p. 600.

499 *Carne-Ross's final word*
**Carne-Ross's final word.** The quotations below conclude Carne-Ross's *Classics and Translation* (2010).
**"I ruined . . . wrote Latin."** Letter to Iris Barry, 7/?/1916; Paige, 87.

*Finally, there is Professor*
**discreditable partisanship.** As in the case of Carne-Ross's review of David Ferry's *Horace* (see p. 600).
**"Pope is . . . translator."** Lang, 90.
**"idiom . . . are poetic."** Steiner (1966), 26.

500 *If Logue's Homer is*
**own review of Logue.** See Wills (1992).

*For a sense of what*
**"thrilling . . . art of verse."** Jim Lewis, "24-Hour War: Is Christopher Logue a Genius or a Madman?" *Slate.* www.slate.com/id/2082824. Web. 5/13/2003.
**Logue is the Jeff Koons.** The most recent Logue-like roughhousing of Homer is Alice Oswald, *Memorial: A Version of Homer's Iliad* (New York and London: W. W. Norton, 2011). The work skims the cream of Homer, "doing" the similes alone in its eighty-one-page plenitude (much in a Poundian "imagist" manner). On Jeff Koons, see Jed Perl, "The Cult of Jeff Koons," *New York Review of Books,* 9/25/2014. Writing on the occasion of the Jeff Koons retrospective (New York, Paris, and Bilbao, 2014–2015), Perl is the last word—wonderfully nasty and immanently quotable—on Koons as the sum of everything vacuous, debased, and fraudulent in today's art world.

501 *Little more may be*
**Lombardo's . . . "Yo, Achilles."** Mendelsohn concludes, or perhaps protests: "Still, the success of so many of Lombardo's choices more than makes up for the false notes."

*The twentieth century's*
**"wanted to know . . . instance."** M. Reynolds, 231. For a similarly commendatory treatment of Logue, see Emily Greenwood, "Logue's Tele-Vision: Reading Homer from a Distance," in Graziosi and Greenwood, eds., 145–176.

*What so distresses about*
**"the proper . . . and matter."** For the quoted definitions of decorum in this paragraph, see Sowerby (2006), 28, 30, and 128. See also V. Cox, noting in the ideal of linguistic decorum "powerful moral and social implications" (56); and compare Dante's rebuke of the "vile jargon" of the Romans of his day, which he relates to the "ugliness of their manners." See Botterill, 27. Linguistic decorum is an ingredient of civility, for Dante no less than for ourselves.

503 *Wills finally notes,*
**The same excuse . . . *Aeneid.*** "Finally, since [C. Day Lewis's] translation was made for broadcasting over the British radio, it can be read aloud more successfully than it can be read silently. In other words, it is a translation for the ear, not the eye, a distinct rarity in an eye-minded age." Lind (1962), xxii. For all his judiciousness elsewhere, Lind here makes a virtue of necessity. The dichotomy he proposes was unknown to Virgil. Though C. Day Lewis's *Aeneid* was a bestseller in its time, one would by now have thought it dead letter. However, the most recent translation of the *Iliad,* by Peter Green, resurrects it, with praise of its "declaimable" quality. Green, as other enthusiasts, glosses the absurdity of Lewis's tone and diction: "The result made for far less boring rhythms, and even a certain verbal springiness." Green (2015), 21–22.

*Of such "freedoms"*
**"reproduces . . . exclude them."** Carne-Ross, review of Fitzgerald (1974).

504 *George Steiner for his*
**"ferocious . . . anyone's guess."** Steiner (1966), 34.

505 *Moving from one travesty*
**"This book . . . classic work."** *The Iliad and Odyssey of Homer* (Radford: Wilder Publications, 2007).
**Western culture . . . source.** The same vilification is apparent in recent efforts by the College Board (in its AP History exam) to "abandon a rigorous insistence on content"

toward downplaying "American citizenship and American world leadership in favor of a more global and transnational perspective." See Michelle Malkin, "The drive to take 'America' out of US history," *New York Post*, 6/3/2015.
**"Triggers are . . . understand."** As quoted in Jennifer Medina, "Warning: The Literary Canon Could Make Students Squirm," *New York Times*, 5/17/2014; cf. Colleen Flaherty, "Trigger Happy," *Inside Higher Ed*, 4/14/2014.
**"safe space" to "recuperate."** See Judith Shulevitz, "In College and Hiding From Scary Ideas," *New York Times* (Sunday Review), 3/22/2015. See also "Campus 'Safe Spaces': Readers discuss whether colleges should be protecting students from distressing ideas," *New York Times* (Letters), 3/29/2015. The next day, the *Times* printed Alexandra Alter, "Grown-Ups Get Out their Crayons and Make Coloring Book a Best Seller," *New York Times* (Business Day), 3/30/2015. The piece makes the follow-up case for coloring books and Play-Doh as antidote, not necessarily to distressing ideas, but to screen stress in a computerized age. Distressing, to be sure.

CHAPTER 34

507 *As Logue was an*
**Roman elegiac poet Propertius.** Elegiac meter alternates between lines of dactylic hexameter and dactylic pentameter. See pp. 234–235. The most accessible introduction to Propertius—and the first book-length study in English—is Margaret Hubble, *Propertius* (London: Duckworth, 1974). See also Steele Commager, *A Prolegomenon to Propertius* (Norman: University of Oklahoma Press, 1974).
**would "liberate" Propertius.** Bettini, 70.
**"in reality . . . being modern."** Bettini, 73.
**"make everyone . . . modern."** Bettini, 74.

508 *Indeed, the twentieth-century*
**Fraser . . . adduces Catullus's.** See Fraser, 31–32, and for the discussion that follows, Howe, 23, 27.
**"The value . . . as we have."** Letter to Iris Barry, 7/27/1916; Paige, 90.
**"comment by juxtaposition."** Schlauch, 263.
**"uses both . . . latter 1930's."** Schlauch, 263.

509 *Propertius needed no remake.*
**Mackail had rhapsodized.** Quotations from Mackail (1895), 124–126, 131 (emphases added).

*In an article entitled*
**"The Roman is . . . youth."** Nitchie, 207.
**"Romantics are . . . uses."** Nitchie, 216.
**the analogy he perceived.** ". . . I may perhaps avoid charges of further mystification and wilful obscurity by saying that [the *Homage*] represents certain emotions as vital to me in 1917, faced with the infinite and ineffable imbecility of the British Empire, as they were to Propertius some centuries earlier, when faced with the infinite and ineffable imbecility of the Roman Empire. These emotions are defined largely, but not entirely, in Propertius's own terms." Letter to the editor, *English Journal*, 1/14/1931; Paige, 231.
**"Among our . . . romantic."** Nitchie, 218–219 (referencing *Poetry*, XIII, 291–299).

510 *In the years immediately*
**"an amatory . . . his time."** Kirby Flower Smith, "Propertius: A Modern in the Augustan Age," *The Sewanee Review*, 25.1 (1917), 20–39. Smith died in 1918, foreclosing a

response to *Homage* (1919). An appreciation of Smith, with special attention to Smith's appreciation of Propertius, appears in G. J. Laing, "IN MEMORIAM: Kirby Flower Smith. 1862–1918," *Classical Journal*, 14.9 (1919), 567–569.
**"is one of the . . . temper."** Kenneth Rexroth, "On Translating Roman Verse" (in *With Eye and Ear*), 146.
**published in 1795 as *Elegien*.** Goethe's *Elegies*, inspired by Karl Ludwig von Knebel's translation of Propertius, was handsomely translated into English by L. R. Lind, *Johann Wolfgang von Goethe's Roman Elegies and Venetian Epigrams. A Bilingual Edition* (Lawrence and Manhattan: Univ. Press of Arkansas, 1974).
**modern . . . Pound's doings.** See, e.g., James Gardner, "Propertius, our contemporary," review of W. G. Shepherd, tr., *Propertius: The Poems*, *The New Criterion*, 4.10 (1986), 73–77.

511 *The Classics' perennial*
**"was riding . . . as troubled."** Barnard, 95.
**"Lucretius . . . ancient poets."** H. St. H. Vertue, "Lucretius, the Poet of Our Time," *Greece & Rome*, 17.50 (1948), 49–64 (opening sentence).
**"modern . . . sincere sorrow."** Lind (1963), x. In his introduction to *Latin Poetry in Verse Translation* (1957), Lind makes a broader case for the modern in Latin poetry—Catullus, Lucretius, Ovid, Juvenal, Silver Latin—and what attracts modern poets to it. The free rein he gives languageless adapters is later tempered in his "On 'Modern' Translation" (1983).
**"And what . . . experience."** Arnold (1868–1869), 306.
**"I am tired . . . violence."** Dorothy Wellesley, ed., *Letters on Poetry from W. B. Yeats to Dorothy Wellesley* (London and New York: Oxford Univ. Press, 1940), 25.

*Says political philosopher*
**"We have . . . truly modern."** Manent, 48. The desire to be modern, while "guid[ing] the entire life of Western societies," has its darker unwieldy underside in anti-Western tendencies, including fascism, as seen, and communism. In the latter instance, Czech-born author Milan Kundera (who has lived in Paris since 1975; naturalized French citizen, 1981; considers himself French) notes that the compulsive wish for newness and the need to be modern lie at the heart of communism, and further, that "the desire to be modern is an archetype, that is, an irrational imperative, anchored deeply within us, a persistent form whose content is changeable and indeterminate: what is modern is what declares itself modern and is accepted as such." Milan Kundera, *The Art of the Novel*, Linda Asher, tr. (New York: Grove Press, 1986), 141.
**synchronic versus diachronic.** See pp. 197–199, 512, 604, 616–617.
**"some famous modern poets."** In the generation that followed, Dryden's contemporaries endorsed what might be called a moderate modernism, "the best of the moderns [being] only the most able imitators of antiquity." Levine, 37–38. See generally Levine, Ch. 3 ("Dryden and the Moderns"), Ch. 4 ("Dryden and the Ancients"), and Ch 5. ("Dryden and the Battle of the Books").
**progressive transformation.** On progressivism in the arts, see pp. 15–18, 342–345.
**nebulous postmodernism.** American art critic and essayist Hilton Kramer (1928–2012) has, in typically trenchant fashion, described postmodernism as "nothing but a mindset of deconstructive attitudes in search of a mission," "modernism gone rancid," a "nihilistic imperative" (Kramer, 40–41); also, "a revolt against the basic traditions of Western civilization." *NYT* obit., 3/27/2012.

512 *We note in this*
**lead article . . . new series.** Peter G. Snyder, "Homer's Apocalypse," *Arion*, n.s. 1 (1973), 67.

**"The logical . . . Pope's.** Lind (1983), 71.
**"so genuine . . . the original."** As concerns this assessment, that Fitzgerald was "so genuine a recreation and yet so faithful to the original," I have endeavored to show precisely the opposite: that "Fitzgerald's importations are insufficient to be transformative, yet sufficient to mislead." See pp. 470–471. Also exalting Fitzgerald above his Greek original is Bagg (1969).

513 *We return to Propertius.*
**present a living figure.** Paraphrase from Letter to A. R. Orage, 4/?/1919; Paige, 148–149.

*Propertius, to the mind*
**"cabalistic type of poetry."** Gilbert Highet (2010), 84, 86, 88 (1st pub. 1957).

514 *Pound converted that which*
**"willful strangeness."** Vincent Katz, tr., *The Complete Elegies of Sextus Propertius* (Princeton: Princeton Univ. Press, The Lockert Library of Poetry in Translation, 2005).
**His libertine *Homage*.** The first—and a most scathing—review of *Homage* was by Classics professor William Gardner Hale, "Pegasus Impounded," *Poetry*, 14 (1949), 52–55. Pound's defensive response appears in correspondence. See letter to A. R. Orage, ?/4/1919; Paige, 149–150 ("My job was to bring a dead man to life, to present a living figure"), and letter to Felix E. Schelling, 8/7/1922; Paige, 178–179 ("No, I have not done a translation of Propertius. That fool in Chicago took the Homage as translation. . . .").
**withdrew . . . *translation*.** Sullivan (1964), 9, 13; Sullivan (1961), 463.
**conceded it was middling.** "It takes no more Latin than I have to know that Divus's Latin is not the Latin of Catullus and Ovid." Pound, "Translators of Greek: Early Translators of Homer," in Eliot, ed. (1918), 264. Pound goes on to commend Divus's sixteenth-century translation of Homer for its crib-like quality.
***cano* 'sing' . . . *canes* 'dogs'.** For this and other examples, see Bettini, 67–68; also, and more systematically, Schlauch, 258–259. The confusion of verb and noun did not merely reflect Pound's misapprehension of Latin, but was characteristic of his English as well. Translator and Pound-supporter Dudley Fitts, in a brief review of Pound's poems, lighted on Pound's syntax, exclaiming, "Those, Reader, are verbs not nouns." Dudley Fitts, "The Tea-Shop Aura," *The New Republic*, 1/4/1954.
**"The 'Homage' . . . words."** Svensson, 122–123 (forcefully advancing an indefensible explanation of Pound's technique and effectiveness in such practices).
**"Yet the . . . accuracy."** Review, *The New Age*, 26 (1919), 62.
**"refuses . . . words mean."** D. S. Carne-Ross, "Conversations with Robert Lowell," *Delos: A Journal of and on Translation*, 1 (1968), 175.
**"Either . . . doesn't have it."** Schlauch, 260.
**a shoddy . . . with bravura.** Pound steadfastly *would not learn*, concealing his disdain beneath carping pronunciamentos that make learning seem impossible or passé. His favored ploy (as in the first three examples) is to posit comparative nonsensicalities. For example, since traditional methods of study are all but impossible, one does better to seize the alternative, whether a crib or one's intuitive sense. Again, and as previously seen:

> Really one DON'T need to know a language. One NEEDS, damn well needs, to know the first few hundred words in the few really good poems that any language has in it. It is far better to know the POIKILOTHRON [i.e., Sappho's "Hymn to Aphrodite"] than to be able to read Thucydides without trouble. . . . [Letter to Iris Barry, 8/24/1916; Paige, 93]

The comparison is wildly inapposite, and precious the few who have ever read Thucydides without trouble. Similarly:

> It is much better that a man should use a crib, and know the content of his authors than that he should be able to recite all the rules in Allen and Greenough's *Grammar*. [Pound (1968), 239]

It is never a matter of such extremes. One begins (and ideally ends) neither with a crib nor with Allen and Greenough. Again:

> A child may be bulldozed into learning almost anything, but man accustomed to some degree of freedom is loath to approach a masterpiece through five hundred pages of grammar. [Pound (1968), 249]

Five hundred pages of grammar are little needed to distinguish *canes* 'dogs' and *canēs* 'you will sing'. "Some degree of freedom" does not foreclose the basics. And finally:

> Education is an onanism of the soul. Philology will be ascribed to De la Sade. [Pound (1968), 241]

Which is to say, masturbatory education will ultimately blind us to the beauty of the Classics; better to emulate the half-baked autodidact that Pound has made of himself. We may note that Pound's abhorred philology suspiciously resembles his much-vaunted *logopoeia*. See Pound (1968), 25; and further, Pound (1968), 240. Otherwise, see Schlauch (1928) and (1949), who was onto Pound from the outset.

*Critic Robert Graves saw*
**"Breathtaking . . . century."** Graves (1955), 213. And further, "Mr. Pound's translation depends on an almost perfect ignorance of Latin, and a guessing at Propertius's sense from the nearest English verbal equivalents." Graves (1965), 53.
**"As if, had . . . shillings."** Letter to Felix E. Schelling, 7/9/1922; Paige, 178. Pound apologist J. P. Sullivan seeks to explain or explain away Pound's mistakes, claiming that "Pound pointed out that he was not doing a crib of the poems," i.e., Pound was not required to be "accurate." Sullivan (1964), 95. But Pound did not say he would have written a crib had he wanted to be accurate. He said that if he wanted to *pretend* to accuracy, he could correct mistakes by checking a crib. That temptation was rare. So also, "The alleged 'howlers' are not mistakes at all in any ordinary sense, but *deliberate* distortions of the original to express what Pound wanted to express in the *Homage as a poem*." Sullivan (1961), 464. Typical of Sullivan's approach is the following: "There seems implicit in certain of Pound's practices a theory that homophones in a language (for example, *canes*—"you will sing" and *canes*—"dogs") somehow infect each other and thus each meaning carries the contagion of the other." Sullivan (1964), 99. The pestilential metaphor could not be more appropriate. The two words are, in any event, not true homophones, as the long *e* in *canēs* 'you will sing' distinguishes its pronunciation from that of *canes* 'dogs'. A reviewer of Sullivan notes candidly as follows: "Pound's misinterpretation [of Propertius] leads even Mr. Sullivan astray" and "one must conclude that Mr. Sullivan claims too much for Pound and is sometimes led to distort Propertius in the process of vindicating his translator." See Thomas Drew-Baer, review of J. P. Sullivan, *Ezra Pound and Sextus Propertius: A Study in Creative Translation, American Literature*, 37.4 (1966), 503–504.
**the most . . . of languages."** Graves (1965), 47.

515 *The manuscripts of Propertius*
**his abnormal Latinity.** Nitchie, 218.
**"We also . . . Propertius."** Elegia quoque Graecos provocamus, cuius mihi tersus

atque elegans maxime videtur auctor Tibullus. Sunt qui Propertium malint (*Inst. Orat.* 10.1.93). See J. P. Elder, "Tibullus: *Tersus Atque Elegans,*" and Archibald W. Allen, "Sunt Qui Propertium Malint, " in J. P. Sullivan, ed., *Critical Essays on Roman Literature: Elegy and Lyric* (Cambridge: Harvard Univ. Press, 1962), 65–105; 106–148. This is not to underestimate the complexities in the manuscript tradition of Tibullus, leading one scholar to conclude that "the poet suffered from brain dysfunction, resulting in random snatches of insight, set in verse." See Robert J. Ball, *Tibullus the Elegist: A Critical Survey* (Göttingen: Vandenhoeck & Ruprecht, Hypomnemata, Heft 77, 1983), 12–13.
**"formal perfection . . . taste."** Archibald W. Allen, "'Sincerity' and the Roman Elegist," *Classical Philology*, 45 (1950), 145.
**paraphrase Gilbert Highet.** Highet (1957), 81–82.

516 *As concerned his view*
**"also resembles . . . writers."** Highet, (1957), 81. Highet here momentarily yields to the notion that harder is better. See also "We have already mentioned Eliot and Pound. Let anyone who believes that poetry must follow a predictable scheme attempt to arrange *The Waste Land* or *The Cantos* in quatrains, or even to account logically for the transitions within these poems as they stand. If he succeeds, he should try Propertius." Highet (1957), 82.
**"Homage to . . . of taste."** Highet (1961), 118, and (1971), 254–255.

517 *Even classicist and Pound*
**Wordsworth . . . "unenglish."** The tendency toward "unenglish" translation arises from time to time. So William Morris's Homer: "It may be argued that, though this is perhaps a translation, it is not English, never was, and never will be." Lang, 91.
**"yet rejected . . . originality."** Venturi, 185 (quoting Fitts [1954]). See also Venturi, 184 ("Fitts evidently felt a deep ambivalence towards modernist translation"); and 186 ("Fitts ignored Pound's concept of interpretive translation," preferring those of Pound's poems that "tended to be written either in a fluent, contemporary English that was immediately intelligible or in a poetic language that seemed to him unobtrusive enough not to interfere with the evocation of a coherent speaking voice").

*Pound's stance toward*
**"If you . . . something."** Letter to Iris Barry, 7/27/1916; Paige, 91. Pound's cavalier statement has been taken to mean that he translated "because he could not find any versions he liked." Balmer (2013), 32, n. 47. Were that the case, Pound would need have translated much of the classical poetic canon. The issue, in any event, is not one of Pound's finding a Propertius he might like. It is doubtful that any likable version would have obviated the *Homage*.
"**Really one . . . trouble.**" Letter to Iris Barry, 8/24/1916; Paige, 93.
**"he prize[d] the . . . else."** Letter to Iris Barry, 8/?/1916; Paige, 91.
**"A fellow named Spenser."** Pound (1938), 145. Pound elsewhere has it that "old Spencer [sic] . . . first declaimed me the Odyssey." Canto 80/52.
**"You . . . translate 'em."** Letter to Iris Barry, 7/27/1916; Paige, 90.

518 *Pound's reliance on*
**"Let the . . . the movement."** Pound (1918), 5.
**"communicating . . . understood."** Eliot (1932), 200.

*Pound's borderline-comprehensible*
**"so unhappy . . . their own."** Sir John Denham, Preface.

**in the classical sense.** For translation in the classical sense as transformative imitation, see pp. 263, 286, 439, 475, 481, 530.
**"second-rater . . . Homer."** See also p. 365.

519 *Much, however, tends*
**"Undoubtedly . . . of life."** Bettini, 69.
**"For every . . . it is read."** Charles Martin, "A Classic in Paraphrase," *Blackbird Archive: an online journal of literature and the arts,* 9.2 (2010), 2.
**"The problem . . . this effect."** Martin, 2.

520 *In sum, too much Pound,*
**"has directed . . . ever could."** Sullivan (1961), 463.

521 *The "instructions" that have*
**"The book . . . willing reader."** John Edward, "Poet or Poo-Bah," review of Hugh Kenner, *The Poetry of Ezra Pound, The Kenyon Review,* 14.4 (1952), 686.
**"does not . . . are answered."** Forster, 118.
**"overtones . . . meaning."** Isaacs, 20.
**"Certain . . . riddles to us."** Isaacs, 21.

*Pound was too busy*
**"misspelling . . . by heart"?** Kenner (1968), 218–219.
**"bad memory . . . Eloquio"?** Logan (1995), 61.

522 *Whatever the typically*
**"Scruples . . . of priorities."** Bettini, 69.
**"It is *not* . . . altogether."** Edgar Allan Poe, "The Poetic Principle," in Louis Untermeyer, ed., *Complete Poems of Edgar Allan Poe* (New York: Heritage Press, 1943), 91.
**"the proper . . . superficial."** Edgar Allan Poe, "The Rationale of Verse," in Untermeyer, ed., 147.

*These doings, according*
**Pound's most ardent advocate.** It was Davenport who first argued Pound's preeminence in the modernist canon. See, e.g., "Pound and Frobenius" in *Motive and Method in the Cantos of Ezra Pound* (New York: Columbia Univ. Press, 1954); and *The Geography of the Imagination* (San Francisco: North Point Press, 1981) (containing four essays on Pound); and numerous journal articles.
**"And look . . . archaic English."** Guy Davenport, "The Symbol of the Archaic," *The Georgia Review,* 28.4 (1974), 650.

523 *Pound was admittedly*
**"Why . . . pleasant season."** Letter to William Carlos Williams, 10/21/1908; Paige, 6.
**"Of all . . . and profound."** Quoted in Eric S. Christianson, *Ecclesiastes Through the Centuries* (Oxford: Wiley-Blackwell, 2007), 70 (from the letter of Wolfe's novelist-protagonist George Weber to friend Fox in *You Can't Go Home Again,* 1940).

524 *Clearly no imitator*
**"an Endeavour . . . Country."** Pope, Preface, *Ovid's Epistles, Translated by Several Hands,* Hooker and Swedenborg, eds., 116. One need not belabor Dryden's above-referenced tripartite distinction: metaphrase (a word-for-word, line-by-line fidelity), paraphrase (meaning rather than words), and imitation. Paraphrase, in the words of

poet Sir John Denham, is the translation not of "Language into Language, but Poesie into Poesie."

524 *The Age of Dryden,*
**critical of A. E. Housman.** See Pound, "Mr. Housman at Little Bethel" (1918, 1968), 70.

*As Dryden did more*
**did more . . . reputation.** Isaacs, 10.
**"Nearly . . . first time."** Rajan, 120.
**"a series . . . of Paradise."** Rajan, 120.
**"never a contemporary poet."** Isaacs, 3.

525 *Milton, moreover, was*
**"perhaps . . . in the language."** Rajan, 126.

*Pound was not yet*
**"To break . . . first heave."** Canto 81/53.
**"traditional . . . our poetry."** Viereck (1953), 7.
**as yet "untapped resources."** For examples, see Viereck (1953), 7.

526 *Indeed, as Dryden and*
**"distinguished . . . Mencius."** Letter to Katue Kitasono, 11/15/1940; Paige, 347.
**"that old . . . gossip of Socrates."** Pound (1938), 307.

*Himself so much the*
**"higher dilettantism" . . . sixties.** Pound (1938), 312–313. For the full rancor of Pound's anti-Aristotelianism, see "And Therefore Tending," Pound (1938), 304–331.
**Aristotle's . . . basic definition.** Butcher (*Poetics* 1450b, VII.27), 31.
**"multitudinous discontinuities."** For this and the sentence's remaining quotations, see Rajan, 279, 294. Rajan's perversely brilliant, ultimately self-defeating chapter "Ezra Pound and the Logocentric Survival" provides the only tenable—one dare not say *logical*—approach to *The Cantos*: that of deconstruction and reader response (both anathema to the traditional belief in artistic design). The deconstructive mode is apparent in Pound's belief that "All knowledge is built up from a rain of factual atoms." Rajan, 274, 291 (citing Pound [1938], 98). To focus on atoms is to deconstruct the whole for its minuscule components, while reader response makes the *reader* the author of the poem's meaning. Thus Rajan, in two of his headily seductive formulations:

> It can even be said that the fragment seeks relationship and that when conventional relationships are shorn away, the effect is to engage the reader more fully with the poem by assigning him the responsibility of joining the fragment to its implicit destiny.
>
> The meaning can be only bestowed, not discovered . . . the only meaning is that which the voyager wrests from experience, from its shifting seas, and from its yielding of a shoreline that has to be both discovered and remembered. [Rajan, 278, 285]

Rajan especially fails where he elaborates on the basis of some literary design or goal which he ascribes to Pound, only to end by saying that Pound was ultimately unable to realize the same.
**"Certainly the . . . used."** Letter to Iris Barry, 8/29/1916; Paige, 95.
**Though the . . . nothing of it."** Cooper, 108.

*"Once the classics*

**"*Once* the classics . . . no go."** Letter to W. H. D. Rouse, 5/?/1937; Paige, 295.

**Leo Frobenius (1873–1938).** See generally Demetres P. Tryphonopoulos and Stephen J. Adams, eds., *The Ezra Pound Encyclopedia* (Westport: Greenwood Press, 2005), 126–127.

**discredited Martin Bernal's.** See Mary Lefkowitz, *Not Out of Africa: How Afrocentrism Became an Excuse to Teach Myth as History* (New York: Basic Books, 1996); Mary Lefkowitz and Guy MacLean Rogers, eds., *Black Athena Revisited* (Chapel Hill: Univ. of North Carolina Press, 1996); and Mary Lefkowitz, *History Lesson: A Race Odyssey* (New Haven and London: Yale Univ. Press, 2008).

**vilify the . . . Battle of Salamis.**

> Since his adopted ideology compels Pound to besmirch all struggles for liberty, and the fraternal heroism engendered in democratic wars of defense, past and present, he undertakes to 'debunk' the Battle of Salamis, since it has been a textbook example for ages of that kind of war. And the device? It is once more the juxtaposition of sordid cash with what claims to be great. We are reminded with repetitious insistence, that "the fleet at Salamis [was] made with money lent by the state to the shipwrights [Canto 74/429]. That is supposed to vilify the entire struggle of the Greeks to protect their homeland from the Persians." [Schlauch, 268]

**"reconfigured by . . . saint."** Tryphonopoulos and Adams, eds., 142.

527 *Though Eliot, by contrast,*

**of Virgil, Dante, Dryden.** See Eliot's essay "John Dryden" (1922), in Eliot (1932), 264–275.

**"approach . . . been tackled."** Isaacs, 1.

**"are taught and . . . of art."** Dalrymple, 134.

**"As satire . . . superfluous."** Dalrymple, 134.

*Pound, by his silence,*

**"Although . . . and Keats."** Isaacs, 4–5.

**"is notable . . . wedding."** Andrew Hadfield, "Why Edmund Spenser Matters," *Huffington Post* (Culture), 6/27/2012.

**a renounced awareness.** Yeats (Pound's friend and often severest critic) was, by contrast, fully appreciative of Spenser. See Brater, 663 ("The figure of Spenser becomes for Yeats an ideal vehicle for the presentation of his own ideas about the function of symbolism and allegory in modern poetry.").

**"an extraordinary parallel."** Richard Burton, *A Strong Song Tows Us: The Life of Basil Bunting* (Oxford: Infinite Ideas Limited, 2013), 472.

528 *All of which suggests that*

**"represents not . . . poet."** Russo (1968), 278.

**the setting of . . . "mood."** Garcia, 20–21.

529 *Pound was also contemptuous*

**"The evil . . . wash lists."** Ezra Pound, "Harold Monro," *The Criterion*, XI.45 (1932), 581–592.

**not merely "controversial."** Viereck, 136.

**"totalitarian synthesis."** Dasenbrock, 171, 172.

*Imitation, as defined by*

**"Hyperbolic . . . 'Pound Era.'"** D. Robinson, 178–179.

**merely dabbled in languages.** Pound was enrolled in the University of Pennsylvania, School of Arts in the College, during the 1901–1902 and 1902–1903 sessions. He transferred to Hamilton College, graduating in 1905. He entered the University of Pennsylvania Graduate School in 1905 and received his master of arts in June 1906. What follows is an overview of Pound's language studies as reflected solely in his academic transcripts. For these I record my special thanks to staff members of University of Pennsylvania Archives, and of Burke Library–Hamilton College, Special Collections. On Pound's academic career, see further A. David Moody, *Ezra Pound: Poet, A Portrait of the Man and His Work, Vol. I: The Young Genius 1885–1920* (Oxford: Oxford Univ. Press, 2007), 14–33; and on Pound's classical education, Peter Liebregts, "The Classics," in Ira B. Nadel, ed., *Ezra Pound in Context* (Cambridge: Cambridge Univ. Press, 2010), 171–180. Pound boosters often rely on a bit of his high-school doggerel—"no more Latin, no more Greek / no more smoking on the sneak"—as evidence of Pound's receiving "a solid grounding" in Latin and Greek. Liebregts, 171; Svensson, 117 ("a student, if not initially an avid one, of both Latin and Greek from an early age onwards"). Such claims are belied both by Pound's Cheltenham transcript and his own avowals of inadequacy.

At the Cheltenham Military Academy (1897–1901), Pound studied the run of high-school courses, including Latin. The space beneath a "Greek" subject matter heading is blank. Pound's handwritten UPenn transcript shows freshman course work in the usual subjects, including Latin and German, with continued Latin in his sophomore year. There are no assigned grades. Pound's handwritten transcript from Hamilton College (to which he transferred) shows coursework, *inter alia*, in German, French, French Provençal, Italian, Spanish, and Old English, his grades erratic even within the same languages (typically *B*'s and *C*'s): an *A* in Old English on one occasion, a *C* on another; an *A* in German on one occasion, a *D* on another; and an *E* in Bible: Job. Pound's M.A. work at UPenn included Old Spanish, Old French/Provençal (as separate entries), Petrarch, and Latin (all ungraded). He was awarded his M.A. upon written examination (the "Thesis: Title" line remaining blank). Pound's one-page application for masters study at UPenn contains the following under "Knowledge of Languages": "Latin, german [sic], French, italian [sic], Spanish, some greek [sic], Anglo-Saxon + Provencal [sic]," with the notation: "German reading knowledge certified from Hamilton College, Prof. Brandt. 3/6/06."

Though "some greek" materializes on Pound's application for M.A. study, Greek nowhere appears on *any* of Pound's academic transcripts. Pound explicator Hugh Kenner, within a small number of pages, makes decidedly mixed claims for Pound's Greek: Greek, to Pound, was "an ancient literature he couldn't read and didn't even have texts for"; and next, Homer's Greek is something "which Pound after all could read." Then, crediting fifteenth-century Byzantine scholars with the introduction of Greek texts into the Latin West, Kenner happily concludes: "But for them, there would have been no Greek classrooms in Pennsylvania for the adolescent Ezra Pound to meet Homer in." See Hugh Kenner, "Ezra Pound's Commedia," in Stuart Y. McDougal, ed., *Dante Among the Moderns* (Chapel Hill and London: Univ. of North Carolina Press, 1985), 41–42. Other boosters of Pound's classicism rely on Pound apologist J. P. Sullivan: "It is not that Pound didn't know Virgil: Pound, as his *Homage to Sextus Propertius* and other works make clear, was thoroughly at home in the Latin classics." Ziolkowski (1993), 191 (citing Sullivan). Similarly reliant on third-party sources are the following: "Pound had been reading Horace since 1902–1903, when as a student at the University of Pennsylvania he studied *Odes, Satires,* and the *Epistles.*" Ziolkowski (2005), 198. The formidable and elsewhere scrupulously well-documented Ziolkowski here cites Ronald Edward Thomas, *The Latin Masks of Ezra Pound* (Ann Arbor: UMI Research Press, 1983), 117–139, "for a complete catalogue of Pound's allusions to Horace." The "catalogue," however, evidences neither the nature nor extent of Pound's study of Horace. Accordingly, those who ardently praise and defend Pound's *Homage* often do so upon the unsubstantiated belief in his full command of each language to which he pretended; see, e.g., May Sinclair, "The Reputation of Ezra Pound," *The North American Review*, 211.774 (1920), 658–668; Clarence A. Forbes, "Ezra Pound and Sextus Propertius," *Classical Journal*, 42.3 (1946), 177–179.

**"one uses . . . lack of respect."** John Simon, "Abuse of Privilege: Lowell as Translator," *The Hudson Review*, 20.4 (1967–1968), 543–562. In his review-essay of Lowell's *Imitations,* Simon notes that "what Lowell has done with Rilke's poem is neither a decent translation nor a good original work, merely a disaster." The same conclusion, by degree, characterizes Simon's view of *Imitations* as a whole.

**Propertius-influenced.** Though translating Propertius only twice (*Elegies* 4.7 and 4.3), Lowell, as revealed by his letters, felt a "peculiar sense of personal connection" with the poet, as persuasively set forth by Talbot (2007). Especially helpful is Talbot's overview of Propertius's challenging thought process and obscurity of allusion vis-à-vis the imputed corruption of the poet's manuscript tradition (142–147).

Talbot creates a misleading picture of Highet as a modernist advocate. Talbot urges that Highet "proceeds to justify [Propertius's] dislocations by appealing to the authority of T. S. Eliot and Ezra Pound (then both ascendant), and so take[s] his place in a line of critics and poets . . . who find in Propertius an anticipation of modernist techniques and attitudes." The "line of critics" culminates, according to Talbot, in D. Thomas Benediktson, *Propertius: Modernist Poet of Antiquity* (1989). The work's thesis is that nobody understood Propertius before Pound. In making this argument, Talbot omits reference both to Highet's view of the modernist technique as one that "*has brought* [the modernist poets] *much abuse*" (emphasis added), and to Highet's excoriating 1961 *volte-face* concerning Pound.

The review of Benediktson by Propertius authority J. L. Butrica is toxic, to say the least. See "Propertius the Modernist?" *Classical Review*, n.s. 40.2 (1990), 266–268 (e.g., "B's attack on textual criticism might carry more conviction if he did not display an absolute ignorance of its principles and methods"; "To enumerate the inadequacies of this volume would itself require a book, for there is little here that is not questionable or patently wrong"; "It is a sad comment upon the state of Propertian scholarship . . . that a book such as this one could ever have been conceived, much less published"). See also J. L. Butrica, "Editing Propertius," *Classical Quarterly*, n.s. 47.1 (1997), 176–208; and *The Manuscript Tradition of Propertius* (*Phoenix* Supplementary Volume 17, 1984).

**the "new sensationalism."** Vendler pp. 558–559, note. None of Lowell's Horace imitations appears in *Imitations*. His imitations of *Odes* 1.4, 1.37, and 2.7 appear in *Near the Ocean: Poems* (New York: Farrar, Straus & Giroux, 1967), the last two also in *New York Review of Books*, 1/28/65.

**"The pressure . . . effect."** Vendler, 558–559.

530 *Pound's Homage was inspiration*

**one and the same for Lowell.** "I believe poetic translation—I would call it an imitation—must be expert and inspired. . . ." (xii).

**"what [his] . . . in America."** Robert Lowell, *Imitations* (New York: Farrar, Straus & Giroux, 1958), xi–xiii.

**"monument . . . bronze."** The reference is to Horace, *Odes* 3.30, in which the poet envisions his immortality:

> Exegi monumentum aere perennius
> regalique situ pyramidum altius. . . .

I have reared a monument more lasting than bronze,
outsoaring the pyramids' regal construction. . . .

531 *Lowell limited his*

**"No, it . . . couldn't tell."** See D. S. Carne-Ross, "Conversations with Robert Lowell," *Delos: A Journal of and on Translation,* 1 (1968), 168–169. Lowell's response anticipates the boorishness of Carne-Ross protégé David Ferry (p. 498).

*It is Pound and Lowell*

**one of the most egregious.** For Davenport's translations from the Greek, see pp. 81–82, 89–90, 115–117. Davenport did not scruple to review others of his own ilk; see "From the Greek," *Poetry,* 108.6 (1966), 416–419 (reviewing Barnard, Barnstone, and Logue).

**a plangent eulogy for Pound.** Guy Davenport, "Ezra Pound 1885–1972," *Arion,* 1.1 (1973), 188–196. Davenport also gave the inaugural lecture at the 1975 opening of the Ezra Pound Papers Collection at Yale's Beinecke Library.

532 *Ten years after his "go"*

**"What, then . . . ignorance."** Nabokov (1969).

***de-te-fabula-narrabitur.*** Future-tense paraphrase of Horace: (*mutato nomine*) *de te / fabula narratur* 'the name changed, of you / the tale is told'. *Sat.* I.1.69–70.

**"If this kind . . . would be."** Nabokov (1969).

533 *Nabokov's vision of*

**Kirkus Reviews, praising.** Review of *Imitations,* by Robert Lowell. www.kirkusreviews.com/book-reviews/robert-lowell-2/imitations (n.d.). Web. 4/17/2014.

**"to treat . . . the original."** Graves (1965), 54–55.

534 *The infatuation with*

**recent review . . . *Montale.*** Jonathan Galassi, "The Great Montale in English," *New York Review of Books,* 11/8/2012.

535 *Scholars remain in thrall*

**Scholars remain in thrall.** Lowell's poetry, for example, is praised for its prosody, even as its meaning mystifies. Thus, e.g., William Arrowsmith, concerning "The Mills of the Kavanaughs": Lowell's "most obvious strength is diction, . . . a bold disregard for logical or metrical pause. . . . More important—I wish I understood the poem. I don't, in any satisfactory, even, way, understand it." Arrowsmith, "A Monotony of Violence," in Michael London and Robert Boyers, eds., *Robert Lowell: A Portrait of the Artist in His Time* (New York: David Lewis, 1971), 32.

The first and principal Pound apologist was J. P. Sullivan (1964), *supra,* who "owe[s] particular thanks to Mr. T. S. Eliot for encouraging [him] to begin this book and to Mr. Ezra Pound for answering some detailed inquiries" (Preface, ix–x). Also by Sullivan: "Ezra Pound's Classical Translations," in "MAKE IT NEW: Articles delivered at a Symposium on Translation and Metrical Innovation: Aspects of Ezra Pound's Work," *The Texas Quarterly,* 10.4 (1967), 57–60; and "Ezra Pound as Latin Translator," *Arion* 3.1 (1964), 100–111 (book review). See also the plangently apologetic introduction to Sullivan's "Ezra Pound on Classics and Classicists," *Arion* 3.1 (1964), 9–22. Sullivan's article, summer 1961 (see Bibliography) either ignores or does not know about Highet's article, January 1961. In his *Ezra Pound and Sextus Propertius* (1964), Sullivan quotes only passingly from Highet. Amid continuing praise of Pound, Sullivan (1967) makes no mention of Highet.

Sullivan's attachment comes strangely from one whose Latin, quite to the contrary of Pound's, was impeccable, and who was otherwise scrupulously devoted to Latin poetry—all despite the relative indifference of classicists to Sullivan's favorite. See Sullivan, *Propertius: A Critical Introduction* (Cambridge: Cambridge Univ. Press, 1976), 53: "Ezra Pound's notorious *Homage to Sextus Propertius* . . . constituted the first genuine critical advance in the study of Propertius. . . . It must be confessed, however, that . . . most scholarly work on Propertius has proceeded along conventional lines." So also Venturi, 186: "British and American poets continued to translate foreign language poetry, of course, but Pound's experimental strategies attracted relatively few adherents." Sullivan's view of Pound's *Homage* as "the first genuine critical advance in the study of Propertius" is contested by Zane Udris, *Classical Philology*, 73.4 (1978), 361–364, who otherwise concludes that Sullivan's "introduction to Propertius . . . is so deeply permeated by the author's prejudices [as to be] recommended to a beginning classicist with great reservation." More recently pro-Poundian is Daniel M. Hooley, "Pound's Propertius, Again," *Comparative Literature*, 100.5 (1985), 1025–1044; and Hooley, *The Classics in Paraphrase: Ezra Pound and Modern Translators of Latin Poetry* (London and Toronto: Susquehanna Univ. Press, 1988).

**"might thus . . . correction."** Anthony Pym, "Overt Translation Strategies in the Histories of Robert Lowell and Ezra Pound." www.usuaris.tinet.cat/apym/-on-line/translation/1995_pound_lowell.pdf (Web. 1/7/2011), published as "Resistant Strategies in Robert Lowell's Imitations and Ezra Pound's Cantos," in Christine Pagnoulle and Ian Mason, eds., *Cross-Words. Issues and Debates in Literary and Non-literary Translating* (Liège, L3—Liège Language and Literature, 1995), 159–171.

Pym's conclusion is a world as much turned upside down as Pound himself might want: "It would be more proper to say," says Pym, "that [Pound and Lowell] sought help and advice, but were then prepared openly to turn their back on criteria of correctness. Their works should thus be . . . analysed in terms of the use of error to construe knowledge from the distance of foreign documents."

**"Never . . . indiscriminately."** George Seferis, "The Cantos," in Peter Russell, ed., *An Examination of Ezra Pound: A Collection of Essays* (Norfolk: New Directions, 1950), 80.

**"prepared . . . on meaning."** Logan (1995), 59.

*Indeed, farraginous*

**Indeed, farraginous innovation.** My paragraph draws from David Kirby, "Lush Life," review of Fitzgerald's *The Late Parade*, in *New York Times Book Review*, 8/4/2013, and William Grimes, "John Hollander, Poet at Ease with Intellectualism and Wit, Dies at 83," *New York Times*, 8/19/2013.

536 *Pound in his own*

**"I resolved . . . for degrees."** Alan Levy, *Ezra Pound: The Voices of Silence* (New York: The Permanent Press, 1983), 11.

**"I have . . . about everything."** Forrest Read, ed., *Pound/Joyce: The Letters of Ezra Pound to James Joyce, with Pound's Critical Essays and Articles About Joyce* (New York: New Directions, 1967), 102. Encyclopedic facility is as much Pound's as his acolytes' signature. To read Davenport, Carne-Ross, and the rest is to encounter an impenetrable literary-cultural thicket. Davenport's attraction to Pound extends back to their common "ancestor," the fourth-century Bordelais rhetorician Ausonius (p. 430). Ausonius, says Davenport, was "half pagan, less than half Christian. He read everything, quoted everybody, and sported an erudition that clearly had for its message that although he lived a great remove from Rome, Alexandria, and Athens, nevertheless we Bordelais are right up with everything. We read books. We have a university. We have travelled. We are witty and well-mannered." Andre Furlani, "Guy Davenport and the Archival Imagination," *New*

*England Review*, 28.1 (2007), 65–66 (quoting Davenport's *Every Force Evolves a Form*). Bordelais Ausonius is none other than the Kentuckian Davenport.

*The damage done Propertius*
**"That there . . . might respond."** Michael Comber, "A Book Made New: Reading Propertius Reading Pound. A Study in Reception," *The Journal of Roman Studies*, 88 (1998), 37–55.
**note in passing that Comber.** See e.g., "Michael Comber," *The Telegraph*, 7/19/2004 (Comber described as a professor with "something of a cult following").

537 *Let us briefly turn*
**(to Mary Barnard).** "If you really learn to write proper quantitative sapphics in the Amurikan langwidge [Poundian snide for "American language"] I shall love and adore you all the days of my life . . . eh . . . provided you don't fill 'em with trype." Letter to Mary Barnard, 1/22/1934; Paige, 252.

538 *The opening stanza*
**"On your . . . soul now?"** John Frederick Nims, *Sappho to Valéry: Poems in Translation* (Princeton: Princeton Univ. Press, 1971), 285.

541 *Matters are otherwise*
**might refer *to Sappho*.** For views on this possibility, see Prentice, 356–357.

*The aforementioned classicist-translator*
**buzz and provocation.** See "*Poetry*'s Opening the Door," in John Timberman Newcomb, *How Did Poetry Survive: The Making of Modern American Verse* (Urbana and Chicago: Univ. of Illinois Press, 2012), 36–39.
**"his own kind . . . urgency."** Jay Parini, "Why WS Merwin deserves his second Pulitzer Prize," *The Guardian* (Books Blog), 4/24/2009.
***Revised and Enlarged Edition.*** (Fayetteville and London: Univ. of Arkansas Press, 1990.)

542 *Pound considered the*
**"No man . . . successors."** Pound (1918), 10.
**"continue[s] . . . the text."** Balmer (2013), 94; cf. Balmer (2009), 47.
**descriptions . . . pause.** See, e.g., Balmer (2013), 95–96.

*We have quoted Pound*
**We have quoted Pound.** See p. 302.
**The fashioner . . . lives.** See, e.g., Glover, 11–16; Eyres, 104–106.

543 *The novice need only*
**need only read Gilbert.** See Highet (2010), 126–137 ("The Odes"). Numerous testimonials have attended the perennial, albeit often begrudging, appreciation of Horace.
**his warmth and worth.** Matthew Arnold also had problems with Horace, but for reasons relating to Horace's lack of faith, enthusiasm, and energy. See *Essays in Criticism*, Third Series (Boston: Ball, 1910), 80–82.
**"*Orazio è sempre attuale.*"** Eyres, 223.
**"I have adored . . . appetite."** Levi, xi.

*Pound would have none*
***Criterion*, IX (1929–1930).** The article seems the fulfillment of an earlier-promised

explanation: "Catullus, Propertius, Horace, and Ovid are the people who matter. Catullus most of all. Martial somewhat. Propertius for beautiful cadence though he uses only one meter. Horace you will not want for a long time. I doubt if he is of any use save to the Latin scholar. I will explain sometime viva voce." Letter to Iris Barry, 7/20/1916; Paige, 87. For other instances of Pound's disparagement of Horace, see Davidson, 28–31.
**'first' (*prima*) . . . last (*finis*).** *El.* 1.1.1–2; 1.12.20–21.
**"the mature . . . be found."** Otis (1967), 14 (on *Odes* 3.29, 14–17).

544 *Similarly, Pound considered*
**"chucking . . . compunction."** Pound (1937), 174. Pindar and Horace were "the chief classical models for the modern formal lyric." See Highet (1949), 119–254.
**"He had . . . Greek meters."** Pound (1930), 226.
**"Horace was . . . pseudonyms."** Kristine Louise Haugen, *Richard Bentley: Poetry and Enlightenment* (Cambridge: Harvard Univ. Press, 2011), 131.
**If Horace . . . Pound's *Cantos*.** Horace's influence on Pound is argued with excessive ingenuity by Lowell Bowditch, "The Horatian Poetics of Ezra Pound and Robert Pinsky," *Classical World*, 89.6 (1996), 451–477.

545 *Dealing with Pound's*
**"wiser, better . . . appetite."** Levi, xi.
**These include subject matter.** Sentence summarized with excerpted phrasing from Davidson, 28–31 (referencing Pound, 1930). Davidson otherwise suggests an anti-establishment bias in Pound's dislike of Horace: "It is perhaps surprising that Pound did not recognize earlier the possibilities of Horace's oblique hints and juxtapositions . . . the rapid shifts of images and ideas. It can only be assumed that the blanket approval accorded to Horace by the English literary establishment blinded Pound to Horace's unconventionality." Davidson, 30–31. Pound, nonetheless, turned to Horace during the later years of his poetic career (1963–1964), rendering *Odes* 1.11, 1.31, and 3.30, the three together "form[ing] . . . as effective a 'crown' to Pound's career, as conclusive a *sphargis* [i.e., seal] as any he could devise." Hooley, 121. Whether Pound's rendering of the famed *Odes* 3.30 (*Exegi monumentum*) is "almost perversely faithful to the original in the imitation of sense and cadence" (Davidson, 41), is debatable, to say the least.
**truisms—or "commonplaces."** The poems' "peculiar rhythms, their charged and demanding word-order, reared upon the so very stable armature of their quite unsurprising thought." Beye (1987), 165.
**Georgian poetry . . . "chuck."** Characteristics shared by Georgian poetry and Horace include: the lack of stridency, the remoteness, and precocity; a certain intimacy of tone, the avoidance of exaltation, an occasional prosiness, familiar countryside scenes and incidents; plainness, honesty, and inner disquiet. See Fraser, 254–256. Georgian poetry was that written during the reign of King George V (1910–1936). *Georgian Poetry* refers to a series of five anthologies published between 1912 and 1922, showcasing the genre and establishing its canon. The period is midway situated between the end of the classicist Victorian Era (death of Queen Victoria, 1901) and the accelerant free-for-all of modernism during and in the aftermath of World War I (war ended, 1918). Among the Georgian poets most recognized today are Rupert Brooke, Robert Graves, D. H. Lawrence, and Siegfried Sassoon. The list excludes A. E. Housman (discussed immediately below), whose most significant poetry, so Georgian in tone, was published in 1896 (*A Shropshire Lad*) and 1922 (*Last Poems*). His exclusion may owe to the fact that he resisted periodic publication until the completion of a book.

*Let us note Professor*
"**[Horace's] . . . outlines.**" Mackail (1895), 114.
**plenus . . . felicissime audax.** Quintilian, *Inst. Orat.* 10.1.96.
**"long since . . . the world."** Moses Stephen Slaughter, "Horace, an Appreciation," *Classical Journal.* 3.2 (1907), 57.

546 *One might have hoped*
**befriending and helping.** One finds an eloquent and heartfelt tribute to Pound as teacher and mentor in the pamphlet-sized tribute of American poet and publisher James Laughlin (1914–1997), *The Master of Those Who Know: Ezra Pound* (San Francisco: City Lights Books, 1986). Laughlin's New Directions, starting in 1963, became the premier publisher of modernist literature. See recently, Charles Simic, "The Godfather of Modernism," *New York Review of Books*, 4/2/2015 (reviews of Laughlin biography and collected poems).
**and found it in Augustus.** There is a Horatian element in Milton's veneration of Oliver Cromwell, "Lord Protector." See Milton's sonnet "To Oliver Cromwell" (1652) and *Second Defence of the English People* (1653). See further p. 654.
**"Linguistic . . . distinctions."** Eyres, 58.

*If any English poetry*
**John W. Stevenson discusses.** See "*A Shropshire Lad* Reappraised," *The Sewanee Review*, 105.2 (1997), 244–250.

*The key here, as*
**"we want . . . as new."** Dorothy Wellesley, ed., *Letters on Poetry from W. B. Yeats to Dorothy Wellesley* (London and New York: Oxford Univ. Press, 1940), 70 (letter of 5/22/1936).
**"a compelling . . . death."** Rica Brenner, *Ten Modern Poets* (New York: Harcourt, Brace, 1930), 176.
**in demand . . . World War I.** Brenner, 176.
**"O woe . . . dead already."** Pound elsewhere condescends to Housman; see "Mr. Housman at Little Bethel" (1918, 1968), 66–73.

547 *Pound especially missed*
**"English . . . not surpassed."** Lucas (1924), 202.
**"the spirit . . . countryside."** Lucas (1924), 203.
**"It is . . . hackneyed meters."** Lucas (1924), 204.
**Some rejecting . . . deprecate."** Lucas (1924), 202.

548 *Pound's take on Horace*
**enjoyed a second life.** Ezra Pound, "Horace," *Arion*, 9.2&3 (1970), 178–187.

*Arion has suffered from*
**"distinctively . . . classics."** Quotations in this and the following paragraph are from: "Editorial Statement," *Arion*, 3rd series, 1.1 (1990), 5–8; Diskin Clay, "William Ayers Arrowsmith: The Years at Johns Hopkins," *Arion*, 3rd series, 2.2&3 (1992–1993), 263–267; and Karl Galinsky, "*Arion*. A Journal of Humanities and the Classics," *International Journal of the Classical Tradition*, 2.1 (1995), 146–147.

*The tumult and torrent*
**That tertium . . . learning.** Editorial, *Arion*, 1.1 (1962).
**the journal's third series.** On *Arion*'s third series, see James W. Halporn, "Arion: A Journal of the Humanities and the Classics," *Bryn Mawr Classical Review*, www.bmcr.

brynmawr.edu/1991/02.04.02.html (Web. 2/19/2015); and Roger Kimball, "Arion: A Journal of the Humanities and the Classics," *Times Literary Supplement*, 3/8/1991. Halporn takes a somewhat jaundiced view. Kimball is more approving.

549 *Carne-Ross wins the*

**Carne-Ross . . . offender.** In further breach of editorial discretion, *Arion* served as a principal venue for the translations of Carne-Ross protégés—the Latinless David Ferry and Greekless Christopher Logue (and for Carne-Ross's laudations of Logue; *Arion*, 1.2 [1962], 27–38). *Arion* also published the page-consuming translations of Alcman, Archilochus, and Menander by the Greekless and Pound-enamored Guy Davenport (*Arion*, 2.2 [1963], 29–53; 6.2 [1967], 169–178; 8.4 [1969], 477–499). Carne-Ross's Ferry laudation appears as "Horace Transplanted," *The New Criterion*, 16.5 (1998), 56–61.

550 *Arion favorite John Talbot*

**Talbot . . . thirty-pager.** John Talbot, "English Ghosts of Callimachus," *Arion*, 3rd series, 12.1 (2004), 139–169.

*The year following*

**"Wrong Meaning . . . Translator."** Steven J. Willett (2005)—a magisterial review by a most perceptive reviewer of classics in translation.

552 *The crack in the façade*

**"If he goes . . . becomes shaky."** Viereck (1986), 125.
**"Modernism . . . road not taken."** Viereck (1986), 125.
**"reform[ing] . . . from without."** Viereck (1986), 126.
**"a tale told . . . Williams."** Viereck (1986), 125.

*Arion is currently*

**"The objects . . . may wither."** Forster, 119.
**"And here . . . everlastingly."** See Helen Waddell, tr., *Mediaeval Latin Lyrics* (New York: W. W. Norton, 1929), 14–15 (from a poem attributed to Petronius Arbiter, c. 27–66 AD).

553 *Elegance, notes Horace,*

**"Then drained . . . day."** *Ep.* 2.1.157–160.

> . . . Sic horridus ille
> defluxit numerus Saturnius, et grave virus
> munditiae pepulere; sed in longum tamen aevum
> manserunt hodieque manent vestigia ruris.

**"to the old . . . all the time."** From Thomas Wolfe, *You Can't Go Home Again* (Book Seven: "A Wind Is Rising, and the Rivers Flow").
**in the New Formalism.** See, e.g., Philip Dacey and David Jauss, *Strong Measures: Contemporary American Poetry in Traditional Forms* (1986); William Baer, *Writing Metrical Poetry: Contemporary Lessons for Mastering Traditional Forms* (2006); William Baer, *The Conservative Poets: A Contemporary Anthology* (2006); X. J. Kennedy, *The Powow River Anthology* (2006); and M. Evans, *The Best of the Barefoot Muse* (2011).
**"debasement . . . language."** Dana Gioia, "Notes on the New Formalism," *The Hudson Review*, 40.3 (1987), 395–408.
**"now that . . . cleared away."** Teachout (1997), 54. Teachout was premature in declaring "mission accomplished." For a brief review of conservative responses to the

avant-garde, see Frederick Turner, *The Culture of Hope: A New Birth of the Classical Spirit* (New York: The Free Press, 1995), Ch. 1 ("The Culture Wars"), and Ch. 2 ("The Failure of the Avant-garde").

*Spearheading the new focus*
**founder... "Derriere Guard."** Aka "derrière-garde," a designation early describing the wonderfully eclectic, though ever classical, composer Alec Wilder (1907–1980). See Whitney Balliett, "The President of the Derrière-garde," *The New Yorker* (PROFILES), 7/9/1973.

554 *A similar neglect essentially*
**"each new shocking . . . culture."** James Panero, "Radical un-chic: On Tom Wolfe & the derrière garde," *The New Criterion,* 26.4 (2007), 27–30 (quoting Turner).
**"a simple virus . . . tradition."** Panero, above (quoting Collins). On Collins's greater recognition and influence since 2004, see James Panero, "The new old school: on the rise of classical realism and its dean, Jacob Collins," *The New Criterion,* 25.1 (2006), 104–107; and by way of corrective and critique, Louis Torres, "Muddying the Waters of Classical Realism," *Aristos* (December 2006).

*The swamp, to be sure,*
**"New York's . . . culture."** Heather Mac Donald, "Rusalka v. regietheater," *The New Criterion*, 32.9 (2014), 56.
**New York Philharmonic.** See Michael Cooper, "What's New? Ask the Philharmonic," *New York Times* (Arts), 5/25/2014.
**the mainstream media?** See Anthony Tommasini, "Beauty is in the Eye of Your Fellow Swine," *New York Times* (Arts), 5/31/2014.

555 *What transpires within*
**"The rapturous . . . tourism."** Martin Filler, "Frank Gehry in Paris," *New York Review of Books*, 1/8/2015.

# Bibliography


Acosta-Hughes, Benjamin, and Susan A. Stephens. *Callimachus in Context: From Plato to the Augustan Poets* (Cambridge: Cambridge Univ. Press, 2012).

Adams, J. N., and R. G. Mayer, eds. *Aspects of the Language of Latin Poetry* (Oxford: Oxford Univ. Press, 1999).

———. *Bilingualism and the Latin Language* (Cambridge: Cambridge Univ. Press, 2003).

Aiken, Conrad. "Disintegration in Modern Poetry" (review of D. H. Lawrence, *Birds, Beasts and Flowers*), *The Dial*, 77 (June, 1924), 535–539.

Alexander, Caroline. *The War That Killed Achilles: The True Story of Homer's Iliad and Trojan War* (New York: Viking Penguin, 2009).

Alter, Robert. *Pen of Iron: American Prose and the King James Bible* (Princeton and Oxford: Princeton Univ. Press, 2010).

Antheil, George. *Bad Boy of Music* (Garden City: Doubleday, Doran, 1945).

Appelbaum, Stanley, tr. and ed. *The New Life: La Vita Nuova, By Dante Alighieri* (Mineola: Dover Publications, 2006). A Dual-Language Book.

Apter, Emily. "Translation with No Original: Scandals of Textual Reproduction," in Bermann and Wood, eds., 159–174.

"Archiloque," *Entretiens sur l'Antiquité Classique* 10 (Genève: Fondation Hardt, 1964). Essays in English, French, and German.

Armstrong, Richard H. "Translating Ancient Epic," in Foley, ed. (2005), 174–195.

———. "Classical Translations of the Classics: The Dynamics of Literary Tradition in Retranslating Epic Poetry," in Lianeri and Zajko, eds. (2008), 169–202.

Arnold, Matthew. *On the Study of Celtic Literature and On Translating Homer* (New York: Macmillan, 1883, 1902). 1st pub. as *On Translating Homer: Three Lectures Given at Oxford* (London: Longman, Green, Longman, and Roberts, 1861).

———. *On Translating Homer, Last Words* (London: Longman, Green, et. al., 1862). Response to F. W. Newman (1861).

———. *Culture and Anarchy*, J. Dover Wilson, ed. (Cambridge: Cambridge Univ. Press, 1966). 1st pub. 1896.

———. "On the Modern Element in Literature," *Macmillan's Magazine* 19 (February, 1869), 304–314. Reprint, *Essays* (1910), 35–86.

———. *Essays in Criticism: Third Series* (Boston: Ball Publishing, 1910).

Arrowsmith, William. "The Decade of Five Iliads," *The Hudson Review*, 5.3 (1952), 432–443.

———, tr. "Jerome on Translation, A Breviary," *Arion*, 2.3 (1975), 358–367.

Atlas, James. "The Men of 1914"(review of Julian Symons, *Makers of the New: The Revolution in Literature, 1912–1939*), *The New Criterion*, 6.7 (1988), 66–68.

Attridge, Derek. *Well-Weighed Syllables: Elizabethan Verse in Classical Meters* (Cambridge: Cambridge Univ. Press, 1974).

Auerbach, Erich. *Mimesis: The Representation of Reality in Western Literature,* Willard R. Trask, tr. (Princeton: Princeton Univ. Press, 1953).

———. *Literary Language and Its Public in Late Latin Antiquity and in the Middle Ages,* Ralph Manheim, tr. (London: Routledge and Keegan Paul, 1965).

Austin, Norman. *Helen and Her Shameless Phantom* (Ithaca: Cornell Univ. Press, 2008).

Austin, R. G. *Some English Translations of Virgil* (Liverpool: Liverpool Univ. Press, 1956).

Ayrton, M., tr. *Archilochos* (London: Secker & Warburg, 1977).

Bagg, Robert. "Love, Ceremony and Daydream in Sappho's Lyrics," *Arion*, 3.3 (1964): 44–82.

———. "Translating the Abyss: On Robert Fitzgerald's *Odyssey*," *Arion*, 8.1 (1969), 51–65.

Bakker, Egbert J., and Ahuvia Kahane, eds. *Written Voices, Spoken Signs: Tradition, Performance, and the Epic Text* (Cambridge: Harvard Univ. Press, 1997).

Bakker, Egbert J., ed. *Pointing to the Past: From Formula to Performance in Homeric Poetics* (Washington, D.C.: Center for Hellenic Studies and Harvard Univ. Press, 2005).

———. *A Companion to the Ancient Greek Language* (Oxford and Malden: Blackwell Publishing, 2010; John Wiley, 2014).

Balmer, Josephine, tr. *Sappho: Poems and Fragments* (London: Brilliance Books, 1984). Reissued, Blooxade, 1992.

———. "What Comes Next? Reconstructing the Classics," in Bassnett and Bush, eds. (2006), 184–195.

———. "Jumping Their Bones: Translating, Transgressing, and Creating," in S. J. Harrison, ed. (2009), 43–64.

———. *Piecing Together the Fragments: Creating Contemporary Poetry* (Oxford: Oxford Univ. Press, 2013).

Barker, Elton T. E., and Joel P. Christensen. "Flight Club: The New Archilochus Fragment and its Resonance with Homeric Epic," *Materiali e discussioni per l'analisi dei testi classici*, 57 (2006), 9–41.

Barnard, Mary. *Sappho: A New Translation* (Berkeley and Los Angeles: Univ. of California Press, 1958).

———. *Assault on Helicon: A Literary Memoir* (Berkeley and Los Angeles: Univ. of California Press, 1984).

———. See *Paideuma* (1994).

Barnstone, Willis. *Greek Lyric Poetry* (New York: Schocken, 1962, 1967).

———. *The Song of Songs, Shir Hashirim* (Athens: Kedros, 1970). Reprint, Green Integer (2002).

———. *Sunday Morning in Fascist Spain: A European Memoir (1948–1958)* (Carbondale: Southern Illinois Univ. Press, 1995).

———. "Sappho Herself" (Letter to the Editor), *New York Review of Books*, 5/26/1996. Response to reviewer D. S. Carne-Ross.

———. "How I Strayed into Asian Poetry," *Manoa*, 12.1 (2000a), 74–78.

———. *With Borges on an Ordinary Evening in Buenos Aires: A Memoir* (Urbana: Univ. of Illinois, 2000b).

———. Letter to the Editor, *Poetry*, 187.2 (2005), 157–159. Response to reviewer Gary Wills (on Santos, tr.). See also Rosanna Warren.

Bassnett, Susan, and Peter Bush, eds. *The Translator as Writer* (London: Continuum, 2006).

Baxter, Elizabeth. "Sappho and Socrates and the Nature of Eros" (Masters Thesis, Dalhousie Univ., Nova Scotia, 2007).

Beach, Christopher. *The Cambridge Introduction to Twentieth-Century American Poetry* (Cambridge: Cambridge Univ. Press, 2003).

Beard, Mary. "Which Thucydides Can You Trust?" *New York Review of Books*, 9/30/2010. Reprint, Mary Beard, *Confronting the Classics: Traditions, Inventions, Innovations* (New York and London: W. W. Norton, 2013), 32–41.

———. "Do the Classics Have a Future?" *New York Review of Books*, 1/12/2012.

Beck, William. "Kleos," in Finkelberg, ed. (2011), Vol. 2, 442–443.

Benardete, Seth. "Achilles and the Iliad," *Hermes*, 91.1 (1963), 1–16.

———. *Achilles and Hector: The Homeric Hero* (South Bend: St. Augustine's Press, 2005).

Bennett, Curtis. "Concerning 'Sappho Schoolmistress,'" *Transactions of the American Philological Association*, 124 (1994), 345–347. Response to Parker, 1993.

Benson, A. C. *English Men of Letters: Edward FitzGerald* (London: Macmillan, 1905).

Bergen, Ann. "Helen's Web: Time and Tableau in the Iliad," *Helios*, 7 (1980), 19–34.

Bermann, Sandra, and Michael Wood, eds. *Nation, Language, and the Ethic of Translation* (Princeton: Princeton Univ. Press, 2005).

Bespaloff, Rachel. *On the Iliad*, Mary McCarthy, tr. (Princeton: Princeton Univ. Press, 1947).

Beye, Charles Rowan. *The Iliad, the Odyssey and the Epic Tradition* (New York: Anchor Books, 1966, 1976).

———. *Ancient Greek Literature and Society* (New York: Anchor Books, 1975, 1987).

———. "Tackling Homer's *Iliad*" (review of Robert Fitzgerald, tr., *The Iliad*), *Parnassus: Poetry in Review*, 2.2 (1975), 137–149.

———. "Reupholstering Greek Tragedy" (review, inter alia, of Robert Fagles, tr., *Aeschylus, The Oresteia*), *Parnassus: Poetry in Review*, 6.1 (1977), 289–304.

———. "Greek Lyrics in and out of Brackets" (review, inter alia, of Guy Davenport, tr., *Archilochos, Sappho, Alkman: Three Lyric Poets*, etc.), *Parnassus: Poetry in Review*, 9.1 (1981), 199–216.

———. "Fitzgerald's *Aeneid*," *Parnassus: Poetry in Review*, 11.2 (1984), 213–235.

———. "Horace in English" (review, inter alia, of Burton Raffel, tr., *The Essential Horace: Odes, Epodes, Satires, and Epistles*), *Parnassus: Poetry in Review*, 14.1 (1987), 164–186.

———. "Logue's Homeric Battles" (review of Christopher Logue, *War Music: An Account of Books 16 to 19 of Homer's Iliad*), *Parnassus: Poetry in Review*, 14.2 (1987–1988), 93–107.

———. *Ancient Epic Poetry: Homer, Apollonius, Virgil, With a Chapter on the Gilgamesh Poems* (Waconda: Bolchazy-Carducci, 2006).

Blake, Warren E. Review of William Smith, tr., *The Iliad of Homer: A Line for Line Translation into Dactylic Hexameters*, in *American Journal of Philology*, 66.2 (1945), 198–202.

Bloch, Ariel, and Chana Bloch, trs. *The Song of Songs* (Berkeley: Univ. of California Press, 1995).

Blondell, Ruby. "'Third Cheerleader From the Left': From Homer's Helen to Helen of Troy," *Classical Receptions Journal*, 1.1 (2009), 4–22.

———. "'Bitch That I Am': Self-Blame and Self-Assertion in the *Iliad*," *Transactions of the American Philological Association*, 140.1 (2010), 1–32.

———. "Refractions of Homer's Helen in Archaic Lyric," *American Journal of Philology*, 131.3 (2010), 349–391.

———. *Helen of Troy: Beauty, Myth, Devastation* (Oxford: Oxford Univ. Press, 2013).

Blunden, Edmund. *War Poets 1914–1918* (Harlow: Longmans, Green, 1958).

Boardman, J., and E. La Rocca. *Eros in Greece* (London: John Murray, 1978).

Bobrick, Benson. *Wide as the Waters: The Story of the English Bible and the Revolution It Inspired* (New York: Simon & Schuster, 2001).

Bogacz, Ted. "'A Tyrrany of Words': Language, Poetry, and Antimodernism in England in the First World War," *Journal of Modern History*, 58.3 (1986), 643–668.

Botterill, Steven, tr. and ed. *Dante: De Vulgari Eloquentia* (Cambridge: Cambridge Univ. Press, Cambridge Medieval Classics, 1996).

Bowersock, Glen. "The Art of Risk" (review of Anne Carson, tr., *Grief Lessons: Four Plays by Euripides*), *New York Review of Books*, 6/14/2007.

Bowie, A. M. *The Poetic Dialect of Sappho and Alcaeus* (New York: Arno, 1981).

Bowra, C. M., and T. F. Higham, eds. *The Oxford Book of Greek Verse in Translation* (Oxford: Clarendon Press, 1938).

———. *Greek Lyric Poetry: From Alcman to Simonides* (Oxford: Oxford Univ. Press, 1961, 1967).

Boyle, A. J., ed. *Roman Epic* (London and New York: Routledge, 1993).

Braden, Gordon, Robert Cummings, and Stuart Gillespie, eds. *The Oxford History of Literary Translation in English (1550–1660), Vol. 2* (Oxford: Oxford Univ. Press, 2010).

Brater, Enoch. "W. B. Yeats: The Poet as Critic," *Journal of Modern Literature*, 4.3 (1975), 651–676.

Bridges, Robert. *Ibant Obscuri: An Experiment in the Classical Hexameter* (Oxford: Clarendon Press, 1916).

Brooten, Bernadette J. *Love Between Women: Early Christian Responses to Female Homoeroticism* (Chicago and London: Univ. of Chicago Press, 1996).

Brown, John Pairman. *Ancient Israel and Greece: Religion, Politics, and Culture* (Minneapolis: Fortress Press, 2003).

Bryant, William Cullen, tr. *The Iliad of Homer, Translated into English Blank Verse* (Boston: Houghton, Mifflin, 1870).

Buchan, Mark. *The Limits of Heroism: Homer and the Ethics of Reading* (Ann Arbor: Univ. of Michigan Press, 2004).

Budelmann, Felix, ed. *The Cambridge Companion to Greek Lyric* (Cambridge: Cambridge Univ. Press, 2009).

Burgess, Jonathan S. "Achilles' Heel: The Death of Achilles in Ancient Myth," *Classical Antiquity*, 14.2 (1995), 217–244.

———. *The Tradition of the Trojan War in Homer and the Epic Cycle* (Baltimore: Johns Hopkins Univ. Press, 2001).

———. "The Epic Cycle and Fragments," in Foley, ed. (2005), 344–352.

Burrow, C. "Virgil in English Translation," in Charles Martindale, ed., *The Cambridge Companion to Virgil* (Cambridge: Cambridge Univ. Press, 1997), 21–37.

Butcher, S. H., tr. *Aristotle's Theory of Poetry and Fine Arts* (New York: Dover Publications, 1951). Greek text, facing translation, commentary, and critical introduction.

Butler, Samuel. *The Authoress of the Odyssey* (London: Jonathan Cape, 1922). Reprint, Univ. of Chicago Press (1967).

Calame, Claude. *Les choeurs de jeunes filles en Grèce archaïque, Vol. 1, Morphologie, fonction religieuse et sociale* (Roma: Edizioni dell' Ateneo & Bizzari, 1977). See also Derek Collins and Janice Orion, trs.

———. "Sappho's Group: An Initiation into Womanhood," in Derek Collins and Janice Orion, trs. (1997). Reprint, Greene, ed. (1996a), 113–124.

Cameron, J. "Sappho's Prayer to Aphrodite," *Harvard Theological Review*, 32.1 (1939), 1–17.

Campbell, David A., ed., tr. *Greek Lyric, Vol. 1, Sappho and Alcaeus* (Cambridge: Harvard Univ. Press, Loeb Classical Library, 1982a).

———, ed. *Greek Lyric Poetry: A Selection of Early Greek Lyric, Elegiac and Iambic Poetry* (London: Bristol Classical Press, 1982b).

———, ed., tr. *Greek Lyric, Vol. 5, The New School of Poetry and Anonymous Songs and Hymns* (Cambridge: Harvard Univ. Press, Loeb Classical Library, 1993).

Cantarella, Eva. *Bisexuality in the Ancient World*, Cormac Ó Cuilleanáin, tr. (New Haven: Yale Univ. Press, 1992).

Carman, William Bliss, tr. *Sappho: One Hundred Lyrics* (Boston: L. C. Page, 1903). Introduction, G. D. Roberts.

Carne-Ross, D. S. "Structural Translation: Notes on Logue's *Patrokleia*," *Arion*, 1.2 (1962), 27–38.

———. "Prima Donna" (review of Barnstone and Davenport, trs.) *New York Review of Books*, 5/3/1966.

———. "On Looking into Fitzgerald's Homer," *New York Review of Books*, 12/12/1974.

———. *Classics and Translation*, Kenneth Haynes, ed. (Lewisburg: Bucknell Univ. Press, 2010).

Carson, Anne. "The Justice of Aphrodite," *Transactions of the American Philological Association*, 110 (1980), 135–142. Reprint, Greene, ed. (1996a), 226–232.

———. *Eros the Bittersweet* (Princeton: Princeton Univ. Press, 1986).

———, tr. *If Not, Winter: Fragments of Sappho* (New York: Vintage, 2003).

Carter, Jane B., and Sarah P. Morris, eds. *The Ages of Homer* (Austin: Univ. of Texas Press, 1995). A Tribute to Emily Townsend Vermeule.

Chadwick, John. "The Descent of Greek Epic," *The Journal of Hellenic Studies*, 110 (1990), 174–177.

Childers, Christopher. "'Brothers' & others: new Sappho poems," *The New Criterion*, 34.6 (2016), 25–30.

Cicero. *Brutus, Orator*, G. L. Hendrickson and H. M. Hubbell, trs. (Cambridge: Harvard Univ. Press, Loeb Classical Library, 1939).

Cingano, Ettore. "A Catalogue Within a Catalogue: Helen's Suitors in the Hesiodic Catalogue of Women (fr. 196–204)," in Richard Hunter, ed., *The Hesiodic Catalogue of Women: Constructions and Reconstructions* (Cambridge: Cambridge Univ. Press, 2005).

Clackson, James, and Geoffrey Horrocks. *The Blackwell History of the Latin Language* (Oxford: Wiley-Blackwell, 2011).

Clader, Linda, and Helen Lee. *The Evolution from Divine to Heroic in Greek Epic Tradition* (Leiden: E. J. Brill, 1976).

Clark, Kenneth. *Civilization: A Personal View* (New York: Harper & Row, 1969).

Clarke, H. W. "In Praise of Pope's Notes," *College Literature*, 3 (1976), 203–218.

Clive, James. *Poetry Notebook: Reflections on the Intensity of Language* (New York: Liveright, 2015). A work echoing many of the concerns of *The Lesbian Lyre*.

Coleman, R. G. G. "Poetic Diction, Poetic Discourse, and the Poetic Register," in Adams and Mayer, eds. (1999), 21–93.

Collins, Derek, and Janice Orion, trs. *Choruses of Young Women in Ancient Greece: Their Morphology, Religious and Social Function* (Lanham: Rowman and Littlefield, 1997). Essentially a corrected, expanded, and updated second edition of Calame, 1977.

Colvin, Stephen. "The Greek *Koine* and the Logic of a Standard Language," in Alexandra Georgakopoulou and Michael Silk, eds., *Standard Languages and Language Standards: Greek, Past and Present,* (Farnham: Ashgate Publishing, 2009).

Commager, Steele. *The Odes of Horace: A Critical Study* (New Haven: Yale Univ. Press, 1962).

Comparetti, Domenico. *Vergil in the Middle Ages*, E. F. M. Benecke, tr. (Princeton: Princeton Univ. Press, 1997). 1st pub. as *Virgilio nel Medio Evo*, 2 vols., 1872.

Conington, John, tr. *The Iliad of Homer, Books XII–XXIV* (Edinburgh: W. Blackwood and Sons, 1868).

———. *The Aeneid of Virgil* (New York: A. C. Armstrong, 1902).

Connolly, T. E. *Swinburne's Theory of Poetry* (Albany: State Univ. of New York Press, 1964).

Cook, Albert Stanburrough. *The Artistic Ordering of Life: An Address* (New Jersey: Rutgers College, 1898).

Cooper, Lane. *The Poetics of Aristotle: Its Meaning and Influence* (Boston: Marshall Jones, 1923).

Copley, Frank O., tr. *The Aeneid: A Verse Translation* (Indianapolis: Bobbs-Merrill, 1965).

Cortiel, Jeanne. *Demand My Writing: Joanna Russ, Feminism, Science Fiction* (Liverpool: Liverpool Univ. Press, 1999).

Cowper, William, tr. *The Iliad of Homer, Translated into English Blank Verse*, Robert Southey, ed., with notes by M. A. Dwight (New York: D. Appleton, 1850).

Cox, Edwin M. *The Poems of Sappho With Historical & Critical Notes, Translations, and a Bibliography* (London: Williams & Norgate; New York: Charles Scribner's Sons, 1925). Update to H. T. Wharton, 1885.

———. *Sappho and the Sapphic Metre in English, with Bibliographical Notes* (London: Chiswick Press, 1916).

Cox, Virginia. *Women's Writing in Italy: 1400–1650* (Baltimore: Johns Hopkins Univ. Press, 2008).

Cramer, Jeffrey S., ed. *Henry D. Thoreau: Walden* (New Haven: Yale Univ. Press, 2004). Annotated edition.

Crossly, Robert. "Pope's *Iliad*: The Commentary and the Translation," *Philological Quarterly*, 56 (1977), 339–357.

Currie, Bruno. "Hesiod and Human History," in Marincola et al., eds. (2012), 37–51.

Cyrino, Monica S. *Aphrodite* (New York: Routledge, 2007).

Dalby, Andrew. *Rediscovering Homer: Inside the Origins of the Epic* (New York: W. W. Norton, 2006).

Dalrymple, Theodore. "Beauty and the Best," in *Farewell Fear* (Nashville: New English Review Press, 2012), 132–137.

Dasenbrock, Reed Way. *Imitating the Italians; Wyatt, Spenser, Synge, Pound, Joyce* (Baltimore and London: Johns Hopkins Univ. Press, 1991).

Davenport, Guy, tr. *Sappho: Poems and Fragments* (Ann Arbor: Univ. of Michigan Press, 1965).

———. *Archilochus, Sappho, Alkman: Three Lyric Poets of the 7th Century B.C.* (Berkeley: Univ. of California Press, 1980).

———. *7 Greeks, Translations of Archilochos, Sappho, Alkman, Anakreon, Herakleitos, Diogenes, and Herodas* (New York: New Directions Books, 1995).

Davidson, James. *The Greeks and Greek Love* (New York: Random House, 2007).

Davidson, Peter. *Ezra Pound and Roman Poetry: A Preliminary Survey* (Amsterdam and Atlanta: Rodopi, 1995).

Davison, J. A. *From Archilochus to Pindar* (London: Macmillan, 1968).

Day, David. *Conquest: How Societies Overwhelm Others* (Oxford: Oxford Univ. Press, 2008).

DeJean, Joan. *Fictions of Sappho, 1546–1937* (Chicago: Univ. of Chicago Press, 1989).

De Laura, David J. "The Place of the Classics in T. S. Eliot's Christian Humanism," in Frederick Will, ed., *HEREDITAS: Seven Essays on the Modern Experience of the Classics* (Austin: Univ. of Texas Press, 1964), 155–197.

Denham, John. "The destruction of Troy, an essay upon the second book of Virgils Aeneis, Written in the Year, 1636" (Printed for Humphrey Moseley, London, 1656). Reprint, Denham, *Poems and Translations* (1668).

Dettmar, Kevin J. H., and Stephen Watt, eds. *Marketing Modernisms: Self-Promotion, Canonization, Rereading* (Ann Arbor: Univ. of Michigan Press, 1996).

D = Diehl, E. *Anthologia Lyrica Graeca* (Leipzig: B. G. Teubneri, 1925, 1953).

Dillon, George, and Edna St. Vincent Millay. *Flowers of Evil, from the French of Charles Baudelaire* (With the Original Texts and with a Preface by Miss Millay) (New York and London: Harper & Brothers, 1956). Millay's thirty-four-page preface echoes many of the concerns of *The Lesbian Lyre.*

Doherty, Lillian E., ed. *Oxford Readings in Classical Studies: Homer's Odyssey* (Oxford: Oxford Univ. Press, 2009).

Donoghue, Denis. *On Eloquence* (New Haven: Yale Univ. Press, 2008).

———. "Three Presences: Yeats, Eliot, Pound," *The Hudson Review,* 62.4 (2010), 563–582.

Donoghue, Emma. *Inseparable: Desire Between Women in Literature* (New York: Alfred A. Knopf, 2010).

Dova, Stamatia. *Greek Heroes in and out of Hades* (Lanham: Lexington Books, 2012).

Dover, Kenneth J. "The Poetry of Archilochus," in "Archiloque," *Entretiens,* etc. (1964), 182–212.

———. *Greek Homosexuality* (London: Duckworth, 1987).

Downes, Jeremy M. *The Female Homer: An Exploration of Women's Epic Poetry* (Newark: Univ. of Delaware Press, 2010).

Downing, Christine. "Lesbian Mythology," *Historical Reflexions,* 20.2 (1994), 169–199.

Drury, Annmarie. "Accident, Orientalism, and Edward FitzGerald as Translator," *Victorian Poetry,* 46.1 (2008), 37–53.

Dryden, John, tr. *The Works of Virgil* (New York: American Book Exchange, 1881).

———. *Virgil's Aeneid* (with Introduction and Notes), *The Harvard Classics,* Vol. 13, Charles W. Eliot, ed. (New York: P. P. Collier & Son, 1909).

———. *Of Dramatic Poesy and Other Critical Essays,* George Watson, ed., 2 vols. (London: J. M. Dent, 1962).

Dubal, David. *The Essential Canon of Classical Music* (New York: Farrar, Straus and Giroux, 2001).

———. "The Piano as Paintbrush: The Wondrous Colors of Debussy," *Wall Street Journal,* 12/19/2012.

Duban, Jeffrey M. "Distortion as a Poetic Device in the 'Pursuit of Hector' and Related Events," *Aevum,* 54 (1980a), 3–22.

———. "Poets and Kings in the *Theogony* Invocation," *Quaderni Ubinati di Cultura Classica,* 33 (1980b), 7–20.

———. "Venus, Epicurus and the *Naturae Species Ratioque,*" *American Journal of Philology,* 103 (1982), 165–177.

———. *Ancient and Modern Images of Sappho: Translations and Studies in Archaic Greek Love Lyric* (Lanham: University Press of America, 1983).

DuBois, Page. *Sappho Is Burning* (Chicago: Univ. of Chicago Press, 1995).

———. Introduction to Roche (1998).

———. *Slaves and Other Objects* (Chicago: Univ. of Chicago Press, 2008).

Dunbar, Henry. *A Complete Concordance to the Odyssey of Homer* (Oxford, 1880). Revised and enlarged by B. Marzullo (Hildesheim and New York: Georg Olms Verlag, 1971).

Durrell, Lawrence. *Sappho: A play in verse* (London: Faber & Faber, 1950).

———. *The Greek Islands* (New York: The Viking Press, 1978).

Dutton, Denis. *The Art Instinct: Beauty, Pleasure, and Human Evolution* (New York and Berlin: Bloomsbury Press, 2009).

Ebbott, Mary. "The Wrath of Helen: Self-Blame and Nemesis in the *Iliad*," in Miriam Carlisle and Olga Levaniouk, eds., *Nine Essays on Homer* (New York and Oxford: Rowman & Littlefield, 1999).

Edmonds, J. M. *Sappho, in the Added Light of the New Fragments, being a paper read before the Classical Society of Newnham College, 22nd February, 1912* (Cambridge: Deighton Bell, 1912).

———, ed., tr. *Lyra Graeca, Vol. 1, Terpander, Alcman, Sappho and Alcaeus* (Cambridge: Harvard Univ. Press, Loeb Classical Library, 1922).

———. *Lyra Graeca, Vols. 1–3* (Cambridge: Harvard Univ. Press, Loeb Classical Library, 1922, 1952).

Edwards, Anthony T. "Kleos Aphthiton and Oral Theory," *Classical Quarterly*, 38.1 (1988), 25–30.

Edwards, Mark. "Homer's Iliad," in Foley, ed. (2005), 302–314.

Einarson, Benedict, and Phillip De Lacy, trs. See *Plutarch, Moralia.*

Eliot, T. S., ed. *Literary Essays of Ezra Pound* (New York: New Directions, 1918).

———. *T. S. Eliot: Selected Essays (1917–1932)* (New York: Harcourt, Brace, 1932).

———. *The Use of Poetry and the Use of Criticism: Studies in the Relation of Criticism to Poetry in England* (New York: Faber & Faber, 1933).

———. *On Poetry and Poets* (London: Faber and Faber, 1943, 1945). Reprint, Farrar, Straus and Giroux (2009).

———. "What is a Classic? an address delivered before the Virgil Society on the 16th of October, 1944," *On Poetry and Poets* (London: Faber and Faber, 1945). Reprint, Farrar, Straus and Giroux (2009), 52–74. See essay of same name by Saint-Beuve.

———. *To Criticize the Critic: Eight Essays on Literature and Education* (New York: Farrar, Straus and Giroux, 1965).

Ellis, William Ashton, tr. *Opera and Drama, Richard Wagner* (Lincoln: Univ. of Nebraska Press, 1995). 1st pub., Kegan, Paul, 1893.

Else, Gerald F. *Aristotle's Poetics: The Argument* (Cambridge: Harvard Univ. Press, 1957).

E-W = Evelyn-White, H. G. *Hesiod, the Homeric Hymns and Homerica* (Cambridge: Harvard Univ. Press; London: William Heinemann, 1914).

Eyres, Harry. *Horace and Me: Life Lessons from an Ancient Poet* (New York: Farrar, Straus & Giroux, 2012).

Fagles, Robert, tr. *The Iliad* (London and New York: Penguin Books, 1990). Bernard Knox, introduction and notes.

Fairclough, H. R. *Horace: Satires, Epistles, Ars Poetica* (Cambridge: Harvard Univ. Press, Loeb Classical Library, 1926).

Falkner, Thomas M. "Slouching Towards Boeotia: Age and Age-Grading in the Hesiodic Myth of the Five Races," *Classical Antiquity*, 8.1 (1989), 42–60.

———. "The Politics and the Poetics of Time in Solon's 'Ten Ages,'" *Classical Journal*, 86.1 (1990), 1–15.

Fantham, Elaine. "The Growth of Literature and Criticism at Rome," in George A. Kennedy, ed., *The Cambridge History of Literary Criticism, Vol. 1, Classical Criticism* (Cambridge: Cambridge Univ. Press, 1989).

Fantuzzi, Marco. *Achilles in Love: Intertextual Studies* (Oxford: Oxford Univ. Press, 2012).

Farnell, G. S. *Greek Lyric Poetry* (London: Longman's Green, 1891).

Farrell, Joseph. "The Origins and Essence of Roman Epic," in Foley, ed. (2005), 417–428.

———, and Michael C. J. Putnam. *A Companion to Vergil's Aeneid and Its Tradition* (Malden: Blackwell Publishing, 2010).

Felson, Nancy, and Laura M. Slatkin. "Gender and Homeric Epic," in Fowler, ed. (2005), 91–116.

Ferkiss, Victor C. "Ezra Pound and American Fascism," *Journal of Politics*, 17.2 (1955), 173–197.

Ferrari, Gloria. *Alcman and the Cosmos of Sparta* (Chicago: Univ. of Chicago Press, 2008).

Filreis, Alan. *Counter-revolution of the Word: The Conservative Attack on Modern Poetry, 1945–1960* (Chapel Hill: Univ. of North Carolina Press, 2008).

Finkelberg, Margalit. "Is Kleos Aphthiton a Homeric Formula?" *Classical Quarterly*, 36.1 (1986), 1–5.

———. *The Birth of Literary Fiction in Ancient Greece* (Oxford: Oxford Univ. Press, 1998).

———, and Guy G. Stroumsa, eds., *Homer, the Bible, and Beyond, Vol. 2* (Leiden: Brill, 2003).

———. *Greeks and Pre-Greeks: Aegean Prehistory and Greek Heroic Tradition* (Cambridge: Cambridge Univ. Press, 2005).

———. "More on *Kleos Aphthiton*," *Classical Quarterly*, 57.2 (2007), 341–350.

———, ed. *The Homeric Encyclopedia, 3 Vols.* (Oxford: Wiley-Blackwell, 2011).

Finley, M. I. *The World of Odysseus* (New York: Viking Press, 1978).

Fiske, Shanyn. *Heretical Hellenism: Women Writers, Ancient Greece, and the Victorian Popular Imagination* (Athens: Ohio Univ. Press, 2008).

FitzGerald, Edward, tr. *The Rubáiyát of Omar Khayyám*, with illustrations by Edmund Dulac (New York: Garden City Books, 1952).

———. *Rubáiyát of Omar Khayyám and the Saláman and Absál of Jámí*, with Biographical Preface by M. K. (New York and Boston: Thomas Y. Crowell, n.d.).

Fitzgerald, Robert, tr. *The Iliad* (Garden City: Anchor Press/Doubleday, 1974).

Fitzgerald, William. *How To Read A Latin Poem, If You Can't Read Latin Yet* (Oxford: Oxford Univ. Press, 2013).

Floyd, Edwin D. "Kleos Aphthiton: An Indo-European Perspective on Early Greek Poetry," *Glotta*, 58.3&4 (1980), 133–157.

Foley, Helene P. "'Reverse Similes' and Sex Roles in the Odyssey," *Arethusa*, 11 (1978), 7–26. Reprint, Harold Bloom, ed., *Modern Critical Interpretations: Homer's the Odyssey* (1988), 87–101. Reprint, Doherty, ed., 189–207.

———, ed. *Reflections of Women in Antiquity* (New York: Gordon and Breach, 1981).

Foley, John Miles. *A Companion to Ancient Epic* (Oxford: Wiley-Blackwell, 2005, 2009).

Ford, Ford Madox. *The March of Literature: From Confucius to Modern Times* (London: Allen & Unwin/Reader's Union, 1947).

Forster, E. M. *Two Cheers for Democracy* (New York and London: Harcourt Brace, 1951).

Fowler, Robert. *The Cambridge Companion to Homer* (Cambridge: Cambridge Univ. Press, 2004).

Fowler, Rowena. "Moments and Metamorphoses: Virginia Woolf's Greece," *Comparative Literature*, 51.3 (1999), 217–242.

Fraenkel, Hermann. *Early Greek Poetry and Philosophy*, M. Hadas and J. Willis, trs. (Oxford: Alden Press, 1963).

———. "Die Zeitauffassung in der frühgriechischen Literatur" [The Concept of Time in Early Greek Literature], in *Wege und Formen frügrichieschen Denkens*, 3rd ed., Franz Tietze, ed. (Munich 1968), 1–22 . Orig. pub., 1931.

Fraser, George Sutherland. *The Modern Writer and His World* (Westport: Greenwood Press, 1975). 1st pub., Frederick A. Praeger, 1965.

Frazer, James George. *Apollodorus, The Library, Vol. II* (Cambridge and London, Harvard Univ. Press, Loeb Classical Library, 1921, 1996).

Friar, Kimon, tr. See Kazantzakis.

Friedrich, Paul. "Sanity and the Myth of Homer: The Problem of Achilles," *Ethos*, 5.3 (1977), 281–305.

———. *The Meaning of Aphrodite* (Chicago: Univ. of Chicago Press, 1978).

Friedrich, Rainer. "'Flaubertian Homer': The *Phrase Juste* in Homeric Diction," *Arion*, 10.2 (2002), 1–13.

Frost, W. "Translating Virgil: Douglas to Dryden," in M. Mack and G. de F. Lord, eds., *Poetic Traditions of the English Renaissance* (New Haven: Yale Univ. Press, 1982).

Fyfe, W. H., tr. See Longinus.

Galinsky, G. Karl. *The Herakles Theme: The Adaptations of the Hero in Literature From Homer to the Twentieth Century* (Oxford: Blackwell, 1972).

Garcia Jr., Lorenzo F. *Homeric Durability: Telling Time in the Iliad* (Washington, D.C.: Center for Hellenic Studies and Harvard Univ. Press, 2013).

G = Gentili, B. *Anacreon* (Roma: Edizioni dell'Ateneo, 1958).

George, Emery. "Translating Poetry: Notes on a Solitary Craft," *The Kenyon Review*, n.s. 4.2 (1982), 33–54.

Gerber, D. D. *Euterpe: An Anthology of Early Greek Lyric, Elegiac, and Iambic Poetry* (Amsterdam: Hakkert, 1970).

Gillespie, Stuart, ed. *John Dryden, Classicist and Translator* (Edinburgh: Edinburgh Univ. Press, 2001).

Glover, T. R. *Horace: A Return to Allegiance* (Cambridge: Cambridge Univ. Press, 1932).

Goethe, Johann Wolfgang von. *The Sorrows of Young Werther and Novella*, Elizabeth Mayer and Louis Bogan, trs.; poems translated and forward by W. H. Auden (New York: Random House, 1971).

Goldberg, Sander M. "Early Republican Epic," in Foley, ed. (2005), 429–439.

Goldhill, Simon. *The Poet's Voice: Essays on Poetics and Greek Literature* (Cambridge and New York: Cambridge Univ. Press, 1991).

———. *Who Needs Greek?: Contests in the Cultural History of Hellenism* (Cambridge: Cambridge Univ. Press, 2002).

González, José M. "The Catalogue of Women and the End of the Heroic Age," *Transactions of the American Philological Association*, 140 (2010), 375–422.

Gordon, Cyrus H. *The Common Background of Greek and Hebrew Civilizations* (New York: W. W. Norton, 1965).

Graver, Bruce. "Wordsworth and the Language of Epic: The Translation of the *Aeneid*," *Studies in Philology*, 83.3 (1986), 261–285.

Graves, Robert. "Dr. Syntax and Mr. Pound," in *The Crowning Privilege: The Clark Lectures, 1954–1955* (London: Cassell, 1955).

———. "Moral Principles in Translation," *Poetry*, XXIV.4 (1965), 47–54.

———. *Poetic Craft and Principle: Lectures and Talks by Robert Graves* (London: The Camelot Press, 1967).

———, ed. *The Greek Myths: Complete and Unabridged in One Volume* (Wakefield: Moyer Bell, 1988).

Graziosi, Barbara, and Emily Greenwood, eds. "Moral Principles in Translation," *Encounter*, 24 (1965), 47–55.

———.*Homer in the Twentieth Century: Between World Literature and the Western Canon* (Oxford: Oxford Univ. Press, 2007).

Green, Peter. "On Fire with Longings" (review of Anne Carson, tr., *If Not, Winter: Fragments of Sappho,* and Stanley Lombardo, tr., *Sappho: Poems and Fragments*), *The New Republic*, 10/7/2002.

———, tr. *The Iliad* (Oakland: Univ. of California Press, 2015). Kudos to Peter Green for his translation of the *Iliad* at age ninety.

Greene, Ellen, ed. *Reading Sappho: Contemporary Approaches* (Berkeley: Univ. of California Press, 1996a).

———. *Re-reading Sappho: Reception and Transmission* (Berkeley: Univ. of California Press, 1996b).

———, and Marilyn B. Skinner, eds. *The New Sappho on Old Age: Textual and Philosophical Issues* (Washington, D.C.: Center for Hellenic Studies and Harvard University Press, 2009).

Grethlein, Jonas. "Homer and Heroic History," in Marincola et al., eds., (2012), 14–36.

Griffen, Roger. *Modernism and Fascism: The Sense of a Beginning under Mussolini and Hitler* (New York: Palgrave Macmillan, 2007).

Griffin, Jasper. "The Epic Cycle and the Uniqueness of Homer," *Journal of Hellenistic Studies*, 97 (1977), 39–53.

Grigson, Geoffrey. *The Goddess of Love: The Birth, Death and Return of Aphrodite* (London: Constable, 1976).

Gross, H. *Sound and Form in Modern Poetry* (Ann Arbor: Univ. of Michigan Press, 1964).

Haeusermann, H. W. "W. B. Yeats's Criticism of Ezra Pound," *The Sewanee Review*, 57.3 (1949), 437–455.

Haines, C. R. *Sappho: The Poems and Fragments* (London: C. Routledge, 1926).

Hall, Edith. "Sensual Sappho," *New York Review of Books,* 3/7/2015. Review of Rayor and Lardinoire (2014).

Hallet, Judith P. "Sappho and Her Social Context: Sense and Sensuality," *Signs: Journal of Women in Culture and Society,* 4 (1979), 447–464. Reprint, Greene, ed. (1996a), 125–142.

———. "Beloved Cleis," *Quaderni Urbinati di Cultura Classica,* n.s. 10 (1982), 21–31.

Hamilton, Edith, and Huntington Cairns, eds. *Plato: The Collected Dialogues* (Princeton: Princeton Univ. Press, Bollingen Series, 1961).

Hanne, Michael. "Metaphors for the Translator," in Bassnett and Bush, eds., 208–224.

Hard, Robin, tr. *Apollodorus, The Library of Greek Mythology* (Oxford: Oxford Univ. Press, Oxford World's Classics, 1997).

Hardie, Alex. "Sappho, the Muses, and Life after Death," *Zeitschrift für Papyrologie und Epigraphik,* 154 (2005), 13–32.

Hardie, Philip. "Spenser's Vergil: The Faerie Queene and the Aeneid," in Farrell and Putnam, eds., 173–185.

Harrison, S. J., ed. *Living Classics: Greece and Rome in Contemporary Poetry in English* (Oxford: Oxford Univ. Press, 2009).

Hartman, C. O. *Free Verse* (Princeton: Princeton Univ. Press, 1980).

Havelock, Ellis A. "The Aeneid and Its Translators," *Hudson Review,* 27 (1974), 338–370.

Hawley, Richard. Review of Page duBois, *Sappho Is Burning,* in *Classical Review,* 49.2 (1999), 342–343.

Hecht, Anthony. *Melodies Unheard: Essays on the Mysteries of Poetry* (Baltimore and London: Johns Hopkins Univ. Press, 2003).

Hendel, Ronald S. "Of Demigods and the Deluge: Toward an Interpretation of Genesis 6:1–4," *Journal of Biblical Literature,* 106.1 (1987), 13–26.

Herington, C. J. "The New Homer," *The Yale Review,* 64 (1975), 568–579.

Heyer, Elfriede, and Roger C. Norton. *Reflections on the Imitation of Greek Works in Painting and Sculpture* (La Salle: Open Court Publishing, 1987).

Highet, Gilbert. *The Classical Tradition: Greek and Roman Influences on Western Literature* (Oxford: Oxford Univ. Press, 1949).

———. *Poets in a Landscape* (New York: Alfred A. Knopf, 1957). Reissued, New York Review of Books, 2010. Introduction, Michael Putnam.

———. "Beer Bottle on the Pediment," *Horizon,* 3.3 (1961), 116–118 (on Pound's *Homage to Sextus Propertius*). Reprint, *Explorations* (1971), 244–256.

———. "The Man in the Grey Velvet Suit," in *Explorations* (1971), 224–232 (on Erik Satie).

———. *Explorations* (New York: Oxford Univ. Press, 1971).

Hobsbaum, Philip. *Metre, Rhythm, and Verse Form* (London and New York: Rutledge, 1996).

Holland, Gary B. "The Name of Achilles: A Revised Etymology," *Glotta,* 71.1&2 (1993), 17–27.

Hooker, Edward Niles, and H. T. Swedenborg, eds. "John Dryden Poems, 1649–1680," in *The Works of John Dryden, Vol. 1* (Berkeley: Univ. of California Press, 1956).

Hooker, J. T. *The Language and Text of Lesbian Poets* (Innsbruck: Institut für Sprachwissenschaft der Univ. Innsbruck, 1977).

Hooley, Daniel H. *The Classics in Paraphrase: Ezra Pound and Modern Translators of Latin Poetry* (London: Associated Univ. Presses, 1988).

Housman, A. E. "The Name and Nature of Poetry" (1933), in John Carter, ed., *A. E. Housman, The Name and Nature of Poetry and Other Selected Prose* (New York: New Amsterdam Books, 1989). 1st. pub., Cambridge Univ. Press, 1961.

Howe, Irving. *Decline of the New* (New York: Harcourt, Brace & World, 1962).

Hubbard, Thomas K., ed. *Homosexuality in Greece and Rome: A Sourcebook of Basic Documents* (Berkeley: Univ. of California Press, 2003).

Hughes-Hallett, Lucy. *Heroes: A History of Hero Worship* (New York: Anchor Books, 2004).

Hunter, Paul J. "The Heroic Couplet: Its Rhyme and Reason," *Ideas from the National Humanities Center*, 4.1 (1966), 22–29.

———. "Seven Reasons for Rhyme," in Lorna Clymer, ed., *Ritual, Routine, and Regime: Repetition in Early Modern British and European Culture* (Toronto: Univ. of Toronto Press, 2006), 172–200.

Hunter, Richard, ed. *The Hesiodic Catalogue of Women: Constructions and Reconstructions* (Cambridge: Cambridge Univ. Press, 2005).

———, and Ian Rutherford, eds. *Wandering Poets in Ancient Greek Culture* (Cambridge: Cambridge Univ. Press, 2009).

Isaacs, J. *The Background of Modern Poetry* (New York: E. P. Dutton, 1952).

Jarratt, Susan C. "Sappho's Memory," *Rhetoric Society Quarterly*, 32.1 (2002), 11–43.

Jay, Peter, and Caroline Lewis, eds. *Sappho Through English Poetry* (London: Anvil Press, 1966).

Jebb, R. C. *Homer: An Introduction to the Iliad and the Odyssey* (Boston and New York: Ginn, 1886).

Johnson, Marguerite. *Sappho* (London: Duckworth, 2007).

Johnson, Samuel. *Lives of the English Poets,* 3 Vols., George Birbeck Hill, ed. (Oxford: Clarendon Press, 1905).

Johnson, Thomas George. *Sappho the Lesbian: A Monograph* (London: Williams and Nougat, 1899).

Johnson, Tore. "Language Change and Metalinguistic Change: Latin to Romance and Other Cases," in Wright, ed. (1996), 19–28.

Johns-Putra, Adeline. *The History of Epic* (New York: Palgrave Macmillan, 2006).

Kahane, Ahuvia. "Hexameter Progression and the Homeric Hero's Solitary State," in Bakker and Kahane, eds., 110–137.

Kaiser, Walter. "A Hero of Translation," *New York Review of Books*, 6/4/2015 (emphasizing consummate Proust translator Charles Scott Moncrieff's schoolboy familiarity with the Classics, English poetry, and the King James Bible).

Katz, Marilyn A. *Penelope's Renown* (Princeton: Princeton Univ. Press, 1991).

———. "Sappho and Her Sisters: Women in Ancient Greece," *Signs: Journal of Women in Culture and Society*, 25.2 (2000), 505–531.

Kazantzakis, Nikos. *The Odyssey: A Modern Sequel, translation into English verse, introduction, synopsis, and notes by Kimon Friar* (New York: Simon and Schuster, 1958). Orig. pub. *Odusseia* (Pyros, Athens, 1938).

Keaney, J. J., and Roberts Lamberton, eds. See Plutarch.

Keener, Frederick, M., ed. *Aeneid, Translated by John Dryden* (London and New York: Penguin, 1997).

Kennedy, George A. "Language and Meaning in Archaic and Classical Greece," in George A. Kennedy, ed., *The Cambridge History of Literary Criticism, Vol. 1: Classical Criticism* (Cambridge: Cambridge Univ. Press, 1989), 78–91.

Kenner, Hugh. *The Pound Era* (Berkeley and Los Angeles: Univ. of California Press, 1971).

———. "Pope's Reasonable Rhymes," *English Literary History*, 41.1 (1974), 74–88.

Kermode, Frank. *The Classic: Literary Images of Permanence and Change* (Cambridge: Harvard Univ. Press, 1983). 1st pub., Viking Press and Faber and Faber, 1975.

Kiernan, V. G. *Horace: Poetics and Politics* (New York: St. Martin's Press, 1999).

Kimball, Roger, and Hilton Kramer eds. *Lengthened Shadows: America and Its Institutions in the Twenty-First Century* (San Francisco: Encounter Books, 2004).

Kirk, Geoffrey S. *The Songs of Homer* (Cambridge: Cambridge Univ. Press, 1962). Edited and shortened as *Homer and the Epic* (Cambridge Univ. Press, 1965).

Kirsch, Adam. *The Modern Element: Essays on Contemporary Poetry* (New York: W. W. Norton, 2008).

Knight, Douglas M. "The Development of Pope's *Iliad* Preface," *Modern Language Quarterly*, 16 (1955), 237–246.

Kramer, Hilton. "Modernism & Its Institutions," in Kimball and Kramer, eds., 25–42.

Kreymborg, Alfred. "American Poetry After the War," *The English Journal*, 22.3 (1933), 175–184, and 22.4 (1933), 263–273.

———. *A History of American Poetry: Our Singing Strength* (New York: Tudor Publishing, 1934).

Kullmann, Wolfgang. "Gods and Men in the *Iliad* and the *Odyssey*," *Harvard Studies in Classical Philology*, 89 (1985), 1–23.

Lang, Andrew. "Homer and the Study of Greek," in *Essays in Little* (New York: Charles Scribner's Sons, 1891; London: Henry, 1891), 77–92.

Lardinois, André. "Lesbian Sappho and Sappho of Lesbos," in J. N. Bremmer, ed., *From Sappho to de Sade: Moments in the History of Sexuality* (London: Routledge, 1989), 15–35.

———. "Subject and Circumstance in Sappho's Poetry," *Transactions of the American Philological Association*, 124 (1994), 57–84. Responding to Holt N. Parker, 1993.

———. "'Someone, I Say, Will Remember Us': Oral Memory in Sappho's Poetry," in E. Anne MacKay, ed., *Orality, Literacy, and Memory in the Ancient Greek and Roman World* (Leiden: Brill Academic Publishers, 2008), 79–96.

Lasserre, F. "Ornements érotiques dans la poésie lyrique archaïque," in J. L. Heller and J. K. Newman, eds., *Serta Turyniana: Studies in Greek Literature and Paleography in Honor of Alexander Turyn* (Urbana: Univ. of Illinois Press, 1974), 5–33.

Lattimore, Richmond, tr. *The Iliad of Homer* (Chicago: Univ. of Chicago Press, 1951).

———, tr. *Greek Lyrics: Translated into Close Approximation of the Original Meter* (Chicago: Univ. of Chicago Press, 1955).

———. *The Poetry of Greek Tragedy* (Baltimore: Johns Hopkins Univ. Press, 1958).

———, tr. *Hesiod: Works and Days, Theogony, Shield of Heracles* (Ann Arbor: Univ. of Michigan Press, 1959).

———, tr. *Greek Lyrics,* 2nd ed. (Chicago: Univ. of Chicago Press, 1960).

———. *Story Patterns in Greek Tragedy* (Ann Arbor: Univ. of Michigan Press, 1964).

———, tr. *The Odyssey of Homer* (New York and London: Harper & Row, 1965).

———, tr. *The Iliad of Homer* (Chicago: Univ. of Chicago Press, 2011). Richard Martin, introduction and notes, 60th anniversary edition.

Lauber, John. "Pound's *Cantos*: A Fascist Epic," *Journal of American Studies,* 12.1 (1978), 3–21.

Leaf, Walter, ed. *The Iliad, Books I–XII, Vol. 1,* edited, with apparatus criticus, prolegomena, notes, and appendices (London: MacMillan & Sons, 1900).

Leighton, Lauren C. "Translation as a Derived Art," *Proceedings of the American Philosophical Society,* 134.4 (1990), 445–454.

Lefkowitz, Mary R. "Cultural Conventions and the Persistence of Mistranslation," *Classical Journal,* 68 (1972), 21–38.

———. "Critical Stereotypes and the Poetry of Sappho," *Greek, Roman, and Byzantine Studies,* 14 (1973), 113–123. Reprint, Greene, ed. (1996a), 26–34.

———. *The Lives of the Greek Poets* (Baltimore: Johns Hopkins Univ. Press, 1982).

Leonard, W. E., tr. *Of the Nature of Things by Lucretius: A Metrical Translation* (New York: Random House, Everyman's Library, 1921).

Lessing, Gotthold Ephraim. *Laocoon: An Essay Upon the Limits of Painting and Poetry,* 6th ed., Ellen Frothingham, tr. (New York: Farrar, Straus & Giroux, 1969).

Levaniouk, Olga. *Eve of the Festival: Making Myth in Odyssey 19* (Washington, D.C.: Center for Hellenic Studies, 2011).

LeVen, Pauline. "New Music and Its Myths: Athenaeus' Reading of the *Aulos* Revolution (*Deipnosophistae* 14.616E–617F)," *Journal of Hellenic Studies,* 130 (2010), 35–37.

Levi, Peter. *Horace: A Life* (London: Gerald Duckworth, 1997).

———, tr. See Pausanias.

Levine, Joseph M. *Between the Ancients and the Moderns: Baroque Culture in Restoration England* (New Haven and London: Yale Univ. Press, 1999).

Lewis, C. Day, tr. *The Aeneid of Virgil* (Oxford: Oxford Univ. Press, 1953).

Lewis, C. S. *A Preface to Paradise Lost* (Oxford: Oxford Univ. Press, 1942).

———, tr. *Aeneid.* See A. T. Reyes.

Lewis, Charlton Thomas. "Mr. Bryant's Translation of the Iliad," *North American Review,* 112.231 (1871), 328–370.

Lianeri, Alexandra and Vanda Zajko, eds. *Translation & The Classic: Identity as Change in the History of Culture* (Oxford: Oxford Univ. Press, 2008).

Lidov, Joel B. "The Second Stanza of Sappho 31: Another Look," *American Journal of Philology*, 114.4 (1993), 503–535.

Lind, L. R. "Traduttore Traditore: The Great Ages of Translation," *Classical Journal*, 44.6 (1949), 371–377.

———, ed. *Latin Poetry in Verse Translation: From the Beginnings to the Renaissance* (Boston: Houghton Mifflin, 1957).

———, tr. *Virgil's Aeneid: An Epic Poem of Rome* (Bloomington: Indiana Univ. Press, 1962).

———. "On 'Modern' Translation," *Classical and Modern Literature*, 3 (1983), 69–74.

Lloyd-Jones, Hugh. "Translating Homer," in *Greek in a Cold Climate* (Savage: Barnes & Noble Books, 1991). 1st pub. as "Welcome Homer!" (reviews of Robert Fagles, *Iliad*; Michael Reck, *Iliad*; and Allen Mandelbaum, *Odyssey*), *New York Review of Books*, 2/14/1991.

Lloyd, Paul M. "Latin Versus Romance: One Language or Two?" *Hispanic Review*, 52.3 (1984), 367–377. Review article of Roger Wright, *Late Latin and Early Romance in Spain and Carolingian France* (Liverpool: Francis Cairns, 1982).

———. "On the Names of Languages (and Other Things)," in Roger Wright, ed., *Latin and the Romance Languages in the Early Middle Ages* (University Park: Pennsylvania State Univ. Press, 1996).

LP = Lobel, Edgar, and Denys L. Page. *Poetarum Lesbiorum Fragmenta* (Oxford: Clarendon Press, 1955, 1968).

Logan, William. "Ezra Pound at the Post Office" (review of nine books of Pound correspondence, 1967–1991), *Parnassus: Poetry in Review*, 20.1&2 (1995), 55–77.

———. *Our Savage Art: Poetry and the Civil Tongue* (New York: Columbia Univ. Press, 2009).

———. "The Unbearable Rightness of Criticism," *The New Criterion*, 30.8 (2012), 21–28.

Logue, Christopher. *War Music: An Account of Homer's Iliad* (New York: Farrar, Straus & Giroux, 2016).

Longinus. *On the Sublime*, W. H. Fyfe, tr., revised by Donald Russell (Cambridge: Harvard Univ. Press, Loeb Classical Library, 1995).

Loraux, Nicole. *The Experiences of Tiresias: The Feminine and the Greek Man* (Princeton: Princeton Univ. Press, 1995).

———, Gregory Nagy, and Laura Slatkin, eds. *Antiquities: Postwar French Thought, Vol. III* (New York: The New Press, 2001).

Lord, Albert B. *The Singer of Tales* (New York: Atheneum, 1968). 1st pub., *Harvard Studies in Comparative Literature 24*, 1960.

Loudon, Bruce. "The Gods in Epic, or the Divine Economy," in Foley, ed. (2005), 90–104.

Lowell, Robert. "Three Letters to Anaktoria," in *Imitations* (London: Faber and Faber, 1962).

Lucas, F. L. "Few but Roses," *The Dial*, 77 (September, 1924), 201–208.

———, tr. *Greek Poetry* (London: J. M. Dent & Sons, Everyman Library, 1966).

Macaulay, Alastair. "Translating Poetry to the Stage, With or Without Words," *New York Times* (Dance), 7/21/2010.

MacCary, Thomas J. *Childlike Achilles: Ontogeny and Phylogeny in the Iliad* (New York: Columbia Univ. Press, 1982).

Mackail, J. W. *Latin Literature* (London: John Murray, 1895).

———. *Lectures on Greek Poetry* (London: Longmans, Green, 1919).

Mackie, Hilary. *Talking Trojan: Speech and Community in the Iliad* (Lanham: Rowman & Littlefield, 1996).

Maegher, Robert Emmet. *The Meaning of Helen: In Search of an Ancient Icon* (Wauconda: Bolchazy-Carducci, 2002).

Maguire, Laurie. *Helen of Troy: From Homer to Hollywood* (Oxford: Wiley-Blackwell, 2009).

Manent, Pierre. "City, Empire, Church, Nation: How the West Created Modernity," *City Journal*, 22.3 (2012), 48–57.

Manguel, Alberto. *Homer's The Iliad and The Odyssey, A Biography* (New York: Grove Press, 2007).

Marincola, John, Lloyd Llewellyn-Jones, and Calum Maciver, eds. *Greek Notions of the Past in the Archaic and Classical Eras: History without Historians* (Edinburgh: Edinburgh Univ. Press, 2012).

Markley, A. A. *Stateliest Measures: Tennyson and the Literature of Greece and Rome* (Toronto: Univ. of Toronto Press, 2004).

Marks, J. "The Junction Between the *Kypria* and the *Iliad*," *Phoenix*, 56.1&2 (2002), 1–24.

Marris, W. S. *The Odes of Horace: Books I–IV & The Secular Hymn, Translated into English Verse* (London and Edinburgh: Oxford Univ. Press, 1912).

Marry, J. D. "Sappho and the Heroic Ideal: *erotos arete*," *Arethusa*, 12 (1979), 71–92.

Martin, Meredith. *The Rise and Fall of Meter: Poetry and English National Culture, 1860–1930* (Princeton and Oxford: Princeton Univ. Press, 2012).

Martin, Richard P. "Similes and Performance," in Bakker and Kahane eds., 138–166.

Marx, Olga, and Ernst Morwitz, trs. *Poems of Alcman Sappho and Ibycus* (New York: Alfred A. Knopf, 1945).

Mason, H. A. *To Homer Through Pope: An Introduction to Homer's Iliad and Pope's Translation* (Great Britain: Harper & Row, 1972).

May, Herbert G., and Bruce M. Metzger, eds. *The Oxford Annotated Bible With the Apocrypha: Revised Standard Version* (Oxford: Oxford Univ. Press, 1962).

Mayer, Kenneth. "Helen and the Dios Boule," *American Journal of Philology*, 117.1 (1996), 1–15.

Maynard, Roy, ed. *Fierce Wars and Faithful Loves: Edmund Spenser's The Faerie Queene, Book 1* (Moscow: Canon Press, 1999).

McEvilley, Thomas. *Sappho* (Putnam: Spring Publications, 2008).

McWilliams Jr., John P. *The American Epic: Transforming a Genre, 1770–1860* (Cambridge: Cambridge Univ. Press, 1989).

Mendelsohn, Daniel. "Yo, Achilles: A Classicist Renders the 'Iliad' in a Contemporary and Colloquial Voice," *New York Times* (Books), 7/20/1997.

———. "Brush Up Your Aeschylus: New translations of classical Greek drama seek to find a contemporary audience," *New York Times* (Books), 7/9/1998.

———. "In Search of Sappho" (review of Anne Carson, *If Not, Winter: Fragments of Sappho*), *New York Review of Books*, 8/14/2003. Reprint, Mendelsohn (2012), 121–138.

———. "A Little Iliad" (review of Benioff/Peterson, *Troy* [2004]), *New York Review of Books*, 6/24/2004.

———. “The Strange Music of Horace,” *New York Review of Books*, 5/13/2004. Reprint, Mendelsohn (2012), 159–178.

———. *Waiting for the Barbarians: Essays From the Classics to Pop Culture* (New York: New York Review of Books, 2012).

———. “Herakles: Punished Again!” *New York Review of Books*, 5/23/2013.

———. “The Bacchae: Ecstasy & Terror,” *New York Review of Books*, 9/25/2014.

———. “Girl, Interrupted: Who Was Sappho,” *The New Yorker*, 3/16/2015. Review of Rayor and Lardinoire (2014).

Menocal, María Rosa. *Shards of Love: Exile and the Origins of the Lyric* (Durham: Duke Univ. Press, 1994).

MW = Merkelbach, R., and M. L. West. *Fragmenta Hesiodea* (Oxford: Oxford Univ. Press, 1967).

Miller, Dean A. *The Epic Hero* (Baltimore: Johns Hopkins Univ. Press, 2000).

Miller, Jeffrey Alan. “Fruit of good labours: Discovering the earliest known draft of the King James Bible,” *Times Literary Supplement*, 10/14/2015.

Miller, Marion Mills, and David Moore Robinson. *The Songs of Sappho* (New York: Frank-Maurice, 1925). Translation into “Rimed Verse” by Miller. Greek texts prepared, annotated, and literally translated into prose by Robinson. Elaborate four-hundred-page edition with “Selected Bibliography Supplementary to Wharton’s.”

Mills, Donald H. *The Hero and the Sea: Patterns of Chaos in Ancient Myth* (Wauconda: Bolchazy-Carducci, 2003).

Monro, David B., and Thomas W. Allen. *Homeri Opera: Iliadis Libri I–XXIV*, 2 Vols. (Oxford: Clarendon Press, 1902, 3rd ed., 1969).

Monro, Harold, ed. *Twentieth Century Poetry: An Anthology Chosen by Harold Monro*. Revised and enlarged by Alida Monro (London: Chatto and Windus, 1929, 1933).

Monsacré, Hélène. “The Erotic Images of War,” in Loraux et al., eds., 276–282. Translated and abridged from “Les images érotiques de la guerre,” in Monsacré, *Les larmes d’Achille: Le héros, la femme et la souffrance dans la poésie d’Homère* (Paris: Éditions Albin Michel, 1984), 63–77.

Morris, William, tr. *The Aeneids of Virgil* (London: Ellis & White, 1876).

M= Most, Glenn W. *The Shield, Catalogue of Women, Other Fragments,* (Cambridge and London: Harvard Univ. Press, Loeb Classical Library, 2007).

Moulton, Carroll. “Similies in the *Iliad*,” *Hermes*, 102.3 (1974), 381–397.

———. *Similes in the Homeric Poems* (Göttingen: Vandenhoeck & Ruprecht, 1977).

Muellner, Leonard. *The Anger of Achilles: Mēnis in Greek Epic* (Ithaca: Cornell Univ. Press, 1996).

Murnaghan, Sheila. “Equal Honor and Future Glory: The Plan of Zeus in the *Iliad*,” in Deborah H. Roberts, Francis M. Dunn, and Don Fowler eds., *Classical Closure: Reading the End in Greek and Latin Literature* (Princeton: Princeton Univ. Press, 1997).

Murray, Gilbert. *The Rise of Greek Epic* (Oxford: The Clarendon Press, 1907, 1911 [2nd ed]., 1924 [3rd ed.]). A course of lectures delivered at Harvard University.

———. “What English Poetry May Still Learn from Greek,” in W. P. Ker, ed., *Essays and Studies by Members of the English Association, Vol. III* (Oxford: The Clarendon Press, 1912), 7–31.

———. *The Classical Tradition in Poetry* (Cambridge: Harvard Univ. Press, 1930).

———. "A Book to Keep," *Journal of Hellenic Studies*, 74 (1954), 49–55.

Nabokov, Vladimir. "On Adaptation," *New York Review of Books*, 4/12/1969.

Nagy, Gregory. "Sappho's Phaon, and the White Rock of Leukas," *Harvard Studies in Classical Philology*, 77 (1973), 137–177. Reprint, Nagy (1990b), 223–262. Revised and retitled, "Phaethon, Sappho's Phaon, and the White Rock of Leukas: 'Reading' the Symbols of Greek Lyric," in Greene, ed. (1996a), 35–57.

———. *Comparative Studies in Greek and Indic Meter* (Cambridge: Harvard Univ. Press, 1974).

———. "The Wedding of Hektor and Andromache: Epic Contacts in Sappho 44LP," in Nagy (1974), 118–139.

———. "Iambos: Typologies of Invective and Praise," in Van Sickle (1976a), 191–205.

———. "Formula and Meter," in B. A. Stolz and R. S. Shannon, eds., *Oral Literature and the Formula* (Ann Arbor: Center for the Coordination of Ancient and Modern Studies, 1976b), 239–260.

———. *The Best of the Achaeans: Concepts of the Hero in Archaic Greek Poetry* (Baltimore: Johns Hopkins Univ. Press, 1979). 2nd ed., new introduction, 1999.

———. "Another Look at *Kleos Aphthiton*." *Würzburger Jahrbücher für die Altertumswissenschaft*, n.f. 7 (1981), 113–116. Response to Floyd.

———. "Hesiod," in T. J. Luce, ed., *Ancient Writers: Greece and Rome* (New York: Charles Scribner's Sons, 1982), Vol. I, 43–74.

———. "Theognis and Megara: A Poet's Vision of His City," in Thomas J. Figueira and Gregory Nagy, eds., *Theognis of Megara: Poetry and the Polis* (Baltimore: Johns Hopkins Univ. Press, 1985).

———. "Early Greek Views of Poets and Poetry," in George A. Kennedy, ed., *The Cambridge History of Literary Criticism, Classical Criticism* (Cambridge: Cambridge Univ. Press, 1989), Vol. I, 1–77.

———. *Pindar's Homer: The Lyric Possession of an Epic Past* (Baltimore: Johns Hopkins Univ. Press, 1990a).

———. *Greek Mythology and Poetics* (Ithaca: Cornell Univ. Press, 1990b).

———. *Homeric Questions* (Austin: Univ. of Texas Press, 1993).

———. "The Name of Achilles: Questions of Etymology and Folk-Etymology," *Illinois Classical Studies*, 19 (1994), 3–9. Response to G. B. Holland, *Glotta*, 71.1&2 (1993), 17–27.

———. "An Evolutionary Model for the Making of Homeric Poetry: Comparative Perspectives," in Carter and Morris, eds. (1995), 163–179.

———. *Poetry as Performance: Homer and Beyond* (Cambridge: Cambridge Univ. Press, 1996).

———. *Plato's Rhapsody and Homer's Music: The Poetics of the Panathenaic Festival in Classical Athens* (Washington, D.C.: Center for Hellenic Studies, 2002).

———. *Homer's Text and Language* (Urbana: Univ. of Illinois Press, 2004a).

———. "Transmission of Archaic Greek Sympotic Songs: From Lesbos to Alexandria," *Critical Inquiry*, 31.1 (2004b), 26–48.

———. "The Epic Hero," in Foley, ed. (2005), 71–89. 2nd ed., Nagy, Vol. I.4 (2012).

———. "Did Sappho and Alcaeus Ever Meet? Symmetries of Myth and Ritual in Performing the Songs of Ancient Lesbos," in Anton Bierl et al., eds., *Literatur und Religion I. Wege zu einer mythisch-rituellen Poetik bei den Griechen* (Berlin: Walter de Gruyter, 2007), 211–269. 2nd ed. revised and corrected, Nagy, Vol. II.14 (2012).

———. *Homer the Classic* (Washington, D.C.: Center for Hellenic Studies, 2009).

———. *Homer the Preclassic* (Berkeley: Univ. of California Press, 2010). Sather Classical Lectures, Vol. 37.

———. "The Aeolic Component in Homeric Diction," in S. W. Jamison, H. C. Melchert, and B. Vine, eds., *Proceedings of the 22nd Annual UCLA Indo-European Conference* (Bremen: Ute Hempen Verlag, 2011), 133–179. Reprint, Nagy, Vol. 1.1 (2012).

———. *Short Writings,* Vols. I–III, online anthologies containing articles by Gregory Nagy (Washington, D.C.: Center for Hellenic Studies, 2012, 2014). www.chs.harvard.edu (online publications).

Nelson, Stephanie. "Hesiod," in Foley, ed. (2005), 330–343.

Newman, Francis W. *Homeric Translation in Theory and Practice, A Reply to Matthew Arnold* (London: Williams and Norgate, 1861).

Nicoll, Allardyce, ed. *Chapman's Homer: The Iliad,* 2 Vols. (Princeton: Princeton Univ. Press, Bollingen Series, 1956). Preface, Garry Wills.

Nikoletseas, Michael M. *The Iliad—Twenty Centuries of Translation: A Critical View* (CreateSpace Independent Publishing Platform, 2012).

———. *The Iliad: The Male Totem* (CreateSpace, 2013).

Nitchie, Elizabeth. "Propertius, Kin to the Romantics," *The Sewanee Review,* 31.2 (1923), 205–219.

O'Hara, John Meyers. *The Poems of Sappho: An Interpretive Rendition into English* (Portland: Smith & Hale, 1924).

Omond, T. S. *English Hexameter Verse* (Edinburgh: David Douglas, 1897).

———. *English Metrists in the Eighteenth and Nineteenth Centuries* (New York and London: Oxford Univ. Press, 1907).

———. Review of H. B. Cotterill, tr., *Homer's Odyssey: A Line-for-Line Translation in the Metre of the Original,* in *The Modern Language Review,* 7.2 (1912), 257–262.

Ormand, Kirk. *The Hesiodic Catalogue of Women and Archaic Greece* (Cambridge: Cambridge Univ. Press. 2014).

Osborne, Robin. "Ordering Women in Hesiod's *Catalogue,*" in Richard Hunter, ed.

Ostler, Nicholas. *Ad Infinitum: A Biography of Latin* (New York: Walker and Company, 2007).

Otis, Brooks. *Virgil: A Study in Civilized Poetry* (Oxford: Clarendon Press, 1963).

———. "Horace and Housman," *Pacific Coast Philology,* 2 (1967), 5–24.

Page, Denys L. *Alcman: The Partheneion* (Oxford: Clarendon Press, 1951).

———. *Sappho and Alcaeus: An Introduction to the Study of Ancient Lesbian Poetry* (Oxford: Clarendon Press, 1955).

———. *History and the Homeric Iliad* (Berkeley and Los Angeles: Univ. of California Press, 1959).

P = ———. *Poetae Melici Graeci* (Oxford: Clarendon Press, 1962).

———. "Archilochus and the Oral Tradition," in "Archiloque," *Entretiens*, etc. (1964), 119–163.

Paglia, Camille. *Sexual Personnae: Art and Decadence From Nefertiti to Emily Dickinson* (New York: Random House, 1990).

*Paideuma: A Journal Devoted to Ezra Pound Scholarship*, 23.1 (1994). Mary Barnard issue.

Paige, D. D., ed. *The Letters of Ezra Pound, 1907–1941* (New York: Harcourt Brace, 1950).

Palmer, Henrietta. *A List of English Editions and Translations of Greek and Latin Classics Printed Before 1641* (London: London Bibliographical Society, 1911).

Parker, Fred. "Classic Simplicity," in Lianeri and Zajko, eds., 227–242.

Parker, Holt N. "Sappho Schoolmistress," *Transactions of the American Philological Association*, 123 (1993), 309–351. Reprint, Greene ed.(1996b), 146–183.

———. "Sappho's Daughter/Clitoris/Lover," *Rheinisches Museum für Philologie*, n.f. 149.1 (2006), 109–112.

Parry, Milman. "Studies in the Epic Technique of Oral Verse-Making: I: Homer and Homeric Style," *Harvard Studies in Classical Philology*, 41 (1930), 73–148.

Pausanias. *Guide to Greece. Vol. 1: Central Greece*, Peter Levi, tr. (Harmondsworth: Penguin Books, 1971).

Pei, Mario. *The Story of Latin and the Romance Languages* (New York: Harper & Row, 1976).

Percy III, William A. *Pederasty and Pedagogy in Archaic Greece* (Urbana: Univ. of Illinois Press, 1996).

Peterson, Linda H. "Sappho and the Making of Tennysonian Lyric," *English Literary History*, 61.1 (1994), 121–137.

Petropoulos, J. C. B. "Sappho the Sorceress—Another Look at Fr. 1 (LP)," *Zeitschrift für Papyrologie und Epigraphik*, 97 (1993), 43–56.

Pfeiffer, Robert H., and William G. Pollard. *The Hebrew Iliad: The History of the Rise of Israel Under Saul and David* (New York: Harper & Brothers, 1957).

Philips, F. Carter. "Heracles," *Classical World*, 71.7 (1978), 431–440.

Plutarch. *Essay on the Life and Poetry of Homer*, J. J. Keaney and Robert Lamberton, eds. (Atlanta: Scholars Press, 1996).

———. *Moralia*, Vol. 14, Benedict Einarson and Phillip De Lacy, trs. (Cambridge: Harvard Univ. Press, Loeb Classical Library, 1967).

———. "On Music," in *Moralia*, Vol. 14, 344–455.

Poochigian, Aaron, tr. *Sappho, Stung with Love: Poems and Fragments* (New York: Penguin Books, 2009).

Pope, Alexander. *The Iliad of Homer*, Steven Shankman, ed. (New York: Penguin Classics, 1996).

Pound, Ezra. "Raphaelite Latin," *Book News Monthly*, 25.1 (1906), 31–34. Pound's first published article, announcing his sacrifice of original poetic form to translated thought, based on the Latin's verbal nuances.

———. *The Spirit of Romance* (London: J. M. Dent, 1910). Reissued, New Directions, 1952, 2005.

———. "Horace," *The Criterion*, IX.35 (1930), 217–227. Reprint, *Arion* 9.2&3 (1970), 178–187.

———. *ABC of Reading* (New York: New Directions, 1934, 2010).

———. *Make It New* (London: Faber and Faber, 1934). Reissued, Yale Univ. Press, 1935.

———. *Polite Essays* (London: Faber and Faber, 1937), Reissued, New Directions, 1940.

———. "How to Read," in *Polite Essays* (1940), 155–192.

———. *Guide to Kultchur* (New York: New Directions, 1938, 1968).

———. *The Letters of Ezra Pound, 1907–1941*; see D. D. Paige, ed. (1950).

———. *Literary Essays of Ezra Pound,* T. S. Eliot, ed. (New York: New Directions, 1954, 1968). Essays, 1918–1937. Introduction, T. S. Eliot.

———. "Early Translators of Homer," in *Literary Essays* (1968), 249–276.

———. "A Retrospect," in *Literary Essays* (1968), 3–14.

Powell, Jim, tr. *Sappho: A Garland: The Poems and Fragments of Sappho* (New York: Farrar, Straus and Giroux, 1993). Abridged and reissued as *The Poetry of Sappho* (Oxford: Oxford Univ. Press, 2007).

Power, Timothy. *The Culture of Kitharôidia* (Washington, D.C.: Center for Hellenic Studies, 2010).

Prendergast, Guy Lushington. *A Complete Concordance to the Iliad of Homer* (London, 1875). Revised and enlarged by B. Marzullo (Hildesheim and New York: Georg Olms Verlag, 1971).

Prentice, William K. "Sappho," *Classical Philology*, 13.4 (1918), 347–360.

Prins, Yopie. "Sappho's Afterlife in Translation," in Greene, ed. (1996b), 36–57.

———. *Victorian Sappho* (Princeton: Princeton Univ. Press, 1999).

———. "Metrical Translation: Nineteenth-Century Homers and the Hexameter Mania," in Bermann and Wood, eds. (2005), 227–257.

Purves, Alex. "Falling into Time in Homer's *Iliad*," *Classical Antiquity*, 25.1 (2006), 179–209.

Putnam, Michael C. J. *The Poetry of the Aeneid: Four Studies in Imaginative Unity and Design* (Cambridge: Harvard Univ. Press, 1966).

———. "The Virgilian Achievement," *Arethusa*, 5 (1972), 53–70. Reprint, Putnam (1995), 9–26.

———. "Catullus 11: The Ironies of Integrity," *Ramus* 3 (1974), 70–86. Reprint, Putnam (1982), 13–29.

———. "*Pius* Aeneas and the Metamorphosis of Lausus," *Arethusa*, 14 (1981), 139–156. Reprint, Putnam (1995), 134–151.

———. *Essays on Latin Lyric, Elegy, and Epic* (Princeton: Princeton Univ. Press, 1982).

———. *Virgil's Aeneid: Interpretation and Influence* (Chapel Hill and London: Univ. of North Carolina Press, 1995).

———. "The Lyric Genius of the 'Aeneid,'" *Arion*, 3.2&3 (1995–1996), 81–101. The influence of Catullus 11 on the *Aeneid*.

———. *The Humanness of Heroes: Studies in the Conclusion of Virgil's Aeneid* (Amsterdam: Amsterdam Univ. Press, 2011).

Raffel, Burton. "Mary Barnard's Sappho," *The Hudson Review*, 18.2 (1965), 236–241.

Rajan, Balachandra. *The Form of the Unfinished: English Poetics from Spenser to Pound* (Princeton: Princeton Univ. Press, 1985).

Rankin, H. D. *Archilochus of Paros* (Park Ridge: Noyes Press, 1977).

Rawson, Claude, ed. *The Cambridge Companion to English Poets* (Cambridge: Cambridge Univ. Press, 2011).

Raymond, M. B. *Swinburne's Poetics: Theory and Practice* (The Hague: Mouton, 1971).

Rayor, Diane J., tr. *Sappho Poems* (Colorado Springs: Press at Colorado College, 1980).

———. *Sappho's Lyre: Archaic Lyric and Women Poets of Ancient Greece* (Oakland: Univ. of California Press, 1991).

———, and André Lardinoire. *Sappho: A New Translation of the Complete Works* (Cambridge: Cambridge Univ. Press, 2014). Reviewed by Mendelsohn (2015), Hall (2015), and Stallings (2015).

Ready, Jonathan L. *Character, Narrator, and Simile in the Iliad* (Cambridge and New York: Cambridge Univ. Press, 2011).

Reck, Michael, tr. *Homer: The Iliad for Speaking* (Breitbrunn am Ammersee: Porpentine Press, 1990).

Reeves, John D. "The Cause of the Trojan War: A Forgotten Myth Revived," *Classical Journal*, 61.5 (1966), 211–214.

———. "The Cause of the War: Addendum," *Classical Journal*, 62.7 (1967), 314–315.

Rexroth, Kenneth. *With Eye and Ear* (New York: Herder and Herder, 1970).

Reyes, A. T., ed. *C. S. Lewis's Lost Aeneid: Arms and the Exile* (New Haven: Yale Univ. Press, 2011). Introduction, T. S. Reyes.

Reynolds, Margaret. *The Sappho History* (New York: Palgrave Macmillan, 2003).

Reynolds, Matthew. *The Poetry of Translation: From Chaucer & Petrarch to Homer & Logue* (Oxford: Oxford Univ. Press, 2011).

Riding, Laura, and Robert Graves. *A Survey of Modernist Poetry* (New York: Haskell House Publishers, 1928, 1969).

Robbins, Emmet I. *Thalia Delighting in Song: Essays in Ancient Greek Poetry*, Bonnie MacLachlan, ed. (Toronto and London: Univ. of Toronto Press, 2013).

Robbins, Ernest. "The Education of Achilles," *Quaderni Urbinati di Cultura Classica*, n.s. 45.3 (1933), 7–20.

Robert, Louis. "Inscriptions from Lesbos," in Loraux et al., eds., 240–248. 1st pub., *Revue des études grecques*, 73 (1960), 285–315.

Roberts, Deborah H., Francis M. Dunn, and Don Fowler. *Classical Closure: Reading the End in Greek and Latin Literature* (Princeton: Princeton Univ. Press, 1997).

Robinson, David M. *Sappho and Her Influence* (Boston: Marshall Jones, 1924).

Robinson, Douglas. *The Translator's Turn* (Baltimore: Johns Hopkins Univ. Press, 1991).

Roche, Paul, tr. *The Love Songs of Sappho* (New York: Mentor Books, 1966). Reprint, Prometheus Books (1998). Introduction, Page duBois.

Rose, H. J. *A Handbook of Latin Literature: From the Earliest Times to the Death of St. Augustine* (Wauconda: Bolchazy-Carducci, 1996). 1st pub., Methuen, 1936.

Rosen, Charles. *Freedom and the Arts: Essays on Music and Literature* (Cambridge: Harvard Univ. Press, 2012).

Rosen, Ralph M. "Aristophanes' Frogs and the Contest of Homer and Hesiod," *Transactions of the American Philological Association*, 134.2 (2004), 285–322.

Rosenmeyer, Patricia A. "Girls at Play in Early Greek Poetry," *American Journal of Philology*, 125 (2004), 163–178.

Rosenwald, Lawrence. "On Not Reading in Translation," *The Antioch Review*, 62.2 (2004), 308–318.

Ross, David O. Preface to A. T. Reyes, ed.

Rubino, Carl, and Cynthia Shelmerdine, eds. *Approaches to Homer* (Austin: Univ. of Texas Press, 1983).

Ruskin, John. *The True and the Beautiful, Part 5, Painting* (New York and Boston: H. M. Caldwell, 1855).

———. "The English Translators of Homer," *The National Review*, 10 (1860), 283–314.

Russ, Joanna. *To Write Like a Woman: Essays in Feminism and Science Fiction* (Bloomington: Indiana Univ. Press, 1995).

Russo, Joseph. "Homer Against His Tradition," *Arion*, 7.2 (1968), 275–295.

———. "Reading the Greek Lyric Poets (Monodists)" (review of Gordon Kirkwood, *Early Greek Monody: The History of a Poetic Type*), *Arion*, n.s. 1.4 (1973/1974), 707–730.

———. "Parry, Milman," in Finkelberg, ed. (2011), Vol. II, 629–631.

Rydbeck, Lars. "Sappho's Phainetai Moi Kēnos," *Hermes*, 97 (1969), 161–166.

Saïd, Suzanne. *Homer and the Odyssey*, Ruth Webb, tr. (Oxford: Oxford Univ. Press, 2011).

Sainte-Beuve, Charles Augustin. "What is a Classic," E. Lee, tr., in Charles W. Eliot, ed., *The Harvard Classics: Literary and Philosophical Essays*, Vol. 32 (New York: P. F. Collier & Son, 1910). See essay of same name by T. S. Eliot.

Santayana, George. *The Sense of Beauty* (New York: Charles Scribner's Sons, 1896).

———. *Three Philosophical Poets: Lucretius, Dante, and Goethe* (Cambridge: Harvard Univ. Press, 1910).

Santos, Sherod. *Greek Lyric Poetry: A New Translation* (New York: W. W. Norton, 2005).

Schein, S. I. *The Mortal Hero: An Introduction to Homer's Iliad* (Berkeley: Univ. of California Press, 1984).

Schlauch, Margaret. "Philology and Undergraduates," *The English Journal*, 17.6 (1928), 487–494.

———. "The Anti-Humanism of Ezra Pound," *Science and Society*, 13.3 (1949), 258–269.

Schmidt, Michael, *Lives of the Poets* (New York: Random House, 1998).

———. *The First Poets: Lives of the Ancient Greek Poets* (New York: Alfred A. Knopf, 2005).

Scodel, Ruth. "The Achaean Wall and the Myth of Destruction," *Harvard Studies in Classical Philology*, 86 (1982), 33–50.

Scott, J. A. "The Assumed Duration of the War of the *Iliad*," *Classical Philology*, 8.4 (1913), 445–456.

Segal, Charles, P. "Eros and Incantation: Sappho and Oral Poetry," *Arethusa*, 7 (1974), 139–160. Reprint, Greene, ed. (1996a), 58–75.

———. *Lucretius on Death and Anxiety, Poetry and Philosophy in the De Rerum Natura* (Princeton: Princeton Univ. Press, 1990).

———. *Oedipus Tyrannus: Tragic Heroism and the Limits of Knowledge* (New York and Oxford: Oxford Univ. Press, 1993, 2001).

———. *Singers, Heroes, and Gods in the Odyssey* (Ithaca: Cornell Univ. Press, 1994).

Sellar, W. Y. *The Roman Poets of the Augustan Age: Virgil* (Oxford: Clarendon Press, 1897).

Shankman, Steven. *Pope's "Iliad": Homer in the Age of Passion* (Princeton: Princeton Univ. Press, 1983).

———. *In Search of the Classic: Reconsidering the Greco-Roman Tradition, Homer to Valéry and Beyond* (University Park: Univ. of Pennsylvania, 1994).

———, ed. *The Iliad of Homer* (1996). See Pope.

Shaw, Philip. *The Sublime* (New York: Routledge, 2006).

Sherry, Vincent, B. "Liberal Measures: Language, Modernism, and the Great War," in Thormählen ed., 7–23.

Shields, Emily Ledyard. *The Cults of Lesbos* (Ph.D. Dissertation, The Johns Hopkins University, 1917; Menasha: George Banta).

Shinan, Avigdor, and Yair Zakovitch. *From Gods to God: How the Bible Debunked, Suppressed, or Changed Ancient Myths & Legends*, Valerie Zakovitch, tr. (Philadelphia: The Jewish Publication Society, 2012). Hebrew pub. 2004, *Lo kakh katuv ba-Tanach 'Not Thus Is It Written in the Bible'.*

Simonsuuri, Kirsti. *Homer's Original Genius: Eighteenth-Century Notions of the Early Greek Epic (1688–1798)* (Cambridge: Cambridge Univ. Press, 1979).

Silk, Michael, Ingo Gildenhard, and Rosemary Barrow. "Translation," in *The Classical Tradition: Art, Literature Thought* (Oxford and Malden: Wiley Blackwell, 2014), 173–198 (with excellent discussion of Keats's "On First Looking into Chapman's Homer").

Skinner, Marilyn. "Women and Language in Archaic Greece," in Nancy Sorkin Rabinowitz and Amy Richlin, eds., *Feminist Theory and the Classics* (New York: Routledge, 1993).

Skutch, Otto. "Alfred Edward Housman (1859–1936)." An Address delivered at the Centenary Celebrations in the University of London during the Third International Congress of Classical Studies (London: The Athlone Press, 1960).

———. "Helen, Her Name and Nature," *Journal of Hellenic Studies*, 107 (1987), 188–193.

Slatkin, Laura M. *The Power of Thetis: Allusion and Interpretation in the Iliad* (Berkeley: Univ. of California Press, 1991).

———. "Homer's *Odyssey*," in Foley, ed. (2005), 315–329.

Smith, Miles. *The Translators to the Reader: The Original Preface to the King James Version of 1611 Revisited*, Erroll F. Rhodes and Liana Lupas, eds. (New York: American Bible Society, 1997).

Smith, Seymour, F. *The Classics in Translation: An Annotated Guide to the Best Translations of the Greek and Latin Classics into English*, with a preface by Henry Bartlett Van Hoesen (New York: Burt Franklin, Bibliography & Reference Series, 1930, 1968).

Smith, William Benjamin, and Walter Miller, trs. *The Iliad of Homer: A Line for Line Translation into Dactylic Hexameters* (New York: Macmillan, 1944). Illustrated with the classical designs of John Flaxman.

Smyth, H. W. *Greek Melic Poets* (London: Macmillan, 1900).

Snodgrass, Anthony. *Archaic Greece: The Age of Experiment* (Berkeley: Univ. of California Press, 1980).

Snyder, Jane McIntosh. *The Woman and the Lyre: Woman Writers in Classical Greece and Rome* (Carbondale: Southern Illinois Univ. Press, 1989).

———. *Lesbian Desire in the Lyrics of Sappho* (New York: Columbia Univ. Press, 1997).

Sowerby, Robin, ed. *Dryden's Aeneid: A Selection With Commentary* (Bristol: Bristol Classical Press, 1986).

———. *The Augustan Art of Poetry: Augustan Translation of the Classics* (Oxford: Oxford Univ. Press, 2006).

Spender, Stephen. "Remembering Eliot," *Encounter*, XXIV.4 (1965), 1–14.

Spenser, Edmund. *The Faerie Queene*, A. C. Hamilton et al., eds. (London & New York: Pearson Longman, 2001, rev. 2007).

Stallings, A.E., tr. *Lucretius, The Nature of Things* (New York: Penguin Classics, 2007).

———. "Classical Intoxications: Love through the Lens of Sappho," *The Weekly Standard*, 7/21/2015. Review of Rayor and Lardinoire (2014), noting, among various commendations, that "What the book lacks is a certain grace: It could do with less whiff of lamp and more attar of Pierian roses."

Stanford, W. B. *The Odyssey of Homer*, edited with general and grammatical introduction, commentary, and indexes, 2 Vols. (London: Macmillan; New York: St. Martin's Press, 1965). 1st ed. 1947; 2nd ed. reprinted with alterations and additions, 1965.

———. *The Sound of Greek* (Berkeley: Univ. of California Press, 1967).

Stehle, Eva. "Sappho's Circle," in *Performance and Gender in Ancient Greece: Nondramatic Poetry in Its Setting* (Princeton: Princeton Univ. Press, 1997), 262–318.

Steiner, George, ed. *The Penguin Book of Modern Verse Translation* (Harmondsworth and Baltimore: Penguin Books, 1966).

———. *After Babel: Aspects of Language and Translation* (Oxford: Oxford Univ. Press, 1975; 3rd ed., 1998).

———. *No Passion Spent: Essays 1978–1995* (New Haven and London: Yale Univ. Press, 1996a).

———, ed. *Homer in English* (London and New York: Penguin Books, 1996b).

———. "Homer in English Translation," in Fowler, ed. (2004), 363–375.

Stewart, Mary, tr. *Selections From Catullus* (Boston: Richard G. Badger, 1915). English verse translation with introduction on the theory of translation.

Stigers, Eva. "Romantic Sensuality, Poetic Sense: A Response to Hallett on Sappho," *Signs: Journal of Women in Culture and Society*, 4 (1979), 465–471.

———. "Sappho's Private World," *Women's Studies*, 8 (1981), 47–63.

Storrs, Ronald. *Ad Pyrrham: A Polyglot Collection of Translations of Horace's Ode to Pyrrha, Book 1, Ode 5* (London: Oxford Univ. Press, 1959).

Sullivan, J. P. "The Poet as Translator: Ezra Pound and Sextus Propertius," *The Kenyon Review*, 23.3 (1961), 462–481.

———. *Ezra Pound and Sextus Propertius: A Study in Creative Translation* (Austin: Univ. of Texas Press, 1964).

Suzuki, Mihoko. *Metamorphoses of Helen: Authority, Difference, and the Epic* (Ithaca: Cornell Univ. Press, 1989).

Svensson, Lars-Håkan. "Modernism and the Classical Tradition: The Examples of Pound and H.D.," in Thormählen, ed. (2003), 112–131.

Swinburne, Algernon Charles. *Swinburne's Poems in Six Volumes* (London: Chatto and Windus, 1909).

———. "Sappho," *Saturday Review*, 117 (1914), 228. Posthumous publication.

Symonds, John Addington. *Studies of the Greek Poets*, Two Vols. (New York: Harper & Brothers, 1882).

Talbot, John. "Twenty-First Century Horace and the End of a Shared Culture" (review of McClatchy: *Horace, The Odes*), *Arion*, 11.2 (2003), 149–192.

———."Robert Lowell's Propertius," *International Journal of the Classical Tradition*, 14.1&2 (2007), 130–147.

———. "Classic Carne-Ross," *The New Criterion*, 29.9 (2011), 4–11.

———. "Speaking for Homer," *The New Criterion*, 31.1 (2012), 24–30.

T = Tarditi, G. *Archilochus* (Roma: Edizioni dell'Ateneo, 1968).

Teachout, Terry. "The New Tonalists," *Commentary*, 12/1997.

———. "Music: Back to the Future," *Time Magazine*, 3/6/2000.

Teasdale, Sara. *Collected Poems* (New York: Macmillan, 1917).

Tennyson, Alfred Lord. *Poems*, Christopher Ricks, ed. (London: Longmans, Green, 1969).

Thoreau, Henry D. *Translations: The Writings of Henry David Thoreau*, R. P. van Anglen, ed. (Princeton: Princeton Univ. Press, 1986).

Thormählen, Marianne. *The Waste Land: A Fragmentary Wholeness* (Lund: LiberLaromede/Gleerup, Lund Studies in English, 1978).

———, ed. *Rethinking Modernism* (New York: Palgrave Macmillan, 2003).

Todorov, Tzvetan. *The Limits of Art (two essays)*, Gila Walker, tr. (London and New York: Seagull Books, 2006). Essay one: "Artists and Dictators," 3–60; essay two: "Art and Ethics," 63–100.

Tomlinson, Charles. "Why Dryden's Translations Matter," *Translation and Literature*, 10.1 (2001), 3–20.

Toner, Jerry. *Homer's Turk: How Classics Shaped Ideas of the East* (Cambridge and London: Harvard Univ. Press, 2013).

Trench, Richard Chenevix. *On the Study of Words: Five Lectures Addressed to the Pupils of Diocesan*, A. L. Mayhew, ed., 29th ed. (London: John W. Parker and Son, 1851). Reprint, Kegan Paul, Trench, Trübner (1914).

———. *The Sonnets of William Wordsworth, Collected in One Volume* (London: Suttaby, 1884).

Trimpi, Wesley. "Horace's 'Ut Pictura Poesis': The Argument for Stylistic Decorum," *Traditio*, 34 (1978), 29–73.

Tucker, T. G. *Sappho: A Lecture Delivered Before the Classical Association of Victoria, 1913* (Melbourne: Thomas C. Lothian, 1914). Reprint, Leopold Classical Library (2015).

Turley, Richard Marggraff. "Indolent Minds, Indolent Men, and 'On First Looking into Chapman's Homer,'" *Review of English Studies*, 50 (1999), 204–207.

Turner, Frank Miller. *The Greek Heritage in Victorian Britain* (New Haven: Yale Univ. Press, 1981).

Vandiver, Elizabeth. "Fireflies in a Jar" (review of Davenport, tr. [1995] and Powell, tr. [1993]), *Parnassus: Poetry in Review*, 21.1&2 (1996), 59–76.

———. *Stand in the Trenches, Achilles: Classical Receptions in British Poetry of the Great War* (Oxford: Oxford Univ. Press, 2010).

Van Sickle, John B. "Archilochus: A New Fragment of an Epode," *Classical Journal*, 71 (1975), 1–15.

———. "The Doctored Text/Translating a New Fragment of Archilochus," *Modern Language Notes*, 90 (1975a), 872–885.

———. "The New Erotic Fragment of Archilochus," *Quaderni Urbinati di Cultura Classica*, 20 (1975b), 123–156.

———, ed. "The New Archilochus," *Arethusa*, 9.2 (1976).

Vendler, Helen. "Recent American Poetry," *The Massachusetts Review*, 8.3 (1967), 541–560.

Venuti, Lawrence. *The Translator's Invisibility: A History of Translation* (Abingdon: Routledge, 1995).

———. *The Scandals of Translation: Towards an Ethic of Difference* (London and New York: Routledge, 1998).

———. *The Translation Studies Reader* (New York: Routledge, 2004).

Vermeule, Emily Townsend. "Jefferson and Homer," *Proceedings of the American Philosophical Society*, 137.4 (1993), 689–703.

Viereck, Peter. "Pure Poetry: The Implications of Ezra Pound and the Bollingen Controversy," in *Dream and Responsibility* (Washington, D.C.: The Univ. Press of Washington, D.C., 1953).

———. "Strict Form in Poetry: Would Jacob Wrestle with a Flabby Angel"? *Critical Inquiry*, 5.2 (1978), 203–222.

———. "Pound, Williams, and the Road Not taken," *Parnassus: Poetry in Review*, 13.2 (1986), 125–139.

Virgil. *Eclogues, Georgics, Aeneid 1–6*, H. R. Fairclough, tr., revised by G. P. Gould (Cambridge: Harvard Univ. Press, Loeb Classical Library, 1916, 1999).

Voigt, E. M. *Sappho et Alcaeus* (Amsterdam: Polak & Van Gennep, 1971). Exhaustive critical edition; supersedes Lobel-Page whose numberings it largely follows.

Volk, Katharina. "Kleos Aphthiton Revisited," *Classical Philology*, 97.1 (2002), 61–68.

Walker, Keith, ed. *John Dryden, The Major Works* (Oxford: Oxford Univ. Press, Oxford World's Classics, 1987).

Warren, Rosanna, ed. *The Art of Translation: voices from the field* (Boston: Northeastern Univ. Press, 1989).

———. "Sappho: Translation as Elegy," in Warren (1989), 199–216, and Warren (2008), 10–26.

———. Letter to the Editor, *Poetry,* 187.2 (2005), 155–157. Response to Garry Wills on Sherod Santos.

———. *Fables of the Self: Studies in Lyric Poetry* (New York and London: W. W. Norton, 2008).

Webb, William Stanford. "Vergil in Spenser's Epic Theory," *English Literary History,* 4.1 (1937), 62–84.

Webster, T. B. L. *From Mycenae to Homer: A Study in Early Greek Literature and Art* (New York: W. W. Norton, 1958).

Weigall, A. *Sappho of Lesbos: Her Life and Times* (New York: Frederick A. Stokes, 1932).

Wertham, Fredric. "The Road to Rapallo," *American Journal of Psychotherapy,* 3.4 (1949), 585–600.

West, M. L. "Hesiodea," *Classical Quarterly,* 11.2 (1961), 130–145.

———, ed. *Hesiod Theogony,* with Prolegomena and Commentary (Oxford: Clarendon Press, 1966).

———, ed. *Fragmenta Hesiodea* (1967a), with R. Merkelbach.

———. "The Contest of Homer and Hesiod," *Classical Quarterly,* 17 (1967b), 433–450.

———. "Burning Sappho," *Maia,* 22 (1970), 307–330.

———, ed. *Works and Days,* with Prolegomena and Commentary (Oxford: Clarendon Press, 1978, 1990).

W = ———. *Delectus ex Iambis et Elegis Graecis* (Oxford: Oxford Univ. Press, 1980).

———. *The Hesiodic Catalogue of Women: Its Nature, Structure, and Origins* (Oxford: Clarendon Press, 1985).

———, tr. *Hesiod: Theogony and Works and Days,* With Introduction and Commentary (Oxford: Oxford Univ. Press, 1988). Reprint, Oxford World's Classics Paperback (1999, 2008).

———. *Greek Lyric Poetry: A New Translation* (Oxford: Oxford Univ. Press, Oxford World's Classics, 1993, 2008).

———. *The East Face of Helicon: West Asiatic Elements in Greek Poetry and Myth* (Oxford: Clarendon Press, 1997).

———. "The View from Lesbos," in Michael Reichel and Antonios Rengakos, eds., *Epea Pteroenta: Beiträge zur Homerforschung* (Stuttgart: Franz Steiner Verlag, 2002), 207–219. Festschrift Wolfgang Kullmann.

W′ = ———, tr. and ed. *Greek Epic Fragments* (Cambridge: Harvard Univ. Press, Loeb Classical Library, 2003).

———. "A New Sappho Poem," *Times Literary Supplement,* 6/29/2005.

———. *The Epic Cycle: A Commentary on the Lost Troy Epics* (Oxford: Oxford Univ. Press, 2013).

Wharton, Henry Thornton. *Sappho: Memoir, Text, Renderings, and a Literal Translation* (London: David Stott, 1885, 1887, 1895; Chicago: A. C. McClurg, 1887).

Whitman, Cedric H. *Homer and the Heroic Tradition* (New York: W. W. Norton, 1958).

———. *Fifteen Odes of Horace* (Lunenburg: Stinehour Press, 1980).

Wilcock, G. D. "Passing Pitefull [i.e., Pitiful] Hexameters: A Study of Quantity and Accent in English Renaissance Verse," *The Modern Language Review*, 29.1 (1934), 1–19.

Will, Frederic. *The Generic Demands of Greek Literature* (Amsterdam: Rodophi, 1976).

Willett, Steven J. Review of Robert Fagles, tr., *Homer, the Odyssey*, in *Classical Journal*, 93.2 (1997–1998), 203–206.

———. Review of David R. Slavitt, tr., *Propertius in Love: The Elegies*, in *Museion*, 3rd series, XLVI.2 (2002), 392–401.

———. "Postmodern Classics," *Academic Questions*, 17.2 (2004) 59–66.

———. "Wrong Meaning, Right Feeling: Ezra Pound as Translator," *Arion*, 3rd series, 12.3 (2005), 149–189.

Williamson, Margaret. *Sappho's Immortal Daughters* (Cambridge: Harvard Univ. Press, 1995).

Wills, Garry. Preface, *Chapman's Homer, the Iliad*; Preface, *Chapman's Homer, the Odyssey*, in Nicoll, ed. (1956).

———. "Sappho 31 and Catullus 51," *Greek, Roman, and Byzantine Studies*, 8 (1967), 167–197.

———. "Homer Alive" (review of Christopher Logue, *Kings: An Account of Books 1 and 2 of Homer's Iliad*), *New York Review of Books*, 4/23/1992.

———. "Slop and Gossip" (review of Sherod Santos, tr., *Greek Lyric Poetry: A New Translation*), *Poetry*, 187.1 (2005), 53–63. On controversy surrounding the review title (chosen by *Poetry* editors), see "Garry Wills Responds" and "Editors' Note," *Poetry*, 187.2 (2005).

———, tr. *Martial's Epigrams, A Selection* (New York: Viking Penguin, 2007).

———. "Closer than Ever to Virgil" (review of Sarah Ruden, tr., *The Aeneid*), *New York Review of Books*, 3/12/2009.

Wilson, Joe. "Homer and the Will of Zeus," *College Literature*, 34. 2 (2007), 150–173.

Wilson, Lyn Hatherly. *Sappho's Sweetbitter Songs: Configurations of Female and Male in Ancient Greek Lyric* (New York: Routledge, 1996).

Windschuttle, Keith. "The Burdens of Empire," in Kimball and Kramer eds., 3–24.

Winkler, Jack. "Gardens of Nymphs: Public and Private in Sappho's Lyrics," in H. P. Foley, ed. (1981), 63–90. Reprint, Greene, ed. (1996a), 89–109.

Woodman, A. J. "Some Implications of Otium in Catullus 51," *Latomus*, 25 (1966), 217–226.

Woolf, Virginia. "On Not Knowing Greek," in Andrew McNeillie, ed., *The Common Reader* (New York: Harcourt, 1925).

Wormell, D. E. W. "Catullus as Translator," in L. Wallach, ed., *The Classical Tradition: Literary and Historical Studies in Honor of Harry Caplan* (Ithaca: Cornell Univ. Press, 1966).

Worsley, Philip Stanhope, tr. *The Iliad of Homer: Translated into English Verse in the Spenserian Stanza* (London: William Blackwood & Sons, 1865–1868).

Wright, Roger, ed. *Latin and the Romance Languages in the Early Middle Ages* (University Park: Penn. State Univ. Press, 1996). 1st pub., Routledge, 1991.

Wright, William Aldis, ed. *Letters of Edward FitzGerald in Two Volumes* (New York: Macmillan, 1894, 1901).

Yeats, W. B. *The Oxford Book of Modern Verse (1892–1935)* (Oxford: Oxford Univ. Press, 1936).

Ziogas, Ioannis. *Ovid and Hesiod: The Metamorphosis of the Catalogue of Women* (Cambridge: Cambridge Univ. Press, 2013).

Ziolkowski, Theodore. "The Literature of Atrocity," *The Sewanee Review*, 85.1 (1977), 135–143.

———. *Virgil and the Moderns* (Princeton: Princeton Univ. Press, 1993).

———. "The Fragmented Text: The Classics and Postwar European Literature," *International Journal of the Classical Tradition*, 6.4 (2000), 549–562.

———. "Uses and Abuses of Horace: His reception since 1935 in Germany and Anglo-America," *International Journal of the Classical Tradition*, 12.2 (2005), 183–215.

Zonana, Joyce. "Swinburne's Sappho: The Muse as Sister-Goddess," *Victorian Poetry*, 28 (1990), 39–50.

# Index

## A

# B

# C

# D

# E

# F

# G

# H

# K



# L

# M

# N



# O

# P

# Q



# R

# S

# T

# U



# V

# W

# X



# Y



# Z

*Map of Ancient Greek world highlighting sites significant to Homer, Sappho, and other Greek lyric poets, and places of general interest.*